FOOD AND ADDICTION

FOOD AND ADDICTION

A Comprehensive Handbook

EDITED BY

KELLY D. BROWNELL

MARK S. GOLD

OXFORD
UNIVERSITY PRESS

OXFORD
UNIVERSITY PRESS

Oxford University Press is a department of the University of Oxford. It furthers
the University's objective of excellence in research, scholarship, and education by publishing
worldwide.

Oxford   New York
Auckland   Cape Town   Dar es Salaam   Hong Kong   Karachi
Kuala Lumpur   Madrid   Melbourne   Mexico City   Nairobi
New Delhi   Shanghai   Taipei   Toronto

With offices in
Argentina   Austria   Brazil   Chile   Czech Republic   France   Greece
Guatemala   Hungary   Italy   Japan   Poland   Portugal   Singapore
South Korea   Switzerland   Thailand   Turkey   Ukraine   Vietnam

Oxford is a registered trademark of Oxford University Press in the UK and certain other countries.

Published in the United States of America by
Oxford University Press
198 Madison Avenue, New York, NY 10016

Library of Congress Cataloging-in-Publication Data
Food and addiction: a comprehensive handbook/edited
By Kelly D. Brownell, Mark S. Gold.—1st ed.
p. cm.
Includes bibliographical references.
ISBN 978–0–19–973816–8
1. Eating disorders.   2. Eating disorders—Animal models.   3. Obesity.
4. Compulsive eating.   5. Drug abuse—Treatment.
I. Brownell, Kelly D.   II. Gold, Mark S.
RC552.E18F65 2012
616.85′26—dc23
2011048217

3 5 7 9 8 6 4
Printed in the United States of America
on acid-free paper

For our wonderful, kind and talented children, Kristy, Kevin, and Matthew;

and Steve, Katie, Kimberly, Dan, Kyle, and Jessica

—Kelly Brownell & Mark Gold

CONTENTS

PART V: *Public Health Approaches and Implications*

PART VI: *Legal and Policy Implications*

PART VII: *Concluding Comments*

ACKNOWLEDGMENTS

There are many important people to thank and acknowledge in the development of this book. We offer special thanks to our colleagues who attended the historic Yale Conference on Food and Addiction held in 2007. This conference brought together the world's experts and debated the strength, weaknesses, and merits of the addiction hypothesis. The very experts from the nutrition, neurobiology, endocrinology, obesity, and addiction fields who came together to discuss this developing concept are represented in this volume. The meeting was a first and gave many in the field a new sense of confidence that this topic deserved much more study and attention. Their intellectual input at a critical stage of our journey was very helpful.

Kelly Brownell's colleagues at the Rudd Center for Food Policy and Obesity at Yale have been instrumental in the intellectual work that encompasses the topic of food and addiction. Marlene Schwartz, deputy director of the Rudd Center, and Rebecca Puhl, director of research, have helped lead a legion of top-rate people working on various aspects of obesity prevention and have been highly supportive of this work. Similarly, Mark Gold's colleagues at the McKnight Brain Institute and the University of Florida College of Medicine deserve much of the credit for the bench-to-bedside program in food and addiction discovery that exists at U.F. today.

Nicole Novak of the Rudd Center and Paula Edge at U.F. have been invaluable in the editorial work on this book. Countless details, editing, and other organizational issues were central to having this book published. Nicole and Paula were there at every stage of the process and were outstanding in every way.

Mark Gold was working on this area on and off for 30 years. Kelly Brownell is newer to the topic of food and addiction and would like to thank two colleagues, Ashley Gearhart and William Corbin, for their role in helping this interest develop. The idea of food addiction was no more than that, an idea, until Ashley, then a graduate student at Yale, and Will, then a psychology department colleague at Yale, began collaborating with him on this topic. Kelly and the Rudd Center reached out to Mark, and a long-term friendship and collaboration began. A wonderful line of research was born, Ashley's career on food addiction was launched, and a wonderful series of collaborative relationships developed.

We thank our families and friends for supporting our scholarly work. Most important, we thank the authors of the chapters in this book. All are leading scholars and have great demands on their time. We appreciate that they found this book compelling enough to contribute.

CONTRIBUTORS

Serge H. Ahmed, PhD
Research Director, CNRS
Institute of Neurogenerative Diseases
University of Bordeaux
Bordeaux, France

Louis J. Aronne, MD
Clinical Professor of Medicine
Weill-Cornell Medical College
Cornell University
New York, NY

Nicole M. Avena, PhD
Research Assistant Professor of Psychiatry
College of Medicine
University of Florida
Gainesville, FL

Colleen L. Barry, PhD
Associate Professor
Department of Health Policy
    and Management
Johns Hopkins Bloomberg School
    of Public Health
Baltimore, MD

Jessica R. Barson, PhD
Postdoctoral Associate
Laboratory of Behavioral Neurobiology
The Rockefeller University
New York, NY

Linda M. Bartoshuk, PhD
Professor of Community Dentistry and
    Behavioral Sciences
Director of Human Research,
    UF Center for Smell and Taste
Member of Plant Innovation Program
College of Dentistry
University of Florida
Gainesville, FL

Hans-Rudolf Berthoud, PhD
Professor of Neurobiology and Nutrition
Pennington Biomedical Research Center
Louisiana State University System
Baton Rouge, LA

Elliott M. Blass, PhD
Professor of Psychology and Behavioral
    Neuroscience
University of Massachusetts
Amherst, MA

Daniel M. Blumenthal, MD, MBA
Resident in Internal Medicine
Massachusetts General Hospital
Harvard Medical School
Boston, MA

Kimberly Blumenthal, MD
Resident in Internal Medicine
Harvard Medical School
Massachusetts General Hospital
Boston, MA

John E. Blundell, PhD
Professor of Biopsychology
Institute of Psychological Sciences
Faculty of Medicine and Health
University of Leeds
Leeds, United Kingdom

Kelly D. Brownell, PhD
Professor of Psychology, Epidemiology,
    and Public Health
Director, Rudd Center for Food Policy and Obesity
Yale University
New Haven, CT

John Cawley, PhD
Professor of Policy Analysis and Management, and
    Economics
Cornell University
Ithaca, NY

Karishma Chandaria, MSc
Senior Policy Officer
Alzheimer's Society
London, UK

Wendy K. Chung, MD, PhD
Assistant Professor of Pediatrics in Medicine
Director of Clinical Genetics Department of
    Pediatrics
Division of Molecular Genetics
College of Physicians and Surgeons
Columbia University
New York, NY

William R. Corbin, PhD
Associate Professor of Psychology
Arizona State University
Tempe, AZ

Michele A. Crisafulli, MA
Graduate Student
Clinical/Community and Applied Social
    Psychology
University of Maryland, Baltimore County
Baltimore, MD

Alain Dagher, MD
Associate Professor of Neurology
Montreal Neurological Institute
McGill University
Montréal, Quebec, Canada

Mary F. Dallman, PhD
Professor Emerita of Physiology
School of Medicine
University of California, San Francisco
San Francisco, CA

Michelle Dalton, BSc
Research Student
Institute of Psychological Sciences
Faculty of Medicine and Health
University of Leeds
Leeds, United Kingdom

Marcelo O. Dietrich, MD
Postdoctoral Associate
School of Medicine
Yale University
New Haven, CT

Robert L. DuPont, MD
President, Institute for Behavior and Health
Clinical Professor of Psychiatry
School of Medicine
Georgetown University
Washington, D.C.

Cara B. Ebbeling, PhD
Associate Director for Research and Training
New Balance Foundation Obesity
    Prevention Center
Children's Hospital Boston
Boston, MA

Elissa S. Epel, PhD
Associate Professor of Psychiatry
School of Medicine
University of California, San Francisco
San Francisco, CA

Daniel P. Evatt, PhD
Department of Psychiatry and
    Behavioral Sciences
Johns Hopkins University School of Medicine
Baltimore, MD

Lucy F. Faulconbridge, PhD
Assistant Professor of Psychology
Perelman School of Medicine
University of Pennsylvania
Philadelphia, PA

Graham Finlayson, PhD
Lecturer in Psychology
Institute of Psychological Sciences
Faculty of Medicine and Health
University of Leeds
Leeds, United Kingdom

Gary D. Foster, PhD
Lauren Carnell Professor of Medicine,
    Public Health, and Psychology
Director, Center for Obesity Research
    and Education
Temple University
Philadelphia, PA

Joanna S. Fowler, PhD
Senior Scientist
Medical Department
Director, Radiotracer Chemistry,
    Instrumentation and Biological Imaging
Brookhaven National Laboratory
Upton, NY

Ashley N. Gearhardt, PhD
Assistant Professor of Psychology
University of Michigan
Ann Arbor, MI

Ian Gilmore, MD
Professor of Medicine
University of Liverpool
Liverpool, UK

Mark S. Gold, MD
Distinguished Professor and Chair of Psychiatry
McKnight Brain Institute
College of Medicine
University of Florida
Gainesville, FL

Shelly F. Greenfield, MD, MPH
Professor of Psychiatry
Harvard Medical School
Boston, MA
Chief Academic Officer
McLean Hospital
Belmont, MA

Roland R. Griffiths, PhD
Professor
Departments of Psychiatry and Neuroscience
Johns Hopkins University School of Medicine
Baltimore, MD

Carlos M. Grilo, PhD
Professor of Psychiatry and Psychology
Director, Program for Obesity, Weight, and Eating
    Research (POWER)
School of Medicine
Yale University
New Haven, CT

Jeffrey W. Grimm, PhD
Professor of Psychology
Department of Psychology and Program in
    Behavioral Neuroscience
Western Washington University
Bellingham, WA

Jennifer L. Harris, PhD, MBA
Director of Marketing Initiatives
Rudd Center for Food Policy and Obesity
Yale University
New Haven, CT

Amanda E. Higley, PhD
Postdoctoral Research Fellow in Clinical
    Neuropsychopharmacology
Scripps Research Institute
La Jolla, CA

Andrew J. Hill, PhD
Professor of Medical Psychology
Academic Unit of Psychiatry & Behavioural
    Sciences
School of Medicine
University of Leeds
Leeds, United Kingdom

Bartley G. Hoebel, PhD
Professor of Psychology
Princeton Neuroscience Institute
Princeton University
Princeton, NJ

Tamas L. Horvath, DVM, PhD
Professor and Chair
Section of Comparative Medicine
Jean and David W. Wallace Professor
    of Biomedical Research
Professor of Neurobiology and Obstetrics,
    Gynecology, and Reproductive Sciences
Director, Yale Program in Integrative
    Cell Signaling and Neurobiology of Metabolism
Yale University School of Medicine
New Haven, CT

Joan Ifland, PhD
Chair
Refined Food Addiction Research Foundation
Houston, TX

Satya P. Kalra, PhD
Distinguished Professor of Neuroscience
McKnight Brain Institute
College of Medicine
University of Florida
Gainesville, FL

Brian K. Kit, MD, MPH
Lieutenant Commander, United States
    Public Health Service
Medical Epidemiologist
National Center for Health Statistics
Centers for Disease Control and Prevention
Hyattsville, MD

Firas H. Kobeissy, PhD
Research Assistant Professor of Psychiatry
Associate Scientific Director,
    Psychoproteomics and Nanotechnology
    Research Center
McKnight Brain Institute
College of Medicine
University of Florida
Gainesville, FL

George F. Koob, PhD
Professor and Chair
Committee on the Neurobiology of Addictive
    Disorders
Scripps Research Institute
La Jolla, CA

Shiriki Kumanyika, PhD, MPH
Professor of Biostatistics and Epidemiology
Perelman School of Medicine
University of Pennsylvania
Philadelphia, PA

Caitlin A. LaGrotte, MEd
Graduate Student
Department of Psychology
LaSalle University
Philadelphia, PA

Molly M. Lamb, PhD
Research Instructor
Department of Epidemiology
Colorado School of Public Health
Aurora, CO

Rudolph L. Leibel, MD
Christopher J. Murphy Professor of Diabetes
    Research
Head, Division of Molecular Genetics
Co-Director, Naomi Berrie Diabetes Center
College of Physicians and Surgeons
Columbia University
New York, NY

Sarah F. Leibowitz, PhD
Research Associate Professor
Laboratory of Behavioral Neurobiology
The Rockefeller University
New York, NY

Yijun Liu, PhD
River Branch Professor
Chief, Global Tobacco, Alcohol, Obesity, &
    Health Research
Department of Psychiatry
College of Medicine and McKnight
    Brain Institute
University of Florida
Gainesville, FL

Tim Lobstein, PhD
Director of Policy and Programmes
International Association for the Study of Obesity
International Obesity TaskForce
London, UK

David S. Ludwig, MD, PhD
Professor of Pediatrics, Harvard Medical School
Professor of Nutrition, Harvard School
    of Public Health
Director, New Balance Foundation Obesity
    Prevention Center
Children's Hospital Boston
Boston, MA

Michael Lutter, MD, PhD
Assistant Professor of Psychiatry
University of Texas at Southwestern
    Medical Center
Dallas, TX

Bess H. Marcus, PhD
Professor and Chair
Department of Family and Preventive Medicine
University of California, San Diego
La Jolla, CA

Barbara J. Mason, PhD
Professor
Director, Laboratory of Clinical
    Psychopharmacology
Co-Director, Pearson Center for Alcoholism
    and Addiction Research
Scripps Research Institute
La Jolla, CA

Brittany L. Mason, PhD
Postdoctoral Fellow
University of Texas at Southwestern
    Medical Center
Dallas, TX

Donna M. Matheson, PhD
Senior Research Scientist
Stanford Prevention Research Center
Stanford University School of Medicine
Stanford, CA

Lisa J. Merlo, PhD, MPE
Assistant Professor of Psychiatry
College of Medicine
University of Florida
Gainesville, FL

Peter M. Monti, PhD
Distinguished Professor of Alcohol and
    Addiction Studies
Director, Center for Alcohol and
    Addiction Studies
Brown University
Providence, RI

Irene Morganstern, PhD
Postdoctoral Associate
Laboratory of Behavioral Neurobiology
The Rockefeller University
New York, NY

Eric J. Nestler, MD, PhD
Professor and Chair of Neuroscience
Director, Friedman Brain Institute
Mount Sinai School of Medicine
New York, NY

Ernest P. Noble, MD, PhD
Professor of Psychiatry and
    Biobehavioral Sciences
David Geffen School of Medicine
University of California, Los Angeles
Los Angeles, CA

Nicole L. Novak, MSc
Research Associate
Rudd Center for Food Policy and Obesity
Yale University
New Haven, CT

Cynthia L. Ogden, PhD
Epidemiologist
National Center for Health Statistics
Centers for Disease Control and Prevention
Hyattsville, MD

Stephanie S. O'Malley, PhD
Professor of Psychiatry and Assistant Chair
    for Clinical Research
Director, Division of Substance Abuse Research
School of Medicine
Yale University
New Haven, CT

Jennifer L. Pomeranz, JD, MPH
Director of Legal Initiatives
Rudd Center for Food Policy and Obesity
Yale University
New Haven, CT

Barry M. Popkin, PhD
W. R. Kenan, Jr. Distinguished Professor of Nutrition
Gillings School of Global Public Health
University of North Carolina
Chapel Hill, NC

Douglas S. Ramsay, DMD, PhD, MSD
Professor and Chair, Oral Health Sciences
School of Dentistry
University of Washington
Seattle, WA

Lara A. Ray, PhD
Assistant Professor of Clinical Psychology
University of California Los Angeles
Los Angeles, CA

Mahdi Razafsha, MD
Department of Psychiatry
Center for Neuroproteomics and Biomarkers
   Research at the Evelyn F. and William L.
   McKnight Brain Institute
University of Florida
Gainesville, FL

Thomas N. Robinson, MD, MPH
Irving Schulman, MD Endowed Professor
   of Child Health
Professor of Pediatrics and of Medicine
Division of General Pediatrics and Stanford
   Prevention Research Center
Director, Center for Healthy Weight
Stanford University School of Medicine
Stanford, CA

Barbara J. Rolls, PhD
Professor and Helen A. Guthrie
   Chair in Nutritional Sciences
The Pennsylvania State University
University Park, PA

Orli Rosen, MD
Instructor, Division of Endocrinology
Mount Sinai Medical Center
New York, NY

Anne Rosenberg, CHF, BSW
Vancouver, British Columbia, Canada

Lainie Rutkow, JD, PhD, MPH
Assistant Professor of Health Policy and
   Management
Bloomberg School of Public Health
Johns Hopkins University
Baltimore, MD

Marina Sánchez, MSc
Department of Kinesiology
Faculty of Medicine
Laval University
Quebec City, Quebec, Canada

Gary J. Schwartz, PhD
Professor of Medicine and Neuroscience
Albert Einstein College of Medicine
   of Yeshiva University
Bronx, NY

Marlene B. Schwartz, PhD
Deputy Director
Rudd Center for Food Policy and Obesity
Yale University
New Haven, CT

Kay Sheppard, MA, LMHC
Certified Eating Disorders Specialist
Palm Bay, FL

Richard L. Shriner, MD
Assistant Clinical Professor of Psychiatry
University of Florida
Gainesville, FL

Rajita Sinha, PhD
Foundations Fund Professor of Psychiatry,
   Neurobiology, and Child Study
Chief, Psychology Section in Psychiatry
Director, Yale Stress Center
School of Medicine
Yale University
New Haven, CT

Dana M. Small, PhD
Associate Fellow, The John B. Pierce Laboratory
Associate Professor, Psychiatry and Psychology
Yale University School of Medicine
New Haven, CT

Derek J. Snyder, PhD
Postdoctoral Associate
Department of Psychology
San Diego State University
San Diego, CA

Eric Stice, PhD
Senior Research Scientist
Oregon Research Institute
Eugene, OR

Ece Tek, MD
Medical Director
Adult Behavioral Health
Cornell Scott Hill Health Center
Assistant Clinical Professor of Psychiatry
School of Medicine
Yale University
New Haven, CT

Stephen P. Teret, JD, MPH
Professor of Health Policy and Management
Director, Center for Law and the Public's Health
Bloomberg School of Public Health
Johns Hopkins University
Baltimore, MD

A. Janet Tomiyama, PhD
Assistant Professor of Psychology and Nutritional
    Sciences
Rutgers University
New Brunswick, NJ

Angelo Tremblay, PhD
Department of Kinesiology
Faculty of Medicine
Laval University
Quebec City, Quebec, Canada

Marion L. Vetter, MD, RD
Assistant Professor of Medicine
Perelman School of Medicine
University of Pennsylvania
Philadelphia, PA

Nora D. Volkow, MD
Director, National Institute on Drug Abuse
National Institutes of Health
Rockville, MD

Thomas A. Wadden, PhD
Professor of Psychology and Psychiatry
Director, Center for Weight and Eating Disorders
Perelman School of Medicine
University of Pennsylvania
Philadelphia, PA

Gene-Jack Wang, MD
Senior Scientist
Chairman, Medical Department
Brookhaven National Laboratory
Upton, NY

Brian Wansink, PhD
Professor of Marketing
Charles H. Dyson School of Applied Economics
    and Management
Cornell University
Ithaca, NY

Kenneth E. Warner, PhD
Avedis Donabedian Distinguished University
    Professor of Public Health
Department of Health Management and Policy
School of Public Health
University of Michigan
Ann Arbor, MI

Philip Werdell, MA
Director, Food Addiction Professional Training
    Program
ACORN Food Dependency Recovery Services
    and The Food Addiction Institute
Sarasota, FL

Marney A. White, PhD, MS
Assistant Professor of Psychiatry and Chronic
    Disease Epidemiology
School of Medicine
Yale University
New Haven, CT

Walter C. Willett, MD
Professor of Epidemiology and Nutrition
Chair, Department of Nutrition
Harvard School of Public Health
Boston, MA

David M. Williams, PhD
Assistant Professor of Behavioral and Social
    Sciences
Brown University
Providence, RI

Noel N. Williams, MD
Associate Professor of Clinical Surgery
Director, Bariatric Surgery Program
Perelman School of Medicine
University of Pennsylvania
Philadelphia, PA

Stephen C. Woods, PhD
Professor of Psychiatry
Director, Obesity Research Center
University of Cincinnati
Cincinnati, OH

H. Theresa Wright, MS, RD, LDN
Renaissance Nutrition Center, Inc.
East Norriton, PA

Jacqueline D. Wright, DrPH
Health Scientist Administrator
National Heart, Lung, and Blood Institute
National Institutes of Health
Bethesda, MD

Sonja Yokum, PhD
Research Associate
Oregon Research Institute
Eugene, OR

Yi Zhang, PhD
Associate Professor
 Life Sciences Research Center
School of Life Sciences and Technology
Xidian University
Xi'an, Shaanxi, China

Zhiqun Zhang, PhD
Adjunct Assistant Professor
Department of Psychiatry
University of Florida
Gainesville, FL

Introduction

KELLY D. BROWNELL AND MARK S. GOLD

FOOD AND ADDICTION: WHY AND WHY NOW?

With obesity's stampeding rate throughout the world, and poor diet affecting longevity in billions of people by increasing risk of other diseases such as cancer and heart disease, there is great concern with promoting healthier eating. Part of this effort involves a search for factors that interfere with this objective. The addictive properties of food may be one such factor.

The concept of food and addiction is firmly established in the popular culture. Terms such as "chocoholic" and "carbohydrate addict" are common. Individuals in day-to-day life use terms such as craving and withdrawal; hence, people "get" the concept. The food industry has capitalized on this in their marketing, with advertisements promising delicious tasting foods that will conquer cravings.

Acceptance in popular culture does not make the food and addiction concept viable and valid. With that said, much can be learned from listening to people. Professionals have long heard the language of addiction in clinical settings. Individuals with an array of eating issues, including obesity, eating disorders, and binge eating, often use terms of addiction to describe their relationship with food. People speak directly about being addicted to food, and in many cases act as if they are. Eating in the presence of untoward consequences, compulsive eating, inability to stop, and a number of other behavioral patterns should have suggested that food might be addictive long before it did.

Clinical anecdote also does not prove the vitality of the food and addiction concept. Ultimately science will determine whether this concept is meaningful and helpful, can be defended with the best scientific methods, and helps describe eating problems beyond our descriptors available already.

MIXED OPINIONS

The two of us met some years back when Kelly Brownell invited Mark Gold to Yale University to speak about his work on food and addiction. Brownell believed that this concept was important, and other than pioneering work by Bartley Hoebel and his colleagues at Princeton University, was not being investigated much in the obesity and nutrition fields. Gold, a substance abuse researcher, was one of the first to address the issue from the perspective of the addiction field.

In 2007, we co-hosted an historic meeting at Yale University that brought together leading researchers in nutrition and obesity with top experts from the addiction field. Research was presented, new concepts were discussed, and there was extensive discussion about whether food and addiction was a concept worth pursuing. There was considerable agreement that the topic was important, that the implications were significant, and that much work remained to be done.

An observation we had from that 2007 meeting was that experts from the nutrition/obesity field were more reticent than those from the addiction field to accept the notion that some foods might act on the brain as addictive substances. At first glance this was not surprising, as more work had been done by addictions researchers, but there was still hesitation among nutrition experts beyond what we expected.

This hesitation has now given way, and leading scientists across both addictions and nutrition/obesity/ingestive behavior fields have kicked into higher gears and research is being published by scholars from a variety of disciplines. We believe the science has reached a critical mass to the point where an edited book is warranted. As in most scientific fields, available work is scattered across a variety of journals representing people from many disciplines, hence the need to have the most up-to-date and comprehensive information available in a single source.

WHY THIS WORK IS SO IMPORTANT

The full implications of work on food and addiction are difficult to predict, as the field is moving rapidly. It is our belief, however, that the way the world deals with issues such as obesity could be heavily affected by this concept and the work surrounding it.

Work on food and addiction could enrich our understanding of why people eat like they do. The confluence of biological, psychological, and social factors such as food marketing have created dietary mayhem. To what extent is food and addiction a player? Such information could be harnessed to develop better treatment programs for eating issues. This could include not only treatments for obesity, which are in dire need of improvement, but also programs designed to educate people about nutrition in general.

Information on food and addiction could be helpful for designing prevention programs. Understanding more clearly which foods should be avoided, removed from institutions such as schools, or targeted by public policy could be informed by research on food and addiction. As one example, agricultural subsidy policies favor the production of certain crops such as corn and soybeans. These are processed into a variety of foods, some referred to as "Frankenfoods" by some nutrition experts, in which a long list of chemicals get processed with commodity crops to form foods that dizzy the imagination with their colors, tastes, smells, textures, and other sensory properties that maximize consumption. As elected leaders consider changes in subsidies, different crops might be subsidized to better defend against vulnerabilities in human biology.

Vast numbers of people could be affected by the addictive effects of food on the brain, regardless of their weight or whether they eat in compulsive ways. When the bell rings and the high school day ends, and teenagers feel they need a sugary beverage, why? If the sugar in those beverages acts on the brain to create craving, withdrawal, or tolerance, one might look to the concept of food and addiction to help explain the ravages of nutrient-poor, calorie-dense foods on the public's health.

One word in particular, one of the most common in our language, has special meaning in this book, "and." We titled this book food *and* addiction rather than food addiction. This may seem like nuance, but it has profound implications. The term "food addiction" conjures up images of individuals who are eating out of control, who are extremely overweight, and who represent the tail end of the distribution of human eating. This book is relevant to that discussion, but ultimately more important is the concept of food *and* addiction—the impact of food on the brain of everyday people in everyday life.

Diseases related to poor diet do not require extreme eating. Small daily increments in calories or nutrients such as saturated fat, sugar, and sodium can increase risk for disease. A florid addictive process, like one might see with classic substances of abuse, may not be necessary for the addictive effects of food on the brain to be important. From a public health perspective, the key question is whether enough foods produce enough of an addictive effect on enough people to affect the health of the population.

This issue of addiction becomes complicated when the substance being considered is food. One must eat; hence, food is necessary for survival, but alcohol, cigarettes, or drugs are not. One might parody the interest in food and addiction by saying that people are also addicted to water and air. But people do not overconsume water and air. This is why the examination of food is so important and we must ask why eating occurs beyond the meeting of biological needs for energy and nutrients. The substance necessary for survival is consumed in ways that interfere with survival.

The aim of this book is to draw together the work of leading experts to highlight what is known on a broad range of topics pertaining to food and addiction. This begins with chapters on basic mechanisms of addiction and body weight regulation, followed by writings by authors who have tackled specifically the issue of the addictive impact of food using both animal and human models. There is also emphasis on the implications and importance of this work, including extension into legal and policy arenas. Consider, for instance, the First Amendment of the US Constitution. The food industry, among other corporate players, has been afforded a great deal of latitude in marketing products to all parts of the population, including children. As it protects political and religious speech, the constitution protects "commercial speech." If certain foods or their constituents could be considered addictive, there might be justification for restricting their marketing, particularly to vulnerable populations, such as youth.

It is our hope that this book shines needed light on this very important topic. Researchers around the world are doing excellent work on this issue, and the implications are beginning to enter the public and policy realms. It is essential that this discourse proceed in a reasoned, thoughtful, and scientifically sound way. This book is designed with that purpose in mind.

PART I

The Neurobiology and Psychology of Addiction

1

Animal Models of Drug Addiction

GEORGE F. KOOB

CONCEPTUAL FRAMEWORK FOR ANIMAL MODELS

Definitions: Addiction and Animal Models

Drug addiction can be defined as a chronically relapsing disorder characterized by (1) compulsion to seek and take the drug, (2) loss of control in limiting intake, and (3) emergence of a negative emotional state (e.g., dysphoria, anxiety, irritability) when access to the drug is prevented. Drug addiction has been conceptualized as a disorder that progresses from impulsivity to compulsivity in a collapsed cycle comprising three stages: *preoccupation/anticipation*, *binge/intoxication*, and *withdrawal/negative affect*.[1]

Much of the recent progress in understanding the mechanisms of addiction has derived from animal models of addiction. Although no animal model of addiction fully emulates the human condition, animal models do permit investigation of specific elements of the drug addiction process. Thus, animal models are most likely to have construct or predictive validity when the model mimics only the specific signs or symptoms associated with the psychopathological condition.[2] Such elements can be defined by models of different systems, models of psychological constructs such as positive and negative reinforcement, models of actual symptoms of addiction outlined by psychiatric nosology, and models of different stages of the addiction cycle.[1,3] For the present chapter, the animal models are organized by the stage of the addiction cycle that they most likely represent. However, it is critical to note that the particular behavior being used for an animal model may or may not be symptomatic of the disorder, but it must be defined objectively and observed reliably. Indeed, the behavior being used may be found both in pathological and nonpathological states but still have predictive validity.

A good example of such a situation is the widespread use of drug reinforcement or reward as an animal model of addiction. Drug reinforcement does not necessarily lead to addiction (e.g., social drinking of alcohol). Self-administration of alcohol has major predictive validity for the *binge/intoxication* stage of addiction, and it is difficult to imagine addiction without alcohol reinforcement.

Validation of Animal Models of Drug Addiction

The most relevant conceptualization of validity for animal models of addiction has been argued to be the concept of *construct validity*.[4] Construct validity refers to the interpretability, "meaningfulness," or explanatory power of each animal model and incorporates most other measures of validity in which multiple measures or dimensions are associated with conditions known to affect the construct.[5] An alternative conceptualization of construct validity is the requirement that models meet the construct of functional equivalence, defined as "assessing how controlling variables influence outcome in the model and the target disorders."[6] The most efficient process for evaluating functional equivalence has been argued to be through common experimental manipulations that should have similar effects in the animal model and the target disorder.[6] This process is very similar to the broad use of *predictive validity*, which refers to the model's ability to lead to accurate predictions about the human phenomenon based on the response of the model system. *Face validity* is often the starting point in animal models in which animal syndromes are produced that resemble those found in humans to study selected parts of the human syndrome but is limited by necessity.[7] *Reliability* refers to the stability and consistency with which the variable of interest can be measured.[8] The present chapter describes animal models that have been shown to be reliable and in many cases to have construct validity for various stages of the addictive process.

ANIMAL MODELS OF THE BINGE/INTOXICATION STAGE OF THE ADDICTION CYCLE

Animals and humans will readily self-administer drugs in the nondependent state. Drugs of abuse have powerful positive reinforcing properties. Animals will perform many different tasks and procedures to obtain drugs, even when not dependent. The positive reinforcing effects of drugs are generally considered to be an important part of the beginning of the addiction cycle, and thus they are included here. The drugs that have positive reinforcing effects, measured by direct self-administration, lowering of brain stimulation reward thresholds, and conditioned place preference in rodents and primates, correspond very well with the drugs that have high abuse potential in humans.[9-11]

Intravenous Drug Self-Administration

Drugs that are self-administered by animals correspond well with those that have high abuse potential in humans, and intravenous drug self-administration has long been considered an animal model that is predictive of abuse potential.[10] Drug self-administration has also been proven to be a powerful tool for exploring the neurobiology of positive reinforcement.[12] Different schedules of reinforcement in intravenous self-administration can provide important control procedures for nonspecific motor actions, such as increases in exploratory activity and locomotion, and motivational effects, such as loss of reinforcement efficacy. Other schedules of reinforcement, referred to as second-order schedules, are used to test the motivational effects of drugs of abuse and have been proven highly useful for the study of the neuropharmacological bases of the positive reinforcing and conditioned reinforcing effects of drugs of abuse.[13] In a multiple schedule of reinforcement, self-administration is one component, and another component may involve a nondrug natural reinforcer. Behavior maintained by food or drug alternately in the same test session and with identical reinforcement requirements has been reported for various species.[14]

Oral Drug Self-Administration

Oral self-administration almost exclusively involves alcohol because of the obvious face validity of oral alcohol self-administration. Two procedures are predominantly used to explore the neurobiological basis of alcohol reinforcement: two-bottle choice and operant self-administration. Most commonly, animals are allowed free choice of drinking solutions in their home cages for successive 24 h periods with simultaneous free access to food.[15] For operant alcohol self-administration, rodents can be trained to lever press for alcohol using a variety of techniques. Many of these approaches are designed to overcome the aversive effects of initial exposure to alcohol, either by slowly increasing the concentration of alcohol or by adding a sweet solution.[16]

Brain Stimulation Reward

Animals will perform a variety of tasks to self-administer short electrical trains of stimulation (approximately 250 ms) to many different brain areas,[17] and the highest rates and preference for stimulation follow the course of the medial forebrain bundle coursing bidirectionally from the midbrain to basal forebrain.[18] The study of the neuroanatomical and neurochemical substrates of intracranial self-stimulation (ICSS) has led to the hypothesis that ICSS directly activates neuronal circuits that are activated by conventional reinforcers (e.g., food, water, sex) and that ICSS may reflect the direct electrical stimulation of the brain systems involved in motivated behavior. Drugs of abuse decrease ICSS thresholds, and there is good correspondence between the ability of drugs to decrease ICSS thresholds and their abuse potential.[19] Two ICSS procedures have been used extensively to measure changes in reward threshold and are not confounded by influences on motor/performance capability: the rate-frequency curve-shift procedure[20] and the discrete-trial, current-intensity procedure.[11]

Conditioned Place Preference

Conditioned place preference, or place conditioning, is a nonoperant procedure for assessing the reinforcing efficacy of drugs using a classical or Pavlovian conditioning procedure. In a simple version of the place preference paradigm, animals experience two distinct neutral environments that are spatially and temporally paired with distinct drug or nondrug states. The animal is then given an opportunity to choose to enter and explore either environment, and the time spent in the drug-paired environment is considered an index of the reinforcing value of the drug. This procedure assesses the conditioning of drug reinforcement and can provide indirect information regarding the positive and negative reinforcing effects of drugs.[21]

Drug Discrimination

Drug discrimination procedures in animals have provided a powerful tool for identifying the relative similarity of the stimulus effects of drugs and, by comparison with known drugs of abuse, the generation of hypotheses regarding the abuse potential of these drugs.[22] Drug discrimination typically involves training an animal to exhibit a particular response in a given drug state for a food reinforcer and to exhibit a different response for the same food reinforcer in the placebo or nondrug state. The choice of response that follows administration of an unknown test compound can provide valuable information about the similarity of that drug's interoceptive cue properties to those of the training drug. Some of the original drug discrimination procedures utilized a T-maze escape procedure.[23] More commonly, an appetitively motivated operant procedure is used in which the rat has access to two levers.[24] An alternative drug discrimination training procedure involves a discrete-trials protocol using avoidance or escape from shock. A major advantage of this aversively maintained responding is that no food restriction is necessary, with no confound from the anorexic effects of the drug.[22]

Genetic Animal Models of High Alcohol Drinking

Many genetically selected lines of rats of high versus low drinking have been developed and include University of Chile A and B rats, Alko alcohol (AA) and Alko nonalcohol (ANA) rats, University of Indiana alcohol-preferring (P) and alcohol-nonpreferring (NP) rats, University of Indiana high-alcohol-drinking (HAD) and low-alcohol-drinking (LAD) rats, and Sardinian alcohol-preferring (sP) and Sardinian-nonpreferring (sNP) rats. P rats have been the most extensively studied and provide a model of some of the most salient features of excessive alcohol consumption.[25]

Summary of Animal Models for the Binge/Intoxication Stage

The procedures outlined earlier have proven reliable and have predictive validity in their ability to understand the neurobiological basis of the acute reinforcing effects of drugs of abuse and the compulsive drug seeking associated with the *binge/intoxication* stage of the addiction cycle. Understanding the neurobiological mechanisms of the positive reinforcing actions of drugs of abuse also provides a framework for understanding the changes in motivational effects of drugs that also result from counteradaptive mechanisms. A strength of the models outlined for this stage is that any of the operant measures used as models for the reinforcing effects of drugs of abuse lend themselves to within-subjects designs, limiting the number of subjects required. Indeed, once an animal is trained, full dose–effect functions can be generated for different drugs, and the animal can be tested for weeks to months. Pharmacological manipulations can be conducted with standard reference compounds to validate any effects. Additionally, a rich literature is available for exploring the hypothetical constructs of drug action and modifications of drug reinforcement by altering the history and contingencies of reinforcement.

The advantage of the ICSS paradigm as a model of drug effects on motivation and reward is that the behavioral threshold provided by ICSS is easily quantifiable. ICSS threshold estimates are very stable over periods of several months.[26] Another considerable advantage of the ICSS technique is the high reliability with which it predicts the abuse liability of drugs. For example, a false positive has never been reported with the discrete trials threshold technique.[11]

The advantages of place conditioning include its high sensitivity to low doses of drugs, its potential utility in studying both positive and negative reinforcing stimuli, the fact that testing for drug reward is done under drug-free conditions, and its allowance for precise control over the interaction of environmental cues with drug administration.[27]

ANIMAL MODELS OF THE *DRUG WITHDRAWAL/ NEGATIVE AFFECT* STAGE OF THE ADDICTION CYCLE

Drug withdrawal from chronic drug administration is usually characterized by responses opposite to the acute initial actions of the drug. Many of these overt physical signs associated with withdrawal from drugs (e.g., alcohol and opiates) can be easily quantified and may provide a marker for the study of the neurobiological mechanisms of dependence. Withdrawal from opiates, nicotine, and alcohol has standard rating scales.[28–30] However, motivational measures of withdrawal have more validity for understanding the counteradaptive mechanisms that drive addiction.[25] Such motivational measures have been proven extremely sensitive to drug withdrawal and powerful tools for exploring the neurobiological bases for the motivational aspects of drug dependence. Animal models of the motivational effects of drug withdrawal have included operant schedules, place aversion, ICSS, the elevated plus maze, drug discrimination, and some of the same motivational measures of drug seeking used to characterize the *binge/intoxication* stage. Many of these models can address different theoretical constructs associated with a given motivational aspect of withdrawal, and some reflect more general malaise.

Intracranial Self-Stimulation, Conditioned Place Aversion, Anxiety-Like Responses, and Amotivational Response

Withdrawal from chronic administration of virtually all major drugs of abuse elevates ICSS thresholds (i.e., decreases reward) in contrast to a lowering of reward thresholds by acute drug administration.[31] The aversive stimulus effects of withdrawal can also be measured with a variant of place conditioning, termed place aversion,[32] in contrast to conditioned place preference.

A common response to acute withdrawal and protracted abstinence from all major drugs of abuse is the manifestation of anxiety-like responses. The dependent variable is often a passive response to a novel or aversive stimulus, such as the open field or elevated plus maze, or an active response to an aversive stimulus, such as defensive burying of an electrified metal probe. Withdrawal from repeated administration of cocaine, opioids, alcohol, nicotine, and Δ^9-tetrahydrocannabinol produces an anxiogenic-like response in the elevated plus maze and defensive burying test.[33–35]

The response-disruptive effects of drug withdrawal measured with operant schedules have also been associated with the "amotivational" state of withdrawal.[36,37] Similarly, drug discrimination can be used to characterize both specific and nonspecific aspects of withdrawal. For alcohol withdrawal, animals have been trained to discriminate the anxiogenic substance pentylenetetrazol from saline,[38] and generalization to the pentylenetetrazol cue during withdrawal has suggested an anxiogenic-like component of the withdrawal syndrome.

Opiate-dependent animals have been trained to discriminate an opiate antagonist from saline,[39] and generalization to an opiate antagonist provides a more general nonspecific measure of opiate withdrawal intensity and time course.[40]

Increased Drug Self-Administration Associated with Dependence

A progressive increase in the frequency and intensity of drug use is one of the major behavioral phenomena characterizing the development of addiction and has face validity with a number of *Diagnostic and Statistical Manual of Mental Disorders*, 4th edition (*DSM-IV*), criteria, but particularly with "The substance is often taken in larger amounts and over a longer period than was intended."[41] Excessive drug intake associated with withdrawal also has face validity with the criteria of "substance is taken to relieve or avoid withdrawal symptoms." A framework with which to model the transition from drug use to drug dependence can be found in recent animal models of prolonged access to drugs. When rats were allowed access to intravenous self-administration of cocaine for 6 h per day (vs. 1 h), drug intake gradually escalated over days.[42] Rats with extended access to cocaine showed an upward shift in the cocaine dose–response function, motivational withdrawal,[42,43] and increases in progressive-ratio responding.[44] Escalation has now been observed with extended access to all major drugs of abuse, including cocaine, methamphetamine, heroin, nicotine, and alcohol.[45] Escalation is also associated with an increase in breakpoint in a progressive-ratio schedule of reinforcement, suggesting enhanced motivation to seek cocaine or enhanced efficacy of drug reward.[45] Rats with extended access to cocaine or individual differences in the propensity for compulsive responding for cocaine do not suppress drug seeking in the presence of an aversive conditioned stimulus.[46,47] From a *DSM-IV* perspective, this observable may fit well with "continued substance use despite knowledge of having a persistent physical or psychological problem."

Historically, animal models of excessive alcohol self-administration in dependent animals have proven difficult, but reliable and useful models of alcohol consumption in dependent rats and mice have been developed, with the critical issue appearing to be that alcohol is first established as a reinforcer in nondependent, limited-access situations, and then the animals are made dependent. Animals are maintained through an alcohol liquid diet or continuous alcohol vapor exposure at blood alcohol levels of 100–200 mg%. When the rats were tested repeatedly following the induction of dependence, they showed reliable increases in self-administration of alcohol during withdrawal.[48] With alcohol, escalation of intake is also observed in rats given intermittent access (3 days/week on alternate days) to alcohol (20% w/v) using a two-bottle choice procedure (alcohol vs. water).[49,50] Both acamprosate and naltrexone showed increased efficacy in rats with escalation in intake.[50]

A robust and reliable feature of animal models of alcohol drinking is an increase in consumption observed after a period of deprivation. Termed the "alcohol deprivation effect," the increase in consumption has been observed in many species.[51] The alcohol deprivation effect in nondependent animals is more robust with extended access to alcohol (> 1 month) in daily limited-access situations.[52] The alcohol deprivation effect is exaggerated in alcohol-preferring rats in which deprivations can increase intake by 200%–300% and over more prolonged periods.[53]

Summary of Animal Models of the Withdrawal/Negative Affect Stage

Motivational measures of drug withdrawal have significant face validity for the motivational measures of drug withdrawal in humans. Symptoms of dysphoria, elements of anhedonia, loss of motivation, anxiety, and irritability are reflected in the animal models described earlier. Additionally, ICSS threshold procedures have high predictive validity for changes in reward valence. Disruption of operant responding during drug abstinence reflects, at a minimum, general malaise, and drug discrimination allows a powerful and sensitive comparison to other drug states. Both procedures provide a basis for further testing. Place aversion is hypothesized to reflect an aversive unconditioned stimulus. As more and more data are generated, thus establishing the neurobiological bases for negative emotional states in animals that correspond to the neurobiological bases for such negative emotional states in humans, these measures will gain construct validity.[54]

The studies outlined in this section illustrate how animal models of addiction have progressed from simple drug reinforcement models to sophisticated models with robust face validity. Escalation in drug intake with extended access has now been observed in numerous laboratories.[55] Thus,

increased drug taking during dependence has been well established with alcohol, cocaine, methamphetamine, heroin, and nicotine and can produce intake sufficient to maintain dependence. Such excessive drug intake has been construct validated as "compulsive" with measures such as increased responding on a progressive-ratio schedule and persistent responding in the face of punishment.

The animal models associated with responding in the face of punishment and the progressive-ratio schedule have both face and construct validity. Numerous studies in humans argue that individuals meeting the criteria for substance dependence will work harder to obtain drugs and as such show increased motivation for drug taking. The behavioral repertoire narrows for drug seeking and taking. Indeed, progressive-ratio studies in humans show patterns of responding that are similar to the animals models.[56] Clearly, responding in the face of punishment and progressive-ratio responding in rodents show individual differences reflecting the same degree of individual differences in the human population.[47] From a construct validity perspective, responding in the face of punishment and progressive-ratio paradigms predict the key role of the midbrain dopamine systems in the reinforcing effects of cocaine.[57] Second-order schedules of a well-established cocaine "habit" revealed a key role for dorsal striatal mechanisms in the increased motivation to work for cocaine.[58]

ANIMAL MODELS OF THE PREOCCUPATION/ ANTICIPATION STAGE OF THE ADDICTION CYCLE

A defining characteristic of addiction is its chronic, relapsing nature. Animal models of relapse fall into three categories of a broad-based conditioning construct: drug-induced reinstatement, cue-induced reinstatement, and stress-induced reinstatement. The general conceptual framework for the conditioning construct is that cues, either internal or external, become associated with the reinforcing actions of a drug or drug abstinence by means of classical conditioning and then can elicit drug use. Human studies have shown that the presentation of stimuli previously associated with drug delivery or drug withdrawal increases the likelihood of relapse as well as self-reports of craving and motivation to engage in drug taking.[59,60] Environmental cues or a drug-predictive discriminative stimulus repeatedly paired with primary reinforcers can acquire reinforcing properties via classical conditioning processes,[61] and these conditioned reinforcing effects have been hypothesized to contribute to drug craving and relapse. Moreover, the response-contingent conditioned stimulus, acting as a conditioned reinforcer, may contribute to the maintenance of subsequent drug-seeking behavior once it is initiated.

Drug-Induced Reinstatement

When noncontingent drug injections are administered after extinction, they produce an increase in responding on the lever that previously delivered drug, and this responding is termed drug-primed reinstatement.[62] After priming with the drug, the latency to reinitiate responding or the amount of responding on the previously extinguished lever is used to reflect the motivation for drug-seeking behavior. Systemic injections of compounds of drug classes other than the training drug are generally less effective in reinstating drug self-administration behavior.[62] The effectiveness of compounds in reinstating drug self-administration decreases as their discriminative stimulus similarity to the training drug decreases.

Cue-Induced Reinstatement

Formerly neutral environmental stimuli or contexts that have been repeatedly associated with drug self-administration or drug administration can acquire reinforcing properties. Cues paired with drug self-administration can reliably and robustly reinstate responding after extinction.[61] Animals are trained to self-administer cocaine or other drugs of abuse via an operant response, usually lever pressing, with a cue that precedes and is continuous with the delivery of the drug. Following stable responding, the animal is subjected to extinction in which lever pressing delivers no drug or cue. In the reinstatement sessions, the animal is allowed to respond for the cue alone. This procedure is widely used for exploring the neurobiological substrates of "relapse."[61] Place conditioning can also be used as a model of cue-induced reinstatement. Conditioned place preference is induced by a drug, extinction is conducted, and then conditioned place preference is again induced by a priming injection.[63]

Context-Induced Reinstatement: "Renewal"

Drug-associated stimuli that signal response-contingent availability of intravenous cocaine versus saline[64] also reliably elicit drug-seeking behavior in experimental animals, and responding for these stimuli is highly resistant to extinction.[64] Another variant of context-induced reinstatement involves reinstatement of drug seeking by an explicit environment that has been paired with drug administration or drug self-administration.[65] Animals acquire self-administration in the presence of a distinct set of environmental stimuli (drug-paired context) that signify the availability of the drug. Drug-reinforced behavior is then subjected to extinction in a different context (extinction context). Reexposure to the drug context then reinstates drug seeking.[65]

Cue-Induced Reinstatment without Extinction: "Relapse"

Another model of drug seeking, termed a "relapse" model, is one in which animals undergo cue-induced exposure following forced abstinence from chronic self-administration without extinction outside of the testing cage.[66] This paradigm is based on the well-established "incubation effect" in which cocaine seeking induced by reexposure to drug-associated cues progressively increases over the first 2 months after withdrawal from cocaine self-administration.[67] Thus, cues paired with drugs robustly increase cocaine seeking after abstinence without extinction. This paradigm has face validity for the human condition because individuals with drug addiction rarely experience explicit extinction of drug seeking related to drug-paired cues.

Stress-Induced Reinstatement

In human studies, situations of stress are the most likely triggers for relapse to drug taking.[68] Animal models of stress-induced reinstatement show that stressors elicit strong recovery of extinguished drug-seeking behavior in the absence of further drug availability.[69] Stressors shown to be effective in reinstating drug seeking include foot shock, food deprivation, restraint stress, tail-pinch stress, swim stress, conditioned fear, social defeat stress, and pharmacological agents, such as α2 noradrenergic receptor antagonists.

Second-Order Schedules of Reinforcement

As noted earlier, second-order schedules of reinforcement involve training animals to work for a previously neutral stimulus that ultimately predicts drug availability.[13] Responses occurring before any drug administration can be used as measures of the conditioned reinforcing properties of drugs. Second-order schedules maintain high rates of responding (e.g., thousands of responses per session in monkeys) and extended sequences of behavior before any drug administration. Thus, potentially disruptive, nonspecific, acute drug and treatment effects on response rates are minimized. High response rates are maintained even for doses that decrease rates during a session on a regular fixed-ratio schedule, indicating that performance on the second-order schedule is unaffected by those acute effects of the drug that disrupt operant responding.[70]

Protracted Abstinence

In human alcoholics, numerous symptoms that can be characterized as components of negative affect can persist long after acute physical withdrawal from drugs and has been termed "protracted abstinence."[71] Relapse to drugs of abuse often occurs even after physical and motivational withdrawal signs have ceased, suggesting perhaps that the neurochemical changes that occur during the development of dependence can persist beyond the overt signs of acute withdrawal. Indeed, animal work has shown that prior dependence lowers the "dependence threshold," such that previously alcohol-dependent animals made dependent again display more severe withdrawal symptoms than groups receiving alcohol for the first time.[72] In rodents, persistent alterations in alcohol self-administration and residual sensitivity to stressors have been arbitrarily defined as a state of "protracted abstinence." Protracted abstinence so defined in the rat spans a period after acute physical withdrawal has disappeared in which elevations in alcohol intake over baseline and increased stress responsivity persist 2–8 weeks after withdrawal from chronic alcohol.[73,74]

Animal Models of Conditioned Withdrawal

Motivational aspects of withdrawal can also be conditioned, and conditioned withdrawal has been repeatedly observed in opiate-dependent animals and humans.[60] Paradigms demonstrating the motivational significance of conditioned withdrawal have also been shown in monkeys and rats.[75] A cue paired with repeated administration of an opioid antagonist elicited increased intravenous self-administration similar to that observed with naloxone alone.[75,76] These results are a powerful demonstration of the negative reinforcing properties of antagonist-precipitated drug withdrawal.

Summary of Animal Models of the Preoccupation/Anticipation Stage

Each of the models outlined thus far has face validity to the human condition and ideally heuristic value for understanding the neurobiological bases for different aspects of the craving stage of the addiction cycle. The *DSM-IV* criteria that apply to the craving stage and loss of control over drug intake include "any unsuccessful effort or persistent desire to cut down or control substance use." The reinstatement procedure can be a reliable indicator of the ability of conditioned stimuli to reinitiate drug-seeking behavior. A second-order schedule has the advantage of assessing the motivational value of a drug infusion in the absence of acute effects of the self-administered drug that could influence performance or other processes that interfere with motivational functions. For example, nonspecific effects of manipulations administered before the stimulus-drug pairings do not directly affect the assessment of the motivational value of the stimuli because the critical test can be conducted several days after the stimulus drug pairings. Moreover, the paradigm contains a built-in control for nonspecific motor effects of a manipulation by its assessment of the number of responses on an inactive lever.

The specificity of conditioning in animal models may have predictive validity with the specificity of conditioned responses in human drug users. An experimental study in human drug users indicated that cocaine-related stimuli were effective in eliciting conditioned physiological responses and self-reported cocaine craving in cocaine users but not in opiate or non–drug users. Furthermore, self-reported cocaine withdrawal-related or neutral stimuli were ineffective in eliciting any conditioned responses.[77] This effect has been confirmed in animal studies. Thus, the noncontingent presentation of drug-paired stimuli, in the absence of drug infusions, also can reinstate drug-seeking behavior after a period of extinction.[78] In addition to general physiological responses, conditioned stimuli associated with drug administration also induce the "psychological" phenomenon of drug craving in humans, even after a period of abstinence.[59,79]

The animal models for the conditioned negative reinforcing effects of drugs are reliable measures and have good face validity. Work in this area, however, has largely been restricted to the opiate field, where competitive antagonists reliably precipitate a withdrawal syndrome. There is general consensus that the animal reinstatement models have face validity.[6,80] However, predictive validity remains to be established. To date, there is some predictive validity for the stimuli that elicit reinstatement in the animal models, but there is little evidence of predictive validity from studies of the pharmacological treatments for drug relapse.[6] Very few clinical trials have tested medications that are effective in the reinstatement model, and very few antirelapse medications have been tested in the animal models of reinstatement. From the perspective of functional equivalence or construct validity, there is some evidence of functional commonalities. For example, drug reexposure or priming, stressors, and cues paired with drugs all produce reinstatement in animal models and promote relapse in humans.

SUMMARY
Most of the animal models discussed in this chapter have predictive validity for some components of the addiction cycle (compulsive use, withdrawal, or craving) and are reliable. For the positive reinforcing effects of drugs, drug self-administration, ICSS, and conditioned place preference have been shown to have predictive validity. Drug discrimination has predictive validity indirectly through generalization to the training drug. Animal models of withdrawal with construct validity involve motivational constructs as opposed to the physical or somatic signs of withdrawal. Animal models of conditioned drug effects are successful in predicting the potential for conditioned drug effects in humans. Predictive validity is more problematic for such concepts as craving, largely because of the inadequate formulation of the concept of "craving" in humans.[81] Virtually all of the measures described herein have demonstrated reliability. Consistency and stability of the measures, small within-subject and between-subject variability, and reproducibility of the phenomenon are characteristic of most of the measures employed in animal models of dependence.

Clearly, much remains to be explored about the face validity and predictive validity of unconditioned positive and negative motivational states, particularly the conditioned positive and negative motivational states associated with drug use and withdrawal. However, particularly important

for the study of the neurobiology of addiction is that animal models have moved away from simple measures of drug reinforcement to measures with strong face validity for the "observable symptoms" of addiction. What remains to be accomplished is to show that both construct validity (functional equivalence) and predictive validity exist for these models. A further challenge for future studies will be the development of "endophenotypes" that cross from animal to human species that will allow further construct validity (functional equivalence) for studies of genetic and environmental vulnerability and the neurobiological mechanisms therein.

ACKNOWLEDGMENTS
This is publication number 20797 from The Scripps Research Institute. Preparation of this chapter was supported by the Pearson Center for Alcoholism and Addiction Research and National Institutes of Health grants AA06420 and AA08459 from the National Institute on Alcohol Abuse and Alcoholism; DA023597, DA04043, and DA04398 from the National Institute on Drug Abuse; and DK26741 from the National Institute of Diabetes and Digestive and Kidney Diseases. The author would like to thank Michael Arends and Mellany Santos for assistance with manuscript preparation.

REFERENCES
1. Koob GF, Le Moal M. Drug abuse: hedonic homeostatic dysregulation. Science 1997;278:52–58.
2. Geyer M, Markou A. Animal models of psychiatric disorders. In: Bloom F, Kupfer D, eds. Psychopharmacology: The Fourth Generation of Progress. New York: Raven Press; 1995:787–798.
3. Koob GF, Sanna PP, Bloom FE. Neuroscience of addiction. Neuron 1998;21:467–476.
4. Ebel R. Must all tests be valid? Am Psychol 1961;16:640–647.
5. Sayette MA, Shiffman S, Tiffany ST, Niaura RS, Martin CS, Shadel WG. The measurement of drug craving. Addiction 2000;95(suppl 2):S189–S210.
6. Katz JL, Higgins ST. The validity of the reinstatement model of craving and relapse to drug use. Psychopharmacol (Berl) 2003;168:21–30.
7. McKinney WT. Models of Mental Disorders: A New Comparative Psychiatry. New York: Plenum; 1988.
8. Geyer M, Markou A. The role of preclinical models in the development of psychotropic drugs. In: Davis K, Charney D, JT C, Nemeroff C, eds. Neuropsychopharmacology: The Fifth Generation of Progress. New York: Lippincott Williams and Wilkins; 2002:445–455.

9. Carr GD, Fibiger HC, Phillips AG. Conditioned place preference as a measure of drug reward. In: Liebman J, Cooper S, eds. *The Neuropharmacological Basis of Reward*. New York: Oxford University Press; 1989:264–319.

10. Collins RJ, Weeks JR, Cooper MM, Good PI, Russell RR. Prediction of abuse liability of drugs using IV self-administration by rats. *Psychopharmacol (Berl)* 1984;82:6–13.

11. Kornetsky C, Esposito RU. Euphorigenic drugs: effects on the reward pathways of the brain. *Fed Proc* 1979;38:2473–2476.

12. Koob GF, Goeders NE. Neuroanatomical substrates of drug self-administration. In: Liebman J, Cooper S, eds. *The Neuropharmacological Basis of Reward*. Oxford, England: Clarendon Press; 1989:214–263.

13. Katz JL, Goldberg SR. Second-order schedules of drug injection: implications for understanding reinforcing effects of abused drugs. *Adv Sub Abuse* 1991;4:205–223.

14. Caine SB, Koob GF. Effects of mesolimbic dopamine depletion on responding maintained by cocaine and food. *J Exp Anal Behav* 1994;61:213–221.

15. Rhodes JS, Best K, Belknap JK, Finn DA, Crabbe JC. Evaluation of a simple model of ethanol drinking to intoxication in C57BL/6J mice. *Physiol Behav* 2005;84:53–63.

16. Samson HH. Initiation of ethanol reinforcement using a sucrose-substitution procedure in food- and water-sated rats. *Alcohol Clin Exp Res* 1986;10:436–442.

17. Olds J, Milner P. Positive reinforcement produced by electrical stimulation of septal area and other regions of rat brain. *J Comp Physiol Psychol* 1954;47:419–427.

18. Gallistel CR, Davis AJ. Affinity for the dopamine D2 receptor predicts neuroleptic potency in blocking the reinforcing effect of MFB stimulation. *Pharmacol Biochem Behav* 1983;19:867–872.

19. Kornetsky C, Bain G. Brain-stimulation reward: a model for durg induced euphoria. In: Adler M, Cowan A, eds. *Testing and Evaluation of Drugs of Abuse*. New York: Wiley-Liss; 1990:211–231.

20. Campbell KA, Evans G, Gallistel CR. A microcomputer-based method for physiologically interpretable measurement of the rewarding efficacy of brain stimulation. *Physiol Behav* 1985;35:395–403.

21. Carboni E, Vacca C. Conditioned place preference: a simple method for investigating reinforcing properties in laboratory animals. In: Wang J, ed. *Drugs of Abuse: Neurological Reviews and Protocols*. Totowa, NJ: Humana Press; 2003:481–498.

22. Holtzman SG. Discriminative stimulus effects of drugs: relationship to potential for abuse. In: Adler M, Cowan A, eds. *Testing and Evaluation of Drugs of Abuse*. New York: Wiley; 1990:193–210.

23. Overton DA. Experimental methods for the study of state-dependent learning. *Fed Proc* 1974;33:1800–1813.

24. Colpaert FC, Lal H, Niemegeers CJ, Janssen PA. Investigations on drug produced and subjectively experienced discriminative stimuli. I. The fentanyl cue, a tool to investigate subjectively experience narcotic drug actions. *Life Sci* 1975;16:705–715.

25. Koob GF, Le Moal M. *Neurobiology of Addiction*. London: Academic Press; 2006.

26. Stellar JR, Stellar E. *The Neurobiology of Motivation and Reward*. New York: Springer-Verlag; 1985.

27. Mucha RF, van der Kooy D, O'Shaughnessy M, Bucenieks P. Drug reinforcement studied by the use of place conditioning in rat. *Brain Res* 1982;243:91–105.

28. Macey DJ, Schulteis G, Heinrichs SC, Koob GF. Time-dependent quantifiable withdrawal from ethanol in the rat: effect of method of dependence induction. *Alcohol* 1996;13:163–170.

29. Malin DH, Lake JR, Newlin-Maultsby P, et al. Rodent model of nicotine abstinence syndrome. *Pharmacol Biochem Behav* 1992;43:779–784.

30. Gellert VF, Holtzman SG. Development and maintenance of morphine tolerance and dependence in the rat by scheduled access to morphine drinking solutions. *J Pharmacol Exp Ther* 1978;205:536–546.

31. Koob GF. Alcoholism: allostasis and beyond. *Alcohol Clin Exp Res* 2003;27:232–243.

32. Stinus L, Le Moal M, Koob GF. Nucleus accumbens and amygdala are possible substrates for the aversive stimulus effects of opiate withdrawal. *Neuroscience* 1990;37:767–773.

33. Koob GF. The role of animal models in reward deficit disorders: views from academia. In: McArthur R, Borsini F, eds. *Animal and Translational Models of CNS Drug Discovery: Vol. 3, Reward Deficit Disorders*. London: Academic Press; 2008:59–89.

34. Sarnyai Z, Biro E, Gardi J, Vecsernyes M, Julesz J, Telegdy G. Brain corticotropin-releasing factor mediates "anxiety-like" behavior induced by cocaine withdrawal in rats. *Brain Res* 1995;675:89–97.

35. Basso AM, Spina M, Rivier J, Vale W, Koob GF. Corticotropin-releasing factor antagonist attenuates the "anxiogenic-like" effect in the defensive burying paradigm but not in the elevated plus-maze following chronic cocaine in rats. *Psychopharmacol (Berl)* 1999;145:21–30.

36. Denoble U, Begleiter H. Response supression on a mixed schedule of reinforcement during alcohol withdrawal. *Pharmacol Biochem Behav* 1976;5:227–229.

37. Gellert VF, Sparber SB. A comparison of the effects of naloxone upon body weight loss and suppression of fixed-ratio operant behavior in morphine-dependent rats. *J Pharmacol Exp Ther* 1977;201:44–54.

38. Gauvin DV, Holloway FA. Cue dimensionality in the three-choice pentylenetetrazole-saline-chlordiazepoxide discrimination task. *Behav Pharmacol* 1991;2:417–428.

39. Emmett-Oglesby MW, Mathis DA, Moon RT, Lal H. Animal models of drug withdrawal symptoms. *Psychopharmacol (Berl)* 1990;101:292–309.

40. Gellert VF, Holtzman SG. Discriminative stimulus effects of naltrexone in the morphine-dependent rat. *J Pharmacol Exp Ther* 1979;211:596–605.

41. American Psychiatric Association. *Diagnostic and Statistical Manual of Mental Disorders.* 4th ed. Washington, DC: American Psychiatric Press; 1994.

42. Ahmed SH, Koob GF. Transition from moderate to excessive drug intake: change in hedonic set point. *Science* 1998;282:298–300.

43. Ahmed SH, Kenny PJ, Koob GF, Markou A. Neurobiological evidence for hedonic allostasis associated with escalating cocaine use. *Nat Neurosci* 2002;5:625–626.

44. Wee S, Mandyam CD, Lekic DM, Koob GF. Alpha 1-noradrenergic system role in increased motivation for cocaine intake in rats with prolonged access. *Eur Neuropsychopharmacol* 2008;18:303–311.

45. Koob GF. Neurobiological substrates for the dark side of compulsivity in addiction. *Neuropharmacol* 2009;56(suppl 1):18–31.

46. Vanderschuren LJ, Everitt BJ. Drug seeking becomes compulsive after prolonged cocaine self-administration. *Science* 2004;305:1017–1019.

47. Deroche-Gamonet V, Belin D, Piazza PV. Evidence for addiction-like behavior in the rat. *Science* 2004;305:1014–1017.

48. Gilpin NW, Koob GF. Neurobiology of alcohol dependence: focus on motivational mechanisms. *Alcohol Res Health* 2008;31:185–195.

49. Wise RA. Voluntary ethanol intake in rats following exposure to ethanol on various schedules. *Psychopharmacologia* 1973;29:203–210.

50. Simms JA, Steensland P, Medina B, et al. Intermittent access to 20% ethanol induces high ethanol consumption in Long-Evans and Wistar rats. *Alcohol Clin Exp Res* 2008;32:1816–1823.

51. Heyser C, Schulteis G, Koob GF. The alcohol deprivation effect: experimental conditions, applications, and treatment. In: Hannigan J, Spear L, Spear N, Goodlett C, eds. *Alcohol and Alcoholism: Effects on Brain and Development.* Mahwah, NJ: Lawrence Erlbaum; 1999:161–176.

52. Heyser CJ, Schulteis G, Koob GF. Increased ethanol self-administration after a period of imposed ethanol deprivation in rats trained in a limited access paradigm. *Alcohol Clin Exp Res* 1997;21:784–791.

53. Rodd-Henricks ZA, Bell RL, Kuc KA, et al. Effects of concurrent access to multiple ethanol concentrations and repeated deprivations on alcohol intake of alcohol-preferring rats. *Alcohol Clin Exp Res* 2001;25:1140–1150.

54. Koob GF, Volkow ND. Neurocircuitry of addiction. *Neuropsychopharmacol* 2010;35:217–238.

55. Ahmed SH, Koob GF. Transition to drug addiction: a negative reinforcement model based on an allostatic decrease in reward function. *Psychopharmacol (Berl)* 2005;180:473–490.

56. Stoops WW. Reinforcing effects of stimulants in humans: sensitivity of progressive-ratio schedules. *Exp Clin Psychopharmacol* 2008;16:503–512.

57. Roberts DC, Loh EA, Vickers G. Self-administration of cocaine on a progressive ratio schedule in rats: dose-response relationship and effect of haloperidol pretreatment. *Psychopharmacol (Berl)* 1989;97:535–538.

58. Belin D, Everitt BJ. Cocaine seeking habits depend upon dopamine-dependent serial connectivity linking the ventral with the dorsal striatum. *Neuron* 2008;57:432–441.

59. Childress A, McLellan A, Ehrman R, O'Brien C. Classically conditioned responses in opioid and cocaine dependence: a role in relapse? In: Ray B, ed. *Learning Factors in Substance Abuse.* Rockville, MD: National Institute on Drug Abuse; 1988:25–43.

60. O'Brien CP, Testa T, O'Brien TJ, Brady JP, Wells B. Conditioned narcotic withdrawal in humans. *Science* 1977;195:1000–1002.

61. Shaham Y, Shalev U, Lu L, De Wit H, Stewart J. The reinstatement model of drug relapse: history, methodology and major findings. *Psychopharmacol (Berl)* 2003;168:3–20.

62. Stewart J, de Wit H. Reinstatement of drug-taking behavior as a method of assessing incentive motivational properties of drugs. In: Bozarth M, ed. *Methods of Assessing the Reinforcing Properties of Abused Drugs.* New York: Springer-Verlag; 1987:211–227.

63. Mueller D, Stewart J. Cocaine-induced conditioned place preference: reinstatement by priming injections of cocaine after extinction. *Behav Brain Res* 2000;115:39–47.

64. Weiss F, Maldonado-Vlaar CS, Parsons LH, Kerr TM, Smith DL, Ben-Shahar O. Control of cocaine-seeking behavior by drug-associated stimuli in rats: effects on recovery of extinguished operant-responding and extracellular dopamine levels in amygdala and nucleus accumbens. *Proc Natl Acad Sci USA* 2000;97:4321–4326.

65. Crombag HS, Bossert JM, Koya E, Shaham Y. Review. Context-induced relapse to drug seeking: a review. *Philos Trans R Soc Lond B Biol Sci* 2008;363:3233–3243.

66. Yahyavi-Firouz-Abadi N, See RE. Anti-relapse medications: preclinical models for drug addiction treatment. *Pharmacol Ther* 2009;124:235–247.

67. Lu L, Grimm JW, Hope BT, Shaham Y. Incubation of cocaine craving after withdrawal: a review of preclinical data. *Neuropharmacol* 2004;47 (suppl 1):214–26.

68. Brown SA, Vik PW, Patterson TL, Grant I, Schuckit MA. Stress, vulnerability and adult alcohol relapse. *J Stud Alcohol* 1995;56:538–545.

69. Shalev U, Highfield D, Yap J, Shaham Y. Stress and relapse to drug seeking in rats: studies on the generality of the effect. *Psychopharmacol (Berl)* 2000; 150:337–46.

70. Katz JL, Goldberg SR. Second-order schedules of drug injection. In: Bozarth M, ed. *Methods of Assessing the Reinforcing Properties of Abused Drugs.* New York: Springer-Verlag; 1987:105–115.

71. Mason BJ, Ritvo EC, Morgan RO, et al. A double-blind, placebo-controlled pilot study to evaluate the efficacy and safety of oral nalmefene HCl for alcohol dependence. *Alcohol Clin Exp Res* 1994;18:1162–1167.

72. Becker HC. Positive relationship between the number of prior ethanol withdrawal episodes and the severity of subsequent withdrawal seizures. *Psychopharmacol (Berl)* 1994;116:26–32.

73. Valdez GR, Zorrilla EP, Roberts AJ, Koob GF. Antagonism of corticotropin-releasing factor attenuates the enhanced responsiveness to stress observed during protracted ethanol abstinence. *Alcohol* 2003;29:55–60.

74. Roberts AJ, Heyser CJ, Cole M, Griffin P, Koob GF. Excessive ethanol drinking following a history of dependence: animal model of allostasis. *Neuropsychopharmacol* 2000;22:581–594.

75. Goldberg SR, Woods JH, Schuster CR. Morphine: conditioned increases in self-administration in rhesus monkeys. *Science* 1969;166:1306–1307.

76. Kenny PJ, Chen SA, Kitamura O, Markou A, Koob GF. Conditioned withdrawal drives heroin consumption and decreases reward sensitivity. *J Neurosci* 2006;26:5894–5900.

77. Ehrman RN, Robbins SJ, Childress AR, O'Brien CP. Conditioned responses to cocaine-related stimuli in cocaine abuse patients. *Psychopharmacol (Berl)* 1992;107:523–529.

78. de Wit H, Stewart J. Reinstatement of cocaine-reinforced responding in the rat. *Psychopharmacol (Berl)* 1981;75:134–143.

79. McLellan AT, Childress AR, Ehrman R, O'Brien CP, Pashko S. Extinguishing conditioned responses during opiate dependence treatment turning laboratory findings into clinical procedures. *J Subst Abuse Treat* 1986;3:33–40.

80. Epstein DH, Preston KL, Stewart J, Shaham Y. Toward a model of drug relapse: an assessment of the validity of the reinstatement procedure. *Psychopharmacol (Berl)* 2006;189:1–16.

81. Tiffany ST, Carter BL, Singleton EG. Challenges in the manipulation, assessment and interpretation of craving relevant variables. *Addiction* 2000;95(suppl 2): S177–S187.

2

Human Laboratory Models of Addiction

BARBARA J. MASON AND AMANDA E. HIGLEY

Palatable food and drugs compete for similar neurotransmitter receptors. This has led to the theory that excessive food consumption may be conceptualized as an addictive behavior.[1,2] Neuroimaging and animal models have demonstrated that excessive food consumption is associated with neurobiological changes in the opiate and dopaminergic systems that parallel changes caused by drugs of abuse.[1,3] Many of the closest connections between food and addictive substances have been drawn between alcohol and high-fat, high-sugar foods. In addition to producing behavioral reinforcement through the same neurobiological pathway, both high-fat sweets and alcohol are frequently used to regulate emotions.[4,5] Research on human eating habits has also found behavioral evidence that maps onto substance dependence criteria such as loss of control, continued use despite negative consequences, and an inability to reduce consumption of calorie-dense foods.[2]

Alcohol use disorders make up the most prevalent category of substance use disorders in the United States, affecting over 18 million Americans.[6] *The Diagnostic and Statistical Manual of Mental Disorders*, fourth edition (*DSM-IV*) characterizes alcohol dependence as a maladaptive pattern of drinking leading to clinically significant impairment, as manifested by a compulsion to drink, a lack of control over the amount of alcohol consumed, and continued drinking despite knowledge of having a persistent physical or psychological problem.[7] Alcoholism is a chronic relapsing disorder that has several stages that contribute to excessive drinking and dependence. Relapse, or the return to alcohol abuse following periods of abstinence, is one of the principal characteristics of dependence on alcohol. Chronic alcohol abuse has been associated with changes in stress and reward pathways that can increase vulnerability to emotional stress and alcohol craving.[8] In human alcoholics, numerous symptoms that can be characterized as "negative affect" persist long after acute physical withdrawal from alcohol. Fatigue and tension have been reported to persist up to 5 weeks post withdrawal[9,10]; anxiety has been shown to persist up to 9 months[11]; and, in 20%–25% of alcoholics, symptoms of anxiety and depression have been shown to persist up to 2 years post withdrawal.[11] These postacute withdrawal symptoms (protracted abstinence) tend to be affective in nature, subsyndromal, and often precede relapses.[12,13]

The addiction cycle can be generally conceptualized as having three components: the preoccupation/anticipation stage, the binge/intoxication stage, and the withdrawal/negative affect stage.[14] The three stages interact with each other, with the withdrawal/negative affect component becoming more intense as the addictive behavior moves from impulsive to compulsive. During the withdrawal/negative affect stage, negative reinforcement mechanisms are in effect rather than positive reinforcement mechanisms. As such, individuals will often take the addictive substance to relieve emotional withdrawal states such as anxiety, irritability or dysphoria, or to self-medicate the negative affect or general malaise. Human laboratory studies provide a powerful means of exploring pharmacological treatment targets for each stage of the addiction cycle prior to the conduct of expensive, double-blind, placebo-controlled clinical trials. Moreover, human laboratory studies can potentially identify efficacy measures for clinical trials of prospective pharmacotherapies for each stage of the addiction cycle and can be extended to investigate real-world constructs such as vulnerability to addiction, impulsivity, craving, and resistance to relapse.

For the binge intoxication phase of the addiction cycle, human laboratory models using self-administration procedures for alcohol, cocaine, heroin, marijuana, and food have been established using operant procedures in which dependent participants make a behavioral response such as pressing a computer key to receive a drug or other substance.[15,16] These self-administration procedures involve administering the addictive substance in the same manner in which it is abused, utilizing different schedules of reinforcement (i.e., choice procedures, fixed or progressive ratio). Impulsivity, which is an important component of the binge/intoxication phase of addiction, can also be examined in the human laboratory paradigms. Impulsivity contributes to an increased likelihood of engaging in initial drug intake, and it may provoke relapse in dependent individuals.[17] Commonly used behavioral measures of impulsivity include the delayed discounting task, where participants must choose between smaller, immediate rewards over larger delayed rewards and the Stop Task,[18] which is a measure of impulse control and reaction time. Importantly, acute and chronic administration of drugs of abuse produce effects on delayed discounting and behavioral inhibition that demonstrate impaired impulse control.[17]

Three major factors are hypothesized to contribute to relapse: priming dose of drug, drug-associated cues, and exposure to stress. Several human laboratory procedures have been developed to reflect these aspects of craving in the preoccupation/anticipation stage. A well-studied model of the drug-associated cue component of craving is the cue-reactivity paradigm. In the cue-reactivity paradigm psychological and physiological reactivity to stimuli associated with drug-taking behavior are measured. Developed initially with nicotine, craving states have been measured that are associated with presentation of cues for smoking, alcohol, and cocaine.[19] Exposure to stimuli or cues associated with drug consumption produces urges to take the drug, conditioned appetitive responses, and changes in autonomic responses. These paradigms link exteroceptive cues such as the sight and smell of alcohol, with interoceptive cues such as affective mood. Exposure to alcohol cues, such as the sight and smell of alcoholic beverages, reliably increases the urge to drink alcohol, increases salivation, and increases attention to cues.[20] This response set is known as cue reactivity and has been found to be more intense in alcoholics than nonalcoholics.[21] Increased reactivity and urge to drink have been found when alcoholics are exposed to their usual

alcoholic beverage in laboratory settings.[19] A relationship has been found between the measure of reactivity and subsequent drinking, which lends support for the predictive validity of cue reactivity as an analog for clinical outcomes.[20,22,23] Moreover, cue reactivity can predict treatment outcome[23] and has been validated in some cases using medications that successfully treat alcoholism. For example, naltrexone, but not toprimate, blocks cue reactivity in alcohol-dependent subjects.[20,24]

The human laboratory model includes measures of reactivity to alcohol and affective cues as analogs of high-risk situations and that can be combined with measures of drinking, mood, and sleep under natural conditions. A real-world aspect to cue reactivity is the association between drug intake, cues in the environment, and vulnerability for addiction. Prior work has shown that subjective and physiological reactivity to the sight and smell of alcohol (i.e., exteroceptive cues) is enhanced by induction of affective states. During the withdrawal/negative affect stage of addiction, individuals are likely to take drugs to relieve the emotional withdrawal state. Individuals self-administer drugs or alcohol to self-medicate the malaise or negative affect associated with protracted abstinence. Using this information, Mason et al (2008)[25] developed a novel approach to study craving in alcoholics during protracted abstinence in which non-treatment-seeking, alcohol-dependent subjects are exposed to affective stimuli that have either positive or negative valence and then are immediately exposed to a beverage cue. A key aspect of the cue-induced paradigm is exposure to alcohol cues (sight and smell of the subject's favorite alcoholic beverage) without the opportunity for consumption. Human models of alcohol cue reactivity use a laboratory setting to re-create risk conditions for relapse similar to those experienced by alcoholics in their natural environment.[26]

The highly standardized human cue reactivity model (Mason et al., 2008)[25] permits sensitive and systematic evaluations of effects of medications on affective states and drinking urges, alone and in combination, that have been reliably associated with drinking relapse. The presence of an alcoholic beverage is an important contributor to relapse,[27] but exposure to alcohol alone does not reflect the emotional factors often associated with relapse. Relapse studies identify negative and positive affective states as the most prevalent relapse precipitants.[27,28] Induction of negative affective states in the cue exposure laboratory has been associated with increased reactivity,[22,29–31] and shorter time to relapse.[23] Positive affective states have also been induced in the laboratory and although less effective than negative states, were associated with significantly greater urges to relapse than neutral affective states.[32]

Using this paradigm, Mason et al. (2008)[25] exposed a sample of non-treatment-seeking alcohol-dependent subjects to affective stimuli that had positive or negative valence and then to a beverage cue, but with no opportunity to self-administer alcohol. Cue reactivity was measured using subjective measures of craving, measures of emotional reactivity, and psychophysiological measures. Both alcohol and the positive or negative valence had the expected effects on subjective and emotional reactivity. Treatment with gabapentin (a calcium channel/GABA modulator) significantly decreased subjective craving and craving that was affectively evoked and improved several measures of sleep quality. Taken together, these results suggest that affective priming, combined with alcohol cue exposure, provides a powerful means to evaluate potential pharmacotherapies for the negative affect and preoccupation/craving phase (i.e., protracted abstinence) of addiction treatment.

Self-administration of alcohol in the laboratory is a useful tool to study effects of potential pharmacotherapies for the binge/intoxication phase of addiction. In one design, subjects are presented with a tray of alcoholic drinks and are invited to consume as many of them as they like, or to receive monetary compensation for each drink they reject. Thus, the total number of drinks, or blood alcohol concentration (BAC), is the outcome measure. This type of experiment is presumably influenced by several distinct factors that may not be affected by drug, including sensitivity and tolerance to alcohol, maintenance or loss of control, taste preferences, personality traits such as impulsivity, and the kinetics of gastrointestinal absorption. A further problem with oral alcohol administration is that even after adjusting dosages for total body weight (thus minimizing the effects of sex and body morphology) and performing the ingestion with identical experimental procedures, the maximum observed BAC and the time of its occurrence after oral ingestion vary about three-fold between subjects.[33] This variability complicates the interpretation of self-administration experiments because subjects ingesting the same sequence of drinks will differ substantially in their brain alcohol exposure. The impact of the many influential factors that contribute to alcohol self-administration cannot be easily dissected; nonetheless, it is a highly valid measure with respect to the binge/intoxication phase because the dependent variable comprises the behavior under question.

Infusing the alcohol intravenously can overcome many of the problems of alcohol self-administration. Plawecki and colleagues[34,35] have developed a physiologically based pharmacokinetic (PBPK) model of alcohol administration and elimination. In this paradigm, the arterial (rather than venous) BAC is controlled, which is a better representation of BAC and can be reliably measured using breath samples.[36] The PBPK model calculates an individualized infusion protocol maintaining arterial BAC within 5 mg% of the target concentration. The same principle was used to achieve rapid linear changes of arterial BAC with minimal experimental variability across subjects.[37] A computer-assisted self-infusion of ethanol (CASE) model has recently been developed that employs the PBPK model to achieve an identical increment in arterial BAC each time a subject chooses to self-infuse, rather than administering a fixed dose with drinking.[38] An important facet of the CASE method is that subjects do not know how much alcohol they have infused or how often they are supposed to push the "drink" button. Therefore, their decisions for or against taking another "drink" are based solely on the pharmacological alcohol effects they perceive. Thus, the effects of a potential pharmacotherapy on the binge/intoxication phase of dependence may be assessed with fewer confounding factors. From a learning theory point of view, another advantage of the CASE paradigm is that the contingency between the behavior (pushing the button to receive a "drink") and its consequences (feeling a change in alcohol effect) is closer than with oral administration for two reasons. First, each button press results in exactly the same amount of arterial BAC increase in every subject at any time throughout the experiment. Second, all these arterial BAC increments follow exactly the same kinetics (i.e., a linear increase over a preset period of time); thus, increments are achieved with much more reliability than would be possible with drinking. Therefore, CASE enables human subjects to gain more direct control over their BAC than with oral self-administration and makes other implications like individual preferences for specific alcoholic beverages, brands, tastes, and/or smells irrelevant.

Converging lines of evidence indicate that stress increases risk of addictive behaviors. Early life stress and childhood maltreatment, chronic cumulative adversity, major life trauma, and negative emotionality are associated with increasing levels of drug use and abuse.[39] Stress and stressors have also been associated with relapse and vulnerability to relapse.[40,41] Stress responses, including changes in the activities of the hypothalamic-pituitary-adrenal (HPA) axis and extrahypothalamic brain stress systems, affect all phases of the addiction cycle. Psychosocial stress-related behaviors also affect dopaminergic pathways.[42] These findings are beginning to provide the molecular basis for how stress and cumulative adversity initiate epigenetic changes that alter the transmission of reward pathways to affect the reinforcing properties of addictive substances. Regular and chronic drug use is associated with stress-related symptoms and changes in mental state that include increased anxiety and negative emotions, changes in sleep and food intake, aggressive behaviors, alterations in attention, concentration, memory, and desire/craving for drug.[43]

Stress-related responses in stress-induced craving have been elicited in individuals with addiction using a model of stress-induced responsivity with an emotional imagery paradigm based on the early work of Lang and colleagues.[44] Sinha and colleagues[45] found that exposure to a 5-minute individualized guided imagery of each subject's own stressful scenario elicited multiple emotions of fear, sadness, and anger when compared with a commonly used social stress task (public speaking) that elicited fear, but no sadness or anger. Additionally, individualized stress imagery resulted in significant increases in drug craving, whereas public speaking did not.[45,46] Using this paradigm, drug craving with mild to moderate levels of physiological arousal and subjective distress was reliably induced in multiple groups of alcohol-, cocaine-, and opioid-dependent individuals engaged in treatment. Moreover, individuals that use greater quantity of cocaine and alcohol, and those recovering from alcohol dependence, showed greater craving and physiological responses to stressors than control counterparts (social drinkers) in this paradigm. Stress-induced cocaine craving in the laboratory could be used to accurately predict time to relapse. Similar results

have been observed for subjects dependent on alcohol or nicotine.[47,48]

Clinical trials have consistently shown that acamprosate and naltrexone are both active agents for the treatment of alcohol dependence. However, each drug seems to work via unique mechanisms of action. Acamprosate inhibits glutamatergic receptor function and may exert its therapeutic action by decreasing an alcoholic's "need" to drink[49,50] by normalizing dysregulation in brain systems caused by chronic alcohol use and withdrawal. In contrast, naltrexone exerts its effect by blockade of opioid receptors, which are involved in alcohol's rewarding effects on the brain.[51] As a result, a patient drinking alcohol while on naltrexone is hypothesized to experience less reinforcing euphoria, resulting in less consumption (i.e., binge/intoxication), which is appropriately measured in the alcohol self-administration paradigm of the human laboratory models. Conversely, acamprosate, a glutamate modulator, is hypothesized to exert its effect by normalizing dysregulated brain stress and reward systems in early abstinence, thereby reducing risk for a return to drinking in the negative affect and preoccupation/craving phase of addiction. Therefore, acamprosate may be most appropriately studied in the cue- or stress-induced paradigms and not in those relying on alcohol administration. When using human laboratory models to screen potential pharmacotherapies for addiction, it is critical to choose the model appropriate for the mechanism of action of the drug under study to avoid false-negative findings.

When opioid receptor blockers, such as naltrexone, are used to block the reward pathway, binge eaters acutely reduce their consumption of sweet, high-fat foods,[52] and alcohol-dependent participants reduce their consumption of alcohol.[53] If the characterization of excessive food consumption as a possible addictive behavior is accurate, there may be important implications for the prevention and treatment of excessive food consumption. Perhaps the most important implication is the potential impact of highly available energy-dense foods and the advertising to promote its consumption. The widespread availability and aggressive advertising of unhealthy foods may play on cue-triggered relapse to derail public health interventions aimed to decrease consumption of these unhealthy foods. With respect to identifying underlying mechanisms and consequent approaches to treatment, empirically validated approaches for substance dependence may have comparable relevance for pathological eating. Interventions for both disorders include identification and avoidances of triggers as a relapse prevention strategy and methods to decrease the severity of a binge if relapse occurs. Studies of underlying mechanisms of obesity and potential pharmacotherapies for pathological eating should exploit the human laboratory models of cue- and stress-induced craving and self-administration described in this review to advance our understanding of the underlying mechanisms of pathological food consumption and the development of potential novel treatments.

REFERENCES

1. Hajnal A, Smith GP, Norgren R. Oral sucrose stimulation increases accumbens dopamine in the rat. *Am J Physiol Regul Integr Comp Physiol* 2004;286:R31–37.
2. Kleiner KD, Gold MS, Frost-Pineda K, Lenz-Brunsman B, Perri MG, Jacobs WS. Body mass index and alcohol use. *J Addict Dis* 2004;23:105–118.
3. Volkow ND, Wang GJ, Maynard L, et al. Brain dopamine is associated with eating behaviors in humans. *Int J Eat Disord* 2003;33:136–142.
4. Canetti L, Bachar E, Berry EM. Food and emotion. *Behav Processes* 2002;60:157–164.
5. Cooper ML, Frone MR, Russell M, Mudar P. Drinking to regulate positive and negative emotions: a motivational model of alcohol use. *J Pers Soc Psychol* 1995;69:990–1005.
6. Grant BF, Hasin DS, Stinson FS, et al. Prevalence, correlates, and disability of personality disorders in the United States: results from the national epidemiologic survey on alcohol and related conditions. *J Clin Psychiatry* 2004;65:948–958.
7. Vanderschuren LJ, Everitt BJ. Drug seeking becomes compulsive after prolonged cocaine self-administration. *Science* 2004;305:1017–1019.
8. Sinha R, Fox HC, Hong KA, Bergquist K, Bhagwagar Z, Siedlarz KM. Enhanced negative emotion and alcohol craving, and altered physiological responses following stress and cue exposure in alcohol dependent individuals. *Neuropsychopharmacology* 2009;34:1198–1208.
9. Garbutt JC, West SL, Carey TS, Lohr KN, Crews FT. Pharmacological treatment of alcohol dependence: a review of the evidence. *JAMA* 1999;281:1318–1325.
10. Martinotti G, Nicola MD, Reina D, et al. Alcohol protracted withdrawal syndrome: the role of anhedonia. *Subst Use Misuse* 2008;43:271–284.
11. Roelofs SM. Hyperventilation, anxiety, craving for alcohol: a subacute alcohol withdrawal syndrome. *Alcohol* 1985;2:501–505.
12. Hershon HI. Alcohol withdrawal symptoms and drinking behavior. *J Stud Alcohol* 1977;38:953–971.
13. Annis HM, Sklar SM, Moser AE. Gender in relation to relapse crisis situations, coping, and outcome among treated alcoholics. *Addict Behav* 1998; 23:127–131.
14. Koob GF, Le Moal M. Drug abuse: hedonic homeostatic dysregulation. *Science* 1997;278:52–58.
15. Haney M, Hart CL, Vosburg SK, Comer SD, Reed SC, Foltin RW. Effects of THC and lofexidine in a human laboratory model of marijuana withdrawal and relapse. *Psychopharmacology (Berl)* 2008; 197:157–168.
16. Weerts EM, Froestl W, Griffiths RR. Effects of GABAergic modulators on food and cocaine self-administration in baboons. *Drug Alcohol Depend* 2005;80: 369–376.
17. de Wit H. Impulsivity as a determinant and consequence of drug use: a review of underlying processes. *Addict Biol* 2009;14:22–31.
18. Logan GD. Spatial attention and the apprehension of spatial relations. *J Exp Psychol Hum Percept Perform* 1994;20:1015–1036.
19. Carter BL, Tiffany ST. Cue-reactivity and the future of addiction research. *Addiction* 1999;94:349–351.
20. Monti PM, Rohsenow DJ, Hutchison KE, et al. Naltrexone's effect on cue-elicited craving among alcoholics in treatment. *Alcohol Clin Exp Res* 1999;23: 1386–1394.
21. Kaplan RF, Meyer RE, Stroebel CF. Alcohol dependence and responsivity to an ethanol stimulus as predictors of alcohol consumption. *Br J Addict* 1983; 78:259–267.
22. Rohsenow DJ, Monti PM, Rubonis AV, et al. Cue reactivity as a predictor of drinking among male alcoholics. *J Consult Clin Psychol* 1994;62:620–626.
23. Cooney NL, Litt MD, Morse PA, Bauer LO, Gaupp L. Alcohol cue reactivity, negative-mood reactivity, and relapse in treated alcoholic men. *J Abnorm Psychol* 1997;106:243–250.
24. Miranda R, Jr., MacKillop J, Monti PM, et al. Effects of topiramate on urge to drink and the subjective effects of alcohol: a preliminary laboratory study. *Alcohol Clin Exp Res* 2008;32:489–497.
25. Mason BJ, Light JM, Escher T, Drobes DJ. Effect of positive and negative affective stimuli and beverage cues on measures of craving in non treatment-seeking alcoholics. *Psychopharmacology (Berl)* 2008; 200:141–150.
26. Litt MD, Cooney NL. Inducing craving for alcohol in the laboratory. *Alcohol Res Health* 1999;23:174–178.
27. Marlatt GA. Taxonomy of high-risk situations for alcohol relapse: evolution and development of a cognitive-behavioral model. *Addiction* 1996;91 (suppl):S37–S49.
28. Lowman C, Allen J, Stout RL. Replication and extension of Marlatt's taxonomy of relapse precipitants: overview of procedures and results. The Relapse Research Group. *Addiction* 1996;91(suppl):S51–S71.

29. Cooney NL, Kadden RM, Litt MD, Getter H. Matching alcoholics to coping skills or interactional therapies: two-year follow-up results. *J Consult Clin Psychol* 1991;59:598–601.

30. Litt MD, Cooney NL, Kadden RM, Gaupp L. Reactivity to alcohol cues and induced moods in alcoholics. *Addict Behav* 1990;15:137–146.

31. Rubonis AV, Colby SM, Monti PM, Rohsenow DJ, Gulliver SB, Sirota AD. Alcohol cue reactivity and mood induction in male and female alcoholics. *J Stud Alcohol* 1994;55:487–494.

32. Tiffany ST, Drobes DJ. Imagery and smoking urges: the manipulation of affective content. *Addict Behav* 1990;15:531–539.

33. Ramchandani VA, O'Connor S. Studying alcohol elimination using the alcohol clamp method. *Alcohol Res Health* 2006;29:286–290.

34. Plawecki MH, Decarlo R, Ramchandani VA, O'Connor S. Improved transformation of morphometric measurements for a priori parameter estimation in a physiologically-based pharmacokinetic model of ethanol. *Biomed Signal Process Control* 2007;2:97–110.

35. Plawecki MH, Han JJ, Doerschuk PC, Ramchandani VA, O'Connor SJ. Physiologically based pharmacokinetic (PBPK) models for ethanol. *IEEE Trans Biomed Eng* 2008;55:2691–700.

36. Lindberg L, Brauer S, Wollmer P, Goldberg L, Jones AW, Olsson SG. Breath alcohol concentration determined with a new analyzer using free exhalation predicts almost precisely the arterial blood alcohol concentration. *Forensic Sci Int* 2007;168:200–207.

37. O'Connor AB, Lang VJ. Baclofen not comparable to diazepam for alcohol withdrawal. *Am J Med* 2007;120:e5; author reply e7.

38. Zimmermann US, Mick I, Vitvitskyi V, Plawecki MH, Mann KF, O'Connor S. Development and pilot validation of computer-assisted self-infusion of ethanol (CASE): a new method to study alcohol self-administration in humans. *Alcohol Clin Exp Res* 2008;32:1321–1328.

39. Nemeroff CB. The corticotropin-releasing factor (CRF) hypothesis of depression: new findings and new directions. *Mol Psychiatry* 1996;1:336–342.

40. Marlatt GA. Cue exposure and relapse prevention in the treatment of addictive behaviors. *Addict Behav* 1990;15:395–399.

41. Koob G, Kreek MJ. Stress, dysregulation of drug reward pathways, and the transition to drug dependence. *Am J Psychiatry* 2007;164:1149–1159.

42. Heinz A, Siessmeier T, Wrase J, et al. Correlation between dopamine D(2) receptors in the ventral striatum and central processing of alcohol cues and craving. *Am J Psychiatry* 2004;161:1783–1789.

43. Sinha R, Fox H, Hong KI, Sofuoglu M, Morgan PT, Bergquist KT. Sex steroid hormones, stress response, and drug craving in cocaine-dependent women: implications for relapse susceptibility. *Exp Clin Psychopharmacol* 2007;15:445–452.

44. Lang PJ, Kozak MJ, Miller GA, Levin DN, McLean A, Jr. Emotional imagery: conceptual structure and pattern of somato-visceral response. *Psychophysiology* 1980;17:179–192.

45. Sinha R, Catapano D, O'Malley S. Stress-induced craving and stress response in cocaine dependent individuals. *Psychopharmacology (Berl)* 1999;142:343–351.

46. Sinha R, O'Malley SS. Craving for alcohol: findings from the clinic and the laboratory. *Alcohol Alcohol* 1999;34:223–230.

47. Breese GR, Overstreet DH, Knapp DJ. Conceptual framework for the etiology of alcoholism: a "kindling"/stress hypothesis. *Psychopharmacology (Berl)* 2005;178:367–380.

48. al'Absi M, Hatsukami D, Davis GL. Attenuated adrenocorticotropic responses to psychological stress are associated with early smoking relapse. *Psychopharmacology (Berl)* 2005;181:107–117.

49. Mason BJ. Acamprosate in the treatment of alcohol dependence. *Expert Opin Pharmacother* 2005;6:2103–2115.

50. Heilig M, Egli M. Pharmacological treatment of alcohol dependence: target symptoms and target mechanisms. *Pharmacol Ther* 2006;111:855–876.

51. Galloway GP, Koch M, Cello R, Smith DE. Pharmacokinetics, safety, and tolerability of a depot formulation of naltrexone in alcoholics: an open-label trial. *BMC Psychiatry* 2005;5:18.

52. Drewnowski A, Krahn DD, Demitrack MA, Nairn K, Gosnell BA. Naloxone, an opiate blocker, reduces the consumption of sweet high-fat foods in obese and lean female binge eaters. *Am J Clin Nutr* 1995;61:1206–1212.

53. O'Malley SS, Krishnan-Sarin S, Farren C, Sinha R, Kreek MJ. Naltrexone decreases craving and alcohol self-administration in alcohol-dependent subjects and activates the hypothalamo-pituitary-adrenocortical axis. *Psychopharmacology (Berl)* 2002;160:19–29.

3

Neuroanatomy of Addiction

GEORGE F. KOOB

CONCEPTUAL FRAMEWORK

Addiction Definitions: Drug Use, Abuse, and Dependence Addiction Cycle

While much of the initial study of the neurobiological mechanisms of drug addiction focused on the acute impact of drugs of abuse (analogous to comparing no drug use to drug use), the focus now is shifting to chronic administration and the acute and long-term neuroadaptive changes in the brain that result in the development, maintenance, and relapse to addiction. Drug addiction is a chronically relapsing disorder that has been characterized by (1) compulsion to seek and take the drug, (2) loss of control in limiting intake, and (3) emergence of a negative emotional state (e.g., dysphoria, anxiety, irritability) reflecting a motivational withdrawal syndrome when access to the drug is prevented (defined as substance dependence by the *Diagnostic and Statistical Manual of Mental Disorders* [DSM]).[1,2] The occasional but limited use of an abusable drug is clinically distinct from escalated drug use, loss of control over limiting drug intake, and the emergence of chronic compulsive drug seeking that characterizes addiction.

The symptoms and syndrome of addiction define different stages described as an addiction cycle: *binge/intoxication, withdrawal/negative affect,* and *preoccupation/anticipation.* These three stages are conceptualized as interacting with each other, becoming more intense, and ultimately leading to the pathological state known as addiction.[2] Much of the recent progress in understanding the neurobiology of addiction has derived from the study of animal models of addiction to specific drugs such as stimulants, opioids, alcohol, nicotine, and Δ^9-tetrahydrocannabinol. Although no animal model of addiction fully emulates the human condition, animal models do permit the investigation of specific elements of the process of drug addiction. The present review focuses on the brain neurocircuitry that is engaged at each stage of the addiction cycle, how the neurocircuitry changes with increasing engagement with drugs of abuse, and how different neurocircuits interact to produce the pathological state known as addiction.

NEUROCIRCUITRY OF ADDICTION: *BINGE/INTOXICATION STAGE*

The understanding of the neurobiological substrates for the reinforcing effects of drugs of abuse can be traced to early work on the identification of a reward system in the brain with the discovery of electrical brain stimulation reward or intracranial self-stimulation by Olds and Milner.[3] The most sensitive sites for eliciting brain stimulation reward, defined by the lowest thresholds, involve the trajectory of the medial forebrain bundle that connects the ventral tegmental area (VTA) to the basal forebrain.[3] All drugs of abuse, when administered acutely, decrease brain stimulation reward thresholds (i.e., increased reward)[4] and when administered chronically increase reward thresholds during withdrawal (i.e., decreased reward). Although much emphasis was focused initially on the role of the ascending monoamine systems in the medial forebrain bundle in reward, first norepinephrine[5] and then dopamine,[6] other nondopaminergic systems in the medial forebrain bundle clearly play a key role in mediating brain stimulation reward.[7] Indeed, much work suggests that activation of the midbrain dopamine system has multiple roles, such as facilitating incentive salience to stimuli in the environment,[8] driving performance of goal-directed behavior,[9] and promoting activation in general.[10] More recently, the hypothesis has been raised that the time course of dopamine signaling is a key factor, with the fastest time course predominantly having a preferential role in reward and valuation of predicted outcomes of behavior and the steady release of dopamine having a preferential role in providing an enabling effect on specific behavior-related systems.[11] Work in the domain of the acute reinforcing effects of drugs of abuse supports this hypothesis in which the mesolimbic dopamine system is critical for the acute rewarding effects of psychostimulant drugs but plays a more enabling function for all drugs of abuse (Fig. 3.1).[12]

Neurochemical Circuitry in Drug Reward

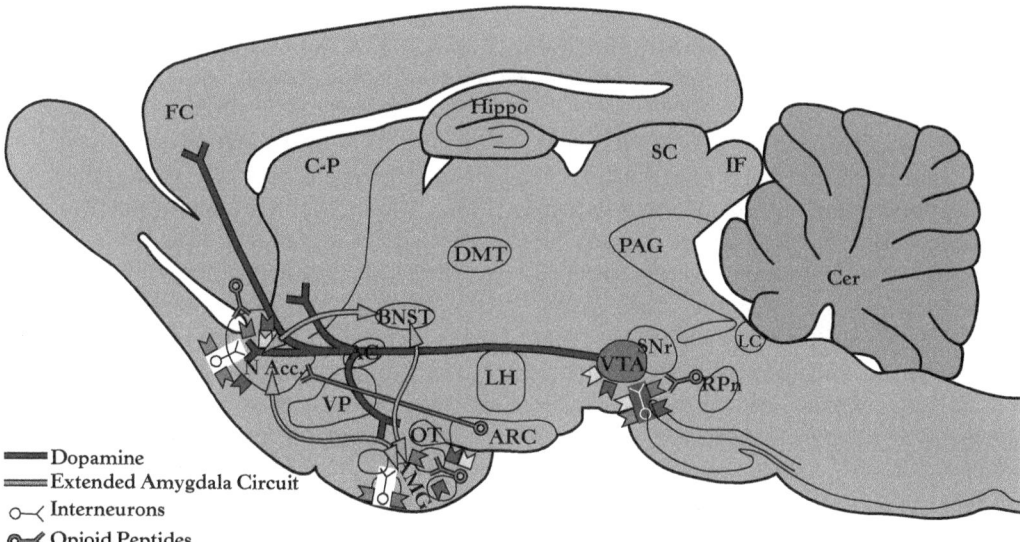

FIGURE 3.1. Sagittal section through a representative rodent brain illustrating the pathways and receptor systems implicated in the acute reinforcing actions of drugs of abuse. Cocaine and amphetamines activate the release of dopamine in the nucleus accumbens and amygdala via direct actions on dopamine terminals. Opioids activate opioid receptors in the ventral tegmental area, nucleus accumbens, and amygdala via direct actions or indirect actions via interneurons. Opioids facilitate the release of dopamine in the nucleus accumbens via an action either in the ventral tegmental area or nucleus accumbens but are also hypothesized to activate elements independent of the dopamine system. Alcohol activates γ-aminobutyric acid-A (GABA$_A$) receptors or GABA release in the ventral tegmental area, nucleus accumbens, and amygdala via either direct actions at the GABA$_A$ receptor or through indirect release of GABA. Alcohol is hypothesized to facilitate the release of opioid peptides in the ventral tegmental area, nucleus accumbens, and central nucleus of the amygdala. Alcohol facilitates the release of dopamine in the nucleus accumbens via an action either in the ventral tegmental area or nucleus accumbens. Nicotine activates nicotinic acetylcholine receptors in the ventral tegmental area, nucleus accumbens, and amygdala, either directly or indirectly, via actions on interneurons. Cannabinoids activate cannabinoid CB$_1$ receptors in the ventral tegmental area, nucleus accumbens, and amygdala. Cannabinoids facilitate the release of dopamine in the nucleus accumbens via an unknown mechanism either in the ventral tegmental area or nucleus accumbens. The blue arrows represent the interactions within the extended amygdala system hypothesized to play a key role in psychostimulant reinforcement. The medial forebrain bundle represents ascending and descending projections between the ventral forebrain (nucleus accumbens, olfactory tubercle, septal area) and the ventral midbrain (ventral tegmental area) (not shown in figure for clarity). AC, anterior commissure; AMG, amygdala; ARC, arcuate nucleus; BNST, bed nucleus of the striaterminalis; Cer, cerebellum; C-P, caudate-putamen; DMT, dorsomedial thalamus; FC, frontal cortex; Hippo, hippocampus; IF, inferior colliculus; LC, locus coeruleus; LH, lateral hypothalamus; N Acc., nucleus accumbens; OT, olfactory tract; PAG, periaqueductal gray; RPn, reticular pontine nucleus; SC, superior colliculus; SNr, substantianigra pars reticulata; VP, ventral pallidum; VTA, ventral tegmental area.

Source: Reprinted from Clinical Neuroscience Research, Volume 5, Koob, The Neurocircuitry of Addiction: Implications for Treatment, 89–101, Copyright (2005), with permission from Elsevier.

Consistent with this hypothesis, brain imaging studies in humans have been instrumental in showing that drug-induced increases in dopamine in the striatum (including the ventral striatum where the nucleus accumbens is located) are associated with subjective descriptors of reward (e.g., pleasure, high, euphoria).[13] Moreover, these studies have shown that fast dopamine changes are associated with the subjective perception of reward, whereas slow and stable dopamine increases do not induce these subjective responses.[14,15]

In animal studies, the mesolimbic dopamine system is activated by acute administration of opioids, ethanol, nicotine, and Δ^9-tetrahydrocannabinol (Δ^9-THC).[16] Using the techniques of intracranial self-administration, opioids, alcohol, phencyclidine, and psychostimulants are rewarding when injected or self-injected into the ventral tegmental area, nucleus accumbens, and frontal cortex. Thus, all drugs of abuse activate the mesolimbic dopamine system, but much evidence suggests that dopamine-independent reinforcement occurs at the level of the nucleus accumbens, suggesting multiple inputs to the activation of critical reinforcement circuitry in these brain regions.[17,18]

A prominent hypothesis is that drugs of abuse, particularly cocaine and amphetamine, increase dopamine release in a more prolonged and unregulated manner than natural stimuli, resulting in changes in synaptic plasticity both within the dopamine system and in dopamine-receptive neurons.[19] Decreased basal release of glutamate also occurs, but sensitized synaptic glutamate release occurs during the reinstatement of extinguished drug seeking in rats.[20] Clinical studies have also shown that the striatal slow dopamine increases induced by acute administration of oral methylphenidate do not elicit craving in cocaine abusers unless they are coupled to drug-associated cues.[21] Thus, concomitant dopamine and glutamate neurotransmission in the dorsal striatum, a region implicated in habit learning and action initiation, may be involved in cue/context-dependent craving (see later discussion).[22]

The central nucleus of the amygdala (CeA) also plays a key role in the acute reinforcing actions of drugs of abuse. Microinjections of dopamine D_1 receptor antagonists into the CeA block cocaine self-administration. The most sensitive site for γ-aminobutyric acid (GABA) and opioid antagonism of oral alcohol self-administration in nondependent rats was the CeA. Lesions of the CeA block oral self-administration of alcohol. Serotonin-3 antagonists injected into the CeA block oral ethanol self-administration in nondependent rats, an effect hypothesized to involve the ability of serotonin-3 receptor antagonists to block drug-induced dopamine release.[23,24]

A major output from the nucleus accumbens is to the ventral pallidum/substantia innominata. Consistent with the nucleus accumbens as a key substrate for drug reward, lesions of the ventral pallidum are particularly effective in blocking the motivation to work for intravenous cocaine and heroin. Additionally, blockade of dopamine and $GABA_A$ receptors in the ventral pallidum block the reinforcing effects of alcohol. Thus, elements of the ventral pallidum may not only be critical for further processing of the drug reward signal but also may be directly modulated by drugs of abuse.[23,24]

The dorsal striatum does not appear to play a major role in the acute reinforcing effects of drugs of abuse but appears to be recruited during the development of compulsive drug seeking.[25] When the nucleus accumbens core was selectively lesioned on one side of the brain, combined with dopamine receptor blockade in the contralateral dorsal striatum, no effect was observed in animals immediately after acquisition, but greatly decreased cocaine seeking was observed in rats with stable responding on a second-order schedule of reinforcement.[26] These results suggest that the dorsal striatum may have a minor role in the acute reinforcing effects of psychostimulant drugs but a key role in the transition to compulsive use.[25]

Data with knockout mice also provide key insights into the role of dopamine in the rewarding effects of drugs of abuse. Genetically altered mice homozygous for a lack of dopamine D_1 receptors do not self-administer cocaine.[27] Transgenic animals that expressed dopamine transporters with functional dopamine reuptake carriers (but that did not bind cocaine) did not show cocaine reward measured by conditioned place preference.[28] These results support the hypothesis of a crucial role of the dopamine transporter in cocaine's reinforcing effects.

Based on this synthesis, an early neurobiological circuit for drug reward was proposed[17] that has been elaborated and expanded[29] (Fig. 3.1).[30,31] The starting point for the reward circuit was the medial forebrain bundle, composed of myelinated fibers connecting bidirectionally the olfactory tubercle and nucleus accumbens with the hypothalamus and VTA[32] and including the ascending monoamine pathways such as the mesocorticolimbic dopamine system. The initial action of drug reward was hypothesized to depend on dopamine release in the nucleus accumbens for cocaine, amphetamine, and nicotine, opioid peptide receptor activation in the VTA (via dopamine activation) and nucleus accumbens (independent of dopamine activation) for opiates, and $GABA_A$ systems in the nucleus accumbens and amygdala for alcohol. The nucleus accumbens is situated strategically to receive important limbic information from the amygdala, frontal cortex, and hippocampus that could be converted to motivational action via its connections with the extrapyramidal motor system. Thus, an early critical role for the nucleus accumbens was established for the acute reinforcing effects of drugs, with a supporting role for the CeA and ventral pallidum (Figs. 3.1 and 3.2), and it is this neurocircuitry that is hypothesized to be critical for the *binge/intoxication* stage.

NEUROCIRCUITRY OF ADDICTION: *WITHDRAWAL/ NEGATIVE AFFECT STAGE*

The neuroanatomical entity termed "the extended amygdala"[33] may represent a common anatomical substrate integrating brain arousal–stress systems with hedonic processing systems to produce the negative emotional states that drive negative reinforcement mechanisms associated with the development of addiction. The extended amygdala is composed of the CeA, bed nucleus of the stria terminalis (BNST), and a transition zone in the medial (shell) subregion of the nucleus accumbens (Fig. 3.2). Each of these regions has cytoarchitectural and circuitry similarities.[33] The extended amygdala receives numerous afferents from limbic structures such as the basolateral amygdala and hippocampus and sends efferents to the medial part of the ventral pallidum and a large projection to the lateral hypothalamus, thus further defining the specific brain areas that interface classical limbic (emotional) structures with the output of the extrapyramidal motor system.[34] The extended amygdala has long been hypothesized to play a key role not only in fear conditioning[35] but also in the emotional component of pain processing.[36]

Compulsive drug use, defined by increased intake of drug with extended access, is accompanied by a chronic perturbation in brain reward homeostasis using measures of brain stimulation reward thresholds. The differential exposure to drug self-administration has dramatic effects on reward thresholds that progressively increase (i.e., decreased reward) in extended-access, but not in limited-access, rats across successive self-administration sessions (Wee et al., unpublished results).[37,38]

Within-system neuroadaptations to chronic drug exposure include decreases in the function of neurotransmitter systems in the neurocircuits implicated in the acute reinforcing effects of drugs of abuse. One prominent hypothesis is that dopamine systems are compromised in crucial phases of the addiction cycle, such as withdrawal, and this dysfunction leads to decreased motivation for non-drug-related stimuli and increased sensitivity to the abused drug.[39] Animals during amphetamine withdrawal show decreased responding on a progressive-ratio schedule for a sweet solution, and this decreased responding was reversed by the dopamine partial agonist terguride,[40] suggesting that low dopamine tone contributes to the motivational deficits associated with psychostimulant withdrawal. Decreases in the activity of the mesolimbic dopamine system and decreases in serotonergic neurotransmission in the nucleus accumbens occur during acute drug withdrawal from all major drugs of abuse in animal studies.[41–43]

Animals with extended access to cocaine are also more sensitive to the blockade of self-administration by dopamine antagonists and partial agonists.[44,45] Indeed, more chronic repeated administration of psychostimulants failed to produce sensitization of mesolimbic dopamine activity in animal models, and human cocaine abusers showed attenuated dopamine responses when challenged with a stimulant drug, which is opposite to that predicted by the enhanced sensitization of mesolimbic dopamine activity.[23]

During protracted withdrawal, once the signs and symptoms of acute withdrawal have subsided, imaging studies have documented hypofunction in dopamine pathways, demonstrated by decreases in D_2 receptor expression and decreases in dopamine release, which may contribute to the hypohedonia (i.e., decreased sensitivity to rewarding stimuli) and amotivation reported by drug-addicted subjects during protracted withdrawal.[46–49] The decreased reactivity of dopamine to reinforcing stimuli is

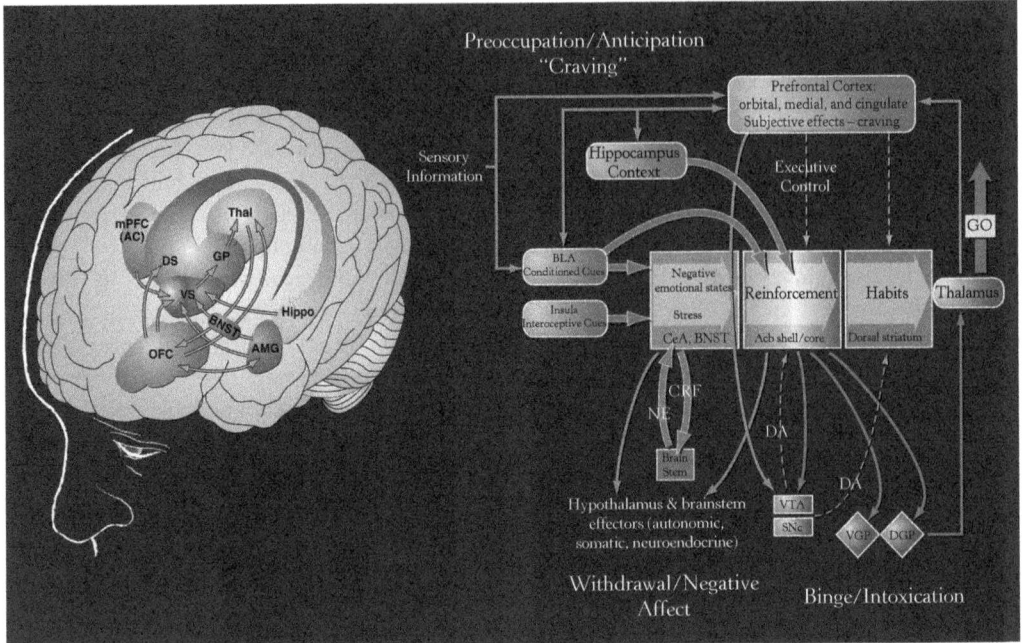

FIGURE 3.2. Neurocircuitry schematic illustrating the combination of neuroadaptations in the brain circuitry for the three stages of the addiction cycle that drive drug-seeking behavior in the addicted state. *Binge/intoxication stage*: Reinforcing effects of drugs may engage associative mechanisms and reward neurotransmitters in the nucleus accumbens shell and core and then engage stimulus-response habits that depend on the dorsal striatum. Two major neurotransmitters mediating the rewarding effects of drugs of abuse are dopamine and opioid peptides. *Withdrawal/negative affect stage*: The negative emotional state of withdrawal may engage the activation of the extended amygdala. The extended amygdala is composed of several basal forebrain structures, including the bed nucleus of the striaterminalis, central nucleus of the amygdala, and possibly a transition area in the medial portion (shell) of the nucleus accumbens. Major neurotransmitters in the extended amygdala hypothesized to play a role in negative reinforcement are corticotropin-releasing factor, norepinephrine, and dynorphin. Major projections of the extended amygdala are to the hypothalamus and brainstem. *Preoccupation/anticipation (craving) stage*: This stage involves the processing of conditioned reinforcement in the basolateral amygdala and the processing of contextual information by the hippocampus. Executive control depends on the prefrontal cortex and includes representation of contingencies, representation of outcomes, and their value and subjective states (i.e., craving and, presumably, feelings) associated with drugs. The subjective effects termed "drug craving" in humans involves activation of the orbital and anterior cingulate cortices and temporal lobe, including the amygdala, in functional imaging studies. A major neurotransmitter involved in the craving stage is glutamate localized in pathways from frontal regions and the basolateral amygdala that project to the ventral striatum. Note the activation of the ventral striatum/dorsal striatum/extended amygdala driven by cues via hippocampal and basolateral amygdala and stress via the insula. The frontal cortex system is compromised, producing deficits in executive function and contributing to the incentive salience of drugs compared with natural reinforcers. Dopamine systems are compromised, and brain stress systems, such as CRF, are activated to further reset the salience of drugs and drug-related stimuli in the context of an aversive dysphoric state. Green/blue arrows, glutamatergic projections; orange arrows, dopaminergic projections; pink arrows, GABAergic projections; Acb, nucleus accumbens; BLA, basolateral amygdala; BNST, bed nucleus of the striaterminalis; CeA, central nucleus of the amygdala; CRF, corticotropin-releasing factor; DGP, dorsal globuspallidus; NE, norepinephrine; PIT, Pavlovian instrumental transfer; SNc, substantianigra pars compacta; VGP, ventral globuspallidus; VTA, ventral tegmental area. (Brain schematic modified from Zald and Kim, 2001.[30])

Source: Adapted with permission from a diagram published in Fundamental Neuroscience, 3rd Edition, G.F. Koob, B.J. Everitt, T.W. Robbins, Reward, Motivation, and Addiction, 987–1016, Copyright Elsevier (2008), and with permission from The Frontal Lobes and Neuropsychiatric Illness, Zald and Kim, Copyright (2001) American Psychiatric Publishing, Inc.

also present after protracted withdrawal from alcohol when acute physical withdrawal has subsided. Brain imaging studies have also revealed decreases in endogenous opioids during cocaine withdrawal, which may contribute to the irritability, malaise, and dysphoria that occur during this phase of motivational withdrawal.[50]

A second functional component hypothesized to be key to the *withdrawal/negative affect* stage is a between-system neuroadaptation. Different neurochemical systems involved in stress modulation may also be engaged within the neurocircuitry of the brain stress and aversive systems in an attempt to overcome the chronic presence of the perturbing drug to restore normal function despite the presence of drug. Both the hypothalamic-pituitary-adrenal axis and the brain stress/aversive system mediated by corticotropin-releasing factor (CRF) are activated during withdrawal from chronic administration of all major drugs with abuse potential, with a common response of elevated adrenocorticotropic hormone, corticosterone, and amygdala CRF during acute withdrawal.[51,52] Acute withdrawal from all drugs of abuse also produces an aversive or anxiety-like state in which CRF and other stress-related systems (such as noradrenergic pathways and dynorphin systems) play key roles.[51]

For example, withdrawal from repeated administration of cocaine produces an anxiogenic-like response in the elevated plus maze and defensive burying test, both of which are reversed by CRF antagonists. Similarly, ethanol withdrawal produces anxiety-like behavior that is reversed by intracerebroventricular administration of CRF_1/CRF_2 peptidergic antagonists, systemic administration of a small molecule CRF_1 antagonist, and microinjection of a peptidergic CRF_1/CRF_2 antagonist into the amygdala.[51] CRF antagonists injected intracerebroventricularly or systemically also block the potentiated anxiety-like responses to stressors observed during protracted abstinence from chronic ethanol, and the effects of CRF antagonists have been localized to the CeA.[51] Precipitated withdrawal from nicotine produces anxiety-like responses that are also reversed by CRF antagonists.[53,54] Much evidence shows that dynorphin is increased in the nucleus accumbens in response to dopaminergic activation and, in turn, that overactivity of the dynorphin systems can decrease dopaminergic function. κ-opioid agonists are aversive, and cocaine, opioid, and ethanol withdrawal is associated with increased dynorphin in the nucleus accumbens and amygdala.[51,55]

A number of other neurotransmitter systems have been hypothesized to modulate the extended amygdala both from the stress-induction domain (vasopressin, substance P, orexin) and the antistress domain (nociceptin, endocannabinoids; for review, see Koob, 2008). Such dysregulation may be a significant contribution to the between-system opponent processes that help maintain dependence and also set the stage for more prolonged state changes in emotionality, such as protracted abstinence.

An interoceptive circuit that most likely interfaces with the extended amygdala and ventral striatum involves the insula. Smokers with damage to the insula were able to stop smoking easily and without experiencing either craving or relapse.[56] The insula, particularly its more anterior regions, is reciprocally connected to several limbic regions (e.g., ventromedial prefrontal cortex, amygdala, and ventral striatum) and appears to play an interoceptive role, integrating autonomic and visceral information with emotion and motivation and providing conscious awareness of these urges. Consistent with this hypothesis, imaging studies demonstrated differential activation in the insula during craving.[57]

Thus, acute withdrawal is associated with within-system changes reflected in a decrease in dopaminergic activity in the mesolimbic dopamine system and with between-system recruitment of neurotransmitter systems that convey stress and anxiety-like effects, such as CRF and dynorphin. Other neurotransmitter systems known to be involved in emotional dysregulation of the motivational effects of drug withdrawal include norepinephrine, substance P, vasopressin, neuropeptide Y, endocannabinoids, and nociceptin.[51]

NEUROCIRCUITRY OF ADDICTION: *PREOCCUPATION/ ANTICIPATION* (CRAVING) STAGE

The *preoccupation/anticipation* or craving stage of the addiction cycle has long been hypothesized to be a key element of relapse in humans and defines addiction as a chronic relapsing disorder. Although often linked to the construct of craving, craving per se has been difficult to measure clinically[58] and often does not correlate well with relapse. Nevertheless, the stage of the addiction cycle in which the individual reinstates drug-seeking behavior after abstinence remains a challenging focus for neurobiological mechanisms and medications development for treatment. Animal models of craving can be divided into two domains: drug seeking induced by drug or stimuli paired with drug taking, and drug seeking induced by an acute stressor or a residual negative emotional state, often a state of stress, termed "protracted abstinence" (see Chapter 1). Neurocircuitry changes associated with drug- and cue-induced reinstatement after extinction have been linked to a glutamatergic pathway from the prefrontal cortex, basolateral amygdala, and hippocampus to the nucleus accumbens core[59] (Fig. 3.2).

Much evidence from animal studies suggests that drug-induced reinstatement is localized to the medial prefrontal cortex/nucleus accumbens/ventral pallidum circuit mediated by the neurotransmitter glutamate.[60] In contrast, cue-induced reinstatement appears to involve the basolateral amygdala as a critical substrate with a possible feedforward mechanism through the prefrontal cortex system involved in drug-induced reinstatement.[61,62] The association of previously neutral stimuli paired with precipitated opioid withdrawal (conditioned withdrawal) also depends critically on the basolateral amygdala,[63] and such stimuli may have motivational significance.[64]

Imaging studies have reported that during detoxification, enhanced sensitivity to conditioned cues occurs. Abstinence from smoking, for example, can dramatically potentiate neural responses to smoking-related cues.[65] Imaging studies evaluating markers of brain function have shown that drug abusers tested during protracted detoxification show evidence of disrupted activity of frontal regions, including dorsolateral prefrontal regions, the cingulate gyrus, and orbitofrontal cortex, which is hypothesized to underlie their impaired inhibitory control and impulsivity and contribute to relapse. Additionally, abnormalities in frontocortical regions may underlie the inability to delay gratification, a trait that is characteristic of addiction and other psychiatric disorders.[66]

Human subjects with cocaine addiction also show impaired performance in tasks involving attention, cognitive flexibility, and delayed reward discounting that are mediated by the medial and orbital prefrontal cortex, as well as spatial, verbal, and recognition memory impairments that are mediated by the hippocampus, and these deficits can predict poor treatment outcomes.[67,68] Parallel animal studies of the orbitofrontal cortex, prefrontal cortex, and hippocampus in addiction using animal models have begun to show some of the deficits reflected in human studies.[69]

Indeed, human neuroimaging studies show that the prefrontal cortex (orbitofrontal, medial prefrontal, prelimbic/cingulate) and basolateral amygdala play critical roles in drug- and cue-induced craving in humans.[70] In prefrontal regions (e.g., cingulate gyrus and orbitofrontal cortex), these changes have been associated with a reduction in striatal dopamine D_2 receptor availability observed in addicted subjects.[46,47,71,72] These associations could either reflect a disruption of frontal brain regions secondary to changes in striatal dopamine activity, or alternatively they could reflect a primary disruption of frontal regions that regulate dopamine cell activity.

In contrast, stress-induced reinstatement of drug-related responding in animal models appears to depend on activation of both CRF and norepinephrine in elements of the extended amygdala (both the CeA and BNST).[73,74] Protracted abstinence, largely described in alcohol dependence models, appears to involve overactive glutamatergic and CRF systems, presumably in the extended amygdala, although to a large extent this remains to be explored.[75,76]

SUMMARY AND CONCLUSIONS

In summary, multiple brain regions and circuits are disrupted in drug addiction and are likely to contribute differentially to the complex phenotype observed in addicted individuals (Fig. 3.2). Some of these functional abnormalities may be present to a greater or lesser extent across all classes of drug addictions. For example, decreases in dopamine D_2 receptors in the striatum are observed in subjects addicted to all of the drugs of abuse that have been investigated, and increased activation of brain stress systems such as CRF have been observed in animal models during acute withdrawal for all types of drugs. Importantly, the neuronal abnormalities that become manifest in an addicted individual and that can be uncovered by imaging or neuropsychopharmacological studies are a reflection of not only a given chronic drug exposure trajectory but also an individual's specific constellation of genetic, developmental, and environmental characteristics.

ACKNOWLEDGMENTS

This is publication number 20803 from The Scripps Research Institute. Preparation of this work was supported by the Pearson Center for Alcoholism and Addiction Research and National Institutes of Health grants AA08459 and AA06420 from the National Institute on Alcohol Abuse and Alcoholism, DA04043, DA04398, DA023597, and DA10072 from the National Institute on Drug Abuse, and DK26741 from the National Institute of Diabetes and Digestive and Kidney Diseases, and 17RT-0095 from the Tobacco-Related Disease Research Program from the State of California. The authors would like to thank Michael Arends for assistance with manuscript preparation.

REFERENCES

1. American Psychiatric Association. *Diagnostic and Statistical Manual of Mental Disorders.* 4th ed. Text rev. Washington, DC: American Psychiatric Press; 2000.
2. Koob GF, Le Moal M. Drug abuse: hedonic homeostatic dysregulation. *Science* 1997;278:52–58.
3. Olds J, Milner P. Positive reinforcement produced by electrical stimulation of septal area and other regions of rat brain. *J Comp Physiol Psychol* 1954;47:419–427.
4. Kornetsky C, Esposito RU. Euphorigenic drugs: effects on the reward pathways of the brain. *Fed Proc* 1979;38:2473–2476.
5. Stein L. Effects and interactions of imipramine, chlorpromazine, reserpine, and amphetamine on self-stimulation: possible neurophysiological basis of depression. *Recent Adv Biol Psychiatry* 1961;4:288–309.
6. Crow TJ. Catecholamine-containing neurones and electrical self-stimulation. 2. A theoretical interpretation and some psychiatric implications. *Psychol Med* 1973;3:66–73.
7. Hernandez G, Hamdani S, Rajabi H, et al. Prolonged rewarding stimulation of the rat medial forebrain bundle: neurochemical and behavioral consequences. *Behav Neurosci* 2006;120:888–904.
8. Robinson TE, Berridge KC. The neural basis of drug craving: an incentive-sensitization theory of addiction. *Brain Res Brain Res Rev* 1993;18:247–291.
9. Salamone JD, Correa M, Farrar A, Mingote SM. Effort-related functions of nucleus accumbens dopamine and associated forebrain circuits. *Psychopharmacol (Berl)* 2007;191:461–482.
10. Le Moal M, Simon H. Mesocorticolimbic dopaminergic network: functional and regulatory roles. *Physiol Rev* 1991;71:155–234.
11. Schultz W. Multiple dopamine functions at different time courses. *Annu Rev Neurosci* 2007;30:259–288.
12. Volkow ND, Wang GJ, Fowler JS, et al. Relationship between psychostimulant-induced "high" and dopamine transporter occupancy. *Proc Natl Acad Sci USA* 1996;93:10388–10392.
13. Koob GF. The neurocircuitry of addiction: implications for treatment. *Clin Neurosci Res* 2005;5:89–101.
14. Grace AA. The tonic/phasic model of dopamine system regulation and its implications for understanding alcohol and psychostimulant craving. *Addiction* 2000;95(suppl 2):S119–S128.
15. Volkow ND, Swanson JM. Variables that affect the clinical use and abuse of methylphenidate in the treatment of ADHD. *Am J Psychiatry* 2003;160:1909–1918.
16. Di Chiara G, Imperato A. Drugs abused by humans preferentially increase synaptic dopamine concentrations in the mesolimbic system of freely moving rats. *Proc Natl Acad Sci USA* 1988;85:5274–5278.
17. Koob GF. Drugs of abuse: anatomy, pharmacology, and function of reward pathways. *Trends Pharmacol Sci* 1992;13:177–184.
18. Nestler EJ. Is there a common molecular pathway for addiction? *Nat Neurosci* 2005;8:1445–1449.
19. Wolf ME. Addiction: making the connection between behavioral changes and neuronal plasticity in specific pathways. *Mol Interv* 2002;2:146–157.
20. Kalivas PW, O'Brien C. Drug addiction as a pathology of staged neuroplasticity. *Neuropsychopharmacol* 2008;33:166–180.
21. Volkow ND, Wang GJ, Telang F, et al. Dopamine increases in striatum do not elicit craving in cocaine abusers unless they are coupled with cocaine cues. *Neuroimage* 2008;39:1266–1273.
22. Volkow ND, Wang GJ, Telang F, et al. Cocaine cues and dopamine in dorsal striatum: mechanism of craving in cocaine addiction. *J Neurosci* 2006;26:6583–6588.
23. Koob GF, Volkow ND. Neurocircuitry of addiction. *Neuropsychopharmacol* 2010;35:217–238 [erratum: 35:1051].
24. Koob GF, Le Moal M. *Neurobiology of Addiction.* London: Academic Press; 2006.
25. Everitt BJ, Belin D, Economidou D, Pelloux Y, Dalley JW, Robbins TW. Review. Neural mechanisms underlying the vulnerability to develop compulsive drug-seeking habits and addiction. *Philos Trans R Soc Lond B Biol Sci* 2008;363:3125–3135.
26. Belin D, Everitt BJ. Cocaine seeking habits depend upon dopamine-dependent serial connectivity linking the ventral with the dorsal striatum. *Neuron* 2008;57:432–441.
27. Caine SB, Thomsen M, Gabriel KI, et al. Lack of self-administration of cocaine in dopamine D1 receptor knock-out mice. *J Neurosci* 2007;27:13140–13150.
28. Chen R, Tilley MR, Wei H, et al. Abolished cocaine reward in mice with a cocaine-insensitive dopamine

transporter. *Proc Natl Acad Sci USA* 2006;103: 9333–9338.

29. Koob GF, Nestler EJ. The neurobiology of drug addiction. *J Neuropsychiatry Clin Neurosci* 1997;9: 482–497.

30. Zald DH, Kim SW. The orbitofrontal cortex. In: Salloway SP, Malloy PF, Duffy JD, eds. *The Frontal Lobes and Neuropsychiatric Illness.* Washington, DC: American Psychiatric Press; 2001:33–70.

31. Koob GF, Everitt BJ, Robbins TW. Reward, motivation, and addiction. In: Squire LG, Berg D, Bloom FE, Du Lac S, Ghosh A, Spitzer N, eds. *Fundamental Neuroscience.* 3rd ed. Amsterdam, The Netherlands: Academic Press; 2008: 987–1016.

32. Nauta JH, Haymaker W. Hypothalamic nuclei and fiber connections. In: Haymaker W, Anderson E, Nauta WJH, eds. *The Hypothalamus.* Springfield, IL: Charles C. Thomas; 1969:136–209.

33. Heimer L, Alheid G. Piecing together the puzzle of basal forebrain anatomy. In: Napier TC, Kalivas PW, Hanin I, eds. *The Basal Forebrain: Anatomy to Function. Advances in Experimental Medicine and Biology,* Vol 295. New York: Plenum Press; 1991:1–42.

34. Alheid GF, De Olmos JS, Beltramino CA. Amygdala and extended amygdala. In: Paxinos G, ed. *The Rat Nervous System.* 2nd ed. San Diego, CA: Academic Press; 1995:495–578.

35. Le Doux JE. Emotion circuits in the brain. *Ann Rev Neurosci* 2000;23:155–184.

36. Neugebauer V, Li W, Bird GC, Han JS. The amygdala and persistent pain. *Neuroscientist* 2004;10:221–234.

37. Ahmed SH, Kenny PJ, Koob GF, Markou A. Neurobiological evidence for hedonic allostasis associated with escalating cocaine use. *Nat Neurosci* 2002;5:625–626.

38. Kenny PJ, Chen SA, Kitamura O, Markou A, Koob GF. Conditioned withdrawal drives heroin consumption and decreases reward sensitivity. *J Neurosci* 2006;26:5894–5900.

39. Melis M, Spiga S, Diana M. The dopamine hypothesis of drug addiction: hypodopaminergic state. *Int Rev Neurobiol* 2005;63:101–154.

40. Orsini C, Koob GF, Pulvirenti L. Dopamine partial agonist reverses amphetamine withdrawal in rats. *Neuropsychopharmacol* 2001;25:789–792.

41. Rossetti ZL, Hmaidan Y, Gessa GL. Marked inhibition of mesolimbic dopamine release: a common feature of ethanol, morphine, cocaine and amphetamine abstinence in rats. *Eur J Pharmacol* 1992;221:227–234.

42. Weiss F, Markou A, Lorang MT, Koob GF. Basal extracellular dopamine levels in the nucleus accumbens are decreased during cocaine withdrawal after unlimited-access self-administration. *Brain Res* 1992;593:314–318.

43. Weiss F, Parsons LH, Schulteis G, et al. Ethanol self-administration restores withdrawal-associated deficiencies in accumbal dopamine and 5-hydroxytryptamine release in dependent rats. *J Neurosci* 1996;16:3474–3485.

44. Ahmed SH, Koob GF. Changes in response to a dopamine antagonist in rats with escalating cocaine intake. *Psychopharmacol (Berl)* 2004;172:450–454.

45. Wee S, Wang Z, Woolverton WL, Pulvirenti L, Koob GF. Effect of aripiprazole, a partial D2 receptor agonist, on increased rate of methamphetamine self-administration in rats with prolonged session duration. *Neuropsychopharmacol* 2007;32:2238–2247.

46. Volkow ND, Wang GJ, Fowler JS, et al. Decreased striatal dopaminergic responsiveness in detoxified cocaine-dependent subjects. *Nature* 1997;386:830–833.

47. Volkow ND, Wang GJ, Telang F, et al. Profound decreases in dopamine release in striatum in detoxified alcoholics: possible orbitofrontal involvement. *J Neurosci* 2007;27:12700–12706.

48. Martinez D, Broft A, Foltin RW, et al. Cocaine dependence and D2 receptor availability in the functional subdivisions of the striatum: relationship with cocaine-seeking behavior. *Neuropsychopharmacol* 2004;29:1190–1202 [erratum: 29: 1763].

49. Martinez D, Gil R, Slifstein M, et al. Alcohol dependence is associated with blunted dopamine transmission in the ventral striatum. *Biol Psychiatry* 2005;58:779–786.

50. Zubieta JK, Gorelick DA, Stauffer R, Ravert HT, Dannals RF, Frost JJ. Increased mu opioid receptor binding detected by PET in cocaine-dependent men is associated with cocaine craving. *Nat Med* 1996;2:1225–1229.

51. Koob GF. A role for brain stress systems in addiction. *Neuron* 2008;59:11–34.

52. Koob GF, Kreek MJ. Stress, dysregulation of drug reward pathways, and the transition to drug dependence. *Am J Psychiatry* 2007;164:1149–1159.

53. Tucci S, Cheeta S, Seth P, File SE. Corticotropin releasing factor antagonist, α-helical CRF(9-41), reverses nicotine-induced conditioned, but not unconditioned, anxiety. *Psychopharmacol (Berl)* 2003;167:251–256.

54. George O, Ghozland S, Azar MR, et al. CRF-CRF1 system activation mediates withdrawal-induced increases in nicotine self-administration in nicotine-dependent rats. *Proc Natl Acad Sci USA* 2007;104: 17198–17203.

55. Wee S, Koob GF. The role of the dynorphin-κ opioid system in the reinforcing effects of drugs of abuse. *Psychopharmacol (Berl)* 2010;210:121–135.

56. Naqvi NH, Rudrauf D, Damasio H, Bechara A. Damage to the insula disrupts addiction to cigarette smoking. *Science* 2007;315:531–534.

57. Naqvi NH, Bechara A. The hidden island of addiction: the insula. *Trends Neurosci* 2009;32:56–67.

58. Tiffany ST, Carter BL, Singleton EG. Challenges in the manipulation, assessment and interpretation of craving relevant variables. *Addiction* 2000;95 (suppl 2):S177–S87.

59. Kalivas PW, O'Brien C. Drug addiction as a pathology of staged neuroplasticity. *Neuropsychopharmacol* 2008;33:166–180.

60. McFarland K, Kalivas PW. The circuitry mediating cocaine-induced reinstatement of drug-seeking behavior. *J Neurosci* 2001;21:8655–8663.

61. Everitt BJ, Wolf ME. Psychomotor stimulant addiction: a neural systems perspective. *J Neurosci* 2002;22: 3312–3320 [erratum: 22(16): 1a].

62. Weiss F, Ciccocioppo R, Parsons LH, et al. Compulsive drug-seeking behavior and relapse: neuroadaptation, stress, and conditioning factors. In: Quinones-Jenab V, ed. *The Biological Basis of Cocaine Addiction. Annals of the New York Academy of Sciences.* Vol 937. New York: New York Academy of Sciences; 2001:1–26.

63. Schulteis G, Ahmed SH, Morse AC, Koob GF, Everitt BJ. Conditioning and opiate withdrawal: the amygdala links neutral stimuli with the agony of overcoming drug addiction. *Nature* 2000;405: 1013–1014.

64. Kenny PJ, Chen SA, Kitamura O, Markou A, Koob GF. Conditioned withdrawal drives heroin consumption and decreases reward sensitivity. *J Neurosci* 2006;26:5894–5900.

65. McClernon FJ, Kozink RV, Lutz AM, Rose JE. 24-h smoking abstinence potentiates fMRI-BOLD activation to smoking cues in cerebral cortex and dorsal striatum. *Psychopharmacol (Berl)* 2009;204: 25–35.

66. Bjork JM, Momenan R, Hommer DW. Delay discounting correlates with proportional lateral frontal cortex volumes. *Biol Psychiatry* 2009;65:710–713.

67. Aharonovich E, Hasin DS, Brooks AC, Liu X, Bisaga A, Nunes EV. Cognitive deficits predict low treatment retention in cocaine dependent patients. *Drug Alcohol Depend* 2006;81:313–322.

68. Bolla KI, Eldreth DA, London ED, et al. Orbitofrontal cortex dysfunction in abstinent cocaine abusers performing a decision-making task. *Neuroimage* 2003;19:1085–1094.

69. George O, Koob GF. Individual differences in prefrontal cortex function and the transition from drug use to drug dependence. *Neurosci Biobehav Rev* May 18, 2010. Available at: http://www.sciencedirect.com/science/article/pii/S0149763410000965. Accessed March 11, 2012.

70. Franklin TR, Wang Z, Wang J, et al. Limbic activation to cigarette smoking cues independent of nicotine withdrawal: a perfusion fMRI study. *Neuropsychopharmacol* 2007;32:2301–2309.

71. Heinz A, Siessmeier T, Wrase J, et al. Correlation between dopamine D2 receptors in the ventral striatum and central processing of alcohol cues and craving. *Am J Psychiatry* 2004;161:1783–1789 [erratum: 161: 2344].

72. Volkow ND, Chang L, Wang GJ, et al. Low level of brain dopamine D2 receptors in methamphetamine abusers: association with metabolism in the orbitofrontal cortex. *Am J Psychiatry* 2001;158:2015–2021.

73. Shaham Y, Shalev U, Lu L, de Wit H, Stewart J. The reinstatement model of drug relapse: history, methodology and major findings. *Psychopharmacol (Berl)* 2003;168:3–20.

74. Shalev U, Grimm JW, Shaham Y. Neurobiology of relapse to heroin and cocaine seeking: a review. *Pharmacol Rev* 2002;54:1–42.

75. de Witte P, Littleton J, Parot P, Koob G. Neuroprotective and abstinence-promoting effects of acamprosate: elucidating the mechanism of action. *CNS Drugs* 2005;19:517–537.

76. Valdez GR, Roberts AJ, Chan K, et al. Increased ethanol self-administration and anxiety-like behavior during acute withdrawal and protracted abstinence: regulation by corticotropin-releasing factor. *Alcohol Clin Exp Res* 2002;26:1494–1501.

4

Genetics of Addiction

ERNEST P. NOBLE

DRD2 AND ALCOHOL DEPENDENCE

In 1990,[1] we published an article in the *Journal of the American Medical Association* in which we searched for the involvement of a number of putative genes in alcoholism. The only gene that associated with alcoholism was the D_2 dopamine receptor gene (*DRD2*). Specifically, using brains of deceased alcoholic and nonalcoholic (control) subjects, we found the *DRD2* A1+ allele (A1A1, A1A2) to be significantly associated with alcoholism.

That study caused controversy because, while some studies could replicate the finding, others could not. A subsequent Swedish study,[2] using the largest number of alcoholic (n = 357) and nonalcoholic (n = 578) subjects to date, did replicate this finding, although it found the effect size of *DRD2* to be small (odds ratio [OR] = 1.34). The authors suggested that there is a need for individual studies to have case-control sets of 300–400 subjects to ensure that they have the statistical power to detect the small effect size of the *DRD2* A1 allele. To collect such a large set of subjects, assess their genotype, and obtain other relevant data is a laborious and an expensive task. To circumvent this problem, a meta-analytic approach has been employed. One such meta-analysis[3] using 21 studies, composed of 1,837 alcoholic subjects and 1,492 controls, found the frequency of the *DRD2* A1+ allele to be significantly higher in the alcoholic subjects than in controls (p = 2.14 × 10⁻⁷, OR = 1.39). A more recent meta-analysis,[4] using 40 studies, composed of 5,305 alcoholic subjects and 3,938 controls, found the frequency of the *DRD2* A1+ allele to be significantly higher in the alcoholic subjects than in controls (p = 4.58 x 10⁻⁸, OR = 1.31). Thus, these meta-analyses, as well as a number of others, showed the *DRD2* A1+ allele frequency to be significantly and strongly associated with alcoholism.

DRD2 AND OTHER SUBSTANCE DEPENDENCE

Is the association of *DRD2* unique to alcoholism, or is this association found also in other substance dependencies? To answer this question, an assessment was made of the relationship of variants of *DRD2* with other substance dependencies.

Cocaine Dependence

The first such study was on cocaine-dependent (CD) subjects.[5] The objective of this study was to examine allele prevalence of two variants of *DRD2*—the A1 allele and the B1 allele—in CD subjects and in non-substance-abusing controls. The results showed that the prevalence of the A1+ allele and B1+ allele (B1B1, B1B2 genotypes), which are in linkage disequilibrium, was each significantly higher in CD subjects (n = 52) than in controls (n = 53). Logistic regression analysis of CD subjects identified potent routes of cocaine use (i.v., free base, and crack) and the interaction of early deviant behaviors and parental alcoholism as significant risk factors associated with the A1+ allele. Data showing association of A1+ and B1+ alleles of *DRD2* with CD subjects suggest that this gene confers susceptibility to cocaine dependence.

Nicotine Dependence

The next study was on nicotine-dependent subjects.[6] The *DRD2* A1+ allele prevalence was examined in current smokers (n = 57), past smokers (n = 115), and nonsmokers (n = 182). The results showed *DRD2* A1+ allele prevalence was significantly different among these three groups. Specifically, the A1+ allele occurred in a significantly larger proportion of current smokers compared to nonsmokers. Furthermore, smokers (past and current combined) had a significantly higher prevalence of the A1+ allele compared to nonsmokers. Linear trend analysis of A1$^+$ allele prevalence in the nonsmoker, past smoker, and current smoker groups, respectively, showed that as smoking severity increased, so did the prevalence of the A1$^+$ allele. This study showed the *DRD2* A1$^+$ allele to be associated with nicotine-dependent subjects. It hypothesizes that *DRD2* is a reward gene and that those who carry the *DRD2* A1$^+$ allele have a deficit in their brain dopamine reward system. By using nicotine, a substance that increases brain dopamine levels, A1$^+$ allele subjects experience enhanced reward or pleasure, a diathesis for developing nicotine dependence.

Opioid Dependence

The association of the *DRD2* A1$^+$ allele with opioid dependence was the objective of our next study.[7] In this investigation, opioid-dependent patients were followed over a 1-year period in an outpatient methadone treatment program. The frequency of the *DRD2* A1$^+$ allele was found to be significantly higher in these patients than in controls free of past and current alcohol and other drug abuse. Twenty-two of these patients dropped out of the methadone treatment program (Group A), 54 had a successful treatment outcome (Group B), and 19 had a poor treatment outcome (Group C). The frequency of the *DRD2* A1$^+$ allele was highest in Group C (42.1%), followed by Group A (22.7%), and was lowest in Group B (9.3%). The more than four-fold higher frequency of the A1$^+$ allele in the poor treatment group compared to the successful treatment group was significant. Moreover, the average use of heroin (grams/day) during the year prior to study entry was significantly and more than two-fold greater in patients with the A1$^+$ allele than those with the A1$^-$ allele (A2A2 genotype). The study suggests the DRD2 A1$^+$ allele is a predictor of heroin use and subsequent methadone treatment outcome and suggests a pharmacogenetic approach to the treatment of opioid dependence.

Obesity

In 1994 we published a study on the association of *DRD2* with obesity.[8] A total of 73 obese subjects, free of alcohol and other drugs of abuse, with an average body mass index (BMI) of 35.1, were studied. The prevalence of the *DRD2* A1$^+$ allele in these subjects was 45.2% and was significantly higher than in controls. This suggests that obesity is also associated with the *DRD2* gene.

The relationship of the *DRD2* A1$^+$ allele to phenotypic characteristics of these obese subjects was determined.

With respect to parental history of obesity, the relationship of A1$^+$ allele prevalence was assessed in four of the obese subjects' parental groups: fathers and mothers nonobese (A1$^+$ prevalence = 31.0%); fathers obese (A1$^+$ prevalence = 43.5%); mothers obese (A1$^+$ prevalence = 51.5%); and fathers and/or mothers obese (A1$^+$ prevalence = 53.7%). Thus, as family density of obesity increased, so did A1$^+$ allele prevalence.

Next, *DRD2* A1 allele association with onset of obesity was determined. A1$^+$ allele prevalence was 25.0% in childhood onset of obesity and progressively increased to 35.5% in adolescent onset of obesity and 56.4% in adult onset of obesity. A1$^+$ allele prevalence was more than twice and significantly higher in adult onset of obesity than the prevalence of this allele in childhood onset of obesity. This suggests that obese subjects with adult onset of obesity are the main contributors to the association of the *DRD2* A1$^+$ allele with obesity.

Comparisons were also made in food preference of these obese individuals. The results showed that obese individuals who preferred carbohydrates had a significantly higher A1$^+$ allele prevalence of 64.3%, compared to the 21.1% prevalence of this allele in those who preferred other foods.

In sum, the *DRD2* A1$^+$ allele was found to be associated with obesity. A unique phenotypic profile, characterized by the presence of parental history and postpuberty onset of obesity as well as carbohydrate preference, was observed in obese subjects carrying the A1$^+$ allele. The study suggests that besides metabolic genes that contribute to obesity, another factor that increases the risk for certain types of obesity is *DRD2*.

DRD2 PHENOTYPES

The positive association of the A1$^+$ allele, but not the A1$^-$ allele (A2A2 genotype), with alcoholism and other substance dependencies raised the question: Do the brains of A1$^+$ and A1$^-$ allele subjects express different phenotypes? To answer this question, the following studies were conducted.

Brain D$_2$ Dopamine Receptors

Having available brains of alcoholic and nonalcoholic subjects from our first study on the association of DRD2 with alcoholism, binding studies were performed on these brains to determine the number of D_2 dopamine receptors in those who had the A1$^+$ allele or the A1$^-$ allele. The results showed that those with the A1$^+$ allele, irrespective of whether they were alcoholic or nonalcoholic subjects, had significantly fewer brain D_2 dopamine receptors than those with the A1$^-$ allele.[9] This finding has been confirmed by other investigators.[10–12]

Basal Brain Glucose Metabolism

Are the reduced brain D2 dopamine receptors that characterize A1$^+$ allele subjects reflected in other aspects of brain function? In a study of non-alcohol-/non-drug-abusing subjects, brain regional glucose metabolic rate (GMR), using positron emission tomography (PET), was determined in A1$^+$ and A1$^-$ allele subjects.[13] The results showed that brain regional GMR was significantly lower in A1$^+$ allele compared to A1$^-$ allele subjects. This reduction was found in the striatum, insula, and other brain regions rich in dopamine, regions associated with drug reinforcement and brain reward. These findings suggest that under basal conditions, subjects with the A1$^+$ allele, compared to those with the A1$^-$ allele, have a deficit in their brain dopamine reward system.

Alcohol-Induced Brain Glucose Metabolism

The next question we asked was as follows: Does alcohol induce differential activation of brain glucose metabolism in A1$^+$ and A1$^-$ allele subjects?

In a study of non-alcohol-/non-drug-abusing subjects,[14] using PET, we ascertained behavior and brain regional GMR in A1$^+$ and A1$^-$ allele subjects following the administration of placebo or ethanol (0.75 ml/kg). The results showed that alcohol significantly decreased fatigue and anxiety in A1$^+$ allele subjects, whereas it significantly increased these behaviors in A1$^-$ allele subjects. With respect to brain regional GMR, alcohol increased activation in A1$^+$ allele subjects in brain regions associated with craving or reinforcement (striatum) and mood (insula), but it reduced activation in A1$^-$ allele subjects in the anterior cingulate, a region associated with cognitive coping. These findings suggest that alcohol is more reinforcing in A1$^+$ allele subjects, thereby providing a possible explanation for their increased risk for developing alcoholism.

DRD2 AND TREATMENT OF ALCOHOLISM

Since the DRD2 A1 allele increases the risk for developing alcoholism and is associated with expression of fewer D_2 dopamine receptors, what would the effect on treatment be if a dopamine receptor agonist were to be administered to alcoholic subjects? To answer this question, we conducted a double-blind study[15] in which bromocriptine (a D_2 dopamine receptor agonist) or placebo was administered to alcoholic subjects who carried the A1$^+$ or A1$^-$ allele. Changes in craving, anxiety, and retention rates were determined over the 6-week period of the trial. The results showed that craving was significantly and almost completely abolished in alcoholic subjects who received bromocriptine (BRO) and had the A1$^+$ allele (A1$^+$), that is, the BRO A1$^+$ group. Little change was found in the other three groups (BRO A1$^-$, placebo A1$^+$, placebo A1$^-$). Similarly, significant decreases in anxiety were found in the BRO A1$^+$ group, with no notable changes in the other three groups. When retention rate was measured, the greatest number of alcoholic subjects who stayed in the trial were those in the BRO A1$^+$ group.

In sum, the A1$^+$ allele alcoholic patients who were treated with bromocriptine were the only group that benefitted from bromocriptine treatment. The feasibility of a pharmacogenetic approach in treating certain types of alcoholics is suggested.

DISCUSSION

DRD2 has been one of the most extensively and intensively studied genes in neuropsychiatric disorders. Herein, we present evidence that alcohol, other drug abuse (cocaine, nicotine, opioids), and food (obesity) dependencies have, through DRD2, a common genetic diathesis for the development of these substance use disorders.

What is unique about DRD2 that makes its association possible with substance use disorders? It is the variants of this gene that manifest themselves as different phenotypes. Specifically, subjects with the DRD2 A1$^+$ allele, compared to those with the A1$^-$ allele, have reduced brain D_2 dopamine receptors. This reduction is reflected in brain activity, where, under basal conditions, subjects with the A1$^+$ allele, compared to those with the A1$^-$ allele, have reduced glucose metabolism in the mesocorticolimbic dopamine reward system. This reduction renders A1$^+$ allele subjects reward or pleasure deficient.[16] To compensate for this deficiency, A1$^+$ allele individuals consume alcohol, which, by increasing brain dopamine levels and stimulating their fewer D$_2$ dopamine receptors, activates brain glucose metabolism in regions associated with craving and reinforcement, resulting in improvement in mood and pleasure. This does not occur in A1$^-$ allele subjects. It is proposed that alcohol is, thus, more reinforcing in A1$^+$ allele subjects, leading to their greater propensity for developing alcoholism.

Since the consumption of other drugs of abuse and food also enhances brain dopamine levels, the reinforcing effect of these substances in A1$^+$ allele subjects may also lead to their greater risk for developing other drug dependencies and obesity.

How does knowledge of a genetic commonality among the various substance use disorders bode for the treatment of these disorders? Here, again, we turn to the prototypic drug: alcohol. As indicated earlier, alcohol consumption enhances the release of dopamine, which, by stimulating D$_2$ dopamine receptors, is more reinforcing in A1$^+$ allele subjects. Unfortunately, the continual use of high amounts of alcohol can lead to the development of alcoholism. What if a drug is used that, like alcohol, similarly activates D$_2$ dopamine receptors but does not have the addictive potential of alcohol? This has been done with bromocriptine, a D$_2$ dopamine receptor agonist. The results showed that this drug had its most salutary effects in the treatment of A1$^+$ allele alcoholics. We suggest that bromocriptine, or other D$_2$ dopamine receptor agonists, can similarly be used in the treatment of other drug dependencies and obesity.

ACKNOWLEDGMENTS

I thank the Christopher D. Smithers Foundation and the National Institutes of Health for their generous support. I am grateful to my many colleagues who collaborated with me in the genetics of substance use disorders. I thank Bonita Porch for her assistance in the preparation of the manuscript.

REFERENCES

1. Blum K, Noble EP, Sheridan PJ, et al. Allelic association of human dopamine D$_2$ receptor gene in alcoholism. *JAMA* 1990;263:2055–2060.
2. Berggren U, Fahlke C, Aronsson E, et al. The Taq1 DRD2 A1 allele is associated with alcohol-dependence although its effect size is small. *Alcohol Alcoholism* 2006:41:479–485.
3. Noble EP. D$_2$ dopamine receptor gene in psychiatric and neurologic disorders and its phenotypes: a review. *Am J Med Genet B Neuropsychiatr Genet* 2003;116B:103–125.
4. Le Foll B, Gallo A, Le Strat Y, Lu L, Garabod P. Genetics of dopamine receptors and drug addiction: a comprehensive review. *Behav Pharmacol* 2009;20:1–17.
5. Noble EP, Blum K, Khalsa ME, et al. Allelic association of the D$_2$ dopamine receptor gene with cocaine dependence. *Drug Alcohol Depend* 1993;33:271–285.
6. Noble EP, St. Jeor ST, Ritchie T, et al. D$_2$ dopamine receptor gene and cigarette smoking: a reward gene? *Med Hypotheses* 1994;42:257–260.
7. Lawford BR, Young RM, Noble EP, et al. The D$_2$ dopamine receptor A$_1$ allele and opioid dependence: association with heroin use and response to methadone treatment. *Am J Med Genet B Neuropsychiatr Genet* 2000;96:592–598.
8. Noble EP, Noble RE, Ritchie T, et al. D$_2$ dopamine receptor gene and obesity. *Int J Eat Disord* 1994;15:205–217.
9. Noble EP, Blum K, Ritchie T, Montgomery A, Sheridan PJ. Allelic association of the D2 dopamine receptor gene with receptor-binding characteristics in alcoholism. *Arch Gen Psychiatry* 1991;48:648–654.
10. Jönsson EG, Nöthen MM, Grünhage F, et al. Polymorphisms in the dopamine D$_2$ receptor gene and their relationships to striatal dopamine receptor density of health volunteers. *Mol Psychiatry* 1999;4:290–296.
11. Pohjalainen T, Rinne JO, Någren K, et al. The A1 allele of the human D$_2$ dopamine receptor gene predicts low D$_2$ receptor availability in healthy volunteers. *Mol Psychiatry* 1998;3:256–260.
12. Thompson J, Thomas N, Singleton A, et al. D2 dopamine receptor gene (DRD2) Taq1 A polymorphism: reduced dopamine D2 receptor binding in the human striatum associated with the A1 allele. *Pharmacogenetics* 1997;7:479–484.
13. Noble EP, Gottschalk LA, Fallon JH, Ritchie TL, Wu JC. D2 dopamine receptor polymorphism and brain regional glucose metabolism. *Am J Med Genet B Neuropsychiatr Genet* 1997;74:162–166.
14. London ED, Berman SM, Mohammadian P, et al. Effect of the TaqI A polymorphism on ethanol response in the brain. *Psychiatry Res* 2009;174(3):163–170.
15. Lawford BR, Young RMcD, Rowell JA, et al. Bromocriptine in the treatment of alcoholics with the D$_2$ dopamine receptor A1 allele. *Nat Med* 1995;1:337–341.
16. Bowirrat A, Oscar-Berman M. Relationship between dopaminergic neurotransmission, alcoholism, and reward deficiency syndrome. *Am J Med Genet B Neuropsychiatr Genet* 2005;132B:29–37.

5

Epigenetic Changes in Addiction and Eating Disorders

FIRAS H. KOBEISSY, MAHDI RAZAFSHA, ZHIQUN ZHANG,
AND MARK S. GOLD

INTRODUCTION

Genes have been well recognized to form and shape human phenotype and are considered to define innate characteristics. However, another major factor in determining self phenotype involves environmental factors that can modulate gene expression.[1] Different studies have focused on the (gene–environment) interaction to elucidate the dynamic effects of how environmental cues can modulate genetic expression, which was later introduced as the field of epigenetics.[1,2] In principle, epigenetics refers to the regulation of genomic functions such as gene expression independent of DNA sequence but rather controlled by potentially reversible chemical modifications occurring on the DNA and/or histones leading to chromatin remodeling and histone modification, inducing alteration in gene expression.[3] In the area of psychiatry, epigenetics studies evaluate how gene–environment interaction contributes to the state of psychiatric disorders. It has been shown that exposure to certain drugs of abuse (amphetamine, cocaine, nicotine, and morphine)[4–9] can induce neuronal structural changes that will remain persistent long after exposure to these drugs, as will be discussed later.

EPIGENETIC MECHANISMS: CHROMATIN REMODELING AND HISTONE MODIFICATION

Recent growing evidence has shown that structural modifications of chromatin can change synaptic connections in a way that ultimately leads to long-term changes in behavior without direct changes in DNA sequence.[10–13] Epigenetics mediates its control via chromatin modification occurring on the DNA and histone levels.[14] Among the epigenetics signature mechanisms, DNA methylation is considered a relatively stable epigenetic marker occurring on the 5′ position of the pyrimidine ring on cytosine guanine dinucleotide (CpG) islands (regions of high GC content [>55%]), catalyzed by several types of DNA methyltransferase.[15–17] These CpG islands are often found around gene promoters and are typically unmethylated.[16]

DNA methylation is thought to repress gene expression by altering different transcription factors' binding affinity to their target sequences, resulting in transcriptional silencing.[18] Furthermore, methylated DNA can also recruit methyl-binding domain-containing proteins, such as methyl-CpG-binding protein 2 (MeCP2), which recruit chromatin-remodeling proteins such as histone deacetylase (HDAC) to deacetylate histones, leading to transcriptional silencing.[19] MeCP2 is an abundant chromosome-binding protein that selectively binds 5-methyl cytosine residues located in the promoter regions of genes subjected to transcriptional silencing after DNA methylation.[20]

On the other hand, histone modification represents another level of epigenetic regulation. Histone proteins are essential for packaging DNA inside the nucleus and play an important role in regulating gene expression. DNA is wrapped around a histone octamer (pairs of the core histone: H2A, H2B, H3, and H4), which is the site for posttranslational modification (PTM) on their N terminal tails as reviewed by Kouzarides.[14] Among the major PTMs carried out by histone-modifying enzymes are acetylation, methylation, and phosphorylation.[14,21] Histone modifications are highly dynamic and regulated via a group of catalytic enzymes, such as histone acetyltransferases (HAT) and histone deacetylases (HDACs), which add or remove acetyl groups, respectively.[22–24] Condensed chromatin (heterochromatin), in which the DNA and histone proteins are tightly packed, acts to block the access of transcription factors. An open chromatin conformation (euchromatin) allows the cell's transcriptional machinery to access DNA and drives transcription. Histone acetylation would reduce interaction between histone proteins and DNA, which relaxes chromatin structure and improves access of transcriptional regulators to DNA.[22–24] Histone modification is related to serve two purposes: first, it functions as a recruitment signal for nonhistone proteins (e.g., transcription factors), which are important in transcriptional activation and silencing[25]; second, it induces chromatin relaxation by disrupting contacts between histone tails and genomic DNA.[14] Recent studies have demonstrated that epigenetic processes have been associated with a range of neurobiological processes, including learning and memory, which may account for a number of psychiatric disorders, including addiction and schizophrenia.[22,33–35]

EPIGENETICS, PLASTICITY, AND DRUG ADDICTION

Although family history has been common among key candidates for psychiatric diseases, advances in the areas of genomic and proteomics have revealed other factors, including epigenetics, contributing to the phenotype of these psychiatric disorders, as will be discussed in the area of drug abuse, addiction, and major psychosis.[18]

Drug addiction is characterized by compulsive drug-seeking behavior coupled with loss of control over drug intake, mediated by stable changes in central reward pathways.[26,27] Drug abusers remain at a high risk of relapse to drugs of abuse long after drug abstinence.[10,13] Such long-lasting effects have been attributed to neuronal plasticity as the result of stable structural and functional changes on the brain circuitry occurring on the cellular and molecular levels.[28,29] Neuronal synaptic plasticity has been implicated as the underlying process of learning and memory.[30–32] Epigenetic regulations have been shown to impose control over dynamic plasticity in neurons.[30,33] Addictive drugs induce structural changes in the dendrites and dendritic spines in brain regions involved in incentive motivation and reward such as the nucleus accumbens (NAc) and the prefrontal cortex.[34]

Recognition of the epigenetic molecular mechanisms in neuroplasticity related to addictive diseases

can alter our understanding about the pathophysiology of compulsive drug-seeking behavior.[35,36] It has been shown that histone-modifying enzymes (deacetylases, methyltransferases, etc.) are pivotal in regulating long-term learning and memory processes. Impairments in HAT enzymes function coupled with a decrease in histone acetylation results in an impaired synaptic plasticity, while elevated histone acetylation (via HDAC inhibition) results in enhanced synaptic plasticity and long-term memory.[13] Of interest, drugs of abuse have been shown to induce chromatin modifications modulating transcription patterns leading to neural and behavioral changes that contribute to the development and persistence of drug addiction.[13]

Among the regulators implicated in drug addiction are the two transcription factors ΔFosB and cyclic adenosine monophosphate response element–binding (CREB) protein, which regulate gene expression after drug exposure.[10] Epigenetic mechanisms have been found to be a key player to the cellular responses to drugs of abuse, which includes transition from acute exposure to chronic exposure, as illustrated by Nestler.[37,38] Drug abuse exposure including cocaine targets the NAc, leading to alteration in gene expression, which has been linked to addictive behavior.[38] Elegant work by Nestler and colleagues on cocaine abuse has shown that different genes are differentially expressed after cocaine exposure and are related to drug addiction.[39–41] A number of these genes, including *FosB*, brain-derived neurotrophic factor (*BDNF*), and cyclin-dependent kinase 5 (*Cdk5*), exhibit differential expression after distinct cocaine exposure (chronic vs. acute).[38] The c-*fos* gene is activated in the acute model, while *FosB* is activated by both acute as well as chronic cocaine exposure. It has been shown that both H4 acetylation and H3 phosphorylation histone PTMs occur at the c-*fos* gene promoter after acute cocaine exposure , which can be seen after 30 minutes and returns to baseline after 3 hours. Based on the finding that acute cocaine exposure would induce global acetylation, the use of different HDAC inhibitors exhibited similar patterns to cocaine exposure in inducing c-fos expression and elevated phosphoacetylated H3 at the c-*fos* gene promoter. These data established a correlation between epigenetic changes and drug abuse exposure.[40]

Interestingly, chronic cocaine exposure appears to be associated with H3 hyperacetylation of the

FosB promoter with no effect on the cFos promoter, while H4 modification shows transient activity at the beginning. In addition, H3 hyperacetylation of Cdk5 and BDNF genes was associated with chronic, but not acute, cocaine administration occurring after 24 hours of cocaine exposure and persisted even 1 week after treatment.[40]

It has been further investigated that the transcription factor ΔFosB , FosB gene product, accumulates upon chronic cocaine exposure. Chronic cocaine-induced ΔFosB has been associated with Cdk5 expression, supporting the hypothesis that induced ΔFosB recruits chromatin remodeling factors, including histone acetylases to induce H3 acetylation with other chromatin remodeling complexes to different gene targets such as Cdk5, which are elevated after cocaine exposure. These findings implicate epigenetic mechanisms in the development of addiction and particularly in the addictive behavioral model of cocaine.[42] Finally, chronic administration of several drugs of abuse such as cocaine,[4] amphetamine,[5] opiates,[6] nicotine,[7] and alcohol[9] have been shown to induce Fos-like proteins in different parts of brain.[43]

In the related area of alcohol dependence, Muschler and colleagues evaluated DNA methylation of the POMC gene promoter in 145 alcohol-dependent patients and 37 healthy controls.[44] DNA methylation of the 5′ promoter of the pro-opiomelanocortine (POMC) gene was evaluated in these two groups. POMC plays an important role in the regulation of the hypothalamic-pituitary-adrenal (HPA) axis and is a substrate for epigenetic regulation due to promoter-related DNA methylation. Interestingly, it was found that DNA methylation correlated with alcohol craving, which may in turn contribute to craving via promoting HPA-axis dysfunction.

Similarly, in the area of tobacco addiction, Launay and colleagues investigated DNA methylation of monoamine oxidase (MAO-B) gene promoter in three experimental groups distributed as current smokers (S), never smokers (NS), and former smokers (FS).[45] Interestingly, it was shown that MAO-B activity was inhibited during smoking coupled with elevated enzyme protein concentration found both in S and FS, indicating that MAO inhibition during smoking was compensated by a higher synthesis. On the molecular levels, it was found that the methylation frequency of the MAOB gene promoter was markedly lower for S and FS versus NS, which was correlated to "cigarette smoke"–induced

increase of nucleic acid demethylase activity. These results demonstrate that epigenetics regulation contributes to tobacco addiction and its long-lasting effects after quitting.[45]

Based on these findings relating addiction and drug-seeking behavior to epigenetic control, one can anticipate that eating disorders, which are one form of addictive disorder, share similar factors that fall among the spectrum of epigenetic regulation. Future research is anticipated in this area, which can reveal the "environment–gene" interaction involved in the area of eating disorders; this also necessitates the need for future research in the area of eating disorders models to identify the differentially altered genes in susceptible individuals, which can represent to be genetic biomarkers indicative of addictive diseases.[46]

EPIGENETIC STUDIES IN EATING DISORDERS

Eating disorders constitute complex disorders that are caused by several genetic and nongenetic risk factors. It has been proposed that environmental factors affecting energy expenditure play a major role in the current emerging eating disorders such as the obesity epidemic, as the population gene pool is unlikely to have been significantly altered within the past generations.[47] This is primarily caused by recent lifestyle changes with the availability of energy-dense fast food and decreased physical activity and exercise.[48] Thus, similar to other psychiatric disorders, gene–environment interaction represents a key factor in the etiology of eating disorders.

Among the various eating disorders, obesity has been widely investigated because its prevalence has reached pandemic proportions. Initially, genetic studies considered obesity as an inherited disease caused by gene mutations and polymorphisms.[49] However, the epigenetic regulation has emerged in the last years as a potential important contributor for obesity incidence. These environmental factors take into account various environmental factors, such as perinatal nutrition, maternal energy status, maternal endocrine status, and oxidative stress. These factors can affect methylation patterns on eating disorder specific genes (epiobesigenes), such as FGF2, PTEN, CDKN1A, and ESR1.[50] It has been shown that maternal calorie restriction is associated with increased methylation of the HRAS gene, and maternal protein deficiency is associated with alterations in epigenetic regulation of the glucocorticoid receptor and peroxisome proliferator activated receptor alpha.[51,52]

Furthermore, neonatal exposure to bisphenol A (DNA-hypomethylating compound) has been associated with higher body weight in the rat model.[53] Dolinoy and colleagues showed that maternal dietary genistein supplement during gestation in the mice model, at levels comparable with humans consuming high-soy diets, induced hypermethylation of six cytosine-guanine sites in *Agouti* gene, decreasing the expression of this gene and protecting offspring from obese phenotype by permanently altering the epigenome status.[54] Taken together, these data suggest that epigenetic mechanism modulated by environmental factors could be involved in obesity susceptibility.

Along the same lines, Frieling and colleagues evaluated genomic and gene-specific DNA altered methylation in a well-defined sample of females with eating disorders. In his study, 22 women with anorexia nervosa (AN) and 24 women with bulimia nervosa (BN) were screened for altered epigenetic regulation in their peripheral blood relevant to their eating disorder. Two genes were evaluated for DNA methylation, which included alpha synuclein gene (SNCA) and the homocysteine-induced endoplasmic reticulum protein (HERP) gene. These genes have been implicated to be epigenetically altered in alcohol dependence previously.[55,56] Interestingly, patients with AN showed a trend toward a lower global methylation coupled with a decreased SNCA expression in patients, which was associated with a DNA hypermethylation of the SNCA promoter. However, the BN group showed no hypermethylation change when compared to controls.[56]

This work was followed by another elegant study that investigated alteration in volume-regulating mechanisms implicated in the pathophysiology of eating disorders, including AN and BN, in relation to appetite-regulating hormones (atrial natriuretic peptide [ANP] and vasopressin).[57] Vasopressin and ANP are implicated to have anxiogenic and axiolitic effects, respectively, and been shown to be altered in AN and BN conditions. Thus, in their work, Frieling and colleagues evaluated mRNA expression and DNA methylation of the vasopressin and the ANP genes.

These two genes were assessed using real-time polymerase chain reaction in AN ($n = 22$) and in BN ($n = 24$) as well as healthy controls ($n = 30$).

Of interest, lower levels of ANP mRNA in both anorexic and bulimic patients were observed. In addition, DNA methylation of the ANP gene promoter was significantly higher in patients with BN compared to healthy patients and patients with AN. To estimate the severity and assess behavioral aspects of AN and BN, Eating Disorder Inventory-2 (EDI-2) was used. Higher scores of EDI-2 indicating more severe disease were associated with more dysregulations in volume-controlling hormones. However, there was no association between these hormones and serum electrolyte and creatinine levels, raising the possibility that other mechanisms may contribute to expression of ANP. Taken together, these studies advance our understanding of the epigenetic mechanisms involved in the pathophysiology of different eating disorders. We believe that these epigenetic-related studies will likely add a novel dimension toward the explanation of the causes leading to the occurrence of different eating disorders.

CONCLUSION

Similar to other novel, emerging fields, such as proteomics, in psychiatric disorders, epigenetic research is developing rapidly.[58,59] The introduction of next generation sequencing and other advanced ChIP-based quantitative DNA methylation profiling techniques would allow investigators to decipher the mechanisms of how environmental factors affect genome regulation. And epigenetics in the area of psychiatric disorders provides new insights for understanding the molecular mechanisms involved in both addiction and other related psychiatric diseases. Thus, it is of great importance to initiate translational epigenetic studies in the areas of addiction and psychiatric disorders for identifying epigenetic signature markers, which can lead to new targets identification that can be applied in therapeutics and prevention.

REFERENCES

1. Oh G, Petronis A. Environmental studies of schizophrenia through the prism of epigenetics. *Schizophr Bull* 2008;34:1122–1129.
2. Rutten BP, Mill J. Epigenetic mediation of environmental influences in major psychotic disorders. *Schizophr Bull* 2009;35:1045–1056.
3. Henikoff S, Matzke MA. Exploring and explaining epigenetic effects. *Trends Genet* 1997;13:293–295.
4. Hope BT, Nye HE, Kelz MB, et al. Induction of a long-lasting AP-1 complex composed of altered Fos-like

proteins in brain by chronic cocaine and other chronic treatments. *Neuron* 1994;13:1235–1244.

5. Conversi D, Bonito-Oliva A, Orsini C, Colelli V, Cabib S. DeltaFosB accumulation in ventro-medial caudate underlies the induction but not the expression of behavioral sensitization by both repeated amphetamine and stress. *Eur J Neurosci* 2008;27:191–201.

6. Zachariou V, Bolanos CA, Selley DE, et al. An essential role for DeltaFosB in the nucleus accumbens in morphine action. *Nat Neurosci* 2006;9:205–211.

7. Marttila K, Raattamaa H, Ahtee L. Effects of chronic nicotine administration and its withdrawal on striatal FosB/[Delta]FosB and c-Fos expression in rats and mice. *Neuropharmacol* 2006;51:44–51.

8. Kontkanen O, Lakso M, Koponen E, Wong G, Castren E. Molecular effects of the psychotropic NMDA receptor antagonist MK-801 in the rat entorhinal cortex: increases in AP-1 DNA binding activity and expression of Fos and Jun family members. *Ann NY Acad Sci* 2000;911:73–82.

9. Ryabinin AE, Wang YM. Repeated alcohol administration differentially affects c-Fos and FosB protein immunoreactivity in DBA/2J mice. *Alcohol Clin Exp Res* 1998;22:1646–1654.

10. McQuown SC, Wood MA. Epigenetic regulation in substance use disorders. *Curr Psychiatry Rep* 2010; 12:145–153.

11. Impey S. A histone deacetylase regulates addiction. *Neuron* 2007;56:415–417.

12. Duman RS, Monteggia LM. A neurotrophic model for stress-related mood disorders. *Biol Psychiatry* 2006;59:1116–1127.

13. Malvaez M, Barrett RM, Wood MA, Sanchis-Segura C. Epigenetic mechanisms underlying extinction of memory and drug-seeking behavior. *Mamm Genome* 2009;20:612–623.

14. Kouzarides T. Chromatin modifications and their function. *Cell* 2007;128:693–705.

15. Jaenisch R, Bird A. Epigenetic regulation of gene expression: how the genome integrates intrinsic and environmental signals. *Nat Genet* 2003;33(suppl): 245–254.

16. Bird AP. CpG-rich islands and the function of DNA methylation. *Nature* 1986;321:209–213.

17. Antequera F. Structure, function and evolution of CpG island promoters. *Cell Mol Life Sci* 2003;60: 1647–1658.

18. Renthal W, Nestler EJ. Chromatin regulation in drug addiction and depression. *Dialogues Clin Neurosci* 2009;11:257–268.

19. Robertson KD, Wolffe AP. DNA methylation in health and disease. *Nat Rev Genet* 2000;1:11–19.

20. Amir RE, Van den Veyver IB, Wan M, Tran CQ, Francke U, Zoghbi HY. Rett syndrome is caused by mutations in X-linked MECP2, encoding methyl-CpG-binding protein 2. *Nat Genet* 1999;23: 185–188.

21. Berger SL. The complex language of chromatin regulation during transcription. *Nature* 2007;447:407–412.

22. Saha RN, Pahan K. HATs and HDACs in neurodegeneration: a tale of disconcerted acetylation homeostasis. *Cell Death Differ* 2006;13:539–550.

23. Renthal W, Maze I, Krishnan V, et al. Histone deacetylase 5 epigenetically controls behavioral adaptations to chronic emotional stimuli. *Neuron* 2007;56: 517–529.

24. Robertson KD, Jones PA. DNA methylation: past, present and future directions. *Carcinogenesis* 2000;21: 461–467.

25. Taverna SD, Li H, Ruthenburg AJ, Allis CD, Patel DJ. How chromatin-binding modules interpret histone modifications: lessons from professional pocket pickers. *Nat Struct Mol Biol* 2007;14:1025–1040.

26. Hyman SE, Malenka RC, Nestler EJ. Neural mechanisms of addiction: the role of reward-related learning and memory. *Annu Rev Neurosci* 2006;29:565–598.

27. Kalivas PW, Volkow N, Seamans J. Unmanageable motivation in addiction: a pathology in prefrontal-accumbens glutamate transmission. *Neuron* 2005;45:647–650.

28. Lamprecht R, LeDoux J. Structural plasticity and memory. *Nat Rev Neurosci* 2004;5:45–54.

29. Robinson TE, Kolb B. Structural plasticity associated with exposure to drugs of abuse. *Neuropharmacol* 2004;47(suppl 1):33–46.

30. Duman RS, Newton SS. Epigenetic marking and neuronal plasticity. *Biol Psychiatry* 2007;62:1–3.

31. Levenson JM, Roth TL, Lubin FD, et al. Evidence that DNA (cytosine-5) methyltransferase regulates synaptic plasticity in the hippocampus. *J Biol Chem* 2006;281:15763–15773.

32. Levenson JM, Sweatt JD. Epigenetic mechanisms: a common theme in vertebrate and invertebrate memory formation. *Cell Mol Life Sci* 2006;63:1009–1016.

33. Levenson JM, Roth TL, Lubin FD, et al. Evidence that DNA (cytosine-5) methyltransferase regulates synaptic plasticity in the hippocampus. *J Biol Chem* 2006;281:15763–15773.

34. Harris KM, Kater SB. Dendritic spines: cellular specializations imparting both stability and flexibility to synaptic function. *Annu Rev Neurosci* 1994;17:341–371.

35. Valjent E, Pagès C, Hervé D, Girault JA, Caboche J. Addictive and non-addictive drugs induce distinct and specific patterns of ERK activation in mouse brain. *Eur J Neurosci* 2004;19(7):1826–1836.

36. Hyman SE. Addiction: a disease of learning and memory. *Am J Psychiatry* 2005;162:1414–1422.

37. Renthal W, Carle TL, Maze I, et al. Delta FosB mediates epigenetic desensitization of the c-fos gene after chronic amphetamine exposure. *J Neurosci* 2008;28:7344–7349.

38. Colvis CM, Pollock JD, Goodman RH, et al. Epigenetic mechanisms and gene networks in the nervous system. *J Neurosci* 2005;25:10379–10389.

39. McClung CA, Nestler EJ. Regulation of gene expression and cocaine reward by CREB and DeltaFosB. *Nat Neurosci* 2003;6:1208–1215.

40. Kumar A, Choi KH, Renthal W, et al. Chromatin remodeling is a key mechanism underlying cocaine-induced plasticity in striatum. *Neuron* 2005;48:303–314.

41. Nestler EJ, Bergson CM, Gultart X, Hope BT. Regulation of neural gene expression in opiate and cocaine addiction. NIDA *Res Monogr* 1993;125:92–116.

42. Jiang Y, Langley B, Lubin FD, et al. Epigenetics in the nervous system. *J Neurosci* 2008;28:11753–11759.

43. Nestler EJ. Molecular basis of long-term plasticity underlying addiction. *Nat Rev Neurosci* 2001;2:119–128.

44. Muschler MA, Hillemacher T, Kraus C, Kornhuber J, Bleich S, Frieling H. DNA methylation of the POMC gene promoter is associated with craving in alcohol dependence. *J Neural Transm* 2010;117:513–519.

45. Launay JM, Del Pino M, Chironi G, et al. Smoking induces long-lasting effects through a monoamineoxidase epigenetic regulation. *PLoS One* 2009;4:e7959.

46. Archer T, Beninger RJ, Palomo T, Kostrzewa RM. Epigenetics and biomarkers in the staging of neuropsychiatric disorders. *Neurotox Res* 2010;18:347–366.

47. Taubes G. As obesity rates rise, experts struggle to explain why. *Science* 1998;280:1367–1368.

48. Andreasen CH, Andersen G. Gene-environment interactions and obesity—further aspects of genomewide association studies. *Nutrition* 2009;25:998–1003.

49. Marti A, Martinez-Gonzalez MA, Martinez JA. Interaction between genes and lifestyle factors on obesity. *Proc Nutr Soc* 2008;67:1–8.

50. Campion J, Milagro FI, Martinez JA. Individuality and epigenetics in obesity. *Obes Rev* 2009;10:383–392.

51. Hass BS, Hart RW, Lu MH, Lyn-Cook BD. Effects of caloric restriction in animals on cellular function, oncogene expression, and DNA methylation in vitro. *Mutat Res* 1993;295:281–289.

52. Burdge GC, Slater-Jefferies J, Torrens C, Phillips ES, Hanson MA, Lillycrop KA. Dietary protein restriction of pregnant rats in the F0 generation induces altered methylation of hepatic gene promoters in the adult male offspring in the F1 and F2 generations. *Br J Nutr* 2007;97:435–439.

53. Rubin BS, Murray MK, Damassa DA, King JC, Soto AM. Perinatal exposure to low doses of bisphenol A affects body weight, patterns of estrous cyclicity, and plasma LH levels. *Environ Health Perspect* 2001;109:675–680.

54. Dolinoy DC, Weidman JR, Waterland RA, Jirtle RL. Maternal genistein alters coat color and protects Avy mouse offspring from obesity by modifying the fetal epigenome. *Environ Health Perspect* 2006;114:567–572.

55. Bleich S, Lenz B, Ziegenbein M, et al. Epigenetic DNA hypermethylation of the HERP gene promoter induces down-regulation of its mRNA expression in patients with alcohol dependence. *Alcohol Clin Exp Res* 2006;30:587–591.

56. Frieling H, Gozner A, Romer KD, et al. Global DNA hypomethylation and DNA hypermethylation of the alpha synuclein promoter in females with anorexia nervosa. *Mol Psychiatry* 2007;12:229–230.

57. Frieling H, Bleich S, Otten J, et al. Epigenetic down-regulation of atrial natriuretic peptide but not vasopressin mRNA expression in females with eating disorders is related to impulsivity. *Neuropsychopharmacol* 2008;33:2605–2609.

58. Hunnerkopf R, Grassl J, Thome J. Proteomics: biomarker research in psychiatry. *Fortschr Neurol Psychiatr* 2007;75:579–586.

59. Kobeissy FH, Sadasivan S, Liu J, Gold MS, Wang KK. Psychiatric research: psychoproteomics, degradomics and systems biology. *Expert Rev Proteomics* 2008;5:293–314.

6

Feeding Systems and Drugs of Abuse

BRITTANY L. MASON, ERIC J. NESTLER, AND MICHAEL LUTTER

We now find that it is wise to eat balanced meals at regular hours, and get the proper amount of sleep without the unhealthy aid of liquor and sleeping pills…The reason for this advice is simple. If we are undernourished and lack rest we become irritable and nervous. In this condition our tempers get out of control, our feelings are easily wounded and we get back to the old and dangerous thought processes.

—A Manual for Alcoholics Anonymous, written and distributed in 1940
by Dr. Bob's Home Group, AA Group No. 1, Akron, Ohio

INTRODUCTION

This advice first provided by Alcoholics Anonymous 70 years ago recognized the importance of food intake in preventing the relapse to alcoholism. This clinical observation is now supported by scientific evidence demonstrating that disruption of feeding can lead to a drive in addictive, drug-seeking behaviors. For example, food deprivation increases the self-administration of drugs of abuse, lowers the threshold dose for the reinforcing properties of drugs, increases behavioral motivation to obtain drugs, and increases the amount of drug finally consumed.[1] Modern neurobiological techniques now make it possible to study the interaction between feeding systems and addictive processes. Many neuropeptides that regulate food intake and body weight, including the proappetite peptides orexin (hypocretin), ghrelin, and neuropeptide Y (NPY) as well as the appetite-suppressing hormones leptin and melanocortin, have also been shown to regulate addiction behaviors. This is reflected in the prominent circuit-level connections between these well-established feeding pathways and the brain's reward regions that mediate the addicting actions of drugs of abuse (Fig. 6.1).

PROAPPETITE SYSTEMS

Orexin System

The lateral hypothalamus (LH) has been implicated in the regulation of many complex behavioral states, including arousal, reward, and motivation.[2]

The peptide orexin, also known as hypocretin, is localized to three contiguous hypothalamic regions: the lateral hypothalamus (LH), the perifornical area, and the dorsomedial hypothalamus, where it is found in two forms, orexin-A and orexin-B.[3–5] Neurons expressing orexin receptors are expressed in numerous anatomical sites known to regulate arousal, motivation, and stress states, including the amygdala, hippocampus, ventral tegmental area (VTA), and medial prefrontal cortex.[6] Two receptors have been identified that bind orexin: OX1R and OX2R. OX1R has a stronger affinity for orexin-A (Km ~30 nM), whereas both orexin-A and orexin–B bind to OX2R with a similar affinity.[2]

The activity of the orexin system is modulated by drugs of abuse. For example, an LH-specific decrease in orexin peptide mRNA expression is seen following administration of cocaine in a "binge"-like paradigm of chronic high-escalating dosage (reaching 90 mg/kg).[7] Orexin neurons are also activated by reward-related stimuli, with a strong correlation between induction of c-Fos (a surrogate marker of neural activity) in orexin-positive neurons and a preference for morphine, cocaine, or food reward in a conditioned place preference (CPP) paradigm.[8] Orexin neuron activation in LH is seen during opiate withdrawal as well.[9] Interestingly, the effects of drugs of abuse on orexin mRNA levels are complex. In alcohol-preferring rats that had access to ethanol, orexin mRNA expression was increased in the lateral, but not medial, hypothalamus.[10] Furthermore,

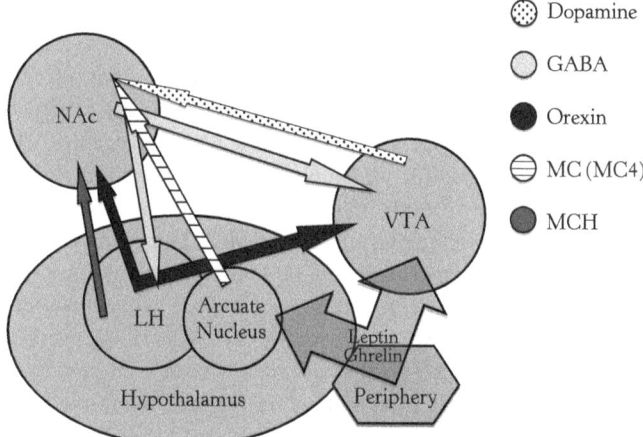

FIGURE 6.1. Innervation of the brain's reward circuitry by feeding peptides. Detailed here are the prominent innervations of two key brain reward regions, the ventral tegmental area (VTA) and the nucleus accumbens (NAc), by peptides classically studied in hypothalamic feeding mechanisms. Orexin, expressed in lateral hypothalamus (LH) and other nearby hypothalamic regions, innervates both the VTA and NAc, among a number of other brain regions. Melanin-concentrating hormone (MCH) (also expressed in the LH) and melanocortin (αMSH or MC, expressed in the arcuate nucleus) densely innervate the NAc and mostly act on reward through the MC4 receptor. Peripherally derived peptides also contribute to the reward pathways. Leptin (derived from adipose tissue) may act on leptin receptors in the VTA (in addition to its classic actions in the hypothalamus), and ghrelin (derived from stomach) also regulates the VTA. The figure also details the dopamineragic projections of the VTA to GABAergic projection neurons in the NAc.

Source: Adapted from Biological Psychiatry, Vol. 59, E.J. Nestler, W. A. Carlezon, The Mesolimbic Dopamine ReqRD Circuit in Depression, 1151–1159, Copyright (2006), with permission from Elsevier.

amphetamine was shown to increase Fos expression in the medial, but not lateral, hypothalamus.[11] Together, these data indicate that orexin neurons are a heterogeneous population that appear to exhibit different responses to different drugs of abuse.

Recently, more insight has been gained on how orexin signaling contributes to drug-induced sensitization. Orexin-A peptide directly infused into the VTA, a key dopaminergic brain reward region, induces synaptic plasticity in dopaminergic neurons.[12] Furthermore, systemic administration of the OX1R antagonist SB334867 blocks the development of sensitization prior to administration of cocaine[12] or amphetamine.[13] Intracerebroventricular (i.c.v.) infusion of orexin-A was found to reinstate previously extinguished cocaine seeking and significantly increased self-administration thresholds, but it did not alter responding to active cocaine self-administration.[14] This finding suggests that orexin may reinstate cocaine seeking by a different mechanism than the primary reinforcing effects due to increased dopamine release.

One possibility is that orexin signaling may promote actions of a drug of abuse, thus heightening drug sensitivity and strengthening the development of a connection between the drug's hedonic effects and the environment or cues connected to receiving this positive effect. This hypothesis is supported by evidence demonstrating that orexin plays a major role in cue-induced, rather than drug-induced, reinstatement of drug seeking in several paradigms. Administration of SB334867 was shown to reduce morphine CPP and direct infusion of rat pancreatic polypeptide (rPP, a Y4 agonist, Y4 being expressed on and activating orexin neurons) into the LH was shown to reinstate extinguished preference.[8] Additionally, orexin-deficient mice are resistant to developing morphine CPP, and intra-VTA injection of the OX1R antagonist SB334867 suppresses morphine CPP.[15] Blockade of the orexin system similarly diminishes the development of opiate physical dependence.[9] SB334867 dose dependently attenuates cue-induced reinstatement of cocaine self-administration, but it does not reduce established cocaine self-administration.[16] SB334867 blocks cue-induced reinstatement of alcohol self-administration and decreases operant responding for ethanol in alcohol-preferring rats.[10,17] Finally, blockade of OX1R in the insular cortex decreases nicotine self-administration in rats.[18] Together, these data indicate that orexin is an important integrator of environmental behavioral cues with consummatory rewards and indicate that the stimulation of orexin neurons may contribute importantly to relapse behavior.

Some evidence suggests one way that orexin may contribute to drug relapse is through integration of stress pathways. Blockade of OX1R prevented footshock-induced reinstatement of extinguished cocaine seeking[14] and attenuated ethanol reinstatement induced by yohimbine, an α2-adrenergic antagonist that induces a stress-like state.[17] However, our understanding of the interactions between the orexin pathway and established stress response systems in brain remains incomplete, as infusion of orexin-A into the VTA reinstates cocaine self-administration, which could be blocked by an OXR1 antagonist but not by an antagonist of corticotrophin-releasing factor (CRF), which mediates the hypothalamic-pituitary-adrenal stress response system.[19] This finding suggests that stress-induced reinstatement of cocaine seeking through orexin and CRF signaling may occur through independent pathways.

Finally, there is minimal evidence to suggest that OX2R plays a role in reward. OX2R signaling is thought to primarily regulate the sleep-wake cycle.[20] Repeated intraperitoneal (i.p.) administration of cocaine was shown to upregulate the expression of OX2R receptors in the nucleus accumbens, which persisted up to 60 days following cessation of cocaine treatment, with no effect on OXR1 or orexin-A or orexin-B levels.[21] However, i.p. administration of an OXR2 antagonist did not reduce cue-induced reinstatement of cocaine self-administration, and it was not able to reduce established cocaine self-administration.[16] In addition, infusion of orexin-B, which preferentially activates OX2R, into the VTA did not reinstate cocaine self-administration.[19] These findings support the view that orexin-B and OX2R do not play a major role in addiction.

Melanin-Concentrating Hormone

Another feeding peptide expressed in the LH that has been shown to have some effect on drug-seeking behavior is melanin-concentrating hormone (MCH). MCH is predominately expressed in the LH with fibers that project throughout the central nervous system. Importantly, MCH-positive neurons project to the shell subregion of the nucleus accumbens (NAcSh), a key brain reward region and target of VTA dopamine neurons, and MCH1R is known to be highly enriched in neurons of the NAcSh.[22] Typhon and colleagues initially reported that MCH1R null mice have no difference in CPP for cocaine or amphetamine compared to wild-type control mice.[23] Recently, however, Chung and colleagues found that MCH1R null mice have attenuated cocaine CPP and blunted development of cocaine sensitization, and that acute blockade of the MCH system by an MCH1R antagonist was able to dose dependently reduce cocaine self-administration and reduce the breakpoint in a self-administration schedule.[22] It should be noted that methodological differences in the CPP paradigms make direct comparison of the two papers difficult. Although a potent effect of the MCH system on the actions of drug of abuse would be expected based on the prominence of MCH innervation of the NAcSh, further work is needed to better understand the role of MCH in drug reward.

Neuropeptide Y

Neuropeptide Y (NPY) is a peptide neurotransmitter expressed throughout the brain. NPY-positive neurons in the arcuate nucleus of the hypothalamus stimulate feeding and are an important target for metabolic hormones from the periphery, including leptin, ghrelin, and insulin. In addition to a role in feeding, NPY signaling has been shown to potently regulate alcohol consumption. A single i.c.v. infusion of NPY in alcohol-preferring rats given free access to ethanol or water was shown to suppress ethanol consumption compared to control rats.[24] Furthermore, this suppression of ethanol intake was enhanced following a 2-week abstinence period from alcohol. A follow-up study demonstrated that when NPY was infused directly into the central nucleus of the amygdala (CeA), it eliminated increases in operant responding for alcohol in rats that were alcohol dependent.[25] Although NPY has been hypothesized to have effects on the consummatory factors, as opposed to the appetitive factors, contributing to alcohol intake, NPY was shown to decrease ethanol intake following involuntary exposure to ethanol vapor.[26] However, it did not reduce time spent drinking or significantly reduce lever pressing in this model.[26]

In contrast to ethanol, NPY seems to have a stimulatory effect on intake of other drugs of abuse. I.c.v. injection of NPY dose dependently increases heroin self-administration and induces reinstatement of extinguished heroin-seeking behavior.[27] NPY administration similarly amplifies cocaine-induced hyperlocomotion and cocaine self-administration.[28] One interesting possibility is that, unlike drugs such as stimulants and opiates, ethanol does have nutritional content. This distinction may account for the observed differences in the effect of NPY, a known appetite-stimulating molecule, on intake of alcohol versus other drugs of abuse.

Ghrelin

Ghrelin is an appetite-stimulating peptide hormone produced by the stomach in response to negative energy balance. Recent studies suggest that ghrelin may also contribute to drug craving, with higher levels of ghrelin increasing the risk of relapse in humans or reinstatement of drug seeking in rodents. In patients with alcohol dependence, a significant positive correlation was found between plasma ghrelin levels and alcohol craving. Alcohol-dependent patients have lower plasma levels of ghrelin compared to healthy controls,[29] although acutely intoxicated alcoholic patients were found to have higher plasma levels of ghrelin compared to nondrinking subjects.[30] Furthermore, alcoholic patients that had quit drinking in the previous 72 hours had even higher plasma ghrelin levels than acutely intoxicated patients,[30] which supports the hypothesis that elevated ghrelin levels may contribute to the risk of relapse.

Several studies in rodents have begun to delineate the neurobiological substrate of ghrelin's actions. Injection of ghrelin into the VTA increased alcohol consumption in wild-type, but not ghrelin receptor–deficient, mice. Additionally, disruption of ghrelin receptor signaling, either by genetic or pharmacological blockade, reduced alcohol CPP, indicating that ghrelin is required for alcohol's rewarding effects.[31] Finally, rats with higher plasma ghrelin levels were shown to be more prone to cocaine reinstatement triggered by a conditioned stimulus compared to their nonconditioned stimulated controls.[32] These observations suggest that ghrelin signaling may influence the addictive actions of several classes of drugs of abuse.

APPETITE-SUPPRESSING SYSTEMS

Leptin

Research on the role of leptin in alcohol abuse has yielded mostly mixed results. One study demonstrated that i.p. injection of leptin increased free-choice ethanol consumption following alcohol withdrawal in mice.[33] However, other studies have yielded inconsistent findings. Pharmacological studies using leptin administration did not report a reduction in alcohol intake in alcohol-preferring rats.[34] Additionally, genetic studies investigating alcohol consumption in leptin-deficient and leptin receptor–deficient mice did find a decreased preference for ethanol; however, i.p. administration of leptin did not restore alcohol consumption in leptin-deficient mice.[35] The authors hypothesized that, while disruptions in the leptin system can disrupt alcohol preference, these disruptions are likely due to compensatory or developmental changes in secondary systems, rather than being mediated directly by leptin.[35]

Studies in human patients have found some evidence for a role of leptin in mediating alcohol craving. In dependent patients recently detoxified from alcohol, plasma leptin levels were positively correlated with relapse to alcohol use with non-alcohol-abstinent patients having a greater increase in serum leptin levels at 4, 8, and 12 weeks from baseline compared to those patients who remained sober.[36] Furthermore, leptin levels were positively correlated with alcohol craving in this group at 4 weeks, suggesting that leptin levels are associated with craving and thus may be indicative of a higher risk of relapse. Consistent with this theory, Hillemacher and colleagues reported that serum leptin levels were positively correlated with self-reported feelings of craving in a large study of patients with alcohol dependence recently detoxified from alcohol.[37] More work is needed to determine whether leptin signaling directly mediates the effect on alcohol craving or whether it is merely a marker for another process such as nutritional status.

There are also several reports of leptin regulation of the brain's reward circuitry and responses to drugs other than alcohol. I.c.v. administration of leptin either increased or decreased the sensitivity to brain-stimulation reward, depending on the site of the stimulation.[38] I.c.v. leptin also blocked the ability of food deprivation to induce relapse to heroin self-administration, an effect not seen for footshock- or heroin-induced relapse.[39] Leptin-deficient mice have been shown to exhibit reduced locomotor responses to acute or chronic amphetamine administration[40] and to show reduced levels of dopamine stores by VTA dopamine neurons.[41]

These various effects of leptin on brain reward may be mediated via direct effects of the hormone on VTA dopamine neurons, since such neurons have been reported to express leptin receptors and be inhibited upon receptor activation.[40,42] Of course, a major question remains as to whether peripherally derived leptin can regulate VTA dopamine neurons in vivo or whether such regulation is primarily indirect through various hypothalamic-VTA circuits.

Melanocortin Signaling

The melanocortin system is an important regulator of food intake and body weight homeostasis. The central melanocortin system consists of melanocortin itself (also known as α-melanocyte stimulating hormone or α-MSH), which is derived from the pro-opiomelanocortin (POMC) gene, and its major receptors in brain, the melanocortin 3- and 4- receptors (MC3R and MC4R). Genetic and pharmacological studies have demonstrated that melanocortin signaling promotes dissipation of excess energy stores by suppressing appetite and increasing metabolic rate.[43] Interestingly, MC4R is highly expressed in nucleus accumbens neurons, which suggests the involvement of the melanocortin system in the regulation of brain reward mechanisms.

Indeed, melanocortin signaling has been implicated directly in setting the threshold for the rewarding properties of drugs of abuse. Several studies in rodents have demonstrated that activation of melanocortin signaling enhances the rewarding properties of drugs of abuse, while blockade of the system reduces their rewarding properties. Lindbolm and colleagues reported an increased ratio of POMC expression to expression of agouti-related peptide (an endogenous antagonist of melanocortin receptors) in rats selectively bred for alcohol preference compared to control animals.[44] Furthermore, they found higher binding of MC3R in the nucleus accumbens as well as in several hypothalamic nuclei, including the arcuate nucleus, paraventricular nucleus, and ventromedial hypothalamus.[44] The combination of an increased agonist/antagonist ratio, coupled with increased MC3R binding, would indicate that alcohol-preferring rats have enhanced melanocortin tone.

Several additional studies have suggested a role for melanocortin signaling in stimulant addiction. I.c.v. injection of the MC3R/MC4R agonist Melanotan II acutely enhanced the threshold-lowering effect of amphetamine in lateral hypothalamic self-stimulation (an indication of increased drug reward).[45] Hsu and colleagues reported that chronic cocaine administration increased the expression of MC4R mRNA in the nucleus accumbens and that infusion of the melanocortin antagonist SHU-9199 into the nucleus accumbens blocked cocaine self-administration and changed a conditioned preference for cocaine into a conditioned avoidance.[46] These results indicate that blockade of MC4R signaling may reduce the conditioned reinforcing effects of drugs of abuse, which is a contributor to some forms of addiction.

CONCLUSIONS

Multiple lines of evidence in both clinical and preclinical studies indicate that feeding systems strongly regulate the expression of addictive processes. Numerous significant effects have been reported; however, no clear picture has yet emerged that satisfactorily explains several discrepancies in the data. Further research will need to be conducted to delineate the precise molecular and cellular pathways that mediate the apparently complex influence of several feeding systems on the induction and expression of drug addiction syndromes.

Moreover, while this review has focused on the role of hypothalamic feeding mechanisms in regulating an individual's responses to drugs of abuse, we know that food and drug rewards also share some common, chronic adaptations at the transcriptional level within the brain's reward circuitry. The best established example of such shared mechanisms is the induction of the Fos family transcription factor, ΔFosB, in nucleus accumbens in response to the chronic consumption of high levels of food, drug, or other rewards.[47,48] Such induction of ΔFosB has been shown to sensitize animals to the rewarding effects of both drug and natural rewards (including food), which further underscores the likely overlap of mechanisms in the brain that mediate drug addiction and disordered food intake.

REFERENCES

1. Carr KD. Chronic food restriction: enhancing effects on drug reward and striatal cell signaling. *Physiol Behav* 2007;91:459–472.
2. Aston-Jones G, Smith RJ, Moorman DE, Richardson KA. Role of lateral hypothalamic orexin neurons in reward processing and addiction. *Neuropharmacol* 2009;56(suppl 1):112–121.
3. Sakurai T, Amemiya A, Ishii M, et al. Orexins and orexin receptors: a family of hypothalamic neuropeptides and

G protein-coupled receptors that regulate feeding behavior. *Cell* 1998;92(4):573–585.

4. de Lecea L, Kilduff TS, Peyron C, et al. The hypocretins: hypothalamus-specific peptides with neuroexcitatory activity. *Proc Natl Acad Sci USA* 1998;95: 322–327.

5. Siegel JM. Hypocretin (orexin): role in normal behavior and neuropathology. *Annu Rev Psychol* 2004;55:125–148.

6. Marcus JN, Aschkenasi CJ, Lee CE, et al. Differential expression of orexin receptors 1 and 2 in the rat brain. *J Comp Neurol* 2001;435:6–25.

7. Zhou Y, Cui CL, Schlussman SD, et al. Effects of cocaine place conditioning, chronic escalating-dose "binge" pattern cocaine administration and acute withdrawal on orexin/hypocretin and preprodynorphin gene expressions in lateral hypothalamus of Fischer and Sprague-Dawley rats. *Neuroscience* 2008;153:1225–1234.

8. Harris GC, Wimmer M, Aston-Jones G. A role for lateral hypothalamic orexin neurons in reward seeking. *Nature* 2005;437:556–559.

9. Georgescu D, Zachariou V, Barrot M, et al. Involvement of the lateral hypothalamic peptide orexin in morphine dependence and withdrawal. *J Neurosci* 2003;23:3106–3111.

10. Lawrence AJ, Cowen MS, Yang HJ, Chen F, Oldfield B. The orexin system regulates alcohol-seeking in rats. *Br J Pharmacol* 2006;148:752–759.

11. Fadel J, Bubser M, Deutch AY. Differential activation of orexin neurons by antipsychotic drugs associated with weight gain. *J Neurosci* 2002;22:6742–6746.

12. Borgland SL, Taha SA, Sarti F, Fields HL, Bonci A. Orexin A in the VTA is critical for the induction of synaptic plasticity and behavioral sensitization to cocaine. *Neuron* 2006;49:589–601.

13. Quarta D, Valerio E, Hutcheson DM, Hedou G, Heidbreder C. The orexin-1 receptor antagonist SB-334867 reduces amphetamine-evoked dopamine outflow in the shell of the nucleus accumbens and decreases the expression of amphetamine sensitization. *Neurochem Int* 2010;56(1):11–15.

14. Boutrel B, Kenny PJ, Specio SE, et al. Role for hypocretin in mediating stress-induced reinstatement of cocaine-seeking behavior. *Proc Natl Acad Sci USA* 2005;102:19168–19173.

15. Narita M, Nagumo Y, Hashimoto S, et al. Direct involvement of orexinergic systems in the activation of the mesolimbic dopamine pathway and related behaviors induced by morphine. *J Neurosci* 2006;26:398–405.

16. Smith RJ, See RE, Aston-Jones G. Orexin/hypocretin signaling at the orexin 1 receptor regulates cue-elicited cocaine-seeking. *Eur J Neurosci* 2009;30:493–503.

17. Richards JK, Simms JA, Steensland P, et al. Inhibition of orexin-1/hypocretin-1 receptors inhibits yohimbine-induced reinstatement of ethanol and sucrose seeking in Long-Evans rats. *Psychopharmacol (Berl)* 2008;199:109–117.

18. Hollander JA, Lu Q, Cameron MD, Kamenecka TM, Kenny PJ. Insular hypocretin transmission regulates nicotine reward. *Proc Natl Acad Sci USA* 2008;105:19480–19485.

19. Wang B, You ZB, Wise RA. Reinstatement of cocaine seeking by hypocretin (orexin) in the ventral tegmental area: independence from the local corticotropin-releasing factor network. *Biol Psychiatry* 2009;65:857–862.

20. Willie JT, Chemelli RM, Sinton CM, et al. Distinct narcolepsy syndromes in Orexin receptor-2 and Orexin null mice: molecular genetic dissection of Non-REM and REM sleep regulatory processes. *Neuron* 2003;38:715–730.

21. Zhang GC, Mao LM, Liu XY, Wang JQ. Long-lasting up-regulation of orexin receptor type 2 protein levels in the rat nucleus accumbens after chronic cocaine administration. *J Neurochem* 2007;103:400–407.

22. Chung S, Hopf FW, Nagasaki H, et al. The melanin-concentrating hormone system modulates cocaine reward. *Proc Natl Acad Sci USA* 2009;106: 6772–6777.

23. Tyhon A, Lakaye B, Adamantidis A, Tirelli E. Amphetamine- and cocaine-induced conditioned place preference and concomitant psychomotor sensitization in mice with genetically inactivated melanin-concentrating hormone MCH(1) receptor. *Eur J Pharmacol* 2008;599:72–80.

24. Gilpin NW, Stewart RB, Murphy JM, Li TK, Badia-Elder NE. Neuropeptide Y reduces oral ethanol intake in alcohol-preferring (P) rats following a period of imposed ethanol abstinence. *Alcohol Clin Exp Res* 2003;27:787–794.

25. Gilpin NW, Misra K, Koob GF. Neuropeptide Y in the central nucleus of the amygdala suppresses dependence-induced increases in alcohol drinking. *Pharmacol Biochem Behav* 2008;90:475–480.

26. Thorsell A, Slawecki CJ, Ehlers CL. Effects of neuropeptide Y on appetitive and consummatory behaviors associated with alcohol drinking in wistar rats with a history of ethanol exposure. *Alcohol Clin Exp Res* 2005;29:584–590.

27. Maric T, Tobin S, Quinn T, Shalev U. Food deprivation-like effects of neuropeptide Y on heroin self-administration and reinstatement of heroin seeking in rats. *Behav Brain Res* 2008;194:39–43.

28. Maric T, Cantor A, Cucciolletta H, Tobin S, Shalev U. Neuropeptide Y augments cocaine self-administration and cocaine-induced hyperlocomotion in rats. *Peptides* 2009;30:721–726.

29. Addolorato G, Capristo E, Leggio L, et al. Relationship between ghrelin levels, alcohol craving, and nutritional status in current alcoholic patients. *Alcohol Clin Exp Res* 2006;30:1933–1937.

30. Kraus T, Schanze A, Groschl M, et al. Ghrelin levels are increased in alcoholism. *Alcohol Clin Exp Res* 2005;29:2154–2157.

31. Jerlhag E, Egecioglu E, Landgren S, et al. Requirement of central ghrelin signaling for alcohol reward. *Proc Natl Acad Sci USA* 2009;106:11318–11323.

32. Tessari M, Catalano A, Pellitteri M, et al. Correlation between serum ghrelin levels and cocaine-seeking behaviour triggered by cocaine-associated conditioned stimuli in rats. *Addict Biol* 2007;12:22–29.

33. Kiefer F, Jahn H, Wolf K, Kampf P, Knaudt K, Wiedemann K. Free-choice alcohol consumption in mice after application of the appetite regulating peptide leptin. *Alcohol Clin Exp Res* 2001;25:787–789.

34. Polidori C, Luciani F, Fedeli A, Geary N, Massi M. Leptin fails to reduce ethanol intake in Marchigian Sardinian alcohol-preferring rats. *Peptides* 2003;24:1441–1444.

35. Blednov YA, Walker D, Harris RA. Blockade of the leptin-sensitive pathway markedly reduces alcohol consumption in mice. *Alcohol Clin Exp Res* 2004;28:1683–1692.

36. Kiefer F, Jahn H, Otte C, Demiralay C, Wolf K, Wiedemann K. Increasing leptin precedes craving and relapse during pharmacological abstinence maintenance treatment of alcoholism. *J Psychiatr Res* 2005;39:545–551.

37. Hillemacher T, Bleich S, Frieling H, et al. Evidence of an association of leptin serum levels and craving in alcohol dependence. *Psychoneuroendocrinol* 2007;32:87–90.

38. Fulton S, Woodside B, Shizgal P. Modulation of brain reward circuitry by leptin. *Science* 2000;287:125–128.

39. Shalev U, Yap J, Shaham Y. Leptin attenuates acute food deprivation-induced relapse to heroin seeking. *J Neurosci* 2001;21:RC129.

40. Fulton S, Pissios P, Manchon RP, et al. Leptin regulation of the mesoaccumbens dopamine pathway. *Neuron* 2006;51:811–822.

41. Roseberry AG, Painter T, Mark GP, Williams JT. Decreased vesicular somatodendritic dopamine stores in leptin-deficient mice. *J Neurosci* 2007;27:7021–7027.

42. Hommel JD, Trinko R, Sears RM, et al. Leptin receptor signaling in midbrain dopamine neurons regulates feeding. *Neuron* 2006;51:801–810.

43. Kishi T, Elmquist JK. Body weight is regulated by the brain: a link between feeding and emotion. *Mol Psychiatry* 2005;10:132–146.

44. Lindblom J, Wikberg JE, Bergstrom L. Alcohol-preferring AA rats show a derangement in their central melanocortin signalling system. *Pharmacol Biochem Behav* 2002;72:491–496.

45. Cabeza de Vaca S, Kim GY, Carr KD. The melanocortin receptor agonist MTII augments the rewarding effect of amphetamine in ad-libitum-fed and food-restricted rats. *Psychopharmacol (Berl)* 2002;161:77–85.

46. Hsu R, Taylor JR, Newton SS, et al. Blockade of melanocortin transmission inhibits cocaine reward. *Eur J Neurosci* 2005;21:2233–2242.

47. Nestler EJ. Review. Transcriptional mechanisms of addiction: role of DeltaFosB. *Philos Trans R Soc Lond B Biol Sci* 2008;363:3245–3255.

48. Wallace DL, Vialou V, Rios L, et al. The influence of DeltaFosB in the nucleus accumbens on natural reward-related behavior. *J Neurosci* 2008;28:10272–10277.

7

Co-Occurring Addiction and Psychiatric Disorders

SHELLY F. GREENFIELD AND MICHELE A. CRISAFULLI

INTRODUCTION

Population-based surveys, as well as studies of clinical populations, have shown that addictive disorders tend to have high rates of co-occurring psychiatric disorders. Having a substance use disorder (SUD) raises the risk for having a psychiatric disorder, and having a psychiatric disorder in turn raises the risk for having an SUD. The high rate of co-occurring disorders is an important factor on the population level in determining burden of illness and treatment services planning and delivery, and on the individual level in considering prognosis, appropriate diagnosis, and treatment planning. Four major epidemiological surveys have examined the co-occurrence of SUDs and psychiatric disorders in the United States: the Epidemiologic Catchment Area study (ECA),[1] the National Comorbidity Survey (NCS),[2] the National Comorbidity Survey Replication (NCS-R),[3] and the National Epidemiologic Survey on Alcohol and Related Conditions (NESARC).[4] These population-based surveys, in addition to studies of clinical populations, indicate that the disorders that most commonly co-occur with SUDs are mood disorders, anxiety disorders including posttraumatic stress disorder (PTSD), eating disorders (EDs), and psychotic and personality disorders. For each of these categories of disorders, we will briefly review the available data from community and clinical populations, discussing basic epidemiology and prognosis in turn.

There is converging evidence that the co-occurrence of an untreated psychiatric disorder with an SUD worsens the prognosis for the SUD, and conversely, co-occurring untreated SUDs worsen the outcome of psychiatric disorders.[5] In general, there are three models of care for co-occurring disorders: sequential, parallel, and integrated. Where empirical studies exist, they tend to support integrated models of care. Insofar as data are available regarding treatment indications for each co-occurring disorder, this evidence will also be briefly reviewed.

MOOD DISORDERS

The large population-based epidemiologic surveys[1-4] have provided prevalence data for mood disorders, including major depression, dysthymia, and bipolar disorder. Among members of the general population, the lifetime prevalence rate of any mood disorder was estimated to be approximately 7.8%,[6] with 12-month prevalence estimates falling between 3.7% and 9.5%.[2,4,6] However, the odds of having a lifetime mood disorder were greater among those with than without a lifetime SUD, with an odds ratio (OR) of 1.9 for those with an alcohol use disorder (AUD) and 4.7 for those with a drug use disorder (DUD).[1] Indeed, 29.7% of respondents with any lifetime SUD were found also to have a lifetime mood disorder.[2] Similarly, among those who reported experiencing an SUD in the past 12 months, an estimated 20.1%–24.5% experienced a mood disorder within the same 12-month period (OR 2.8).[2,4] In general, risk ratios tended to be higher for bipolar disorder compared with unipolar depression, substance dependence compared with abuse, and drug use disorders compared with alcohol use disorders.[4]

In addition to mood disorders being especially prevalent among those with SUDs, SUDs are also especially prevalent among those with mood disorders. Epidemiologic studies indicate that 32%–41.2% of individuals with lifetime mood disorders and 19.9% of those with 12-month mood disorders have lifetime and 12-month SUDs, respectively.[1,2,4] Risk ratios indicate that the odds of someone with a mood disorder having an SUD are 2.6 times higher than someone without a mood disorder.[1] Of note, those with manic episodes were especially likely to have a co-occurring SUD. Of those who had a manic episode in the past 12 months, 27.9%–37.1% also met criteria for an SUD in that period[2,4]; of those who had experienced mania in their lifetime, 60.7%–71% had met criteria for an SUD at some point.[1,2]

A number of studies provide evidence that those who have both a mood disorder and an SUD tend to have a worse prognosis relative to those who have only one disorder. In one study, those with only bipolar disorder were compared to those with co-occurring SUDs, and the group with co-occurring substance use and bipolar disorders was found to have higher scores on anxiety scales, as well as higher rates of attempted suicide.[7] Similarly, among those with both unipolar depression and an alcohol use disorder, improvement in substance use is associated with more sustained remission from depression.[8]

Mood disorders may be more difficult to diagnose among active substance users because symptoms of intoxication and withdrawal often mimic symptoms of mood disorders. However, the NESARC study demonstrated that mood disorders that are purely substance-induced account for a very small percentage of mood disorders among all those with SUDs.[4] With regard to treatment of co-occurring substance use and bipolar disorders, Weiss et al.'s Integrated Group Therapy[9] showed superior outcomes to a comparison group that received nonintegrated treatments for bipolar and substance use disorders. On the other hand, there is currently no evidence-based integrated treatment for co-occurring unipolar depression and SUD and no clear evidence supporting the use of any particular psychosocial or pharmacologic method over another.[10] However, Westermeyer[11] strongly advocates for integrated models where both disorders are addressed simultaneously and preferably by the same treatment team.

ANXIETY DISORDERS

Several population-based epidemiologic studies[1–4] have established the prevalence of anxiety disorders, including panic disorder (with and without agoraphobia), social phobia, specific phobia (or, in the case of the ECA study, simple phobia), and generalized anxiety disorder, while only two studies[1,3] examined obsessive-compulsive disorder and PTSD. The estimated 12-month prevalence of anxiety disorders in the general population ranged from 11.1% to 18.1%.[3,4]

As was the case with mood disorders, rates of anxiety disorders were elevated for those with SUDs. Among those with 12-month SUDs, estimates of 12-month anxiety disorders ranged from 17.8% in the NESARC, which did not include PTSD, to 35.6% in the NCS, which did include PTSD.[2,4] Among those with any lifetime SUD, 40.7% had a lifetime anxiety disorder, including PTSD.[2] Overall, the odds ratio for having any anxiety disorder (excluding PTSD) if one has an SUD (compared with those without an SUD) was 1.9.[4] Although respondents with SUDs were more likely to have a specific phobia than any other anxiety disorder,[4] this may be due to the relatively high base rate of specific phobias in the general population. Compared with those without specific anxiety disorders, the risk of having an SUD for those with anxiety disorders was greater and especially high for panic disorder with agoraphobia (3.1 times as likely) and generalized anxiety disorder (2.3 times as likely).[4] In general, the odds of having these anxiety disorders tended to be higher among those with substance dependence than abuse, and among those with DUDs than AUDs.[4]

Just as anxiety disorders were common among those with SUDs, SUDs were also common among those with anxiety disorders. Estimates of 12-month occurrence of an SUD in respondents with an anxiety disorder were approximately 15%.[2,4] Among those with any lifetime anxiety disorder, an estimated 23.7% to 37.8% had one or more lifetime SUDs,[1,2] which corresponds to an OR of 1.7.[1] Across studies, rates of SUDs appeared to be particularly elevated in those with panic disorder and generalized anxiety disorder.[1,2,4]

Rates of co-occurring disorders were especially high for those who had sought treatment for their disorder. In the NESARC sample, 33.4% of those who reported being treated for an AUD and 42.6% of those who reported being treated for a DUD had at least one independent (i.e., not substance induced) anxiety disorder, which is approximately double the rates reported among non-treatment seekers.[4] Similarly, the NCS found that respondents with an anxiety disorder who also had an addictive disorder were significantly more likely than their non-substance-abusing counterparts to seek treatment (37.0% vs. 24.6%).[2] Overall, about 20% of patients who seek specialty treatment for an anxiety disorder also have a co-occurring SUD, which points to the need for comprehensive assessment and treatment.[2]

Similar to mood disorders, diagnosis of anxiety disorders in the presence of a co-occurring SUD (particularly during acute intoxication or withdrawal phases) can be complicated, although Grant et al.[4] note that a very small percentage of anxiety disorders that co-occur with SUDs are purely substance induced. With regard to treatment of co-occurring SUD and anxiety disorders (not including PTSD), empirical evidence is generally lacking.[12] Efficacy data have come almost entirely from outcome studies examining treatments designed for a single illness, and consequently, most guidelines and recommendations for treatment of this population are based on expert opinion and many inconsistencies (e.g., whether the use of benzodiazepines to treat anxiety in this population is ever warranted) remain.[12] All available guidelines and recommendations advocate for "integrated" treatment, but at this point the nature of "integrated" treatment with this population has yet to be clearly defined.[12]

POSTTRAUMATIC STRESS DISORDER

Relative to mood and other anxiety disorders, data from large-scale epidemiologic studies on the comorbidity of PTSD and SUDs are less available. Nonetheless, data from one population-based study that did examine PTSD and SUDs, as well as many smaller studies conducted with clinical populations, suggest that these disorders frequently co-occur. According to results from the NCS-R, the 12-month prevalence of PTSD in the general population is 3.5%.[3] On the other hand, among those with 12-month and lifetime SUDs, the prevalence of PTSD is 8.3% and 12.9%, respectively.[2] Perhaps even more strikingly, among those with 12-month PTSD, the prevalence of SUD is 17.7%, and lifetime occurrence of SUDs among those with PTSD is 45.2%.[2] Because of the high prevalence of SUDs among those with PTSD, PTSD is reviewed separately from the other anxiety disorders.

PTSD and SUD each confer a poor prognosis for the other disorder. In one study of SUD patients with and without PTSD, those with PTSD reported more psychological distress, more social and role disability due to emotional disability, and poorer health perceptions than did those without PTSD, even if they had other co-occurring psychiatric disorders.[13] Similarly, Jacobsen et al.[14] note that those patients with SUDs who also have PTSD tend to have higher rates of other co-occurring Axis I and II disorders, psychosocial and medical problems, substance-related hospitalizations, and substance use relapses than their counterparts without PTSD. Likewise, patients with PTSD who also have a co-occurring SUD often experience more severe avoidance and arousal symptoms.[15]

As with other co-occurring disorders, evidence generally tends to support integrated treatments for those with PTSD and SUDs, especially among women.[16] One manualized, integrated intervention for co-occurring SUDs and PTSD that has received particular attention in the literature is Seeking Safety,[17] which has been rigorously evaluated and tends to show improvements in PTSD symptoms that are at least equivalent, if not superior, to various comparison groups.[18]

EATING DISORDERS

Like PTSD, EDs have not tended to be examined in large epidemiologic studies; of the four major studies reviewed here, EDs were only assessed in the NCS-R and then only as a disorder of secondary interest (i.e., they were only assessed in a probability subsample). In this study, lifetime prevalence rates of EDs in the general population were 0.6% for anorexia nervosa (AN), 1.0% for bulimia nervosa (BN), and 2.8% for binge eating disorder; for females, these rates were 0.9%, 1.5%, and 3.5%, respectively.[19] From the same study, 12-month prevalence estimates for BN were 0.3% overall and 0.5% for women and for BED were 1.2% overall and 1.6% for women; no one in the sample met for current AN.[19]

To our knowledge, no epidemiological studies have examined the presence of EDs among those whose primary problem is an SUD, and even in smaller community or clinical samples such studies are rare.[20] With regard to rates of SUDs among those with EDs, the NCS-R showed that of those with lifetime AN, BN, and BED (modified 3-month criteria), 27%, 36.8%, and 23.3%, respectively, met for a lifetime SUD.[19] The odds ratios were 3.0, 4.6, and 2.1, indicating that the odds of having a lifetime ED for those with a lifetime SUD were double to quadruple the odds for those without a lifetime SUD.[19]

As is the case with many disorders, rates of co-occurring EDs and SUDs were elevated in clinical populations. According to one review, rates of lifetime AN and BN among those with SUDs range from 2% to 10% and from 8% to 40.7%, respectively, with a median rate of about 20%.[20] Similarly, in an international sample of individuals with lifetime EDs, between 16.8% and 46.1% (depending on the specific ED) had a lifetime AUD,[21] and in a 9-year longitudinal study of women seeking treatment for EDs, a lifetime history of DUD was reported by 17.1%.[22] Of note, although SUDs tend to be fairly uncommon in individuals with restricting AN, rates among those with AN binge-purge subtype are comparable to rates among those with BN.[21,22]

Co-occurrence of EDs and SUDs tends to complicate the diagnosis and treatment of these disorders and is associated with greater psychiatric disturbance, greater medical risks, and increased mortality.[23,24] Nonetheless, research on how to best treat co-occurring EDs and SUDs is almost entirely lacking[23], and consequently, treatment of these disorders remains largely fragmented. In one survey of publicly funded substance abuse treatment programs in the United States, only about half of the programs assessed for EDs at intake, and even among those who did assess, most programs did not attempt to treat or even provide referrals for EDs.[25] Typically, addiction programs that do provide ED treatment attempt to integrate treatment,[25] but again, evidence-based models of care are not yet available.[23] In the absence of such models, Grilo et al.[23] provide a theoretical argument for using cognitive-behavioral therapy, coping skills, or dialectical-behavioral therapy as "starting points" in treating this population.

PSYCHOTIC DISORDERS

Although psychotic disorders were assessed to some extent in all four of the major epidemiological studies discussed, the specific disorders assessed and the methods of assessment varied substantially between studies. These differences notwithstanding, estimates of lifetime prevalence of psychotic disorders tended to be quite similar, ranging from 0.9% to 1.5% of the general population.[1,26,27] Rates of psychotic disorders among individuals with SUDs were not reported in any of these studies.

Rates of SUDs among those with psychotic disorders tend to be higher than in the general population. For example, rates of lifetime SUDs for those with a lifetime diagnosis of psychotic disorder ranged from 28.6% to 47.0%, with ORs ranging from 2.3 to 4.6.[1,26,27] Rates of 12-month co-occurrence were estimated to be 15.6%, corresponding to an OR of 5.2 for those with a psychotic disorder versus without.[26]

For those patients with psychotic disorders, having a co-occurring SUD is associated with a variety of negative outcomes, including reduced social contact, housing instability, increased family conflict, violent behavior, financial difficulties, earlier onset of mental health problems, psychotic relapse, exacerbation of mental health problems, increased risk of HIV, risk of sexual/physical abuse, increased hospitalization, medication adherence problems, reduced effects of antipsychotics, and increased use of services (summarized by Maslin[28]). Given relatively high rates and important consequences of co-occurring psychotic and SUDs, McMillan et al.[27] recommend that clinicians make it a practice to screen for SUDs when treating patients with psychotic disorders, as SUDs may be amenable to treatment, which may in turn produce improvements in quality of life for these patients. With regard to treatments to be used, Drake et al.[29] provide a review of recent treatment outcome studies and note that integrated treatments consistently demonstrate equivalent or superior outcomes to nonintegrated treatments.

PERSONALITY DISORDERS

Most epidemiologic studies that have examined co-occurring substance use and personality disorders (PDs) have focused on antisocial PD.[30] However, two more recent studies examined a broader range of PDs and their associations with SUDs.[30,31] According to the one study that examined all 10 DMS-IV PDs,[31] approximately 10% of US adults in the general population have a diagnosable PD. By contrast, among those with a 12-month SUD (including tobacco), 28.5% had any PD, with 9.4% having a Cluster A PD (paranoid, schizotypal, schizoid), 8.2% having a Cluster B PD (antisocial, borderline, histrionic, narcissistic), and 10.2% having a Cluster C PD (avoidant, dependent, obsessive-compulsive).[31] Similarly, in the NESARC study, 28.6% of respondents with a 12-month AUD and 47.7% of respondents with a 12-month DUD had at least 1 PD.[30] In general, rates of PDs tended to be higher among those with substance dependence than abuse.[30]

Among those with PDs, rates of SUDs are generally higher than in the general population. Specifically, of those with at least one 12-month PD, an estimated 22.6% met for any 12-month SUD,[31] with 16.4% and 6.5% meeting for a current AUD or DUD, respectively.[30] Rates of SUDs among those with antisocial PD are particularly high, with lifetime estimates ranging from 78.7% to 83.6%.[1,2] The 12-month conditional probability of an SUD among those with antisocial PD is 40.5%, which corresponds to an OR of 7.2.[31] Rates of SUDs also tend to be notably elevated among those with borderline PD, with an estimated 38.2% of those currently meeting for this PD also meeting for a current SUD (OR = 7.9).[31]

Treatment for those with co-occurring SUDs and PDs can be expected to be more extensive and of longer duration than for those with either disorder alone.[30] Antisocial PD confers poor prognosis on those with a SUD.[32] In addition, Zanarini et al.[33] demonstrated that absence of an SUD is associated with more rapid time to recovery from borderline PD, more so than absence of any other Axis I disorder. An integrated treatment of dialectical behavior therapy for women with co-occurring borderline PD and SUD has shown promise.[34,35]

CONCLUSIONS

The rates of current and lifetime co-occurrence between SUDs and other psychiatric disorders in community and treatment-seeking populations are high, especially for mood, anxiety, posttraumatic stress, eating, psychotic, and personality disorders. Rates of these disorders are elevated among those with SUDs, and rates of SUDs are elevated among those with these disorders. This elevation is particularly pronounced in treatment-seeking populations. As such, assessments for each of these disorders should routinely include screening for SUDs, and vice versa.

In most research studies, the presence of a co-occurring psychiatric disorder is a poor prognostic indicator associated with a variety of negative outcomes. Despite widespread recognition of a need to address co-occurring disorders, development of treatments specifically designed to address co-occurring disorders is still in its nascent stages. Where empirically supported treatments do exist (as in the case of PTSD and bipolar disorder), the evidence tends to favor integrated, as opposed to sequential or parallel, forms of treatment. Research designed to develop and test effective integrated treatments for individuals with co-occurring substance use and other psychiatric disorders, as well as to enhance our health care delivery system's ability to provide

these treatments, will improve care, increase prognosis, and decrease lifetime adverse consequences for this vulnerable population.

ACKNOWLEDGMENTS

The authors would like to acknowledge grant K24DA019855 (SFG) from the National Institute on Drug Abuse.

REFERENCES

1. Regier DA, Farmer ME, Rae DS, et al. Co-morbidity of mental disorders with alcohol and other drug abuse: results from the epidemiologic catchment area (ECA) study. *JAMA* 1990;264:2511–2518.
2. Kessler RC, Nelson CB, McGonagle KA, Edlund MJ, Frank RG, Leaf PJ. The epidemiology of co-occurring addictive and mental disorders. *Am J Orthopsychiatry* 1996;66:17–31.
3. Kessler RC, Chiu WT, Demler O, Walter EE. Prevalence, severity, and comorbidity of 12-month DSM-IV disorders in the National Comorbidity Survey Replication. *Arch Gen Psychiatry* 2005;62:617–627.
4. Grant BF, Stinson FS, Dawson DA, et al. Prevalence and co-occurrence of substance use disorders and independent mood and anxiety disorders: results from the National Epidemiologic Survey on Alcohol and Related Conditions. *Arch Gen Psychiatry* 2004;61(8):807–816.
5. Greenfield SF. Assessment of mood and substance use disorders. In: Westermeyer JJ, Weiss RD, Ziedonis D, eds. Integrated treatment for mood and substance use disorders. Baltimore, MD: Johns Hopkins University Press; 2003:100–116.
6. Weissman MW, Bruce ML, Leaf PJ, Florio LP, Holzer III. C. Affective disorders. In: Robins LN, Regier DA, eds. Psychiatric disorders in America: the Epidemiologic Catchment Area study. New York: The Free Press; 1991:53–80.
7. Feinman JA, Dunner DL. The effect of alcohol and substance abuse on the course of bipolar affective disorder. *J Affect Disord* 1996;37:43–49.
8. Hasin DS, Tsai W, Endicott J, Mueller TI, Coryell W, Keller M. Five-year course of major depression: effects of comorbid alcoholism. *J Affect Disord* 1996;41:63–70.
9. Weiss RD, Griffin ML, Kolodziej ME, et al. A randomized trial of integrated group therapy versus group drug counseling for patients with bipolar disorder and substance dependence. *Am J Psychiatry* 2007;164:100–107.
10. Ross S. The mentally ill substance abuser. In: Galanter M, Kleber HD, eds. *The American Psychiatric Publishing Textbook of Substance Abuse Treatment.* 4th ed. Arlington, VA: American Psychiatric Publishing; 2008:537–554.

11. Westermeyer JJ. Addressing co-occurring mood and substance use disorders. In: Westermeyer JJ, Weiss RD, Ziedonis D, Ziedoniz DM, eds. Integrated treatment for mood and substance use disorders. Baltimore, MD: The Johns Hopkins University Press; 2003:1–16.

12. Watkins KE, Hunter SB, Pincus HA, Nicholson G. Review of treatment recommendations for persons with a co-occurring affective or anxiety and substance use disorder. Psychiatr Serv 2005;56:913–926.

13. Ouimette PC, Goodwin E, Brown PJ. Health and well being of substance use disorder patients with and without posstraumatic stress disorder. Addict Behav 2006;31:1415–1423.

14. Jacobsen LK, Southwick SM, Kosten TR. Substance use disorders in patients with posttraumatic stress disorder: a review of the literature. Am J Psychiatry 2001;158:1184–1190.

15. Ouimette P, Brown P, Najavits L. Course and treatment of patients with both substance use and posttraumatic stress disorders. Addict Behav 1998;23: 785–795.

16. Morrissey JP, Jackson EW, Ellis AR, Amaro H, Brown VB, Najavits LM. Twelve-month outcomes of trauma-informed interventions for women with co-occurring disorders. Psychiatr Serv 2005;56:1213–1222.

17. Najavits L. Seeking Safety: A Treatment Manual for PTSD and Substance Abuse. New York: Guilford Press; 2002.

18. Hien DA, Wells EA, Jiang H, et al. Multisite randomized trial of behavioral interventions for women with co-occurring PTSD and substance use disorders. J Consult Clin Psychol 2009;77:607–619.

19. Hudson JI, Hiripi E, Pope HGJ, Kessler RC. The prevalence and correlates of eating disorders in the National Comorbidity Survey Replication. Biol Psychiatry 2007;61:348–358.

20. Holderness CC, Brooks-Gunn J, Warren MP. Comorbidity of eating disorders and substance abuse: review of the literature. Int J Eat Disord 1994; 16(1):1–34.

21. Bulik CM, Klump KL, Thornton L, et al. Alcohol use disorder comorbidity in eating disorders: a multicenter study. J Clin Psychiatry 65(7):1000–1006.

22. Herzog DB, Franko DL, Dorer DJ, Keel PK, Jackson S, Manzo MP. Drug abuse in women with eating disorders. Int J Eat Disord 2006;39:364–368.

23. Grilo CM, Sinha R, O'Malley SS. Eating disorders and alcohol use disorders. Alcohol Res Health 2002;26(2):151–160.

24. Keel PK, Dorer DJ, Eddy KT, Franko D, Charatan DL, Herzog DB. Predictors of mortality in eating disorders. Arch Gen Psychiatry 2003;60:179–183.

25. Gordon SM, Johnson AJ, Greenfield SF, Cohen L, Killeen T, Roman PM. Assessment and treatment of co-occurring eating disorders in publicly funded addiction treatment programs. Psychiatr Serv 2008;59(9): 1056–1059.

26. Kessler RC, Birnbaum H, Demler O, et al. The prevalence and correlates of nonaffective psychosis in the National Comorbidity Survey Replication (NCS-R). Biol Psychiatry 2005;58:668–676.

27. McMillan KA, Enns MW, Cox BJ, Sareen J. Comorbidity of axis I and II mental disorders with schizophrenia and psychotic disorders: findings from the National Epidemiologic Survey on Alcohol and Related Conditions. Can J Psychiat 2009;54: 477–486.

28. Maslin J. Substance misuse in psychosis: contextual issues. In: Graham HL, Copello A, Birchwood MJ, Mueser KT, eds. Substance Misuse in Psychosis: Approaches to Treatment and Service Delivery. Hoboken, NJ: Wiley; 2003:3–23.

29. Drake RE, Mueser KT, Brunette MF, McHugo GJ. A review of treatments for people with severe mental illnesses and co-occurring substance use disorders. Psychiatr Rehabil J 2004;27(4):360–374.

30. Grant BF, Stinson FS, Dawson DA, Chou SP, Ruan WJ, Pickering RP. Co-occurrence of 12-month alcohol and drug use disorders and personality disorders in the United States: results from the National Epidemiologic Survey on Alcohol and Related Conditions. Arch Gen Psychiatry 2004;61:361–368.

31. Lenzenweger MF, Lane MC, Loranger AW, Kessler RC. DSM-IV personality disorders in the National Comorbidity Survey Replication. Biol Psychiatry 2007;62:553–564.

32. Hesselbrock MN. Gender comparison of antisocial personality disorder and depression in alcoholism. J Subst Abuse 1991;3:205–219.

33. Zanarini MC, Frankenburg FR, Hennen J, Reich DB, Silk KR. Axis I comorbidity in patients with borderline personality disorder: 6-year follow-up and prediction of time to remission. Am J Psychiatry 2004;161:2108–2114.

34. Linehan MM, Schmidt H, Dimeff LA, Craft JC, Kanter J, Comtois KA. Dialectical behavior therapy for patients with borderline personality disorder and drug-dependence. Am J Addiction 1999;8:279–292.

35. Linehan MM, Dimeff LA, Reynolds SK, et al. Dialectical behavior therapy versus comprehensive validation therapy plus 12-step for the treatment of opioid dependent women meeting criteria for borderline personality disorder. Drug Alcohol Depend 2002;67:13–26.

8

The Study of Craving and Its Role in Addiction

PETER M. MONTI AND LARA A. RAY

INTRODUCTION

Although the notion of craving and its association with addiction has been around since antiquity, it has only been the purview of scientific study for the past 60 years or so.[1] Craving for a substance is defined as a strong desire to consume that substance, which in turn has been associated with *The Diagnostic and Statistical Manual of Mental Disorders* (*DSM-IV*) criterion of loss of control over substance use, one of the seven criteria for substance dependence. Craving itself represents a criterion for substance dependence in the current version of the *International Classification of Diseases* (*ICD-10*). A longitudinal study of alcoholism course and chronicity found that craving was associated with the highest relative risk of all *ICD-10* criteria for alcohol dependence.[2] Furthermore, recent studies have advanced our understanding of the genetic bases of craving. Many of these studies use one or a combination of the following: self-report data in family-based designs,[3] experimental laboratory paradigms,[4] and more recently, neuroimaging techniques.[5] Pharmacological studies have also leveraged craving paradigms to screen[6] and to test[7,8] promising medications for alcoholism. In short, the construct of craving has been successfully applied to the study of addiction etiology and treatment.

This review of the scientific study of craving and substance use will begin with a discussion of the phenomenology and assessment of craving, followed by a review of selective studies on craving neurobiology and genetics. We will then briefly discuss clinical applications and will conclude by highlighting limitations of the extant research and by providing directions for future inquiry in the field.

PHENOMENOLOGY AND ASSESSMENT

Although the operational definition of craving has been debated over the years, craving is inherently a subjective experience, best described as a state of desire or wanting.[9] Patients trying to abstain from alcohol or drugs often describe craving as an unpleasant state that challenges their commitment to abstinence and is often associated with relapse.[10] In fact, while in a craving state, individuals frequently show impaired cognitive processing. For example, we have shown craving to both increase reaction time [11] and interfere with cognitive resource allocation.[12] Further, while craving, individuals often overestimate the duration and intensity of their own future urges.[13] This is consistent with Marlatt's conceptualization of cravings as ocean waves that gradually build, peak, and then subside.[14] To that end, scientists and practitioners alike are interested in helping patients surf those waves of craving without consuming substances of abuse. Importantly, craving has been shown to impair working memory, which is a cognitive process related to effective decision making.[15]

It is also of interest that imagery is emerging as an important variable in the study of craving. The work of Kavanagh and colleagues suggests that imagery across sensory channels is critical to the experience of craving.[16] For example, a recent study showed that visualizations and other forms of sensory imagery were observed in cravings across a range of substances, including food.[17,18] This line of work makes a case for intensive thoughts forming a "gateway" to episodes of craving, and convincing data are presented across substances of abuse as well as food. Clearly, identifying the psychological and neurobiological underpinnings of craving has vast implications for addiction etiology and treatment and perhaps also for the study of food as an addiction.

The assessment of craving has received a great deal of attention in the addiction literature over the past three decades. For a review, see Rosenberg.[19] Although a number of self-report paper-and-pencil measures have been developed to assess craving for substances of abuse,[20,21] the cue-exposure paradigm represents the gold standard in the experimental assessment of craving. This paradigm consists of systematically exposing individuals to alcohol or drug cues and assessing their associated urge to drink/use. For example, during alcohol cue exposure, participants are asked to hold and smell a glass of water as a standard procedure to control for the effects of simple exposure to any potable liquid. Participants are then presented with their preferred alcoholic beverage and asked to hold and smell the beverage for the same number of trials.[22] Experimenter observation and prerecorded instructions further standardize the procedure. In addition to recording self-reported urge to drink, this protocol measures physiological reactivity to cues, such as heart rate, blood pressure, and salivation. These procedures have been found to elicit craving among heavy drinkers and alcohol-dependent individuals [22] and to yield valid and reliable measures of cue-induced craving [23] that are predictive of treatment outcome.[24]

Variations of these procedures include the presentation of alcohol/drug stimuli via pictures, imagery, and small taste cues. Different modes of cue presentation and methodological approaches may be more or less suited for different research questions and scientific designs, including brain imaging studies, and may be uniquely informative in experimental and clinical settings. For instance, a treatment study comparing two measures of craving (cue-elicited vs. just self-reported) found that cued craving was uniquely and positively associated with total number of drinks per drinking occasion, suggesting that cue-elicited craving may capture loss of control over drinking during recovery.[25]

From a theoretical standpoint, the cue-reactivity paradigm is largely predicated on Pavlovian conditioned responses. Specifically, repeated pairing of alcohol/drug cues (e.g., sight, smell, and taste of the alcoholic beverage or drug) with alcohol/drug consumption over time produced a conditioned reinforcement such that over time, alcohol/drug cues become conditioned stimuli, which in turn elicit craving for that substance. These learned processes have been well documented in both human [26] and animal [27] models. The argument can also be made that a variety of stimuli, including external and internal states, may become conditioned stimuli and therefore elicit craving. This is consistent with both the theoretical framework and the clinical phenomenology of craving as well as clinical anecdotes from patients in recovery.[1]

The study of craving has recently been advanced by ecological momentary assessment (EMA), the near real-time assessment of experiences and behavior in the natural environment using, for example, palm-top computers. While EMA has been predominately used in the assessment of smoking and smoking relapse,[28] it is increasingly being used in the study of alcohol use and has recently been incorporated into a pharmacotherapy study for cannabis use in our lab at Brown University. For example, Litt et al. showed that the magnitude and frequency of craving in the natural environment is associated with consumption in alcohol-dependent individuals.[29] Our laboratory has been using EMA as an adjunct to laboratory-based procedures such as cue reactivity and alcohol challenge procedures.[30,31] While lab-based procedures offer a measure of control that is not possible in the real world (for example, the careful study of blood alcohol concentration and the biphasic effects of alcohol), EMA allows us to capture more general contextual factors, such as the presence of others in the drinking environment.[32] In short, the selection of assessment instrument should be driven by the experimental question of interest. Much as the study of craving for substances of abuse has benefited by both lab-based and EMA technologies, so too should the study of craving for food.

NEUROBIOLOGY AND GENETICS

Cue-induced craving is essentially the result of associative learning. The neural basis of this learned association is supported and highlighted in the most prominent neurobiological theories of addiction.[33,34] Specifically, the neurobiology of addiction focuses primarily on three brain regions: the amygdala, prefrontal cortex, and nucleus accumbens. The activation of dopaminergic pathways through this circuitry is thought to be essential to alcohol/drug seeking, and recent research has shown that conditioned stimuli, such as alcohol or drug cues that predict substance availability and use, will independently trigger the release of dopamine in these brain areas.[35] Dopamine release into the core of the nucleus accumbens in response to stimuli that predict a biologically rewarding event, such as substance use, is thought to modulate the expression of adaptive behaviors, contribute to the assignment of salience to cues, and facilitate the development of learned associations.[33] In brief, cue-induced craving has well-characterized neural bases, and learned processes play a prominent role in the neurobiology of addiction.

The concept of incentive-sensitization, emphasized in the theoretical work of Robinson and Berridge, has focused on neuroadaptations in the brain reward circuitry, leading to brain sensitization to drugs or drug-associated stimuli.[36] In this model, craving is best described as "wanting," or in other words, as a measure of incentive-salience that is distinct from "liking" of a substance and consistent with the neural dissociation of the reward.[37] The assignment of incentive salience at the neural level, in turn, represents an essential determinant of compulsive and disordered patterns of drug-seeking behavior.[38] One of the remarkable features of the neuroadaptation and resulting incentive-sensitization processes is their persistence over time. This is consistent with the phenomenology of craving and patient reports of strong ("spontaneous") craving response to alcohol/drug-related stimuli, even after years of recovery. This is also in line with the increasing recognition that permanent changes in brain function take place as a result of addiction, and that these neuroadaptations render individuals vulnerable to relapse for extended periods of time.[33]

Neurobiological theories of addiction have consistently emphasized the role of dopamine in the assignment of incentive value to alcohol or drug cues. In later stages of addiction, glutamatergic projections from the orbitofrontal cortex to the nucleus accumbens are seen as essential to the maintenance of addictive disorders.[33] Behavioral genetic and neuroimaging studies of craving have been informed by these neurobiological theories and, as a result, have focused on these neural pathways. Behavioral genetic studies have capitalized on the cue-reactivity paradigm to capture craving for alcohol as an endophenotype for alcoholism. To that end, studies have found that the Long allele of the dopamine D_4 receptor (DRD4) gene was associated with greater craving for alcohol[4] and cigarettes.[39] Interestingly, and pertinent to the theme of this book, these findings have been extended to cue-induced craving for food.[40]

Brain imaging studies, following up on the genetic association findings, have reported greater neural activation of the brain reward circuitry in response to smoking[41] and alcohol[5] cues, among carriers of the Long allele of the DRD4 VNTR. Although encouraging, the association between this polymorphism and cue-induced craving in the laboratory has not been uniformly supported.[42] In addition to experimental studies of cue-induced craving, a recent genetic study using a family-based design found that variation in the α-synuclein (SNCA) gene, which plays a central role in dopamine synthesis, was associated with craving for alcohol, measured in a semistructured interview.[3] Taken together, these findings underscore the utility of the craving phenotype in addictions research, particularly by advancing inquiries into learning, as well as the neurobiological and genetic underpinnings of addiction.

CLINICAL APPLICATIONS

An important clinical application of the scientific work on cue-induced craving is the development of cue-exposure treatment (CET) approaches. In brief, these approaches consist of employing repeated unreinforced exposures to alcohol- or drug-related stimuli in an attempt to extinguish the conditioned response of craving and subsequent use. These approaches are often combined with cognitive-behavioral techniques, such as coping skills training.[43] A meta-analysis of cue-exposure addiction treatment outcome studies showed no consistent evidence for the efficacy of cue-exposure treatment, as originally implemented.[44] These findings have led some to draw attention to the need for advances in assessment and greater appreciation for the role of contextual factors in conditioning and extinction.[45]

Indeed, as Conklin and Tiffany point out, we know from basic research on learning that extinction is not the erasure of learning (unlearning), but rather new learning that reflects sophisticated relationships between stimuli in the form of context-dependent learning, or differential learning dependent upon environmental context.[44] Thus, more attention to phenomena such as context-dependent learning could help inform cue-exposure treatments in addictive behaviors and in the study of craving for food.

In light of these findings, recent directions in studies of craving and addiction include leveraging craving paradigms to screen[6] and to test[8] promising medications for addiction. Moreover, efforts that combine cue-exposure and urge specific coping skills training with pharmacotherapies for addiction[46] or with more comprehensive addiction treatment programs [47] may prove especially useful.

More recent and considerably less developed clinical applications of cue exposure–based approaches include those based in the elaborated intrusion (EI) theory of desire and in virtual reality approaches. The EI theory[16] distinguishes between the initial associative processes that prompt intrusive thoughts about an appetitive target (e.g. alcohol) and those controlled cognitive elaboration processes that follow and have stronger affective links. Although there are few data from controlled trials based on this approach, it does represent a promising departure from existing cue exposure–based approaches. Basically, this approach argues that for dysfunctional coping, in vivo demonstration of the ineffectiveness of thought suppression and the promotion of acceptance is likely to have a positive effect. Kavanagh et al. suggest that if acceptance is adopted by the client, then he or she should apply competing imagery on tasks with high working memory load to discourage elaboration and enhance functional coping.[16]

Virtual reality (VR)–based approaches are receiving a great deal of attention in the experimental literature and more recently in clinical application. VR has been defined as "high-end user-computer interface that involves real-time simulation and interactions through multiple sensorial channels."[48] Baumann and Sayette (2006) are among several researchers who have suggested the use of VR to help smokers extinguish conditioned responses to smoking cues.[49] Further, as we have noted,[45] VR technologies have the potential to reduce the context dependency of extinction (i.e., the extent to which extinction is specific to the treatment environment), one of the major limitations of cue-based extinction approaches.

SUMMARY AND CONCLUSIONS

While it is clear that the scientific study of craving has advanced substantially over the past two decades, it is equally true that we have a long road ahead. Advances in assessment, neurobiology, and genetics and contributions from learning theory and pharmacotherapy have been exciting, indeed. However, treatment approaches have been only moderately effective. If we are to enhance the treatment for

craving, we must emphasize the application of scientific findings. We have attempted to bridge this gap in this chapter as we have elsewhere.[31] For example, in the case of psychotherapeutic approaches, we have emphasized,[45] the importance of contextual factors and recommended leveraging new technologies and methods from basic research to enhance treatment. Similarly, for pharmacological approaches, there is both a need to understand how our current treatments work as well as a need for new pharmacotherapies. Craving paradigms will be useful in both instances. Finally, cue-based treatments can benefit from innovative approaches, such as those derived from the EI and VR models. As we have argued elsewhere,[50] the scientific and clinical enterprises must become completely transdisciplinary if we are to improve on the efficacy and effectiveness of our treatments. This will require more than just collaboration, but rather true communication between clinicians and scientists. Only then can we hope to gain insight into the complexities of craving and its role in addiction.

REFERENCES

1. Drummond DC. Theories of drug craving, ancient and modern. *Addiction* 2001;96:33–46.
2. de Bruijn C, van den Brink W, de Graaf R, Vollebergh WA. Alcohol abuse and dependence criteria as predictors of a chronic course of alcohol use disorders in the general population. *Alcohol Alcoholism* 2005;40:441–446.
3. Foroud T, Wetherill LF, Liang T, et al. Association of alcohol craving with alpha-synuclein (SNCA). *Alcohol Clin Exp Res* 2007;31:537–545.
4. Hutchison KE, McGeary J, Smolen A, Bryan A, Swift RM. The DRD4 VNTR polymorphism moderates craving after alcohol consumption. *Health Psychol* 2002;21:139–146.
5. Filbey FM, Ray L, Smolen A, Claus ED, Audette A, Hutchison KE. Differential neural response to alcohol priming and alcohol taste cues is associated with DRD4 VNTR and OPRM1 genotypes. *Alcohol Clin Exp Res* 2008;32:1113–1123.
6. Mason BJ, Light JM, Williams LD, Drobes DJ. Proof-of-concept human laboratory study for protracted abstinence in alcohol dependence: effects of gabapentin. *Addict Biol* 2009;14:73–83.
7. Hutchison KE, Ray L, Sandman E, et al. The effect of olanzapine on craving and alcohol consumption. *Neuropsychopharmacol* 2006;31:1310–1317.
8. Miranda R, Jr., MacKillop J, Monti PM, et al. Effects of topiramate on urge to drink and the subjective effects of alcohol: a preliminary laboratory study. *Alcohol Clin Exp Res* 2008;32:489–497.

The Study of Craving and Its Role in Addiction   57

9. Monti PM, Tidey J, Czachowski CL, et al. Building bridges: the transdisciplinary study of craving from the animal laboratory to the lamppost. *Alcohol Clin Exp Res* 2004;28:279–287.

10. Oslin DW, Cary M, Slaymaker V, Colleran C, Blow FC. Daily ratings measures of alcohol craving during an inpatient stay define subtypes of alcohol addiction that predict subsequent risk for resumption of drinking. *Drug Alcohol Depend* 2009;103:131–136.

11. Sayette MA, Monti PM, Rohsenow DJ, et al. The effects of cue exposure on reaction time in male alcoholics. *J Stud Alcohol* 1994;55:629–633.

12. Sayette MA, Hufford MR. Effects of cue exposure and deprivation on cognitive resources in smokers. *J Abnorm Psychol* 1994;103:812–818.

13. Sayette MA, Loewenstein G, Kirchner TR, Travis T. Effects of smoking urge on temporal cognition. *Psychol Addict Behav* 2005;19:88–93.

14. Marlatt G. Addiciton, mindfulness, and acceptance. In: Hayes S, Jacobson, NS, Follette, VM, Dougher, MJ, ed. *Acceptance and Change: Content and Context in Psychotherapy*. Reno, NV: Context Press; 1994:175–197.

15. Bechara A, Martin EM. Impaired decision making related to working memory deficits in individuals with substance addictions. *Neuropsychol* 2004;18:152–162.

16. Kavanagh DJ, Andrade J, May J. Imaginary relish and exquisite torture: the elaborated intrusion theory of desire. *Psychol Rev* 2005;112:446–467.

17. May J, Andrade J, Panabokke N, Kavanagh D. Images of desire: cognitive models of craving. *Memory* 2004;12:447–461.

18. Smeets E, Roefs A, Jansen A. Experimentally induced chocolate craving leads to an attentional bias in increased distraction but not in speeded detection. *Appetite* 2009;53(3):370–375.

19. Rosenberg H. Clinical and laboratory assessment of the subjective experience of drug craving. *Clin Psychol Rev* 2009;29:519–534.

20. Moak DH, Anton RF, Latham PK. Further validation of the Obsessive-Compulsive Drinking Scale (OCDS). Relationship to alcoholism severity. *Am J Addict* 1998;7:14–23.

21. MacKillop J. Factor structure of the alcohol urge questionnaire under neutral conditions and during a cue-elicited urge state. *Alcohol Clin Exp Res* 2006;30:1315–1321.

22. Monti PM, Binkoff JA, Abrams DB, Zwick WR, Nirenberg TD, Liepman MR. Reactivity of alcoholics and nonalcoholics to drinking cues. *J Abnorm Psychol* 1987;96:122–126.

23. Payne TJ, Rychtarik RG, Rappaport NB, et al. Reactivity to alcohol-relevant beverage and imaginal cues in alcoholics. *Addict Behav* 1992;17:209–217.

24. Rohsenow DJ, Monti PM, Rubonis AV, et al. Cue reactivity as a predictor of drinking among male alcoholics. *J Consult Clin Psychol* 1994;62:620–626.

25. Ray LA, Hutchison KE, Bryan A. Psychosocial predictors of treatment outcome, dropout, and change processes in a pharmacological clinical trial for alcohol dependence. *Addict Disorders Treat* 2006;5:179–190.

26. O'Brien CP, Childress AR, McLellan T, Ehrman R. Integrating systemic cue exposure with standard treatment in recovering drug dependent patients. *Addict Behav* 1990;15:355–365.

27. Rodd ZA, Bell RL, Sable HJ, Murphy JM, McBride WJ. Recent advances in animal models of alcohol craving and relapse. *Pharmacol Biochem Behav* 2004;79:439–450.

28. Shiffman S, Gwaltney CJ, Balabanis MH, et al. Immediate antecedents of cigarette smoking: an analysis from ecological momentary assessment. *J Abnorm Psychol* 2002;111:531–545.

29. Litt MD, Cooney NL, Morse P. Reactivity to alcohol-related stimuli in the laboratory and in the field: predictors of craving in treated alcoholics. *Addiction* 2000;95:889–900.

30. Tidey JW, Monti PM, Rohsenow DJ, et al. Moderators of naltrexone's effects on drinking, urge, and alcohol effects in non-treatment-seeking heavy drinkers in the natural environment. *Alcohol Clin Exp Res* 2008;32:58–66.

31. Monti PM. Translational research on craving: promises, problems, and potential. In: Baltimore, MD: Research Society on Alcoholism; 2006.

32. Ray LA, Miranda R, Tidey J, et al. Polymorphisms of the mu-opioid receptor and dopamine d4 receptor genes and subjective responses to alcohol in the natural environment. *J Abnorm Psychol* 2010;119(1):115–125.

33. Kalivas PW, Volkow ND. The neural basis of addiction: a pathology of motivation and choice. *Am J Psychiatry* 2005;162:1403–1413.

34. Koob GF, Le Moal M. Addiction and the brain anti-reward system. *Annu Rev Psychol* 2008;59:29–53.

35. Phillips PE, Stuber GD, Heien ML, Wightman RM, Carelli RM. Subsecond dopamine release promotes cocaine seeking. *Nature* 2003;422:614–618.

36. Robinson TE, Berridge KC. Review. The incentive sensitization theory of addiction: some current issues. *Philos Trans R Soc Lond B Biol Sci* 2008;363:3137–146.

37. Berridge KC, Robinson TE, Aldridge JW. Dissecting components of reward: "liking," "wanting," and learning. *Curr Opin Pharmacol* 2009;9:65–73.

38. Robinson TE, Berridge KC. The neural basis of drug craving: an incentive-sensitization theory of addiction. *Brain Res Brain Res Rev* 1993;18:247–291.

39. Hutchison KE, LaChance H, Niaura R, Bryan A, Smolen A. The DRD4 VNTR polymorphism influences reactivity to smoking cues. *J Abnorm Psychol* 2002;111:134–143.

40. Sobik L, Hutchison K, Craighead L. Cue-elicited craving for food: a fresh approach to the study of binge eating. *Appetite* 2005;44:253–261.

41. McClernon FJ, Hutchison KE, Rose JE, Kozink RV. DRD4 VNTR polymorphism is associated with transient fMRI-BOLD responses to smoking cues. *Psychopharmacol (Berl)* 2007;194:433–441.

42. van den Wildenberg E, Janssen RG, Hutchison KE, van Breukelen GJ, Wiers RW. Polymorphisms of the dopamine D4 receptor gene (DRD4 VNTR) and cannabinoid CB1 receptor gene (CNR1) are not strongly related to cue-reactivity after alcohol exposure. *Addict Biol* 2007;12:210–220.

43. Monti PM, Rohsenow DJ, Rubonis AV, et al. Cue exposure with coping skills treatment for male alcoholics: a preliminary investigation. *J Consult Clin Psychol* 1993;61:1011–1019.

44. Conklin CA, Tiffany ST. Applying extinction research and theory to cue-exposure addiction treatments. *Addiction* 2002;97:155–167.

45. Monti PM, MacKillop J. Advances in the treatment of craving for alcohol and tobacco. In: Miller PM, Kavanagh DJ, eds. *Translation of Addictions Science into Practice*. Amsterdam, The Netherlands: Elsevier Press; 2007:209–238.

46. Monti PM, Rohsenow DJ, Swift RM, et al. Naltrexone and cue exposure with coping and communication skills training for alcoholics: treatment process and 1-year outcomes. *Alcohol Clin Exp Res* 2001;25:1634–1647.

47. Rohsenow DJ, Monti PM, Rubonis AV, et al. Cue exposure with coping skills training and communication skills training for alcohol dependence: 6- and 12-month outcomes. *Addiction* 2001;96:1161–1174.

48. Burdea GC, Cioffet P, eds. *Virtual Reality Technology*. 2nd ed. Hoboken, NJ: Wiley Interscience; 2003.

49. Baumann SB, Sayette MA. Smoking cues in a virtual world provoke craving in cigarette smokers. *Psychol Addict Behav* 2006;20:484–489.

50. Monti PM, Rohsenow DJ, Hutchison KE. Toward bridging the gap between biological, psychobiological and psychosocial models of alcohol craving. *Addiction* 2000;95(suppl 2):S229–S236.

9

Stress and Addiction

A Brief Overview

RAJITA SINHA

Engaging in rewarding and pleasurable behaviors is a natural part of human existence. Consuming highly palatable foods, engaging in sex, smoking cigarettes, drinking alcohol, and taking illicit and/or prescription drugs are among the behaviors that are vulnerable to excess, overconsumption, and addiction. But not all individuals develop addictive behaviors, and hence there are at least two sets of questions critical to the problem of addiction. First, who and under what conditions and contexts are humans most susceptible to develop addictive behaviors, and second, once addicted, which individuals and what conditions and contexts contribute to the high rates of relapse commonly seen in addiction. To address these two questions, this chapter focuses on stress and the integral role that stress mechanisms play in the development of addiction and in addiction relapse risk. The concept of stress and allostasis as it pertains to addiction vulnerability is discussed, followed by an overview of the literature linking types of stress to addiction. The neurobiological mechanisms that could drive this association is presented and this is followed by an overview of the effects of regular and chronic engagement in addictive behaviors and their concomitant allostatic changes on stress coping and addiction relapse.

STRESS, ALLOSTASIS, AND ADDICTION VULNERABILITY

Most simply, *stress* may be defined as any highly challenging emotional or physiological event or series of events that result in adaptive and maladaptive processes required to regain homeostasis and/or stability.[1,2] Examples of emotional stressors include interpersonal conflict, loss of relationship, death of a close family member, and loss of a child.

Some common physiological stressors are hunger or food deprivation, sleep deprivation or insomnia, high levels of psychoactive drug effects, extreme hyperthermia or hypothermia and drug withdrawal states. Stress-related adaptation has been extended to include the concept of *allostasis*, which is the ability to achieve physiological stability through change in internal milieu and to maintain apparent stability at a new physiological set point.[3] According to McEwen and colleagues, health functioning requires ongoing adjustments of internal milieu, with fluctuations in physiology, mood, and activity as individuals respond and adapt to environmental demands.[2-4] Excessive stress to the system, termed as increased *allostatic load*, results in "wear and tear" of the adaptive regulatory systems and biological alterations that weaken stress adaptation and increase disease susceptibility.[4-6] For brief periods and in the short term, the allostatic response to environmental demands or stressors is adaptive, for example, increased energy producing food intake during periods of stress.[7] However, repeated and chronic stress with resultant increased allostatic load over time leads to a dysregulated neural, physiological, behavioral, and social state that is maintained outside the homeostatic range.

The perception and appraisal of stress relies on individual-level factors such as the specific presenting external or internal stimuli, personality traits, availability of internal resources, including physiological condition of the individual (e.g., sleep deprivation, altered mental state), prior emotional state, including beliefs and expectancies expressed via responses of specific brain regions mediating the appraisal of stimuli as distressing and the resulting physiological, behavioral, and emotional experiences and adaptive responses. Brain regions such as the amygdala, hippocampus, insula, orbitofrontal cortex, medial prefrontal, cingulate, temporal, and parietal cortices are involved in the perception and appraisal of emotional and stressful stimuli and the brainstem (locus ceruleus and related arousal regions), hypothalamus, thalamus, striatal, and limbic regions are involved in the physiological,emotional and behavioral responses and together these regions contribute to the experience and regulation of stress.

The physiological responses are manifested through two interacting stress pathways, namely the corticotropin-releasing factor (CRF) released from the paraventricular nucleus (PVN) of the hypothalamus, which stimulates adrenocorticotrophin hormone (ACTH) from the anterior pituitary, which subsequently stimulates the secretion of cortisol/corticosterone from the adrenal glands, and the autonomic nervous system ,which is coordinated via the sympathoadrenal medulary (SAM) systems and the concomitant changes in the inflammatory cytokine and immune system markers.[8] In addition, CRF has extensive influence in extrahypothalamic regions across the corticostriatal-limbic regions and plays a critical role in modulating the subjective and behavioral stress responses.[9] Furthermore, central catecholamines, particularly noradrenaline and dopamine, are involved in modulating brain motivational pathways (including the ventral tegmental area [VTA], nucleus accumbens [NAc], and the medial prefrontal [mPFC] regions) that are important in regulating distress, exerting cognitive and behavioral control, and negotiating behavioral and cognitive responses critical for adaptation and homeostasis.[10-12] The hypothalamic and extrahypothalamic CRF pathways and central catechoamines target brain motivational and cognitive pathways, with interactive effects on brain glutamate, GABA, opioids, and several other regulatory neuropeptides and neurosteroids to critically affect adaptive and homeostatic processes. For example, the medial and lateral components of the prefrontal cortex (PFC) are involved in higher cognitive or executive control functions, and high stress alters structural and functional responses in these brain regions.[12-15] These findings are consistent with behavioral and clinical research showing that with high levels of stress or negative affect, there is decreased emotional and behavioral control, increases in impulsivity,[16-18] which in turn is associated with greater engagement in alcohol, smoking, and other drug abuse,[19-25] as well as increased intake of rich and highly palatable foods.[26-30] Thus, the motivational brain pathways are key targets for the brain and body's stress chemicals, thereby providing important clues for how stress affects addiction vulnerability.

STRESS, CHRONIC ADVERSITY, AND INCREASED VULNERABILITY TO ADDICTIVE BEHAVIORS

Considerable evidence from population-based and clinical studies indicates that psychosocial adversity, especially highly stressful and uncontrollable events, and chronic distress states increase addiction vulnerability. Negative life events such as loss of parent; parental divorce and conflict; low parental support; isolation and deviant affiliation; abandonment; forced to live apart from parents; loss of child by death or removal; unfaithfulness of significant other; loss of home to natural disaster; death of a close one; emotional abuse or neglect; sexual abuse; rape; physical abuse by parent, caretaker, family member, spouse, or significant other; victim of gun shooting or other violent acts; and observing violent victimization have all been associated with increased risk of substance abuse in adolescent and adult samples.[2] Similarly, there is growing evidence to support the significant association between high uncontrollable stress, chronic stress, and adiposity, high body mass index (BMI), and weight gain.[31,32]

Overlapping Neurobiology of Stress and Reward

Neurobiological research indicates that early and repeated adversity and chronic levels of stress, particularly at specific developmental stages, results in persistent and long-lasting changes in brain stress pathways, which in turn alters stress responsivity throughout adulthood.[33-36] More recent evidence further supports this earlier data and indicates gene expression changes in CRF, GC, and noradrenergic and serotoninergic signaling in critical cortico-limbic-striatal brain regions that are integral to these alterations in stress responses.[37] Furthermore, early and chronic stress related alterations in glutamate, GABA, noradrenergic, dopamine, and opioid pathways in mesolimbic striatal and prefrontal regions are associated with neurochemical and behavioral sensitization of stress responsivity.[15,38-40]

There is clear evidence that drugs of abuse and highly palatable foods activate the brain reward pathways that are involved in the reinforcing effects of natural primary (food, sex) and secondary (drugs, money, etc.) hedonic stimuli.[41] However, stress activation also stimulates mesolimbic dopamine transmission[2] and enhances self-administration of abusive substances and the intake of highly palatable fatty foods.[42–46] Stress-related increases in the stress hormone (cortisol) and resulting changes in glucocorticoid (GC) signaling alter energy balance and, combined with insulin, affect brain reward regions (e.g., NAc) to amplify incentive motivation and increase the intake of rich, fatty foods.[47] Abolishing biological stress responses such as cortisol, or attenuating extrahypothalamic CRF or inhibiting brain catecholamine, decreases self- administration of psychoactive drugs and prevents stress-induced return to drug seeking and food seeking.[48–53]

There is also evidence that like drugs of abuse, stress and concomitant increases in CRF and GCs enhance glutamate activity in the VTA, which in turn, enhances activity of dopaminergic neurons.[54–57] Human brain imaging studies have further shown that stress-related increases in cortisol are associated with dopamine accumulation in the ventral striatum,[58,59] and some evidence also reveals that amphetamine-induced increases in cortisol are associated with both dopamine binding in the ventral striatum and with ratings of amphetamine-induced euphoria.[60] Given that both stress and drugs of abuse activate the mesolimbic pathways, it is not surprising that each results in synaptic adaptations in VTA dopamine neurons and in morphological changes in the mPFC.[13,55,61,62] New evidence indicates that there are specific subgroups of neurons in the VTA projecting to the NAc and the PFC that are specifically responsive to stress while others are responsive to reward signals. However, high exposure to either set of stimuli alters the basal firing, responsiveness, and recovery rates of these neurons to both sets of stimuli.[63] These mechanisms have begun to explain the converging evidence indicating that drugs of abuse and stress can each result in behavioral, neurochemical, and neuronal cross-sensitization of stress and drugs of abuse.[55,64] High levels of stress exposure and concomitant increases in corticosterone and early life stress-related changes in GCs both alter the sensitivity and responsiveness of mesolimbic dopamine responses as well as hypothalamic CRF and extrahypothalamic CRF, and metabolic factors such that each set of stimuli show increased responsiveness to the other, thereby setting up a feed-forward facilitatory system that promotes and strengthens stress-related seeking of addictive behaviors.

ADDICTIVE HABITS AND SUSCEPTIBILITY TO COMPULSIVE SEEKING AND STRESS-INDUCED ENGAGEMENT IN HEDONIC BEHAVIORS

In addition to chronic stress impacting allostasis, chronic abuse of substances and high intake of rich, fatty foods are also persistent challenges that apply *allostatic load* to psychophysiological systems, similar to chronic stress. Increased load in physiological systems influences the nervous system and brain stress and reward pathways that are involved in physiological and behavioral coping responses.[7] In addition to physiological systems responding to load, there are concomitant adaptations in the behavioral coping and adaptive systems as well. Thus, chronic abuse of substances or specific types of foods (e.g. rich, fatty foods) and metabolic states (e.g., high BMI, metabolic syndrome) result in a dysregulation in the reward or hedonic set point of affected individuals,[3,65–68] as well as altered basal stress tone and stress responsivity.[2,69,70] Such dysregulation in reward and stress circuits can lead to increased "salience" of drug or specific food cues that can result in the compulsive engagement in addictive behaviors, the organism's behavioral response to maintain hedonic homeostasis in the context of a compromised physiological state.[18,71,72] This hypothesis is consistent with evidence of adaptations in brain reward and stress circuits and in local physiology (e.g. energy balance) that may facilitate addictive processes like cravings, reduced self-control, and a compulsive engagement in addictive behaviors.[18,41,72–74]

The aforementioned line of thinking would predict that with increasing severity of chronic drug abuse and or increasing BMI representative of high metabolic load, there would be increases in craving for preferred hedonic stimuli, compulsive seeking of those stimuli, and susceptibility for addiction relapse. Furthermore, stress and high hedonic cue contexts would serve to be particularly "toxic" environments that increase compulsive seeking and risk of addiction relapse in those with overconsumption of such hedonic stimuli. There is growing evidence from human and basic science studies to support these hypotheses. Alcohol-, nicotine-, and drug-abusing individuals report higher basal levels of craving for their preferred drugs and enhanced and persistent craving with laboratory exposure to stress- and drug-related cues.[69,75] The increased salience of food cues in behavioral and neural responses is more evident among individuals with high BMI than those with BMIs in the normal range.[76-79] High levels of stress, stress- and cue-related craving, and real-world craving as measured by ecological momentary assessment (EMA) techniques as well as altered stress responses have each been associated with addiction relapse risk and weight gain.[2,31,32,80-84]

On the other hand, acute, regular, and chronic exposure to drugs results in "sensitization" or enhanced behavioral and neurochemical response to drugs and to stress. Synaptic alterations in the VTA, NAc, and medial PFC modulated by glutamate effects on dopamine neurons, and CRF and noradrenergic effects on DA and non-DA pathways contribute to behavioral sensitization of stress and drugs of abuse.[71,85-88] Similarly, chronic intake of fatty foods exacerbates stress responsiveness and increase plasma GC levels.[47,89] In addition, increased levels of brain-derived neurotrophic factor (BDNF) in the mesolimbic dopamine regions has been associated with increases in drug seeking during abstinence from chronic drug use.[90,91] Furthermore, behavioral sensitization observed with drugs of abuse and with stress are associated with synaptic changes in mesolimbic dopamine regions, particularly the VTA, NAc, and the amygdala, and such changes contribute to compulsive drug seeking.[92,93] Furthermore, stress-induced increases in drug seeking and food seeking are associated with upregulated extrahypothalamic CRF expression and increases in glutamate and BDNF signaling.[52,57,68,94] Thus, there are significant physiological, neurochemical, and behavioral alterations in stress and dopaminergic pathways associated with chronic drug use and overeating of highly palatable foods, which in turn, could affect craving and compulsive seeking, maintenance of overconsumption of drugs and food, and relapse risk.

INDIVIDUAL DIFFERENCE VARIABLES AFFECTING STRESS AND ADDICTION

While the main thrust of this chapter has been on stress and adverse environmental contexts and their significant role in addiction vulnerability

and relapse risk, it is important to highlight two additional vulnerability factors and how they may interact with the stress and addiction association. The first is genetic and familial influences on stress vulnerability and risk of specific addictions, such as alcoholism, nicotine, other drug abuse, food addiction, and obesity risk. Adverse environments are known to alter gene expression in stress, metabolic, and reward pathways, and on a cellular level, these factors influence the mechanisms linking stress to high addiction risk.[40,95-97] Depending on the level of stress (magnitude and chronicity) and developmental stage of exposure to adversity, such cellular and molecular changes influence development of brain systems involved in executive function, negative emotionality, behavioral/self-control, impulsivity, or risk taking and other personality factors that can alter the initial sensitivity to rewarding effects of hedonic stimuli like drugs and food.[2,97] The second is that chronic exposure to drugs or highly palatable foods and their associated metabolic state alters specific gene expression that not only influences the risk of engaging in those hedonic behaviors but also alter the vulnerability to stress and stress-induced seeking of hedonic stimuli.[69] These individual differences are integral to the manifestation of the strength of association between stress and addiction vulnerability, thereby contributing significantly to this complex association.

SUMMARY AND FUTURE DIRECTIONS

This chapter provides an overview of the growing evidence from preclinical, clinical, and population studies that stress increases addiction vulnerability and risk of relapse. Highly stressful events that are uncontrollable and unpredictable, cumulative and persistent psychosocial adversity, and physiological load all increase risk of addiction for both children and adults. Exposure to such stressors early in life and cumulative adversity (stress load) without adequate amounts of stress-buffering factors (social support, high IQ and education, healthy diet, individual biological and psychological factors, and enriched environment) results in neuroendocrine, physiological, behavioral, and subjective changes that tend to be long lasting and adversely affect development of brain systems involved in learning, motivation, and stress-related adaptive behaviors. Neurobiological effects of high stress load on the brain reward pathways are described to identify possible mechanisms that may begin to explain the important relationship between stress and addiction. Regular and chronic use of addictive substances and rich highly palatable foods result in allostatic changes in stress and reward pathways that promote compulsive seeking and increase relapse risk. Significant clinical implications include assessment of individuals who are susceptible to stress-related increases in addiction and those who are at most risk for stress-induced relapse. Finally, there are no specific medications that target withdrawal-related anxiety, stress-induced compulsive seeking, and stress-related relapse risk, development of which is desperately needed to decrease the addiction epidemic in the United States.

It is important to underscore the point that high stress exposure and chronic distress debilitates stress adaptive coping mechanisms, and hence treatments that rely on improving coping may not be as beneficial to those with greatest stress-related risk factors. Development of new interventions that target stress vulnerability and improve self-control, especially in the context of stress, is needed. Systematic research on these questions will lead to a greater understanding of how stress is associated with addiction risk and relapse. Furthermore, such research may be significant in developing new treatment targets to reduce relapse, both in the area of medication development as well as in developing behavioral treatments that specifically target the effects of stress on continued overconsumption of drugs and food and high relapse risk.

REFERENCES

1. McEwen BS. Physiology and neurobiology of stress and adaptation: central role of the brain. *Physiol Rev* 2007;87(3):873–904.
2. Sinha R. Chronic stress, drug use, and vulnerability to addiction. *Ann NY Acad Sci* 2008;1141:105–130.
3. McEwen BS. Allostasis and allostatic load: implications for neuropsychopharmacology. *Neuropsychopharmacol* 2000;22(2):108–124.
4. Seeman TE, Singer BH, Rowe JW, Horwitz RI, McEwen BS. Price of adaptation—allostatic load and its health consequences. MacArthur studies of successful aging. *Arch Intern Med* 1997;157(19):2259–2268.
5. MacArthur Foundation Research Network on Socioeconomic Status and Health. Allostatic load notebook—chapter 9: heart rate variability. 1997. Available at http://www.macses.ucsf.edu/research/allostatic/heartrate.php. Accessed March 11, 2012.
6. Lampert R, Shusterman V, Burg MM, et al. Effects of psychologic stress on repolarization and relationship to autonomic and hemodynamic factors. *J Cardiovasc Electr* 2005;16(4):372–377.
7. McEwen BS. Protection and damage from acute and chronic stress: allostasis and allostatic overload and relevance to the pathophysiology of psychiatric disorders. *Ann NY Acad Sci* 2004;1032:1–7.
8. Kyrou I, Tsigos C. Stress mechanisms and metabolic complications. *Horm Metab Res* 2007;39(6):430–438.
9. Heinrichs S. Behavioral consequences of altered cortiocotropin-releasing factor activation in brain: a functionalist view of affective neuroscience. In: Steckler T, Kalin NH, Reul JMHM, eds. *Handbook of stress and the Brain. Part 1: The Neurobiology of Stress.* Dusseldorf, Germany: Elsevier; 2005:155–177.
10. Phan KL, Fitzgerald DA, Nathan PJ, Moore GJ, Uhde TW, Tancer ME. Neural substrates for voluntary suppression of negative affect: a functional magnetic resonance imaging study. *Biol Psychiat* 2005;57(3):210–219.
11. Paulus MP. Decision-making dysfunctions in psychiatry—altered homeostatic processing? *Science* 2007;318(5850):602–606.
12. Arnsten AF. Stress signalling pathways that impair prefrontal cortex structure and function. *Nat Rev Neurosci* 2009;10(6):410–422.
13. Liston C, Miller MM, Goldwater DS, et al. Stress-induced alterations in prefrontal cortical dendritic morphology predict selective impairments in perceptual attentional set-shifting. *J Neurosci* 2006;26(30):7870–7874.
14. Liston C, McEwen BS, Casey BJ. Psychosocial stress reversibly disrupts prefrontal processing and attentional control. *P Natl Acad Sci USA* 2009;106(3):912–917.
15. Dias-Ferreira E, Sousa JC, Melo I, et al. Chronic stress causes frontostriatal reorganization and affects decision-making. *Science* 2009;325(5940):621–625.
16. Mischel W. *From Good Intentions to Willpower.* New York: Guildford Press; 1996.
17. Tice DM, Bratslavsky E, Baumeister RF. Emotional distress regulation takes precedence over impulse control: if you feel bad, do it! *J Pers Soc Psychol* 2001;80(1):53–67.
18. Sinha R. How does stress increase risk of drug abuse and relapse? *Psychopharmacol* 2001;158(4):343–359.
19. Fishbein DH, Herman-Stahl M, Eldreth D, et al. Mediators of the stress-substance-use relationship in urban male adolescents. *Prev Sci* 2006;7(2):113–126.
20. Baler RD, Volkow ND. Drug addiction: the neurobiology of disrupted self-control. *Trends Mol Med* 2006;12(12):559–566.
21. Wills TA, Stoolmiller M. The role of self-control in early escalation of substance use: a time-varying analysis. *J Consult Clin Psych* 2002;70(4):986–997.
22. Wills TA, Walker C, Mendoza D, Ainette MG. Behavioral and emotional self-control: relations to substance use in samples of middle and high

school students. *Psychol Addict Behav* 2006;20(3): 265–278.

23. Wills TA, Ainette MG, Mendoza D, Gibbons FX, Brody GH. Self-control, symptomatology, and substance use precursors: test of a theoretical model in a community sample of 9-year-old children. *Psychol Addict Behav* 2007;21(2):205–215.

24. Laucht M, Treutlein J, Blomeyer D, et al. Interaction between the 5-HTTLPR serotonin transporter polymorphism and environmental adversity for mood and anxiety psychopathology: evidence from a high-risk community sample of young adults. *Int J Neuropsychoph* 2009;12(6):737–747.

25. Fields S, Leraas K, Collins C, Reynolds B. Delay discounting as a mediator of the relationship between perceived stress and cigarette smoking status in adolescents. *Behav Pharmacol* 2009;20(5–6):455–460.

26. Klein L, Faraday N, Grunberg M. Gender differences in eating after exposure to noise stressor. *Ann Behav Med* 1996;18:S103.

27. Willner P, Benton D, Brown E, et al. "Depression" increases "craving" for sweet rewards in animal and human models of depression and craving. *Psychopharmacol* 1998;136(3):272–283.

28. Epel EE, Moyer AE, Martin CD, et al. Stress-induced cortisol, mood, and fat distribution in men. *Obes Res* 1999;7(1):9–15.

29. Epel E, Lapidus R, McEwen B, Brownell K. Stress may add bite to appetite in women: a laboratory study of stress-induced cortisol and eating behavior. *Psychoneuroendocrinol* 2001;26(1):37–49.

30. Roberts CJ. The effects of stress on food choice, mood and body weight in healthy women. *Nutr Bull* 2008;33(1):33–39.

31. Adam TC, Epel ES. Stress, eating and the reward system. *Physiol Behav* 2007;91(4):449–458.

32. Block JP, He Y, Zaslavsky AM, Ding L, Ayanian JZ. Psychosocial stress and change in weight among US adults. *Am J Epidemiol* 2009;170(2):181–192.

33. Meaney MJ, Bhatnagar S, Larocque S, et al. Individual differences in the hypothalamic-pituitary-adrenal stress response and the hypothalamic CRF system. *Ann NY Acad Sci* 1993;697:70–85.

34. Plotsky PM, Thrivikraman KV, Meaney MJ. Central and feedback regulation of hypothalamic corticotropin-releasing factor secretion. *Ciba Found Symp* 1993;172:59–75.

35. Coplan JD, Andrews MW, Rosenblum LA, et al. Persistent elevations of cerebrospinal fluid concentrations of corticotropin-releasing factor in adult nonhuman primates exposed to early-life stressors: implications for the pathophysiology of mood and anxiety disorders. *Proc Natl Acad Sci USA* 1996;93(4):1619–1623.

36. Plotsky PM, Meaney MJ. Early, postnatal experience alters hypothalamic corticotropin-releasing factor (CRF) mRNA, median eminence CRF content and

stress-induced release in adult rats. *Brain Res Mol Brain Res* 1993;18(3):195–200.

37. Liu D, Diorio J, Tannenbaum B, et al. Maternal care, hippocampal glucocorticoid receptors, and hypothalamic-pituitary-adrenal responses to stress. *Science* 1997;277(5332):1659–1662.

38. Brake WG, Zhang TY, Diorio J, Meaney MJ, Gratton A. Influence of early postnatal rearing conditions on mesocorticolimbic dopamine and behavioural responses to psychostimulants and stressors in adult rats. *Eur J Neurosci* 2004;19(7):1863–1874.

39. Gratton A, Sullivan RM. Role of prefrontal cortex in stress responsivity. In: Steckler T, Kalin NH, Reul JMHM, eds. *Handbook of Stress and the Brain. Part 1: The Neurobiology of Stress*. Dusseldorf, Germany: Elsevier, 2005:838.

40. Olsen CM, Huang Y, Goodwin S, et al. Microarray analysis reveals distinctive signaling between the bed nucleus of the stria terminalis, nucleus accumbens, and dorsal striatum. *Physiol Genomics* 2008; 32(3):283–298.

41. Kalivas PW, Volkow ND. The neural basis of addiction: a pathology of motivation and choice. *Am J Psychiat* 2005;162(8):1403–1413.

42. Ramsey NF, Van Ree JM. Emotional but not physical stress enhances intravenous cocaine self-administration in drug-naive rats. *Brain Res* 1993;608(2):216–222.

43. Haney M, Maccari S, Le Moal M, Simon H, Piazza PV. Social stress increases the acquisition of cocaine self-administration in male and female rats. *Brain Res* 1995;698(1–2):46–52.

44. Miczek KA, Mutschler NH. Activational effects of social stress on IV cocaine self-administration in rats. *Psychopharmacol* 1996;128(3):256–264.

45. Piazza PV, Barrot M, Rouge-Pont F, et al. Suppression of glucocorticoid secretion and antipsychotic drugs have similar effects on the mesolimbic dopaminergic transmission. *Proc Natl Acad Sci USA* 1996;93(26):15445–15450.

46. Goeders NE. A neuroendocrine role in cocaine reinforcement. *Psychoneuroendocrinol* 1997;22(4): 237–259.

47. Pecoraro N, Gomez F, Dallman MF. Glucocorticoids dose-dependently remodel energy stores and amplify incentive relativity effects. *Psychoneuroendocrinol* 2005;30(9):815–825.

48. Shaham Y, Stewart J. Exposure to mild stress enhances the reinforcing efficacy of intravenous heroin self-administration in rats. *Psychopharmacol* 1994;114(3):523–527.

49. Shaham Y, Stewart J. Effects of opioid and dopamine receptor antagonists on relapse induced by stress and re-exposure to heroin in rats. *Psychopharmacol* 1996;125(4):385–391.

50. Stewart JA. *Pathways to Relapse: Factors Controlling the Reinitiation of Drug Seeking after Abstinence*. Lincoln: University of Nebraska Press; 2003.

51. Weiss F. Neurobiology of craving, conditioned reward and relapse. *Curr Opin Pharmacol* 2005;5(1):9–19.
52. Ghitza UE, Gray SM, Epstein DH, Rice KC, Shaham Y. The anxiogenic drug yohimbine reinstates palatable food seeking in a rat relapse model: a role of CRF1 receptors. *Neuropsychopharmacol* 2006;31(10): 2188–2196.
53. Cottone E, Guastalla A, Pomatto V, et al. Interplay of the endocannabinoid system with neuropeptide Y and corticotropin-releasing factor in the goldfish forebrain. *Ann NY Acad Sci* 2009;1163:372–375.
54. Overton PG, Tong ZY, Brain PF, Clark D. Preferential occupation of mineralocorticoid receptors by corticosterone enhances glutamate-induced burst firing in rat midbrain dopaminergic neurons. *Brain Res* 1996;737(1–2):146–154.
55. Saal D, Dong Y, Bonci A, Malenka RC. Drugs of abuse and stress trigger a common synaptic adaptation in dopamine neurons. *Neuron* 2003;37(4): 577–582.
56. Ungless MA, Singh V, Crowder TL, Yaka R, Ron D, Bonci A. Corticotropin-releasing factor requires CRF binding protein to potentiate NMDA receptors via CRF receptor 2 in dopamine neurons. *Neuron* 2003;39(3):401–407.
57. Wang B, Shaham Y, Zitzman D, Azari S, Wise RA, You ZB. Cocaine experience establishes control of midbrain glutamate and dopamine by corticotropin-releasing factor: a role in stress-induced relapse to drug seeking. *J Neurosci* 2005;25(22):5389–5396.
58. Pruessner JC, Champagne F, Meaney MJ, Dagher A. Dopamine release in response to a psychological stress in humans and its relationship to early life maternal care: a positron emission tomography study using [11C]raclopride. *J Neurosci* 2004;24(11):2825–2831.
59. Oswald LM, Wong DF, McCaul M, et al. Relationships among ventral striatal dopamine release, cortisol secretion, and subjective responses to amphetamine. *Neuropsychopharmacol* 2005;30(4):821–832.
60. Wand GS, Oswald LM, McCaul ME, et al. Association of amphetamine-induced striatal dopamine release and cortisol responses to psychological stress. *Neuropsychopharmacol* 2007;32(11):2310–2320.
61. Robinson TE, Kolb B. Alterations in the morphology of dendrites and dendritic spines in the nucleus accumbens and prefrontal cortex following repeated treatment with amphetamine or cocaine. *Eur J Neurosci* 1999;11(5):1598–1604.
62. Cleck JN, Blendy JA. Making a bad thing worse: adverse effects of stress on drug addiction. *J Clin Invest* 2008;118(2):454–461.
63. Brischoux F, Chakraborty S, Brierley DI, Ungless MA. Phasic excitation of dopamine neurons in ventral VTA by noxious stimuli. *Proc Natl Acad Sci USA* 2009;106(12):4894–4899.
64. Wang HL, Morales M. Corticotropin-releasing factor binding protein within the ventral tegmental area is expressed in a subset of dopaminergic neurons. *J Comp Neurol* 2008;509(3):302–318.
65. Koob GF, Le Moal M. Drug abuse: hedonic homeostatic dysregulation. *Science* 1997;278(5335):52–58.
66. Koob GF. Alcoholism: allostasis and beyond. *Alcohol Clin Exp Res* 2003;27(2):232–243.
67. Dallman MF, Pecoraro NC, la Fleur SE. Chronic stress and comfort foods: self-medication and abdominal obesity. *Brain Behav Immun* 2005;19(4):275–280.
68. Cottone P, Sabino V, Roberto M, et al. CRF system recruitment mediates dark side of compulsive eating. *Proc Natl Acad Sci USA* 2009;106(47): 20016–20020.
69. Sinha R, Fox HC, Hong KA, Bergquist K, Bhagwagar Z, Siedlarz KM. Enhanced negative emotion and alcohol craving, and altered physiological responses following stress and cue exposure in alcohol dependent individuals. *Neuropsychopharmacol* 2009;34(5):1198–1208.
70. van Dijk G, Buwalda B. Neurobiology of the metabolic syndrome: an allostatic perspective. *Eur J Pharmacol* 2008;585(1):137–146.
71. Robinson TE, Berridge KC. The psychology and neurobiology of addiction: an incentive-sensitization view. *Addiction* 2000;95(suppl 2):S91–S117.
72. Koob GF, Ahmed SH, Boutrel B, et al. Neurobiological mechanisms in the transition from drug use to drug dependence. *Neurosci Biobehav Rev* 2004;27(8):739–749.
73. Kalivas PW, Pierce RC, Cornish J, Sorg BA. A role for sensitization in craving and relapse in cocaine addiction. *J Psychopharmacol* 1998;12(1):49–53.
74. Dallman MF, Akana SF, Strack AM, et al. Chronic stress-induced effects of corticosterone on brain: direct and indirect. *Ann NY Acad Sci* 2004;1018: 141–150.
75. Fox HC, Talih M, Malison R, Anderson GM, Kreek MJ, Sinha R. Frequency of recent cocaine and alcohol use affects drug craving and associated responses to stress and drug-related cues. *Psychoneuroendocrinol* 2005;30(9):880–891.
76. Saelens BE, Epstein LH. Reinforcing value of food in obese and non-obese women. *Appetite* 1996;27(1):41–50.
77. Fedoroff IC, Polivy J, Herman CP. The effect of pre-exposure to food cues on the eating behavior of restrained and unrestrained eaters. *Appetite* 1997; 28(1):33–47.
78. Fedoroff I, Polivy J, Herman CP. The specificity of restrained versus unrestrained eaters' responses to food cues: general desire to eat, or craving for the cued food? *Appetite* 2003;41(1):7–13.
79. Simansky KJ. NIH symposium series: ingestive mechanisms in obesity, substance abuse and mental disorders. *Physiol Behav* 2005;86(1–2):1–4.
80. Sinha R, Garcia M, Paliwal P, Kreek MJ, Rounsaville BJ. Stress-induced cocaine craving and hypothalamic-

pituitary-adrenal responses are predictive of cocaine relapse outcomes. *Arch Gen Psychiat* 2006;63(3): 324–331.

81. Sinha R, Li CS. Imaging stress- and cue-induced drug and alcohol craving: association with relapse and clinical implications. *Drug Alcohol Rev* 2007;26(1):25–31.

82. Epstein DH, Marrone GF, Heishman SJ, Schmittner J, Preston KL. Tobacco, cocaine, and heroin: craving and use during daily life. *Addict Behav* 2009;35(4):318–324.

83. al'Absi M, Hatsukami D, Davis GL. Attenuated adrenocorticotropic responses to psychological stress are associated with early smoking relapse. *Psychopharmacol* 2005;181(1):107–117.

84. Tasca GA, Illing V, Balfour L, et al. Psychometric properties of self-monitoring of eating disorder urges among treatment seeking women: ecological momentary assessment using a daily diary method. *Eat Behav* 2009;10(1):59–61.

85. Nestler EJ, Hope BT, Widnell KL. Drug additction: a model for the molecular basis of neural plasticity. *Neuron* 1993;11:995–1006.

86. Robinson TE, Berridge KC. The neural basis of drug craving: an incentive-sensitization theory of addiction. *Brain Res* 1993;18(3):247–291.

87. White F, Xiu Y-H. Neurophysiological alterations in the mesocortiolimbic dopamine system during repeated cocaine administration. In: Hammer RP, ed. *The Neurobiology of Cocaine Addiction*. Boca Raton, FL: CRC Press; 1995:99–120.

88. Pierce RC, Kalivas PW. A circuitry model of the expression of behavioral sensitization to amphetamine-like psychostimulants. *Brain Res* 1997;25(2): 192–216.

89. Bolanos CA, Barrot M, Berton O, Wallace-Black D, Nestler EJ. Methylphenidate treatment during pre- and periadolescence alters behavioral responses to emotional stimuli at adulthood. *Biol Psychiat* 2003;54(12): 1317–1329.

90. Grimm JW, Shaham Y, Hope BT. Effect of cocaine and sucrose withdrawal period on extinction behavior, cue-induced reinstatement, and protein levels of the dopamine transporter and tyrosine hydroxylase in limbic and cortical areas in rats. *Behav Pharmacol* 2002;13(5–6):379–388.

91. Lu L, Grimm JW, Hope BT, Shaham Y. Incubation of cocaine craving after withdrawal: a review of preclinical data. *Neuropharmacol* 2004;47(suppl 1): 214–226.

92. Hyman SE, Malenka RC, Nestler EJ. Neural mechanisms of addiction: the role of reward-related learning and memory. *Ann Rev Neurosci* 2006;29:565–598.

93. Kauer JA, Malenka RC. Synaptic plasticity and addiction. *Nat Rev Neurosci* 2007;8(11):844–858.

94. Shaham Y, Hope BT. The role of neuroadaptations in relapse to drug seeking. *Nat Neurosci* 2005;8(11): 1437–1439.

95. Kaufman J, Yang BZ, Douglas-Palumberi H, et al. Brain-derived neurotrophic factor-5-HTTLPR gene interactions and environmental modifiers of depression in children. *Biol Psychiat* 2006;59(8):673–680.

96. Kreek MJ, Nielsen DA, Butelman ER, LaForge KS. Genetic influences on impulsivity, risk taking, stress responsivity and vulnerability to drug abuse and addiction. *Nat Neurosci* 2005;8(11):1450–1457.

97. Sinha R. Stress and addiction: a dynamic interplay of genes, environment, and drug intake. *Biol Psychiat* 2009;66(2):100–101.

PART II

Regulation of Eating and Body Weight

10

The Changing Face of Global Diet and Nutrition

BARRY M. POPKIN

INTRODUCTION

Many view dietary and body composition changes as occurring fairly slowly and believe that the shift toward great obesity has occurred and will now slow down. In fact, there are some surveys from France and Stockholm that lead the investigators to state that child obesity has reached a plateau and a biological limit and will not increase.[1-3] The evidence on this is minimal and typically based on localized data rather than systematic national surveys. There are data, however, from a few countries such as the United States that are nationally representative and show leveling off for selected age-gender groupings at the national level.[4] I have found the same for the 95th centile body mass index (BMI) level in some countries.[5] At the same time, analysis of dietary changes in some of these same countries and of body composition in others shows an acceleration of changes seen as potentially detrimental to energy imbalance and subsequently obesity.[6-9]

In this chapter I review current nationally representative data on obesity dynamics across the globe with a focus on trends and annualized changes in prevalence. I then present information on dietary trends across a range of eating behaviors and follow with a discussion of the underlying common changes reflected in these global shifts.

SHIFTS IN BODY MASS INDEX AND OBESITY

Is There a Leveling Off in Child or Adult Obesity or Both?

There are limited data that allow us to state there is a leveling off. There are surveys for limited geographic areas such as Stockholm and other areas across the world. The only nationally representative data that provide some indicator of this leveling off is the US NHANES data for the 2003–2008 period,[4,10-12] the French data for kids aged 7–9,[2] and Brazilian data

for women in the southern half of the country representing about 56% of Brazilian women.[13]

Prevalance Data across the Globe

A map of the world provides some sense of the large proportion of countries where over half the population is overweight (see Fig. 10.1). In this map I do not have nationally representative data for the few countries in white, but all the others are seen to have high levels of overweight and obesity. North America stands out as do Russia and Eastern Europe, parts of Latin America, all the Gulf States and Egypt of the Middle East, the United Kingdom, and Australia for over half of the adults being overweight or obese. Among the other countries where over half of the adults are overweight and obese we find Canada, all the countries on the western side of South America (e.g., Columbia, Peru), Spain, Germany, Turkey, Russia, and South Africa.

There are a number of large high- and low-income countries where over half of all adult women are overweight and obese. These include the United States, United Kingdom, and Australia, Egypt, South Africa, and Mexico.

In general, the prevalence of adult overweight and obesity is greater among women than men. The gender gap is largest in the Middle East and narrowest in Asia.

Similarly across the globe there is more overweight among adults than children. We cannot exactly compare adult and child measures of overweight and can truly only compare trends in the annualized prevalence rate (see later). Child overweight appears to be rising across the globe except for the limited exceptions noted earlier.[5,14-17]

Annualized Change in the Prevalence Rates for Children and Adults

In a few countries, we have adequate data to show that rates of change are accelerating. This means that

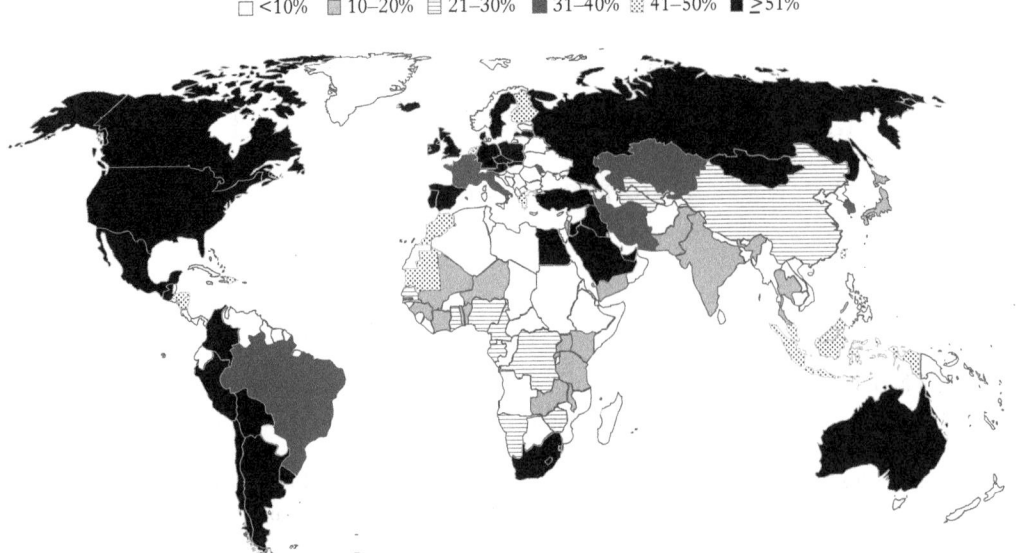

□ <10%   ▦ 10–20%   ▤ 21–30%   ■ 31–40%   ▨ 41–50%   ■ ≥51%

FIGURE 10.1. Patterns of overweight and obesity globally for nationally representative samples (percentage over-weight + obese).

we have shown that the percentage of both adults and children in the United States who become overweight and obese each year has increased from the decades before 1994. The rate of increase for children is not as rapid as the rate for adults, but nonetheless it is very high.[17] About 0.5% of all children in most high- and moderate-income countries are becoming overweight each year. Thus, since 2006 there were about 1.8 billion children in these moderate- and low-income countries of the world with more than 9 million additional children each year becoming overweight. And there are about 3 billion adults in these same countries where 1% are becoming overweight each year; this would be 30 million new overweight adults each year. While my proportions of people who are children and adults are not exactly precise to the million, we get some idea of the number of adults and children added to the number of overweight children and adults each year.

Importantly, in the higher income countries, we have evidence that the increases in overweight have been occurring for much of the century.[18] One of the most useful studies looked at children in Denmark over the 1930 to 1983 period.[19] These scholars went back in the Copenhagen municipality school records to study annual recorded measurements of children aged 7–13 years over this period. They found that overweight and obesity increased

steadily from 1930 until the 1950s, reached a plateau in the 1950–60 period, and rose again rapidly after that. A Nobel Laureate in economics and others have shown similar evidence for adults over a much longer period.[20–21] Thus, for higher income countries we can focus on the large increases beginning in the 1970s or 1980s, though we do not have insights into the earlier periods. In contrast, the lower income world was a world of poverty, hunger, and malnutrition with very little overweight until the last several decades.

Is Obesity a Problem of Rich Countries and Individuals?

Overweight and obesity is not just a problem of the affluent, economically more developed world, however. My colleagues and I have obtained nationally representative surveys from 38 of the poorest nations in the world in one study and 43 in another. All these data were collected in an identical manner and the women of child-bearing age were weighted and measured identically. It tells us that in the poorest countries of sub-Saharan Africa, 5%, 10%, or even 15% of the surveyed adult women are overweight.[22] Furthermore, in the past decade the proportion of overweight has increased greatly across all of the low- and middle-income world of Asia, Africa, and Latin America, so the total numbers in the globe are approaching 2 billion overweight and obese.[23-25] Out of these 38 lower income countries, we find in both urban and rural areas that more women are overweight than are underweight. Rural areas in India, Haiti, and just a few other very poor sub-Saharan African countries are the exceptions to this finding. What is remarkable also is that this set of studies was based on women aged 18–49 years. Older women aged 50–65 years are usually more overweight than women during their child-bearing years and then there is a drop-off among much older women.

My work with Brazilian colleagues shows that more lower income and less educated people are overweight in that country than are the higher income and better educated populace—a finding that is replicated globally in all moderate-income and higher income countries.[26-27] Even China, with its much lower income, has this same economic class disparity.[23,25,28]

This issue of the poor being more overweight than the rich is a phenomenon we have lived with for decades in the United States and Western Europe. In our countries, obesity, heart disease, and diabetes are all problems of the poor much more than of the rich.[29-34] In the United States we undertook research where we identified public and private recreation facilities over a large geographic area and linked these facilities and their distances from the homes of 20,000 youth from our National Longitudinal Study of Adolescent Health. We found that low-income and minority youth were much less likely to live near (within

5 miles) either public facilities such as parks, basketball courts, playgrounds, and YMCAs and private facilities such as private gyms and pools.[32] We found that additional new facilities were associated with large decreases in the likelihood of obesity and large increases in being highly active in physical terms for these youth. However, additional food resources have not necessarily improved diet as readily[35-36]

Body Mass Index at the 95th Centile

Elsewhere I present the methods and data used to examine the mean BMI level for individuals from the United States, China, Australia, and the United Kingdom at the 95th BMI centile.[5] The analysis provided results for all ages; however, in Figure 10.2, I present the data for children aged 6 years old and do not present the data for adults. In unreported results I show that at ages 9 and older you see that the BMI levels of children in the United States are much higher at the 95th centile. From this, one assumes that these cohorts of children will lead to much higher adult BMIs in the United States. Elsewhere, we present data for adults from these same countries and show more rapid increases in middle-aged adult BMI in the United Kingdom and Australia to show that this is not necessarily the case for adults at all ages.

It is only when you look at age 6 that you see a marked shift upward in BMI for Chinese children. This has occurred very rapidly and recently for the Chinese children aged 6–12 years. It is indicative of

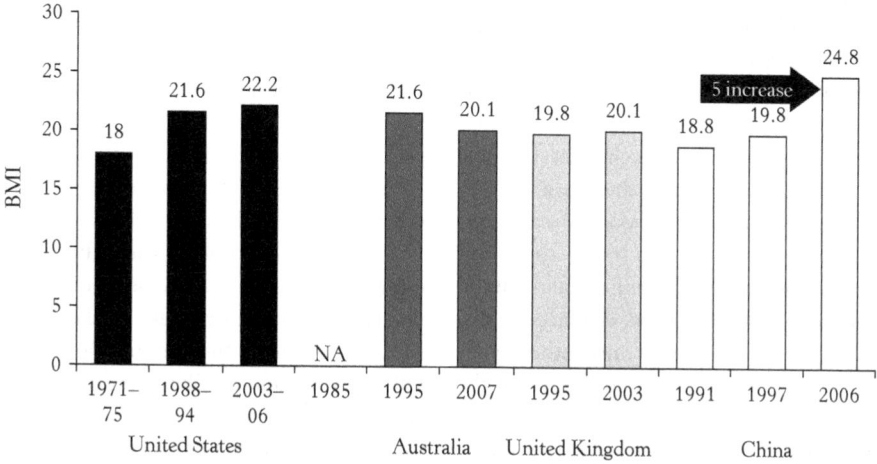

FIGURE 10.2. The shift in body mass index (BMI) levels at the 95th centile for children aged 6.

Source: Reprinted from The American Journal of Clinical Nutrition, Vol 91, B.M. Popkin, Recent dynamics suggest selected countries catching up to US obesity, p. 287S, Copyright (2010), with permission from American Society for Nutrition.

a large cohort increase for Chinese that is likely, if it continues, to mean that in the future higher BMI levels are going to be found for Chinese adolescents. Figure 10.2 highlights this marked BMI shift upward for Chinese children at the 95th centile. In contrast, it also shows the new data just released in July 2009 for Australia shows that child BMI at the 95th centile has leveled off.

GLOBAL SHIFTS IN DIET

Common Changes across the Globe: Sweetening of Diets and Frequency of Eating

Initially the major sweetening of the world's diet was seen consistently in our food supply in the last three to four decades, [37] while today there is increasing proportions of caloric sweeteners used in beverages.[38-41] It began slightly earlier in high-income countries; however, today processed foods across the globe contain one or more of the world's many modes of adding caloric sweeteners to food. There are only a few countries with published studies of these trends of the exact foods where added caloric sweeteners are found; the United States and South Africa are two of these countries.[37,38,42-45] It is important to note that there is a vast array of options for providing caloric sweeteners and often foods contain three to four types of these sweeteners. There are two major sugar crops: sugar beets and sugar cane. Sugar and syrups are also produced from the sap of certain species of maple trees, from sweet sorghum when cultivated explicitly for making syrup, and from sugar palm. Under the name "sweeteners," the Food and Agriculture Organization (FAO) includes products used for sweetening that are either derived from sugar crops, cereals, fruits, or milk, or produced by insects. This category includes a wide variety of monosaccharides (glucose and fructose) and disaccharides (sucrose and saccharose), which exist either in a crystallized state as sugar or in thick liquid form as syrups. Included in sweeteners are maple sugar and syrups, caramel, golden syrup, artificial and natural honey, maltose, glucose, dextrose, isoglucose (also known as high-fructose corn syrup), other types of fructose, sugar confectionery, and lactose. In the last several decades, increasingly larger quantities of cereals (primarily maize) have been used to produce sweeteners derived from starch as high fructose corn syrup or as other corn-based types of syrup. In addition, more recently fruit juice concentrate is

being used in about 11% of the commercial foods in the US food supply.[46]

In another publication, we have used food disappearance data to document the worldwide increase in caloric sweeteners to the diet. We show that, as national income (gross national product [GNP]) per capita and the proportion of the population residing in urban areas increased, sugar intake also increased.[37] The changes are larger for lower income and middle-income countries. Urbanization and national income per capita are correlated highly in the developing world countries that have access to processed foods higher in sugar. Urbanization is also linked with greater access to modern mass media, to better transportation systems, and to larger, modern supermarkets dominated by multinational corporations.[47,48] While increases in income per capita have occurred hand in hand (usually with urbanization), it plays a powerful, separate role in food consumption decisions—in particular related to the consumption of more processed foods.

In the United States, calorically sweetened beverages (e.g., soft drinks and fruit drinks) account for more than half of the increase in added caloric sweeteners in the past several decades; the foods responsible for caloric sweetener intake in South Africa are much more varied than in the United States.[37,42-45,49]

The role of sugar-sweetened beverages (SSBs) in the global and US diets has increased dramatically.[38,40-41] In the United States the proportion of sugar from beverages is now over 65%. In the United States this is just a huge increase in SSB consumption and not a decrease in consumption of sugars used in foods. This may come from traditional soft drinks and fruit drinks. It may be apple juice, where the process involves combining apple flavoring with 100% sweetener derived from concentrated fructose from the apple so it can be called 100% apple juice. Or it might be sugar-sweetened waters, coffees, and energy drinks.

Despite all the concern voiced by scholars about increased intake of SSBs across the globe, there are few large-scale dietary intake studies to document this.[37,50-52] One of these noted large increases in SSB consumption in China, India, Vietnam, Thailand, and other Southeast Asian countries.[52] This same study presented Beverage World International data that showed large per capita consumption of soft drinks across all of the Americas, Germany, Australia, Spain, and Great Britain.[52] Some smaller food consumption studies back up this point and add many other countries as varied as Japan and New Zealand.[53-57] One large-scale study in urban South Africa found children 6–9 and 10 years and older consumed 122 and 175 ml of SSBs in 2002.[45] In the Cebu metropolitan region of the Philippines over 3% of energy came from SSBs.[58] However, for detailed individual beverage consumption data that are carefully measured there are only a few nationally representative studies. A study just published shows the very large increase in sales in kilojoule terms of Pepsi and Coca-Cola sugar-sweetened beverages in Brazil and China.[59]

The best sources of nationally representative patterns and trends of SSBs come from the United States, the United Kingdom, and Mexico, where large-scale dietary intake surveys have been repeated in the last decade and are fairly up to date.[38,40,60-62]

Mexico is the country that is experiencing a large increase in total caloric intake from SSBs. Traditionally this country consumed limited amounts of agua frescas, beverages with some fruit juice and extensive added sugar. A rapid shift toward increased intake of these beverages as well as all SSBs and other caloric beverages is under way across all age groups. All age groups in Mexico consume more than 20% of their total energy intake from caloric beverages. A large increase between 1999 and 2006 has been documented from dietary intake surveys and is backed up by food expenditure and other national data.[61]

The second component common to all countries is the increased intake of snacks. Studies in China and the United States have shown marked increases in snacking over the past decade.[63-65] I think from my reading of the literature and from the large number of anecdotal press articles that snacking increases represent a major new shift in global eating behavior. In China we will show in one new paper a tripling of the proportion of all ages snacking just between 2004 and 2006.[66]

Shifts More Prominent in Low- and Middle-Income Transitional Countries: Edible Oil, Animal Source Foods

There have been changes that are unique to low-income and middle-income countries in the past three to four decades.[25] These are changes that occurred earlier in the high-income countries rather than changes unique to low-income countries only. One is the large increased intake of edible oils (vegetable oils).[67] In the 1950s and 1960s as concern about heart disease and intake of butter and lard and other saturated fats emerged, there was a surge in research and ultimately major technological breakthroughs in ways to extract oil from oil seeds and the breeding of higher oil versions of the same seeds. This combination led first in the higher income world and more recently in the low- and middle-income world to a large shift toward these oils. The major difference is that today these oils are much cheaper in real terms and income-constrained individuals and countries have shown a much greater tendency to consume these.[68] Pricing reductions have been accelerated by the World Trade Organization's push to remove barriers on importation of edible oils.[69-70]

Across Asia, urban Africa, and the Middle East we have seen particularly large shifts in intake of vegetable oils. In China, for example, over 13% of total energy intake comes from vegetable oils and over half of the population fry over 30% of all calories consumed. The latter was a large shift from steaming and boiling to frying in China.[63]

The consumption of what we term "animal source foods," namely meat, poultry, dairy, and fish/seafood and their products, is very low across the developing world.[25,71] Higher income countries consume more than double the amount of meat per capita and triple the amount of milk, though the more rapid increase in per capita meat and milk consumption has been occurring in the developing world.[72] We provide elsewhere some detail on the shifts in China in animal source food intake.[73]

Shifts in Higher Income: Portion Sizing, Constant Eating

There are two dietary shifts that seem to be more pronounced in higher income countries, namely the shift toward much larger portion sizes and the movement toward eating very frequently. Others have documented in the United States, for example, the increased size of various food items at fast food restaurants.[74,75] In the United States, we have used actual food consumption intake to document a similar intake in the 1990s.[76] More recently we have some research that shows a slightly lower portion size for salty snacks. Furthermore, we have some research that shows a slight drop in portion sizes for desserts and SSBs.[8,77] At the same time, frequency of these items is increasing, so the decline in portion sizes does not mean a decline in total caloric intake from these foods. In addition, this research finds very large 100–200 kcal increases in the portion sizes of pizza and Mexican dishes. While there is a campaign against large portion sizes in the United Kingdom, I am not aware of studies of trends in UK portion sizes. There is some concern in the United Kingdom and elsewhere in Europe, but cross-sectional studies are all that exist.[78,79]

The concept of constant eating is a concern that the proportion of eating events is at the point of constancy for at least 20%–35% of Americans, whereby they consume food hourly or every hour and a half.[6] Essentially, this means that we might be losing our physiological basis for hunger and food intake and undertake what Brian Wansink terms "mindless eating" on a large population level.[80]

UNDERLYING COMMONALITIES: GLOBAL FOOD DISTRIBUTION, MEDIA, TRANSPORTATION, AND FOOD PRICE CHANGES

Common global changes include (a) the worldwide shifts in trade of technology innovations that affect energy expenditures during leisure, transportation, and work; (b) globalization of modern food processing, marketing, and distribution techniques (most frequently linked with Westernization of the world's diet); (c) vast expansion of the global mass media; and (d) other changes that constitute the rubric of impacts resulting from an increased opening of our world economy.

Globalization has certainly enhanced the interconnectedness of the world in terms of trade in goods, technology, services, and spread of the modern mass media. These changes began in the last half of the previous century and were accelerated by the push from the higher income countries for more open markets for these items. During this period, international agencies (e.g., the International Monetary Fund [IMF] and the World Bank) and most of the higher income countries, have promoted a "free trade" agenda as the panacea for the ills of the developing world. This article does not focus on the exact linkages between each aspect of globalization and how it affects the increased trade in services, commodities, processed products, technology, and investments; rather, the focus is on understanding how technological and other shifts are linked to, and affect, diet, activity, and obesity throughout the world. Since it is impossible at this

time, with the available databases, to fully link each aspect of globalization exactly to each one of these elements, we can, however, document many threads of change that clearly relate to their global shifts.

Work Technology

Beginning in the 1990s, quite pervasive shifts in the technological innovations for performing work in urban areas have been provided and observed to be increasing in rural areas. In a new document prepared for Nike and several international organizations in preparation for a major global launch of physical activity promotion activities and funding, Ng and Popkin showed the very rapid decline in activity in China, India, and Brazil, with the most rapid future decline coming in India. Furthermore, we showed sedentary time is rapidly increasing in these countries.[81] While there are several major shifts occurring—a global increase in the proportion of service sector jobs and a reduction of efforts required by each job, it is the change of energy expended in each occupation that appears to be most important. In China, where the China Health and Nutrition Survey has been longitudinally observing 16,000 adults and children since 1989 using six panel surveys, the shifts in activity among the adults have been carefully documented.[82,83]

The following relationships have been observed in China:

- Adults who purchased motor scooters/motor bikes or cars to travel to work doubled their likelihood of becoming overweight, in comparison to those who made no change in their mode of transportation.[84]
- Occupational changes accounted for a significant proportion of the weight gain and incident overweight of Chinese adults, especially in urban areas.[82]
- In a 4-year period, 16% of Chinese adults' overall work-related physical activity patterns in urban areas shifted significantly to lighter activity, a shift related to significant increases in BMI and overweight.[82,85]
- The proportion of Chinese adults, aged 20–45 years, performing light physical activity work increased from 24% to 34% during the 1989 to 2000 period. Most of the shift toward lighter work occurred in urban areas, while concurrent changes found many in the rural sector increasing their activity patterns.

Global Food Systems Are Rapidly Changing

Three important examples of the changes in the global food system are found in (a) the rapid increase in consumption of low-cost edible vegetable oils noted briefly and elaborated here; (b) the way large supermarkets and supermarket chains have gained control of food distribution; and (c) the vast shift toward processed and ultraprocessed food intake concomitant with an explosion in the number of processed and packaged food purchased across the globe.

The edible vegetable oils story is particularly important as its effects have been quite profound. Until the decade following World War II, the majority of fats available for human consumption were animal fats, milk, butter, and meat. Subsequently, a revolution in the production and processing of oilseed-based fats occurred. Principal vegetable oils include soybean, sunflower, rapeseed, palm, and peanut oil. Technological breakthroughs in the development of high-yield oilseeds and in the refining of high-quality vegetable oils greatly reduced the cost of baking and frying fats, margarine, butter-like spreads, salad oils, and cooking oils in relation to animal-based products.[86] A number of major economic and political initiatives led to the development of oil crops, not only in Europe and the United States, but in Southeast Asia (palm oils), in Brazil, and in Argentina (soybean oils). The net effect was that from 1945 to 1965, there was almost a fourfold increase in the US production of vegetable oils, while animal fat production increased by only 11%.[87]

In developing nations, one of the earliest shifts toward a higher fat diet began with major increases in the domestic production and imports of oilseeds and vegetable oils, rather than increased imports of meat and milk. At this stage, vegetable oils contributed far more energy to the human food supply than meat or animal fats.[88] With the exception of peanut oil, global availability of the vegetable oils (i.e., soybean, sunflower, rapeseed, and palm) has approximately tripled from 1961 to 1990. Soybeans now account for the bulk of vegetable oil consumption worldwide. It is also important to note that many of these processed oils are not regulated well and some of the new edible oils or other foods are highly pathogenic.[89]

The other important change in the global food system is occurring in food distribution. There is no research to date that can provide any analysis of the consequences of these food distribution shifts on dietary intake patterns. The fresh (wet) market is disappearing as the major source of supply for food in the developing world. They are being replaced by multinational, regional, and local large supermarkets—supermarkets that are usually part of larger chains (e.g., Carrefour or Walmart) or in other countries such as South Africa and China local domestic chains patterned to function and look like these global chains. Increasingly, large megastores are found. For example, in Latin America, supermarkets' share of all retail food sales increased from 15% in 1990 to 60% by 2000.[47,90] For comparison, 80% of retail food sales in the United States in 2000 occurred in supermarkets. In one decade, the role of supermarkets in Latin America has expanded equivalent to about a half century of expansion in the United States. Supermarket use has spread across both large and small countries, from capital cities to rural villages, and from upper- and middle-class families to the working class.[91] This same process is also occurring at varying rates and different stages in Asia, Eastern Europe, and Africa.[48]

There are many factors causing this food system phenomenon.[92,93] Consumer demand for processed and safer foods is on the rise in developing countries. Additionally, as countries modernize, the opportunity cost of women's time has grown; building a market for time-saving, prepared foods has become more important. Transportation and access to technology, such as refrigerators, has also played a role in the demand for, and access to, supermarkets. Other factors include the liberalization of direct foreign investment, trade liberalization, and the saturation of Western markets that has pushed growing companies into other locales. Furthermore, improvements in the logistics and procurement systems used by the supermarkets have allowed them to compete on cost with the more typical outlets in developing countries: the small "mom-and-pop" stores and wet markets (open public markets) for fruits, vegetables, and all other products.

Supermarkets are large providers of processed higher fat, added sugar, and salt-laden foods in developing countries, but they have also been the purveyors of some good. For example, supermarkets (a) were instrumental in the development of ultra heat treatment (UHT) milk, giving it a long shelf life and providing a safe source of milk for all income groups and (b) were key players in establishing food safety standards.[90] Most important, they have solved the cold chain and in many instances have brought higher quality produce to the urban consumer throughout the year.

It remains to be understood how the shift in food marketing to these mega supermarkets will affect the structure of the diet and also the amount of total food consumed. There needs to be research on the ways these new food markets affect overall prices as well as relative prices of different food group categories. Furthermore, other research needs to be done on how this shifts the consumption of refined versus complex carbohydrates, calorically sweetened foods, animal source foods, fruits and vegetables, among other key issues.

The shift toward increased processing of food is concomitant with the shift in availability not only of supermarkets but also convenience stores.[94] As Monteiro has most articulately laid out, the availability and marketing of ultraprocessed foods with excessive refined carbohydrates, added sugar, fat, and sodium represents a major concern for global health.[95,96] This concept, which suggests that these ultraprocessed refined carbohydrates are bad for health, goes hand in hand with the research that has shown that complex carbohydrate-based meals and diets (diets low in refined foods) are linked with reduced weight gain and weight loss.[97-103]

Mass Media Changes

One of the least discussed and least understood areas of change affecting dietary and physical activity patterns is the role of the modern mass media. Throughout the developing world, there has been a profound increase in the ownership of television sets and the penetration of modern television, magazine, and other modes of media. This has been accompanied by a proliferation of modern magazines and ready access to DVDs of Western movies. Many scholars accuse television viewing as being directly responsible for child obesity, due both to its effect on energy expenditure as well as to the direct marketing of food on the television. This remains to be studied in most developing countries in a rigorous causal manner. Programming and advertisements have been rapidly shifting toward more modern and Western content. For instance, the first TV advertisements began with one advertisement in 1979 on a Shanghai TV station and only began

in earnest with a large increase in the 1990s. Today, China is considered the world's fastest growing advertising market and India and other markets are close behind.[104]

SUMMARY

Clearly, large-scale rapid shifts like those noted in this chapter in obesity and related to both poor diets and reduced physical activity will have profound effects on current and future health problems across the globe.[25,81] For instance, a large 5-year set of meta-analyses of the factors that can prevent cancer found that the most preventable cause of cancer was obesity or abdominal obesity.[105] The economic and health consequences of this shift are profound for low- and middle-income countries.[106-108]

REFERENCES

1. Salanave B, Peneau S, Rolland-Cachera MF, Hercberg S, Castetbon K. Stabilization of overweight prevalence in French children between 2000 and 2007. *Int J Pediatr Obes* 2009;4:66–72.
2. Peneau S, Salanave B, Maillard-Teyssier L, et al. Prevalence of overweight in 6- to 15-year-old children in central/western France from 1996 to 2006: trends toward stabilization. *Int J Obes (Lond)* 2009;33:401–407.
3. Sundblom E, Petzold M, Rasmussen F, Callmer E, Lissner L. Childhood overweight and obesity prevalences levelling off in Stockholm but socioeconomic differences persist. *Int J Obes* 2008;32: 1525–3150.
4. Flegal KM, Carroll MD, Ogden CL, Curtin LR. Prevalence and trends in obesity among us adults, 1999-2008. *JAMA* 2010;303:235-241.
5. Popkin BM. Recent dynamics suggest selected countries catching up to US obesity. *Am J Clin Nutr* 2010;91:284S-288S.
6. Popkin BM, Duffey KJ. Does hunger and satiety drive eating anymore? Increasing eating occasions and decreasing time between eating occasions in the United States. *Am J Clin Nutr* 2010;91: 1342–1347.
7. Piernas C, Popkin BM. Snacking increased among U.S. adults between 1977 and 2006. *J Nutr* 2010;140: 325–332.
8. Piernas C, Popkin BM. Food portion patterns and trends among U.S. children and the relationship to total eating occasion size, 1977–2006. *J Nutri* 2011;141(6):1159–1164.
9. Duffey KJ, Popkin BM. Energy density, portion size, and eating occasions: contributions to increased energy intake in the United States, 1977–2006. *PLoS Med* 2011;8:e1001050.

10. Flegal KM, Carroll MD, Ogden CL, Curtin LR. Prevalence and trends in obesity among US adults, 1999–2008. *JAMA* 2010;303:235–241.

11. Flegal KM, Ogden CL, Yanovski JA, et al. High adiposity and high body mass index-for-age in US children and adolescents overall and by race-ethnic group. *Am J Clin Nutr* 2010;91:1020–1026.

12. Ogden CL, Carroll MD, Curtin LR, Lamb MM, Flegal KM. Prevalence of high body mass index in US children and adolescents, 2007–2008. *JAMA* 2010;303: 242–249.

13. Monteiro CA, Conde WL, Popkin BM. Income-specific trends in obesity in Brazil: 1975–2003. *Am J Public Health* 2007;97:1808–1812.

14. Wang Y, Lobstein T. Worldwide trends in childhood overweight and obesity. *Int J Pediatr Obes* 2006;1:11–25.

15. Lobstein T, Baur L, Uauy R. Obesity in children and young people: a crisis in public health. *Obes Rev* 2004;5:4–97.

16. Lobstein T, Frelut ML. Prevalence of overweight among children in Europe. *Obes Rev* 2003;4:195–200.

17. Popkin BM, Wolney C, Ningqi H, Carlos M. Is there a lag globally in overweight trends for children as compared to adults? *Obesity* 2006;14:1846–1853.

18. Popkin BM. *The World Is Fat—The Fads, Trends, Policies, and Products That Are Fattening the Human Race.* New York: Avery-Penguin Group; 2008.

19. Bua J, Olsen LW, Sorensen TIA. Secular trends in childhood obesity in Denmark during 50 years in relation to economic growth. *Obesity* 2007;15:977–985.

20. Fogel RW. Economic growth, population theory, and physiology: the bearing of long-term processes on the making of economic policy. *Am Econ Rev* 1994;84:369.

21. Fogel RW, ebrary Inc. The escape from hunger and premature death, 1700–2100 Europe, America, and the third world. In: *Cambridge Studies in Population, Economy, and Society in Past Time.* Vol. 38. New York: Cambridge University Press; 2004: 191.

22. Mendez M, Monteiro C, Popkin B. Overweight exceeds underweight among women in most developing countries. *Am J Clin Nutr* 2005;81:714–721.

23. Jones-Smith J, Gordon-Larsen, P. ,Siddiqi, A. Popkin, Barry Cross-national comparisons of time trends in overweight inequality by socioeconomic status among women using repeated cross-sectional surveys from 37 developing countries, 1989–2007. *Am J Epidemiol* 2011;173:667–675.

24. Jones-Smith JC, Gordon-Larsen P, Siddiqi A, Popkin BM. Is the burden of overweight shifting to the poor across the globe? Time trends among women in 39 low- and middle-income countries (1991–2008). *Int J Obes* 2011. doi: 10.1038/ijo.2011.179. [Epub ahead of print.]

25. Popkin BM, Adair, Linda, Ng, Shu Wen. Global nutrition transition and the pandemic of obesity in developing countries. *Nutr Rev* 2012;70:3–21.

26. Monteiro CA, Moura EC, Conde WL, Popkin BM. Socioeconomic status and obesity in adult populations of developing countries: a review. *Bull World Health Org* 2004;82:940–946.

27. Monteiro CA, Conde WL, Lu B, Popkin BM. Obesity and inequities in health in the developing world. *Int J Obes Rel Metabolic Dis* 2004;28:1181–1186.

28. Jones-Smith JC, Gordon-Larsen P, Siddiqi A, Popkin BM. Emerging disparities in overweight by educational attainment in Chinese adults (1989–2006). *Int J Obes* 2011. doi: 10.1038/ijo.2011.134. [Epub ahead of print.]

29. Sobal J, Stunkard AJ. Socioeconomic status and obesity: a review of the literature. *Psychol Bull* 1989;105: 260–275.

30. Davis SK, Winkleby MA, Farquhar JW. Increasing disparity in knowledge of cardiovascular disease risk factors and risk-reduction strategies by socioeconomic status: implications for policymakers. *Am J Prevent Med* 1995;11:318–323.

31. Kaufman JS, Cooper RS, McGee DL. Socioeconomic status and health in blacks and whites: the problem of residual confounding and the resiliency of race. *Epidemiol* 1997;8:621–628.

32. Gordon-Larsen P, Nelson MC, Page P, Popkin BM. Inequality in the built environment underlies key health disparities in physical activity and obesity. *Pediatrics* 2006;117:417–424.

33. Neumark-Sztainer D, Croll J, Story M, Hannan PJ, French SA, Perry C. Ethnic/racial differences in weight-related concerns and behaviors among adolescent girls and boys: findings from Project EAT. *J Psychosom Res* 2002;53:963–974.

34. Wang Y, Beydoun MA. The obesity epidemic in the United States—gender, age, socioeconomic, racial/ethnic, and geographic characteristics: a systematic review and meta-regression analysis. *Epidemiol Rev* 2007;29:6–28.

35. Boone-Heinonen J, Gordon-Larsen P, Kiefe CI, Shikany JM, Lewis CE, Popkin BM. Fast food restaurants and food stores: longitudinal associations with diet in young to middle-aged adults: the CARDIA Study. *Arch Intern Med* 2011;171:1162–1170.

36. Richardson AS, Boone-Heinonen J, Popkin BM, Gordon-Larsen P. Neighborhood fast food restaurants and fast food consumption: A national study. *BMC Public Health* 2011;11:543.

37. Popkin BM, Nielsen SJ. The sweetening of the world's diet. *Obes Res* 2003;11:1325–1332.

38. Duffey KJ, Popkin BM. High-fructose corn syrup: is this what's for dinner? *Am J Clin Nutr* 2008;88: 1722S–1732S.

39. Malik VS, Popkin BM, Bray GA, Despr'Es J-P, Willett WC, FB H. Sugar-sweetened beverages and risk of metabolic syndrome and type 2 diabetes: a meta-analysis. *Diabetes Care* 2010;33:2477–2483.

40. Ng SW, Ni Mhurchu C, Jebb SA, Popkin PM. Patterns and trends of beverage consumption among children and adults in Great Britain, 1986–2009. *Br J Nutr* 2011. [Epub ahead of print]

41. Duffey KI, Huybrecht T, Mouratidou M, et al. Beverage consumption among European adolescents in the HELENA Study. *Eur J Clin Nutr* 2012;66:244–252.

42. Bray G, Nielsen S, Popkin B. High fructose corn sweeteners and the epidemic of obesity. *Am J Clin Nutr* 2002;79:537–543.

43. Nielsen SJ, Popkin BM. Changes in beverage intake between 1977 and 2001. *Am J Prev Med* 2004;27:205–210.

44. Steyn NP, Nel JH, Casey A. Secondary data analyses of dietary surveys undertaken in South Africa to determine usual food consumption of the population. *Public Health Nutr* 2003;6:631–644.

45. Steyn NP, Myburgh NG, Nel JH. Evidence to support a food-based dietary guideline on sugar consumption in South Africa. *Bull World Health Organ* 2003;81:599–608.

46. Ng SW, Slining MM, Popkin BM. Sweeteners in the US food supply and the role of fruit juice concentrate. Unpublished data. 2011.

47. Reardon T, Berdegué J. The rapid rise of supermarkets in Latin America: challenges and opportunities for development. *Dev Policy Rev* 2002;20:371–388.

48. Reardon T, Timmer P, Berdegue J. The rapid rise of supermarkets in developing countries: induced organizational, institutional, and technological change in agrifood systems. *E J Ag Dev Econ* 2004;1:168–183.

49. Popkin BM. Patterns of beverage use across the lifecycle. *Physiol Behav* 2010;100:4–9.

50. WHO/FAO. *Expert Consultation on Diet, Nutrition and the Prevention of Chronic DiseasesReport of the joint WHO/FAO expert consultation*. Geneva: World Health Organization; 2003.

51. WHO. Obesity: preventing and managing the global epidemic. Report of a WHO consultation. *World Health Organ Tech Rep Ser*. 2000;894:i–xii, 1–253.

52. Ismail A, Tanzer, JM, Dingle, JL. Current trends of sugar consumption in developing societies. *Comm Dent Oral Epidemiol* 1997;25:438–443.

53. Sanigorski AM, Bell AC, Swinburn BA. Association of key foods and beverages with obesity in Australian schoolchildren. *Public Health Nutr* 2007;10:152–157.

54. Libuda L, Alexy U, Sichert-Hellert W, et al. Pattern of beverage consumption and long-term association with body-weight status in German adolescents—results from the DONALD study. *Br J Nutr* 2008;99:1370–1379.

55. Sichert-Hellert W, Kersting M, Manz F. Fifteen year trends in water intake in German children and adolescents: results of the DONALD Study.

Dortmund Nutritional and Anthropometric Longitudinally Designed Study. *Acta Paediatr* 2001;90:732–737.

56. Yamada M, Murakami K, Sasaki S, Takahashi Y, Okubo H. Soft drink intake is associated with diet quality even among young Japanese women with low soft drink intake. *J Am Diet Assoc* 2008;108:1997–2004.

57. Chacko E, McDuff I, Jackson R. Replacing sugar-based soft drinks with sugar-free alternatives could slow the progress of the obesity epidemic: have your Coke and drink it too. *N Z Med J* 2003;116:U649.

58. Adair LS, Popkin BM. Are child eating patterns being transformed globally? *Obes Res* 2005;13:1281–1299.

59. Kleiman S, Ng, Shu WEn, Popkin, Barry. Drinking to our health: can beverage companies cut calories while maintaining profits? *Obes Rev* 2012;13:258–274.

60. Rivera JA, Muñoz-Hernández O, Rosas-Peralta M, Aguilar-Salinas CA, Popkin BM, Willett WC. Consumo de bebidas para una vida saludable: recomendaciones para la población [Beverage consumption for a healthy life: recommendations for the Mexican population]. *Salud Publica Mexico* 2008;50:173–195.

61. Barquera S, Hernández L, Tolentino ML, et al. Energy from beverages is on the rise among Mexican adolescents and adults. *J Nutr* 2008;138:2454–2461.

62. Duffey K, Popkin BM. Shifts in patterns and consumption of beverages between 1965 and 2002. *Obesity* 2007;15:2739–2747.

63. Wang Z, Zhai F, Shufa D, Popkin BM. Dynamic shifts in Chinese eating behaviors. *Asia Pacific J Clin Nutr* 2008;17:123–130.

64. Piernas C, Popkin B. Snacking increased among U.S. adults between 1977 and 2006. *J Nutr* 2010;140(2):325–332..

65. Piernas C, Popkin BM. Trends in snacking among U.S. children. *Health Aff* 2010;29:3398–3404.

66. Wang Z, Zhai F, Du S, Popkin B. Snacking trends in China. Unpublished data.

67. Popkin B, Drewnowski A. Dietary fats and the nutrition transition: new trends in the global diet. *Nutr Rev* 1997;55:31–43.

68. Ng SW, Zhai F, Popkin BM. Impacts of China's edible oil pricing policy on nutrition. *Soc Sci Med* 2008;66:414–426.

69. China's Reform of the Edible Oil Circulation System. 2004. Available at: http://www.chinagate.cn/english/2125.htm. Accessed March 12, 2012.

70. Hsu H, Tuan F. China's accession to WTO would boost world trade of edible oils. In: *Agricultural Trade with China in the New Economic and Policy Environment*. Proceedings WERA101: Assessing the Chinese Market for U.S. Agricultural Products Annual Meeting, Washington. 2001

71. Popkin BM. Reducing meat consumption has multiple benefits for the world's health. *Arch Intern Med* 2009;169:543–545.

72. Food and Agricultural Organization of the United Nations. *Livestock's Long Shadow: Environmental Issues and Options*. Rome: Food and Agricultural Organization United Nations; 2007.

73. Popkin BM, Du S. Dynamics of the nutrition transition toward the animal foods sector in China and its implications: a worried perspective. *J Nutr* 2003;133:3898S-906S.

74. Young LR, Nestle M. Expanding portion sizes in the US marketplace: implications for nutrition counseling. *J Am Diet Assoc* 2003;103:231-234.

75. Young LR, Nestle M. The contribution of expanding portion sizes to the US obesity epidemic. *Am J Public Health* 2002;92:246-249.

76. Nielsen SJ, Popkin BM. Patterns and trends in food portion sizes, 1977-1998. *JAMA* 2003;289: 450-453.

77. Piernas C, Popkin BM. Increased portion sizes from energy-dense foods affect total energy intake at eating occasions in US children and adolescents: patterns and trends by age group and sociodemographic characteristics, 1977-2006. *Am J Clin Nutr* 2011;94:1324-1332.

78. Howell DO, Suleiman S, Nicholas J, et al. Food portion weights in primary and secondary school lunches in England. *J Hum Nutr Diet* 2008;21:46-62.

79. Lioret S, Volatier JL, Lafay L, Touvier M, Maire B. Is food portion size a risk factor of childhood overweight? *Eur J Clin Nutr* 2009;63:382-391.

80. Wansink B. *Mindless Eating—Why We Eat More Than We Think*. New York: Bantam-Dell; 2006.

81. Ng SW, Popkin B. Time use and physical activity: a shift away from movement across the globe. *Obes Rev*, in press .

82. Bell AC, Ge, K., Popkin, B. M. Weight gain and its predictors in Chinese adults. *Int J Obes Relat Metab Disord* 2001;25:1079-1086.

83. Ng SW, Norton E, Popkin BM. Why have physical activity levels declined among Chinese adults? Findings from the 1991-2006 China health and nutrition surveys. *Soc Sci Med* 2009;68:1305-1314.

84. Bell AC, Ge, K., Popkin, B. M. The road to obesity or the path to prevention: motorized transportation and obesity in China. *Obes Res* 2002;10:277-283.

85. Paeratakul S, Popkin BM, Ge K, Adair LS, Stevens J. Changes in diet and physical activity affect the body mass index of Chinese adults. *Int J Obes Relat Metab Disord* 1998;22:424-431.

86. Williams GW. Development and future direction of the world soybean market. *Quart J Int Ag* 1984;23:319-337.

87. US Department of Agriculture. *1996 U.S. Fats and Oils Statistics*. Washington, DC: ERS; 1966.

88. Morgan N. World vegetable oil consumption expands and diversifies. *Food Rev* 1993;16:26-30.

89. Wallingford JC, Yuhas, R, Du, S, Zhai, F, Popkin, BM. Fatty acids in Chinese edible oils: evidence for unexpected impact in changing diet. *Food Nutr Bull* 2004;25:330-336.

90. Balsevich F, Berdegue JA, Flores L, Mainville D, Reardon T. Supermarkets and produce quality and safety standards in Latin America. *Am J Ag Econ* 2003;85:1147-1154.

91. Hu D, Reardon T, Rozelle S, Timmer P, Wang H. The emergence of supermarkets with Chinese characteristics: challenges and opportunities for China's agricultural development. *Dev Pol Rev* 2004;22: 557-586.

92. Wilkinson J. The food processing industry, globalization and developing countries. *E J Ag Dev Econ* 2004;1:184-201.

93. Wilkinson J. The food processing industry, globalization and developing countries. *E J Ag Dev Econ* 2004;1:184-201.

94. Ng SW, Popkin BM. Monitoring foods and nutrients sold and consumed in the United States: Dynamics and challenges. *J Acad Nutr Diet* 2012;112: 41-45.

95. Monteiro CA, Gomes FS, Cannon G. The snack attack. *Am J Public Health* 2010;100:975-981.

96. Monteiro C. The big issue is ultra-processing. *J World Public Health Nutr Assoc* 2010;6:237-239.

97. Sacks FM, Bray GA, Carey VJ, et al. Comparison of weight-loss diets with different compositions of fat, protein, and carbohydrates. *N Engl J Med* 2009;360: 859-873.

98. Jacobs DR, Jr., Slavin J, Marquart L. Whole grain intake and cancer: a review of the literature. *Nutr Cancer* 1995;24:221-229.

99. Jacobs DR, Jr., Meyer KA, Kushi LH, Folsom AR. Is whole grain intake associated with reduced total and cause-specific death rates in older women? The Iowa Women's Health Study. *Am J Public Health* 1999;89:322-329.

100. Jacobs DR, Pereira MA, Meyer KA, Kushi LH. Fiber from whole grains, but not refined grains, is inversely associated with all-cause mortality in older women: the Iowa Women's Health Study. *J Am Coll Nutr* 2000;19:326S-330S.

101. Liu S, Manson JE, Stampfer MJ, et al. Whole grain consumption and risk of ischemic stroke in women: a prospective study. *JAMA* 2000;284:1534-1540.

102. Slavin J. Why whole grains are protective: biological mechanisms. *Proc Nutr Soc* 2003;62:129-134.

103. Jacobs DR, Jr., Gallaher DD. Whole grain intake and cardiovascular disease: a review. *Curr Atheroscler Rep* 2004;6:415-423.

104. Weber IG. Challenges facing China's television advertising industry in the age of spiritual civilization: an industry analysis. *Int J Advert* 2000;19:259-281.

105. WCRF. *Food, Nutrition, Physical Activity and the Prevention of Cancer: a Global Perspective*. Washington, DC: World Cancer Research Fund in association with the American Institute for Cancer Research; 2007

106. Popkin BM, Kim S, Rusev ER, Du S, Zizza C. Measuring the full economic costs of diet, physical activity and obesity-related chronic diseases. *Obes Rev* 2006;7:271–293.

107. Popkin BM, Horton S, Kim S. The nutrition transition and prevention of diet-related chronic diseases in Asia and the Pacific. *Food Nutr Bull* 2001;22: 1–58.

108. Popkin BM, Horton S, Kim S-W, Mahal A, Jin S-G. Trends in diet, nutritional status, and diet-related noncommunicable diseases in China and India: the economic costs of the nutrition transition. *Nutr Rev* 2001;59:379–390.

11

Weight and Diet among Children and Adolescents in the United States, 2005–2008

CYNTHIA L. OGDEN, MOLLY M. LAMB, BRIAN K. KIT,
AND JACQUELINE D. WRIGHT

Obesity remains a major public health priority in the United States. Over the last 30 years, the prevalence of obesity increased in both adults and children throughout the world.[1-6] In the United States, the prevalence of obesity among children and adolescents has more than tripled in recent decades from approximately 5% to 16.9%.[2,7] While the prevalence of obesity may now be leveling off with no significant increases between 1999–2000 and 2007–2008, it remains high.[7] Excess weight in childhood is a public health concern because of immediate consequences related to psychosocial problems, elevated blood pressure, adverse lipids, and abnormal glucose tolerance.[8,9] In addition, obesity in childhood tracks to adulthood,[10,11] and it may put an individual at increased risk for the chronic diseases associated with adult obesity, such as diabetes, cardiovascular disease, and certain cancers.[12]

Obesity is a result of an imbalance between dietary intake and energy expenditure. However, studies generally have found that among children there is not a strong relationship between overweight and total caloric intake using current dietary assessment methods (which may not accurately measure total caloric intake).[13,14] Consequently, attention has turned to *what* children eat. A number of recent studies have found that consumption of sugar-sweetened beverages (SSBs),[15,16] energy-dense foods (foods high in fat and/or sugar),[17,18] and fruits and vegetables may impact body mass index (BMI).[19,20] This chapter provides an overview of obesity and consumption of total calories, SSBs, energy-dense foods, and fruits and vegetables in US children and adolescents using data from the National Health and Nutrition Examination Survey (NHANES) from 2005–2008. The association between obesity and these dietary behaviors is presented.

DATA SOURCE, DEFINITIONS, AND METHODS

NHANES is a multistage probability sample of the US civilian, noninstitutionalized population conducted by the National Center for Health Statistics, Centers for Disease Control and Prevention (CDC).[21] In 2005–2008, Mexican Americans and non-Hispanic Blacks (among other groups) were oversampled. The survey consists of a home interview followed by a physical examination in a mobile examination center. The physical exam includes standardized measurements of weight and height along with two 24-hour dietary recalls (one in-person interview followed by an interview on the telephone 3–7 days later). This analysis is based on data from 6,989 children age 2–19 years (92% of those interviewed and examined in this age group) who had complete weight, height, and dietary data from at least one 24-hour recall. The overall response rates for children and adolescents in NHANES 2005–2008 were over 81% for all age groups.

Excess weight, or obesity, is defined based on a BMI (weight in kilograms divided by height in meters squared) ≥95th percentile of the age- and sex-specific 2000 CDC growth charts.[22-24]

Data from the in-person 24-hour dietary recall interview were used to estimate mean daily total caloric intake, mean daily percent of calories consumed from SSBs, mean daily percent of calories consumed from foods with added fats and sugars (energy-dense foods), and mean daily intake of fruits and vegetables in cup equivalents (referred to as cups) for the population. In this chapter, SSBs are defined as fruit drinks, sodas, energy drinks, sports drinks, and sweetened bottled waters, consistent with definitions reported by the National Cancer Institute.[25] Percent of calories consumed from energy-dense foods and cups of fruits and vegetables consumed were calculated from the US Department of Agriculture's MyPyramid equivalents database,[26] which is based on the Dietary Guidelines for Americans.[27] SSBs are included in the energy-dense food definition as a source of added sugars.

Prevalence of obesity and mean values of total caloric intake, percent of calories from SSBs, percent of calories from energy-dense foods, and fruit and vegetable consumption are presented by sex, age group (2–5 years, 6–11 years, and 12–19 years), and race/ethnicity (non-Hispanic White, non-Hispanic Black, and Mexican American). Differences between race/ethnic groups were tested using t-tests with a Bonferonni adjustment for multiple comparisons. With this conservative approach, $p = .01$ was considered significant. Differences by age were tested using trend tests. To consider the contribution of consumption of SSBs, energy-dense foods, and fruits and vegetables on the prevalence of obesity, sex-specific logistic regression models were estimated separately for each of the three dietary behaviors of interest. Percent of calories from SSBs, percent of calories from energy-dense foods, and fruit and vegetable consumption were included in the models as tertiles of consumption and tested as continuous variables. Each model was adjusted for age group and race/ethnicity. The model with fruit and vegetable consumption was also adjusted for total caloric intake. The other two models were not adjusted for total caloric intake because the SSB and energy-dense food variables were analyzed as the percent of total caloric intake and thus were already adjusted for calories.

WEIGHT STATUS

In 2005–2008, approximately 16% (SE 1.0) of US children and adolescents 2–19 years of age were obese. There were significant disparities in prevalence of obesity by age and race/ethnicity. Preschool-age children 2–5 years of age were less likely to be obese compared to older children ($p < .01$). Over 9% (SE 0.9) of 2- through 5-year-old preschool-age children were obese, while 15.7% (SE 1.3) of 6- through 11-year-olds and 18.6% (SE 1.4) of 12- through 19-year-olds were obese. Non-Hispanic Blacks ($p < .01$) and Mexican Americans ($p < .01$) were disproportionately affected by obesity compared to non-Hispanic Whites. Fourteen percent (SE 1.5) of non-Hispanic Whites were obese, while 20.2% (SE 1.1) of non-Hispanic Blacks and 20.6% (SE 1.2) of Mexican Americans were obese.

Differences in obesity prevalence by age and race/ethnicity can be seen in Figure 11.1. The prevalence of obesity among boys was significantly higher among Mexican Americans compared to

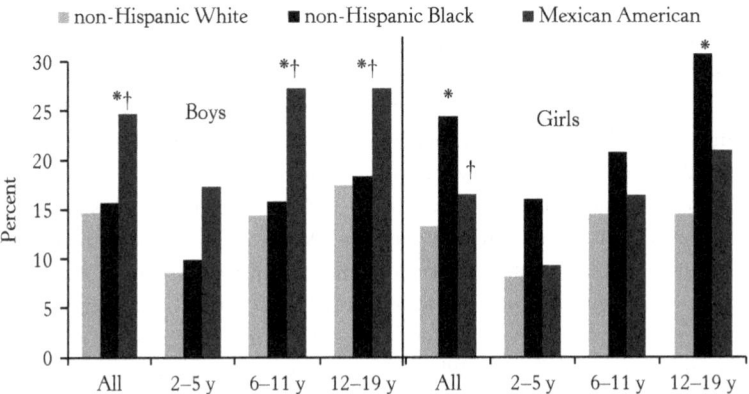

FIGURE 11.1. Prevalence of obesity, US children and adolescents, 2005–2008. *Significantly different from non-Hispanic Whites (p < .01); +Significantly different from non-Hispanic Blacks (p < .01); significant increasing trends by age among non-Hispanic Black and non-Hispanic White boys and non-Hispanic Black and Mexican American girls (p < .01). Note that obesity is defined as BMI-for-age ≥ 95th percentile of the sex-specific 2000 CDC growth charts.

Source: Centers for Disease Control and Prevention, National Center for Health Statistics, National Health and Nutrition Examination Survey.

non-Hispanic Whites and non-Hispanic Blacks ($p < .01$). Among girls, non-Hispanic Blacks were significantly more likely to be obese compared to non-Hispanic Whites and Mexican Americans ($p < .01$). Age trends, where the youngest children are less likely to be obese compared to adolescents, were significant for non-Hispanic Black and non-Hispanic White boys ($p < .01$) and non-Hispanic Black and Mexican American girls ($p < .01$). Trends among Mexican American boys ($p = .011$) and non-Hispanic White girls ($p = .016$) were approaching significance.

Trends in body weight are evident when comparing median weight in 2005–2008 to the median (50th percentile) on the CDC growth charts. The CDC growth charts were created using nationally representative data from the 1960s through the early 1990s, so a comparison of these medians shows a change over time. Figure 11.2 illustrates this comparison. For both boys and girls throughout childhood, the median weight in 2005–2008 was consistently greater than the median of the CDC growth charts.

DIETARY INTAKE

Estimated mean caloric intakes do not explain the disparities in prevalence of obesity. As expected, mean total caloric intake among US children and adolescents increased significantly with age among all groups ($p < .01$) except Mexican American girls

($p = .016$). There were no statistically significant differences in mean total caloric intake between race/ethnic groups among girls. Among boys, however, non-Hispanic Whites consumed significantly more calories than did non-Hispanic Blacks and Mexican Americans ($p < .01$). Figure 11.3 shows the mean caloric intake for each subgroup.

Analyses related to specific dietary behaviors reveal more than analyses of total caloric consumption, but they still do not fully explain race/ethnic differences in prevalence of obesity. In 2005–2008, US children and adolescents 2–19 years of age consumed an average 7.6% (SE 0.3) of daily calories from SSBs. Figure 11.4 shows the mean percent of calories from SSBs by sex, age, and race/ethnic group. The percent of calories obtained from SSBs increased linearly with age among both boys and girls in each race/ethnic group ($p < .01$). No statistically significant differences between race/ethnic groups were found among boys. Among girls, mean intake of SSBs was higher among non-Hispanic Blacks than among Mexican Americans-. Differences between non-Hispanic White and non-Hispanic Black 6- through 11-year-old girls approached significance ($p = .016$) as did differences between non-Hispanic Black and Mexican American 12- through 19-year-old adolescent girls ($p = .019$).

On average, US children and adolescents consumed more than one-third (36.0% SE 0.2) of their daily calories from energy-dense foods. Race/ethnic and age

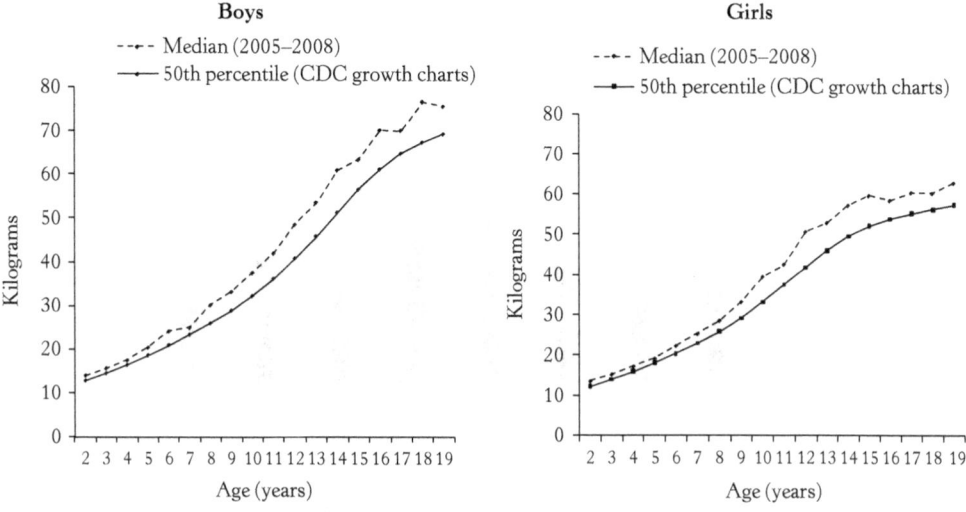

FIGURE 11.2. Median weight (kg), children and adolescents, 2005–2008 versus CDC growth charts.

Source: Centers for Disease Control and Prevention, National Center for Health Statistics, National Health and Nutrition Examination Survey; http://www.cdc.gov/growthcharts.

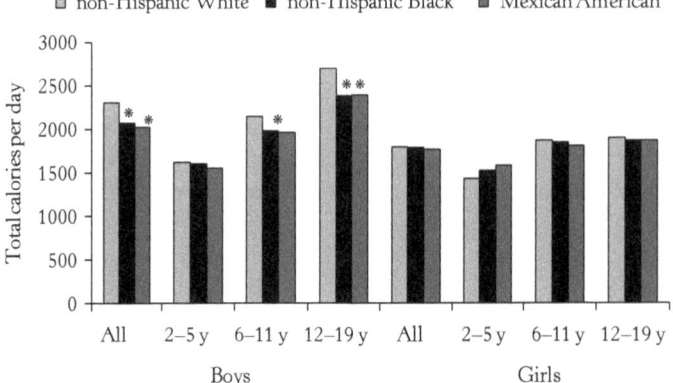

FIGURE 11.3. Mean total daily caloric intake, US children and adolescents, 2005–2008. *Significantly different from non-Hispanic Whites ($p < .01$); significant increasing trends by age for all sex race/ethnic groups except Mexican American girls ($p < .01$).

Source: Centers for Disease Control and Prevention, National Center for Health Statistics, National Health and Nutrition Examination Survey.

differences in the consumption of energy-dense foods were seen (Fig. 11.5). Mexican American boys and girls ate, on average, fewer energy-dense foods as a percent of total calories than did non-Hispanic White or non-Hispanic Black children and adolescents ($p < .01$). There were significant increasing trends by age in energy-dense food intake among non-Hispanic White and non-Hispanic Black girls and boys ($p < .01$) but not among Mexican Americans.

Mean fruit and vegetable consumption was 2.1 (SE 0.04) cups per day in all US children and adolescents.

Consumption did not vary significantly by race/ethnicity. However, the difference between Mexican American and non-Hispanic White girls 6–11 years of age approached significance ($p = 0.016$) with Mexican Americans consuming on average more fruits and vegetables than non-Hispanic White girls. Among all girls there was a significant decreasing trend by age ($p < 0.01$) in fruit and vegetable consumption. Figure 11.6 shows mean consumption for each sex, age, and race/ethnic subgroup similar to those subgroups presented for other dietary behaviors.

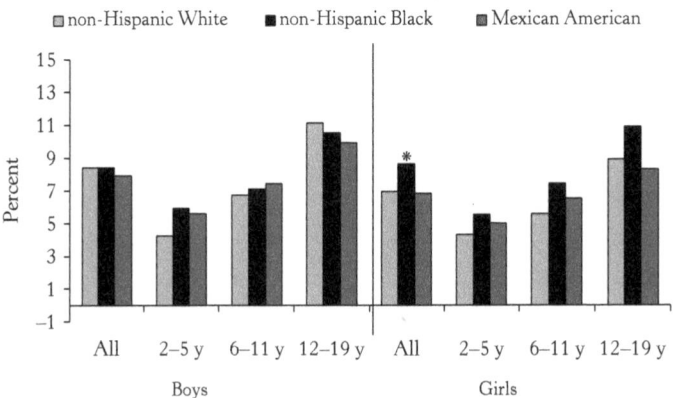

FIGURE 11.4. Mean daily percent of calories from sugar sweetened beverages, US children and adolescents, 2005–2008. *Significantly different from Mexican Americans. Significant increasing trends by age for all sex race/ethnic groups ($p < .01$).

Source: Centers for Disease Control and Prevention, National Center for Health Statistics, National Health and Nutrition Examination Survey.

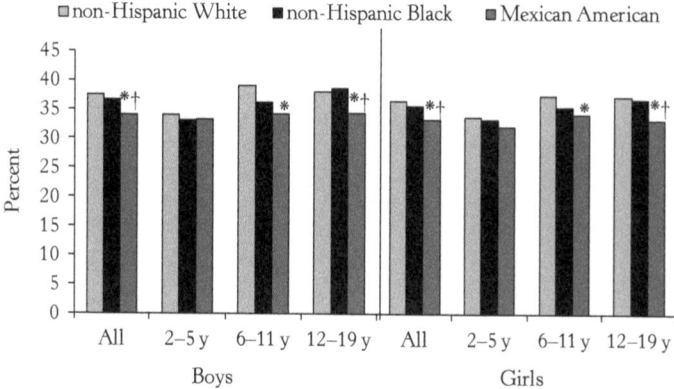

FIGURE 11.5. Mean daily percent of calories from energy-dense foods, US children and adolescents, 2005–2008. *Significantly different from non-Hispanic Whites ($p < .01$); †Significantly different from non-Hispanic Blacks ($p < .01$); significant increasing trends by age for non-Hispanic Black and non-Hispanic White boys and girls ($p < .01$).

Source: Centers for Disease Control and Prevention, National Center for Health Statistics, National Health and Nutrition Examination Survey.

WEIGHT STATUS AND DIETARY INTAKE

Separate multiple logistic regression models indicate that SSB consumption was positively related to obesity. Among girls, percent of calories from SSBs was positively related to obesity after adjusting for age and race/ethnicity (OR: 1.19, 95% CI: 1.01–1.40). Percent of calories from energy-dense foods and fruit and vegetable consumption were not significantly associated to obesity in either boys or girls. Table 11.1 shows these results.

DISCUSSION

Prevalence of obesity remains high with approximately 16% of US children and adolescents at or above the 95th percentile of BMI for age. Significant disparities in obesity currently exist between age groups and race/ethnic groups. Total caloric consumption appears to vary by age, and among boys by race/ethnicity. But the differences are not consistent with disparities in obesity and, in fact, caloric consumption was lower in Mexican American boys while obesity prevalence was higher in this group. Significant differences by age and race/ethnicity also exist for specific food behaviors such as consumption of SSBs and energy-dense foods, but, again, the differences are not all consistent with the disparities in prevalence of obesity. SSB consumption appears to be positively associated with obesity. Percent of calories from SSBs was positively

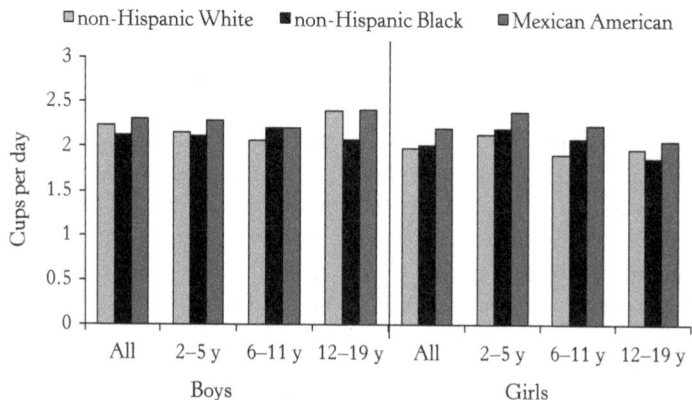

FIGURE 11.6. Mean daily cups of fruits and vegetables, US children and adolescents, 2005–2008.

Source: Centers for Disease Control and Prevention, National Center for Health Statistics, National Health and Nutrition Examination Survey.

TABLE 11.1. ODDS OF OBESITY BASED ON LOGISTIC REGRESSION MODELS,
UNITED STATES, 2005–2008

	Odds Ratio (95% Confidence Interval)		
	SSB Consumption	Energy-Dense Food Consumption	Fruits and Vegetable Consumption[a]
Boys			
Dietary behavior (tertiles)	1.01 (0.86–1.19)	0.90 (0.74–1.09)	0.98 (0.85–1.13)
Age (years)			
2–5	0.41 (0.26–0.64)	0.40 (0.26–0.60)	0.37 (0.25–0.56)
6–11	0.78 (0.56–1.09)	0.78 (0.56–1.08)	0.75 (0.52–1.06)
12–19	Reference	Reference	Reference
Race/ethnicity			
Non-Hispanic White	Reference	Reference	Reference
Non-Hispanic Black	1.10 (0.82–1.47)	1.10 (0.82–1.47)	1.08 (0.81–1.44)
Mexican American	2.03 (1.54–2.68)	1.98 (1.49–2.64)	1.99 (1.53–2.60)
Girls			
Dietary behavior (tertiles)	1.19 (1.01–1.40)	1.04 (0.87–1.24)	1.10 (0.90–1.35)
Age (years)			
2–5	0.52 (0.39–0.69)	0.49 (0.37–0.65)	0.45 (0.33–0.61)
6–11	0.86 (0.65–1.16)	0.84 (0.63–1.12)	0.83 (0.63–1.11)
12–19	Reference	Reference	Reference
Race/ethnicity			
Non-Hispanic White	Reference	Reference	Reference
Non-Hispanic Black	2.06 (1.30–3.28)	2.15 (1.34–3.44)	2.14 (1.34–3.42)
Mexican American	1.31 (0.84–2.05)	1.35 (0.85–2.15)	1.33 (0.85–2.08)

Note: Obesity defined as BMI-for-age ≥ 95th percentile of the sex-specific 2000 CDC growth charts.
[a]Adjusted for total caloric intake.
SSBs, sugar-sweetened beverages.
Source: CDC/NCHS National Health and Nutrition Examination Survey.

associated with obesity in girls after adjusting for age and race/ethnicity.

Energy intake appears to have increased over the last decades with individuals snacking and eating out of the home more often.[28,29] However, in most epidemiologic studies little association has been found between total caloric intake and obesity in children.[13,14] Specific dietary behaviors such as SSB consumption and energy-dense food consumption have been linked to weight gain in children.16 Our results related to SSBs are consistent with these findings.

SSB consumption has recently become a major focus of childhood obesity research. Among children and adolescents, consumption of SSBs has increased dramatically in the 1980s and 1990s,[30,31] however, in the last decade mean soda intake has decreased.[32] Recent studies suggest that consuming SSBs or soft drinks may contribute to weight gain in children and teens,[33,34] potentially through increased caloric intake.[35] SSBs comprised almost 8% of the childhood diet based on NHANES 2005–2008 data presented here.

Results based on the NHANES 2005–2008 do not show a significant association between energy-dense foods and obesity, but mean intake of 36% of total calories from energy-dense foods is much higher than the 5%–15% the US 2010 Dietary Guidelines state "can be reasonably accommodated in the USDA Food Patterns, which are designed to meet nutrient needs within calorie limits."[36] Frequent snacking on energy-dense foods may contribute to excess energy intake of children and teens, and high childhood BMI.[37,38]

Fruit and vegetable consumption has been shown to have significant health benefits, including in relation to weight management.[20] However, fruit and vegetable consumption among children and adolescents is low. Data from the National Youth Risk Behavior Surveillance System suggest that most children and adolescents in the United States consume fruits and vegetables fewer than five times per day.39 In 2009, only 22.3% of high school students reported that they ate fruits and vegetables five or more times per day during the previous 7 days. The evidence of an inverse relationship between fruit and vegetable consumption and obesity in childhood is mixed. Some studies have found an association between low fruit and vegetable consumption and obesity.[40,41] However, consistent with our results, one review found no association between fruit and vegetable intake and obesity in childhood.[42]

The results reported here are subject to certain limitations. Dietary intake data were self-reported and thus are subject to recall bias. One 24-hour recall can adequately represent the mean intake of a population for most nutrients and widely consumed foods, but day-to-day variation in intake causes large within-person variation that can distort estimates of the distribution of intakes. A recently published study suggests methods for use in modeling of nutrient intakes with health-related outcome measures.[43] In this chapter, consumption of SSBs, energy-dense foods, and fruits and vegetables were examined, all of which are broad food groups and not episodically consumed foods. All of these food categories are commonly consumed.

Survey data suggest that total caloric intake does not explain disparities in prevalence of obesity or increases in prevalence of obesity among children. However, *what* children are eating is changing, and certain dietary behaviors such as increased consumption of SSBs may contribute to obesity in childhood. The conversation about diet and obesity has begun to include the concept of food addiction, although the concept is still controversial. The scientific literature is beginning to contain papers[44,45] related to food addiction and obesity. An argument has been made that compulsive overeating is similar to conventional drug addiction.[45] Future research could explore this concept in relation to SSB consumption among US children and adolescents.

AUTHOR'S NOTES

Jacqueline D. Wright's contribution to this chapter was completed at the National Center for Health Statistics, Centers for Disease Control and Prevention.

Molly M. Lamb's contribution to this chapter was completed while she was in the Epidemic Intelligence Service, Office of Surveillance, Epidemiology, and Laboratory Services, Centers for Disease Control and Prevention (CDC) assigned to the Analysis Branch, Division of Health and Nutrition Examination Surveys, National Center for Health Statistics, CDC.

REFERENCES

1. Flegal KM, Carroll MD, Ogden CL, Johnson CL. Prevalence and trends in obesity among US adults, 1999–2000. *JAMA* 2002;288:1723–1727.
2. Ogden CL, Flegal KM, Carroll MD, Johnson CL. Prevalence and trends in overweight among US children and adolescents, 1999–2000. *JAMA* 2002;288: 1728–1732.
3. Ogden CL, Carroll MD, Curtin LR, McDowell MA, Tabak CJ, Flegal KM. Prevalence of overweight and obesity in the United States, 1999–2004. *JAMA* 2006;295:1549–1555.
4. Silventoinen K, Sans S, Tolonen H, et al. Trends in obesity and energy supply in the WHO MONICA Project. *Int J Obes Relat Metab Disord* 2004;28:710–718.
5. Wang Y, Monteiro C, Popkin BM. Trends of obesity and underweight in older children and adolescents in the United States, Brazil, China, and Russia. *Am J Clin Nutr* 2002;75:971–977.
6. Zaninotto P, Head J, Stamatakis E, Wardle H, Mindell J. Trends in obesity among adults in England from 1993 to 2004 by age and social class and projections of prevalence to 2012. *J Epidemiol Community Health* 2009;63:140–146.
7. Ogden CL, Carroll MD, Curtin LR, Lamb MM, Flegal KM. Prevalence of high body mass index in US children and adolescents, 2007–2008. *JAMA* 2010;303:242–249.
8. Daniels SR. The consequences of childhood overweight and obesity. *The Future of Children* 2006;16:47–67.
9. Cali AM, Caprio S. Obesity in children and adolescents. *J Clin Endocrinol Metab* 2008;93:S31–S36.
10. Serdula MK, Ivery D, Coates RJ, Freedman DS, Williamson DF, Byers T. Do obese children become obese adults? A review of the literature. *Prev Med* 2005;22:167–177.
11. Deshmukh-Taskar P, Nicklas TA, Morales M, Yang SJ, Zakeri I, Berenson GS. Tracking of overweight status from childhood to young adulthood: the Bogalusa Heart Study. *Eur J Clin Nutr* 2006;60:48–57.
12. Clinical guidelines on the identification, evaluation, and treatment of overweight and obesity in adults—the evidence report. National Institutes of Health. *Obes Res* 1998;6 (suppl 2):51S-209S.

13. Eck LH, Klesges RC, Hanson CL, Slawson D. Children at familial risk for obesity: an examination of dietary intake, physical activity and weight status. *Int J Obes Relat Metab Disord* 1992;16:71–78.

14. Troiano RP, Briefel RR, Carroll MD, Bialostosky K. Energy and fat intakes of children and adolescents in the united states: data from the national health and nutrition examination surveys. *Am J Clin Nutr* 2000;72:1343S-1353S.

15. Ludwig DS, Peterson KE, Gortmaker SL. Relation between consumption of sugar-sweetened drinks and childhood obesity: a prospective, observational analysis. *Lancet* 2001;357:505–508.

16. Malik VS, Schulze MB, Hu FB. Intake of sugar-sweetened beverages and weight gain: a systematic review. *Am J Clin Nutr* 2006;84:274–288.

17. Epstein LH, Paluch RA, Beecher MD, Roemmich JN. Increasing healthy eating vs. reducing high energy-dense foods to treat pediatric obesity. *Obesity (Silver Spring)* 2008;16:318–326.

18. Phillips SM, Bandini LG, Naumova EN, et al. Energy-dense snack food intake in adolescence: longitudinal relationship to weight and fatness. *Obes Res* 2004;12:461–472.

19. Bradlee ML, Singer MR, Qureshi MM, Moore LL. Food group intake and central obesity among children and adolescents in the Third National Health and Nutrition Examination Survey (NHANES III). *Public Health Nutr* 2009;13:1–9.

20. Buijsse B, Feskens EJ, Schulze MB, et al. Fruit and vegetable intakes and subsequent changes in body weight in European populations: results from the project on Diet, Obesity, and Genes (DiOGenes). *Am J Clin Nutr* 2009;90:202–209.

21. CDC/NCHS. National Health and Nutrition Examination Survey. 2009. Available at: http://www.cdc.gov/nchs/nhanes/nhanes_questionnaires.htm, accessed 5 April 2012.

22. Kuczmarski RJ, Ogden CL, Guo SS, et al. 2000 CDC growth charts for the United States: methods and development. *Vital Health Stat 11* 2002;1–190.

23. Krebs NF, Himes JH, Jacobson D, Nicklas TA, Guilday P, Styne D. Assessment of child and adolescent overweight and obesity. *Pediatrics* 2007;120 (suppl 4):S193-S228.

24. Himes JH, Dietz WH. Guidelines for overweight in adolescent preventive services: recommendations from an expert committee. The Expert Committee on Clinical Guidelines for Overweight in Adolescent Preventive Services. *Am J Clin Nutr* 1994;59:307–316.

25. Reedy J, Krebs-Smith SM. Dietary sources of energy, solid fats, and added sugars among children and adolescents in the United States. *J Am Diet Assoc* 2010;110:1477–1484.

26. Agricultural Research Service, United States Department of Agriculture. MyPyramid Equivalents Database.. 2009. Available at: http://www.ars.usda.gov/Services/docs.htm?docid=17563, accessed 5 April 2012.

27. US Department of Health and Human Services and US Department of Agriculture. *Dietary Guidelines for Americans, 2005.* 6th ed. Washington, DC: US Government Printing Office; 2005.

28. Sebastian RS, Cleveland LE, Goldman JD, Moshfegh AJ. Trends in the food intakes of children 1977–2002. *Consumer Interests Ann* 2006;52. Available at: http://www.consumerinterests.org/i4a/pages/index/cfm?pageid=4145. Accessed March 12, 2012.

29. Nielsen SJ, Siega-Riz AM, Popkin BM. Trends in energy intake in U.S. between 1977 and 1996: similar shifts seen across age groups. *Obes Res* 2002;10:370–378.

30. French SA, Lin BH, Guthrie JF. National trends in soft drink consumption among children and adolescents age 6 to 17 years: prevalence, amounts, and sources, 1977/1978 to 1994/1998. *J Am Diet Assoc* 2003;103:1326–1331.

31. Wang YC, Bleich SN, Gortmaker SL. Increasing caloric contribution from sugar-sweetened beverages and 100% fruit juices among US children and adolescents, 1988–2004. *Pediatrics* 2008;121:e1604–e1614.

32. Welsh JA, Sharma AJ, Grellinger L, Vos MB. Consumption of added sugars is decreasing in the United States. *Am J Clin Nutr* 2011;94:726–734.

33. Fiorito LM, Marini M, Francis LA, Smiciklas-Wright H, Birch LL. Beverage intake of girls at age 5 y predicts adiposity and weight status in childhood and adolescence. *Am J Clin Nutr* 2009;90:935–942.

34. Vartanian LR, Schwartz MB, Brownell KD. Effects of soft drink consumption on nutrition and health: a systematic review and meta-analysis. *Am J Public Health* 2007;97:667–675.

35. Wang YC, Ludwig DS, Sonneville K, Gortmaker SL. Impact of change in sweetened caloric beverage consumption on energy intake among children and adolescents. *Arch Pediatr Adolesc Med* 2009;163:336–343.

36. US Department of Agriculture and US Department of Health and Human Services. *Dietary Guidelines for Americans, 2010.* 7th ed. Washington, DC: US Government Printing Office; 2010.

37. Fox MK, Dodd AH, Wilson A, Gleason PM. Association between school food environment and practices and body mass index of US public school children. *J Am Diet Assoc* 2009;109:S108–S117.

38. Taveras EM, Berkey CS, Rifas-Shiman SL, et al. Association of consumption of fried food away from home with body mass index and diet quality in older children and adolescents. *Pediatrics* 2005;116:e518–e524.

39. Eaton DK, Kann L, Kinchen S, et al. Youth risk behavior surveillance—United States, 2009. *MMWR Surveill Summ* 2010;59:1–142.

40. Neumark-Sztainer D, Story M, Resnick MD, Blum RW. Correlates of inadequate fruit and vegetable consumption among adolescents. *Prev Med* 1996;25:497–505.
41. Lin BH, Morton RM. Higher fruit consumption linked with lower body mass index. *Food Rev* 2002;25:28–32.
42. Janssen I, Katzmarzyk PT, Boyce WF, et al. Comparison of overweight and obesity prevalence in school-aged youth from 34 countries and their relationships with physical activity and dietary patterns. *Obes Rev* 2005;6:123–32.
43. Kott PS, Wagstaff DA, Guenther PM, Juan WY, Kranz S. Fitting a linear model to survey data when the long-term average daily intake of a dietary component is an explanatory variable. *Survey Res Methods* 2009;3:157–165.
44. Dagher A. The neurobiology of appetite: hunger as addiction. *Int J Obes (Lond)* 2009;33(Suppl 2):S30–S33.
45. Davis C, Carter JC. Compulsive overeating as an addiction disorder. A review of theory and evidence. *Appetite* 2009;53:1–8.

12

Genetics of Body Weight Regulation

WENDY K. CHUNG AND RUDOLPH L. LEIBEL

Recent emphasis on the contributions of environmental, socioeconomic, and early developmental factors to the secular trend of increasing adiposity has dampened (and to some extent been a reaction to) earlier emphasis on the role of genes in determining susceptibility to obesity. Increasingly, these perspectives have been dichotomized into biologically untenable and therapeutically naïve formulations. In actuality, the phenotype of body composition (adiposity) represents a classic example of the resolution of complex genetic, developmental, and environmental forces whose relative contributions vary by age, demography, race-ethnicity, diet, and possibly even infectious disease history. One of the defining features of a "complex trait" to which genetic variation contributes—for example, height, blood pressure, coronary heart disease, cancer, and so on—is that the qualitative and quantitative aspects of the genetic contributions are powerfully influenced by the environmental (in the broadest sense) contexts in which they are examined.

With rare exception, obesity is not a state most people wish upon themselves. Repeatedly, the adverse psychological, socioeconomic, and medical consequences of obesity have been detailed, suggesting strongly that few would willingly choose this phenotype. The fact that apparently voluntary activities—eating and physical activity—strongly influence energy balance has led to the notion, still prevalent in many quarters, that individuals become obese solely by acts of free will and choice. While there may be some perverse righteous satisfaction in this formulation, the biology does not suggest this.

Using a variety of techniques—most convincingly based on differences in concordance of adiposity among monozygous and dizygous twins,

and adopted versus biological children and their parents—the "heritability" (proportion of phenotype attributable to genetics) for obesity *within a specific environment* is estimated to be between 40% and 70%.[1] A critical qualifying stipulation is that environment must be taken into account in making such estimates. This proviso is based upon the fact that the biologic salience of the contributory genes varies substantially depending upon the environmental circumstances in which they are examined. For example, the genes important for preservation of relative adiposity in an environment of famine may have a different effect in an environment with a surfeit of calories. Also, based upon evolutionary considerations, including the critical importance of maintaining sufficient fat stores to support reproduction and nurturing of young, it seems likely that humans (and other animals) are currently endowed with alleles of genes more effective at defense against weight loss than weight gain.

CLASSICAL LINKAGE ANALYSIS

For inherited phenotypes related to simple, highly penetrant (phenotype virtually always apparent when mutation is present) gene mutations (e.g., Huntington's disease, cystic fibrosis) the pattern of "segregation" of the phenotype can be related to known DNA sequence variants located throughout the genome. This is classical "linkage analysis." Linkage analysis is an effective strategy of gene identification for diseases in which single genes account for disease within families, or when such genes account for a significant fraction of the increased risk for the disease within a population. Linkage analysis has not proven successful in obesity largely because the underlying genetic architecture is more complex, with contributions of large numbers of genes—many of which are common but have small effects[2] and others which have large effects but are relatively rare.[3-6] A large number of linkage studies for obesity have been performed, including linkage studies in population isolates that are more likely to be genetically homogeneous and have a smaller number of contributing genes. However, no genes for obesity have been successfully identified by this strategy.

CANDIDATE GENE ASSOCIATION STUDIES

Based largely upon work in rodents, beginning with the molecular analysis of the causes of monogenic obesity, and then the analysis of genes using gene expression arrays and gene knockout and overexpression techniques, nearly 100 genes have been implicated in aspects of physiology determining body weight.[7] In association studies of candidate genes using polymorphic markers, over 20 genes have been repeatedly implicated in aspects of energy homeostasis. These genes, acting mainly, though certainly not exclusively, in the central nervous system (primarily the hypothalamus and brain stem), affect unconscious and conscious aspects of food intake and energy expenditure, and include genes mediating brain sensing of fat stores (*Leptin, Leptin Receptor, Serotonin 5-HT-2C Receptor*), fluxes of calories in the gut (*Glucagon Like Peptide; Peptide YY*), hedonic responses to specific foods, adipose tissue metabolism and development (*Hormone Sensitive Lipase, Peroxisome Proliferator Activated Receptor Gamma*), rates of energy expenditure (*Uncoupling Protein 1; Peroxisome Proliferator Activated Receptor Gamma Coactivator 1 Alpha*), tendency to oxidize specific metabolites, and even inclination to physical activity. Among the genes analyzed in this manner, 22 genes have consistently been reported positive in five or more studies.[7]

DIRECT ANALYSIS OF CANDIDATE GENES

Direct mutation screening using DNA sequencing methods has shown that mutations in one of these genes, *Melanocortin 4 Receptor* (*MC4R*)—which conveys hypothalamic signals suppressing food intake and increasing energy expenditure (as well as effects on hepatic glucose production)—account

for 3%–5% of severe obesity (BMI > 40 kg/m^2) in children and adults in some populations.[4,8] Families tend to have unique mutations private to their family, underscoring the need to directly analyze (e.g., sequence) the gene rather than utilizing surrogate markers as is the case in linkage and association studies. However, analyses in humans of other genes important by virtue of their apparent physiologic roles in energy balance have generally failed to show reproducible effects of this magnitude.

Thus, the so-called candidate gene approach to identifying the major genes responsible for the regulation of human body weight has not been particularly fruitful if measured by success in identifying genes of major effect in large numbers of individuals. There are several possible reasons for this failure to identify genes of major effect in broad clinical relevance:

1. For a phenotype so physiologically complex and critical to survival, no single gene or even handful of genes is likely to have a dispositive role. Additionally, the relative impact of specific genes may vary with age, yet most studies are cross-sectional, measuring adiposity at a single time point.

2. Gene–gene interactions among these candidates are difficult to examine without very large numbers (tens of thousands) of subjects.

3. The candidate genes provided by the rodent models and gene expression studies are not the most important genes for heritability of adiposity in humans.

4. Complex and subtle contributions to ultimate body weight of areas (and constituent molecules/structures) of the brain mediating hedonic, affective, and memory-related responses to food are hard to model in animals. The tools to examine these phenotypes in humans are now being expanded by the availability of functional magnetic resonance imaging (fMRI) and sophisticated testing strategies for mapping—behaviorally and by image analysis—these critical aspects of human responses to food and the contexts in which it is available.[9-17]

Even though a molecule may be critical for energy homeostasis physiologically, it is not necessarily the case that genetic variation in that gene accounts for variation in adiposity within the population. For example, while the enzyme HMGCoA reductase is critical in enabling feedback control of hepatic cholesterol synthesis, genetic variation in this molecule does not contribute significantly to the genetics of cholesterol homeostasis in humans. Likewise, leptin and its receptor, though clearly central elements in the regulation of body weight, mutations and genetic variation do not appear to play a major role in the determination of adiposity in humans in the general population, although rare highly penetrant mutations have been identified for both these genes in small numbers of individuals. These genes, nonetheless, are excellent examples of important therapeutic targets whose salience derives from the molecular physiologic pathways in which they participate rather than a primary contribution to obesity of their respective genetic variants. In fact, evolutionary considerations suggest that functionally critical genes would have heavy selective pressures to eliminate such genetic variation from the population.

GENOME-WIDE ASSOCIATION

An alternative approach to finding the genes responsible for complex traits such as obesity susceptibility is to take a hypothesis-free approach to gene discovery. Sequencing of the human genome revealed the presence of single-nucleotide polymorphisms (SNPs) occurring at a high frequency (~1/1,000 base pairs) throughout the genome. Over 1 million of these are present at >5% frequency in most populations, allowing the generation of molecular maps with SNP "sign posts" every ~ 3,000 bp. Most of these SNPs, as expected, occur in noncoding regions of their respective genes. The availability of high throughput genotyping technologies to analyze large panels of SNPs across the genome in thousands of DNA samples at modest (and declining) cost (~$500/ million SNPs), has driven the rapid explosion of genome-wide association studies (GWASs) for many diseases, including obesity. Individuals with and without the phenotype of interest (obesity, diabetes, hypercholesterolemia, etc.) are genotyped for the panel of SNPs, and the statistical association of SNPs with the phenotype is ascertained.

Given the heavy statistical penalty for multiple testing given the large number of markers genotyped, the samples sizes for the most credible studies are large and number in the thousands of samples for each ethnic group. Furthermore, due to the high probability of a type I error, these associations require independent replication. The large samples sizes required for these studies have resulted in unprecedentedly large collaborative efforts and meta-analyses to combine data sets, producing highly statistically significant results. GWAS for type 2 diabetes identified the first of the obesity loci, *Fat Mass and Obesity Associated* (*FTO*).[18,19] The GWAS approach was then utilized specifically for obesity in three studies, one with over 90,000 individuals, identifying a total of 10 additional regions associated with obesity, including *Fat Mass and Obesity Associated* (*FTO*), *Melanocortin 4 Receptor* (*MC4R*), *SH2B Adaptor Protein 1* (*SH2B1*), and *Neuronal Growth Regulator 1* (*NEGR1*).[20–22] Subsequently, an even larger study of ~250,000 individuals confirmed 14 previously identified regions and identified 18 novel loci associated with obesity.[2] Several of the genes implicated through these unbiased studies (*Melanocortin 4 Receptor, Proopiomelanocortin, SH2B Adaptor Protein 1, and Brain Derived Neurotrophic Factor*) act primarily in the central nervous system—particularly the hypothalamus—and emphasize the important neurological/ behavioral aspects of body weight regulation. Additionally, there is an apparent paucity of genes related to adipose tissue development and biochemistry and to cellular mechanism of energy expenditure within the regions implicated by GWAS studies. The majority of the newly implicated loci have been novel and not previously implicated by earlier candidate gene association studies with the notable exception of *MC4R*. It is important to note that GWAS identify genetic regions that contain genes contributing to a phenotype, not the gene(s) *per se*. There are generally multiple genes in the implicated region(s), and causal inferences based on nominal functions of genes in the interval must be tested by direct sequence analysis of these genes.

Despite the high statistical significance of the results of the GWAS, the newly identified loci have quite small effects on adiposity (body mass index [BMI]) or risk of obesity. *FTO* has been repeatedly shown to have the largest effect on BMI, yet its effect is small with each risk allele increasing body weight by only 1–2 kg in the average adult.[23] The *FTO* risk allele is, however, common in Caucasians with 63% of the population carrying one risk allele and 16% of the population carrying two risk alleles, leading to the high population-attributable risk of 20%, suggesting that 20% of the population's adiposity could be reduced if the effects of this locus were neutralized. At a population level, the *FTO* risk allele has a large effect because it is so common and therefore has effects on the majority of individuals within the population, although the effect size in specific individuals is modest. The effect sizes for other replicated loci are even more modest and increase population BMIs by 0.06 to 0.26 kg/m^2. Furthermore, a combination of eight of the statistically strongest genetic variants related to adiposity explains only 0.84% of the variance in BMI in the population, and the predictive value of these variants is limited. The area under the receiver-operator curve, a graphical plot of the true-positive rate, versus false-positive rate, used to predict the adiposity of an individual given the genotypes at these eight loci is only 0.548 and only marginally greater than the minimal value of 0.50.[22,24]

COPY NUMBER VARIANTS

Genetic variation in the number of copies of genes—referred to as copy number variants (CNVs)—has only recently been shown to be far more ubiquitous than previously appreciated. CNVs have been previously associated with a wide variety of neurological and psychiatric disorders, including intellectual disability, autism, and schizophrenia.[25–28] Many of the genotyping platforms for GWAS now also include the capability to detect and analyze copy number by virtue of the addition of probes targeted to regions of copy number variation and due to the addition of algorithms to measure signal intensity, which is proportionate to copy number. Thus, with the widespread adoption of GWAS methods, data on CNVs in obesity cohorts are increasingly available. By focusing on early onset, severe obesity, particularly in those patients with intellectual disabilities, large (> 1 Mb) rare (<1% population frequency) contiguous gene deletions/duplications were identified in approximately 10% of patients.[29] Similar strategies in children with modest obesity without intellectual disabilities found no increase in large, rare CNVs compared with controls,[30] whereas analysis of a cohort of moderately to extremely obese adults demonstrated that 1.3% of cases had large, rare CNVs.[31] By identifying genomic regions of CNVs associated with obesity, it is straightforward to define the boundaries of the CNV and to inventory the genes within these regions. By comparing multiple individuals with overlapping CNVs, it is possible to define the minimal overlapping critical region common to all the individuals with obesity, and thereby to identify novel candidate genes for obesity. Among the CNVs, the most common CNV consistently associated with obesity is a deletion in chromosome 16p11.2 observed to occur both *de novo* and to segregate with obesity within families.[29,32,33] The size of the deletion is somewhat variable, but one critical region includes *SH2B1*, a gene also previously identified and replicated by GWAS. The deletions of *SH2B1* suggest that haploinsufficiency (absence of one allele) results in increased adiposity, and that common variants in *SH2B1* may alter regulation of *SH2B1* to affect body weight.

In the aggregate, the candidate gene, GWAS, and copy number analyses can account for only a small fraction of the large genetic contribution to obesity risk indicated by the twin and adoption studies alluded to earlier. There are several major possibilities for this discrepancy:

1. These heritability estimates may be inaccurate (too high).
2. Obesity susceptibility is conveyed by a large number of genes, any one of which has a minimum influence. The relevant gene groupings may vary depending on race/ethnicity, environment, or developmental influences.
3. Major effects may be conveyed by rare alleles (e.g., present in < 1% of individuals in a population) of genes already implicated by candidate gene and GWAS studies, and/or by additional genes not yet detected in this way due to the rarity of their dispositive alleles.
4. Some combination of the above with the relative contributions depending on environment, race/ethnicity, and development.

The possibility that rare alleles of human genes play a role in determining adiposity can now be assessed by literally sequencing the entire coding and noncoding regions of these genes in individuals. Such studies have been made possible by the rapidly falling cost of DNA sequencing due to the development of new methods of sequencing, including single molecule sequencing, improved computational algorithms for sequence alignment, and rapidly increasing numbers of reference human genome sequences for comparison.[34] Initial studies utilizing this strategy will likely be focused on individuals with severe and/or early-onset obesity. If height and weight are collected on normal, control subjects used as controls for other genetic studies, associations with obesity could be tested cost effectively. The ultimate answers to these questions await the conduct of such studies in very large numbers (hundreds of thousands) of subjects, and the conjoint analysis of many genes/alleles in individual subjects, and may require bioinformatic analyses based upon pathways and gene interactions to dissect the complex genetics of obesity.

OTHER CONSIDERATIONS

Here we have emphasized "classical" genetic effects on adiposity, and in that context, primarily efforts to identify genes that promote obesity. This approach is based on the reasonable inference that evolutionary pressures have favored the selection of obesity-promoting alleles of such genes. However, the observation that some individuals appear to be defended against the obesity-promoting environmental pressures to which others are susceptible suggests that it might be fruitful to search—using the techniques described earlier—for alleles that favor relative slimness.[35] Careful screening of very slim individuals is required to eliminate those with underlying illness, but the genes identified might be of substantial therapeutic interest.

Nonclassical genetic influences on adiposity include so-called epigenetic effects on gene expression. Imprinting of genes by methylation and histone modification can lead to inheritance of phenotypes in parent-of-origin, non-mendelian modes of transmission as in Prader-Willi syndrome.[36] More subtle versions of such effects are difficult to detect in standard genetic analyses, since the epigenetic "marks" are not apparent in such studies. There also appear to be effects of intrauterine and postnatal environment on gene expression that may promote obesity in offspring.[37] Such effects might also be conveyed by actual induced structural changes in the parts of the brain regulating food intake and energy expenditure.[38-40] Such effects, which are biologically plausible, would also confound efforts to identify genes related to obesity, and they could account for some of the missing "heritability" implied by twin studies.

CONCLUSION

Clearly the underlying genetic basis for obesity in humans is complex and involves a substantial number of genes that likely differ between individuals in terms of number of relevant genes and their effect sizes, interactions among genes, interactions with the environment, which is in flux, and possibly maternal and postnatal effects (on brain structure and levels of gene expression) on the developing brain. While these complexities are challenging to disarticulate, the tools for analysis are improving rapidly and should allow for more comprehensive genomic analyses on larger numbers of subjects. The goal of these genetic studies is ultimately to provide insight into the underlying mechanisms of body weight regulation and provide potential targets for novel therapeutic and preventative strategies. Thus, although the multitude of genetic studies to date have not identified genes that account for a large proportion of the heritability of obesity, they have identified a large number of novel genes that may provide therapeutic strategies even for patients without genetic lesions in those genes, just as insulin can be used for diabetic patients even though most diabetics do not have *Insulin* gene mutations.

ACKNOWLEDGMENT

This work is supported by NIH Grant RO1-DK52431.

REFERENCES

1. Maes HH, Neale MC, Eaves LJ. Genetic and environmental factors in relative body weight and human adiposity. *Behav Genet* 1997;27:325–351.
2. Speliotes EK, Willer CJ, Berndt SI, et al. Association analyses of 249,796 individuals reveal 18 new loci associated with body mass index. *Nat Genet* 2010;42:937–948.
3. Clement K, Vaisse C, Lahlou N, et al. A mutation in the human leptin receptor gene causes obesity and pituitary dysfunction. *Nature* 1998;392:398–401.
4. Farooqi IS, Keogh JM, Yeo GS, Lank EJ, Cheetham T, O'Rahilly S. Clinical spectrum of obesity and muta-

tions in the melanocortin 4 receptor gene. *N Engl J Med* 2003;348:1085–1095.

5. Montague CT, Farooqi IS, Whitehead JP, et al. Congenital leptin deficiency is associated with severe early-onset obesity in humans. *Nature* 1997;387: 903–908.

6. Strobel A, Issad T, Camoin L, Ozata M, Strosberg AD. A leptin missense mutation associated with hypogonadism and morbid obesity. *Nat Genet* 1998;18: 213–215.

7. Bouchard C. Gene-environment interactions in the etiology of obesity: defining the fundamentals. *Obesity (Silver Spring)* 2008;16(suppl 3):S5–S10.

8. Vaisse C, Clement K, Durand E, Hercberg S, Guy-Grand B, Froguel P. Melanocortin-4 receptor mutations are a frequent and heterogeneous cause of morbid obesity. *J Clin Invest* 2000;106:253–262.

9. Aarts H, Custers R, Marien H. Preparing and motivating behavior outside of awareness. *Science* 2008; 319:1639.

10. Berthoud HR, Morrison C. The brain, appetite, and obesity. *Annu Rev Psychol* 2008;59:55–92.

11. DelParigi A, Chen K, Salbe AD, et al. Successful dieters have increased neural activity in cortical areas involved in the control of behavior. *Int J Obes (Lond)* 2007;31:440–448.

12. Pessiglione M, Schmidt L, Draganski B, et al. How the brain translates money into force: a neuroimaging study of subliminal motivation. *Science* 2007;316:904–906.

13. Rosenbaum M, Sy M, Pavlovich K, Leibel RL, Hirsch J. Leptin reverses weight loss-induced changes in regional neural activity responses to visual food stimuli. *J Clin Invest* 2008;118:2583–2591.

14. Rothemund Y, Preuschhof C, Bohner G, et al. Differential activation of the dorsal striatum by high-calorie visual food stimuli in obese individuals. *Neuroimage* 2007;37:410–421.

15. Stice E, Spoor S, Bohon C, Small DM. Relation between obesity and blunted striatal response to food is moderated by TaqIA A1 allele. *Science* 2008;322:449–452.

16. van Gaal S, Ridderinkhof KR, Scholte HS, Lamme VA. Unconscious activation of the prefrontal no-go network. *J Neurosci* 2010;30:4143–4150.

17. Zheng H, Lenard NR, Shin AC, Berthoud HR. Appetite control and energy balance regulation in the modern world: reward-driven brain overrides repletion signals. *Int J Obes (Lond)* 2009;33(suppl 2):S8–S13.

18. Frayling TM, Timpson NJ, Weedon MN, et al. A common variant in the FTO gene is associated with body mass index and predisposes to childhood and adult obesity. *Science* 2007;316:889–894.

19. Hinney A, Nguyen TT, Scherag A, et al. Genome wide association (GWA) study for early onset extreme obesity supports the role of fat mass and obesity associated gene (FTO) variants. *PLoS One* 2007;2:e1361.

20. Meyre D, Delplanque J, Chevre JC, et al. Genome-wide association study for early-onset and morbid adult obesity identifies three new risk loci in European populations. *Nat Genet* 2009;41:157–159.

21. Thorleifsson G, Walters GB, Gudbjartsson DF, et al. Genome-wide association yields new sequence variants at seven loci that associate with measures of obesity. *Nat Genet* 2009;41:18–24.

22. Willer CJ, Speliotes EK, Loos RJ, et al. Six new loci associated with body mass index highlight a neuronal influence on body weight regulation. *Nat Genet* 2009;41:25–34.

23. Loos RJ. Recent progress in the genetics of common obesity. *Br J Clin Pharmacol* 2009;68:811–829.

24. Li S, Zhao JH, Luan J, et al. Cumulative effects and predictive value of common obesity-susceptibility variants identified by genome-wide association studies. *Am J Clin Nutr* 2010;91:184–190.

25. McCarthy SE, Makarov V, Kirov G, et al. Microduplications of 16p11.2 are associated with schizophrenia. *Nat Genet* 2009;41:1223–1227.

26. Sebat J, Lakshmi B, Malhotra D, et al. Strong association of de novo copy number mutations with autism. *Science* 2007;316:445–449.

27. Wagenstaller J, Spranger S, Lorenz-Depiereux B, et al. Copy-number variations measured by single-nucleotide-polymorphism oligonucleotide arrays in patients with mental retardation. *Am J Hum Genet* 2007;81:768–779.

28. Walsh T, McClellan JM, McCarthy SE, et al. Rare structural variants disrupt multiple genes in neurodevelopmental pathways in schizophrenia. *Science* 2008;320:539–543.

29. Bochukova EG, Huang N, Keogh J, et al. Large, rare chromosomal deletions associated with severe early-onset obesity. *Nature* 2010;463:666–670.

30. Glessner JT, Bradfield JP, Wang K, et al. A genome-wide study reveals copy number variants exclusive to childhood obesity cases. *Am J Hum Genet* 2010;87:661–666.

31. Wang K, Li WD, Glessner JT, Grant SF, Hakonarson H, Price RA. Large copy-number variations are enriched in cases with moderate to extreme obesity. *Diabetes* 2010;59:2690–2694.

32. Bachmann-Gagescu R, Mefford HC, Cowan C, et al. Recurrent 200-kb deletions of 16p11.2 that include the SH2B1 gene are associated with developmental delay and obesity. *Genet Med* 2010;12:641–647.

33. Walters RG, Jacquemont S, Valsesia A, et al. A new highly penetrant form of obesity due to deletions on chromosome 16p11.2. *Nature* 2010;463: 671–675.

34. Durbin RM, Abecasis GR, Altshuler DL, et al. A map of human genome variation from population-scale sequencing. *Nature* 2010;467:1061–1073.

35. Jacquemont S, Reymond A, Zufferey F. Mirror extreme BMI phenotypes associated with gene dosage at the chromosome 16p11.2 locus. *Nature* 2011;478:97–102.

36. Chung WK, Leibel RL. Molecular physiology of syndromic obesities in humans. *Trends Endocrinol Metab* 2005;16:267–272.

37. Pankevich DE, Mueller BR, Brockel B, Bale TL. Prenatal stress programming of offspring feeding behavior and energy balance begins early in pregnancy. *Physiol Behav* 2009;98:94–102.

38. Carmody JS, Wan P, Accili D, Zeltser LM, Leibel RL. Respective contributions of maternal insulin resistance and diet to metabolic and hypothalamic phenotypes of progeny. *Obesity (Silver Spring)* 2010;19:492–499.

39. Kral JG, Biron S, Simard S, et al. Large maternal weight loss from obesity surgery prevents transmission of obesity to children who were followed for 2 to 18 years. *Pediatrics* 2006;118:e1644–e1649.

40. Levin BE. Metabolic imprinting: critical impact of the perinatal environment on the regulation of energy homeostasis. *Philos Trans R Soc Lond B Biol Sci* 2006;361:1107–1121.

13

Central Regulation of Hunger, Satiety, and Body Weight

HANS-RUDOLF BERTHOUD

DEFENSE OF OPTIMAL ENERGY STORES AND BODY WEIGHT: FLEXIBLE AND ADAPTIVE REGULATION

In a given environment, body weight is kept remarkably constant during most of adult human life in spite of a large total calorie turnover. Furthermore, weight loss and weight gain induced by experimental under- and overfeeding are rapidly corrected by compensatory adjustments in energy intake and energy expenditure in both rodents and humans.[1-3] These observations suggested a long time ago that body weight and perhaps fat mass are regulated in a homeostatic fashion, similar to other physiological parameters like blood glucose, but the specific mechanisms involved became clearer only after the discovery of leptin and a leptin-responsive neural system with a hot spot in the basomedial hypothalamus.

Unfortunately, this "homeostatic regulator" of body weight/adiposity has often been interpreted in a rigid, isolated fashion that does not reflect the powerful impact of environmental and other modulatory influences throughout every day and the entire life span. For example, the term "set point" was often used to mean that adiposity is kept at a constant level, like room temperature regulated by a thermostat, and it was suggested that the cause of the modern obesity crisis is inevitably linked to pathology of the homeostatic regulator. These extreme viewpoints started to crack when it became clear that although the lower limits of fat reserves and body weight are very powerfully defended, the mechanisms defending weight gain are relatively weak and can be easily overridden by modulatory influences.[4] Because fat (energy) reserves had a strategic reservoir function in the changing environment throughout evolution, they should be expected to vary considerably over time. Thus, homeostatic regulation is not rigid but flexible and adaptive, taking advantage of the brain's powerful cognitive functions.

APPETITIVE PHASE OF EATING: STRONG BASIC DRIVE TO FIND FOOD DEPENDS ON MULTIPLE NEURAL SYSTEMS WITH COGNITIVE FUNCTIONS PLAYING A MAJOR ROLE

One of the fundamental neurological paradigms involved in ingestive behavior is finding a good food source, remembering it, and finding it again. As simple as this sounds, it is a neurological tour de force, with just about the entire brain participating. Much of the brain has evolved to take care of hunger and other fundamental biological functions. Although procuring food in our modern world is no longer difficult or potentially hazardous, it was a demanding task for most of the last 5 million years. Each ingestive episode consists in (1) shifting behavioral attention induced by metabolic and/or environmental cues, (2) retrieving memorial representations of former experience with a particular food source or food, (3) navigation to the source, (4) consummation of the food, and (5) updating the memorial representation, if necessary. Thus, key neural functions are rapid learning, sensitive visual, auditory, olfactory, and gustatory perception, as well as strong basic motivation. Importantly, all of these functions are strongly modulated by the level of metabolic "hunger" (see Fig. 13.1).

All types of memory, explicit (episodic) and implicit (habits/skills, classical conditioning, and nonassociative learning), as well as working (short-term) and long-term memory, are involved in ingestive behavior. Key systems are the hippocampal complex and associated cortical areas involved in spatial orientation and explicit memory functions, the striatum primarily involved in habit and skills learning, and the amygdala involved in emotional learning.

Reward from food is processed by a complex neural system that includes the nucleus accumbens and ventral pallidum in the ventral striatum, the ventral tegmental area located in the midbrain and projecting through the mesolimbic dopamine system back to the nucleus accumbens, the prefrontal cortex, the hippocampus, and amygdala. Besides neural circuits in the hindbrain, the nucleus accumbens and ventral pallidum in the limbic forebrain are key components of the distributed neural network mediating "liking" of palatable foods. The

mu-opioid and cannabinoid receptors appear to play a crucial role.[5] To consciously experience and give subjective ratings of pleasure from palatable foods (liking), humans appear to also use areas in the prefrontal and cingulate cortex.[6]

Although "liking" a food is typically followed by "wanting" and eating it, "wanting" is a dissociable process that has a distinct underlying neural substrate comprising the mesolimbic dopamine system. With projections from the ventral tegmental area to the nucleus accumbens and prefrontal cortex, the mesolimbic dopamine system is the most crucial component of the implicit or subconscious "wanting" system.[7] Manipulation of this dopamine system powerfully influences "wanting" but not "liking" of foods.[8-10] The lateral hypothalamus is also involved in "wanting" as electrical stimulation of this area induces rats to vigorously self-stimulate and eat ("want") food, even though it does not

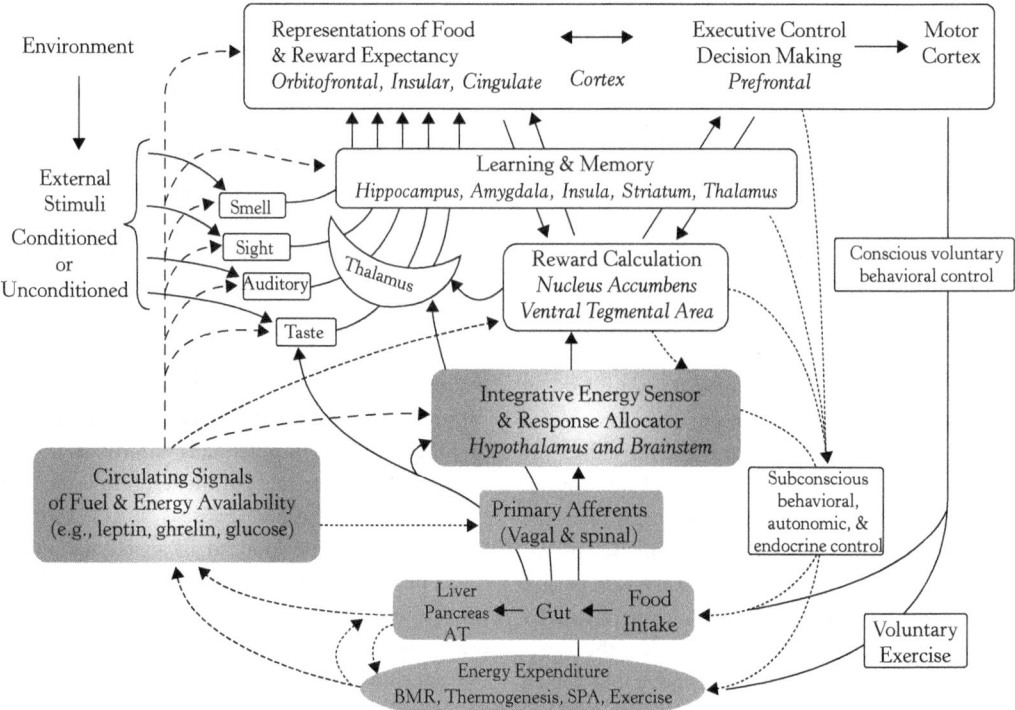

FIGURE 13.1. Schematic flow diagram showing the relationship between the classical "homeostatic regulator" (dark gray boxes) and neural systems involved in reward, cognitive, and executive functions (light gray boxes). Note that humoral (broken lines with open arrows) and neural (full lines with open arrows) signals from peripheral organs handling energy assimilation and metabolism not only feed back to the hypothalamus and brainstem but also to sensory and cortico-limbic structures. Similarly, effector pathways can be accessed not only from hypothalamus and brainstem but also from a number of cortico-limbic structures (broken lines with closed arrows).

Source: Berthoud 2011.

make them "like" the food more.[11] Wanting also has a conscious component most likely depending on areas of the orbitofrontal, cingulate, and insular cortex, as well as the dorsolateral prefrontal cortex known to play an important role in decision making and executive control (see further discussion later).

That even bland food tastes good and is more rewarding when we are really hungry has already been noted by Aristotle[12] and was systematically analyzed by Cabanac and colleagues.[13] However, the underlying neural mechanisms are far from being clearly understood. The main reason for this is that although several specific brain areas have been implicated in processing reward, we still have no clear understanding of how these areas work together and how they are embedded in overall behavioral control. The traditional view of homeostatic regulation originating from centers in the hypothalamus assumed that the attribution of incentive value happened within this area, specifically in the lateral hypothalamus. Eating and reward elicited by electrical stimulation of the lateral hypothalamus was shown to be modulated by metabolic signals such as leptin, insulin, cytoglucopenia, and gastric fill.[14–16] However, the mechanisms by which these disparate metabolic signals modulate lateral hypothalamic activity were not revealed by these studies.

More recently, considerable evidence has accumulated for a number of circulating hormones that are indicators of metabolic state to modulate information processing in the neural circuits orchestrating the appetitive phase of ingestive behavior. These circulating hormones act directly or indirectly on sensory processing, reward, and cognitive functions. On the sensory side, olfactory and taste perception is modulated by leptin, insulin, and gut hormones.[17–21] These findings suggest that low levels of leptin or absence of leptin signaling dramatically heightens olfactory and gustatory detection of food. The gut hormone ghrelin has been shown to directly act on hippocampal neurons and induce formation of new synapses in the CA1 region, resulting in enhanced spatial learning.[22] These findings are consistent with the idea that ghrelin is involved in the appetitive phase of ingestive behavior when it is important to find food in the environment. It is plausible that the ghrelin-induced changes in hippocampal function facilitate the recall of stored representations of prior experience with food.[23]

Nutritionally relevant hormones can also modulate activity of the mesolimbic dopamine system thought to be responsible for the wanting of food. Leptin can directly inhibit mesolimbic dopamine neurons and suppress food intake, whereas local inhibition of leptin signaling or leptin deficiency does the reverse.[24–27]

THE CONSUMMATORY AND SATIATING PHASE OF EATING: FROM PRIMARY AFFERENTS TO BRAINSTEM, HYPOTHALAMUS, AND CORTICO-LIMBIC SYSTEMS

Once a meal is initiated, attention shifts more and more to interoceptive mechanisms to control meal size, energy partitioning, glucose homeostasis, as well as the behavioral transition to satiety and other behaviors. As discussed earlier, these same interoceptive mechanisms also play a crucial role in generating the "hungry" brain when nutrient stores are depleted. Thus, this mainly internally and metabolically driven system is usually referred to as the "homeostatic regulator," consisting of three basic components, (1) a nutrient sensing system providing feedback for the regulated parameters, (2) an integrator making sense of all the internal signals in a given environment, and (3) behavioral, autonomic, and endocrine effector pathways leading to changes in energy intake, efficiency, and expenditure.

Different components of ingested foods interact with mechano- and chemosensors all along the alimentary canal that send neural signals via sensory nerves and/or humoral signals via the bloodstream to the brain (for a more detailed discussion, see Berthoud 2008[28]). Once absorbed, macronutrients and their metabolites are partitioned into either storage or immediate metabolism in various tissues, including the brain. The pancreas plays a special role in that circulating fuels and certain gastrointestinal hormones, the incretins, determine the release of the pancreatic hormones insulin, glucagon, amylin, and pancreatic polypeptide, all signaling to the brain.[29] Similarly, adipose tissue is another key organ sending hormonal signals to the brain and other organs,[30] although the stimuli and mechanisms determining the release of leptin, adiponectin, resistin, and other adipose tissue-derived cytokines are less clear. It is also likely that the other major metabolically active tissues, muscle and liver, produce hormonal signals used for energy balance regulation and these are just starting to be explored.[31,32]

Clearly, the hypothalamus is a key player in the control of food intake and energy balance. The arcuate nucleus, in particular, is a major hub for integrating nutritionally relevant information originating from all peripheral organs and mediated through circulating hormones and metabolites and/or neural pathways mainly from the brainstem. Nutritional information is then further integrated with other important information from the internal and external world, such as the diurnal clock and the presence of predators. Nutritional information also competes with other motivated behaviors such as thermoregulatory, fluid homeostatic, reproductive, and aggressive/defensive behaviors represented in the hypothalamus. Finally, the resulting optimal adaptive responses chosen are executed through behavioral, autonomic, and endocrine output pathways. Some of the key neuronal populations have been identified in the arcuate nucleus and much of the molecular mechanisms of intracellular integration of various hormonal and nutrient signals are currently under intensive investigation. The neuroanatomical layout,[33,34] molecular machinery,[35,36] and genes[37] constituting the hypothalamic energy balance regulator have been reviewed extensively in the past, and here we will draw attention to only a few important unsolved questions.

The homeostatic regulator in the hypothalamus and brainstem has three effector arms available to influence energy balance, behavior, autonomic, and endocrine outflow. Besides the arcuate nucleus, the paraventricular nucleus of the hypothalamus and lateral hypothalamus serve as major integration and output hubs. In contrast to the central organization of autonomic and endocrine outflow, our understanding of the neural pathways leading to ingestive behavior is much less clear, because behavioral activation typically requires more or less involvement of extrahypothalamic structures. Although there are some evolutionarily conserved pathways linking hypothalamus directly to brainstem and spinal cord responsible for fight and flight and primitive ingestive behaviors, an eating episode in humans typically engages the limbic system, thalamus, and cortex, with their complex loops and interactions. This makes it extremely difficult to point to the exact path of neural signaling for a given eating episode.

ENERGY EXPENDITURE: WELL-KNOWN EFFECTOR MECHANISMS BUT ELUSIVE CENTRAL CONTROLS AND COUPLING TO ENERGY INTAKE

An important feature of homeostatic energy balance regulation is that both arms of the effector (intake and expenditure) can be used to achieve the desired corrective response. To efficiently correct an energy deficit, intake should be stimulated and expenditure suppressed (anabolic mode), and the reverse should happen (catabolic mode) to correct an energy surplus. While this balanced response pattern appears straightforward, its neurological organization is somewhat complicated by at least two factors. First, energy expenditure can be achieved through several mechanisms, each with its own neural controls. Basal metabolism, thermogenesis, and physical activity are each controlled by vastly different pathways and effector organs. Furthermore, thermogenesis itself is a multifaceted process with several effector organs and control circuits, and physical activity has a spontaneous and a voluntary component with fundamentally different neural pathways. Second, certain environmental and metabolic conditions may require exceptions to the basic response pattern.

There is some evidence that the evolutionarily conserved brain-specific transcription factor Bsx[38] and ghrelin act on the hypothalamic NPY/AGRP system to couple increased food intake to increased locomotor behavior. Furthermore, the hypothalamic peptide orexin plays an important role in orchestrating foraging behavior.[39–41]

THE EXECUTIVE BRAIN: CONSCIOUS AND SUBCONSCIOUS MECHANISMS

Although humans have the ability to make conscious, voluntary decisions and choices, most of our actions have a subconscious component that escapes voluntary control.[42] This is why we eat palatable food such as chocolate in the absence of any metabolic need, even if we "know" better not to do it. The right prefrontal cortex appears to play a critical role in behavioral restraint and moral self-control by keeping reward-generating mechanisms in check.[43,44] The prefrontal cortex receives sensory information from inside and outside the body as well as emotional and cognitive information from the limbic system, and it is intimately connected to cortical areas involved in motor planning and execution. It is thus in an ideal position to translate all available homeostatic and environmental information into adaptive behavioral responses—in brief, to make choices and decisions.[45,46] Modern neuroimaging studies also support the importance of a balanced control by distinct areas of the prefrontal cortex in the control of food intake. Successful dieters who have significantly higher levels of dietary restraint compared to nondieters show increased neural activity in the right dorsolateral prefrontal cortex in response to food consumption.[47] In contrast, obese subjects show less activation of the left dorsolateral prefrontal cortex in response to food,[48,49] and patients suffering from the Prader-Willi syndrome who show severe disturbances in appetite control resulting in hyperphagia and obesity also show increased activity in the ventromedial prefrontal cortex when viewing pictures of food after glucose consumption.[50] This latter finding is consistent with a role of the ventromedial prefrontal cortex in the mediation of food intake driven by conditioned (learned) motivational cues in sated rats.[51]

In conclusion, the vital importance of ingestive behavior is reflected in the complexity and redundancy of the underlying neural circuitry. Extensive interactions between internal metabolic and external, environmental demands allow the system to regulate energy homeostasis in a more flexible and adaptive manner. Unfortunately, this architecture also makes it more challenging to find effective therapies to treat obesity and eating disorders.

REFERENCES

1. Bandini LG, Schoeller DA, Edwards J, Young VR, Oh SH, Dietz WH. Energy expenditure during carbohydrate overfeeding in obese and nonobese adolescents. *Am J Physiol* 1989;256:E357–E367.

2. Siervo M, Fruhbeck G, Dixon A, et al. Efficiency of autoregulatory homeostatic responses to imposed caloric excess in lean men. *Am J Physiol Endocrinol Metab* 2008;294:E416–E424.

3. Keesey RE, Corbett SW. Adjustments in daily energy expenditure to caloric restriction and weight loss by adult obese and lean Zucker rats. *Int J Obes* 1990;14:1079–1084.

4. Schwartz MW, Woods SC, Seeley RJ, Barsh GS, Baskin DG, Leibel RL. Is the energy homeostasis system inherently biased toward weight gain? *Diabetes* 2003;52:232–238.

5. Kelley AE, Bakshi VP, Haber SN, Steininger TL, Will MJ, Zhang M. Opioid modulation of taste hedonics within the ventral striatum. *Physiol Behav* 2002;76:365–377.

6. Kringelbach ML. Food for thought: hedonic experience beyond homeostasis in the human brain. *Neurosci* 2004;126:807–819.

7. Dayan P, Balleine BW. Reward, motivation, and reinforcement learning. *Neuron* 2002;36:285–298.

8. Berridge KC, Robinson TE. Parsing reward. *Trends Neurosci* 2003;26:507–513.

9. Pecina S, Cagniard B, Berridge KC, Aldridge JW, Zhuang X. Hyperdopaminergic mutant mice have higher "wanting" but not "liking" for sweet rewards. *J Neurosci* 2003;23:9395–9402.

10. Cannon CM, Palmiter RD. Reward without dopamine. *J Neurosci* 2003;23:10827–10831.

11. Berridge KC, Valenstein ES. What psychological process mediates feeding evoked by electrical stimulation of the lateral hypothalamus? *Behav Neurosci* 1991;105:3–14.

12. Ross CR. trans-ed. *Aristotle: De Sensu and de Memoria.* Cambridge, England: Cambridge University Press; 1906 (originally published ca. 330 b.c.).

13. Cabanac M. Physiological role of pleasure. *Science* 1971;173:1103–1107.

14. Berthoud HR, Baettig K. Effects of insulin and 2-deoxy-D-glucose on plasma glucose level and lateral hypothalamic eating threshold in the rat. *Physiol Behav* 1974;12:547–556.

15. Berthoud HR, Baettig K. Effects of nutritive and nonnutritive stomach loads on plasma glucose level and lateral hypothalamic eating threshold in the rat. *Physiol Behav* 1974;12:1015–1019.

16. Fulton S, Woodside B, Shizgal P. Modulation of brain reward circuitry by leptin. *Science* 2000;287:125–128.

17. Julliard AK, Chaput MA, Apelbaum A, Aime P, Mahfouz M, Duchamp-Viret P. Changes in rat olfactory detection performance induced by orexin and leptin mimicking fasting and satiation. *Behav Brain Res* 2007;183:123–129.

18. Getchell TV, Kwong K, Saunders CP, Stromberg AJ, Getchell ML. Leptin regulates olfactory-mediated behavior in ob/ob mice. *Physiol Behav* 2006;87:848–856.

19. Shigemura N, Ohta R, Kusakabe Y, et al. Leptin modulates behavioral responses to sweet substances by influencing peripheral taste structures. *Endocrinology* 2004;145:839–847.

20. Ketterer C, Heni M, Thamer C, Herzberg-Schafer SA, Haring HU, Fritsche A. Acute, short-term hyperinsulinemia increases olfactory threshold in healthy subjects. *Int J Obes (Lond)* 2010;35:1135–1138.

21. Martin B, Dotson CD, Shin YK, et al. Modulation of taste sensitivity by GLP-1 signaling in taste buds. *Ann NY Acad Sci* 2009;1170:98–101.

22. Diano S, Farr SA, Benoit SC, et al. Ghrelin controls hippocampal spine synapse density and memory performance. *Nat Neurosci* 2006;9:381–388.
23. Schmid DA, Held K, Ising M, Uhr M, Weikel JC, Steiger A. Ghrelin stimulates appetite, imagination of food, GH, ACTH, and cortisol, but does not affect leptin in normal controls. *Neuropsychopharmacol* 2005;30:1187–1192.
24. Figlewicz DP. Adiposity signals and food reward: expanding the CNS roles of insulin and leptin. *Am J Physiol Regul Integr Comp Physiol* 2003;284:R882–R892.
25. Hommel JD, Trinko R, Sears RM, et al. Leptin receptor signaling in midbrain dopamine neurons regulates feeding. *Neuron* 2006;51:801–810.
26. Fulton S, Pissios P, Manchon RP, et al. Leptin regulation of the mesoaccumbens dopamine pathway. *Neuron* 2006;51:811–822.
27. Farooqi IS, Bullmore E, Keogh J, Gillard J, O'Rahilly S, Fletcher PC. Leptin regulates striatal regions and human eating behavior. *Science* 2007;317(5843):1355.
28. Berthoud HR. Vagal and hormonal gut-brain communication: from satiation to satisfaction. *Neurogastroenterol Motil* 2008;20(suppl 1):64–72.
29. Woods SC, Schwartz MW, Baskin DG, Seeley RJ. Food intake and the regulation of body weight. *Annu Rev Psychol* 2000;51:255–277.
30. Trayhurn P, Bing C, Wood IS. Adipose tissue and adipokines—energy regulation from the human perspective. *J Nutr* 2006;136:1935S-1939S.
31. Flores MB, Fernandes MF, Ropelle ER, et al. Exercise improves insulin and leptin sensitivity in hypothalamus of Wistar rats. *Diabetes* 2006;55:2554–2561.
32. Kumar KG, Trevaskis JL, Lam DD, et al. Identification of adropin as a secreted factor linking dietary macronutrient intake with energy homeostasis and lipid metabolism. *Cell Metab* 2008;8:468–481.
33. Elmquist JK. Hypothalamic pathways underlying the endocrine, autonomic, and behavioral effects of leptin. *Physiol Behav* 2001;74:703–708.
34. Berthoud HR, Morrison C. The brain, appetite, and obesity. *Annu Rev Psychol* 2008;59:55–92.
35. Myers MG, Cowley MA, Munzberg H. Mechanisms of leptin action and leptin resistance. *Annu Rev Physiol* 2008;70:537–556.
36. Hofbauer KG. Molecular pathways to obesity. *Int J Obes Relat Metab Disord* 2002;26(suppl 2):S18–S27.
37. Lenard NR, Berthoud HR. Central and peripheral regulation of food intake and physical activity:

pathways and genes. *Obesity (Silver Spring)* 2008;16 (suppl 3):S11–S22.
38. Sakkou M, Wiedmer P, Anlag K, et al. A role for brain-specific homeobox factor bsx in the control of hyperphagia and locomotory behavior. *Cell Metab* 2007;5:450–463.
39. Kotz CM. Integration of feeding and spontaneous physical activity: role for orexin. *Physiol Behav* 2006;88:294–301.
40. Thorpe AJ, Teske JA, Kotz CM. Orexin A-induced feeding is augmented by caloric challenge. *Am J Physiol Regul Integr Comp Physiol* 2005;289:R367-R372.
41. Rodgers RJ, Ishii Y, Halford JC, Blundell JE. Orexins and appetite regulation. *Neuropeptides* 2002;36:303–325.
42. Aarts H, Custers R, Marien H. Preparing and motivating behavior outside of awareness. *Science* 2008;319:1639.
43. Alonso-Alonso M, Pascual-Leone A. The right brain hypothesis for obesity. *JAMA* 2007;297:1819–1822.
44. Lee D, Rushworth MF, Walton ME, Watanabe M, Sakagami M. Functional specialization of the primate frontal cortex during decision making. *J Neurosci* 2007;27:8170–8173.
45. Balleine BW. *The neural basis of choice and decision making.* J Neurosci 2007;27:8159–8160.
46. Murray EA, O'Doherty JP, Schoenbaum G. What we know and do not know about the functions of the orbitofrontal cortex after 20 years of cross-species studies. *J Neurosci* 2007;27:8166–8169.
47. DelParigi A, Chen K, Salbe AD, et al. Successful dieters have increased neural activity in cortical areas involved in the control of behavior. *Int J Obes (Lond)* 2007;31:440–448.
48. Le DS, Pannacciulli N, Chen K, et al. Less activation of the left dorsolateral prefrontal cortex in response to a meal: a feature of obesity. *Am J Clin Nutr* 2006;84:725–731.
49. Batterink L, Yokum S, Stice E. Body mass correlates inversely with inhibitory control in response to food among adolescent girls: an fMRI study. *Neuroimage* 2010;52:1696–1703.
50. Miller JL, James GA, Goldstone AP, et al. Enhanced activation of reward mediating prefrontal regions in response to food stimuli in Prader-Willi syndrome. *J Neurol Neurosurg Psychiatry* 2007;78:615–619.
51. Petrovich GD, Ross CA, Holland PC, Gallagher M. Medial prefrontal cortex is necessary for an appetitive contextual conditioned stimulus to promote eating in sated rats. *J Neurosci* 2007;27:6436–6441.

14

Peripheral Regulation of Hunger and Satiety

GARY J. SCHWARTZ

The presence of nutrients in the gastrointestinal tract gives rise to a wide range of neurohumoral signals that contribute to the control of food intake. These signals arise at multiple sites along the gut and hepatic portal system during ongoing ingestion of a meal, and they have been classified by Smith as "direct controls."[1] The gastrointestinal muscle and mucosa is richly innervated with sensory nerve fibers that extend within the gut wall as well as to the brain, making it possible to convey gastrointestinal meal-related direct control signals to the central nervous system sites critical in the control of food intake, digestion, and metabolism.

In addition to direct controls, indirect controls of feeding have also been proposed. These indirect controls function to determine meal size by modulating the potency of the direct controls of ingestion. Examples of indirect controls might include the circulating levels of adiposity hormones, secreted from fat tissue in proportion to whole body adiposity, or the neural consequences of prior experience with the oral and post-oral effects of ingested foods. This chapter provides a general classification of the types and distribution of meal-related gut direct control signals important in determining food intake, and it briefly characterizes some of the ways in which indirect controls may modulate the feeding inhibitory potency of such direct control signals.

Three general classes of meal-related stimuli generate direct control signals important in the control of food intake and meal size: mechanical, nutrient/chemical, and gut neuropeptide. Mechanical stimuli include both stretch and tension receptors localized to the muscular and serosal surfaces of the stomach and intestines, as well as mucosal receptors that are sensitive to discrete mechanical manipulation.[2] Stretch and tension receptors dose-dependently respond to increasing volumes of gastrointestinal loads, and they vary across the gastrointestinal tract in (1) the threshold amount of stimulation required to activate them and (2) in their maximal response rates. The functional significance of this variation is unknown, but it may contribute not only to the negative feedback control of ingestion but also to the reflex control of gastrointestinal motility and gastric emptying required for the appropriate digestion and absorption of nutrients consumed during a meal. Stretch and tension receptors typically adapt slowly to ongoing stimulation, and, after adaptation, increased volume or distension is required to reinitiate neural activity in sensory nerves supplying these receptors.

The slowly adaptive properties of such mechanoreceptors suggest that the behavioral effects of gastrointestinal volume in the control of food intake may be limited to the time during which incoming nutrients and secretions accrue during ingestion of a meal. On the other hand, mucosal receptors typically have small receptive fields along the intestinal or gastric luminal surface, adapt quite rapidly to stimulation, and have been proposed to mediate the reflex controls of the stomach and peristaltic movement of the intestines important in the mixing, digestion, and absorption of foods. Taken together, these receptors provide critical information to local intrinsic gastrointestinal neuromuscular reflexes via the enteric nervous system, as well as longer loop reflexes, via the central nervous system. These reflexes not only coordinate the motor and secretory events required for digestion of food but also importantly (1) determine the rate of nutrient delivery to gut nutrient sensors that feed back to the central nervous system sites regulating feeding, and (2) promote the release of gut neuropeptides that act locally on gut sensory nerves or via a humoral route in the central nervous system to modulate food intake.

Luminal infusions of individual macronutrient stimuli, such as fatty acids, carbohydrates, and amino acid or protein solutions, have each been reported to promote short latency, robust activation of gastrointestinal sensory nerve fibers. Intestinal infusions of each of these have also been shown to reduce food intake, either during real feeding, or during sham feeding, when ingested nutrients are permitted to drain from the stomach during ongoing feeding. The presence of intestinal nutrients has also recently been demonstrated to trigger the local intestinal synthesis of fatty acids, fatty acid ethanolamines, and endogenous cannabinoids, each of which may act as a stimulus for gut vagal sensory fibers innervating the gastrointestinal wall. Exogenous administration of the fatty acid ethanolamine oleoylethalnolamide (OEA) promotes satiety by increasing the latency to feed and increasing the interval between the end of one meal and the beginning of the next.[3] Ingestion of fatty acids promotes the intestinal biosynthesis of endogenous fatty acids as well as OEA.[4] Furthermore, the afferent vagus expresses receptors for fatty acid ethanolamides and cannabinoids, such as OEA[5] and anadamide,[6] which have been demonstrated to have feeding modulatory actions. Such nutrient-derived signals likely provide additional important sources of peripheral negative feedback in the control of ingestion.

The gut also has the ability to sense nonnutrient chemical properties derived from ingested foods, such as the osmolarity and pH of the gastrointestinal contents, and chemosensitive sensory nerve endings lining the mucosa are activated by low pH as well as by supraphsyiological osmolarity. The roles for these signals in the control of meal size are poorly documented and variable, but it is clear that increasing intestinal osmolarity can lead to decreases in short-term food intake during scheduled feeding episodes. Other nonnutrient chemosensation has also been reported in gastrointestinal sensory nerves, including vagal afferent sensitivity to intestinal alcohol and capsaicin, an active component of hot pepper extracts contributing to oral heat sensation. However, the contributions of these modes of chemosensation to the peripheral control of hunger and satiety have not been established.

The transduction mechanisms responsible for the ability of intestinal nutrients and to directly activate local vagal or splanchnic sensory nerve fibers have not been elucidated. Selective nutrient transporters, such as sodium-linked glucose transporters or the fatty acid transporter CD36, have been proposed to mediate intestinal nutrient signal transduction; expression of these transporters in the gut expression is nutritionally regulated and is important for the ability of gut nutrients to limit meal size.[4,7] Understanding the functional bases for the linkage between these transporters and the activation of gut afferents will be essential for targeting therapeutic strategies to modulate sensory feedback and eating behavior.

Important support for the role of gut vagal afferent signals in the negative feedback control of food intake comes from rodent studies evaluating the ability of extrinsic gut sensory nerve interruption to block the feeding inhibitory effects of intestinal nutrients. For example, intestinal administration of the sensory neurotoxin capsaicin limits the ability of intestinal lipid infusions to reduce subsequent meal size.[8] Furthermore, surgical transection of all gut vagal afferent fibers blocks the ability of intestinal infusions of fat and carbohydrates to reduce feeding.[9] From a genetic perspective, mice lacking neurotrophin-4, essential for the normal development of the vagal extrinsic sensory innervation of the gut, have larger meal size and meal duration, and are less responsive to the inhibition of food intake produced by gastrointestinal nutrient exposure.[10] While many of these results underscore the importance of gut vagal afferent feedback in the control of ingestion, nonvagal, splanchnic gut afferents also contribute to this control, as surgical transection of these nonvagal fibers blocks the ability of intestinal fat and carbohydrate infusions to limit food intake.[9]

Within the stomach and small intestine, ingested food also promotes the production of feeding modulatory neuropeptides released by endocrine cells of the gut during ingestion of a meal. Gut and portal vagal afferents have been demonstrated to express receptors for and/or respond to many of these meal-stimulated hormones. These include the satiety peptides cholecystokinin (CCK) and peptide Y (PYY), as well the incretin glucagon-like peptide (GLP-1). Results from CCK studies provide the most well-developed, coherent examples of how peripheral meal-induced gut peptides drive gut-brain neural signals important in the control of meal size.[11] CCK is released by the presence of intestinal nutrients, particularly fats and proteins, and plasma CCK levels are rapidly elevated in response to a meal. Exogenous CCK reduces gastric emptying, promotes gastric fill and gastric distension, and reduces food intake by limiting meal size. Pharmacological blockade of CCKA receptors promotes food intake[12] and blocks the ability of exogenous CCK to limit meal size. CCKA receptors are expressed by vagal sensory neurons in the nodose ganglion and are transported in vagal sensory nerve fibers.[13] Local gut vascular application of CCK at feeding inhibitory doses rapidly and dose-dependently activates gastroduodenal mechanosensitive and mucosal afferent fibers, and these effects are blocked by CCKA receptor antagonists.[14] Gut sensory vagotomy alone chronically increases meal size,[15] and obese rats lacking CCKA receptors are hyperphagic at each meal,[16] findings consistent with role for gut vagal CCKA receptor activation as a critical signal in the negative feedback control of meal size. Accordingly, gut sensory vagotomy significantly blocks the satiety effects of peripherally administered CCK as well.[17] These findings are consistent with the idea that, during a meal, vagal gut peptide signaling provides an index of intestinal nutrient availability that contributes to the negative feedback control of ingestion.

Peripheral gut vagal afferents not only respond to but can also integrate multiple modalities of meal-related stimuli important in the negative feedback control of ingestion. Both gastric distension and plasma CCK levels increase during the course of a meal, and combinations of gastric distending loads and CCK administration can be shown to reduce meal size to a greater degree than either stimulus when administered alone.[18] Gut vagal sensory nerves may also mediate these additive effects, in that combined application of gastric load stimuli and exogenous CCK activate gastric distension-sensitive afferents to a greater degree than either stimulus alone.[19] Thus, CCK increases the vagal excitatory and feeding inhibitory potencies of meal-related distension signals.

While it is clear from the previous discussion that intestinal nutrient exposure is an important gut neuroendocrine stimulus in the peripheral control of feeding, meal-stimulated gastric gut peptide release from the stomach has also recently been implicated in this control. The stomach is a source of the adiposity hormone leptin,[20] and gastric and plasma leptin levels are elevated during a meal. Local infusions of leptin into the gastrointestinal blood supply are sufficient to reduce food intake and meal size.[21] ObRb, the long form of the leptin receptor implicated in leptin's actions on feeding and energy balance, has been localized to vagal sensory

nerves supplying the stomach and small intestine, and exogenous application of leptin increases neural activity in these fibers.[22] Furthermore, destruction of unmyelinated gut vagal afferents using the selective neurotoxin capsaicin, or selective surgical transection of the vagal celiac branch fibers supplying the upper gut, blocks the satiety effects of leptin.[21] Taken together, these data support the idea that meal-elicited gastric leptin release is a short-term direct control of feeding via a peripheral gut sensory pathway.

Feeding excitatory peripheral gut peptides are also present in the stomach and are released by gastric endocrine cells. The growth hormone receptor ligand ghrelin, the only known peripheral feeding stimulatory peptide, is processed into its bioactive, acylated form in the stomach. Ghrelin secretion and release are nutritionally regulated; plasma acyl-ghrelin levels increase during fasting and are rapidly decreased by feeding or intestinal infusions of fats, carbohydrates, and proteins. Exogenous administration of ghrelin increases food intake by rapidly promoting meal initiation,[23] suggesting it may act via gut sensory nerves. Indeed, ghrelin receptors have been demonstrated to be expressed on vagal afferent nodose ganglion cell bodies and transported in vagal afferent fibers, where ghrelin binding occurs.[24] Ghrelin has also been shown to decrease the neural vagal afferent responses to some gut mechanical tension stimuli, consistent with a potential role for the sensory vagus in ghrelin's feeding stimulatory effects.[25] Capsaicin treatment, and transection of the entire sensorimotor gastric or subdiaphragmatic branches of the vagus nerve, have each been reported to block the feeding stimulatory effects of peripheral ghrelin,[24] but total gut sensory vagal denervation does not,[26] suggesting that distinct populations of sub- and supradiaphragmatic vagal afferents may be implicated in ghrelin's ability to promote feeding. Taken together, these findings support the idea that meal-stimulated peripheral gut hormones help determine both meal size and meal initiation by modulating the levels of vagal afferent activity.

Gut vagal and nonvagal afferent signals arising from the mechanical, chemical, and humoral consequences of food intake converge on the nucleus of the solitary tract, the first central nervous system target of neural meal-related negative feedback. This nucleus, located in the caudal brainstem, also receives neural signals arising from gustatory stimulation of the oral cavity. Furthermore, it is adjacent to the area postrema, a circumventricular organ with a relatively porous blood–brain barrier. Motor neurons critical for the oral acts of ingestion (chewing, licking, swallowing) as well as gastrointestinal secretomotor function, are in close physical proximity to and make synaptic contacts with solitary nucleus neurons relaying meal-related gut feedback signals. This set of features gives rise to the possibility that blood-borne nutrients and hormones, released by the gastrointestinal presence of food during a meal, can influence the neuronal circuitry important in ongoing ingestion. Consistent with this suggestion, gut peptides such as leptin, GLP-1, and ghrelin are transported across the blood–brain barrier, and brainstem injections of these peptides have been shown to recapitulate the feeding effects of peripheral peptide administration.[27-29] Finally, brainstem neurons, similar to their peripheral gut sensory counterparts, have the capacity to integrate gut sensory neural input with local neuropeptide signals. For example, central administration of leptin can potentiate the feeding inhibitory and brainstem neuronal activation resulting from both gastric distending loads and peripheral CCK, two prototypical peripheral satiety stimuli.[30-32] Taken together, these data support a role for the caudal brainstem as a critical locus of convergence of direct and indirect controls in the peripheral regulation of hunger and satiety.

ACKNOWLEDGMENT

The author would like to acknowledge support from NIH DK 020541 Einstein Diabetes Research And Training Center and NIH DK026667 NY Obesity Research Center.

REFERENCES

1. Smith GP. The direct and indirect controls of meal size. *Neurosci Biobehav Rev* 1996;20:41–46.
2. Page AJ, Martin CM, Blackshaw LA. Vagal mechanoreceptors and chemoreceptors in mouse stomach and esophagus. *J Neurophysiol* 2002;87:2095–2103.
3. Fu J, Gaetani S, Oveisi F, et al. Oleylethanolamide regulates feeding and body weight through activation of the nuclear receptor PPAR-alpha. *Nature* 2003;425:90–93.
4. Schwartz GJ, Fu J, Astarita G, et al. The lipid messenger OEA links dietary fat intake to satiety. *Cell Metab* 2008;8:281–288.
5. Wang X, Miyares RL, Ahern GP. Oleoylethanolamide excites vagal sensory neurones, induces visceral pain and reduces short-term food intake in mice via capsaicin receptor TRPV1. *J Physiol* 2005;564:541–547.
6. Burdyga G, Varro A, Dimaline R, Thompson DG, Dockray GJ. Expression of cannabinoid CB1 receptors by vagal afferent neurons: kinetics and role in influencing neurochemical phenotype. *Am J Physiol Gastrointest Liver Physiol* 2010;299:G63–G69.
7. Raybould HE. Nutrient sensing in the gastrointestinal tract: possible role for nutrient transporters. *J Physiol Biochem* 2008;64:349–356.
8. Tamura CS, Ritter RC. Intestinal capsaicin transiently attenuates suppression of sham feeding by oleate. *Am J Physiol* 1994;267:R561–R568.
9. Sclafani A, Ackroff K, Schwartz GJ. Selective effects of vagal deafferentation and celiac-superior mesenteric ganglionectomy on the reinforcing and satiating action of intestinal nutrients. *Physiol Behav* 2003;78:285–294.
10. Fox EA, Phillips RJ, Baronowsky EA, Byerly MS, Jones S, Powley TL. Neurotrophin-4 deficient mice have a loss of vagal intraganglionic mechanoreceptors from the small intestine and a disruption of short-term satiety. *J Neurosci* 2001;21:8602–8615.
11. Moran TH, Ladenheim EE, Schwartz GJ. Within-meal gut feedback signaling. *Int J Obes Relat Metab Disord* 2001;25(suppl 5):S39–S41.
12. Reidelberger RD, Varga G, Solomon TE. Effects of selective cholecystokinin antagonists L364,718 and L365,260 on food intake in rats. *Peptides* 1991;12:1215–1221.
13. Moran TH, Smith GP, Hostetler AM, McHugh PR. Transport of cholecystokinin (CCK) binding sites in subdiaphragmatic vagal branches. *Brain Res* 1987;415:149–152.
14. Schwartz GJ, McHugh PR, Moran TH. Pharmacological dissociation of responses to CCK and gastric loads in rat mechanosensitive vagal afferents. *Am J Physiol* 1994;267:R303–R308.
15. Schwartz GJ, Salorio CF, Skoglund C, Moran TH. Gut vagal afferent lesions increase meal size but do not block gastric preload-induced feeding suppression. *Am J Physiol* 1999;276:R1623–R1629.
16. Moran TH, Katz LF, Plata-Salaman CR, Schwartz GJ. Disordered food intake and obesity in rats lacking cholecystokinin A receptors. *Am J Physiol* 1998;274:R618–R625.
17. Moran TH, Baldessarini AR, Salorio CF, Lowery T, Schwartz GJ. Vagal afferent and efferent contributions to the inhibition of food intake by cholecystokinin. *Am J Physiol* 1997;272:R1245–R1251.
18. Schwartz GJ, Netterville LA, McHugh PR, Moran TH. Gastric loads potentiate inhibition of food intake produced by a cholecystokinin analogue. *Am J Physiol* 1991;261:R1141–R1146.
19. Schwartz GJ, McHugh PR, Moran TH. Integration of vagal afferent responses to gastric loads and cholecystokinin in rats. *Am J Physiol* 1991;261:R64–R69.
20. Bado A, Levasseur S, Attoub S, et al. The stomach is a source of leptin. *Nature* 1998;394:790–793.

21. Peters JH, McKay BM, Simasko SM, Ritter RC. Leptin-induced satiation mediated by abdominal vagal afferents. *Am J Physiol Regul Integr Comp Physiol* 2005;288:R879–R884.

22. Peters JH, Ritter RC, Simasko SM. Leptin and CCK selectively activate vagal afferent neurons innervating the stomach and duodenum. *Am J Physiol Regul Integr Comp Physiol* 2006;290:R1544–R1549.

23. Cummings DE. Ghrelin and the short- and long-term regulation of appetite and body weight. *Physiol Behav* 2006;89:71–84.

24. Date Y, Murakami N, Toshinai K, et al. The role of the gastric afferent vagal nerve in ghrelin-induced feeding and growth hormone secretion in rats. *Gastroenterol* 2002;123:1120–1128.

25. Page AJ, Slattery JA, Milte C, et al. Ghrelin selectively reduces mechanosensitivity of upper gastrointestinal vagal afferents. *Am J Physiol Gastrointest Liver Physiol* 2007;292:G1376–G1384.

26. Arnold M, Mura A, Langhans W, Geary N. Gut vagal afferents are not necessary for the eating-stimulatory effect of intraperitoneally injected ghrelin in the rat. *J Neurosci* 2006;26:11052–11060.

27. Grill HJ, Schwartz MW, Kaplan JM, Foxhall JS, Breininger J, Baskin DG. Evidence that the caudal brainstem is a target for the inhibitory effect of leptin on food intake. *Endocrinology* 2002;143:239–246.

28. Hayes MR, Skibicka KP, Grill HJ. Caudal brainstem processing is sufficient for behavioral, sympathetic, and parasympathetic responses driven by peripheral and hindbrain glucagon-like-peptide-1 receptor stimulation. *Endocrinology* 2008;149:4059–4068.

29. Faulconbridge LF, Cummings DE, Kaplan JM, Grill HJ. Hyperphagic effects of brainstem ghrelin administration. *Diabetes* 2003;52:2260–2265.

30. Huo L, Maeng L, Bjorbaek C, Grill HJ. Leptin and the control of food intake: neurons in the nucleus of the solitary tract are activated by both gastric distension and leptin. *Endocrinology* 2007;148:2189–2197.

31. Emond M, Ladenheim EE, Schwartz GJ, Moran TH. Leptin amplifies the feeding inhibition and neural activation arising from a gastric nutrient preload. *Physiol Behav* 2001;72:123–128.

32. Schwartz GJ, Moran TH. Leptin and neuropeptide y have opposing modulatory effects on nucleus of the solitary tract neurophysiological responses to gastric loads: implications for the control of food intake. *Endocrinology* 2002;143:3779–3784.

15

Food Intake and Metabolism

DOUGLAS S. RAMSAY AND STEPHEN C. WOODS

INTRODUCTION

What controls food intake? Stated another way, what factors or stimuli determine when a meal will occur, and what stimuli determine when it will end and how much will have been eaten? The answers to such questions are vitally important for trying to understand the etiology and potential treatments of the worldwide prevalence of obesity, and they were historically thought to be deceptively simple.

Early conceptualizations considered the stomach to be key. When the stomach was empty, hunger occurred and an individual ate so long as food was available; and as food accumulated in the stomach, causing distension during a meal, hunger waned and satiation took over, eventually causing eating to stop. Observations such as the continuous eating by animals with open gastric fistulas, where ingested food exited the body and precluded filling the stomach,[1] supported the concept; and bariatric procedures such as gastric banding that reduce the functional volume of the stomach when swallowing are at least partly based on the premise that distending the remaining pouch is instrumental in eating less food.[2]

An alternative possibility, and the one championed by most lay people, is that some correlate of energy storage or metabolism governs the start and end of meals. For example, Jean Mayer's glucostatic hypothesis held that the critical controller was the rate of metabolism of glucose by specialized sensory cells in the ventral hypothalamus.[3] With a limited capacity to store glucose, brain cells rely on a steady influx of energy-rich glucose molecules from the blood to drive their cellular activities; hence, low blood glucose (hypoglycemia) was considered sufficient to trigger the sensation of hunger and to elicit eating. Consistent with this, procedures that lower blood glucose, such as administering insulin, elicit the onset of eating.[4] The critical stimulus is not the level of glucose in the blood, however, but rather the ability of some brain cells to derive sufficient energy from glucose. This can be demonstrated by administering drugs like 2-deoxyglucose (2DG) that interfere with brain intracellular glucose metabolism, raising blood glucose while simultaneously eliciting eating.[5]

While there is no doubt that drastically lowering glucose metabolism in the brain is sufficient to cause eating, this experimentally induced phenomenon bears little relationship to normal eating since virtually all meals begin when blood glucose and brain glucose metabolism are at much higher levels. Hence, eating in response to insulin or 2DG is considered an emergency response, a vital reflex to be activated to enhance long-term survival.[4] Likewise, elevations of available glucose or glucose utilization are not considered to be major controllers of satiation during most ongoing meals.

BRAIN AND METABOLISM

In recent years, the possibility that metabolic signals act in the brain to influence food intake has broadened considerably.[6,7] Glucose received most historical attention as it is the primary energy source for most brain cells, and the signaling activity of some glucose-sensitive neurons in the hypothalamus (as well as elsewhere in the brain) changes in association with changes in local glucose.[8] There is now compelling evidence that neurons in the same areas of the hypothalamus, and perhaps even the glucose-sensitive neurons themselves, also change their signaling activity in response to local changes of some fatty acids[9]; and unlike neurons in general, these cells synthesize the enzymes necessary to synthesize and metabolize fatty acids; and changes in these cellular processes are known to influence cell signaling and to influence food intake.[10] The ventral hypothalamus has also recently been found to be sensitive to local changes of some amino acids, such as leucine.[11] The point is that an area of the hypothalamus known to be important in the regulation of energy homeostasis and body weight contains neurons sensitive to molecules representing all three classes of energy-rich compounds: carbohydrates, fats, and proteins. Furthermore, under some conditions, local manipulations of the metabolism of any of these compounds can influence food intake.

A picture that has emerged in recent years is that this area of the hypothalamus can be considered a general energy sensor that integrates information on the metabolism (or potential metabolism) of all major molecular sources of energy.[6,12,13] While this concept is not new,[14,15] what is perhaps novel is the recognition that most cells in the body share common energy-sensitive enzymatic systems that control their local activity. For example, when ample energy is available from the circulation, a cell is able to put effort into growth and repair as well as carrying out its unique functions. When energy is scarce, nonessential activities are attenuated and energy is targeted into simply staying alive.[6,7]

Two molecules have been identified that determine whether metabolic activity of cells is aimed at growth, maintenance, or survival. AMP-activated protein kinase (AMPK) activity increases during energy need (e.g., during hypoglycemia), whereas mammalian target of rapamycin (mTOR) activity increases during energy excess. Increased AMPK or decreased mTOR locally within the ventral hypothalamus increases food intake and vice versa, and the balance is influenced by cellular energy metabolism.[6,7]

FOOD INTAKE AND THE REGULATION OF BODY FAT

The amount of fat stored in the body is signaled to the brain by means of hormones whose rate of secretion and levels in the blood are proportional to stored fat.[16,17] The best-known such adiposity signals are leptin, which is secreted by fat cells, and insulin, which is secreted by pancreatic β-cells. Both hormones are transported from the circulation into the brain, and specific receptors for each are expressed by neurons in the ventral hypothalamus as well as elsewhere in the brain.[16,17] Hence, the brain area that is sensitive to local energy-rich fuels and their metabolism is also sensitive to molecules that signify body fat storage. Leptin and

insulin increase hypothalamic mTOR and decrease AMPK and vice versa, leading to decreased food intake and weight loss.[6,18,19] There is compelling evidence (reviewed in several chapters in this book) that total body fat itself is regulated in the sense that when it is decreased, homeostatic reflexes are activated to restore fat to normal, and that when it is increased, reflexes with opposite actions are activated to elicit weight loss. These processes account for the relatively stable maintenance of body weight over long intervals.

CONTROL OF FOOD INTAKE

Food intake (i.e., the behavioral act of eating) is not a regulated variable; rather, food intake is an effector or response mechanism that can be recruited or turned off in the regulation of body fat.[20] Brain circuits that regulate body weight/fat have several effectors at their command, including exercise/general physical activity and whole-body metabolic rate as well as food intake. When body fat is higher or lower than normal, any of these effectors might be recruited, the exact process(es) depending upon other activities and constraints. An important point is that food intake and other effectors can also be recruited in the service of other regulated variables. Blood glucose and glucose metabolism by some cells in the brain are homeostatically regulated, and as discussed earlier, when they are experimentally decreased, eating is elicited.[20,21] Analogously, body temperature is also homeostatically regulated, and when it is decreased, increased physical activity, peripheral vasoconstriction, or whole-body metabolism is recruited to defend normothermia.[21,22] Because of their overlapping and redundant consequences, activating any particular effector is likely to influence multiple regulated variables.

In sum, numerous homeostatic reflexes are available to maintain certain vital parameters in the body within strict limits. When these limits are exceeded in one direction or the other, a subset of available reflexes is recruited, the exact effectors used depending upon environmental and internal conditions.[21] For example, if glucose metabolism decreases, initial defenses might include the secretion of catecholamines or glucagon to increase acute glucose secretion into the blood from the liver; if the hypoglycemia is more persistent, more chronically acting hormones such as cortisol/corticosterone might be secreted. Increased eating may be recruited, but its glucose restorative ability is relatively slow, and any benefit in terms of increasing available glucose is not immediate. In fact, eating in the face of hypoglycemia might better be viewed as precluding future glucose shortages than correcting an existing one.[4,23]

When body weight is displaced from its usual level, the first effector typically activated is altered food intake. For example, individuals who have dieted and lost weight tend to eat more food (typically larger meals) until weight is restored. Changes of metabolic rate or of exercise are less preferred strategies as they come with other costs, impacting other regulated parameters. Nonetheless, if an individual's weight is above or below the weight the brain is striving to maintain (sometimes called a set point or settling point for weight), and appropriate changes of food intake are not possible, then changes of metabolism and/or exercise are recruited as effectors[24,25]; and although they may require more time than changes of food intake, they eventually get the job done.

NEGATIVE FEEDBACK VERSUS FEED-FORWARD CONTROL

To summarize, food intake is influenced by metabolic activity in hypothalamic neurons and elsewhere; by hormones that signal the body's fat content to the brain; and by other homeostatic-need situations such as low blood glucose. All of these represent instances of negative feedback. If brain metabolism is too low or too high, eating is impacted; if body fat is too low or too high, eating is impacted; if blood glucose is too low or too high, eating is impacted; and so on. All are examples of eating being an effector recruited in response to a challenge to a homeostatically regulated variable. However, this conception fails to capture the predominant influences over eating; that is, rather than eating being a reflex to correct a homeostatic perturbation, it is better viewed as anticipating and thus circumventing homeostatic perturbations.[20,21,26]

EATING AS AN ANTICIPATORY BEHAVIOR

As discussed elsewhere, it is maladaptive to have to rely upon changes in vital parameters and subsequent recruitment of corrective reflexes as a primary mode of regulation.[27] Rather, at least at the behavioral level, most regulation is anticipatory, providing what might be needed before any

need arises. In this light, eating can be viewed as stockpiling ample energy-laden nutrients to meet future metabolic needs.

Rather than reacting to homeostatic perturbations through negative feedback, effector activity can be calibrated based on past experience and thereby prevent significant homeostatic deviations from ever occurring. With regard to eating, meal size, meal frequency, and dietary choice are highly flexible effector mechanisms that can be adjusted to best maintain body adiposity, blood glucose, brain metabolism, and other regulated variables. For example, imposing restrictions that temporally limit food availability (e.g., changing from free food access to a single daily window of time when food is available) results in dramatically increased meal size that mitigates reductions in body fat.[28,29] For this preventive strategy to be effective, animals use past experience to accurately anticipate environmental challenges so that corrective or compensatory effector activity can be initiated prior to any actual homeostatic perturbation. Learning is the adaptive mechanism enabling these effector changes to be controlled in this way. Learned cues such as the time of day signal a pending change in conditions so that effector activity can be adjusted appropriately to meet the demands of the situation.

This feed-forward strategy has important implications. A highly flexible behavioral effector like food intake can present major challenges to metabolism. As an example, if the environment dictates that in order to maintain body weight, an individual becomes "meal fed" and must eat only one very large meal each day, it adapts by learning to make anticipatory responses to increase the efficiency and capacity of the digestive system, and at the same time to limit the impact of absorbing so much new energy into the blood at one time.[26,30]

EATING AND DRUG TAKING

Pertinent to the theme of this volume, like eating, drug taking presents major challenges to homeostatically regulated variables; that is, the value of learning to activate effectors to prevent regulated variables from being overly perturbed is as relevant to drug taking as it is to ingestion. The use of effector mechanisms to progressively diminish perturbations caused by drug effects is described as drug tolerance that permits the escalation of drug taking. We have argued[21,26,27] that tolerance also develops to foods in that the physiological disturbances caused by eating can be mitigated by the well-synchronized activation of controlled effectors made possible by learning. An important implication is that highly conditioned individuals, whether tolerant or addicted to drugs or else trained on an extreme meal-feeding schedule, are vulnerable to metabolic mishaps. Making anticipatory responses but failing to get the anticipated drug or food creates symptoms of withdrawal and can lead to an escalating spiral of dependence on both the anticipatory responses and the drug/food effects.[21]

CONCLUSION

Metabolic processes are intimately intertwined with food intake. Changes in both can be adequately adjusted to the environment to preclude major perturbations in homeostatically regulated systems, but only if the environment is predictable. Learning plays a critical role in adapting these processes to specific situations. The regulatory context plays a critical role in how metabolism and food intake interact.

ACKNOWLEDGMENTS

The Helen Riaboff Whiteley Center at Friday Harbor Laboratories is gratefully acknowledged for providing an ideal setting to write this chapter. Supported in part by National Institutes of Health grants DK 067550 and DA 023484.

REFERENCES

1. Davis JD, Smith GP. Learning to sham feed: behavioral adjustments to loss of physiological postingestional stimuli. *Am J Physiol* 1990;259(6 Pt 2):R1228–R1235.

2. Thaler JP, Cummings DE. Minireview: hormonal and metabolic mechanisms of diabetes remission after gastrointestinal surgery. *Endocrinology* 2009;150(6): 2518–2525.

3. Mayer J. Regulation of energy intake and the body weight: the glucostatic and lipostatic hypothesis. *Ann NY Acad Sci* 1955; 63:14–42.

4. Langhans W. Metabolic and glucostatic control of feeding. *Proc Nutr Soc* 1996;55:497–515.

5. Smith GP, Epstein AN. Increased feeding in response to decreased glucose utilization in rat and monkey. *Am J Physiol* 1969; 217:1083–1087.

6. Sandoval DA, Cota D, Seeley RJ. The integrative role of CNS fuel-sensing mechanisms in energy balance and glucose regulation. *Ann Rev Physiol* 2007;70:513–535.

7. Woods SC, D'Alessio DA. Central control of body weight and appetite. *J Clin Endocrinol Metab* 2008;93(11 suppl 1):S37–S50.

8. Levin BE, Routh VH, Kang L, Sanders NM, Dunn-Meynell AA. Neuronal glucosensing: what do we know after 50 years? *Diabetes* 2004;53(10):2521–2528.

9. Obici S, Feng Z, Morgan K, Stein D, Karkanias G, Rosetti L. Central administration of oleic acid inhibits glucose production and food intake. *Diabetes* 2002;51(2):271–275.

10. Obici S, Rossetti L. Minireview: nutrient sensing and the regulation of insulin action and energy balance. *Endocrinology* 2003;144(12):5172–5178.

11. Cota D, Proulx K, Smith KA, et al. Hypothalamic mTOR signaling regulates food intake. *Science* 2006;312(5775):927–930.

12. Konner AC, Klockener T, Bruning JC. Control of energy homeostasis by insulin and leptin: targeting the arcuate nucleus and beyond. *Physiol Behav* 2009;97(5): 632–638.

13. Woods SC, Seeley RJ, Cota D. Regulation of food intake through hypothalamic signaling networks involving mTOR. *Annu Rev Nutr* 2008;28: 295–311.

14. Friedman MI. Control of energy intake by energy metabolism. *Am J Clin Nutr* 1995;62(5 suppl): 1096S–1100S.

15. Nicolaidis S, Even P. Physiological determinant of hunger, satiation, and satiety. *Am J Clin Nutr* 1985;42 (5 suppl):1083–1092.

16. Schwartz MW, Woods SC, Porte D Jr, Seeley RJ, Baskin DG. Central nervous system control of food intake. *Nature* 2000;404(6778):661–671.

17. Woods SC, Seeley RJ, Porte D Jr, Schwartz MW. Signals that regulate food intake and energy homeostasis. *Science* 1998; 280(5368):1378–1383.

18. Kahn BB, Alquier T, Carling D, Hardie DG. AMP-activated protein kinase: ancient energy gauge provides clues to modern understanding of metabolism. *Cell Metab* 2005;1(1):15–25.

19. Kahn BB, Myers MG Jr. mTOR tells the brain that the body is hungry. *Nat Med* 2006;12(6):615–617.

20. Woods SC. The control of food intake: behavioral versus molecular perspectives. *Cell Metab* 2009;9(6): 489–498.

21. Ramsay DS, Woods SC. Biological consequences of drug administration: implications for acute and chronic tolerance. *Psychol Rev* 1997;104:170–193.

22. Kaiyala KJ, Ramsay DS. Assessment of heat production, heat loss, and core temperature during nitrous oxide exposure: a new paradigm for studying drug effects and opponent responses. *Am J Physiol Regul Integr Comp Physiol* 2005;288(3):R692–R701.

23. Woods SC. The house economist and the eating paradox. *Appetite* 2002;38:161–165.

24. Bernardis LL, Frohman LA. Effect of lesion size in the ventromedial hypothalamus on growth hormone and insulin levels in weanling rats. *Neuroendocrinology* 1970;6(5):319–328.

25. Bi S, Moran TH. Actions of CCK in the controls of food intake and body weight: lessons from the CCK-A receptor deficient OLETF rat. *Neuropeptides* 2002;36:171–181.

26. Woods SC, The eating paradox: how we tolerate food. *Psychol Rev* 1991;98:488–505.

27. Woods SC, Ramsay DS. Homeostasis: beyond Curt Richter. *Appetite* 2007;49(2):388–398.

28. Collier G, Johnson DF, Mathis C. The currency of procurement cost. *J Exp Anal Behav* 2002;78(1):31–61.

29. West DB, Fey D, Woods SC. Cholecystokinin persistently suppresses meal size but not food intake in free-feeding rats. *Am J Physiol* 1984;246 (5 Pt 2):R776–R787.

30. Drazen DL, Vahl TP, D'Alessio DA, Seeley RJ, Woods SC. Effects of a fixed meal pattern on ghrelin secretion: evidence for a learned response independent of nutrient status. *Endocrinology* 2006;147:23–30.

16

Neuroendocrine Regulation of Energy Balance

MARCELO O. DIETRICH AND TAMAS L. HORVATH

In mammals, energy balance is dictated by energy intake and expenditure. The former is mostly derived from food consumption, even though modern societies have seen an increase in the use of high-calorie (energy) drinks that provide an additional source of energy (drink intake). Mammals cannot derive energy from other sources, even though other biological systems can. For example, plants extract energy from sunlight through the process of photosynthesis. Thus, the regulation of energy intake in mammals is quite simple, since only food or drink supplies the energy. On the other hand, energy expenditure is a more complex part of the equation consisting of a basal expenditure that is utilized for autonomic functions, as well as an activity-dependent expenditure that is determined by the individual.

The whole organism is involved in the regulation of energy balance, accomplished through crosstalk between the peripheral organs and the central nervous system to regulate momentary and long-term energy balance. This is a very tightly maintained system, evidenced by the fact that minimal disruptions in energy balance can generate severe consequences to body metabolism. For example, if a typical human consumes 2,000 calories (Cal) per day, and expends 1,970 Cal, he or she will have a net positive balance of 30 Cal per day (less than a bite of a chocolate bar). This minimal amount of positive balance per day will generate an approximately 12,000 Cal positive energy balance over the course of a year. Because this "extra" energy mainly deposits into the adipose tissue of mammals, it is expected that this 12,000 Cal will do just that. One gram of fat contains approximately 9 Cal; thus, this positive balance of 10,000+ Cal will accumulate more than 1 kg of fat over 1 year. If this persists, during the course of 10 years, this person will have a very large fat depot as a consequence of a "small" daily positive energy balance. The nature of this imbalance is unknown; however, a modern lifestyle in which high calorie consumption comes mainly from fat and simple sugars and is combined with low energy expenditure (sedentary society) is likely to be a major contributor. Other factors are also implicated, such as high levels of stress and/or sleep deprivation, which are prevalent in today's society. This chapter touches upon these issues and delineates our current understanding and some state-of-the-art ideas as to how the brain contributes to the regulation of energy balance (and its imbalance).

THE BRAIN AS A CENTRAL REGULATOR OF ENERGY BALANCE

Even though various brain areas are essential for the regulation of both energy intake and expenditure, it is noteworthy that several other tissues produce a myriad of substances (hormones, cytokines, etc.) that will in turn affect the central nervous system. Thus, appropriate signaling between peripheral organs and the brain is critical to maintaining the physiological regulation of energy balance.

As a side note, it is worth looking at this from an evolutionary perspective in that neural cells did not compose the first individuals, or, at least, neural cells were not the first cells to emerge on the evolutionary scale. This fact implies that these cells are a consequent specialization of the evolutionary process based upon a predecessor. Thus, it is a plausible idea that during the course of evolution, not only did brain cells emerge, but the ability of these cells to sense factors being released by other cells of the body did as well. This concept has been explored over the past decades in biological systems and has proven to be correct.

The brain can be described as being composed of a complex network of nuclei that communicate with each other to dictate behavior as well as regulate bodily functions. The first studies to elucidate some of the brain structures that are important in the regulation of energy balance date back to the early 1900s. These earlier findings suggested that the basal part of the brain was involved in the regulation of homeostatic functions. More detailed examinations identified the precise nuclei that regulate energy balance in mammals. Lesions to more medial parts of the basal hypothalamus were found to cause hyperphagia and obesity.[1-4] This region, the ventromedial hypothalamic nucleus (VMH), was then considered to be the "satiety center" of the brain. On the other hand, bilateral lesions to more lateral areas of the hypothalamus led to a complete cessation of feeding, distinguishing it as the "hunger center."[3,4]

This classic "two-center" hypothesis is still in use today and several reports have confirmed these data using more advanced techniques. Later, chemical lesions caused by monosodium glutamate identified the arcuate nucleus (ARC) within the hypothalamus as a key region in the regulation of food intake.[5-7] Rodents treated with monosodium glutamate became obese, an observation that highlighted the significance of cells within the ARC that were sensitive to this chemical as having an anorexigenic tone. Together with lesion data showing that whole ARC damage causes very little change in energy balance, these results raised the idea of the existence of another group of cells in the ARC with orexigenic properties (not sensitive to monosodium glutamate). This important observation was the earliest footprint of the subsequent elucidation of the melanocortin system of the ARC (see next section).

THE ARC MELANOCORTIN SYSTEM AS A KEY METABOLIC SENSOR

The ARC is located in the most basal part of the brain and is a key region in the regulation of several neuroendocrine responses and homeostatic signals.[8] The putative lack of a blood–brain barrier in this part of the brain indicates that it can serve as a sensor for peripheral signals.[9-12] Within the ARC are located two groups of neurons that have singular importance in the regulation of energy homeostasis. One of these groups of neurons expresses neuropeptide-y (Npy) and the agouti-related protein (Agrp).[13] The Npy/Agrp neurons exert an orexigenic tone (stimulate food intake)

by sending projections to several brain areas, most important the paraventricular nucleus of the hypothalamus (PVN)[14-17] and the parabrachial nucleus in the brainstem (PBN).[18] These neurons have been shown to be inhibitory cells, utilizing GABA as a neurotransmitter.[19]

The other population of cells located in the ARC is known to express proopiomelanocortin (POMC) derived peptides, such as alpha-MSH and CART. The POMC cells exert an anorexigenic tone; thus, their activation leads to cessation of feeding and satiety.[20] The contrasting nature of these two cell populations within the ARC helps explain why lesions to the whole ARC have little effect on food intake. It is also worth emphasizing the intricate network that exists between these cell groups in the ARC, such that the Npy/Agrp neurons send GABAergic projections to the POMC cells.[21-23] Thus, an orexigenic stimulus can induce food intake by activating Npy/Agrp cells and concomitantly inhibiting the neighboring POMC cells. This seemingly redundant network is an important evolutionary outcome comprising a constitutive mechanism by which an orexigenic response is preferred over one which is anorexigenic. This organization of the ARC connections was likely important during periods of limited food availability, maintaining a status of hunger as the default in the brain. As indicated in the next section, the connectivity of these cells in the ARC fluctuates depending on hormone levels and according to energy availability, thus providing evidence of a mechanism by which the brain senses peripheral signals to coordinate energy balance.

SYNAPTIC PLASTICITY MODULATES THE NEUROENDOCRINE RESPONSE IN THE ARC: HOW THE BRAIN SENSES HORMONES

Earlier studies indicated that peripheral factors were acting in the brain to promote satiety. Indeed, two centuries ago, the famous English physiologist Sir Charles Sherrington proposed that food intake (and energy expenditure) could be regulated in a similar way as respiration, where peripheral organs produce substances that travel through the blood to signal the brain. Further breakthroughs came in the 1950s with several findings from studies of the obese and diabetic phenotype of the naturally occurring *ob/ob* and *db/db* mice, respectively. The *ob/ob* mice were first described by Jackson Laboratories as mice with a massive obese phenotype.[24] The inheritability of this mutant followed a recessive ratio according to Mendel's law.[24] The *obese* (*ob/ob*) gene was later found to occur on chromosome 6 of these mice.

In the wake of this discovery, some of the first experiments on this mutant mouse provided insight into how the earlier physiologists identified the mechanisms implicated in energy homeostasis. In the 1950s–1970s, parabiosis was one of the few techniques available to identify blood factors that could influence physiology. Using this method it was possible to combine the blood circulation of two animals and study whether a humoral factor from one could affect the other. Research headed by Coleman utilized parabiosis to investigate the missing factor in the *ob/ob* mouse.[25,26] When an *ob/ob* mouse was conjoined with a normal mouse, the body weight of the obese mouse slowly approached normal, indicating that a circulating factor from the control mouse was able to signal the obese animal to lose weight. A similar experiment was done using the diabetic mouse (*db/db*). In this case, the *db/db* mouse had no major modification of its phenotype; however, the normal mouse lost weight, so much so that it nearly starved.[25,26] In this case, a factor produced in the *db/db* mouse was traveling into the blood of the control, causing it to stop eating.

Years later, utilizing more advanced techniques, researchers lead by Dr. Jeffrey Friedman (1994) using point mutation identified the gene involved in the obese phenotype of the *ob/ob* mouse.[27,28] The protein encoded by this gene was called leptin, from the greek *leptos*, meaning thin.[28] Not long after this discovery, the gene missing in the *db/db* mouse was also revealed and was found to be the receptor for leptin,[27,29,30] thus explaining the findings of the parabiosis studies of Coleman.[25,26] Moreover, leptin was found to be produced mainly by the fat tissue, and the *db/db* mouse, which was obese, had high levels of circulating leptin. Thus, in the parabiosis studies, leptin crossed the circulation from the *db/db* mouse and acted in the normal mouse, leading it to starve.[25–27]

The discovery of this important anorexigenic protein, leptin, led to a better understanding of how hormones could act in the brain to modulate energy metabolism. Ten years after its discovery, another important finding by the laboratory of Dr. Tamas Horvath (2004) shed light on the brain

mechanisms implicated in the sensing of peripheral stimuli.[23] Utilizing POMC-GFP and Npy/Agrp-GFP transgenic mice (mice in which green fluorescent protein is under the transcriptional control of either the POMC or Npy genomic sequence), they found that leptin induces a rapid rearrangement of the ARC neuronal circuitry that is responsible for governing energy balance.[23] When leptin-deficient mice (*ob/ob*, i.e., *Lep*$^{-/-}$) were compared to wild-type mice, they exhibited an increased number of excitatory inputs on the Npy/Agrp cells, with a concomitant decrease in the number of inhibitory inputs on these cells. The opposite profile was observed for the POMC neurons of the ARC. Interestingly, leptin replacement to the *Le*$^{-/-}$ mice reversed these neuroanatomical adaptations so that they were like that of the wild-type phenotype, thus indicating that these connections were sensitive to peripheral hormones and could modulate energy balance by orchestrating the synaptic inputs onto the ARC neurons.[23] Following this work, another study raised the possibility of targeting this mechanism of synaptic remodeling to treat eating disorders. By administering estrogen to obese mice, Gao and collaborators mimicked the effects of leptin on the synaptic inputs of POMC and Npy/Agrp cells, resulting in decreased body adiposity over time.[31]

The discovery of the brain as a tissue that undergoes constant remodeling[23,31–35] opened avenues for several lines of thinking about how brain can adapt and regulate energy homeostasis. One of these very interesting hypotheses that takes into account the plasticity of the adult brain is the postulation that newly formed neurons in the hypothalamus can have an effect on regulating food intake. The first report to raise this possibility showed that treatment with CNTF, a cytokine known to decrease body weight, induces the proliferation of cells in the hypothalamus.[36] Many of these cells differentiated into neurons that were responsive to hormones, such as leptin. The anorexigenic effect of CNTF was counteracted by the elimination of cell proliferation in the brain, emphasizing the likely importance of cell division in the adult brain under certain circumstances to modulate energy metabolism.[36,37] This study was followed by a recent publication showing that slow ablation of Agrp neurons in the ARC induces cell proliferation in the same area, and part of these new cells differentiate into Agrp neurons.[38] When cell proliferation was inhibited in the brain containing the ablated

Agrp neurons, the mice lost weight and decreased their body adiposity. Overall, these data indicate that the hypothalamus is capable of neurogenesis even in the adult brain, and that this process is important for the regulation of food intake.[36–38]

HORMONAL CROSS-TALK BETWEEN PERIPHERAL ORGANS AND THE BRAIN

So far, this chapter has described the effects of leptin as a model of an anorexigenic molecule that allows for communication between the fat tissue and the brain. However, leptin is not the only hormone important in the regulation of energy metabolism. Indeed, there are a growing number of peptides, proteins, hormones, and cytokines being described as modulators of energy balance.

Contrasting the effects of leptin is a well-known orexigenic peptide, ghrelin. Ghrelin consists of 28 amino acids and is released by the gut.[39,40] Its release from the stomach is mainly at times of negative energy balance. Ghrelin reaches the blood and signals the ARC neurons to induce food intake through the G-protein-coupled growth hormone secretagog receptor (GHSR).[41–43] Interestingly, ghrelin is produced as a larger peptide, which is cleaved into at least two small molecules.[39,44–46] The other part of the pre-ghrelin cleavage has been described to have opposite actions to ghrelin, promoting satiety.[46] This peptide has been named obestatin and is just one example of the complexity of the hormonal network involved in the regulation of energy balance.[45,46] Moreover, the involvement of ghrelin to modulate appetite and metabolism has been a target of intense investigation, leading to new concepts in neuroendocrinology. First, it has been shown that the effect of ghrelin to promote appetite is dependent upon fatty acid metabolism in the hypothalamus.[47] This effect was reliant upon mitochondrial energy metabolism, indicating for the first time that a peripheral hormone can alter brain bioenergetics, and thus, can ultimately change energy balance.[47] Intriguingly, fatty acid metabolism through beta-oxidation has been neglected as a pathway involved in the production of energy by neuronal cells. These studies challenge this classic concept and provide more insight into the flexibility of the brain to adapt to different environmental conditions. Another interesting fact about the physiology of ghrelin is that it needs to be modified to be active. The acylation of ghrelin by the enzyme, GOAT, transforms it from its inactive to its active form.[48–51] The availability of GOAT has been shown to be dependent upon the presence of specific lipids in the diet, thereby linking the ingestion of lipids with energy balance.[52]

Leptin as a classic anorexigenic molecule and ghrelin as a representative orexigenic molecule are just a couple of examples of substances involved in the intricate field of metabolic integration of energy balance. Innumerable new molecules that play a role in modulating energy metabolism are regularly being described, thus adding to the already complex neuroendocrine network that regulates food intake and energy expenditure.

REFERENCES

1. Hetherington A, Ranson S. The relation of various hypothalamic lesions to adiposity in the rat. *J Comp Neurol* 1942;76:475–499.
2. Hetherington A. Non-production of hypothalamic obesity in the rat by lesions rostral or dorsal to the ventro-medial hypothalamic nuclei. *J Comp Neurol* 1944;80:33–45.
3. Anand B, Brobeck J. Hypothalamic control of food intake in rats and cats. *Yale J Biol Med* 1951;24:123–140.
4. Anand B, Brobeck J. Localization of a "feeding center" in the hypothalamus of the rat. *Proc Soc Exp Biol Med* 1951;77:323–324.
5. Olney J. Brain lesions, obesity, and other disturbances in mice treated with monosodium glutamate. *Science* 1969;164:719–721.
6. Olney J, Sharpe L. Brain lesions in an infant rhesus monkey treated with monsodium glutamate. *Science* 1969;166:386–388.
7. Olney J, Adamo N, Ratner A. Monosodium glutamate effects. *Science* 1971;172:294.
8. Cone R. Anatomy and regulation of the central melanocortin system. *Nat Neurosci* 2005;8:571–578.
9. Brightman M, Broadwell R. The morphological approach to the study of normal and abnormal brain permeability. *Adv Exp Med Biol* 1976;69:41–54.
10. Broadwell R, Brightman M. Entry of peroxidase into neurons of the central and peripheral nervous systems from extracerebral and cerebral blood. *J Comp Neurol* 1976;166:257–283.
11. Broadwell R, Balin B, Salcman M, Kaplan R. Brain-blood barrier? Yes and no. *Proc Natl Acad Sci USA* 1983;80:7352–7356.
12. Norsted E, Gömüç B, Meister B. Protein components of the blood-brain barrier (BBB) in the mediobasal hypothalamus. *J Chem Neuroanat* 2008;36:107–121.
13. Hahn T, Breininger J, Baskin D, Schwartz M. Coexpression of Agrp and NPY in fasting-activated hypothalamic neurons. *Nat Neurosci* 1998;1:271–272.

14. Bai F, Yamano M, Inagaki S, et al. Distribution of neuropeptides in the hypothalamo-hypophyseal system in the rat: an immunohistochemical observation. *Cell Mol Biol* 1984;30:437–452.

15. Bai F, Yamano M, Shiotani Y et al. An arcuato-paraventricular and -dorsomedial hypothalamic neuropeptide Y-containing system which lacks noradrenaline in the rat. *Brain Res* 1985;331:172–175.

16. Lu D, Willard D, Patel I et al. Agouti protein is an antagonist of the melanocyte-stimulating-hormone receptor. *Nature* 1994;371:799–802.

17. Fan W, Boston B, Kesterson R, Hruby V, Cone R. Role of melanocortinergic neurons in feeding and the agouti obesity syndrome. *Nature* 1997;385:165–168.

18. Wu Q, Boyle M, Palmiter R. Loss of GABAergic signaling by AgRP neurons to the parabrachial nucleus leads to starvation. *Cell* 2009;137:1225–1234.

19. Horvath T, Bechmann I, Naftolin F, Kalra S, Leranth C. Heterogeneity in the neuropeptide Y-containing neurons of the rat arcuate nucleus: GABAergic and non-GABAergic subpopulations. *Brain Res* 1997;756:283–286.

20. Zigman J, Elmquist J. Minireview: from anorexia to obesity—the yin and yang of body weight control. *Endocrinology* 2003;144:3749–3756.

21. Horvath T, Naftolin F, Kalra S, Leranth C. Neuropeptide-Y innervation of beta-endorphin-containing cells in the rat mediobasal hypothalamus: a light and electron microscopic double immunostaining analysis. *Endocrinology* 1992;131:2461–2467.

22. Cowley M, Smart J, Rubinstein M, et al. Leptin activates anorexigenic POMC neurons through a neural network in the arcuate nucleus. *Nature* 2001;411:480–484.

23. Pinto S, Roseberry A, Liu H, et al. Rapid rewiring of arcuate nucleus feeding circuits by leptin. *Science* 2004;304:110–115.

24. Ingalls A, Dickie M, Snell G. Obese, a new mutation in the house mouse. *J Hered* 1950;41:317–318.

25. Coleman D. Effects of parabiosis of obese with diabetes and normal mice. *Diabetologia* 1973;9:294–298.

26. Coleman D, Hummel K. Effects of parabiosis of normal with genetically diabetic mice. *Am J Physiol* 1969;217:1298–1304.

27. Coleman D. Obese and diabetes: two mutant genes causing diabetes-obesity syndromes in mice. *Diabetologia* 1978;14:141–148.

28. Zhang Y, Proenca R, Maffei M, Barone M, Leopold L, Friedman J. Positional cloning of the mouse obese gene and its human homologue. *Nature* 1994;372:425–432.

29. Hummel K, Dickie M, Coleman D. Diabetes, a new mutation in the mouse. *Science* 1966;153:1127–1128.

30. Chen H, Charlat O, Tartaglia L, et al. Evidence that the diabetes gene encodes the leptin receptor: identification of a mutation in the leptin receptor gene in db/db mice. *Cell* 1996;84:491–495.

31. Gao Q, Mezei G, Nie Y, et al. Anorectic estrogen mimics leptin's effect on the rewiring of melanocortin cells and Stat3 signaling in obese animals. *Nat Med* 2007;13:89–94.

32. Matsumoto A, Arai Y. Synaptogenic effect of estrogen on the hypothalamic arcuate nucleus of the adult female rat. *Cell Tissue Res* 1979;198:427–433.

33. Garcia-Segura L, Baetens D, Naftolin F. Synaptic remodelling in arcuate nucleus after injection of estradiol valerate in adult female rats. *Brain Res* 1986;366:131–136.

34. Garcia-Segura L, Olmos G, Tranque P, Naftolin F. Rapid effects of gonadal steroids upon hypothalamic neuronal membrane ultrastructure. *J Steroid Biochem* 1987;27:615–623.

35. Olmos G, Aguilera P, Tranque P, Naftolin F, Garcia-Segura L. Estrogen-induced synaptic remodelling in adult rat brain is accompanied by the reorganization of neuronal membranes. *Brain Res* 1987;425:57–64.

36. Kokoeva M, Yin H, Flier J. Neurogenesis in the hypothalamus of adult mice: potential role in energy balance. *Science* 2005;310:679–683.

37. Kokoeva M, Yin H, Flier J. Evidence for constitutive neural cell proliferation in the adult murine hypothalamus. *J Comp Neurol* 2007;505:209–220.

38. Pierce A, Xu A. De novo neurogenesis in adult hypothalamus as a compensatory mechanism to regulate energy balance. *J Neurosci* 2010;30:723–730.

39. Kojima M, Hosoda H, Date Y, Nakazato M, Matsuo H, Kangawa K. Ghrelin is a growth-hormone-releasing acylated peptide from stomach. *Nature* 1999;402:656–660.

40. Date Y, Kojima M, Hosoda H, et al. Ghrelin, a novel growth hormone-releasing acylated peptide, is synthesized in a distinct endocrine cell type in the gastrointestinal tracts of rats and humans. *Endocrinology* 2000;141:4255–4261.

41. Wren A, Small C, Ward H, et al. The novel hypothalamic peptide ghrelin stimulates food intake and growth hormone secretion. *Endocrinology* 2000;141:4325–4328.

42. Tang-Christensen M, Vrang N, Ortmann S, Bidlingmaier M, Horvath T, Tschöp M. Central administration of ghrelin and agouti-related protein (83–132) increases food intake and decreases spontaneous locomotor activity in rats. *Endocrinology* 2004;145:4645–4652.

43. Williams D, Cummings D. Regulation of ghrelin in physiologic and pathophysiologic states. *J Nutr* 2005;135:1320–1325.

44. Hosoda H, Kojima M, Matsuo H, Kangawa K. Purification and characterization of rat des-Gln14-Ghrelin, a second endogenous ligand for the growth hormone secretagogue receptor. *J Biol Chem* 2000;275:21995–2000.

45. Hosoda H, Kojima M, Matsuo H, Kangawa K. Ghrelin and des-acyl ghrelin: two major forms of rat
ghrelin peptide in gastrointestinal tissue. *Biochem
Biophys Res Commun* 2000;279:909–913.

46. Zhang J, Ren P, Avsian-Kretchmer O, et al. Obestatin, a peptide encoded by the ghrelin gene, opposes
ghrelin's effects on food intake. *Science* 2005;310:
996–999.

47. Andrews Z, Liu Z, Walllingford N, et al. UCP2 mediates ghrelin's action on NPY/AgRP neurons by lowering free radicals. *Nature* 2008;454:846–851.

48. Gutierrez J, Solenberg P, Perkins D et al. Ghrelin
octanoylation mediated by an orphan lipid trans-
ferase. *Proc Natl Acad Sci USA* 2008;105:6320–6325.

49. Yang J, Brown M, Liang G, Grishin N, Goldstein J.
Identification of the acyltransferase that octanoylates
ghrelin, an appetite-stimulating peptide hormone.
Cell 2008;132:387–396.

50. Yang J, Zhao T, Goldstein J, Brown M. Inhibition of
ghrelin O-acyltransferase (GOAT) by octanoylated
pentapeptides. *Proc Natl Acad Sci USA* 2008;105:
10750–10755.

51. Chen C, Asakawa A, Fujimiya M, Lee S, Inui A. Ghrelin gene products and the regulation of food intake and
gut motility. *Pharmacol Rev* 2009;61:430–481.

52. Kirchner H, Gutierrez J, Solenberg P, et al. GOAT
links dietary lipids with the endocrine control of
energy balance. *Nat Med* 2009;15:741–745.

17

Prenatal Programming of Obesity

Role of Macronutrient-Specific Peptide Systems

IRENE MORGANSTERN, JESSICA R. BARSON, AND
SARAH F. LEIBOWITZ

Accumulating clinical evidence indicates that the specific nutritional environment during early development can affect later feeding behavior as well as the metabolic state of the offspring.[1] Also, high maternal dietary intakes may stimulate specific food preferences in children.[1] Similar findings are obtained in rodent studies, showing prenatal exposure to diets rich in fat or carbohydrate or exposure to nicotine to increase food intake, body weight, and vulnerability toward obesity, as well as affect macronutrient preferences in the offspring.[2] Although the exact mechanisms underlying these prenatal effects are not clear, animal studies suggest that intrauterine factors may program appetite-regulating hormones and neurochemicals in the hypothalamus and that this occurs in a macronutrient-specific manner. Collectively, the studies described in this review demonstrate that nutritional status during gestation may program hypothalamic peptides that enhance consumption of specific dietary substances and contribute to an increased vulnerability toward obesity later in life.

NUTRIENT-SPECIFIC CONTROL OF FEEDING BEHAVIOR BY BRAIN PEPTIDES

Peptide systems of the hypothalamus function in the tight regulation of energy balance, by responding to peripheral hunger and satiety signals. Expression of orexigenic peptides, such as neuropeptide Y (NPY) and agouti-related peptide (AgRP) in the arcuate nucleus (ARC) and orexin (OX) and melanin-concentrating hormone (MCH) in the perifornical lateral hypothalamus (PFLH), is elevated during periods of starvation, and central injections of these same peptides are found to further stimulate feeding behavior.[3]

Additional evidence suggests that the regulation of energy balance by these hypothalamic peptides is macronutrient specific, differentially affected by foods rich in carbohydrates or fats. In the ARC where neurons are highly responsive to fluctuations in energy levels, NPY is found to be stimulated by consumption of carbohydrates such as sucrose rather than fat and to preferentially stimulate the ingestion of carbohydrates,[3,4] and AgRP has a role in relation to both sucrose and fat consumption.[5–7] These peptides in the ARC contrast with galanin (GAL) and opioid peptides enkephalin (ENK) and dynorphin (DYN) in the paraventricular nucleus (PVN), as well as OX and possibly MCH in the PFLH, which are more closely related to the consumption of dietary fat and preferentially stimulate intake of a high-fat diet.[8,9] In addition to fat, these peptides in the PVN and PFLH are also strongly, positively related to circulating levels of lipids, particularly triglycerides (TGs), which are invariably stimulated by fat consumption.[3,8,9] Given the important role these peptides play in both normal and excessive feeding behavior, they may be prime substrates for the prenatal programming of obesity. The studies described later in this chapter demonstrate how nutrient-specific manipulations of the intrauterine environment can differentially affect these peptide systems within the hypothalamic ARC, PVN, and PFLH regions, thereby resulting in distinct patterns of consummatory behavior and food preferences and long-term consequences for energy balance.

PERINATAL UNDERNUTRITION AND OVERNUTRITION

Early studies on prenatal and perinatal programming of obesity focused on gross nutritional status. In both clinical and preclinical studies, perinatal malnutrition was found to produce hyperphagia, weight gain, and metabolic disturbances in the offspring after weaning and into adulthood,[10,11] despite a reduction in early life body weight.[10] Energy-sensing peptide systems in the hypothalamus appear to be affected by perinatal undernutrition and may explain the changes in postnatal body weight. The offspring from protein-restricted dams, a model of gross undernutrition, consistently show an increase in hypothalamic expression of NPY during embryonic and adult stages.[12,13] Similarly, underfed pups raised in larger litters also exhibit increased NPY mRNA in the ARC.[14] Together, these studies suggest that animals malnourished prenatally or soon after birth become hyperphagic and heavier in adulthood, possibly due to increased expression of NPY, which is known to promote consumption specifically of carbohydrate-rich diets.

Similar to the effects of undernutrition, perinatal overnutrition can also have long-term consequences in the offspring. One often-employed model of overnutrition is a reduced litter size, which leads to adult hyperphagia along with increased body weight, body fat, circulating levels of lipids and satiety signals, such as leptin and insulin.[15,16] The elevated leptin and insulin can lead to resistance to these critical regulatory factors, thus disrupting energy balance and producing metabolic disturbances associated with obesity.[17] Similar to undernourished rats, these offspring show increased expression of NPY as well as AgRP mRNA in the ARC.[14] In addition, they have an increased density of hypothalamic GAL neurons, which is positively correlated with insulin levels and body weight.[15] Other changes in these animals prenatally exposed to overnutrition include increased expression of orexigenic peptides in the ARC nucleus, as well as a down-regulation of the leptin receptor that may be one possible mechanism of leptin resistance that promotes obesity.[14] The finding that undernutrition and overnutrition have some of the same long-term consequences on feeding behavior and hypothalamic peptide expression suggests that poor nutrition can come not only from a lack of calories but also from general overeating or consumption of imbalanced diets that are high in carbohydrates or fat.

PRENATAL CARBOHYDRATE-RICH DIET

Prenatal exposure to a carbohydrate-rich environment, like that occurring with prenatal sucrose

exposure or gestational diabetes, has been found to increase adiposity and obesity in adult offspring, with no alterations in TGs or free fatty acids.[18–20] Animal studies demonstrate that these disturbances may also be related to the stimulation of orexigenic peptides in utero. In adult rats exposed prenatally and until weaning to a high-carbohydrate diet as compared to a control diet, basal concentration of NPY in the ARC and PVN is unchanged, but responsiveness to the feeding-stimulatory effect of NPY is increased.[21,22] Moreover, dams bred to exhibit diet-induced obesity show a reduced number of glucose-inhibited cells in the hypothalamus after consumption of a sucrose-rich, high-energy diet.[23] Similar to these effects with sucrose, offspring from diabetic rats exhibit an increased number of NPY and GAL neurons in the ARC,[24] while offspring cross-fostered to diabetic dams after birth show enhanced NPY- and AgRP-immunoreactive cells in the ARC.[25] This programming of peptide systems may be specific to carbohydrate-sensitive hypothalamic regions, as the number of neurons in the PVN is either unaffected or reduced under these same conditions.[26] Additional behavioral studies demonstrate that animals from dams consuming a high-carbohydrate diet also show a strong preference for this macronutrient as adults.[22] Together, these studies suggest that offspring exposed to a prenatal environment of increased carbohydrate or elevated glucose levels have disturbances in energy- and carbohydrate-related peptides of the ARC, which are distinct from changes reported in fat-sensitive regions, such as the PVN, and may themselves enhance consumption of a carbohydrate diet.

PRENATAL HIGH-FAT DIET

Exposure to a high-fat diet during gestation and lactation causes disturbances in hypothalamic peptide systems and metabolic processes in offspring that again increase their propensity to develop obesity in adulthood.[27–29] This same in utero and early life exposure to a fat-rich diet results in increased expression in weanling rats of fat-sensitive peptides, such as GAL and ENK in the PVN and OX and MCH in the PFLH.[8,29] Epigenetic mechanisms of in utero fat exposure have recently been proposed, with evidence that perinatal fat consumption leads to promotor DNA hypomethylation of specific genes related to dopamine and ENK and that this effect is accompanied by increased expression of ENK, mu opioid receptors, and the dopamine transporter in mesocorticolimbic and hypothalamic brain regions.[30] While this high-fat diet exposure fails to stimulate NPY- and AgRP-expressing cells in the ARC of offspring from normal-weight dams,[8] studies using dams that have become obese on the high-fat diet describe enhanced expression of these peptides,[27,28,31] suggesting that this effect may be a consequence of the obese state and resistance to the satiety hormones, rather than an effect of the high-fat diet. With the dams already obese during pregnancy as indicated by elevated levels of circulating insulin and leptin, the proliferative effects of in utero high-fat diet exposure may involve the actions of these hormones. This is supported by evidence that insulin can increase DNA, RNA, and protein synthesis in cell culture[32] and neuronal density in hypothalamic regions, such as the PVN.[33] Similarly, leptin, which is also increased by a high-fat diet, can act as a growth factor and increase neurogenesis in vivo.[34] Although these studies clearly demonstrate that high-fat diet exposure may have long-term effects on hypothalamic gene expression in embryonic, young and adult life stages, an interesting question to address is whether fat ingestion limited specifically to gestation, with no change in body weight or adiposity hormones, might have similar effects in the offspring.

Our laboratory has recently demonstrated that a brief, 2-week period of prenatal high-fat diet exposure, in addition to increasing body weight, caloric intake, and preference for dietary fat in the offspring, stimulates expression of a variety of peptides in the hypothalamus in postnatal offspring cross-fostered immediately after birth to dams consuming a balanced diet.[8] This same study was the first to report a stimulatory effect of 2-week, prenatal high-fat diet consumption on hypothalamic neuronal differentiation, proliferation, and migration in utero, providing a key step toward understanding mechanisms of fetal programming. Offspring (at postnatal day 21) from high-fat diet exposed dams demonstrated a significantly higher proportion of newly generated neurons and an increased number expressing the fat-responsive orexigenic peptides, OX and MCH in the PFLH (Fig. 17.1) and also ENK, DYN, and GAL in the PVN.[8] Further examination of the neuroepithelium during embryonic day 14, a time of increased neurogenesis in the hypothalamus, revealed a stimulatory effect of in utero high-fat diet exposure on the density of progenitor cells as well as on mature new neurons

and migrating neurons in and around the third ventricle, the place of origin of hypothalamic neurons (Fig. 17.2). Although the exact mechanism for these in utero changes induced by a high-fat diet is not yet understood, lipids circulating in the blood may be involved. The lipids, TGs, and fatty acids are increased by maternal consumption of a high-fat diet and readily pass through the placenta,[8,35] while levels of insulin and leptin are not affected.[8] This lipid-based mechanism is supported by evidence that fatty acids can stimulate neuronal proliferation and differentiation both in vivo and in vitro.[36,37] In addition, an essential fatty acid, docosahexaenoic acid, derived from foods as well as breast milk, is also known to enhance neurite outgrowth in neuronal cell culture.[38] These studies collectively demonstrate that fat-sensitive peptides within the PVN and PFLH are more responsive to in utero exposure to a fat-rich rich diet and are programmed, perhaps by circulating lipids, to enhance further fat consumption in offspring, thereby contributing to an obese state later in life.

PRENATAL NICOTINE EXPOSURE

A large body of literature in humans and a few in animals shows that prenatal nicotine exposure, similar to fat, leads to increased body weight and obesity.[39,40] In humans, this effect is dose dependent, becomes more apparent with age, and occurs independently of maternal weight and socioeconomic status.[41] In rats, it can be shown to occur with no change in litter size.[42] It is interesting that adult rats prenatally exposed to nicotine, similar to results obtained with dietary fat, have elevated plasma levels of TGs.[43] They also show increased insulin and leptin resistance,[40] which due to reduced satiety signaling may promote greater food intake. Although most studies with prenatal nicotine exposure have generally described a reduction in neuronal survival and cell number, these effects are more likely to occur at higher doses.[44,45] There are also two studies in rats with prenatal exposure to nicotine that examine changes in hypothalamic functioning. The first describes an increase in concentration of norepinephrine in the PVN,[46] where injection of this neurotransmitter can strongly enhance food consumption.[47] The second study shows a decrease in NPY mRNA in rhesus macaques,[48] similar to effects observed with prenatal fat consumption.[8] While not yet tested, prenatal nicotine could also

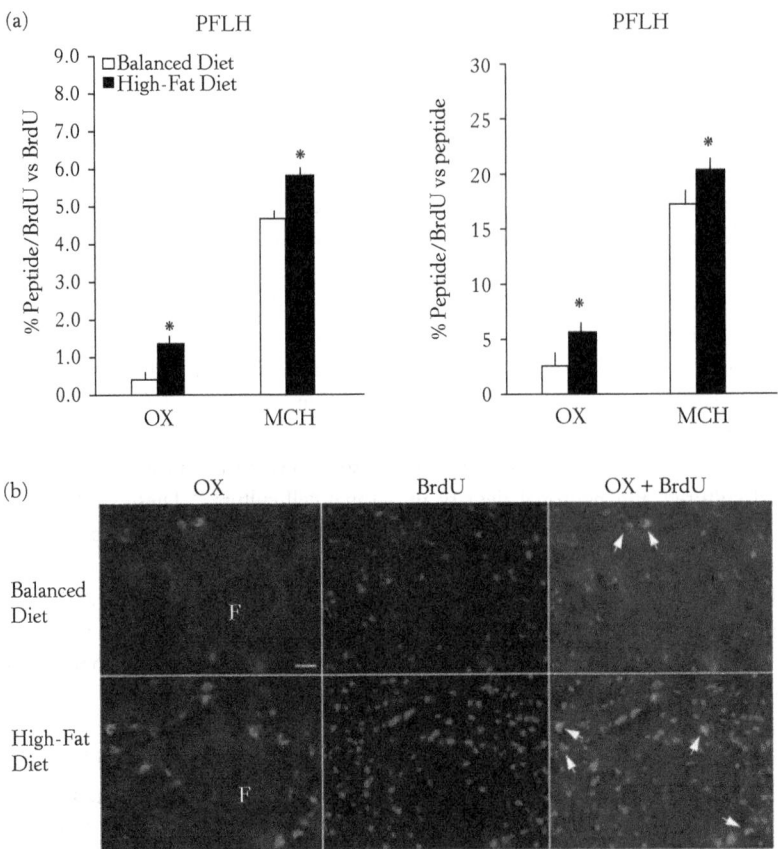

FIGURE 17.1. Prenatal high-fat diet increased neurogenesis in the perifornical lateral hypothalamus (PFLH) at postnatal age 21, specifically neurons that express orexigenic peptides. This is shown by (A) increased (*, $p < .01$) double-labeling of OX and MCH peptide with BrdU in PFLH neurons in high-fat diet compared to balanced diet offspring, as revealed by double-labeling immunofluorescence. Data (mean ± SEM) are expressed as % double-labeled cells relative to the total single-labeled BrdU+ cells (left) or peptide+ neurons (right); and (B) photomicrographs of offspring illustrating single-labeled OX-synthesizing neurons (green), single-labeled BrdU-immunoreactive cells (red), and double-labeled OX+ + BrdU+ neurons (green + red) in the PFLH, in the area of the fornix (F). Image is taken from our publication.

Source: Reprinted from Journal of Neuroscience, Vol 28, G. Q. Chang, V. Gaysinskaya, O. Karatayev & S. F. Leibowitz, Maternal high-fat diet and fetal programming: increased proliferation of hypothalamic peptide-producing neurons that increase risk for overeating and obesity , 12107–12119, Copyright (2008), with permission from Society for Neuroscience.

affect the development of fat-sensitive peptides, as injection of nicotine in adult rats increases ENK expression in the PVN[49] and OX activation in the PFLH.[50] Thus, prenatal exposure to cigarettes and nicotine appears to increase a drive toward food intake, possibly by enhancing hypothalamic fat-sensitive peptides in utero, which can eventually lead to an increased incidence of obesity.

CONCLUSION

Manipulations of the intrauterine environment with diet or nicotine can have long-lasting effects on body weight and obesity. These effects are mediated by changes in circulating hormones and in hypothalamic systems controlling food intake. The expression of orexigenic peptides, particularly the carbohydrate-sensitive peptide NPY and fat-sensitive peptides, OX, GAL, and ENK, is enhanced by prenatal exposure to carbohydrate- or fat-rich diets or exposure to nicotine in a nutrient-specific manner. In line with clinical studies,[1] the reviewed animal literature suggests that maternal consumption of diets rich in fat or carbohydrate stimulates a preference for these same substances in the offspring, which may be determined by increased neuronal proliferation and differentiation in utero.

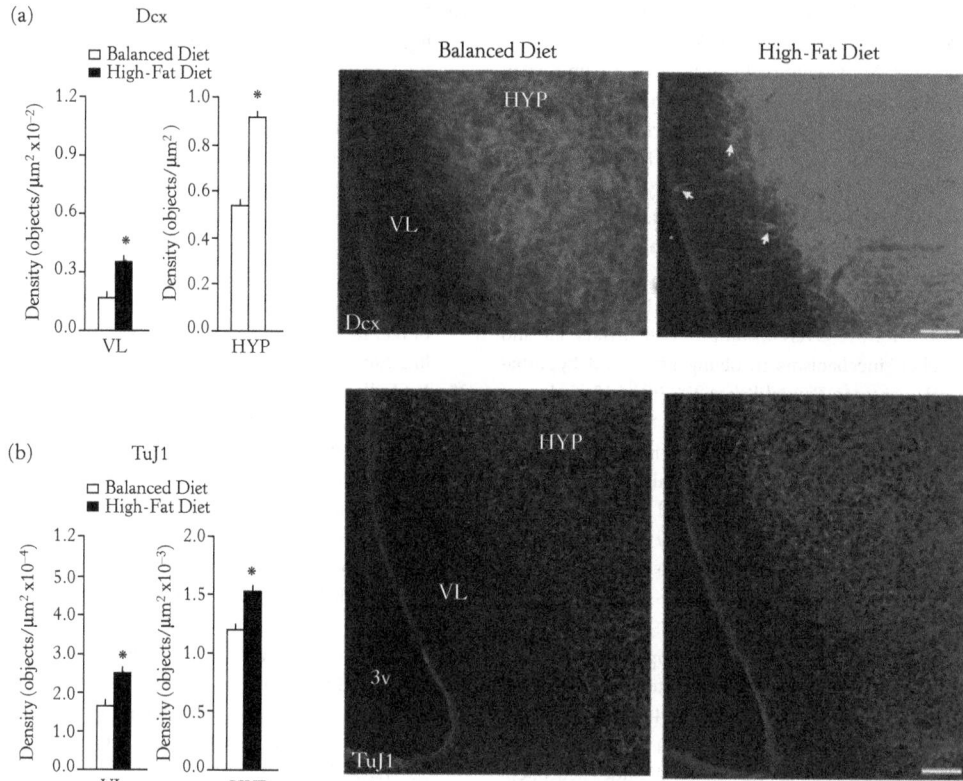

FIGURE 17.2. Embryos of high-fat diet dams at embryonic age 14 exhibited an increase in the development of neuronal precursor cell phenotype compared to embryos of balanced diet dams. This is demonstrated by single-labeling immunofluorescence, which revealed (A) an increased density (*, $p < .05$) in the high-fat diet embryos of Dcx$^+$ neurons in the ventral neuroepithelial lobe (VL) of the third ventricle (3v) and surrounding hypothalamic (HYP) area (left). This is illustrated to the right by photomicrographs of Dcx$^+$ neurons (green) that are considerably more dense in the HYP while still evident in the VL of high-fat diet embryos but not balanced diet embryos; and (B) an increased density (*, $p < .05$) of TuJ1$^+$ neuronal precursor cells in the VL and HYP (left), as illustrated to the right by photomicrographs of TuJ1$^+$ cells (red) in these areas surrounding the 3v.

Source: Reprinted from Journal of Neuroscience, Vol 28, G. Q. Chang, V. Gaysinskaya, O. Karatayev & S. F. Leibowitz, Maternal high-fat diet and fetal programming: increased proliferation of hypothalamic peptide-producing neurons that increase risk for overeating and obesity , 12107–12119, Copyright (2008), with permission from Society for Neuroscience.

We conclude that the prenatal environment is responsible for programming hypothalamic systems in a nutrient- and peptide-specific manner, which prepares the offspring for survival and growth in a similar environment after birth. However, when the offspring are born into an environment that has an overabundance of palatable and energy-rich foods, these peptide changes are detrimental and are likely to contribute to the worldwide obesity epidemic.

REFERENCES

1. Brion MJ, Ness AR, Rogers I, et al. Maternal macronutrient and energy intakes in pregnancy and offspring intake at 10 y: exploring parental comparisons and prenatal effects. *Am J Clin Nutr* 2010;91:748–756.
2. Metges CC. Early nutrition and later obesity: animal models provide insights into mechanisms. *Adv Exp Med Biol* 2009;646:105–112.
3. Leibowitz SF, Wortley KE. Hypothalamic control of energy balance: different peptides, different functions. *Peptides* 2004;25:473–504.
4. Beck B. Neuropeptide Y in normal eating and in genetic and dietary-induced obesity. *Phil Trans Royal Soc London* 2006;361:1159–1185.
5. Tracy AL, Clegg DJ, Johnson JD, Davidson TL, Benoit SC. The melanocortin antagonist AgRP (83–132) increases appetitive responding for a fat, but not a carbohydrate, reinforcer. *Pharmacol Biochem Behav* 2008;89:263–271.
6. Wang H, Storlien LH, Huang XF. Effects of dietary fat types on body fatness, leptin, and ARC leptin

receptor, NPY, and AgRP mRNA expression. *Am J Physiol* 2002;282:E1352–E1359.

7. Wirth MM, Giraudo SQ. Effect of Agouti-related protein delivered to the dorsomedial nucleus of the hypothalamus on intake of a preferred versus a non-preferred diet. *Brain Res* 2001;897:169–174.

8. Chang GQ, Gaysinskaya V, Karatayev O, Leibowitz SF. Maternal high-fat diet and fetal programming: increased proliferation of hypothalamic peptide-producing neurons that increase risk for overeating and obesity. *J Neurosci* 2008;28:12107–12119.

9. Leibowitz SF. Overconsumption of dietary fat and alcohol: mechanisms involving lipids and hypothalamic peptides. *Physiol Behav* 2007;91:513–521.

10. Orozco-Solis R, Lopes de Souza S, Barbosa Matos RJ, et al. Perinatal undernutrition-induced obesity is independent of the developmental programming of feeding. *Physiol Behav* 2009;96:481–492.

11. Ravelli GP, Stein ZA, Susser MW. Obesity in young men after famine exposure in utero and early infancy. *N Engl J Med* 1976;295:349–353.

12. Plagemann A, Waas T, Harder T, Rittel F, Ziska T, Rohde W. Hypothalamic neuropeptide Y levels in weaning offspring of low-protein malnourished mother rats. *Neuropeptides* 2000;34:1–6.

13. Terroni PL, Anthony FW, Hanson MA, Cagampang FR. Expression of agouti-related peptide, neuropeptide Y, pro-opiomelanocortin and the leptin receptor isoforms in fetal mouse brain from pregnant dams on a protein-restricted diet. *Brain Res* 2005;140: 111–115.

14. Lopez M, Seoane LM, Tovar S, et al. A possible role of neuropeptide Y, agouti-related protein and leptin receptor isoforms in hypothalamic programming by perinatal feeding in the rat. *Diabetologia* 2005;48:140–148.

15. Plagemann A, Harder T, Rake A, Melchior K, Rohde W, Dorner G. Increased number of galanin-neurons in the paraventricular hypothalamic nucleus of neonatally overfed weanling rats. *Brain Res* 1999;818:160–163.

16. Plagemann A, Heidrich I, Gotz F, Rohde W, Dorner G. Obesity and enhanced diabetes and cardiovascular risk in adult rats due to early postnatal overfeeding. *Exp Clin Endocrinol* 1992;99:154–158.

17. Morrison CD, Huypens P, Stewart LK, Gettys TW. Implications of crosstalk between leptin and insulin signaling during the development of diet-induced obesity. *Biochem Biophys Acta* 2009;1792: 409–416.

18. Ahlsson F, Lundgren M, Tuvemo T, Gustafsson J, Haglund B. Gestational diabetes and offspring body disproportion. *Acta Paediatr* 2010;99:89–93.

19. Plagemann A, Harder T, Franke K, Kohlhoff R. Long-term impact of neonatal breast-feeding on body weight and glucose tolerance in children of diabetic mothers. *Diabetes Care* 2002;25:16–22.

20. Sedova L, Seda O, Kazdova L, et al. Sucrose feeding during pregnancy and lactation elicits distinct metabolic response in offspring of an inbred genetic model of metabolic syndrome. *Am J Physiol* 2007;292:E1318–E1324.

21. Kozak R, Burlet A, Burlet C, Beck B. Dietary composition during fetal and neonatal life affects neuropeptide Y functioning in adult offspring. *Brain Res Dev Brain Res* 2000;125:75–82.

22. Kozak R, Richy S, Beck B. Persistent alterations in neuropeptide Y release in the paraventricular nucleus of rats subjected to dietary manipulation during early life. *Euro J Neurosci* 2005;21:2887–2892.

23. Le Foll C, Irani BG, Magnan C, Dunn-Meynell A, Levin BE. Effects of maternal genotype and diet on offspring glucose and fatty acid-sensing ventromedial hypothalamic nucleus neurons. *Am J Physiol Regul Integr Comp Physiol* 2009;297:R1351–R1357.

24. Plagemann A, Harder T, Rake A, et al. Hypothalamic insulin and neuropeptide Y in the offspring of gestational diabetic mother rats. *Neuroreport* 1998;9: 4069–4073.

25. Fahrenkrog S, Harder T, Stolaczyk E, et al. Cross-fostering to diabetic rat dams affects early development of mediobasal hypothalamic nuclei regulating food intake, body weight, and metabolism. *J Nutr* 2004;134:648–654.

26. Plagemann A, Harder T, Janert U, et al. Malformations of hypothalamic nuclei in hyperinsulinemic offspring of rats with gestational diabetes. *Dev Neurosci* 1999;21:58–67.

27. Chen H, Morris MJ. Differential responses of orexigenic neuropeptides to fasting in offspring of obese mothers. *Obesity (Silver Spring)* 2009;17: 1356–1362.

28. Page KC, Malik RE, Ripple JA, Anday EK. Maternal and postweaning diet interaction alters hypothalamic gene expression and modulates response to a high-fat diet in male offspring. *Am J Physiol Regul Integr Comp Physiol* 2009;297:R1049–R1057.

29. Beck B, Kozak R, Moar KM, Mercer JG. Hypothalamic orexigenic peptides are overexpressed in young Long-Evans rats after early life exposure to fat-rich diets. *Biochem Biophys Res Comm* 2006;342: 452–458.

30. Vucetic Z, Kimmel J, Totoki K, Hollenbeck E, Reyes TM. Maternal high-fat diet alters methylation and gene expression of dopamine and opioid-related genes. *Endocrinology* 2010;151:4756–4764.

31. Gupta A, Srinivasan M, Thamadilok S, Patel MS. Hypothalamic alterations in fetuses of high fat diet-fed obese female rats. *J Endocrinol* 2009;200: 293–300.

32. Nakamura H, Shitara N, Takakura K. Insulin binds to specific receptors and stimulates macromolecular synthesis in C6 glioma cells. *Acta Neurochirurgica* 1988;93:10–12.

33. Plagemann A, Harder T, Rake A, et al. Morphological alterations of hypothalamic nuclei due to intra-hypothalamic hyperinsulinism in newborn rats. *Int J Dev Neurosci* 1999;17:37–44.

34. Simerly RB. Hypothalamic substrates of metabolic imprinting. *Physiol Behav* 2008;94:79–89.

35. Srinivasan M, Katewa SD, Palaniyappan A, Pandya JD, Patel MS. Maternal high-fat diet consumption results in fetal malprogramming predisposing to the onset of metabolic syndrome-like phenotype in adulthood. *Am J Physiol* 2006;291:E792–E799.

36. Kamata Y, Shiraga H, Tai A, Kawamoto Y, Gohda E. Induction of neurite outgrowth in PC12 cells by the medium-chain fatty acid octanoic acid. *Neuroscience* 2007;146:1073–1081.

37. Kawakita E, Hashimoto M, Shido O. Docosahexaenoic acid promotes neurogenesis in vitro and in vivo. *Neuroscience* 2006;139:991–997.

38. Innis SM. Dietary (n-3) fatty acids and brain development. *J Nutr* 2007;137:855–859.

39. Salsberry PJ, Reagan PB. Taking the long view: the prenatal environment and early adolescent overweight. *Res Nurs Health* 2007;30:297–307.

40. Somm E, Schwitzgebel VM, Vauthay DM, et al. Prenatal nicotine exposure alters early pancreatic islet and adipose tissue development with consequences on the control of body weight and glucose metabolism later in life. *Endocrinology* 2008;149:6289–6299.

41. Oken E, Levitan EB, Gillman MW. Maternal smoking during pregnancy and child overweight: systematic review and meta-analysis. *Int J Obes* 2008;32:201–10.

42. Newman MB, Shytle RD, Sanberg PR. Locomotor behavioral effects of prenatal and postnatal nicotine exposure in rat offspring. *Behav Pharmacol* 1999;10:699–706.

43. Pausova Z, Paus T, Sedova L, Berube J. Prenatal exposure to nicotine modifies kidney weight and blood pressure in genetically susceptible rats: a case of gene-environment interaction. *Kidney Int* 2003;64:829–835.

44. Chen WJ, King KA, Lee RE, Sedtal CS, Smith AM. Effects of nicotine exposure during prenatal or perinatal period on cell numbers in adult rat hippocampus and cerebellum: a stereology study. *Life Sci* 2006;79:2221–2227.

45. Vaglenova J, Parameshwaran K, Suppiramaniam V, Breese CR, Pandiella N, Birru S. Long-lasting teratogenic effects of nicotine on cognition: gender specificity and role of AMPA receptor function. *Neurobiol Learn Mem* 2008;90:527–536.

46. Jansson A, Andersson K, Fuxe K, Bjelke B, Eneroth P. Effects of combined pre- and postnatal treatment with nicotine on hypothalamic catecholamine nerve terminal systems and neuroendocrine function in the 4-week old and adult male and female diestrous rat. *J Neuroendocrinol* 1989;1:455–464.

47. Leibowitz SF, Shor-Posner G, Brennan G, Alexander JT. Meal pattern analysis of macronutrient intake after PVN norepinephrine and peripheral clonidine administration. *Obes Res* 1993;1:29–39.

48. Grove KL, Sekhon HS, Brogan RS, Keller JA, Smith MS, Spindel ER. Chronic maternal nicotine exposure alters neuronal systems in the arcuate nucleus that regulate feeding behavior in the newborn rhesus macaque. *J Clin Endocrinol Metab* 2001;86:5420–5426.

49. Loughlin SE, Islas MI, Cheng MY, Lee AG, Villegier AS, Leslie FM. Nicotine modulation of stress-related peptide neurons. *J Comp Neurol* 2006;497:575–588.

50. Corrigall WA. Hypocretin mechanisms in nicotine addiction: evidence and speculation. *Psychopharmacol* 2009;206:23–37.

18

The Biology and Psychology of Taste

LINDA M. BARTOSHUK AND DEREK J. SNYDER

ORAL SENSATIONS

The term "taste" in ordinary conversation refers to sensations evoked from foods or beverages. With this usage, "taste" is essentially interchangeable with "flavor." However, flavor sensations actually result from true taste plus "retronasal olfaction." Retronasal olfaction is produced when we chew and swallow food. The odorants emitted by the food are forced up behind the palate into the nasal cavity, where they rise to the top, pass through a small opening (the olfactory cleft), and finally contact the olfactory receptors buried in the olfactory mucosa. In ordinary conversation, "smell" refers to what the specialist calls orthonasal olfaction; sniffing draws odorants through the nostrils into the nasal cavity, where they rise to the top and thereafter follow the same path as odorants introduced retronasally. We now know, thanks to functional magnetic resonance imaging studies, that orthonasal and retronasal olfaction are not processed in exactly the same brain areas.[1]

To the specialist, "taste" refers to the sensations evoked by stimulation of taste buds. Taste buds on the tongue are not visible but rather are buried in the tissue of papillae (fungiform papillae on the anterior tongue). Fungiform papillae are innervated by cranial nerve (CN) VII (chorda tympani, taste) and CN V (trigeminal, oral burn and touch).[2] Thus, any variation in density of fungiform papillae means variation in burn and touch. Fats in foods produce touch sensations (consider our descriptors for fats: oily, viscous, thick, and creamy).

The Four Basic Tastes and Affect

The most salient characteristic of sweet, salty, sour, and bitter (the "four basic tastes") is hard-wired affect. We are born liking sweet and disliking bitter. Salt receptors are not mature at birth in some mammals, but once they are, salt is liked. Note that the affect guides survival; sugar is an important energy source and sodium is essential to muscle and nerve function. Bitter appears to have evolved for poison detection. Sour is less well understood. Although strong acids are clearly dangerous to tissue, some have speculated that aversions to less concentrated acids might play a role in avoiding unripe fruit. Umami, the taste of glutamate, is sometimes called a fifth basic taste (see more in next section). However, it is noteworthy that glutamate taste is not universally liked.

Much is now known about the receptors that recognize the four basic tastes.[3–5] Perhaps most salient in the context of food and weight is the sweet receptor. Two genes (*TAS1R2* and *TAS1R3*) express proteins that twist together forming a heterodimer that contains multiple binding sites for various sweeteners.[6] However, if this were the sole sweet receptor, all sweet molecules would produce the same sweet quality; as most who have tasted saccharin can attest, the sweet is not identical to that of sucrose. However, *TAS1R3* may function as a sweet receptor capable of responding only to high concentrations of sugars.[7] This could account for the difference in sweetness of sugars and artificial sweeteners.

Are Umami and Fat Additional Basic Tastes?

Our survival depends on our abilities to regulate the intake of nutrients. The early history of regulatory studies was dominated by Curt Richter's "wisdom of the body" (see Moran & Schulkin, 2000): a deficit in a nutrient motivated an organism to search for that nutrient, ingest it, and bring the body back into homeostasis. This theory was supported by research with sodium and glucose. Note that without receptors to detect the nutrient, hard-wired wisdom of the body must fail. The theory worked only for sodium and glucose. The pioneering work of Rozin[8] revealed another type of regulation: conditioned aversions based on symptoms of illness generated by deficits. Organisms learned to avoid the sensations produced by deficient diets. Rozin and his colleagues went on to show the other side of the coin: organisms learned to prefer the sensations produced by diets with benefits (especially calories).[9]

Protein and fat are important nutrients. Not surprisingly, there has been an active search for oral receptors for protein and fat that could allow organisms to detect and thus regulate them. Unfortunately, protein and fat molecules are too large to stimulate either taste or olfaction. However, proteins and fats are broken into smaller molecules by digestion; proteins yield their constituent amino acids (one of those is glutamate) and fats yield fatty acids. Some of that digestive process can begin in the mouth. Receptors for glutamate[10] and fatty acids[11] have been found in the mouth, but they have also been found in the digestive tract.[12,13] Sensations evoked by glutamate and fatty acids in the mouth may play some role in regulation of protein and fat; however, the major role may well be played in the gastrointestinal (GI) tract. When protein or fat are consumed, digestion leads to stimulation of the GI receptors for glutamate and fatty acids. This input allows the brain to produce conditioned preferences for the oral sensations evoked by the consumed foods. We learn to like the sensations evoked by foods containing protein and fat (e.g., bacon, cheese, roast beef, etc.)

Taste Qualities: Detection of Nutrients

The two major taste quality-coding theories (patterning vs. labeled lines) were both initiated by Pfaffmann. Pfaffmann first proposed patterning (the idea that taste quality was coded by a pattern of activation over many taste nerve fibers) because he failed to find fibers specific to a single taste quality.[14] However, as studies accumulated, fiber types were identified.[15] Furthermore, it became clear that the properties of taste mixtures were not adequately explained by patterning. Sensory mixtures can be classified as analytic (the component qualities can be recognized as in a musical chord) or synthetic (the component qualities yield to a new quality as in the mixing of red and green light to produce yellow light). Although some tried to argue for synthetic taste mixtures, the data overwhelmingly support

analytic mixing in taste.[16] Analytic mixing is characteristic of labeled-line coding while synthetic mixing is characteristic of pattern coding. Pfaffmann ultimately rejected patterning in favor of labeled lines.[17] Incidentally, the analytic nature of taste insures that organisms can recognize sodium, sugars, and poisons even when they are in mixtures.

Olfactory Qualities: A Labeling System for Objects That Emit Odors

Olfaction has a very different biological function than does taste. Taste identifies specific nutrients that are crucial to survival with specific receptors. Olfaction identifies objects; retronasal olfaction identifies orally sensed objects. Briefly, the olfactory periphery is wired to send to the brain a simple picture of the chemical structure of a molecule.[18] Olfactory receptors bind salient parts of molecules (e.g., functional groups, carbon chains, etc.). There are nearly 400 receptor types.[19] All nerve fibers innervating a specific type project to a particular place in the olfactory brain (a structure called a "glomerulus"). Thus, looking across the glomeruli, a pattern emerges that forms a picture of the structural components of molecules. Interestingly, the human has more glomeruli than other mammals; the significance of this is not yet known but might "contribute to more robust odor representation" in the human.[20] The picture labels olfactory objects, but we must learn whether these objects are good or bad for us. Nausea appears to be the most important cue for learned aversion;[21] an odorant (perceived retronasally) that precedes nausea can become aversive with one exposure. Positive conditioning tends to take multiple exposures. A variety of consequences appear to be able to produce conditioned preferences (e.g., calories, pleasure like that induced by drugs, etc.).

Taste Variation: We Do Not All Live in the Same Taste Worlds

To understand oral sensory variation, we have to have psychophysical tools that provide valid comparisons across individuals/groups. Unfortunately, the conventional visual analog and category scales used in an earlier era failed to produce valid comparisons.[22-24] New psychophysical tools corrected the earlier errors and led to the discovery that some individuals experience taste intensities two to three times as intense as those experienced by others; those individuals are called "supertasters."[25] Supertasters tend to have larger numbers of fungiform papillae than do others.[26] This anatomical variation is thought to be genetic, but the mechanism is unknown. Supertasters show a variety of differences in dietary behavior that are relevant to weight. For example, supertasters show more extreme affective reactions to foods.[27]

In addition to anatomical variation, there is genetic variation in the receptors for taste. Bitter taste is mediated by about 30 different receptors.[3] The stimuli that excite each of these are not yet completely known. The first bitter receptor discovered was that expressed by PTC gene *TAS2R38* on chromosome 7. This genetic characteristic has been the subject of many subsequent studies and has been shown to influence preferences for important foods/beverages (e.g., vegetables[28,29] and alcohol[30]).

Taste Pathology
Sensory Interactions in the Mouth
Taste input via the chorda tympani appears to normally inhibit both taste from other nerves and trigeminal sensations (burn, touch). Although retronasal olfaction does not actually originate from the mouth, it is perceptually localized to the mouth. Taste can intensify retronasal olfaction. As the food industry has long known, addition of sugar can intensify the flavor of a beverage like fruit juice.[31] Removing taste with anesthesia causes retronasal sensations to diminish.[32] These interactions mean that damage to taste can reduce flavor.[33]

Taste Loss and Oral Phantoms
Much is yet to be learned, but an overview of what is currently known follows. Taste input passes from the periphery to the cortex through the conventional synapses: peripheral nerves, medulla, thalamus, and then cortex; the projection in humans is essentially ipsilateral.[34] Taste presumably crosses the midline at the cortex; descending pathways are at least in part inhibitory.[35,36]

Behavioral evidence for inhibition in taste comes from clinical observations as well as lab studies. One of the earliest cases of taste damage was documented in the nineteenth century by Brillat-Savarin.[37] In an interview (in writing), an ex-prisoner whose tongue was amputated as punishment for an escape attempt said, "that he still possessed the ability to taste fairly well; that he could tell, with other

more normal men, what was pleasant or unappetizing; but that very sour or bitter things caused him unbearable pain." Bull[38] reported patient observations following the unilateral severing of the chorda tympani during stapedectomies (middle ear surgery to improve hearing). He reported, "The most constant symptom referable to taste was that of a metallic sensation on the tongue, this occurred at one time or another in all 101 patients presenting with symptoms." Other sensations reported were "bitter," "salty," and "sore." We call such sensations "phantoms" because they occur in the absence of stimulation. In our clinical experience, patients who complain of taste phantoms virtually always show localized taste losses.

In the laboratory, damage to the chorda tympani simulated with anesthesia supports and extends these observations; unilateral anesthesia of the chorda tympani has little effect on whole mouth taste but actually intensifies taste evoked by stimulation of the contralateral glossopharyngeal nerve.[39–41] This intensification compensates for the loss at the anesthetized nerve, thus producing whole mouth taste constancy. For organisms depending on taste, taste constancy could aid survival. Unilateral anesthesia of the chorda tympani nerve also intensifies oral burn on the contralateral anterior tongue, but this occurs only for supertasters.[42] This taste–pain interaction may also aid survival. In an animal with a mouth injury, eating would stimulate taste and thus reduce oral pain, possibly permitting an animal to eat.

During the anesthesia experiments, about half of the subjects reported taste phantoms, again supporting the clinical observation that taste damage produces these phantoms. Interestingly, burning mouth syndrome (BMS, pain perceived in the absence of visible pathology) is associated with damage to the chorda tympani.[43] BMS may be an oral pain phantom induced by taste damage.

TASTE AND WEIGHT
Relation between Taste Damage and Body Mass Index
The inhibition model of taste damage explains an observation we made some years ago: individuals with moderate to severe histories of ear infections had significantly higher body mass indexes (BMIs). Subsequent studies suggested that an interaction between taste and trigeminal perception played a

role; the sequence of events appears to be something like this. The chorda tympani nerve passes through the middle ear, where it is vulnerable to damage from the pathogens associated with ear infections. Because the damage is restricted to the anterior tongue (the innervation field of the chorda tympani), whole mouth taste is not diminished. However, chorda tympani input normally inhibits trigeminal sensations, so damage will intensify them; indeed, subjects with histories of ear infections experienced intensified oral touch sensations (e.g., thickness, creaminess) from foods containing fats[44] and also rated the palatability of energy-dense foods greater than did those without the history.[45] Thus, it appears that damage to the chorda tympani may be an environmental source of increased BMI mediated by the intensification of the palatability of energy-dense foods.

Oral Sensation, Affect, and Obesity

Given damage to taste as one source of weight gain, we might expect to find taste loss among obese individuals. However, studies dating back to Pangborn's classic work[46] seemed to show no difference in oral sensation across obese and thin individuals. Furthermore, although the obese are known to prefer fat more than do thin individuals, sweet preference appeared to be equivalent; in fact, a few studies even claimed that the obese like sweet less than do the thin. However, these early studies were done with psychophysical methodology that we now know fails to show important sensory/affective differences. Correcting those errors showed that the obese, on average, show some taste loss. Once we accounted for this and made valid comparisons of liking sweet, we found that sweet liking rose with BMI.[27]

REFERENCES

1. Small DM, Prescott J. Odor/taste integration and the perception of flavor. *Exp Brain Res* 2005;166: 345–357.

2. Whitehead MC, Beeman CS, Kinsella BA. Distribution of taste and general sensory nerve endings in fungiform papillae of the hamster. *Am J Anat* 1985;173:185–201.

3. Behrens M, Meyerhof W. Mammalian bitter taste perception. In: Meyerhof W, Korsching S, eds. *Chemosensory Systems in Mammals, Fishes, and Insects.* Heidelberg, Germany: Springer; 2009:1–18.

4. Termussi PA. Sweet, bitter and umami receptors: a complex relationship. *Trends Biochem Sci* 2009;34: 296–302.

5. Lyall V, Phan T-HT, Mummalaneni S, et al. Effect of nicotine on chorda tympani responses to salty and sour stimuli. *J Neurophysiol* 2007;98:1662–1674.

6. Li X, Staszewski L, Xu H, Durick K, Zoller M, Adler E. Human receptors for sweet and umami taste. *Proc Natl A Sci USA* 2002;99:4692–4696.

7. Fushan AA, Simon CT, Slack JP, Manichaikul A, Drayna DT. Allelic polymorphism withhin the TAS1R3 promoter is associated with human taste sensitivity to sucrose. *Curr Biol* 2009;19:1288–1293.

8. Rozin P. Specific aversions as a component of specific hungers. *J Comp Physiol Psychol* 1967;64:237–242.

9. Zellner DA, Rozin P, Aron M, Kulish C. Conditioned enhancement of human's liking for flavor by pairing with sweetness. *Learn Motiv* 1983;14:338–350.

10. Chaudhari N, Landin AM, Roper SD. A metabotropic glutamate receptor variant functions as a taste receptor. *Nat Neurosci* 2000;3:113–119.

11. Gilbertson TA. Gustatory mechanisms for the detection of fat. *Curr Opin Neurobiol* 1998;8:447–452.

12. Uneyama H, Niijima A, San Gabriel AM, Torii K. Luminal amino acid sensing in the rat gastric mucosa. *Am J Physiol Gastrointest Liver Physiol* 2006;291:G1163–G1170.

13. Wellendorph P, Johansen LD, Bräuner-Osborne H. Molecular pharmacology of promiscuous seven transmembrane receptors sensing organic nutrients. *Mol Pharmacol* 2009;76:453–465.

14. Pfaffmann C. Gustatory afferent impulses. *J Cell Comp Physiol* 1941;17:243–258.

15. Frank M. An analysis of hamster afferent taste nerve response functions. *J Gen Physiol* 1973;61:588–618.

16. Bartoshuk LM, Gent JF. Taste mixtures: an analysis of synthesis. In: Pfaff D, ed. *Taste and Olfaction and the Central Nervous System.* New York: Rockefeller University Press; 1985:210–232.

17. Pfaffmann C. The sensory coding of taste quality. *Chem Sens Flav* 1974;1:5–8.

18. Shepherd GM. Outline of a theory of olfactory processing and its relevance to humans. *Chem Sens* 2005; 30(suppl 1):i3–i5.

19. Olender T, Lancet D, Nebert DW. Update on the olfactory receptor (OR) gene superfamily. *Hum Genomics* 2008;3:87–97.

20. Maresh A, Gil DR, Whitman MC, Greer CA. Principles of glomerular organization in the human olfactory bulb—Implications for odor processing. *PLoS ONE* 2008;3:1–6.

21. Pelchat ML, Rozin P. The special role of nausea in the acquisition of food dislikes by humans. *Appetite* 1982;3:341–351.

22. Bartoshuk LM, Duffy VB, Fast K, Green BG, Prutkin JM, Snyder DJ. Labeled scales (e.g., category, Likert, VAS) and invalid across-group comparisons. What we have learned from genetic variation in taste. *Food Qual Pref* 2002;14:125–138.

23. Bartoshuk LM, Fast K, Snyder D. Differences in our sensory worlds: invalid comparisons with labeled scales. *Curr Dir Psychol Sci* 2005;14:122–125.

24. Snyder DJ, Prescott J, Bartoshuk LM. Modern psychophysics and the assessment of human oral sensation. In: Hummel T, Welge-Lüssen A, eds. *Taste and Smell: An Update*. Basel, Switzerland: Karger; 2006:221–241.

25. Bartoshuk LM, Duffy VB, Green BG, et al. Valid across-group comparisons with labeled scales: the gLMS vs magnitude matching. *Physiol Behav* 2004;82:109–114.

26. Hayes JE, Bartoshuk LM, Kidd JR, Duffy VB. Supertasting and PROP bitterness depends on more than the TAS2R38 gene. *Chem Sens* 2008;33:255–265.

27. Bartoshuk LM, Duffy VB, Hayes JE, Moskowitz H, Snyder DJ. Psychophysics of sweet and fat perception in obesity: problems, solutions and new perspectives. *Philos Trans Royal Soc B* 2006;361:1137–1148.

28. Dinehart ME, Hayes JE, Bartoshuk LM, Lanier SL, Duffy VB. Bitter taste markers explain variability in vegetable sweetness, bitterness, and intake. *Phys Behav* 2006;87:304–313.

29. Sandell MA, Breslin PA. Variability in a taste-receptor gene determines whether we taste toxins in food. *Curr Biol* 2006;16:R792-4.

30. Duffy VB, Davidson AC, Kidd JR, et al. Bitter receptor gene (TAS2R38), 6-n-propylthiouracil (PROP) bitterness and alcohol intake. *Alcohol Clin Exp Res* 2004;28:1629–1637.

31. Noble AC. Taste-aroma interactions. *Trends Food Sci Technol* 1996;7:439–444.

32. Snyder DJ, Clark CJ, Catalanotto FA, Mayo V, Bartoshuk LM. Oral anesthesia specifically impairs retronasal olfaction. *Chem Sens* 2007;32:A15.

33. Bartoshuk LM, Snyder DJ, Grushka M, Berger AM, Duffy VB, Kveton JF. Taste damage: previously unsuspected consequences. *Chem Sens* 2005;30 (suppl 1):i218-i219.

34. Pritchard TC, Macaluso DA, Eslinger PJ. Taste perception in patients with insular cortex lesions. *Behav Neurosci* 1999;113:663–671.

35. DiLorenzo P. Corticofugal influence on taste responses in the parabrachial pons of the rat. *Brain Res* 1990;530:73–84.

36. DiLorenzo PM, Monroe S. Corticofugal influence on taste responses in the nucleus of the solitary tract in the rat. *J Neurophysiol* 1995;74:258–272.

37. Brillat-Savarin JA. Physiologie du goût. Paris: Sautelet et Cie, 1826.

38. Bull TR. Taste and the chorda tympani. *J Laryngol Otol* 1965;79:479–493.

39. Catalanotto FA, Bartoshuk LM, Östrum KM, Gent JF, Fast K. Effects of anesthesia of the facial nerve on taste. *Chem Sens* 1993;18:461–470.

40. Lehman CD, Bartoshuk LM, Catalanotto FC, Kveton JF, Lowlicht RA. The effect of anesthesia of the chorda tympani nerve on taste perception in humans. *Physiol Behav* 1995;57:943–951.

41. Yanagisawa K, Bartoshuk LM, Catalanotto FA, Karrer TA, Kveton JF. Anesthesia of the chorda tympani nerve and taste phantoms. *Physiol Behav* 1998;63:329–335.

42. Tie K, Fast K, Kveton J, et al. Anesthesia of chorda tympani nerve and effect on oral pain. *Chem Sens* 1999;24:609.

43. Grushka M, Bartoshuk LM. Burning mouth syndrome and oral dysesthesias. *Can J Diagnosis* 2000;17:99–109.

44. Catalanotto FA, Broe ET, Bartoshuk LM, Mayo VD, Snyder DJ. Otitis media and intensification of nontaste oral sensations. *Chem Sens* 2009;34:A120.

45. Snyder DJ, Bartoshuk LM. Epidemiological studies of taste function. *Ann NY Acad Sci* 2009;1170:574–580.

46. Pangborn RM, Simone M. Body size and sweetness preference. *J Am Diet Assoc* 1958;34:924–928.

19

Leptin Gene Therapy for Hyperphagia, Obesity, Metabolic Diseases, and Addiction

A New Opportunity

SATYA P. KALRA

INTRODUCTION

Close associations between hyperphagia and meta-bolic diseases, such as obesity and the attendant disease cluster of metabolic syndrome, with sub-stance abuse have been described in ancient scrip-tures and writings. Recently it has become evident that the innate human desire to improve the quality of daily life and advances in science and technology have jointly, but quite unintentionally and imper-ceptibly, conspired to boost the adverse health consequences of energy imbalance to epidemic pro-portions worldwide.[1–3] Since the times of formative environment of ancestral hunter-gatherers, a com-plex interplay of those changes in daily lifestyle and habits that have progressively orchestrated these disorders are as follows: (1) hyperphagia, that is, compulsive consumption of easily accessible, energy-dense meals enriched with palatable addictive nutri-ents; (2) urban lifestyle, rise in income supporting increased comfort punctuated by less physically demanding work, adoption of automated technol-ogy for transport and living comforts; (3) increased passive pursuits benefited by marked improvement in health delivery; and (4) pharmacologic therapies for psychiatric disorders and drug abuse.[3–11]

NEURAL AND HORMONAL CIRCUITS IN INTEGRATION OF ENERGY HOMEOSTASIS

Instinctual urges promote positive energy balance in the body by modulating the appetitive drive, energy expenditure, and storage of unexpended energy on a daily basis. Normally, the interplay of the appe-tite-regulating network (ARN) and the energy-reg-ulating network in the hypothalamus, and neural relays from the reward and food discriminating extrahypothalamic circuit, integrate energy homeo-stasis on a moment-to-moment basis.[4,7,12–15]

Within the ARN, neuropeptide Y (NPY), ago-uti-related peptide, and γ-aminobutyric acid coex-pressing neurons in the arcuate nucleus (ARC) that innervates the paraventricular nucleus (PVN) and neighboring hypothalamic regions are involved in propagation of the appetitive drive.[12–21] The ante-cedent release of NPY and cohorts in the ARC-PVN axis under the direction of afferent hormonal signals, anorexigenic leptin secreted primarily by white adipose tissue (WAT) and orexigenic gastric ghrelin, evoke appetite in a timely fashion.[12–14,20,22]

During the intermeal intervals, leptin restrains appetitive drive in two ways, directly by repressing NPY efflux in the ARC-PVN axis and indirectly both by countering the orexigenic effects of ghrelin on the hypothalamic ARN and by suppressing ghre-lin secretion from the stomach.[12,22–24] The evidence of reciprocal fluctuations in circulating concentra-tions of leptin and ghrelin during the intermeal, preprandial and postprandial intervals is consistent with the notion that optimal leptin signaling to the hypothalamus is necessary to sustain episodic appetitive drive.[22–25] In addition, leptin plays a sig-nificant role in integration of energy homeostasis by regulating signal relays along the hypothalamic efferents to (1) repress insulin secretion from pan-creas, (2) impose euglycemia by an intricate control on glucose metabolism and disposal in liver, skele-tal muscles, WAT, and brown adipose tissue (BAT), and (3) promote energy expenditure by activating nonshivering thermogenesis in BAT.[12,13,16,26–29] Thus, a dynamic dialogue between circulating leptin con-centrations and the hypothalamic ARC-NPY axis is mandatory for energy homeostasis.

LEPTIN INSUFFICIENCY SYNDROME

Indeed, absence of leptin signaling to the ARN, either due to lack of leptin or leptin receptors, leads to incessant hyperphagia, unceasing fat accumulation, dyslipidemia, hyperinsulinemia, hyperglycemia, diabetic cardiomyopathy, low-grade systemic inflammation, and several other metabolic ailments (Figs. 19.1 and 19.2).[2,4,5,13,30]

More recently, insufficiency in leptin feedback conferred by restricted leptin transport across the blood–brain barrier (BBB) due to hyperleptinemia was shown to recapitulate these diverse metabolic afflictions.[3,31] Evidently, it is not the leptin resistance as generally believed,[4,5] but the central leptin insufficiency that underlies the pathogenesis of varied peripheral and central ailments observed in association with rising leptin titers accompanying the increased rate of visceral fat accrual, either gradually in an age-related fashion or rapidly in response to consumption of calorie-dense macronutrients (Figs. 19.1 and 19.2).[3]

LEPTIN GENE THERAPY TO OVERCOME CENTRAL LEPTIN INSUFFICIENCY

Since current pharmacologic therapies to suppress hyperphagia and excess fat accumulation and to prevent the attending disease cluster of metabolic syndrome on a long-term basis have been unsuccessful,[3] the new insight that central leptin insufficiency is a common causal factor in the pathogenesis of these afflictions offers a novel avenue to design therapeutic strategies that can stably and safely overcome central leptin insufficiency and, thereby, curtail or forestall the current epidemic of chronic metabolic diseases.

In this context, increased supply of leptin selectively within the hypothalamus was found feasible by instilling leptin transgene expression with viral vectors.[32–34] We observed that the replicative-deficient, nonimmunogenic and nonpathogenic, clinically safe,[35,36] recombinant adeno-associated viral vector encoding the leptin gene (rAAV-lep) stably augmented leptin transgene expression through the lifetime of rodents after either a single injection intracerebroventricularly (icv) or microinjection in a discrete hypothalamic site.[16,26,32–34,37] Consequently, a spectrum of health benefits conferred by stable leptin signaling in the hypothalamus, with the aid of central rAAV-lep therapy in various experimental paradigms, are enumerated briefly in the following section.

Hyperphagia, Fat Accumulation, and Energy Expenditure

A single icv injection of rAAV-lep suppressed hyperphagia in leptin-deficient *ob/ob* mice[24,38,39] and

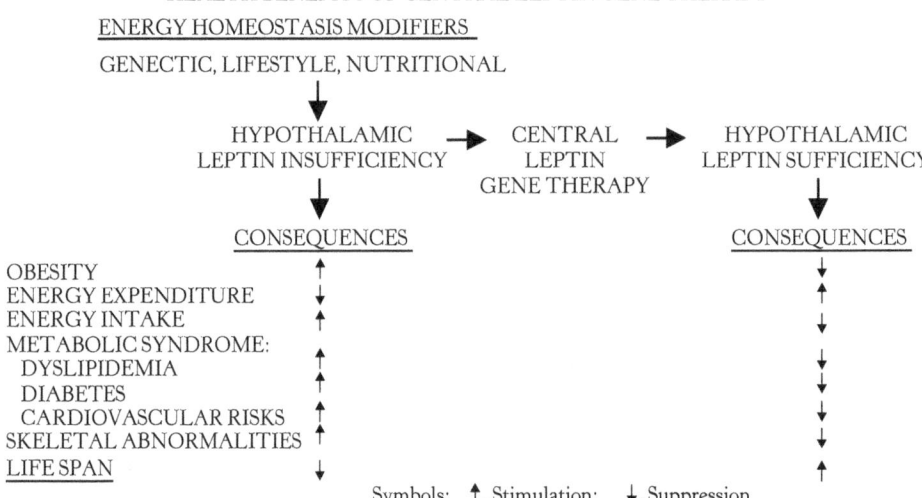

FIGURE 19.1. Increased leptin supply to hypothalmus by gene therapy confers lifelong benefits on energy homeostasis, disease cluster of metabolic syndrome—diabetes type 1 and 2, dyslipidemia, and cardiovascular ailments—and bone remodeling.

Source: Reprinted with kind permission from Springer Science+Business Media. Copyright (2009), S. P. Kalra.

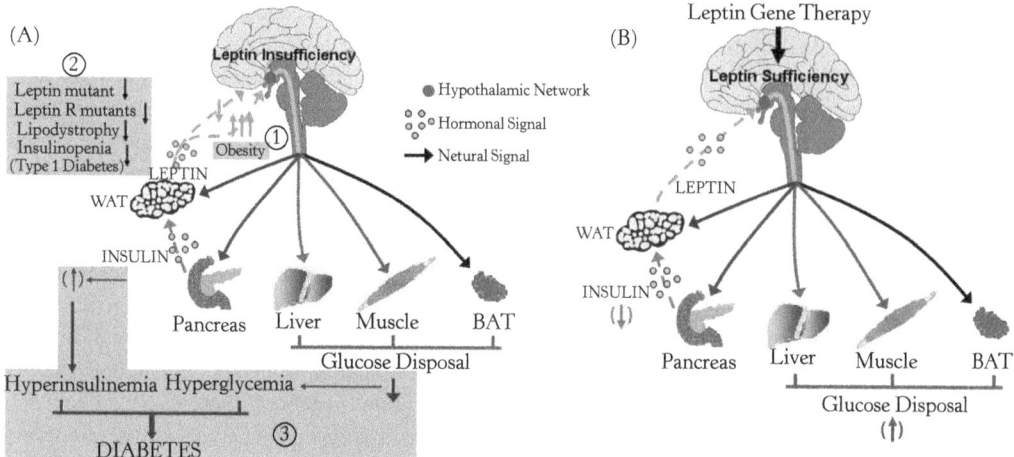

FIGURE 19.2. The independent course traversed by leptin-responsive pathways emanating from the hypothalamus and descending caudally through the brainstem to innervate the WAT, pancreas, liver, skeletal muscle, and BAT in the periphery. The information relay along these tracts regulates episodic adipocyte leptin and pancreatic insulin secretion and glucose metabolism in the liver, skeletal muscle, and BAT, as detailed in the text. (A) Leptin insufficiency in the hypothalamus due to restriction on transport by blood–brain barrier induced by hyperleptinemia associated with obesity (as shown ②) and other factors (as shown in ①) results in hyperinsulinemia due to diminution of hypothalamic restraint on pancreatic insulin release and hyperglycemia due to suppression of glucose disposal by liver, muscle, and BAT (as shown ③). (B) Leptin sufficiency produced by adequate leptin supply with the aid of leptin gene therapy reverses the imbalance in energy homeostasis shown in (A). BAT, brown adipose tissue; WAT, white adipose tissue.

Source: Adapted from Nutrition, Vol. 24, S.P. Kalra, Disruptioini in the leptin-NPY link underlies the pandemic of diabetes and metabolic syndrome: New therapeutic approaches, 820–826. Copyright (2008), with permission from Elsevier.

insulinopenic Akita mice.[39,40] Similarly, increased leptin transgene expression in the hypothalamus dose-dependently reduced daily food intake through the duration of the experiments in wild-type (WT) rodents maintained on either a rodent chow or high-fat diet (HFD).[16,25,26,32–34,37,39,41,42] Reduction in BW, near complete blockade of WAT accrual and markedly reduced circulating levels of the adipokines leptin, tumor necrosis factor α (TNFα), interleukin-6 (IL-6), and triglycerides and free fatty acids accompanied the reduced food intake in these rodents. Furthermore, suppression of fat accrual was attributable largely to upregulation of energy expenditure, as shown by enhanced uncoupling protein mRNA expression in BAT, a response that manifested independently of effects on daily food intake (Figs. 19.1 and 19.2).[16,26,28,32–34,37–39,41–45]

AMELIORATION OF DIABETES
Repression of Pancreatic Insulin Secretion

An additional outcome of central leptin gene therapy, also independent of the effects on food intake

and adiposity, was the amelioration of diabetes in various rodent paradigms.[13,16,26,28,32–34,37–39] Since insulin is obesogenic, coexistence of hyperinsulinemia with increasing adiposity is attributed to promotion of adipogenesis by insulin. We observed that central leptin gene therapy suppressed episodic tonic and postprandial insulin hypersecretion in conjunction with depletion of fat depots. The clamp on insulin efflux in WT and *ob/ob* rodents consuming either normal rodent chow or HFD was apparently imposed by activation of descending efferents to pancreatic β-cells (Figs. 19.1 and 19.2). In addition, insulin resistance, a major risk factor for diabetes type 2, was abrogated. Insulin sensitivity was reinstated in conjunction with suppressed blood levels of adiponectin and TNFα, the adipokines implicated in imparting insulin sensitivity.[24,28,38,39,41–45]

Glucose Homeostasis

In this context, persistent euglycemia was an unanticipated outcome, even in the absence of insulin.[28] By augmenting glucose metabolism and disposal through increased neural relay along the descending tracts to peripheral targets, WAT, BAT, skeletal muscles, and liver (Figs. 19.1 and 19.2), central rAAV-lep injection rapidly suppressed hyperglycemia and imposed euglycemia for extended periods in lean and obese WT rodents, ob/ob mice, and hyperglycemic, insulinopenic Akita mice and those suffering from insulitis.[3,28,29,39,40,44,46–48] Consequently, this durability of central rAAV-lep to impose euglycemia, independent of existing fat depots and severe insulinopenia, clearly unraveled a new therapeutic approach to ameliorate type 1 and 2 diabetes for a lifetime.[28]

Bone Remodeling

A similar stable supply of leptin in the hypothalamus also decreased cancellous bone volume, promoted femur length and volume, and promoted total bone growth in association with enhanced secretion of osteoblast-specific osteocalcin, a hormone implicated in improving skeletal architecture and remodeling processes.[44,49,50] Evidently, leptin-induced signal relay along the neural efferents from the hypothalamus can stimulate osteocalcin secretion by osteoblasts and, thereby, facilitate bone remodeling and abate osteoporosis.[29,44]

Cardiovascular Disease Risks

A causal association of cardiovascular disease risk factors, such as systemic low-grade inflammation and progressive cardiomyopathy, with obesity and diabetes is well known.[3–5,13] In response to increased neural outflow to WAT and liver in rodents expressing leptin transgene in the hypothalamus, blood levels of proinflammatory adipokine, the cytokine IL-6 and hepatic C-reactive protein, fell markedly, a response indicative of abrogation of low-grade systemic inflammation (Figs. 19.1 and 19.2).[43] Similarly, stable leptin supply in the hypothalamus, concomitant with normalized blood glucose levels, decelerated cardiomyopathy and deterioration of heart function and decreased oxidative stress and apoptosis in cardiac muscle in obese, diabetic, and lean insulinopenic diabetic rodents.[51]

Impact of Leptin Transgene Expression in the Hypothalamus on Imprinting and Life Span
Imprinting

The metabolic environment in utero can irreversibly modify the hypothalamic hardcore wiring involved in integration of energy homeostasis.[52] We observed that, despite reduced daily food intake, adiposity, and circulating levels of leptin, insulin and lipids conferred by icv rAAV-lep injection in adult female rats, estrous cycles were normal during pregestation and, thereafter, gestation, parturition, and lactation were unaffected.[52] However, whereas the litter size was also unchanged, the body weight of the pups delivered by rAAV-lep-injected lean mothers was not only significantly lower than those delivered by mothers treated with control vector, but the low birth weight of F1 generation persisted during postnatal, prepubertal, pubertal, and adult (3 months old) periods. Seemingly, sustenance of low body weight and adiposity together with diminution in metabolic hormonal signals in rAAV-lep-injected females reorganized the hypothalamic circuitry of F1 progeny to presumably impel maintenance of body weight at levels lower than their control counterparts (Fig. 19.3).[52]

Clearly then, the in utero metabolic environment conferred by reduced fat depots, blood hormones leptin and insulin, and lipids can structurally and functionally reorganize the weight-regulating neural circuitry in the brain of F1 progeny through epigenesis.[52]

Life Span

Morbid obesity and the attending disease cluster of metabolic syndrome shorten life span.[3,45] Since central leptin gene therapy can suppress obesity and ameliorate comorbidities, the efficacy of optimal supply of leptin in the hypothalamus on life span of obese ob/ob mice afflicted with similar comorbidities was assessed.[45] In association with normalized body weight and blood-borne indices of the disease cluster of metabolic syndrome, stable leptin signaling in the hypothalamus prevented early mortality and normalized life span in ob/ob mice (Fig. 19.1).[45] Seemingly, circumventing leptin insufficiency in the hypothalamus alone is sufficient to reverse the adverse consequences of morbid obesity on health and longevity.[3,45]

Craving for Food Versus Drugs of Abuse

The notion that the worldwide escalation in the prevalence of obesity is a consequence of not only increased craving for palatable food but compulsive urges for addictive drugs of abuse that mobilize those very neurochemical circuits that normally propagate appetitive drive and hyperphagia, has drawn considerable attention.[7,8] Indeed,

FIGURE 19.3. Physical appearance at weaning of a pup delivered by rAAV-GFP-treated (left) and rAAV-lep-treated (right) female rats.
Source: Reprinted from Peptides, Vol. 26, A. Lecklin, M.G. Dube, R.N. Torto, P.S. Kalra, S.P. Kalra, Perigestational suppression of weight gain with central leptin gene therapy results in lower weight F1 generation, 1176–1187. Copyright (2005), with permission from Elsevier.

a breakdown in neural signaling in any locus in the ARN has been shown to invariably evoke hyperphagia and not anorexia.[12,13,19,21] Clinically, relentless hyperphagia, that is, compulsive eating, regardless of the hedonic nature of the food, underlies morbid obesity in genetic disorders of Prader-Willi syndrome, Alstrom syndrome, WAGR syndrome, Fragile X syndrome, and Bardet-Biedl syndrome.[53]

On the other hand, investigations spanning decades show that hyperphagia in laboratory rodents maintained on regular chow is of rare occurrence and it manifests only in response to defective central leptin restraint on appetite, ablation of critical hypothalamic leptin target sites, and varied genetic mutation in components of ARN.[4,5,12,19,29,45] The question of whether defective leptin signaling predisposes rodents for increased craving for drugs, as for food, has recently been addressed.[7–11] It is quite possible that the impact of various drugs of abuse on appetite may be due to overlapping signaling pathways and/or the commonality in intracellular signaling for expression of the drive for food and drug addiction.[7,8]

Altered circulating levels of leptin in drug addicts and propensity of leptin receptors on dopaminergic neurons in the ventral tegmental area (VTA), a component of the reward-related behavioral circuitry, have been reported.[9,10] Intriguingly, leptin insufficiency is also associated with modified mesoaccumbens and dopamine function. Since VTA neurons project to nucleus accumbens, it is possible that this extrahypothalamic leptin responsive circuitry may participate in drug addiction.[7–11] Furthermore, it is reasonable to speculate that

central leptin insufficiency may also underlie eating disorders, increased fat accrual, and disease cluster of metabolic syndrome observed in response to psychotropic drug therapies for schizophrenia and bipolar depression.[3] If this is the case, then we propose restoration of optimal leptin signaling in neurocircuitry associated with expression of craving and psychiatric illnesses would be beneficial.

CONCLUDING REMARKS

A better understanding of the neurobiology of leptin has unraveled leptin insufficiency in the hypothalamus as a common mechanism in the etiology of diverse metabolic diseases (Figs. 19.1 and 19.2).[3] A convergence of recent evidence affirms that a state of "reward deficiency" in drug addiction may similarly be dependent upon inadequate leptin signaling at loci within the neurocircuitry of addiction. Research spanning over a decade has demonstrated the safety and tolerability of central leptin gene therapy to restrain appetitive drive and to curtail obesity, diabetes, and attending metabolic comorbidities for the lifetime of rodents (Fig. 19.1).[2,28,29,44] Collectively, bioavailability of leptin by gene therapy is potentially a powerful strategy for preclinical and clinical trials aimed at reinstating adequate leptin signaling to alleviate the pathophysiological sequalae responsible for the worldwide epidemic of metabolic ailments and drug addiction.

ACKNOWLEDGEMENT

Supported by a grant from the National Institutes of Health (DK37273).

REFERENCES

1. Bray GA. Historical framework for the development of ideas about obesity. In: Bray GA, Bouchard C, James WPT, eds. *Handbook of Obesity*. New York: Marcel Dekker; 1998:1–29.

2. Kalra SP, Kalra PS. Gene transfer technology: a preventive neurotherapy to curb obesity, ameliorate metabolic syndrome and extend life-expectancy. *Trends Pharmacol Sci* 2005;26:488–495.

3. Kalra SP. Central leptin insufficiency syndrome: an interactive etiology for obesity, metabolic and neural diseases and for designing new therapeutic interventions. *Peptides* 2008;29:127–138.

4. Friedman JM. Obesity: causes and control of excess body fat. *Nature* 2009;459:340–342.

5. O'Rahilly S, Farooqi IS, Yeo GS, Challis BG. Minireview: human obesity-lessons from monogenic disorders. *Endocrinology* 2003;144:3757–3764.

6. Eckel RH. Clinical practice. Nonsurgical management of obesity in adults. *N Engl J Med* 2008;358: 1941–5190.

7. Kalra SP, Kalra PS. Overlapping and interactive pathways regulating appetite and craving. In: Gold MS, ed. *Eating Disorders, Overeating, and Pathological Attachment to Food*. Binghamton, NY: The Haworth Medical Press; 2004:5–21.

8. Gold MS, ed. *Eating Disorders, Overeating, and Pathological Attachment to Food*. Binghamton, NY: The Haworth Medical Press, 2004.

9. Corwin RL, Grigson PS. Symposium overview—food addiction: fact or fiction? *J Nutr* 2009;139:617–619.

10. Lutter M, Nestler EJ. Homeostatic and hedonic signals interact in the regulation of food intake. *J Nutr* 2009;139:629–632.

11. Thakore J, Leonard BE, eds. Metabolic effects of psychotropic drugs. Basel, Switzerland: S. Karger AG, 2009.

12. Kalra SP, Dube MG, Pu S, Xu B, Horvath TL, Kalra PS. Interacting appetite-regulating pathways in the hypothalamic regulation of body weight. *Endocr Rev* 1999;20:68–100.

13. Kalra SP, Kalra PS. NPY and cohorts in regulating appetite, obesity and metabolic syndrome: beneficial effects of gene therapy. *Neuropeptides* 2004;38: 201–211.

14. Kalra SP, Kalra PS. Neuropeptide Y: a conductor of the appetite-regulating orchestra in the hypothalamus. In: Kastin AJ, ed. *Handbook of Biologically Active Peptides*. Amsterdam, The Netherlands: Elsevier Press; 2006:889–894.

15. Clark JT, Kalra PS, Crowley WR, Kalra SP. Neuropeptide Y and human pancreatic polypeptide stimulate feeding behavior in rats. *Endocrinology* 1984;115:427–429.

16. Bagnasco M, Dube MG, Kalra PS, Kalra SP. Evidence for the existence of distinct central appetite and energy expenditure pathways and stimulation of ghrelin as revealed by hypothalamic site-specific leptin gene therapy. *Endocrinology* 2002;143:4409–4421.

17. Pu S, Jain MR, Horvath TL, Diano S, Kalra PS, Kalra SP. Interactions between neuropeptide Y and gamma-aminobutyric acid in stimulation of feeding: a morphological and pharmacological analysis. *Endocrinology* 1999;140:933–940.

18. Dietrich MO, Horvath TL. GABA keeps up an appetite for life. *Cell* 2009;137:1177–1179.

19. Dube MG, Xu B, Kalra PS, Sninsky CA, Kalra SP. Disruption in neuropeptide Y and leptin signaling in obese ventromedial hypothalamic-lesioned rats. *Brain Res* 1999;816:38–46.

20. Kalra SP, Dube MG, Sahu A, Phelps CP, Kalra PS. Neuropeptide Y secretion increases in the paraventricular nucleus in association with increased appetite for food. *Proc Natl Acad Sci USA* 1991;88: 10931–10935.

21. Dube MG, Kalra SP, Kalra PS. Low abundance of NPY in the hypothalamus can produce hyperphagia and obesity. *Peptides* 2007;28:475–479.

22. Kalra SP, Bagnasco M, Otukonyong EE, Dube MG, Kalra PS. Rhythmic, reciprocal ghrelin and leptin signaling: new insight in the development of obesity. *Regul Pept* 2003;111:1–11.

23. Otukonyong EE, Dube MG, Torto R, Kalra PS, Kalra SP. Central leptin differentially modulates ultradian secretory patterns of insulin, leptin and ghrelin independent of effects on food intake and body weight. *Peptides* 2005;26:2559–2566.

24. Ueno N, Dube MG, Inui A, Kalra PS, Kalra SP. Leptin modulates orexigenic effects of ghrelin and attenuates adiponectin and insulin levels and selectively the dark-phase feeding as revealed by central leptin gene therapy. *Endocrinology* 2004;145:4176–4184.

25. Otukonyong EE, Dube MG, Torto R, Kalra PS, Kalra SP. High fat diet-induced ultradian leptin and insulin hypersecretion and ghrelin is absent in obesity-resistant rats. *Obes Res* 2005;13:991–999.

26. Bagnasco M, Dube MG, Katz A, Kalra PS, Kalra SP. Leptin expression in hypothalamic PVN reverses dietary obesity and hyperinsulinemia but stimulates ghrelin. *Obes Res* 2003;11:1463–1470.

27. Kalra SP. Appetite and body weight regulation: is it all in the brain? *Neuron* 1997;19:227–230.

28. Kalra SP. Central leptin gene therapy ameliorates diabetes type 1 and 2 through two independent hypothalamic relays; a benefit beyond weight and appetite regulation. *Peptides* 2009;30:1957–1963.

29. Kalra SP. Disruption in the leptin-NPY link underlies the pandemic of diabetes and metabolic syndrome: new therapeutic approaches. *Nutrition* 2008;24: 820–826.

30. Keen-Rhinehart E, Kalra SP, Kalra PS. AAV mediated leptin receptor installation improves energy balance

and the reproductive status of obese female Koletsky rats. *Peptides* 2005;26:2567–2578.

31. Kastin AJ, Pan W. Intranasal leptin: blood-brain barrier bypass (BBBB) for obesity? *Endocrinology* 2006;147:2086–2087.

32. Dhillon H, Ge Y, Minter RM, et al. Long-term differential modulation of genes encoding orexigenic and anorexigenic peptides by leptin delivered by rAAV vector in ob/ob mice. Relationship with body weight change. *Regul Pept* 2000;92:97–105.

33. Dhillon H, Kalra SP, Kalra PS. Dose-dependent effects of central leptin gene therapy on genes that regulate body weight and appetite in the hypothalamus. *Mol Ther* 2001;4:139–145.

34. Dhillon H, Kalra SP, Prima V, et al. Central leptin gene therapy suppresses body weight gain, adiposity and serum insulin without affecting food consumption in normal rats: a long-term study. *Regul Pept* 2001;99:69–77.

35. Kaplitt MG, Feigin A, Tang C, et al. Safety and tolerability of gene therapy with an adeno-associated virus (AAV) borne GAD gene for Parkinson's disease: an open label, phase I trial. *Lancet* 2007;369:2097–2105.

36. Wilson JM. Progress in the commercial-scale production of adeno-associated viral vectors. *Hum Gene Ther* 2009;20:695.

37. Beretta E, Dube MG, Kalra PS, Kalra SP. Long-term suppression of weight gain, adiposity, and serum insulin by central leptin gene therapy in prepubertal rats: effects on serum ghrelin and appetite-regulating genes. *Ped Res* 2002;52:189–198.

38. Boghossian S, Dube MG, Torto R, Kalra PS, Kalra SP. Hypothalamic clamp on insulin release by leptin-transgene expression. *Peptides* 2006;27:3245–3254.

39. Ueno N, Inui A, Kalra SP, Kalra PS. Leptin transgene expression in the hypothalamus enforces euglycemia in diabetic, insulin-deficient nonobese Akita mice and leptin-deficient obese ob/ob mice. *Peptides* 2006;27:2332–2342.

40. Wang J, Takeuchi T, Tanaka S, et al. A mutation in the insulin 2 gene induces diabetes with severe pancreatic beta-cell dysfunction in the Mody mouse. *J Clin Invest* 1999;103:27–37.

41. Dube MG, Beretta E, Dhillon H, Ueno N, Kalra PS, Kalra SP. Central leptin gene therapy blocks high fat diet-induced weight gain, hyperleptinemia and hyperinsulinemia: effects on serum ghrelin levels. *Diabetes* 2002;51:1729–1736.

42. Boghossian S, Lecklin AH, Torto R, Kalra PS, Kalra SP. Suppression of fat deposition for the life time of rodents with gene therapy. *Peptides* 2005;26:1512–1519.

43. Dube MG, Torto R, Kalra SP. Increased leptin expression selectively in the hypothalamus suppresses inflammatory markers CRP and IL-6 in leptin-deficient diabetic obese mice. *Peptides* 2008;29:593–598.

44. Kalra SP. Increased leptin supply to hypothalamus by gene therapy confers life-long benefits on energy homeostasis, disease cluster of metabolic syndrome-diabetes type 1 and 2, dyslipidemia and cardiovascular ailments-and bone remodeling. In: Shioda S, Homma I, Kato N, eds. Transmitters and modulators in health and disease. Tokyo: Springer; 2009:19–30.

45. Boghossian S, Ueno N, Dube MG, Kalra P, Kalra S. Leptin gene transfer in the hypothalamus enhances longevity in adult monogenic mutant mice in the absence of circulating leptin. *Neurobiol Aging* 2007;28:1594–15604.

46. Kojima S, Akihiro A, Inui A, Kalra SP. Leptin as a substitute for insulin therapy in insulin-deficient diabetes-correction of hyperglycemia and hyperphagia and promotion of survival without diabetic complications. Paper presented at: 90th Annual Meeting of The Endocrine Society; June 15–18, 2008; San Francisco.

47. Kojima S, Asakawa A, Amitani H, et al. Central leptin gene therapy, a substitute for insulin therapy to ameliorate hyperglycemia and hyperphagia, and promote survival in insulin-deficient diabetic mice. *Peptides* 2009;30:962–966.

48. Yu X, Park BH, Wang MY, Wang ZV, Unger RH. Making insulin-deficient type 1 diabetic rodents thrive without insulin. *Proc Natl Acad Sci USA* 2008;105:14070–14075.

49. Iwaniec UT, Boghossian S, Lapke PD, Turner RT, Kalra SP. Central leptin gene therapy corrects skeletal abnormalities in leptin-deficient ob/ob mice. *Peptides* 2007;28:1012–1019.

50. Kalra SP, Dube MG, Iwaniec UT. Leptin increases osteoblast-specific osteocalcin release through a hypothalamic relay. *Peptides* 2009;30:967–973.

51. Malhotra A, Vashistha H, Yadav VS, et al. Inhibition of p66ShcA redox activity in cardiac muscle cells attenuates hyperglycemia-induced oxidative stress and apoptosis. *Am J Physiol Heart Circ Physiol* 2009;296:H380–388.

52. Lecklin AH, Dube MG, Torto R, Kalra PS, Kalra SP. Perigestational suppression of weight gain with central leptin gene therapy results in lower weight F1 generation. *Peptides* 2005;26:1176–1187.

53. Goldstone AP. The hypothalamus, hormones, and hunger: alterations in human obesity and illness. *Prog Brain Res* 2006;153:57–73.

20

Lessons from Prader-Willi Syndrome and Pathological Brain Reinforcement

YIJUN LIU AND YI ZHANG

INTRODUCTION

Obesity is a worldwide problematic phenomenon that has been the center of much scientific debate and research. Causes of obesity are multiple and troublesome to identify as very few good human genetic models for obesity exist, such as Prader-Willi syndrome (PWS) and Gourmand syndrome. Monogenic forms of obesity have been identified to be associated with defects in the hypothalamic leptin-melanocortin pathway[1]; examples of which include PWS, microdeletion syndromes such as Wilms' tumor,[2] and Bardet-Biedl syndrome.[3] In addition, common obesity appears to be linked to the FTO (fat mass and obesity associated) gene.[4]

PWS is a genetic imprinting disorder that results in profound hyperphagia and childhood-onset obesity. One hallmark characteristic of this human disease is a marked impulsive drive to over-eat, even though not happening during early infant time, which could result from excessive, pathological reinforcement produced by the ingested items themselves.[5] This description indicates that PWS may be associated with a substance dependence disorder or addiction,[6] which is defined by *The Diagnostic and Statistical Manual of Mental Disorders*, fourth edition (*DSM-IV*) as "a maladaptive pattern of substance use, leading to clinically significant impairment or distress."[7] Hence, it can be implied that PWS patients appear to have a form of addiction to food.

A broader understanding of the genetic causes of hyperphagia and appetite control may aid in distinguishing the differences between normal eating and aberrant eating disorders. A limited number of studies have been conducted on PWS in order to shed more light on how external and internal food cues regulate appetite in these individuals as compared to normal obese patients.[8-11] PWS is an ideal mechanistic model since these individuals have a higher drive for food consumption despite physiological and emotional satiety. Neuroimaging studies using functional magnetic resonance imaging (fMRI) are crucial in determining whether this type of behavior is a possible model for food addiction. In this review, we will address how environmental cues affect PWS and normal obese patients.

OBESITY AND PRADER-WILLI SYNDROME

Numerous studies in the past decade have attempted to shed light on not only resolving but also preventing obesity in both animals and humans.[12-15] Joranby et al. defined obesity as "an imbalance between energy input and energy expenditure,"[6] while Goldstone et al. state that obesity is "usually associated with the metabolic syndrome, consisting of a spectrum of detrimental phenotypes, including insulin resistance and hypertriglyceridemia, with increased risk of diabetes mellitus and cardiovascular disease, particularly mediated by increased visceral adiposity."[16] Obesity is a complex condition that consists of the interaction between genetics, diet, infectious agents, environmental conditions, behaviors, cultures, and societies. Obese individuals overeat with respect to the amount of energy necessary for maintaining homeostasis,[17] though the overall etiology is not well explained. There is still more research needed to elucidate genetic variants that cause obesity.

A genetic imprinting disorder, PWS results in profound hyperphagia and early childhood onset obesity caused by excessive and pathological overeating.[8-11,18] PWS patients are identified as being genetically obese since childhood. About 70% of cases are caused by a paternal genetic deletion on chromosome 15 (15q11-13), whereas

25% are from a maternal uniparental disomy of chromosome 15.[19] The remaining 1%–5% of PWS cases result from certain imprinting defects, which have a 50% risk potential to recur in future offspring.[5] There is a loss of specific brain genes such as *MAGEL2, MKRN3, NDN, SNURF-SNRPN,* and sno-RNA that are misrouted or lost, resulting in abnormal cortical development in patients diagnosed with PWS.[20] These genetic anomalies can be detected by DNA methylation analysis and in situ hybridization of the alleles.[5]

Individuals with PWS are characterized as having dolichocephaly, almond-shaped eyes, small mouth, hands, and feet, decreased muscle tone,[21] infantile hypotonia, hypogonadia, short stature, and early onset of obesity due to central dysfunction (around 18 to 36 months of age).[22] They also show major disturbances in appetite, sleep, breathing, and metabolism regulation. Abnormal eating behavior is manifested by delayed satiety, premature return of hunger after eating a meal, seeking and hoarding food and food-related objects, and ingesting inanimate items,[9] as well as excessive daytime drowsiness, poor ventilation, hypercapnia, and dental cavities.[23] Overall, many systems are affected by PWS such as the central nervous system (CNS), gastrointestinal, urogenital, cardiovascular, respiratory, and integumentary, resulting in numerous medical conditions and disorders.[5]

Miller et al.[9] hypothesized that the irregular reward processing of food stimuli in brain pathways caused the aberrant appetite, and these pathways involved the hypothalamus, frontal cortex, insula, and limbic/paralimbic areas. Furthermore, postmortem analyses have shown a decreased number of cells in the paraventricular nucleus (PVN).[24] This is a crucial evidence for explaining why satiety is difficult to attain, since PVN is the hunger center of the brain that controls appetite.[24] Using the conditional Granger causality method, the preliminary results of our group demonstrated that there is strong causal influence of the amygdala (AMY) on the anterior cingulated cortex (ACC), which is more highly activated during an emotional task associated with feeding[9] compared to the normal subjects during the resting state.

It is important to note that PWS is one of very few human genetic models for studying obesity. PWS has been associated with substance dependence and then was chosen as a well-defined genetic model since it may help explain certain neurophysiological and neuropathological mechanisms that affect appetite and food addiction.[25] Thus, this model can be investigated more comprehensively and applied to obesity research in a way better than using animal models of obesity, especially as a neuroimaging model.[26]

FOOD ADDICTION AND SHARED BRAIN PATHWAYS

In the past, traditional addiction research focused on drugs of abuse, such as cocaine, nicotine, morphine, and alcohol. It implied that both physiological and psychological dependence were often referred to "substance dependence," as defined in the *DSM-IV-TR*.[7] However, beginning with pathological gambling, a category of so-called process addictions (including gambling, sex, technology, and food) gained support in the literature.[27–29] In general, food addiction is associated with substance-related disorders[30] as well as eating disorders, although there is no clear definition for such a condition. It has been noted in the *DSM-V*'s proposed revision (http://www.dsm5.org) that a recommendation for binge eating disorder to be recognized as a free-standing diagnosis. It is also being recommended that the category of Eating Disorders be renamed as Eating and Feeding Disorders to reflect the proposed inclusion of feeding disorders. From a scientific standpoint, food addiction can be defined as a chronic relapsing problem caused by various fundamental factors that increase craving for food or food-related substances leading to a state of heightened pleasure, energy, or excitement.[15] There are also clinical accounts in which self-identified food addicts used food to self-regulate in order to escape a negative mood state.[31] One of the most commonly studied food cravings is carbohydrate craving, and the authors found that the combination of increased liking for carbohydrates in the context of decreased mood effects paralleled other addiction processes.[32] Most food addiction results in the loss of control, impulsive and/or compulsive behavior arising from emotional and environmental conditions, and a psychological dependence on food. Eating behaviors are similar to those of other addiction behaviors since both affect the levels of dopamine (DA) in the mesolimbic dopaminergic system.[15]

The neurobiological regulation of feeding is much more complex than the regulation of drug abuse, since food consumption is controlled not only by reward but also by multiple peripheral, endocrinological, and central factors beyond those that participate in reward.[33] Volkow hypothesized that adaptation in the reward circuit and also in the motivational, memory, and control circuits that occur with repeated exposure to large quantities of highly palatable food is similar to that which one observes with repeated drug exposures.[33]

Reward/Saliency Circuitry

Drug addiction has significant reduction DA D_2 receptor availability in striatum that persists months after protracted detoxification. Drug abusers (cocaine and alcohol) also show decreased DA release, which is likely to reflect reduced DA cell firing.[33] Results in one study showed that subjects with the lower amount of D_2 receptors had higher body mass index (BMI).[34]

Inhibitory Control/Emotional Reactivity Circuit

Reductions in striatal D_2 receptors in the detoxified drug-addicted subjects were associated with decreased metabolic activity in orbitofrontal cortex (OFC), anterior cingulate cortex (ACC), and dorsolateral prefrontal cortex (DLPFC).[35] Since these regions are involved with inhibitory control and with emotional processing, improper regulation by DA in addicted subjects could underlie their loss of control over drug intake and their poor emotional self-regulation.[36] D_2 receptor availability was associated with metabolism in DLPFC, medial OFC, and ACC in obese subjects,[33] which contribute to overeating in part through deregulation of prefrontal regions implicated in inhibitory control and emotional regulation.

Motivation/Drive Circuit

During cocaine intoxication or as the intoxication subsides, the drug-induced DA increases in striatum activate OFC and ACC, which result in craving and compulsive drug intake. However, when food-related stimuli are given to obese subjects, medial prefrontal cortex is activated and cravings are reported.[9]

Memory, Conditioning, and Habits

Circuits underlying memory and learning have been proposed to be involved in drug addiction. The effects of drugs on memory systems suggest ways that neutral stimuli can acquire reinforcing properties and motivational salience through conditioned incentive learning.[33] DA regulates food consumption not only through modulation of its rewarding properties but also by facilitating conditioning to food stimuli that then drive the motivation to consume the food.[33]

In addition, Avena has developed a rat model of sucrose bingeing, in which rats are maintained on a diet of 12-h access to a 10% sucrose solution (or 25% glucose in earlier studies) and standard rodent chow, then followed by 12 h of sucrose and chow deprivation for a period of about 1 month. The findings of this model relate to a variety of factors associated with addictive behavior and with sugar classified as an addictive substance [37] because it follows the typical stages of the human addiction pathway of bingeing, withdrawal, craving, and bingeing in a never-ending cycle.

THE REWARD SYSTEM HYPOTHESIS AND PATHOLOGICAL BRAIN REINFORCEMENT

The reward system hypothesis states that drugs and food compete for the same brain pathways. It was discovered that the globus pallidus, thalamus, and subgenual cingulate were associated with immediate rewards, while the caudate, insula, and ventral prefrontal cortex responded to reward consequences.[38] The mesolimbic reward system is a common pathway in response to food intake (consummatory food reward),[39] which may reinforce craving behavior and increase risk for overeating.[8] This is similar to the reinforcement sensitivity model of substance abuse, which postulates that certain people show greater reactivity of reward circuitry to psychoactive drugs. Thus, reward processing is linked to addiction, and it is processed only if it can promote the craving of seeking food as a positive reward rather than facing the consequences of the reward behavior.[24]

On the other hand, obesity is a "reward deficiency syndrome"[40] since DA D_2 receptors are mediators of reinforcement and compulsiveness, and obese subjects were found to have lower levels of these receptors in the striatum.[15] In a study with subjects of normal weight, DA D_2 availability in the striatum modulated eating behavioral patterns, and DA D_2 receptor availability negatively correlated with the tendency to eat when exposed to negative emotion.[41] Another hypothesis postulates that greater anticipated reward from food intake (anticipatory food reward)[39] increases the risk for overeating. Stice tested the hypothesis that obese individuals experience greater reward from food consumption (consummatory food reward) and anticipated consumption (anticipatory food reward) than lean individuals. Results suggested that individuals with increased activation in the gustatory cortex and somatosensory regions and decreased activation in the striatum in response to anticipation and consumption of food may be at risk for overeating and consequent weight gain.[39] In addition, Stice investigated the difference between emotional and nonemotional eaters during negative versus neutral mood states. Results indicated that emotional eating is related to increased anticipatory and consummatory food reward, but only during the negative mood state.[39] Most important, the common pathway for addiction involves the mesolimbic frontocortical dopamine system, which is a reward pathway that controls eating behavior. Addictive behaviors cause the release of DA in the reward pathway, causing almost immediate positive reinforcement.[14] Increased activation in the somatic parietal areas in food-addicted individuals suggests that enhanced activity in these regions involves sensory processing of food, which may make food even more rewarding.[42] Morris and Dolan [42] showed that the state of hunger can influence the memory associated with food-related stimuli in fasting individuals. Joranby and colleagues[6] found that the localization of brain activation was dependent on the stimulus received. For example, the right anterior OFC had a variable response to all stimuli, despite hunger, while the right posterior OFC had different response only with food-related stimuli during hunger. Thus, the posterior area was associated with general rewards, while the anterior part was associated with abstract and goal-oriented rewards.

CONCLUSION

Hyperphagia is thought to be a contributing factor to increased caloric intake and hence obesity. PWS is a human genetic model for hyperphagia as demonstrated by fMRI for explaining obesity. Functional neuroimaging would be the most logical tool in precisely locating the brain regions responsible for controlling appetite and for the reward centers of food addiction. In past studies, using food-related pictures or other visual means to elicit neural responses has been a standard method of determining valid mechanisms that delineate brain reinforcement and the path to obesity. Hence, the fMRI-supported hypothesis that PWS is a naturally occurring human genetic model for food addiction or loss of control of eating or absence of satiety would be crucial for further studies.

ACKNOWLEDGMENTS

This work was supported in part by grants from the National Institutes of Health (NS045518 and DA016221).

REFERENCES

1. Blakemore AI, Froguel P. Is obesity our genetic legacy? *J Clin Endocrinol Metab* 2008;93:S51–S56.
2. Gray J, Yeo G, Cox J. Hyperphagia, severe obesity, impaired cognitive function, and hyperactivity associated with functional loss of one copy of the brain-derived neurotrophic factor (BDNF) gene. *Diabetes* 2006;55:S51–S56.
3. Adams M, Smith UM, Logan CV, Johnson CA. Recent advances in the molecular pathology, cell biology and genetics of ciliopathies. *J Med Genet* 2008;45: 257–267.
4. Frayling TM, Timpson NJ, Weedon MN, et al. A common variant in the FTO gene is associated with body mass index and predisposes to childhood and adult obesity. *Science* 2007;316:889–894.
5. Benarroch F, Hirsch HJ, Genstil L, Landau YE, Gross-Tsur V. Prader-Willi syndrome: medical prevention and behavioral challenges. *Child Adolesc Psychiatr Clin N Am* 2007;16:695–708.
6. Joranby L, Pineda K, Gold M. Addiction to food and brain reward systems. *Sex Addict Compuls* 2005;12:201–217.
7. American Psychiatric Association. *Diagnostic and Statistic Manual of Mental Disorder*. 4th ed. Washington, DC: American Psychiatric Association, 2000.
8. Shapira NA, Lessig MC, He AG, James GA, Driscoll DJ, Liu Y. Satiety dysfunction in Prader-Willi syndrome demonstrated by fMRI. *J Neurol Neurosurg Psychiatry* 2005;76:260–262.
9. Miller JL, James GA, Goldstone AP, et al. Enhanced activation of reward mediating prefrontal regions in response to food stimuli in Prader-Willi syndrome. *J Neurol Neurosurg Psychiatry* 2007;78:615–619.
10. Dimitropoulos A, Schultz RT. Food-related neural circuitry in Prader-Willi syndrome: response to high- versus low-calorie foods. *J Autism Dev Disord* 2008;38:1642–1653.
11. Holsen LM, Zarcone JR, Chambers R, et al. Genetic subtype differences in neural circuitry of food motivation in Prader-Willi syndrome. *Int J Obes (Lond)* 2009;33:273–283.
12. Avena NM. The study of food addiction using animal models of binge eating. *Appetite* 2010;55:734–737.

13. Dietrich MO, Horvath TL. Feeding signals and brain circuitry. *Eur J Neurosci* 2009;30:1688–1696.
14. Gold MS, Graham NA, Cocores JA, Nixon SJ. Food addiction? *J Addict Med* 2009;3:42–45.
15. Wang GJ, Volkow ND, Thanos PK, Fowler JS. Imaging of brain dopamine pathways: implications for understanding obesity. *J Addict Med* 2009;3:8–18.
16. Goldstone AP, Patterson M, Kalingag N, et al. Fasting and postprandial hyperghrelinemia in Prader-Willi syndrome is partially explained by hypoinsulinemia, and is not due to peptide YY3-36 deficiency or seen in hypothalamic obesity due to craniopharyngioma. *J Clin Endocrinol Metab* 2005;90:2681–2690.
17. Hays NP, Bathalon GP, McCrory MA, Roubenoff R, Lipman R, Roberts SB. Eating behavior correlates of adult weight gain and obesity in healthy women aged 55–65 y. *Am J Clin Nutr* 2002;75:476–483.
18. Mantoulan C, Payoux P, Diene G, et al. PET scan perfusion imaging in the Prader-Willi syndrome: new insights into the psychiatric and social disturbances. *J Cereb Blood Flow Metab* 2011;31:275–282.
19. Gunay-Aygun M, Schwartz S, Heeger S, O'Riordan MA, Cassidy SB. The changing purpose of Prader-Willi syndrome clinical diagnostic criteria and proposed revised criteria. *Pediatrics* 2001;108:E92.
20. Pagliardini S, Ren J, Wevrick R, Greer JJ. Developmental abnormalities of neuronal structure and function in prenatal mice lacking the prader-willi syndrome gene necdin. *Am J Pathol* 2005;167:175–191.
21. Cassidy SB. Prader-Willi syndrome. *J Med Genet* 1997;34:917–923.
22. Goldstone AP. Prader-Willi syndrome: advances in genetics, pathophysiology and treatment. *Trends Endocrinol Metab* 2004;15:12–20.
23. Nixon GM, Brouillette RT. Sleep and breathing in Prader-Willi syndrome. *Pediatr Pulmonol* 2002;34:209–217.
24. Kalra SP, Kalra PS. Overlapping and interactive pathways regulating appetite and craving. *J Addict Dis* 2004;23:5–21.
25. Gearhardt AN, Yokum S, Orr PT, Stice E, Corbin WR, Brownell KD. Neural correlates of food addiction. *Arch Gen Psychiatry* 2011;68:808–816.
26. Zhang Y, von Deneen KM, Tian J, Gold MS, Liu Y. Food addiction and neuroimaging. *Curr Pharm Des* 2011;17:1149–1157.
27. Bancroft J, Vukadinovic Z. Sexual addiction, sexual compulsivity, sexual impulsivity, or what? Toward a theoretical model. *J Sex Res* 2004;41:225–234.
28. Comings DE, Gade-Andavolu R, Gonzalez N, et al. The additive effect of neurotransmitter genes in pathological gambling. *Clin Genet* 2001;60:107–16.
29. Liu Y, von Deneen K, Kobeissy F, Gold M. Food addiction and obesity: evidence from bench to bedside. *J Psychoactive Drugs* 2010;42:133–145.
30. Warren MW, Gold MS. The relationship between obesity and drug use. *Am J Psychiatry* 2007;164:1268, 1268–1269.
31. Ifland JR, Preuss HG, Marcus MT, et al. Refined food addiction: a classic substance use disorder. *Med Hypotheses* 2009;72:518–526.
32. Corsica JA, Spring BJ. Carbohydrate craving: a double-blind, placebo-controlled test of the self-medication hypothesis. *Eat Behav* 2008;9:447–454.
33. Volkow ND, Wang GJ, Fowler JS, Telang F. Overlapping neuronal circuits in addiction and obesity: evidence of systems pathology. *Philos Trans R Soc Lond B Biol Sci* 2008;363:3191–3200.
34. Haltia LT, Rinne JO, Merisaari H, et al. Effects of intravenous glucose on dopaminergic function in the human brain in vivo. *Synapse* 2007;61:748–756.
35. Volkow ND, Wang GJ, Telang F, et al. Profound decreases in dopamine release in striatum in detoxified alcoholics: possible orbitofrontal involvement. *J Neurosci* 2007;27:12700–12706.
36. Goldstein RZ, Volkow ND. Drug addiction and its underlying neurobiological basis: neuroimaging evidence for the involvement of the frontal cortex. *Am J Psychiatry* 2002;159:1642–1652.
37. Avena NM. The study of food addiction using animal models of binge eating. *Appetite* 2010;55:734–737.
38. Elliott R, Friston KJ, Dolan RJ. Dissociable neural responses in human reward systems. *J Neurosci* 2000;20:6159–6165.
39. Stice E, Spoor S, Bohon C, Veldhuizen MG, Small DM. Relation of reward from food intake and anticipated food intake to obesity: a functional magnetic resonance imaging study. *J Abnorm Psychol* 2008;117:924–935.
40. Blum K, Braverman ER, Holder JM, et al. Reward deficiency syndrome: a biogenetic model for the diagnosis and treatment of impulsive, addictive, and compulsive behaviors. *J Psychoactive Drugs* 2000;32(suppl):1–112.
41. Volkow ND, Wang GJ, Maynard L, et al. Brain dopamine is associated with eating behaviors in humans. *Int J Eat Disord* 2003;33:136–142.
42. Morris JS, Dolan RJ. Involvement of human amygdala and orbitofrontal cortex in hunger-enhanced memory for food stimuli. *J Neurosci* 2001;21:5304–5310.

21

Environmental Toxins as Triggers for Obesity

ANGELO TREMBLAY AND MARINA SÁNCHEZ

INTRODUCTION

It is not necessarily obvious for a physiologist interested in toxicology to present a message that is of entire relevance regarding the study of addiction in obesity. However, if one considers the addiction of humankind for everything that could be a source of pleasure and easiness, even chemical toxins become a relevant issue.

The increased prevalence of obesity has forced a thorough examination of what may explain the apparent proneness of people to store spontaneously more fat under free-living conditions. In this regard, there is a consensus among health professionals and scientists about the idea that environmental changes have promoted what has been ultimately described as an epidemic. These changes have also been proposed to represent a toxic environment by making reference to the suboptimal compatibility between what is offered by the socio-psycho-economic context of living and what is needed by the human body to reach an optimal functionality.[1] This notion also reminds us that the environment favors the exposure to nonnatural compounds that exert a genuine toxic effect. In this chapter, this question is addressed by mainly referring to the case of lipid soluble contaminants and their potential negative effect on energy balance.

ARE WE AND OUR FOOD POLLUTED?

Many reports have shown that the body substance bears a large amount of nonnatural compounds. In most cases, it is difficult to evaluate the risk associated with this contamination, which is frequently low compared to the concentrations having been declared as safe in animals. However, our own experience with the study of the environmental persistence of organochlorines (OCs) suggests

that theoretically safe levels of body accumulation can produce subtle significant effects under circumstances that represent free-living conditions in obese individuals.

The issue of accumulation of chemicals is relevant in the study of potential determinants of obesity. A relevant example of such a possibility is the case of OC compounds,[2] which have been traditionally used as efficient insecticides in agriculture and lubricants in other industrial sectors. OCs are lipid soluble and their half-life is generally long, reaching several decades for some compounds. Accordingly, body accumulation is greater in obese than in lean people,[3] at least partly because the dilution space provided by their large fat mass presumably reduces their clearance rate over time.[4]

Even though OCs were banned several decades ago in Canada and the United States for their use in agriculture, they remain detectable in the food chain, particularly in animal foods like dairy products, meat, and fish. This was indeed made clear several years ago when Atlantic salmon was shown to still bear significant body loads of some contaminants, including OCs.[5,6] In this case, feeding salmon with pellets containing contaminated fish oil appeared as the main cause of this problem. It was also viewed as a practice contributing to the perpetuation of the accumulation of OCs in the food chain. Other studies also suggest that OCs penetrating the food chain can come from elsewhere since they can be transported by air to be deposited on cold surfaces of the planet.[7,8]

In summary, these observations indicate that the persistence of chemicals in the environment, including the human body substance, may remain significant beyond the time of their formal withdrawal. As discussed in the next sections, they represent a source of metabolic disturbance that can favor a positive energy balance.

TOXINS AND ENERGY BALANCE

The environment that favors obesity and its underlying state of positive energy balance has been described as toxic[1] because of its effect to promote practices that are not compatible with optimal body functioning and body weight stability. Specifically, these practices may include the consumption of cheap low nutrient foods that complicate appetite control and favor overfeeding. These practices also promote sedentariness and its corollaries such as reduced energy expenditure and body stimulation. With respect to chemical toxins, their effects are more subtle, as it is the case for their impact on thyroid function. Indeed, animal research has demonstrated that chemicals such as OCs impair the development of the thyroid gland and reduce the blood levels of thyroid hormones.[9,10,11] In addition, the thyroid gland is further handicapped by OCs due to their stimulation of the UDP-glucoronosyltransferase enzyme, which is known to accentuate the body clearance of these hormones.[12,13] In humans, our research experience is concordant since we have found a negative relationship between circulating levels of triiodothyronine (T3), a thyroid hormone, and OCs.[14] Thus, although chemical toxins do not a priori modify consumer's practice regarding obesity-related phenotypes, they nevertheless have the potential to affect them via more discrete strategies.

WHEN BODY WEIGHT LOSS BECOMES A PROBLEM

A major preoccupation for health professionals intervening with obese individuals is to reduce body fat stores in order to improve metabolic fitness and thus attenuate the risk of diseases such as diabetes and cardiovascular diseases. For the toxicologist, body fat loss refers to another reality regarding the management of body concentrations of lipophilic toxins. In this context, a weight-reducing program is a strategy that results in a decrease in the dilution space of these toxins.

About 30 years ago, Backman and Kolmodin-Hedman documented for the first time that weight loss induced by a bariatric surgery increases the plasma concentration of OC compounds such as DDT and DDE.[15] More recently, we confirmed this observation by showing that obese patients subjected to a biliopancreatic diversion displayed a 388% increase in total plasma OC concentration 1 year after the surgical intervention.[16]

Our investigations of weight loss induced by diet restriction combined with physical exercise contributed to better understand some metabolic effects of weight loss. In response to a diet-exercise program leading to resistance to further lose fat, we collected blood and adipose tissue samples from which fluctuations of OC concentrations were measured. As expected, a significant increase in both plasma and adipose tissue (AT) OC concentrations was noted.[17] It is also important to emphasize that body weight loss was significantly correlated with changes in plasma OCs, indicating that the greater the success in terms of weight loss, the greater was the increase in the level of circulating pollutants. A further analysis of these effects revealed that changes in OCs within abdominal AT, femoral AT, and blood were highly positively correlated.[18] This is in agreement with the idea that total body fat can be viewed in this case as a global dilution space in which changes in OCs proceed in a uniform manner in response to a caloric deficit leading to fat loss.

Beyond the demonstration that weight/fat loss predicts the severity of the OC hyperconcentration, we have also shown that it is predictive of its related metabolic changes. Indeed, in response to the diet/exercise-induced fat loss, the changes in the concentration of some compounds were correlated to a greater than predicted decrease in plasma T3[19] and skeletal muscle oxidative enzymes.[20] Accordingly, the main predictor of the decrease in resting metabolic rate was also the increase in plasma OCs.[19] More recently, we repeated this analysis by using sleeping metabolic rate measured in a respiratory chamber as a dependent variable to further document this issue. As expected, the body weight loss induced a significant decrease in sleeping metabolic rate, which was greater than what would have been predicted by the natural variation of SMR in relation to body weight in a reference population.[21] The difference between the predicted and measured change in SMR, also called adaptive thermogenesis, was also mostly predicted by changes in plasma OCs.

In summary, these observations suggest that body weight loss is an intervention that is useful to investigate the impact of variations in body lipophilic pollutants on energy metabolism. This vision is reinforced by the fact that the quantitative importance of their variations predicts the severity of the deterioration of the body's metabolic "furnace." Furthermore, the extent to which these variations can predict weight regain in ex-obese individuals has not been documented and might remain unconsidered due to the methodological difficulties that such an investigation may pose.

Finally, the results described thus far impose the question as to how obesity should be perceived. Indeed, while it is generally perceived as the unfortunate outcome of the exposure to a "toxic" environment,[1] these observations open a different perspective focusing on some protective effects of body fat gain. In this case, the protection comes from the buffering effect of fat on OC toxins with the beneficial effect that target cells are less exposed to their detrimental effects. After all, when body weight loss becomes a problem, it is certainly relevant to reconsider our vision of variations in body fat regarding the maintenance of body homeostasis.

IS THERE A DECONTAMINATING SOLUTION?

The experience of testing that we have accumulated over time regarding the body clearance of organochlorines has led us to examine this issue under different conditions. As an attempt to investigate the long-term effect of regular aerobic exercise on the concentration of OC pollutants, we recruited endurance athletes having accumulated thousands of training hours over many years.[3] Their plasma OC concentrations were slightly lower than those observed in sedentary lean controls, which represents an observation that is opposite to initial expectations. Indeed, considering that their high training regimen had probably increased considerably their food intake without substantial changes in fat mass, it was logical to postulate that these athletes would be more contaminated. Thus, it would not be unrealistic to hypothesize that regular exercising over many years might accentuate the clearance of OC compounds.

The plasma OC concentrations have also been measured in vegans maintaining rigorous food habits since more than 10 years. Their plasma OC profile suggested that chronic nonconsumption of any animal foods, including meat, fish, eggs, and dairy products, was associated with only small decreases in some OC compounds.[14]

Several studies have shown that the nondigestible compound olestra has the potential to considerably reduce the blood levels of some contaminants.

This was found in severely contaminated individuals[22] as well as in subjects displaying a habitual body load of pollutants.[23] These observations prompted us to postulate that the olestra supplementation during the course of a weight-reducing program could prevent the hyperconcentration of OCs resulting from fat loss. Unfortunately, olestra did not induce this effect for most contaminants, with the exception that it contributed to a significant attenuation of the increase in β-Hexachlorocyclohexane (β-HCH), which remains one of the most detectable lipid soluble pollutants in the body.[14]

Taken together, these observations emphasize the difficulty to successfully accelerate the clearance of some body toxins such as OC.

CONCLUSION

Environmental toxins are not primarily considered when addiction is discussed in relation to obesity. However, they are part of a global lifestyle for which humankind displays a great attraction. In this chapter, the authors use their experience in the study of OCs to illustrate the subtle and potentially detrimental effects of pollutants when tested after their withdrawal for common use. Since the search of productivity and profitability remains dominant in the preoccupations of industrialized countries, it might well be possible that the same story is also valid for other compounds.

REFERENCES

1. Brownell KD, Horgen KB. *Food Fight: The Inside Story of the Food Industry, America's Obesity Crisis, and What We Can Do About It.* New York: McGraw-Hill/Contemporary Books, 2004.
2. Kutz FW, Wood PH, Bottimore DP. Organochlorines pesticides and polychlorinated biphenyls in human adipose tissue. *Rev Environ Contam T* 1991;120:1–82.
3. Pelletier C, Despres JP, Tremblay A. Plasma organochlorine concentrations in endurance athletes and obese individuals. *Med Sci Sports Exer* 2002;34:1971–1975.
4. Jung D, Becher H, Edler L, et al. Elimination of beta-hexachlorocyclohexane in occupationally exposed persons. *J Toxicol Environ Health* 1997;51:23–34.
5. Easton MD, Luszniak D and Von der GE. Preliminary examination of contaminant loadings in farmed salmon, wild salmon and commercial salmon feed. *Chemosphere* 2002;46:1053–1074.
6. Hites RA, Foran JA, Carpenter DO, Hamilton MC, Knuth BA, Schwager SJ. Global assessment of organic contaminants in farmed salmon. *Science* 2004;303:226–229.

7. Barrie LA, Gregor D, Hargrave B, et al. Arctic contaminants: sources, occurrence and pathways. *Sci Total Environ* 1992;122:1–74.

8. Wilkinson AC, Kimpe LE, Blais JM. Air-water gas exchange of chlorinated pesticides in four lakes spanning a 1,205 meter elevation range in the Canadian Rocky Mountains. *Environ Toxicol Chem* 2005;24:61–69.

9. Barsano CP. Environmental factors altering thyroid function and their assessment. *Environ Health Perspect* 1981;38:71–82.

10. Bastomsky CH, Murthy PV. Enhanced in vitro hepatic glucuronidation of thyroxine in rats following cutaneous application or ingestion of polychlorinated biphenyls. *Can J Physiol Pharmacol* 1976;54:23–26.

11. Byrne JJ, Carbone JP, Hanson EA. Hypothyroidism and abnormalities in the kinetics of thyroid hormone metabolism and rats treated chronically with polychlorinated biphenyls and polybrominated biphenyls. *Endocrinology* 1987;121:520–527.

12. Barter RA, Klaassen CD. UDP-glucuronosyltranferase inducers reduce thyroid hormone levels in rats by an extrathyroidal mechanism. *Toxicol Appl Pharmacol* 1992;113:36–42.

13. Barter RA, Klaassen CD. Reduction of thyroid hormone levels and alteration of thyroid function by four representative UDP-glucuronosyltranferase inducers in rats. *Toxicol Appl Pharmacol* 1994;128:9–17.

14. Arguin H, Sanchez M, Bray GA, et al. Impact of adopting a vegan diet or an olestra supplementation on plasma organochlorine concentrations: results from a case-control and a 9-month interventional study. *Br J Nutr* 2010;103(10):1433–1441.

15. Backman L, Kolmodin-Hedman B. Concentration of DDT and DDE in plasma and subcutaneous adipose tissue before and after intestinal bypass operation for treatment of obesity. *Toxicol Appl Pharmacol* 1978;46:663–669.

16. Hue O, Marcotte J, Berrigan F, et al. Increased plasma levels of toxic pollutants accompanying weight loss induced by hypocaloric diet or by bariatric surgery. *Obes Surg* 2006;16:1145–1154.

17. Chevrier J, Dewailly E, Ayotte P, Mauriège P, Després JP, Tremblay A. Body weight loss increases plasma and adipose tissue concentrations of potentially toxic pollutants in obese individuals. *Int J Obes Relat Metab Disord* 2000;24:1272–1278.

18. Pelletier C, Imbeault P, Tremblay A. Energy balance and pollution by organochlorines and polychlorinated biphenyls. *Obes Rev* 2003;4:17–24.

19. Pelletier C, Doucet E, Imbeault P, Tremblay A. Associations between weight loss-induced changes in plasma organochlorine concentrations, serum $T(3)$ concentration, and resting metabolic rate. *Toxicol Sci* 2002;67:46–51.

20. Imbeault P, Tremblay A, Simoneau JA, Joanisse DR. Weight loss-induced rise in plasma pollutant is associated with reduced skeletal muscle oxidative capacity. *Am J Physiol Endocrinol Metab* 2002;282: E574–E579.

21. Tremblay A, Pelletier C, Doucet E, Imbeault P. Thermogenesis and weight loss in obese individuals: a primary association with organochlorine pollution. *Int J Obes Relat Metab Disord* 2004;28:936–939.

22. Redgrave TG, Wallace P, Jandacek RJ, Tso P. Treatment with a dietary fat substitute decreased Arochlor 1254 contamination in an obese diabetic male. *J Nutr Biochem* 2005;16:383–384.

23. Moser GA, McLachlan MS. A non-absorbable dietary fat substitute enhances elimination of persistent lipophilic contaminants in humans. *Chemosphere* 1999;39:1513–1521.

22

The Special Case of Sugar-Sweetened Beverages

CARA B. EBBELING, WALTER C. WILLETT, AND DAVID S. LUDWIG

INTRODUCTION

Sugar-sweetened beverages (SSBs) include not only conventional carbonated beverages, often known as sodas, but also noncarbonated beverages such as fruit drinks, sports drinks, energy drinks, enhanced waters, and highly sweetened coffees and teas. Consumption of SSBs is remarkably high, representing an estimated 10%–15% of total energy needs across a wide age range.[1,2] The energy in SSBs typically is in the form of high-fructose corn syrup or sucrose. Emerging data indicate that consuming SSBs has a uniquely adverse effect on dietary quality that, in turn, alters metabolism and increases risk for obesity, type 2 diabetes, cardiovascular disease (CVD), and other conditions such as gout and dental caries (Fig. 22.1). The purpose of this chapter is to summarize the evidence for a link between consuming SSBs and disease risk, and to consider plausible dietary and metabolic pathways for these effects relating to four properties of SSBs (energy in liquid form, high glycemic load, high sweetness intensity, and sugar content).

CONSUMING SUGAR-SWEETENED BEVERAGES AND DISEASE RISK

Obesity

Multiple longitudinal cohort studies indicate a positive relationship between consumption of SSBs and weight gain in children and adults, as summarized in recent systematic reviews.[3,4] For example, in a study of 10,904 preschool children, Welsh et al.[5] noted that those who were overweight or obese were approximately two times more likely to become or remain obese if they consumed SSBs during 1 year of observation. In a prospective study of 548 middle school students, Ludwig et al.[6] found that risk for becoming obese over two academic years increased by 60% for every additional serving

of SSBs consumed per day. In an 8-year prospective study of 51,603 women in the Nurses' Health Study II, Schulze et al.[7] observed an 8-kg weight gain among those who increased consumption of SSBs during the initial 4 years and maintained the increase over the subsequent 4 years compared to a 2.8-kg gain among those who decreased consumption of SSBs and maintained the decrease. Results of several other studies, mainly employing a weaker, cross-sectional design, are equivocal.[4]

To date, randomized trials designed to evaluate the effects of SSBs on body weight have focused on children and adolescents, with body mass index (BMI) as the primary outcome. James et al.[8] conducted a school-based study using a cluster randomized design among 644 students aged 7 to 11 years in England. The intervention comprised four educational sessions to encourage reduced consumption of all carbonated beverages. The incidence of obesity decreased significantly over 1 year among students in the intervention versus control group, but absolute change in BMI was not significant in response to the low-intensity intervention. In another school-based study, Sichieri et al.[9] used a cluster randomized design among 1,140 students aged 9 to 12 years in Brazil. The intervention focused on reducing consumption of SSBs and increasing consumption of water over one academic year. BMI decreased significantly among overweight girls in the intervention versus control group, but the group difference was not significant in the full cohort. Employing an intervention that relied on weekly home delivery of noncaloric beverages as a strategy for reducing consumption of SSBs, Ebbeling et al.[10] conducted a 25-week randomized controlled trial among 103 high school students. BMI decreased significantly in the intervention versus control group among overweight adolescents, but the effect was not significant in the full cohort that also included lean students.

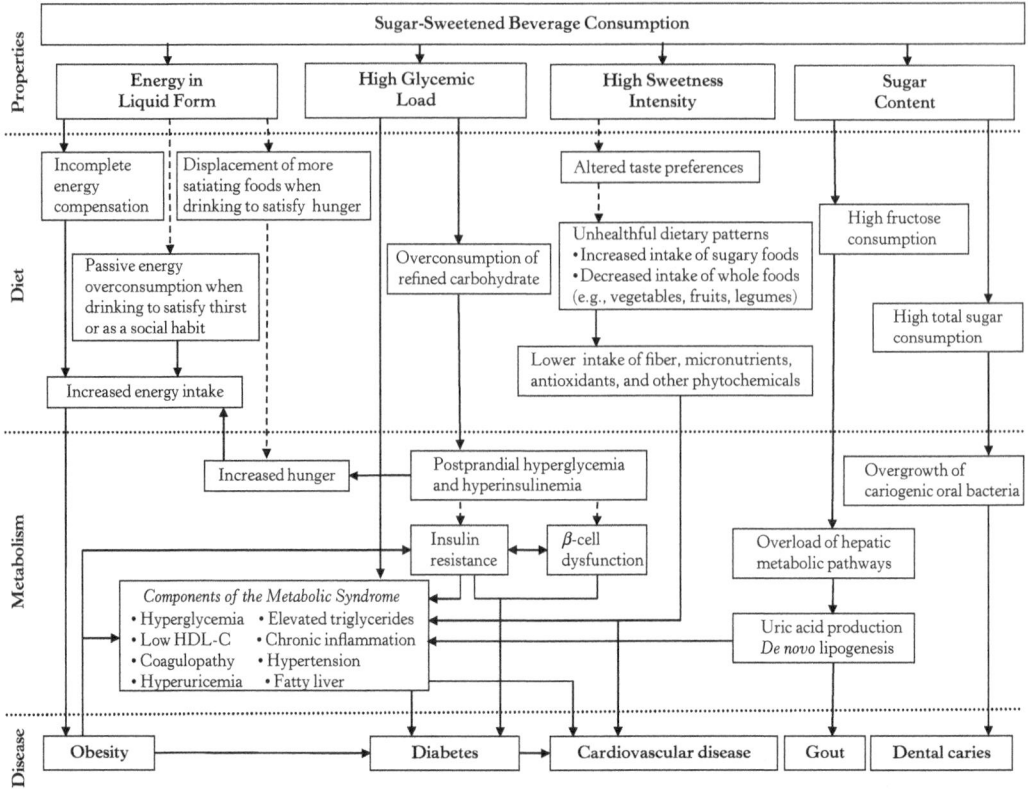

FIGURE 22.1. Mechanisms by which properties of sugar-sweetened beverages may adversely affect diet, metabolism, and risk for disease.

Solid lines indicate pathways supported by published data, and dashed lines indicate pathways warranting further investigation.

Source: Copyright, D Ludwig & W Willett, Harvard School of Public Health, 2009.

Type 2 Diabetes and Cardiovascular Disease

Several prospective observational studies suggest that consuming SSBs may increase risk for type 2 diabetes and cardiovascular disease (CVD) via weight-dependent and weight-independent pathways.[11] In an analysis of 6,039 person-observations from the Framingham Heart Study, Dhingra et al.[12] observed an odds ratio of 1.44 for incident metabolic syndrome during a mean follow-up period of 4 years among middle-aged participants consuming ≥1 serving of SSBs per day. Moreover, this level of consumption also was associated with elevated risk for developing individual components of the syndrome (obesity, increased waist circumference, impaired fasting glucose, hypertriglyceridemia, low high-density lipoprotein cholesterol). Montonen et al.[13] reported a 67% increased risk of diabetes among 4,304 middle-aged Finnish men and women over 12 years, comparing highest to lowest quartiles for consumption of SSBs and adjusting for

potentially confounding variables, including body mass index (BMI). Palmer et al.[14] found an association between consuming SSBs and diabetes among 59,000 African American women over 6 years, a relationship that was partially but not totally attributable to BMI. In the aforementioned study by Schulze et al.,[7] among young adult women in the Nurses' Health Study II, those who consumed ≥1 serving of SSBs per day had an 83% increased risk of diabetes, with BMI accounting for only half of the increase. In a meta-analysis of 11 prospective studies, persons with the highest consumption of SSBs, usually 1–2 servings per day, had a 26% increased risk of type 2 diabetes (RR = 1.26 [95% CI 1.12–1.41]).[15] Fung et al.,[16] analyzing data from 88,520 women the Nurses' Health Study, found that consuming ≥2 servings of SSBs per day was associated with a 35% increased risk of incident coronary heart disease (nonfatal myocardial infarction and fatal coronary heart disease) over a 24-year period, after adjustment for potential confounders. Further adjustment for BMI attenuated but did not fully explain the association.

Data from interventional studies examining risk for diabetes and CVD are limited. One 10-week study, presented in two reports,[17–18] was designed to examine the effects of consuming sucrose (28% of total energy) versus artificial sweetener, primarily as beverages, in 41 overweight individuals. Systolic and diastolic blood pressures increased significantly more in the sucrose group, with net group effects of 6.9 and 5.3 mmHg, respectively.[17] Likewise, measures of chronic inflammation (serum haptoglobin and transferrin) increased significantly more with sucrose, even after adjusting for changes in body weight.[18]

Other conditions

Consuming SSB adversely affects other conditions, including gout and dental caries, that are not the focus of this chapter but have substantial public health importance. Regarding gout, a form of inflammatory arthritis related to hyperuricemia, Choi et al.[19] reported that consuming just 1 serving of SSB per day increased risk of incident gout by 45% among 46,393 men in the Health Professionals Follow-up Study and by 74% among 78,906 women in the Nurses' Health Study. Consumption of SSB has been directly associated with dental caries in primary and permanent teeth.[20–22] Using National Health and Nutrition Examination data from the 1970s, Ismail et al.[22] noted that at- or between-meal consumption of SSB was independently association with DMFT (decayed\missing\filled teeth) score. In a two-year study of low-income children aged 3-5 years, Lim et al.[21] found that the DMFT score for those who increased daily consumption of soft drinks from about 0.5 liter to over 1 liter was 1.75 times higher compared to their counterparts who did not increase consumption.

PLAUSIBLE BIOLOGICAL PATHWAYS FOR THE ADVERSE EFFECTS OF SUGAR-SWEETENED BEVERAGES

Energy in Liquid Form

A conventional 12-ounce serving of carbonated beverage contains approximately 150 kcal. Medium and large portions of SSBs sold in fast food establishments, convenience stores, and theaters often contain 300–500 kcal. Consuming energy in liquid form may elicit incomplete energy compensation, displacement of more satiating foods, and passive calorie overconsumption, thereby promoting weight gain and obesity.

Several lines of evidence, from observational and experimental studies, indicate that modification of dietary intake to compensate for energy consumed as a clear beverage is less complete than for energy consumed in the form of solid food. For example, when evaluating beverage consumption among 1,810 children and adolescents, Harnack et al.[23] observed that those who drank 9 ounces or more of SSBs per day, on average, consumed nearly 200 kcal per day more than their counterparts who did not drink SSBs. Wang et al.,[24] using a within-person comparison of reported diet among 3,098 children and adolescents, found that each additional 8-ounce serving of SSBs corresponded to a net increase of 106 kcal. Mattes[25] showed that total energy intake among 16 young adults was greater during a day when a SSB was given at lunch, compared to the preceding day, with extra energy intake closely approximating the energy in the SSB. In another study of 16 young adults, DiMeglio and Mattes[26] observed precise energy compensation under free-living conditions when sugar was consumed in solid form (jelly beans) but no compensation when the same amount of sugar was consumed in liquid form (SSBs). Maurao et al.[27] contrasted responses in 120 adults to an ad libitum lunch containing standardized portions of a solid food (watermelon fruit) versus beverage (watermelon juice), controlled for energy and carbohydrate content. Although energy consumed during lunch was not dependent on the form in which energy was provided, intake was 193 kcal greater following the lunch containing juice, suggesting adverse effects on satiety. Based on a secondary analysis of data from a dietary intervention trial of 810 middle-aged adults, Chen et al.[28] noted that reducing energy consumed in liquid versus solid form was more effective for weight loss. In particular, reducing consumption of SSBs by only 1 serving per day was associated with weight loss of 0.49 kg at 6 months and 0.65 kg at 18 months.

Drinking SSBs to satisfy hunger or thirst may have unintended consequences. *Hunger* refers to sensations that initiate ingestion of food to meet energy needs, and *thirst* refers to sensations that initiate ingestion of fluids to maintain adequate hydration.[29] When consumed in response to hunger, SSBs may displace more satiating foods, thereby promoting increased hunger (possibly due to high glycemic load, discussed later). Moreover, consuming energy-containing beverages to satisfy thirst may compromise homeostatic regulatory mechanisms that control energy balance, resulting in passive calorie overconsumption. However, evaluating links between hunger, thirst, consumption of SSBs, and positive energy balance poses a challenge because ratings of hunger and thirst vary widely both within and between individuals and do not reliably predict dietary behaviors.[29] Indeed, many individuals consume foods and beverages as a social habit or to alleviate emotions,[30–31] irrespective of the physiologic sensations defining hunger and thirst.

High Glycemic Load

The term *glycemic load* is used to describe the effects of dietary intake on postprandial glycemia.[32–33] After ingestion of most refined carbohydrate, as during an oral glucose tolerance test, blood glucose and insulin levels increase rapidly.[34] Elevation of circulating insulin relative to glucagon stimulates glucose uptake by insulin-sensitive tissues, resulting in a rapid drop in blood glucose to concentrations below fasting during the later postprandial period for many individuals.[34] Hunger increases due to limited availability of metabolic fuels, often with heightened preference for products containing refined carbohydrate.[34] A similar response is likely to occur following consumption of SSBs in large portions, particularly given that SSBs are often consumed alone, apart from other foods, and contain no protein, fat, or fiber to attenuate the carbohydrate-induced rise in blood glucose.[35]

In susceptible individuals, recurrent swings in blood glucose, hormones, and metabolic responses with frequent consumption of SSBs may have adverse effects on numerous health outcomes. Findings from a meta-analysis of prospective observational studies indicate that dietary glycemic load is independently associated with risk for diabetes and CVD.[36] Moreover, observational studies also suggest a direct relationship between dietary glycemic load and insulin resistance,[37] elevated triglycerides and low high-density lipoprotein cholesterol,[38] and chronic inflammation.[39] Interventional studies suggest that lowering dietary glycemic load, by decreasing or eliminating refined carbohydrate from sources such as SSBs, may be efficacious for promoting weight loss, improving insulin resistance and β-cell function, and alleviating components of

the metabolic syndrome.[35] For example, replacing dietary carbohydrate with fat consistently causes a decrease in serum triglyceride concentration and an increase in HDL-cholesterol level[40]; and replacing carbohydrate with monounsaturated fat or protein also may have a beneficial effect on blood pressure.[41] The relevance of dietary glycemic load on metabolism and disease processes remains a subject of debate, though the benefit of reducing postprandial glycemia has been clearly demonstrated in studies of alpha-glucosidase inhibitors in the prevention of diabetes and cardiovascular disease.[42,43] As with research on most dietary factors, observational studies may not fully control for confounding factors, and interventional studies may lack specificity and treatment fidelity. Nevertheless, recent large clinical trials and meta-analyses provide growing confidence regarding the scientific and public health importance of this dietary factor.[44–48]

High Sweetness Intensity

Stimulation of sweetness receptors on the tongue causes an acute sensation equated with pleasure.[49] Moreover, excessive stimulation, as with habitual consumption of SSBs, may have chronic effects on taste preferences and food acceptance. Pepino and Mennella[50] noted that children aged 6 to 10 years who were routinely fed sweetened water as infants preferred solutions with higher concentrations of sucrose (0.66 M) than their counterparts who were not exposed to this feeding practice. Liem and de Graaf[51] found that repeated consumption of a beverage sweetened with sucrose (0.42 M) for 8 days enhanced beverage preference in a group of 39 children. Using a rat model to study the rewarding effect of sweetness, Lenoir et al.[52] noted that animals chose sweetened water over cocaine, suggesting that the high sweetness intensity of SSBs may be addictive in susceptible individuals.

The high primordial palatability of SSBs may disrupt the complex homeostatic mechanisms that regulate hunger, satiety, and food intake.[53] Individuals who habitually consume SSBs may develop cravings for sweet foods, with limited interest in whole foods that are more nutritious and satiating but less sweet (e.g., vegetables, fruits, legumes). Indeed, several observational studies indicate that SSBs are a component of unhealthful dietary patterns[54–55] and associated with compromised nutrient intake[7,12]; though whether consumption of SSBs is on the causal pathway leading to lower overall dietary quality remains unresolved. Nevertheless, dietary patterns that include consumption of SSBs are lower in fiber, micronutrients, antioxidants, and other phytochemicals and have been associated with increased energy intake,[55] weight gain,[56–57] prevalence of the metabolic syndrome,[55] and risk for diabetes[54] and CVD.[58]

Sugar content

Much debate focuses on the metabolic effects of fructose, whether consumed in the form of high-fructose corn syrup (typically composed of about 55% fructose and 45% glucose in monomeric form) or sucrose (50% fructose and 50% glucose in dimeric form). Some evidence suggests that fructose may have beneficial effects on appetite and insulin secretion when compared to glucose, possibly due to hepatic uptake and attenuation of postprandial glycemia.[59,60] However, other studies have linked fructose consumption to the metabolic syndrome, in part through stimulation of hepatic metabolic pathways including *de novo* lipogenesis and uric acid production.[60,61] Consumption of SSB *per se* has been associated with the severity of fatty liver in patients from a hepatology clinic[62] and with increased serum uric acid in nationally representative samples of adolescents[63] and adults.[64]

Regarding dental caries, in vitro studies provide strong evidence for the erosive potential of SSB on tooth enamel,[65–67] an effect mediated by beverage acidogenicity.[68] The sugar in SSB stimulates overgrowth of oral cariogenic bacteria and thereby release of acidic metabolic products. Regular cola and non-cola beverages have greater erosive potential in vitro than respective diet alternatives with similar ingredients and pH but without sugar.[66] Moreover, levels of bacteria in plaque and saliva samples increase when exposed to high sugar intake, for example in "nursing bottle caries,"[69] and decrease with dietary intervention to reduce sugar consumption.[70]

CONCLUSION

Emerging data support a strong case for a uniquely adverse effect of consuming SSBs on disease risk through plausible dietary and metabolic pathways. Replacing SSBs with artificially sweetened beverages would reduce intake of energy in liquid form, lower dietary glycemic load, and decrease dietary fructose. However, the high sweetness intensity of artificial sweeteners may have adverse effects on taste preferences.[71] Additional research is warranted to determine whether SSBs can be safely replaced with artificially sweetened beverages. In the interim, recommending unsweetened or minimally sweetened beverages, with no more than 1 gram of added sugar per ounce, would seem to be prudent.

REFERENCES

1. Wang YC, Bleich SN, Gortmaker SL. Increasing caloric contribution from sugar-sweetened beverages and 100% fruit juices among US children and adolescents, 1988–2004. *Pediatrics* 2008;121:e1604–e1614.
2. Duffey KJ, Popkin BM. Shifts in patterns and consumption of beverages between 1965 and 2002. *Obesity (Silver Spring)* 2007;15:2739–2747.
3. Malik VS, Schulze MB, Hu FB. Intake of sugar-sweetened beverages and weight gain: a systematic review. *Am J Clin Nutr* 2006;84:274–288.
4. Vartanian LR, Schwartz MB, Brownell KD. Effects of soft drink consumption on nutrition and health: a systematic review and meta-analysis. *Am J Public Health* 2007;97:667–675.
5. Welsh JA, Cogswell ME, Rogers S, Rockett H, Mei Z, Grummer-Strawn LM. Overweight among low-income preschool children associated with the consumption of sweet drinks: Missouri, 1999–2002. *Pediatrics* 2005;115:e223–e229.
6. Ludwig DS, Peterson KE, Gortmaker SL. Relation between consumption of sugar-sweetened drinks and childhood obesity: a prospective, observational analysis. *Lancet* 2001;357:505–508.
7. Schulze MB, Manson JE, Ludwig DS, et al. Sugar-sweetened beverages, weight gain, and incidence of type 2 diabetes in young and middle-aged women. *JAMA* 2004;292:927–934.
8. James J, Thomas P, Cavan D, Kerr D. Preventing childhood obesity by reducing consumption of carbonated drinks: cluster randomised controlled trial. *BMJ* 2004;328:1237.
9. Sichieri R, Paula Trotte A, de Souza RA, Veiga GV. School randomised trial on prevention of excessive weight gain by discouraging students from drinking sodas. *Public Health Nutr* 2009;12:197–202.
10. Ebbeling CB, Feldman HA, Osganian SK, Chomitz VR, Ellenbogen SJ, Ludwig DS. Effects of decreasing sugar-sweetened beverage consumption on body weight in adolescents: a randomized, controlled pilot study. *Pediatrics* 2006;117:673–680.
11. Hu FB, Malik VS. Sugar-sweetened beverages and risk of obesity and type 2 diabetes: epidemiologic evidence. *Physiol Behav* 2010;100:47–54.
12. Dhingra R, Sullivan L, Jacques PF, et al. Soft drink consumption and risk of developing cardiometabolic risk factors and the metabolic syndrome in middle-aged adults in the community. *Circulation* 2007;116:480–488.
13. Montonen J, Jarvinen R, Knekt P, Heliovaara M, Reunanen A. Consumption of sweetened beverages

and intakes of fructose and glucose predict type 2 diabetes occurrence. *J Nutr* 2007;137:1447–1454.

14. Palmer JR, Boggs DA, Krishnan S, Hu FB, Singer M, Rosenberg L. Sugar-sweetened beverages and incidence of type 2 diabetes mellitus in African American women. *Arch Int Med* 2008;168:1487–1492.

15. Malik VS, Popkin BM, Bray GA, Després JP, Willett WC, Hu FB. Sugar sweetened beverages and risk of metabolic syndrome and type 2 diabetes: a meta-analysis. *Diabetes Care* 2010;33:2477–2483.

16. Fung TT, Malik V, Rexrode KM, Manson JE, Willett WC, Hu FB. Sweetened beverage consumption and risk of coronary heart disease in women. *Am J Clin Nutr* 2009;89:1037–1042.

17. Raben A, Vasilaras TH, Moller AC, Astrup A. Sucrose compared with artificial sweeteners: different effects on ad libitum food intake and body weight after 10 wk of supplementation in overweight subjects. *Am J Clin Nutr* 2002;76:721–729.

18. Sorensen LB, Raben A, Stender S, Astrup A. Effect of sucrose on inflammatory markers in overweight humans. *Am J Clin Nutr* 2005;82:421–427.

19. Choi HK, Willett W, Curhan G. Fructose-rich beverages and risk of gout in women. *JAMA* 2010;304:2270–2278.

20. Marshall TA, Levy SM, Broffitt B, et al. Dental caries and beverage consumption in young children. *Pediatrics* 2003;112:e184–e191.

21. Lim S, Sohn W, Burt BA, et al. Cariogenicity of soft drinks, milk and fruit juice in low-income african-american children: a longitudinal study. *J Am Dent Assoc* 2008;139:959–967.

22. Ismail AI, Burt BA, Eklund SA. The cariogenicity of soft drinks in the United States. *J Am Dent Assoc* 1984;109:241–245.

23. Harnack L, Stang J, Story M. Soft drink consumption among US children and adolescents: nutritional consequences. *J Am Diet Assoc* 1999;99:436–441.

24. Wang YC, Ludwig DS, Sonneville K, Gortmaker SL. Impact of change in sweetened caloric beverage consumption on energy intake among children and adolescents. *Arch Pediatr Adolesc Med* 2009;163:336–343.

25. Mattes RD. Dietary compensation by humans for supplemental energy provided as ethanol or carbohydrate in fluids. *Physiol Behav* 1996;59:179–187.

26. DiMeglio DP, Mattes RD. Liquid versus solid carbohydrate: effects on food intake and body weight. *Int J Obes Relat Metab Disord* 2000;24:794–800.

27. Mourao DM, Bressan J, Campbell WW, Mattes RD. Effects of food form on appetite and energy intake in lean and obese young adults. *Int J Obes* 2007;31:1688–1695.

28. Chen L, Appel LJ, Loria C, et al. Reduction in consumption of sugar-sweetened beverages is associated with weight loss: the PREMIER trial. *Am J Clin Nutr* 2009;89:1299–1306.

29. McKiernan F, Houchins JA, Mattes RD. Relationships between human thirst, hunger, drinking, and feeding. *Physiol Behav* 2008;94:700–708.

30. Salvy SJ, Howard M, Read M, Mele E. The presence of friends increases food intake in youth. *Am J Clin Nutr* 2009;90:282–287.

31. Spring B, Schneider K, Smith M, et al. Abuse potential of carbohydrates for overweight carbohydrate cravers. *Psychopharmacol* 2008;197:637–647.

32. Salmeron J, Manson JE, Stampfer MJ, Colditz GA, Wing AL, Willett WC. Dietary fiber, glycemic load, and risk of non-insulin-dependent diabetes mellitus in women. *JAMA* 1997;277:472–477.

33. Brand-Miller JC, Thomas M, Swan V, Ahmad ZI, Petocz P, Colagiuri S. Physiological validation of the concept of glycemic load in lean young adults. *J Nutr* 2003;133:2728–2732.

34. Ludwig DS. The glycemic index: physiological mechanisms relating to obesity, diabetes, and cardiovascular disease. *JAMA* 2002;287:2414–2423.

35. Ludwig DS. Clinical update: the low-glycaemic-index diet. *Lancet* 2007;369:890–892.

36. Barclay AW, Petocz P, McMillan-Price J, et al. Glycemic index, glycemic load, and chronic disease risk— a meta-analysis of observational studies. *Am J Clin Nutr* 2008;87:627–637.

37. McKeown NM, Meigs JB, Liu S, Saltzman E, Wilson PW, Jacques PF. Carbohydrate nutrition, insulin resistance, and the prevalence of the metabolic syndrome in the Framingham Offspring Cohort. *Diabetes Care* 2004;27:538–546.

38. Liu S, Manson JE, Stampfer MJ, et al. Dietary glycemic load assessed by food-frequency questionnaire in relation to plasma high-density-lipoprotein cholesterol and fasting plasma triacylglycerols in postmenopausal women. *Am J Clin Nutr* 2001;73:560–566.

39. Liu S, Manson JE, Buring JE, Stampfer MJ, Willett WC, Ridker PM. Relation between a diet with a high glycemic load and plasma concentrations of high-sensitivity C-reactive protein in middle-aged women. *Am J Clin Nutr* 2002;75:492–498.

40. Mensink RP, Zock PL, Kester AD, Katan MB. Effects of dietary fatty acids and carbohydrates on the ratio of serum total to HDL cholesterol and on serum lipids and apolipoproteins: a meta-analysis of 60 controlled trials. *Am J Clin Nutr* 2003;77:1146–1155.

41. Appel LJ, Sacks FM, Carey VJ, et al. Effects of protein, monounsaturated fat, and carbohydrate intake on blood pressure and serum lipids: results of the OmniHeart randomized trial. *JAMA* 2005;294:2455–2464.

42. Chiasson JL, Josse RG, Gomis R, Hanefeld M, Karasik A, Laakso M. Acarbose treatment and the risk of cardiovascular disease and hypertension in patients with impaired glucose tolerance: the STOP-NIDDM trial. *JAMA* 2003;290:486–494.

43. Chiasson JL, Josse RG, Gomis R, Hanefeld M, Karasik A, Laakso M. Acarbose for prevention of type 2 diabetes mellitus: the STOP-NIDDM randomised trial. *Lancet* 2002;359:2072–2077.

44. Larsen TM, Dalskov SM, van Baak M, et al. Diets with high or low protein content and glycemic index for weight-loss maintenance. *N Engl J Med* 2010;363:2102–2113.

45. Papadaki A, Linardakis M, Larsen TM, et al. The effect of protein and glycemic index on children's body composition: the DiOGenes randomized study. *Pediatrics* 2010;126:e1143–e1152.

46. Barclay AW, Petocz P, McMillan-Price J, et al. Glycemic index, glycemic load, and chronic disease risk—a meta-analysis of observational studies. *Am J Clin Nutr* 2008;87:627–637.

47. Thomas D, Elliott EJ. Low glycaemic index, or low glycaemic load, diets for diabetes mellitus. *Cochrane Database Syst Rev* 2009:CD006296.

48. Thomas DE, Elliott EJ, Baur L. Low glycaemic index or low glycaemic load diets for overweight and obesity. *Cochrane Database Syst Rev* 2007:CD005105.

49. Levine AS, Kotz CM, Gosnell BA. Sugars: hedonic aspects, neuroregulation, and energy balance. *Am J Clin Nutr* 2003;78:834S–842S.

50. Pepino MY, Mennella JA. Factors contributing to individual differences in sucrose preference. *Chem Senses* 2005;30(suppl 1):i319–i320.

51. Liem DG, de Graaf C. Sweet and sour preferences in young children and adults: role of repeated exposure. *Physiol Behav* 2004;83:421–429.

52. Lenoir M, Serre F, Cantin L, Ahmed SH. Intense sweetness surpasses cocaine reward. *PloS One* 2007;2:e698.

53. Erlanson-Albertsson C. How palatable food disrupts appetite regulation. *Basic Clin Pharmacol Toxicol* 2005;97:61–73.

54. McNaughton SA, Mishra GD, Brunner EJ. Dietary patterns, insulin resistance, and incidence of type 2 diabetes in the Whitehall II Study. *Diabetes Care* 2008;31:1343–1348.

55. Sonnenberg L, Pencina M, Kimokoti R, et al. Dietary patterns and the metabolic syndrome in obese and non-obese Framingham women. *Obes Res* 2005;13:153–162.

56. Mozaffarian D, Hao T, Rimm EB, Willett WC, Hu FB. Changes in diet and lifestyle and long-term weight gain in women and men. *N Engl J Med* 2011;364:2392–2404.

57. Schulze MB, Fung TT, Manson JE, Willett WC, Hu FB. Dietary patterns and changes in body weight in women. *Obesity (Silver Spring)* 2006;14:1444–1453.

58. Fung TT, Stampfer MJ, Manson JE, Rexrode KM, Willett WC, Hu FB. Prospective study of major dietary patterns and stroke risk in women. *Stroke* 2004;35:2014–2019.

59. Moyer AE, Rodin J. Fructose and behavior: does fructose influence food intake and macronutrient selection? *Am J Clin Nutr* 1993;58:810S–814S.

60. Johnson RJ, Perez-Pozo SE, Sautin YY, et al. Hypothesis: could excessive fructose intake and uric acid cause type 2 diabetes? *Endocrine Rev* 2009;30:96–116.

61. Lim JS, Mietus-Snyder M, Valente A, Schwarz JM, Lustig RH. The role of fructose in the pathogenesis of NAFLD and the metabolic syndrome. *Nat Rev Gastroenterol Hepatol* 2010;7:251–264.

62. Abid A, Taha O, Nseir W, Farah R, Grosovski M, Assy N. Soft drink consumption is associated with fatty liver disease independent of metabolic syndrome. *J Hepatol* 2009;51:918–924.

63. Nguyen S, Choi HK, Lustig RH, Hsu CY. Sugar-sweetened beverages, serum uric acid, and blood pressure in adolescents. *J Pediatr* 2009;154:807–813.

64. Choi JW, Ford ES, Gao X, Choi HK. Sugar-sweetened soft drinks, diet soft drinks, and serum uric acid level: the Third National Health and Nutrition Examination Survey. *Arthritis Rheumat* 2008;59:109–116.

65. Owens BM, Kitchens M. The erosive potential of soft drinks on enamel surface substrate: an in vitro scanning electron microscopy investigation. *J Contemp Dent Pract* 2007;8:11–20.

66. Jain P, Nihill P, Sobkowski J, Agustin MZ. Commercial soft drinks: pH and in vitro dissolution of enamel. *Gen Dent* 2007;55:150–154.

67. von Fraunhofer JA, Rogers MM. Effects of sports drinks and other beverages on dental enamel. *Gen Dent* 2005;53:28–31.

68. Tahmassebi JF, Duggal MS, Malik-Kotru G, Curzon MEJ. Soft drinks and dental health: a review of the current literature *J Dent* 2006;34:2–11.

69. van Houte J, Gibbs G, Butera C. Oral flora of children with "nursing bottle caries." *J Dent Res* 1982;61:382–385.

70. Wikner S. An attempt to motivate improved ugar discipline in a 12-year-old high caries-risk group. *Community Dent Oral Epidemiol* 1986;14:5–7.

71. Hampton T. Sugar substitutes linked to weight gain. *JAMA* 2008;299:2137–2138.

23

The Impact of Portion Size and Energy Density on Eating

BARBARA J. ROLLS

The prevalence of obesity has surged in recent years. One possible explanation is that the eating environment in Westernized societies has altered, so that overconsumption of energy has become easier. At the same time, opportunities for physical activity have declined. Thus, it is increasingly difficult for individuals to match energy intake to energy output in order to maintain a healthy body weight. Some of the changes in the eating environment that encourage overeating are the ready availability of inexpensive high-energy-dense foods, the wide variety of palatable foods, the increasing frequency of meals consumed outside of the home, and the rise in portion sizes.[1,2] This review focuses on the effects of portion size and energy density on energy intake and the implications of these findings.

COULD PORTION SIZE PLAY A ROLE IN THE DEVELOPMENT OF OBESITY?

Since the 1970s the portion sizes of many foods and beverages have increased, a trend that has been observed in a variety of settings, including restaurants, supermarkets, and homes.[3–6] These increases in portion size have occurred in parallel with the rise in the prevalence of obesity, suggesting that portion size could play a role.[2,3] A crucial step in establishing a causal link is to determine whether portion size affects energy intake. Multiple, laboratory-based studies have shown that providing participants with larger portions increases energy intake.

When adults were served different portions of macaroni and cheese on different days, the bigger the portion, the more they ate.[7] The influence of portion size is not limited to foods amorphous in shape, such as pasta, for which it is difficult to judge the size. Variations in the portion size of foods with clearly defined shapes or units, such as sandwiches and packaged snacks, also had a systematic and significant effect on intake.[8,9] Studies in natural eating environments confirm that food portions influence energy intake. When the portion size of a pasta entrée served in a campus cafeteria was increased by 50%, customers rated the standard and larger portions as equally appropriate, and most ate all of the bigger portion.[10] This is similar to the findings of a survey of more than 1,000 adults in which the majority of respondents reported that, when dining out, they finish their entrées all or most of the time.[11] Many respondents stated that they base the amount they eat on the amount they are used to eating. This supports the hypothesis that exposure to large portions affects consumption norms or the amount considered appropriate to eat.[12]

Critical questions are whether after a bout of overeating in response to large portions consumers will compensate by eating less later, and whether, if large portions are continuously available, the effect will be sustained over time. In several studies, the effect has been shown to persist over 2 to 4 days.[13–15] In a longer study, when men and women were provided with all of their foods and beverages during two 11-day periods, increasing the portion size by 50% led to a 16% increase in mean daily energy intake.[16] Overconsumption was sustained over the 11 days, resulting in a mean cumulative increase in intake of 4,636 kcal. An intervention conducted at a work site indicated that doubling the portion size of lunch significantly increased intake with no indication of a compensatory reduction in intake over a 1-month intervention.[17] These data demonstrate that portion size can have persistent effects over multiple days, resulting in substantial increases in energy intake. Thus, characteristics of the eating environment such as the ready availability of large portions of energy-dense foods can override the regulation of energy balance over prolonged periods.

The persistent effects of portion size on energy intake suggest that the widespread availability of large portions is likely to be contributing to the increased incidence of obesity. Recent population-based studies also suggest an association between portion size and weight status. Of particular interest is the indication from these analyses that it is large portions of foods high in energy density that are related to excess body weight.[18,19]

STRATEGIES TO MODERATE THE EFFECT OF PORTION SIZE

A number of strategies have been proposed to counter the effects of portion size; however, it is not clear which are likely to be both acceptable and effective.[1,20] Portion-controlled meals can be a useful tool for weight management. Providing patients with preportioned liquid meal replacements was associated with better compliance and greater weight loss compared with self-selected diets for periods as long as 4 years.[21] Other possible approaches include education and consumer awareness campaigns, food labels that provide clear information about portion size, more point-of-purchase nutrition information, and incentives to the food industry to reduce portion sizes or to offer a greater variety of portions.[2] The impact of these suggestions needs to be established since it is not easy to anticipate consumer responses in our complex eating environment.

In the current environment of huge portions of energy-dense foods, it is difficult for many individuals to eat appropriate amounts of food. Getting intake back in synchrony with energy needs will be challenging since consumers equate large portions with good value and they have a distorted idea of how much food is appropriate.[1,2,12] If people were to heed the frequently offered advice simply "to eat less," and were to reduce the portion size of all the foods consumed, they would probably feel deprived and would not sustain this eating pattern. A promising approach that would allow people to eat satisfying portions would be to reduce the energy density of the diet or at least of selected foods.

ENERGY DENSITY AND ENERGY INTAKE

Energy density refers to the amount of energy in a given weight of food (kcal/g). Of the components of foods, water has the greatest influence on energy density since it adds substantial weight without adding energy. Fat, because of its high energy content (9 kcal/g), has a greater influence on the energy density of a food than either carbohydrates or protein (4 kcal/g). Not all high-fat foods have a high energy density; the incorporation of water lowers the energy density even of high-fat foods. A growing body of evidence indicates that reducing the energy density of foods by increasing the water content or by decreasing the proportion of fat can reduce energy intake.[22–25]

The energy density of food influences satiety or the feeling of fullness that occurs after food has been eaten. To study satiety, a fixed amount of a defined food (a preload) is consumed and the effect of the preload on subsequent intake of a test meal is measured. Studies using preloads such as milkshakes and soups have demonstrated that adding water to the preload (thus increasing volume and decreasing energy density) leads to a significant reduction in subsequent energy intake.[26–28] Interestingly, drinking water as a beverage along with a food did not as effectively enhance satiety as did incorporating it into the food to lower the energy density.[27] While consumption of low-energy dense foods at the start of a meal can significantly affect energy intake, few studies have explored the utility of "high-satiety" foods over multiple meals to decrease energy intake, or as a tool for weight management.

Energy density can influence energy intake not only by enhancing satiety but also through effects on ad libitum intake. Ad libitum intake is an indicator of satiation, or the processes leading to the termination of eating during a meal. In controlled studies, when adults were offered ad libitum access to meals in which the energy density was reduced by increasing the proportion of water-rich vegetables, they ate a consistent weight of food. This meant that energy intake varied directly with changes in energy density. Subjects reported similar ratings of hunger and fullness even when reductions in energy density led to a decrease in energy intake of approximately 25% over 2 days.[14,29] That the response to energy density emerges early in life is indicated by studies in preschool children showing they too consumed significantly less energy when the energy density of the available foods was lowered.[30,31] This suggests the possibility of using reductions in energy density strategically to prevent excess energy intake in young children as well as in adults.

DIETARY ENERGY DENSITY AND BODY WEIGHT

Advice to reduce the energy density of the diet has been shown to be an effective approach for weight management. In a year-long trial, daily incorporation of a low-energy-dense food (soup) into a reduced-energy diet increased the magnitude of the weight loss compared to the incorporation of snack foods higher in energy density.[32] In another year-long trial, obese women who were counseled to reduce dietary energy density by increasing intake of fruits and vegetables along with reducing intake of fat had greater weight loss than those who were advised just to reduce fat intake.[33] Over the course of the year, participants randomly assigned to the lower energy-dense diet (higher in fruits and vegetables) reported consuming an average of 25% more food and reported less hunger than those in the fat-reduction group. In addition, the results from a multicenter intervention (the PREMIER trial) indicated that changes in dietary energy density after 6 months were related to changes in body weight.[34] Participants received one of three lifestyle interventions that included information on physical activity, diet, and weight loss. Participants who achieved a relatively large reduction in dietary energy density reduced their energy intake and lost more weight than those with a modest reduction or those with little change in energy density. Furthermore, participants with both large and modest decreases in energy density increased the amount of food they consumed. Increasing the amount of food consumed while decreasing energy intake could contribute to the long-term acceptability of a low-energy-dense eating pattern since it could help to control hunger. While data from clinical trials suggest that reducing dietary energy density can facilitate weight management, more long-term multicenter trials are needed to understand how to implement this approach and facilitate the maintenance of low-energy-dense eating habits.[35]

The association between energy density and body weight is supported by both longitudinal and epidemiological studies that have tracked dietary patterns. In a 6-year longitudinal study, it was observed that young women who reported a diet higher in energy density gained two and a half times as much weight as those reporting a diet lower in energy density.[36] Longitudinal studies in children have also found an association between dietary energy density and changes in body fatness.[37–39]

Population-based studies in adults provide additional support for associations between energy density and energy intake, the amount of food consumed, diet quality, and weight status. Surveys of self-reported intakes by free-living adults have shown that normal-weight individuals consume diets with a lower energy density than obese individuals.[40,41] Furthermore, increases in dietary energy density were associated with greater weight gain in a prospective study of 50,000 middle-aged women over 8 years.[42]

COMBINED EFFECTS OF PORTION SIZE AND ENERGY DENSITY

Since individuals under free-living conditions have access to foods that vary simultaneously in both portion size and energy density, it is important to understand how these factors work together to affect energy intake. In studies of satiety, the energy density and portion size of the preload combine to determine energy intake at the meal.[43] In general, when choosing a first course, the greatest enhancement of satiety and reduction in overall meal intake is likely with large portions of foods low in energy density such as salad, soup, or fruit.[28,43,44]

Portion size and energy density also combine to affect satiation or ad libitum consumption.[14,45,46] When women were served a variety of popular foods such as pizza and sandwiches to consume ad libitum at all meals over 2 days, a 25% decrease in portion size led to a 10% decrease in energy intake, and a 25% decrease in energy density led to a 24% decrease in energy intake.[14] The effects were independent and when combined, daily energy intake was reduced by 32%. Not only was the effect of the energy density manipulation stronger than that of portion size, the participants were less likely to notice the changes in energy density. Food providers could combine reductions in energy density with small decreases in portion size to produce foods that would help consumers eat fewer calories.

Our eating environment has become increasingly characterized by an abundance of energy-dense foods in portions determined more by consumer demands and expectations than by calorie content.[47,48] Particularly problematic is that many meals are composed of small portions of low-energy-dense options such as vegetables and fruits along with large portions of energy-dense meats, starches, and grains, a combination that promotes excess energy intake. In recent studies, we found that increasing the portion size of a low-energy-dense vegetable[49] served at a meal significantly increased vegetable intake, and when substituted for more energy-dense meal components, also reduced energy intake. These studies suggest that increases in portion size of low-energy-dense foods can be used beneficially to influence the types and amounts of foods consumed at a meal.

CONCLUSION

In recent years significant progress has been made in understanding how characteristics of the food environment can affect energy intake and how they can be varied strategically to improve nutritional status. Both changes in the portion size and the energy density of foods show potential to be used either independently or in combination to counter overconsumption. Encouraging larger portions of foods low in energy density such as vegetables and fruits, while limiting portions of high-energy-dense foods, would not only improve diet quality but could also reduce energy intake. The effectiveness of this strategy will depend upon altering the current food environment so that lower energy density choices are easily accessible, appealing, and affordable.

ACKNOWLEDGMENTS

This research was supported by the National Institute of Diabetes and Digestive and Kidney Diseases grants DK039177, DK059853, and DK082580, and by the Robert Wood Johnson Foundation.

REFERENCES

1. Rolls BJ. The supersizing of America: portion size and the obesity epidemic. *Nutr Today* 2003;38:42–53.
2. Ledikwe JH, Ello-Martin JA, Rolls BJ. Portion sizes and the obesity epidemic. *J Nutr* 2005;135:905–909.
3. Young LR, Nestle M. The contribution of expanding portion sizes to the US obesity epidemic. *Am J Public Health* 2002;92:246–249.
4. Nielsen SJ, Popkin BM. Patterns and trends in food portion sizes, 1977–1998. *JAMA* 2003;289:450–453.
5. Smiciklas-Wright H, Mitchell DC, Mickle SJ, Goldman JD, Cook A. Foods commonly eaten in the United States, 1989–1991 and 1994–1996: are the portion sizes changing? *J Am Diet Assoc* 2003;103:41–47.
6. Young LR, Nestle M. Portion sizes and obesity: responses of fast-food companies. *J Public Health Policy* 2007;28:238–248.
7. Rolls BJ, Morris EL, Roe LS. Portion size of food affects energy intake in normal-weight and overweight men and women. *Am J Clin Nutr* 2002;76:1207–1213.
8. Rolls BJ, Roe LS, Kral TV, Meengs JS, Wall DE. Increasing the portion size of a packaged snack increases energy intake in men and women. *Appetite* 2004;42:63–69.
9. Rolls BJ, Roe LS, Meengs JS, Wall DE. Increasing the portion size of a sandwich increases energy intake. *J Am Diet Assoc* 2004;104:367–372.
10. Diliberti N, Bordi P, Conklin MT, Roe LS, Rolls BJ. Increased portion size leads to increased energy intake in a restaurant meal. *Obes Res* 2004;12:562–568.
11. American Institute for Cancer Research. *Awareness and Action: AICR Surveys on Portion Size, Nutrition and Cancer Risk*. Washington, DC: American Institute for Cancer Research, 2003.
12. Wansink B, van Ittersum K. Portion size me: downsizing our consumption norms. *J Am Diet Assoc* 2007;107:1103–1106.
13. Rolls BJ, Roe LS, Meengs JS. Larger portion sizes lead to sustained increase in energy intake over two days. *J Am Diet Assoc* 2006;106:543–549.
14. Rolls BJ, Roe LS, Meengs JS. Reductions in portion size and energy density of foods are additive and lead to sustained decreases in energy intake. *Am J Clin Nutr* 2006;83:11–17.
15. Kelly MT, Wallace JM, Robson PJ, et al. Increased portion size leads to a sustained increase in energy intake over 4 d in normal-weight and overweight men and women. *Br J Nutr* 2009;16:1–8.
16. Rolls BJ, Roe LS, Meengs JS. The effect of large portion sizes on energy intake is sustained for 11 days. *Obesity* 2007;15:1535–1543.
17. Jeffery RW, Rydell S, Dunn CL, et al. Effects of portion size on chronic energy intake. *Int J Behav Nutr Phy* 2007;4:27.
18. Berg C, Lappas G, Wolk A, et al. Eating patterns and portion size associated with obesity in a Swedish population. *Appetite* 2009;52:21–26.
19. Lioret S, Volatier JL, Lafay L, Touvier M, Maire B. Is food portion size a risk factor of childhood overweight? *Eur J Clin Nutr* 2009;63:382–391.
20. Steenhuis IH, Vermeer WM. Portion size: review and framework for interventions. *Int J Behav Nutr Phys* 2009;6:58.
21. Heymsfield SB, van Mierlo CA, van der Knaap HC, Heo M, Frier HI. Weight management using a meal replacement strategy: meta and pooling analysis from six studies. *Int J Obes Relat Metab Disord* 2003;27:537–549.
22. Rolls BJ, Drewnowski A, Ledikwe JH. Changing the energy density of the diet as a strategy for weight management. *J Am Diet Assoc* 2005;105:S98–S103.
23. Ledikwe JH, Blanck HM, Kettel Khan L, et al. Reductions in dietary energy density as a weight management strategy. In: Kushner RF, Bessesen DH, eds. *Treatment of the Obese Patient*. Totowa, NJ: Humana Press; 2007:265–280.

24. Hetherington MM, Rolls BJ. From protocols to populations: establishing a role for energy density of food in the obesity epidemic. In: Blass EM, ed. *Obesity: Causes, Mechanisms, Prevention, and Treatment.* Sunderland, MA: Sinauer Associates; 2008:301–318.

25. Rolls BJ. The relationship between dietary energy density and energy intake. *Physiol Behav* 2009;97:609–615.

26. Rolls BJ, Castellanos VH, Halford JC, et al. Volume of food consumed affects satiety in men. *Am J Clin Nutr* 1998;67:1170–1177.

27. Rolls BJ, Bell EA, Thorwart ML. Water incorporated into a food but not served with a food decreases energy intake in lean women. *Am J Clin Nutr* 1999; 70:448–455.

28. Flood JE, Rolls BJ. Soup preloads in a variety of forms reduce meal energy intake. *Appetite* 2007;49: 626–634.

29. Bell EA, Castellanos VH, Pelkman CL, Thorwart ML, Rolls BJ. Energy density of foods affects energy intake in normal-weight women. *Am J Clin Nutr* 1998; 67:412–420.

30. Fisher JO, Liu Y, Birch LL, Rolls BJ. Effects of portion size and energy density on young children's intake at a meal. *Am J Clin Nutr* 2007;86:174–179.

31. Leahy KE, Birch LL, Rolls BJ. Reducing the energy density of multiple meals decreases the energy intake of preschool-age children. *Am J Clin Nutr* 2008;88: 1459–1468.

32. Rolls BJ, Roe LS, Beach AM, Kris-Etherton PM. Provision of foods differing in energy density affects long-term weight loss. *Obes Res* 2005;13:1052–1060.

33. Ello Martin JA, Roe LS, Ledikwe JH, Beach AM, Rolls BJ. Dietary energy density in the treatment of obesity: a year-long trial comparing 2 weight-loss diets. *Am J Clin Nutr* 2007;85:1465–1477.

34. Ledikwe JH, Rolls BJ, Smiciklas-Wright H, et al. Reductions in dietary energy density are associated with weight loss in overweight and obese participants in the PREMIER trial. *Am J Clin Nutr* 2007;85: 1212–1221.

35. Lowe MR, Tappe KA, Annunziato RA, et al. The effect of training in reduced energy density eating and food self-monitoring accuracy on weight loss maintenance. *Obesity* 2008;16:2016–2023.

36. Savage JS, Marini M, Birch LL. Dietary energy density predicts women's weight change over 6 y. *Am J Clin Nutr* 2008;88:677–684.

37. Johnson L, Mander AP, Jones LR, Emmett PM, Jebb SA. Energy-dense, low-fiber, high-fat dietary pattern is associated with increased fatness in childhood. *Am J Clin Nutr* 2008;87:846–854.

38. Johnson L, Mander AP, Jones LR, Emmett PM, Jebb SA. A prospective analysis of dietary energy density at age 5 and 7 years and fatness at 9 years among UK children. *Int J Obes* 2008;32:586–593.

39. McCaffrey TA, Rennie KL, Kerr MA, et al. Energy density of the diet and change in body fatness from childhood to adolescence; is there a relation? *Am J Clin Nutr* 2008;87:1230–1237.

40. Kant AK, Graubard BI. Energy density of diets reported by American adults: association with food group intake, nutrient intake, and body weight. *Int J Obes* 2005;29:950–956.

41. Ledikwe JH, Blanck HM, Kettel-Khan L, et al. Dietary energy density is associated with energy intake and weight status in US adults. *Am J Clin Nutr* 2006;83:1362–1368.

42. Bes-Rastrollo M, van Dam RM, Martinez-Gonzalez MA, Li TY, Sampson LL, Hu FB. Prospective study of dietary energy density and weight gain in women. *Am J Clin Nutr* 2008;88:769–777.

43. Rolls BJ, Roe LS, Meengs JS. Salad and satiety: energy density and portion size of a first course salad affect energy intake at lunch. *J Am Diet Assoc* 2004;104:1570–1576.

44. Flood-Obbagy JE, Rolls BJ. The effect of fruit in different forms on energy intake and satiety at a meal. *Appetite* 2009;52:416–422.

45. Kral TVE, Rolls BJ. Energy density and portion size: their independent and combined effects on energy intake. *Physiol Behav* 2004;82:131–138.

46. Kral TVE, Roe LS, Rolls BJ. Combined effects of energy density and portion size on energy intake in women. *Am J Clin Nutr* 2004;79:962–968.

47. Condrasky M, Ledikwe JH, Flood JE, Rolls BJ. Chefs' opinions of restaurant portion sizes. *Obesity* 2007;15:2086–2094.

48. Obbagy JE, Condrasky M, Roe LS, Sharp JL, Rolls BJ. Chefs' opinions about reducing the calorie content of menu items in restaurants. *Obesity* 2011;19:332–337.

49. Rolls BJ, Roe LS, Meengs JS. Portion size can be used strategically to increase vegetable consumption in adults. *Am J Clin Nutr* 2010;91:913–922.

24

Specific Environmental Drivers of Eating

BRIAN WANSINK

All of us eat the amount we do, in part, because of what is around us. We overeat not only due to hunger but also due to family and friends, packages and plates, names and numbers, labels and lights, colors and candles, shapes and smells, distractions and distances, cupboards and containers. This list is almost as endless as it is invisible to us.

Food choice decisions are not the same as intake volume decisions.[1] That is, the former determine *what* we eat (soup or salad); the latter determine *how much* we eat (half of the bowl or all of it). A great deal of money, time, and intelligence has been invested in understanding the physiological mechanisms influencing food *choice*.[2,3] Much less has been invested in understanding how and why our environment influences food consumption *volume*.[4–6]

One of the ironies of food research is that most of us are largely unaware of what factors influence how much we eat. Dozens of studies involving thousands of people show that people wrongly think that what they eat is mainly determined by how hungry they are, how much they like the food, and what mood they are in.[7] We all think we are too smart to be tricked by plates, packages, or lighting. This suggests that people may be influenced at an unmonitored, basic level of which they are not even aware. Understanding drivers of consumption volume has immediate implications for research, nutrition education, and consumer welfare.[8,9] This chapter aims to explain what environmental factors unknowingly influence eating and why they do so.

ENVIRONMENTAL DRIVERS OF OVEREATING

It has often been suggested that we overeat from larger portions because we tend to "clean our plate."[10] While this may *describe* why many people eat what they are served, it does not *explain* why they do so or why they may overserve themselves at all. Figure 24.1 suggests why portion size may have a ubiquitous, almost automatic influence on how much we eat: first, portion sizes create consumption norms; second, we underestimate the calories in large portions.

DINNERWARE CREATES ILLUSION, WHICH INCREASES SERVING SIZE AND INTAKE

Nearly 72% of a person's calorie intake is comprised of foods dished out from serving aids such as bowls, plates, glasses, or spoons.[11] Though seemingly innocuous, one's selection of dishware unconsciously drives one's serving and intake behavior. In the context of drinking glasses, when people examine how much they have poured into a glass, there is a fundamental tendency to focus on the height of the liquid and to downplay its width. To prove this, Wansink and van Ittersum conducted a study with teenagers at weight loss camps (as well as a subsequent study with nondieting adults) and showed that this basic visual bias caused teenagers to pour 88% more juice or soda (and subsequently consume more) into short, wide glasses than into tall, narrow glasses that held the same volume.[12] These teenagers believed, however, that they poured half as much as as much as they actually did. The same was found with expert pourers—Philadelphia bartenders. When asked to pour 1.5 ounces of gin, whiskey, rum, and vodka into short, wide (tumbler) glasses, these bartenders poured 26% more than when pouring into tall, narrow (highball) glasses. Experience or confidence in one's estimations (the bartenders had both) cannot supersede the fundamental susceptibility to the vertical-horizontal illusion.

Now consider plates. The size-contrast illusion suggests that if we spoon 4 ounces of mashed potatoes onto a 12-inch plate and 4 ounces onto an 8-inch plate, we will underestimate the total amount spooned onto the larger plate because of its greater negative space, even though they contain exactly the same amount.[13] That is, the size contrast between the potatoes and the plate is greater when the plate is 12 inches than when it is 8 inches. A study at an ice cream social showed similar results. People who were randomly given 24-ounce bowls dished out and consumed 15%–38% more ice cream than those who were given 16-ounce bowls.[14] The same appears to be true with spoon sizes. With plates, bowls, and spoons, there is a basic tendency to use their size as an indication of how much should be served and consumed.

Unfortunately, the size of dishware has steadily increased in our homes. The average size of dinner plates from 1900 to 2010 increased 22% from 9.625 inches to 11.75 inches.[15] Even historically, depictions of plate size in the paintings of *The Last Supper* have increased by 67% over the prior millennium.[16] Interestingly, this increase in plate size approximately mirrors increases in portion size and the availability and affordability of food. While it would be foolish to advocate that food be less available and less affordable, as these two factors increase, so may the surrounding cues that prompt food intake or subtly suggest larger portions.[17,18]

THE SIZE OF PACKAGES, PLATES, AND PORTIONS SUGGEST CONSUMPTION NORMS

Just as the size of dinnerware has increased in homes, there is overwhelming evidence that the size of food packaging and portions has steadily increased over the past 30 years.[19,20] This trend has many implications for consumption, as it well known that the size of a package can increase consumption,[21] as can the portion sizes in kitchens[22,23] and restaurants.[24] Interestingly, package and portion size have also been shown to increase consumption of unfavorable foods. For instance, when movie-goers were given either medium- or large-sized containers of stale, 5-day-old popcorn, individuals provided large-sized containers ate 38% more despite its poor quality.[25] Clearly, environmental cues can, in some situations, influence intake as much influence as the taste of the food itself.

One likely explanation of why large packages and portions increase consumption may be because they suggest larger consumption norms (recall Fig. 24.1). These norms implicitly suggest what is a "normal" or "appropriate" amount to consume. Even if one does not clean his or her plate or finish the contents of a package, the amount of the food presented gives one liberty to consume past the point where he or she might have stopped with a smaller, but still unconstrained, supply.

Since 1970 portion sizes have steadily increased in supermarkets and homes.[26,27] We even find increased portion sizes in classic home recipes. Over the past 70 years, the calories per serving size of some entrées in *The Joy of Cooking* cookbook has increased an average of 42%, with a third of those being attributable to increased portion size.[28]

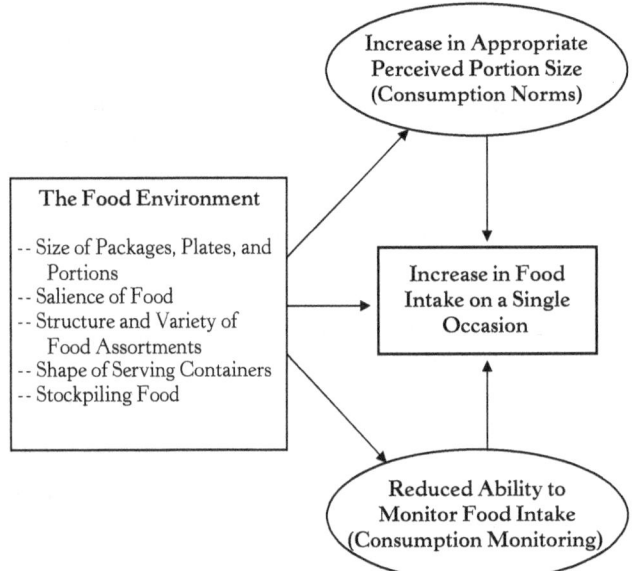

FIGURE 24.1. Selected environmental antecedents of consumption volume.

Source: Reprinted from Physiology & Behavior, Vol. 100, B. Wansink, From mindless eating to mindlessly eating better, 454–463, Copyright (2010), with permission from Elsevier.

SALIENT FOOD PROMOTES SALIENT HUNGER

Food can powerfully influence our visual and olfactory senses, and the mere presence of food can prompt unplanned consumption even when we are not hungry.[29,30] For instance, when 30 chocolate kisses were placed on the desks of secretaries, 46% more were consumed from clear candy dishes than opaque ones.[31] Similarly, people given sandwich quarters wrapped in transparent wrap ate more than those who were given sandwiches in opaque wrap.[32]

The increased intake of visible foods may occur because their salience served as a constant consumption reminder. This effect is partially cognitively based and partially physiological. That is, simply seeing or smelling a favorable food can increase reported hunger[33-36] and can stimulate salivation, which is correlated with greater consumption.[37] Some physiological evidence suggests that the visibility of a tempting food can enhance actual hunger by increasing the release of dopamine, a neurotransmitter associated with pleasure and reward.[38] Such cues can be particularly strong with unrestrained eaters.[39]

STRUCTURE AND PERCEIVED VARIETY INCREASE FOOD INTAKE

When offered a plate containing three different flavors of yogurt, individuals consume an average of 23% more yogurt than if offered only one flavor.[40] This trend of greater consumption as prompted by greater variety of a food[41,42] has been found across a wide range of ages.[43]

More recently, however, Kahn and Wansink have shown that simply increasing the *perceived variety* of an assortment can increase consumption. In one study, people were given an assortment of 300 chocolate-covered M&M candies that were presented in either seven or ten different colors. Although the candies were identical in taste, people who had each been given a bowl with ten colors ate 43% more (91 vs. 64 candies) than those who were given bowls with seven colors. Interestingly, ten colors is 43% more colors than seven. In another study, participants were offered two assortments of six flavors of jelly beans, one arranged by color and the other mixed together. Those offered the disorganized assortment rated the assortment as having more variety, and they ate 69% more jelly-beans (22 vs. 13) than those offered the organized assortment.[44]

These studies suggest that simply changing a food's arrangement (such as its organization, duplication, and symmetry) without an actual increase in variety can increase consumption. One reason this occurs is because increases in perceived variety make a person believe he or she will enjoy the assortment more. Another reason is that increasing the perceived variety can concurrently suggest an appropriate amount to consume (consumption norm) in a particular situation.

For researchers, it is important to know that perceptions of variety[45-47]—and not just actual variety—can influence consumption. For consumers, it is more important to keep in mind that our immediate food environments are malleable and can be adjusted and designed to better control intake.

STOCKPILED FOOD IS QUICKLY CONSUMED

The presence of large stockpiles of food products at home (such as multiunit packages purchased at wholesale club stores) can make those products more visible and salient than those contained in singular or smaller packages. Not only are stockpiled products by their very nature visually conspicuous, they are often stored in salient locations until they are depleted to more manageable levels. Because visibility and salience can stimulate consumption frequency, bulk buying or stockpiling food can cause overconsumption and may promote obesity.

To investigate this, Chandon and Wansink directly stockpiled peoples' homes with either large or moderate quantities of eight different foods. Each family's consumption of these foods was monitored for 2 weeks. It was found that when convenient, ready-to-eat foods were initially stockpiled, they were eaten at an average of 112% faster rate as nonstockpiled foods.[48] After the eighth day, however, the consumption of these stockpiled foods was similar to that of the less stockpiled foods, even though plenty of both remained in stock. Part of this eventual decrease was due to "burnout" or taste satiation,[49] but another factor was that the inventory level of these foods dropped to the point where they became much less visually salient.

To investigate the link between the visibility of stockpiled food and obesity, Terry and Beck[50] compared food storage habits in homes of obese and nonobese families. Curiously, their first study showed that stockpiled food tended to be visible in

TABLE 24.1 HOW TO ALTER ONE'S PERSONAL ENVIRONMENT TO HELP REDUCE FOOD INTAKE

The Food Environment	How One's Personal Environment Can Be Altered to Help Reduce Consumption
Dinnerware creates illusions → greater serving sizes and intake	• Use smaller bowls, plates, and servingware. • Use smaller packaging or break large packaging into subpackages. • Replace short, wide glasses with tall, narrow ones. • Use small spoons when serving oneself or when eating from a bowl.
The size of packages and portions suggests consumption norms: larger packages and portions → greater consumption	• Repackage foods into smaller containers to suggest smaller consumption norms. • Plate smaller dinner portions in advance. • Never eat from a package. Always transfer a food to a (small) plate or bowl in order to make portion estimation easier.
Salient food promotes salient hunger: greater visibility → greater consumption	• Replace the cookie jar with a fruit bowl. • Store tempting foods in foil or opaque containers. • Place healthier, low-density foods in the front of the refrigerator and less healthy foods in the back.
Structure and perceived variety of food assortments: greater *perceived* variety → greater consumption	• At a high-variety environment (ex. parties, buffets, and receptions)… • Avoid having multiple bowls of the same food. • Don't serve more than two foods on a platter. • Arrange foods in organized patterns. • *Conversely*, arrange foods in less organized patterns to stimulate consumption in retirement homes and hospitals.
Stockpiled food → faster consumption	• Out of sight is out of mind. Reduce visibility by moving stockpiled foods to the basement or cupboard immediately after purchase. • Reduce the convenience of stockpiled foods. Box or freeze them. • Stockpile healthy foods to stimulate their consumption and to leave less room for their unhealthy counterparts.

the homes of obese families, but their second study showed the opposite. In general, though, more studies show that stockpiled products tend to be visually salient, an important reason why they are frequently consumed.

CONCLUSION

Consumption occurs within a context wherein understanding fundamental behavior has immediate implications for consumer welfare. However, simply knowing the relationship between environmental factors and consumption will not eliminate its effects on consumers. People are often surprised at how much they consume, and this indicates that they may be influenced at a subliminal level of which they are unaware. Yet in the same way our immediate personal environment often leads us to overeat, it can be redesigned to encourage us to eat less (see Table 24.1).

We are at a point of development wherein much of the incremental improvement in our life span and our quality of life is likely to come more from behavioral lifestyle changes than from new medical treatments. When it comes to contributing to length and quality of life in the next generations, well-intentioned marketers may be in a prime position to help lead the movement toward behavior change.[51] Obesity is a good place to start.[52]

REFERENCES

1. de Castro JM. When, how much and what foods are eaten are related to total daily food intake. *Br J Nutr* 2009;102:1228–1237.
2. Hill JO. Can a small-changes approach help address the obesity epidemic? A report of the Joint Task Force of the American Society for Nutrition, Institute of Food Technologists, and International Food Information Council. *Am J Clin Nutr* 2009;89: 477–484.

3. Cutler DM, Glaeser EL, Shapiro JM. Why have Americans become more obese? *J Econ Perspectives* 2003;17:93–118.

4. Levitsky DA. The control of food intake and the regulation of body weight in humans. In: Harris RBS, Mattes RD, eds. *Appetite and Food Intake: Behavioral and Physiological Considerations.* Boca Raton, FL: CRC Press; 2008:21–42.

5. Pliner P, Martins Y. The effects of meal cues and amount consumed on predictions of future eating in others. *Pers Soc Psychol B* 2002;28:1354–1365.

6. Stroebele N, de Castro J. Environmental stimuli influence people's food intake; are there individual differences? *Obes Res* 2004;12.

7. Wansink B, Payne CR, Chandon P. Internal and external cues of meal cessation: the French paradox redux? *Obesity (Silver Spring)* 2007;15:2920–2924.

8. Meiselman HL. Obstacles to studying real people eating real meals in real situations. *Appetite* 1992;19:84–86.

9. Rozin P, Tuorila H. Simultaneous and temporal contextual influences on food acceptance. *Food Qual Pref* 1993;4:11–20.

10. Birch LL, McPhee L, Shoba BC, Steinberg L, Krehbiel R. Clean up your plate: effects of child feeding practices on the conditioning of meal size. *Learn Motiv* 1987;18:301–317.

11. Wansink B. *Marketing Nutrition.* Champaign: University of Illinois Press; 2004.

12. Wansink B, Van Ittersum K. Bottoms up! Peripheral cues and consumption volume. *J Consum Res* 2003;30:311–319.

13. Van Ittersum K, Wansink B. Plate size and color suggestibility: the Delboeuf illusion's bias on serving and eating behavior. *J Consum Res* 2012. Available at http://www.jstor.org/stable/10.1086/662615.

14. Wansink B, van Ittersum K, Painter JE. Ice cream illusions bowls, spoons, and self-served portion sizes. *Am J Prev Med* 2006;31:240–243.

15. Wansink B. From mindless eating to mindlessly eating better. *Physiol Behav* 2010;100(5):454–463.

16. Wansink B, Wansink CS. The largest last supper: depictions of food portions and plate size increased over the millennium. *Int J Obesity* 2010;34(5):943–944.

17. Blundell J, de Graaf C, Hulshof T, et al. Appetite control: methodological aspects of the evaluation of foods. *Obes Rev* 2010;11:251–270.

18. Shepherd R. Influences on food choice and dietary behavior. *Forum Nutr* 2005;57:36–43.

19. Young LR, Nestle M. The contribution of expanding portion sizes to the US obesity epidemic. *Am J Public Health* 2002;92:246–249.

20. Rolls BJ. The supersizing of America: portion size and the obesity epidemic. *Nutr Today* 2003;38:42–53.

21. Wansink B. Can package size accelerate usage volume? *J Marketing* 1996;60:1–14.

22. Nisbett RE. Determinants of food intake in human obesity. *Science* 1968;159:1254–1245.

23. Rolls BJ, Morris EL, Roe LS. Portion size of food affects energy intake in normal-weight and overweight men and women. *Am J Clin Nutr* 2002;76:1207–1213.

24. Edelman B, Engell D, Bronstein P, Hirsch E. Environmental effects on the intake of overweight and normal-weight men. *Appetite* 1986;7:71–83.

25. Wansink B, Kim J. Bad popcorn in big buckets: portion size can influence intake as much as taste. *J Nutr Educ Behav* 2005;37:242–245.

26. Young LR. *The Portion Teller: Smartsize Your Way to Permanent Weight Loss.* New York: Morgan Road Books; 2005.

27. Schwartz J, Byrd-Bredbenner C. Portion distortion: typical portion sizes selected by young adults. *J Am Diet Assoc* 2006;106:1412–1418.

28. Wansink B, Payne CR. The joy of cooking too much: 70 years of calorie increases in classic recipes. *Ann Intern Med* 2009;150:291–292.

29. Cornell CE, Rodin J, Weingarten H. Stimulus-induced eating when satiated. *Physiol Behav* 1989;45:695–704.

30. Boon B, Stroebe W, Schut H, Jansen A. Food for thought: cognitive regulation of food intake. *Brit J Health Psych* 1998;3:27–40.

31. Wansink B, Painter JE, Lee YK. The office candy dish: proximity's influence on estimated and actual consumption. *Int J Obesity* 2006;30:871–875.

32. Johnson WG. Effect of cue prominence and subject weight on human food-directed performance. *J Pers Soc Psychol* 1974;29:843–848.

33. Klajner F, Herman CP, Polivy J, Chhabra R. Dieting rather than obesity predicts the anticipatory salivary response to palatable food. *Physiol Behav* 1981;27:195–198.

34. Bossert-Zaudig S, Laessle R, MeilleR C, Ellring H. Hunger and appetite during visual perception of food in eating disorders. *Eur Psychiat* 1991;6:237.

35. Staiger P, Dawe S, McCarthy R. Responsitivity to food cues in bulimic women and controls. *Appetite* 2000;35:27–33.

36. Jansen A, Van den Hout M. On being led into temptation: "counterregulation" of dieters after smelling a "preload." *Addict Behav* 1991;5:247–253.

37. Nederkoorn C, Jansen A. Cue reactivity and regulation of food intake. *Eat Behav* 2002;3:61–72.

38. Volkow ND, Wang GJ, Fowler JS, et al. "Nonhedonic" food motivation in humans involves dopamine in the dorsal striatum and methylphenidate amplifies this effect. *Synapse* 2002;44:175–180.

39. Jansen A, Broekmate J, Heymans M. Cue-exposure vs self-control in the treatment of binge eating: a pilot study. *Behav Res Ther* 1992;30:235–241.

40. Rolls BJ, Rowe EA, Rolls ET, Kingston B, Megson A, Gunary R. Variety in a meal enhances food intake in man. *Physiol Behav* 1981;26:215–221.

41. Rolls BJ. Sensory-specific satiety. *Nutr Rev* 1986;44:93–101.

42. Miller DL, Bell EA, Pelkman CL, Peters JC, Rolls BJ. Effects of dietary fat, nutrition labels, and repeated consumption on sensory-specific satiety. *Physiol Behav* 2000;71:153–158.

43. Rolls BJ, McDermott TM. Effects of age on sensory-specific satiety. *Am J Clin Nutr* 1991;54:988–996.

44. Kahn BE, Wansink B. The influence of assortment structure on perceived variety and consumption quantities. *J Consum Res* 2004;30:519–533.

45. Hoch SJ, Bradlow ET, Wansink B. The variety of an assortment. *Market Sci* 1999;18:527–546.

46. Hoch SJ, Bradlow ET, Wansink B. Rejoinder to "The variety of an assortment: an extension to the attribute-based approach." *Market Sci* 2002;21:342–346.

47. van Herpen E, Pieters R. The variety of an assortment: an extension to the attribute-based approach. *Market Sci* 2002;21:331–341.

48. Chandon P, Wansink B. When are stockpiled products consumed faster? A convenience-salience framework of postpurchase consumption incidence and quantity. *J Marketing Res* 2002;39:321–335.

49. Inman JJ. The role of sensory-specific satiety in attribute-level variety seeking. *J Consum Res* 2001;28:105–120.

50. Terry K, Beck S. Eating style and food storage habits in the home—assessment of obese and nonobese families. *Behav Modif* 1985;9:242–261.

51. Chandon P, Wansink B. Is food marketing making us fat? A multi-disciplinary review. *Found Trend Market* 2011;5(3):113–196.

52. Wansink B, Huckabee M. De-marketing obesity. *Calif Manage Rev* 2005;47(4):6–18.

PART III

Research on Food and Addiction

25

Food Addiction and Diagnostic Criteria
for Dependence

ASHLEY N. GEARHARDT AND WILLIAM R. CORBIN

Rates of obesity in the United States and internationally have reached epidemic proportions and there are no signs of slowing. Approximately 66% of American adults are now overweight or obese,[1] and rates of childhood obesity continue to grow at an alarming rate.[2] Increases in obesity in the United States and other developed nations have been paralleled by major changes in the food environment. Specifically, there has been an influx of highly processed foods that are rich in fat and sugar. These foods are typically cheap, easily accessible, and highly advertised. The correspondence between changes in the food environment and increased rates of obesity have led some to argue that these highly processed, high-fat and high-sugar foods are addictive.[3] Such a model might help explain why so many people struggle to control their weight despite repeated attempts, much like smokers trying to quit.

Consistent with this hypothesis, animal models and neuroimaging studies in humans have identified striking similarities between excess food consumption and addictive behaviors.[4,5] Specifically, the opioid and dopaminergic systems are implicated in both obesity and substance dependence.[6] Although data on shared biological mechanisms for food and substances of abuse suggest a possible addictive process, based on the diagnostic criteria outlined in *The Diagnostic and Statistical Manual for Mental Disorders*, fourth edition, text revision (*DSM-IV-TR*),[7] substance dependence is a behavioral disorder defined by the experience of the individual rather than his or her physiology. Thus, it is critical to examine behavioral indicators of food dependence that correspond to the criteria for substance dependence.

BEHAVIORAL INDICATORS OF SUBSTANCE DEPENDENCE

The *DSM-IV-TR* states that a diagnosis of substance dependence should be given when three (or more) of seven diagnostic criteria are experienced in a 12-month period.[7] Additionally, clinically significant impairment or distress must be present.[7] In the remainder of this chapter, we will discuss the current state of the research for each of the seven diagnostic criteria. We will also report the prevalence of each symptom in the initial validation of the Yale Food Addiction Scale (YFAS),[8] which was developed to measure the existence of substance dependence diagnostic criteria as applied to eating behavior.

TOLERANCE AND WITHDRAWAL

Tolerance occurs when the effects of a substance become less pronounced with repeated use, or when an individual needs to consume larger amounts to receive the desired effects.[7] Withdrawal is defined as the development of physiological or cognitive symptoms in response to periods of abstinence of reduced consumption of a substance.[7] Withdrawal can also be identified by the consumption of a substance to prevent symptoms from occurring.[7] Although tolerance or withdrawal was required to meet a diagnosis of substance dependence under earlier versions of the *DSM*, neither is necessary for a diagnosis of substance dependence under the *DSM-IV-TR*. Rather, individuals reporting tolerance and withdrawal are classified as having substance dependence *with physical dependence.*[7]

The use of tolerance as an indicator of dependence has received some criticism, because the development of tolerance is not unique to addiction, but rather, accompanies frequent use of a substance regardless of dependence symptoms.[9] For example, habitual coffee drinkers will develop signs of tolerance (and withdrawal) over time, but caffeine dependence is not included in the diagnostic criteria because physical dependence does not typically cause distress or impairment.[7] Thus, it is possible to exhibit signs of physical dependence on a substance without receiving a diagnosis of substance dependence. Although evidence of withdrawal is more consistently an indicator of physical dependence on a substance, withdrawal is not associated with all addictive substances. For example, cannabis, hallucinogens, and inhalants do not trigger a withdrawal syndrome.[7] Thus, it is not necessary for a drug to trigger withdrawal to be addictive. Despite the aforementioned issues with physical signs of substance dependence, tolerance and withdrawal are among the seven diagnostic indicators of substance use disorders and must therefore be considered in evaluating food dependence.

Little experimental research on tolerance to food has been conducted, perhaps due in part to the methodological obstacles associated with conducting this type of research. Unlike other drugs of abuse, consumption of highly palatable foods typically begins *very* early in life, in some cases within the first 12 months.[10] Thus, examination of food tolerance during infancy or early childhood may be most informative. Although we are aware of no such studies to date, research on sugar and pain may provide indirect evidence for the development of tolerance to specific foods. Sugar-rich solutions have been found to work as an effective analgesic for infants and young children, but not adults.[11] In addition, a recent study by Pepino and colleagues[12] found that sugar was a less effective analgesic for overweight children (or those at risk for becoming overweight) than for normal weight children. The authors hypothesized that this reduced effect of sucrose could be due to differential consumption of carbohydrates or sweets, which could potentially modify the dopaminergic and opioid systems.

Although there is also limited research on food tolerance in adults, we are aware of one study in which the results were suggestive of tolerance. Brown et al.[13] found that illness duration among individuals with bulimia nervosa (BN) was related to larger and more frequent binges, possibly reflecting signs of tolerance. Although interesting, participants were not specifically asked if the increased binges were

due to the diminished effect of food consumption. To our knowledge, the YFAS validation study is the only study to date that directly assessed tolerance to foods believed to have addictive properties. In this sample of undergraduate students, 13.5% of participants reported food-related tolerance.[8] This study provides preliminary evidence for tolerance to certain foods, but it will be important in future studies to determine whether tolerance develops to all high-risk foods or only to certain types of foods, such as those high in fat or sugar.

We are not aware of any empirical investigations of withdrawal related to reduced consumption of certain types of food (e.g., sugar, fat) in humans. There are, however, anecdotal reports that certain diets cause withdrawal-like symptoms. For example, Atkins warns in his popular low-carbohydrate diet book that reducing sugar and carbohydrates can cause "fatigue, faintness, palpitations, headaches, and cold sweats."[14] In the YFAS validation sample, 16.3% of participants met criteria for withdrawal,[8] though it is important to note that reliance on self-reports increases the likelihood that discomfort associated with dieting could be attributed to a withdrawal syndrome. To better characterize withdrawal to food, it will be necessary to conduct controlled lab-based studies that examine the physiological and psychological effects of cutting down on sugar and fat.

LOSS OF CONTROL

Loss of control is defined by the frequent consumption of a substance in greater amounts or over longer periods of time than was initially intended.[7] Although we are not aware of any studies examining loss of control over food as defined in the diagnostic criteria for substance abuse, loss of control over eating has been well documented among individuals with eating disorders. In particular, loss of control is central to the diagnosis of binge eating disorder (BED) and BN.[7] Eating binges are generally triggered by exposure to or consumption of foods that are often high in fat and/or sugar,[15] and they can result in very large quantities of food being consumed, sometimes as much as 5,000 calories.[16] Thus, there is substantial evidence that clinically relevant loss of control can occur with respect to eating behavior.

Although the term "loss of control" is important in both substance dependence and eating disorders, there are subtle differences in the meaning across the two disorders. The criterion for binge eating episodes is only met when a large quantity of food is consumed in a discrete period of time and is accompanied by a feeling of loss of control.[7] In contrast, the loss of control criterion is met in substance dependence if consumption occurs in a larger quantity or over a longer period of time than is intended.[7] Thus, less emphasis is placed on the subjective experience of control and the period of time over which the behavior occurs. For example, planning to smoke only after meals but instead "chain" smoking throughout the day would be characterized as loss of control from an addictions perspective despite the lack of a discrete episode of overconsumption. It is worth noting that such behavior is captured within the criteria for Eating Disorder Not Otherwise Specified (EDNOS),[7] which is the most frequently diagnosed eating disorder.[17] It will be important in future studies to see how many individuals within the EDNOS category meet the diagnostic criteria for food dependence. In the preliminary validation of the YFAS, 21.7% of participants met the loss of control criterion as defined for food addiction.[8]

A DESIRE OR REPEATED FAILED ATTEMPTS TO REDUCE OR STOP CONSUMPTION

This criterion is associated with the high rates of chronic relapse in substance dependence. High rates of relapse are also pervasive with respect to eating behavior. Attempts to create a diet or dieting aid that results in long-term success have often failed.[17] Although the development of a successful dieting strategy remains elusive, the desire to lose weight remains pervasive. For example, approximately 30% of American adults are actively trying to lose an average of 30 pounds.[18] Data from the preliminary validation of the YFAS also speak to the ubiquitous nature of this criterion. In this study, 71.3% of participants met the criteria for unsuccessful attempts at reducing their consumption of certain foods.[8]

A GREAT DEAL OF TIME SPENT IN ACTIVITIES NECESSARY TO OBTAIN, USE, OR RECOVER

This criterion attempts to capture the role that substance use plays in the patient's life. Like withdrawal, this criterion does not apply equally to all addictive substances. Nicotine provides a good case in point. Although social attitudes and policies surrounding nicotine are changing, for many years it was legal,

cheap, easily accessible, and socially acceptable to smoke at any time and in any place. Additionally, nicotine does not result in a significant intoxication syndrome that reduces functioning in the same way as other substances.[8] Thus, while it is illegal to drive a car under the influence of most other drugs, it is perfectly legal to drive while using nicotine. Furthermore, nicotine withdrawal causes few physical symptoms, which makes recovery from nicotine less severe than other drugs.[8] Many of these characteristics are also true of consumption of high-calorie foods. These foods are legal, cheap, easily accessible, and socially acceptable. Furthermore, consuming large quantities of high-fat/high-sugar foods does not cause intoxication in a manner that is similar to heroin or alcohol. Although further research on withdrawal is needed, cutting down on high-fat/high-sugar foods does not appear to cause severe physical debilitation. Thus, like nicotine, excess consumption of certain foods may not be captured appropriately by this criterion. Despite concerns about this criterion for substances like nicotine and food, 24.0% of participants in the YFAS validation sample reported that they spent a great deal of time either consuming these foods, feeling sluggish or fatigued due to excess consumption, or spending time seeking out highly palatable foods.[8]

GIVING UP OTHER IMPORTANT ACTIVITIES

This criterion also addresses the extent to which substance use impacts daily functioning. Although research has found that binge eating is related to significant disability, impairment, and distress,[19] there has been little examination of the activities that may be given up due to excess food consumption. In the preliminary validation of the YFAS, 10.3% of participants reported giving up other important activities, such as spending time with friends and family, to either consume food or to recover from the consequences of excess food consumption. Participants also reported they had avoided professional or social situations because they would not be able to consume a desired food or would be tempted to overeat.[8]

CONTINUED USE DESPITE PHYSICAL OR PSYCHOLOGICAL PROBLEMS

Patients who are substance dependent typically continue use in the face of legal, financial, interpersonal, and health problems.[8] In the case of nicotine, the most common problem is serious health problems. This pattern of consequences is also evident in excess food consumption. Obesity and a diet high in fat and sugar are widely acknowledged to cause a wide range of health problems, such as diabetes, cancer, and heart disease.[20] Additionally, obesity is associated with depression, anxiety, and widespread weight-based discrimination.[21,22] Thus, there is compelling evidence for excess food consumption in the face of serious negative consequences. In the preliminary validation of the YFAS, 28.3% of participants reported continued consumption of high-calorie foods in the face of physical and psychological problems.[8]

DIAGNOSTIC THRESHOLD AND CLINICALLY SIGNIFICANT IMPAIRMENT OR DISTRESS

In considering the diagnostic criteria for food dependence, it is important to note that the diagnostic threshold for substance dependence requires that three (or more) symptoms must occur *within a 12 month period*.[7] Additionally, a diagnosis of substance dependence is not given unless *clinically significant impairment or distress* is present.[7] Studies using self-report criteria for substance dependence often fail to address the issue of impairment and distress and may therefore inflate prevalence estimates. Data from the YFAS highlight the importance of this specification. Although 17.2% of participants in the validation study reported meeting three or more of the seven diagnostic criteria, only 11.4% of participants met the full diagnostic criteria with the inclusion of the requirement of impairment or distress.[8] Although it is important to ensure that a substance dependence diagnosis is only given when appropriate, high rates of subclinical symptoms of addiction to food would also have major public health ramifications. As has been the case with alcohol and nicotine, environmental factors (e.g., accessibility, marketing, and price) have a major impact on the levels of both subclinical and clinical substance-related problems.[23] This is almost certainly true for food as well. Thus, altering environmental factors may result in a reduction of food-related problems.

AREAS OF FUTURE RESEARCH

In conclusion, there is significant evidence for three food-related substance dependence criteria: loss of control, unsuccessful efforts to reduce consumption, and continued use despite negative consequences. Furthermore, there are self-report data to support the idea that a great deal of time is spent, and that other important activities are given up, due to excess consumption of food. Tolerance and withdrawal have received little research attention and are in need of further study. Further exploration is also needed to understand the role that subclinical symptoms of food addiction may have on public health. Finally, food addiction and eating disorders, such as BED and BN, share many overlapping characteristics. It will be important to more fully understand the relationship between these disorders and the extent to which they are distinct disorders as opposed to different manifestations of a single underlying problem.

REFERENCES

1. Freid VM, Prager K, MacKay AP, Xia H. *Health, United States, 2003: with chartbook on trends in the health of Americans.* Hyattsville, MD.: National Center for Health Statistics, 2003:169, 212, 228. (DHHS publication no. 2003-1232.)
2. Lobstein T, Baur L, Uauy R. Obesity in children and young people: a crisis in public health. *Obes Rev* 2004;5:4–104.
3. Gold MS, Frost-Pineda K, Jacobs WS. Overeating, binge eating, and eating disorders as addictions. *Psychiat Ann* 2003;33:117–122.
4. Davis C, Carter JC. Compulsive overeating as an addiction disorder: a review of theory and evidence. *Appetite* 2009;53:1–8.
5. Volkow ND, Wang RA. How can drug addiction help us understand obesity. *Lancet* 2005;357:354–357.
6. Avena NM, Rada P, Hoebel BG. Evidence for sugar addiction: behavioral and neurochemical effects of intermittent, excessive sugar intake. *Neurosci Biobehav Rev* 2008;32:20–39.
7. Amercican Psychiatric Association. *Diagnostic and Statistical Manual of Mental Disorders.* 4th ed. Washington DC: American Psychiatric Association, 2000.
8. Gearhardt AG, Corbin WR, Brownell KD. Preliminary validation of the Yale Food Addiction Scale. *Appetite* 2009;52:32–36.
9. O'Brien CP, Volkow NV, Li T-K. What's in a word? Addiction versus dependence in DSM-V. *Am J Psychiat* 2006;163:764–765.
10. Lande B, Frost-Andersen L, Veierød MB, et al. Breast-feeding at 12 months of age and dietary habits among breast-fed and non-breast-fed infants. *Public Health Nutr* 2004;7:495–503.
11. Harrison DM. Oral sucrose for pain management for infants: myths and misconceptions. *J Neonatal Nurs* 2008;14:39–46.

12. Pepino MY, Mennella JA. Sucrose-induced analgesia is related to sweet preferences in children but not adults. *Pain* 2005;119:210–218.

13. Brown AJ, Spanos A, Devlin MJ, Walsh BT. Bulimia nervosa as an addiction: evidence for a tolerance effect in patterns of binge eating over the course of illness. Poster presented at: International Conference of Eating Disorders; June 21, 2007; Baltimore, MD.

14. Atkins RC. *Dr. Atkins' New Diet Revolution.* North Yorkshire, England: Guill, 2002.

15. Vanderlinden J, Dalle Grave R, Vandereycken W, Noorduin C. Which factors do provoke binge eating? An exploratory study in female students. *Eat Behav* 2001;2:79–83.

16. Mitchell JE, Pyle RL, Eckert ED. Frequency and duration of binge-eating episodes in patients with bulimia. *Am J Psychiatry* 1981;138:835–836.

17. Anderson T, Stokholm KH, Backer OG, Quadde F. Long-term (5-year) results after either horizontal gastroplasty or very-low-calorie diet for morbid obesity. *Int J Obes* 1988;12:277–284.

18. William DF, Serdula MK, Anda RF, Levy A, Byers T. Weight loss attempts in adults: goals, duration, and rate of weight loss. *Am J Public Health* 1992;82:1251–1257.

19. Johnson JG, Spitzer RL, Williams JBW. Health problems, impairment and illnesses associated with bulimia nervosa and binge eating disorder among primary care and obstetric gynaecology patients. *Psych Med* 2001;31:1455–1466.

20. Mokdad AH, Marks JS, Stroup MF, Gerberding JL. Actual causes of death in the United States. *JAMA* 2004;291:1238–1245.

21. Marcus MD, Wilde JE. Obesity: is it a mental disorder? *Int J Eat Disord* 2009;42(8):739–753.

22. Puhl RM, Brownell KD. Confronting and coping with weight stigma: an investigation of overweight and obese adults. *Obesity* 2006;14:1802–1815.

23. Room R, Babor T, Rehm J. Alcohol and public health. *Lancet* 2005;365:519–530.

26

Phylogenetic and Ontogenetic Contributions to Today's Obesity Quagmire

ELLIOTT M. BLASS

All animals, including humans, until recently, must successfully meet the challenge of obtaining enough food to successfully mate and raise offspring, evolution's currency. While this may seem obvious, the magnitude of the challenge is anything but. A thought experiment, originally exercised by Darwin,[1] evaluates the time that it would take elephants living in a hypothetical world to cover the earth's surface. This hypothetical paradise is free of rate-limiting constraints, such as food supply, predators, or disease. My model animal, the Norway rat, lives closer to home. I have calculated the number of direct descendants that this familiar, smaller, more fecund mammal can expect to enjoy in her hypothetical habitat of unlimited food and freedom from predators and disease.

Over 1 trillion, 4 billion F6 offspring will have been born under these halcyon conditions within 21 months of the progenitor female's own birth. She will deliver her first litter of 12 before her own 3-month birthday. She will immediately become sexually receptive and conceive within hours of giving birth. This reproductive strategy allows her, her daughters, indeed all female rats of reproductive age to rear two litters simultaneously during their 9 months (at least) of fecundity; one litter in utero, the other, ex utero. Her offspring, making the reasonable assumption that a typical adult rat will average 8 inches from snout to rump, and 4 inches across at its widest part, then circa 32 inches^2 are occupied by each animal for a total of 72,000 miles^2 for the lot of them, or about 2% of the continental US land mass. The real numbers are kept down to about 300 million, that is, roughly one per human through inadequate food supplies, predation, disease, and pest control. Because the rate-limiting factor of population growth is food supply, it follows that strategies would evolve to maximize harvesting, storing, and utilizing available food. If such *strategies have evolved for dealing with the hard times*, it follows that animals, especially humans that suddenly find themselves in the artificial warp of technologically produced excess food, might explosively become obese. This chapter argues on empirical grounds that all aspects of mammalian feeding systems are geared toward overfeeding. Under normal circumstances in which food availability limits individual obesity, population obesity is held in check, by an inadequate food supply and *not* by homeostatic constraints. In contrast a seemingly *unlimited* supply of readily available, cheap, energy-dense foods fabricated for taste, makes the principled evolutionary prediction that a significant portion of the population partaking of that cornucopia will become obese. Here we are: one-third of the population is obese (body mass index ≥ 30), another one-third overweight (body mass index ≥ 25 < 30).

What evidence supports these assertions? First, energy-dense foods such as sugars and fats please our palates. In fact, elaborate sweet receptors on tongue and palate that extend into the esophageal region code sweet with remarkable fidelity, including artificial substances fabricated at concentrations that far exceed any natural substance. This remarkable capacity has been established through electrophysiological research in animals and taste psychophysics in humans.[2] This information has not escaped the attention of the food industry.

One can understand this functionality: sweeter, more energy-dense fruits will be more avidly sought in nature, will be eaten more frequently, and their seeds will spread further in a rich matrix as healthier animals expand their range. This establishes a positive feed-forward system of mutual benefit to both animals and plants. Laboratory studies support this idea; sweet foods and solutions are preferred to nonsweet ones. Indeed, in very brief taste tests, in which very little is tasted in rat studies,[3] or, tasted and spit out in human studies,[2] more concentrated solutions are preferred.

The paradox of progressively *decreased* intake of freely available hypertonic sucrose solutions was resolved in a classic study by DG Mook.[4] For hypertonic sugars like sucrose, diminished intake reflects the dehydration caused by ingesting large volumes of osmotically concentrated material that sequesters water out of cells and the gastrointestinal tract, making it unavailable to the general circulation. When this consequence is avoided experimentally by having animals sham drink so that the fluid exits through an esophageal fistula, avoiding systematic dehydration, sucrose intake is linear to concentration. The same held when the lost concentrated solution was replaced by gastric infusions of hydrating water or isotonic saline. The essential data have been replicated in humans in taste and preference tests.[2] Ominously, artificial substances fabricated to exploit the fidelity of taste transduction, have been put into force by the food industries, for the sole purpose of enhancing taste and exaggerating food intake, a luxury that consumers, already sporting unhealthy body mass indexes can ill afford. This practice does not apparently concern either the food manufacturers or the United States Department of Agriculture (USDA) and Food and Drug Administration (FDA) regulatory bodies.

Second, fullness sensations that normally shut meals down are easily overridden by attractive tastes, as in Thanksgiving desserts even in turkey-stuffed eaters. Clearly mammals encumbered with the *strategy* of eating more energy-dense foods than needed for immediate use, and banking the excess in fat depots for the long-term predictable shortages, are vulnerable in today's "surround-sound" unlimited artificially flavored calorically dense foods. To make things worse, food variety itself independently disinhibits feeding in sated individuals. In an important series of studies, Barbara Rolls[5] has shown that individuals who had stopped eating one food would reengage when a second food was presented, even one equally or less palatable. The most telling study in this regard by Mook[6] demonstrated that rats that had stopped eating chow pellets would resume when the chow was crushed into powder form. This opens the philosophical issue of "identity" or sameness. From the rat's perspective, powdered food differs from pellets; even powder

fashioned by crushing the pellets is accepted after "satiation" on pellets. The boundaries that terminate feeding are permeable and easily crossed, a tendency that effectively counters moderating intake of unlimited energy-dense, nutritionally empty foods.

Overeating tendencies in nature are seasonal. A variety of cues, contracted day length especially,[7] trigger overeating to bulk up for winter's advent. Signals from gastric distension or changes in gastrointestinal inhibitory hormones are functionally diminished; eating *in the absence of need*, breaks through otherwise effective hormonal/mechanical barriers. As we know from walks in woods of changing colors, small mammals are very busy socking in winter's supplies. Thus, in addition to feeding control being waved by the tastes and flavors of energy-dense foods and by food variety, anticipation of seasonal shortage also pushes food storage and intake, a parallel to shopping at Costco and other purveyors of massive portion sizes. The most extreme manifestations of winter preparation are the thousand[s] mile animal migrations and hibernation or torpor through lowered body temperatures. The former avoid cold and find sustaining food supplies; the latter save considerable energy otherwise expended to maintain normal body temperature levels.

Other important factors that contribute to overeating include social facilitation that reflects increased intake when animals, including human, eat together. According to Hermann and Polivy,[8] human food intake increases linearly when eating with friends and relatives and decreases when eating with strangers or people with whom we are uncomfortable or do not like.

The final major suspension of inhibitory control occurs during lactation and pregnancy, when the fetuses/sucklings literally eat off of the mother. The nursing/suckling relationship is what defines us as mammals.[9] For this to occur seamlessly requires an adequate nutrient supply that allows the dam to provide enough food for her eager young to drain. Absent an enabling food supply a number of scenarios follow. In one, the young survive, but they are so runted as to render them defenseless and incapable of establishing and defending territories. In a second script, hungry females spend a dangerous amount of time away from the nest, resulting in infant hypothermia, or more likely, cannibalism by predators. Driven to seek food, the adult herself becomes dinner. In other scenarios of food shortage, puberty is delayed or implantation is thwarted. In anorexic humans, menarche is "reversed" and women can become amenoriac.

Taken together, we quickly appreciate how the potential of over a trillion offspring for the lucky rat in our example is quickly diminished. In my view the default is driven by the historical urgency of inadequate food so that we come into the world prepared to opportunistically harvest energy. The evolutionary asset of feeding opportunism, conversion to and storage of fat, however, becomes a liability when confronted by the lure of low-priced tasty foods served in boat-sized portions that are unrelentingly pushed in the media.

Understanding the evolutionary web of feeding determinism and the previous inadequate resources that contributed to "overeating" selection starts to provide a rational orientation toward a basis for identifying obesity's causes, and preventing and treating obesity. As AJ Stunkard[10] has demonstrated repeatedly in behavioral and epidemiological studies, and as EP Noble[11] has provided a genetic basis for in people with deficient D2 receptor gene, the tendency toward obesity is strongly biased genetically both from the perspective of overeating and from metabolic differences that can be reflected in differential weight loss.[12]

Developmental, ontogenetic perspectives on energy-saving mechanisms are complementary and provide proximal mechanisms through which mothers conserve infant energy. First, almost all mammalian mothers are attracted to their infants and spend considerable time in contact with them[13]; rabbits being an exception.[14] This contact, often preliminary to allowing infants to suckle, severely reduces the infant's surface-to-mass ratio, thereby reducing radiant and conductive heat loss. Maternal body contact also induces infant analgesia in both rats[15] and humans.[16]

Second, suckling per se, even when not yielding milk, also calms human infants[17] and powerfully blocks pain afferents.[18] Both qualities also save energy. Indeed, calories saved by crying reduction through calming or analgesia can be brought to the service of somatic and, especially, brain growth.[19]

Third, sweet taste and milk flavor of mother's milk also calm[20] and mitigate pain.[21] The magnitude of the calming effect is substantial. Sucrose,[22] glucose, and fats are all effective,[21] as is milk of course. These reductions cannot be explained through either contact or the suckling act per se because the

material was introduced into the mouth by direct infusion from a syringe that did not elicit sucking movements. The descending dorsolateral funiculus spinal pathway, mature at birth,[23] is engaged by sweet taste and fat flavor to target the dorsal horn and intercept pain afferents at their point of central nervous system entry. Inhibiting afferent pain pathways blocks or reduces pain information from synapsing in the spinal gray and turning upstream in the spinothalamic tract.[18] The "painful" episode is not felt. One might ask—so what if infant pain is prevented through nursing? Of what advantage is it to block pain? What is gained by calming a crying infant and normalizing heart rate?

One benefit accrues through energy savings. The distinguished pediatrician Madu Rao of Downstate Medical Center in Brooklyn, our colleagues, and I evaluated energy savings in term and preterm infants while directly recording heat loss in an infant metabolic chamber.[19] Heat loss in all 38 spontaneously crying infants was lowered by a 1/10 ml drop of sucrose within seconds of delivery, and it remained low. Crying did not return nor did heat loss increase. In fact, there was a mean 13% savings in heat loss from the crying state.

These studies among others speak to a hardwired biology of energy conservation that is available and functional at birth, likely before.[24] The system is conserved phylogenetically: both rats and humans are calmed by tastes of energy-dense substances, by touch, and especially by suckling, and seemingly by the same mechanisms. The power of the behavioral intervention is impressive: sucrose on a pacifier mitigates the pain of circumcision in day 2. Crying was reduced by 60%.[25]

Analgesia and calming are conferred through opioid and cannabanoid pathways. In rats, both sucrose calming and analgesia are blocked by naloxone, a potent opioid antagonist delivered systemically[26] or in microgram quantities to brain lateral ventricles.[27] Sucrose and, presumably, other tastes and flavors therefore target central mechanisms. These biologically driven analgesic systems are redundant and powerful; contact, suckling, and taste/flavor mechanisms combine in the genesis of analgesia at a time when human infants appear to be insensitive to pain-relieving substances, other than opioids, that will later be very effective in infants and children.[28]

Analgesic redundancy of milk extends to an intrinsic postingestive mechanism. The endogenous milk-borne opioid *beta-casomorphine* is cleaved from the casein protein in milk. Systemic *beta-casomorphine* increased heat escape latencies, an effect blocked by intracranial injections of naloxone,[29] demonstrating a potential central target for milk's enduring energy-conserving effects. Whether *beta-casomorphine* cleaved from casein and liberated from the gut at physiological levels reaches these central mechanisms remains an issue open to empirical exploration.

The big picture of nursing-suckling energetics looks like this. Tasting sucrose, fats, or other energy-dense foods triggers five fundamental changes in individual affect, behavior, physiology neurology, and memory that coalesce to obtain, conserve, and store energy. All of these changes are initiated centrally through opioid and cannabanoid[30] mechanisms. First, tasting these substances produces positive affect that creates a greater urgency to consume more. The technical term for this rush is *priming*, a phenomenon that has been well documented in the experimental psychology literature and that we all recognize when eating a tasty appetizer, artfully presented to whet our appetites. This rush sustains feeding.[31]

Second, central opioid and cannabanoid states are motive states.[31] Mammals, including humans, work to engage them either directly through drugs, tobacco, or alcohol, or indirectly, but *naturally*, by eating energy-dense foods, all of which are sweet or fatty. More is eaten; the urge to eat sustains seeking food and serves as a basis for accessing memories of food location. Because there is never enough food to go around and because sugar and sweetness in ingested natural foods are never at addicting levels, food maximization works with no "downside" of sustained energy surfeit. That which is banked is soon spent either in winter or nursing the kids.

Human and rat newborns are engaged by sweet tastes and fatty flavors. Each is rewarding in the conventional sense of the word.[32] They sustain linkage between an odor and sweet taste so that normally aversive odors are preferred for having been linked to fats or sweets. Linkage can be blocked by naloxone at the time of exposure to odor and sweet/fat solutions. Moreover, expression of odor preference can be blocked with naloxone administered for the first time at testing. Absent capacity for endogenous opioid recruitment, the aversive qualities of the odor predominate and the odor is avoided.

Third, endogenous opioids target the gastrointestinal tract to facilitate food passage and absorption.[33] To my knowledge, this has not been studied in infants. The effects in adults, however, have been well established. Interestingly, individuals in the throes of breaking a morphine addiction are notoriously constipated during the recovery process until enough endogenous opioids can be synthesized to offset the withdrawal of exogenous opiates.

Fourth, sweets, fats, and exogenous opioids are calming. They are the "comfort" in "comfort foods." We have demonstrated this in rats through naloxone blockade established centrally or peripherally. Blass and Ciamiatero[34] have shown that infants born to women who had been maintained on methadone during pregnancy could not be comforted by even concentrated solutions of sucrose. Yet these infants were calmed by holding and by sucking a pacifier. This exactly parallels findings in rats; naloxone blocks sucrose-induced calming, but it has no effect on calming induced by maternal contact.[15] Like many vital physiological systems, such as water and salt conservation, cardiac regulation, and so on,[35] redundancy is an integral feature of energy conservation.

Finally, taste/flavor and contact are analgesic. Redundancy again rules. Analgesia through maternal contact or nonnutritive suckling survived even very large doses of naloxone in a paradigm when an exposed paw was touched with a heated stylus.[15] Much smaller doses compromise taste-induced analgesia.[27]

Energy attainment and conservation are common to each integrative system identified herein. Each system though triggered by the same sensory event follows anatomically distinct neural and physiological pathways. Some, like the pain-inhibiting pathways, are laid down early and cannot be modified in their spinal trajectories; likewise for gastric actions. Others, however, are considerably more open ended. They bear the hallmarks of all motivated behaviors: flexibility; persistence; and use of different motor, perceptual, and memorial systems to the service of obtaining the energy source.

Together these complementary pathways have evolved to function in an energy-poor environment, in which production cannot sustain all of its potential citizens. We assume that the Darwinian edge came to those able to locate energy-dense foods, eat them, and remember their cache location and defend it. Redundant energy-conserving systems, opioid and nonopioid alike, contribute to energy conservation, diminishing squandering this commodity. Today's ambiance of energy surfeit in which exercise is not encouraged antiquates these biological strategies that we "bring to the table." Despite the well-publicized consequences of poor diet, abstinence (or even moderation) from the energy-dense cornucopia has proven difficult to achieve. Compulsively taking harmful substances characterizes every addiction that has been identified.[31] Moreover, as others in this volume have demonstrated, overeating energy-dense foods has many primary features of addictive behaviors whether assessments are behavioral, neurological, or functional. Overeating also fulfills bioassay criteria that have been established for addictive drugs and agents.[35] Current approaches to weight loss are remarkably ineffective, in large part, I believe, because rather than maintain biological integrity, weight loss centers and pharmaceutical houses are trying to overthrow it through dieting and drugs. Different, rational approaches are called for, ones that provide barriers, real and imagined, between us and energy-dense foods.

Our task as health professionals is made more manageable by recognizing extreme obesity as a form of drug addiction, a maladaptive behavioral/physiological/cognitive constellation that is notoriously difficult to break. Because we can legitimately draw on the principles of organization established here and in the other chapters of this compendium, our efforts to curb overeating-caused obesity are strengthened. Establishing high-density foods as a legitimate addicting agent empowers concerned citizens to petition and use political leverage to seek changes in USDA subsidy structure, advertising and marketing practices, and tax structures that will curb accessibility to these harmful substances. Neighborhood groups and organizations can use boycott and demonstration powers locally to effect change in purchasing, advertising, and selection procedures used by their local stores. Recognizing the hurt and damage suffered by children whose genetic vulnerability to the evolutionary and developmental events described earlier, empowers parents to curb their own excesses in food shopping patterns for their children. Obesity has sneaked up on us in a wink of evolutionary time. We have been blindsided by the events. No more. In addition to taking preventive actions in our personal lives, we can now act coordinately against institutions that have promoted this situation and government agencies that have allowed this major health problem to flourish.

REFERENCES

1. Darwin C. On the Origin of the Species by Means of Natural Selection. New York: D. Appleton & Co, 1888.
2. Snyder DG, Bartoshuk LM. The logic of sensory and hedonic comparisons: are the obese different? In: Blass EM, ed. Obesity: Causes, Mechanisms, Prevention and Treatment. Sunderland, MA: Sinauer & Associates; 2008: 139–162.
3. Young PT. Studies of food preference, appetite and dietary habit. Com Psych Mon 1949;19:1–74.
4. Mook DG. Oral and postingestional determinants of various solutions in rats with esophageal fistulas. J Comp Physiol Psychol 1963;56:645–659.
5. Rolls BJ. Sensory specific satiety. Nutr Rev 1986;44: 93–101.
6. Mook DG. Satiety, specifications and stop rules: feeding as a voluntary act. In: Epstein AN, Morrison AR, eds. Progress in Psychobiology and Physiological Psychology. Vol. 14. New York: Academic Press; 1990: 1–65.
7. Nelson RJ. An Introduction to Behavioral Endocrinology. 2nd ed. Sunderland, MA: Sinauer Associates, 2000.
8. Herman CP, Polivy J. Normative influences on food intake. Physiol Behav 2005;86:762–772.
9. Blass EM, Teicher MH. Suckling. Science 1980;210: 15–22.
10. Stunkard AJ, Haris JR, Pedersen NL, McClearn GE. The body mass index of twins who have been reared apart. N Engl J Med 1990;322:1483–1487.
11. Noble EP, Noble RE, Ritchie T. D2 dopamine receptor gene and obesity. Int J Eating Dis 1994;15: 205–217.
12. Bouchard C, Tremblay A, Despres JP, et al. The response to long-term overfeeding in identical twins. New Engl J Med 1990;322:1477–1481.
13. Alberts JR, Cramer CP. Ecology and experience: sources of means and meaning of developmental change. In: Blass EM, ed. Handbook of Behavioral Neurobiology. Vol 9, Developmental Psychobiology and Behavioral Ecology. New York: Plenum Press; 1988: 1–40.
14. Zarrow MX, Denenberg VH, Anderson CO. Rabbit: frequency of suckling in the pup. Science 1965;150:1835–1836.
15. Blass EM, Fillion TJ, Weller A, Brunson L. Separation of opioid from non-opioid mediation of affect in neonatal rats: non-opioid mechanisms mediate maternal contact influences. Behav Neurosci 1990;104:625–636.
16. Gray L, Watt L, Blass EM. Skin-to-skin contact is analgesic in healthy newborns. i 1999;105:e14.

17. Gray L, Miller LW, Phillip BL, Blass EM. Breast-feeding is analgesic in healthy newborns. *Pediatrics* 2002;109:590–593.
18. Ren K, Blass EM, Zhou Q-Q, Dubner R. Suckling and sucrose ingestion suppress persistent hyperalgesia and spinal Fos expression after forepaw inflammation in infant rats. *Proc Natl Acad Sci USA* 1997;104:1471–1477.
19. Rao M, Blass EM, Brignol MM, Marino L, Glass L. Reduced heat loss following sucrose ingestion in premature and normal human newborns. *Ear Hum Devel* 1997;48:109–116.
20. Blass EM, Fitzgerald E, Kehoe P. Interactions between sucrose, pain and isolation distress. *Pharm Biochem Behav* 1987;26:483–489.
21. Blass EM, Fitzgerald E. Milk-induced analgesia and comforting in 10-day-old rats: opioid mediation. *Pharm Biochem Behav* 1988;29:9–13.
22. Blass EM, Watt L. Suckling and sucrose-induced analgesia in human newborns. *Pain* 1999;83:611–623.
23. Fitzgerald M. The development of descending brainstem control of spinal cord sensory processing. In: Hanson M, ed. *Fetal and Neonatal Brainstem: Developmental and Clinical Issues.* Cambridge, England: Cambridge University Press; 1991: 127–136.
24. Smith BA, Blass EM. Taste-mediated calming in premature, preterm, and full-term human infants. *Dev Psychol* 1996;32:1084–1089.
25. Kaufman G, Cimo S, Watt LW, Blass EM. An evaluation of the effects of sucrose on neonatal pain with two commonly used circumcision methods. *Am J Ob Gyn* 2002;186:564–568.
26. Kehoe P, Blass EM. Behaviorally functional opioid systems in infant rats: II. Evidence for pharmacological, physiological and psychological mediation of pain and stress. *Behav Neurosci* 1986;100:624–630.
27. Kehoe P, Blass EM. Central nervous system mediation of positive and negative reinforcement in neonatal albino rats. *Devel Br Res* 1986;27:69–75.
28. Blass EM, Barr RG. Evolutionary biology and the practice of medicine: the case of management of infant pain experience. *J Dev Behav Ped* 2000;21:283–284.
29. Blass EM, Blom J. Betacasomorphin causes hypoalgesia in 10-day-old rats: evidence for central mediation. *Ped Res* 1996;39:199–203.
30. Kirkham TC, Williams CM. Endogenous cannabinoids and appetite. *Nutr Res Rev* 2001;14:65–86.
31. Wise R. Obesity and addiction. In: Blass EM, ed. *Obesity: Causes, Mechanisms, Prevention and Treatment.* Sunderland, MA: Sinauer & Associates; 2008:111–138.
32. Shide DJ, Blass EM. Opioid mediation of odor preferences induced by sugar and fat in 6-day-old rats. *Physiol Behav* 1991;50: 961–966.
33. Blass EM. The ontogeny of ingestive behavior. In: Morrison A, Fluharty S, eds. *Progress in Psychobiology and Physiological Psychology.* New York: Academic Press; 1995: 1–51.
34. Blass EM, Ciaramitaro V. Oral determinants of state, affect, and action in newborn humans. *Mon Soc Res Ch Devel* 1994;59:I–V, 1–86.
35. Fitzsimons JT. *The Physiology of Thirst and Sodium Appetite.* New York: Cambridge University Press, 1979.

27

Food Reward

DANA M. SMALL

INTRODUCTION

What is food reward? Scientists and philosophers have been grappling with, and often clashing over, what constitutes *reward* for centuries, if not millennia.[1] The concept of pleasure as an organizing principle for behavior was introduced by the hedonists of antiquity and echoed throughout the ages, most notably in Freud's pleasure principle. Psychophysical experiments have established that humans can reliably introspect about the perceived pleasure of sensory experiences and report this subjective experience as a rating, thus quantifying pleasure and allowing it to be subject to experimental inquiry.[2,3] With respect to food, it has long been established that there is a clear relationship between subjective ratings of food pleasantness and food consumption.

The behaviorist definition of reward, by contrast, casts reward in terms of observable behavioral contingencies that can be easily measured in animals. *Reward* is defined as a stimulus that has the property of eliciting approach responses, and *reinforcement* as the tendency for stimuli to strengthen learned stimulus-response tendencies,[4] which is usually measured by assessing the willingness of an animal to work for a reward. It has been well established that the pleasure elicited by a food and its reinforcing properties are dissociable behaviorally and biologically.[5-9] For example, overweight subjects may work harder for a food than their healthy weight counterparts but rate the food as equally pleasant. Indeed, the incentive sensitization hypothesis proposed by Berridge and Robinson posits that addiction is characterized by increases in the incentive properties of drug (or food) cues (i.e., their ability to reinforce) rather than excess pleasure experienced during consumption (of a drug or food).[10] Our definition of reward must therefore include the concepts of pleasure, reward, and reinforcement.

The rewarding value of foods and the pleasure they elicit is also closely tied to their postingestive effects.[11] Rodents[11,12] and humans[13,14] develop preferences for flavors paired with calories. The question then becomes, how do we incorporate all of these processes into a cohesive definition of food reward? In a recent review de Araujo proposes that food reward be considered a "summation of relatively independent 'layers of reward' that act to sustain positive energy balance." More specifically, three layers of reward signal are proposed: (1) proximal signals associated with food consumption (e.g., taste/flavor); (2) distal signals, associated with the postingestive effects produced by nutrients; and (3) preingestive signals, such as visual or olfactory cues that predict the proximal and distal rewards.[15] According to this view, sugars, for example, can be considered as "bilayered" rewards consisting of energy-carrying molecules (distal signal) that are also highly palatable (proximal signal). Critically, these three layers are posited to be unified by their common ability to engage the dopamine system.[16-21]

Here I adopt this definition and briefly review the neural correlates of food reward in healthy-weight humans. The relationship between adiposity and brain response to food is addressed in other chapters in this volume (see Chapters 13–18). I also propose an additional layer: "top-down" signals, such as brand [22] and cost,[23] and stimulus identity,[24,25] which for humans, living in the age of neuromarketing, may constitute yet another layer of reward.

BRAIN REPRESENTATION OF FOOD REWARD

Proximal Signals

Proximal food sensation refers to the flavors of food and drink, which result from the integration of taste, oral somatosensation, and retronasal olfaction.[26] Overlapping responses in human anterior insular cortex have been documented to taste and astringency and oral burn,[27,28] temperature and taste,[29] taste and retronasal odors,[30-32] and taste, fat, and viscosity.[33] It has therefore been proposed that this region represents and integrated oral sensory modality.[28,34] Indeed, simultaneous sensation of a taste and a retronasal odor that "go together," such as vanilla odor and sweet taste, produce supra-additive responses in the insula, indicative of sensory integration.[35] It is therefore likely that insular cortex plays a critical role in binding the discrete components of flavors into unitary flavor or food percepts.[26] However, while insula responses often reflect perceptual dimensions of oral stimuli, such as viscosity,[33] or intensity,[36] which may influence perceived pleasantness,[37-39] they may[25,40,41] or may not[29,42,43] reflect perceived pleasantness. One possibility is that the insula contributes to pleasantness coding by relaying neural computations related to sensation to the orbitofrontal cortex and anterior cingulate cortex, where valuation computations are performed. Supporting this suggestion, studies examining the interaction between brain regions during food sensation show that the insular cortex preferentially interacts with orbital cortex during pleasantness evaluations.[44] Likewise, insular cortex may integrate sensory and homeostatic signals. Resting insular response is greater during states of hunger compared to satiety, and this difference correlates positively with plasma insulin concentrations.[45] As such, insular response to food decreases as a function of eating the food to satiety.[46] The insula also preferentially interacts with the hypothalamus and ventral striatum during the consumption of potentially nutritive versus potentially harmful oral stimuli.[28] Thus, several lines of evidence highlight insular cortex as a neural hub regulating the interaction of oral sensory signals with homeostatic and reward centers.

In contrast to the insula, there is general consensus that the anterior ventral cingulate cortex (AVC) and orbitofrontal cortex (OFC) play a critical role in encoding the perceived pleasantness of the proximal food sensations. In general, the more pleasant a taste,[36,43,47] temperature,[29] or flavor[30,48,49] of an oral stimulus is reported to be, the greater is the response in these regions of the brain. These responses may be independent of other perceptual dimensions that influence pleasantness, such as intensity,[36] and they may also reflect sensory

integration and flavor enhancement. McCabe and Rolls, for example, found that the perceived pleasantness of a glutamate taste and savory odor was greater than the sum of its parts. Mirroring this supra-additive perceptual effect, response in the medial OFC and AVC was greater to the combined sensation of glutamate taste and savory odor compared to the summed responses to their independent stimulation. These supra-additive responses also correlated with the pleasantness ratings of the flavor. This finding is important because overall flavor pleasantness is not a simple function of adding affective responses to individual components. Rather, affective integration appears to be nonlinear and highly dependent upon the components involved (see Chapter 18), with the OFC and AVC critical for orchestrating this complicated valuation process.

The insula, OFC, and AVC also all show sensitivity to the devaluation of oral sensory cues by eating,[46,49-51] a processed termed *alliesthesia*.[52] Small and colleagues, for example, used positron emission tomography (PET) to measure regional cerebral blood flow changes evoked during the consumption of chocolate to beyond satiety.[46] Response evoked by the chocolate in the insula, AVC, OFC, thalamus, hippocampus, temporal neocortex, dorsal striatum, and midbrain correlated positively with the pleasantness ratings, indicating that these regions were sensitive to the devaluation of the food stimulus by eating.

Also, critical to de Araujo's proposal that dopamine unites the various layers of reward is the fact that there is indirect evidence that the palatability of food is associated with dopamine release in humans. PET was used to measure carbon 11 raclopride binding potential before and after consumption of a favorite meal in six healthy-weight participants.[17] Raclopride is a D2 receptor antagonist, and dopamine release is inferred when binding potential decreases significantly from baseline as a result of an experimental challenge. A significant reduction in striatal binding potential was observed in the fed compared to the hungry state and the magnitude of binding potential change correlated positively with the perceived pleasantness of the meal eaten, but not with hunger or ratings of desire to eat. Although indirect, and based only upon six subjects, the effect does suggest that proximal reward signals are associated with dopamine release in humans. In addition to dopamine, there is clear evidence for the opioid system in regulating food palatability in humans[53-55] and animals alike.[56]

Distal Signals

The distal food reward signals include pre- and postabsorptive postingestive effects.[15] These signals may promote or inhibit eating. The most critical preabsorptive event is gastric distention and the associated stimulation of the nerve terminal sensors throughout the gut epithelium.[57,58] Signals about gastric distension reach the hypothalamus via the vagus nerve[57] and can exert powerful inhibitory influences on food intake.[59] Several groups have examined the neural correlates of gastric distension.[60-66] Interestingly, these studies by and large implicate the same network representing proximal food sensations, that is, the insula, overlying operculum, AVC, and OFC.

The postabsorptive effects include physiological responses that follow nutrient absorption by the gut such as fuel oxidation or deposition, along with increases in plasma hormonal levels.[15] These signals reach the brain and modulate reward circuitry so that an association is formed between proximal oral sensations and their rewarding postingestive effects.[11] This process, termed *flavor nutrient conditioning*, allows organisms to learn to prefer foods that are biologically useful. Injection of dopamine antagonists into the amygdala, nucleus accumbens, and prefrontal cortex disrupts flavor nutrient conditioning and establishes a critical role for dopamine in this conditioning.[11] Lesion studies also implicate the pontine parabrachial nucleus and lateral hypothalamus.[11] Although the existence of the phenomenon is clearly established in humans,[14,67,68] the neural correlates in humans remain unknown.

Not surprisingly there is consistent evidence that the hypothalamus plays a critical role in representing distal reward. Several studies have shown that feeding reduces hypothalamic response.[69-72] This response reduction is delayed relative to meal initiation and is correlated with the fasting plasma insulin,[69] suggesting that the response reflects glucose metabolism, which is thought to be the critical postingestive reward signal.[19] Hormonal signals have also been shown to modulate brain responses beyond the hypothalamus.[73-75] In particular, infusion of ghrelin, which is an important orexigenic hormone that increases food intake by acting on dopamine neurons,[76] increases brain response to food pictures in the amygdala, OFC, anterior insula, and striatum.

Preingestive Signals

The primary role of preingestive signals is to provide information about food availability and quality. Whereas proximal food cues influence intake via sensory pleasure, preingestive signals provide cues that stimulate motivation, appetitive behavior, and guide choice. The sight and aroma of foods constitute the two primary sensory preingestive signals. However, location and time of day may also serve. Like proximal and distal food reward signals, the sight and smell of food recruits the anterior insula, OFC, and AVC.[32,77-81] However, there is also evidence that proximal and preingestive signals recruit separable networks,[81-82] which may map onto Berridge's (1996) proposal for separate substrates for food wanting and food liking. In particular, food cues tend to preferentially recruit regions that are dopamine source and target areas demonstrated to be important for reward learning such as the amygdala, midbrain, ventral striatum, and OFC. These regions are also sensitive to the devaluation of predictive food cues by eating,[83-86] and the energy content of the food,[78] indicating that the value of the incentive is being coded.

Many studies have also examined the impact of the caloric or macronutrient content of food pictures on brain response and shown generally that responses are greater to the more energetic stimulus.[41,78,79,87-89] Also of interest is the fact that the brain appears to track the energetic content of foods within milliseconds of the stimulus coming into view, indicating very rapid implicit tagging of the predicted distal reward signified by preingestive cues.[90]

Once the food cues have been sensed, decisions to eat or not to eat must be made. The OFC may play a critical role in orchestrating decisions about hedonic eating. The OFC is specifically engaged when subjects must choose between selecting two attractive menu options.[91] In addition, although neural response in the hypothalamus predicts feeding in hungry individuals, after administration of peptide YY, which mimics the satiated state, it is the OFC that predicts feeding, indicating that orbital cortex plays a key role in eating for pleasure in the absence of hunger.[73]

Top-Down Signals

Finally, given that we are under constant bombardment by advertising messages, it is important to consider the role of top-down signals on food reward. An odor labeled "cheddar cheese" when sniffed will produce remarkably different pleasantness ratings and orbitofrontal responses compared to when it is labeled as "body odor."[24] Likewise, an extremely bitter taste will result in less insular response if the subject is misled into thinking that the solution was the less intense of two possible bitter solutions.[25] More provocative, information about the brand of a soda has been shown to disrupt the relationship between response in the ventral medial prefrontal cortex (OFC/AVC juncture) and the perceived pleasantness of the sodas when they were presented anonymously.[22] In other words, subjects' preferences changed depending upon whether the soda was anonymous or associated with a brand name and that whereas anonymous preference correlated with response in the ventral medial prefrontal cortex, brand-derived preferences were associated with response, in more lateral aspects of the frontal lobe, implicated in higher order decision making. This finding illustrates the ability of brand to override sensory signals and control behavior. More recently, a similar effect was shown with price.[23] Increasing the price of a wine parametrically increased subjective reports of flavor pleasantness as well as response in the ventromedial prefrontal cortex. An important future avenue for research will be to determine whether changes in value produced by top-down signals are associated with dopamine signaling.

SUMMARY

Food reward is multifaceted. There are proximal, pre- and postingestive signals that have distinct mechanisms and purposes, but they are hypothesized to be united by their uniform reliance upon dopamine signaling.[15] In addition, top-down signals generated by expectations and beliefs modulate central responses to the sensation and consumption of foods, resulting in modulation of their perceptions and thus their reward impact. Determining the precise role of dopaminergic mechanisms on these processes is likely a fruitful avenue for further research given that food reward is expected to contribute to overeating and hence the obesity epidemic [92] and because obesity has been reliably associated with alterations in dopamine signaling.[93,94]

REFERENCES

1. Marks LE. A brief history of sensation and reward. In: Gottfried JA, ed. *The Neurobiology of Sensation and Reward*. Boca Raton, FL: Taylor & Francis Group; 2011: 15–44.
2. Wundt W. *Outlines of Psychology*. Leipzig: Wilhelm Engelmann; 1897.
3. Lim J, Wood A, Green BG. Derivation and evaluation of a labeled hedonic scale. *Chem Senses* 2009;34: 739–751.
4. White NM. Reward or reinforcement: what's the difference? *Neurosci Biobehav Rev* 1989;13:181–186.
5. Berridge KC. Food reward: brain substrates of wanting and liking. *Neurosci Biobehav Rev* 1996;20:1–25.
6. Clark JJ, Bernstein IL. Sensitization of salt appetite is associated with increased "wanting" but not "liking" of a salt reward in the sodium-deplete rat. *Behav Neurosci* 2006;120:206–210.
7. Epstein LH, Leddy JJ, Temple JL, Faith MS. Food reinforcement and eating: a multilevel analysis. *Psychol Bull* 2007;133:884–906.
8. Epstein LH, Wright SM, Paluch RA, et al. Relation between food reinforcement and dopamine genotypes and its effect on food intake in smokers. *Am J Clin Nutr* 2004;80:82–88.
9. Saelens BE, Epstein LH. Reinforcing value of food in obese and non-obese women. *Appetite* 1996;27: 41–50.
10. Robinson TE, Berridge KC. Incentive-sensitization and addiction. *Addiction* 2001;96:103–114.
11. Sclafani A. Oral and postoral determinants of food reward. *Physiol Behav* 2004;81:773–779.
12. Sclafani A. Post-ingestive positive controls of ingestive behavior. *Appetite* 2001;36:79–83.
13. Mobini S, Chmbers LC, Yoemans MR. Interactive effects of flavour-flavour and flavour-consequence learning in development of liking for sweet-paired flavours in humans. *Appetite* 2007;48:20–28.
14. Birch LL, McPhee L, Steinberg L, Sullivan S. Conditioned flavor preferences in young children. *Physiol Behav* 1990;47:501–505.
15. de Araujo IE. Multiple reward layers in food reinforcement. In: Gottfried JA, ed. *The Neurobiology of Sensation and Reward*. Boca Raton, FL: Taylor & Francis Group; 2011: 253–275.
16. Hajnal A, Smith GP, Norgren R. Oral sucrose stimulation increases accumbens dopamine in the rat. *Am J Physiol Regul Integr Comp Physiol* 2004;286:R31–R37.
17. Small DM, Jones-Gotman M, Dagher A. Feeding-induced dopamine release in dorsal striatum correlates with meal pleasantess ratings in healthy human volunteers. *Neuroimage* 2003;19:1709–1715.
18. de Araujo IE, Oliveira-Maia AJ, Sotnikova TD, et al. Food reward in the absence of taste receptor signaling. *Neuron* 2008;57:930–941.
19. Ren X, Ferreira JG, Zhou L, Shammah-Lagnado SJ, Yeckel CW, de Araujo IE. Nutrient selection in the absence of taste receptor signaling. *J Neurosci* 2010;30:8012–8023.
20. Schultz W. Predictive reward signal of dopamine neurons. *J Neurophysiol* 1998;80:1–27.

21. Schultz W, Dayan P, Montague PR. A neural substrate of prediction and reward. *Science* 1997;275:1593–1599.

22. McClure SM, Li J, Montague LM, Montague PR. Neural correlates of behavioral preference for culturally familiar drinks. *Neuron* 2004;44:379–387.

23. Plassmann H, O'Doherty J, Shiv B, Rangel A. Marketing actions can modulate neural representations of experienced pleasantness. *Proc Natl Acad Sci USA* 2008;105:1050–1054.

24. de Araujo IE, Rolls ET, Velazco MI, Margot C, Cayeux I. Cognitive modulation of olfactory processing. *Neuron* 2005;46:671–679.

25. Nitschke JB, Dixon GE, Sarinopoulos I, et al. Altering expectancy dampens neural response to aversive taste in primary taste cortex. *Nature Neurosci* 2006;9:435–442.

26. Small DM. Flavor and the formation of category-specific processing in olfaction. *Chemosens Percep* 2008;1:136–146.

27. Cerf-Ducastel B, Van de Moortele PF, MacLeod P, Le Bihan D, Faurion A. Interaction of gustatory and lingual somatosensory perceptions at the cortical level in the human: a functional magnetic resonance imaging study. *Chem Senses* 2001;26:371–383.

28. Rudenga K, Green BG, Nachtigal D, Small DM. Evidence for an intgrated oral sensory module in the human ventral insula. *Chem Senses* 2010;35:693–703.

29. Guest S, Grabenhorst F, Essick G, et al. Human cortical representation of oral temperature. *Physiol Behav* 2007;92:975–984.

30. de Araujo E, Rolls Et, Kringelbach ML, McGlone F, Phillips N. Taste-olfactory conergence, and the representation of the pleasantness of flavour in the human brain. *Eur J Neurosci* 2003;18:2059–2068.

31. Marciani L, Pfeiffer JC, Hort J, et al. Improved methods for fMRI studies of combined taste and aroma stimuli. *J Neurosci Methods* 2006;158:186–194.

32. Veldhuizen MG, Nachtigal D, Teulings L, Gitelman DR, Small DM. The insular taste cortex contributes to odor quality coding. *Front Human Neurosci* 2010;4:58.

33. de Araujo E, Rolls ET. Representation in the human brain of food texture and oral fat. *J Neurosci* 2004;24:3086–3093.

34. De Araujo I, Simon SA. The gustatory cortex and mulitsensory integration. *Int J Obes* 2009;33:S23–S43.

35. Small DM, Voss J, Mak YE, Simmons KB, Parrish TB, Gitelman DR. Experience-dependent neural integration of taste and smell in the human brain. *J Neurophysiol* 2004;92:1892–1903.

36. Small DM, Gregory MD, Mak YE, Gitelman D, Mesulam MM, Parrish T. Dissociation of neural representation of intensity and affective valuation in human gustation. *Neuron* 2003;39:701–711.

37. Delwiche JF, Heffelfinger AL. Cross-modal additivity of taste and smell. *J Sens Stud* 2005;20:512–25.

38. Moskowitz HR. Sensations, measurement and pleasantness: confessions of a latent introspectionist. In: Weiffenbach JM, ed. *Taste and Development: The Genesis of Sweet Preference.* DHEW Publication No (NIH) 77-1068. Bethesda, MD: US Dept Health, Educ, and Welfare; 1977: 282–294.

39. Moskowitz HR, et al. Effects of hunger, satiety and glucose load upon taste intensity and taste hedonics. *Physiol Behav* 1976;16:471–475.

40. Berns GS, McClure SM, Pagnoni G, Montague PR. Predictability modulates human brain response to reward. *J Neurosci* 2001;21:2793–2798.

41. Frank GK, Oberndorfer TA, Simmons AN, et al. Sucrose activates human taste pathways differently from artificial sweetener. *Neuroimage* 2008;39:1559–1569.

42. de Araujo IE, Rolls ET, Kringelbach ML, McGlone F, Phillips N. Taste-olfactory convergence, and the representation of the pleasantness of flavour, in the human brain. *Eur J Neurosci* 2003;18:2059–2068.

43. O'Doherty J, Rolls ET, Francis S, Bowtell R, McGlone F. Representation of pleasant and aversive taste in the human brain. *J Neurophysiol* 2001;85:1315–1321.

44. Bender G, Veldhuizen MG, Meltzer JA, Gitelman DR, Small DM. Neural correlates of evaluative compared with passive tasting. *Eur J Neurosci* 2009;30:327–338.

45. Tataranni PA, Gautier JF, Chen K, et al. Neuroanatomical correlates of hunger and satiation in humans using positron emission tomography. *Proc Natl Acad Sci USA* 1999;96:4569–4574.

46. Small DM, Zatorre RJ, Dagher A, Evans AC, Jones-Gotman M. Changes in brain activity related to eating chocolate: from pleasure to aversion. *Brain* 2001;124:1720–1733.

47. O'Doherty JP, Deichmann R, Critchley HD, Dolan RJ. Neural responses during anticipation of a primary taste reward. *Neuron* 2002;33:815–826.

48. McCabe C, Rolls ET. Umami: a delicious flavor formed by convergence of taste and olfactory pathways in the human brain. *Eur J Neurosci* 2007;25:1855–1864.

49. Kringelbach ML, O'Doherty J, Rolls ET, Andrews C. Activation of the human orbitofrontal cortex to a liquid food stimulus is correlated with its subjective pleasantness. *Cerebral Cortex* 2003;13:1064–1071.

50. Haase L, Cerf-Ducastel B, Murphy C. Cortical activation in response to pure taste stimuli during the physiological states of hunger and satiety. *Neuroimage* 2009;44:1008–1021.

51. Smeets PA, de Graaf C, Stafleu A, van Osch MJ, Nievelstein RA, van der Grond J. Effect of satiety on brain activation during chocolate tasting in men and women. *Am J Clin Nutr* 2006;83:1297–1305.

52. Cabanac M. Physiological role of pleasure. *Science* 1971;173:1103–1107.

53. Yeomans MR, Gray RW. Effects of naltrexone on food intake and changes in subjective appetite during

eating: evidence for opioid involvement in the appetizer effect. *Physiol Behav* 1997;62:15–21.

54. Yeomans MR, Gray RW. Opioid peptides and the control of human ingestive behaviour. *Neurosci Biobehav Rev* 2002;26:713–728.

55. Yeomans MR, Wright P. Lower pleasantness of palatable foods in nalmefene-treated human volunteers. *Appetite* 1991;16:249–259.

56. Kelley AE, Bakshi VP, Haber SN, Steininger TL, Will MJ, Zhang M. Opioid modulation of taste hedonics within the ventral striatum. *Physiol Behav* 2002;76:365–377.

57. Anand BK, Pillai RV. Activity of single neurones in the hypothalmic feeding centres: effect of gastric distension. *J Physiol Lond* 1967;192:63–77.

58. Andrews PLR, Grundy D, Scratcherd T. Vagal afferent discharge from mechanoreceptors in different regions of the ferret stomach. *J Physiol Lond* 1980;298:513–524.

59. Geliebter A, Westreich S, Pierson RN, Jr., Van Itallie TB. Extra-abdominal pressure alters food intake, intragastric pressure, and gastric emptying rate. *Am J Physiol* 1986;250:R549–R552.

60. Ladabaum U, Minoshima S, Hasler WL, Cross D, Chey WD, Owyang C. Gastric distention correlates with activation of multiple cortical and subcortical regions. *Gastroenterol* 2001;120:369–376.

61. Ladabaum U, Roberts TP, McGonigle DJ. Gastric fundic distension activates fronto-limbic structures but not primary somatosensory cortex: a functional magnetic resonance imaging study. *Neuroimage* 2007;34:724–732.

62. Lu CL, Wu YT, Yeh TC, et al. Neuronal correlates of gastric pain induced by fundus distension: a 3T-fMRI study. *Neurogastroenterol Motil* 2004;16:575–587.

63. Stephan E, Pardo JV, Faris PL, et al. Functional neuroimaging of gastric distention. *J Gastrointest Surg* 2003;7:740–749.

64. Vandenbergh J, Dupont P, Fischler B, et al. Regional brain activation during proximal stomach distention in humans: a positron emission tomography study. *Gastroenterol* 2005;128:564–573.

65. Wang G-J, Tomasi D, Backus W, et al. Gastric distention activates satiety circuitry in the human brain. *Neuroimage* 2008;39:1824–1831.

66. Wang G-J, Yang J, Volkow ND, et al. Gastric stimulation in obese subjects activates the hippocampus and other regions involved in brain reward circuitry. *Proc Natl Acad Sci USA* 2006;103:15641–15645.

67. Yeomans MR, Leitch M, Gould NJ, Mobini S. Differential hedonic, sensory and behavioral changes associated with flavor-nutrient and flavor-flavor learning. *Physiol Behav* 2008;93:798–806.

68. Yeomans MR, Mobini S. Hunger alters the expression of acquired hedonic but not sensory qualities of food-paired odors in humans. *J Exp Psychol Anim Behav Process* 2006;32:460–466.

69. Liu Y, Gao JH, Liu HL, Fox PT. The temporal response of the brain after eating revealed by functional MRI. *Nature* 2000;405:1058–1062.

70. Matsuda M, Liu Y, Mahankali S, et al. Altered hypothalamic function in response to glucose ingestion in obese humans. *Diabetes* 1999;48:1801–1806.

71. Smeets PA, de Graaf C, Stafleu A, van Osch MJ, van der Grond J. Functional MRI of human hypothalamic responses following glucose ingestion. *Neuroimage* 2005;24:363–368.

72. Smeets PA, de Graaf C, Stafleu A, van Osch MJ, van der Grond J. Functional magnetic resonance imaging of human hypothalamic responses to sweet taste and calories. *Am J Clin Nutr* 2005;82:1011–1016.

73. Batterham RL, ffytche DH, Rosenthal JM, et al. PYY modulation of cortical and hypothalamic brain areas predicts feeding behaviour in humans. *Nature* 2007;450:106–109.

74. Guthoff M, Grichisch Y, Canova C, et al. Insulin modulates food-related activity in the central nervous system. *J Clin Endocrinol Metab* 2009;95:748–755.

75. Malik S, McGlone F, Bedrossian D, Dagher A. Ghrelin modulates brain activity in areas that control appetitive behavior. *Cell Metabolism* 2008;7:400–409.

76. Abizaid A, Liu ZB, Andrews J, et al. Ghrelin increases food intake by modulating the activity of dopaminergic neuruons in the VTA. *J Clin Invest* 2006;116:3229–3239.

77. Bragulat V, Dzemidzic M, Bruno C, et al. Food-related odor probes of brain reward circuits during hunger: A pilot fMRI study. *Obesity* 2010; doi:10.1038/oby.2010.57.

78. Schur EA, Kleinhans NM, Goldberg J, Buchwald D, Schwartz MW, Maravilla K. Activation in brain energy regulation and reward centers by food cues varies with choice of visual stimulus. *Int J Obes (Lond)* 2009;33:653–661.

79. Siep N, Roefs A, Roebroeck A, Havermans R, Bonte ML, Jansen A. Hunger is the best spice: an fMRI study of the effects of attention, hunger and calorie content on food reward processing in the amygdala and orbitofrontal cortex. *Behav Brain Res* 2009;198:149–158.

80. Simmons WK, Martin A, Barsalou LW. Pictures of appetizing foods activate gustatory cortices for taste and reward. *Cerebral Cortex* 2005;15:1602–1608.

81. Small DM, Gerber J, Mak YE, Hummel T. Differential neural responses evoked by orthonasal versus retronasal odorant perception in humans. *Neuron* 2005;47:593–605.

82. Small DM, Felsted J, Veldhuizen MG, Mak YE, McGlone F. Separable to anticipatory and consummatory chemosensation of food. *Neuron* 2008; 57:786–797.

83. Gottfried JA, O'Doherty J, Dolan RJ. Encoding predictive reward value in human amygdala and orbitofrontal cortex. *Science* 2003;301:1104–1107.

84. LaBar KS, Gitelman DR, Parrish TB, Kim YH, Nobre AC, Mesulam MM. Hunger selectively modulates corticolimbic activation to food stimuli in humans. *Behav Neurosci* 2001;115:493–500.

85. Mohanty A, Gitelman DR, Small DM, Mesulam MM. The spatial attention network interacts with limbic and monoaminergic systems to modulate motivation-induced attentional shifts. *Cerebral Cortex* 2008; doi:10.1093/cercor/bhn021.

86. O'Doherty J, Rolls ET, Francis S, et al. Sensory-specific satiety-related olfactory activation of the human orbitofrontal cortex. [republished in Neuroreport 2000 Mar 20;11(4):893–897]. Neuroreport 2000;11:399–403.

87. Killgore WD, Young AD, Femia LA, Bogorodzki P, Rogowska J, Yurgelun-Todd DA. Cortical and limbic activation during viewing of high- versus low-calorie foods. *Neuroimage* 2003;19:1381–1394.

88. Rothemund Y, Preuschhof C, Bohner G, et al. Differential activation of the dorsal striatum by high-calorie visual food stimuli in obese individuals. *Neuroimage* 2007;37:410–421.

89. Stoeckel LE, Weller RE, Cook Iii EW, Twieg DB, Knowlton RC, Cox JE. Widespread reward-system activation in obese women in response to pictures of high-calorie foods. *NeuroImage* 2008;41:636–647.

90. Toepel U, Knebel J-F, Hudry J, le Coutre J, Murray MM. The brain tracks the energetic value in food images. *Neuroimage* 2009;44:967–974.

91. Arana FS, Parkinson JA, Hinton E, Holland AJ, Owen AM, Roberts AC. Dissociable contributions of the human amygdala and orbitofrontal cortex to incentive motivation and goal selection. *J Neurosci* 2003;23:9632–9638.

92. Volkow ND, Wise RA. How can drug addiction help us understand obesity? *Nature Neurosci* 2005;8: 555–560.

93. Wang GJ, Volkow ND, Logan J, et al. Brain dopamine and obesity. *Lancet* 2001;357:354–357.

94. Johnson PM, Kenny PJ. Dopamine D2 receptors in addiction-like reward dysfunction and compulsive eating in obese rats. *Nature Neurosci* 2010;13: 635–641.

28

Dopamine Deficiency, Eating, and Body Weight

GENE-JACK WANG, NORA D. VOLKOW, AND JOANNA S. FOWLER

INTRODUCTION

Obesity can derive from a variety of causes (i.e., genes, culture, nutrition intake, physical activity).[1] Although maintenance of an appropriate body weight requires balance between caloric intake and physical activity, genetic factors play an important role in both energy requirements and general activity levels. Obesity reflects an imbalance between energy intake and expenditure. However, the core pathophysiological mechanisms responsible for maintaining this balance are not well understood. The hypothalamus and its various circuits are thought to be the principal homeostatic brain regions responsible for the regulation of body weight.[2] Brain imaging studies show that obese individuals have significant deficits in regulation of energy homeostasis (i.e., delayed response to peripheral metabolic signals in the hypothalamus).[3] Brain circuits that regulate normal eating behavior (i.e., hunger, satiety, motivation, reward, emotion, learning, memory, and inhibitory control) also play a significant role in obesity.[4]

EATING BEHAVIOR AND BRAIN NEUROTRANSMITTERS

Eating is a highly reinforcing behavior. In fact, some ingredients in palatable food (i.e., sugar, corn oil) are compulsively consumed, and this loss of control over food intake is similar to what is observed with compulsive consumption of substances of abuse.[5] Behavioral studies show similarities among certain patterns of overeating and other excessive behaviors such as overconsumption of alcohol and compulsive gambling. These behaviors activate brain circuitry that involves reward, motivation, decision making, learning, and memory. Indeed, ingestion of sugar induces brain release of opioids and dopamine (DA), which are neurotransmitters traditionally associated with the rewarding effects of drugs

of abuse. In certain conditions (i.e. intermittent, excessive sugar intake) rats can display behavioral and neurochemical changes that resemble those observed in animal models of drug dependence.[6] From an evolutionary perspective, animals would benefit from a neural mechanism (circuitry) that supports an animal's ability to pursue natural rewards (food, water, sex). These circuits, however, are sometimes dysfunctional, leading to various types of disorders.

Endogenous opioids are expressed throughout the limbic system and contribute to processing of reinforcing signals, and palatable foods increase endogenous opioid gene expression.[7] Furthermore, injection of mu-opioid agonists in the nucleus accumbens potentiates the intake of palatable foods.[8] Opioid antagonists, on the other hand, reduce food ratings of pleasantness without affecting hunger.[9] It is likely that the opioid system is involved with the liking and the pleasurable responses to food that might promote the intake of highly palatable foods such as those consumed in a high-fat and high-sugar diet.[10]

Other neurotransmitters (e.g., acetylcholine, gamma-aminobutyric acid, serotonin, cannabinoids, and glutamine) are also involved in eating behaviors.[11,12] For example, acetylcholine and dopamine (DA) play opposite role in the nucleus accumbens in feeding behavior. DA in the nucleus accumbens can increase appetite but as feeding slows down toward the end of a meal, extracellular acetylcholine increases.[13] In addition, other mechanisms such as stress can also modulate eating behavior and contribute to obesity[14] by increasing the consumption of high energy density food.[15] Neurotransmitter imaging studies for obesity and overeating behaviors in humans have mostly investigated the DA system, and a few studies have also assessed the serotonin system.

EATING BEHAVIOR AND BRAIN DOPAMINE SYSTEM

DA is a neurotransmitter known to play a major role in motivation that is involved with reward and prediction of reward. The mesocorticolimbic DA system projects from the ventral tegmental area to the nucleus accumbens, with inputs from various components of the limbic system, including the amygdala, hippocampus, hypothalamus, striatum, orbitofrontal cortex, and the prefrontal cortex. DA has been shown to mediate the reinforcing effects of natural rewards (i.e., sucrose).[16] DA pathways make food more reinforcing and are also associated with the reinforcing responses to drugs of abuse (i.e., alcohol, methamphetamine, cocaine, heroin).[17] The mesencephalic DA system regulates pleasurable and motivating responses to food intake and stimuli,[18] which affects and alters behavioral components of energy homeostasis. The mesencephalic DA system can respond to food stimuli even in the presence of postprandial satiety factors.[19] When that occurs, the regulation of eating behavior can be switched from a homeostatic state to a hedonic corticolimbic state.

DA regulates food intake via the mesolimbic circuitry apparently by modulating appetitive motivational processes.[20] There are projections from the nucleus accumbens to the hypothalamus that directly regulate feeding.[21] Other forebrain DA projections are also involved. DAergic pathways are critical for survival since they help influence the fundamental drive for eating. Brain DA systems are necessary for wanting incentives, which is a distinct component of motivation and reinforcement.[22] It is one of the natural reinforcing mechanisms that motivate an animal to perform a given behavior such as seeking food. The mesolimbic DA system mediates incentive learning and reinforcement mechanisms associated with positive reward such as palatable food in a hungry animal.[22]

DAergic neurotransmission is mediated by five distinct receptor subtypes, which are classified into two main classes of receptors termed *D1-like* (D1 and D5) and *D2-like* (D2, D3, and D4). In the case of drug self-administration, activation of D2-like receptors has been shown to mediate the incentive to seek further cocaine reinforcement in animals. In contrast, D1-like receptors mediate a reduction in the drive to seek further cocaine reinforcement.[23] Both the D1- and D2-like receptors

act synergistically when regulating feeding behaviors. Nevertheless, the precise involvement of DA receptor subtypes in mediating eating behavior is still not clear. DA D1-like receptors play a role in reward learning and translation of new reward to action.[24] The D2-like receptors have been associated with feeding and addictive behaviors in animal and human studies. Most of human imaging studies of eating behaviors have mainly used positron emission tomography (PET) studies with [11C]raclopride, a reversible DA D2/D3 receptor radioligand that is sensitive to changes in extracellular DA.

MOLECULAR IMAGING OF EATING BEHAVIOR AND BRAIN DOPAMINE SYSTEM

Many animal studies have evaluated mixed D2/D3 receptor antagonists or agonists on food-seeking behaviors.[25] DA D2 receptor (D2R) antagonists block food-seeking behaviors that depend on history association (reinforcement) between the cues and the reward they predict as well as on palatable foods.[26] When food is no longer priming and rewarding for an animal, D2 agonists can be used to reinstate extinguished reward-seeking behavior.[27] Simple carbohydrates such as sugar are a major nutritional source and contribute to about one-fourth of total energy intake. Animal studies have demonstrated that glucose modulates DA neuronal activity in the ventral tegmental area and substantia nigra directly.[28] Daily bingeing on sugar repeatedly releases DA in the nucleus accumbens.[29] A human PET study with [11C]raclopride that measured DA release in the striatum following intravenous administration blindly of glucose solution (300 mg/kg) showed significant DA release in fasting men but not in women.[30]

SENSORY EXPERIENCE OF FOOD AND ITS RELATION TO EATING BEHAVIORS

Sensory processing of food and food-related cues plays an important role in the motivation for food and it is especially important in the selection of a varied diet. A PET study that used [11C]raclopride to measure DA release in the striatum following the consumption of a favorite food showed that the amount of striatal DA release correlated with the ratings of meal pleasantness.[31]

It is likely that the reward related to eating is not only associated with food ingredient (i.e., sugar) but also associated with other stimuli (i.e., sensory experience of food). Sensory inputs of taste, vision, olfaction, temperature, and texture are first sent to the primary sensory cortices (i.e., insula, primary visual cortex, pyriform, primary somatosensory cortex) and then to the orbitofrontal cortex and amygdala.[32] The hedonic reward value of food is closely linked to the sensory perception of the food. DA in these brain regions is associated with sensory perception of food.[32]

Imaging studies in humans and animals from our laboratory and others showed enhanced activation in brain regions related to sensory processing of food in obese individuals. A functional magnetic resonance imaging (fMRI) study of adolescent girls showed obese girls had greater activation in insula and gustatory somatosensory cortex than lean girls in response to anticipated food intake and to actual consumption of food.[33] Our study using PET and 2-deoxy-2-[18F]fluoro-D-glucose (FDG) to measure regional brain glucose metabolism (marker of brain function) found that morbidly obese subjects had higher than normal baseline metabolism (without stimulation) in the gustatory somatosensory cortex.[34] We also showed that food stimulation (viewing and smelling without consumption) enhanced thalamic activation in obese Zucker rats more than in lean littermates.[35]

These activated/enhanced regions are implicated in sensory (somatosensory, visual cortices, thalamus) and hedonic (insula) aspects of the food cue. Opioid circuits in the ventral striatum also play a role in hedonic aspect of food cue and intake.[36] The input and output nuclei of the striatum interact with areas of the thalamus and cortices involved in processing sensory stimuli.[37] There is evidence that DA also plays a role in modulating activity in the somatosensory cortex,[38] including facilitation of neuroplasticity.[39] Moreover, we recently showed an association between striatal D2R availability and glucose metabolism in the somatosensory cortex of obese subjects.[40] Neurons in the sensory thalamus play an essential role in relaying information about the external environment to the cerebral cortex. Corticothalamic feedback between the thalamus and cortices influence sensory processing of vision, auditory, and somatosensation.[41] The thalamus is also a key region in modulating attention and wakefulness.[41] The striatal-thalamo-cortical circuits connect to prefrontal cortex (including anterior

cingulate gyrus) and play an important role in attention and learning.[37] DA stimulation signals saliency and facilitates conditioning.[42] DA's modulation of neural processing of food cues in the sensory cortices and thalamus to food stimuli might enhance their saliency, which is likely to play a role in the formation of conditioned associations between food and food-related environmental cues.

IMAGING EXPECTATION AND PREDICTION OF FOOD REWARD

DA D2 receptors play a role in reward seeking, prediction, expectation, and motivation.[20] Food seeking is initiated by hunger; however, it is food-predictive cues that activate DA cell firing and motivate animals.[43] Food deprivation potentiates the rewarding effects of food.[44] During fasting, the role of DA is not selective for food but rather signals the salience for a variety of potential biological rewards and cues that predict rewards.[45] Chronic food deprivation also potentiates the rewarding effects of most addictive drugs.[46] The striatum, orbitofrontal cortex, and amygdala, which are brain regions that receive DA projections, are activated during the expectation of food.[47] PET and [11C]raclopride were used to evaluate the changes in extracellular DA in striatum in response to the expectation of receiving an intravenous sugar solution when subjects received a placebo and revealed DA increases in the ventral striatum (where the nucleus accumbens is located) in food-deprived men but not in women.[37] These findings suggested that DA releases in the ventral striatum mediate the placebo response in the context of glucose expectation.

Using food cues (presentation of palatable food) in food-deprived subjects, we showed significant increases in extracellular DA in the dorsal striatum but not in the ventral striatum.[48] The DA increases were significantly correlated with the increases in self-reports of hunger and desire for food. These results provided evidence that in a food-deprived human subject, food conditioned-cues trigger DA release in the dorsal striatum. The involvement of DA in the dorsal striatum appears to be crucial for enabling the motivation required to consume the food that is necessary for survival.[49] It is different from the activation in the nucleus accumbens, which may be related more to motivation associated with food palatability.[20]

MOLECULAR IMAGING OF BRAIN DOPAMINE SYSTEM ON OBESITY

Excessive and repeated food intake in obese subjects might lead to a down-regulation of DA signaling in the reward circuitry. An fMRI study with consumption of anticipated food showed decreased activation in caudate nucleus in response to food consumption in adolescent obese girls.[50] Thus, hyposensitivity to food stimuli in brain regions modulated by DA in obese individuals could increase their risk of overeating. In fact, our (Fig. 28.1)[51] and other[30] PET studies with [11C]raclopride have documented a reduction in striatal D2/D3 receptor availability in obese subjects that was inversely related to body mass index (BMI).

To assess whether low D2/D3 receptors in obesity reflected the consequences of food overconsumption as opposed to a vulnerability that preceded obesity, we assessed the effect of food intake on D2/D3 receptor in Zucker rats (a genetically leptin-deficient rodent model of obesity) using autoradiography.[52] The animals had free access to food for 3 months and the D2/D3 receptor levels were evaluated at 4 months old. Results showed that Zucker obese (fa/fa) rats had lower D2/D3 receptor levels than the lean (Fa/Fa or Fa/fa) rats and that food restriction increased D2/D3 receptors both in the lean and the obese rats, indicating that low D2/D3 reflects in part the consequences of food overconsumption. Similar to the human

study, we also found an inverse correlation of D2/D3 receptor levels and body weight in these obese rats. The relationship between BMI and brain DA transporter levels has also been investigated. Rodent studies demonstrated significant decreases in DA transporter densities in the striatum of obese mice.[53] In humans, a recent study using single photon emission tomography and [99mTc] TRODAT-1 to study 50 Asians (BMI: 18.7–30.6) in the resting state showed that BMI was inversely associated with striatal DA transporter availability.[54] These studies suggest the involvement of an understimulated DA system in excessive weight gain. Since the DA pathways have been implicated in reward (predict reward) and motivation, these studies suggest that deficiency in DA pathways may lead to pathological overeating as a means to compensate for an understimulated reward system.

INHIBITORY CONTROL AND OBESITY

Impaired inhibitory control may contribute to behavioral disorders such as addiction and pathological overeating. We evaluated the responses of the brain when subjects were exposed to appealing food either with or without a prior directive to suppress the desire for food (cognitive inhibition).[55] Regional brain metabolic responses to food stimulation with and without cognitive inhibition were assessed with PET and FDG. Specifically, with cognitive inhibition as compared with no

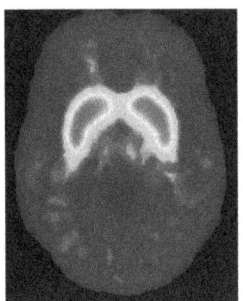 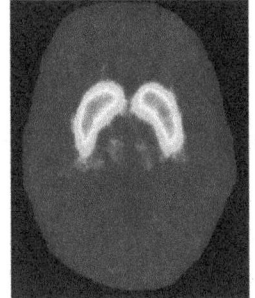 

Control Subjects   Obese Subjects

FIGURE 28.1. Lower dopamine D2 receptor (D2R) availability in obese subjects. Group averaged images of [11C] raclopride positron emission tomography (PET) scans for obese and control subjects at the level of the basal ganglia. The images are scaled with respect to the maximum value (distribution volume) obtained on the control subjects and presented using the rainbow scale. Red represents the highest value (2.0), and dark violet represents the lowest value (0 ml/g). The obese subjects have lower D2R as compared to the control subjects.

Source: Adapted from The Lancet, Vol. 357, G-J. Wang, N.D. Volkow, J. Logan, N. R. Pappas, C. T. Wong, N. Zhu, N. Netusll, J.S. Fowler, Brain Dopamine and Obesity, 354–357, Copyright (2001), with permission from Elsevier.

inhibition, male subjects (but not females) showed significant decreases in metabolism in anterior cingulate gyrus, left orbitofrontal cortex, left amygdala, and right striatum. These regions, which decreased metabolism, had been shown by prior studies to be activated by food stimuli when the subjects were presented via pictures, smells, taste, recall, or a combination of these. The suppressed activation of the orbitofrontal cortex with inhibition was also associated with decreases in self-reports of hunger, which corroborates the involvement of this region in processing the conscious awareness of the drive to eat. This finding suggests a mechanism by which cognitive inhibition decreases the desire for food.

In our laboratory we have tested the hypothesis that individuals with dysfunction in the prefrontal cortex may be at greater risk for compulsive behaviors, including obesity. Using PET and FDG in a group of healthy volunteers (BMI range: 19 to 37 kg/m^2) tested during baseline condition (no stimulation),[56] we showed a significant negative correlation between BMI and metabolic activity in prefrontal regions but not in other cortical or subcortical regions. The metabolism in these prefrontal regions was positively associated with performance in tests of memory and executive function. These findings suggest that the deleterious effects of excessive weight on cognitive function in healthy individuals may be mediated in part via its association with decreased activity of prefrontal regions.

There are several genes related to DA transmission that play important roles in drug reward and inhibitory control.[57] For example, polymorphisms in the D2R gene in healthy subjects are associated with behavioral measures of inhibitory control. Individuals with the gene variant that is linked with lower D2R expression had lower inhibitory control than individuals with the gene variant associated with higher D2R expression.[58] These behavioral responses are associated with differences in activation of the anterior cingulate gyrus and dorsolateral prefrontal cortex, which are brain regions that have been implicated in various components of inhibitory control.[59] Prefrontal regions also participate in the inhibition of tendencies for inappropriate behavioral responses.[60] The significant association between D2R availability and metabolism in prefrontal regions is observed in our studies in drug-addicted subjects (cocaine, methamphetamine, and alcohol).[61–63] We found that the reduction in D2R

availability in these subjects was associated with decreased metabolism in prefrontal cortical regions, which are involved in regulating impulse control, self-monitoring, and goal-directed behaviors.[64,65] A similar observation was documented in individuals at high familial risk for alcoholism.[66] These behaviors could influence the ability of an individual to self-regulate his or her eating behavior. Previous work with PET using [^{11}C]raclopride and FDG to evaluate the association between DA activity and brain metabolism in morbidly obese subjects (BMI > 40 kg/m^2)[40] found that D2/D3 receptor was associated with glucose metabolism in dorsolateral prefrontal, orbitofrontal cortex, and cingulate cortices (Fig. 28.2). The findings suggested that D2/D3 receptor–mediated dysregulation of regions implicated in inhibitory control in the obese subjects might underlie their inability to control food intake despite their conscious attempts to do so. This led us to consider the possibility that the low D2/D3 receptor modulation of the risk for overeating in the obese subjects could also be driven by its regulation of the prefrontal cortex.

APPLICATIONS TO OTHER AREAS OF HEALTH AND DISEASE

Obesity is associated with abnormal eating behaviors. Brain imaging studies show that obese individuals have significant deficits in circuits that regulate abnormal eating behavior (i.e., motivation, reward, emotion, learning, memory, and inhibitory control). The results from these studies suggest that multiple but similar brain circuits are disrupted in obesity and drug addiction. These brain imaging studies have the potential to facilitate understanding the mechanisms underlying obesity and overeating behaviors and provide scientific bases for the assessment of disorders related to understimulated reward circuits, the efficacy of drug treatments, and for the development of novel pharmacological approaches. For example, prevalence of overweight is reported in children and adolescents with attention-deficit/hyperactivity disorder. Attention-deficit disorder is also observed among adults in obesity treatment. It is possible that attention-deficit/hyperactivity disorder and obesity are related through deficits in the brain DA system. In fact, our study in drug-naive attention-deficit/hyperactivity disorder subjects reveals reduced striatal D2 receptors and DA transporters, which is similar to the findings in chronic

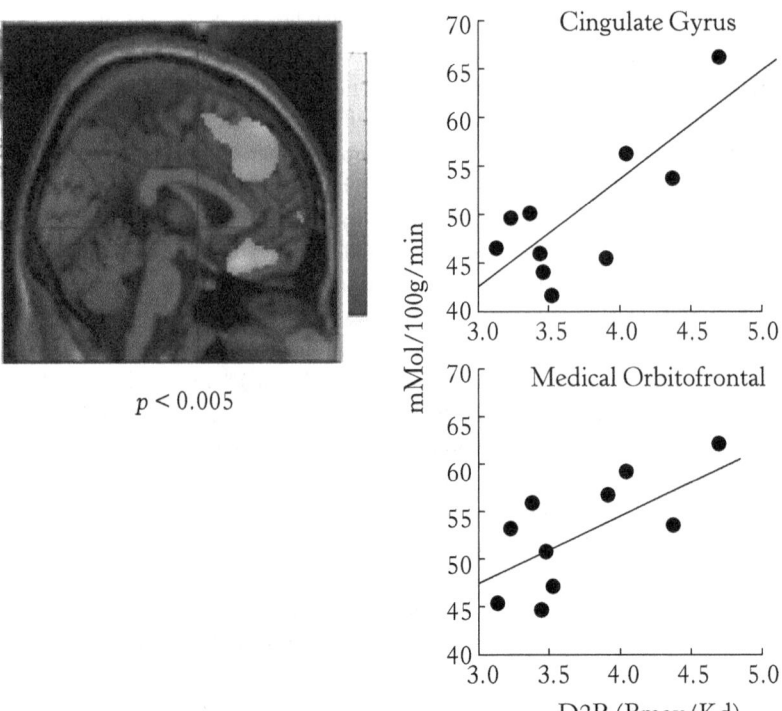

FIGURE 28.2. Association between D2 receptor (D2R) and prefrontal metabolism in obese subjects. Brain map obtained using statistical parametric mapping showing a correlation between D2R and brain metabolism in obese subjects. The areas that metabolic measures are significantly correlated with D2R are displayed in orange and superimposed onto a sagittal plane of brain magnetic resonance images (grayscale). The association between D2R and metabolism in orbitofrontal cortices and cingulate gyrus suggests that D2R-mediated dysregulation of regions implicated in inhibitory control may underlie the inability to control food intake despite conscious attempts to do so.

Source: Adapted from NeuroImage, Vol. 42, N.D. Volkow, G-J. Wang, F. Telang, J.S. Fowler, P.K. Thanos, J. Logan, D. Alexoff, Y. Ding, W. Wong, Y. Ma, K. Pradhan, Low dopamine striatal D2 receptors are associated with prefrontal metabolism in obese subjects: Possible contributing factors, 1537–1543, Copyright (2008), with permission from Elsevier.

drug-abusing subjects and severely obese subjects.[67] These observations suggest that the early identification of subjects with reward deficit–related disorders and the initiation of lifestyle modification (i.e., education concerning nutrition, aerobic exercise, effective stress reduction) in the early childhood would attenuate its impact on brain development and prevent development of metabolic disorders. Drug therapies, in addition to lifestyle modulations, can also be developed to improve weight loss maintenance and to reduce obesity-related medical consequences. For example, DA reuptake inhibitors (i.e., bupropion), opioid antagonists (i.e., naltrexone), or a combination of other drugs that modulate DA activity (i.e., zonisamide, topiramate) have been reported to promote weight loss in obese subjects.[68]

SUMMARY

1. Striatal D2R availability is reduced in obese subjects, which is similar to drug-addicted subjects. Decreases in D2R might predispose obese subjects to seek food to temporarily compensate for understimulated reward circuits.

2. Obese subjects have increased metabolism in the somatosensory cortex, which suggests an enhanced sensitivity to the sensory properties of food.

3. The reduction in D2R in obese subjects coupled with the enhanced sensitivity to food palatability could put them at risk for compulsive eating.

4. Decreased D2R in the obese subjects is also associated with decreased metabolism

in prefrontal regions involved in inhibitory control that may underlie their inability to control food intake.

5. The results of imaging studies have the potential to facilitate understanding the mechanisms underlying obesity and overeating behaviors as well as the development of strategies for prevention and treatment.

ACKNOWLEDGMENTS

The brain imaging studies were carried out at Brookhaven National Laboratory with infrastructure support from the US Department of Energy OBER (DE-AC02-98CH10886) and under support in part by the National Institute of Health: R01DA7092-01 (GJW), R01DA00280 (GJW), R01MH66961 (GJW), Z01AA000550 (NDV) and M01RR10710 (the General Clinical Research Center of Stony Brook University).

REFERENCES

1. Bessesen DH. Update on obesity. *J Clin Endocrinol Metab* 2008;93(6):2027–2034.
2. Morrison CD, Berthoud HR. Neurobiology of nutrition and obesity. *Nutr Rev* 2007;65 (12 Pt 1):517–534.
3. Matsuda M, Liu Y, Mahankali S, et al. Altered hypothalamic function in response to glucose ingestion in obese humans. *Diabetes* 1999;48(9):1801–1806.
4. Volkow ND, Wang GJ, Fowler JS, Telang F. Overlapping neuronal circuits in addiction and obesity: evidence of systems pathology. *Philos Trans R Soc Lond B Biol Sci* 2008a;363(1507):3191–3200.
5. Avena NM, Rada P, Hoebel BG. Sugar and fat bingeing have notable differences in addictive-like behavior. *J Nutr* 2009;139(3):623–628.
6. Avena NM, Rada P, Hoebel BG. Evidence for sugar addiction: behavioral and neurochemical effects of intermittent, excessive sugar intake. *Neurosci Biobehav Rev* 2008;32(1):20–39.
7. Will MJ, Franzblau EB, Kelley AE. Nucleus accumbens mu-opioids regulate intake of a high-fat diet via activation of a distributed brain network. *J Neurosci* 2003;23(7):2882–2888.
8. Woolley JD, Lee BS, Fields HL. Nucleus accumbens opioids regulate flavor-based preferences in food consumption. *Neuroscience* 2006;143(1):309–317.
9. Yeomans MR, Gray RW. Effects of naltrexone on food intake and changes in subjective appetite during eating: evidence for opioid involvement in the appetizer effect. *Physiol Behav* 1997;62(1):15–21.
10. Will MJ, Pratt WE, Kelley AE. Pharmacological characterization of high-fat feeding induced by opioid stimulation of the ventral striatum. *Physiol Behav* 2006;89(2):226–234.
11. Gaetani S, Kaye WH, Cuomo V, Piomelli D. Role of endocannabinoids and their analogues in obesity and eating disorders. *Eat Weight Disord* 2008;13(3):e42–e48.
12. Kelley AE, Baldo BA, Pratt WE, Will MJ. Corticostriatal-hypothalamic circuitry and food motivation: integration of energy, action and reward. *Physiol Behav* 2005;86(5):773–795.
13. Avena NM, Rada P, Moise N, Hoebel BG. Sucrose sham feeding on a binge schedule releases accumbens dopamine repeatedly and eliminates the acetylcholine satiety response. *Neuroscience* 2006;139(3):813–820.
14. Adam TC, Epel ES. Stress, eating and the reward system. *Physiol Behav* 2007;91(4):449–458.
15. Dallman MF, Pecorraro N, Akana SF, et al. Chronic stress and obesity: a new view of "comfort food." *Proc Natl Acad Sci USA* 2003;100(20):11696–11701.
16. Smith GP. Accumbens dopamine mediates the rewarding effect of orosensory stimulation by sucrose. *Appetite* 2004;43(1):11–13.
17. Di Chiara G, Bassareo V. Reward system and addiction: what dopamine does and doesn't do. *Curr Opin Pharmacol* 2007;7(1):69–76.
18. Volkow ND, Wise RA. How can drug addiction help us understand obesity? *Nat Neurosci* 2005;8(5):555–560.
19. Batterham RL, ffytche DH, Rosenhall JM, et al. PYY modulation of cortical and hypothalamic brain areas predicts feeding behaviour in humans. *Nature* 2007;450(7166):106–109.
20. Wise RA. Role of brain dopamine in food reward and reinforcement. *Philos Trans R Soc Lond B Biol Sci* 2006;361(1471):1149–1158.
21. Baldo BA, Kelley AE. Discrete neurochemical coding of distinguishable motivational processes: insights from nucleus accumbens control of feeding. *Psychopharmacol (Berl)* 2007;191(3):439–459.
22. Robinson S, Rainwater AJ, Hnasko TS, Palmiter RD. Viral restoration of dopamine signaling to the dorsal striatum restores instrumental conditioning to dopamine-deficient mice. *Psychopharmacol (Berl)* 2007;191(3):567–578.
23. Self DW, Barnhart WJ, Lehman DA, Nestler EJ. Opposite modulation of cocaine-seeking behavior by D1- and D2-like dopamine receptor agonists. *Science* 1996;271(5255):1586–1589.
24. Trevitt JT, Carlson BB, Nowend K, Salamone JD. Substantia nigra pars reticulata is a highly potent site of action for the behavioral effects of the D1 antagonist SCH 23390 in the rat. *Psychopharmacol (Berl)* 2001;156(1):32–41.
25. Missale C, Nash SR, Robinson SW, Jaber M, Caron MG. Dopamine receptors: from structure to function. *Physiol Rev* 1998;78(1):189–225.
26. McFarland K, Ettenberg A. Haloperidol does not affect motivational processes in an operant runway model of food-seeking behavior. *Behav Neurosci* 1998;112(3):630–635.

27. Wise RA, Murray A, Bozarth MA. Bromocriptine self-administration and bromocriptine-reinstatement of cocaine-trained and heroin-trained lever pressing in rats. *Psychopharmacol (Berl)* 1990;100(3): 355–360.

28. Levin BE. Glucose-regulated dopamine release from substantia nigra neurons. *Brain Res* 2000;874(2): 158–164.

29. Rada P, Avena NM, Hoebel BG. Daily bingeing on sugar repeatedly releases dopamine in the accumbens shell. *Neuroscience* 2005;134(3):737–744.

30. Haltia LT, Rinne JO, Merisaari H, et al. Effects of intravenous glucose on dopaminergic function in the human brain in vivo. *Synapse* 2007;61(9):748–756.

31. Small DM, Jones-Gotman M, Dagher A. Feeding-induced dopamine release in dorsal striatum correlates with meal pleasantness ratings in healthy human volunteers. *Neuroimage* 2003;19(4):1709–1715.

32. Rolls ET. Sensory processing in the brain related to the control of food intake. *Proc Nutr Soc* 2007; 66(1):96–112.

33. Stice E, Spoor S, Bohon C, Veldhuizen MG, Small DM. Relation of reward from food intake and anticipated food intake to obesity: a functional magnetic resonance imaging study. *J Abnorm Psychol* 2008; 117(4):924–935.

34. Wang GJ, Volkow ND, Felder C, et al. Enhanced resting activity of the oral somatosensory cortex in obese subjects. *Neuroreport* 2002;13(9):1151–1155.

35. Thanos PK, Michaelides M, Gispert JD, et al. Differences in response to food stimuli in a rat model of obesity: in-vivo assessment of brain glucose metabolism. *Int J Obes (Lond)* 2008;32(7):1171–1179.

36. Pecina S. Opioid reward "liking" and "wanting" in the nucleus accumbens. *Physiol Behav* 2008;94(5):675–680.

37. Herrero MT, Barcia C, Navarro JM. Functional anatomy of thalamus and basal ganglia. *Childs Nerv Syst* 2002;18(8):386–404.

38. Huttunen J, Kahkonen S, Kaakkola S, Ahveninen J, Pekkonen E. Effects of an acute D2-dopaminergic blockade on the somatosensory cortical responses in healthy humans: evidence from evoked magnetic fields. *Neuroreport* 2003;14(12):1609–1612.

39. Kuo MF, Paulus W, Nitsche MA. Boosting focally-induced brain plasticity by dopamine. *Cereb Cortex* 2008;18(3):648–651.

40. Volkow ND, Wang GJ, Telang F, et al. Low dopamine striatal D2 receptors are associated with prefrontal metabolism in obese subjects: possible contributing factors. *Neuroimage* 2008;42(4):1537–1543.

41. Coull JT. Neural correlates of attention and arousal: insights from electrophysiology, functional neuroimaging and psychopharmacology. *Prog Neurobiol* 1998;55(4):343–361.

42. Zink CF, Pagnoni G, Martin ME, Dhamala M, Berns GS. Human striatal response to salient nonrewarding stimuli. *J Neurosci* 2003;23(22):8092–8097.

43. Watanabe M, Cromwell HC, Tremblay L, Hollerman JR, Hikosaka K, Schultz W. Behavioral reactions reflecting differential reward expectations in monkeys. *Exp Brain Res* 2001;140(4):511–518.

44. Cameron JD, Goldfield GS, Cyr MJ, Doucet E. The effects of prolonged caloric restriction leading to weight-loss on food hedonics and reinforcement. *Physiol Behav* 2008;94(3):474–480.

45. Carr KD. Chronic food restriction: enhancing effects on drug reward and striatal cell signaling. *Physiol Behav* 2007;91(5):459–472.

46. Carr KD. Augmentation of drug reward by chronic food restriction: behavioral evidence and underlying mechanisms. *Physiol Behav* 2002;76(3):353–364.

47. Schultz W. Neural coding of basic reward terms of animal learning theory, game theory, microeconomics and behavioural ecology. *Curr Opin Neurobiol* 2004;14(2):139–147.

48. Volkow ND, Wang GJ, Fowler JS, et al. Nonhedonic food motivation in humans involves dopamine in the dorsal striatum and methylphenidate amplifies this effect. *Synapse* 2002;44(3):175–180.

49. Palmiter RD. Dopamine signaling in the dorsal striatum is essential for motivated behaviors: lessons from dopamine-deficient mice. *Ann NY Acad Sci* 2008;1129:35–46.

50. Stice E, Spoor S, Bohon C, Veldhuizen MG, Small DM. Relation of reward from food intake and anticipated food intake to obesity: a functional magnetic resonance imaging study. *J Abnorm Psychol* 2008; 117(4):924–935.

51. Wang GJ, Volkow ND, Logan J, et al. Brain dopamine and obesity. *Lancet* 2001;357(9253):354–357.

52. Thanos PK, Michaelides M, Piyis YK, Wang GJ, Volkow ND. Food restriction markedly increases dopamine D2 receptor (D2R) in a rat model of obesity as assessed with in-vivo muPET imaging ([11C] raclopride) and in-vitro ([3H] spiperone) autoradiography. *Synapse* 2008;62(1):50–61.

53. Geiger BM, Behr GG, Frank LE, et al. Evidence for defective mesolimbic dopamine exocytosis in obesity-prone rats. *Faseb J* 2008;22(8):2740–2746.

54. Chen PS, Yang YK, Yeh TL, et al. Correlation between body mass index and striatal dopamine transporter availability in healthy volunteers--a SPECT study. *Neuroimage* 2008;40(1):275–279.

55. Wang GJ, Volkow ND, Telang F, et al. Evidence of gender differences in the ability to inhibit brain activation elicited by food stimulation. *Proc Natl Acad Sci USA* 2009;106(4):1249–1254.

56. Volkow ND, Wang GJ, Telang F, et al. Inverse association between BMI and prefrontal metabolic activity in healthy adults. *Obesity (Silver Spring)* 2009;17(1):60–65.

57. Hurd YL. Perspectives on current directions in the neurobiology of addiction disorders relevant to genetic risk factors. *CNS Spectr* 2006;11(11):855–862.

58. Klein TA, Neumann J, Reuter M, Hennig J, von Cramon DY, Ullsperger M. Genetically determined differences in learning from errors. *Science* 2007;318(5856):1642–1645.

59. Dalley JW, Cardinal RN, Robbins TW. Prefrontal executive and cognitive functions in rodents: neural and neurochemical substrates. *Neurosci Biobehav Rev* 2004;28(7):771–784.

60. Goldstein RZ, Volkow ND. Drug addiction and its underlying neurobiological basis: neuroimaging evidence for the involvement of the frontal cortex. *Am J Psychiatry* 2002;159(10):1642–1652.

61. Volkow ND, Fowler JS, Wang GJ, et al. Decreased dopamine D2 receptor availability is associated with reduced frontal metabolism in cocaine abusers. *Synapse* 1993;14(2):169–177.

62. Volkow ND, Chang L, Wang GJ, et al. Low level of brain dopamine D2 receptors in methamphetamine abusers: association with metabolism in the orbitofrontal cortex. *Am J Psychiatry* 2001;158(12):2015–2021.

63. Volkow ND, Wang GJ, Telang F, et al. Profound decreases in dopamine release in striatum in detoxified alcoholics: possible orbitofrontal involvement. *J Neurosci* 2007;27(46):12700–12706.

64. Brewer JA, Potenza MN. The neurobiology and genetics of impulse control disorders: relationships to drug addictions. *Biochem Pharmacol* 2008;75(1):63–75.

65. Grace AA, Floresco SB, Goto Y, Lodge DJ. Regulation of firing of dopaminergic neurons and control of goal-directed behaviors. *Trends Neurosci* 2007;30(5):220–227.

66. Volkow ND, Wang GJ, Begleiter H, et al. High levels of dopamine D2 receptors in unaffected members of alcoholic families: possible protective factors. *Arch Gen Psychiatry* 2006;63(9):999–1008.

67. Volkow ND, Wang GJ, Kollins SH, et al. Evaluating dopamine reward pathway in ADHD: clinical implications. *JAMA* 2009;302(10):1084–1091.

68. Aronne LJ, Wadden T, Isoldi KK, Woodworth KA. When prevention fails: obesity treatment strategies. *Am J Med* 2009;122(4 suppl 1):S24–S32.

29

Genes and Reward Circuitry as Predictors of Eating and Weight Gain

SONJA YOKUM AND ERIC STICE

INTRODUCTION

Theorists have posited that obesity results from abnormalities in reward processing. Some posit that hyperresponsivity of the mesolimbic and mesocortical circuitry to food cues and food intake increases risk for overeating.[1,2] Others hypothesize that obese individuals experience less activation of the mesolimbic reward system in response to food intake, resulting in less subject reward from food intake, which may prompt some individuals to overeat in an effort to overcome this reward deficit.[3,4]

RELATION OF FOOD REWARD CIRCUITRY TO EATING AND WEIGHT GAIN

Accumulating data suggest that obese individuals show a hyperresponsiveness of reward circuitry. A positron emission tomography (PET) study found that obese relative to lean adults show greater resting metabolic activity in the oral somatosensory cortex, a region that encodes sensation in the mouth, lips, and tongue.[4] Only a few brain imaging studies have compared obese and lean individuals using paradigms assessing brain regions implicated in food reward. Obese versus lean women showed increased activation in the parietal and temporal cortices.[5] Furthermore, obese binge eaters showed greater activation of frontal and prefrontal regions in response to food images than lean non-binge-eating individuals.[6] In addition, obese versus lean adults show greater activation in the orbitofrontal cortex (OFC), amygdala, striatum, medial prefrontal cortex, insula, anterior cingulate cortex, ventral pallidum, and hippocampus in response to high-calorie versus low-calorie food images.[7,8] In our lab, we found that body mass index (BMI) correlated positively with activation in the putamen, lateral OFC, and frontal operculum in response to images

of appetizing food versus unappetizing food and glasses of water.[9] In a preliminary functional magnetic resonance imaging (fMRI) study using an attention network task involving food stimuli, we found that BMI correlated positively with activation in the anterior cingulate and ventrolateral prefrontal cortex during exposure to appetizing food versus unappetizing food images.[10]

Other studies have used a paradigm with which anticipation and consumption of food was investigated. Delparigi and colleagues[11] found increased activation in the mid insula, midbrain, and greater decreases in posterior cingulate, temporal, and orbitofrontal cortices in obese versus lean adults during a liquid meal. Furthermore, the authors found that the mid dorsal insula, midbrain, and posterior hippocampus remain abnormally responsive to food consumption in previously obese individuals compared to lean individuals.[12] Extending the findings of Wang and colleagues,[4] we found that obese adolescents showed greater activation in the oral somatosensory cortex and gustatory cortex in response to food consumption.[13]

Other findings are more consistent with the hypothesis that obese individuals show hyporesponsivity of reward circuitry. In two fMRI studies conducted by our lab, activation in the striatum was *negatively* related to food consumption as a function of BMI.[13,14] Because we measured BOLD response, we can only speculate that the effects reflect lower D2 receptor density. This interpretation seems reasonable because the presence of the Taq1A A1 allele, which has been associated with reduced dopaminergic signaling in several postmortem and PET studies,[15,16] significantly moderated the observed BOLD effects. That is, activation in this region showed a strong inverse relation to concurrent BMI for those with the Taq1A A1 allele, and a weaker relation to

BMI for those without this allele.[14] Yet the blunted striatal activation may also implicate altered down-regulation of dopamine receptors caused by overeating, versus an initial vulnerability factor.

To our knowledge, only three studies have tested the relation between response in the reward circuitry and future weight gain. In our preliminary study using an attention network task involving food stimuli, young women who showed greater activation in response to cues for appetizing vs. unappetizing food images in a region of OFC that encodes the reward value of stimuli, showed elevated future weight gain.[10] Although the degree of activation of the striatum in response to food consumption did not show a main effect in predicting weight gain, the relation between abnormal striatum activation and future weight gain was moderated by the A1 allele of the Taq1A gene.[14] In addition, activation in the frontal operculum, striatum, and lateral OFC during appetizing food versus unappetizing food images was negatively related to future weight gain for participants with the A1 allele, but positively related to future weight gain for participants without this allele.[9]

In sum, the abovementioned data suggest that obese relative to lean individuals show hyperresponsivity in the gustatory cortex and somatosensory cortex but show hyporesponsivity in the dopamine-based reward circuitry[11,14] in response to food intake. Furthermore, preliminary data suggest that activation in the reward circuitry in response to food consumption interacts with the TaqIA A1 allele in its prediction of future weight gain. Thus, the findings do not accord with a simple hyperresponsiveness model or a simple hyporesponsiveness model for food intake in obesity. The findings with regard to the presentation of food stimuli seem to be more consistent. Extant data suggest that obese individuals show increased activation of reward and attention regions during the presentation of food stimuli compared to lean individuals. Moreover, preliminary data suggest that increased response in the regions implicated in attention and reward during exposure to food cues predicts future weight gain. Thus, obesity may arise as a consequence of a hyperresponsiveness in the anticipatory "wanting" system.

We believe the field would benefit from imaging studies that directly test whether obese individuals show evidence of greater anticipatory food reward in response to presentation of actual food

as opposed to food that is not obtainable. This is important, especially because theorists have posited that the core issue in obesity does not relate so much to food consumption, but to the anticipatory phase, with greater anticipated reward from food increasing the risk for overeating and obesity.[17] The incentive salience theory posits that consummatory and anticipatory reward operate in tandem in the development of reinforcing value of food, but that with repeated intake of a food, hedonics decrease, while anticipatory reward increases.[18] Via conditioning, food images and cues come to activate reward circuitry, leading to food cravings, overeating, and weight gain.[17] This motivational state, mediated by increased dopamine in reward circuitry, draws attention to food and should therefore result in attentional bias for food stimuli.[19] There is some support for this hypothesis in the animal literature[20], with some initial objective behavioral evidence for this thesis emerging in studies with humans.[21,22] As noted, only one study has used an objective brain imaging paradigm to investigate these relations.[10]

Another priority for future research will be to test whether activations in the reward circuitry in response to food reward predict increases of weight gain and risk for obesity onset. These studies should help distinguish abnormalities that are vulnerability factors for unhealthy weight gain versus consequences of a history of overeating or elevated body fat.

RELATION BETWEEN DOPAMINE BINDING IN THE REWARD CIRCUITRY AND WEIGHT GAIN

Dopamine plays a key role in reward circuitry and is involved in food reward.[23] Data suggest that deficiencies in dopamine receptors and dopamine release play a role in obesity. Animal research implicates that obese rats have lower basal dopamine levels and reduced D2 receptor expression than lean rats,[24] yet obese rats show more phasic release of dopamine during feeding than lean rats.[25] D2 receptor blockade causes obese but not lean rats to overeat,[24] suggesting that blockade of already low D2 receptor availability may sensitize obese rats to food.[26] In a PET study, D2 receptors are reduced in the striatum in morbidly obese individuals in proportion to their body mass.[27] In an independent study, obese versus lean humans show reduced striatal D2 receptor density.[28]

It is hypothesized that obese individuals show lower striatal D2 receptor binding and weaker dopamine signal transduction in response to food intake, which leads them to overeat to compensate for this deficiency.[3,4] If reduced striatal D2 receptor availability produces attenuated subjective reward, it is unclear why individuals with lower D2 binding report that psychostimulants are more subjectively rewarding. In addition, these data also seem to be in contrast with the findings of the brain imaging studies reviewed in the previous section, as some neuroimaging studies suggest that obese versus lean individuals show hyperresponsivity of reward regions. Therefore, it is unclear to what extent the fMRI results are dependent on dopamine mechanisms, as has been theorized. A possible explanation of the aforementioned findings is that consumption of a high-fat, high-sugar diet leads to down-regulation of D2 receptors.[29] Animal studies suggest that repeated intake of sweet and fatty foods results in down-regulation of postsynaptic D2 receptors, increased D1 receptor binding, and decreased D2 sensitivity and α-opioid receptor binding[30,31]—changes that also occur in response to chronic substance abuse. To date, no PET imaging study has tested whether obese humans showed greater dopamine release in response to food intake relative to lean humans. However, there is evidence that women who showed weight gain evidence a reduced striatal response to palatable food receipt relative to baseline and women who did not gain weight.[32] Accordingly, it will be important to investigate dopamine release in response to food intake in obese versus lean individuals. In addition, it is crucial for future studies to characterize the dopaminergic synaptic function in humans and to examine their effects on future weight gain.

GENETIC VARIATIONS IN DOPAMINERGIC REWARD IN HUMANS

Given that dopamine plays a key role in reward circuitry and is involved in food reward,[23] it follows that genetic polymorphisms that affect dopamine signaling may influence reward during or in anticipation of eating. Several genes have been associated with dopamine functioning and BMI.

The Taq1A A1 Polymorphism of the ANKK1 Gene

The Taq1A polymorphism has three allelic variants: A1/A1, A1/A2, and A2/A2. Postmortem and PET studies suggest that individuals with one or two copies of the A1 allele have 30%–40% fewer D2 receptors and altered brain dopamine signaling compared to those without an A1 allele.[15,16]

Frequencies of the A1 genotype range from 26% in young women with a range of body weights,[14] to 30% in individuals with binge eating disorder,[33] to 45% in obese individuals.[34] The A1 allele is correlated with BMI in some studies,[35,36] but others have not found a significant main effect between A1 allele status and BMI.[37,38] One possible explanation of this pattern of finding is that the A1 allele status interacts with reward sensitivity to predict obesity. Epstein and colleagues[39] found that the greatest ad lib food intake occurred in those who reported more reinforcement from food and who had the A1 allele. As noted, we also found an interaction between activation in the reward circuitry in response to food images and food intake and future weight gain.[9,14]

Variants in the DRD4 Gene

DRD4 is a postsynaptic dopamine receptor whose principal action is to inhibit the second messenger, adenylate cyclase. D4 receptors are predominantly localized in the prefrontal cortex, cingulate gyrus, and insula.[40] Presence of the DRD4-L allele has been associated with higher maximum BMI in humans at risk for obesity.[41] Adults with versus without the DRD4-L allele have shown stronger food cravings in response to food cues.[42] Weaker activation of the frontal operculum in response to the images of appetizing food versus unappetizing food and glasses of water predicted elevated weight gain for those with the DRD4-L allele.[9]

Variants in the Dopamine Transporter

Phasically released dopamine is normally eliminated by rapid reuptake into presynaptic terminals through the dopamine transporter (DAT). Lower DAT expression, which is associated with a 10 repeat allele (DAT-L), may reduce synaptic clearance and produce higher basal, or tonic, dopamine levels and blunted phasic dopamine release.[43] Peciña and colleagues[44] found that a DAT knockdown mouse with increased extracellular dopamine displayed increased energy intake and preference for palatable foods. In a study of normal mice, feeding a high-fat diet significantly decreased dopamine density in the caudate and putamen compared to a low-fat diet.[45] Lower striatal DAT levels also have been associated with elevated BMI in humans.[46] DAT-L has been associated with obesity in African American smokers versus smokers of other ethnic groups.[47]

Variants in the Catechol-*O*-Methyltransferase Gene

Catechol-*O*-methyltransferase (COMT) regulates extrasynaptic dopamine breakdown, which occurs in both the prefrontal cortex and the striatum.[48] A single nucleotide exchange in the COMT gene, a valine to methionine substitution (Val/Met-158), is associated with a four-fold reduction in COMT activity in humans. Individuals with the Met allele (low enzyme activity) had relatively higher tonic dopamine levels in prefrontal and striatal regions but reduced phasic dopamine release in the striatum.[49] One study found that eating-disordered individuals with the Met-allele reported more elevated bulimic symptoms than those without this allele.[50] Another study found that individuals with bulimia nervosa were marginally less likely to have a Met-allele than were control individuals.[51]

CONCLUSIONS AND DIRECTIONS FOR FUTURE RESEARCH

In this chapter we reviewed findings from studies that have investigated whether reward circuitry and genes related to dopamine functioning correlate with concurrent BMI and future unhealthy weight gain. Overall, the studies using brain imaging suggests that obese versus lean individuals anticipate greater reward from food intake. The literature also suggest that obese compared to lean individuals show greater activation in the gustatory cortex and somatosensory cortex in response to food receipt, which may imply that consuming food is more pleasurable from a sensory perspective. However, obese versus lean individuals show less activation in the dorsal striatum and OFC in response to food intake relative to lean individuals, suggesting a blunted activation of reward circuitry. Thus, as noted, extant data do not lend clear support to a simple hyperresponsivity or a simple hyporesponsivity model of obesity. Future research should strive to resolve the apparently inconsistent findings suggesting that obese individuals show hyperresponsiveness of some brain regions to food intake, but hyporesponsiveness of other brain regions, relative to lean individuals. Furthermore, there is a particular need

to integrate measurement of dopamine functioning with functional MRI measures of striatal and cortical responses to food. The literature suggests that dopamine functioning is linked to differences in food reward sensitivity. However, because existing studies in humans have either used fMRI measures of responses to food, or PET measures of dopamine binding, but have never measured both in the same participants, it is unclear to what extend the fMRI findings are dependent on dopamine mechanisms and whether this explains the differential responsivity in obese versus lean individuals. Furthermore, a priority for future research will be to test whether abnormalities in brain reward circuitry increase risk for unhealthy weight gain and onset of obesity. Specifically, future studies should examine whether reward circuitry disturbances are primary or secondary to a chronic intake of a high-fat, high-sugar diet. Finally, future research should continue exploring factors that moderate the risk conveyed by abnormalities in reward circuitry in response to food consumption and anticipated consumption to increase risk for unhealthy weight gain.

REFERENCES

1. Davis C, Strachan S, Berkson M. Sensitivity to reward: implications for overeating and overweight. *Appetite* 2004;42(2):131–138.
2. Dawe S, Loxton NJ. The role of impulsivity in the development of substance use and eating disorders. *Neurosci Biobehav Rev* 2004;28(3):343–351.
3. Blum K, Braverman ER, Holder JM, et al. Reward deficiency syndrome: a biogenetic model for the diagnosis and treatment of impulsive, addictive, and compulsive behaviors. *J Psychoactive Drugs* 2000;32 (suppl: i–iv):1–112.
4. Wang GJ, Volkow ND, Fowler JS. The role of dopamine in motivation for food in humans: implications for obesity. *Expert Opin Ther Targets* 2002;6(5):601–609.
5. Karhunen LJ, Lappalainen RI, Vanninen EJ, Kuikka JT, Uusitupa MI. Regional cerebral blood flow during food exposure in obese and normal-weight women. *Brain* 1997;12(pt 9):1675–1684.
6. Karhunen L, Vanninen EJ, Kuikka JT, Lappalainen RI, Tiihonen J, Uusitupa MI. Regional cerebral blood flow during exposure to food in obese binge eating women. *Psychiat Res* 2000;99(1):29–42.
7. Rothemund Y, Preuschhof C, Bohner G, et al. Differential activation of the dorsal striatum by high-calorie visual food stimuli in obese individuals. *Neuroimage* 2007;37(2):410–421.
8. Stoeckel LE, Weller RE, Cook EW, 3rd, Twieg DB, Knowlton RC, Cox JE. Widespread reward-system activation in obese women in response to pictures

of high-calorie foods. *Neuroimage* 2008;41(2): 636–647.

9. Stice E, Yokum S, Bohon C, Marti N, Smolen A. Reward circuitry responsivity to food predicts future weight gain: moderating effects of DRD2 and DRD4. *Neuroimage* 2010;50(4):1618–1625.

10. Yokum S, Ng J, Stice E. Attentional bias for food images associated with elevated weight and future weight gain: An fMRI study. *Obesity* 2011;19:1775–1783.

11. DelParigi A, Chen K, Salbe AD, Reiman EM, Tataranni PA. Sensory experience of food and obesity: a positron emission tomography study of the brain regions affected by tasting a liquid meal after a prolonged fast. *Neuroimage* 2005;24(2):436–443.

12. DelParigi A, Chen K, Salbe AD, et al. Persistence of abnormal neural responses to a meal in postobese individuals. *Int J Obes Relat Metab Disord* 2004; 28(3):370–377.

13. Stice E, Spoor S, Bohon C, Veldhuizen M, Small DM. Relation of reward from food intake and anticipated intake to obesity: a functional magnetic resonance imaging study. *J Abnorm Psychol* 2008;117(4):924–935.

14. Stice E, Spoor S, Bohon C, Small DM. Relation between obesity and blunted striatal response to food is moderated by TaqIA A1 allele. *Science* 2008; 322(5900):449–452.

15. Jönsson EG, Nöthen MM, Grünhage F, Farde L, Nakashima Y, Propping P, Sedvall GC. Polymorphisms in the dopamine D2 receptor gene and their relationships to striatal dopamine receptor density of healthy volunteers. *Mol Psychiatry* 1999;4:290–296.

16. Tupala E, Hall H, Bergström K, et al. Dopamine D2 receptors and transporters in type 1 and 2 alcoholics measured with human whole hemisphere autoradiography. *Hum Brain Mapp* 2003;20(2):91–102.

17. Berridge KC. "Liking" and "wanting" food rewards: brain substrates and roles in eating disorders. *Physiol Behav* 2009;97(5):537–550.

18. Robinson TE, Berridge KC. Intra-accumbens amphetamine increases the conditioned incentive salience of sucrose reward: enhancement of reward "wanting" without enhanced "liking" or response reinforcement. *J Neurosci* 2000;20:s91–s117.

19. Castellanos EH, Charboneau E, Dietrich MS, et al. Obese adults have visual attention bias for food cue images: evidence for altered reward system function. *Int J Obes* 2009;33(9):1063–1073.

20. Schultz W, Apicella P, Ljungberg T. Responses of monkey dopamine neurons to reward and conditioned stimuli during successive steps of learning a delayed response task. *J Neurosci* 1993;13(3):900–913.

21. Braet C, Crombez G. Cognitive interference due to food cues in childhood obesity. *J Clin Child Adolesc* 2003;32(1):32–39.

22. Grossberg JM, Grant BF. Obese-normal differences in visual stimulus detection as a function of cue salience. *J Pers* 1976;44(4):645–653.

23. Yamamoto T. Neural substrates for the processing of cognitive and affective aspects of taste in the brain. *Arch Histol Cytol* 2006;69(4):243–255.

24. Fetissov SO, Meguid MM, Sato T, Zhang LH. Expression of dopaminergic receptors in the hypothalamus of lean and obese Zucker rats and food intake. *Am J Physiol* 2002;283(4):R905–R910.

25. Yang ZJ, Meguid, MM. LHA dopaminergic activity in obese and lean Zucker rats. *Neuroreport* 1995;6(8):1191–1194.

26. Epstein LH, Leddy, JJ, Temple JL, Faith, MS. Food reinforcement and eating: a multilevel analysis. *Psychol Bull* 2007;133(5):884–906.

27. Wang GJ, Volkow ND, Logan J, et al. Brain dopamine and obesity. *Lancet* 2001;357(9253):354–357.

28. Volkow ND, Wang GJ, Telang F, et al. Low dopamine striatal D2 receptors are associated with prefrontal metabolism in obese subjects: possible contributing factors. *Neuroimage* 2008;42(4):1537–1543.

29. Small DM, Jones-Gotman M, Dagher A. Feeding-induced dopamine release in dorsal striatum correlates with meal pleasantness ratings in healthy human volunteers. *Neuroimage* 2003;19(4):1709–1715.

30. Bello NT, Lucas LR, Hajnal A. Repeated sucrose access influences dopamine D2 receptor density in the striatum. *Neuroreport* 2002;13(12):1575–1578.

31. Kelley AE, Will MJ, Steininger TL, Zhang M, Haber SN. Restricted daily consumption of a highly palatable food (chocolate Ensure(R)) alters striatal enkephalin gene expression. *Eur J Neurosci* 2003;18(9): 2592–2598.

32. Stice E, Yokum S, Blum K, Bohon C. Weight gain associated with reduced striatal response to palatable food. *J Neurosci* 2010;30:13105–13109.

33. Davis C, Levitan RD, Kaplan AS, et al. Reward sensitivity and the D2 dopamine receptor gene: a case-control study of binge eating disorder. *Prog Neuro-Psychoph* 2008;32(3):620–628.

34. Noble EP, Noble RE, Ritchie T, et al. D2 dopamine receptor gene and obesity. *Int J Eat Disord* 1994; 15(3):205–217.

35. Spitz MR, Detry MA, Pillow P, et al. Variant alleles of the D2 dopamine receptor gene and obesity. *Nutr Res* 2000;20:371–380.

36. Thomas GN, Tomlinson B, Critchley JA. Modulation of blood pressure and obesity with the dopamine D2 receptor gene TaqI polymorphism. *Hypertension* 2000;36(2):177–182.

37. Jenkinson CP, Hanson R, Cray K, et al. Association of dopamine D2 receptor polymorphisms Ser311Cys and TaqIA with obesity or type 2 diabetes mellitus in Pima Indians. *Int J Obes Relat Metab Disord* 2000;24(10):1233–1238.

38. Southon A, Walder K, Sanigorski AM, et al. The Taq IA and Ser311 Cys polymorphisms in the dopamine D2 receptor gene and obesity. *Diabetes Nutr Metab* 2003;16(1):72–76.

39. Epstein LH, Wright SM, Paluch RA, et al. Relation between food reinforcement and dopamine genotypes and its effect on food intake in smokers. *Am J Clin Nutr* 2004;80(1):82–88.

40. Noaín D, Avale ME, Wedemeyer C, Calvo D, Peper M, Rubinstein M. Identification of brain neurons expressing the dopamine D4 receptor gene using BAC transgenic mice. *Eur J Neurosci* 2006;24(9): 2429–2438.

41. Levitan RD, Masellis M, Lam RW, et al. Childhood inattention and dysphoria and adult obesity associated with the dopamine D4 receptor gene in overeating women with seasonal affective disorder. *Neuropsychopharmacol* 2004;29(1):179–186.

42. Sobik L, Hutchison K, Craighead L. Cue-elicited craving for food: a fresh approach to the study of binge eating. *Appetite* 2005;44(3):253–261.

43. Brody AL, Mandelkern MA, Olmstead RE, et al. Gene variants of brain dopamine pathways and smoking-induced dopamine release in the ventral caudate/nucleus accumbens. *Arch Gen Psychiat* 2006; 63(7):808–816.

44. Peciña S, Cagniard B, Berridge KC, Aldridge JW, Zhuang X. Hyperdopaminergic mutant mice have higher "wanting" but not "liking" for sweet rewards. *J Neurosci* 2003;23(28):9395–9402.

45. South T, Huang, X.F. High-fat diet exposure increases dopamine D2 receptor and decreases dopamine transporter receptor binding density in the nucleus accumbens and caudate putamen of mice. *Neurochem Res* 2008;33(3):598–605.

46. Chen PS, Yang YK, Yeh TL, et al. Correlation between body mass index and striatal dopamine transporter availability in healthy volunteers—a SPECT study. *Neuroimage* 2008;40(1):275–279.

47. Epstein LH, Jaroni JL, Paluch RA, et al. Dopamine transporter genotype as a risk factor for obesity in African-American smokers. *Obes Res* 2002;10(12): 1232–1240.

48. Matsumoto M, Weickert CS, Beltaifa S, et al. Catechol O-methyltransferase (COMT) mRNA expression in the dorsolateral prefrontal cortex of patients with schizophrenia. *Neuropsychopharmacol* 2003;28(8): 1521–1530.

49. Bilder RM, Volavka J, Lachman HM, Grace AA. The catechol-O-methyltransferase polymorphism: relations to the tonic-phasic dopamine hypothesis and neuropsychiatric phenotypes. *Neuropsychopharmacol* 2004;29(11):1943–1961.

50. Frieling H, Römer KD, Wilhelm J, et al. Association of catecholamine-O-methyltransferase and 5-HTTLPR genotype with eating disorder-related behavior and attitudes in females with eating disorders. *Psychiat Genet* 2006;16(5):205–208.

51. Mikolajczyk E, Smiarowska M, Grzywacz A, Samochowiec J. Association of eating disorders with catechol-o-methyltransferase gene functional polymorphism. *Neuropsychobiol* 2006;54(1):82–86.

30

Hormones, Hunger, and Food Addiction

ALAIN DAGHER

INTRODUCTION

The conceptual link between drug addiction and feeding rests on multiple lines of evidence. Here we review one of these: gut and adipose tissue hormones that provide short- and long-term energy balance signals, which regulate food intake, act on brain systems also involved in drug addiction, most notably mesolimbic dopamine neurons and their projection sites. The major anorexigenic hormones, leptin, insulin, and PYY, and the single known orexigenic hormone, ghrelin, all appear to exert their effects predominantly through the modulation of brain circuitry involved in incentive motivation. In addition, the secretion by the periphery of these hormones is itself partly controlled by the brain, forming a gut-brain feed-forward loop that controls appetite. This chapter will outline the animal and human neuroimaging data that support these statements.

THE APPETITIVE BRAIN NETWORK: A COMMON NEURAL SUBSTRATE FOR DRUGS OF ABUSE AND FOOD

Appetite, the tendency to eat, consists of several behavioral, cognitive, and neural phenomena: arousal and autonomic activation; attention to, and learning about, food-predictive cues; motivation, or the willingness to expend effort and take risks to obtain food; and the sensation of hunger. Animal studies and human neuroimaging experiments have identified a brain network for appetite that centers around four interconnected regions: the amygdala/hippocampus, the orbitofrontal cortex (OFC) and nearby ventromedial prefrontal cortex (vmPFC), the striatum, and the insula. Neural activity in these areas is modulated by food cues (the sight, smell, and taste of food), food thoughts, hunger, and also by peripheral signals that relate the energetic state of the body (hormones, blood-borne nutrients such as glucose, and neural afferents from the gut). All of these brain regions are innervated by dopamine neurons originating in the ventral tegmental area (VTA), and they receive direct or indirect input from the arcuate and lateral nuclei of the hypothalamus,[1] which are both involved in feeding. Dopamine plays an important role in the individual's response to rewards, be they foods or drugs. Food and addictive drugs both promote dopamine release.[2] Incentive learning, whereby a neutral stimulus paired repeatedly with food (or other reward) acquires incentive properties, is dopamine dependent[3] and critically involves the striatum,[4] amygdala and OFC,[5] and insula,[6] all dopamine projection sites.

The amygdala and OFC encode the current incentive value of food cues: lesions of either structure, or their disconnection, impair an animal's ability to assign motivational value to cues and to act appropriately to obtain rewards.[7] The amygdala is thought to assign incentive value to sensory stimuli and to pass that information on to the OFC and adjacent vmPFC, where predictions are made about the potential reward associated with the cue or related action, and where the trade-off between effort and reward is computed.[8] In a recent functional magnetic resonance imaging (fMRI) study, the willingness to pay for junk food items (candy, chips, etc.) correlated with brain activity in the medial OFC and vmPFC.[9]

The anterior insula is the first cortical relay of information from taste receptors in the oral cavity, but neurons there also respond to other properties of foods, such as texture, temperature, and olfactory and visual properties, which is why it is often referred to as "ingestive cortex."[10] The insula is also the sensory cortex for visceral information from the gut.[11] Insula activity is modulated by cognitive and emotional factors, including hunger and attention, and by gut peptides such as ghrelin.[12] The multi-modal sensory features of foods in the mouth are encoded by neuronal ensembles within the insula, and this activity is modulated by hunger and satiety.[13] The insula plays a crucial role in learning about the nutritional effects of ingested foods[14] and thus aids in the ability of food cues to become conditioned. Animals with insula lesions fail to attribute incentive value to calorie-rich foods.[6] Stimulation of the anterior insula during epilepsy surgery triggers gustatory, olfactory, and epigastric sensations.[15]

The striatum is crucially implicated in motivated behaviors and incentive learning. It is thought to form a link between motivation and action,[16] and conditioned cues exert their incentive properties via the mesolimbic dopamine system.[17] Initially, unexpected food rewards trigger dopamine neuron firing; however, with time, the response is transferred to conditioned cues paired with reward.[18] Conditioned cues do more than signal available rewards; they also energize the individual by creating an incentive state, motivating it to approach and consume food or other rewards with great vigor, a phenomenon that also appears to be mediated by dopamine.[17]

The ability of cues to trigger appetite may be a component of the obesogenic environment, which bombards us with foods, odors, advertising, brand names, and logos. A neutral stimulus or environment paired repeatedly with food or drug acquires the ability to trigger consumption of the food or drug. Kelley and colleagues have mapped gene expression changes in animals exposed to an environment previously paired with rewards.[19] For both food and addictive drugs, the paired environments caused activation in the prefrontal cortex (PFC), anterior cingulate cortex, insula, striatum, and amygdala. In humans, pictures of drugs of abuse (shown to addicts) or food (shown to anyone) both activate regions of the appetitive network. Activation of this network likely reflects craving for and motivation to consume the drug or food. Indeed, in animals, a conditioned cue previously paired with food triggers feeding, even in sated animals.[12,20] This phenomenon reflects craving rather than a nonspecific increase in appetite, since it is only the food that was paired with the conditioned stimulus that is consumed. A similar phenomenon is described in humans, where food odors or thoughts cause increased consumption of the target food.[21] Similarly, drug cues do not cause a nonspecific incentive state, but a specific craving for the drug itself. Key components of cue-potentiated feeding include the amygdala, lateral hypothalamus, and OFC.

A ROLE FOR GUT SIGNALS BEYOND THE HOMEOSTATIC/HEDONIC DICHOTOMY

It has been suggested that there are two parallel systems driving food intake: a homeostatic one that responds to energy signals from the body (humoral, hormonal, mechanical), transmitted mainly via the circulation and the vagus nerve, and acting via the hypothalamus, and a hedonic one in which food cues (odors, thoughts, the sight of food) have the ability to stimulate appetite in the absence of metabolic need. Overeating can be viewed as a failure of homeostasis, or as being driven by pleasure, which overwhelms homeostasis. Interestingly, a homeostatic dysregulation model has been proposed to explain drug addiction.[22]

Note, however, that homeostatic and hedonic responses are closely intertwined. First, in order to affect behavior, homeostatic signals must act via drive and motivation. It is well known that hunger increases the incentive value of food. In animals and humans, the homeostatic signals ghrelin, leptin, insulin, and PYY have all been found to act on amygdala, hippocampus, OFC, insula, and striatum,[12,23–25] the key components of a motivational system also implicated in drug addiction.

Conversely, hedonic signals, such as odors, food thoughts, and cravings, can affect the homeostatic system via the cephalic response. Food cues trigger the cephalic phase of ingestive behavior, which consists of increased gastrointestinal motility, gut hormone secretion, and autonomic arousal; for example, exposure to food increases plasma ghrelin in humans.[26] Exposure to food cues also increases the desire for food as measured by prospectively chosen portion sizes.[27] Thus, ghrelin may form part of a feed-forward loop for feeding: food cues processed in the central nervous system promote ghrelin release from the stomach via the vagus nerve. Ghrelin returns to the brain via the circulation to activate feeding centers in the hypothalamus and VTA and augment incentive salience by its action on the appetitive network. Factors that increase or decrease the cue-induced release of ghrelin could therefore affect food intake. Likely modulators of ghrelin secretion include stress[28] and negative energy balance.[26,29] This feed-forward model of the gut/brain response to food cues is relevant to obesity, as a component of the obesogenic environment is the daily bombardment with enticing foods, for example, through advertising. The insula may be a central node in this response, as it is activated by food cues,[12] and components of the cephalic phase response such as salivation, chewing, swallowing, and epigastric sensations can be triggered by electrical stimulation of the insula.[15] A similar cue-reactivity model has been proposed for drug addiction. In humans, drug cues (e.g., photographs of cigarettes) cause drug craving and activate the insula, amygdala, striatum, and OFC.[30,31] Interestingly, cigarette smokers who suffer insula damage (e.g., from stroke) found it easy to quit smoking,[32] possibly due to disruption of cue-induced drug craving.

LEARNING AND MOTIVATION

Animals must learn about food in their environment, and they are better at this when hungry.[33] Dopamine neurons are thought to encode a learning signal,[18] which has been shown in numerous animal and human studies to resemble the reward prediction error (RPE) signal of temporal difference models of machine learning.[18] In the computer models, RPE promotes learning by modulating synaptic strength, whereas, in humans, dopamine both resembles an RPE in its temporal pattern and modulates synaptic plasticity.[34] This dopamine learning signal favors learning and memory through projections to the striatum,[18] hippocampus,[35] and amygdala.[36] The dopamine signal serves two purposes: during cue exposure it is an anticipatory and motivating signal (reward prediction), while after feedback it is a reward prediction error signal used for learning.[37] Through their actions on dopamine neuron firing, gut hormones can impact both of these neural processes.

GUT PEPTIDES AND INCENTIVE MOTIVATION

Ghrelin is the only known appetite-stimulating (orexigenic) hormone.[38] It is a peptide secreted by the stomach and small intestine[39] prior to meals, and it triggers hunger and feeding.[38] Ghrelin secretion is suppressed by ingested nutrients, proportional to their caloric content.[40] Chronic administration of ghrelin to rodents leads to increased food intake and body weight,[41] while antagonism reduces feeding. Ghrelin levels are inversely proportional to body weight: elevated following weight loss or in anorexia nervosa, and reduced in obesity,[29] suggesting an important role in the defense of body weight.

The ghrelin receptor is found mainly in the brain, most notably the hypothalamus (arcuate nucleus), on VTA dopamine neurons, and in the hippocampus and amygdala.[23,42,43] In the hypothalamus it stimulates NPY/AgRP neurons,[43] which are key promoters of food intake.

Ghrelin directly and indirectly activates mesolimbic dopamine neurons (indirectly via orexin neurons in the lateral hypothalamus). In this way it can act on systems involved in motivation and drive. Local injections of ghrelin into the rodent VTA promote locomotor activity, striatal dopamine release, and feeding, while systemically administered ghrelin causes VTA dopamine neuron firing and simultaneous feeding behavior.[23,44] Intra-VTA delivery of a selective ghrelin antagonist blocks the orexigenic effect of circulating ghrelin and blunts rebound feeding following fasting, supporting a key role for dopamine in ghrelin's appetitive effects. Dopamine increases the incentive salience of food (and drug) cues and the willingness of animals to work for food (or drug).[45] It is a key regulator of appetitive drive, mediating arousal, foraging behavior, risk taking, and food anticipation. Indeed, ghrelin null mice fail to show the normal anticipatory locomotion to scheduled meals,[46] a dopamine-dependent phenomenon. In sum, ghrelin acts on the mesolimbic dopamine system and the orexin system, both of which are central targets of addictive drugs and food reward.[2,47]

Ghrelin is thus a prime candidate for modulating food-related reward signals and incentive learning: it is elevated during hunger and increases phasic dopamine neuron firing,[23] which should allow it to amplify the learning signal. Ghrelin increases the response to food pictures in the dopaminergic midbrain, striatum, amygdala, hippocampus, insula, and OFC.[12] Moreover, ghrelin increases recognition for the food cues (tested 24 hours later) compared to the food cues tested in a placebo condition. The ability of conditioned cues to act as incentives for drug seeking is a keystone of neural models of addiction. When ghrelin is present in high concentrations, food cues, such as the sight, smell, and taste of food, but possibly also food thoughts, exert greater attraction for the individual, increasing the motivation to eat. Interestingly, activation of the same appetitive brain network in drug users in response to drug cues is also predictive of imminent drug use.[30] Moreover, activation of these brain areas in response to food cues correlates with a personality measure called Behavioral Activation,[48] a measure of an individual's reactivity to potential rewards, and a risk factor for both obesity and drug addiction.

PYY is implicated in satiety and meal termination. It is released into the circulation from intestinal cells after meal ingestion, proportional to caloric load and to subsequent satiety.[49] In obese individuals, postmeal PYY secretion and satiety are proportionally reduced,[50] and postprandial PYY predicts future weight gain, suggesting that it participates in long-term energy homeostasis in addition to short-term meal termination. PYY also reduces ghrelin levels. Circulating PYY crosses the blood–brain barrier and acts on the hypothalamus, where it has anorectic effects.[49] However, functional neuroimaging in humans demonstrates a distributed effect on the entire appetitive network. Batterham et al. administered synthetic PYY to human volunteers as they underwent fMRI.[25] Brain regions where neural activity covaried with serum PYY included the lateral hypothalamus, VTA, OFC, insula, ACC, ventral striatum, and lateral frontal lobe. On days when subjects received saline injection prior to scanning, neural activity in the hypothalamus predicted subsequent food intake (from a free choice buffet). However, on days when subjects received PYY, activity in the OFC predicted subsequent food intake. It is reasonable to conclude that PYY exerts its anorectic effects in part by reducing the incentive value of food. Interestingly, OFC activation in drug addicts may also predict subsequent drug use.[31]

Leptin is another anorexic signal, and it is a key regulator of long-term energy balance. It is secreted by adipocytes and its levels reflect the body's energy stores.[51] Leptin receptors are found in the hypothalamus but also on VTA dopamine neurons, a site of action that allows leptin to directly impact brain reward function. Transgenic animals that lack leptin are hyperphagic and obese, but they also demonstrate anomalies in dopamine signaling and deficient locomotor response to amphetamine.[24] A single neuroimaging study in humans with congenital leptin deficiency confirmed the mesolimbic dopamine system as a site of action of leptin.[52]

Finally, insulin is also thought to be an anorectic feedback signal: it is increased immediately following meals, and there are insulin receptors in the hypothalamus, VTA, amygdala, and hippocampus. Insulin appears to affect the rewarding properties of food.[53] In a recent fMRI experiment, intranasal insulin, which directly increases brain insulin levels without affecting peripheral metabolism, led to reduced response to food pictures in the fusiform gyrus and hippocampus,[54] consistent with a role in down-regulating the appetitive response to the cues.

CONCLUSION

The appetitive network is responsive to peripheral signals of energy balance. It integrates information on energy stores and gut contents to control feeding behavior. Central to this network's function is dopamine, which signals the presence of rewards, motivates the individual to seek these rewards, and promotes learning about rewards and reward-associated cues. Drugs of abuse also target this system, largely through the VTA dopamine neuron. That appetite-controlling hormones act on the same neural systems implicated in drug addiction is further evidence that viewing obesity from the standpoint of addiction neuroscience is a potentially fruitful avenue of research. The links between addiction and feeding have implications for the clinical management of obesity and for public policy addressing the obesity epidemic.

REFERENCES

1. Saper CB, Chou TC, Elmquist JK. The need to feed: homeostatic and hedonic control of eating. *Neuron* 2002;36:199–211.
2. Di Chiara G, Imperato A. Drugs abused by humans preferentially increase synaptic dopamine concentrations in the mesolimbic system of freely moving rats. *Proc Natl Acad Sci USA* 1988;85:5274–5278.
3. Wise RA. Dopamine, learning and motivation. *Nat Rev Neurosci* 2004;5:483–494.
4. Balleine BW. Neural bases of food-seeking: affect, arousal and reward in corticostriatolimbic circuits. *Physiol Behav* 2005;86:717–730.
5. Cardinal RN, Parkinson JA, Hall J, Everitt BJ. Emotion and motivation: the role of the amygdala, ventral striatum, and prefrontal cortex. *Neurosci Biobehav Rev* 2002;26:321–352.
6. Balleine BW, Dickinson A. The effect of lesions of the insular cortex on instrumental conditioning: evidence for a role in incentive memory. *J Neurosci* 2000;20:8954–8964.

7. Holland PC, Gallagher M. Amygdala-frontal interactions and reward expectancy. *Curr Opin Neurobiol* 2004;14:148–155.

8. Murray EA, Izquierdo A. Orbitofrontal cortex and amygdala contributions to affect and action in primates. *Ann NY Acad Sci* 2007;1121:273–296.

9. Plassmann H, O'Doherty J, Rangel A. Orbitofrontal cortex encodes willingness to pay in everyday economic transactions. *J Neurosci* 2007;27:9984–9988.

10. Scott TR, Plata-Salaman CR. Taste in the monkey cortex. *Physiol Behav* 1999;67:489–511.

11. Craig AD. How do you feel? Interoception: the sense of the physiological condition of the body. *Nat Rev Neurosci* 2002;3:655–666.

12. Malik S, McGlone F, Bedrossian D, Dagher A. Ghrelin modulates brain activity in areas that control appetitive behavior. *Cell Metab* 2008;7:400–409.

13. de Araujo IE, Gutierrez R, Oliveira-Maia AJ, Pereira A, Jr., Nicolelis MA, Simon SA. Neural ensemble coding of satiety states. *Neuron* 2006;51:483–494.

14. de Araujo IE, Simon SA. The gustatory cortex and multisensory integration. *Int J Obes (Lond)* 2009; 33(suppl 2):S34–S43.

15. Penfield W, Faulk ME, Jr. The insula; further observations on its function. *Brain* 1955;78:445–470.

16. Mogenson GJ, Jones DL, Yim CY. From motivation to action: functional interface between the limbic system and the motor system. *Prog Neurobiol* 1980;14:69–97.

17. Phillips PE, Stuber GD, Heien ML, Wightman RM, Carelli RM. Subsecond dopamine release promotes cocaine seeking. *Nature* 2003;422:614–618.

18. Schultz W. Behavioral theories and the neurophysiology of reward. *Annu Rev Psychol* 2006;57:87–115.

19. Kelley AE, Schiltz CA, Landry CF. Neural systems recruited by drug- and food-related cues: studies of gene activation in corticolimbic regions. *Physiol Behav* 2005;86:11–14.

20. Petrovich GD, Gallagher M. Control of food consumption by learned cues: a forebrain-hypothalamic network. *Physiol Behav* 2007;91:397–403.

21. Fedoroff I, Polivy J, Herman CP. The specificity of restrained versus unrestrained eaters' responses to food cues: general desire to eat, or craving for the cued food? *Appetite* 2003;41:7–13.

22. Koob GF. A role for brain stress systems in addiction. *Neuron* 2008;59:11–34.

23. Abizaid A, Liu ZW, Andrews ZB, et al. Ghrelin modulates the activity and synaptic input organization of midbrain dopamine neurons while promoting appetite. *J Clin Invest* 2006;116:3229–239.

24. Fulton S, Pissios P, Manchon RP, et al. Leptin regulation of the mesoaccumbens dopamine pathway. *Neuron* 2006;51:811–822.

25. Batterham RL, ffytche DH, Rosenthal JM, et al. PYY modulation of cortical and hypothalamic brain areas predicts feeding behaviour in humans. *Nature* 2007;450:106–109.

26. Monteleone P, Serritella C, Martiadis V, Maj M. Deranged secretion of ghrelin and obestatin in the cephalic phase of vagal stimulation in women with anorexia nervosa. *Biol Psychiatr* 2008;64:1005–1008.

27. Ferriday D, Brunstrom JM. How does food-cue exposure lead to larger meal sizes? *Br J Nutr* 2008;100:1325–1332.

28. Kristenssson E, Sundqvist M, Astin M, et al. Acute psychological stress raises plasma ghrelin in the rat. *Regul Pept* 2006;134:114–117.

29. Wiedmer P, Nogueiras R, Broglio F, D'Alessio D, Tschop MH. Ghrelin, obesity and diabetes. *Nat Clin Pract End Met* 2007;3:705–712.

30. McBride D, Barrett SP, Kelly JT, Aw A, Dagher A. Effects of expectancy and abstinence on the neural response to smoking cues in cigarette smokers: an fMRI study. *Neuropsychopharmacol* 2006;31:2728–2738.

31. Wilson SJ, Sayette MA, Fiez JA. Prefrontal responses to drug cues: a neurocognitive analysis. *Nat Neurosci* 2004;7:211–214.

32. Naqvi NH, Rudrauf D, Damasio H, Bechara A. Damage to the insula disrupts addiction to cigarette smoking. *Science* 2007;315:531–534.

33. Dickinson A, Balleine B. Motivational control of goal-directed action. *Anim Learn Behav* 1994;22:1–18.

34. Shen W, Flajolet M, Greengard P, Surmeier DJ. Dichotomous dopaminergic control of striatal synaptic plasticity. *Science* 2008;321:848–851.

35. Wittmann BC, Schott BH, Guderian S, Frey JU, Heinze H-J, Düzel E. Reward-related fMRI activation of dopaminergic midbrain is associated with enhanced hippocampus-dependent long-term memory formation. *Neuron* 2005;45:459–467.

36. Paton JJ, Belova MA, Morrison SE, Salzman CD. The primate amygdala represents the positive and negative value of visual stimuli during learning. *Nature* 2006;439:865–870.

37. McClure SM, Daw ND, Montague PR. A computational substrate for incentive salience. *Trends Neurosci* 2003;26:423–428.

38. Cummings DE. Ghrelin and the short- and long-term regulation of appetite and body weight. *Physiol Behav* 2006;89:71–84.

39. Kojima M, Hosoda H, Date Y, Nakazato M, Matsuo H, Kangawa K. Ghrelin is a growth-hormone-releasing acylated peptide from stomach. *Nature* 1999;402:656–660.

40. Callahan HS, Cummings DE, Pepe MS, Breen PA, Matthys CC, Weigle DS. Postprandial suppression of plasma ghrelin level is proportional to ingested caloric load but does not predict intermeal interval in humans. *J Clin Endocrinol Metab* 2004;89:1319–1324.

41. Tschop M, Smiley DL, Heiman ML. Ghrelin induces adiposity in rodents. *Nature* 2000;407:908–913.

42. Cowley MA, Smith RG, Diano S, et al. The distribution and mechanism of action of ghrelin in the CNS demonstrates a novel hypothalamic circuit regulating energy homeostasis. *Neuron* 2003;37:649–661.

43. Nakazato M, Murakami N, Date Y, et al. A role for ghrelin in the central regulation of feeding. *Nature* 2001;409:194–198.

44. Jerlhag E, Egecioglu E, Dickson SL, Douhan A, Svensson L, Engel JA. Ghrelin administration into tegmental areas stimulates locomotor activity and increases extracellular concentration of dopamine in the nucleus accumbens. *Addict Biol* 2007;12:6–16.

45. Berridge KC, Robinson TE. What is the role of dopamine in reward: hedonic impact, reward learning, or incentive salience? *Brain Res Brain Res Rev* 1998;28:309–369.

46. Blum ID, Patterson Z, Khazall R, et al. Reduced anticipatory locomotor responses to scheduled meals in ghrelin receptor deficient mice. *Neuroscience* 2009;164(2):351–359.

47. Aston-Jones G, Smith RJ, Sartor GC, et al. Lateral hypothalamic orexin/hypocretin neurons: a role in reward-seeking and addiction. *Brain Res* 2010;1314:74–90.

48. Beaver JD, Lawrence AD, van Ditzhuijzen J, Davis MH, Woods A, Calder AJ. Individual differences in reward drive predict neural responses to images of food. *J Neurosci* 2006;26:5160–5166.

49. Karra E, Chandarana K, Batterham RL. The role of peptide YY in appetite regulation and obesity. *J Physiol* 2009;587:19–25.

50. le Roux CW, Batterham RL, Aylwin SJ, et al. Attenuated peptide YY release in obese subjects is associated with reduced satiety. *Endocrinol* 2006; 147:3–8.

51. Farooqi IS, O'Rahilly S. Leptin: a pivotal regulator of human energy homeostasis. *Am J Clin Nutr* 2009;89:980S–984S.

52. Farooqi IS, Bullmore E, Keogh J, Gillard J, O'Rahilly S, Fletcher PC. Leptin regulates striatal regions and human eating behavior. *Science* 2007;317:1355.

53. Figlewicz DP, Benoit SC. Insulin, leptin, and food reward: update 2008. *Am J Physiol Regul Integr Comp Physiol* 2009;296:R9–R19.

54. Guthoff M, Grichisch Y, Canova C, et al. Insulin modulates food-related activity in the central nervous system. *J Clin Endocrinol Metab* 2010;95(2): 748–745.

31

Bingeing, Withdrawal, and Craving

An Animal Model of Sugar Addiction

NICOLE M. AVENA AND BARTLEY G. HOEBEL

WHY STUDY SUGAR ADDICTION?

In light of the recent publicity surrounding the obesity epidemic, the concept of "food addiction" has been popularized. In particular, clinical accounts of "sugar addiction" have been the topic of many books and popular diet programs.[1–5] In these accounts, people describe symptoms of withdrawal when they deprive themselves of sugar-rich foods, and these feelings are combined with food craving, particularly for carbohydrates, chocolate, and sugar, which can trigger impulsive eating. This leads to a vicious cycle of self-medication with sweet foods that, for some people, may result in obesity or an eating disorder. Although food addiction has been popular in the media and proposed to be based on brain neurochemistry,[6,7] this phenomenon has only recently been systematically studied in the laboratory.

Based on these clinical accounts of "sugar addiction" in people, it is clear that sweet taste can be a powerful reinforcer. This is further validated by studies of laboratory animals.[8] Rats born with a strong tendency to drink saccharin more rapidly learn to self-administer cocaine,[9] and rats will even prefer sugar over cocaine in some situations.[10] The concept of addiction in animals and the means by which it can be studied are rooted in the classical drug addiction literature. We have used models that were developed with rats for studying drug dependence and adapted them to test for signs of sugar dependence. In our animal model, rats are food deprived daily for 12 h, then are given food and a sugar solution (25% glucose or 10% sucrose) after a delay of 4 h into their normal circadian-driven active period to stimulate a large meal.[11] As a result, rats drink the sugar solution copiously, especially when it first becomes available each day (i.e., they binge),

and they ultimately enter a state that resembles drug dependence on several dimensions.

BEHAVIORAL EVIDENCE OF ADDICTION IN RATS BINGEING ON SUGAR

Before describing our data, it is best to define and qualify the terms we are using. The diagnostic criteria for dependence can be grouped into three stages.[12,13] *Bingeing* is defined as a high proportion of intake at one time, usually after a period of voluntary abstinence or forced deprivation. Signs of *withdrawal* become apparent when the abused substance is no longer available or chemically blocked. We will discuss withdrawal in terms of opiate withdrawal, which has a clearly defined set of behavioral signs.[14,15] *Craving* occurs when motivation to obtain a particular substance is enhanced, usually after a period of abstinence.

After a month on the intermittent, binge eating schedule outlined above, rats show a series of behaviors that resemble the effects of drugs of abuse (Table 31.1). These rats escalate their sugar intake and increase their intake during the first hour of daily access, which we define as a binge. In contrast, animals with ad libitum access to a sugar solution tend to drink it throughout the day, including during their inactive period. Both groups increase their overall intake, but the bingeing rats consume as much sugar in 12 h as the ad libitum-fed animals do in 24 h (Fig. 31.1). The bingeing rats regulate caloric intake by decreasing their chow consumption to compensate for the extra calories obtained from sugar, which results in a normal body weight.[16,17]

When administered a relatively high dose of the opioid antagonist naloxone, somatic signs

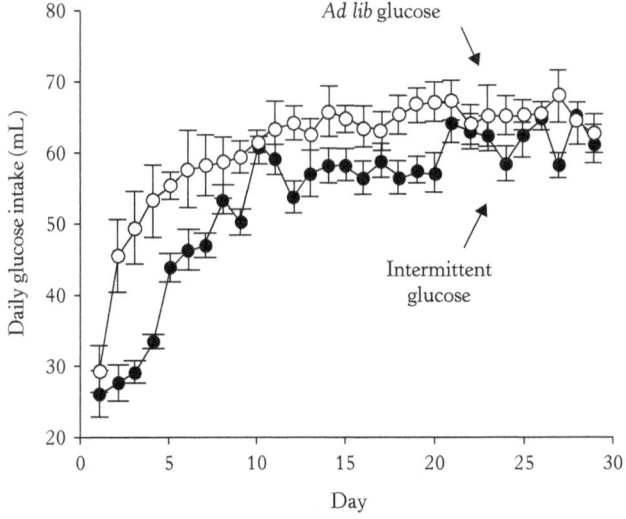

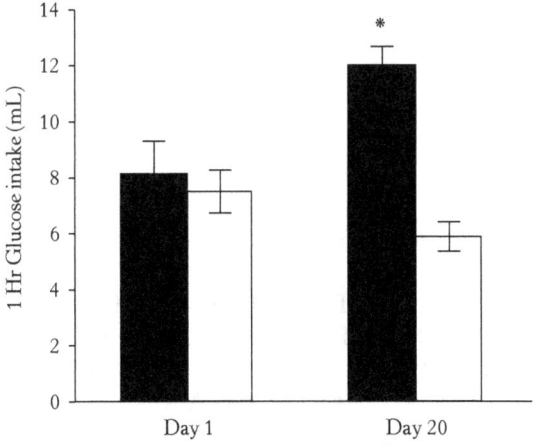

FIGURE 31.1. (A) Escalation of glucose intake. The mean volume of 25% glucose solution ingested by animals during daily intermittent 12-h access to glucose and chow (closed symbols) is similar to a group receiving ad libitum glucose solution and chow (open symbols). (B) The daily glucose intake during the first hour of access is the same on day 1 for the two groups, but by day 20, the bingeing rats (black bars) consumed more glucose in a 1-h binge compared to the rats that were fed glucose ad libitum ($*p < .05$).

Source: Adapted from Neuroreport, Vol. 12, C. Colantuoni et al, Excessive Sugar Intake Alters Binding to Dopamine and Mu-Opioid Receptors in the Brain, Copyright (2001), with permission from Wolters Kluwer Health.

of withdrawal, such as teeth chattering, forepaw tremor, and head shakes are observed in rats that have been bingeing on sugar for approximately 1 month.[17] These animals are also anxious, as measured by reduced time spent on the exposed arm of an elevated plus-maze.[17] Signs of opiate-like withdrawal also emerge when all food is removed for 24 h; this includes somatic signs such as teeth chattering, forepaw tremor, head shaking,[17] and anxiety as measured with an elevated plus-maze (Fig. 31.2).[11] The removal of sugar has been reported to decrease body temperature in rats,[18] which is another sign of opioid-like withdrawal, and signs of aggressive behavior have been noted in animals with history of intermittent sugar access.[19]

Craving is measured in rats as enhanced responding for sugar during sugar abstinence.[20] As

a measure of motivation, rats were trained to bar press for aliquots of 10% sucrose, and they pressed for sugar in a binge-like manner, just like animals with free access to a bottle of 10% sucrose.[11] We used operant conditioning and the "deprivation effect" paradigm to investigate consumption of sugar after abstinence in rats that had been bingeing on sugar for approximately 1 month. After 2 weeks of forced abstinence, these rats lever pressed for 23% more sugar than they ever did before (Fig. 31.3).[20] These results suggest a change in the motivational impact of sugar that persists throughout 2 weeks of abstinence, leading to enhanced intake. Research from other laboratories suggests that the motivation to obtain sugar appears to "incubate," or grow, with the duration of abstinence.[21] Using operant conditioning, Grimm and

TABLE 31.1. FINDINGS THAT SUGGEST MULTIPLE SIMILARITIES BETWEEN SUGAR ADDICTION IN ANIMAL SUBJECTS AND DRUG ADDICTION

Substance Dependence	Animal Model of Sugar Dependence
A. *DSM-IV-TR*	
Tolerance	Escalation of daily sugar intake (Colantuoni et al., 2001)
Signs of withdrawal	Somatic signs (teeth chattering, tremor)
	Anxiety measured by plus-maze
	Ultrasonic distress vocalizations (Colantuoni et al., 2002)
Consuming more than intended	Deprivation effect (Avena et al., 2005)
B. Behavioral Signs	
Locomotor cross-sensitization	Amphetamine (Avena and Hoebel, 2003)
Proclivity to consume other drugs of abuse	Alcohol (Avena et al., 2004)
C. Neurochemical Changes in the NAc	
Repeated release of DA	Rada et al., 2005; Avena et al., 2006
↑ D1 receptor binding	Colantuoni et al., 2001
↓ D2 receptor binding	Colantuoni et al., 2001
↑ D3 receptor mRNA	Spangler et al., 2004
↓ preproenkephalin mRNA	Spangler et al., 2004
DA/ACh imbalance during withdrawal	Colantuoni et al., 2002

ACh, acetylcholine; DA, dopamine; NAc, nuclear accumbens.

colleagues[22] find that sucrose seeking (measured by lever pressing for a sucrose-paired cue) increases during abstinence, and responding for the cue is greater after 30 days of sugar abstinence than after 1 week or 1 day. These results suggest that excessive motivation is generated by sugar self-administration on a binge-inducing schedule and then persists, even grows, as a result of abstinence.

Forced abstinence in sugar-bingeing rats has deleterious effects. In addition to causing increased motivation for sugar, abstinence causes a tendency to become hyperactive and to substitute another drug of abuse if made available. Hyperactivity as a sign of dopaminergic sensitization was shown in sugar-bingeing rats that were abstinent from sugar for 9 days, then given a low dose of amphetamine.[23] Sugar-induced sensitization of the dopamine (DA) system was confirmed by Gosnell,[24] using cocaine instead of amphetamine. In real-life contexts, this hyperactivity is probably channeled into searching for the substance of abuse, as illustrated by the enhanced lever pressing for sugar described above.

If sugar is not available, sugar-bingeing rats will ingest another substance of abuse. Rats with previous access to bingeing on sugar drank more 9% alcohol compared to the control groups with access to ad libitum sugar, ad libitum chow, or binge chow only (12 h of chow).[25] Thus, sugar appears to act as a gateway to enhanced alcohol use.

ADDICTIVE-LIKE NEUROCHEMICAL CHANGES IN RESPONSE TO BINGEING ON SUGAR

Unlike drugs of abuse, which effect DA release each time they are administered,[26,27] the effect of eating palatable food on DA release wanes with repeated access to a food, unless the animal is food deprived.[28–30] For example, control rats fed sugar or chow ad libitum, binge chow, or rats that taste sugar only two times develop a blunted DA response as is typical of a food that loses it novelty. Sugar bingeing rats, however, release DA every day, as measured on days 1, 2 and 21 of access,[30] and this release of DA seems to be elicited by the taste of sucrose as revealed by sham feeding, in which ingested food is drained from the stomach.[31] These results are supported by findings of alterations in accumbens DA turnover and DA transporter in rats maintained on an intermittent sugar-feeding schedule.[32,33]

Thus, intermittent access to sugar causes recurrent increases in extracellular DA in a manner that is more like a drug of abuse than a food. Consequently, changes in the expression or availability of DA receptors emerge.[34,35] Autoradiography reveals

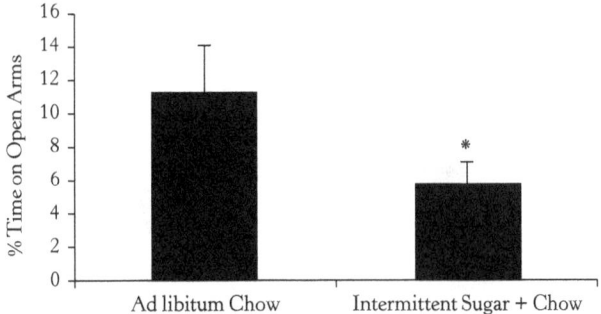

FIGURE 31.2. Percent of time spent on the open arm of the elevated plus-maze.

Rats that had been previously bingeing on sucrose (intermittent sugar + chow) spent significantly less time on the open arm following 36 h of fasting compared with an equally deprived ad libitum chow group. This suggests anxiety (*$p < .05$).

Source: Adapted from Physiology & Behavior, Vol. 94, N.M. Avena, et al, After daily bingeing on sucrose solution, food deprivation induces anxiety and accumbens dopamine/acetylcholine imbalance, 309–315, Copyright (2008), with permission from Elsevier.

increased D_1 in the nucleus accumbens (NAc) and decreased D_2 receptor binding in the striatum.[34] Others have reported a decrease in D_2 receptor binding in the NAc of rats with intermittent access to sucrose.[36] Rats bingeing on sugar show decreases in D_2 receptor mRNA in the NAc and increased D_3 receptor mRNA in the NAc and caudate-putamen, compared with ad libitum chow controls.[35]

Regarding opioid receptors, mu-receptor binding is increased in response to cocaine and morphine,[37–39] and enkephalin mRNA in the striatum and the NAc is decreased in response to repeated injections of morphine.[40–42] Likewise, in sugar-bingeing rats, mu-opioid receptor binding is significantly enhanced in the accumbens shell, cingulate, hippocampus, and locus coeruleus after 3 weeks of

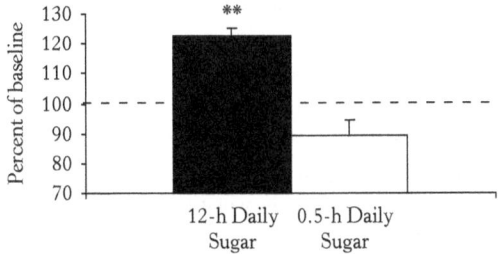

FIGURE 31.3. After 14 days of abstinence from sugar, the bingeing rats (Long-Access group; 12 h glucose/day) showed a significant increase in bar pressing for glucose; the control group (Short-Access group; 30-min glucose access/day) did not (**$p < 0.01$).

Source: Adapted from Physiology & Behavior, Vol. 84, N.M. Avena et al, Sugar-dependent rats show enhanced responding for sugar after abstinence. Evidence of a sugar deprivation effect, 359–362, Copyright (2005), with permission from Elsevier.

access, compared with rats given ad libitum chow.[34] Rats bingeing on sugar also have a significant decrease in enkephalin mRNA,[35] which is consistent with findings in rats with limited daily access to a sweet-fat, liquid diet.[43] Assuming this decrease in mRNA results in less enkephalin peptide being synthesized and released, this could account for a compensatory increase in mu-opioid receptors.

We find that drug withdrawal is usually accompanied by alterations in DA/acetylcholine (ACh) balance in the NAc. Abstinence from an abused substance is also sufficient to elicit a decrease in extracellular DA in the NAc.[44,45] During withdrawal, extracellular DA decreases while ACh release is increased.[46–48] This imbalance has been shown during withdrawal with several drugs of abuse, including morphine, nicotine, and alcohol.[49–51] Rats that have intermittent access to sugar and chow show the same neurochemical imbalance in DA/ACh during withdrawal. This is produced (1) when they are given naloxone to precipitate opioid withdrawal,[17] and (2) after 36 h of total food deprivation (Fig. 31.4).[16] It is possible that deprivation-induced withdrawal releases opioids, and the rat experiences the same type of withdrawal as when the up-regulated mu-opioid receptors are blocked with naloxone.

CLINICAL IMPLICATIONS AND CONCLUSIONS

We propose the theory that intermittent, excessive intake of sugar can have dopaminergic, cholinergic, and opioid effects that are similar to those seen in response to some drugs of abuse, albeit smaller in magnitude. Based on the behavioral

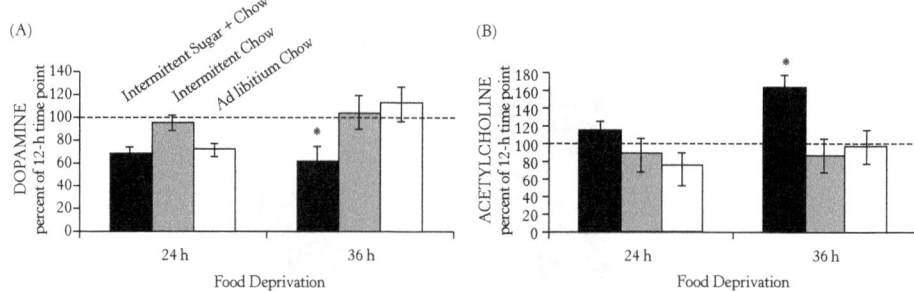

FIGURE 31.4. Extracellular dopamine (DA) and acetylcholine (Ach) in the nucleus accumbens (NAc) following 24 and 36 h of fasting. (A) After 36 h of fasting, DA release in the bingeing rats (intermittent sugar+chow group; black bar) was significantly less than both the intermittent chow (gray bar) and ad libitum chow (white bar) control groups. (B) Extracellular ACh was significantly increased in the bingeing rats (intermittent sugar+chow group) at the 36 h fasting point compared with both control groups. *$p < .05$ compared with both intermittent chow and ad libitum chow.
Source: Adapted from Physiology & Behavior, Vol. 94, N.M. Avena, et al, After daily bingeing on sucrose solution, food deprivation induces anxiety and accumbens dopamine/acetylcholine imbalance, 309–315, Copyright (2008), with permission from Elsevier.

and neurochemical similarities between the effects of intermittent sugar access and drugs of abuse, we suggest that sugar meets the criteria for a substance of abuse and may be "addictive" for some individuals when consumed in a binge-like manner. Changes in limbic system neurochemistry that are similar for drugs and sugar reinforce this conclusion. Although the effects are smaller in magnitude than those produced by a drug of abuse such as cocaine or morphine, the fact that these behaviors and neurochemical changes can be elicited with a natural reinforcer is convincing.

The binge eating schedule we have employed shares some characteristics of the behavioral pattern of people diagnosed with binge-eating disorder or bulimia. Bulimics often restrict intake early in the day and then binge later in the evening, usually on palatable foods.[52,53] Bulimic patients have low β-endorphin levels,[54,55] which might foster eating with a preference or craving for sweets. They also show decreased mu-opioid receptor binding in the insula compared with controls, which correlates with recent fasting behavior.[56] Bulimic patients will binge on excessive amounts of noncaloric sweeteners.[57] These patients later purge the food, either by vomiting, using laxatives, or, in some cases, by engaging in strenuous exercise.[12] We used the sham feeding preparation mentioned earlier to mimic the purging associated with bulimia and found that in response to the sweet taste of sugar, bingeing repeatedly released DA.[31] This finding may help in understanding the bingeing behaviors associated with bulimia. It has been reported that bulimic

patients have low central DA activity as reflected in analysis of DA metabolites in the spinal fluid, which may indicate a role for DA in their abnormal responses to food.[58]

Obesity is one of the leading preventable causes of death in the United States.[59] Several studies have correlated a rise in the incidence of obesity with an increase in sugar consumption.[60–63] The US Department of Agriculture has reported that per capita soft drink consumption has increased by almost 500% in the past 50 years.[64] However, as noted in the beginning of this chapter, after 1 month on the diet using 10% sucrose or 25% glucose, sugar-bingeing rats do not become overweight, although others have reported aspects of metabolic syndrome,[65] a loss of fuel efficiency,[66] and an increase in body weight in rats fed sucrose[67,68] and glucose.[18] It is important to note that most studies of sugar intake and body weight do not use a binge-inducing diet. In our model the rats compensate for sucrose or glucose calories by decreasing chow intake.[16] Bingeing on sucrose or glucose appears to result in a normal body weight, but this may not be true for all sugars.[69] Once obese, animals[70] and people [71] show low DA function and low D_2 receptor binding, like drug- or sugar-dependent animals. Thus, some of the characteristics of addiction we have described for bingeing rats may also occur as a result of obesity.

In conclusion, certain people, including some obese and bulimic patients in particular, may develop an unhealthy dependence on palatable food that interferes with well-being. The rise in obesity, coupled with the scientific evidence of similarities between drugs of abuse and sugar, has given credibility to this idea. The model described in this chapter provides evidence that supports the theory that, in some circumstances, intermittent access to sugar can lead to behavioral and neurochemical changes that resemble the effects of a substance of abuse. This constitutes evidence for sugar addiction.

ACKNOWLEDGMENTS

This research was supported by USPHS grant MH-65024 (B. G. H.), DA-10608 (B. G. H.), AA-12882, DA-079793 and DA-03123 (N. M .A).

REFERENCES

1. Appleton N. *Lick the Sugar Habit.* Santa Monica, CA: Avery Publishing Group, 1996.
2. Rufus EB. *Sugar Addiction: A Step-by-Step Guide to Overcoming Sugar Addiction.* Bloomington, IN: AuthorHouse, 2004.
3. DesMaisons K. *Your Last Diet! The Sugar Addict's Weight-Loss Plan.* Toronto: Random House, 2001.
4. Katherine A. *Anatomy of a Food Addiction: An Effective Program to Overcome Compulsive Eating.* Carlsbad, NM: Gurze Books, 1996.
5. Bennett C, Sinatra S. *Sugar Shock!* New York: Penguin Group, 2007.
6. Hoebel BG, Hernandez L, Schwartz DH, Mark GP, Hunter GA. Microdialysis studies of brain norepinephrine, serotonin, and dopamine release during ingestive behavior. Theoretical and clinical implications. *Ann NY Acad Sci* 1989;575:171–191.
7. Le Magnen J. A role for opiates in food reward and food addiction. In: Capaldi PT, ed. *Taste, Experience, and Feeding.* Washington, DC: American Psychological Association; 1990: 241–252.
8. Bonacchi KB, Ackroff K, Sclafani A. Sucrose taste but not polycose taste conditions flavor preferences in rats. *Physiol Behav* 2008;95(1–2):235–244.
9. Perry JL, Nelson SE, Anderson MM, Morgan AD, Carroll ME. Impulsivity (delay discounting) for food and cocaine in male and female rats selectively bred for high and low saccharin intake. *Pharmacol Biochem Behav* 2007;86(4):822–837.
10. Lenoir M, Serre F, Cantin L, Ahmed SH. Intense sweetness surpasses cocaine reward. *PloS One* 2007; 2(1):e698.
11. Avena NM, Bocarsly ME, Rada P, Kim A, Hoebel BG. After daily bingeing on a sucrose solution, food deprivation induces anxiety and accumbens dopamine/acetylcholine imbalance. *Physiol Behav* 2008;94(3): 309–315.
12. American Psychiatric Association. *Diagnostic and Statistical Manual of Mental Disorders.* 4th ed. Washington, DC: American Psychiatric Association, 2000.
13. Koob GF, Le Moal M. Drug abuse: hedonic homeostatic dysregulation. *Science* 1997;278(5335):52–58.
14. Martin WR, Wikler A, Eades CG, Pescor FT. Tolerance to and physical dependence on morphine in rats. *Psychopharmacologia* 1963;4:247–260.
15. Way EL, Loh HH, Shen FH. Simultaneous quantitative assessment of morphine tolerance and physical dependence. *J Pharmacol Exp Ther* 1969;167(1):1–8.
16. Avena NM, Rada P, Hoebel BG. Evidence for sugar addiction: behavioral and neurochemical effects of intermittent, excessive sugar intake. *Neurosci Biobehav Rev* 2008;32(1):20–39.
17. Colantuoni C, Rada P, McCarthy J, et al. Evidence that intermittent, excessive sugar intake causes endogenous opioid dependence. *Obes Res* 2002;10(6): 478–488.
18. Wideman CH, Nadzam GR, Murphy HM. Implications of an animal model of sugar addiction, withdrawal and relapse for human health. *Nutr Neurosci* 2005;8(5–6):269–276.
19. Galic MA, Persinger MA. Voluminous sucrose consumption in female rats: increased "nippiness" during periods of sucrose removal and possible oestrus periodicity. *Psychol Rep* 2002;90(1):58–60.
20. Avena NM, Long KA, Hoebel BG. Sugar-dependent rats show enhanced responding for sugar after abstinence: evidence of a sugar deprivation effect. *Physiol Behav* 2005;84(3):359–362.
21. Shalev U, Morales M, Hope B, Yap J, Shaham Y. Time-dependent changes in extinction behavior and stress-induced reinstatement of drug seeking following withdrawal from heroin in rats. *Psychopharmacol* 2001;156(1):98–107.
22. Grimm JW, Fyall AM, Osincup DP. Incubation of sucrose craving: effects of reduced training and sucrose pre-loading. *Physiol Behav* 2005;84(1):73–79.
23. Avena NM, Hoebel BG. Amphetamine-sensitized rats show sugar-induced hyperactivity (cross-sensitization) and sugar hyperphagia. *Pharmacol Biochem Behav* 2003;74(3):635–639.
24. Gosnell BA. Sucrose intake enhances behavioral sensitization produced by cocaine. *Brain Res* 2005; 1031(2):194–201.
25. Avena NM, Carrillo CA, Needham L, Leibowitz SF, Hoebel BG. Sugar-dependent rats show enhanced intake of unsweetened ethanol. *Alcohol* 2004;34 (2–3):203–209.
26. Pothos E, Rada P, Mark GP, Hoebel BG. Dopamine microdialysis in the nucleus accumbens during acute and chronic morphine, naloxone-precipitated withdrawal and clonidine treatment. *Brain Res* 1991; 566(1–2):348–350.
27. Wise RA, Newton P, Leeb K, Burnette B, Pocock D, Justice JB, Jr. Fluctuations in nucleus accumbens dopamine concentration during intravenous cocaine self-administration in rats. *Psychopharmacol* 1995; 120(1):10–20.

28. Bassareo V, Di Chiara G. Modulation of feeding-induced activation of mesolimbic dopamine transmission by appetitive stimuli and its relation to motivational state. *Eur J Neurosci* 1999;11(12):4389–4397.

29. Di Chiara G, Tanda G. Blunting of reactivity of dopamine transmission to palatable food: a biochemical marker of anhedonia in the CMS model? *Psychopharmacol* 1997;134(4):351–353.

30. Rada P, Avena NM, Hoebel BG. Daily bingeing on sugar repeatedly releases dopamine in the accumbens shell. *Neurosci* 2005;134(3):737–744.

31. Avena NM, Rada P, Moise N, Hoebel BG. Sucrose sham feeding on a binge schedule releases accumbens dopamine repeatedly and eliminates the acetylcholine satiety response. *Neurosci* 2006;139:813–820.

32. Hajnal A, Norgren R. Repeated access to sucrose augments dopamine turnover in the nucleus accumbens. *Neuroreport* 2002;13(17):2213–2216.

33. Bello NT, Sweigart KL, Lakoski JM, Norgren R, Hajnal A. Restricted feeding with scheduled sucrose access results in an upregulation of the rat dopamine transporter. *Am J Physiol* 2003;284(5):R1260–R1268.

34. Colantuoni C, Schwenker J, McCarthy J, et al. Excessive sugar intake alters binding to dopamine and mu-opioid receptors in the brain. *Neuroreport* 2001;12(16):3549–3552.

35. Spangler R, Wittkowski KM, Goddard NL, Avena NM, Hoebel BG, Leibowitz SF. Opiate-like effects of sugar on gene expression in reward areas of the rat brain. *Brain Res Mol Brain Res* 2004;124(2):134–142.

36. Bello NT, Lucas LR, Hajnal A. Repeated sucrose access influences dopamine D2 receptor density in the striatum. *Neuroreport* 2002;13(12):1575–1578.

37. Bailey A, Gianotti R, Ho A, Kreek MJ. Persistent upregulation of mu-opioid, but not adenosine, receptors in brains of long-term withdrawn escalating dose "binge" cocaine-treated rats. *Synapse* 2005;57(3):160–166.

38. Vigano D, Rubino T, Di Chiara G, Ascari I, Massi P, Parolaro D. Mu opioid receptor signaling in morphine sensitization. *Neurosci* 2003;117(4):921–929.

39. Unterwald EM, Kreek MJ, Cuntapay M. The frequency of cocaine administration impacts cocaine-induced receptor alterations. *Brain Res* 2001;900(1):103–109.

40. Uhl GR, Ryan JP, Schwartz JP. Morphine alters preproenkephalin gene expression. *Brain Res* 1988;459(2):391–397.

41. Turchan J, Lason W, Budziszewska B, Przewlocka B. Effects of single and repeated morphine administration on the prodynorphin, proenkephalin and dopamine D2 receptor gene expression in the mouse brain. *Neuropeptides* 1997;31(1):24–28.

42. Georges F, Stinus L, Bloch B, Le Moine C. Chronic morphine exposure and spontaneous withdrawal are associated with modifications of dopamine receptor and neuropeptide gene expression in the rat striatum. *Eur J Neurosci* 1999;11(2):481–490.

43. Kelley AE, Will MJ, Steininger TL, Zhang M, Haber SN. Restricted daily consumption of a highly palatable food (chocolate Ensure(R)) alters striatal enkephalin gene expression. *Eur J Neurosci* 2003;18(9):2592–2598.

44. Acquas E, Di Chiara G. Depression of mesolimbic dopamine transmission and sensitization to morphine during opiate abstinence. *J Neurochem* 1992;58(5):1620–1625.

45. Rossetti ZL, Hmaidan Y, Gessa GL. Marked inhibition of mesolimbic dopamine release: a common feature of ethanol, morphine, cocaine and amphetamine abstinence in rats. *Eur J Pharmacol* 1992;221(2–3):227–234.

46. Rada P, Pothos E, Mark GP, Hoebel BG. Microdialysis evidence that acetylcholine in the nucleus accumbens is involved in morphine withdrawal and its treatment with clonidine. *Brain Res* 1991;561(2):354–356.

47. Fiserova M, Consolo S, Krsiak M. Chronic morphine induces long-lasting changes in acetylcholine release in rat nucleus accumbens core and shell: an in vivo microdialysis study. *Psychopharmacol* 1999;142(1):85–94.

48. Hoebel BG, Avena NM, Rada P. Accumbens dopamine-acetylcholine balance in approach and avoidance. *Curr Opin Pharmacol* 2007;7(6):617–627.

49. Rada P, Jensen K, Hoebel BG. Effects of nicotine and mecamylamine-induced withdrawal on extracellular dopamine and acetylcholine in the rat nucleus accumbens. *Psychopharmacol* 2001;157(1):105–110.

50. Rada P, Johnson DF, Lewis MJ, Hoebel BG. In alcohol-treated rats, naloxone decreases extracellular dopamine and increases acetylcholine in the nucleus accumbens: evidence of opioid withdrawal. *Pharmacol Biochem Behav* 2004;79(4):599–605.

51. Rada PV, Mark GP, Taylor KM, Hoebel BG. Morphine and naloxone, i.p. or locally, affect extracellular acetylcholine in the accumbens and prefrontal cortex. *Pharmacol Biochem Behav* 1996;53(4):809–816.

52. Drewnowski A, Krahn DD, Demitrack MA, Nairn K, Gosnell BA. Taste responses and preferences for sweet high-fat foods: evidence for opioid involvement. *Physiol Behav* 1992;51(2):371–379.

53. Gendall KA, Sullivan PE, Joyce PR, Carter FA, Bulik CM. The nutrient intake of women with bulimia nervosa. *Int J Eat Disorder* 1997;21(2):115–127.

54. Waller DA, Kiser RS, Hardy BW, Fuchs I, Feigenbaum LP, Uauy R. Eating behavior and plasma beta-endorphin in bulimia. *Am J Clin Nutr* 1986;44(1):20–23.

55. Brewerton TD, Lydiard RB, Laraia MT, Shook JE, Ballenger JC. CSF beta-endorphin and dynorphin in bulimia nervosa. *Am J Psychiat* 1992;149(8):1086–1090.

56. Bencherif B, Guarda AS, Colantuoni C, Ravert HT, Dannals RF, Frost JJ. Regional mu-opioid receptor binding in insular cortex is decreased in bulimia ner-

vosa and correlates inversely with fasting behavior. *J Nucl Med* 2005;46(8):1349–1351.

57. Klein DA, Boudreau GS, Devlin MJ, Walsh BT. Artificial sweetener use among individuals with eating disorders. *Int J Eat Disord* 2006;39(4):341–345.

58. Jimerson DC, Lesem MD, Kaye WH, Brewerton TD. Low serotonin and dopamine metabolite concentrations in cerebrospinal fluid from bulimic patients with frequent binge episodes. *Arch Gen Psychiatry* 1992;49(2):132–138.

59. Mokdad AH, Marks JS, Stroup DF, Gerberding JL. Actual causes of death in the United States, 2000. *JAMA* 2004;291(10):1238–1245.

60. Bray GA, York B, DeLany J. A survey of the opinions of obesity experts on the causes and treatment of obesity. *Am J Clin Nutr* 1992;55(1 suppl): 151S-154S.

61. Ludwig DS, Peterson KE, Gortmaker SL. Relation between consumption of sugar-sweetened drinks and childhood obesity: a prospective, observational analysis. *Lancet* 2001;357(9255):505–508.

62. Elliott SS, Keim NL, Stern JS, Teff K, Havel PJ. Fructose, weight gain, and the insulin resistance syndrome. *Am J Clin Nutr* 2002;76(5):911–922.

63. Howard BV, Wylie-Rosett J. Sugar and cardiovascular disease: a statement for healthcare professionals from the Committee on Nutrition of the Council on Nutrition, Physical Activity, and Metabolism of the American Heart Association. *Circulation* 2002;106(4): 523–527.

64. Putnam J, Allhouse JE. *Food Consumption, Prices, and Expenditures, 1970–1997.* Washington, DC: Food and Consumers Economics Division, Economics Research Service, U. S. Department of Agriculture, 1999. Statistical Bulletin No. SB-965.

65. Toida S, Takahashi M, Shimizu H, Sato N, Shimomura Y, Kobayashi I. Effect of high sucrose feeding on fat accumulation in the male Wistar rat. *Obes Res* 1996;4(6):561–568.

66. Levine AS, Kotz CM, Gosnell BA. Sugars: hedonic aspects, neuroregulation, and energy balance. *Am J Clin Nutr* 2003;78(4):834S–842S.

67. Bock BC, Kanarek RB, Aprille JR. Mineral content of the diet alters sucrose-induced obesity in rats. *Physiol Behav* 1995;57(4):659–668.

68. Kawasaki T, Kashiwabara A, Sakai T, et al. Long-term sucrose-drinking causes increased body weight and glucose intolerance in normal male rats. *Brit J Nutr* 2005;93(5):613–618.

69. Bocarsly ME, Powell E, Avena NM, Hoebel BG. High-fructose corn syrup causes characteristics of obesity in rats: increased body weight, body fat and triglyceride levels. *Pharmacol Biochem Behav* 2010;97(1):101–106.

70. Geiger BM, Behr GG, Frank LE, et al. Evidence for defective mesolimbic dopamine exocytosis in obesity-prone rats. *FASEB J* 2008;22(8):2740–2746.

71. Wang GJ, Volkow ND, Thanos PK, Fowler JS. Similarity between obesity and drug addiction as assessed by neurofunctional imaging: a concept review. *J Addict Dis* 2004;23(3):39–53.

32

Incubation of Sucrose Craving in Animal Models

JEFFREY W. GRIMM

The "obesity epidemic" now has a global reach. Over 1 billion of the world's adult population is overweight with the number of obese above 300 million.[1] Childhood overweight and obesity prevalence doubled to tripled from 1980 to 2006.[2] Blame for the dramatic increase in overweight and obese individuals has fallen primarily on increased consumption of highly palatable, calorie-dense foods,[1–3] along with decreased physical activity.[1,2] Almost by definition of overweight or obese, the increased caloric consumption is eating outside of caloric need.

Factors that drive this excess consumption include the "obesigenic environment," where not only are rich foods readily available but reminders of their existence are in place in media and in social environments, including schools and the workplace. Most people are well aware of how advertising and social situations can lead them to eat when they are not hungry. These environmental cues are frustrating for healthy individuals watching their weight, but for obese individuals and/or individuals that suffer from compulsive overeating regardless of body weight, they can serve as an overwhelming push to eat—further contributing to their disease.

The propensity to seek and consume foods rich in energy is considered to be an adaptation to an environment where food is not consistently plentiful.[4] To survive in such an environment, for example, across seasonal variation in vegetation, an individual would require the ability to identify food resources that have high nutritional value, remember the type and locations of the food, and in some instances ingest quantities of the food far in excess of current caloric need. Most studied in mammals, although rudimentary forms have been identified in other non-chordate phyla, including Drosophila[5] and planaria,[6] these adaptive behaviors map on to memory and motivational brain systems often referred to as the brain reward system.[7] Elements of this system that

include limbic brain regions tied to motivated behavioral output [8] have drawn the interest of drug addiction researchers in the past several decades. Within this framework, much progress has been made in elucidating the neurobiology of drug addiction.

Drug self-administration by nonhuman animals, as a model of clinical addiction, has often been presented as a special case of motivated behavior. In fact, it is not uncommon to find food self-administration studies conducted in parallel with drugs to serve as a "control" to isolate drug-specific effects. In some cases there is the implication that the rewarding effects of food and drug are therefore served by different neurobehavioral systems. Certainly each has its particular substrates, for example, putative glucose-sensing neurons in the hypothalamus [9] versus cocaine acting directly on dopamine transporter protein in the nucleus accumbens,[7] but what is more likely is that the general neurobehavior is conserved. Interestingly, much of the original concept of the reward system came from non-drug research, in particular electrical brain self-stimulation and food self-administration.[10,11] As drug addiction is characterized by extremes, it would be expected that an addiction to food would also lead to pertubations in the reward system.

Evidence for this has already been identified in rat studies. For example, a high-fat diet enhances the motivation to consume sucrose,[12] and a dam fed a high-fat diet produces offspring that have hypothalamic neurons (part of the reward system) that are increased in sensitivity to glucose and production of orexigenic peptides, neurotransmitters that promote feeding.[9,13] Furthermore, treatment of a food addiction would be a more daunting challenge compared to drug addiction in some respects as the reward system in question likely evolved selective for food. There would be less flexibility in this system in regard to food. Thereby food as a control condition for drug addiction may have many limitations. Better yet, food may best serve as a target of addiction research in its own right.

It is clear that there are several features of uncontrolled eating that resemble criteria for addiction to drugs as defined by the American Psychiatric Association. For example, addiction to drugs is characterized by intense craving and ensuing compulsive drug-seeking.[14] Individuals who have trouble avoiding excessive food intake also experience intense craving and will focus their behaviors on acquiring food.[15] Much remains to be done to validate food addiction within the scientific and clinical communities, although progress is being made on both fronts.[16,17] To this end, from a basic science perspective, we and a handful of other laboratories have been examining sucrose as a substance with addictive qualities. In our laboratory we have focused on sucrose craving as the addiction behavior of interest. As indicated earlier, intense craving is part of the definition of addiction.

Craving is, however, a rather complicated phenomenon to define and therefore measure in humans.[18] In addition, at least for alcohol, subjective indications of craving are often poor predictors of subsequent relapse.[19] Tiffany has suggested a cognitive model to account for this discrepancy, where an unconscious reaction to drug-predictive stimuli engages drug seeking within the individual. This reaction then may or may not activate cognitive awareness and, if so, this would be experienced as craving.[20] We and others[21,22] argue that the unconscious reaction, an unconscious craving, is an important target for basic research with the goal of translational therapies for addiction. A recent brain imaging study lends support for unconscious reaction to either drug or nondrug appetitive stimuli. Not surprisingly, circuits within the reward system are activated upon exposure of an individual to these cues outside of conscious awareness.[23]

It is reasonable to assume that this type of reaction could contribute to increased approach and consumption of food following exposure to food-predictive cues. This unconscious craving behavior would therefore be a key element of relapse behavior. As rats are without the self-awareness of humans, yet share the reward system, they provide a strong model system for study of craving, including food craving. Our particular approach has been to characterize sucrose-craving behavior in rats utilizing a rat model of relapse initially designed to examine cocaine relapse. Rats learn to self-administer either

drug or food in daily self-administration sessions wherein responding on a lever delivers both the reward and a tone + light stimulus. Craving behavior is then examined in a subsequent test session wherein the reward is no longer available. In this session, rats will reliably respond for presentations of the tone + light stimulus.[24] This responding serves as our operational definition of craving.

INCUBATION OF CRAVING

One element of craving that we have identified in the animal model to be of great potential relevance to human food addiction behaviors is how the length of time following reward self-administration influences reward craving. Specifically, over several weeks of abstinence from a reward, rats respond progressively more for the reward-paired cue upon returning to the reward self-administration environment. We first described this effect, an "incubation of craving" in rats that had self-administered cocaine. This first discovery was that rats in prolonged abstinence from cocaine self-administration will work harder pressing a lever for the presentation of a tone + light cue (no drug) that was previously paired with their cocaine compared to rats in very early abstinence (Fig. 32.1).[25]

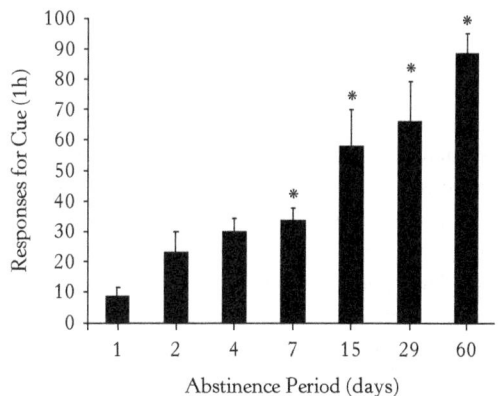

FIGURE 32.1. Incubation of cocaine craving in rats. Rats first had 10 days of 6 h/day access to cocaine self-administration (0.5 mg/kg per infusion) in operant chambers. After 1 to 60 days of forced abstinence in the home cage, rats were allowed to respond for a cocaine-paired stimulus in the operant chambers for 1 h. Asterisk indicates significant difference from day 1, $p < 0.05$, $n = 9$–11 per group.

Source: Reprinted by permission from Macmillan Publishers Ltd: *Nature*, Vol. 412, J.W. Grimm, et al, Neuroadaptation: Incubation of cocaine craving after withdrawal, Copyright (2001), Nature Publishing Group.

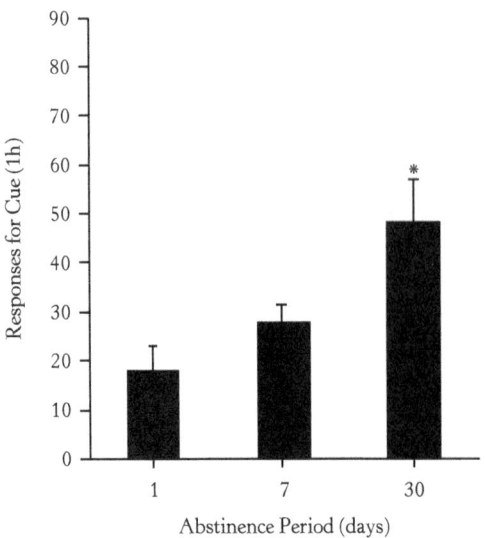

FIGURE 32.2. Incubation of sucrose craving in rats. Rats first had 10 days of 6 h/day access to 10% sucrose self-administration in operant chambers. After 1, 7, or 30 days of forced abstinence in the home cages, rats were allowed to respond for a sucrose-paired stimulus in the operant chambers for 1 h. Asterisk indicates significant difference from day 1, $p < 0.05$, $n = 8-9$ per group.

Source: Reprinted from Physiology & Behavior, Vol. 84, J.W. Grimm, et al, Incubation of sucrose craving: effects of reduced training and sucrose pre-loading, 7, Copyright (2005), wither permission from Elsevier.

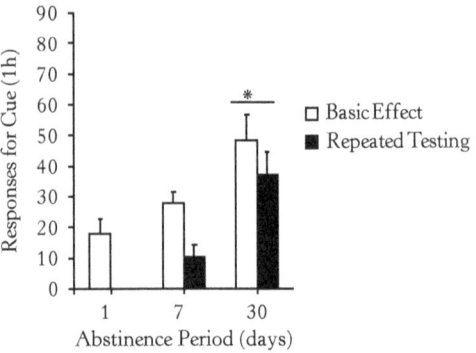

FIGURE 32.3. Effect of repeated craving testing on incubation of sucrose craving. Rats were trained as described in Figure 32.2. Black bars indicate that rats were then allowed to respond for a sucrose-paired stimulus in the operant chambers for 1 h on days 1, 7, and 30 of forced abstinence. White bars indicate independent group testing as depicted in Figure 32.2. Asterisk indicates significant difference from day 1 (both groups), $p < 0.05$, $n = 8-9$ per group.

Source: Reprinted from Physiology & Behavior, Vol. 84, J.W. Grimm, et al, Incubation of sucrose craving: effects of reduced training and sucrose pre-loading, 7, Copyright (2005), with permission from Elsevier.

INCUBATION OF SUCROSE CRAVING

We subsequently observed incubation of craving for sucrose (Fig. 32.2).[26] In these studies, rats had previously self-administered sucrose by drinking a drop of sucrose solution. As with the cocaine study, each delivery of sucrose depended on pressing a lever and each delivery was accompanied by a tone + light cue.[27]

Incubation of sucrose craving is an extremely robust phenomenon. For example, we see this time-dependent increase in responding for a sucrose-paired cue even when the rats are tested multiple times (Fig. 32.3).[26] Modern learning theory would predict that repeated exposure to the testing condition would lead to a decrease in responding over time, otherwise known as extinction.

In addition, prolonged access to sucrose ("satiety") up to the beginning of a test session was without effect at reducing incubation of sucrose craving (Fig. 32.4).[26] This finding supports a hypothesis that craving in response to sucrose-paired cues

becomes dissociated from sucrose itself. If this is true, it helps to explain how cues activate food craving and associated seeking (and intake) even when the individual feels "full."

We have also looked for evidence of incubation of craving with a nonnutritive sweetener as recent findings from both rat and human studies indicate that these sweeteners in "diet" foods may actually increase caloric intake from other sources.[28,29] We found an incubation of craving for sucralose (Splenda®) in animals that had self-administered sucralose solution in the same procedure we have used to examine sucrose craving (Fig. 32.5).

As noted earlier, the brain substrates of drug and food craving have substantial overlap as they both characterize the brain reward system.[30] The nexus of these cravings may be circuits in the brain that rely on the neurotransmitter dopamine.[31] These circuits include connections both in the higher order thinking parts of the brain, the cortex, and in subcortical structures that mediate our behavioral output, including how we respond to signals in the environment indicating availability of drugs or food.[24] Using our animal model of craving, we have performed several studies to identify the neural substrates of the incubation of craving for both cocaine and sucrose. For example, we found that

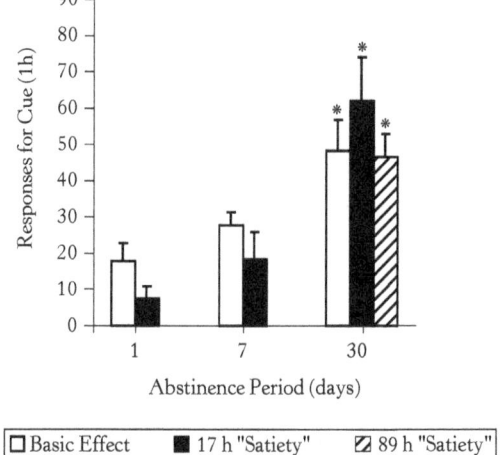

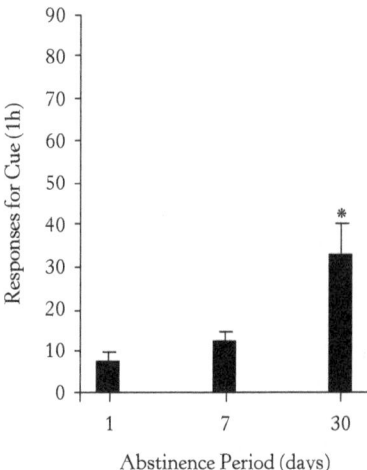

FIGURE 32.4. Effect of 17 h (black bars) or 89 h (striped bar) free consumption of sucrose immediately prior to a sucrose craving test session after either 1, 7, or 30 days of forced abstinence from sucrose self-administration. Other than the "satiety" manipulation, training and testing parameters were as described in Figure 32.2. * indicates significant difference from day 1, basic effect, $p < 0.05$, $n = 8$–9 per group.
Source: Reprinted from Physiology & Behavior, Vol. 84, J.W. Grimm, et al, Incubation of sucrose craving: effects of reduced training and sucrose pre-loading, 7, Copyright (2005), wither permission from Elsevier.

FIGURE 32.5. Incubation of sucralose (Splenda®) craving in rats. Rats first had 10 days of 6 h/day access to 1.25% sucralose self-administration in operant chambers. After 1, 7, or 30 days of forced abstinence in the home cages, rats were allowed to respond for a sucralose-paired stimulus in the operant chambers for 1 h. Asterisk indicates significant difference from day 1, $p < 0.05$, $n = 7$–8 per group.
Source: Reprinted from Physiology & Behavior, Vol. 84, J.W. Grimm, et al, Incubation of sucrose craving: effects of reduced training and sucrose pre-loading, 7, Copyright (2005), wither permission from Elsevier.

acute cocaine was less effective at potentiating craving in rats 1 month versus 1 day into forced abstinence.[32] We interpret this finding as a tolerance of the response of the mesolimbic dopamine system to cocaine, perhaps due to already elevated levels of dopamine related to the incubation of craving. In other ongoing studies, we have found evidence indicating that the basolateral amygdala mediates cue-induced craving for both drug and food, and that the nucleus accumbens contributes to the time-dependent increase in craving for both drug and food.[33] These brain regions are components of the subcortical circuits, noted earlier, that mediate how we respond to signals in the environment indicating availability of drugs or food. In addition, both of these structures are activated by the neurotransmitter dopamine. We have thus far found that while systemic injection of a dopamine D1 receptor antagonist preferentially decreases sucrose craving after 1 versus 30 days of forced abstinence, injection of the antagonist into subregions of the nucleus accumbens reduces sucrose craving to a similar extent at both forced abstinence time points.[34] It is possible that incubation of craving is

mediated by dopamine receptors in sites outside of the nucleus accumbens, and it also has been shown that neurotransmitter systems in other brain regions contribute to the effect. For example, our colleagues at the National Institutes of Health have found a critical role for metabotropic glutamate receptors in the central nucleus of the amygdala in the incubation of sucrose craving.[35]

In other studies examining the incubation of sucrose craving at a more general behavioral and pharmacological level, we have found that incubation of sucrose craving can be attenuated by an opiate antagonist,[36] and also by 1 month of environmental enrichment.[37] In a recent study we have found that a conditioned taste aversion is effective at reducing sucrose craving only after several weeks of forced abstinence—indicating that some aspect(s) of the reward system changes along with, or due to, the incubation of craving.[38]

INCUBATION OF CRAVING AND FOOD ADDICTION

Incubation of sucrose craving has not *yet* been documented in humans. It is fact, though, that many obese dieters actually gain weight,[39] and it is possible that incubation of craving accounts for some portion of diet recidivism. Incubation of craving for cocaine,[40,41] heroin,[42] and cigarettes[43-45] has been observed. Given the overlap between behavioral and neural substrates of drug and food craving, it is likely incubation of sucrose (and other food) craving occurs and has an important role in unhealthy eating behaviors. Related to this point, we have observed in several of our studies that actual sucrose consumption *increases* after several weeks of abstinence. If there is such a coemergence of incubation of sucrose craving and consumption in humans, it is not surprising that abstaining from sugar may become an unachievable goal in some food addicts. We hope that gaining a basic science understanding of behavioral and neurobiological aspects of the incubation of craving will be of use for developing effective therapies for food addiction and related diseases such as obesity.

REFERENCES

1. World Health Organization. Obesity and overweight. 2011. Available at: http://www.who.int/mediacentre/factsheets/fs311/en/. Accessed April 5, 2012.
2. Centers for Disease Control and Prevention. Childhood overweight and obesity. 2011. Available at: http://www.cdc.gov/obesity/childhood/index.html. Accessed April 5, 2012,
3. Drewnowski A. The real contribution of added sugars and fats to obesity. *Epidemiol Rev* 2007;29:160–171.
4. Ulijaszek SJ. Obesity: a disorder of convenience. *Obes Rev* 2007;8(suppl 1):183–187.
5. Tempel BL, Bonini N, Dawson DR, Quinn WG. Reward learning in normal and mutant Drosophila. *Proc Natl Acad Sci USA* 1983;80:1482–1486.
6. Kusayama T, Watanabe S. Reinforcing effects of methamphetamine in planarians. *Neuroreport* 2000;11: 2511–2513.
7. Wise RA. Dopamine, learning and motivation. *Nat Rev Neurosci* 2004;5:483–494.
8. Mogenson GJ, Yang CR. The contribution of basal forebrain to limbic-motor integration and the mediation of motivation to action. *Adv Exp Med Biol* 1991;295:267–290.
9. Le Foll C, Irani BG, Magnan C, Dunn-Meynell AA, Levin BE. Effects of maternal genotype and diet on offspring glucose and fatty acid sensing ventromedial hypothalamic nucleus neurons. *Am J Physiol Regul Integr Comp Physiol* 2009;297(5):R1351–R1357.
10. Olds J. Hypothalamic substrates of reward. *Physiol Rev* 1962;42:554–604.
11. Wise RA, Spindler J, deWit H, Gerberg GJ. Neuroleptic-induced "anhedonia" in rats: pimozide blocks reward quality of food. *Science* 1978;201:262–264.
12. Figlewicz DP, Bennett JL, Naleid AM, Davis C, Grimm JW. Intraventricular insulin and leptin decrease sucrose self-administration in rats. *Physiol Behav* 2006;89:611–616.
13. Chang GQ, Gaysinskaya V, Karatayev O, Leibowitz SF. Maternal high-fat diet and fetal programming: increased proliferation of hypothalamic peptide-producing neurons that increase risk for overeating and obesity. *J Neurosci* 2008;28:12107–12119.
14. American Psychiatric Association. *Diagnostic and Statistical Manual of Mental Disorders*. 4th ed. Washington, DC: American Psychiatric Association, 2000.
15. Hill AJ. The psychology of food craving. *Proc Nutr Soc* 2007;66:277–285.
16. Volkow ND, O'Brien CP. Issues for DSM-V: should obesity be included as a brain disorder? *Am J Psychiatry* 2007;164:708–710.
17. Gearhardt AN, Corbin WR, Brownell KD. Preliminary validation of the Yale Food Addiction Scale. *Appetite* 2009;52:430–436.
18. Tiffany ST, Carter BL, Singleton EG. Challenges in the manipulation, assessment and interpretation of craving relevant variables. *Addiction* 2000;95 (suppl 2):S177–S187.
19. Rohsenow DJ, Monti PM. Does urge to drink predict relapse after treatment? *Alcohol Res Health* 1999;23:225–232.
20. Tiffany ST, Conklin CA. A cognitive processing model of alcohol craving and compulsive alcohol use. *Addiction* 2000;95(suppl 2):S145–S153.
21. Grimm JW. Animal models of craving. In: Olmstead MC, ed. *Animal Models of Drug Addiction* 2011; 331–336. New York: Springer-Verlag.
22. Berridge KC, Robinson TE. The mind of the addicted brain: neural sensitization of wanting versus liking. *Curr Dir Psychol Sci* 1995;4:71–76.
23. Childress AR, Ehrman RN, Wang Z, et al. Prelude to passion: limbic activation by "unseen" drug and sexual cues. *PLoS One* 2008;3:e1506.
24. Shalev U, Grimm JW, Shaham Y. Neurobiology of relapse to heroin and cocaine seeking: a review. *Pharmacol Rev* 2002;54:1–42.
25. Grimm JW, Hope BT, Wise RA, Shaham Y. Neuroadaptation. Incubation of cocaine craving after withdrawal. *Nature* 2001;412:141–142.
26. Grimm JW, Fyall AM, Osincup DP. Incubation of sucrose craving: effects of reduced training and sucrose pre-loading. *Physiol Behav* 2005;84:73–79.
27. Grimm JW, Barnes J, North K, Collins S, Weber R. A general method for evaluating incubation of sucrose craving in rats. *J Vis Exp* 2011;57:e3335. doi: 10.3791/3335.
28. Swithers SE, Davidson TL. A role for sweet taste: calorie predictive relations in energy regulation by rats. *Behav Neurosci* 2008;122:161–173.
29. Swithers SE, Baker CR, Davidson TL. General and persistent effects of high-intensity sweeteners on

body weight gain and caloric compensation in rats. *Behav Neurosci* 2009;123:772–780.

30. Volkow ND, Wise RA. How can drug addiction help us understand obesity? *Nat Neurosci* 2005;8:555–560.

31. Wang GJ, Volkow ND, Thanos PK, Fowler JS. Similarity between obesity and drug addiction as assessed by neurofunctional imaging: a concept review. *J Addict Dis* 2004;23:39–53.

32. Grimm JW, Buse C, Manaois M, Osincup D, Fyall A, Wells B. Time-dependent dissociation of cocaine dose-response effects on sucrose craving and locomotion. *Behav Pharmacol* 2006;17:143–149.

33. Grimm JW, Manaois M, Osincup D, Fyall A, Wells B. Time-dependent dissociation between accumbal and amygdalar mediation of cue-induced cocaine seeking. Poster session at: Annual Meeting of the American College on Neuropsychopharmacology; December 13, 2005; Waikoloa, Hawaii.

34. Grimm JW, Harkness JH, Ratliff C, Barnes J, North K, Collins S. Effects of systemic or nucleus accumbens-directed dopamine D1 receptor antagonism on sucrose seeking in rats. *Psychopharmacol (Berl)* 2011;216:219–233.35. Uejima JL, Bossert JM, Poles GC, Lu L. Systemic and central amygdala injections of the mGluR2/3 agonist LY379268 attenuate the expression of incubation of sucrose craving in rats. *Behav Brain Res* 2007;181:292–296.

36. Grimm JW, Manaois M, Osincup D, Wells B, Buse C. Naloxone attenuates incubated sucrose craving in rats. *Psychopharmacol (Berl)* 2007;194:537–544.

37. Grimm JW, Osincup D, Wells B, et al. Environmental enrichment attenuates cue-induced reinstatement of sucrose seeking in rats. *Behav Pharmacol* 2008;19:777–785.

38. Harkness JH, Webb S, Grimm JW. Abstinence-dependent transfer of lithium chloride-induced sucrose aversion to a sucrose-paired cue in rats. *Psychopharmacol (Berl)* 2010;208:521–530.

39. Mann T, Tomiyama AJ, Westling E, Lew AM, Samuels B, Chatman J. Medicare's search for effective obesity treatments: diets are not the answer. *Am Psychol* 2007;62:220–233.

40. Kosten TR, Kosten TA, Poling J, Oliveto A. "Incubation" of cocaine relapse during a disulfiram clinical trial. Poster presented at: Meeting of the College on Problems of Drug Dependence; June 21, 2005; Orlando, Florida.

41. Bergquist KL, Paliwal P, Hyman SM, Sinha R. Changes in cocaine craving, mood and stress in cocaine-dependent individuals during inpatient treatment and outpatient follow-up. Poster presented at: Meeting of the College on Problems of Drug Dependence; June 19, 2006; Scottsdale, Arizona.

42. Nava F, Caldiroli E, Premi S, Lucchini A. Relationship between plasma cortisol levels, withdrawal symptoms and craving in abstinent and treated heroin addicts. *J Addict Dis* 2006;25:9–16.

43. Bedi G, Preston KL, Epstein DH, Heishman SJ, Marrone GF, Shaham Y, de Wit H. Incubation of cue-induced cigarette craving during abstinence in human smokers. *Biol Psychiatry* 2011;69:708–711.

44. Piasecki TM, Fiore MC, Baker TB. Profiles in discouragement: two studies of variability in the time course of smoking withdrawal symptoms. *J Abnorm Psychol* 1998;107:238–251.

45. Piasecki TM, Niaura R, Shadel WG, et al. Smoking withdrawal dynamics in unaided quitters. *J Abnorm Psychol* 2000;109:74–86.

33

Liking versus Wanting Food in Human Appetite

Relation to Craving, Overconsumption, and "Food Addiction"

GRAHAM FINLAYSON, MICHELLE DALTON, AND JOHN E. BLUNDELL

INTRODUCTION

In recent years there has been a strong tendency for hedonic processes of appetite control to be regarded as exerting a more powerful influence over real-world food consumption than homeostatic mechanisms. This has been reflected in a number of articles comparing the two domains[1-3] and describing their neural substrates.[4] However, the most persuasive arguments arise from observations that the increasing palatability of food stimulates an orexigenic drive and that this potent oro-sensory stimulus—apparently independent from hunger or energy need—can lead to overconsumption. Eating is a reliable source of pleasure for most people, and reward plays an important role in the pattern of consumption from food selection to the initiation, maintenance, and cessation of each eating episode. The semantics of language describing eating-related pleasure imply that food hedonics are more than simply liking the taste of a food. We also talk about wanting, craving and desiring food. In addition to this, research in nonhuman studies has demonstrated neural-chemical dissociations between the mediation of affective responses to the hedonic impact of primary reinforcers (e.g., food), and those substrates responsible for attributing stimuli with motivational significance.[4] This suggests that reward is not a unitary process but may consist of subcomponents. In broad terms, distinct psychological components can be identified according to "liking" (hedonic pleasure or affect) and "wanting" (hedonic motivation or desire), these dual processes provide a theoretical framework for studying drugs of abuse and other natural pleasures such as palatable food. Recently a view has emerged that eating behavior, driven by the attractiveness of high-fat, highly rewarding food, could lead to forms of disordered eating that resonate with the concept of "food addiction."[6] This chapter will examine the notion of liking versus wanting as separable components of reward in human eating behavior: challenges and solutions in the definition and measurement of these processes; their relation to food craving and overconsumption; and their involvement in "food addiction."

LIKING AND WANTING AS PSYCHOLOGICAL COMPONENTS OF REWARD

Liking and wanting are often discussed in relation to subjective states or feelings that correspond to the ordinary understanding of these terms (and their synonyms) in the context of food choice and food intake. Wanting may refer to subjective states of desire, craving, or literally to feel a "lack [of] something desirable or necessary (esp. a quality or attribute)."[7] While liking is usually understood as the perceived impact of a food or its sensory properties on subjective affect or some judgment of the pleasure it elicits. Although it is assumed that the intensity and valence of our subjective experience of reward are reflective of changes in underlying biological processes, the link between subjective sensations and objective neurobiological events is far from understood. There are instances where subjective reports are weakly associated with objective measures of ingestive behavior as well as situations where the perceived urge to eat or the experienced taste of food is clearly linked to consumption.

The nature of subjective forms of liking and wanting is that they are consciously experienced and subject to interference from other thoughts and subjective states. Therefore, their relationship to human behavior is frequently obscured. The distinction between human subjective experience of liking and wanting and behavior influenced by reward processes that operate outside awareness suggests it is necessary to delineate these processes. It cannot be claimed that processes that control the expression of eating habits are necessarily explicit. This distinction between implicit and explicit processes may enhance understanding of the expression of food reward and particularly the concepts of liking and wanting and their importance for human appetite control. This means that they have much greater resolving potential for understanding the role of reward on eating.[8] Therefore, liking and wanting should be viewed as intervening variables operating at implicit (unconscious, automatic) and explicit (conscious, introspective) levels that imply motivational strength but cannot be directly observed. Identifying these variables is useful because it has the potential to explain and organize our thinking about the causes of behavior. A formidable, but surmountable, challenge for psychologists is how these components can be measured in the context of real-world food consumption.

MEASUREMENT OF LIKING AND WANTING IN HUMANS

While liking and wanting cannot be directly measured, as with all psychological constructs, they can be operationalized. Fortunately there are many different ways that this might be accomplished. In research in nonhuman animals, liking has previously been operationalized by counting the frequency of positive and negative behavioral reactions to the taste of food. These reactions are thought to be universal expressions of affect because some of them can also be observed in primates and human infants.[9] However, in older children and adults, facial reactions to tastes are less reliable, making them unsuitable as objective measures. Most commonly, liking for food is assessed explicitly by subjective psychological tools, including Likert scales, Labelled Magnitude scales,[10] and Visual Analogue scales. Questions such as "How palatable is this food?" "How pleasant is the taste of this food?" and "How much do you like this food now?" are often used. Explicit forms of wanting can also be captured using subjective scales. Questions such as "How strong is your desire to eat this food?" "How much do you want this food?" or questions relating to how much effort one would go to in order to obtain a food have all been employed in previous studies. These tools are limited by the accuracy of self-reporting and methodological issues such as "end avoidance" and social desirability. However, if used carefully, they can be quite sensitive to even subtle experimental manipulations, and they frequently predict ingestive behavior.

In contrast to explicit forms of liking and wanting, implicit wanting concerns the core motivational aspects of reward-seeking behavior. Therefore, measures that reflect motivational responses to food and food-related cues can be said to contain at least an element of wanting. The more spontaneous the response, the closer that behavior is likely to reflect the core process of wanting without contamination from subjective processes. Importantly, wanting may not be adequately captured by the nonspecific desire for food in general. Wanting implies a target with a direction, not just a force.

METHODOLOGICAL PLATFORM: LEEDS FOOD PREFERENCE QUESTIONNAIRE

In recent years our laboratory has devoted time to the theoretical and methodological understanding of liking and wanting food behavior in humans. The outcome has been the development of a methodological platform for detecting variation in liking and wanting hedonic responses. The Leeds Food Preference Questionnaire (LFPQ) assesses explicit liking and wanting for an array of well-defined common food items and incorporates a reaction time based measure of implicit wanting using the same item array. Participants are required to evaluate each item according to their explicit liking and wanting value using Visual Analogue Scales. Then in an adjacent task they are presented with randomized pairs of food items and required to select between them as quickly and accurately as possible. The speed with which the choices are made for each item relative to alternatives provides a measure of "implicit wanting" that contributes to a category score. Scores can then be compared between explicit and implicit measures made for the same foods. The platform is highly versatile and has been used in a number of experimental scenarios, including sensory, physiological, and pharmacological manipulations.[11–17] The procedures can be used to help identify hedonic susceptibility to overconsumption.[18] They also reveal the dual role of liking and wanting as intervening variables in actual food consumption.

EXPERIENCE OF CRAVINGS AS A MARKER FOR SENSITIZED WANTING

Liking and wanting appear to have separate and disproportionate roles in overconsumption. In terms of liking, some individuals at risk of weight gain may experience an exaggerated hedonic response to palatable foods, so that foods are enjoyed more and therefore eaten in greater amounts for longer periods of time.[19,20] On the other hand, a reward deficiency hypothesis has been proposed[21,22] that suggests a diminished ability to experience pleasure from food and thereby consumption of palatable food is driven up to satisfy an optimum level of stimulation.[23-26] However, processes of wanting have attracted more speculation and research aimed at understanding hedonic susceptibility to overconsumption. For example, vulnerability to weight gain may be characterized by an increased reactivity toward cues signaling the availability of food.[27,28] Alternatively, a maintained motivation to eat high fat, energy dense foods when satiated could explain episodes of hedonic overconsumption.[29,30] These scenarios describe features that are common to the experience of food craving; the former occurring during abstinence from the desired food and the latter occurring during the eating episode—sometimes described as "moreishness."[31]

Food cravings are defined as an intense desire to eat a specific food and estimated to occur in 52%–100% of the population.[32,33] Food cravings have also been described as an intense simultaneous expression of implicit and explicit wanting for a food (or type of food).[34] In overweight dieters, experience of food cravings was shown to be predictive of failure to comply to a low-calorie diet.[35,36] Furthermore, general tendency to experience cravings has been associated with body weight[37,38] and binge eating in obese individuals.[39] The implication is that while liking may be important in establishing the motivational properties of food, susceptible individuals whether through predisposition or adaptation are characterized by pathologically elevated levels of wanting—experienced periodically as food cravings—which promote overconsumption in a food-rich environment.

CAN CHRONIC EXCESSIVE FOOD INTAKE LEAD TO ENHANCED WANTING?

An interesting question raised by some researchers is whether reward-related sensitization—evidenced by enhanced food wanting[5,40]—can occur after prolonged excessive food intake in humans. The suggestion is that individuals who might develop neural sensitization with repeat consumption of palatable foods and drinks would come to experience exaggerated food wanting that is no longer in step with their food liking, hence promoting overconsumption and weight gain. Finlayson et al.[41] reviewed some of the early studies that interpreted their findings on eating behavior through the framework of dissociated liking and wanting. Among these, one study investigated daily consumption of chocolate over a 15-day period.[42] Participants were given 0 g (control), 67 g (fixed), or increasing amounts from 57–86 g (variable) to consume each day, while ad libitum intake of chocolate was assessed on day 1, 8, and 15. The authors found that subjective ratings of pleasantness and desire to eat chocolate declined over time consistent with stimulus satiation or monotony (no change in the control group). However, ad libitum intake of chocolate increased over time. Furthermore, subjects in the fixed and variable conditions had significantly gained weight over the exposure period. The authors concluded: "This apparent dissociation between ratings and intake of chocolate may reflect differences in 'liking' and 'wanting.' The separation of these processes reflects research evidence from intake and taste reactivity patterns in animals by Kent Berridge and his colleagues of different neural systems underlying 'liking' and 'wanting'" (p. 27).[42] More recently, with methodology developed to test measures of liking and wanting, further evidence for enhanced wanting after repeated exposure to food has been published.[43] In this study obese and nonobese women were randomly assigned to consume 0, 100, or 300 kcal of a favorite snack food each day for 14 days. Relative reinforcing value of food (wanting) and subjective measure of liking for the snack food was taken at baseline and after the exposure period. The results showed that liking for the food had decreased in obese and nonobese groups after 14-day repeated consumption. However, for the measure of wanting, there was an interaction between obese status, portion size, and exposure period. The authors noted that daily consumption of 300 kcal of snack food resulted in enhanced wanting in the obese women only. These findings support the notion that a form of incentive sensitization may have developed in the obese women after chronic exposure to large quantities of palatable food.

ARE LIKING AND WANTING INVOLVED IN FOOD ADDICTION?

Currently a number of research reports have been accompanied by a powerful rhetoric encouraging the view that eating behavior, driven by the attractiveness of high-palatability, high-energy foods, could engender a form of "food addiction." In turn, this and other evidence could lead to the characterization of obese people as food addicts.

At the present time the human evidence on this issue arises almost exclusively from research conducted in North America, and from authors and researchers embedded in this sociocultural landscape. The food environment in North America is indeed highly specialized to promote excessive consumption; however, this food is contained within a socioeconomic system that encourages purchasing and consumption of many items (not only food) without limits. Therefore, it may be premature to regard addiction to foods as a universal phenomenon that has global penetration. Before extending the concept further it seems sensible to gather cross-cultural data to discover whether the "addiction" to foods exists in cultures whose food habits and food repertoires differ from those in North America (or Western Europe where industrialized foods exist in similar form and scale to those in the United States). At the moment it is not possible to detect whether the avid overconsumption of certain foods in the North American food supply arises solely from the oro-sensory properties of these foods or from the way in which this overconsumption is legitimized and promoted by prevailing values in the surrounding culture.[44]

Whether or not the term "addiction" should be applied, it certainly can be recognized that the hedonic response to food is a psychological and biological reality and that the pleasure derived from eating forms an important part of the quality of life for many human beings—in whichever culture they live. Oro-sensory qualities of food can only engender a human emotional response if brain processes exist to mediate this physical impact on subjective state. These brain processes are the subject of intense scrutiny.[45,46] The hedonic "hot spots" and dopamine pathways within this circuitry (identified with animal experiments) have been regarded as providing a neural basis for processes of liking and wanting.[47] This approach has facilitated understanding of how the hedonic

system may function physiologically and has added sensitivity to the experimental study of hedonically driven eating. The terms liking and wanting can be dissociated semantically (although they are often used as synonyms in common speech), and this gives further substance to the separation of the processes through experimental analysis and observational scrutiny. The validity of such a distinction can be demonstrated through the experimental dissociation of functional effects ascribed to liking and wanting.[13,15–17,27,44] The separate identities for liking and wanting provide increasing analytical power to explore the complexities of the effects of food hedonics on eating. The further distinction (experimentally validated) between explicit and implicit processes adds theoretical justification to commonly observed self-statements about appetite ("I've just got to have that food—I don't know why but I have to"; "implicit wanting").

Our current position is that separate processes (that we refer to as liking and wanting) can exert separate (and sometimes conjoint) effects on eating, and therefore can contribute to overconsumption. We argue that liking and wanting contribute to what can be termed "hedonically driven eating" and that these processes can represent risk factors or susceptibility factors for overconsumption and some forms of disorderly eating. However, we await further evidence before regarding all overconsumption as a form of addictive behavior.

REFERENCES

1. Blundell JE, Finlayson G. Is susceptibility to weight gain characterized by homeostatic or hedonic risk factors for overconsumption? *Physiol Behav* 2004; 82(1):21–25.
2. Saper CB. Hypothalamic connections with the cerebral cortex. *Prog Brain Res* 2000;126:39–48.
3. Schwartz MW, Woods SC, Porte D Jr., Seeley RJ, Baskin DG. Central nervous system control of food intake. *Nature* 2000;404(6778):661–671.
4. Berthoud H-R. Interactions between the "cognitive" and "metabolic" brain in the control of food intake. *Phys Behav* 2007;91(5):486–498.
5. Berridge KC, Robinson TE. The mind of an addicted brain: neural sensitization of wanting versus liking. *Cur Direct Psych Sci* 1995;4(3):71–76.
6. Gearhardt AN, Grilo CM, DiLeone RJ, Brownell KD, Potenza MN. Can food be addictive? Public health and policy implications. *Addiction* 2011;106:1208–1212.
7. Fulton S, Pissios P, Manchon RP, et al. Leptin regulation of the mesoaccumbens dopamine pathway. *Neuron* 2006;51(6):811–822.

8. Booth DA. How not to think about immediate dietary and postingestional influences on appetites and satieties. *Appetite* 1990;14(3):171–179.

9. Simpson JA, Weiner ESC. *The Oxford English Dictionary.* 2nd ed. Oxford, England: Clarendon Press, 1989.

10. Berridge KC. Measuring hedonic impact in animals and infants: microstructure of affective taste reactivity patterns. *Neurosci Biobehav Rev* 2000;24(2): 173–198.

11. Brignell C, Griffiths T, Bradley BP, Mogg K. Attentional and approach biases for pictorial food cues. Influence of external eating. *Appetite* 2009;52(2): 299–306.

12. Finlayson G, King N, Blundell J. The role of implicit wanting in relation to explicit liking and wanting for food: implications for appetite control. *Appetite* 2008;50:120–127.

13. Finlayson G, Marsaux C, Barrilet P. Implicit wanting determines incidental eating when hunger is suppressed. *Appetite.* 2011;57(2):537.

14. Griffioen-Roose S, Finlayson G, Mars M, Blundell J, de Graaf C. Measuring food reward and the transfer effect of sensory specific satiety. *Appetite* 2010; 55(3):648–655.

15. Cameron JD, Finlayson G, Blundell J, Doucet E. Impact of a 24-hour complete fast on food preference and explicit and implicit hedonic measures of food reward. Paper presented at: The Obesity Society Annual Meeting; October 8-10 2010; San Diego, CA.

16. Verschoor E, Finlayson G, Blundell J, Markus CR, King NA. Effects of an acute alpha-lactalbumin manipulation on mood and food hedonics in high- and low-trait anxiety individuals. *Br J Nutr* 2010;104(4): 595–602.

17. Finlayson G, Bryant E, Blundell JE, King NA. Acute compensatory eating following exercise is associated with implicit hedonic wanting for food. *Physiol Behav* 2009;97(1):62–67.

18. Finlayson G, Arlotti A, Dalton M, King N, Blundell J. Implicit wanting and explicit liking are markers for trait binge eating–a susceptible phenotype for overeating. *Appetite* 2007; doi:10.1016/j.appet.2011.08.012.

19. Finlayson G, Caudwell P, Gibbons C, Hopkins M, King N, Blundell J. Low fat loss response after medium-term supervised exercise in obese is associated with exercise-induced increase in food reward. *J Obes* 2011;2011. pii 615624. Epub 2010 Sep 20.

20. Berridge KC. "Liking" and "wanting" food rewards: brain substrates and roles in eating disorders. *Physiol Behav* 2009;97(5):537–550.

21. Blundell JE, Stubbs RJ, Golding C, et al. Resistance and susceptibility to weight gain: individual variability in response to a high-fat diet. *Physiol Behav* 2005;86(5):614–622.

22. Blum K, Sheridan PJ, Wood RC, et al. The D2 dopamine receptor gene as a determinant of reward deficiency syndrome. *J Roy Soc Med* 1996;89(7):396–400.

23. Comings DE, Blum K. Reward deficiency syndrome: genetic aspects of behavioral disorders. *Prog Brain Res* 2000;126:325–341.

24. Davis C, Levitan RD, Kaplan AS. Dopamine transporter gene (DAT1) associated with appetite suppression to methylphenidate in a case-control study of binge eating disorder. *Neuropsychopharmacol* 2007;32: 2199–2206.

25. Davis C, Strachan S, Berkson M. Sensitivity to reward: implications for overeating and overweight. *Appetite* 2004;42(2):754–766.

26. Stice E, Spoor S, Bohon C, Veldhuizen MG, Small DM. Relation of reward from food intake and anticipated food intake to obesity: a functional magnetic resonance imaging study. *J Abnorm Psychol* 2008;117(4): 924–935.

27. Epstein LH, Leddy JJ, Temple JL, Faith MS. Food reinforcement and eating: a multilevel analysis. *Psychol Bull* 2007;133(5):884–906.

28. Wang GJ, Volkow ND, Thanos PK, Fowler JS. Similarity between obesity and drug addiction as assessed by neurofunctional imaging: a concept review. *J Addict Dis* 2004;24:39–53.

29. Nijs IMT, Muris P, Euser AS, Franken IHA. Differences in attention to food and food intake between overweight/obese and normal-weight females under conditions of hunger and satiety. *Appetite* 2010;54(2): 243–254.

30. Nasser JA, Evans SM, Foltin RW. The relationship between self-reported eating behavior and performance in a behavioral task assessing food reinforcement. *Appetite* 2002;39:93A.

31. Yeomans MR. Palatability and the micro-structure of feeding in humans: the appetizer effect. *Appetite* 1996;27(2):119–133.

32. Rogers PJ. Food craving and addictions—fact and fallacy? In: Carr T, Descheemaeker K, eds. *Nutrition and Health: Current topics III.* Antwerp, Belgium: Garant Publishers; 2003: 69–76.

33. Gilhooly CH, Das SK, Golden JK, et al. Food cravings and energy regulation: the characteristics of craved foods and their relationship with eating behaviors and weight change during 6 months of dietary energy restriction. *Int J Obes* 2007;31(12):1849–1858.

34. Pelchat ML. Of human bondage: food craving, obsession, compulsion, and addiction. *Physiol Behav* 2002;76(3):347–352.

35. Robinson TE, Berridge KC. The neural basis of drug craving: an incentive-sensitization theory of addiction. *Brain Res Rev* 1993;18(3):247–291.

36. Fedoroff I, Polivy J, Herman CP. The specificity of restrained versus unrestrained eaters' responses to food cues: general desire to eat, or craving for the cued food? *Appetite* 2003;41(1):7–13.

37. Sitton SC. Role of craving for carbohydrates upon completion of a protein-sparing fast. *Psychol Rep* 1991;69(2):683–686.

38. Franken IH, Muris P. Individual differences in reward sensitivity are related to food craving and relative body weight in healthy women. *Appetite* 2005;45: 198–201.

39. White MA, Whisenhunt BL, Williamson DA, Greenway FL, Netemeyer RG. Development and validation of the food-craving inventory. *Obes Res* 2002;10(2):107–114.

40. Robinson, TE, Berridge KC. The psychology and neurobiology of addiction: an incentive–sensitization view. *Addiction* 2000;95(8):91–117.

41. Finlayson G, King N, Blundell JE. Liking vs. wanting food: importance for human appetite control and weight regulation. *Neurosci Biobehav Rev* 2007;31(7):987–1002.

42. Hetherington MM, Pirie LM, Nabb S. Stimulus satiation: effects of repeated exposure to foods on pleasantness and intake. *Appetite* 2002;38:19–28.

43. Temple JL, Bulkley AM, Badawy RL, Krause N, McCann S, Epstein LH. Differential effects of daily snack food intake on the reinforcing value of food in obese and nonobese women. *Am J Clin Nutr* 2009; 90(2):304–313.

44. Park M-I, Camilleri M. Gastric motor and sensory functions in obesity. *Obes Res* 2005;13(3): 491–500.

45. Phan KL, Wager T, Taylor SF, Liberzon I. Functional neuroanatomy of emotion: a meta-analysis of emotion activation studies in PET and fMRI. *Neuroimage* 2002;16(2):331–348.

46. Kessler D. *The End of Overeating: Taking Control of the Insatiable American Appetite*. New York: Rodale Books, 2009.

47. Berridge KC. Pleasures of the brain. *Brain Cogn* 2003;52(1):106–128.

34

The Psychology of Food Cravings

ANDREW J. HILL

Surveys find food cravings are extremely common events, experienced by the majority of young adults. Food craving is closely associated with liking since the most commonly craved foods are highly palatable.[1] But craving is not synonymous with increased consumption. Foods are frequently eaten without being craved, and craved foods are not always eaten. Likewise, hunger is not a precondition for craving. The purpose of this chapter is to overview these quintessentially psychological phenomena, to look at the impact of energy restriction, and consider underlying psychological mechanisms.

THE NATURE OF FOOD CRAVINGS

What do people understand by the term "food craving"? Most researchers have focused on the subjective experience of craving, of which strength and specificity are the core components. Accordingly, a food craving is both an intense experience *and* directed at a particular food or taste. It follows that prevalence estimates vary according to the elements required. One study found that 58% of their sample of adult women reported ever having experienced a food craving (85% of whom had a craving in the past 3 months).[2] This proportion reduced to 42% when moderate to strong intensity was a requirement and to 21% when it was limited to strong intensity.

There are useful parallels with fear. Some 20%–30% of people have mild fears about things like spiders, dogs, thunder, or blood, and their feelings are reflected in altered behavior regarding these objects or events. But only 1% has a severe phobia, a state of extreme fear typified by absolute avoidance of the feared object or event. Similarly, a great majority of the population can identify a time when they have experienced a distinct urge to eat a particular food. For a much smaller proportion, these urges feel irresistible and their behavioral or emotional

consequences are serious. Food cravings therefore should be seen on a continuum of experience that ranges from mild to extreme.

THE TARGETS OF CRAVINGS

Chocolate is the most commonly craved food, regularly accounting for around half of craving experiences.[2–4] Chocolate has advantageous orosensory features that confer high palatability and, being associated with celebration and romance, is a food with special social status. Unsurprisingly, it is a food associated, by consumers and some advertisers, with addiction.[5] More women than men crave chocolate[6] and although there is evidence these cravings increase prior to menstruation, they do not disappear post menopause, suggesting something other than hormonal determination.[7]

Craving for sweet foods such as cakes, cookies, and desserts, or just "something sweet," is often the next most common target category. However, savory foods, including snacks, meals, and takeaway foods, rival sweet food craving frequencies in some studies of women and are the most common category in studies of men.[8] Food craving changes with age. Elderly participants report fewer cravings and for a more limited number of foods, and craving for sweets has also been observed to decline.[9]

There is very limited information on cultural differences in food craving. The foods craved by North Americans and Europeans appear indistinguishable. Interviews with young and older Egyptian adults reveal that more savory than sweet foods are craved.[10] The authors note that Egyptian Arabic has no single word that describes food cravings for anyone other than pregnant women. There is also the likelihood that cultural differences in cuisine are reflected in the foods craved. Using an inventory of familiar Japanese foods, the cravings of young Japanese women fell into five statistically determined groups: sweets, snacks (mostly savory),

Western foods (again savory), sushi, and rice.[11] Rice is a staple food across Asia. Whether this familiarity makes rice more frequently craved than chocolate in countries other than Japan is open to investigation.

ASSESSMENT OF FOOD CRAVINGS

The approaches used to measure food cravings fall into four broad categories. The first focuses on the foods craved in list or inventory form. Using foods representative of the groups described earlier, the Food-Craving Inventory[12] has been developed from craving frequency ratings of US adults. Factor analysis revealed four food categories: high-fat (all savory), sweets, starches, and fast food fat. The strength of this approach is its directionality, food groupings organized by sensory and/or nutritional composition. A weakness is that geographic and cultural differences in food use demand variation in the foods listed.

Questionnaire assessments form the second category. The most established is the Food Craving Questionnaire.[13] Divided into trait and state versions, this assessment adheres to a multidimensional conceptualization of craving, evaluating the experience within a broader context of affect, hunger, and reward associated with eating. As such, this is a lengthy but psychometrically robust measure translated into several European languages, and with published data from different participant groups.[14]

The third category is the simple, often single, rating scale approach that has remained popular given its ease of use and sensitivity to moment-to-moment change. These are features shared by most fixed point or visual analog scales directed at subjective experience and, unsurprisingly, they are commonly used in experimental evaluations of craving where current strength or intensity of craving is of primary interest.

Fourth is what might be described as descriptive approaches to assessment. These range from the interviews referred to earlier, to freely written accounts and template records of craving. To illustrate the latter two approaches, researchers asked a sample of undergraduates to recall their last experience of a food craving, remembering it as if it was happening right now, and writing a short paragraph about the experience as well as completing ratings of its intensity and character.[15] The second is built into an incident approach to food craving. This differs from the continuous sampling afforded by single rating scales in that participants are asked to note every occurrence of a food craving and to complete a detailed account of the experience once it has passed. The information is noted on a food craving record, a list of 18 or more questions and ratings of the event detailing information on context, affect (before and after craving), strength, resistibility, craving target, and behavior.[4] The detail obtained and capacity to conduct quasi-prospective, real-life monitoring of cravings are the main strengths of descriptive approaches.

EFFECTS OF ENERGY RESTRICTION

If food cravings are psychological registrations of the body's energy depletion, then an association between dieting and food craving frequency or strength would be expected. Accordingly, fasting impacts on food craving, although the direction of change is unexpected. Both in the short term[16] and long term,[17] fasting is associated with *fewer* food craving experiences. This decrease in craving is generalized across all food groups and does not appear to rebound during refeeding.[17,18] While such interventions are effective at bringing about weight loss, there is no relationship between the amount of weight lost and reduction in food craving.

This suppression of food craving is consistent with other observations of reduced appetite during weight loss on very low calorie diets (VLCDs). The paradox "Less food, less hunger" reports the effect of obese patients following a VLCD (500 or 1200 kcal/day) over 3 months.[19] In fact, the suppression of hunger was modest and overshadowed by a marked increase in physical symptoms such as constipation, dizziness, and fatigue. Reduced hunger is also found in patients with eating disorders who have similarly low levels of daily energy intake.[20]

Studies of dieting or dietary restraint are more equivocal. In a mini-symposium on food craving, two of the three of the studies failed to find the expected cross-sectional relationship,[1,21] while the third described a weak association between dietary restraint and craving strength.[22] Monitoring a small group of normal weight women and men on an energy-restricted diet for a period of 2 weeks (1,200 and 1,500 kcal/day, respectively) revealed an increase in being preoccupied with thoughts about food or eating and feeling a strong urge to eat.[23] In a community sample of women, two-thirds of whom were members of a commercial slimming group, current dieters reported significantly more cravings during the week of monitoring than nondieters, while watchers (dieting to maintain current weight) did not differ from either group.[24] The craving experiences recorded by dieters were significantly stronger, more difficult to resist, and slower to disappear than those of nondieters. Unsurprisingly, success in resisting cravings and not eating the craved foods has been associated with greater weight loss over a 6-month weight management program.[25]

Dieters do not only deprive themselves of potential food energy, they deprive themselves of foods they enjoy eating, and they may lose variety in their daily menu. Both monotony and self-restriction are associated with increased food cravings. Consuming a nutritionally adequate, sweet, monotonous liquid diet for 5 days resulted in an increase in food cravings compared to baseline but in young rather than elderly adults.[26] Interestingly, the increase was for meal foods and not sweets, those foods that differed in sensory quality to the liquid diet and that participants were denied the opportunity to eat.

Attempted restriction over eating was one of the best discriminators between dieters, watchers, and nondieters in the study described earlier.[24] There was no difference between the groups in terms of the types of food craved. Rather, dieters rated their cravings as for foods they had recently tried to restrict eating. Watchers scored intermediate on this scale and nondieters very low. Paradoxically, dieters' attempts at resisting eating certain foods appear to have led to cravings for the same foods, and their consumption on 70% of craving occasions.

This association between restriction or deprivation and food craving has also been studied in the laboratory. Cravings and consumption were monitored following a week when participants were required to refrain from eating foods containing either chocolate or vanilla.[27] Chocolate-deprived high-restraint participants ate more chocolate in the taste test situation than either those vanilla-deprived or non-flavor-deprived participants. Vanilla deprivation had no comparable effect. Highly restrained eaters also reported a stronger desire to eat chocolate at the start of the session and abandoned a psychological test earlier believing they could access chocolate sooner. Interestingly, restrained eaters reported more food cravings generally. Using a similar methodology revealed a selective effect of short-term (3-day) carbohydrate or protein restriction on craving for these food types but without an effect of restraint.[28]

This suggests either restriction-induced craving is a phenomenon that dieters have more life experience of, or that there is something special about chocolate that is not shared by bread or chicken.

CRAVING AND DISORDERED EATING

While women with a history of anorexia nervosa have been found not to differ from non-eating-disordered women in recent or lifetime occurrence of food cravings, a greater proportion report strong and irresistible cravings.[29] Moreover, those who experienced cravings were significantly more likely to have had past diagnosis of bulimia nervosa. Looking at food cravings and their relationship to binge eating in women with bulimia nervosa shows a strong influence of mood. Food cravings leading to a binge were associated with higher tension and lower mood than cravings that did not lead to a binge, and post binge there was a further substantial deterioration of post-craving mood.[30] In contrast, mood improved significantly when there was no subsequent binge. Interestingly, rated hunger was significantly lower when craving led to a binge and reduced regardless of whether a binge occurred.

Other naturalistic research has shown dietary restriction to precede the urge to binge but not to be a direct antecedent of binge episodes.[31] In an eating disorder context, craving and subsequent eating appear more affect driven than hunger oriented. This description is consistent with the functional view of binge eating as an emotionally regulating behavior that occurs more often in a context of negative affect. It is also consistent with more moderate mood states associated with food cravings seen in women without disordered eating.[4,22]

PSYCHOLOGICAL EXPLANATIONS FOR FOOD CRAVINGS

Various mechanisms have been proposed to account for food cravings, many of them summarized in other sections of this handbook. Simple associations with nutrient deficiency are compelling[32] but are unrepresentative of the diet and nutritional status of people in the developed world and who contribute to the literature cited here. The following are pointers to the different psychological mechanisms applied to food cravings.

The idea that some people choose and eat foods to intentionally regulate mood has a long history.

Several biological pathways have been proposed, the most prominent involving brain serotonin and endogenous opioids. Learned regulation of mood through food, or emotionally instrumental eating, is not restricted to eating-disordered individuals. Monitoring momentary emotional state and motivation to eat over 6 consecutive days showed that during negative emotion participants tended to eat to provide distraction, to relax, and to feel better.[33] Extending this to food craving, it is plausible that some individuals eat a specific food, and crave it, for reasons of negative reinforcement—that is, consumption reduces aversive mood states such as boredom and depression. Applied to foods such as chocolate, however, the ambivalence associated with overeating is more likely to prolong than ameliorate dysphoric mood.[34]

The process of cue reactivity is described in Chapter 8. Attentional bias is a cognitive component describing selective attention, in this case, to food-related cues. Negative mood induction leads to faster response times to pictures of foods than control pictures and increased urge to eat, suggesting a mood-associated increase in the reward value of foods.[35] In addition, chocolate cravers and those induced to crave chocolate show an attentional bias to chocolate that is not shared by other highly desirable food cues.[36] These findings demonstrate the complex interplay between affect and environmental cue salience.

Cravings for restricted foods referred to earlier are consistent with ironic process accounts of cognitive control that describe how, under certain conditions, efforts to avoid thinking about a situation or stimulus actually lead to an increase in their salience.[37,38] Applying this to food craving, participants (including chocolate cravers) instructed to try not to think about chocolate performed better on a computer task that yielded chocolate rewards.[39] While the thought suppression task reduced the number of verbalized thoughts about chocolate, the opportunity to access chocolate immediately afterward showed an ironic spillover (or rebound) into performance and chocolate-reward driven behavior. Similarly, obese adolescents asked to button press each time a thought about food and eating came to mind successfully suppressed these thoughts. But in the period immediately afterward, when they were told to think about anything they liked, they showed the characteristic ironic rebound of increased food and eating thoughts.[40]

The ambivalence shown toward the object of craving suggests a further psychological process. A craving can be an attribution to account for why a food was eaten.[41] Having overconsumed, people search for a reason why and choose between the food and themselves as agents of this behavior. Blaming the food is a personally and socially acceptable justification that resonates with reasoning about why people smoke cigarettes and drink alcohol. It also illustrates a bias in self-attributions, where, for events with negative outcomes, the cause is more often seen as external or situational (the food) rather than the result of internal, psychological features.[42]

CONCLUSIONS

Food cravings are moving away from being cast as personal peccadilloes to shared common experience that is often benign but, on occasion, emotionally costly. Although desire to eat is a defining component of food craving, craving strength is neither a metric nor analog of hunger. Circumstances have been described where food cravings are more likely when hunger is reduced. However, neither are they independent of hunger. It is likely that the more extreme or intense cravings deviate most from a normal hunger experience and have strong acquired associations with mood. A challenge will be to translate experimental evidence on manipulations that reduce cravings[43] into interventions that help in their management.

REFERENCES

1. Pelchat ML. Of human bondage: food craving, obsession, compulsion, and addiction. *Physiol Behav* 2002;76:347–352.
2. Gendall KA, Joyce PR, Sullivan PF. Impact of definition on prevalence of food cravings in a random sample of young women. *Appetite* 1997;28:63–72.
3. Weingarten HP, Elston D. Food cravings in a college population. *Appetite* 1991;17:167–175.
4. Hill AJ, Heaton-Brown L. The experience of food craving: a prospective investigation in healthy women. *J Psychosom Res* 1994;38:801–814.
5. Hetherington MM, Macdiarmid JI. "Chocolate addiction": a preliminary description and report of its relationship to problem eating. *Appetite* 1993;21:233–246.
6. Osman JL, Sobal J. Chocolate cravings in American and Spanish individuals: biological and cultural influences. *Appetite* 2006;47:290–301.
7. Hormes JM, Rozin P. Perimenstrual chocolate craving. What happens after the menopause? *Appetite* 2009;53:256–259.
8. Zellner DA, Garriga-Trillo A, Rohm E, Centeno S, Parker S. Food liking and craving: a cross-cultural approach. *Appetite* 1999;33:61–70.
9. Pelchat ML. Food cravings in young and elderly adults. *Appetite* 1997;28:103–113.

10. Parker S, Kamel N, Zellner D. Food craving patterns in Egypt: comparisons with North America and Spain. *Appetite* 2003;40:193–195.

11. Komatsu S. Rice and sushi cravings: a preliminary study of food craving among Japanese females. *Appetite* 2008;50:353–358.

12. White MA, Whisenhunt BL, Williamson DA, Greenway FL, Netemeyer RG. Development and validation of the Food-Craving Inventory. *Obes Res* 2002;10:107–114.

13. Cepeda-Benito A, Gleaves DH, Fernandez MC, Vila J, Reynoso J. The development and validation of the state and trait food cravings questionnaire. *Behav Ther* 2000;31:151–173.

14. Moreno S, Rodgriguez S, Carmen Fernandez M, Tamez J, Cepeda-Benito A. Clinical validation of the trait and state versions of the Food Craving Questionnaire. *Assessment* 2008;15:375–387.

15. Tiggemann M, Kemps E. The phenomenology of food cravings: the role of mental imagery. *Appetite* 2005;45:305–313.

16. Lappalainen R, Sjödén PO, Hursti T, Vesa V. Hunger/craving responses and reactivity to food stimuli during fasting and dieting. *Int J Obes* 1990;14:679–688.

17. Harvey J, Wing RR, Mullen M. Effects on food cravings of a very low calorie diet or a balanced, low calorie diet. *Appetite* 1993;21:105–115.

18. Martin CK, O'Neil PM, Pawlow L. Changes in food cravings during low-calorie and very-low-calorie diets. *Obesity (Silver Spring)* 2006;14:115–121.

19. Wadden TA, Stunkard AJ, Day SC, Gould RA, Rubin CJ. Less food, less hunger: reports of appetite and symptoms in a controlled study of a protein-sparing modified fast. *Int J Obes* 1987;11:239–249.

20. Halmi KA, Sunday SR. Temporal patterns of hunger and fullness ratings and related cognitions in anorexia and bulimia. *Appetite* 1991;16:219–237.

21. Rodin J, Mancuso J, Granger J, Nelback E. Food cravings in relation to body mass index, restraint and estradiol levels: a repeated measures study in healthy women. *Appetite* 1991;17:177–185.

22. Hill AJ, Weaver CFL, Blundell JE. Food craving, dietary restraint and mood. *Appetite* 1991;17:187–197.

23. Warren C, Cooper PJ. Psychological effects of dieting. *Brit J Clin Psychol* 1988;27:269–270.

24. Massey A, Hill AJ. Dieting and food craving. A descriptive, quasi-prospective study. *Appetite* 2012;58:781–785.

25. Gilhooly CH, Das SK, Golden JK, et al. Food cravings and energy regulation; the characteristics of craved foods and their relationship with eating behaviours and weight change during 6 months of dietary energy restriction. *Int J Obes* 2007;31:1849–1858.

26. Pelchat ML, Schaefer S. Dietary monotony and food cravings in young and elderly adults. *Physiol Behav* 2000;68:353–359.

27. Polivy J, Coleman J, Herman CP. The effect of deprivation on food cravings and eating behaviour in restrained and unrestrained eaters. *Int J Eat Disord* 2005;38:301–309.

28. Coelho JS, Polivy J, Herman CP. Selective carbohydrate or protein restriction: effects on subsequent food intake and cravings. *Appetite* 2006;47:352–360.

29. Gendall KA, Sullivan PF, Joyce PR, Bulik CM. Food cravings in women with a history of anorexia nervosa. *Int J Eat Disord* 1997;22:403–409.

30. Waters A, Hill A, Waller G. Bulimics' responses to food cravings: is binge-eating a product of hunger or emotional state? *Behav Res Therap* 2001;39:877–886.

31. Engelberg MJ, Gauvin L, Steiger H. A naturalistic evaluation of the relation between dietary restraint, the urge to binge, and actual binge eating: a clarification. *Int J Eat Disord* 2005;38:355–360.

32. Louw VJ, du Preez P, Malan A, van Deventer L, van Wyk D, Joubert G. Pica and food craving in adult patients with iron deficiency in Bloemfontein, South Africa. *S African Med J* 2007;97:1069–1071.

33. Macht M, Simons G. Emotions and eating in everyday life. *Appetite* 2000;35:65–71.

34. Parker G, Parker I, Brotchie H. Mood effects of chocolate. *J Affect Disord* 2006;92:149–159.

35. Hepworth R, Mogg K, Brignell C, Bradley BP. Negative mood increases selective attention to food cues and subjective appetite. *Appetite* 2010;54(1):134–142.

36. Kemps E, Tiggemann M. Attentional bias for craving-related (chocolate) food cues. *Exp Clin Psychopharmacol* 2009;17:425–433.

37. Wegner DM. When the antidote is the poison: ironic mental control processes. *Psychol Sci* 1997;8:148–150.

38. Mann T, Ward A. Forbidden fruit: does thinking about a prohibited food lead to its consumption? *Int J Eat Disord* 2001;29:319–327.

39. Johnston L, Bulik CM, Anstiss V. Suppressing thoughts about chocolate. *Int J Eat Disord* 1999;26:21–27.

40. Soetens B, Braet C. "The weight of a thought": food-related thought suppression in obese and normal-weight youngsters. *Appetite* 2006;46:309–317.

41. Rogers PJ, Smit HJ. Food craving and food "addiction": a critical review of the evidence from a biopsychosocial perspective. *Pharmacol Biochem Behav* 2000;66:3–14.

42. Malle BF. The actor-observer asymmetry in attribution: a (surprising) meta-analysis. *Psychol Bull* 2006;132:895–919.

43. Kemps E, Tiggemann M. Modality-specific imagery reduces cravings for food: an application of the elaborated intrusion theory of desire to food craving. *J Exp Psychol Appl* 2007;13(2):95–104.

35

Is Sugar as Addictive as Cocaine?

SERGE H. AHMED

In contemporary affluent societies, people report consuming sugar-sweetened foods and beverages not only to get calories but also to experience pleasant sensations, to cope with stress or fatigue, to enhance cognition, and/or to ameliorate mood (e.g., relief of negative affect). As a result, sweetened foods and drinks have often been metaphorically likened to certain drugs of abuse, including psychostimulants and opiates. However, it is not until recently after having taken full measure of the rapid "sweetening of the world's diet"[1] and the associated obesity epidemic that serious concerns have begun to emerge about the real addictive potential of sugar-sweetened goods.[2-5] There is also a rapidly rising issue about the potential long-term impact of overconsumption of sugar-sweetened diets during infant and adolescent development on subsequent adult psychosocial functioning (e.g., impulse control, motivation).[6,7]

Most, though not all, of the satisfaction or gratification that is derived from sugar-sweetened foods and drinks comes from the sense of taste. In virtually all mammals, including humans, the taste of sweet is unique in being an innately and intensely rewarding primary sensory modality that is hardwired to the brain reward system.[8] There is now compelling evidence that sweet taste, along other primary taste modalities, is mediated by a "distinct and strictly segregated population of taste receptor cells."[8] Thus, for instance, if a non-taste-receptor is ectopically expressed in sweet cells in the taste buds of mutant mice, they will drink a solution containing a normally tasteless ligand.[9] More strikingly, in fruit flies, feeding behavior can be initiated by a light stimulus when their sweet receptor neurons have been genetically engineered to express a light-sensitive ionic channel.[10] At a more central level, sweet taste activates brain systems that are also targeted by drugs of abuse. For instance, consumption of sweetened water activates midbrain dopamine neurons,[11] which then release dopamine in the ventral striatum[12]—a neurochemical event that plays a major role in reinforcement learning and associated functions, including decision making and action selection. Sweet taste also activates other components of the brain reward circuitry that is affected by drugs of abuse, such as the ventral striatum,[13] the ventral pallidum,[14] and the orbitofrontal cortex.[15,16] The orbitofrontal cortex—which is anatomically and functionally linked to the insular gustatory cortex—is currently conceptualized as a general valuation system that allows a subject to represent and to compare the values of different kinds of rewards to determine choice.[17] It is intriguing to note that the valuation system of the brain— that is also recruited during moral judgments—is probably evolutionarily and functionally related to the gustatory cortex.

Thus, there exist clear behavioral, psychological, and neurobiological commonalities between sweet diets and drugs of abuse. Little is known, however, about the relative rewarding and addictive potential of the former compared to the latter. For instance, is sweetness as addictive as cocaine, the current prototypical drug of abuse? This information will be useful in updating the hierarchy of addictive substances and activities and to prioritize public health action. In the recent past the direct comparison of nicotine—which was initially thought to be nonaddictive—with cocaine contributed substantially to change public awareness about its addictive potential.[18,19] In light of the difficulties inherent in conducting direct comparisons between sweet goods and drugs of abuse in humans, we began to address this question in laboratory rats. Rats are, by far, the most frequently used animal model in experimental research on addiction. Like humans, rats have a sweet tooth, and they self-administer most major drugs of abuse (e.g., cocaine, heroin). Finally, most breakthrough advances in the neurobiology of drugs of abuse have been initially obtained through research using rats.[20]

To assess the relative rewarding and addictive value of sweet taste, rats that were not hungry or thirsty were allowed to choose between drinking water sweetened with a near optimal concentration of saccharin (0.2%) or taking an intravenous bolus of cocaine (0.25 mg per injection).[21] Saccharin—a nonnutritive sweetener—was chosen to study the unique contribution of taste sweetness on preference. However, similar findings have been obtained with sucrose[21]—a natural sugar that is more rewarding than saccharin.[22] Cocaine, especially when it is delivered rapidly to the brain following smoking or intravenous injection, induces intense rewarding sensations that are thought to contribute to its addictive liability. At the neurobiological level, cocaine boosts dopamine signaling in the ventral striatum by inhibiting the dopamine transporter[23] and also by activating midbrain dopamine neurons through an as-yet-undetermined interoceptive conditioning mechanism.[24] In addition to these acute effects, extended use of cocaine also induces long-lasting structural and functional changes in several brain regions[20,25,26] that may explain some of the behavioral symptoms of addiction, including escalation of cocaine use,[27] increased effort to obtain cocaine,[28] and continued cocaine use despite potential negative consequences.[29]

To make their choice, rats had to press one of two levers, one associated with sweetened water, the other with cocaine. Each daily choice session consisted of several discrete, spaced trials and was divided into two successive phases: sampling and choice.[21] During sampling, each lever was presented alternatively, thereby allowing rats to separately learn the value of each reward before making their choice. In contrast, during choice, the cocaine- and sweet-associated levers were presented simultaneously and rats were free to respond on either lever to obtain the corresponding reward. When one reward was selected, the two levers retracted simultaneously until the next trial. As a result, selecting one reward excluded the alternative reward, thereby allowing rats to express their preference (i.e., choice was mutually exclusive or either/or). Naïve rats were initially tested in the choice procedure under three reward conditions. The first two reward conditions were control conditions aimed at separately measuring the effectiveness of each type of reward. In those control conditions, only responding on

one lever was rewarded by the corresponding reward (cocaine or saccharin); responding on the other lever remained unrewarded. In the third, experimental condition, responding on one lever was rewarded by cocaine and responding on the alternate lever was rewarded by sweetened water.

As expected, when only one response was rewarded by either cocaine or sweet water, rats developed a significant preference for it and ignored the nonrewarded lever (Fig. 35.1a). This result demonstrates that when presented alone, each type of reward effectively and selectively reinforced and maintained responding. Surprisingly, however, the rate of preference acquisition (i.e., number of days to reach a stable preference) was slower when behavior was rewarded with cocaine than with sweetened water (Fig. 35.1b), suggesting that the former reward is probably less efficacious than the latter. This interpretation is confirmed by the outcome of the experimental condition. When responding on either lever was rewarded, rats developed a rapid and marked preference for sweetened water and almost completely ignored cocaine (Fig. 35.1a,b), a finding that is consistent with previous research in rats with concurrent access to cocaine and saccharin.[30,31] Interestingly, sweet preference was acquired and persisted despite near maximal sampling of the cocaine lever.[21] Finally, the latency to choose sweet water was shorter than the latency to choose cocaine (Fig. 35.1c). Since the latency to respond is generally inversely related to the magnitude of the upcoming reward (i.e., the more intense the reward, the shorter the latency), this outcome provides additional, independent confirmation that the reward value of cocaine is weaker than that of sweetened water in rats.

The preference for sweetened water was not surmountable by increasing the dose of cocaine (i.e., up to the subconvulsive dose of 1.5 mg), suggesting that the reward value of sweet water is higher than the maximal reward value of cocaine.[21] In addition, once acquired, preference for sweet taste did not persist because of some sort of behavioral inertia, unrelated to the reward value of sweetness. For instance, it could be argued that since rats rapidly learned to choose sweet water almost exclusively, they would subsequently have little opportunity to change their preference in favor of cocaine. To address this important issue, rats were first trained in the choice procedure with no alternative to cocaine. Once they developed a stable preference

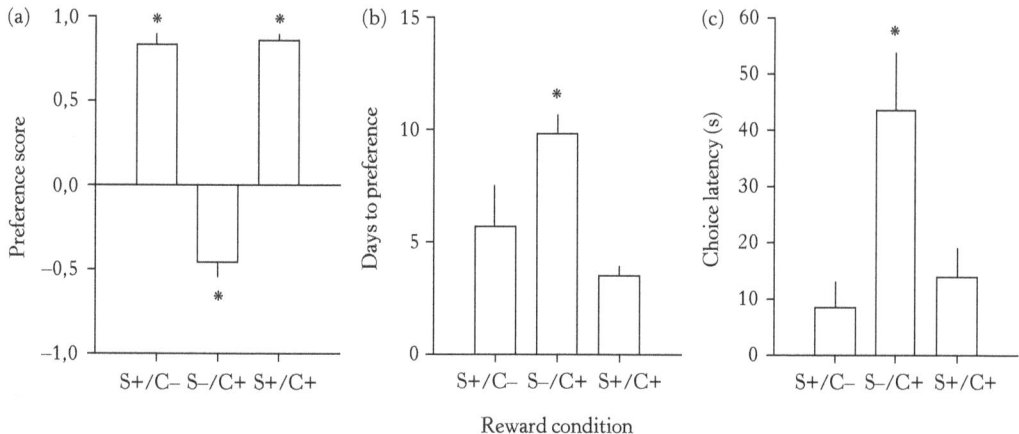

FIGURE 35.1. The effects of choice on cocaine self-administration. (a) Choice (mean ± SEM) between the saccharin-associated lever (S) and the cocaine-associated lever (C) across reward conditions (S+/C−: only responses on lever S are rewarded; S−/C+: only responses on lever C are rewarded; S+/C+: responses on both levers are rewarded). Preference scores were normalized as described previously.[21] The horizontal dotted line at 0 indicates the indifference level. Scores above 0 indicate a preference for sweet water, while values below 0 indicate a preference for cocaine. Asterisk indicates difference from the indifference level ($p < .05$). (b) Number of days (mean ± SEM) before stabilization of preference scores (i.e., at least three consecutive sessions of stable preference). Asterisk indicates differences from the other two reward conditions. (c) Latency (mean ± SEM) of choice making in seconds ($p < .05$). Asterisk indicates difference from the other two reward conditions ($p < .05$).
Source: Adapted from Lenoir et al., 2007.

for the cocaine lever, they were then offered the choice between cocaine and sweetened water. Subjects rapidly shifted their preference away from cocaine toward sweetened water (Fig. 35.2a), suggesting that behavioral inertia is unlikely a significant factor in sweet preference.[21] To further address this issue, other rats were first trained on alternate days to lever press to self-administer either cocaine or saccharin. The number of rewards was limited to 30 per session to equal the number of pairings of each lever with its corresponding reward. After acquisition and stabilization of cocaine and saccharin self-administration, rats were then trained in the choice procedure. Surprisingly, prior fixed-ratio (FR) training accelerated, rather than retarded, the expression of sweet preference.[32] In fact, rats presented a significant preference for sweet water on the first day of testing (Fig. 35.2b). This outcome shows that during FR training, rats had independently attributed a higher value to the saccharin lever compared to the cocaine lever, a process that does not support a role for behavioral inertia in sweet preference. Finally, to definitively rule out behavioral inertia, rats were trained in a modified choice procedure. Briefly, the sampling period was replaced by 1 h of continuous

access to cocaine. Thus, every day before choice testing, rats were allowed to self-administer cocaine continuously. If behavioral inertia played a significant role in choice performance, then one should expect that rats will continue—at least transiently—to respond on the cocaine lever during choice. Contrary to this prediction, however, rats normally self-administered cocaine during the first hour, but they almost immediately shifted their response to the lever associated with sweet water during choice.[21] The fact that rats quickly reoriented their behavior away from cocaine to sweet water clearly demonstrates that the persistence of sweet preference is not attributable to behavioral inertia.

Overall, the research reviewed earlier demonstrates that the reward value of sweet taste is greater than that of intravenous cocaine. But what is exactly the magnitude of this difference in reward value? To address this question, the number of responses or amount of effort required to earn sweetened water was gradually increased above that of cocaine until a reversal of preference and thus identification of the indifference point (or point of subjective equality). The latter provides a quantitative estimation of the relative value of cocaine compared to sweet water.

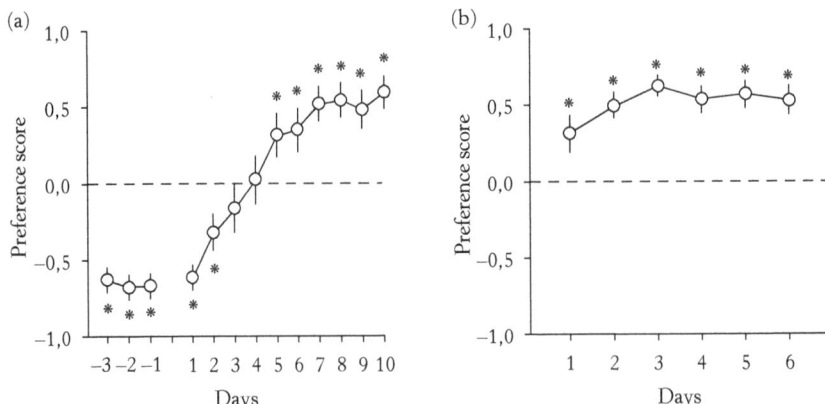

FIGURE 35.2. Sweet preference is not due to behavioral inertia. (a) Reversal of preference in rats that had first acquired a preference for lever C under the S–/C+ condition. The first 3 days (–3 to –1) correspond to baseline choice under the S–/C+ condition. The next 10 days correspond to choice after the shift to the S+/C+ reward condition. (b) Immediate expression of sweet preference in rats previously trained to stably self-administer cocaine and sweet water on alternate days under a continuous reinforcement schedule. Asterisk indicates difference from the indifference level ($p < .05$).

Source: Panel (a) was adapted from Lenoir et al 2007); Panel (b) was adapted from Cantin et al., 2010.

As one would expect, when the amount of effort for sweetened water increased, rats progressively shifted their preference to cocaine.[32] At the highest amount of effort (i.e., 16 times that for cocaine), virtually all rats shifted their preference to cocaine. Importantly, the point of indifference was reached when the effort demanded for sweetened water was about 8 times that for cocaine.[32] This large ratio of effort suggests that the reward value of sweet water is about one order of magnitude higher than that of cocaine.

Preference for sweet water was observed in either initially cocaine-naïve rats or in rats with a limited experience with cocaine. As mentioned earlier, following extended access to cocaine, most rats escalate their consumption of cocaine and work harder for and take more risk to obtain the drug, suggesting an increased drug value.[32] Thus, a key issue is whether sweet preference can be overridden by this increase in cocaine value. To answer this question, rats were first allowed to have daily extended access to cocaine self-administration during several weeks before choice testing (i.e., 6 hours per day, 6 days a week). As expected, following extended access to cocaine self-administration, most rats escalated their consumption of cocaine (Fig. 35.3a). Surprisingly, however, when offered a choice between cocaine and sweet water, most rats rapidly acquired a strong preference for the latter regardless of the cocaine dose available

(Fig. 35.3b). In fact, sweet preference reached statistical significance as early as the second day of testing, a rate of acquisition that was comparable to that seen in initially naïve rats.[21] Thus, although the value of cocaine definitively increases during extended drug self-administration, this increase was apparently not sufficient to override sweet preference, at least in the majority of individuals.

In summary, in nonhungry, nonthirsty rats, the taste sensation associated with the ingestion of sweetened water is clearly more rewarding than the artificial sensations of intravenous cocaine, independent of prior cocaine history. Recently, this conclusion was generalized to intravenous heroin, with one notable difference[33,34]: heroin was more potent than cocaine in competing with sweet taste, especially following extended heroin use.[34] This difference is consistent with epidemiological research in humans suggesting that heroin is more addictive than cocaine.[35] Nevertheless, when offered a choice, most heroin-dependent rats eventually cut down heroin use to drink more sweet water.[34] This observation further underscores the importance of sweet taste reward in driving and controlling preference. Other recent research has also uncovered a major role of other palatability factors (i.e., other than taste quality) in determining preference. For instance, Kippin and colleagues have recently shown using a similar choice procedure to that described here that hungry rats rapidly stop using cocaine to prefer standard

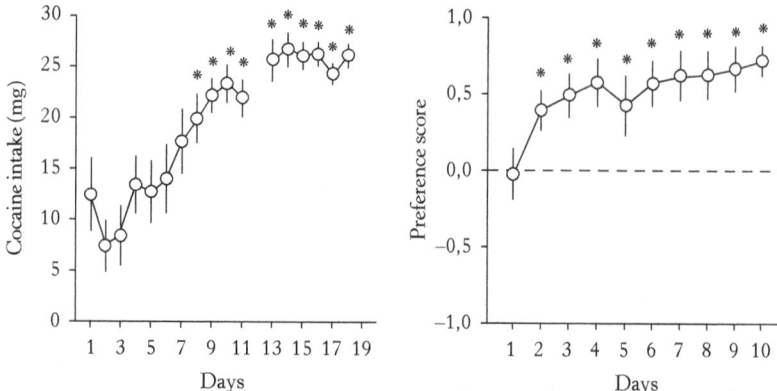

FIGURE 35.3. Sweet preference following extended cocaine self-administration. (a) Escalation of cocaine self-administration during extended access to a high dose of cocaine (0.75 mg per injection). Data corresponding to the 12th day are missing due to a computer failure. Asterisk indicates difference from the first day ($p < .05$). (b) Choice between cocaine and sweet water (mean ± SEM) after cocaine intake escalation. Asterisk indicates difference from the indifference level ($p < .05$). *Source:* Adapted from Lenoir et al., 2007.

food pellets (nonsweet, nonfat), an effect that is partially sex dependent.[36] Similarly, using a behavioral economic approach, it was recently estimated that the reward value of standard food pellets or sucrose is much greater than that of intravenous cocaine in hungry rats from different strains.[37-39] This difference in value persists even following chronic cocaine self-administration and evidence for escalated cocaine use.[40] These observations are also consistent with older, though often overlooked, experiments showing that under some circumstances, palatable food or sweetened water can compete with direct electrical stimulation of the brain reward circuit.[41-44] More recently, it was found using optogenetic methods that mice largely prefer drinking sucrose over direct stimulation of midbrain dopamine cells.[45] This finding reminds us that sucrose intake activates more than dopamine neurons in the brain which may explain why it is such a compelling stimulus even when compared to cocaine. Finally, though little is known about the neural correlates of sugar preference over cocaine, clues are beginning to emerge. A recent in vivo electrophysiological recording study in rats self-administering cocaine or sucrose found that sucrose-selective neurons outnumber by a large margin cocaine-selective neurons in the ventral striatum (70% versus 5%)[46]—a finding that corroborates previous research in monkeys.[47] This predominance of sugar-selective cells in the ventral striatum may represent the neural correlate of rats' preference for sugar over cocaine. All together these different findings suggest that palatable diets, in general,

and sweet diets, in particular, can clearly be more rewarding—and thus potentially more addictive—than intravenous cocaine and heroin in laboratory rats. Though one cannot, of course, directly extrapolate these findings to humans, they should nevertheless contribute to prompt a serious reconsideration of the hierarchy of potentially addictive substances and activities, with certain foods and drinks possibly taking precedence over major drugs of abuse.

ACKNOWLEDGMENTS

This work was supported by grants from the French Research Council (CNRS), Université Victor-Segalen Bordeaux 2, the National Research Agency (ANR), the Mission Interministérielle de Lutte contre la Drogue et la Toxicomaine (MILDT), and the Fondation pour la Recherche Médicale (FRM). I thank Dr. Kelly Clemens for her comments on a previous draft of this book chapter.

REFERENCES

1. Popkin BM, Nielsen SJ. The sweetening of the world's diet. *Obes Res* 2003;11:1325–1332.
2. Ifland JR et al. Refined food addiction: a classic substance use disorder. *Med Hypotheses* 2009;72:518–526.
3. Gearhardt AN, Corbin WR, Brownell KD. Preliminary validation of the Yale Food Addiction Scale. *Appetite* 2009;52:430–436.
4. Corwin RL, Grigson PS. Symposium overview—Food addiction: fact or fiction? *J Nutr* 2009;139:617–619.
5. Avena NM, Rada P, Hoebel BG. Evidence for sugar addiction: behavioral and neurochemical effects of intermittent, excessive sugar intake. *Neurosci Biobehav Rev* 2008;32:20–39.

6. Moore SC, Carter LM, van Goozen S. Confectionery consumption in childhood and adult violence. *Br J Psychiatry* 2009;195:366–367.

7. Frazier CR, Mason P, Zhuang X, Beeler JA. Sucrose exposure in early life alters adult motivation and weight gain. *PLoS One* 2008;3:e3221.

8. Yarmolinsky DA, Zuker CS, Ryba NJ. Common sense about taste: from mammals to insects. *Cell* 2009;139:234–244.

9. Zhao GQ, et al. The receptors for mammalian sweet and umami taste. *Cell* 2003;115:255–266.

10. Gordon MD, Scott K. Motor control in a Drosophila taste circuit. *Neuron* 2009;61:373–384.

11. Mirenowicz J, Schultz W. Preferential activation of midbrain dopamine neurons by appetitive rather than aversive stimuli. *Nature* 1996;379:449–451.

12. Hajnal A, Norgren R. Accumbens dopamine mechanisms in sucrose intake. *Brain Res* 2001;904:76–84.

13. Roitman MF, Wheeler RA, Carelli RM. Nucleus accumbens neurons are innately tuned for rewarding and aversive taste stimuli, encode their predictors, and are linked to motor output. *Neuron* 2005;45:587–597.

14. Tindell AJ, Smith KS, Pecina S, Berridge KC, Aldridge JW. Ventral pallidum firing codes hedonic reward: when a bad taste turns good. *J Neurophysiol* 2006;96:2399–2409.

15. Kravitz AV, Peoples LL. Background firing rates of orbitofrontal neurons reflect specific characteristics of operant sessions and modulate phasic responses to reward-associated cues and behavior. *J Neurosci* 2008;28:1009–1018.

16. Critchley HD, Rolls ET. Olfactory neuronal responses in the primate orbitofrontal cortex: analysis in an olfactory discrimination task. *J Neurophysiol* 1996;75:1659–1672.

17. Kable JW, Glimcher PW. The neurobiology of decision: consensus and controversy. *Neuron* 2009;63:733–745.

18. Stolerman IP, Jarvis MJ. The scientific case that nicotine is addictive. *Psychopharmacol (Berl)* 1995;117:2–10; discussion 14–20.

19. Pich EM, et al. Common neural substrates for the addictive properties of nicotine and cocaine. *Science* 1997;275:83–86.

20. Koob GF, Le Moal M. *Neurobiology of Addiction* San Diego, CA: Academic Press, 2006: p. 490.

21. Lenoir M, Serre F, Cantin L, Ahmed SH. Intense sweetness surpasses cocaine reward. *PLoS One* 2007;2:e698.

22. Smith JC, Sclafani A. Saccharin as a sugar surrogate revisited. *Appetite* 2002;38:155–160.

23. Giros B, Jaber M, Jones SR, Wightman RM, Caron MG. Hyperlocomotion and indifference to cocaine and amphetamine in mice lacking the dopamine transporter. *Nature* 1996;379:606–612.

24. Wise RA, Wang B, You ZB. Cocaine serves as a peripheral interoceptive conditioned stimulus for central glutamate and dopamine release. *PLoS One* 2008;3:e2846.

25. Nestler EJ. Is there a common molecular pathway for addiction? *Nat Neurosci* 2005;8:1445–1449.

26. Robinson TE, Kolb B. Structural plasticity associated with exposure to drugs of abuse. *Neuropharmacology* 2004;47 Suppl 1:33–46.

27. Ahmed SH, Koob GF. Transition from moderate to excessive drug intake: change in hedonic set point. *Science* 1998;282:298–300.

28. Paterson NE, Markou A. Increased motivation for self-administered cocaine after escalated cocaine intake. *Neuroreport* 200314:2229–2232.

29. Vanderschuren LJ, Everitt BJ. Drug seeking becomes compulsive after prolonged cocaine self-administration. *Science* 2004;305:1017–1019.

30. Carroll ME, Lac ST, Nygaard SL. A concurrently available nondrug reinforcer prevents the acquisition or decreases the maintenance of cocaine-reinforced behavior. *Psychopharmacol (Berl)* 1989;97:23–29.

31. Carroll ME, Lac ST. Autoshaping i.v. cocaine self-administration in rats: effects of nondrug alternative reinforcers on acquisition. *Psychopharmacol (Berl)* 1993;110:5–12.

32. Cantin L, et al. Cocaine is low on the value ladder of rats: possible evidence for resilience to addiction. *PLoS One* 2010;5:e11592.

33. Ahmed SH. Imbalance between drug and non-drug reward availability: a major risk factor for addiction. *Eur J Pharmacol* 2005;526:9–20.

34. Lenoir M, Cantin L, Serre F, Ahmed SH. The value of heroin increases with extended use but not above the value of a non-essential alternative reward. Paper presented at 38th annual meeting of the Society for Neuroscience; November 15-19 2008; Washington DC.

35. Substance Abuse and Mental Health Services Administration. Results from the 2002 National Survey on Drug Use and Health: National Findings. in *NHSDUA Series H-22, DHHS Publication No. SMA 03-3836*; 2003; Rockville, MD: Office of Applied Studies.

36. Kerstetter KA, Wade MA, Gonzalez SG, Kneib JB, Kippin TE. Selecting between food and cocaine reinforcement. Paper presented at 39th annual meeting of the Society for Neuroscience; October 17-21 2009; Chicago, IL.

37. Christensen CJ, Kohut SJ, Handler S, Silberberg A, Riley AL. Demand for food and cocaine in Fischer and Lewis rats. *Behav Neurosci* 2009;123:165–171.

38. Christensen CJ, Silberberg A, Hursh SR, Huntsberry ME, Riley AL. Essential value of cocaine and food in rats: tests of the exponential model of demand. *Psychopharmacol (Berl)* 2008;198:221–229.

39. Koffarnus MN, Woods JH. Individual differences in discount rate are associated with demand for self-administered cocaine, but not sucrose. *Addict Biol* 2011 Aug 4. doi: 10.1111/j.1369-1600.2011.00361.x. [Epub ahead of print]

40. Christensen CJ, Silberberg A, Hursh SR, Roma PG, Riley AL. Demand for cocaine and food over time. *Pharmacol Biochem Behav* 2008;91:209–216.

41. Hursh SR, Natelson BH. Electrical brain stimulation and food reinforcement dissociated by demand elasticity. *Physiol Behav* 1981;26:509–515.

42. Phillips AG, Morgan CW, Mogenson GJ. Changes in self-stimulation preference as a function of incentive of alternative rewards. *Can J Psychol* 1970;24:289–297.

43. Conover KL, Shizgal P. Differential effects of postingestive feedback on the reward value of sucrose and lateral hypothalamic stimulation in rats. *Behav Neurosci* 1994;108:559–572.

44. Conover KL, Shizgal P. Competition and summation between rewarding effects of sucrose and lateral hypothalamic stimulation in the rat. *Behav Neurosci* 1994;108:537–548.

45. Domingos AI, et al. Leptin regulates the reward value of nutrient. *Nat Neurosci* 2011;14:1562–1568.

46. Cameron CM, Carelli RM. Cocaine abstinence alters nucleus accumbens firing dynamics during goal-directed behaviors for cocaine and sucrose. *Eur J Neurosci* 2012;35:940–951.

47. Bowman EM, Aigner TG, Richmond BJ. Neural signals in the monkey ventral striatum related to motivation for juice and cocaine rewards. *J Neurophysiol* 1996;75:1061–1073.

36

Caffeine, Addiction, and Food Consumption

DANIEL P. EVATT AND ROLAND R. GRIFFITHS

INTRODUCTION

Caffeine, the most widely used psychoactive drug in the world, is usually consumed in beverages and foods. It is a natural constituent of at least 60 species of plants, including coffee, tea, cocoa, cola nut, and yerba maté. Tea consumption dates back at least two millennia in China. Coffee, tea, and cocoa consumption became widespread in Europe and elsewhere in the seventeenth and eighteenth centuries with the development of worldwide trading routes. In the United States, 87% of the population regularly consume caffeinated foods and beverages.[1] Mean daily dietary caffeine intake among all caffeine users is 193 mg/day; caffeine consumption is greatest among men aged 35–54 years, who consume, on average, 336 mg/day.[1]

Although caffeine is most usually prepared and consumed directly from its natural plant forms (e.g., coffee and tea), caffeine has a long history of being used in combination with food products. Legend holds that the ancient Galla tribe of Ethiopia combined coffee cherries with animal fat to create small edible balls to provide sustenance during wartime raids.[2] The practice of adding sugar to coffee and tea dates back at least several hundred years.

This review will first discuss several clinical effects of caffeine that are important to understanding the role of caffeine in food consumption: subjective effects, reinforcing effects, conditioned flavor preferences, tolerance, withdrawal, and clinical dependence (i.e., addiction). The final sections will discuss caffeine as a promoter of weight loss, caffeine as an added as well as a naturally occurring ingredient in beverages and foods, and children and adolescents as a vulnerable population.

CAFFEINE SUBJECTIVE EFFECTS, REINFORCEMENT, AND CONDITIONED FLAVOR PREFERENCE EFFECTS

Studies show that low to moderate doses of caffeine generally produce increased ratings of positive (i.e., pleasant) subjective effects, such as increased well-being, alertness, and energy. At higher doses, caffeine generally produces various unpleasant effects, including anxiety and upset stomach. The positive subjective effects of caffeine are robust, occurring both in nonhabitual caffeine users as well as in regular caffeine users who have been briefly caffeine deprived (e.g., overnight).[3-5]

The reinforcing effects of caffeine have been demonstrated in numerous double-blind studies using a variety of methodological approaches (i.e., variations of self-administration and choice procedures), in various subject groups (e.g., adult and adolescents), and when caffeine was tested in various vehicles (e.g., coffee, soft drinks, and capsules).[5-7] A review of caffeine reinforcement studies showed that approximately 40% of normal caffeine users demonstrate caffeine reinforcement.[5]

Experimental studies using a conditioned flavor preference paradigm have provided indirect evidence of caffeine reinforcement. In these studies, repeated exposure to a novel flavored beverage paired with caffeine resulted in increased ratings of drink pleasantness, relative to exposure to a different flavor paired with placebo.[8-10] It seems plausible that such conditioned flavor preferences play an important role in the development of consumer preferences for different types of caffeine-containing beverages.

Studies suggest that avoidance of abstinence-associated withdrawal symptoms (discussed later) represents a primary pharmacological mechanism underlying the habitual consumption of caffeinated beverages. This important role of caffeine withdrawal has been demonstrated in survey studies as well as controlled experimental studies of caffeine subjective effects, caffeine reinforcement, and beverage flavor preferences.[9,11-13]

CAFFEINE TOLERANCE

Acquired tolerance to the physiological, subjective, and sleep-disrupting effects of caffeine is well documented.

Tolerance to caffeine can be expected to vary according to the caffeine dose, frequency of dosing, and individual differences in elimination rate.[14] Complete tolerance to the subjective, pressor, and neuroendocrine effects of caffeine has been observed in individuals consuming 750–1200 mg of caffeine daily.[11,15] One recent study at lower doses (400 mg/day) suggested that tolerance to subjective effects (e.g., ratings of lively, full of pep, and friendly) was more likely to occur than tolerance to physiological effects.[16]

Survey data suggest that self-reported prevalence of caffeine tolerance among current caffeine users varies considerably, with reported rates ranging between 8%[17] and 50%.[18] Prevalence of self-reported tolerance is much higher (70%–92%) in studies of caffeine-dependent individuals.[19–21]

CAFFEINE WITHDRAWAL

In the last two decades, strong empirical evidence has emerged that caffeine withdrawal is a discrete syndrome occurring in some chronic caffeine users following abstinence. The World Health Organization recognizes caffeine withdrawal as a valid diagnosis in *ICD-10*[22] and the American Psychiatric Association includes caffeine withdrawal as a proposed research diagnosis in *DSM-IV-TR*.[23] A review of 66 studies found evidence for five valid clusters of symptoms for describing the caffeine-withdrawal syndrome: (1) headache; (2) fatigue or drowsiness; (3) dysphoric mood, depressed mood, or irritability; (4) difficulty concentrating; and (5) flu-like somatic symptoms, nausea, vomiting, or muscle pain/stiffness.[12] Headache is the most common symptom of caffeine withdrawal, although a withdrawal syndrome can occur without headache.[24,25] In experimental studies of caffeine withdrawal, 50% of subjects report headache and 13% of subjects report clinically significant distress or functional impairment.[12]

After cessation of caffeine, onset of caffeine withdrawal typically occurs within 12 to 24 hours, with symptoms usually reaching maximal intensity between 20 and 51 hours.[12] After reaching peak intensity, withdrawal symptoms usually diminish to prewithdrawal levels over 2 to 9 days. Severity of withdrawal is an increasing function of caffeine dose, with symptoms occurring after cessation of doses of as low as 100 mg/day.[24] The readministration of caffeine can rapidly and completely reverse the symptoms of caffeine withdrawal.[24] There is considerable variability between people in the onset, time course, and severity of withdrawal symptoms.[12]

CAFFEINE DEPENDENCE

In recent years, a growing literature has emerged that clearly documents that some caffeine users manifest clinically significant symptoms of substance dependence applied to caffeine (i.e., addiction).[17–21] Substance dependence (commonly referred to as drug addiction) is a clinically significant syndrome characterized by problematic use of a psychoactive substance. Caffeine dependence is an official diagnosis in *ICD-10*[22], although *DSM-IV-TR*[23] currently excludes caffeine dependence as a substance dependence diagnosis.

Of particular relevance to the use of caffeinated beverages are findings from two survey studies in the general population that indicate that 56%[17] or 45%[18] of caffeine users endorse the criterion "a persistent desire or unsuccessful efforts to cut down or control substance use." These same studies reported rates of 28%[17] and 45%[18] for caffeine users endorsing "the substance is often taken in larger amounts or over a longer period than intended," and 18%[17] and 77%[18] for endorsing withdrawal (as described earlier) or taking the substance "to relieve or avoid withdrawal." In addition, these studies reported rates of 14%[17] and 43%[18] for caffeine users endorsing "substance use is continued despite knowledge of having a persistent or recurrent physical or psychological problem that is likely to have been caused or exacerbated by the substance." Finally, the Hughes et al. survey[17] also reported that 15% of caffeine consumers endorsed the *ICD-9* criterion that drug use had become so regular that a person would not change when or how much they used, no matter what they were doing or where they were. Rates of past year caffeine dependence in the general population are not trivial. Depending on the specific *DSM-IV-TR* substance dependence criteria applied, the rate of caffeine dependence has been estimated to be between 9%[17] and 30%[18] of caffeine consumers. The diagnosis has clinical utility in that it predicts the inability to quit caffeine and is associated with high rates of functional impairment during withdrawal.[18,19]

Development of caffeine dependence is not restricted to coffee consumers. A recent investigation of individuals who were seeking treatment for problematic caffeine use found that coffee was the primary source of caffeine for 50% of the sample, while soft drinks were the primary source of caffeine for 37% of the sample, with 74% of the sample consuming soft drinks every day[26]. Although participants who primarily drank coffee consumed more daily caffeine relative to participants who primarily drank soft drinks, there was no difference in prevalence of caffeine dependence between coffee drinkers and soft drink consumers.[26]

CAFFEINE AND WEIGHT LOSS

Caffeine is a common ingredient in over-the-counter weight loss medications. Several investigations suggest that caffeine may reduce weight via stimulation of thermogenic effects.[27] Experimental studies in habitual caffeine consumers that compared a caffeine administration condition to a caffeine-free (i.e., withdrawal) condition have consistently demonstrated that caffeine administration is associated with greater energy expenditure.[28–31] However, these findings should be interpreted cautiously because it is not clear whether the difference reported is due to caffeine increasing thermogenic effects and/or caffeine withdrawal decreasing thermogenesis. Furthermore, even if it is assumed that caffeine has thermogenic effects, these studies do not address whether tolerance to such effects occurs with daily caffeine exposure. As described earlier, tolerance to various caffeine effects has been well demonstrated. Finally, the clinical applicability of possible thermogenic effects of caffeine may be limited by the observation that the effects of caffeine on energy expenditure may be greater in lean, relative to obese, individuals.[31]

Caffeine could also reduce weight by reducing appetite and decreasing food intake. One study found that, following a 12-hour fast, administration of 300 mg of caffeine reduced subsequent food intake in men, but not women.[32] A residential laboratory study revealed that the readministration of caffeine reduced caloric intake relative to the preceding 2-day caffeine abstinent period.[33] Another study found that caffeine enhanced the anorectic effect of nicotine on ratings of hunger, but it did not affect food consumed in men who had been overnight abstinent from both caffeine and nicotine.[34] Taken together, these findings suggest that caffeine may reduce appetite and caloric intake. Although caffeine withdrawal seemingly did not affect caloric intake in the Comer et al. study, the confounding effects of caffeine withdrawal cannot

be entirely ruled out. Also, as with the caffeine thermogenic findings discussed earlier, these studies do not address whether regular caffeine users develop tolerance to the effects of caffeine on appetite or caloric intake.

Prospective epidemiological studies have found that caffeine intake is negatively associated with weight gain.[35,36] However, there are few placebo-controlled, prospective, long-term outcome investigations of the effects of caffeine alone on weight loss. One randomized placebo-controlled study in obese patients over 24 weeks showed no effect of caffeine alone (200 mg, t.i.d.) on weight loss.[37]

Several investigations have examined the effects of caffeine in combination with other drugs or products on weight loss outcomes. Studies typically reveal an efficacious effect of combined ephedrine/caffeine on weight loss outcomes.[38] However, the Food and Drug Administration has banned use of ephedra alkaloids because of adverse events.[39] Some studies suggest that consumption of green tea or green tea extract that contain both caffeine and catechin polyphenols can increase thermogenesis and weight loss, and can reduce weight regain.[27,38] The specific role of caffeine in these effects is unclear. One placebo-controlled study showed that administration of caffeine and catechins prevented weight regain following a period of dieting in low, but not high, caffeine consumers.[40]

CAFFEINE AS AN INGREDIENT IN BEVERAGES AND FOODS

Caffeine as an Added Ingredient in Beverages and Foods

Caffeine, which has a bitter taste, has been an added ingredient in commercially available soft drinks for over 100 years. Although bitter-tasting foods may be unpalatable, sugar, fat, and other flavors can be added to bitter foods to effectively mask or obscure the bitter taste profile.[41] Indeed, it has been suggested that sugar is commonly used as a means to increase the palatability of the bitter taste of coffee in novice users.[42] Although beverage manufacturers have claimed that caffeine is added to soft drinks as a flavor enhancer, studies show that most people are unable to detect a flavor difference between sugar-sweetened cola beverages with and without added caffeine at the caffeine concentration of most marketed soft drinks.[43,44]

As documented in previous sections, caffeine can function as a reinforcer, produce conditioned flavor preferences, produce a withdrawal syndrome that promotes habitual daily consumption, and produce a drug dependence syndrome (i.e., addiction) that result in habitual daily use. It is not surprising, therefore, that many widely consumed beverages contain caffeine. In 2008, 14.4 billion gallons of carbonated soft drink were sold in the United States, which is the equivalent to approximately 507 cans for every man, woman, and child. The great majority of these products contain caffeine.[43,45] In addition to soft drinks, manufacturers are increasingly adding caffeine to other food products, including candy, potato chips, beef jerky, and energy drinks. In the last several years, the sugar-sweetened energy drink market has grown exponentially and hundreds of new caffeinated energy drinks have been introduced.[46]

A growing body of literature suggests that the regular use of sugary drinks is associated with weight gain and obesity.[47] A recent review and meta-analysis of 88 studies found a positive relationship between soft drink consumption and energy intake and body weight.[48] Importantly, experimental studies showed that when soft drink consumption is increased, people do not compensate for the increased caloric intake (i.e., do not reduce their remaining diet). In fact, one study showed that soft drink consumption resulted in daily energy intake even greater (17%) than could be accounted for by the additional energy content of the soft drinks consumed.[49]

Studies have also shown associations between sugary drink consumption and other adverse health outcomes. The strongest and most consistent finding is that sugary drink consumption is associated with the development of type 2 diabetes.[47,48] Some studies suggest positive relationships between sugar-sweetened beverage consumption and hypocalcemia, urinary or kidney stones, systolic and diastolic blood pressure, and hypertension. Moreover, studies have found an association between sugary drink consumption and reduced intake of healthy foods and essential nutrients.[48]

Naturally Occurring Caffeine-Containing Beverages with Added Sugar and Fat

Although adding sugar to coffee has occurred for hundreds of years, a significant recent trend in the United States has been the proliferation of specialty coffee outlets marketing high-calorie, high-fat specialty coffee beverages. Moreover, the widespread and habitual consumption of highly sugared caffeine-containing tea, or Sweet Tea, is prevalent in the Southeastern United States. It is plausible that these calorie-containing beverages may be associated with the same types of health risks discussed earlier for caffeinated sugary soft drinks (e.g., weight gain, obesity, type 2 diabetes). However, the long-term health consequences of the consumption of these specific types of beverages have not been rigorously evaluated.

CHILDREN AND ADOLESCENTS AS A VULNERABLE POPULATION

In considering the role of caffeine in foods and beverages, it is important to note that children and adolescents, to whom caffeinated beverages are often aggressively marketed, represent a vulnerable population. Analogous to concerns that have surrounded the marketing of tobacco products, it seems likely that children and adolescents are more susceptible than adults to advertising and promotion of caffeine-containing products. Sugar-sweetened beverage consumption has been associated weight gain and obesity in children, and it may displace milk and other nutritious foods in the diet of children and adolescents.[47] Studies have also demonstrated that children are susceptible to both caffeine withdrawal[50] and caffeine dependence.[20,51]

CONCLUSION

Caffeine is a widely used psychoactive drug that is both a natural and an added constituent of many beverages and foods. The human pharmacological profile of caffeine has many features in common with classic drugs of addiction. Caffeine produces positive subjective effects, functions as a reinforcer, produces conditioned flavor preferences, produces tolerance, produces a withdrawal syndrome that promotes habitual daily consumption, and results in a classic substance dependence syndrome characterized by inability to quit or cut down and harmful use. Both naturally occurring and added caffeine is a significant factor in the high rates of consumption of many beverages and foods. Consumption of sugary beverages is associated with adverse health outcomes such as weight gain, obesity, and type 2 diabetes. Thus, the apparent central role of caffeine in engendering habitual consumption of sugary drink consumption is troubling, and children and adolescents may represent a particularly vulnerable population. There is some evidence that caffeine may reduce weight, possibly via thermogenic or anorectic effects; however, findings are mixed and the long-term efficacy of caffeine as a weight loss aid has not been established.

REFERENCES

1. Frary CD, Johnson RK, Wang MQ. Food sources and intakes of caffeine in the diets of persons in the United States. *J Am Diet Assoc* 2005;105:110–113.
2. Weinberg BA, Bealer BK. *The World of Caffeine: The Science and Culture of the World's Most Popular Drug.* New York: Routledge, 2001.
3. Lieberman HR, Wurtman RJ, Emde GG, Coviella IL. The effects of caffeine and aspirin on mood and performance. *J Clin Psychopharm* 1987;7:315–320.
4. Griffiths RR, Evans SM, Heishman SJ, et al. Low-dose caffeine discrimination in humans. *J Pharmacol Exp Ther* 1990;255:1123–1132.
5. Griffiths RR, Juliano LM, Chausmer AL. Caffeine pharmacology and clinical effects. In: Graham AW, Schultz TK, Mayo-Smith MF, Ries RK, Wilford BB, eds. *Principles of Addiction Medicine.* 3rd ed. Chevy Chase, MD: American Society of Addiction Medicine; 2003: 193–224.
6. Griffiths RR, Woodson PP. Reinforcing effects of caffeine in humans. *J Pharmacol Exp Ther* 1988;246: 21–29.
7. Hughes JR, Oliveto AH, Bickel WK, Higgins ST, Badger GJ. Caffeine self-administration and withdrawal: incidence, individual differences and interrelationships. *Drug Alcohol Depen* 1993;32:239–246.
8. Rogers PJ, Richardson NJ, Elliman NA. Overnight caffeine abstinence and negative reinforcement of preference for caffeine-containing drinks. *Psychopharmacol* 1995;120:457–462.
9. Yeomans MR, Spetch H, Rogers PJ. Conditioned flavour preference negatively reinforced by caffeine in human volunteers. *Psychopharmacol* 1998;137: 401–409.
10. Tinley EM, Yeomans MR, Durlach PJ. Caffeine does not reinforce conditioned flavour liking in fully abstinent caffeine consumers. *Psychopharmacol* 2003;166:416–423.
11. Evans SM, Griffiths RR. Caffeine tolerance and choice in humans. *Psychopharmacol* 1992;108: 51–59.
12. Juliano LM, Griffiths RR. A critical review of caffeine withdrawal: empirical validation of symptoms and signs, incidence, severity, and associated features. *Psychopharmacol* 2004;176:1–29.
13. Chambers L, Mobini S, Yeomans MR. Caffeine deprivation state modulates expression of acquired

liking for caffeine-paired flavors. *Q J Exp Psychol* 2007;60:1356–1366.
14. Shi J, Benowitz NL, Denaro CP, Sheiner LB. Pharmacokinetic-pharmacodynamic modeling of caffeine: tolerance to pressor effects. *Clin Pharmacol Ther* 1993;53:6–14.
15. Robertson D, Wade D, Workman R, Woosley RL, Oates JA. Tolerance to the humoral and hemodynamic effects of caffeine in man. *J Clin Invest* 1981;67: 1111–1117.
16. Sigmon SC, Herning RI, Better W, Cadet JL, Griffiths RR. Caffeine withdrawal, acute effects, tolerance, and absence of net beneficial effects of chronic administration: cerebral blood flow velocity, quantitative EEG, and subjective effects. *Psychopharmacol* 2009;204:573–585.
17. Hughes JR, Oliveto AH, Liguori A, Carpenter J, Howard T. Endorsement of DSM-IV dependence criteria among caffeine users. *Drug Alcohol Depen* 1998;52:99–107.
18. Svikis DS, Berger N, Haug NA, Griffiths RR. Caffeine dependence in combination with a family history of alcoholism as a predictor of continued use of caffeine during pregnancy. *Am J Psychiat* 2005;162:2344–2351.
19. Strain EC, Mumford GK, Silverman K, Griffiths RR. Caffeine dependence syndrome: evidence from case histories and experimental evaluations. *JAMA* 1994;272:1043–1048.
20. Oberstar JV, Bernstein GA, Thuras PD. Caffeine use and dependence in adolescents: one-year follow-up. *J Child Adol Psychopharmacol* 2002;12:127–135.
21. Jones HE, Lejuez CW. Personality correlates of caffeine dependence: the role of sensation seeking, impulsivity and risk taking. *Exp Clin Psychopharmacol* 2005;13:259–266.
22. World Health Organization. *The ICD-10 Classification of Mental and Behavioral Disorder: Clinical Descriptions and Diagnostic Guidelines.* Geneva, Switzerland: WHO, 1992.
23. American Psychiatric Association. *Diagnostic and Statistical Manual of Mental Disorders.* 4th ed. Washington, DC: APA, 2000.
24. Evans SM, Griffiths RR, Caffeine withdrawal: a parametric analysis of caffeine dosing conditions. *J Pharmacol Exp Ther* 1999;289:285–294.
25. Garrett BE, Griffiths RR, Physical dependence increases the relative reinforcing effects of caffeine versus placebo. *Psychopharmacol* 1998;139:195–202.
26. Juliano, LM, Evatt, DP, Richards, BD, Griffiths, RR. Characterization of individuals seeking treatment for caffeine dependence. *Psychology of Addictive Behaviors* 2012; 27.
27. Diepvens K, Westerterp KR, Westerterp-Plantenga MS. Obesity and thermogenesis related to the consumption of caffeine, ephedrine, capsaicin, and

green tea. *Am J Physiol Regul Integr Comp Physiol* 2007;292:R77–R85.

28. Hollands MA, Arch JRS, Phil D, Cawthorne MA. A simple apparatus for comparative measurements of energy expenditure in human subjects: the thermic effect of caffeine. *Am J Clin Nutr* 1981;34:2291–2294.

29. Dulloo AG, Geissler CA, Horton T, Collins A, Miller DS. Normal caffeine consumption: influence on thermogenesis and daily energy expenditure in lean and postobese human volunteers. *Am J Clin Nutr* 1989;49:44–50.

30. Astrup A, Toubro S, Cannon S, Hein P, Breum L, Madsen J. Caffeine: a double-blind, placebo-controlled study of its thermogenic, metabolic, and cardiovascular effects in healthy volunteers. *Am J Clin Nutr* 1990;51:759–767.

31. Bracco D, Ferrarra JM, Arnaud MJ, Jequier E, Schutz Y. Effects of caffeine on energy metabolism, heart rate, and methylxanthine metabolism in lean and obese women. *Am J Physiol* 1995;269:E671–E678.

32. Tremblay A, Masson E, Leduc S, Houde A, Despres JP. Caffeine reduces spontaneous energy intake in men but not in women. *Nutr Res* 1988;8:553–558.

33. Comer SD, Haney M, Foltin RW, Fischman MW. Effects of caffeine withdrawal on humans living in a residential laboratory. *Exp Clin Psychopharmacol* 1997;5:399–403.

34. Jessen A, Buemann B, Toubro S, Skovgaard IM, Astrup A. The appetite-suppressant effect of nicotine is enhanced by caffeine. *Diabetes Obes Metab* 2005;7:327–333.

35. Greenberg JA, Axen KV, Schnoll R, Boozer CN. Coffee, tea and diabetes: the role of weight loss and caffeine. *Int J Obes* 2005;29:1121–1129.

36. Lopez-Garcia E, van Dam RM, Rajpathak S, Willett WC, Manson JE, Hu FB. Changes in caffeine intake and long-term weight change in men and women. *Am J Clin Nutr* 2006;83:674–680.

37. Astrup A, Breum L, Toubro S, Hein P, Quaade F. The effect and safety of an ephedrine/caffeine compound compared to ephedrine, caffeine and placebo in obese subjects on an energy restricted diet. A double blind trial. *Int J Obes Relat Metab Disord* 1992;16:269–277.

38. Kovacs EMR, Mela DJ. Metabolically active functional food ingredients for weight control. *Obes Rev* 2006;7:59–78.

39. Haller CA, Benowitz NL. Adverse cardiovascular and central nervous system events associated with dietary supplements containing ephedra alkaloids. *N Engl J Med* 2000;343:1833–1838.

40. Westerterp-Plantenga MS, Lejeune MPGM, Kovacs EMR. Body weight loss and weight maintenance in relation to habitual caffeine intake and green tea supplementation. *Obes Res* 2005;13:1195–1204.

41. Drewnoski A, Gomez-Carneros C. Bitter taste, phytonutrients, and the consumer: a review. *Am J Nutr* 2000;72:1424–1435.

42. Rozin P, Vollmecke TA. Food likes and dislikes. *Annu Rev Nutr* 1986;6:433–466.

43. Griffiths RR, Vernotica VM. Is caffeine a flavoring agent in cola soft drinks? *Arch Fam Med* 2000;9:727–734.

44. Keast RSJ, Riddell LJ. Caffeine as a flavor additive in soft-drinks. *Appetite* 2007;49:255–259.

45. Beverage Digest Company. *Beverage Digest Special Issue: Top 10 CSD Results for 2008.* Bedford Hills, NY: Beverage Digest Company, 2009.

46. Reisig CJ, Strain EC, Griffiths RR. Caffeinated energy drinks—a growing problem. *Drug Alcohol Depen* 2009;99:1–10.

47. Malik VS, Schulze MB, Hu FB. Intake of sugar-sweetened beverages and weight gain: a systematic review. *Am J Clin Nutr* 2006;84:274–288.

48. Vartanian LR, Schwartz MB, Brownell KD. Effects of soft drink consumption on nutrition and health: a systematic review and meta-analysis. *Am J Public Health* 2007;4:667–675.

49. DiMeglio DP, Mattes RD. Liquid versus solid carbohydrate: effects on food intake and body weight. *Int J Obes Relat Metab Disord* 2000;24:794–800.

50. Bernstein GA, Carroll ME, Dean NW, Crosby RD, Perwien AR, Benowitz NL. Caffeine withdrawal in normal school-aged children. *J Am Acad Child Psychiatry* 1998;37:858–865.

51. Bernstein GA, Carroll M, Thuras PD, Cosgrove KP, Roth ME. Caffeine dependence in teenagers. *Drug Alcohol Depen* 2002;66:1–6.

37

Interactions between Smoking, Eating, and Body Weight

MARNEY A. WHITE AND STEPHANIE S. O'MALLEY

The influence of cigarette smoking on energy expenditure and body weight has been long recognized.[1,2] For nearly a century, the cigarette industry has capitalized on the perceived ability of smoking to control body weight.[3] Indeed, for some individuals the desire to lose weight may motivate smoking initiation,[4] and concerns about weight gain may prevent successful smoking cessation.[5,6] Smoking rate and frequency have been linked with weight concerns and the subjective belief in the effectiveness of smoking as a weight control measure.[7,8] Importantly, after quitting, many people resume smoking following modest weight gain.[9]

This chapter will review the evidence from a variety of sources (i.e., epidemiological, human treatment studies, animal, lab, and neurobiological research) regarding the interactions between smoking and eating and weight. Research on the interactive nature of smoking and binge eating is also discussed. Finally, a review of treatments to address smoking cessation–related weight gain is provided.

EPIDEMIOLOGICAL FINDINGS

On the population level, smokers tend to weigh less than nonsmokers,[10] and the prevalence of obesity is lower among smokers.[11] While the prevalence of smoking has declined in recent years, the incidence of obesity has increased, leading some to question whether the obesity epidemic can be partially explained by smoking cessation and declining smoking rates. That smokers tend to gain weight following cessation lends some credibility to this hypothesis. In addition to the immediate weight gain following cessation, former smokers may be at elevated risk of subsequent weight gain. A large epidemiological study found that individuals who had recently quit smoking were more likely to gain weight over a 10-year period than were nonsmokers and current smokers.[11] However, at the population level, decreased smoking prevalence has very little impact on the prevalence of obesity; it has been estimated that despite large reductions in smoking prevalence in recent decades, the impact on obesity rates is less than 1%.[12]

While there is a slightly lower prevalence of smoking in overweight and obese groups than in normal-weight counterparts, recent estimates report a substantial portion of overweight (24.3%) and obese (20.2%) people currently smoke.[13] Despite overall lower body mass index, smokers have greater central adiposity than nonsmokers,[14] and they are therefore at heightened risk for diabetes mellitus due to greater abdominal fat. In addition, the combined effect of smoking and obesity on health outcomes is interactive rather than additive. For example, cardiovascular risk is an estimated 3.5 to 5 times greater for obese individuals who also smoke.[15] Overall, although smokers tend to weigh less than nonsmokers, a substantial portion of smokers are overweight and obese. In addition, the health benefits of lower weight are greatly offset by the negative health impact of smoking.

WEIGHT GAIN FOLLOWING SMOKING CESSATION

Smoking cessation is associated with modest weight gain.[16] The amount of weight gain tends to average 10–13 pounds in the first year after quitting, with most of this occurring within the first 6 months of abstinence.[17] The mechanism through which cigarette smoking influences energy expenditure and body weight is likely a combination of several factors, including increased energy intake, decreased resting metabolic rate, and changes in enzyme activity influencing fat storage.[18]

In general, smoking serves as an appetite suppressant, and appetite increases during withdrawal from nicotine. Following smoking cessation, the hedonic properties of food increase due to improved sensory perception; in short, food tastes and smells better, and individuals tend to consume more in the immediate months following cessation.[19] Among current smokers, short-term abstinence from smoking is associated with heightened cravings for cigarettes and food, as well as increased calorie and fat intake.[20] With regard to motivational states, some smoking abstinence literature indicates that short-term abstainers report heightened cravings for foods, especially sweets, but this urge does not translate to increased consumption. Rather heightened cravings *for cigarettes* are associated with increased food intake,[20] indicating that some misattribution or substitution may occur in the effort to satisfy the cravings. Finally, research on the reward value of food has found that during short-term nicotine abstinence, the reward incentive of food is elevated, independent of hunger and palatability.[21] In this study, smokers deprived of nicotine worked harder for access to preferred snack foods.

Animal studies provide additional evidence for the interactive nature of food intake and smoking. In one animal study, rats administered nicotine reduced meal size and overall food intake compared to control animals,[22] and in turn they lost weight over the course of nicotine administration. The effect of nicotine on food intake may be moderated by type of diet. In a separate study, rats administered nicotine on a high-fat diet reduced intake by significantly more than those on a normal chow diet. However, following nicotine withdrawal, the high-fat and regular chow groups did not gain weight at different rates.[23] Comparison animals that did not receive nicotine gained more weight over the course of the trial than those receiving nicotine; that is, the weight suppression effect of nicotine persisted even after withdrawal and even when factoring in the withdrawal-related weight gain. Additional animal research[24] has paralleled the human findings of weight gain following nicotine withdrawal. In addition, the relationship between food intake and nicotine is reciprocal; while nicotine withdrawal enhances responding for food, food deprivation also enhances an animal's responding for nicotine.[25]

NEUROBIOLOGICAL EVIDENCE

It appears that food and nicotine activate common brain reward circuitry, with much of the overlap focused on the dopamine and endogenous opioid systems.[26] Decreased levels of dopamine receptors predispose vulnerability for an individual to seek reinforcers, which may be appetitive behaviors such as nicotine and binge eating.[27] Indeed, increased food intake during smoking abstinence may serve to stimulate the dopamine reward pathway in the absence of nicotine.[28] The dopamine reward system has also been implicated in theories of obesity, also with the suggestion that food intake may be used as a means of self-medication through enhanced dopamine activation.[29] Animal studies confer the role of dopamine in smoking and overeating, with increases in dopamine following both nicotine administration[30–32] and overeating on familiar foods.[30] Similarly, the noradrenergic system has been implicated in both smoking[33] and eating[34] behaviors, although the exact mechanism of these complex systems is not fully understood.

Functional imaging studies have found that the brain regions involved in food craving have also been reported in drug craving studies[27] and in animal studies of food and drug administration.[35] Collectively, various forms of research (i.e., from psychological, neuroimaging, and animal learning paradigms) suggest a shared system of craving and reward for food and nicotine, such that a common vulnerability—potentially involving dopaminergic function—may predispose both overeating and smoking.

CIGARETTE SMOKING IN BINGE-EATING DISORDER

A discussion of binge-eating disorder (BED) is particularly relevant to cigarette smoking and food addiction (for elaboration, see Chapter 49). In brief, BED is a type of eating disorder not otherwise specified, is associated with obesity, and is marked by recurrent episodes of consuming unusually large amounts of food with the subjective sense of loss of control over eating. To date, few studies have reported the prevalence of current cigarette smoking in BED. A large-scale epidemiological study of broadly defined BED in the Norwegian twin registry reported increased odds of *lifetime* smoking in the binge-eating sample compared to controls, which was attenuated in women after adjusting for body mass index.[36] Among obese women with BED, a history of cigarette smoking is associated with higher comorbid Axis I psychopathology[37] and a general worsening of eating pathology specific to binge eating.[38] Therefore, among individuals with BED, cigarette smoking appears to engender a more severe clinical profile, suggesting that different mechanisms may be involved in the pathophysiology and maintenance of binge eating.

A review of the literature on cigarette smoking and binge eating reveals some common themes; for example, *cravings* are viewed as antecedents to both behaviors. Cravings are defined as strong (difficult to resist) urges to consume a substance. While the literature is mixed, scant evidence of a physiological basis (i.e., in terms of nutritional deficit) of food cravings exists. Although a biochemical component drives cravings and physiological addiction to nicotine, subjective reports of cravings remain elevated long after physical withdrawal of nicotine has occurred.[39] Therefore, it seems that something other than physical addiction contributes to the continued experience of cravings. Several theories have been proposed for the development of cravings for a particular substance that transcend physical addiction. Perhaps the most compelling of these explain maintenance of cravings as conditioned responses to learning histories that associate various environmental and internal cues with consuming the desired substance and receiving positive or negative reinforcement. With regard to positive reinforcement, the hedonic properties of food, or the stimulating effects of nicotine, activate reward systems and generate pleasure. Smoking may also serve to heighten positive affect.[40] In the case of negative reinforcement, both binge eating[41] and smoking[42] serve as a temporary escape from negative affect. Finally, unlike other substances of "abuse," individuals can smoke or eat throughout the day without interfering with consciousness or resulting in an observable "high." Also of note, the motor components of both smoking and eating (i.e., "hand-to-mouth" movements and oral stimulation) share common properties as well. Finally, smokers report cravings associated with hunger and satiety cues, for example, the desire to smoke following a meal. As a result, a wide range of internal states, situations, and environments can subsequently serve as conditioned cues that will elicit craving.

SMOKING TREATMENTS TARGETING POSTCESSATION WEIGHT GAIN

In an effort to improve smoking treatment outcome, a number of research groups have employed behavioral strategies designed to address weight gain.[43] While it had been hypothesized that behavioral weight control interventions administered concurrently with smoking cessation treatment would increase quit rates by reducing postcessation weight gain, results have been inconsistent.[44] A recent review concluded that although there is a short-term advantage of behavioral weight control treatment on smoking outcomes and weight gain, these effects do not persist in the long term (i.e., 1 year following treatment or beyond).[43] Based on the hypothesis that overconcern about weight gain rather than actual weight gain leads to smoking relapse in weight concerned women, Perkins et al.[45] tested a cognitive-behavioral intervention focused on ameliorating maladaptive concerns about weight. This intervention, administered in the context of a behavioral smoking cessation trial, discouraged dieting and was compared to a concurrent behavioral weight control program and a standard treatment for smoking cessation that avoided discussion of weight and weight concerns.[45] As predicted, participants receiving the cognitive behavioral treatment for weight concerns had significantly higher continuous abstinence rates and had the lowest weight gain following cessation. This finding suggests that efforts to reduce concern about weight gain can have beneficial effects on weight as well as smoking cessation.

Pharmacotherapy has been moderately successful in treating nicotine dependence,[46] but the effects on minimizing postcessation weight gain have been mixed. For instance, nicotine replacement therapy is fairly effective in enhancing smoking cessation success rates but does not reduce hunger or weight gain significantly.[47] The effects of nicotine gum on delaying weight gain are stronger than nicotine patch, but the size of this difference is modest.[48] Sustained-release bupropion hydrochloride has proven effective in increasing smoking cessation success rates and is moderately successful in helping to reduce weight gain. For instance, Hurt et al.[49] reported weight gain of 3.3 pounds with bupropion compared to 6.4 pounds with placebo at the end of 6 weeks of treatment. Varenicline is also an efficacious smoking cessation medication, but it does not significantly reduce postcessation weight gain.[50] Thus, current Food and Drug Administration–approved pharmacological treatments for smoking cessation are modestly successful in assisting smokers to quit, but only bupropion consistently attenuates postcessation weight gain while taking the medication. No smoking cessation pharmacotherapy exists that attenuates long-term postcessation weight gain after discontinuation of the drug treatment.

SUMMARY

This chapter has reviewed evidence from a variety of sources highlighting the interactive nature of smoking, eating, and body weight. Nicotine is a known appetite suppressant, and smoking cessation is associated with modest weight gain. Despite the weight-suppressing effects of cigarette smoking, a substantial portion of smokers are overweight and are at elevated health risks due to the synergistic effects of having both negative lifestyle factors. The next generation of treatments for smoking and weight should consider both factors in order to prevent cessation-related weight gain.

REFERENCES

1. Hofstetter A, Schutz Y, Jequier E, Wahren J. Increased 24-hour energy expenditure in cigarette smokers. *N Engl J Med* 1986;314(2):79–82.
2. Klesges RC, Klesges LM, Meyers AW. Relationship of smoking status, energy balance, and body weight: analysis of the Second National Health and Nutrition Examination Survey. *J Consult Clin Psychol* 1991;59(6):899–905.
3. Carpenter CM, Wayne GF, Connolly GN. Designing cigarettes for women: new findings from the tobacco industry documents. *Addiction* 2005;100(6):837–851.
4. French SA, Perry CL, Leon GR, Fulkerson JA. Weight concerns, dieting behavior, and smoking initiation among adolescents: a prospective study. *Am J Public Health* 1994;84:1818–1820.
5. John U, Meyer C, Hapke U, Rumpf HJ, Schumann A. Nicotine dependence, quit attempts, and quitting among smokers in a regional population sample from a country with a high prevalence of tobacco smoking. *Prev Med* 2004;38(3):350–358.
6. Pirie PL, Murray DM, Luepker RV. Gender differences in cigarette smoking and quitting in a cohort of young adults. *Am J Public Health* 1991;81(3):324–327.
7. Copeland AL, Carney CE. Smoking expectancies as mediators between dietary restraint and disinhibition and smoking in college women. *Exp Clin Psychopharmacol* 2003;11(3):247–251.

8. Klesges RC, Elliot VE, Robinson LA. Chronic dieting and the belief that smoking controls body weight in a biracial, population-based adolescent sample. *Tob Control* 1997;6:89–94.
9. Office on Smoking and Health, Centers for Disease Control and Prevention. Women and smoking: a report of the Surgeon General. 2001. Available at: http://www.ncbi.nlm.nih.gov/bookshelf/br.fcgi?book=womsmk. Accessed August 18, 2010.
10. Klesges RC, Meyers AW, Klesges LM, La Vasque ME. Smoking, body weight, and their effects on smoking behavior: a comprehensive review of the literature. *Psychol Bull* 1989;106(2):204–230.
11. Flegal KM, Troiano RP, Pamuk ER, Kuczmarski RJ, Campbell SM. The influence of smoking cessation on the prevalence of overweight in the United States. *N Engl J Med* 1995;333(18):1165–1170.
12. Flegal KM. The effects of changes in smoking prevalence on obesity prevalence in the United States. *Am J Public Health* 2007;97(8):1510–1514.
13. Gregg EW, Cheng YJ, Cadwell BL, et al. Secular trends in cardiovascular disease risk factors according to body mass index in US adults. *JAMA* 2005;293(15):1868–1874.
14. Canoy D, Wareham N, Luben R, et al. Cigarette smoking and fat distribution in 21,828 British men and women: a population-based study. *Obes Res* 2005;13(8):1466–1475.
15. Freedman DM, Sigurdson AJ, Rajaraman P, Doody MM, Linet MS, Ron E. The mortality risk of smoking and obesity combined. *Am J Prev Med* 2006;31(5):355–362.
16. Perkins KA. Weight gain following smoking cessation. *J Consult Clin Psychol* 1993;61(5):768–777.
17. Hall SM, Ginsberg D, Jones RT. Smoking cessation and weight gain. *J Consult Clin Psychol* 1986;54(3):342–346.
18. Filozof C, Fernandez Pinilla MC, Fernandez-Cruz A. Smoking cessation and weight gain. *Obes Rev* 2004;5(2):95–103.
19. Caan B, Coates A, Schaefer C, Finkler L, Sternfeld B, Corbett K. Women gain weight 1 year after smoking cessation while dietary intake temporarily increases. *J Am Diet Assoc* 1996;96(11):1150–1155.
20. Ogden J. Effects of smoking cessation, restrained eating, and motivational states on food intake in the laboratory. *Health Psychol* 1994;13(2):114–121.
21. Spring B, Pagoto S, McChargue D, Hedeker D, Werth J. Altered reward value of carbohydrate snacks for female smokers withdrawn from nicotine. *Pharmacol Biochem Behav* 2003;76(2):351–360.
22. Miyata G, Meguid MM, Varma M, Fetissov SO, Kim HJ. Nicotine alters the usual reciprocity between meal size and meal number in female rat. *Physiol Behav* 2001;74(1–2):169–176.

23. Wellman PJ, Bellinger LL, Cepeda-Benito A, Susabda A, Ho DH, Davis KW. Meal patterns and body weight after nicotine in male rats as a function of chow or high-fat diet. *Pharmacol Biochem Behav* 2005;82(4): 627–634.

24. Fornari A, Pedrazzi P, Lippi G, Picciotto MR, Zoli M, Zini I. Nicotine withdrawal increases body weight, neuropeptide Y and Agouti-related protein expression in the hypothalamus and decreases uncoupling protein-3 expression in the brown adipose tissue in high-fat fed mice. *Neurosci Lett* 2007;411(1):72–76.

25. Lang WJ, Latiff AA, McQueen A, Singer G. Self administration of nicotine with and without a food delivery schedule. *Pharmacol Biochem Behav* 1977;7(1): 65–70.

26. Volkow ND, Wise RA. How can drug addiction help us understand obesity? *Nat Neurosci* 2005;8(5): 555–560.

27. Wang GJ, Volkow ND, Thanos PK, Fowler JS. Similarity between obesity and drug addiction as assessed by neurofunctional imaging: a concept review. *J Addict Dis* 2004;23(3):39–53.

28. Lerman C, Berrettini W, Pinto A, et al. Changes in food reward following smoking cessation: a pharmacogenetic investigation. *Psychopharmacol (Berl)* 2004;174(4):571–577.

29. Davis C, Fox J. Sensitivity to reward and body mass index (BMI): evidence for a non-linear relationship. *Appetite* 2008;50(1):43–49

30. Avena NM. Examining the addictive-like properties of binge eating using an animal model of sugar dependence. *Exp Clin Psychopharmacol* 2007;15(5): 481–491.

31. Benwell ME, Balfour DJ. The effects of acute and repeated nicotine treatment on nucleus accumbens dopamine and locomotor activity. *Br J Pharmacol* 1992;105(4):849–856.

32. Corrigall WA, Coen KM, Adamson KL. Self-administered nicotine activates the mesolimbic dopamine system through the ventral tegmental area. *Brain Res* 1994;653(1–2):278–284.

33. Goodwin R, Hamilton SP. Cigarette smoking and panic: the role of neuroticism. *Am J Psychiatry* 2002;159(7):1208–1213.

34. Wellman PJ. Modulation of eating by central catecholamine systems. *Curr Drug Targets* 2005;6(2): 191–199.

35. Kelley AE, Berridge KC. The neuroscience of natural rewards: relevance to addictive drugs. *J Neurosci* 2002;22:3306–3311.

36. Reichborn-Kjennerud T, Bulik CM, Sullivan PF, Tambs K, Harris JR. Psychiatric and medical symptoms in binge eating in the absence of compensatory behaviors. *Obes Res* 2004;12(9):1445–1454.

37. White MA, Grilo CM. Psychiatric comorbidity in binge-eating disorder as a function of smoking history. *J Clin Psychiatry* 2006;67(4):594–599.

38. White MA, Grilo CM. Symptom severity in obese women with binge eating disorder as a function of smoking history. *Int J Eat Disord* 2007;40(1):77–81.

39. Robinson TE, Berridge KC. The neural basis of drug craving: an incentive-sensitization theory of addiction. *Brain Res Brain Res Rev* 1993;18(3):247–291.

40. Cook JW, Spring B, McChargue D, Hedeker D. Hedonic capacity, cigarette craving, and diminished positive mood. *Nicotine Tob Res* 2004;6:39–47.

41. Heatherton TF, Baumeister RF. Binge eating as escape from self-awareness. *Psychol Bull* 1991;110:86–108.

42. Nil R. A psychopharmacological and psychophysiological evaluation of smoking motives. *Rev Environ Health* 1991;9(2):85–115.

43. Spring B, Howe D, Berendsen M, et al. Behavioral intervention to promote smoking cessation and prevent weight gain: a systematic review and meta-analysis. *Addiction* 2009;104(9):1472–1486.

44. Hall SM, Tunstall CD, Vila KL, Duffy J. Weight gain prevention and smoking cessation: cautionary findings. *Am J Public Health* 1992;82:799–803.

45. Perkins KA, Marcus MD, Levine MD, et al. Cognitive-behavioral therapy to reduce weight concerns improves smoking cessation outcome in weight-concerned women. *J Consult Clin Psychol* 2001;69:604–613.

46. Fiore MC, Jaén CR, Baker TB, et al. *Treating Tobacco Use and Dependence: 2008 Update. Clinical Practice Guideline.* Rockville, MD: US Department of Health and Human Services, Public Health Service, 2008.

47. Abelin T, Buehler A, Muller P, Vesanen K, Imhof P. Controlled trial of transdermal nicotine patch in tobacco withdrawal. *Lancet* 1989;1:7–10.

48. Doherty K, Militello FS, Kinnunen T, Garvey AJ. Nicotine gum dose and weight gain after smoking cessation. *J Consult Clin Psychol* 1996;64:799–807.

49. Hurt RD, Sachs DP, Glover ED, et al. A comparison of sustained-release bupropion and placebo for smoking cessation. *N Engl J Med* 1997;337(17):1195–1202.

50. Jorenby D, Hays J, Rigotti N, et al. Efficacy of varenicline, an alpha-4-beta-2 nicotinic acetylcholine receptor partial agonist, vs. placebo or sustained-release bupropion for smoking cessation: a randomized controlled trial. *JAMA* 2006;296:56–63.

38

Interactions between Alcohol Consumption, Eating, and Weight

ASHLEY N. GEARHARDT AND WILLIAM R. CORBIN

Excess alcohol and food consumption are both major causes of psychological distress and poor physical health. Researchers have recently begun to explore the relationship between food and alcohol intake more thoroughly. This has led to a more comprehensive understanding of the shared psychological and biological factors associated with excess food and alcohol consumption. Research has also clarified the nature of the interplay between alcohol and food intake. A better understanding of the complex relations between food and alcohol consumption has important implications for prevention and intervention efforts designed to reduce harm associated with both alcohol use disorders and disordered patterns of eating.

PSYCHOLOGICAL RISK FACTORS

Many of the same risk factors are implicated in excess food and alcohol consumption. For example, individuals who are low in behavioral control (e.g., high in impulsivity and novelty seeking) have been found to be at heightened risk for problems with both alcohol and overeating.[1] Furthermore, excess food and alcohol consumption are both related to higher anxiety and depressive symptoms,[2,3] as well as related but more stable traits like harm avoidance.[4] These more distal influences on consumption of food and alcohol also seem to operate through similar proximal influences such as motives for consumption. Food and alcohol are consumed for many of the same motives, such as reward and stress reduction,[5] and motivations associated with negative emotion management have been implicated in both problematic food and alcohol consumption.[6,7] Thus, individuals who experience strong negative affect may learn to eat or drink alcohol as a way to cope with negative emotions, placing themselves at increased risk for developing disordered patterns of eating or alcohol consumption.

NEUROBIOLOGICAL SIMILARITIES

In addition to common psychological factors, alcohol and food consumption share many neurobiological similarities. Animal research has found that food and alcohol consumption both activate the mesolimbic dopaminergic and opioid systems.[8,9] In addition, animals that are genetically bred to prefer alcohol demonstrate enhanced preferences for certain foods. An alcohol-preferring rat will consume greater quantities of sugar than a non-alcohol-preferring rat.[10] This effect may be driven by neurobiological differences in the opioid system that result in greater reinforcement from both alcohol and sweet-tasting foods.[9,10] Human research has also implicated the dopamine and opioid systems in both alcohol and food consumption. Brain areas associated with dopaminergic release, such as the ventral striatum and the orbitofrontal cortex, are activated in response to both food cues and alcohol cues.[11-13] These same brain regions are also associated with craving for alcohol and palatable foods.[14,15] Finally, the administration of an opioid antagonist, such as naltrexone, is capable of reducing preferences for and consumption of both alcohol and high-fat sweets.[16,17]

RELATIONS BETWEEN ALCOHOL AND SUGAR CONSUMPTION

In addition to evidence for shared psychological and neurobiological processes, there is more direct evidence for relations between alcohol consumption and food intake. Research using animal models has found that patterns of sugar consumption impact future alcohol consumption. For example, Pian et al.[18] found that adolescent rats that consumed large amounts of sugar drank more alcohol in adulthood. Furthermore, when sugar is removed from sugar-addicted rats, they consume significantly greater quantities of alcohol than nonaddicted rats.[19]

Human research has also found a link between alcohol and sugar consumption. First, a personal history of substance dependence has been associated with an increased preference for sugar. For example, Kampov-Polevoy and colleagues[20] found that 65% of participants recovering from alcohol dependence had a preference for intense levels of sweetness, whereas only 16% of controls preferred this same level of sweetness. A family history of alcoholism is also related to sweet preference. Previous research found that participants with a family history of alcoholism, but no personal history of alcoholism, were 2.5 times more likely to prefer sweets than participants without a family history of alcoholism.[21] These findings suggest that the shared preference for alcohol and sugar may be at least partially heritable.

Sugar consumption has also been identified as a factor in recovery from alcohol dependence. Anecdotally, Alcoholics Anonymous instructs its members to consume sugar-rich foods, such as candy bars, to reduce alcohol cravings.[22] There is some evidence that this advice may be useful. For example, approximately one-quarter of alcoholic men reported that consumption of high-sugar foods helped them abstain from alcohol consumption.[23] Furthermore, Yung and colleagues[24] found that alcohol dependent participants with the highest rates of sobriety were those with the highest rates of sugar intake. These findings support the theory that sugar consumption may be effective in promoting abstinence by providing an alcohol substitute.

ALCOHOL AND WEIGHT GAIN

A common feature of both the animal and human studies we have reviewed is that they do not focus on concurrent alcohol and sugar intake. Rather, they suggest that prior consumption of one substance predicts later consumption of the other, or that discontinued use of one substance (e.g., treatment for alcohol dependence) predicts increased preference for the other substance (e.g., sweet tastes). These findings suggest that concurrent levels of alcohol and sugar (or other high-calorie foods) may be

inversely related. In other words, high levels of alcohol consumption may be associated with decreased consumption of calorie-dense foods. At the same time, alcoholic beverages themselves can be high in calories, potentially leading to weight gain.

Despite the added calories associated with the consumption of alcohol, research has shown that alcohol-dependent individuals typically lose a substantial amount of weight and in some cases can become malnourished.[25] Conversely, recovery from substance dependence is associated with significant weight gain.[26] Similar findings have been reported in the obesity field. For example, body mass index (BMI) was found to be inversely associated with alcohol consumption in overweight and obese participants. Among obese participants awaiting bariatric surgery, 35.4% consumed alcohol in the last year, whereas 62.5% of nonobese participants consumed alcohol in the same time period.[27] Evidence for an inverse relation between alcohol consumption and BMI has also been demonstrated in nonclinical populations.[28-30] These findings have led to the theory that food and alcohol compete for similar neurotransmitter receptors in the dopamine and opioid pathways. Thus, when alcohol or food is consumed in excess, it occupies the shared system and blocks the desire for the other substance.[27]

In an effort to more directly test the shared biological vulnerability hypothesis, Gearhardt and Corbin[31] examined the impact of a family history of alcohol problems on the relation between BMI and alcohol consumption. The primary hypothesis was that a family history of alcoholism would confer risk for the development of alcohol problems for nonobese participants, but not for obese participants. The lack of a family history effect for obese participants would suggest that excess food consumption was occupying the shared reward pathway, decreasing motivation to consume alcohol in this high-risk group. Analyses from the National Epidemiological Survey on Alcohol and Related Conditions (NESARC) dataset found support for the study hypothesis. A family history of alcohol problems was associated with increased frequency and quantity of alcohol consumption, but only in nonobese participants. In other words, the risk associated with a family history of alcohol problems was attenuated in obese participants. In addition, participants with a family history but no personal history of alcohol problems had a significantly higher BMI than participants without a family history of alcohol problems or those with a family history and a personal history of alcohol problems.[32] These findings provide further support that food and alcohol compete for access to similar neurobiological systems and that excess food and alcohol consumption may have a shared biological basis.

Although the evidence for a relationship between alcohol and food consumption is striking, many unanswered questions remain. The majority of the existing research has focused specifically on the relation between alcohol and sugar intake. Additional studies examining other highly palatable foods (e.g., processed high-fat foods like potato chips) are much needed, as it is possible that these foods also activate reward pathways in the brain. In addition, although sugar clearly activates reward pathways, the extent to which food is addictive is a current topic of debate with important implications both for treating obesity and for public health efforts designed to reduce obesity at the population level.

An addiction model of excess food consumption has important implications for conceptual models of overeating that may impact the way society views obesity. Alcohol dependence is widely believed to be a disease that is a direct result of the excess consumption of a highly addictive substance, rather than any innate characteristic of the individual.[33] The disease model of alcohol dependence has reduced stigma by reducing the belief that excess alcohol consumption is the result of a lack of willpower or a failure to take personal responsibility for one's behavior. In contrast, beliefs that obesity is the result of the same personal shortcomings that were once attributed to alcohol dependence remain widespread.[34] Increased attention to the similarities between excess food and alcohol consumption may help reduce weight-related bias in the same way that the disease model reduced the stigma associated with substance dependence.

The implications of food addiction for policy related to the availability of potentially addictive foods are also substantial. Policies regarding access to alcohol are well established given the addiction potential of the drug, and the highest risk forms of alcohol are typically the most restricted. For example, in many states liquor can only be sold in state-licensed stores and during restricted hours, whereas beer is accessible in grocery stores and gas stations.[35] A parallel regarding potency may also be relevant to food consumption. Although

food consumption is necessary for survival, there is variation among foods in both nutritional content and abuse potential. Highly processed foods high in fat and sugar are more likely to be consumed in excess and to result in negative health consequences, whereas low-fat and low-sugar foods are seldom implicated in problematic eating patterns.[36] Unlike alcohol, however, foods with greater abuse potential are more easily accessible and less expensive then low-risk, nutrition-dense foods.[37] Thus, public health approaches that have been useful in reducing alcohol-related problems, such as reduced access and taxation, could also be useful in reducing excess food consumption. The essential nature of food consumption might also lead to policies that encourage consumption of nutritious foods. For example, nutritious foods could be subsidized to reduce price, which may result in increased consumption of these foods and decreased consumption of higher risk foods.[38]

Although policies are in place to control access to alcohol, the common perception is that alcohol can be consumed in moderation by most people and that draconian efforts to restrict access are not necessary.[39] In contrast, nicotine is widely believed to have such high addiction potential that regular use almost inevitably leads to addiction. This difference in conceptualization has led to more of a public health approach: to restrict access, increase price, and reduce marketing of tobacco products.[40] The public health approach has led to reduced social acceptance of tobacco use and lower rates of use.[41] In contrast, rates of alcohol use have remained relatively stable in recent years.[42] The differential effectiveness of these approaches may speak to the most useful way of reducing food-related problems. Although the disease model may reduce weight-related stigma, it also may lead to reduced industry-related responsibility. In contrast, the public health approach may be more effective in facilitating large-scale changes to the food environment, which would likely have a widespread effect in reducing clinical and subclinical food-related problems.

Addiction models of excess food consumption also have obvious implications for treating individuals who are struggling to control their eating behavior. Although treatments based on the concept of food addiction are already widespread, there is little research on the efficacy of these approaches. Future research is needed to determine which aspects of addiction treatments might be effectively applied to eating-related problems (e.g., relapse prevention, cue exposure, motivational interviewing). In addition, it will be important to examine the relative efficacy of approaches derived from addiction models relative to approaches designed for the treatment of eating disorders (e.g., binge eating disorder).

CONCLUSION

In summary, there is evidence to suggest that excess food and alcohol consumption share many psychological risk factors. Furthermore, there is evidence for similar neurobiological systems associated with excess alcohol and food consumption. Finally, there is evidence that food and alcohol consumption may compete for the same neurotransmitter receptors, resulting in an inverse relation between alcohol consumption and BMI. Additional research is needed to more fully understand the impact of diet on alcohol-related problems and treatment. Evidence for shared mechanisms of overconsumption of food and alcohol suggests that an addiction model of excess food consumption is worth investigating and preliminary studies support such a model. Additional evidence for food addiction would have important implications for public policy and for treatment of overeating. Efforts to reduce overeating at both the individual and societal levels might benefit from approaches that have been successfully employed with other addictive substances, including alcohol and nicotine.

REFERENCES

1. Dawe S, Loxton NJ. The role of impulsivity in the development of substance use and eating disorders. *Neurosci BioBehav Rev* 2004;28:343–351.
2. Heatherton TF, Baumeister RF. Binge eating as escape from self-awareness. *Psychol Bull* 1991;110:86–108.
3. Grant BF, Stinson FS, Dawson DA, et al. Prevalence and co-occurrence of substance use disorders and independent mood and anxiety disorders. *Arch Gen Psychiat* 2004;61:607–816.
4. Loxton NJ, Dawe S. Alcohol abuse and dysfunctional eating in adolescent girls: the influence of individual differences in sensitivity to reward. *Int J Eat Disord* 2001;29:455–462.
5. Anderson DA, Simmons AM, Martens MP, Ferrier AG, Sheehy MJ. The relationship between disordered eating behavior and drinking motives in college-age women. *Eat Behav* 2006;7:419–422.
6. Holahan CJ, Moos RH, Holahan CK, Cronkite RC, Randall PK. Drinking to cope, emotional distress and alcohol use and abuse: a ten-year model. *J Stud Alcohol* 2001;62:190–198.
7. Eldredge KL, Agras WS. Weight and shape overconcern and emotional eating in binge eating disorder. *Int J Eat Disorder* 1994;19:73–82.
8. Di Chiara G, Acquas E, Tanda G. Ethanol as a neurochemical surrogate of conventional reinforcers: the dopamine-opioid link. *Alcohol* 1996;13:13–17.
9. Avena NM, Rada P, Hoebel BG. Evidence for sugar addiction: behavioral and neurochemical effects of intermittent, excessive sugar intake. *Neurosci BioBehav Rev* 2008;32:20–39.
10. Kampov-Polevoy AB, Garbutt JC, Janowsky DS. Association between preference for sweets and excessive alcohol intake: a review of animal and human studies. *Alcohol Alcoholism* 1999;34:386–395.
11. O'Doherty JP, Buchanan TW, Seymour B, Dolan RJ. Predictive neural coding of reward preference involves dissociable responses in human ventral midbrain and ventral striatum. *Neuron* 2006;49:157–166.
12. Small DM, Jones-Gotman M, Dagher A. Feeding-induced dopamine release in dorsal striatum correlates with meal pleasantness ratings in healthy human volunteers. *Neuroimage* 2003:19:1709–1715.
13. Grüsser SM, Wrase J, Klein S, et al. Cue-induced activation of the striatum and medial prefrontal cortex is associated with subsequent relapse in abstinent alcoholics. *Psychopharmacol* 2004;175:296–302.
14. Heinz A, Seissmeier T, Wrase J, et al. Correlation between dopamine D_2 receptors in the ventral striatum and the central processing of alcohol cues and craving. *Am J Psychiat* 2004;161:1783–1789.
15. Pelchat ML, Johnson A, Chan R, Valdez J, Ragland JD. Images of desire: food-craving activation during fMRI. *Neuroimage* 2004;23:1486–1493.
16. O'Malley SS, Krishnan-Sarin S, Farren C, Sinja R, Kreek M. Naltrexone decreases craving and alcohol self-administration in alcohol-dependent subjects and activates the hypothalamo-pituitary-adrenocortical axis. *Psychopharmacol* 2002;160:19–29.
17. Drewnowski A, Krahn DD, Demitrack MA, Nairn K, Gosnell BA. Naloxone, an opiate blocker, reduces the consumption of sweet high-fat foods in obese and lean female binge eaters. *Am J Clin Nutr* 1995;61:1206–1212.
18. Pian JP, Criado JR, Walker BM, Ehlers CL. Milk consumption during adolescence decreases alcohol drinking in adulthood. *Pharmacol Biochem Behav* 2009;94:179–185.
19. Avena NM, Carillo CA, Needham L, Leibowitz SF, Hoebel BG. Sugar-dependent rats show enhanced intake of unsweetened ethanol. *Alcohol* 2004;34:203–209.
20. Kampov-Polevoy A, Garbutt JC, Janowsky D. Evidence of preference for a high-concentration sucrose solution in alcoholic men. *Am J Psychiatry* 1997;154:269–270.
21. Kampov-Polevoy AB, Garbutt JC, Khalitov E. Family history of alcoholism and response to sweets. *Alcohol Clin Exp Res* 2003;27:1743–1749.

22. Alcoholics Anonymous. *Living Sober*. New York: Alcoholics Anonymous World Services, 1987.

23. Farkas ME, Dwyer J. Nutrition education for alcoholic recovery homes. *J Nutr Educ* 1984;16:123–124.

24. Yung L, Gordis E, Holt J. Dietary choices and likelihood of abstinence in and out patient clinic. *Drug Alcohol Depend* 1983;12:355–362.

25. Gloria L, Cravo M, Camilo ME, et al. Nutritional deficiencies in chronic alcoholics: relation to dietary intake and alcohol consumption. *Am J Gastroenterol* 1997;92:485–489.

26. Hodgkins CC, Jacobs WS, Gold MS. Weight gain after adolescent drug addiction treatment and supervised abstinence. *Psychiat Ann* 2003;32:112–116.

27. Kleiner KD, Gold MS, Frost-Pineda K, Lenz-Brunsman B, Perri MG, Jacobs WS. Body mass index and alcohol use. *J Addictive Dis* 2004;23:105–118.

28. Lahiti-Koski M, Pietinen P, Heliovaara M, Vartiainen E. Association of body mass index and obesity with physical activity, food choices, alcohol intake, and smoking in the 1982–1997 FINRISK studies. *Am J Clin Nutr* 2002;75:809–817.

29. Liu S, Serdula MK, Williamson DF, Mokdad AH, Byers T. A prospective study of alcohol intake and change in body weight among US adults. *Am J Epidemiol* 1994;140:912–920.

30. Rohrer JE, Rohland BM, Denison A, Way A. Frequency of alcohol use and obesity in community medicine patients. *BMC Fam Pract* 2005;6:17.

31. Gearhardt AN, Corbin WC. Body mass index and alcohol consumption: family history of alcoholism as a moderator. *Psychol Addict Behav* 2009;23:216–225.

32. Gearhardt AN, Corbin WR. The effect of a positive family history of alcoholism on body mass index. Poster presented at: 41st Annual Convention of the Association for Behavioral and Cognitive Therapies; November 16, 2007; Philadelphia, PA.

33. Grant BR. Barriers to alcoholism treatment: reasons for not seeking treatment in a general population sample. *J Stud Alcohol* 1997;58:365–371.

34. Puhl R, Brownell KD. Ways of coping with obesity stigma: review and conceptual analysis. *Eat Behav* 2003;4:53–78.

35. Toomey TL, Wagenaar AC. Policy options for prevention: the case of alcohol. *J Public Health Pol* 1999;20:192–213.

36. Drewnowski A, Kurth C, Holden-Wiltse J, Saari, J. Food preferences in human obesity: carbohydrates versus fats. *Appetite* 1992;18:207–221.

37. Drewnowski A. Obesity and the food environment: dietary energy density and diet costs. *Am J Prev Med* 2004;27:154–162.

38. Brownell KD, Frieden TR. Ounces of prevention—the public policy case for taxes on sugared beverages. *New Engl J Med* 2009;360:1805–1808.

39. Latimer WW, Harwood EM, Newcomb MD, Wagenaar AC. Measuring public opinion on alcohol policy: a factor analytic study of a US probability sample. *Addict Behav* 2003;28:301–313.

40. Levy DT, Bauer JE, Lee, H-R. Simulation modeling and tobacco control: creating more robust public health policies. *Am J Public Health* 2006;96:61–65.

41. Levy DT, Gitchell JG, Chaloupka F. The effects of tobacco control policies on smoking rates: a tobacco control scorecard. *J Public Health Man* 2004;10:338–351.

42. Johnston, LD, O'Malley, PM, Bachman, JG, Schulenberg, JE. *Monitoring the Future: National Survey Results on Drug Use, 1975–2008. Volume II: College Students and Adults Ages 19–50*. Bethesda, MD: National Institute on Drug Abuse, 2009. NIH Publication No. 09-7403.

39

Relationships between Drugs of Abuse and Eating

DANIEL M. BLUMENTHAL AND MARK S. GOLD

INTRODUCTION

Food is essential to life and health. Yet consumption of certain types of food, or in excess quantities, can be detrimental to health.[1] Of course, the trouble is that many of the foods that are most dangerous are also intensely pleasurable to consume. This tradeoff between health and homeostasis on the one hand, and hedonism on the other hand, highlights an inherent tension with respect to the role that food should play in our daily lives.

Food's dual and sparring identities are perhaps more evident today than at any other time in history. Indeed, while citizens of wealthier, developed nations rarely lack access to food, and are constantly presented with opportunities to fulfill hedonic desires or urges, residents of less wealthy, developing countries struggle to meet their own homeostatic requirements.

As a result, we have witnessed firsthand that consistently consuming too much food—particularly the types of highly palatable, high-fat, high-sugar, and high-salt foods that stimulate hedonic impulses—can have health consequences that are every bit as severe as those of consuming too little food.[1,2] Underscoring the danger that overeating poses to public health, in 2004 the World Health Organization declared that obesity has outstripped malnutrition as the most significant nutrition problem in the world.[3] Obesity is associated with an increased risk of heart disease, non-insulin-dependent diabetes mellitus, osteoarthritis, cancer, and many other systemic diseases.[4] The prevalence of obesity has nearly doubled over the past two decades, and one in three Americans over the age of 20 years is currently overweight.[4,5] If obesity rates increase at current rates for two more decades, 51% of all US adults will be obese by 2030, and all African American women will be obese by 2034.[6] If current childhood obesity rates remain unchecked, the number of obese US children will double by

2030. Paralleling this expansion of America's collective waist lines, health care costs due to obesity will swell to a projected 860–950 billion dollars per decade by 2030, an estimated 17% of total health care expenditures.[6]

But if health care providers and public health experts agree that being obese is not healthy, why do peoples' waistlines continue to grow? While numerous biological theories and cognitive explanations have been put forward to explain rising rates of overweight and obesity, recent research strongly implicates both psychological and biological processes in the development of these conditions. Moreover, these studies have demonstrated a number of striking, and disturbing, similarities between how humans and animals respond to certain foods and to substances of abuse—including cocaine, heroin, nicotine, and alcohol. This chapter, which is divided into three sections, explores this relationship between food and drugs of abuse. Section one presents the *DSM-IV* definition of substance dependence and the clinical stages of addiction. Section two highlights important clinical, neurobiological, and social evidence that food addiction occurs and should be recognized as a neurobiobehavioral disease. The third and final section of this chapter presents an argument for using alcohol dependence as a model for furthering our understanding of food dependence.

DEFINING SUBSTANCE DEPENDENCE AND ADDICTION

Substance dependence lies on a continuum of patterns of substance use that have common origins but often disparate drivers. Almost all cases of repeated substance use begin with a pleasurable response to experimental use. This pleasurable response—which can be thought of as a positive reward for use—stimulates a desire to use the substance again.

While some individuals never progress beyond this initial experimentation phase to regular use, substance abuse, and/or full-blown dependence, others do. In those individuals who do develop substance use disorders, this experimentation phase is followed by "preoccupation, escalation, tolerance, denial, a series of medical, psychological, and social consequences that related directly to the continued use, and what has been referred to as a 'fatal attraction' between the substance (or activity, e.g., gambling) and the patient."[7]

The *DSM-IV* defines substance dependence (addiction) as a "maladaptive pattern of substance use, leading to clinically significant impairment or distress, as manifested by three (or more) of... [seven signs and symptoms], occurring at any time in the same 12 month period" (see Table 39.1).[8] Substance dependence is also a progressive disorder, with three distinct stages: Stage 1 is characterized by bingeing, or "the escalation of intake with a high proportion of intake at one time, usually after a period of voluntary abstinence or forced deprivation."[9] Withdrawal (as defined by the *DSM-IV*) is the signature element of stage 2. Physical withdrawal is a physiological phenomenon that results from a decrease in stimulation of cellular receptors that have become conditioned to consistent stimulation by a certain substance. Withdrawal thus occurs when a substance is no longer available for use, or when the biochemical effects of this substance are prevented with pharmacologic agents that oppose the substance's activity at the cellular level.[9] Substance cravings are the characteristic feature of stage 3. While the concept of a "craving" has not yet been thoroughly defined in the addiction literature, experts, including this author (M. S. G.), generally agree that cravings possess at least two common features: First, cravings occur after a period of abstinence from substance use. Second, cravings greatly enhance a user's motivation to seek out, and use, the craved substance.[9] Importantly, substance cravings, and the behaviors that they motivate, lie in direct opposition to behaviors that are prompted by "natural rewards" and that are vital to our own survival and health.[10] Additionally, cravings are, at least in part, a behavioral manifestation of chronic cellular and molecular changes in the brain "that mediate enduring associations between drugs and associated stimuli."[10]

While not included in the three stages of substance dependence, "sensitization" can serve as an important marker of susceptibility to drug dependence, and in certain cases it may also precipitate substance use disorders. Sensitization includes both behavioral sensitization, or "increased locomotion in response to repeated administrations of a drug," as well as cross-sensitization, in which animals or humans who have used one substance react to a new and different substance as though they had used this substance before.[9] Likewise, stress predisposes to addiction.[11]

Bingeing is a characteristic pattern of substance use that is tightly linked to dependence. For example, rats that have access to cocaine for 6 hours/day will administer the largest single dose within the first 10 minutes of access to this drug.[12,13] Similarly, people with unlimited access to cocaine will self-administer the drug in periodic binges.[14]

Binge eating, which is characterized by consumption of a portion of food larger than most Americans would eat "under similar circumstances" in less than 2 hours.[8,15] Binge eating also implies a loss of control over food consumption.[15] Importantly, binge eating is beneficial, in environments where food availability is unpredictable, and the impulse to binge may thus be an evolutionary adaptation that helped humans to survive during times of food scarcity.[1,15] While our evolutionary instinct to overconsume still exists, nonhomeostatic feeding is no longer essential to survival for the majority of people who live in the developed world and have consistent access to food.[1]

People and animals binge on foods that are high in sugar, fat, and/or carbohydrates.[16] Indeed, just as rats do not binge on lab chow, humans are far less prone to bingeing on fruits and vegetables.[16] Not surprisingly, binge eating in childhood is associated with higher body fat percentages, and with a greater risk for obesity in adulthood.[15]

Both animals and people who regularly consume hedonic foods have been shown to exhibit, or describe, withdrawal syndromes in response to abstinence from these foods. For example, rats who have been given intermittent access to a sucrose solution demonstrate signs of withdrawal—including tremors, head shaking, and teeth chattering—not only when deprived of sucrose for 24 hours but also when treated with a high dose of naloxone, an opioid antagonist.[9] Similarly, anecdotal evidence indicates that people who typically consume high-fat, high-sugar foods experience anxiety, food cravings, and dysphoria when abstaining from hedonic food.

TABLE 39.1. *DSM-IV* DIAGNOSTIC CRITERIA FOR SUBSTANCE DEPENDENCE

A maladaptive pattern of substance use, leading to clinically significant impairment or distress, as manifested by three (or more) of the following, occurring at any time in the same 12-month period:

1. Tolerance, as defined by either of the following: (1) a need for markedly increased amounts of the substance to achieve intoxication or the desired affect; (2) markedly diminished effect with continued use of the same amount of the substance.
2. Withdrawal, as manifested by either of the following:
   i. The characteristic withdrawal syndrome for the substance
   ii. The same (or a closely related) substance is taken to relieve or avoid withdrawal symptoms.
3. The substance is often taken in larger amounts or over a longer period than was intended.
4. There is a persistent desire or unsuccessful efforts to cut down or control substance use.
5. A great deal of time is spent in activities necessary to obtain the substance (e.g., visiting multiple doctors or driving long distances), use the substance (e.g. chain-smoking), or recover from its effects.
6. Important social, occupational, or recreational activities are given up or reduced because of substance use.
7. The substance use is continued despite knowledge of having a persistent or recurrent physical or psychological problem that is likely to have been caused or exacerbated by the substance (e.g., current cocaine use despite recognition of cocaine-induced depression, or continued drinking despite recognition that an ulcer was made worse by alcohol consumption)[1]

Source: From APA, *Diagnostic and statistical manual of mental disorders*, 4th ed. Washington, DC: American Psychiatric Association, 2000.

Stress not only induces or heightens cravings for drugs of abuse but also impacts eating patterns. Most people—approximately 70%—eat more food on a daily basis when they are under stress. Additionally, stress also appears to heighten people's desire to consume calorically dense, highly palatable foods.[11] The hypothalamic-pituitary-adrenal (HPA) axis not only mediates the stress response but also regulates the release of hormones—including cortisol, glucocorticoids, leptin, insulin, and neuropeptide Y—which control energy storage, distribution, and usage. This regulatory system often becomes unbalanced under chronic stress. Not surprisingly, this combination of increased food consumption and dysregulation of energy storage and distribution that accompanies states of persistent stress predisposes to visceral fat accumulation and weight gain.[11]

CLINICAL EVIDENCE FOR CROSS-SENSITIZATION AND COMMON NEUROBIOLOGY

Significant research on addiction over the past few decades has led experts in this field to recognize that a common neurobiology for reinforcement underlies addiction to all drugs. We now understand, for example, that the neurotransmitter dopamine plays a critical role in reinforcing use of all drugs. This author (M. S. G.) proposed the critical role of dopamine in cocaine reinforcement and the heuristic value of considering cocaine, and not opiates or alcohol, as the model drug of abuse.[14,17] Additionally, we have come to understand that the process of addiction is also driven by a "fatal attraction" between the drug and the person, which is often a more powerful motivator of continued drug use than is a "withdrawal syndrome."[18] The notion that a "fatal attraction" to a drug can be a more significant driver of drug use than an avoidance of withdrawal syndrome is critical for both understanding and validating addictions to gambling, sex, and food, pathologies that may not result in significant physiological withdrawal if stopped.[19,20]

The ability to administer drugs to laboratory animals, particularly rats, has allowed neuroscientists to develop and study "animal models" for addiction. These animal models, which are often "addicted rats," have dramatically improved our understanding of the neuroanatomy and neuropharmacology of drug reinforcement, withdrawal, and reinstatement, and have allowed us to develop new tools and to test new hypotheses and treatments.[21]

Animal studies exemplify the reality that drug-drug and food-drug cross-sensitization indeed occur. In 2005, Gosnell reported cross-sensitization between psychostimulants and sucrose, reporting that sucrose intake in rats enhances behavioral sensitization from cocaine (i.e., the effects of cocaine were prolonged among those consuming sucrose).[22] Similarly, in 2006, Le Merrer and Stephens[23] showed that the effects of cocaine and morphine on locomotor activity were potentiated among food-conditioned rodents. Interestingly, the administration of naltrexone, an opioid antagonist, suppressed this food-conditioned and increased locomotor activity. These studies strongly support a common meso-telecephalic neuroanatomy and common neurobiology for all drugs of abuse. The treatment approach of Alcoholics Anonymous (AA), the oldest, and arguably most effective, substance abuse treatment program reflects this notion. Indeed, AA has long taught its members that abstinence from alcohol should be accompanied by abstinence from all drugs of abuse, because if you are addicted to alcohol you can just as easily become addicted to any other drug.[24] While AA's leadership, sponsors, and members likely did not understand the neurobiological evidence to back this claim, they most certainly had ample anecdotal evidence to support it. Cross-sensitization is a reality of modern day treatment and recovery.[25] For example, treatment experts interpret drug use during recovery to be trigger for relapse.

Animal studies are helpful in understanding substance addiction and treatment, particularly because animal models provide a rare opportunity to study one drug or substance in an otherwise controlled system. However, it is quite difficult to find people who only use one substance. Smokers drink and drinkers smoke.[26] Caffeine and alcohol, cannabis and hallucinogens or psychostimulants, and cocaine and opiates are some of the commonly used combinations.[27] When opiates are not available to an addict, in a snowstorm, for example, the addict will drink large quantities of alcohol (if available).[28] Moreover, if their drug of choice is not available, addicts appear to prefer other drugs that are structurally and neurobiologically similar to their drug of choice. Cocaine addicts may prefer methylphenidate and amphetamines, for example, which have effects that are quite different from those of alcohol and opiates. These examples also provide strong clinical and anecdotal evidence that cross-sensitization is a powerful driver of substance abuse in humans.

Food and drugs also appear to be cross-sensitizing. For example, food can reduce drug self-administration in lab animals, and food consumption reduces drug cravings and self-administration in people.[29] While food is not a treatment for drug addiction, and drugs of abuse are not a treatment for food addiction, both food and drugs can acutely ameliorate cravings for, and withdrawal from, their counterparts.

Drug addiction and obesity are diseases that begin early in life.[30] Exposure to drugs in utero, early childhood, or during adolescence can change the brain and key neuronal systems, increasing the odds of drug experimentation and dependence later in life.[31] Exposure to high-density, highly reinforcing, hedonic foods during pregnancy, early childhood, or adolescence could provide the same catalytic effect, altering gene expression and proteins and making overeating and food addiction more likely. In addition, bad habits developed early in life become relatively impervious to higher brain or other control mechanisms, and are very difficult to extinguish during adulthood, or for that matter, at all.

Food is not only ubiquitous, but it is also exciting to consume. Food consumption releases dopamine in the brain and activates the same reward pathways that drugs co-opt in addicts. Dopamine has been reported to be released, and increased, in the nucleus accumbens in anticipation of both drug use and food consumption. This finding highlights that both food and drugs exert strong reinforcing effects through dopamine channels.[32] While dopamine may drive anticipation of food, and reinforcement during consumption, people's affective state, memory for foods, and conditioned cues are significant drivers of overeating. Indeed, in obese individuals, overeating usually is accompanied by a loss of higher cortical inhibition over the compulsion to eat. The earlier in life these unhealthy patterns of food consumption begin, the more difficult it is for the orbitofrontal cortex to regain control over the compulsion and drive to eat.[33] Food and drugs of abuse share many common properties and features, including similarities in their mechanisms of reward, the role of stress in stimulating cravings and relapse, and the role of learning in allowing users to associate drug or food use with certain consistent outcomes.[34] Yet while the mesotelecephalic dopamine pathways mediate cravings for both hedonic foods and drugs, food appears to exert its reinforcing effects via more complex and diffuse pathways, which involve endorphins, cannabinoids, and many other messengers and hormones that originate from different parts of the body. For example, ghrelin, a hormone secreted by the gut, appears to play an important role in activating the centrally controlled neuronal pathways that regulate hunger and food consumption. In one recent study of the effects of ghrelin on hunger, healthy volunteers who received intravenous ghrelin prior to viewing pictures of food reported more intense hunger ratings than controls. Furthermore, functional magnetic resonance imaging (fMRI) performed during this experiment demonstrated that patients who received ghrelin experienced increased activation of parts of the brain that control hunger, satiety, and consumption drive.[1] While systemic ghrelin levels typically fall after feeding, their consistent elevation in patients with Prader-Willi syndrome, a disorder that is characterized by hyperphagia and obesity, suggests that dysregulation of ghrelin production may be an important driver of pathologic overeating.[1] Thus, while regulation of drug use occurs predominately in the central nervous system, the entire human body is involved in the management of food consumption. Food addiction is more complex than drug addiction for at least one additional reason: food is necessary for survival (and other drugs of abuse are not), and abstinence from food is therefore not a viable treatment for this disorder. fMRI[35] and positron emission tomography (PET) results support the notion that chronic dopamine reinforcement is associated with the down-regulation of D2 receptors in cocaine, alcohol, and food addicts. If overstimulation from drug use and food consumption results in similar changes in the brain—which these studies suggest that they do— then the brain may take months-years to recover from these. In all addicts, including food addicts, the somatosensory cortex changes over time to overrepresent the functions that facilitate eating and its pleasurable effects. Once the neuronal networks that regulate an activity and its rewarding response are organized, the behavior is very difficult to extinguish.[36,37] These studies also allude to why overeating is so difficult to reverse, and why obese patients have great difficulty losing weight, and often relapse. Overeating and weight gain also lengthen the lag time between the onset of feeding and the arrival in the brain of glucose—the body's major signal that feeding has begun and calories are being repleted. During this "lag time," which may be 12 minutes in a thin person, and more than 25 minutes in an obese individual, the brain does not regulate food consumption because it has no information about how many calories have been consumed relative to the number that are needed to meet the body's homeostatic needs. Thus, the longer this unregulated feeding period lasts, the easier it is to consume excess calories before experiencing a signal from the brain to stop eating. This "lag time" also indicates that homeostatic eating should be painfully slow, purposeful, and mindful.[38]

Food Consumption during Substance Abuse Recovery

As residential treatment programs like The Florida Recovery Center (FRC) have focused more intensely on providing long-term residential treatment and recovery programs for addicts, addiction specialists have decided to extend follow-up and outcome research to years instead of months.[39] We have also followed populations who can be closely monitored for 5 years with drug testing, and psychosocial and medical evaluations.[40] This work has allowed us to gain insight into addicts' postdetoxification experiences.[41] We have learned, for example, that just as smokers usually gain weight when they quit smoking, most addicts experience rebound hyperphagia and weight gain when they stop using drugs. In 2007, Hodgkins, Frost-Pineda, and Gold studied the eating patterns of adolescents living at a residential treatment setting while receiving treatment for drug addiction. When allowed to eat ad lib, this cohort overate consistently and gained weight. Those patients who relapsed to drugs experienced decreased appetite and lost weight.[42]

Postaddiction overeating has independently changed addiction treatment approaches and programs throughout the United States. Treatment programs like the Florida Recovery Center, Hazelden, and The Betty Ford Center have developed treatment models that include measures to prevent postdetoxification overeating. These facilities provide patients with access to a dietician, emphasize exercise, and help patients to plan for expected changes in eating and the reinforcing effects of food. Why do recovering addicts gain weight? Some experts have argued that taste returns in the postdrug state. Another possible, and indeed likely, explanation is that drugs exert such a strong reinforcing influence on reinforcement pathways in the brain that weaker reinforcing signals, like those from food, are ignored and fail to motivate behavior. Under the influence of drugs, eating becomes as elective an activity as socializing or performing community service.

Influence of Tobacco on Weight

Cigarette smoking has long been reported to cause loss of appetite, loss of taste, and weight loss. Marketing of tobacco to women began with an emphasis on this association, and it has continued with Virginia Slims (and the tennis tournament by that name). Smoking cigarettes, like chewing coca leaves or taking other drugs, reduces hunger, craving, and drive for food.[43] Likewise, smoking cessation is associated with food cravings and an average weight gain of 3–5 kilograms.[44] In fact, weight gain is so common following smoking cessation that fear of gaining more weight has led many patients to relapse.[44,45] With so few pharmacological treatments for obesity, and none as effective as smoking over the long term, it is not surprising that many smokers start and continue to smoke in order to lose weight and control food intake. Rimonabant, a cannabinoid antagonist used to promote weight loss, is the only drug shown to significantly decrease postcessation weight gain over more than 3 months.[44] Bupropion, a dopamine and norepinephrine reuptake inhibitor, does initially attenuate weight gain following cessation, but it does not help patients to keep this weight off over the long term.[46]

Competition for Dopamine Pathways

Drugs and food appear to compete for control over the same neuronal pathways in the brain and behaviors that reinforce their respective uses. Ample research and clinical evidence exist to support this assertion. In animals and humans, food deprivation appears to intensify the reinforcing effects of drugs.[47–49] Cocaine and methamphetamine users are almost always thin and have no urge to eat when high. Additionally, addicts, and some drug rehabilitation clinics, use high-sugar foods—including candy, cake, and cookies—to treat drug cravings. The third edition of the *Alcoholics Anonymous Big Book*[50] notes that "One of the many doctors who had the opportunity of reading this book in manuscript form told us that the use of sweets was often helpful" [in controlling alcohol cravings].... He added that occasionally in the night a vague craving would arouse that would be satisfied by candy. "Many of us have noticed a tendency to eat sweets and have found this practice beneficial."[50] Some AA chapters teach recovering alcoholics an acronym, HALT, which represents four dangers for relapsing: hunger, anger, loneliness, and tiredness.

Overeating also appears to blunt drug reinforcement. Obese people rarely use other addictive substances: they smoke fewer cigarettes and use fewer drugs of abuse than virtually every other population we have studied. Addiction patients often joke that fewer people do drugs on Thanksgiving than on any other day of the year because they are just too full to waste their money on drugs.

Collectively, these examples strongly support the idea that food and drugs of abuse exist along a spectrum of substances that compete for access to the same dopamine-mediated reinforcement sites in the brain. When one of these substances is being used or consumed, it will temporarily extinguish drives for other substances. If many substances are being used at once, the most powerful will dominate.

Similarities between Pharmacological Treatments for Addiction and Obesity

Pharmacological treatments for obesity share many similarities with those used to treat addiction. Stimulants like Phentermine, an amphetamine, remain the pharmacological treatment mainstays for obesity. Stimulants promote weight loss by stimulating dopamine pathways, resulting in appetite suppression. These drugs can be abused and are therefore not prescribed to patients with a history of drug abuse.

Both obesity and alcohol dependence can be treated with medications that act by preventing a target substance—fat, in the case of obesity, and alcohol in the case of alcoholism—from entering into the bloodstream. For example, Orlistat promotes weight loss by blocking fat absorption in the small intestine. Similarly, Antabuse cross-reacts with ingested alcohol, causing severe physical illness and expulsion of ingested alcohol through violent retching. Fear of this reaction also creates a powerful disinclination to consume alcohol.[51]

Many of the best pharmacological treatments for drug abuse address anhedonia and poor impulse control, and recent clinical trials indicate that they hold significant promise in treating obesity.[52] Indeed, opioid antagonists such as naloxone and naltrexone, which are the pillars of addiction treatment for opiate and alcohol dependence, act by disrupting the opioid-mediated reinforcing effects of these two drugs.[53–55] Contrave, a sustained-release combination of bupropion and naltrexone, is currently in

Phase III clinical trials for the treatment of obesity, and it is reported to increase energy expenditure and reduce appetite.[56]

COMPARING PATTERNS OF USE, NEUROBIOLOGY, PUBLIC HEALTH BURDENS, AND THE LEGAL REGULATION OF FOOD, ALCOHOL, AND TOBACCO

Alcohol, tobacco, and food share many similarities that distinguish them from other substances of abuse. For example, alcohol, tobacco, and food consumption patterns share a number of important similarities. For example, tobacco use, alcohol dependence, and obesity are more prevalent among the poor than the wealthy.[57,58] In addition, smoking, drinking, or pathologic overeating during childhood and adolescence, when the brain is still highly plastic, is highly associated with nicotine dependence, alcohol dependence, and obesity later in life, respectively. Indeed, just as early bingeing on alcohol increases one's risk of becoming an alcoholic, binge eating early in life predisposes to pathologic eating patterns and obesity during adulthood. Smokers, alcoholics, and pathologic overeaters are susceptible to similar triggers or "cues" to binge, or relapse, including the sight of others smoking, eating, or drinking, the taste or smell of cigarette smoke, food, or alcohol.[59,60] Moreover, alcohol, tobacco, and food are intricately interwoven into mechanisms that people have developed to cope with negative emotions, including stress, anxiety, and depression. Indeed, these mood disturbances are associated with increased use of tobacco, alcohol, and food, and they predict relapse in those who have quit.[60-62] Examples of these associations abound in the medical literature. Research has shown, for example, that alcohol-dependent individuals frequently experience strong cravings for alcohol after being exposed to a simulated personal stress.[53] Additionally, a recent study found that stressed individuals with access to two different food options—red grapes and M&M's—were more likely to eat M&M's than were unstressed controls.[62] A qualitative study of food consumption habits concluded that people consume greater amounts of calorie-dense, sweet, and fatty foods when stressed, and that this consumption often occurs between meals.[63] People use food, alcohol, and tobacco "to modulate mood states in the absence of more adaptive ways of coping with intense emotional states," to mask, or self-medicate against depression, loneliness, anger, frustration, and other negative emotions.[62] Importantly, these maladaptive patterns of coping with adversity begin to develop early in life.

While no amount of smoking is healthy, and overconsumption of food and alcohol is deleterious to one's health, judicious consumption of alcohol and food—including certain hedonic foods—has important health benefits: for example, moderate alcohol consumption (one drink/night for a woman and two drinks/night for a man) is associated with a decreased risk of coronary heart disease.[64] Similarly, daily consumption of modest amounts of olive oil—a highly palatable food and the major source of fat in the "Mediterranean diet"—has also been shown to reduce rates of cardiovascular disease.[65]

We also have strong evidence that tobacco, food, and alcohol generate their reinforcing effects through similar neurobiological pathways. Most important, the rewarding properties of all three substances are mediated by dopamine release in the nucleus accumbens.[66-68] Moreover, alcohol, tobacco, and highly palatable foods—particularly those high in sugar and fat—induce endogenous opioid release, producing a feeling of anxiolysis and fortifying the pleasurable effects of each of these substances.[67,69] Tobacco, alcohol, and food also lead to release of a number of other neurotransmitters in the brain, including acetylcholine, norepinephrine, GABA, glutamate, and serotonin.[67,69]

Underscoring the significant similarities between the neurobiological effects of alcohol, tobacco, and food, many of the pharmacological treatments for alcoholism and nicotine dependence may prove to be beneficial in treating pathological overeating. As mentioned earlier, bupropion, an antidepressant and first-line treatment for smoking cessation, and naltrexone, a mainstay in treating alcohol dependence, have shown promise in promoting weight loss. Recent clinical trials have demonstrated that while both drugs are somewhat effective as monotherapies, when administered together they appear to act synergistically to decrease food consumption and promote weight loss.[70] Naltrexone's utility in treating alcohol dependence and promoting weight loss highlights the similarities between how hedonic eating and opiate consumption affect endogenous opioid production.[70] While these findings certainly warrant further confirmation, they are highly encouraging, and evidence that buproprion and naltrexone are effective in treating obesity highlights three important ideas: First, naltrexone's ability to block the pleasurable response associated with the consumption of hedonic foods, and thereby to promote weight loss, provides powerful evidence that endogenous opioids play a significant role in reinforcing pathological overeating. Second, bupropion's efficacy in treating obesity both emphasizes that dopaminergic pathways play a central role in reinforcing pathological food consumption and suggests that nicotine and food may play similar roles in attempting to offset dysregulations in mood. Mood disorders are associated with higher rates of alcohol abuse, nicotine dependence, eating disorders, and obesity, and withdrawal from alcohol, tobacco, and food can result in anhedonia and negative affect.[57,71] Third, the synergy of these two drugs in treating obesity, and bupropion's lack of efficacy in the treatment of alcoholism, suggest that the neurobiology underlying the reinforcing effects of hedonic foods may be more complex than those that mediate the action of either alcohol or tobacco. Additionally, the neuronal pathways involved in the response to food consumption may overlap considerably with the pathways that mediate the effects of alcohol and tobacco.

Food, tobacco, and alcohol are big business. All three can be legally purchased (though different countries put different minimum age limits on buying and using tobacco and alcohol),[64] are produced and sold by for-profit companies, face heavy competition from similar products, and are heavily marketed to consumers. In these businesses, brand loyalty is the key to building profits; products that do not stimulate their own taking do not succeed, and companies use a product's packaging, taste, smell, and image to build sensory, cognitive, and physiological reinforcements of product consumption.[3] Moreover, while minors cannot legally purchase alcohol or tobacco, they are a critical source of revenues for the companies that produce alcohol, cigarettes, and food. Indeed, the majority of smokers begin smoking before turning 18 years old.[72] Over 10 million adolescents use alcohol each year (minors use alcohol more commonly than any other substance of abuse),[73] and children ages 5–14 influence $200–500 billion of consumer spending each year, much of which goes toward food.[74]

Obesity, smoking, and alcoholism also pose significant, and in many ways comparable, public health challenges. While the benefits of smoking, drinking to excess, and eating unhealthily large quantities of food are immediate, clear, and tangible, many of their most serious risks are deferred, often unfamiliar, and difficult to comprehend. Alcohol dependence, tobacco dependence, and obesity are all associated with chronic systemic health problems that result in significant morbidity and mortality and place a tremendous burden on health care systems. Chronic alcohol use is associated with the development of heart disease, pancreatitis, kidney disease, peptic ulcer disease, bone disease (osteoporosis), and chronic liver disease (cirrhosis), which in turn can lead to hepatocellular carcinoma.[75] Smoking is associated with innumerable systemic illnesses over the long term—including lung cancer, emphysema, heart disease, and vascular disease—and is the leading cause of death in the United States.[72] The weight gain and obesity that result from continued overeating predispose to non-insulin-dependent diabetes mellitus, cardiovascular disease, asthma, bone disease (osteoarthritis), nonalcoholic fatty liver disease and liver cirrhosis, and many different forms of cancer.[76] Smoking, obesity-overweight, and alcohol use all rank among the top 10 causes of preventable death in the United States: smoking is ranked first, obesity/overweight is third, and alcohol is ninth.[77] Yet because these dangerous sequelae may not manifest until many years after substance use begins, the threat that they pose to individuals' health is often of little use in motivating changes in behavior. Furthermore, in the absence of an urgent reason to advocate for a behavior change, doctors may postpone interventions that have critical long-term benefits on morbidity and mortality.

A more focused comparison of tobacco and food, and the tobacco and food industries, reveals a number of striking similarities between the production of tobacco and food, and the tactics that the food and tobacco industries have used to challenge claims that their merchandise is harmful to health. Of course, considerable differences between tobacco and food do exist, and they warrant acknowledgment: tobacco is not essential to life, while food certainly is. And, while years of research have clearly elucidated how and why tobacco dependence develops, we are still refining our understanding of the relationship between food and addiction.[3,74] Minors cannot legally purchase tobacco products, but they can buy food. Tobacco companies produce a limited array of products for public sale, while food companies fill convenience and grocery stores with countless numbers of edible items, many of which are healthy.[3]

Nonetheless, the similarities between the public health consequences of smoking and obesity, and how the food and tobacco industries have responded to claims that their products are unhealthy, are quite remarkable. The food industry's "food scientists" are eerily reminiscent of big tobacco's cadre of scientific "experts," who were tasked with making cigarettes more addictive (by manipulating nicotine levels) and pleasant to smoke (for example, by adding menthol) and with poking holes in research that linked cigarettes to lung cancer and addiction.[3] After all, what for-profit food producer would employ scientists to engineer foods that no one wanted to eat over and over again? The food industry's organized strategy to rebut claims that they are partly responsible for the worldwide obesity epidemic utilizes many of the same arguments that big tobacco used to distance itself from the health problems associated with smoking. For example, both big tobacco and food companies have argued that smoking and eating are personal choices, and that people must take responsibility for their own health. Similarly, both industries have questioned whether regulating tobacco and food consumption would infringe upon individual rights. Perhaps most insidiously, food companies contend that "there are no good foods or bad foods."[3] To support this claim, they cite research conducted by the American Dietetic Association (ADA), an organization that, not coincidentally, receives funding from Wendy's, the Tri-Lamb Group, the Hershey Center for Health and Nutrition, the Distilled Spirits Council, and the Wrigley Science Institute (as in Wrigley gum), and which recently partnered with Coca-Cola.[3] This assertion, which credible scientific research has disproven time and again—studies revealing the dangers of trans-fats are just one recent example—echo big tobacco's initial contention that "smoking per se was not bad, only "excess" smoking."[3] Like big tobacco, the food industry has created a powerful lobbying machine that spends billions of dollars each year to support its interests in political arenas across the nation.[3] Just as big tobacco used independent, industry-funded "front groups" to generate studies that questioned the dangers of smoking, so has the food industry funded similar efforts by groups like the American Beverage Association (ABA), the Obesity Society, the ADA, and the Center for Consumer Freedom.[3]

Big tobacco responded to public apprehensions about the health effects of smoking with "low-tar" and low-nicotine cigarettes, which turned out to be just as deadly as their predecessors.[3] Similar public fears about fatty foods have led snack food makers to produce low-fat alternatives, which, while healthier in terms of fat content, will still cause weight gain if consumed in excessive amounts.

These parallels between the food and tobacco industries—the mounting neurobiological, clinical, and behavioral evidence that food addiction does occur, and the dramatic, and enlarging, burden that obesity places on health care systems—are alarming. They should compel us to do everything that we can to better understand why, how, and what people eat, and how we can rein in our voracious appetites and enlarging waist lines in the pursuit of a better public health.

REFERENCES

1. Malik S, McGlone F, Bedrossian D, Dagher A. Ghrelin modulates brain activity in areas that control appetitive behavior. *Cell Metab* 2008;7(5):400–409.
2. Kessler DA. *The End of Overeating*. New York: Rondale Books, 2009.
3. Brownell KD, Warner KE. The perils of ignoring history: Big Tobacco played dirty and millions died. How similar is Big Food? *Milbank Q* 2009; 87(1):259–294.
4. James GA, Gold MS, Liu Y. Interaction of satiety and reward response to food stimulation. *J Addict Dis* 2004;23(3):23–37.
5. Lyznicki JM, Young DC, Riggs JA, Davis RM. Obesity: assessment and management in primary care. *Am Fam Physician* 2001;63(11):2185–2196.
6. Wang Y, Beydoun MA, Liang L, Caballero B, Kumanyika SK. Will all Americans become overweight or obese? Estimating the progression and cost of the US obesity epidemic. *Obesity* 2008;16(10): 2323–2330.
7. Gold MS, Graham NA, Cocores JA, Nixon SJ. Food addiction? *J Addict Med* 2009;3(1):42–45.
8. American Psychiatric Association. *Diagnostic and Statistical Manual of Mental Disorders*. 4th ed. Washington, DC: American Psychiatric Association, 2000.
9. Avena NM, Rada P, Hoebel BG. Evidence for sugar addiction: behavioral and neurochemical effects of intermittent, excessive sugar intake. *Neurosci Biobehav Rev* 2008;32(1):20–39.
10. Weiss F. Neurobiology of craving, conditioned reward and relapse. *Curr Opinion Pharmacol* 2005;5(1): 9–19.
11. Adam TC, Epel ES. Stress, eating and the reward system. *Physiol Behav* 2007;91(4):449–458.

12. Ahmed SH, Koob GF. Transition from moderate to excessive drug intake: change in hedonic set point. *Science* 1998;282(5387):298–300.

13. Bozarth MA, Wise RA. Toxicity associated with long-term intravenous heroin and cocaine self-administration in the rat. *JAMA* 1985;254(1):81–83.

14. Dackis CA, Gold MS. New concepts in cocaine addiction: the dopamine depletion hypothesis. *Neurosci Bio Rev* 1985;9:469–477.

15. Avena NM. Examining the addictive-like properties of binge eating using an animal model of sugar dependence. *Exp Clin Psychopharmacol* 2007;15(5):481–491.

16. Avena NM, Rada P, Hoebel BG. Sugar and fat bingeing have notable differences in addictive-like behavior. *J Nutr* 2009;139(3):623–628.

17. Gold MS, Dackis CA. New insights and treatments: opiate withdrawal and cocaine addiction. *Clin Ther* 1985;7(1):6–21.

18. Dackis CA, Gold MS. New concepts in cocaine addiction: the dopamine depletion hypothesis. *Neurosci Bio Rev* 1985;9(3):469–477.

19. Jonas JM, Gold MS. Cocaine abuse and eating disorders. *Lancet* 1986;1(8477):390–391.

20. Joranby L, Frost-Pineda K, Gold MS. Addiction to food and brain reward systems. *Sex Addict Compuls* 2005;12(2):201–217.

21. Robinson TE. Addicted rats. *Science* 2004;305: 951–953.

22. Gosnell BA. Sucrose intake enhances behavioral sensitization produced by cocaine. *Brain Res* 2005; 1031(2):194–201.

23. Le Merrer J, Stephens DN. Food-induced behavioral sensitization, its cross-sensitization to cocaine and morphine, pharmacological blockade, and effect on food intake. *J Neurosci* 2006;26(27):7163–7171.

24. Chung T, Martin CS, Clark DB. Concurrent change in alcohol and drug problems among treated adolescents over three years. *J Stud Alcohol Drugs* 2008; 69(3):420–429.

25. Fattore L, Deiana S, Spano SM, et al. Endocannabinoid system and opioid addiction: behavioural aspects. *Pharmacol Biochem Behav* 2005;81(2):343–359.

26. Harrison EL, Desai RA, McKee SA. Nondaily smoking and alcohol use, hazardous drinking, and alcohol diagnoses among young adults: findings from the NESARC. *Alcohol Clin Exp Res* 2008;32(12): 2081–2087.

27. Grov C, Kelly BC, Parsons JT. Polydrug use among club-going young adults recruited through time-space sampling. *Subst Use Misuse* 2009;44(6):848–864.

28. Petry NM. A behavioral economic analysis of polydrug abuse in alcoholics: asymmetrical substitution of alcohol and cocaine. *Drug Alcohol Depen* 2001;62(1):31–39.

29. Emmett-Oglesby MW, Mathis DA, Moon RT, Lal H. Animal models of drug withdrawal symptoms. *Psychopharmacol* 1990;101(3):292–309.

30. Miller J, Gold MS, Silverstein J. Pediatric overeating and obesity: an epidemic. *Psychiatr Ann* 2003;33(2):95–99.

31. Rhodes P, Craigon J, Gray C, Rhind SM, Loughna PT, Gardner DS. Adult-onset obesity reveals prenatal programming of glucose-insulin sensitivity in male sheep nutrient restricted during late gestation. *PloS One* 2009;4(10):e7393.

32. Anselme P. The effect of exposure to drugs on the processing of natural rewards. *Neurosci Biobehav Rev* 2009;33(3):314–335.

33. Volkow ND, Li TK. Drug addiction: the neurobiology of behaviour gone awry. *Nat Rev* 2004;5(12): 963–970.

34. Volkow ND, Wise RA. How can drug addiction help us understand obesity? *Nat Neurosci* 2005;8(5): 555–560.

35. Liu Y, Gold MS. Human functional Magnetic Resonance Imaging (fMRI) of eating and satiety in eating disorders and obesity. *Psychiatr Ann* 2003;33(2): 127–132.

36. Volkow ND, Fowler JS, Wang GJ, Swanson JM. Dopamine in drug abuse and addiction: results from imaging studies and treatment implications. *Mol Psychiatry* 2004;9(6):557–69.

37. Volkow ND, Wang GJ, Fowler JS, Telang F. Overlapping neuronal circuits in addiction and obesity: evidence of systems pathology. *Philos Trans R Soc Lond* 2008;363(1507):3191–3200.

38. Andrade AM, Greene GW, Melanson KJ. Eating slowly led to decreases in energy intake within meals in healthy women. *J Am Diet Assoc* 2008;108(7): 1186–1191.

39. DuPont RL, McLellan AT, White WL, Merlo LJ, Gold MS. Setting the standard for recovery: Physicians Health Programs. *J Subst Abus Treat* 2009; 36(2):159–171.

40. Merlo LJ, Gold MS. Prescription opioid abuse and dependence among physicians: hypotheses and treatment. *Harv Rev Psychiatry* 2008;16(3):181–194.

41. McLellan AT, Skipper GS, Campbell M, DuPont RL. Five year outcomes in a cohort study of physicians treated for substance use disorders in the United States. *BMJ* 2008;337:1–6.

42. Hodgkins C, Frost-Pineda K, Gold MS. Weight gain during substance abuse treatment: the dual problem of addiction and overeating in an adolescent population. *J Addict Dis* 2007;26(suppl 1):41–50.

43. Paczynski RP, Gold MS. Cocaine and crack. In: Ruiz P, Strain E, eds. *Lowinson & Ruiz's Substance Abuse: A Comprehensive Textbook.* 5th ed. Baltimore, MD: Lippincott Williams & Wilkins; 2010: 191–213.

44. Rigotti NA, Gonzales D, Dale LC, Lawrence D, Chang Y. A randomized controlled trial of adding the nicotine patch to rimonabant for smoking cessation: efficacy, safety and weight gain. *Addiction* 2009;104(2):266–276.

45. White MA, Masheb RM, Grilo CM. Self-reported weight gain following smoking cessation: a function of binge eating behavior. *Int J Eat Disorder* 2010; 43:572–575.

46. Holm KJ, Spencer CM. Bupropion: a review of its use in the management of smoking cessation. *Drugs* 2000;59(4):1007–1024.

47. Maric T, Tobin S, Quinn T, Shalev U. Food deprivation-like effects of neuropeptide Y on heroin self-administration and reinstatement of heroin seeking in rats. *Behav Brain Res* 2008;194(1):39–43.

48. Shalev U, Finnie PS, Quinn T, Tobin S, Wahi P. A role for corticotropin-releasing factor, but not corticosterone, in acute food-deprivation-induced reinstatement of heroin seeking in rats. *Psychopharmacol* 2006;187(3):376–384.

49. Gold MS. Eating disorders, overeating, and pathological attachment to food: independent or addictive disorders? *J Addict Dis* 2004;23(3):1–3.

50. Anonymous. Sweets vs. cravings. In: *Alcoholics Anonymous*. 3rd ed. New York: Alcoholics Anonymous World Services; 1976: 1–162.

51. Rothman RB, Blough BE, Baumann MH. Dual dopamine/serotonin releasers as potential medications for stimulant and alcohol addictions. *AAPS J* 2007;9(1):E1–E10.

52. Sum CF. Pharmacotherapy and surgery in the treatment of obesity: evaluating risks and benefits. *Asia Pac J Clin Nutr* 2002;11(suppl 8):S722–S725.

53. Morley JE, Levine AS, Yim GK, Lowy MT. Opioid modulation of appetite. *Neurosci Biobehav Rev* 1983;7(2):281–305.

54. Yuan CS, Wang CZ, Attele A, Zhang L. Methylnaltrexone reduced body weight gain in ob/ob mice. *J Opioid Manage* 2009;5(4):213–218.

55. Jonas JM, Gold MS. The use of opiate antagonists in treating bulimia: a study of low-dose versus high-dose naltrexone. *Psychiatry Res* 1988;24(2):195–199.

56. Padwal R. Contrave, a bupropion and naltrexone combination therapy for the potential treatment of obesity. *Curr Opin Investig Drugs* 2009;10(10):1117–1125.

57. McCarty CA, Kosterman R, Mason WA, et al. Longitudinal associations among depression, obesity and alcohol use disorders in young adulthood. *Gen Hosp Psychiatry* 2009;31(5):442–450.

58. Harwood GA, Salsberry P, Ferketich AK, Wewers ME. Cigarette smoking, socioeconomic status, and psychosocial factors: examining a conceptual framework. *Public Health Nurs* 2007;24(4):361–371.

59. Weiner S. The addiction of overeating: self-help groups as treatment models. *J Clin Psychol* 1998;54(2):163–167.

60. Sinha R, Fox HC, Hong KA, Bergquist K, Bhagwagar Z, Siedlarz KM. Enhanced negative emotion and alcohol craving, and altered physiological responses following stress and cue exposure in alcohol dependent individuals. *Neuropsychopharmacol* 2009;34(5):1198–1208.

61. Zhou X, Nonnemaker J, Sherrill B, Gilsenan AW, Coste F, West R. Attempts to quit smoking and relapse: factors associated with success or failure from the ATTEMPT cohort study. *Addict Behav* 2009;34(4):365–373.

62. Zellner DA, Loaiza S, Gonzalez Z, et al. Food selection changes under stress. *Physiol Behav* 2006;87(4):789–793.

63. Steptoe A, Lipsey Z, Wardle J. Stress, hassles and variations in alcohol consumption, food choice, and physicial exercise: a diary study. *Br J Health Psychol* 1998;3:51–63.

64. Rimm EB, Williams P, Fosher K, Criqui M, Stampfer MJ. Moderate alcohol intake and lower risk of coronary heart disease: meta-analysis of effects on lipids and haemostatic factors. *BMJ* 1999;319(7224):1523–1528.

65. Perez-Jimenez F, Alvarez de Cienfuegos G, Badimon L, et al. International conference on the healthy effect of virgin olive oil. *Eur J Clin Invest* 2005;35(7):421–424.

66. George TP, Weinberger AH. Nicotine and tobacco. In: Galanter M, Kleber HD, eds. *The American Psychiatric Publishing Textbook of Substance Abuse Treatment*. 4th ed. Washington, DC: American Psychiatric Publishing; 2008: 201–214.

67. Knapp CM, Ciraulo DA, Kranzler HR. Neurobiology of alcohol. In: Galanter M, Kleber HD, eds. *American Psychiatric Publishing Textbook of Substance Abuse Treatment*. 4th ed. Washington, DC: American Psychiatric Publishing; 2008: 111–129.

68. Rada P, Avena NM, Hoebel BG. Daily bingeing on sugar repeatedly releases dopamine in the accumbens shell. *Neuroscience* 2005;134(3):737–744.

69. Benowitz NL. Neurobiology of nicotine addiction: implications for smoking cessation treatment. *Am J Med* 2008;121(4 suppl 1):S3–S10.

70. Plodkowski RA, Nguyen Q, Sundaram U, Nguyen L, Chau DL, St Jeor S. Bupropion and naltrexone: a review of their use individually and in combination for the treatment of obesity. *Expert Opin Pharmacol* 2009;10(6):1069–1081.

71. Goldbacher EM, Bromberger J, Matthews KA. Lifetime history of major depression predicts the development of the metabolic syndrome in middle-aged women. *Psychosom Med* 2009;71(3):266–272.

72. Rivara FP, Ebel BE, Garrison MM, Christakis DA, Wiehe SE, Levy DT. Prevention of smoking-related deaths in the United States. *Am J Prev Med* 2004;27(2):118–125.

73. Hingson RW. The legal drinking age and underage drinking in the United States. *Arch Pediat Adol Med* 2009;163(7):598–600.

74. Brownell K, Horgen KB. *Food Fight*. New York: Contemporary Books, 2004.

75. Mannelli P, Pae CU. Medical comorbidity and alcohol dependence. *Curr Psychiatr Rep* 2007;9(3):217–224.

76. Guh DP, Zhang W, Bansback N, Amarsi Z, Birmingham CL, Anis AH. The incidence of co-morbidities related to obesity and overweight: a systematic review and meta-analysis. *BMC Public Health* 2009;9:88.

77. Danaei G, Ding EL, Mozaffarian D, et al. The preventable causes of death in the United States: comparative risk assessment of dietary, lifestyle, and metabolic risk factors. *PLoS Med* 2009;6(4):e1000058.

40

Stress and Reward

Neural Networks, Eating, and Obesity

ELISSA S. EPEL, A. JANET TOMIYAMA, AND MARY F. DALLMAN

INTRODUCTION

Stress is increasingly recognized as a factor leading to overeating and obesity. Here we present the evidence that stress-related eating follows well-defined neural pathways that involve control over volitional behavior (prefrontal cortex [PFC]), and subcortical areas controlling stress arousal and energy storage (limbic hypothalamic-pituitary-adrenal [L-HPA] axis) and strong motivational drive and impulsivity (nucleus accumbens [NAcc]). The PFC and limbic system inhibit activity in each other, promoting a balance between slower reflective analytic reasoning, necessary to promote goal-directed behavior, and quick reactive survival instincts. Shifts in activity of this neural network, what we call here the "PFC/limbic balance," has well-demonstrated effects on cognition and behavior during acute stress.[1] It is now becoming clear that this neural network shapes eating behavior. We propose that a low PFC/limbic balance can lead to energy imbalance and, in particular, abdominal obesity.

We first review neural and hormonal control of eating during basal conditions and then under stressful circumstances, showing that in large part = stress affects activation of reward pathways and impairs attempts to control eating. We conclude with suggestions for treatment of this widespread common behavior.

BASIC MECHANISMS UNDERLYING HOMEOSTATIC EATING AND STRESS-RELATED OVEREATING

We are equipped with highly evolved regulatory systems that monitor the amount of stored energy and are attuned to the need to find and eat more calories. In chordates, this system resides primarily in the brainstem and hypothalamus, and it is sensitive to hormonal and nutrient signals acting directly on receptors decorating the neurons within this network. Regulation of homeostatic eating is covered in detail elsewhere.[2] Left alone, the homeostatic regulation of feeding behaviors is remarkably accurate and over weeks, months, and years the organism neither gains nor loses much weight. Despite the complex coordination between gut, pancreas, vagus, and brain, this regulatory system is easily overridden by our emotions. As more brain was added to mammals, such as limbic and cortical networks, regulation of food intake became far more complicated and far less driven by maintenance of energy stores. Higher brain structures also innervate the brainstem and hypothalamic network and, at each level, can subvert or reinforce their normal operations of maintaining energy homeostasis. In particular, eating for reward, or hedonic eating, contributes to a large proportion of our caloric intake. We posit that stress is a major factor that promotes hedonic eating and strengthens networks toward tonic hedonic overeating. This makes sense in that the stress response is likely a mere subset of the metabolic networks that maintain caloric balance, our primary survival need.[3] The focus of this review is the mechanisms for stress eating and the outcomes of energy balance and fat distribution.

Stress Drives Specific Intake of Comfort Food

Both acute, single stressors and chronic, sustained stressors are likely to change feeding behaviors in people and rats. Roughly 40% of people reduce and 40% increase their total caloric intake during stressors, with only 20% maintaining intake at normal levels.[4,5] Rats and mice, given only chow to eat, uniformly decrease food intake during stressors. This is an important observation to note, as historically it was assumed that stress led to weight loss in animals. However, if supplied with highly palatable foods to eat, rats still decrease chow intake but maintain intake of the same or more palatable food, as people do. Whether they decrease or increase caloric intake, people change the type of food ingested, with negative emotion driving a shift away from healthy foods toward highly palatable food—usually sweet, sometimes salty, and high fat, and sometimes moderated by high dietary restraint.[6-9]

THE STRESS-HEDONIC EATING MODEL

In Figure 40.1, we pose a simplified version of the neural networks regulating stress-induced hedonic eating. There are interactive connections between structures regulating eating—the limbic system, reward system, basal ganglia, and PFC. Differential patterns of activation shape two distinct types of eating behavior—stress-induced hedonic eating (S-EAT) versus homeostatic eating (H-EAT), which is eating solely in response to caloric need.

Limbic Structures, Stress, and Regulation by the Stress Hormone Cortisol

Stressors engage a network of limbic (phylogenetically ancient) structures that reflect interoceptive as well as exteroceptive inputs: the insula, extended amygdala, and anterior cingulate cortex, as well as thalamic, hypothalamic, and lower brainstem sites.[10] This recruitment of the stress network appears to depend on the actions of glucocorticoids secreted from the adrenal cortex in response to stressors, and the network is engaged to a large extent through the positive actions of glucocorticoids on corticotropin releasing factor (CRF) expression in extrahypothalamic neurons. Acute cortisol reactivity appears to acutely promote comfort food intake both in the lab and naturalistically.[11,12]

Both acute and chronic stressors increase synapses and dendritic bushing in the amygdala and anterior cingulate cortex, and they reduce synaptic contacts with dendritic atrophy in the hippocampus and PFC,[13-15] further sculpting the chronic stress network toward limbic-biased stress responses. Chronic stress effects on the brain may alter eating tonically toward greater comfort food. Women reporting greater chronic stress report greater hunger drive and greater high-fat intake.[16]

Stress Stimulates the Reward System

Exposure to psychological stressors can induce a hefty immediate stress response. Stress activates limbic CRF, in particular from the amygdala and hypothalamus, and consequently the L-HPA axis. Activation of the L-HPA is linked to activation of the mesolimbic reward area activity. There are several examples of the tight interconnection between stress and reward areas. Anatomically, increased CRF secretion resulting from activation of this central stress response network impinges on dopamine neurons in the ventral tegmental area and increases dopamine secretion over the NAcc that is stimulated by drugs, and possibly stressors.[17,18] Stress is linked to craving and drug addiction in people (see Chapter 9). In humans exposed to a lab stressor during a positron emission tomography study, stress

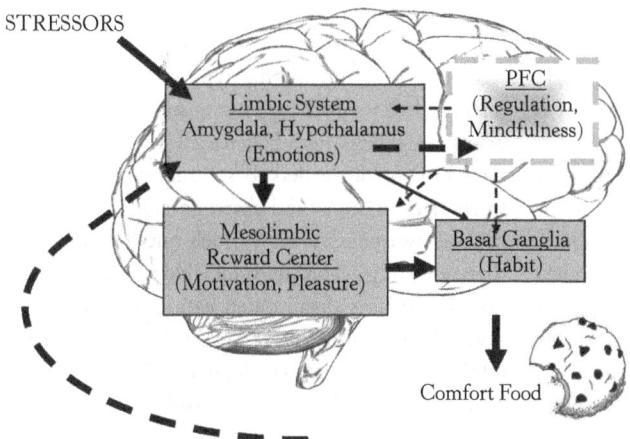

STRESSORS

Limbic System
Amygdala, Hypothalamus
(Emotions)

PFC
(Regulation,
Mindfulness)

Mesolimbic
Reward Center
(Motivation, Pleasure)

Basal Ganglia
(Habit)

Comfort Food

FIGURE 40.1. Stress-induced hedonic eating. PFC, prefrontal cortex.

exposure, as well as cortisol release, both enhanced dopamine release from the NAcc.[19] In another study on acute stress, those who responded with greater cortisol reactivity released more dopamine in the ventral striatum, showing a very strong coupling of the two.[20]

In turn, the experience of dopamine stimulation is one of craving or drive for pleasure, and food is the most available and inexpensive drug around—a "natural" reward. For example, rats that had opioids injected into their reward area respond by overeating.[21]

Stress Eating Is Maintained through Negative Feedback: Short-Term Gain to Well-Being with Long-Term Cost to Health

Stress eating may be motivated by negative reinforcement, seeking distraction from distress or a stressful situation,[22] or seeking reward and relaxation. In rat studies, eating palatable foods reduces both subsequent stress-induced behavioral and neuroendocrine responses[23–26] and eating also makes people feel better.[27,28] Eating palatable foods triggers increased dopamine secretion in the mesolimbic pathway, from the ventral tegmental area to the NAcc—a highly rewarding pleasurable experience, activating dopamine and opioid secretion from neurons throughout the homeostatic feeding network. Thus, as shown in Figure 40.1, eating palatable foods after a stressor reduces activity in the central stress response network and serves as feedback to sharpen the activity of the network and reduce the duration of its activity. Indeed, people who eat more comfort food have damped down HPA axis responses.[29] The long-term cost of S-EAT is high: abdominal fat deposition and related metabolic derangements.

Stress Eating Can Promote Habit-Driven Comfort Food Eating in the Absence of Active Stress

These strong opioid and dopamine responses in the reward center during stress promote encoding of habits in the basal ganglia, the home of habit.[30] Thus, either acute or chronic stressors might augment wanting, pleasure, and memories associated with palatable food intake. Memories of responses to stimuli are stored both in the cortex, where flexibility of response is engendered by the knowledge

of outcome, and in the basal ganglia, where habit is expressed, and a learned response follows the stimulus.[31–33]

Stress Subjugates the Prefrontal Cortex: Impaired Prefrontal Cortex/Limbic Balance

The PFC is a key player in stress neural networks. During normal conditions, the PFC reigns, and cognition is dominated by reflective cognition. During stress, however, the thoughtful PFC activity is dampened and the amygdala and limbic circuitry dominate, promoting automatic behavior geared toward survival, including being vigilant for food cues. In rats, PFC neurons inhibit both dopamine from the NAcc and the L-HPA axis cortisol response.[34]

Conversely, stressors lead both to reduction of PFC function and increased habit expression,[1,30,13] thus reinforcing the likelihood of seeking and eating sweet foods after a stressor regardless of whether the stressed individual ranks highly on dietary restraint.[6,26] The stressed brain expresses both strong drive to eat and impaired capacity to inhibit eating—a potent formula for obesity.

DIETARY RESTRAINT: ADAPTIVE REGULATOR OR ADDITIONAL STRESSOR?

The construct of dietary restraint is an important individual difference that moderates many of the relationships in Figure 40.1. Dietary restraint is defined as voluntary cognitive control over one's eating to restrict food intake to control body weight.[35] Some restraint is necessary to have in our abundantly palatable food environment, but high levels are linked to overeating in states of stress.

A critical distinction is the difference between flexible versus rigid restraint.[36] We propose that high PFC/limbic balance is related to high levels of "adaptive restraint," or the type of flexible dietary restraint behaviors that promote appropriate control over eating. This high balance allows the volitional flexible control needed to self-monitor and adjust to changes in one's food environment and behavior, such as awareness of how much one has eaten and then adjusting accordingly. Flexible restraint is associated with less disinhibited eating, less frequent/severe binge eating, lower weight, and lower energy intake.[36] In contrast, maladaptive or "rigid restraint" reflects severe behaviors to control eating, based on inflexible cognitive rules such as having forbidden foods, and skipping meals. Rigid restraint is associated with disinhibited eating, higher body mass index, greater binge eating, and greater chronic stress[16,36] Those high in rigid restraint, therefore, may reflect low PFC/limbic balance and be particularly vulnerable to S-EAT processes.[37,38]

Rigid restraint may *itself* serve as a stressor, since rigid restraint represents frequent cognitive load or demands on attention and working memory, and violations of one's desires to eat less. General measures of restraint have been associated with perceived stress as well as increased cortisol.[39,40] Furthermore, subjective and objective indices of chronic stress are associated with greater rigid and lower flexible restraint.[16] While high stress may promote more rigid restraint, it is also likely that high levels of rigid restraint chronically activate the L-HPA pathways, leading to physiological stress and strengthening the low PFC/high limbic imbalance, promoting a vicious cycle of overcontrol and loss of control.

PUTTING IT ALL TOGETHER: CONTRASTING STRESS EATING VERSUS HOMEOSTATIC EATING

Ingestive behavior can involve many processes, from hunger and satiety detection, to food choice, to cessation of eating. Given that eating is largely a habitual behavior, often done unintentionally with little awareness,[41] it is regulated in part by the PFC/limbic balance, and thus it is affected by states of stress. Table 40.1 summarizes how eating processes are regulated differently under stress versus nondemanding conditions.

The PFC, particularly the right frontal PFC, plays a crucial role in eating behavior, as demonstrated by certain neurological conditions.[42] Interoceptive awareness of hunger and satiety cues uses somatosensory perception, relying on the anterior insula cortex[10] and, for satiety, the orbitofrontal cortex.[43] PFC also promotes inhibition of undesired responses, so it is crucial in controlling over eating. Those with successful weight loss maintenance have higher activity in certain frontal regions and secondary visual cortex in response to food images than those who are obese.[44-46] The dorsolateral PFC also drives top-down decision making about food choices, enabling one to plan for healthy choices based on goals and nutrition knowledge.

In contrast, stress can disinhibit aspects of PFC circuitry that are so necessary for self-regulation of eating. Emotional states can be misinterpreted as hunger. The limbic brain, amygdala, and hypothalamus drive salience for survival-related cues, making food cues salient and increasing the arousal drive to consume.[2] Stress may thwart careful self-regulation (flexible control) over food portions. Conversely, people with rigid control tend to lose that control under stress, and overeat, at least in laboratory studies.[38] Instead of being a result of thoughtful decisions, S-EATing is driven by ventral tegmental area–driven impulse, and habit circuitry, housed in the basal ganglia.[31,47] For the stressed brain, food "choices" seem to become predetermined or habitual search for dense calories or highly palatable food, rather than a conscious choice.

TABLE 40.1. CONTRASTING EATING-RELEVANT BEHAVIOR IN HOMEOSTATIC EATING VERSUS STRESS EATING

Process	Homeostatic Eating (H-EAT) (PFC Driven, Somatosensory Cortex)	Stress Eating (S-EAT) (Amygdala, Limbic, Hypothalamus Driven)
Hunger	Awareness of hunger level, sensitivity to somatosensory cues	Confusion of emotions with hunger (arousal drive), blunted awareness of somatosensory cues
Control over onset and cessation of eating	Flexible restraint	Rigid restraint and loss of control
Decision making about food choices	Reflective eating enables healthy choices (goal-directed behavior)	Reflexive eating of highly palatable food, pursuit of comfort food (habit-driven behavior)
Satiety	Awareness of sensations of satiety, physical cues	Blunted sensitivity to satiety and physical cues

CONSEQUENCES OF A CHRONICALLY STRESSED SOCIETY AND INTERVENTIONS FOR STRESS EATING

Living in increasingly stressful times creates a potent formula for low PFC/limbic balance, impaired flexible restraint, and sustained excess energy intake, preferentially stored as "stress fat," in the visceral area. Although it is hard to determine how pervasive S-EATING versus H-EATING may be, it could account for a large proportion of our societal caloric excess and the obesity epidemic. Given that S-EAT patterns may be maintained by historical stressors, or provoked by the mildest of daily stressors, and masquerade as habit, it is hard to identify the unique contribution of S-EATING to one's total caloric intake, at least in humans.

Psychoeducational strategies are not enough to counter the strong habitual forces of S-EAT, especially when the food environment is likely the most powerful influence on eating behavior. Exercise improves function of the PFC,[42] but it may not be enough to counter the epidemic. Retraining of the brain to pay effortful attention to eating and to emotions is probably a necessary but not sufficient component in any obesity intervention. Experimental work supports the potential role of techniques that work on reappraisal of emotional stressors, and even simply labeling emotions verbally, in establishing a stronger PFC/limbic balance and control over eating. Mindfulness, or nonjudgmental attention to the present moment, promotes more reflective cognition, awareness of emotions, and separation of emotions from hunger. Mindful eating can reduce binge eating.[48] People high on dispositional mindfulness show stronger PFC/limbic balance (high PFC, low amygdala activity) when simply labeling emotions.[49] Structural data show that meditation is associated with greater volume of right orbital prefrontal cortex, insula, and hippocampus, which are important in self-control.[50,51] We are currently testing whether mindful eating and mindful stress reduction can reduce S-EAT in obesity. However, given the pervasive exposure of both the toxic food environment and societal-wide chronic stress, it is likely that policies that reduce the toxic food environment and societal stress are both necessary to tide the epidemic.

REFERENCES

1. Arnsten AF. Stress signalling pathways that impair prefrontal cortex structure and function. *Nat Rev Neurosci* 2009;10:410–422.
2. Dallman MF. Stress-induced obesity and the emotional nervous system. *Trends Endocrinol Metab* 2010;21(3):159–165.
3. Dallman MF, Hellhammer DH. Stress and the brain: hormonal and autonomic regulation. In: Contrada R, Baum A, eds. *The Handbook of Stress Science: Psychology, Medicine, and Health.* New York: Springer; 2010: 11–36.
4. Mikolajczyk RT, El Ansari W, Maxwell AE. Food consumption frequency and perceived stress and depressive symptoms among students in three European countries. *Nutr J* 2009;8:31.
5. Block JP, He Y, Zaslavsky AM, Ding L, Ayanian JZ. Psychosocial stress and change in weight among US adults. *Am J Epidemiol* 2009;170:181–192.
6. Habhab S, Sheldon JP, Loeb RC. The relationship between stress, dietary restraint, and food preferences in women. *Appetite* 2009;52:437–444.
7. Adam TC, Epel ES. Stress, eating and the reward system. *Physiol Behav* 2007;91:449–458.
8. Wardle J, Steptoe A, Oliver G, Lipsey Z. Stress, dietary restraint and food intake. *J Psychosom Res* 2000;48:195–202.
9. Torres SJ, Nowson CA. Relationship between stress, eating behavior, and obesity. *Nutrition* 2007;23:887–894.
10. Craig AD. How do you feel—now? The anterior insula and human awareness. *Nat Rev Neurosci* 2009; 10:59–70.
11. Epel E, R. Lapidus, et al. Stress may add bite to appetite in women: a laboratory study of stress-induced cortisol and eating behavior. *Psychoneuroendocrinol* 2001;26:37–49.
12. Newman E, O'Connor D B, Conner M. Daily hassles and eating behaviour: the role of cortisol reactivity status. *Psychoneuroendocrinol* 2007;32(2):125–132.
13. Holmes A, Wellman CL. Stress-induced prefrontal reorganization and executive dysfunction in rodents. *Neurosci Biobehav Rev* 2009;33:773–783.
14. Vyas A, Mitra R, Shankaranarayana Rao BS, Chattarji S. Chronic stress induces contrasting patterns of dendritic remodeling in hippocampal and amygdaloid neurons. *J Neurosci* 2002;22:6810–6818.
15. Wellman CL. Dendritic reorganization in pyramidal neurons in medial prefrontal cortex after chronic corticosterone administration. *J Neurobiol* 2001;49: 245–253.
16. Groesz L, McCoy S, Carl J, Saslow L, Adler N, Laraia B, Epel E. What's eating you? Stress and the drive to eat. *Appetite*, 2012;58:17–21.
17. Wanat MJ, Hopf FW, Stuber GD, Phillips PE, Bonci A. Corticotropin-releasing factor increases mouse

ventral tegmental area dopamine neuron firing through a protein kinase C-dependent enhancement of Ih. *J Physiol* 2008;586:2157–2170.

18. Lodge DJ, Grace AA. Acute and chronic corticotropin-releasing factor 1 receptor blockade inhibits cocaine-induced dopamine release: correlation with dopamine neuron activity. *J Pharmacol Exp Ther* 2005; 314:201–206.

19. Wand GS, Oswald LM, McCaul ME, et al. Association of amphetamine-induced striatal dopamine release and cortisol responses to psychological stress. *Neuropsychopharmacol* 2007;32:2310–2320.

20. Pruessner JC, Champagne F, Meaney MJ, Dagher A. Dopamine release in response to a psychological stress in humans and its relationship to early life maternal care: a positron emission tomography study using [^{11}C]raclopride. *J Neurosci* 2004;24:2825–2831.

21. Kelley AE, Bakshi VP, Fleming S, Holahan MR. A pharmacological analysis of the substrates underlying conditioned feeding induced by repeated opioid stimulation of the nucleus accumbens. *Neuropsychopharmacol* 2000;23:455–467.

22. Macht M, Haupt C, Ellgring H. The perceived function of eating is changed during examination stress: a field study. *Eat Behav* 2005;6:109–112.

23. la Fleur SE, Houshyar H, Roy M, Dallman MF. Choice of lard, but not total lard calories, damps adrenocorticotropin responses to restraint. *Endocrinology* 2005;146:2193–2199.

24. Minor TR, Saade S. Poststress glucose mitigates behavioral impairment in rats in the "learned helplessness" model of psychopathology. *Biol Psychiatry* 1997;42:324–334.

25. Pecoraro N, Reyes F, Gomez F, Bhargava A, Dallman MF. Chronic stress promotes palatable feeding, which reduces signs of stress: feedforward and feedback effects of chronic stress. *Endocrinology* 2004;145(8):3754–3762.

26. Foster MT, Warne JP, Ginsberg AB, et al. Palatable foods, stress, and energy stores sculpt corticotropin-releasing factor, adrenocorticotropin, and corticosterone concentrations after restraint. *Endocrinology* 2009;150:2325–2333.

27. Dallman MF, Pecoraro NC, la Fleur SE. Chronic stress and comfort foods: self-medication and abdominal obesity. *Brain Behav Immun* 2005;19:275–280.

28. Kotz CM, Glass MJ, Levine AS, Billington CJ. Regional effect of naltrexone in the nucleus of the solitary tract in blockade of NPY-induced feeding. *Am J Physiol Regul Integr Comp Physiol* 2000;278:R499–R503.

29. Tomiyama A J, Dallman MF, Epel ES. Comfort food is comforting to those most stressed: Evidence of the chronic stress response network in high stress women. *Psychoneuroendocrinol* 2010;36:1513–1519, PMID: 21906885.

30. Wickens J, Horvitz J, Costa R, Killcross S. Dopaminergic mechanisms in actions and habits. *J Neurosci* 2007;27:8181–8183.

31. Schwabe L, Wolf OT. Stress prompts habit behavior in humans. *J Neurosci* 2009;29:7191–7198.

32. Yin HH, Knowlton BJ. The role of the basal ganglia in habit formation. *Nat Rev Neurosci* 2006;7:464–476.

33. Graybiel AM. Habits, rituals, and the evaluative brain. *Annu Rev Neurosci* 2008;31:359–387.

34. Brake W, Flores G, Francis D, Meaney M, Srivasta L, Gratton A. Enhanced nucleus accumbens dopamine and plasma corticosterone stress responses in adult rats with neonatal excitotoxic lesions to the medial prefrontal cortex. *Neuroscience* 2000;96:687–695.

35. Lowe MR, Kral TV. Stress-induced eating in restrained eaters may not be caused by stress or restraint. *Appetite* 2006;46:16–21.

36. Westenhoefer J, Broeckmann P, Munch AK, Pudel V. Cognitive control of eating behaviour and the disinhibition effect. *Appetite* 1994;23:27–41.

37. Greeno C, Wing R. Stress-induced eating. *Psychol Bull* 1994;115:444–464.

38. Gibson LE. Emotional influences on food choice: sensory, physiological and psychological pathways. *Physiol Behav* 2006;89(1):53–61.

39. Rutters F, Nieuwenhuizen AG, Lemmens SG, Born JM, Westerterp-Plantenga MS. Hyperactivity of the HPA axis is related to dietary restraint in normal weight women. *Physiol Behav* 2009;96:315–319.

40. McLean JA, Barr SI, Prior JC. Cognitive dietary restraint is associated with higher urinary cortisol excretion in healthy premenopausal women. *Am J Clin Nutr* 2001;73:7–12.

41. Cohen D, Farley TA. Eating as an automatic behavior. *Prev Chronic Dis* 2008;5:A23.

42. Alonso-Alonso M, Pascual-Leone A. The right brain hypothesis for obesity. *JAMA* 2007;297:1819–1822.

43. Rolls ET. Sensory processing in the brain related to the control of food intake. *Proc Nutr Soc* 2007;66:96–112.

44. Le DS, Pannacciulli N, Chen K, et al. Less activation in the left dorsolateral prefrontal cortex in the reanalysis of the response to a meal in obese than in lean women and its association with successful weight loss. *Am J Clin Nutr* 2007;86:573–579.

45. Del Parigi A, Chen K, Reiman EM. Is the brain representation of hunger normal in the Prader-Willi syndrome? *Int J Obes* 2007;31:390–391.

46. McCaffery JM, Haley AP, Sweet LH, et al. Differential functional magnetic resonance imaging response to food pictures in successful weight-loss maintainers relative to normal-weight and obese controls. *Am J Clin Nutr* 2009;90:928–934.

47. Everitt BJ, Robbins TW. Neural systems of reinforcement for drug addiction: from actions to habits to compulsion. *Nat Neurosci* 2005;8:1481–1489.

48. Kristeller J, Wolever R, Sheets V. Mindfulness-Based Eating Awareness Treatment (MB-EAT) for binge eating disorder: a randomized clinical trial. Unpublished data 2009.

49. Creswell JD, Way BM, Eisenberger NI, Lieberman MD. Neural correlates of dispositional mindfulness during affect labeling. *Psychosom Med* 2007;69:560–565.

50. Lazar SW, Kerr CE, Wasserman RH, et al. Meditation experience is associated with increased cortical thickness. *Neuroreport* 2005;16:1893–1897.

51. Luders E, Toga AW, Lepore N, Gaser C. The underlying anatomical correlates of long-term meditation: larger hippocampal and frontal volumes of gray matter. *Neuroimage* 2009;13:13.

41

Public Attitudes about Addiction as a Cause of Obesity

COLLEEN L. BARRY

Obesity has become a pressing global public health problem. Excess body weight is the fifth most important risk factor contributing to the burden of disease in developed countries.[1] In the United States, between 1980 to 2006, the rate of obesity among American children ages 6 to 11 years more than doubled (6.5% to 17%) while the rate among American adolescents ages 12 to 19 years more than tripled (5% to 17.6%).[2] Over this time period, obesity has increasingly gained attention among the American public. Over 90% of the public believe that most Americans are overweight; 67% think that obesity is a major public issue; and 90% think that those who are overweight face discrimination or other ill treatment.[3] And most Americans believe that the health consequences of being obese can be serious.[4] Widespread attention may reflect the personal significance that the issue has for much of the public given that two-thirds of all Americans are considered to be overweight.

This chapter examines public attitudes about food addiction as a cause of obesity. It is vital to understand beliefs about this issue since public opinion can greatly affect policymaker views about the appropriateness and feasibility of enacting public policies aimed at solving the problem of obesity. Oliver and Lee[5] found that individuals who attributed obesity primarily to bad personal choices were significantly less likely to support government obesity prevention policies than those who recognized factors external to the individual (e.g., societal, economic) as important contributors.

The concept of food addiction is probably familiar to most Americans. Popular cultural references to food addiction abound. Many of us think of ourselves as "chocoholics" or worry about becoming "addicted" to sugar, and best-selling diet guides make reference to carbohydrate addicts[6] and sugar addicts.[7] And clinicians note that obese patients often discuss their relationship to food in terms of cravings and withdrawal, using the language of addiction.

Yet despite popular culture references to food addiction, few Americans are likely aware of scientific advances toward understanding the addictive properties of foods.[8,9] Likewise, the discussion of food addiction is still mostly absent in journalistic portrayals of the causes of obesity. While news media coverage of obesity has grown dramatically over the last decade, research indicates that discussion of food addiction as a cause of obesity is uncommon.

With colleagues, I analyzed the content of a 20% random sample of news articles focused on childhood obesity in 18 prominent news sources, including national and regional newspapers, national news magazines, and national and network cable news shows from 2000 to 2009.[10,i] While 53% of news stories identified individual behavior (i.e., parent or child behaviors related to food/beverages or exercise) as a cause of childhood obesity, we found that only 1% of news stories mentioned food addiction as a potential cause. This evidence suggests that the news media has not yet focused on food addiction as an important cause of increasing obesity rates. This has bearing on public opinion since news media framing can strongly influence how the public thinks about societal problems.[11]

Various public opinion polls confirm that most Americans attribute obesity primarily to personal behaviors, including poor eating habits and insufficient physical activity.[4,5,12] Fewer Americans identify factors external to the individual, such as environmental and societal factors, as important causes of increasing rates of obesity.[4] However, little evidence is available to help us understand Americans' beliefs about food addiction as a cause of obesity, or how these views affect support for public policies to curb obesity rates. One public opinion poll from 1978 suggests a long-standing concern on the part of Americans about safety risks associated with the manipulation of food content. The Tobacco Institute asked respondents to identify two of three things on a list of 14 items that concerned them in terms of their possible effects on the health, safety, and welfare of themselves or their family members. Twenty-three percent identified food additives as a concern (notably, as compared with only 13% identifying cigarette smoking and 17% identifying automobile safety).[ii] However, no current polls provide data on how many Americans view the concept of food addiction as important in explaining increasing rates of obesity.

To address this gap, my colleagues and I included a few questions in the Yale Rudd Center Public Opinion on Obesity Survey ($N = 1,009$), a nationally representative Web sample surveyed from the Knowledge Networks panel in 2006/2007, to assess public attitudes about food addiction as a cause of obesity and public support for policies aimed at addressing food addiction. Knowledge Networks, an internet survey research firm, employs random-digit dialing to recruit their online research panel, which has been shown to be representative of the US population.[13] Unlike other telephone- and Internet-based research, Knowledge Networks surveys are based on a sampling frame that includes both listed and unlisted phone numbers and provides Internet/computer access to those panel members. The strength of its sampling frame and high completion rates have made Knowledge Networks an increasingly common mode for data collection in studies published across a number of academic disciplines.[14-16] The purpose of this survey was to examine whether individuals' beliefs about the causes of obesity affected support for specific policies aimed at stemming obesity rates. This survey was pretested to assess the reliability and validity of the instrument in November 2006. The survey completion rate was 75%.[iii]

To assess public attitudes about the causes of increasing rates of obesity, we showed respondents eight narratives as possible explanations for why Americans are more overweight today than in the past.[12] Each narrative included a causal explanation

for increasing rates of obesity, a fairness judgment, and a related emotional response to overweight individuals. One narrative describing food addiction as a cause read:

A big problem in the U.S. is that people get hooked on certain things and just can't quit. When people get used to eating sugary, fatty foods, some can't keep themselves from eating more and more so they become overweight. It's not fair that this is true for some people, but others can eat whatever they want and not gain weight. People who are heavy must feel so helpless, having lost control over their own bodies.

I compared this narrative with other narratives emphasizing internal (e.g., bad individual choices) and external (e.g., a toxic food environment) factors to explain why Americans are more overweight today than in the past. The individual behavior narrative read:

A big problem with America is that people are unwilling to work hard or control their impulses. People who are overweight aren't even trying to get healthier. Fat people can't do their jobs well and cost us all more for their health care. So it's unfair when those people make others pay for their lack of effort. When I see people who are overweight, they disgust me.

The toxic food environment narrative read:

A big problem in this country is that we're surrounded by choices that are cheap and easy, but not good for us. We have become so used to eating fatty, sugary foods that healthy foods are lost in a sea of unhealthy alternatives. So people are overweight because processed foods displace natural foods and large restaurant portions replace reasonable meals. It's not fair that it's become so hard to find healthy foods at a reasonable price. When I see a person who's overweight, I get angry at our society for allowing bad food choices to drive out the good ones.

For each narrative, respondents were asked, "[O]ut of every 100 Americans with weight problems, for how many do you think that this account explains a lot about why they are overweight?" They were directed to assign a number between 1 and 100 for each narrative. If a respondent assigned a given narrative a score of 10 or greater, the response was coded as an "important" explanation, and a score of 25 or greater was coded as a "very important" explanation.

Despite the lack of attention in news media coverage, the public viewed the food addiction narrative as important in explaining why Americans are overweight. Seventy-one percent of respondents viewed the food addiction narrative as an important explanation and 16% viewed it as a very important explanation. These proportions are comparable to views about the individual behavior narrative (i.e., 50% viewed it as important and 18% viewed it as very important) and toxic food environment narrative (i.e., 77% viewed it as important and 24% viewed it as very important).

Next, respondents were asked about their support for two obesity prevention policies related to food addiction. They were asked to identify on an ordinal scale whether they strongly supported, somewhat supported, neither supported nor opposed, somewhat opposed, or strongly opposed each policy.

Policy 1: To require warning labels on foods with high sugar or fat content, indicating that such foods may be addictive.
Policy 2: To use government funds to establish a national network of obesity treatment programs modeled on treatment for other addictions.

Policy 1, a regulatory policy, was assumed to require no additional taxes. For policy 2, respondents were asked whether they would support the policy if it meant that they would need to pay an additional $50 per year in taxes.

Sixty-three percent of the public supported requiring warning labels on foods with high sugar or fat content, indicating that such foods may be addictive. Only 40% supported the policy to use government funds to establish a national network of obesity treatment programs modeled on treatment for other addictions. A lower level of support for this policy was consistent with expectations given that it would require a tax increase.

Next, ordered logit regression models were used to examine how respondents' health characteristics and political attitudes were associated with support for the two addiction-related policies controlling for individual demographic characteristics. Table 41.1 displays these results. Interestingly, one's own personal health status (i.e., body mass index, exercise level, and self-reported health) appears to play a minimal role in explaining variation in support for these policies. However, political ideology and political party identification were important predictors of support for policies to address food addiction as a cause of obesity. Moderates were more likely than conservatives, and Democrats and Independents were more likely than Republicans to support the warning label policy. Likewise, moderates and liberals were more likely than conservatives, and Democrats were more likely than Republicans to support the tax-based addiction treatment program policy. In separate regression models that included respondents' views about the narratives as well as all demographic and health characteristics and political attitudes, individuals scoring the food addiction narrative as important (as defined earlier) were more likely to support both policies compare with those scoring the individual behavior narrative as important. (Results are not shown, but they are available from author upon request.)

CONCLUSION

Our findings suggest that Americans are open to thinking about food addiction as an important cause of obesity despite the lack of attention to this factor in news media coverage of the obesity epidemic. These results are consistent with research suggesting that the public thinks about obesity as a complex, multicausal problem.[10] However, which aspects of a complex problem Americans are most focused on can have a big impact on policy outcomes. The public may focus disproportionately on one aspect of an issue—in the case of obesity, overweight individuals' poor choices related to eating and exercise—to the exclusion of other causal factors. If new aspects of an issue that have received less attention are demonstrated to be important, public support for policy may shift.

Therefore, a relevant question for the public health community is whether to and how to encourage the public to think more about food addiction as a cause of obesity. Framing obesity in terms of food addiction is attractive in that it does not absolve individuals of responsibility—we all need to make an effort to eat well and exercise—but

TABLE 41.1. REGRESSION RESULTS ON PUBLIC SUPPORT FOR FOOD
ADDICTION POLICIES

	Warning Labels (Policy 1)	Addiction Treatment Programs (Policy 2)
Health characteristics[a]		
BMI 25-29	-0.157	0.0144
	[0.150]	[0.147]
BMI 30+	0.0167	0.269*
	[0.151]	[0.152]
Good health	−0.127	−0.318**
	[0.132]	[0.132]
Fair/poor health	0.0155	0.000620
	[0.191]	[0.192]
Exercise 1–2 times per week	0.132	0.258
	[0.162]	[0.158]
Exercise <1 time per week	0.141	0.0645
	[0.142]	[0.140]
Political characteristics[b]		
Moderate	0.303**	0.499***
	[0.149]	[0.148]
Liberal	0.129	0.558***
	[0.175]	[0.175]
Undecided/independent	0.627**	−0.320
	[0.295]	[0.292]
Democrat	0.421***	0.588***
	[0.144]	[0.144]

Note. Absolute value of t statistics in parentheses; * significant at 10%; ** significant at 5%; *** significant at 1%. Models adjust for individual demographic characteristics, including gender, age, race/ethnicity, education level, income level, employment status, and region of residence.
[a]The reference category for body mass index is <25. Reference category for self-reported health is excellent/very good. Reference category for self-reported exercise is 3+ times per week.
[b]The reference category for ideology is conservative, and reference category for political party identification is Republican.
BMI, body mass index.

acknowledges the importance of external factors. Both differing individual propensities toward addiction and detrimental practices by the food and beverage industry to increase the addictiveness of food products contribute to the problem. Future lab-based experimental research can be useful in testing empirically the extent to which individual exposure to messages framing food addiction as an important contributor to obesity can help to increase public support for obesity prevention policies, including regulations targeting food content and to lower stigma toward obese individuals.

NOTES

i. News sources included the three highest circulation national newspapers in the United States (*USA Today,* *Wall Street Journal, New York Times*); two high circulation regional newspapers in the Northeast (*New York Daily News, Boston Globe*), the Midwest (*Cleveland Plain Dealer, Minneapolis Star-Tribune*), the South (*Atlanta Journal Constitution, Houston Chronicle*), and the West (*San Francisco Chronicle, Denver Post*); the two highest circulation news magazines (*Newsweek, Time*); transcripts from morning and evening news programs for the three television networks (*ABC Good Morning America* and *World News Tonight, NBC Today Show* and *Nightly News,* and *CBS Early Show* and *Evening News*), a cable news program (*Fox Special Report*), and a PBS news program (*NewsHour with Jim Lehrer*).

ii. Survey by The Tobacco Institute. Methodology: Interviews conducted by Roper Organization, March 4–March 11, 1978 and based on 2,511 personal interviews. Sample: national adult. (USROPER.78SMOKE.R06).

iii. We report a sample completion rate rather than a sample response rate as is typical with Web-based panels.

REFERENCES

1. World Health Organization. *World Health Report 2002: Reducing Risks, Promoting Healthy Life.* Geneva, Switzerland: World Health Organization, 2002.

2. Ogden CL, Carroll MD, Flegal KM. High body mass index for age among US children and adolescents, 2003–2006. *J Am Med Assoc* 2008;299:2401–2405.

3. Taylor P, Funk C, Craighill P. *Americans See Weight Problems Everywhere but in the Mirror.* Philadelphia, PA: Pew Foundation Social Trends Report, 2006.

4. Bleich S, Blendon RJ. Public opinion and obesity. In: Blendon R, Brodie M, Altman DE, Benson J, eds. *American Public Opinion and Health Care.* Washington, DC: CQ Press; 2010.

5. Oliver JE, Lee T. Public opinion and the politics of obesity in America. *J Health Polit Policy Law* 2005;30(5):923–954.

6. Heller RF, Heller RF. *The Carbohydrate Addict's Diet: The Lifelong Solution to Yo-Yo Dieting.* New York: Signet, 1993.

7. Desmaisons K. *The Sugar Addict's Total Recovery Program.* New York: Ballantine Books, 2008.

8. Avena NM, Rada P, Hoebel BG. Evidence for sugar addiction: behavioral and neurochemical effects of intermittent, excessive sugar intake. *Neurosci Biobehav Rev* 2007;32:20–39.

9. Volkow ND, Wise RA. How can drug addiction help us understand obesity? *Nat Neurosci* 2005;8(5):555–560.

10. Barry CL, Jarlenski M, Grob R, Schlesinger M, Gollust S. News media framing and childhood obesity in the United States from 2000 to 2009. *Pediatrics* 2011;128(1):132–145.

11. Hilgartner H, Bosk C. The rise and fall of social problems: a public arenas model. *Am J Sociol* 1988;94:53–78.

12. Barry CL, Brescoll VL, Brownell K, Schlesinger M. Obesity metaphors: how do beliefs about the causes of obesity affect support for public policy? *Milbank Q* 2009;87(1):7–47.

13. Baker L, Bundorf MK, Singer S, Wadner T. *Validity of the Survey of Health and Internet and Knowledge Network's Panel and Sampling.* Stanford, CA: Stanford University, 2003.

14. Davis MM and Fant K. Coverage of vaccines in private health plans: what does the public prefer? *Health Affair* 24(5):770–779.

15. Harris KM. How do patients choose physicians? Evidence from a national survey of enrollees in employment-related health plans. *Health Serv Res* 2003;38(2):711–732.

16. Lerner J, Gonzalez R, Small D, Fischhoff B. Effects of fear and anger on perceived risks of terrorism: a natural experiment. *Psychol Sci* 14(2):144–150.

PART IV

Clinical Approaches and Implications

42

Clinical Assessment of Food and Addiction

ASHLEY N. GEARHARDT AND WILLIAM R. CORBIN

Spurred by provocative findings in animal models and human neuroimaging studies, the topic of food and addiction has received increased attention by researchers in both the addictions and eating disorders fields. The idea of food addiction has also entered the public consciousness and has been proposed as one possible explanation for increased rates of obesity. Although research on food addiction is still in its nascent stages, application of the food addiction concept in treating obesity is gaining a foothold, and programs based on addiction models are in early stages of evaluation.

Critical to both clinical intervention and research is a clear definition of food addiction as well as a valid approach to assessing its presence or absence. In the limited number of research studies assessing food addiction, self-identification has often been used.[1] In other words, individuals are simply asked whether they think they are addicted to food or particular types of food (e.g., chocolate). In clinical settings, multiple-item screening tools are often used, but it is not clear how the items were derived and there is generally no evidence for the reliability or validity of the measures that are used. In the remainder of this chapter, we will examine how food addiction is currently being assessed in clinical and research settings, and we will review recent studies designed to develop valid tools for the assessment of food addiction. We will conclude with a discussion of limitations of existing approaches, and we will highlight future directions in the assessment of food addiction.

ASSESSMENT OF FOOD ADDICTION IN CLINICAL AND RESEARCH SETTINGS

Despite the fact that food addiction is not currently recognized as a clinical disorder in *The Diagnostic and Statistical Manual of Mental Disorders*, fourth edition, text revision (*DSM-IV-TR*), a variety of interventions have been developed for "food addicts." Available clinical approaches to treating food addiction include diet books, self-help groups, 12-step programs (based on Alcoholics Anonymous), as well as outpatient and inpatient treatment programs.

These approaches use a variety of methods to identify potential "food addicts." For example, according to their Web site, Food Addicts in Recovery Anonymous assesses food addiction by asking questions about behaviors, including eating outside of hunger, eating to escape problems, and eating large quantities of food.[1] The Web site states that an affirmative answer to any of a series of 20 questions may signify that one is a food addict. An inpatient food addiction treatment center, the Women's Center for Healthy Living, also provides warning signs to facilitate the identification of food addiction in both adults and children. They provide six warning signs indicative of food addiction, ranging from failure to control food intake to binge eating in response to emotion.[2] Again, potential clients are told that an affirmative answer to any one of these questions may indicate the presence of food addiction. Although the items provided by these organizations appear consistent with conceptualizations of food addiction, neither organization indicates how these items were derived or provides information about the validity of these screening tools in identifying food addiction.

Although researchers have begun to search for potential correlates of food addiction, the development of valid tools for the assessment of food addiction has received little attention until quite recently. The assessment of food addiction in research settings has typically relied upon self-identification as a "food addict," "chocoholic," or "carbohydrate craver."[3–5] For example, Tuomisto and colleagues (1997)[3] conducted a study in which they examined the physiological and psychological traits of self-identified chocolate addicts. They found that, relative to control participants, chocolate addicts exhibited increased cravings and greater arousal and negative affect in response to external chocolate cues. In addition, chocolate addicts consumed more chocolate during the task and experienced more eating pathology overall. Although such results are intriguing, the lack of formal assessment calls into question whether the self-identified chocolate addicts were truly experiencing signs of dependence, typically characterized by symptoms such as tolerance, withdrawal, or continued use despite negative consequences.

SENSITIVITY AND SPECIFICITY OF SELF-IDENTIFICATION AND SCREENING MEASURES

Relative to the true classification of individuals as food addicts or non-food addicts, the use of self-identification or screening measures may lead to different types of misclassification. For example, those who are not truly food addicts might be identified as food addicts resulting in "false positives." In contrast, existing measures might fail to identify individuals who are truly food addicts, resulting in "misses." Another way to think about classification accuracy is in terms of sensitivity and specificity. A measure with good sensitivity but poor specificity will correctly identify most true food addicts but will also yield a high number of false positives. In contrast, a measure with good specificity, but poor sensitivity, will reduce the occurrence of false positives but will miss many individuals who are truly food addicts.

It seems likely that self-identification and screening measures with liberal thresholds (e.g., an affirmative response to a single item classifies an individual as a food addict) will have high sensitivity but low specificity. The use of addiction terms in relation to eating behavior in popular culture (e.g., "chocoholics") could lead people who occasionally overindulge or crave certain foods to self-identify as food addicts, particularly if they struggle with controlling their weight. The use of screening measures suggesting that meeting any of the questions in the assessment is sufficient for a diagnosis of dependence is also likely to overidentify food addiction relative to clinical diagnostic assessments that have much more stringent thresholds. For example, according to the *DSM-IV-TR*, a diagnosis of substance dependence should only be given when a patient exhibits three or more of seven symptoms and reports clinically significant impairment or distress.[6] Thus, the low threshold of current assessment strategies is likely to reduce the specificity of the food addiction concept.

Although low specificity is probably the biggest concern with existing measures, it is important to recognize that "misses" may also occur. Substance dependence is sometimes associated with a lack of insight into the severity of problems associated with use,[7] and this might also be true for food dependence. Thus, someone may be experiencing multiple symptoms of food dependence, but he or she may attribute his or her eating problems to a lack of willpower rather than an addiction.

In addition to problems related to sensitivity and specificity, there may be problems with the reliability of widely used measures of food addiction given the small number of items used in most assessments. In addition, the use of widely varying measures across studies and clinical settings makes it difficult to compare rates. This may lead to erroneous conclusions about differences in rates of food addiction across populations. Given the potential problems with self-identification and screening tools, it is critical to develop diagnostic measures with established psychometric properties (e.g., reliability and validity).

YALE FOOD ADDICTION SCALE

Recently, the Yale Food Addiction Scale (YFAS)[8] was developed as a measure of food addiction that is based upon the *DSM-IV-TR*[6] diagnostic criteria for substance dependence as applied to eating behavior. The YFAS is scored to provide both a symptom count and a food addiction diagnosis. A diagnosis of food addiction is only given when someone has met the diagnostic criteria of three or more symptoms as well as clinically significant impairment or distress.

The preliminary validation of the scale found that the YFAS exhibited good reliability, as well as convergent and discriminant validity. In a sample of obese participants diagnosed with binge eating disorder, the YFAS also demonstrates strong psychometric properties and predicts the frequency of binge eating episodes above and beyond other measures.[9] Moreover, endorsement of food addiction is associated with anticipatory and consummatory neural activation in brain regions implicated in other types of addiction (e.g., medial orbitofrontal cortex, caudate).[10] Finally, an examination of the relation between self-identified food addiction and the YFAS found that self-identification resulted in a false-positive rate of 74.07%.[11] In other words, 74.0% of those who self-identified as food addicts did not meet the diagnostic criteria for dependence as measured by the YFAS. Further exploration of the false-positive group suggested that, although these individuals have eating concerns, they do not appear to experience clinically significant eating pathology. Thus, the preoccupation with weight and shape in American culture may lead a significant number of individuals to pathologize their own behavior and lead addiction terms to be incorrectly applied to eating behavior.

FUTURE DIRECTIONS

Although the creation of the YFAS was an important first step in improving our ability to validly assess food addiction, additional research on the measure is needed. First, obesity and compulsive eating patterns are also problematic for children and adolescents.[12,13] Therefore, it will also be important to develop valid food addiction assessment tools that are appropriate for younger samples. The YFAS may also serve as a guide, in conjunction with existing substance dependence diagnostic assessment tools, in developing additional measures, including in-person diagnostic interviews (e.g., Structured Clinical Interview for DSM Disorders).[14] This is a potentially important step as research on eating disorders has shown that interview-led assessments, such as the Eating Disorder Examination,[15] are more valid than self-report assessments, such as the Eating Disorder Examination-Questionnaire.[16] Finally, the assessment of substance dependence has benefited from the development of validated brief measures of substance dependence, such as the CAGE, B-MAST, and AUDIT.[17-19] The development of brief validated food addiction assessments may reduce participant burden and provide an efficient screening tool for clinical and public health applications.

Although there is still work to be done in establishing the validity of the YFAS and other measures of food addiction, these measures will ultimately be critical in understanding how food addiction relates to established clinical disorders with considerable conceptual overlap. Of primary importance, there is significant overlap between the proposed diagnostic criteria for food addiction and binge eating disorder (BED). Although, there is evidence that food addiction may be associated with more frequent binge-eating episodes for BED patients,[9] it will also be necessary in future studies to evaluate whether food addiction is distinct from and has clinical and practical utility above and beyond the concept of BED. For example, it may be possible that an individual can be addicted to food without experiencing periods of discrete binges (i.e., chronically snack in a manner that is similar to a chain smoker). Such questions are critical to differentiating BED and food addiction. If the two constructs are ultimately found not to be distinct, important questions about the fundamental nature of loss of control over food consumption (e.g., addiction versus eating disorder) will need to be addressed.[20,21]

REFERENCES

1. Food Addicts in Recovery Anonymous. Are you a food addict? Available at: http://foodaddicts.org/quiz.html. Accessed October 22, 2009.
2. The Garrison Center for Healthy Living. Food addiction. Available at: http://www.garrisoncenter.org/p6.html. Accessed April 3, 2012.
3. Tuomisto T, Lappalainen R, Heterington M, Moris MF, Tuomisto MT. Affective, physiological and overt behavioral response to chocolate in self identified "chocolate addicts." *Int J Psychophysiol* 1997;25:38–39.
4. Benford R, Gough B. Defining and defending practices "unhealthy" practices: a discourse analysis of chocolate "addicts" accounts. *J Health Psychol* 2006;11:427–440.
5. Spring B, Schneider K, Smith M, et al. Abuse potential of carbohydrates for overweight carbohydrate cravers. *Psychopharmacol* 2008;197:637–647.
6. American Psychiatric Association. *Diagnostic and Statistical Manual of Mental Disorders.* 4th ed. Washington, DC: American Psychiatric Association, 2000.
7. Farid B, Clark M, Williams R. Health locus of control in problem drinkers with and without liver disease. *Alcohol Alcohol* 1998;33:184–187.
8. Gearhardt AN, Corbin WR, Brownell KD. Preliminary validation of the Yale Food Addiction Scale. *Appetite* 2009;52:32–36.
9. Gearhardt AN, White MA, Masheb RM, Morgan PT, Crosby RD, Grilo CM. An examination of the food addiction construct in obese patients with binge eating disorder. *Int J Eat Disord* doi: 10.1002/eat.20957.

10. Gearhardt AN, Yokum S, Orr PT, Stice E, Corbin WR, Brownell KD. Neural correlates of food addiction. *Arch Gen Psychiatry* 2011;68:808–816.

11. Gearhardt AN, Corbin WR. Self-identification as a "food addict": implications for research and practice. Poster presented at: Annual Conference of the Association for Behavioral and Cognitive Therapies; November 20, 2009; New York.

12. Marcus M, Kalarchian. Binge eating in children and adolescents. *Int J Eat Disord* 2003;34:47–57.

13. Lobstein T, Baur L, Uauy. Obesity in children and young people: a crisis in public health. *Obes Rev* 2004;5:4–104.

14. First MB, Spitzer RL, Gibbon M, Williams JBW. *Structured Clinical Interview for DSM-IV-TR Axis I (SCID-I).* New York: Biometrics Research, New York State Psychiatric Institute, 2002.

15. Cooper Z, Fairburn CG. The Eating Disorder Examination: a semi-structured interview for the assessment of the specific psychopathology of eating disorders. *Int J Eat Disord* 1987;6:1–8.

16. Fairburn CG, Berglin SJ. Assessment of eating disorders: interview or self-report questionnaire? *Int J Eat Disord* 1994;16:363–370.

17. Mayfeild D, McLeod G, Hall P. The CAGE questionnaire: validation of a new alcohol screening instrument. *Am J Psychiatry* 1974;121:1121–1123.

18. Pokorny AD, Miller BA, Kaplan HB. The brief MAST: a shortened version of the Michigan Alcoholism Screening Test. *Am J Psychiatry* 1972;3:118.

19. Saunders JB, Aasland OG, Babor TF, de la Fuente JR, Grant M. Development of the Alcohol Use Disorders Identification Test (AUDIT): WHO collaborative project on early detection of personas with harmful alcohol consumption-II. *Addiction* 1993;88:791–804.

20. Gold MS, Frost-Pineda K, Jacobs WS. Overeating, binge eating, and eating disorders as addictions. *Psychiatry Ann* 2003;33:117–122.

21. Davis C, Carter JC. Compulsive overeating as an addiction disorder. A review of theory and evidence. *Appetite* 2009;53:1–8.

43

Psychological Treatments for Substance Use Disorders

LISA J. MERLO

Although alcohol and other drugs negatively impact virtually every human organ system, it is clear that these substances exert profound effects upon the brain. Specific substance-related deficits in frontal lobe functioning include problems with impulse control, delay of gratification, decision making, and planning.[1] Substance use also impairs cognition (e.g., memory and reasoning),[2] preventing individuals from rationally evaluating and coping with situations or adequately engaging in problem solving. In addition, substance use significantly affects behavior. Drugs and alcohol compete with natural reinforcers to drive drug-seeking and drug-taking behavior, and addiction is believed to result, in part, from the positively and negatively reinforcing effects of repeated drug use.[3] Indeed, the substance use disorders (SUDs) are diagnosed on the basis of behavioral indicators.[4]

Recovery from an SUD is extremely challenging because it requires changing deeply embedded behaviors. Many patients do not have adequate coping skills or social support to be successful on their own. So psychological treatments target a number of different goals (e.g., helping the patient understand the nature of addiction, initiating/maintaining sobriety, improving patient functioning across lifestyle domains, repairing relationships, and returning to a productive lifestyle). Relapse prevention is another crucial component of psychological treatment, because substance use disorders are chronic conditions, and relapse is a common concern. The preferred type and intensity of psychological treatment for each individual with an SUD will depend upon his or her personal and situational characteristics. For example, marital and/or family therapy may be needed to salvage or repair important relationships, participation in group therapy or self-help groups may help to combat denial and shame, and individual therapy may be needed to address underlying psychological issues. In addition, the severity of substance use, presence of comorbid medical/psychiatric conditions, and the quality of the individual's social, intellectual, and financial resources will impact treatment decisions. As a result, good treatment should begin with adequate assessment.

SCREENING, BRIEF INTERVENTION, AND REFERRAL TO TREATMENT

Given that identification of an SUD represents the first step toward recovery, many clinics, agencies, and other organization (e.g., SAMHSA, NIDA, NIAAA) are now advocating the use of screening, brief intervention, and referral to treatment (SBIRT) by health care providers from various professions (e.g., medicine, mental health, nursing, dentistry, etc.). SBIRT involves asking every patient about substance use, identifying problematic levels of use, and implementing an intervention or referral appropriate to the patient's current level of risk.[5] Depending on the severity of the SUD, interventions may range from brief patient education/counseling regarding substance use and the nature of addiction, to referral for inpatient treatment. Regardless of the approach utilized, the provider should follow up with the patient to determine whether any steps have been taken toward recovery. Research has demonstrated the efficacy of the SBIRT approach in decreasing drug and alcohol use.[6]

BRIEF INTERVENTION

In general, "brief interventions" involve motivational discussions targeted toward changing mildly to moderately risky substance use behaviors. They typically last 5–25 minutes and can be completed within one or two office visits (or other patient interactions). Brief interventions are most suitable for patients at the beginning stages of problematic substance use. For example, a college student who binge drinks on occasion, but does not display symptoms of alcohol abuse or dependence, would be a good candidate for a brief intervention.

Promoting Self-Change

Many individuals who display mild to moderate levels of problematic substance use are able to cut down or quit without formal treatment.[7] This "self-change" is common among individuals recovering from problematic drinking, smoking, and drug use. However, the process of self-change may be facilitated and/or accelerated via brief intervention.[8] Using methods grounded in motivational interviewing,[9] clinicians explore the patient's view of his or her situation, pros and cons of continuing the problematic substance use, and goals for the future. In promoting self-change, the clinician may also provide psychoeducation, efficacy support, and suggestions regarding effective methods of change.

FRAMES Method

Another common, user-friendly option for brief intervention is the FRAMES method (i.e., Feedback, Responsibility, Advice, Menu of options, Empathy, Self-efficacy).[10] This approach is similar in some ways to motivational interviewing, but it requires less formal training for proficiency. Using FRAMES, the clinician first gives the patient *feedback* regarding his or her substance use, educating the patient about population norms and adverse effects of such use. Next, the provider emphasizes that only the patient can choose whether to change his or her substance use habits (i.e., *responsibility*). The provider gives the patient *advice* regarding the benefits of quitting or cutting down on substance use and offers several suggestions (i.e., a *menu of options*) regarding ways to make the change. Throughout the exchange, the health care provider strives to communicate *empathy* to the patient, acknowledging the reasons for substance use and the difficulty of cutting down or quitting. However, the provider also supports the patient's *self-efficacy*, in order to increase confidence in his or her ability to make the change. The FRAMES approach has demonstrated increased efficacy when compared to simple advice offered by physicians.[11]

Brief Treatment

Brief treatments differ from brief interventions, in that they typically involve multiple sessions and are administered by a clinician with specialized training in substance use disorders or psychotherapy. Treatments typically span 4–20 sessions of 45–60 minutes each. Like brief intervention, patient education and motivation are key foci. Skill building, problem solving, and solicitation of social support are also highly emphasized.

Motivational Enhancement Therapy

Traditionally, treatments for SUDs involved a clinician expert confronting the patient's denial and correcting the patient's mistaken ideas regarding substance use. This approach is effective for some patients, but it can be experienced as overly punitive and unpleasant by others, who may drop out of treatment prior to making adequate gains. On the other hand, Miller and Rollnick's motivational interviewing (MI)[9,12] approach is a "collaborative, person-centered form of guiding to elicit and strengthen motivation for change."[13] Clinicians utilizing MI emphasize the patient's autonomy, while striving to maintain a collaborative relationship and evoking the patient's personal reasons and goals related to changing his or her substance use behaviors. Motivational enhancement therapy (MET) combines motivational interviewing with the provision of feedback regarding the patient's current level of substance use, in order to assist the patient in moving toward change.[14] MET was developed to span four sessions over 12 weeks, with research demonstrating equivalent outcomes compared to more intense interventions (e.g., CBT and 12-step facilitation).[15] There is also evidence that MI/MET interventions may be most efficacious when combined with another treatment.[16,17]

Cognitive-Behavioral Therapy

Cognitive-behavioral therapy (CBT) provides the foundation for many treatment programs for SUD patients. Most outpatient CBT interventions are designed to last 12–20 sessions. Clinicians utilize psychoeducation, functional analysis, environmental modification and contingency management, cognitive restructuring, skill building, and other methods, in order to help patients effect the cognitive and behavioral changes necessary to recover from SUDs.[18] Psychoeducation is considered an essential part of treatment, and clinicians may provide in-session teaching, assign readings, and/ or encourage attendance at special lectures. Clinicians will also help patients to identify and change dysfunctional beliefs, environmental triggers, and conditioned reinforcers that promote substance use. Learning cognitive restructuring techniques, coping strategies, refusal skills, and methods of engaging social support are primary tasks in CBT, as these skills will help the individual to maintain a life of recovery after achieving sobriety. CBT has demonstrated positive outcomes[19] that were generally equivalent to other forms of brief treatment.[15]

Contingency Management

Research has consistently demonstrated that substances of abuse activate the brain's reward system, exerting stronger effects than natural reinforcers and making it difficult for individuals with SUDs to refrain from substance use.[20] Contingency management interventions explicitly reward abstinence from substances of abuse, and withhold reward following use, in order to compete with this process. For example, voucher-based reinforcement therapy (VBRT) allows patients to earn vouchers for desired items/prizes each time their abstinence is confirmed (via urine drug screening, breathalyzer testing, etc.).[21] This typically occurs 2–3 times per week for 12–16 weeks. Most VBRT programs implement an escalating value schedule, such that patients receive increasingly larger rewards as the period of abstinence grows. If the patient produces a sample that is positive for substance use, he or she receives no reward, and the value of the voucher is typically reset to the entry level for the next negative test result. VBRT has demonstrated efficacy in helping individuals, particularly those in the initial phase of abstinence, to refrain from using cocaine and other stimulants, opioids, marijuana, tobacco, and alcohol.[22] It may also help to improve outcome when used as an adjunct to MET and/or CBT.[23]

Another method of contingency management is utilized with impaired health care professionals, who are required to undergo frequent urine drug screening as part of monitoring programs for impaired professionals. However, rather than earning prizes, individuals who continue to produce substance-negative specimens usually earn the right to retain their license to practice. This approach, combined with other treatments, has demonstrated exceptional success rates, with over 70% of physicians undergoing monitoring remaining substance free after 5 years.[24]

12-Step Facilitation

Participation in 12-step fellowships (e.g., Alcoholics Anonymous and Narcotics Anonymous) has been positively associated with sobriety and recovery across multiple studies,[25] including those involving patients with comorbid psychiatric conditions.[26] Though there are many barriers to 12-step participation (e.g., attitudes or beliefs, anxiety, embarrassment/shame), clinicians may assist patients in initiating involvement in these programs by providing a "12-step facilitation" intervention.[27] Using this approach, the clinician typically meets with the patient on a weekly basis for 12 weeks, focusing discussion on three "core topics," as well as some elective topics. The clinician may also assign the patient readings from various 12-step publications, which can be discussed during their sessions. The primary tasks of 12-step facilitation include (1) introducing the patient to the 12-step philosophy, (2) working with the patient to complete the first three steps, and (3) encouraging the patient to become actively involved in a 12-step program. Early in their sessions, the clinician may describe what to expect at meetings in order to lessen anxiety about attending. Later, the clinician will encourage the patient to begin attending 12-step meetings, to form a connection with other group members, and to identify a sponsor.

Long-Term Management

Patients with severe SUDs will generally require participation in an intensive, specialized program and typically benefit most from a longer period of treatment. This may include participation in an inpatient, residential, or partial-hospitalization program, where they continue to receive treatment based in the methods described earlier (e.g., MI/ MET, CBT, 12-step facilitation, etc.). In addition, patients may participate in adjunctive psychological treatments to increase the likelihood of achieving sustained recovery.

Couples/Family Therapy

A substance users' social context (e.g., family, peer network, neighborhood contacts, religious/spiritual community, work colleagues, therapeutic relationship, treatment community, 12-step group, etc.) can serve as both a risk factor and a protective factor for substance use.[28] Important relationships also tend to be negatively affected during active addiction. As a result, participation in couples or family therapy can help to repair relationships that have been damaged by the chaos, broken trust, and financial strain that are common to addiction, and to increase the likelihood of sustained recovery. Couples therapy may help the patient and his or her partner improve communication, restore mutual trust, and work through negative feelings (e.g., guilt, resentment, anger). Family therapy may be particularly useful when children are involved. Involvement of family members also tends to increase the patient's involvement in and commitment to treatment. Indeed, research has demonstrated that these interventions can greatly help SUD patients in their attempts to achieve a stable recovery lifestyle.[29] The interventions can also restore positive social support, providing patients with greater resources for coping.

Relapse Prevention

A critical component of SUD treatment is preparing patients for challenges they will face in their attempts to maintain a sober lifestyle. Relapse prevention[30] is a method of intervention that facilitates this process. Using this approach, patients are taught to think of abstinence violations as a "lapse" rather than a "relapse," in order to reduce the shame that could otherwise trigger more substance use. The clinician also provides psychoeducation regarding relapse and helps the patient to identify potential risk factors that could contribute to a lapse.[31] An additional focus of sessions includes supporting the patient's confidence in his or her ability to refuse substances and maintain sobriety. Useful coping skills are introduced and practiced, and the patient is encouraged to adjust expectancies regarding the recovery lifestyle. Research has demonstrated that inclusion of relapse prevention techniques during treatment helps individuals to maintain sobriety.[32]

Treatment of Psychiatric Conditions

Many patients with an SUD also suffer from comorbid psychiatric conditions. Once the patient has been detoxified and is substance free long enough to determine that the symptoms were not substance induced, some attention should shift to psychological and/or pharmacological treatment of the psychiatric condition, because untreated psychiatric symptoms represent a significant risk factor for relapse. Nace and Tinsley[33] offer suggestions for

clinicians who treat patients with SUDs, including (1) screen all patients for dual diagnosis, (2) recognize that SUDs and psychiatric conditions are separate disorders that may require distinct treatments, (3) remain flexible in your treatment approach in order to minimize risk to the patient,while at the same time guarding against premature termination from treatment, (4) remember that lapses are common and should be met with empathy and adjustments to treatment, and (5) acknowledge that psychiatric medication may be necessary for your patient and that this does not constitute an abstinence violation.

CONCLUSION

In general, psychosocial treatments are associated with improved outcome among patients with SUDs[34]; however, outcome can vary greatly among individuals. Some will achieve stable recovery following a brief intervention or treatment; others may continue a chronic cycle of relapse throughout their lives. The psychological treatment of choice will be based on the individual's personal needs and level of substance abuse. Longer treatment retention is associated with more positive outcome, and achieving a longer period of sustained abstinence during treatment also predicts better outcome.[35] For most individuals with substance dependence, abstinence from all mind-altering substances, including alcohol and some over-the-counter drugs, is an important aspect of recovery.[36] Finally, treatments targeting patient motivation, as well as family factors and other environmental or psychiatric factors, may assist patients in maintaining sobriety once it is achieved.

REFERENCES

1. Goldstein RZ, Volkow ND. Drug addiction and its underlying neurobiological basis: neuroimaging evidence for the involvement of the frontal cortex. *Am J Psychiatry* 2002;159:1642–1652.
2. Schrimsher GW, Parker JD, Burke RS. Relation between cognitive testing performance and pattern of substance use in males at treatment entry. *Clin Neuropsychol* 2007;21:498–510.
3. Kreek MJ, Koob GF. Drug dependence: stress and dysregulation of brain reward pathways. *Drug Alcohol Depen* 1998;51:230–247.
4. American Psychiatric Association. *Diagnostic and Statistical Manual of Mental Disorders.* 4th ed. Washington, DC: American Psychiatric Association, 2000.
5. Babor TF, McRee BG, Kassebaum PA, Grimaldi PL, Ahmed K, Bray J. Screening, brief intervention,

and referral to treatment (SBIRT): toward a public health approach to the management of substance abuse. *Subst Abus* 2007;28:7–30.

6. Madras BK, Compton WM, Avula D, Stegbauer T, Stein JB, Clark HW. Screening, brief interventions, referral to treatment (SBIRT) for illicit drug and alcohol use at multiple healthcare sites: comparison at intake and 6 months later. *Drug Alcohol Depen* 2009;99:280–295.

7. Klingemann H, Sobell LC, eds. *Promoting Self-Change from Addictive Behaviors: Practical Implications for Policy, Prevention, and Treatment.* New York: Springer, 2007.

8. Samet JH, Rollnick S, Barnes H. Beyond CAGE: a brief clinical approach after detection of substance abuse. *Arch Intern Med* 1996;156:2287–2293.

9. Miller WR, Rollnick S. *Motivational Interviewing: Preparing People for Change* (2nd ed.). New York: Guilford Press, 2002.

10. Bien TH, Miller WR, Tonigan JS. Brief interventions for alcohol problems: a review. *Addiction* 1993;88:315–336.

11. Pal HR, Yadav D, Mehta S, Mohan I. A comparison of brief intervention versus simple advice for alcohol use disorders in a North India community-based sample followed for 3 months. *Alcohol Alcohol* 2007;42:328–332.

12. Miller WR, Rollnick S. *Motivational Interviewing: Preparing People to Change Addictive Behavior.* New York: Guilford Press, 1991.

13. Miller WR, Rollnick S. What makes it MI? In: *Motivational Interviewing Network of Trainers Forum; June 2009.* Sitges, Spain 2009.

14. Miller WR, Zweben A, DiClemente CC, Rychtarik RC. *Motivational Enhancement Therapy Manual: A Clinical Research Guide for Therapists Treating Individuals with Alcohol Abuse and Dependence.* Rockville, MD: National Institute on Alcohol Abuse and Alcoholism, 1992.

15. Project MATCH Research Group. Matching Alcoholism Treatments to Client Heterogeneity: project MATCH posttreatment drinking outcomes. *J Stud Alcohol* 1997;58:7–29.

16. Burke BL, Arkowitz H, Menchola M. The efficacy of motivational interviewing: a meta-analysis of controlled clinical trials. *J Consult Clin Psych* 2003;71:843–861.

17. Hettema JM, Steele J, Miller WR. Motivational interviewing. *Ann Rev Clin Psychol* 2005;1:91–111.

18. Kadden R, Carroll K, Donovan DM, et al. *Cognitive-Behavioral Coping Skills Therapy Manual.* Rockville, MD: National Institute on Alcohol Abuse and Alcoholism, 2003.

19. Waldron HB, Kaminer Y. On the learning curve: the emerging evidence supporting cognitive-behavioral therapies for adolescent substance abuse. *Addiction* 2004;99:93–105.

20. Volkow ND, Li TK. Drug addiction: the neurobiology of behaviour gone awry. *Nat Rev Neurosci* 2004;5:963–970.

21. Higgins ST, Alessi SM, Dantona RL. Voucher-based incentives: a substance abuse treatment innovation. *Addict Behav* 2002;27:887–910.

22. Higgins ST, Silverman K, Heil SH, eds. *Contingency Management in Substance Abuse Treatment.* New York: Guildford Press, 2008.

23. Budney AJ, Higgins ST, Radonovich KJ, Novy PL. Adding voucher-based incentives to coping skills and motivational enhancement improves outcomes during treatment for marijuana dependence. *J Consult Clin Psych* 2000;68:1051–1061.

24. DuPont RL, McLellan AT, White WL, Merlo LJ, Gold MS. Setting the standard for recovery: Physicians' Health Programs. *J Subst Abus Treat* 2009;36:159–171.

25. Chappel JN, DuPont RL. Twelve-step and mutual-help programs for addictive disorders. *Psych Clin North Am* 1999;22:425–446.

26. Bogenschutz MP, Geppert CMA, George J. The role of twelve-step approaches in dual diagnosis treatment and recovery. *Am J Addiction* 2006;15:50–60.

27. Nowinski J, Baker S. *The Twelve-Step Facilitation Handbook: A Systematic Approach to Early Recovery from Alcoholism and Addiction.* New York: Lexington Books, 1992.

28. Gifford E, Humphreys K. The psychological science of addiction. *Addiction* 2007;102:352–361.

29. Stanton MD, Shandish WR. Outcome, attrition, and family couples treatment for drug abuse: a meta-analysis and review of the controlled comparative studies. *Psychol Bull* 1997;22:170–191.

30. Marlatt GA, Gordon JR, eds. *Relapse Prevention: Maintenance Strategies in the Treatment of Addictive Behaviors.* New York: Guilford Press, 1985.

31. Larimer ME, Palmer RS, Marlatt GA. Relapse prevention. An overview of Marlatt's cognitive-behavioral model. *Alcohol Res Health* 1999;23:151–160.

32. Irvin JE, Bowers CA, Dunn ME, Wang MC. Efficacy of relapse prevention: a meta-analytic review. *J Consult Clin Psych* 1999;67:563–570.

33. Nace EP, Birkmayer F, Sullivan MA, et al. Socially sanctioned coercion mechanisms for addiction treatment. *Am J Addiction* 2007;16:15–23.

34. Dutra L, Stathopoulou G, Basden SL, Leyro TM, Powers MB, Otto MW. A meta-analytic review of psychosocial interventions for substance use disorders. *Am J Psychiat* 2008;165:179–187.

35. Higgins ST, Badger GJ, Budney AJ. Initial abstinence and success in achieving longer term cocaine abstinence. *Exper Clin Psychopharmacol* 2000;8:377–386.

36. DeLeon G. What psychologists can learn from addiction treatment research. *Psychol Addict Behav* 1993;7:103–109.

44

Behavioral Treatments for Obesity

CAITLIN A. LAGROTTE AND GARY D. FOSTER

PURPOSE

The purpose of this chapter is to describe the behavioral treatment for obesity, its principles and practices, defining characteristics, and outcomes.

BACKGROUND AND PHILOSOPHY

Historically, behavioral treatment of obesity developed from the belief that obesity was the result of maladaptive eating and exercise habits, which could be corrected by the application of learning principles.[1] It is now widely recognized that body weight is affected by factors other than behavior. These include genetic, metabolic, and hormonal influences[2–4] that probably predispose some persons to obesity and may well set the range of possible weights that an individual can achieve. Some individuals may never be thin, despite Herculean efforts to modify eating and activity habits. Behavior therapy, however, can help such individuals develop a set of skills (such as eating a low-calorie diet) to achieve a healthier weight, even if they cannot attain an ideal one.

PRINCIPLES AND PRACTICES

Behavioral treatment is based primarily on principles of classical conditioning, which posit that eating is often prompted by antecedent events (i.e., cues) that become strongly linked to food intake.[1] Behavioral treatment, as described later, helps patients identify cues that trigger inappropriate eating (and activity) and learn new responses to them.[5,6] Treatment also seeks to reinforce (or reward) the adoption of positive behaviors. While the reinforcement of positive behaviors (operant conditioning) is a reasonable strategy, it can be challenging when trying to modify targets (sedentary behavior, consumption of highly palatable,

energy-dense foods) that are immediately and specifically reinforcing. The dilemma is that the very behaviors we are attempting to decrease (consuming a delectable dessert, hitting the snooze button) are much more reinforcing in the short term than the behaviors we are attempting to increase (choosing a low-calorie dessert or getting up early to be physically active). Therefore, many behavioral approaches use strategies based on classical conditioning. This approach involves disconnecting cues on antecedents (times, places, activities, emotions, and people) from unwanted behaviors.

In the past 20 years, cognitive therapy also has been incorporated in the behavioral treatment of obesity. The underlying assumption of cognitive therapy is that thoughts (or cognitions) directly affect feelings and behaviors.[7] Negative thoughts frequently are associated with negative outcomes, as in the case of an individual who overeats thinks, "I've blown my diet," and then proceeds to eat even more secondary to feelings of failure and hopelessness. With cognitive techniques, patients learn to set realistic goals for weight and behavior change, to realistically evaluate their progress in modifying eating and activity habits, and to correct irrational, often negative thoughts that occur when they do not meet their goals.[8–10] Cognitive interventions for weight management[11–13] are based on those developed for the treatments of depression, anxiety, and bulimia nervosa.

CHARACTERISTICS OF BEHAVIORAL TREATMENT

Behavioral treatment has several distinguishing characteristics.[14] First, it is goal directed. It specifies very clear goals in terms that can be easily measured. This is true whether the goal is walking four times per week, lengthening meal duration by 10 minutes, or decreasing the number of self-critical comments. Specific goals facilitate a clear assessment of success.

Second, treatment is process oriented. It is more than helping people to decide what to change (i.e., eating, activity, and thinking habits); it is helping them identify how to change.[9] Thus, once a goal is specified, patients are encouraged to examine factors that will facilitate or hinder goal achievement. In cases in which the desired behavior is not implemented, problem-solving skills are used to identify new strategies to overcome barriers. In this view, successful weight management is based on skills that can be learned and practiced, in the same manner that an individual can learn to play the piano through frequent practice. Skill power, not willpower, is the key to success.

Third, the behavioral approach advocates small rather than large changes. This is based on the learning principle of successive approximation in which incremental steps are taken to achieve more distant goals. Making small changes gives patients successful experiences on which to build rather than attempting drastic changes that are typically short lived.[9]

The behavior change process is facilitated through the use of a variety of problem-solving tools. The behavior chain, an illustration that visually depicts the chain of events that lead to an unwanted behavior such as overeating, is one of the tools commonly used in treatment (Fig. 44.1). By examining the cues and events that lead up to an overeating episode, one can identify areas in which

modifications in behavior can be made to break the chain of events and prevent an overeating episode from occurring in the future. For example, if a patient has identified television watching as part of the sequence of events leading up to an overeating episode, limiting eating to a more appropriate location (i.e., table in the kitchen or dining room) can be an effective strategy for weakening the association between eating and television watching. The more often the patient refrains from eating in front of the television, the less likely that television watching will automatically trigger eating (i.e., extinction).

THE BEHAVIORAL PACKAGE

Behavioral treatment usually includes multiple components, such as keeping food and activity records (i.e., self-monitoring), controlling cues associated with eating (i.e., stimulus control), nutrition education, slowing eating, physical activity, problem solving, and cognitive restructuring (i.e., cognitive therapy).[5,6] These components comprise the "behavioral package" that has been summarized in manuals such as the *LEARN Program for Weight Management 2000*.[8] Studies have shown that two components, self-monitoring[15,16] and physical activity,[17,18] are consistently associated with better weight control in the short and long term, respectively. Additional research is needed to identify the most potent components of the package, as well as additional interventions that might be added (such as body image therapy) to improve efficacy, espe-

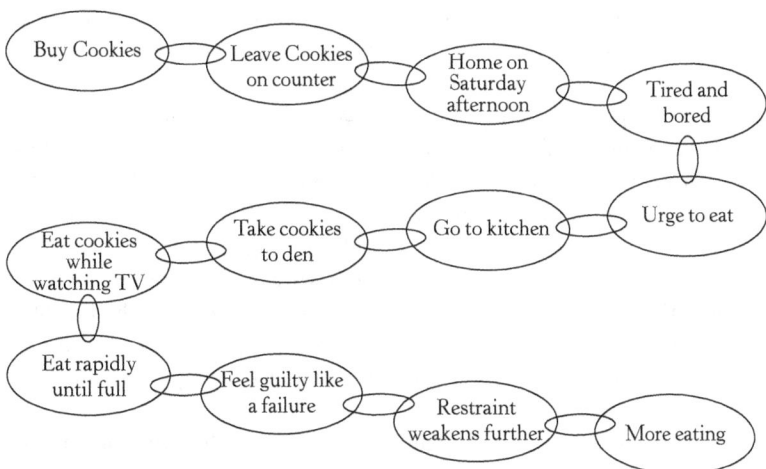

FIGURE 44.1. Behavior chain.
Source: Adapted from Brownell, 2000.

cially in the long term. In the interim, researchers and practitioners probably will continue to use the behavioral package because it is well validated, as a whole, and different patients are drawn to different components of the intervention.

SHORT-TERM RESULTS OF BEHAVIORAL TREATMENT

A large number of clinical studies have been conducted examining the effects of behavioral treatment on weight loss. The typical design of most behavioral treatment weight loss studies is group meetings weekly for the initial treatment phase ($\approx$3–6 months), biweekly (every other week) meetings for the maintenance phase (6–12 months), and monthly or bimonthly for the later phases of the study (12–24 months).[19,20]

Wing et al.[21] reviewed behavioral weight loss studies from 1996 to 1999, which resulted in a mean short-term weight loss of 10.6% (9.6 kg) during the treatment phase (21 weeks) and 8.6% (6.0 kg) at follow-up (18 months). Studies over the last decade have produced roughly similar results.[20,22–24]

OUTCOMES FOR BEHAVIORAL TREATMENT

Although behavioral treatment provides individuals with a set of skills to handle barriers to eating healthy and being active, overcoming barriers is a difficult endeavor in a fast-paced environment that encourages overconsumption of energy-dense, palatable, low-cost foods and promotes energy-saving devices[25,26] A healthy lifestyle requires significant planning, proficiency in making healthy choices and estimating portion sizes, and diligence in monitoring caloric intake and activity, all of which take time to develop and maintain. As such, strategies for simplifying and making this process more practical have been investigated and are described in the following sections. In general, these strategies provide structure and reduce time spent in meal planning and decision making.

Food Provision

Jeffery et al.[27] examined the impact of food provision on weight loss outcome in 202 overweight individuals. Participants who received food along with standard behavioral treatment lost more weight at 6 months (–10.1 vs. –7.7 kg), 12 months (–9.1 vs. –4.5 kg), and 18 months (–6.4 vs. –4.1 kg) than those who were prescribed a reduced calorie diet

and standard behavioral treatment. In a subsequent study, Wing et al.[28] sought to determine whether food provision itself or limited dietary decision making affected weight loss outcome. In this study, 163 overweight women were randomly assigned to one of four interventions: (1) standard behavioral treatment, (2) standard behavioral treatment plus written meal plans and grocery lists for five breakfasts and dinners each week, (3) standard behavioral treatment plus foods for a charge of $25.00/week, and (4) standard behavioral treatment plus foods free of charge. Data were collected for $\approx$90% of participants at the end of active treatment (i.e., 6 months) and at 1 year follow-up (i.e., 18 months after randomization). Weight loss was greater in groups that received food and meal plans compared with the group that received standard behavioral treatment at 6 and 18 months; however, no differences in weight loss were observed between the groups that were provided food and the group that received meal plans and grocery lists.

Meal Replacements

Similar findings are observed in studies that compared meal replacements[29–31] or prepackaged entrees[32,33] with self-selected diets. These studies suggested that replacing two of three meals with a liquid and/or solid meal replacement or at least two meals with a portion-controlled entrée resulted in greater weight loss than self-selected diets. Although some weight regain was observed over time, a greater reduction in weight was observed even up to 4 years in individuals receiving meal replacements.[30] Based on a meta-analysis by Heymsfield et al.,[34] individuals consuming meal replacements lose $\approx$7%–8% body weight, whereas those on a standard self-selected diet lose 3%–7% body weight at 1 year. It is unclear whether meal replacements are superior to other structured weight loss approaches that provide menus and recipes, however. Noakes et al.[35] found similar decreases in weight in individuals using meal replacements (–9.0 kg or –9.4% body weight) and those following structured diets (–9.2 kg or –9.3% body weight) at 6 months. These findings suggest that increasing structure may improve dietary compliance.

Pharmacotherapy

Another method used to enhance weight loss outcomes is to couple behavioral and pharmacotherapy approaches. It can be argued that behavioral treatment modifies the external environment, whereas pharmacologic approaches modify the internal environment either centrally (i.e., phentremine) or peripherally (i.e., orlistat). To test this hypothesis, Wadden et al.[36] compared weight loss in 224 obese adults randomly assigned to one of four groups: (1) 15 mg of sibutramine alone, given by a primary care provider in eight visits of about 10 minutes; (2) 30 group lifestyle-modification counseling sessions; (3) sibutramine plus 30 group lifestyle-modification counseling sessions (i.e., combined therapy); or(4) sibutramine plus brief lifestyle-modification counseling delivered by a primary care provider in eight visits of 10 minutes each. All subjects followed a calorie-controlled diet of 1,200 to 1,500 kcal per day with a weekly exercise regimen. After 1 year, subjects who received combined therapy had significantly greater weight losses than all other groups. These data suggest that the combination of medication and group lifestyle modification resulted in more weight loss than either lifestyle modification or medication alone. These findings may highlight the importance of combining weight loss medications and lifestyle modification.

Commercial Weight Loss Programs

Most research on behavior treatment has been conducted in university-based clinic programs. Although such studies are important, they tell us little about the effectiveness of these approaches in settings outside of specialized clinics. Womble et al.[37] reviewed the available literature on commercial approaches and found, in general, that weight losses were less than those observed in the clinical setting. In a study that evaluated the effectiveness of the Weight Watchers program, Heshka et al.[38] found that those in Weight Watchers lost more weight than those assigned to a self-help group (4.6 vs. 1.7%) after 1 year and after 2 years (3.1 vs. 0.2%). A recent, short-term study[39] assessed the effects of a commercially available weight loss program on weight and glycemic control among obese patients with type 2 diabetes. The study compared a portion-controlled diet (PCD; NutrisystemD) plan to a traditional Diabetes Support and Education (DSE) program. After 3 months, those in the PCD group lost significantly more weight than the DSE group (7.1 ± 4% vs. 0.4 ± 2.3%; $p < .0001$). Those in the PCD group had significantly greater reductions in HbA_{1C} than the DSE group (−0.88 ± 1.1 vs. 0.03 ± 1.09; $p < .001$).

Counseling Skills

Although behavioral change is the responsibility of the patient, it is the responsibility of the health care provider to facilitate change through effective counseling.[40] Counseling is not an innate talent; it requires practice and fine-tuning. Many providers may feel that their primary role is to give advice to patients about healthy methods of weight control. Although some education and advice is useful, most weight control patients are well aware of what they "should" eat; the problem is doing so in an environment that encourages otherwise. Therefore, an emphasis on asking questions to clarify barriers and their solutions is more effective than giving advice about how to "fix" the problem. The former approach models for patients the manner in which a problem can be managed effectively rather than depending on getting the right advice. As a rough indicator, the more a clinician speaks during the session, the less effective the session will be for the patient. If the clinician is talking >50% of the session, it is important to reassess the balance between advice giving and problem solving.[40]

WEIGHT MAINTENANCE

One of the main challenges in weight loss of overweight or obese people is how to maintain the weight loss. Approximately one-third of the weight that was lost is often regained within in the first year after treatment and more weight is regained over time.[41] Recent literature reviews propose that weight loss maintenance may be improved by the following methods: drug therapy with either orlistat or sibutramine in combination with lifestyle modification, caffeine or protein supplementation, consumption of a low-fat diet, commitment to physical activity regimens, continued contact with participants, problem-solving therapy, and even alternative treatments (i.e., acupressure).[42] Wing et al.'s recent data support that self-regulation models that incorporate regular weighing can be useful for facilitating weight loss maintenance. Despite these positive signals, it is important to note that the most frequent outcome of weight loss treatment is weight regain.

FUTURE DIRECTIONS

Health care providers can provide a great service to obese patients by reminding them that their worth is not measured on the scale. Patients should be encouraged to take themselves, their health, and, thus, their weight seriously rather than attempting to lose weight so they can like themselves. Reaffirming the patient's self-worth, independent of body weight, is perhaps one of the most powerful interventions a health care provider can provide an obese patient. As Stunkard[43] suggests, "As with any chronic illness, we rarely have an opportunity to cure, but we do have an opportunity to treat the patient with respect. Such an experience may be the greatest gift that [we] can give an obese patient."

ACKNOWLEDGMENTS

All authors contributed to the writing of this manuscript.

REFERENCES

1. Stuart RB. Behavioral control of overeating. *Behav Ther* 1967;5:357–365.

2. Bell CG, Walley AJ, Froguel P. The genetics of human obesity. *Nature Rev* 2005;6:221–234.

3. Weiss BE, Kim F, Schwartz MW. An integrative view of obesity. *Science* 2009;318:928–929.

4. Morton GJ, Cummings DE, Baskin DG, Barsh GS, Schwartz MW. Central nervous system control of food intake and body weight. *Nature* 2006;443:289–295.

5. Wing RR. Behavioral approaches to the treatment of obesity. In: Bray GA, Bouchard C, eds. *Handbook of Obesity: Clinical Applications*. 3rd ed. New York: Informa Healthcare; 2008: 227–248.

6. Makris AP, Foster GD, Astrup AA. Diet composition and weight loss. In: Bray GA, Bouchard C, eds. *Handbook of Obesity: Clinical Applications*. 3rd ed. New York: Informa Healthcare; 2008: 269–290.

7. Beck AT. *Cognitive Therapy and the Emotional Disorders*. New York: International Universities Press, 1976.

8. Brownell KD. *The LEARN Program for Weight Management 2000*. Dallas, TX: American Health Publishers, 2000.

9. Foster GD. Goals and strategies to improve behavior-change effectiveness. In: Bessesen DH, Kushner RF, eds. *Evaluation and Management of Obesity*. Philadelphia, PA: Hanley & Belfus; 2002: 29–32.

10. Foster GD, Wadden TA, Vogt RA, Brewer G. What is a reasonable weight loss? Patients' expectations and evaluations of obesity treatment outcomes. *J Consult Clin Psychol* 1997; 65: 79–85.

11. Beck, JS. *Cognitive Therapy for Challenging Problems: What to Do When the Basics Don't Work*. New York: Guilford Press, 2005.

12. Beck, JS. *The Beck Diet Solution*. Birmingham, AL: Oxmoor House, 2008.

13. Beck, JS. *The Complete Beck Diet for Life*. Birmingham, AL: Oxmoor House, 2008

14. Wadden TA, Foster GD. Behavioral treatment of obesity. *Med Clin North Am* 2000;84:441–461.

15. Baker RC, Kirschenbaum DS. Self-monitoring may be necessary for successful weight control. *Behav Ther* 1993;24:377–394.

16. O'Neil PM. Assessing dietary intake in the management of obesity. *Obes Res* 2001;9(suppl):361S–366S.

17. Jakicic JM. The effect of physical activity on body weight. *Obesity* 2009;17:S34-S38.

18. Wadden TA, West DS, Neiberg RH, et al. One-year weight losses in the Look AHEAD study: factors associated with success. *Obesity* 2009;17:713–722.

19. The Look AHEAD Research Group, Wadden TA, West DS, et al. The Look AHEAD Study: a descriptive of the lifestyle intervention and the evidence supporting it. *Obesity* 2006;14:737–752.

20. Foster GD, Wyatt HR, James O. Hill JO, et al. Weight and metabolic outcome after two years on a low-carbohydrate vs. low-fat diet: a randomized trial. *Ann Inten Med* 2010;153:147–157.

21. Wing RR. Behavioral weight control. In: Wadden TA, Stunkard AJ, eds. *Handbook of Obesity Treatment*. New York: Guilford Press; 2002: 301–316.

22. Look AHEAD Research Group, Pi-Sunyer X, Blackburn G, et al. Reduction in weight and cardiovascular disease risk factors in individuals with type 2 diabetes: one-year results of the look AHEAD trial. *Diab Care* 2007;30:1374–1383.

23. Jeffrey RW, Wing RR, Sherwood NE, Tate DF. Physical activity and weight loss: does prescribing higher physical activity goals improve outcome? *Am J Clin Nutr* 2003;78:684–689.

24. West DS, Gorin AA, Subak LL, et al. A motivation-focused weight loss maintenance program is an effective alternative to a skill-based approach. *Int J Obes* 2010;35(2):1–11.

25. Swinburn B, Egger G. Analyzing and influencing obesogenic environments. In: Bray GA, Bouchard C, eds. *Handbook of Obesity: Clinical Applications*. 3rd ed. New York: Informa Healthcare; 2008: 177–194.

26. Drewnowski A. Obesity, diets, and social inequalities. *Nutr Rev* 2009;67:S36-S39.

27. Jeffery RW, Wing RR, Thorson C, Burton LR. Strengthening behavioral interventions for weight loss: a randomized trial of food provision and monetary incentives. *J Consult Clin Psychol* 1993;6:1038–1045.

28. Wing RR, Jeffery RW, Burton LR, Thorson C, Nissinoff KS, Baxter JE. Food provision vs structured meal plans in the behavioral treatment of obesity. *Int J Obes Relat Metab Disord* 1996;20:56–62.

29. Heymsfield SB. Meal replacements and energy balance. *Physiol Behav* 2010;100:90–94.

30. Ditschuneit HH, Flechtner-Mors M, Johnson TD, Adler G. Metabolic and weight loss effects of a long-term dietary intervention in obese patients. *Am J Clin Nutr* 1999;69:198–204.

31. Ashley JM, St Jeor ST, Perumean-Chaney S, Schrage J, Bovee V. Meal replacements in weight intervention. *Obes Res* 2001;9:312S–320S.

32. Hannum SM, Carson L, Evans EM, et al. Use of portion-controlled entrees enhances weight loss in women. *Obes Res* 2004;12:538–546.

33. Metz JA, Stern JS, Kris-Etherton P, et al. A randomized trial of improved weight loss with a prepared meal plan in overweight and obese patients. *Arch Intern Med* 2000;160:2150–2158.

34. Heymsfield SB, van Mierlo CAJ, van der Knaap HCM, Heo M, Frier HI. Weight management using meal replacement strategy: meta and pooling analysis from six studies. *Int J Obes* 2003;27:537–549.

35. Noakes M, Foster PR, Keogh JB, Clifton PM. Meal replacements are as effective as structured weight-loss diets for treating obesity in adults with features of metabolic syndrome. *J Nutr* 2004;134:1894–1899.

36. Wadden TA, Berkowitz RI, Womble LG, et al. Randomized trial of lifestyle modification and pharmacotherapy. *N Engl J Med* 2005;353:2111–2120.

37. Womble LG, Wang SS, Wadden TA. Commercial and self-help weight loss programs. In: Wadden TA, Stunkard AJ, eds. *Handbook of Obesity Treatment*. New York: Guilford Press; 2002: 395–415.

38. Heshka S, Anderson JW, Atkinson RL, et al. Weight loss with self-help compared with a structured commercial program. *JAMA* 2003;289: 1792–1798.

39. Foster GD, Borradaile KE, Vander Veur SS, et al. The effects of a commercially available weight loss program among obese patients with Type 2 diabetes: a randomized study. *Postgrad Med J* 2009;121(5): 113–118.

40. Foster GD, Makris A. Behavioral treatment: practical applications. In: Foster GD, Nonas CA, eds. *Managing Obesity: A Clinical Guide*. Chicago: American Dietetic Association; 2004: 76–90.

41. Turk MW, Yang K, Hravnak M, Sereika SM, Ewing LJ, Burke LE. Randomized clinical trials of weight loss maintenance: a review. *J Cardiovasc Nurs* 2009; 24(1):58–80.

42. Perri MG, Foreyt JP, Anton SD. Preventing weight regain after weight loss. In: Bray GA, Bouchard C, eds. *Handbook of Obesity: Clinical Applications*. 3rd ed. New York: Informa Healthcare; 2008: 249–268.

43. Stunkard AJ. Talking with patients. In: Stunkard AJ, Wadden TA, eds. *Obesity: Theory and Therapy*. 2nd ed. New York: Raven Press; 1993: 355–363.

45

Pharmacotherapy of Addictive Disorders

ECE TEK AND STEPHANIE S. O'MALLEY

Recent advances in genomic and molecular biology, genetic manipulation, and psychopharmacological neuroimaging have helped scientists to identify the pharmacokinetic sites of action for many drugs of abuse. Building upon this knowledge, pharmacological treatments have been evaluated for their ability to facilitate abstinence, restore homeostasis, and prevent relapse.

Pharmacological treatments of addiction have their effects through a variety of mechanisms. Agonist drugs act on the same receptors as a drug of abuse, produce similar effects, and are often used to treat withdrawal or as maintenance replacement therapy. Partial agonists typically have mild agonist effects in the absence of drug, thereby relieving withdrawal. However, these agents also antagonize or "block" the effects of the abused drug. Antagonists bind to the pharmacological site of action but do not stimulate or produce the same reinforcing effect. Other medications could have indirect modes of action; for example, they indirectly influence the firing of dopamine, a neurotransmitter considered central to the reinforcing effects of drugs. Immune therapies use vaccines that cause the body to produce antibodies to the drug of abuse. These antibodies bind to the drug, resulting in a molecule too large to pass through the blood–brain barrier, thereby reducing the reinforcing effects of the drug of abuse.

This chapter provides a brief review of medications that are currently approved by the Food and Drug Administration (FDA) for the treatment of substance use disorders and medications under investigation for alcohol, nicotine, opiates, stimulants, and marijuana. Information about dosing, adverse events, and contraindications are presented briefly in tables, but the reader should refer to the product information on each medication for complete information.

ALCOHOL

Although most individuals with alcohol dependence can quit drinking without serious complications, withdrawal can be a potentially fatal medical condition for those with severe dependence. The withdrawal syndrome is in part due to the unopposed activity of glutamate once alcohol is no longer stimulating the inhibitory neurotransmitter gamma-aminobutyric acid (GABA).[1]

Benzodiazepines

Benzodiazepines, which increase the activity of GABA, are the standard of care for treating alcohol withdrawal. Benzodiazepines are used to initiate abstinence and prevent complicated alcohol withdrawal. Thiamine is often added to the detoxification regimen to prevent alcohol-related encephalopathy. Benzodiazepines are not feasible for long-term use because quick tolerance easily develops.[2] Antiepileptics, such as carbamazepine, valproate, and gabapentin, have also been tested for alcohol withdrawal.[3] Carbamazepine[4] and gabapentin[5] appear to reduce alcohol drinking beyond the initial withdrawal period.

There are four FDA-approved pharmacotherapies for relapse prevention: disulfiram, baltrexone, extended-release naltrexone, and acamprosate (see Table 45.1).

Disulfiram

Disulfiram alters the metabolism of alcohol, resulting in an aversive response to drinking. The alcohol-disulfiram reaction usually begins within 10 minutes of drinking and symptoms include flushing, headaches, anxiety, sweating, nausea, vomiting, dizziness, palpitations, hyperventilation, and confusion. Knowledge of the ethanol-disulfiram reaction serves as a deterrent to drinking and supports the patient's commitment to abstinence.

TABLE 45.1. FDA-APPROVED MEDICATIONS FOR ALCOHOL DEPENDENCE

Medication	Mechanism of Action	Dose	Common Side Effects	Contraindications
Disulfiram (Antabuse)	Inhibits metabolism of acetaldehyde and produces aversive reaction if alcohol is consumed	25–50 mg once daily	Metallic aftertaste, dermatititis, fatigue, psychotic symptoms	Acute psychosis, severe myocardial disease
Naltrexone (oral, intramuscular [IM] depot forms)	Opioid antagonist Blocks reward received from alcohol; reduces craving	Oral: 50 mg once daily IM: 380 mg once monthly	Nausea, vomiting, abdominal pain, nervousness, anorexia, headache; injection site reactions	Opiate use, liver failure
Acamprosate (Campral)	May enhance GABA and reduce glutamate function; reduces craving.	666 mg three times daily	Abdominal pain, diarrhea, flatulence, headache	Kidney impairment

Having a family member or a health professional observe administration, however, is often essential to enhance adherence and effectiveness.[6]

Naltrexone

Naltrexone, an opioid antagonist approved for the treatment of alcohol dependence in 1994, does not have aversive interactions with alcohol, but it may reduce the amount consumed during a lapse in abstinence. A meta-analysis indicated that oral naltrexone has modest efficacy over 3 months on preventing relapse to heavy drinking, return to any drinking, and medication discontinuation.[7] Longer treatment can be helpful.[8] The efficacy of naltrexone may be most apparent when combined with less intensive behavioral therapy that can be used by primary care providers.[9] Compliance is an important factor in the success of naltrexone therapy.

Extended-release naltrexone was developed to minimize problems with adherence and requires only a once-per-month injection.[10] Participants who had achieved at least 4 days of abstinence prior to starting treatment maintained abstinence at higher rates with extended-release naltrexone (32%) compared to placebo (11%).[11]

Acamprosate

Although the exact mechanism of acamprosate is unknown, it is hypothesized to normalize the balance between excitatory and inhibitory pathways altered by chronic alcohol consumption.[12] A meta-analysis comprising 13 studies of acamprosate and 19 studies of naltrexone found that acamprosate helped maintain abstinence in alcohol-dependent individuals who had stopped drinking.[13] Two multisite studies in the United States were negative,[9,14] and efforts are under way to identify predictors of response. As acamprosate is poorly absorbed, three times a day dosing is required. Most individuals tolerate acamprosate well, with diarrhea being the most common side effect.

Medications in Development

Other medications with promise include (1) topiramate, which both augments GABA and inhibits glutamate activity; (2) ondansetron, selective serotonin 3 receptor antagonist; (3) baclofen, a GABA-B receptor agonist; (4) mecamylamine, a nicotinic receptor antagonist; (5) varenicline, a nicotinic receptor partial agonist; and(6) medications that alter stress responses. Topiramate has the most empirical support, including a multisite study that demonstrated efficacy in very heavy drinking, alcohol-dependent patients who were not required to be abstinent prior to starting therapy.[15]

Various combinations of treatments for relapse prevention have been tested. While the evidence has not been generally encouraging,[9] a recent study found that combining naltrexone with sertraline for the treatment of individuals with depression and alcohol dependence was more effective than either medication alone.[16]

OPIOIDS

Pharmacotherapies for opioid addiction are classified in three groups: agonists (methadone), partial agonists (buprenorphine), and antagonists (naltrexone, naloxone) of opiate receptors. Withdrawal from opiates is usually not life threatening, but it is a very uncomfortable experience. While undergoing detoxification the aim is to alleviate patient discomfort, thus decreasing early treatment discontinuation. Options for opiate detoxification include administration and slow taper of methadone, administration of buprenorphine, or symptomatic treatment with nonopioid agents such as clonidine alone or clonidine in combination with naltrexone to shorten the withdrawal period (see Table 45.2).[17]

Methadone

Methadone maintenance is one of the most successful interventions in addictions.[18] Methadone is longer acting than most abused opiates such as heroin. Substitution of the abused opiates with methadone prevents drug-seeking behavior, breaks the cycle of euphoria and withdrawal, replaces unsafe use of illicit drugs, and enables the patient to engage in counseling and an active life. Methadone replacement therapy, initially introduced as a bridge to sobriety, is more often considered a long-term treatment for a chronic illness as relapse to intravenous heroin use occurs in 70% to 80% of clients who discontinue methadone maintenance.[19] Methadone is highly regulated in the United States and must be dispensed in specialized programs.

Buprenorphine

Buprenorphine is a partial opiate agonist that has less risk for respiratory depression and overdose than methadone while preventing opiate withdrawal and blocking the reinforcing effects of illicit opioids. Physicians can prescribe buprenorphine in office-based treatment, which makes it accessible for patients. There are two sublingual formulations: buprenorphine mono product (Subutex) and buprenorphine naloxone combination (Suboxone). Naloxone is inactive in sublingual form but can precipitate opiate withdrawal if injected. Thus, the combination formulation is used to prevent intravenous abuse of the medication. Mono buprenorphine is preferred in pregnancy.[20] New formulations of buprenorphine that provide long-term delivery are being investigated.[21]

Naltrexone

Naltrexone, a long-acting opioid antagonist, was developed for maintenance of opiate abstinence. Before initiation of the treatment with naltrexone, patients must be medically detoxified and opioid-free for several days to prevent withdrawal symptoms. High dropout rates occur in unselected patients. Oral naltrexone requires supervised administration and is best suited for highly motivated patients (e.g., physicians who must be drug free to reinstate their license) and who are away from drug-related environments.[22] Recently the FDA approved extended-release naltrexone, which requires only a monthly injection and should improve adherence over the oral formulation.

NICOTINE

Pharmacotherapy interventions for smoking cessation have a long tradition. Indeed, practice guidelines[23] recommend that all smokers be offered pharmacotherapy and outline several first-line therapies, including nicotine replacement therapy (NRT), bupropion, varenicline, and combination treatment with a nicotine patch + a short-acting NRT or nicotine patch + bupropion.

NRTs replace the nicotine obtained from tobacco with a pharmaceutical form with less reinforcing effects in order to prevent withdrawal symptoms and make it easier to abstain from tobacco. Six NRTs are FDA approved: nicotine transdermal patch systems; nicotine nasal spray; and nicotine delivery through the oral mucosa, including gum, lozenge, sublingual tablet, and vapor inhaler. Transdermal patch provides steady levels of nicotine and is effective in reducing nicotine withdrawal; other forms can be titrated by the user to prevent withdrawal as well as to manage cravings. Typically, NRT starts on the "quit day" when smoking cessation begins. Combined NRT provides a higher degree of nicotine substitution by utilization of longer acting (i.e., patch) and intermittent delivery systems (e.g., gum or lozenge) and can increase efficacy (see Table 45.3).[24,25]

Varenicline

Varenicline (Chantix) is an oral partial agonist selective for alpha-4 beta-2 nicotinic acetylcholine receptors. It binds to nicotinic receptors with weak agonist activity, thus preventing withdrawal and reducing craving, while preventing nicotine from binding to these receptors. Treatment with varenicline begins 1–2 weeks prior to the quit date, which may facilitate quitting by reducing the reinforcing value of smoking. Varenicline increases the odds of

TABLE 45.2. FDA-APPROVED MEDICATIONS FOR OPIATE DEPENDENCE

Medication	Mechanism of Action	Dose	Common Side Effects	Contraindications
Methadone	Oral opioid agonist. Replacement therapy for shorter acting illicit opioids. Prevents euphoria peaks followed by withdrawal, reduce drug seeking behavior.	Titrated until withdrawal symptoms are prevented for 24 hr. Daily dose: 60 mg to 120 mg	Cardiac rhythm problems, respiratory depression, nausea, vomiting, constipation, dizziness, sedation	Acute asthma attack, severe respiratory depression, paralytic ileus
Buprenorphine	Partial opiate agonist— prevents withdrawal, replaces illicit opioids; antagonizes opiate reward in response to illicit opioids or at higher dose of itself.	4 to 24 mg once daily	Nausea, vomiting, sedation, dizziness, somnolence, vertigo	Hypersensitivity to buprenorphine
Buprenorphine/ Naloxone combination	Combination provides the same benefits of oral buprenorphine but naloxone, which is active only when injected, serves as a deterrent to injection.	4 to 24 mg daily	Sweating, abdominal pain, nausea, vomiting, constipation, headache	Hypersensitivity to buprenorphine or naloxone
Naltrexone (oral, intramuscular [IM] forms)	Opioid antagonist. Completely blocks euphoria and reward received from illicit opioid use.	Oral: 50 mg once daily. IM: 380 mg once monthly	Nausea, vomiting, abdominal pain, nervousness, anorexia, headache, injection site reactions	Liver failure

smoking cessation success three-fold compared to placebo.[26] The most common side effects are gastrointestinal and sleep disturbances. However, due to reports of behavior change (i.e., depression, hostility, and suicidality) in the postmarketing period, the FDA has required a black box warning for this medication. A recent cohort study from the United Kingdom revealed that there was no clear evidence that varenicline was associated with an increased risk of self-harm.[27]

Bupropion

Bupropion (Zyban, Wellbutrin) is a dopaminergic antidepressant also approved for smoking cessation. The mechanism of action involves blockade of dopamine and norepinephrine reuptake as well as antagonism of high-affinity nicotinic acetylcholine receptors.[28] Bupropion may work by reducing craving, nicotine reinforcement, and by reducing postcessation symptoms such as depression. Bupropion carries the same black box warning as varenicline, although its antidepressant efficacy is established. Similar to varenicline, the quit day is 1–2 weeks after the start of bupropion. Bupropion can be combined with NRTs to improve quit rates.[29]

If first-line therapies fail, second-line therapies can be considered, including clonidine, approved as an antihypertensive agent, and nortriptiline, approved as an antidepressant. The potential of nicotine vaccines in promoting smoking cessation appears promising.[30]

STIMULANTS (COCAINE, AMPHETAMINE)

Numerous medications have been tested (>60); however, there are no FDA-approved treatments.[31] Although psychostimulants are known to have their effect through dopaminergic mechanisms, dopamine agonists have been ineffective. Drugs that indirectly increase dopamine have some evidence of efficacy.

TABLE 45.3. FDA-APPROVED TREATMENTS FOR SMOKING CESSATION

Product	Mechanism	Dose	Common Side Effects	Contraindications
Nicotine replacement products	Replace nicotine from cigarettes Reduces withdrawal, attenuates craving	*Patches:* 7, 14, 21 mg/24 hr *Gum/lozenge:* 2, 4 mg used at least 9 times/day *Nicotine Inhaler:* 10 mg 6 cartridges/day up to 16/day *Spray:* 0.5 mg metered spray; 1–2 mg per hour up to 40 mg daily	Irritation at the site of NRT (nose, skin) Gastrointestinal (gum, lozenge) Sleep disturbance	Caution within 2 weeks post–myocardial infarction period, serious arrhythmias or serious/worsening angina
Bupropion (Zyban)	Blocks reuptake of dopamine and norepinephrine Decreases craving, nicotine withdrawal symptoms, including depression	Days 1–3: 150 mg daily Days 4 on: 150 mg twice per day	Insomnia Dry mouth	Factors that increase risk of seizures Taking Wellbutrin or recent use of MAO inhibitors anorexia or bulimia nervosa
Varenicline (Chantix)	Partial agonist of nicotinic acetylcholine receptors Attenuates withdrawal and reinforcement from smoking	Days 1–3: 0.5 mg daily Days 4–7: 0.5 mg 2× daily Weeks 2–: 1 mg 2× daily	Nausea Constipation Flatulence Reports of allergic reactions and serious neuropsychiatric adverse events	Patients with a known history of hypersensitivity to Chantix

Disulfiram, which inhibits dopamine metabolism, increases cocaine abstinence,[32] but safety concerns related to adverse interactions with cocaine and alcohol have limited development of this compound for cocaine addiction. Modafinil, originally developed for narcolepsy because of its role in increasing dopamine in nucleus accumbens and its effect in promoting wakefulness[33] has been found to decrease cocaine use compared with placebo.[34]

In addition to dopamine, cocaine addiction involves multiple neurobiological systems, including serotonin, norepinephrine, glutamate, GABA, and endocannabinoids and these have been areas for research. Ondansetron, topiramate, baclofen, and vigabatrin are promising medications. Ondansetron is a 5-HT3 blocker that is widely used for nausea and vomiting. One pilot study found a reduction in cocaine use and improvement in treatment retention.[35] One clinical study supported the use of N-Acetyl cysteine as a treatment for cocaine dependence with the idea that this medication inhibits cocaine cue reactivity.[36] Finally, there is enthusiasm for a new cocaine vaccine, which is a cocaine derivative coupled with recombinant cholera toxin B causing cocaine-specific antibodies by binding the circulating cocaine. The cocaine-antibody complex cannot enter the brain; thus, pleasurable effects of cocaine are suppressed.[30,37]

MARIJUANA

Despite the epidemiological results stating that cannabis is the most common illicit drug of abuse, there have not been too many clinical trials for cannabis use disorder in the literature. The development of pharmacotherapies is in its early stage. CB1 cannabinoid receptor agonist, dronabinol (Marinol), and CB1 antagonist, rimonabant, have been evaluated for the treatment.[38] Neuropsychiatric adverse events associated with rimonabant limit the likelihood that this compound will be developed.

REFERENCES

1. Vengeliene V, Bilbao A, Molander A, et al. Neuropharmacology of alcohol addiction. *Br J Pharmacol* 2008;154:299–315.

2. Griffiths RR, Wolf B. Relative abuse liability of different benzodiazepines in drug abusers. *J Clin Psychopharmacol* 1990;10:237–243.

3. Minozzi S, Amato L, Vecchi S, Davoli M. Anticonvulsants for alcohol withdrawal. *Cochrane Database Syst Rev* 2010;(3):CD005064.

4. Malcolm R, Myrick H, Roberts J, et al. The effects of carbamazepine and lorazepam on single versus multiple previous alcohol withdrawals in an outpatient randomized trial. *J Gen Intern Med* 2002;17(5):349–355.

5. Myrick H, Malcolm R, Randall PK, et al. A double-blind trial of gabapentin versus lorazepam in the treatment of alcohol withdrawal. *Alcohol Clin Exp Res* 2009;33(9):1582–1588.

6. Krampe H, Ehrenreich H. Supervised disulfiram as adjunct to psychotherapy in alcoholism treatment. *Curr Pharm Des* 2010;16(19):2076–2090.

7. Srisurapanont M, Jarusuraisin N. Naltrexone for the treatment of alcoholism: a meta-analysis of randomized controlled trials. *Int J Neuropsychopharmacol* 2005;8(2):267–280.

8. O'Malley SS, Rounsaville BJ, Farren C, et al. Initial and maintenance naltrexone for alcohol dependence using primary care vs. specialty care: a nested sequence of three randomized studies. *Arch Internal Med* 2003;163:1695–1704.

9. Anton RF, O'Malley SS, Ciraulo DA, et al. Combined pharmacotherapies and behavioral interventions for alcohol dependence: the COMBINE study: a randomized controlled trial. *JAMA* 2006;295(17):2003–2017.

10. Garbutt JC, Kranzler HR, O'Malley SS, et al. Efficacy and tolerability of long-acting injectable naltrexone for alcohol dependence: a randomized controlled trial. *JAMA* 2005;293(13):1617–1625.

11. O'Malley SS, Garbutt JC, Gastfriend DR, et al. Efficacy of extended-release naltrexone in alcohol-dependent patients who are abstinent before treatment. *J Clin Psychopharmacol* 2007;27(5):507–512.

12. Littleton J, Zieglgänsberger W. Pharmacological mechanisms of naltrexone and acamprosate in the prevention of relapse in alcohol dependence. *Am J Addict* 2003;12(suppl 1):S3–S11.

13. Bouza C, Angeles M, Muñoz A, et al. Efficacy and safety of naltrexone and acamprosate in the treatment of alcohol dependence: a systematic review. *Addiction* 2004;99(7):811–828.

14. Mason BJ, Goodman AM, Chabac S, et al. Effect of oral acamprosate on abstinence in patients with alcohol dependence in a double-blind, placebo-controlled trial: the role of patient motivation. *J Psychiatr Res* 2006; 40(5):383–393.

15. Johnson BA, Rosenthal N, Capece JA, et al. Topiramate for treating alcohol dependence: a randomized controlled trial. *JAMA* 2007;298(14):1641–1651.

16. Pettinati HM, Oslin DW, Kampman KM, et al. A double-blind, placebo-controlled trial combining sertraline and naltrexone for treating co-occurring depression and alcohol dependence. *Am J Psychiatry* 2010;167(6):668–675.

17. Kosten TR, O'Connor PG. Management of drug and alcohol withdrawal. *N Engl J Med* 2003;1786–1795.

18. Mattick RP, Kimber J, Breen C, Davoli M. Buprenorphine maintenance versus placebo or methadone maintenance for opioid dependence. *Cochrane Database Syst Rev* 2008;(2):CD002207.

19. Des Jarlais DC, Joseph H, Dole VP. Long-term outcomes after termination from methadone maintenance treatment. *Ann NY Acad Sci* 1981;362:231–238.

20. Johnson RE, Jones HE, Fischer G. Use of buprenorphine in pregnancy: patient management and effects on the neonate. *Drug Alcohol Depend* 2003; 70(2 suppl):S87–S101.

21. Heidbreder C. Novel pharmacotherapeutic targets for the management of drug addiction. *Eur J Pharmacol* 2005;526(1–3):101–112.

22. Washton AM, Pottash AC, Gold MS. Naltrexone in addicted business executives and physicians. *J Clin Psychiatry* 1984;45(9 pt 2):39–41.

23. Fiore MC, Jaen CR, Baker TB, et al. *Treating Tobacco Use and Dependence: 2008 Update. Clinical Practice Guideline.* Rockville, MD: US Department of Health and Human Services, 2008.

24. Piper ME, Smith SS, Schlam TR, et al. A randomized placebo-controlled clinical trial of 5 smoking cessation pharmacotherapies. *Arch Gen Psychiatry* 2009;66(11):1253–1262.

25. Silagy C, Lancaster T, Stead L, et al. Nicotine replacement therapy for smoking cessation. *Cochrane Database Syst Rev* 2004;(3):CD000146.

26. Gonzales D, Rennard SI, Nides M, et al. Varenicline, an alpha4beta2 nicotinic acetylcholine receptor partial agonist, vs. sustained-release bupropion and placebo for smoking cessation: a randomized controlled trial. *JAMA* 2006;296(1):47–55.

27. Coleman T, Agboola S, Leonardi-Bee J, et al. Relapse prevention in UK Stop Smoking Services: current practice, systematic reviews of effectiveness and cost-effectiveness analysis. *Health Technol Assess* 2010;14(49):1–152, iii–iv.

28. Ascher JA, Cole JO, Colin JN, et al. Bupropion: a review of its mechanism of antidepressant activity. *J Clin Psychiatry* 1995;56(9):395–401.

29. Jorenby DE, Leischow SJ, Nides MA, et al. A controlled trial of sustained-release bupropion, a nicotine
patch, or both for smoking cessation. *N Engl J Med*
1999;340(9):685–691.

30. Orson FM, Kinsey BM, Singh RA, et al. Substance
abuse vaccines. *Ann NY Acad Sci* 2008;1141:257–269.

31. Penberthy JK, Ait-Daoud N, Vaughan M, et al.
Review of treatment for cocaine dependence. *Curr
Drug Abuse Rev* 2010;3(1):49–62.

32. Carroll KM, Fenton LR, Ball SA, et al. Efficacy
of disulfiram and cognitive behavior therapy in
cocaine-dependent outpatients: a randomized placebo-controlled trial. *Arch Gen Psychiatry* 2004;
61(3):264–272.

33. Ferraro L, Antonelli T, O'Connor WT, et al. Modafinil:
an antinarcoleptic drug with a different neurochemical
profile to d-amphetamine and dopamine uptake blockers. *Biol Psychiatry* 1997;42:1181–1183.

34. Dackis CA, Kampman KM, Lynch KG, et al.
A double-blind, placebo-controlled trial of modafinil
for cocaine dependence. *Neuropsychopharmacol* 2005;
30(1):205–211.

35. Johnson BA, Roache JD, Ait-Daoud N, et al. A preliminary randomized, double-blind, placebo-controlled
study of the safety and efficacy of ondansetron in
the treatment of cocaine dependence. *Drug Alcohol
Depend* 2006;84(3):256–263.

36. Mardikian PN, LaRowe SD, Hedden S, et al. An
open-label trial of N-acetylcysteine for the treatment
of cocaine dependence: a pilot study. *Prog Neuropsychopharmacol Biol Psychiatry* 2007;31(2): 389–394.

37. Martell BA, Mitchell E, Poling J, et al. Vaccine pharmacotherapy for the treatment of cocaine dependence. *Biol Psychiatry* 2005;58(2):158–164.

38. Elkashef A, Vocci F, Huestis M, et al. Marijuana neurobiology and treatment. *Subst Abus* 2008;29(3):17–29.

46

Pharmacotherapy for Obesity

Current and Future Treatments

ORLI ROSEN AND LOUIS J. ARONNE

Weight loss with a low-calorie diet, exercise, and behavior modification is often difficult for patients to achieve because as food intake is limited, the body's complex counterregulatory mechanisms cause an increase in appetite and a reduction in energy expenditure.[1] Pharmacological agents can be effective adjunctive treatment options to help patients in their battle against obesity and associated comorbidities.

The National Heart, Lung, and Blood Institute (NHLBI) of the National Institutes of Health (NIH) recommends the use of pharmacotherapy in conjunction with a diet and exercise program if lifestyle changes alone do not promote weight loss after 6 months for patients with a body mass index (BMI) of 30 kg/m² or with a BMI of 27 kg/m² if comorbidities are present. Once pharmacotherapy is initiated, if a patient does not lose 2 kg after 4 weeks of treatment, the dosage should be adjusted or the drug should be discontinued, as it is unlikely that the patient will benefit from continued treatment. If weight is lost within the first 6 months of treatment, or if weight is maintained after initial weight loss, then treatment may continue. The NHLBI further recommends that patients return for follow-up visits initially every 2 to 4 weeks, then monthly for 3 months, and then every 3 months during the first year of drug therapy to monitor weight, vital signs, and side effects as part of a long-term treatment strategy that is similar to the treatment of hypertension or type 2 diabetes.[2]

The current pharmacologic options for treating obesity are limited, as it has only been in the last 10 to 15 years that our understanding of weight-regulating mechanisms has improved to the point that drugs to target certain mechanisms have been developed. At present only one drug is approved for use by the US Food and Drug Administration (FDA) for the long-term management of obesity: orlistat, which was approved in 1999. Sibutramine, approved by the FDA in 1997, was withdrawn from the market in 2010. Phentermine, a sympathomimetic amine, was given FDA approval in 1959, but due to a lack of long-term data, it is only approved for the short-term treatment of obesity. However, in many cases, obesity specialists have used it in the long term.

Other medications such as metformin, exenatide, pramlintide, bupropion, topiramate, and zonisamide, which are currently FDA approved for indications other than obesity, have shown efficacy as weight loss agents and have been prescribed "off label" for that purpose. Combinations of these medications are currently in development.

SIBUTRAMINE

Sibutramine (Meridia; Abbott Laboratories, Abbott Park, IL) is a combined norepinephrine and serotonin reuptake inhibitor that reduces body weight by decreasing appetite, increasing satiety, and reducing food intake[1] while raising energy expenditure by 3% to 5%.[3] Sibutramine was withdrawn from the market in 2010 based on research showing increased risk for cardiovascular events such as heart attack and stroke. We discuss it here, as it is illustrative of the advantages and limitations of pharmacotherapy for obesity and provides evidence for a medication with particular mechanisms of action.

The starting dose is 10 mg/day, but if intolerable side effects occur, the dosage may be reduced to 5 mg/day. If the patient does not respond to the

10-mg dose, then the dosage may be increased to 15 mg/day. A meta-analysis of five sibutramine trials reported a pooled mean difference in weight loss of 4.45 kg (95% confidence interval [CI], 3.62 to 5.29 kg) at 12 months, relative to placebo.[4] Patients in the sibutramine group were 20% to 30% more likely to lose 5% of their body weight than patients in the placebo group.

Sibutramine not only promotes weight loss but also prevents weight regain. The Sibutramine Trial of Obesity Reduction and Maintenance (STORM) study involved an initial 6-month acute weight loss period of sibutramine treatment plus an individualized 600-kcal deficit diet per day, followed by randomization of patients to either sibutramine or placebo for the remaining 18 months of the trial. Of the sibutramine-treated patients who completed the trial, 43% maintained 80% of their initial weight loss compared to only 16% of patients in the placebo group (odds ratio, 4.64; $p < .001$).[5]

The STORM study also demonstrated that sibutramine improves some components of metabolic syndrome such as waist circumference and helped maintain reductions in triglycerides, very low-density lipoprotein cholesterol, and insulin achieved in the initial 6-month weight loss period. High-density lipoprotein cholesterol was also increased 20.7% in the sibutramine group versus 11.7% in the placebo group. Following randomization, patients in the placebo group had immediate weight regain, suggesting that sibutramine therapy should be utilized as part of a long-term obesity treatment strategy to be most effective.[5]

A 1-year randomized trial conducted in the primary care setting demonstrated that sibutramine treatment combined with intensive lifestyle counseling appears to have an additive weight loss effect. Obese adults ($n = 224$) were randomized to receive either sibutramine (15 mg/day) alone, delivered in eight visits of 10 minutes each; intensive lifestyle modification counseling alone (30 group sessions); sibutramine plus intensive lifestyle modification counseling (30 group sessions); or sibutramine plus brief lifestyle counseling, delivered in eight visits of 10 to 15 minutes duration. At 12 months, the patients who received sibutramine combined with intensive lifestyle counseling had a larger mean weight loss of 12.1 kg, as compared with the sibutramine alone, lifestyle modification alone, or sibutramine plus brief lifestyle counseling groups, which had smaller mean weight losses of 5.0, 6.7, and 7.5 kg, respectively. These results emphasize the importance of administering weight loss medication in combination with lifestyle changes in order to improve adherence, which results in more successful outcomes.[4]

The most commonly reported side effects of sibutramine treatment are dry mouth, insomnia, headaches, nervousness, nausea, and constipation.[1,3] Increases in blood pressure (2 to 4 mm Hg) and pulse rate (4 beats/min) can also occur.[1] Therefore, sibutramine should not be used in patients with uncontrolled hypertension or in patients with a history of arrhythmia or coronary artery disease. However, sibutramine is safe in obese patients with well-controlled hypertension[3] since it does not significantly increase blood pressure in patients taking angiotensin-converting enzyme (ACE) inhibitors, beta blockers, or calcium channel blockers. Conversely, the effects of sibutramine on weight loss will be inhibited by beta blockers and diuretic-based antihypertensive medications. Patients beginning sibutramine treatment should initially have their vital signs monitored on a monthly basis until weight stabilizes and then every 3 months thereafter.[6] The weight and cardiometabolic risk–reducing benefits of sibutramine treatment appear to outweigh the potentially harmful effects it may have on blood pressure and pulse rate.[5] Sibutramine has not been associated with valvular heart disease or pulmonary hypertension, as was the case with the serotonergic weight loss agents, fenfluramine and dexfenfluramine, which ultimately led to their withdrawal from the market in 1997.[6] Sibutramine is contraindicated with monoamine oxidase inhibitors or other serotonin reuptake inhibitors as their concomitant use may lead to an increased risk of serotonin syndrome, a potentially fatal condition caused by excess serotonergic activity in the central nervous system.[1,3] Recently, an outcome study of sibutramine, SCOUT, demonstrated a statistically significant increased risk of mortality in those subjects with both type 2 diabetes and cardiovascular disease who took sibutramine compared to placebo, leading the FDA to add contraindications for patients with a history of cardiovascular disease (coronary artery disease, stroke or transient ischemic attack, heart arrhythmias, congestive heart failure, uncontrolled hypertension). In Europe, the European Medicines Agency's action led to withdrawal of sibutramine from the market.

PHENTERMINE

Phentermine (Adipex-P; Gate Pharmaceuticals) was the first FDA-approved medication for weight loss and is the drug most commonly used today. Phentermine is a sympathomimetic amine of the B-phenethylamine family that promotes anorexia. There is only one longer term controlled trial of phentermine, which dates back to 1968. The study involved 64 patients, who were allocated to receive either placebo, 30 mg/day of phentermine, or 30 mg/day of phentermine alternating with placebo. At 36 weeks, the phentermine groups each lost approximately 13% of their initial body weight compared with the placebo group, which lost approximately 5%. A meta-analysis of nine randomized controlled trials of 2 to 24 weeks duration showed that patients treated with phentermine lost an average of 3.6 kg (95% CI, 0.6 to 6.0 kg) compared with the placebo-treated patients.[1]

Side effects of phentermine use include insomnia, palpitations, tachycardia, dry mouth, constipation, restlessness, euphoria, nervousness, increased pulse rate, and elevated blood pressure. Phentermine treatment is contraindicated in patients with hypertension, cardiovascular disease, or a history of drug abuse. Patients should also not take phentermine if they are taking monoamine oxidase inhibitors.[1] Due to a lack of long-term safety and efficacy studies, phentermine is only approved by the FDA for the short-term treatment of obesity of up to 12 weeks, and any treatment beyond 12 weeks is considered "off label,"[6] despite the drug's long history of chronic use.

ORLISTAT

Orlistat (Xenical: Hoffman-LaRoche, Nutley, NJ; Alli: GlaxoSmithKline, Research Triangle Park, NC) promotes weight loss by inhibiting pancreatic and gastrointestinal lipases.[1] Orlistat binds to lipases in the gut, which partially inhibits the hydrolysis of triglycerides into absorbable free fatty acids and monoacylglycerols. This leads to 30% of consumed dietary and caloric fat being excreted in bowel movements, ultimately reducing fat absorption. Orlistat is usually taken as 120-mg doses with meals or up to 1 hour after meals.[5] Alli, an over-the-counter version of orlistat, was granted FDA approval in February 2007. Alli is available as half the standard prescription dose, or 60 mg three times per day, which makes it slightly less effective but also results in diminished gastrointestinal side effects.[3]

A meta-analysis of 22 randomized controlled trials showed a mean weight change of 2.75 kg (95% CI, 3.31 to 2.20 kg) in orlistat-treated patients compared with placebo, assessed at 52 weeks.[4] In addition, patients treated with orlistat also have significant improvements in blood glucose, insulin, HbA1c, and low-density lipoprotein cholesterol levels as compared to placebo.[6] In the 4-year XENical in the Prevention of Diabetes in Obese Subjects Study (XENDOS), 3,305 obese patients with either normal (79%) or impaired (21%) glucose tolerance were randomized to receive lifestyle changes plus 120 mg t.i.d. orlistat, or lifestyle changes plus matching placebo. The cumulative incidence of diabetes was 9.0% and 6.2% for the placebo and orlistat-treated groups, respectively, producing a reduction in disease risk of 37.3% ($p= .0032$).[3]

Systemic side effects are very uncommon with orlistat therapy as it is minimally absorbed. However, orlistat treatment is associated with adverse effects, which are mostly gastrointestinal in nature, due to the mechanism of action of the drug. These side effects can lead to cessation of treatment, although they are sometimes part of a self-correcting mechanism whereby patients learn to reduce the amount of fat they ingest and are thus less likely to have unwanted side effects, ultimately leading to reduction in overall calorie consumption and side effects. Because orlistat limits the absorption of fat-soluble vitamins, patients should take a daily multivitamin 2 hours before or after a dose of orlistat to prevent serum vitamin levels from falling below the normal range. Orlistat may also disrupt the absorption of cyclosporine and amiodarone, and it may augment the effect of warfarin; therefore, discretion should be used when considering orlistat therapy for patients taking these drugs. Orlistat should also be avoided in patients with cholestasis or malabsorptive disorders.[3]

DIABETES MEDICATIONS THAT CAUSE WEIGHT LOSS
Metformin

Metformin (Glucophage; Bristol-Myers Squibb, New York, NY) is an antihyperglycemic agent that acts by suppressing hepatic glucose production.[6] Metformin can reduce body weight and improve other cardiometabolic risk factors, but it is not approved as a weight loss agent. Nonetheless, a meta-analysis of 31 randomized controlled trials of at least 8 weeks duration in persons at risk for diabetes found that metformin decreased BMI −5.3% (95% CI, −6.7 to −4.0), fasting glucose −4.5% (95% CI, −6.0 to −3.0), fasting insulin −14.4% (95% CI, −19.9 to −8.9), calculated insulin resistance −22.6% (95% CI, −27.3 to −18.0), triglycerides −5.3% (95% CI, −10.5 to −0.03), and low-density lipoprotein cholesterol −5.6% (95% CI, −8.3 to −3.0) and increased high-density lipoprotein cholesterol 5.0% (95% CI, 1.6 to 8.3), compared to placebo or no treatment. Importantly, the incidence of new-onset diabetes was decreased by 40% (odds ratio 0.6; 95% CI, 0.5 to 0.8), with an absolute risk reduction of 6% (95% CI, 4 to 8) during an average trial duration of 1.8 years.[7]

The most frequently reported adverse effects of metformin are nausea, abdominal discomfort, diarrhea, flatulence, and bloating.[7] Lactic acidosis is a rare (1/100,000) but serious side effect.[6]

Glucagon-Like Peptide-1 Analogs

Exenatide (Byetta; Amylin Pharmaceuticals, San Diego, CA and Eli Lilly and Company, Indianapolis, IN) and liraglutide (Victoza; Novo-Nordisk, Princeton, NJ) are injectable antidiabetic medications that act by mimicking the incretin hormone glucagon-like peptide-1 (GLP-1), thereby increasing insulin secretion and suppressing glucose-dependent glucagon release.[5] Exenatide is FDA approved for patients with type 2 diabetes who have failed to achieve adequate glycemic control on oral antidiabetic medications. Exenatide improves glycemic control, slows gastric emptying, decreases food intake, enhances satiety, and reduces body weight when used to treat type 2 diabetes.[3] In addition to significant improvements in HbA1c, exenatide-treated patients also exhibited dose-dependent weight losses of 2.8 kg in the 10 μg group and 1.6 kg in the 5 μg group.[5] Several long-term trials of exenatide have also shown improvements in lipid profile and blood pressure in patients taking exenatide.

The most common side effects of exenatide are nausea, diarrhea, and vomiting, but they are usually mild to moderate and rarely lead to discontinuation of treatment. Cases of hypoglycemia have been seen with exenatide treatment; however, it usually occurs when exenatide is coadministered with other agents that cause hypoglycemia, such as sulfonylureas, but not with metformin.[3] The hypoglycemic events reported with exenatide therapy are usually mild to moderate in severity.

MEDICATIONS CURRENTLY IN DEVELOPMENT
Qnexa

Qnexa (phentermine/topiramate, Vivus, Mountain View, CA) is an investigational weight loss medication, which combines low doses of phentermine and topiramate. Phentermine, a previously approved weight loss medication, is described earlier in this chapter. Topiramate is approved as an antiepilepsy agent and for migraine prophylaxis, but it has been observed to be effective as a weight loss agent. Combining the two drugs has produced greater efficacy with lower doses of each component thereby minimizing side effects. This combination medication is thought to address two main mechanisms that impact weight: appetite and satiety. Studies suggest that Qnexa induces significantly greater weight loss than either individual compound. Qnexa has been evaluated as a once daily pill in three different doses of phentermine and controlled release topiramate, respectively: 15/92 mg, 7.5/46 mg, and 3.75/23 mg. In an intention to treat analysis, the 1 year Phase 3 EQUIP trial, which randomized subjects with a mean BMI of 41 to placebo, low-dose Qnexa, or full-dose Qnexa, demonstrated a weight loss of 1.6%, 5.2%, and 11.08%, respectively (p < .0001) in the intent-to-treat analysis. Completers had a weight loss of 7.0% and 14.7% in the low- and full-dose Qnexa groups, respectively (p < .001).[8] The Phase 3 CONQUER trial randomized overweight and obese patients with hypertension, hypercholesterolemia, or type 2 diabetes to 53 weeks of treatment with either mid-dose or full-dose Qnexa versus placebo. Intent-to-treat analysis demonstrated a 10.4% (p < .0001) and 8.4% (p < .0001) mean weight loss in the full-dose arm and mid-dose arm, respectively, versus a 1.8% mean weight loss with placebo. Statistically significant reductions in systolic and diastolic blood pressure, lipid levels, glucose levels, and hemoglobin A1c levels compared to placebo were observed in the Qnexa-treated arm.[8]

The most commonly reported side effects of Qnexa were dry mouth, tingling, altered taste, insomnia, and constipation.[8]

Contrave

Contrave (bupropion SR/naltrexone SR, Orexigen, La Jolla, CA) is a fixed-dose, sustained-release, combination of bupropion and naltrexone. Bupropion, which is approved for depression and smoking cessation, is thought to increase dopamine activity at specific receptors in the brain, which may lead to a reduction in appetite. Naltrexone is approved for treatment of alcohol and opioid addiction, and works by blocking opioid receptors in the brain, thus inhibiting the reinforcing aspects of addictive substances. It has been observed in prior studies that it may negatively alter the taste of many foods. In a Phase 3 trial, intention to treat analysis, obese patients treated with Contrave (bupropion SR 360 mg/naltraxone SR 32 mg) achieved a 6.1% weight loss ($p < 0.001$) at both 28 weeks and 56 weeks of treatment, compared to a 1.3% weight loss with placebo. Forty-eight percent ($p < 0.001$) of patients treated with Contrave achieved a 5% or greater weight loss, compared to only 17.4% with placebo. Patients treated with a lower dose of Contrave, which contains lower dose naltrexone (16 mg) achieved a statistically significant weight loss of 5.0% at 56 weeks. A second Phase 3 trial, which evaluated obese patients with type 2 diabetes revealed a 5.0% ($p < 0.001$) weight loss in those treated with Contrave at 56 weeks, versus a 1.8% weight reduction with placebo. There was no significant change in blood pressure between the two groups.[9]

The most frequently observed adverse events were nausea, constipation and headache. Seven serious adverse events were reported, which included cholecyctitis, seizure, palpitations, paresthesia, and vertigo.[9]

Empatic

Empatic (zonisamide SR/bupropion SR, Orexigen, La Jolla, CA) is a combination, fixed dose of zonisamide, an antiepileptic therapy, and bupropion, described previously. Recent Phase 2 data demonstrated that patients who completed 24 weeks of treatment with Empatic (zonisamide SR 360 mg/bupropion SR 360 mg) lost 9.9% of their baseline

body weight compared to 1.7% in patients treated with placebo ($p < .001$). Patients treated with Empatic also demonstrated significantly greater weight loss than those treated with either of the components alone.[10]

The most commonly reported adverse events were headache, insomnia, and urticaria.[10]

Pramlintide

Pramlintide (Symlin; Amylin Pharmaceuticals, San Diego, CA) is an injectable antihyperglycemic agent that mimics the pancreatic hormone amylin and in conjunction with insulin regulates postprandial glucose control. Pramlintide was FDA approved in 2005 for the treatment of type 1 diabetes or type 2 diabetes and can be prescribed along with insulin or metformin,[3,5] but it is not currently approved as a weight loss agent. Pramlintide may promote weight loss by increasing satiety and reducing food intake.[11] A Phase 2, multicenter trial in 204 non-insulin-treated obese subjects with or without type 2 diabetes showed that pramlintide produced a placebo-corrected weight loss of 3.7 ± 0.5% ($p \leq .001$) and a reduction in waist circumference of 3.6 ± 1.1 cm ($p \leq 0.01$). Also, about 31% of patients treated with pramlintide achieved a 5% reduction in weight, compared with only 2% of the placebo-treated patients ($p \leq .001$).

The most frequently reported adverse effects of pramlintide were mild, transient nausea and injection-related adverse events. Mild hypoglycemic events, which resolved without medical intervention, were reported in 8% of the pramlintide-treated patients; however, there were no reports of moderate or severe hypoglycemia.[11]

Pramlintide/Metreleptin

Pramlintide/metreleptin (Amylin Pharmaceuticals, San Diego, CA) is a combination of pramlintide, a synthetic analog of the neurohormone amylin, which is known to play a key role in the regulation of appetite, food intake, and postprandial glucose concentration, and metreleptin, an analog of the neurohormone leptin, which plays a role in the regulation of energy homeostasis, fat and glucose metabolism, and body weight. A Phase 2 study revealed that overweight and obese patients treated with a combination of pramlintide and metreleptin had weight loss on average of 11% ($p < .01$) over 24 weeks, which was significantly greater than placebo or either agent alone.[12]

The most common side effects were injection site adverse events and nausea.[12]

Lorcaserin

Lorcaserin (Arena Pharmaceuticals, San Diego, CA) is a novel single agent currently undergoing Phase 3 clinical trials. This drug targets the serotonin 5HT2C receptor, which is expressed in the brain, including the hypothalamus. Stimulation of this receptor is thought to be associated with feeding behavior and satiety. Patients treated with lorcaserin 10 mg twice daily achieved statistically significant mean weight loss of 5.8%–5.9% ($p < .0001$) based on intention to treat analysis in the BLOOM and BLOSSOM Phase 3 trials. Weight loss after 52 weeks of treatment with placebo ranged from 2.2% to 2.8%. In the BLOOM trial, 47.5% of patients treated with lorcaserin lost greater than or equal to 5% of their body weight from baseline compared to 20.3% in the placebo group. Treatment with lorcaserin demonstrated favorable trends compared to placebo when blood pressure and lipid levels were evaluated.[13]

Overall, lorcaserin was well tolerated. The most frequently reported adverse events were upper respiratory infection, nasopharyngitis, and headache. However, no adverse event rate in the lorcaserin-treated group exceeded the placebo group by more than 4%. Echocardiographic safety data revealed no risk of valvulopathy in either trial.[13]

Tesofensine

Tesofensine (NeuroSearch, Ballerup, Denmark) is a serotonin-noradrenaline-dopamine reuptake inhibitor, which is currently under investigation as a possible appetite suppressant. This drug was initially developed for the treatment of Parkinson's disease and Alzheimer's dementia, but it was shown to have limited effectiveness. However, studies demonstrated significant weight loss among patients treated with tesofensine. Phase 2 data have demonstrated an average weight loss of 6.5%, 11.2%, and 12.6% among patient treated with 0.25 mg, 0.5 mg, and 1.0 mg of tesofensine, respectively, for 24 months ($p < .0001$). Patients treated with placebo lost an average of 2% of their body weight.[14]

The most common adverse events experienced by patients in this trial and in an extension trial in which patients in the initial trial were continued on 0.5 mg of tesofensine for another 24 weeks, were dry mouth, insomnia, constipation, headache, diarrhea, disturbed sleep, fatigue, and nausea.[15] Tesofensine is a promising drug as current trials show that it produces a weight loss twice that of currently approved antiobesity drugs. At this time, plans are under way for Phase 3 trials.

REFERENCES

1. Korner J, Aronne LJ. Pharmacological approaches to weight reduction: therapeutic targets. *J Clin Endocrinol Metab* 2004;89(6):2616–2621.
2. National Heart, Lung and Blood Institute Obesity Education Initiative. The practical guide: identification, evaluation, and treatment of overweight and obesity in adults. 2000. Available at: http://www.nhlbi.nih.gov/guidelines/obesity. Accessed May 10, 2008.
3. Neff LM, Aronne LJ. Pharmacotherapy for obesity. *Curr Atheroscler Rep* 2007;9(6):454–462.
4. Aronne LJ, Brown WV, Isoldi KK. Cardiovascular disease in obesity: a review of related risk factors and risk-reduction strategies. *J Clin Lipidol* 2007;1(6):575–582.
5. Aronne, LJ. Therapeutic options for modifying cardiometabolic risk factors. *Am J Med* 2007;120(3):S26–S34.
6. Aronne LJ, Waitman J, Isoldi KK. The pharmacotherapy of obesity. 2008. Available at: http://www.endotext.org/obesity/obesity15b/obesity15b.htm. Accessed March 21, 2012.
7. Salpeter SR, Buckley NS, Kahn JA, Salpeter EE. Meta-analysis: metformin treatment in persons at risk for diabetes mellitus. *Am J Med* 2008;121(2):149–57.e2.
8. Vivus, Inc. VIVUS announces positive results from two phase 3 studies; obese patients on Qnexa achieve average weight loss up to 14.7% and significant improvements in co-morbidities. 2009. Available at: http://ir.vivus.com/releasedetail.cfm?ReleaseID=407933. Accessed October 10, 2009.
9. Orexigen Therapeutics, Inc. Contrave(R) obesity research phase 3 program meets co-primary and key secondary endpoints; exceeds FDA efficacy benchmark for obesity treatments. 2009. Available at: http://ir.orexigen.com/phoenix.zhtml?c=207034&p=irol-newsArticle&ID=1308920&highlight=. Accessed October 22, 2009.
10. Orexigen Therapeutics, Inc. Orexigen(R) Therapeutics phase 2b trial for Empatic(TM) meets primary efficacy endpoint demonstrating significantly greater weight loss versus comparators in obese patients. 2009. Available at: http://ir.orexigen.com/phoenix.zhtml?c=207034&p=irol-newsArticle&ID=1336796&highlight=. Accessed October 22, 2009.
11. Aronne LJ, Fujioka K, Aroda V, et al. Progressive reduction in body weight after treatment with the amylin analog pramlintide in obese subjects: a phase 2,

randomized, placebo-controlled, dose-escalation study. *J Clin Endocrinol Metab* 2000;92(8):2977–2983.

12. Ravussin E, Smith SR, Mitchell JA, et al. Enhanced weight loss with pramlintide/metreleptin: an integrated neurohormonal approach to obesity pharmacotherapy. *Obesity* 2009;7(9):1736–1743.

13. Arena Pharmaceuticals. Arena Pharmaceuticals reports positive, highly significant BLOSSOM trial results for weight management; NDA submission on track for December. 2009. Available at: http://

invest.arenapharm.com/releasedetail.cfm? ReleaseID=410040. Accessed October 22, 2009.

14. Tesofensine. Ballerup, Denmark: NeuroSearch, 2009. Available at: http://neurosearch.com/Default. aspx?ID=8265. Accessed April 10, 2012.

15. Astrup A, Madsbad S, Breum L, Jensen TJ, Kroustrup JP, Larsen TM. Effect of tesofensine on bodyweight loss, body composition, and quality of life in obese patients: a randomized, double-blind, placebo-controlled trial. *Lancet* 2008;372(9653):1906–1913.

47

Surgical Treatments for Obesity

MARION L. VETTER, LUCY F. FAULCONBRIDGE,
NOEL N. WILLIAMS, AND THOMAS A. WADDEN

INTRODUCTION

The twin epidemics of obesity and diabetes threaten the health and well-being of millions of Americans. As these conditions rise in tandem, bariatric surgery has become an increasingly popular treatment option. In the United States alone, over 220,000 bariatric surgery procedures were performed in 2008.[1] At present, bariatric surgery is the only therapy that produces mean long-term weight losses of 15% or more of initial weight.[2]

Current guidelines from the National Institutes of Health (NIH) recommend bariatric surgery as a treatment option for individuals with a body mass index (BMI) $\geq$ 40 kg/m^2, or $\geq$ 35 kg/m^2 in the presence of comorbidities, including type 2 diabetes, hypertension, and sleep apnea.[3] Nonsurgical interventions should be implemented first, with surgery reserved for individuals who fail to achieve clinically significant weight loss. Some investigators have suggested that surgery be extended to appropriate patients with a BMI as low as 30 kg/m^2.[4–6] However, there are not sufficient safety and efficacy data at this time to support such practice.

TYPES OF BARIATRIC PROCEDURES

Bariatric surgery was initially classified as a restrictive or malabsorptive procedure (or the combination of the two), based on its purported mechanism of inducing weight loss.[7] Recent evidence suggests that the mechanisms are less clear than were originally thought and likely involve multiple pathways. Restrictive procedures reduce the volume of the stomach dramatically to limit food intake, while leaving the gastrointestinal tract intact. Malabsorptive procedures shorten the small intestine to decrease nutrient absorption, while combined operations incorporate elements of both types of procedures (see Fig. 47.1).

Restrictive Procedures

Laparoscopic Adjustable Gastric Banding

The laparoscopic adjustable silicone gastric band (LAGB) has become increasingly popular since it was approved in 2001 by the Food and Drug Administration and is now the most commonly performed restrictive procedure worldwide.[8] An inflatable silicone band is placed around the fundus of the stomach to create a 30 cc proximal pouch and a large distal remnant. The diameter of the band can be adjusted by adding or removing saline from a subcutaneous port. Gastrointestinal anatomy remains intact, and gastric emptying is not affected.[9] Complications include band erosions or slippage, esophageal dilations, port problems, wound infection, and gastric reflux.[2] Approximately 22% of patients who undergo gastric banding will require a revision or a repeat surgery.[2]

Vertical Sleeve Gastrectomy

Vertical sleeve gastrectomy (VSG) is a relatively new restrictive procedure in which approximately 75% of the stomach is removed, including virtually all of the gastric fundus.[2] This procedure was originally developed as the first stage of a two-part procedure, which is followed later by conversion to either a gastric bypass or duodenal switch. However, increasing evidence suggests that VSG induces weight loss comparable to other bariatric surgeries (including gastric bypass), and VSG is now being performed alone.[10–13] Although the pyloric valve is left intact, the rate of gastric emptying is accelerated.[14,15] Complications include postsurgical leakage and vomiting due to overeating. As the procedure carries a lower risk than Roux-en-Y gastric bypass and biliopancreatic diversion (described later), VSG may be most appropriate for high-risk

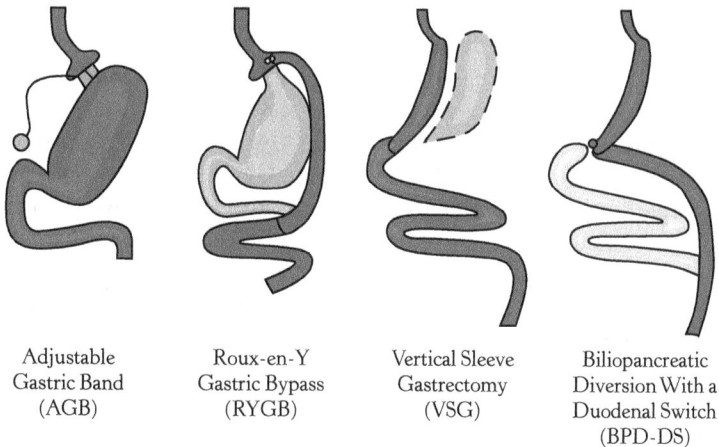

| Adjustable Gastric Band (AGB) | Roux-en-Y Gastric Bypass (RYGB) | Vertical Sleeve Gastrectomy (VSG) | Biliopancreatic Diversion With a Duodenal Switch (BPD-DS) |

FIGURE 47.1. Bariatric and metabolic surgical operations.
Image credit: Walter Pories, MD, FACS. *Source:* NIDDK, 2010.

patients, including those with multiple comorbidities or a BMI > 60 kg/m² (i.e., super obesity).

Malabsorptive Procedures
Biliopancreatic Diversion with Duodenal Switch

Biliopancreatic diversion (BPD) involves a partial gastrectomy to create a 150–200 cc gastric sleeve, which is anastomosed to the distal 250 cm of small intestine. The excluded portion of the small intestine that serves as the conduit for bile and pancreatic juices is attached 100 cm proximal to the ileocecal valve. In the duodenal switch variation (BPD-DS), the antrum of the stomach, the pylorus, and a short portion of the duodenum are left intact, and vagal nerve activity is preserved to decrease the risk of dumping syndrome.[16] This condition occurs when undigested nutrients are rapidly delivered to the small bowel, causing nausea, bloating, cramping, diarrhea, and vomiting.[2] Despite the impressive amount of weight loss, BPDS is associated with a significant number of complications, including leaks and ulceration at the site of anastomosis, chronic loose stools, protein malnutrition, vitamin deficiencies, and anemia.[2] BPDS accounts for only 5% of bariatric procedures performed in the United States and is usually reserved for patients with BMIs greater than 50 kg/m².[16]

Combined Procedures
Roux-en-Y Gastric Bypass

The Roux-en-Y gastric bypass (RYGB) remains the most common bariatric procedure performed worldwide and is considered the gold standard treatment for extreme obesity.[16–18] The stomach is divided to create a gastric pouch roughly 30 cc in volume, and the distal jejunum is anastomosed to the pouch. The proximal jejunum is reattached 75–150 cm below the gastro-jejunal anastomosis, resulting in bypass of 95% of the stomach, the entire duodenum, and most of the jejunum.[16] Although malabsorption may occur transiently after surgery, the remaining small bowel undergoes villous hypertrophy to compensate for the shortened segment, such that clinically significant malabsorption does not usually occur.[6] More than half of RYGB are now performed laparoscopically.[18] Complications of RYGB include leaks at the site of anastomosis, acute gastric dilatation, ulceration, wound hernias, vomiting, and the dumping syndrome.[2]

Weight Loss with Various Procedures

Comparison of bariatric data has been difficult due to the lack of standardization in reporting weight loss.[2,17–19] In the surgical literature, weight loss is typically expressed as percentage of excess weight lost (EWL), in which excess weight is defined as total preoperative weight minus ideal weight. The percentage of EWL is defined as [(weight loss/excess weight) × 100].[20] Percentage change in total weight and percentage change in BMI have also been reported.[7–20] In the largest meta-analysis to date, Buchwald and colleagues[21] evaluated the effect of bariatric surgery on weight loss and obesity-related comorbidities in 135,246 patients. An overall EWL of 55.9% was reported for all procedures, while individual rates associated with each procedure varied. On average, bariatric surgery has been found to result in a 10–15 kg/m^2 reduction in BMI and a weight loss of 30–50 kg.[18,20] Two randomized controlled trials reported greater weight loss with RYGB than LAGB.[22,23] A recent trial that included 250 participants randomly assigned to RYGB or LAGB reported a mean percent EWL of 68.4% and 45.4%, respectively, at 4 years after surgery.[23] These results were confirmed in an earlier, smaller randomized trial that provided 5 years of follow-up; mean EWL at that time was 66.6% in participants who underwent RYGB, compared to 47.5% in those who underwent LAGB.[22] Comparable weight loss was reported at 3 months in one small, randomized trial that compared VSG and RYGB.[12] A second randomized trial reported greater percent EWL with VSG compared to RYGB at 12 months (69.7% vs. 60.5%, respectively; $p = .05$).[13]

Maximal weight loss is typically achieved by 12 to 18 months after the procedure.[17] However, recent evidence suggests that some patients regain a significant amount of weight several years after surgery, as observed in the Swedish Obese Subjects (SOS) Study, a prospective cohort study that

included 4,047 obese participants who underwent a variety of bariatric surgery procedures or nonsurgical, conventional weight management. Figure 47.2 shows that mean total weight loss decreased from 32% at 1 year to 25% at 10 years in the RYGB group, from 25% to 18% in patients who received gastroplasty (a restrictive procedure that is rarely performed anymore) group, and from 20% to 13% at 10 years in the gastric banding group.[24] Despite this weight regain, all three procedures were associated with far greater weight loss at 10 years than was conventional intervention.

Improvement in Comorbidities and Mortality

Patients who undergo bariatric surgery frequently experience remission or significant improvements in several comorbid conditions. In a recent meta-analysis that included 3,188 participants with type 2 diabetes, 78.1% achieved remission (defined as the ability to maintain normglycemia after all diabetes medications were discontinued), and another 8.5% were improved.[21] Comparable rates

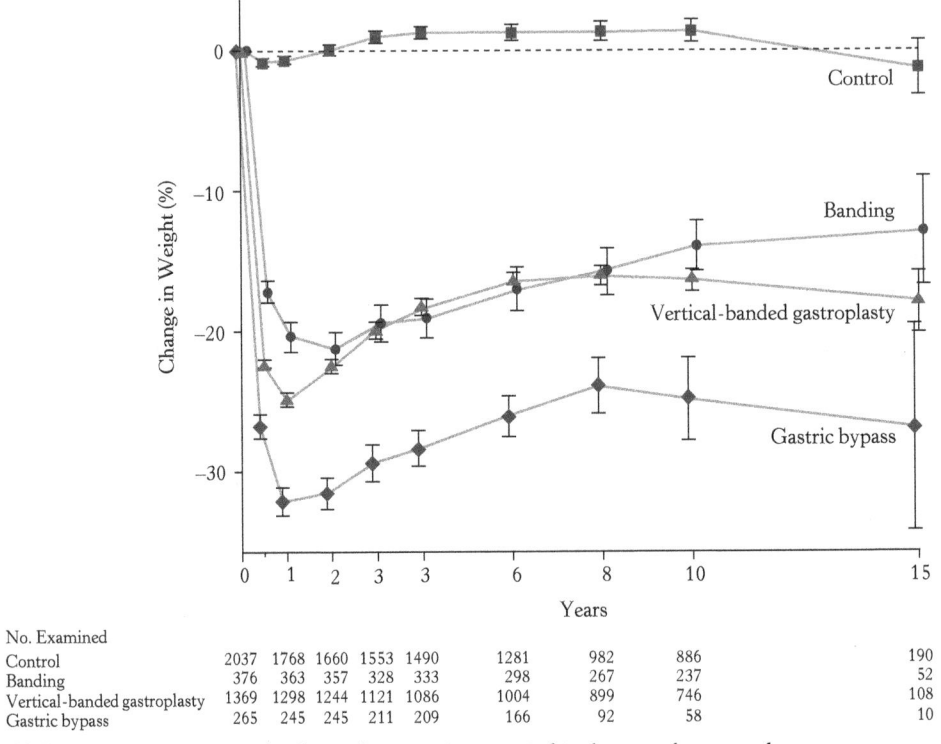

No. Examined									
Control	2037	1768	1660	1553	1490	1281	982	886	190
Banding	376	363	357	328	333	298	267	237	52
Vertical-banded gastroplasty	1369	1298	1244	1121	1086	1004	899	746	108
Gastric bypass	265	245	245	211	209	166	92	58	10

FIGURE 47.2. Mean percent weight change during a 15-year period in the control group and surgery group, according to the method of bariatric surgery. Bars indicate 95% confidence intervals.

Source: Reprinted with permission from The New England Journal of Medicine, Vol. 10.1056, Sjöström et al, Lifestyle, Diabetes, and Cardiovascular Risk Factors 10 Years after Bariatric Surgery, Copyright (2004), NJM.

of remission and improvement were reported in an earlier meta-analysis (by the same authors) that included data from 22,094 patients.[20] In the latter report, hypertension was found to resolve in 61.7% of patients, hyperlipidemia improved in 70%, and obstructive sleep apnea resolved in 85.7%, examining across procedures. Individual rates of remission are reported for each procedure in Table 47.1.

The SOS study observed a significant reduction in overall mortality among participants who underwent bariatric surgery, as compared with matched obese controls in the conventional treatment group.[25] The unadjusted hazard ratio was 0.76 ($p = .04$). The observed reduction in the rate of death remained significant after adjustment for sex, age, and risk factors ($p = .01$). A reduction in mortality was also reported in a recent retrospective cohort study that included 9,949 patients who had undergone gastric bypass surgery, compared to a control group that did not undergo surgery.[26] The adjusted long-term mortality from any cause decreased by 40% in the surgery group, as compared to the control group (37.6 vs. 57.1 deaths per 10,000 person-years; $p < .001$). Cause-specific mortality in the surgery group decreased by 56% for coronary artery disease, by 92% for diabetes, and by 60% for cancer.

Safety and Complications

Perioperative and postoperative complications are generally low after bariatric surgery procedures, although procedures performed using a traditional incision (i.e., open) carry a higher risk than laparoscopically performed procedures.[27] A recent prospective observational study that included 4,776 patients who underwent bariatric surgery at 10 clinical sites across the United States reported a 30-day death rate of 0.3%.[27] At least one complication occurred in 4.3% of patients within 30 days of surgery. Common early complications typically include deep venous thrombosis, venous thromboembolism, infection, and anastomotic leaks.[28] Late complications include incisional hernias, gallstones, failure to lose weight, and the dumping syndrome (which is specific to RYGB). Vitamin and mineral deficiencies can also occur if individuals are not compliant with supplements after surgery, with deficiencies of B_{12} and iron occurring most frequently.[28] The overall mortality rates for each procedure are provided in Table 47.1. We note that the low rates of complication, reported earlier, were observed in patients who were treated by highly skilled surgeons who typically performed 100 or more bariatric surgeries per year. Higher complication rates can be expected with surgeons who do not have as much experience with the procedures.

Limitations in the Quality of Evidence

Few high-quality randomized controlled trials have been performed to evaluate the safety and efficacy of bariatric surgery.[2] The majority of studies consist of uncontrolled case series and low-quality cohort studies, which are limited by incomplete reporting of data.[2,17–18] In the meta-analysis by Maggard[18] a quarter of these studies did not report whether consecutive patients were studied, and less than 50% reported on the percentage of original patients included in follow-up data. In light of the limited evidence and the generally poor quality of trials, caution is advised when evaluating the

TABLE 47.1 IMPROVEMENT IN COMORBIDITIES AND MORTALITY ASSOCIATED WITH VARIOUS BARIATRIC PROCEDURES

	Restrictive (LAGB)	Malabsorptive (BPD)	Combined (RYGB)
Excess weight loss (%)	48	70	62
Resolution of comorbid conditions (%)			
Type 2 diabetes	48	98	84
Hypertension	38	81	75
Hyperlipidemia (improved)	71	100	94
Sleep apnea	95	95	87
Operative mortality rate (%)	0.1	1.1	0.5

*Mean values from a meta-analysis of 22,094 patients. Data from ref. 20.
BPD, biliopancreatic diversion; LAGB, laparoscopic adjustable gastric banding; RYGB, Roux-en-Y gastric bypass; VBG, vertical banded gastroplasty.

comparative safety and effectiveness of bariatric surgery procedures.

ENTEROENDOCRINE FACTORS AND THE REGULATION OF BODY WEIGHT: EFFECT OF BARIATRIC SURGERY

LAGB and RYGB result in distinctly different effects on the secretion of orexigenic (i.e., appetite-inducing) and anorexigenic (i.e., appetite-reducing) gut peptides that interact with appetitive centers in the brain to control energy homeostasis.[6] These neuroendocrine factors are secreted by the gut mucosa in response to ingestion of nutrients, neural signals, and the nutrient status of the body. They include the satiety factors, glucagon-like peptide-1 (GLP-1) and peptide YY (PYY), as well as the orexigenic hormone, ghrelin. Many of these peptides also influence glycemic control by modulating insulin secretion. Several peptides that regulate satiety and appetite are thought to be blunted in obese individuals and may be improved following surgery.[29]

Because LAGB leaves the gastrointestinal tract intact and does not significantly alter the rate of gastric emptying, changes in gut hormones occur in response to weight loss only, and they are less pronounced than changes following malabsorptive or combined procedures. RYGB excludes the proximal gut and expedites nutrient delivery to the distal ileum, resulting in altered secretion of the enteroendocrine factors described later.[13] Similar changes in the secretion of gut peptides are observed after BPDS.[30] As VSG is a relatively new procedure, few studies have examined its effects on the secretion of gut peptides. Emerging evidence in both animal models and humans suggests that VSG induces changes comparable to RYGB in the secretion of gut peptides, despite its being primarily a restrictive procedure.[12,13,31] Changes in the secretion of gut peptides associated with the individual procedures are shown in Table 47.2.

Ghrelin

Ghrelin, secreted primarily by the gastric fundus and proximal small intestine, acts in several feeding-regulatory areas of the brain to increase appetite.[32] It is the only known orexigenic hormone produced in the periphery and is associated with the anticipatory response to food ingestion.[33] Systemic levels of ghrelin rise before a meal and fall after food ingestion. Weight loss by any means increases ghrelin levels, suggesting that ghrelin is a key mediator of the long-term regulation of body weight.[34] Paradoxically, circulating ghrelin levels are decreased in obese individuals.[35]

Suppression of ghrelin has been postulated as a potential mechanism for the generalized loss of hunger that is associated with RYGB, as observed by Cummings and other investigators.[36-38] However, other investigators have reported no change[39] or minimal changes in ghrelin,[40] despite substantial weight loss. Different surgical techniques may account for the inconsistent findings in ghrelin after gastric bypass.[34] As ghrelin secretion may be mediated in part via the vagus nerve, circulating levels may be affected by the integrity of the nerve after surgery and the amount of intact residual ghrelin-producing tissue in the fundus.

In contrast to procedures that bypass segments of the intestine, ghrelin levels increase after weight loss with restrictive procedures that leave the fundus and the vagal nerve intact.[41] The elevated ghrelin

TABLE 47.2 OVERVIEW OF ALTERED SECRETION OF GUT PEPTIDES IN RESPONSE TO DIFFERENT BARIATRIC PROCEDURES

Hormone	Type of Bariatric Surgery			
	LAGB	**BPD**	**RYGB**	**VSG**
Ghrelin	Increases	Decreases	Decreases	Decreases
Glucagon-like peptide-1	No change	Increases	Increases	Increases
Peptide YY	No change	Increases	Increases	Increases

BPD, biliopancreatic diversion; LAGB, laparoscopic adjustable gastric band; VSG, vertical sleeve gastrectomy; RYGB, Roux-en-Y gastric bypass.

levels observed following restrictive procedures may explain the smaller weight losses associated with LAGB compared with RYGB and BPD. Because most of the fundus is removed in VSG, ghrelin levels are suppressed following this procedure.[12,13]

Glucagon-Like Peptide-1

Glucagon-like peptide-1 (GLP-1), a potent satiety signal and insulin secretagogue, is secreted by the L-cells of the distal ileum in response to ingested nutrients and neural signals arising from the proximal gut.[42] Circulating levels rise in the short term upon eating and decline over the course of the meal. Known as the "ileal brake," GLP-1 inhibits gastrointestinal motility, decreases gastrointestinal secretions, and slows gastric emptying to regulate the transit of nutrients through the gut. GLP-1 also binds to receptors in the brainstem, hypothalamus, and periphery to induce satiety. Multiple studies have demonstrated that peripheral infusion of GLP-1 significantly enhances satiety and reduces food intake in both normal weight and obese individuals.[43] Basal levels of GLP-1 are decreased in obesity, and the postprandial response is blunted.[43]

Multiple studies following RYGB and BPD have demonstrated a markedly enhanced GLP-1 response.[44–47] This increase appears to be independent of weight loss, as demonstrated by a study by Laferrère and colleagues that compared postprandial GLP-1 levels in subjects who had undergone RYGB to those of matched obese controls who had lost an equivalent amount of weight on a hypocaloric diet.[44] Supraphysiologic GLP-1 levels were seen in the post-RYGB patients, whereas a nonsignificant increase was observed in the controls. Moreover, GLP-1 levels remain persistently elevated after RYGB, with levels increased even a year after surgery.[45] Enhanced GLP-1 levels may promote weight loss after RYGB by several mechanisms. GLP-1 suppresses gastrointestinal motility and delays gastric emptying, which induces subsequent reductions in food intake.[48] Additionally, GLP-1 acts as a satiety factor and may play a role in early meal termination.

In contrast, LAGB does not alter GLP-1 levels, in part, because the rate of gastric emptying is not altered.[49] Kornet and colleagues showed that postprandial GLP-1 increased three-fold after RYGB but remained unchanged after gastric banding.[50] Significant increases in GLP-1 have been reported after VSG, which is consistent with increased nutrient delivery to the distal ileum as a consequence of accelerated gastric emptying.[12]

Peptide YY

Peptide YY (PYY) is a satiety signal that is co-secreted with GLP-1 from the L-cells of the distal ileum in response to nutrients. Peptide YY inhibits food intake and delays gastric emptying through interaction with neuropeptide Y-receptor subtypes in both the peripheral and central nervous system.[51] Intravenous administration of PYY_{3-36} (a cleaved molecule of PYY) increases satiety and decreases food intake in humans.[51] Like GLP-1, basal and postprandial levels of PYY levels are decreased in obese individuals.[52]

Procedures that expedite nutrient delivery to the distal ileum, such as RYGB, result in an exaggerated PYY response to nutrient ingestion. Korner and colleagues reported a 10-fold postprandial increase in PYY in post-RYGB participants, compared to a much smaller increase in lean and obese, nonsurgical controls.[50] Karamanakos and colleagues found, in a randomized trial, that VSG and RYGB resulted in comparable elevation of PYY for the first 6 months following surgery.[13] However, PYY secretion decreased significantly by 12 months following LSG, whereas the response was maintained months after RYGB. The authors postulated that physiologic adaptation of the gastric remnant over time may account for the decreased secretion of PYY after LSG.

In contrast to the procedures described earlier, the PYY response to nutrient ingestion remains blunted after LAGB.[50] This observation is not surprising, because LAGB does not alter the rate of gastric emptying.[9] The additive effect of the enhanced PYY and GLP-1 response may contribute to the enhanced satiety and earlier meal termination seen after RYGB. Data consistent with this hypothesis were provided by a study which found that that poor responders to RYGB (weight loss <25%) had a lesser PYY and GLP-1 response than did good responders (weight loss > 30%).[53]

CONCLUSIONS

Bariatric surgery is currently the most effective and durable treatment option for extreme obesity. Restrictive procedures induce early satiety by reducing gastric size but leave the intestinal tract intact. Gastrointestinal diversionary procedures (including malabsorptive and hybrid procedures) bypass segments of the gut and are typically associated with greater weight loss than purely restrictive procedures. This phenomenon may be, in part, explained by differential effects on the secretion of gut peptides involved in appetite, glucoregulation, and body weight. Further research is needed to identify the specific mechanisms by which the various procedures induce weight loss and ameliorate glycemic control, as well as to compare the efficacy, safety, and cost-effectiveness of the different procedures to each other and to nonsurgical weight loss interventions.

REFERENCES

1. Taylor K. Metabolic and bariatric surgery fact sheet. American Society for Metabolic & Bariatric Surgery. Available at http://asmbs.org/asmbs-press-kit/. Accessed April 3, 2012.
2. Colquitt JL, Picot J, Loveman E, Clegg AJ. Surgery for obesity. Cochrane Database Syst Rev 2009;(2): CD003641.
3. National Institutes of Health. Gastrointestinal surgery for severe obesity. National Institutes of Health Consensus Development Conference Statement. Am J Clin Nutr 1992;55:615S-619S.
4. Dixon JB, O'Brien PE, Playfair J, et al. Adjustable gastric banding and conventional therapy for type 2 diabetes: a randomized controlled trial. JAMA 2008;299:316-323.
5. O'Brien PE, Dixon JB, Laurie C, et al. Treatment of mild to moderate obesity with laparoscopic adjustable gastric banding or an intensive medical program: a randomized trial. Ann Intern Med 2006;144:625-633.
6. Cummings DE Overduin J, Shannon MH, Foster-Schubert KE. Hormonal mechanisms of weight loss and diabetes resolution after bariatric surgery. Surg Obes Rel Dis 2005;1:358-368.
7. NIDDK Weight-Control Information Network. Bariatric surgery for severe obesity. 2011. Available at: http://win.niddk.nih.gov/publications/gastric.htm. Accessed March 21, 2012.
8. Schneider BE, Mun EC. Surgical management of morbid obesity. Diabetes Care 2005;28:475-480.
9. de Jong JR, van Ramshorst B, Gooszen HG, Smout AJ, Tiel-Van Buul MM. Weight loss after laparoscopic adjustable gastric banding is not caused by altered gastric emptying. Obes Surg 2009;19:287-292.
10. Moy J, Pomp A, Dakin G, Parikh M, Gagner M. Laparoscopic sleeve gastrectomy for morbid obesity. Am J Surg 2008;196:e56-e59.
11. Strain GW, Gagner M, Pomp A, et al. Comparison of weight loss and body composition changes with four surgical procedures. Surg Obes Rel Dis 2009;5:582-487.
12. Peterli R, Wölnerhanssen B, Peters T, et al. Improvement in glucose metabolism after bariatric surgery: comparison of laparoscopic Roux-en-Y gastric bypass and laparoscopic sleeve gastrectomy: a prospective randomized trial. Ann Surg 2009;250:234-241.
13. Karamanakos SN, Vagenas K, Kalfarentzos F, Alexandrides TK. Weight loss, appetite suppression, and changes in fasting and postprandial ghrelin and peptide-YY levels after Roux-en-Y gastric bypass and sleeve gastrectomy: a prospective, double-blind study. Ann Surg 2008;247:401-407.
14. Braghetto I, Davanzo C, Korn O, et al. Scintigraphic evaluation of gastric emptying in obese patients submitted to sleeve gastrectomy compared to normal subjects. Obes Surg 2009;19:1515-1521.
15. Melissas J, Koukouraki S, Askoxylakis J, et al. Sleeve gastrectomy: a restrictive procedures? Obes Surg 2007;17:57-62
16. Rubino F. Bariatric surgery: effects on glucose homeostasis. Curr Opin Clin Nutr Metab Care 2006: 9:497-507.
17. Shah M, Simha V, Garg A. Review: long-term impact of bariatric surgery on body weight, comorbidities, and nutritional status. J Clin Endocrinol Metab 2006;91:4223-4231.
18. Maggard M, Shugarman LR, Suttorp M, et al. Meta-analysis: surgical treatment of obesity. Ann Intern Med 2005;142:547-559.
19. Ferchak CV, Meneghini LF. Obesity, bariatric surgery, and type 2 diabetes: a systematic review. Diabetes Metab Res Rev 2004:20:438-445.
20. Buchwald H, Avidor Y, Braunwald E, et al. Bariatric surgery: a systematic review and meta-analysis. JAMA 2004;292:1724-1737.
21. Buchwald H, Estok R, Fahrback K, et al. Weight and type 2 diabetes after bariatric surgery: systematic review and meta-analysis. Am J Med 2009;122: 248-256.
22. Angrisani L, Lorenzo M, Borrelli V. Laparoscopic adjustable gastric banding versus Roux-en-Y gastric bypass: 5-year results of a prospective randomized trial. Surg Obes Relat Dis 2007;3:127-132.
23. Nguyen NT, Slone JA, Nguyen XM, Hartman JS, Hoyt DB. A prospective randomized trial of laparoscopic gastric bypass versus laparoscopic adjustable gastric banding for the treatment of morbid obesity: outcomes, quality of life, and costs. Ann Surg 2009;250(4):631-641.
24. Sjöström L, Lindroos AK, Peltonen M, et al. Lifestyle, diabetes, and cardiovascular risk factors 10 years after bariatric surgery. N Engl J Med 2004;351: 2683-2693.
25. Sjöström L, Narbro K, Sjöström D, et al. Effects of bariatric surgery on mortality in Swedish obese subjects. N Engl J Med 2007;357:741-752.

26. Adams TD, Gress RE, Smith SC, et al. Long-term mortality after gastric bypass surgery. *N Engl J Med* 2007;357:753–761.

27. Longitudinal Assessment of Bariatric Surgery (LABS) Consortium, Flum DR, Belle SH, et al. Perioperative safety in the longitudinal assessment of bariatric surgery. *N Engl J Med* 2009;361:445–454.

28. Bult MJ, van Dalen T, Muller AF. Surgical treatment of obesity. *Eur J Endocrinol* 2008;158:135–145

29. Vollmer K, Holst JJ, Baller B, et al. Predictors of incretin concentrations in subjects with normal, impaired, and diabetic glucose interolance. *Diabetes* 2008;57:678–687.

30. Guidone C, Manco M, Valera-Mora E, et al. Mechanisms of recovery from type 2 diabetes after malabsorptive bariatric surgery. *Diabetes* 2006;55: 2025–2041.

31. Li F, Zhang G, Liang J, Ding X, Cheng Z, Hu S. Sleeve gastrectomy provides better control of diabetes by decreasing ghrelin in the diabetic goto-kakizaki rats. *J Gastrointest Surg* 2009;13:2302–2308.

32. Cummings DE, Overduin J. Gastrointestinal regulation of food intake. *J Clin Invest* 2007;117:13–23.

33. Cummings DE, Purnell JO, Fravo RS, Schmidova K, Wiesse B, Weigle DS. A prandial rise in plasma ghrelin suggests a role in meal initiation in humans. *Diabetes* 2001;50:1714–1719.

34. Cummings DE, Shannon MH. Ghrelin and gastric bypass: is there a hormonal contribution to surgical weight loss? *J Clin Endocrinol Metab* 2003;88: 2999–3002.

35. Tschöp M, Weyer C, Tataranni PA, Devanarayan V, Ravussin E, Heiman ML. Circulating ghrelin levels are decreased in human obesity. *Diabetes* 2001;50(4): 707–709.

36. Cummings DE, Weigle DS, Frayo RS, et al. Human plasma ghrelin levels after diet-induced weight loss and gastric bypass surgery. *N Engl J Med* 2002;346: 1623–1630.

37. Geloneze B, Tambascia MA, PIlla VF, Geloneze SR, Repetto EM, Pareja JC. Ghrelin: a gut-brain homone: effect of gastric bypass surgery. *Obes Surg* 2003;13:17–22.

38. Fruhbeck G, Diez-Caballero A, Gil MJ, et al. Plasma ghrelin concentrations following bariatric surgery depend on the functional integrity of the fundus. *Int J Obesity* 2004;14:606–612.

39. Faraj M, Havel PJ, Phelis S, Blank D, Sniderman AD, Cianflone K. Plasma acylation-stimulating protein, adiponectin, leptin, and ghrelin before and after weight loss induced by gastric bypass surgery in morbidly obese subjects. *J Clin Endocrinol Metab* 2003;88:1594–1602.

40. Holdstock C, Engstrom BE, Obrvall M, Lind L Sundborn M, Karlsson FA. Ghrelin and adipose tissue regulatory peptides: effect of gastric bypass surgery in obese humans. *J Clin Endocrinol Metab* 2003;88:3177–3183.

41. Nijhuis J, van Dielen FM, Buurman, WA, Greve JW. Ghrelin, leptin, and insulin levels after restrictive surgery: a 2 year follow-up study. *Obes Surg* 2004;14: 783–787.

42. Strader AD, Woods SC. Gastrointestinal hormones and food intake. *Gastroenterol* 2005;128:175–191.

43. Holst JJ. The physiology of glucagon-like peptide-1. *Physiol Rev* 2007;87:1409–1439.

44. Laferrère B, Teixeira J, McGinty J, et al. Effect of weight loss by gastric bypass surgery versus hypocaloric diet on glucose and incretin levels in type 2 diabetes. *J Clin Endocrinol Metab* 2008;93: 2379–2385.

45. Laferrère B, Tran H, Egger J, et al. The increase in GLP-1 levels and incretin effect after Roux-en-Y gastric bypass surgery (RYGBP) persists up to 1 year in patients with type 2 diabetes mellitus (T2DM). *Obesity* 2007;15:7 (Abstr).

46. Laferrère B, Heshka S, Wang K, et al. Incretin levels and effect are markedly enhanced 1 month after Roux-en-Y gastric bypass surgery in obese patients with type 2 diabetes. *Diabetes Care* 2007;30: 1709–1716.

47. Naslund E, Gryback P, Backman L, et al. Distal small bowel hormones: correlation with fasting antroduodenal motility and gastric emptying. *Dig Dis Sci* 1998;43:945–952.

48. Cummings DE, Overduin J, Shannon MH, Foster-Schubert KE. Hormonal mechanisms of weight loss and diabetes resolution after bariatric surgery. *Surg Obes Rel Dis* 2005;1:358–368.

49. Horowitz M, Collins PJ, Catteron BE, Harding PE, Watts JM, Shearman DJ. Gastric emptying after gastroplasty for morbid obesity. *Br J Surg* 1984;71: 435–437.

50. Korner J, Bessler M, Inabnet W, Taveras C, Holst JJ. Exaggerated glucagons-like peptide-1 and blunted glucose-dependent insulinotropic peptide secretion are associated with Roux-en-Y gastric bypass but not adjustable gastric banding. *Surg Obes Relat Dis* 2007;3:597–601.

51. Ballantyne GH. Peptide YY (1–36) and peptide YY (3–36): Part II. Changes after gastrointestinal surgery and bariatric surgery. *Obes Surg* 2006;16:795–803.

52. le Roux CW, Batterham RL, Aylwin SJ, et al. Attenuated peptide YY release in obese subjects is associated with reduced satiety. *Endocrinol* 2006; 147:3–8.

53. Le Roux CW, Welbourn R, Werling M, et al. Gut hormones as mediators of appetite and weight loss after Roux-en-Y gastric bypass. *Ann Surg* 2007;246: 780–785.

48

Treatment of Alcohol and Drug Dependence in 2011 and Relevance to Food Addiction

KIMBERLY BLUMENTHAL, ROBERT L. DUPONT,
AND MARK S. GOLD

The diagnosis and treatment of addictive disorders as well as the understanding of the biology of addiction have been profoundly reshaped in recent years by the recognition of the enormity of the public health challenges of addiction and by the exploding knowledge of brain science. The recognition of the central role of disturbances in brain reward in addictions has led to a redefinition of a wide range of behavior disorders, seeing them increasingly as analogous to the addiction to alcohol and other drugs of abuse. This paradigm shift, based on shared brain biology, has been especially productive in the understanding and treatment of tobacco use and eating disorders. In thinking about the addictions beyond substance, it is useful to understand the current status of the prevention and treatment of substance use disorders.

Although substance abuse treatment today has been profoundly affected by the modern understanding of the brain biology of addiction, the core treatment approach retains many elements of earlier twentieth-century innovations, including a focus on the disease as lifelong and orienting treatment to the goal of lifelong recovery. While all organized treatments are for economic and other practical reasons relatively brief, mostly measured in weeks or months, the exemplary substance abuse treatments commonly rely on 12-step programs for lifetime recovery support. They all have the goal of "abstinence," meaning no use of alcohol or other drugs of abuse.

The standard for long-term good outcomes comes from substance use disorders state physician health programs (PHPs), which are distinguished because they do not seek to find the lowest costs but the best long-term outcomes. These remarkable programs, run by dedicated physicians who meet with their colleagues on a regular basis, do not themselves deliver treatment services. Instead, they require physicians with addictive disorders to purchase treatment from a short list of treatment providers that they have found to produce excellent results. In this way, they not only identify best practices in treatment but they encourage the treatment providers to innovate to stay at the top of their best-practices lists.

The PHPs, while each unique, are generally distinguished by several elements. They (1) use the best treatment available anywhere in the country; (2) establish a no-use, zero-tolerance standard for any use of alcohol or other drugs, which is randomly monitored using the latest technology; (3) intervene when there is any violation of their requirements, including any use of alcohol or other drugs, typically taking the physicians out of the practice of medicine and putting them in more intensive and longer duration therapy; (4) require continuous and active use of community support, mostly the 12-step programs of Alcoholics Anonymous and Narcotics Anonymous (NA); (5) identify and treat coexisting conditions both physical and mental; and (6) continue monitoring, typically lasting for 5 years or longer.

This chapter focuses on the model of current abstinence-based addiction treatment and recovery services provided at treatment centers such as the Betty Ford Center, the Florida Recovery Center, or Hazelden. These programs are commonly used by the state PHPs.

BEHAVIORAL TREATMENTS
Motivational Interviewing

Substance abuse treatment often starts with motivational interviewing and, for some, this may be enough to incite change. Indeed, many persons with food addictions or substance abuse choose to change their behavior on their own. However, simply buying a diet or recovery book or joining a gym is rarely treatment. For those who are not ready to change, motivational interviewing approaches may help. Motivational interviewing is a brief, patient-centered, directive approach that emphasizes personal choice and responsibility. It has demonstrated efficacy with addiction populations related to both quitting/cutting down on substance use or accepting formal treatment. In addition, research has shown that contingency management techniques, like voucher-based reinforcement therapy (VBRT), can help patients achieve abstinence from various substances of abuse. A treatment intervention where patients receive vouchers or incentives exchangeable for good and services in the community, contingent upon completion of a specified treatment goal, VBRT has also shown efficacy in promoting adherence to pharmacotherapy.

Cognitive-Behavioral Therapy

Current addiction treatment often includes cognitive-behavioral therapy (CBT). CBT is a relatively brief treatment approach that often serves as the foundation of psychosocial intervention for patients with addictions. CBT typically combines psychoeducation, functional analysis, skill building, environmental modification and contingency management, examination of dysfunctional thinking, and coping skills training along with other techniques. The therapist will teach and encourage more adaptive thinking, work with the patient to address barriers to sobriety, teach alternative coping strategies, and assist the patient to identify and elicit social support. These interventions and treatments have been used with addicts and alcoholics as well as patients with eating and binge eating disorders.

12-Step Programs

In the early twentieth century, members of the Oxford Group, a movement popular in the United States and Europe, "practiced a formula of self-improvement by performing self-inventory, admitting wrongs, making amends, using prayer and meditation, and carrying this message to others."[3] In 1935, "Bill W." received this message and after reflecting on this philosophy from Dr. Bob S., Alcoholics Anonymous (AA) was born. By 1939, they had helped 99 men and 1 woman recover and had written the Big Book.[4] AA is considered by its members as a fellowship. It is an experience of service, helping, honest sharing, studying, and working the "steps" with a willingness to change rather than a specific prescribed program of activities. There are no dues or obligations but the assumption is that by sharing experiences and life stories everyone will gain strength and hope. In the 1980s, the work of Harvard's George Vaillant confirmed what others had guessed, that AA was the most effective way to achieve and maintain sobriety.[5,6] Table 48.1 addresses each of the twelve steps and their goals.

AA is currently the most popular mutual-help group or 12-step program. Participation in a 12-step program (e.g., AA or NA, Double Trouble in Recovery) is beneficial for many individuals with an addictive disorder.[7,8] The 12-step approach has also helped many patients with process additions (e.g., gambling, sex, or food). Overeaters Anonymous (OA) and AA share the essential features. Although some individuals are hesitant to join these groups, health professionals can assist these patients through "12-step facilitation."[9] This approach involves providing psychoeducation and focusing on three core topics:

1. Introducing the patient to the 12-step philosophy.
2. Working with the patient to complete the first three steps.
3. Encouraging the patient to become actively involved in a 12-step program.

Participation in a 12-step program is associated with increased abstinence and spirituality. Participants who help others show lower rates of relapse, and most participants in the later stages of recovery continue to help other addicts.[10,11] Group treatments, like "Weight Watchers" or OA, also appear to work for many with obesity.

The 12-step approach often includes eating and food advice to help prevent a relapse. *HALT* is the acronym taught to recovering patients. The H in HALT stands for hungry. Never get too hungry and relapse will be prevented. Recovering patients often carry around hard, sugar-filled candy, and AA meetings are notorious for their cakes and cookies. The idea of feeding an addiction craving is a crossover concept between addictions to drugs and addiction to food. Sugar pills are so effective that some studies of nicotine discontinuation showed

TABLE 48.1 THE TWELVE STEPS OF ALCOHOLICS ANONYMOUS (AA)

No.	Step	Goal	Comments
	We:	To:	
1	*Admitted we were powerless over alcohol—that our lives had become unmanageable.*	Accept self as an addict by confronting denial through self-examination. Doing it "my way" has failed and will continue to fail.	This step is the most difficult for many because denial is so strong. Selfishness and self-centeredness are at the heart of addiction.
2	*Came to believe that a Power greater than ourselves could restore us to sanity.*	Come to believe that a Higher Power outside of self could restore "sanity" to our insane lives of addiction. Recognize that help is desperately needed and addict is unable to help him/herself. Coming to AA and working the "steps" will bring hope for change	By "sanity," the addict means abstinence; use is recognized as prolonging the insanity or negative effects. The path to serenity lies outside of ourselves.
3	*Made a decision to turn our will and our lives over to the care of God as we understood Him.*	Decision to turn life over to the care of Higher Power. Have faith in the process, that things will work out, and that cravings/anxiety can be managed one day at a time.	Rather than being seen as religious, this step affirms faith and hope for the future and supports letting go. Accepting guidance from the 12-step fellowship as manifestation of the Higher Power.

Steps 1–3 involve admission and acceptance of the fact that you are an addict, powerless, and that drugs/alcohol have made your life a total mess. Surrender your will and work the program is the next message.
Steps 4–10 deal with therapy, self-examination, amends, and restitution.

No.	Step	Goal	Comments
4	*Made a searching and fearless moral inventory of ourselves.*	Make an honest self-appraisal. Honestly and fearlessly catalogue "insane" acts that have harmed others.	The sponsor plays a key role in this step, much like what happens in psychotherapy. Dishonesty is the core of addiction; honesty is the core of recovery.
5	*Admitted to God, to ourselves, and to another human being the exact nature of our wrongs.*	Directly and honestly put into words the results of the moral inventory to self, another human being (e.g., the sponsor, a home group member, or the clergy), and God.	This step work is usually accompanied by shame, disgust, anxiety, and fears of rejection. Making the moral inventory explicit makes it no longer avoidable and starts healing.
6	*Were entirely ready to have God remove all these defects of character.*	Recognize that even with all of the progress, there are still characterological and personality problems. Be ready and willing to abandon the defects of character.	This step focuses on H. O. W. (honesty, open-mindedness, willingness). Called "How to change"
7	*Humbly asked Him to remove our shortcomings.*	Ask for help in managing these character defects to remove selfishness, dishonesty, and dysfunctional behaviors. Recognizing own fallibility.	Antisocial, borderline, narcissistic, and other personality problems can slowly be managed by a human being who is humbly asking for help. Character defects that promote selfishness and that bring harm to others can be overcome by humility and honesty.

(continued)

TABLE 48.1 (CONTINUED)

No.	Step	Goal	Comments
	We:	To:	
8	*Made a list of all persons we had harmed, and became willing to make amends to them all.*	In this step, the goal is for the addict to work with his or her sponsor to repair damaged relationships and say I am sorry for what I have said, done, or not done. Get away from generalities and into specific harms to specific persons.	Essentially, it is an activity that helps develop and repair relationships at the same time as it promotes empathy for the people used and abused along the addict's way. Saying we are "sorry" perpetuates our selfish, addicted ways. Amends are different—a changed life, not just empty and dishonest words.
9	*Made direct amends to such people wherever possible, except when to do so would injure them or others.*	The goal is for the addict to make amends and restitution directly to those people injured under the guidance of the sponsor. Get real, walk the walk of recovery.	Amends and restitution requires sponsor support and guidance to protect everyone involved in this explosive process of healing. It helps the addict repair damage, reduce guilt, and start over.
10	*Continued to take personal inventory and when we were wrong promptly admitted it.*	Self-regulation through self-observation, honesty, and admission of problems. Getting well is a continuing process, not an endpoint.	Focus is long-term perseverance and attention to relationship building, intimacy, and recovery. Honesty and struggling against selfishness and dishonesty is a way of living.
	The final two steps are all recovery, service and more service to the process and Group.		
11	*Sought through prayer and meditation to improve our conscious contact with God as we understood Him, praying only for knowledge of His will for us and the power to carry that out.*	The goal is to quiet the self whether through prayer or meditation in order to be open to a spiritual awakening.	The power of surrender of the will, spiritual awareness, and tolerance of all others leads to tolerance of self and solving one's problems.
12	*Having had a spiritual awakening as the result of these steps, we tried to carry this message to alcoholics, and to practice these principles in all our affairs.*	The goal is for the addict to get his or her mind off of him/herself and avoid being egotistic or self-centered. Hope and help are achieved by service and helping others. Only by sharing can recovery be sustained.	Helping others is defined as sharing their experiences of recovery and doing good. Humility is the antidote to denial (the greatest enemy of recovery), as well as shame, guilt, narcissism, and grandiosity.

Source: The Twelve Steps are reprinted with permission of Alcoholics Anonymous World Services, Inc. ("AAWS"). Permission to reprint the Twelve Steps does not mean that AAWS has reviewed or approved the contents of this publication, or that AAWS necessarily agrees with the views expressed herein. AA is a program of recovery from alcoholism only—use of the Twelve Steps in connection with programs and activities which are patterned after AA, but which address other problems, or in any other non-AA context, does not imply otherwise. Wording of the 12 steps was taken from http://www.aa.org/bigbookonline/en_bigbook_chapt5.pdf.

significant efficacy for high-dose sugar pills or "placebos" compared to nicotine. More recently, O'Malley showed that tobacco relapse was aggravated with nicotine exposure or hunger.[12] Drugs of abuse are preferred to eating and most often active abusers and addicts forget to eat. Usually, alcoholics, cocaine addicts, and amphetamine addicts are quite thin when they are admitted to treatment. Once they are detoxified and abstinent, we commonly see rebound hyperphagia and overeating.[13,14] Weight gain during abstinence, if unchecked, can lead to obesity.

THE DEFINITION OF RECOVERY

Although sobriety is considered to be necessary for recovery, it is not considered as sufficient. Recovery is recognized universally as being multidimensional,[15] involving more than simply the elimination of substance use.[16-22] *Recovery* may be the best word to summarize all the positive benefits to physical, mental, and social health that can happen when alcohol- and other drug-dependent individuals get the help they need. Those who are in recovery are typically sober, working, and tax-paying parents and neighbors.[15] The recovering addict or alcoholic should have gratitude for relief from pain and suffering, for the restoration of hope and dignity, and for the chance to help and heal others. With this gratitude, the addicts remind themselves to stay humble, often by doing service work like setting up for meetings, making coffee, greeting people, making 12-step calls, or serving on committees. The expectation is to help with no expectation of recognition or reward.

TREATMENT TODAY

Changes in thinking and approach to alcohol abusers and addicts emerged between 1944 and 1970, which led to a system of specialty treatment programs. These included outpatient alcoholism clinic models pioneered in Connecticut (1944), including the short-term residential/inpatient "Minnesota Model" of alcoholism treatment.[23-25] With the exception of the alcoholism clinics and methadone maintenance programs, treatments were delivered in hospital or residential settings,[26-27] followed by 12-steps or AA to some extent. Most programs used recovering addicts as volunteers or counselors in intensive counseling sessions, designed as a counterbalance to the addicts' denial and repeated Step 1 ("powerlessness over alcohol") failures. Denial and outright resistance to the "loss of control" concept became the focal point for entry into the treatment system. Once entered and attending meetings, fellowship and working the program promoted a willingness and commitment to sustained abstinence, leading to broader behavioral change.

The twenty-first-century addiction treatment system is still using most of the same original group and individual therapy methods originated in the 1930s, but changes in national priorities and cost-consciousness left the substance abuse treatment system focused on outpatient (80%+),

very short-term, detoxification, and overall delaying access and obfuscating outcomes. Generally, follow-up after treatment is nonexistent or short term without testing or other objective checks on substance use (e.g., urine testing) or the effectiveness of treatment.[28]

Given that drug discontinuation and abstinence cause rebound hyperphagia and weight gain, most abstinence-based drug treatment programs have mandatory diet counseling and exercise programs. Exercise is now a mainstay of addiction recovery, and research has begun to demonstrate a profound action in stabilizing mood, helping with sleep, and reducing drug craving.[29-31]

Succeeding in a 12-step program of recovery is not easy. It requires a home group, sponsor, and help from others. Twelve-step programs promote sobriety, intimacy, and integrity. Several common models pioneered in alcoholic treatment are in widespread use in the treatment of patients with other addictions, disordered eating, binge eating, and obesity.

Physicians and other health professionals do not enjoy experiencing their patients' failures and relapses. We have no cure for obesity; it is a chronic relapsing medical problem. Physicians often provide directives and confront the patient, but they rarely provide the kind of intervention that promotes change. The medical care system is often centered on the physician's diagnostic and analytical skills. Neither is at a premium in obesity. Diagnosis is easy, which may frustrate health professionals who enjoy differential diagnosis and testing. With just a height and weight, we know a patient's body mass index (BMI). However, despite this ease, most research suggests that physicians fail to recognize obesity as a medical problem.[32-34] For a patient with substance abuse disorders, diagnosis can be more difficult as the patient often denies the association between his or her drug or alcohol use and health problems, marital and relationship deterioration, job loss, or financial ruin. Still, in drug or food addiction, diagnosis is rarely the problem.

Next, motivation to change is a common problem. As drugs or food insinuate themselves into the fabric of daily life, they make living without them seem impossible or difficult to visualize. Once diagnosis and motivation to change come together, the next problem is what is evidence-based treatment?[35] Many health professionals have never learned about addiction interventions or treatment in the same way that they learn how to deliver babies. They do learn in a classroom or read a textbook, but that learning approach would not help them very much when faced with a mother about to deliver. Surgeries for morbid obesity, the fastest growing procedures in the United States, are evidence based and effective for many. However, there is usually a very long course from a BMI of 25 to >40, thus representing copious failures in treatment, with relapses the norm. Similarly, long-term residential treatment for alcoholics and drug addicts is quite effective but costly.

BARRIERS TO RECOVERY

The most well-known barrier to recovery in cigarette smoking cessation is weight gain. While a number of good clinical examples like this exist, extrapolation to food, food addictions, and pathological eating is not an exact science. Certainly, overeating and obesity are major public health problems that have escalated as food has become more manufactured, fast food more commonplace, and exercise less routine. While binge eating is a psychiatric diagnosis commonly found in obese patients, it may have been an essential behavior in hunter-gatherer populations when the kill had to be eaten before it became rotten, spoiled, and parasite infested. Today, binge eating is defined as recurrent episodes of eating more food than normal during a short period of time and accompanied by feeling uncomfortably full; eating large amounts of food when not hungry; eating more rapidly than normal; eating alone because of embarrassment over the amount of food consumed; feeling disgusted, depressed, or guilty after overeating; and having anxiety or depression regarding binge eating. Most binge eaters do not meet criteria for the *DSM* disorder.

THE PHYSICIAN HEALTH PROGRAM: A TREATMENT AND RESEARCH MODEL FOR TREATMENT AND RECOVERY

One of the most exciting changes in treatment has been the PHP model, where the 12 steps are the core part of the long-term treatment of impaired health professionals. Study of impaired health professionals has allowed comprehensive 5-year outcome studies to be conducted in a variety of states and reported first at a Betty Ford Institute meeting and then in the literature in *The Journal of Substance*

Abuse Treatment and the *British Medical Journal*.[36,37] The models developed for impaired professionals could work for any addict if the essential components of the "treatment" were faithfully applied.

Thus, we have focused on impaired health professionals as a model of evidenced-based intervention and also to help define essential ingredients of successful addiction treatment programs over the long term. Five-year outcome is the norm for the PHPs around the United States.[38] PHPs provide active case management, monitoring, and supervision of physicians who have signed formal, binding contracts extending for 5 years. The PHPs have leverage through their relationships with the state medical licensing boards, physicians, and hospitals. The boards often accept the care of the PHP in lieu of imposing other disciplinary action for physicians. Typically, the PHP contracts stipulate treatment accompanied by long-term monitoring. Monitoring includes substance use through random drug testing as well as unscheduled work site visits for extended periods—typically 5 or more years. The treatment, supervision, and monitoring plans for these physicians are individualized around a core approach that dominates the PHP model.[39] Physicians who refuse the terms of the contract and/or are found to continue substance use may ultimately be forced to surrender their licenses.

Following the signing of a PHP contract and after a full evaluation, most physicians engage in formal addiction substance abuse treatment. All PHPs share a complete abstinence approach to the treatment of addiction. Most PHPs operate under the principles espoused by AA and other 12-step programs; and virtually all physicians are expected to attend AA and/or NA meetings. This treatment approach typically has two phases that differ in intensity and frequency of services.

Physicians must withdraw from medical practice during this initial period of addiction treatment. The first phase of treatment typically begins with residential or intensive outpatient treatment. Participating physicians are given a choice of treatment providers. The PHP selects treatment programs and other service providers (e.g., organizations that monitor the physicians) that the PHP trusts to provide excellent services. If there is evidence of slippage in the performance of a particular treatment program or other service provider, it can be removed from the list of approved options for participating physicians.

The second phase of formal treatment is continued outpatient addiction treatment for 6 to 12 months. Families are also involved in this care and coached on how to support recovery and to spot early signs of relapse. Physicians often resume practice during this phase of care but under close supervision by the PHP. During and following the outpatient phase of treatment, the PHPs exercise one of their more distinctive functions: intensive random drug testing.

In practice, participating physicians must call a phone number each morning of the workweek to see whether they are to be tested that day. The yes-or-no decision is made by random computer assignment and generally continues for 5 years or longer. The frequency of testing generally is greater at the beginning of the contract period (weekly or twice weekly) and lesser at the end of PHP monitoring (monthly); unless there is evidence of relapse, in which case the frequency of drug testing is increased. Monitoring over the 5 years of the typical PHP contract is not confined to drug testing but typically also involves assessment of the physicians' work environments and compliance with their specific treatment plans.

"Relapse" includes any use of alcohol or other drugs used nonmedically, but it also includes failure to attend treatment sessions and other signs of noncompliance, or even lying about some aspect of care or recovery. A relapse may be failure to attend an AA meeting, failure to report promptly for a drug test, or evidence that the participant has been lying about participation in treatment. A relapse episode will typically lead to an additional evaluation and intensified treatment and monitoring. The participants who relapse find that the PHPs give them more care and monitoring.

A case management system similar to the PHP model has been used for commercial airline pilots and lawyers, as well as other health care professionals, including nurses, dentists, and veterinarians.

The individual elements that comprise the PHP model have been be summarized by Dupont et al. (JSAT)[36]:

1. *Contingency management aspects of PHP care.* For physicians enrolled in a PHP program, there are both significant positive (continued ability to practice medicine; reduction of pending charges against them) and significant negative consequences (loss of license, professional disgrace) to noncompliance with PHP treatment and monitoring requirements. There is a robust and rapidly growing body of knowledge supporting the view that addiction treatment programs that utilize "socially sanctioned coercion mechanisms"[40] by providing consequences for early termination of treatment or positive drug tests results strongly improve the outcome in addiction treatment.[41-43]

2. *Frequent testing.* When drug testing is used in substance abuse treatment, the test results are seldom linked to meaningful consequences or with the intensity that typifies PHP case management. Recovering physicians frequently report that knowing they would be subject to drug screening is a powerful motivator to avoid using substances of abuse.[44] In fact, it has been suggested that random urine screening actually serves as a behavioral intervention for the recovering physicians, reminding them of the potential consequences of substance use[44,45] and may be the most effective component of treatment. In the State of Florida, the impaired physician calls an 800 number every day during the initial phase of his or her contract and is randomized to drug test or no test. Thus, evidence of relapse is kept current. Indeed, failure to call in for randomization is a prognostic indicator of impending relapse.[46] Such a calling system may be a form of telehealth therapy at no cost to the state. In addition, research has demonstrated that the addition of drug-testing to addiction treatment can improve outcomes, with 96% of physicians who were tested maintaining sobriety, compared to only 64% of physicians who were not routinely tested.[47]

3. *Tight linkage with the 12-step programs AND with the abstinence standard espoused by these fellowships.* The PHP programs are abstinence based, and they require abstinence from all mood-altering drugs, not just the physician's drug(s) of choice. Research has repeatedly demonstrated the efficacy of the 12-step approach for physicians with substance use disorders[48-51] and

participation in a 12-step group, such as AA, is associated with improved self-efficacy for abstinence.[52] Combining AA and professionally directed addiction treatment has also been found to generate better recovery outcomes than is found in participating only in AA or only in treatment.[53]

4. *Active management of relapses by intensified treatment and monitoring.* Relapses do not typically lead to discharge from PHP care. They do routinely lead to intensive reevaluations of the treatment plans and to the implementation of additional care. For example, in this sample, the majority of physicians who provided a urine specimen positive for drug use were reevaluated.

5. *A continuing care approach.* Treatment, support, and monitoring in traditional addiction programs may be limited to a few days, or detox, or at most 30 days. Specifically, acute care–oriented, short-term approaches have little evidence of success. The PHPs have sustained continuity of care and focused much of their professional resources on sustaining therapeutic contact over 5 years.

6. *Focus on lifelong recovery.* Mere abstinence is seldom sufficient for PHP care. Rather, the physicians are expected to significantly improve the quality of their lifestyles, both in their personal lives and in their practice of medicine. This is considered an important aspect of their PHP care. Thus, treatment programs for physicians with substance use disorders generally include comprehensive assessment (including co-occurring medical and psychiatric conditions) and a wide spectrum of services, including educational lectures, individual therapy, group therapy, and family therapy, as well as a performance-based assessment of competency to return to work and participation in continuing medical education as necessary.[54]

7. Results of PHP studies (in *The Journal of Substance Abuse Treatment* and the *British Medical Journal*) also suggest that "addiction" is a fairly general condition, and that drug of choice may not significantly affect treatment choice or outcome. Rarely did a biological intervention or treatment have an impact like working the program.

Lessons and Usefulness

PHP treatment elements can potentially inform all mainstream addiction treatment, including food addiction treatment.[54] Both drugs of abuse and food have similarities seen in basic science models. There is increasing support for the food addiction hypotheses proposed by a variety of scientists to explain pathological association between the over-eating person and food.[55,56] Food cravings and craving-related changes are quite similar between obese and drug-addicted people.[57] Dopamine release in the nucleus accumbens is increased in anticipation of eating a great meal or upon seeing a drug of choice.[58] Highly palatable or great food is highly valued and reinforcing.

Food addictions are not a large leap from the basic science and translational data available and recently reviewed by Blumenthal and Gold.[59] Binge foods are often desserts, ice cream, or candy, but they also include pasta, bread, and fatty or salty foods. Sugars have been studied and appear to have different effects on the brain and behavior than fats.[60] Hoebel and other groups have used sugar solutions to study binge eating.[61] Animals will also binge on vegetable fat and shortening. Sugar-fat mixtures or cookies have also induced binge eating and have been studied in laboratory settings. This model produces both bingeing and also significant body weight increases.[62]

The obese and alcoholics have dopamine receptor down-regulation as evidenced by a reduction in D2 receptor availability on positron emission tomography imaging. Binges or starvation causes changes in brain and behavior with craving–related changes but also changes in brain opioid activity. Avena has shown similarities between sugar binge and drug taking in laboratory models in a number of elegant studies. Rats bingeing on sugar develop locomotor cross-sensitization to amphetamine[63] and also rebound alcohol self-administration during sugar abstinence. Sugar withdrawal can be provoked by removing sugar from the diet[64] and also acute administration of opioid antagonist naltrexone or naloxone. So rats will self-administer glucose or fructose or cheesecake or burgers, binge, use more and more (thus losing control), show cross-tolerance to drugs of abuse, and have a clear abstinence syndrome when sugar is unavailable or withdrawal provoked by naloxone or naltrexone. In clinical practice, too, we see that neonatal intensive care units use a sucrose solution as an anesthetic during minor painful procedures in young infants, with a large body of supportive evidence demonstrating the analgesic efficacy of sugar.[65] The science has been strong and consistent, but the clinical follow through has been lacking. What have we learned about addictions that can help people with binge eating and obesity?[66]

Clearly a first step has been to try to train addiction professionals to try to evaluate and treat food addicts. Use existing treatment resources and experience to develop a model that is long term and relevant for the chronic disease of overeating and obesity. CBT, prescriptive psychology, 12-step groups, and medications for addiction can and will be tried in obesity. Pharmacological therapies used for alcoholism or tobacco smoking appear to show some promise of becoming approved, safe, and effective in both drug addiction and in patients with obesity. This area, reviewed by Blumenthal and Gold,[59] is promising in both approach and outcomes. The obesity treatment system, if one exists, needs to take a detailed look at PHPs and develop a long-term approach with an emphasis on early detection, with a range of services from inpatient and residential to low intervention, and testing or frequent weights and diet evaluation. It should also focus on active management, lifelong recovery, exercise, and treatment of comorbid disorders. Adopting approaches that have proved successful in drug addiction may be successful in food addiction and help solve our global obesity problem.

REFERENCES

1. Miller WR, Rollnick S. *Motivational Interviewing: Preparing People for Change.* New York: Guilford Press, 2002.
2. Higgins ST, Silverman K, Heil SH, eds. *Contingency Management in Substance Abuse Treatment.* New York: Guilford Press, 2008.
3. Alcoholics Anonymous. Origins. Available at: http://www.aa.org/aatimeline/. Accessed September 7, 2010.
4. Alcoholics Anonymous. The big book online. 4th ed. Available at: http://www.aa.org/bigbookonline/. Accessed September 20, 2010.
5. Vaillant GE, Clark W, Cyrus C, et al. Prospective study of alcohol treatment: eight year follow up. *Am J Med* 1983;75(3):455–463.
6. Vaillant GE. *The Natural History of Alcoholism Revisited.* Cambridge, MA: Harvard University Press, 1995.
7. Miller NS, Gold MS, Pottash AC. A 12-step treatment approach for marijuana (cannabis) dependence. *J Subst Abuse Treat* 1989;6(4):241–250.
8. Chappel JN, DuPont RL. Twelve-step and mutual help programs for addictive disorders. *Psych Clin North Am* 1999;22(2):425–446.
9. Nowinski J, Baker S. *The Twelve-Step Facilitation Handbook: A Systematic Approach to Early Recovery from Alcoholism and Addiction.* New York: Lexington Books, 1992.
10. Zemore SE, Kaskutas LA. Helping, spirituality, and Alcoholics Anonymous in recovery. *J Stud Alcohol* 2004;65(3):383–391.
11. Pagano ME, Friend KB, Tonigan JS, Stout RL. Helping other alcoholics in Alcoholics Anonymous and drinking outcomes: findings from Project MATCH. *J Stud Alcohol* 2004;65(6):766–773.
12. Leeman RF, O'Malley SS, White MA, McKee SA. Nicotine and food deprivation decrease the ability to resist smoking. *Psychopharmacol (Berl)* 2010;212(1):25–32.
13. Hodgkins CC, Cahill KS, Seraphine AE, Frost-Pineda K, Gold MS. Adolescent drug addiction treatment and weight gain. *J Addict Dis* 2004;23(3):56–65.
14. Hodgkins CC, Frost-Pineda K, Gold MS. Weight gain during substance abuse treatment: the dual problem of addiction and overeating in an adolescent population. *J Addict Dis* 2007;26(suppl 1):41–50.
15. Betty Ford Institute Consensus Panel. What is recovery? A working definition from the Betty Ford Institute. *J Subst Abuse Treat* 2007;33(3):221–228.
16. DeLeon IG, Anders BM, Rodriguez-Catter V, Neidert PL. The effects of noncontingent access to single- versus multiple-stimulus sets on self-injurious behavior. *J Appl Behav Anal* 2000;33(4):623–626
17. Kurtz JB. Virucidal effect of alcohols against echovirus 11. *Lancet* 1979;1(8114):496–497.
18. Laudet AB. What does recovery mean to you? Lessons from the recovery experience for research and practice. *J Subst Abuse Treat* 2007;33(3):243–256.
19. Laudet AB, Morgen K, White WL. The role of social supports, spirituality, religiousness, life, meaning and affiliation with 12-Step fellowships in quality of life satisfaction among individuals in recovery from alcohol and drug problems. *Alcohol Treat Q* 2006;24(1–2):33–73.
20. Tiebout HM. Surrender versus compliance in therapy, with special reference to alcoholism. *Q J Stud Alcohol* 1953;14(1):58–68.
21. White WL, Reis T. Images from the Brown University Alcohol and Addiction Studies collections. *Addiction* 2006;101(6):788–792.
22. White WL. The new recovery advocacy movement in America. *Addiction* 2007;102(5):696–703.
23. White WL. *Slaying the Dragon: The History of Addiction Treatment and Recovery in America.* Bloomington, IL: Chesnut Health Systems, 1998.
24. Musto DF. The mystery of addiction. *Lancet* 1999; 354(suppl):SIV1.

25. Musto DF. *The American Disease: Origins of Narcotic Control*. 3rd ed. Oxford, England: Oxford University Press, 1999

26. Dackis CA, Gold MS. Treatment of addiction on a psychiatric unit. In: Giannini AJ, Slaby AE, eds. *Drugs of Abuse*. New York: Medical Economics Books; 1989: 367–379.

27. Dackis CA, Gold MS. Inpatient treatment of drug and alcohol addiction. In: Miller NS, ed. *Comprehensive Handbook of Drug and Alcohol Addiction*. New York: Marcel Dekker; 1991: 1233–1244.

28. McLellan AT, Carise D, Kleber HD. Can the national addiction treatment infrastructure support public's demand for quality case? *J Subst Abuse Treat* 2003;25:117–121.

29. Lee IM, Djousse L, Sesso HD, Wang L, Buring JE. Physical activity and weight gain prevention. *JAMA* 2010;303(12):1173–1179.

30. Angelo DL, Tavares H, Bottura HM, Zilberman ML. Physical exercise for pathological gamblers. *Rev Bras Psiquiatr* 2009;31(1):76.

31. Janse Van Rensburg K, Taylor A, Hodgson T, Benattayallah A. Acute exercise modulates cigarette cravings and brain activation in response to smoking-related images: an fMRI study. *Psychopharmacol* 2009;203(3):589–598.

32. van Gerwen M, Franc C, Rosman S, Le Vaillant M, Pelletier-Fleury N. Primary care physicians' knowledge, attitudes, beliefs and practices regarding childhood obesity: a systematic review. *Obes Rev* 2009;10(2):227–236.

33. Persky S, Eccleston CP. Medical student bias and care recommendations for an obese versus non-obese virtual patient. *Int J Obes* 2011;35:728–735.

34. Sawbridge DT, Fitzgerald R. "Lazy, slothful and indolent": medical and social perceptions of obesity in Europe to the eighteenth century. *Vesalius* 2009;5(2):59–70.

35. Cannon CP, Kumar A. Treatment of overweight and obesity: lifestyle, pharmacologic, and surgical options. *Clin Cornerstone* 2009;9(4):55–68.

36. DuPont RL, McLellan AT, White WL, Merlo LJ, Gold MS. Setting the standard for recovery: Physicians' Health Programs. *J Subst Abuse Treat* 2009;36(2):159–171.

37. McLellan AT, Skipper GS, Campbell M, DuPont RL. Five year outcomes in a cohort study of physicians treated for substance use disorders in the United States. *Brit Med J* 2008;337:1–6.

38. Pomm RM, Harmon L. Evaluation and posttreatment monitoring of the impaired physician. *Psychiatric Ann* 2004;34(10):786–789.

39. Merlo LJ, Gold MS. Prescription opioid abuse and dependence among physicians: hypotheses and treatment. *Harv Rev Psychiatry* 2008;16(3):181–194.

40. Nace EP, Birkmayer F, Sullivan MA, et al. Socially sanctioned coercion mechanisms for addiction treatment. *Am J Addict* 2007;16(1):15–23.

41. Fowlie DG. Doctors' drinking and fitness to practise. *Alcohol Alcohol* 2005;40(6):483–484.

42. Monahan G. Drug use/misuse among health professionals. *Subst Use Misuse* 2003;38(11–13):1877–1881.

43. Marlowe DB, Wong CJ. Contingency management in adult criminal drug courts. In: Higgins ST, Heil SH, eds. *Contingency Management in Substance Abuse Treatment*. New York: Guilford Press; 2008: 334–354.

44. Simpson DD, Joe GW. Motivation as a predictor of early dropout from drug-abuse treatment. *Psychother* 1993;30:357–368.

45. Jacobs WS, Repetto M, Vinson S, Pomm R, Gold MS. Random urine testing as an intervention for drug addiction. *Psychiatric Ann* 2004;34(10):781–784.

46. Jacobs WS, Hall JD, Pomm R, et al. Prognostic factors for physician addiction outcomes at five years. Paper presented at: American Society of Addiction Medicine Annual Medical-Scientific Meeting; April 24, 2004; Washington, DC.

47. Shore JH. The Oregon experience with impaired physicians on probation. An eight-year follow-up. *JAMA* 1987;257(21):2931–2934

48. Gallegos KV, Lubin BH, Bowers C, et al. Relapse and recovery: five to ten year follow-up study of chemically-dependent physicians. The Georgia experience. *Md Med J* 1992;41:315–319.

49. Lloyd G. One hundred alcoholic doctors: a 21-year follow-up. *Alcohol Alcohol* 2002;37(4):370–374.

50. Galanter M, Talbott D, Gallegos K, Rubenstone E. Combined Alcoholics Anonymous and professional care for addicted physicians. *Am J Psychiatry* 1990;147(1):64–68.

51. Moos RH, Moos BS. Paths of entry in to Alcoholics Anonymous: consequences for participation and remission. *Alcohol Clin Exp Res* 2005;29(10):1858–1868.

52. Bogenschutz MP, Tonigan JS, Miller WR. Examining the effects of alcoholism typology and AA attendance on self-efficacy as a mechanism of change. *J Stud Alcohol* 2006;67:562–567.

53. Fiorentine R, Hillhouse MP. Drug treatment and 12-step program participation: the additive effects of integrated recovery activities. *J Subst Abuse Treat* 2000;18(1):65–74.

54. Merlo LJ, Gold MS. Elements of successful treatment programs for physicians with addictions. *Psychiatric Times* 2008;14:76–81.

55. Gold MS. Introduction: eating disorders, overeating, and pathological attachment to food: independent or addictive disorders? *J Addict Dis* 2004;23(3):1–3.

56. Gold MS, Graham NA, Cocores JA, Nixon SJ. Food addiction? *J Addict Med* 2009;3(1):42–45.

57. Cocores JA, Gold MS. The salted food addiction hypothesis may explain overeating and the obesity epidemic. *Med Hypotheses* 2009;73(6):892–899.

58. Joranby L, Frost-Pineda K, Gold MS. Addiction to food and brain reward systems. *Sex Addict Compuls* 2005;12(2):201–217.

59. Blumenthal DM, Gold MS. Neurobiology of food addiction. *Curr Opin Clin Nutr Metab Care* 2010; 13(4):359–365.

60. Avena NM, Rada P, Hoebel BG. Sugar and fat bingeing have notable differences in addictive-like behavior. *J Nutr* 2009;139(3):623–628.

61. Avena NM, Rada P, Hoebel BG. Evidence for sugar addiction: behavioral and neurochemical effects of intermittent, excessive sugar intake. *Neurosci Biobehav Rev* 2008;32(1):20–39.

62. Avena NM, Rada P, Moise N, Hoebel BG. Sucrose sham feeding on a binge schedule releases accumbens dopamine repeatedly and eliminates the acetylcholine satiety response. *Neurosci* 2006;139: 813–820.

63. Avena NM, Hoebel BG. Amphetamine-sensitized rats show sugar-induced hyperactivity (cross-sensitization) and sugar hyperphagia. *Pharmacol Biochem Behavior* 2003;74(3):635–639.

64. Avena NM, Long KA, Hoebel BG. Sugar-dependent rats show enhanced responding for sugar after abstinence: evidence of a sugar deprivation effect. *Physiol Behav* 2005;84(3):359–362.

65. Harrison DM. Oral sucrose for pain management in infants: myths and misconceptions. *J Neonat Nur* 2008;14(2):39–46.

66. McKay JR, Carise D, Dennis ML, et al. Extending the benefits of addiction treatment: practical strategies for continuing care and recovery. *J Subst Abuse Treat* 2009;36(2):127–130.

49

Treatment of Binge Eating Disorder

CARLOS M. GRILO

The *Diagnostic and Statistical Manual of Mental Disorders*, fourth edition (*DSM-IV*)[1] includes two well-characterized "formal" eating disorder diagnoses (anorexia nervosa [AN] and bulimia nervosa [BN]) and a poorly characterized "general" diagnostic category (eating disorder not-otherwise-specified [EDNOS]) for those with clinically significant problems but who do not meet criteria for either AN or BN. In addition, the *DSM-IV* includes binge eating disorder (BED), a specific example of EDNOS, as a "research category" with provisional research diagnostic criteria as an appendix. This chapter provides a brief overview of the diagnosis, distribution, and clinical features of BED followed by a critical overview of the current status of the treatment literature.

BINGE EATING DISORDER

Binge Eating Disorder Diagnosis

BED is defined primarily by recurrent episodes of binge eating without the regular use of inappropriate weight-compensatory methods (such as purging behaviors, extreme dietary restriction, or excessive exercise) that are defining features of BN and the binge-purge subtype of AN. Binge eating is defined as eating unusually large amounts of food during discrete periods of time (i.e., within 2 hours) while experiencing a subjective sense of loss of control. The research criteria also require the presence of at least three of five behavioral indicators that reflect loss of control: eating much more rapidly than normal; eating until uncomfortably full; overeating in the absence of hunger; eating alone due to embarrassment about quantity; or negative emotional sequelae such as disgust, depression, or guilt after overeating. The research criteria also require "marked distress" about the binge eating and that the binge eating occurs regularly, that is, at least 2 days per week, on average, over the past 6 months.

Research has supported the distinctiveness of BED from other eating disorders (e.g., BN),[2,3] from other forms of disordered eating (e.g., night eating syndrome),[4] and from obesity without coexisting binge eating.[3] A critical review of the literature concluded that sufficient empirical evidence supports the validity of BED and its inclusion as a distinct and formal eating disorder diagnosis in the *DSM-5*.[5] Although the clinical significance and validity of BED have generally been supported, there remain questions regarding the further refinement of the diagnostic criteria. Research findings are mixed with regard to some of the specifics of the criteria (e.g., the twice-weekly frequency and the unusually large "size" requirement for binge episodes),[6] and there is no empirical basis for others (i.e., the 6-month duration stipulation). In addition, unlike the diagnoses of AN and BN, the *DSM-IV* does not include a cognitive criterion pertaining to disturbed body image (i.e., overvaluation of shape or weight) for the diagnosis of BED. Recent research has found that BED has similar levels of these cognitive body image features as BN and that their presence in BED is associated with heightened levels of both eating disorder and general psychopathology.[2,3,7]

Binge Eating Disorder Distribution and Clinical Features

The recent National Comorbidity Replication Survey reported a lifetime prevalence rate for BED of roughly 2.8%–4.0% in adults, which is greater than AN and BN combined.[8] The distribution of BED is broader and more diverse than the other eating disorders. BED is found evenly distributed throughout adulthood, is common in both men and women, and is found across ethnic and racial groups. BED is strongly associated with obesity, which is not a required diagnostic criterion,[8] and thus with increased medical morbidity due to obesity.

Patients with BED have significantly elevated rates of medical problems and disability compared to obese patients without BED.[9] BED is also associated with significantly elevated psychiatric comorbidities, most notably mood and anxiety disorders.[10] The presence of heightened negative/depressive affect, which occurs in a sizeable minority of patients with BED, signals a more disturbed subgroup of patients with greater psychiatric comorbidity, eating-disorder severity, and general psychopathology.[11] The excess weight in patients with BED is thought to be due to a combination of regular binge eating in addition to the absence of dietary restriction that characterizes the other eating disorders. Many patients with BED report chaotic and overeating behaviors in addition to their binge eating. Patients with BED who seek treatment are typically older than patients with other eating disorders despite the fact that most report a long-standing duration of binge eating[12] along with multiple failed diet attempts often dating back to adolescence.[13] Unlike the other eating disorders, which typically begin following restrictive dieting, roughly half of patients with BED report that the onset of their binge eating preceded their first diet.

TREATMENT OF BINGE EATING DISORDER

Treatments for BED have evolved over time from the obesity and eating disorder fields, which historically interacted little prior to the inclusion of this research diagnosis in the *DSM-IV*. The first generation of treatment studies grew from the obesity field and produced equivocal findings.[14] Mixed findings from obesity treatments for obese binge eaters fueled concerns about the appropriateness of interventions that encouraged dietary restriction for this subgroup of obese patients with co-occurring eating disorder psychopathology. Such concerns stimulated the next stage of treatment studies, which evolved primarily from the research literature for BN, most notably pharmacological interventions (e.g., antidepressant medications) and specialized psychological treatments such as cognitive-behavioral therapy (CBT) and interpersonal psychotherapy (IPT).

Pharmacotherapy-Only Treatments

Most, but not all, randomized placebo-controlled trials testing pharmacotherapy for BED have reported statistically significant findings relative to placebos and have concluded that pharmacotherapy has efficacy for BED. However, a more conservative view of the findings seems indicated in light of typical effect sizes and, most important, that the longer term effects of pharmacotherapy are unknown.

Reas and Grilo,[15] based on a meta-analysis of controlled trials evaluating pharmacotherapy-only for BED which included 14 studies with 1,279 patients, concluded that the medications tested overall have a clinically significant advantage over placebo for producing short-term remission from binge eating and for short-term weight loss. Across different medication classes, a mean attrition rate of 30% was observed, which did not differ from placebo, and 48.7% of patients receiving pharmacotherapy versus 28.5% of patients receiving placebo stopped binge eating (based on last week end-point data). An overall relative risk (RR) of 0.74 was found, which indicates that the medications tested reduce the risk of nonremission by 26%. Effect sizes varied across the different classes of medication for achieving binge eating abstinence. For selective serotonin reuptake inhibitor (SSRI) medications, the RR was 0.81, and for antiepileptic medications the RR was 0.63. Overall, pharmacotherapy also showed evidence of a significant weight reduction of 3.4 kg greater than placebo (i.e., mean weight losses = 3.56 kg versus 0.08 kg) as indicated by a significant effect size (weighted mean difference [WMD] = −3.42). This overall mean weight loss translates approximately to 3.2% of original body weight for the average patient in these studies, which is unlikely to be clinically meaningful for most of the obese patients. The effect sizes across the different medication classes varied somewhat, ranging from modest effects (WMD = −1.7) for SSRIs to larger effects for the antiepileptics (WMD = −4.6).

Two randomized placebo-controlled trials of topiramate reported fairly consistent findings, suggesting clinically meaningful effects for reducing both binge eating and weight. McElroy and colleagues[16] reported that topiramate (median dosing of 212 mg/day) was significantly superior to placebo for producing binge abstinence (based on 1-week end-point) (64% versus 30%) and weight loss (5.9 kg versus 1.2 kg). These findings were replicated and extended in a subsequent larger multisite study, also funded by the drug manufacturer.[17] In the second randomized placebo-controlled trial, topiramate had greater binge remission based on last-week endpoint (58% versus 29%) and weight loss (4.5 kg versus 0.2 kg) than placebo. The multisite replication suggests the positive short-term outcome effects attributable to topiramate are generalizable.[17] However, it is also worth noting that cautious interpretation of conclusions from randomized controlled trials funded by industry may be indicated[18] in light of empirical reports showing associations between industry sponsorship and positive findings.[19,20]

Very little is known regarding the longer term effects of pharmacotherapy-only for BED. To date, only one randomized placebo-controlled trial has included a follow-up[21] and that study, which tested an antiobesity medication subsequently withdrawn from the market due to safety concerns, reported high relapse rates soon after medication discontinuation. A recent uncontrolled open-label study testing the effectiveness of extending treatment with topiramate reported nearly universal noncompliance and attrition due primarily to side effects.[22] These findings,[22] which highlight the need for further studies with both longer treatments and with follow-up designs, suggest the need for caution when interpreting findings regarding the short-term efficacy of topiramate.[16] Lastly, one open-label comparative trial found that two SSRIs (fluoxetine and fluvoxamine) failed to significantly reduce binge eating and weight and were both significantly inferior to CBT-only, CBT-plus-fluoxetine, and CBT-plus-fluvoxamine at posttreatment and 12-month follow-up.[23] Thus, longer term studies of the effects of pharmacotherapy-only represent a pressing research need. Such studies are needed to determine the durability of medication effects, to inform optimal treatment length and timing of medication discontinuation, and determine the risk and timing for relapse.

Collectively, the recent findings for pharmacotherapy-only treatment for BED suggest an update to the specific guidelines offered previously by the National Institute of Clinical Excellence (NICE).[24] The more recent meta-analytic findings[15] suggest the potential efficacy of specific antiobesity (i.e., sibutramine) and antiepiletic (i.e., topiramate) medications but suggest, unlike NICE,[24] that the SSRIs have little utility given their small effects on binge eating and no effect on weight. Importantly, the anti-obesity medication sibutramine has since been withdrawn from the market due to safety concerns. Clinically, a circumspect review of the existing literature suggests that certain medications can cause some patients to stop or reduce binge eating in the short term, resulting in some weight loss that is unlikely to be substantial, but that the longer term effects of these medications are unknown.

Psychological Treatments

A variety of psychological inventions have been tested as treatments for BED. These psychological approaches have generally been slightly adapted versions of the treatment protocols that received some empirical support for BN.[25] NICE,[24] based on meta-analysis, concluded that CBT-BED, a slightly adapted version of CBT-BN,[26] represents the treatment of choice. This clinical recommendation was assigned a methodological "A grade," reflecting strong supporting empirical evidence. Noteworthy is that was the first instance that a psychological therapy was recommended by NICE[24] as the initial treatment of choice for any psychiatric disorder. Subsequent studies have supported this recommendation.[25]

CBT-BED, delivered in either group or individual therapy formats, consistently produces remission rates (defined as at least 1 month of abstinence from binge eating) of 50%-60% and substantial improvements in associated eating disorder psychopathology and broad psychological and psychosocial domains. Unfortunately, CBT does not produce significant weight loss. Various research groups have found that the benefits of CBT-BED appear to be durable and well-maintained through 12 months after completion of treatment.[23,27–29] Research has also documented the effectiveness guided-self-help (GSH) approaches for the delivery of CBT (CBT-GSH), which is very important given the limited availability of clinicians with specialized training in CBT. The NICE[24] guidelines concluded, with a methodological "B grade," that patients with BED could be encouraged to follow a CBT self-help program. Recent randomized controlled trials have provided further support for the effectiveness of CBT-GSH,[30] including its superiority to behavioral weight loss-GSH[31,32] and excellent maintenance through 24-month follow-up.[32] Comparative studies have provided evidence regarding the specificity of CBT effects, including significant differences in time courses[27,33,34] and outcomes between CBT and other treatments.[31,32] In addition, a double-blind study[35] and an open-label study[23] found that CBT was significantly superior to SSRI medications for BED.

Two other specialized psychological approaches, interpersonal psychotherapy (IPT) and dialectical behavior therapy (DBT), have also received empirical support for the treatment of BED. Both of these therapies were tested for BED after receiving some support for BN. The NICE[24] guidelines assigned a "B grade" for the use of these two specific manualized treatments for BED. Unlike CBT-BED, which targets the disordered eating directly, both of these focal therapies target non-ED-specific problems thought to maintain the binge eating (e.g., interpersonal deficits in IPT and emotional regulation deficits in DBT). Research has documented robust short-term and longer term IPT outcomes that are very similar to CBT[29,32] despite their marked conceptual differences. Both IPT and DBT, like CBT, fail to produce weight loss. Further research is needed to replicate these findings by other research groups and to determine whether these specialized interventions can be widely disseminated and delivered effectively by practicing clinicians.

Behavioral Weight Loss Therapy

The NICE[24] guidelines suggested that behavioral weight loss therapy (BWL) with moderate caloric restriction has utility (methodological "B grade") for BED, especially because of the need to reduce weight, which other psychological treatments fail to do. In contrast to early concerns regarding possible negative effects of BWL for this patient group,[14] research has convincingly demonstrated that caloric restriction as part of a comprehensive BWL does not exacerbate binge eating and may be clinically beneficial. Nonetheless, findings for BWL are mixed and a number of controlled trials of BWL have reported no weight loss,[36,37] and others report substantial weight regain following treatment.[38] Recent randomized controlled trials comparing BWL versus other psychological treatments have reported mixed findings in regard to the nature of the various improvements as well as the amount of weight losses, which tend to be small. Wilson and colleagues[32] reported that BWL resulted in greater weight—albeit modest—losses than either IPT or CBT-GSH but that these two treatments had better long-term binge outcomes. Two other randomized controlled trials also reported that BWL resulted in significantly greater—albeit modest—weight losses than CBT but that CBT resulted in significantly greater initial improvements in binge eating at post-treatment but not at 12-month follow-ups.[27,28] The

reasons for such unexpectedly little weight loss in BED patients receiving BWL (and other treatments) across multiple research centers represents a pressing research question.

Combination and Sequenced Treatments

Various combination approaches to treating BED have been tested without much success. NICE[24] concluded, with a methodological "C grade," that little is known about combination or sequenced approaches for BED. Since that review, several trials have found little to no clinical advantage to combining or intensifying treatments. Devlin and colleagues[36] reported that adding CBT—but not antidepressant medication—to BWL enhanced binge eating outcomes, but neither additive treatment enhanced weight loss. De Zwaan and colleagues[38] found that adding CBT to a comprehensive obesity treatment (BWL plus very-low-calorie diet) did not enhance outcomes or slow weight regain. Grilo and colleagues[27] reported that a sequential treatment approach consisting of CBT followed by BWL treatments was not superior to either CBT or BWL. Combining pharmacotherapy and psychological approaches has also generally failed to result in significantly improved outcomes. Reas and Grilo[15] in their review of eight studies testing combination approaches concluded that combining medications with psychological or behavioral treatments did not significantly enhance binge eating outcomes in any study nor did the addition of various antidepressant medications significantly enhance weight losses. However, adding topiramate[39] or orlistat to CBT[30] or BWL[40] significantly increased weight losses, although the weight losses were quite modest.

Predictors, Moderators, and Mediators of Change

Unfortunately, little is known about predictors, moderators, and mediators of treatment outcomes for BED and other eating disorders.[41] Predictors refer to pretreatment variables that predict treatment response across treatments and, if identified, could guide clinicians to patients who might require extra focus. Moderators refer to pretreatment variables that differentially predict outcomes and, if identified, could guide treatment prescription such as matching treatments to patients. Mediators refer to intervening variables during treatment that statistically account to some extent for the relationship between treatment and outcome. Mediators of change could provide clues about potential mechanisms through which treatments achieve their effects.

Reliable predictors of BED outcome have yet to be conclusively identified, although recent studies have reported some support for several significant predictors including overall eating disorder psychopathology, overvaluation of shape/weight, negative affect, self-esteem, and interpersonal problems predict outcomes.[32,42,43,44] Several recent studies have found that early rapid response to treatment (i.e., a treatment process, not a patient characteristic) consistently predicts treatment outcome.[33,34,45,46] Moreover, Grilo and colleagues[33,45,46] reported that early rapid reductions in the frequency of binge eating during the first month of treatment prospectively predicted significant subsequent weight loss during the remaining course of treatment. This finding sheds further light on other reports that abstinence from binge eating is associated with significant, albeit modest, weight loss in those with BED.[29,36] Little is known regarding moderators of BED outcome across different treatment methods. For different psychological treatments, two studies were unable to identify significant moderators of treatment[42,43] whereas a larger study found that lower self-esteem and higher eating disorder severity moderated treatment outcomes, with findings suggesting that IPT was more effective than either BWL or CBT-GSH for patients with those characteristics.[32] Grilo and colleagues[44] reported that overvaluation of shape/weight, lower self-esteem, and higher negative affect signaled significantly greater improvements for patient receiving CBT than patients receiving medication for BED.

Future Research to Improve Treatments
Despite the progress in developing promising treatments for BED in recent years, roughly half of patients do not remit or fail to improve sufficiently even with the best available treatments delivered at specialized programs. Many pressing research questions remain, including (a) how to help nonresponders; (b) are existing treatments effective with groups underrepresented in randomized controlled trials (e.g., minorities, younger patients, patients with medical or psychiatric comorbidities); (c) effectiveness of treatments delivered in non-research clinical settings; (d) effective methods for training and dissemination of evidence-based treatments; and (e) whether generalists can effectively deliver specialty-based treatments.

Future randomized controlled trials should include planned analyses of moderators and mediators of outcomes. A better understanding of such treatment factors has greater potential for contributing to the development of improved treatments than traditional research approaches of combining treatments.

REFERENCES
1. American Psychiatric Association. *Diagnostic and Statistical Manual of Mental Disorders.* Washington, DC: American Psychiatric Association, 1994.
2. Grilo CM, Crosby RD, Masheb RM, et al. Overvaluation of shape and weight in binge eating disorder, bulimia nervosa, and subthreshold bulimia nervosa. *Behav Res Ther* 2009;47:692–696.
3. Grilo CM, Masheb RM, White MA. Significance of overvaluation of shape/weight in binge eating disorder: comparative study with overweight and bulimia nervosa. *Obesity (Silver Spring)* 2010;18(3):499–504.
4. Allison KC, Grilo CM, Masheb RM, Stunkard AJ. Binge eating disorder and night eating syndrome: a comparative study of disordered eating. *J Consult Clin Psychol* 2005;73:1107–1115.
5. Striegel-Moore RH, Franko DL. Should binge eating disorder be included in the DSM-V? A critical review of the state of the evidence. *Ann Rev Clin Psychol* 2008;4:305–324.
6. Roberto CA, Grilo CM, Masheb RM, White MA. Binge eating, purging, or both: eating disorder psychopathology findings from an internet community survey. *Int J Eat Disord* 2010;43(8):724–731.
7. Grilo CM, Hrabosky JI, Allison KC, Stunkard AJ, Masheb RM. Overvaluation of shape and weight in binge eating disorder and overweight controls: refinement of a diagnostic construct. *J Abn Psychol* 2008;117:414–419.
8. Hudson JI, Hiripi E, Pope HG, Kessler RC. The prevalence and correlates of eating disorders in the NCS Replication. *Biol Psychiatry* 2007;61:348–358.
9. Johnson JG, Spitzer RL, Williams JBW. Health problems, impairment and illness associated with bulimia nervosa and binge eating disorder among primary care and obstetric gynaecology patients. *Psychol Med* 2001;31:1455–1466.
10. Grilo CM, White MA, Masheb RM. DSM-IV psychiatric disorder comorbidity and its correlates in binge eating disorder. *Int J Eat Disord* 2009;42:228–234.
11. Grilo CM, Masheb RM, Wilson GT. Subtyping binge eating disorder. *J Consult Clin Psychol* 2001;69:1066–1072.
12. Pope HG, Lalonde JK, Pindyck LJ et al. Binge eating disorder: a stable syndrome. *Am J Psychiatry* 2006;163:2181–2183.
13. Roehrig M, Masheb RM, White MA, Grilo CM. Dieting frequency in obese patients with binge eating disorder: behavioral and metabolic correlates. *Obesity* 2009;17:689–697.

14. Yanovski SZ. Binge eating disorder: current knowledge and future directions. *Obesity Res* 1993;1:306–324.

15. Reas DL, Grilo CM. Review and meta-analysis of pharmacotherapy for binge eating disorder. *Obesity* 2008;16:2024–2038.

16. McElroy SL, Arnold LM, Shapira NA, et al. Topiramate in the treatment of binge eating disorder associated with obesity: a randomized placebo-controlled trial. *Am J Psychiatry* 2003;160:255–261.

17. McElroy SL, Hudson JI, Capece JA et al. Topiramate for the treatment of binge eating disorder associated with obesity: a placebo-controlled study. *Biol Psychiatry* 2007;61:1039–1048.

18. Chan AW, Hrobjartsson A, Haahr MT, Gotzsche PC, Altman DG. Empirical evidence for selective reporting of outcomes in randomized trials: comparison of protocols to published articles. *JAMA* 2004;291:2457–2465.

19. Perlis RH, Perlis CS, Wu Y, Hwang C, Joseph M, Nierenberg AA. Industry sponsorship and financial conflict of interest in the reporting of clinical trials in psychiatry. *Am J Psychiatry* 2005;162:1957–1960.

20. Als-Nielsen B, Chen W, Gluud C, Kjaergard LL. Association of funding and conclusions in randomized drug trials: a reflection of treatment effect or adverse events? *JAMA* 2003;290:921–928.

21. Stunkard AJ, Berkowitz R, Tanrikut C, Reiss E, Young L. D-Fenfluramine treatment of binge eating disorder. *Am J Psychiatry* 1996;153:1455–1459.

22. McElroy SL, Shapiro NA, Arnold LM, et al. Topiramate in the long-term treatment of binge eating disorder associated with obesity. *J Clin Psychiatry* 2004;65:1463–1469.

23. Ricca V, Mannucci E, Mezzani B, et al. Fluoxetine and fluvoxamine combined with individual cognitive-behavioral therapy in binge eating disorder: a one-year follow-up study. *Psychother Psychosom* 2001;70:298–306.

24. National Institute for Clinical Excellence (NICE). *Eating Disorders—Core Interventions in the Treatment and Management of Anorexia Nervosa, Bulimia Nervosa and Related Eating Disorders.* London: NICE, 2004. NICE Clinical Guideline No. 9.

25. Wilson GT, Grilo CM, Vitousek K. Psychological treatments for eating disorders. *Am Psychologist* 2007;62:199–216.

26. Fairburn CG, Marcus MD, Wilson GT. Cognitive behaviour therapy for binge eating and bulimia nervosa: a comprehensive treatment manual. In CG Fairburn, GT Wilson (Eds.), *Binge Eating: Nature, Assessment and Treatment.* New York: Guilford Press; 1993: 361–404.

27. Grilo CM, Masheb RM, Wilson GT, Gueorguieva R,White MA. Cognitive-behavioral therapy, behavioral weight loss, and sequential treatment for obese patients with binge-eating disorder: a randomized controlled trial. *J Consult Clin Psychol* 2011;79(5):675–685.

28. Munsch S, Biedert E, Meyer A, et al. A randomized comparison of cognitive behavioral and behavioral weight loss treatments for overweight individuals with binge eating disorder. *Int J Eat Disord* 2007;40:102–113.

29. Wilfley DE, Welch RR, Stein RI, et al. A randomized comparison of group cognitive-behavioral therapy and group interpersonal psychotherapy for the treatment of overweight individuals with binge eating disorder. *Arch Gen Psychiatry* 2002;59:713–721.

30. Grilo CM, Masheb RM, Salant SL, Cognitive behavioral therapy guided self-help and orlistat for the treatment of binge eating disorder: a randomized, double-blind, placebo-controlled trial. *Biol Psychiatry* 2005;57:1193–1201.

31. Grilo CM, Masheb RM. A randomized controlled comparison of guided self-help cognitive behavioral therapy and behavioral weight loss for binge eating disorder. *Behav Res Ther* 2005;43:1509–1525.

32. Wilson GT, Wilfley DE, Agras WS, Bryson SW. Psychological treatments for binge eating disorder. *Arch Gen Psychiatry* 2010;67(1):94–101.

33. Grilo CM, Masheb RM, Wilson GT. Rapid response to treatment for binge eating disorder. *J Consult Clin Psychol* 2006;74:602–613.

34. Masheb RM, Grilo CM. Rapid response predicts treatment outcomes in binge eating disorder: implications for stepped care. *J Consult Clin Psychol* 2007;75:639–644.

35. Grilo CM, Masheb RM, Wilson GT. Efficacy of cognitive behavioral therapy and fluoxetine for the treatment of binge eating disorder: a randomized double-blind placebo-controlled comparison. *Biol Psychiatry* 2005;57:301–309.

36. Devlin MJ, Goldfein JA, Petkova E, et al. Cognitive behavioral therapy and fluoxetine as adjuncts to group behavioral therapy for binge eating disorder. *Obes Res* 2005;13:1077–1088.

37. Goodrick KG, Poston WSC, Kimball KT, Reeves, RS, Foreyt JP. Nondieting versus dieting treatment for overweight binge-eating women. *J Consult Clin Psychol* 1998;66:363–368.

38. de Zwaan M, Mitchell JE, Crosby RD, et al. Short-term cognitive behavioral treatment does not improve outcome of a comprehensive very-low-calorie diet program in obese women with binge eating disorder. *Behav Ther* 2005;36:89–99.

39. Claudino AM, de Oliveira IR, Appolinario JC, et al. Double-blind, randomized, placebo-controlled trial of topiramate plus cognitive-behavior therapy in binge eating disorder. *J Clin Psychiatry* 2007;68:1324–1332.

40. Golay A, Laurent-Jaccard A, Habicht F, et al. Effect of orlistat in obese patients with binge eating disorder. *Obes Res* 2005;13:1701–1708.

41. Kraemer HC, Wilson GT, Fairburn CG, Agras WS. Mediators and moderators of treatment effects in randomized clinical trials. *Arch Gen Psychiatry* 2002;59:877–883.

42. Hilbert A, Saelens B, Stein R, et al. Pretreatment and process predictors of outcome in interpersonal and cognitive behavioral psychotherapy for binge eating disorder. *J Consult Clin Psychol* 2007;75:645–651.

43. Masheb RM, Grilo CM. Examination of predictors and moderators for self-help treatments of binge eating disorder. *J Consult Clin Psychol* 2008;76:900–904.

44. Grilo CM, Masheb RM, Crosby RD. Predictors and moderators of response to cognitive behavioral therapy and medication for the treatment of binge eating disorder. *J Consult Clin Psychol* 2012 Mar 6; (Epub ahead of print)

45. Grilo CM, Masheb RM. Rapid response predicts binge eating and weight loss in binge eating disorder: findings from a controlled trial of orlistat with guided self-help cognitive behavioral therapy. *Behav Res Ther* 2007;45:2537–2550.

46. Grilo CM, White, Wilson GT, Gueorguieva R, Masheb RM. Rapid response predicts 12-month post-treatment outcomes in binge eating disorder; theoretical and clinical implications. *Psychol Med* 2012;42:807-817.

50

Exercise Addiction and Aversion

Implications for Eating and Obesity

DAVID M. WILLIAMS AND BESS H. MARCUS

Regular physical activity leads to numerous health benefits, both directly and through its impact on weight loss/maintenance. In addition to its health benefits, popular media publications often proclaim that exercise results in the release of endorphins leading to euphoria, often described as a "runner's high." Moreover, there is evidence that some individuals display behaviors consistent with addiction to physical exercise. However, prevalence rates of regular physical activity among the general population are low, especially among overweight and obese adults. The low rates of physical activity are consistent with recent research showing that physically inactive adults actually tend to experience exercise as aversive.

In this chapter we review evidence regarding affective response to exercise, ranging from euphoria to aversion, and associated patterns of physical activity behavior, ranging from exercise addiction to physical inactivity. Additionally, we discuss the relationships between exercise behavior, eating, and obesity. We begin with an overview of basic information on physical activity and exercise.

OVERVIEW OF PHYSICAL ACTIVITY AND EXERCISE

Physical activity (PA) is defined as "any bodily movement produced by the contraction of skeletal muscles that result in a substantial increase over resting energy expenditure."[1] Cleaning the gutters, doing laundry, and walking to the store are all forms of PA. Exercise, however, "is a type of PA consisting of planned structured and repetitive bodily movement done to improve or maintain...physical fitness."[1] For example, walking on a treadmill, swimming laps, or going for a walk on a track are likely to be considered exercise. Thus, all exercise is PA, but not all PA is exercise.

Regardless of whether PA is performed for purposes of improving fitness (i.e., exercise), the benefits of regular PA are numerous, including decreased risk of cardiovascular disease,[2] type 2 diabetes,[3] and osteoporosis,[4] as well as cancers of the breast[5] and colon.[6] Moreover, an inverse linear relationship exists between volume of PA (i.e., frequency by duration by intensity) and all-cause mortality.[7] Evidence suggests that regular PA can positively impact health outcomes independent of its effects on weight control.[8–10] However, PA also has the potential to positively impact health *through* its effects on body weight. Indeed, a recent position stand by the American College of Sports Medicine indicated that regular PA can (a) lead to modest weight loss as a stand-alone intervention (i.e., without dietary intervention), (b) increase the efficacy of dietary weight loss interventions, (c) help prevent weight regain among those who have previously lost weight, and (d) help prevent initial weight gain.[11]

Across each of these outcome categories, the extent to which PA is effective depends on the volume of PA performed, with more PA generally resulting in more favorable health and weight loss/maintenance outcomes.[11] Recent publications by the American College of Sports Medicine, American Heart Association, and US Department of Health and Human Services recommend a minimum of 150 minutes/week of moderate intensity PA (i.e., brisk walking or equivalent; 3–6 metabolic equivalents) or 75 minutes/week of vigorous intensity PA (i.e., jogging or equivalent; > 6 metabolic equivalents) to obtain significant health benefits.[12,13] Additional PA may be necessary for weight loss/maintenance, with recent guidelines recommending up to 300 minutes/week of moderate-intensity

PA to accrue enhanced weight loss/maintenance benefits.[11]

"EXERCISE FEELS GOOD"

In addition to the health benefits of regular physical activity, another widely accepted benefit of exercise is that it "feels good." Indeed, the "runner's high" is an often-used label for the feeling of euphoria that some people have described during exercise—most typically during a prolonged period of endurance running.[14] Occurrence of the runner's high is inconsistent. For example, many endurance athletes report never having experienced a runner's high, and those who have experienced a runner's high report that it does not occur during every exercise session.[15] Thus, while there does appear to be sufficient evidence that some people experience a state of euphoria during prolonged endurance exercise, the phenomenon of the runner's high is likely not as widespread as portrayed in the popular media.

Evidence in support of the "endorphin hypothesis"[16]—a popular explanation for the runner's high—is even more limited. Although several studies have shown increased beta-endorphin concentrations in blood plasma immediately following exercise, these findings fall short of providing an explanation for the runner's high.[15] The most prominent weakness in the findings is that beta-endorphins do not cross the blood–brain barrier, and thus release of endorphins in the peripheral blood stream is unlikely to directly result in the feelings of euphoria experienced during exercise.[15] Additionally, at least one study showed that beta-endorphin concentration in the peripheral blood stream during exercise was not correlated to increases in pain tolerance—an often cited subjective experience of the runner's high.[17] Despite the accumulating skepticism among researchers,[15] a recent pioneering study using positron emission tomography at rest and immediately following a 2-hour run showed both increased beta-endorphin concentration in the brain post exercise, and correlations between beta-endorphin concentration in the brain and subjective reports of euphoria among the 10 male endurance athletes who participated in the study.[18] Additionally, there is growing evidence that endogenous cannabinoids, rather than opioids, may be responsible for the runner's high.[15] Taken together, research is ongoing regarding a biological basis for the runner's high; however, support for the endorphin hypothesis is far from conclusive despite the widespread media portrayal and acceptance by the lay public.

Perhaps most important, because the runner's high is typically experienced by trained endurance athletes in response to prolonged endurance exercise, it is not relevant to the broader population. Nonetheless, there is a large body of research showing that people of varying fitness levels consistently report a mild enhancement of positive affective valence (i.e., greater pleasure versus displeasure) immediately following acute bouts of exercise of varying durations and intensities.[19] This mild but consistent positive shift in affective valence appears to be a different phenomenon than the reportedly more intense experience of the runner's high; however, it is unclear as to whether the two phenomena are triggered by the same underlying mechanisms. Finally, a third body of research has shown that a sustained period of regular exercise over a period of 8–16 weeks can result in decreases in depressive symptoms among clinically depressed adults.[20]

In summary, there are three lines of research that may be contributing to the widely accepted notion that exercise feels good. These include (a) the runner's high and associated endorphin hypothesis that applies primarily to prolonged endurance exercise, (b) the more mild positive shift in affective valence that occurs among the general population immediately following physical activity of various durations and intensities, and (c) the decrease in depressive symptoms associated with sustained exercise programs among clinically depressed adults. While these three phenomena are clearly distinct, they are all consistent with the notion that physical activity feels good.

EXERCISE ADDICTION

Consistent with other behaviors that lead to intensely pleasurable experiences (e.g., drug use), there is a growing body of research indicating that a small proportion of people who exercise regularly may actually become addicted to exercise. Originally, exercise addiction was considered a "positive addiction" because of the benefits of exercise[21]; however, later research revealed that, as with other behavioral addictions (gambling, sex, Internet use), exercise addiction can significantly interfere with adaptive functioning.[22] Exercise addiction (also referred to as exercise dependence or obligatory exercise) has been defined variously, but it typically includes biological (i.e., withdrawal and tolerance) and behavioral (i.e., interference, salience, loss of control) components.[23–25] These features of exercise addiction distinguish it from commitment to regular exercise, though there has not always been careful discrimination between exercise addiction and exercise commitment in the literature.[23] Another distinction is between primary and secondary exercise addiction, with the latter referring to exercise addiction that is secondary to an eating disorder.[25] The literature on exercise addiction lacks large-scale epidemiological studies with representative samples; however, small-scale studies among select samples have led researchers to estimate the prevalence of exercise addiction (primary and secondary combined) to be 1%–5% of regular exercisers.[23,26,27]

There have been various conceptualizations of exercise addiction,[23,28] but most involve some variation of the affect regulation hypothesis often applied to nicotine addiction.[29] That is, those who are addicted to exercise use exercise to regulate their mood. Most often this is conceptualized as relief from negative affect upon exercise, rather than seeking positive affect that is often associated with the runner's high,[23] although greater sensitivity to the release of endorphins during exercise has been implicated in exercise addiction.[28] Unfortunately, there have been few empirical studies to test such conceptualizations, though there is some evidence of greater relief from negative affect among dependent versus nondependent exercisers.[30]

EXERCISE AVERSION AND PHYSICAL INACTIVITY

On the opposite extreme from exercise addiction is the sobering fact that only 32% of US adults meet national PA guidelines.[31] Moreover, PA prevalence rates among overweight and obese individuals are lower than among normal-weight adults,[32,33] with the most recent national data indicating only 20% of overweight or obese adults in the United States meet the minimum recommendations.[34] Additionally, attrition, among those who begin PA programs, is often higher among overweight or obese than normal-weight persons.[35,36]

If physical activity leads to a pleasant affective experience and results in numerous health benefits, then why are rates of regular physical activity so low? More recent research has provided a solution to this apparent paradox. That is, inactive adults—who are the target of efforts to increase population rates of physical activity—report positive affect (i.e., feeling good) upon completion of an exercise bout but find their experience *during exercise* to be unpleasant.[37] This pattern of findings is especially prominent among obese adults.[38] Generally speaking, displeasure experienced during exercise becomes more intense as the intensity of the exercise increases. However, research has shown that, at least among obese women, even moderate intensity exercise (i.e., brisk walking) is often experienced as unpleasant.[38,39]

Thus, for most people it is true that PA "feels good"; it's just that the good feelings come only after the displeasure experienced during the PA has ended. Numerous theorists have observed that humans are notoriously bad at delaying gratification.[40] Thus, it is perhaps not surprising that many people tend to have difficulty engaging in a behavior (physical activity) that tends to be immediately aversive, despite the positive affective (e.g., feeling good afterward) and instrumental (e.g., improved health) outcomes that follow the behavior.[41]

PHYSICAL ACTIVITY AND WEIGHT LOSS/ MAINTENANCE

As indicated earlier, regular physical activity can enhance the efficacy of dietary weight loss programs and aid in effort to maintain weight following weight loss and prior to significant weight gain.[11] Although engaging in physical activity clearly assists with weight loss/maintenance through its impact on energy balance, the effects of physical activity on weight status are not so straightforward. For example, a growing body of research has shown that there a number of processes that compensate for increases in energy expenditure brought about by increased physical activity. For example, increasing physical activity may also lead to increased energy intake, and thus it may limit the extent to which increased energy expenditure creates an overall energy deficit.[42,43] There are two potential pathways through which this may occur. First, acute exercise may increase appetite.[44] Second, engaging in exercise may lead people to believe that they can eat more.[42] In addition to increasing energy intake, the effect of increased energy expenditure (i.e., physical activity) on energy deficit is blunted by metabolic compensatory responses, including reductions in resting metabolic rate and reduced energy cost of exercise (i.e., the body becomes more efficient at exercise with increasing fitness).[42] Finally, there is some evidence to indicate that increased energy expenditure through structured exercise can lead to compensatory decreases in non-exercise activity thermogenesis (or NEAT), thus reducing total energy expenditure.[45]

The presence and magnitude of the compensatory processes varies across individuals.[46,47] Although research on these moderation effects is in its infancy, there appears to be differences based on gender, overweight status, and eating pattern (restrained, unrestrained, disinhibited[48]). For example, exercise may be more likely to create a negative energy balance in restrained relative to unrestrained eaters[49] and in men relative to women.[43] Complicating the picture further are data showing that habitual exercise may actually help people to better match their energy intake with their energy expenditure, thus helping them to maintain energy balance.[43] The latter phenomenon may be a mechanism through which regular exercise helps people to maintain previous weight loss.[50]

CONCLUSIONS AND IMPLICATIONS

In this chapter, we reviewed evidence showing that affective response to physical activity is a complex phenomenon ranging from euphoria to displeasure, and it may be directly responsible for both exercise addiction among a small percentage of exercisers and physical inactivity among the broader population. Additionally, data from epidemiological studies and clinical trials convincingly show that physical activity assists with weight loss maintenance; however, more fine-grained analysis shows that the effects of physical activity on creation of energy deficits are blunted by physiological and behavioral compensatory processes.

A commonality across all of the phenomena discussed is the considerable individual variability in these processes. More research is needed that integrates the complex interplay between physical activity (i.e., energy expenditure) and eating (i.e., energy intake) and takes into consideration the individual variability in these processes. For example, can energy balance interventions be tailored to take advantage of variability in affective response to exercise and compensatory responses to increases in energy expenditure?

Likewise, more research is needed that examines the sources for individual variability in affective response to exercise of varying intensities. Such research might uncover ways in which to harness the euphoric response to exercise to help increase exercise behavior and thus better regulate energy balance. Additionally, such research may discover ways in which exercise can substitute for the reinforcing properties of eating, while avoiding the potentially addictive properties of exercise.

These research agendas can only be addressed through integration of typically isolated methodologies, including behavioral clinical trials, experimental laboratory research, and sophisticated imaging and physiological assessment techniques to name a few. Moreover, research must focus on the sources of individual variability in addition to mean responses among groups of research participants.

REFERENCES

1. American College of Sports Medicine. *ACSM's Guidelines for Exercise Testing and Prescription.* 8th ed. Philadelphia, PA: Lippincott, Williams & Wilkins, 2010.
2. Thompson PD, Buchner D, Pina IL, et al. Exercise and physical activity in the prevention and treatment of atherosclerotic cardiovascular disease: a statement from the Council on Clinical Cardiology (Subcommittee on Exercise, Rehabilitation, and Prevention) and the Council on Nutrition, Physical Activity, and Metabolism (Subcommittee on Physical Activity). *Circulation* 2003;107:3109–3116.
3. Knowler WC, Barrett-Connor E, Fowler SE, et al. Reduction in the incidence of type 2 diabetes with lifestyle intervention or metformin. *N Engl J Med* 2002;346:393–403.
4. Vuori IM. Health benefits of physical activity with special reference to interaction with diet. *Public Health Nutr* 2001;4:517–528.
5. McTiernan A, Kooperberg C, White E, et al. Recreational physical activity and the risk of breast cancer in postmenopausal women: the Women's Health Initiative Cohort Study. *JAMA* 2003;290:1331–1336.
6. Slattery ML. Physical activity and colorectal cancer. *Sports Med* 2004;34:239–252.
7. Lee IM, Skerrett PJ. Physical activity and all-cause mortality: what is the dose-response relation? *Med Sci Sport Exer* 2001;33:S459–S471.
8. Blair SN, Brodney S. Effects of physical inactivity and obesity on morbidity and mortality: current evidence and research issues. *Med Sci Sport Exer* 1999;31:S646–S662.
9. Boule NG, Haddad E, Kenny GP, Wells GA, Sigal RJ. Effects of exercise on glycemic control and body mass in type 2 diabetes mellitus: a meta-analysis of controlled clinical trials. *JAMA* 2001;286:1218–1227.
10. Fagard RH. Physical activity in the prevention and treatment of hypertension in the obese. *Med Sci Sport Exer* 1999;31:S624–S630.

11. Donnelly JE, Blair SN, Jakicic JM et al. Appropriate physical activity intervention strategies for weight loss and prevention of weight regain for adults. *Med Sci Sport Exer* 2009;41(2):459–471.

12. Haskell WL, Lee IM, Pate RR, et al. Physical activity and public health: updated recommendation for adults from the American College of Sports Medicine and the American Heart Association. *Med Sci Sport Exer* 2007;39:1423–1434.

13. Physical Activity Guidelines Advisory Committee. *Physical Activity Guidelines Advisory Committee Report, 2008*. Washington, DC:United States Department of Health and Human Services, 2008.

14. Partin C. Runner's "high." *JAMA* 1983;249:21.

15. Dietrich A, McDaniel WF. Endocannabinoids and exercise. *Brit J Sport Med* 2004;38:536–541.

16. Morgan WP. Affective beneficence of vigorous physical activity. *Med Sci Sport Exer* 1985;17:94–100.

17. Oktedalen O, Solberg EE, Haugen AH, Opstad PK. The influence of physical and mental training on plasma beta-endorphin level and pain perception after intensive physical exercise. *Stress Health* 2001; 17:121–127.

18. Boecker H, Sprenger T, Spilker ME, et al. The runner's high: opioidergic mechanisms in the human brain. *Cereb Cortex* 2008;18:2523–2531.

19. Reed J, Buck S. The effect of regular aerobic exercise on positive-activated affect: a meta-analysis. *Psychol Sport Exerc* 2009;10:581–594.

20. Stathopoulou G, Powers MB, Berry AC, Smits JAJ, Otto MW. Exercise interventions for mental health: a quantitative and qualitative review. *Clin Psychol-Sci Pr* 2006;13:179–193.

21. Glasser W. *Positive Addiction*. New York: Harper & Row, 1976.

22. Morgan W. Negative addiction in runners. *Physician Sportsmed* 1979;7:57–70.

23. Allegre B, Souville M, Therme P, Griffiths M. Definitions and measures of exercise dependence. *Addict Res Theory* 2006;14:631–646.

24. Hausenblas HA, Downs DS. Exercise dependence: a systematic review. *Psychol Sport Exerc* 2002;3:89–123.

25. Veale DMW. Does primary exercise dependence really exist? In Annett J, Cripps B, Steinberg H, eds. *Exercise Addiction: Motivation for Participation in Sport and Exercise*. Leicester, England: The British Psychological Society; 1995: 1–5.

26. Terry A, Szabo A, Griffiths M. The exercise addiction inventory: a new brief screening tool. *Addict Res Theory* 2004;12:489–499.

27. Szabo AGM. Exercise addiction in British sport science students. *Int J Ment Health Addiction* 2007; 5:25–28.

28. Hamer M, Karageorghis CI. Psychobiological mechanisms of exercise dependence. *Sports Med* 2007; 37:477–484.

29. Tomkins S. *A Modified Model of Smoking Behaviour*. Chicago: Aldine, 1968.

30. Rosa DA, De Mello MT, Negrao AB, De Souza-Formigoni MLO. Mood changes after maximal exercise testing in subjects with symptoms of exercise dependence. *Percept Motor Skill* 2004;99:341–353.

31. Centers for Disease Control and Prevention. 1988–2008 No leisure-time physical activity trend chart. 2009. Available at: http://www.cdc.gov/nccdphp/dnpa/physical/stats/leisure_time.htm. Accessed March 22, 2012.

32. Cooper AR, Page A, Fox KR, Misson J. Physical activity patterns in normal, overweight and obese individuals using minute-by-minute accelerometry. *Eur J Clin Nutr* 2000;54:887–894.

33. King GA, Fitzhugh EC, Bassett DR, Jr., et al. Relationship of leisure-time physical activity and occupational activity to the prevalence of obesity. *Int J Obes Relat Metab Disord* 2001;25:606–612.

34. MMWR. Prevalence of leisure-time physical activity among overweight adults—United States, 1998. *Morb Mort Weekly Rep* 2000;49:326–330.

35. King NA, Lluch A, Stubbs RJ, Blundell JE. High dose exercise does not increase hunger or energy intake in free living males. *Eur J Clin Nutr* 1997;51: 478–483.

36. Kriska AM, Bayles C, Cauley JA, LaPorte RE, Sandler RB, Pambianco G. A randomized exercise trial in older women: increased activity over two years and the factors associated with compliance. *Med Sci Sport Exer* 1986;18:557–562.

37. Ekkekakis P. Pleasure and displeasure from the body: perspectives from exercise. *Cognition Emotion* 2003;17:213–239.

38. Ekkekakis P, Lind E. Exercise does not feel the same when you are overweight: the impact of self-selected and imposed intensity on affect and exertion. *Int J Obesity* 2006;30:652–660.

39. Mattsson E, Larsson UE, Rossner S. Is walking for exercise too exhausting for obese women? *Int J Obes Relat Metab Disord* 1997;21:380–386.

40. Metcalfe J, Mischel W. A hot/cool-system analysis of delay of gratification: dynamics of willpower. *Psychol Rev* 1999;106:3–19.

41. Williams DM. Exercise, affect, and adherence: an integrated model and a case for self-paced exercise. *J Sport Exerc Psychol* 2008;30:471–496.

42. King NA, Caudwell P, Hopkins M, et al. Metabolic and behavioral compensatory responses to exercise interventions: barriers to weight loss. *Obesity* 2007;15:1373–1383.

43. Martins C, Morgan L, Truby H. A review of the effects of exercise on appetite regulation: an obesity perspective. *Int J Obes* 2008;32:1337–1347.

44. Finlayson G, Bryant E, Blundell JE, King NA. Acute compensatory eating following exercise is associated

with implicit hedonic wanting for food. *Physiol Behav* 2009;97:62–67.

45. Colley R, Byrne N, Hills A. Quantifying the effect of physical activity on total energy expenditure in obese women. *Obes Res* 2005;13:A24.

46. King NA, Hopkins M, Caudwell P, Stubbs RJ, Blundell JE. Individual variability following 12 weeks of supervised exercise: identification and characterization of compensation for exercise-induced weight loss. *Int J Obes* 2008;32:177–184.

47. King NA, Caudwell PP, Hopkins M, Stubbs JR, Naslund E, Blundell JE. Dual-process action of exercise on appetite control: increase in orexigenic drive but improvement in meal-induced satiety. *Am J Clin Nutr* 2009;90:921–927.

48. Hill JO, Melby C, Johnson SL, Peters JC. Physical activity and energy requirements. *Am J Clin Nutr* 1995;62:1059S-1066S.

49. Lluch A, King NA, Blundell JE. No energy compensation at the meal following exercise in dietary restrained and unrestrained women. *Br J Nutr* 2000;84:219–225.

50. Catenacci VA, Ogden LG, Stuht J, et al. Physical activity patterns in the National Weight Control Registry. *Obesity* 2008;16:153–161.

51

New Treatments for Obesity Based on Addiction Models

RICHARD L. SHRINER

Two-thirds of Americans are overweight, and one-third are obese.[1] Even more penetrating is the statistic that type 2 diabetes is the leading cause of death, and obesity is the major factor.[2] New treatments and new paradigms for treatment are obviously needed to address the obesity epidemic. This chapter outlines some of these new treatments. We also argue for a new paradigm that might help in future modeling of effective antiobesity interventions.

Practical approaches to date that have been used to treat obesity include the following: (1) food relationship paradigms, like The Structure House[3]; (2) food formula paradigms, such as Jenny Craig[4]; and addiction model paradigms like Overeaters Anonymous.[5,6] As Gold[7] and others have pointed out, Alcoholics Anonymous (AA) influenced "recovery centers," which form the central core for successful treatment of addictions. In terms of defining recovery as a dignifying and healing process, The Betty Ford Institute offers the following definition for *recovery*: "a voluntary maintained lifestyle composed and characterized by sobriety, personal health, and citizenship."[8] Embracing this model for addiction and recovery, DuPont, McLellan, White, Merlo, and Gold,[9] have outlined a prototypical therapeutic environment or "setting" for recovery. In their treatment population of some 904 physicians admitted to 16 state physicians' health programs (PHPs), these researchers studied the outcomes of care over a 5-year period. Importantly, Gold[10] and others[11,12] report that PHP programs have a 70%–96% long-term recovery rate. The PHP program model may be successful, in part, due to six key elements: contingency management, drug testing, 12-step programing, active management of relapse, continuing care, and a focus on lifelong recovery.

At the University of Florida, our Florida Recovery Center (FRC) has been highly successful in terms of executing these core features of the PHP concept, following the Betty Ford definition of recovery.[7]

Despite the significant utility of the addiction model for the treatment of obesity, proper initial triage of patients is paramount. For the morbidly obese (i.e., those individuals with a body mass index [BMI] > 40, or a BMI > 35 with metabolic stressors such as diabetes), bariatric surgery is increasingly being advocated as a sensible and cost-effective option.[13–15] Bariatric surgery is for many the only viable means to initiate a successful antiobesity program.

In terms of state-of-the-art pharmacology, given the colocalization of dopamine and opioid synaptic circuits in the nucleus accumbens and other reward centers of the brain, Plodkowski et al.[16] have reviewed the drug Contrave which is in Phase III trials for the treatment of obesity. This drug includes bupropion for its dopamine reuptake inhibitor effects (delivering increased dopamine to POMC neurons), which via α-MSH stimulates MC4 receptors effectuating an extended anorexigenic response, reportedly more effective than either drug (bupropion or naltrexone) when used alone. Experimentally, rat data have opened up the field of bariatric pharmacology to a whole host of possible candidates for antiobesity pharmacotherapy including growth hormone fragment,[17] PYY 3-36,[18] and oleoylestrone.[19] Another novel putative antiobesity agent might be acamprosate, which Han et al.[20] showed in humans reduced food cravings. Liraglutide (a GLP-1 analog) has been shown by Astrup et al.[21] in randomized, double-blind, placebo-controlled studies to be an effective weight loss medication that has yet to be approved in the United States. CB1 receptor antagonists such as rimonabant continue to intrigue, even though their neuropsychiatric side effects (depression) loom problematic to date. Despite this, Janero et al.[22] argue that novel CB1 receptor ligands that are peripherally directed and/or exhibit neutral antagonism in terms of exacerbating unwanted mood-altering side effects are clearly yet discoverable and deserve further research. Perhaps even more appealing in terms of clinical application, Kirkham et al.[23] were able to show that *food deprivation* in rats resulted in a two- to three-fold increase in limbic endocannabinoids, while Bambico et al.[24] were able to demonstrate the mood-elevating (antidepressant) qualities of de novo endocannabinoids by way of their ability to increase serotonin and noradrenergic firing activity. This sets up the interesting paradox that food deprivation, itself, via the CB1 receptor may actually effectuate an antidepressant response. We discuss the ramifications of this to novel treatments for obesity later.

Exercise has been given a thorough risk-to-benefit analysis by many investigators.[25] Total daily energy expenditure (TDEE) is made up of three basic components: resting metabolic rate, diet-induced thermogenesis, and activity thermogenesis.[26] Although relatively small in the overall contribution to TDEE, activity thermogenesis is divided on the basis of planned and unplanned activities (the latter called spontaneous physical activity [SPA] or nonexercise activity thermogenesis [NEAT]). Redman and Ravussin[26] cite Levine's[27] important work that demonstrated how obese individuals participate in less NEAT than normal-weight controls. Levine[27] showed that by increasing NEAT, obese patients could increase their need energy expenditure by up to 500 kcal/day, or equivalent to about 2 hours of a brisk walk! Obviously, cognitive therapies that could enhance the proportion of NEAT could have a direct therapeutic impact on the treatment of obesity.

The traditional model for obesity can be decomposed into the contributions of nutrition and theromogenesis. The food addiction model adds an important third factor called "perception," which contributes to the nonhomeostatic or "hedonic" aspects of food addictions, including rat models for "binge eating."[28] Our nontraditional model for food addiction, NEP, stands for Nutrition, Energy, and Perception. Nutrition is characterized by the types of energy-rich foods we ingest. At present there is ongoing discussion regarding the relative contribution that fats, carbohydrates, or proteins play in the current obesity epidemic. Germane to type 2 diabetes are the various processes that kindle vascular and organelle damage (e.g., β-cell oxidative damage to pancreatic islets causing diabetes), which traditionally have been characterized by the term "inflammation." To this end, both "glucotoxicity" and "lipotoxicity" can be shown to play major roles in type 2 diabetes. Stored triacylglycerols are typically the chief source of energy for muscle contraction, and an inability to oxidize fatty acids from triacylglycerols has serious consequences for health.[29] Whether fat is stored via fatty acid synthesis or undergoes fatty acid β-oxidation is determined by the net influence of insulin versus glucagon.[26] Insulin surges after carbohydrate absorption in the gut favoring fatty acid synthesis, while carbohydrate deprivation stimulates glucagon release. Therefore, there is a literal "fork in the road" favoring either lipid storage or oxidation that is determined, in part, by net carbohydrate intake. This is consistent with data that show over the last 30 years, in synch with the obesity epidemic, net carbohydrate consumption has gone up while net fat consumption has gone down.[30]

Our choice of foodstuffs, carbohydrates versus fats, via their influence on competitive endocrine mediators (insulin versus glucagon) will either effectuate net fatty acid removal from the adipocyte or fatty acid synthesis and storage in the adipocyte, liver, pancreas, and so on, over time. In turn, as others have argued elsewhere,[31] the excessive storage of fat in the adipocyte and in other cells of the endocrine axis, such as pancreatic cells, can cause lipotoxic lymphocyte mediated inflammation, reactive oxidations, and eventual damage to the islet cells of the pancreas, causing diabetes. In addition, excessive glucose loading can damage the β-cells of the pancreas, leading to diabetes. This latter process is called "glucotoxicity" and has been described in detail by Raghavan et al.[32] Finally, Mithieux[33] found that a mechanism exists whereby fasting and high-protein diets induce satiety (via a "portal vein glucose-sensing mechanism"), which stimulates hypothalamic regions controlling food intake. This investigator was able to substantiate that intestinal gluconeogenesis (i.e., de novo synthesis of glucose by the liver) is induced during postabsorption in rats fed on protein-enriched diets, which decreased hunger and subsequent food intake.[34] More recently, Veldhorst, Neiu-wenhuizen, et al.[35] studied human responses to protein supplements and found that a 25% protein whey protein was superior to either casein or soy proteins in triggering GLP-1 response. These investigators confirm that dietary protein plays a role in body weight regulation, partly because of its effects on appetite.

Samaha et al.[36] found that severely obese subjects with diabetes and/or metabolic syndrome lost more weight on low-carbohydrate than on low-fat diets. Haimoto et al.[37] report that a 30% carbohydrate diet over 6 months led to significant reduction in HbA1c even in severe type 2 diabetes stating, "The effectiveness of the diet may be comparable to that of insulin therapy." Johnstone et al.[38] showed that high-protein, low-carbohydrate ketogenic diets reduce hunger and lower intake significantly more than high-protein, medium-carbohydrate nonketogenic diets. Comparing the four most popular diets (Atkins, Zone, Ornish, and Learn), Gardner et al.[39] found that Atkins was superior to the other three diets in terms of its "metabolic effects" and that a low-carbohydrate, high-protein diet was a feasible alternative for weight loss. Thomas and Elliott [40] performed a critical meta-analysis on 11 randomized controlled trials involving 402 participants suffering from either type 1 or 2 diabetes and found that a low glycemic index diet can improve glycemic control in diabetes without compromising hypoglycemic events. And finally, dispelling the often commonly held belief that losing weight on low-carbohydrate diets is just a matter of losing the weight of water of hydration of stored glycogen, Boden et al.[41] found that his subjects on a low-carbohydrate diet lost weight that was primarily due to reduction of adipose tissue, not loss of water. For all the aforementioned reasons, our NEP model would suggest that a low-carbohydrate/moderately high-protein diet probably holds the most promise for containing the obesity epidemic now and in the future.

Moving on to the "E" component of the NEP model, the traditional way we characterize thermogenesis is by the static, linear model: energy$_{taken in}$ − total energy$_{expended}$ = net weight. In our nonlinear NEP model, this equation is transformed into: energy$_{from outside}$ + energy$_{stored}$ − total energy expended = dynamic weight. Consistent with nonlinear models, there is more than one solution set (subject) for the same weight or multiple solution sets (weights) for the same subject. When that solution set results in a dynamic weight that is unhealthy, it is called allobariac. Healthy solution sets are called eubariac.

An example of a eubariac process would be pregnancy, where a woman may be in a state of eubariac metabolic balance or homeostasis, even though she weighs three different weights before, during, and after pregnancy. In this case, the varying energy$_{stored}$ component serves a dynamic and adaptive purpose.

An example of an allobariac state versus a eubaric state in the same animal (i.e., two solution sets for the same animal weighing the same weight) would be two genetically identical rats that both weigh the same weight but one is at its eubariac weight, while the other rat (suffering from a pharmaceutically compensated metabolic syndrome) is not. In this case, the rat that is in a eubariac state will often be eating foodstuffs (usually low-carbohydrate/high-protein), which leaves the energy$_{stored}$ component at its adaptive dynamic weight. This low-carbohydrate/high-protein regimen results in maximum β-oxidation of body fats, which optimizes the energy$_{stored}$ component to maximize survival in any particular environment. On the other hand, the allobariac rat might be on a high-carbohydrate/low-protein diet that is subsidized by thiazolidinediones, which actually prevents aggressive β-oxidation of body fats. Early on, both rats may have the same weight, but with the passage of time, the allobariac rat will progressively store more and more fat (i.e., its energy$_{stored}$ component is no longer optimized), which will lead to a maladaptive or allobariac dynamic weight. At present, this latter allobariac condition of "apparent health" typifies the current state of metabolic imbalance that we find in millions of Americans.

The last factor in our nonlinear NEP model stands for "P" or perception. Perception forms the basis of hendonic homeostasis, which can easily override natural homeostasis that would otherwise prevent the organism from becoming obese. This latter component (the power of reward that affects and effects "food perceptions") affords the food addiction model its robustness and utility. Hoebel [28] argues that feeding rats episodic boluses of either glucose (25%) or sucrose (10%)—to simulate a "sugar binge"—alternating with normal chow, leads to subsequent escalations of sugar intake. The binge alternating with normal chow schedule creates feeding behaviors that are indistinguishable from the binge eating we often see in humans. Importantly, this does not happen if genetically similar rats are given constant access to these same carbohydrate solutions ad libitum. Apparently, it is the "space time" intervalization that seems to prime the pump of binge-eating sugar addiction.

This research has an obvious impact on the way we view food addictions in humans. In terms of reaffirming the sugar addiction model, Hoebel [28] found that if these same rats that had been made binge prone (by a few weeks of scheduled intermittent sugar feedings) were suddenly robbed of sugar access, they showed classical signs of opioid-like withdrawal. Interestingly, the fat binged rats *did not* show this same type of carbohydrate-induced, opioid-like withdrawal. To this end, Gold,[42] Hoebel,[28] Mathes,[43] Zheng,[44] Dagher,[45] and others have all argued that this hedonic hegemony (or what we have chosen to call the allobariac state) has become highly relevant to the study and treatment of obesity, diabetes, and the metabolic syndrome. It demands an appreciation for the fact that carbohydrates, in particular, may be just as addicting as cocaine, opioids, alcohol, and so on. In all these substances, the same dopamine/opioid channels that stimulate the nucleus accumbens and other neurocircuits of reward and addiction share a common end. More recently, Cocores and Gold [46] have argued rather convincingly that "salt" may also play an important part as a key nutrient of addiction. Gleaning from rat model research, perception (immediate food reward) is everything, and everything is perception. And it is this maladaptive perception that drives the current global obesity epidemic.

At the University of Florida, Springhill Health Center, we are studying the practical applications of the NEP model that embrace an AA-type fellowship group experience and a nonblaming, shame-free treatment environment. We are experimenting with supervised time-limited fasting via a brief partial hospitalization that uses a low-carbohydrate/high-protein detoxification strategy. As per Kirkham,[23] and Bambico,[24] this may involve de novo endocannabinoid rescue of mood, while simultaneously allowing for the initial resetting of allobariac metabolic function. If followed by an ongoing low- to moderate-carbohydrate/high-protein "creative" diet, we have found this may be the most effective way to assist patients in their recovery from obesity.

Our overall approach melds cognitive psychotherapy, group fellowship, and focused creative nutrition with effective antiobesity pharmaceutical intervention. This is the only way to effectuate a body-brain-mind long-term emancipation from obesity. Pharmaceutical interventions include naltrexone and wellbutrin combined therapy, the option for time-limited stimulant augmentation strategies, and more traditional antidepressant/antianxiety medications to address comorbid neuropsychiatric illness that typically plagues obese and/or type 2 diabetic patients. We emphasize a "one day at a time" approach that recognizes the potential for lifelong relapse. Our bench work experience with animal models at the McKnight Brain Institute is applied to everyday clinical practice on a continuous and ongoing basis. Our therapeutic model emphasizes to patients their own unique style of food perception called IGS,[47,48] along with the dangers of episodic food avoidance, which only exacerbates binge-eating behaviors. In summary, all our patients must learn to "live with food," rather than try to avoid it. Our intervention first begins by having patients learn how they perceive food. Then, they are evaluated for appropriate medical treatments. Finally, through a fellowship addiction group model, they discover effective pathways to achieve and maintain recovery.

REFERENCES

1. Flegal KM, Carroll MD, Ogden CL, Johnson CL. Prevalence and trends in obesity among US adults, 1999–2000. *JAMA* 2002;288(14):1723–1727.
2. Cooper HD. *The Washington Manual of Medical Therapeutics.* 32nd ed. Baltimore, MD: Lippincott Williams & Wilkins, 2007.
3. Musante GJ. *The Structure House Weight Loss Plan.* New York: Fireside, 2007.
4. Craig J. *What Have You Got to Lose?* Roseville, CA: Prima Publishing, 1997.
5. Schenker MD. *A Clinician's Guide to 12-Step Recovery.* New York: W.W. Norton & Company, 2009.
6. Overeaters Anonymous. *Overeaters Anonymous.* New York: Overeaters Anonymous, 2001.
7. Merlo LJ, Gold MS. Successful treatment of physicians with addictions. *Psychiatric Times* 2009;26(9). Available at: http://www.psychiatrictimes.com/display/article/10168/1444802. Accessed on March 22, 2012.
8. Betty Ford Institute Consensus Panel. What is recovery? A working definition from the Betty Ford Institute. *J Subst Abuse Treat* 2007;33(3):221–228.
9. DuPont RL, McLellan AT, White WL, Merlo LJ, Gold MS. Setting the standard for recovery: Physicians' Health Programs. *J Subst Abuse Treat* 2009;36(2):159–171.
10. Gold MS, Aronson M. Treatment of alcohol abuse and dependence. In: *CD ROM Educational Program.* Cambridge, MA: Harvard University; 2004.
11. Domino KB, Hornbein TF, Polissar NL, Renner G. Risk factors for relapse in health care

professionals with substance use disorders. *JAMA* 2005;293(12):1453–1460.

12. Gastfriend DR. Physician substance abuse and recovery: what does it mean for physicians—and everyone else? *JAMA* 2005;293(12):1513–1515.

13. DeMaria EJ, Jamal MK. Laparoscopic adjustable bastric banding: evolving clinical experience. *Surg Clin N Am* 2005;85(4):773–787.

14. Leslie D, Kellogg T, Ikramuddin S. Bariatric surgery primer for the internist: keys to the surgical consultation. *Med Clin N Am* 2007;91(3):353–381.

15. Mitchell JE, de Zwaan M. *Bariatric Surgery.* New York: Routledge, 2005.

16. Plodkowski RA, Nguyen Q, Sundaram U, Nguyen L, Chau DL, St Jeor S. Bupropion and naltrexone: a review of their use individually and in combination for the treatment of obesity. *Expert Opin Pharmacol* 2009;10(6):1069–1081.

17. Halford JC. Obesity drugs in clinical development. *Curr Opin Invest Drugs* 2006;7(4):312–318.

18. Brandt G, Sileno A, Quay S. Intranasal peptide YY 3-36: phase 1 dose ranging and dose sequencing studies. *Obes Res* 2004;12(suppl):A28.

19. Alemany M, Fernandez-Lopez JA, Petrobelli A, Granada M, Foz M, Remesar X. Weight loss in a patient with morbid obesity under treatment with oleoylestrone. *Med Clin-Barcelona* 2003;121(13):496–499.

20. Han DH, Lyool IK, Sung YH, Lee SH, Renshaw PF. The effect of acamprosate on alcohol and food craving in patients with alcohol dependence. *Drug Alcohol Depen* 2008;93(3):279–283.

21. Astrup A, Rossner S, Van Gaal L, et al. Effects of liraglutide in the treatment of obesity: a randomised, double-blind, placebo-controlled study. *Lancet* 2009;374(9701):1606–1616.

22. Janero DR, Makriyannis A. Cannabinoid receptor antagonists: pharmacological opportunities, clinical experience, and translational prognosis. *Expert Opinion Emerg Dr* 2009;14(1):43–65.

23. Kirkham TC, Williams CM, Fezza F, Di Marzo V. Endocannabinoid levels in rat limbic forebrain and hypothalamus in relation to fasting, feeding and satiation: stimulation of eating by 2-arachidonoyl glycerol. *Brit J Pharmacol* 2002;136(4):550–557.

24. Bambico FR, Duranti A, Tontini A, Tarzia G, Gobbi G. Endocannabinoids in the treatment of mood disorders: evidence from animal models. *Curr Pharm Design* 2009;15(14):1623–1646.

25. Ehrman JK, Gordon PM, Visich PS, Keteyian SJ. *Clinical Exercise Physiology.* 2nd ed. Champaign, IL: Human Kinetics, 2009.

26. Redman LM, Ravussin E. Energy expenditure in obesity. In: *Contemporary Endocrinology: Treatment of the Obese Patient.* New York: Humana Press, 2007: 151–174.

27. Levine JA, Eberhardt NL, Jensen MD. Role of nonexercise activity thermogenesis in resistance to fat gain in humans. *Science* 1999;283(5399):212–214.

28. Hoebel BG, Avena NM, Bocarsly ME, Rada P. Natural addiction: a behavioral and circuit model based on sugar addiction in rats. *J Addict Med* 2009;3(1):33–41.

29. Nelson NL, Cox MC. *Lehninger Principles of Biochemistry.* 4th ed. New York: W. H. Freeman & Company, 2005.

30. Centers for Disease Control and Prevention. Trends in intake of energy and macronutrients—United States, 1971–2000. *Morb Mortal Weekly Rep* 2004;53(4):80–82.

31. Duez H, Lewis FG. Fat metabolism in insulin resistance and type 2 diabetes. In: Feinglos MN, Bethel, MA, eds. *Type 2 Diabetes Mellitus.* New York: Humana Press; 2008: 49–74.

32. Raghavan VA, Garber AJ. Postprandial hyperglycemia. In: Feinglos MN, Bethel, MA, eds. *Type 2 Diabetes Mellitus.* New York: Humana Press; 2008: 97–114.

33. Mithieux G. Glucose sensing: from gut to brain. *B Acad Nat Med Paris* 2007;191(4–5):911–920.

34. Mithieux G, Misery P, Magnan C, et al. Portal sensing of intestinal gluconeogenesis is a mechanistic link in the diminution of food intake induced by diet protein. *Cell Metab* 2005;2(5):321–329.

35. Veldhorst MA, Nieuwenhuizen AG, Hochstenbach-Waelen A, et al. Dose-dependent satiating effect of whey relative to casein or soy. *Physiol Behav* 2009; 96(4–5):675–682.

36. Samaha FF, Iqbal N, Seshadri P, et al. A low-carbohydrate as compared with a low-fat diet in severe obesity. *N Engl J Med* 2003;348(21):2074–2081.

37. Haimoto H, Sasakabe T, Wakai K, Umegaki H. Effects of a low-carbohydrate diet on glycemic control in outpatients with severe type 2 diabetes. *Nutr Metab* 2009;6:21.

38. Johnstone AM, Horgan GW, Murison SD, Bremner DM, Lobley GE. Effects of a high-protein ketogenic diet on hunger, appetite, and weight loss in obese men feeding ad libitum. *Am J Clin Nutr* 2008; 87(1):44–55.

39. Gardner CD, Kiazand A, Alhassan S, et al. Comparison of the Atkins, Zone, Ornish, and LEARN diets for change in weight and related risk factors among overweight premenopausal women: the A TO Z Weight Loss Study: a randomized trial. *JAMA* 2007; 297(9):969–977.

40. Thomas D, Elliott EJ. Low glycaemic index, or low glycaemic load, diets for diabetes mellitus. *Cochrane Database Sys Rev* 2009;(1):CD006296.

41. Boden G, Sargrad K, Homko C, Mozzoli M, Stein TP. Effect of a low-carbohydrate diet on appetite, blood glucose levels, and insulin resistance in obese patients with type 2 diabetes. *Ann Int Med* 2005; 142(6):403–411.

42. Von Deneen KM, Gold MS, Liu Y. Food addiction and cues in Prader-Willi Syndrome. *J Addict Med* 2009;3(1):19–25.

43. Mathes WF, Brownley KA, Mo X, Bulik CM. The biology of binge eating. *Appetite* 2009;52(3):545–553.

44. Zheng H, Lenard NR, Shin AC, Berthoud HR. Appetite control and energy balance regulation in the modern world: reward-driven brain overrides repletion signals. *Int J Obes* 2009;33(suppl 2):S8–S13.

45. Dahl JP, Weller AE, Kampman KM, et al. Confirmation of the association between a polymorphism in the promoter region of the prodynorphin gene and cocaine dependence. *Am J Med Genet B Neuropsychiatr Genet* 2005;139B(1):106–108.

46. Cocores JA, Gold MS. The Salted Food Addiction Hypothesis may explain overeating and the obesity epidemic. *Med Hypotheses* 2009;73(6):892–899.

47. Shriner RL. Solutions in managed care: IT and Inforisk. *Eur Hosp Manag J* 1996;3(2):27.

48. Shriner RL. Metabolic syndrome. The Zone Magazine: Tampa Bay, FL., Sept/Oct 2008:20.

52

From the Front Lines

The Impact of Refined Food Addiction on Well-Being

JOAN IFLAND, KAY SHEPPARD, AND H. THERESA WRIGHT

It's like someone takes over my body and I can't stop eating. I want to be locked up. I can't keep living this way.

From our clinical standpoint, refined food addiction impacts people as extensively as do other addictions. Refined food addiction is characterized by behaviors described under the diagnostic criteria in *The Diagnostic and Statistical Manual of Mental Disorders*, fourth edition (*DSM-IV*) for substance use disorders. Refined food addiction is characterized by cognitive, behavioral, and physiological symptoms, including increased tolerance for the substance; withdrawal symptoms when the substance is withheld; unintended use; failure to cut back; time spent obtaining, consuming, and recovering; missed social activities; and use in spite of knowledge of consequences. Because of the distracting characteristic of excessive adipose tissue (obesity), the nature and scope of refined food addiction are often overlooked.

In decades past, the extent of adverse consequences associated with addiction in general was also largely unrecognized. This lack of awareness gave rise to The Addiction Severity Index (ASI), which serves as an instrument for gathering data on the full constellation of consequences of addiction. Considered the gold standard for assessing addiction severity, the ASI is broadly accepted and validated for a variety of addictions across cultures.[1,2] Thus, the ASI provides an appropriate vehicle for organizing a comprehensive description of refined food addiction and illustrating that obesity is only one consequence of this disorder, and not necessarily the most important.

Herein a group of clinicians report their clinical observations of self-identified food addicts. Clinical observations are a valid, indispensable source of data in the early stages of describing and defining psychiatric diseases.[3] Our observations span 30 years of assessment and treatment of self-identified food addicts.

OBSERVATION DATA

We have organized our observations according to ASI categories—medical, employment, alcohol and drug use (modified for food use), legal, family/social, and psychiatric. We added "other considerations" for issues specific to refined food addiction. The term "abstinence" is defined as the elimination from the diet of refined foods that cause loss of control over eating for that individual. The consequences that we discuss in this section apply to refined food addicts as a group; the particular constellation of consequences for any given patient is highly variable, and it comprises only a subset of the potential consequences.

Medical

We find that our clients have been hospitalized for diabetes, heart disease, depression (including suicide attempts), cancer, bariatric surgery, and complications from these conditions. In recent years, complications of bariatric surgery are noted, such as binging and vomiting, compromised nutrient absorption, and weight regain. Psychiatric symptoms in individuals we see for food addiction are common, ranging from irritability to rage, anxiety to panic, and guilt to debilitating shame. In abstinence, however, clients usually report diminishment or even elimination of these symptoms.

Endocrine system issues include hyper- or hypothyroidism, diabetes, polycystic ovarian syndrome, and infertility. Again, in abstinence, clients frequently report being restored to regular menses and fertility. Common immune system issues include recurring infections such as sinusitis, pharyngitis, and even pneumonia; as well as yeast infections in the digestive system, reproductive system, and skin folds. Rheumatologic conditions reported most commonly are fibromyalgia, arthralgia, and joint swelling (e.g., ankles, knees). Infections and inflammatory conditions also tend to remit within the first month of abstinence and to recur in relapse.

Many clients present with chronic digestive system conditions, including irritable bowel syndrome, diverticulitis, and gluten intolerance, which often clear up in the first month of abstinence and recur in relapse. Circulatory system issues include rapid heartbeat and hypertension, which show significant improvement in the first 10 days of abstinence and recur almost immediately in relapse. Elevated cholesterol often normalizes in 2–6 months. We find that excessive weight is associated with a wide range of musculoskeletal disorders, such as sciatica; neck, shoulder, and back pain; as well as osteoarthritis. Osteoporosis is also commonly observed.

Many of our clients take a large number of medications; these have been predominantly prescribed for depression, anxiety, dyspepsia, pain, thyroid disease, diabetes, hypercholesterolemia, and/or hypertension. Interestingly, these medication requirements typically decrease rapidly in abstinence, often unrelated to the rate of weight loss.

Employment/Support Status

Our clients are likely to have given up on education and career advancement. Many are disabled from some combination of the medical and psychiatric disorders noted earlier. In particular, depression, arthritis, and obesity contribute directly to disability. Moreover, learning disabilities, "brain fog," fatigue, and somnolence seriously interfere with the ability to function at work. Those clients who are able to hold jobs, therefore, tend to miss work often. Many describe a syndrome comprised of nonspecific gastrointestinal symptoms, headache, and generalized malaise that seems to us similar to an alcoholic hangover. Such symptoms often abate early in abstinence, enabling our clients to return to school or find better careers. Because our clients are largely self-pay, they may represent a subpopulation of refined food addicts with a higher level of education and skills.

Substance Use: Modified for Refined Foods

Food addicts report two general eating patterns: eating frequently throughout the day or episodic binging, with many variations on each theme. Some may have a weekly pattern, as reported by a client who lost weight Monday through Thursday and gained it back over the weekend. Regardless of the temporal pattern, clients characteristically eat refined carbohydrates, foods cooked in large amounts of cooking oil (e.g., french fries), refined foods high in salt content or heavily salted, and high-fat dairy (e.g., ice cream). In addition, they drink caffeinated, artificially or sugar-sweetened drinks. Insofar as people abuse substances in order to change how they feel, it appears that sugar provides a transient energy boost, flour produces a sedative effect, and high-fat dairy generates a numbing or calming feeling.

Clients often have been unable to establish abstinence because of misinformation about what effective abstinence entails. They have extensive experience with failed attempts at partial abstinence in the form of diets, fasts, or moderate consumption of refined foods. In our opinion, these diets fail due to the stimulation of cravings—followed by uncontrolled eating—that are caused by ingestion of refined foods to which the client is addicted.

One indicator of the initiation of a food plan that is truly abstinent is that clients report a distinct withdrawal syndrome. In our experience, the characteristics of this withdrawal syndrome, which can last 3–7 days, include nausea, headaches, shakiness, disorientation, cravings, frequent urination, irritability, disrupted sleep, nightmares, and lethargy.

Our food-addicted client population has extensive residential and outpatient treatment histories. They report a broad range of treatment failures, including eating only a specific food (e.g., the grapefruit diet), restricted calories, diet pills, prepared meal plans, 12-step groups, eating disorders treatment, exercise, fasting, hypnosis, bariatric surgery, and purging. They have been blamed for these failures by uninformed health professionals. The experience of failure exacerbates the cycle of shame and food abuse. Bariatric surgery appears to fail, for example, when addiction thwarts the surgery through the abuse of ice cream or alcohol.

Thus, the people we see have regained weight after bariatric surgery.[4]

Clients underestimate how much they spend on food. They take advantage of cheap sources such as discount ice cream, baked goods, and cookies. Nonetheless, working clients may report vending machine expenditures of $70 or more per week. Fast food seems inexpensive until volume spending is considered. One client reported spending "the entire day driving from one restaurant to the next." Others have reported thousands of dollars of credit card debt for food.

We see clients who are so troubled by their pathological relationship with food that they have made plans for suicide, as has been well described in other substance use disorders.

Legal

We rarely observe legal problems because virtually no aspect of food addiction is illegal (except for stealing food). However, recidivist criminals have been found to have hypoglycemia,[5] which may also be symptomatic of refined food addiction.

Family/Social

Blood relatives of our clients often have eating problems, alcoholism, or other addictions, as well as diet-related medical conditions such as heart disease or diabetes. Food abuse is common in our clients' home and workplace environments. An abstinent client reported that her office birthday celebration included a big coffee cake in the morning, huge desserts at lunch, and later cake and ice cream.

Much of our clients' "free time" is consumed with planning what to eat, obtaining food, eating it, and then recovering from the eating episode by sleeping or watching TV. We observe that our clients have acquaintances but few intimate friends. They have serious problems getting along with others, including family members. This may be in part because emotional, physical, and/or sexual abuse appears to be endemic in our clients' families of origin.

Psychiatric

Treatment for chronic psychological and emotional problems (e.g., depression, irritability, anxiety, and shame) is common in our clients, often involving the use of medication. Unfortunately, despite repeated and often long-term treatment, symptoms rarely resolve until abstinence is achieved.

Debilitating mood disorders reported by our clients are consistent with ASI criteria: a significant period of time during which they experienced serious depression, sadness, hopelessness, loss of interest, difficulty with daily functioning, anxiety, worry, or inability to relax. This is almost universal, often starting in childhood; but it can remit with abstinence. Our clients also experience trouble controlling verbal and physical abuse. A self-report is: "I'm glad I'm in treatment so I'm not screaming at my children." Another is: "I am so ashamed about the way I beat my husband." Road rage is common and we observe that this seems to correlate with the use of caffeine, in combination with high-fat diary, sugar, or syrups. About 25% of clients have considered suicide. One client notes, "In abstinence, my internal negative dialogue is gone."

Self-described refined food addicts suffer from obsessive thinking about food, anxiety about others' opinions of them, and distorted ideas about the effects of eating. They rationalize their self-destructive food choices and the resultant harmful consequences and poor life choices. They sometimes demonstrate rapid thoughts, pressured speech, and compulsive talking. They often have difficulty with comprehension, concentration, and memory. They may forget how to shop, prepare food, or even find our offices. A typical report is: "I was in such a fog, I couldn't conduct my business." We have found that there is a consistent reaction, which occurs on about the fourth day of withdrawal from refined food, that clients describe as "a fog lifting."

Other Considerations
Chronic Obesity

Usually, but not always, our clients are overweight or obese. In abstinence, weight loss occurs at 1–2 lb per week. Obesity limits mobility, affects hygiene, and is a direct or indirect cause of many of the medical problems described earlier. In advanced stages of illness, our clients cannot fly, drive a car, find and afford clothing, or even find shoes that fit because their feet are so wide. The prominence of adipose tissue creates a distraction from the underlying addictive disease and limits the perception of required treatment. Furthermore, fatigue and depression present barriers to physical activity that otherwise might help.

Age of Onset

Typically, our clients have been subjected to addictive food substances from infancy. Our clients report addictive behavior in early childhood such as manipulating adults, stealing, and hiding refined foods. We speculate that refined food addiction in early childhood may be a precursor to drugs and alcohol later in life, in addition to persisting as refined food addiction.

Literature Survey

Our observations as to the comprehensive nature of the pathology of refined food addiction are supported by the medical literature. Presently, most of the literature focuses on the adverse health consequences of overweight and obesity. Hypertension, diabetes, dyslipidemia,[6] cancer,[7] sudden death, gall bladder disease, osteoarthritis, sleep apnea,[8] asthma,[9] and allergies[10] are associated with obesity. Increased inflammation markers[11] and psoriasis[12] have been found. Obese men show erectile dysfunction.[13]

Obese women exhibit more depression[14-16] and increasingly in an aging obese population.[17] The obese have more anxiety,[18] panic,[16] stress markers,[19] bipolar,[16] dementia,[20] and fatigue.[21] Obesity is twice as prevalent in psychiatric populations,[22] and it is associated with loss of life up to 25–30 years.[23] Pathological loss of control over eating according to the *DSM-IV* criteria for substance use disorders has been documented.[24-26]

Accident-related mortality and complication rates are approximately twice as high for the obese.[27] The obese are 20% more likely to die from a variety of causes.[28]

Health professionals exhibit antiobese bias.[29] The obese are perceived as lazy.[30] Obese people internalize antifat bias,[31] suffer mental distress,[32] and are the least desirable sex partners.[33] They are discriminated in workplaces,[34] making lower wages with the disparity increasing with age.[35]

DISCUSSION

Clinical observations of food addicts were organized into the ASI categories, revealing a syndrome with a broad range of pathologies. We highlighted many of the ways in which refined food addiction causes illness, pain, and suffering in a variety of different ways, some of which are obvious and some of which are subtle, easy to miss, and easy to deny.

These observations lead to two key questions: (1) How does the severity of refined food addiction compare to other addictions? (2) Does the alleged existence of refined food addiction suggest new approaches to the obesity epidemic?

Comparative severity can be discussed on three levels: individual, family, and society. On an individual level, the impact of refined food addiction appears to be as severe as other addictions, insofar as it seriously and adversely affects physical, emotional, and mental health. The full range of addiction-related medical and psychiatric illnesses, pathological behaviors, and social dysfunction that have been described in other addictive disorders are also present in those with refined food addiction. Although the social consequences are notably not criminal, the impact on occupational and social functioning is quite prominent.

In one important aspect, food addiction may be worse than others, as no other addiction starts so early in life or is so insidiously promoted throughout the entire life span by family and society. This childhood-onset addiction is further compounded by painful stigmatization.[36,37] For all ages, the impact of being "fat" cannot be overstated. Our clients experience severe distress over the inability to perform certain acts of personal hygiene, to dress presentably, to travel comfortably, and, in advanced stages, even to move normally. Yet they find themselves unable to stop their disordered eating.

As with other addictions, family system dysfunction caused by the inability to relate to family members is comparable for refined food–addicted families. Behavioral patterns similar to those of a drug and/or alcohol addict such as manipulation, lying, stealing, hiding, drama, blaming, shaming, threats, violence, and martyrdom are acted out. Isolation and shame may make it more difficult for a family system to get help.

In the society, tools are lacking to identify, assess, and treat refined food addiction. Inappropriate, even harmful, treatment is a significant factor in refined food addiction as opposed to other addictions because it is physiologically more difficult to lose weight after a lose/gain cycle.[38] Because neither the substances nor the consequences are illegal, the legal system does not intervene to stop the cycle of abuse.

Furthermore, like tobacco in the twentieth century, refined food is affordable, available, attractive, and liberally advertised. Compounding the problem, refined foods are almost always processed in combination, presenting the addict with an array of "polysubstance" products (e.g., sugar + salt, or sugar + fat, or sugar + fat + dairy, etc.). This polysubstance presentation may make refined foods comparatively more addictive because a single prepared food product may activate a range of reward neuropathways.[39-44]

The overall impact of refined food addiction on individuals and society may be worse than that of tobacco because the size and profitability of the refined food market is even greater than tobacco. Similar to the situation with tobacco, advertisements present deceptive, confusing messages about the addictive properties of refined foods, and then society blames the individual for the failure to control substance use. In the case of refined food, the situation is further exacerbated by unrealistic expectations of the role of exercise in controlling obesity.

If refined food addiction is understood to be an addictive disorder, as presented here, then a more comprehensive, aggressive, and focused approach to the treatment of obesity can be undertaken. Although not all obesity is a result of refined food addiction, and not all refined food addicts are obese, we believe that the majority of obese individuals also suffer from refined food addiction and need to be treated accordingly. Direction for effective public policy with regard to addictive refined food substances may be drawn from the experience of regulating tobacco. Such policies have included initiatives involving education, pricing, taxation, farm subsidies, availability, labeling, litigation, nonsmoking areas, and advertising.

In conclusion, the ASI was used to organize clinical observations regarding the phenomenology of refined food addiction in humans. Further development of the ASI for refined food addiction would be useful because it would facilitate the clinical documentation of this as-yet-unrecognized disorder, leading to more effective assessment, treatment, and public policy. We have also argued that unless and until the obesity epidemic is understood to be primarily a consequence of refined food addiction, afflicted individuals will continue to suffer from a litany of medical and psychiatric disorders that are refractory to current treatment approaches.

ACKNOWLEDGMENTS

The authors gratefully acknowledge the editorial assistance of William Kadish, MD, and Jennifer Gibson, PhD.

REFERENCES

1. Makela K. Studies of the reliability and validity of the Addiction Severity Index. *Addiction* 2004;99(4): 398–410.

2. McLellan AT, Cacciola JC, Alterman AI, Rikoon SH, Carise D. The Addiction Severity Index at 25: origins, contributions and transitions. *Am J Addiction* 2006;15(2):113–124.

3. Andreasen N, Black D. *Introductory Textbook of Psychiatry.* 4th ed. Arlington, VA: American Psychiatric Publishing, 2006.

4. Magro DO, Geloneze B, Delfini R, Pareja BC, Callejas F, Pareja JC. Long-term weight regain after gastric bypass: a 5-year prospective study. *Obes Surg* 2008; 18(6):648–651.

5. Virkkunen M, De Jong J, Bartko J, Goodwin FK, Linnoila M. Relationship of psychobiological variables to recidivism in violent offenders and impulsive fire setters. A follow-up study. *Arch Gen Psychiat* 1989;46(7):600–603.

6. Wyatt SB, Winters KP, Dubbert PM. Overweight and obesity: prevalence, consequences, and causes of a growing public health problem. *Am J Med Sci* 2006; 331(4):166–174.

7. Hjartaker A, Langseth H, Weiderpass E. Obesity and diabetes epidemics: cancer repercussions. *Adv Exp Med Biol* 2008;630:72–93.

8. Bray GA, Bellanger T. Epidemiology, trends, and morbidities of obesity and the metabolic syndrome. *Endocrine* 2006;29(1):109–117.

9. Stanley AH, Demissie K, Rhoads GG. Asthma development with obesity exposure: observations from the cohort of the National Health and Nutrition Evaluation Survey Epidemiologic Follow-up Study (NHEFS). *J Asthma* 2005;42(2):97–99.

10. Basit A, Hakeem R, Hydrie MZ, Ahmedani MY, Masood Q. Relationship among fatness, blood lipids, and insulin resistance in Pakistani children. *J Health Popul Nutr* 2005;23(1):34–43.

11. Panagiotakos DB, Pitsavos C, Yannakoulia M, Chrysohoou C, Stefanadis C. The implication of obesity and central fat on markers of chronic inflammation: the ATTICA study. *Atherosclerosis* 2005;183(2): 308–315.

12. Setty AR, Curhan G, Choi HK. Obesity, waist circumference, weight change, and the risk of psoriasis in women: Nurses' Health Study II. *Arch Int Med* 2007;167(15):1670–1675.

13. Matfin G, Jawa A, Fonseca VA. Erectile dysfunction: interrelationship with the metabolic syndrome. *Curr Diabetes Rep* 2005;5(1):64–69.

14. Ho RC, Niti M, Kua EH, Ng TP. Body mass index, waist circumference, waist-hip ratio and depressive symptoms in Chinese elderly: a population-based study. *Int J Geriatr Psych* 2008;23(4):401–408.

15. Lim W, Hong S, Nelesen R, Dimsdale JE. The association of obesity, cytokine levels, and depressive symptoms with diverse measures of fatigue in healthy subjects. *Arch Int Med* 2005;165(8):910–915.

16. Simon GE, Von Korff M, Saunders K, et al. Association between obesity and psychiatric disorders

in the US adult population. *Arch Gen Psychiatry* 2006;63(7):824–830.

17. Vogelzangs N, Kritchevsky SB, Beekman AT, et al. Depressive symptoms and change in abdominal obesity in older persons. *Arch Gen Psychiatry* 2008;65(12): 1386–1393.

18. Jorm AF, Korten AE, Christensen H, Jacomb PA, Rodgers B, Parslow RA. Association of obesity with anxiety, depression and emotional well-being: a community survey. *Aust NZ J Publ Heal* 2003;27(4):434–440.

19. Brydon L, Wright CE, O'Donnell K, Zachary I, Wardle J, Steptoe A. Stress-induced cytokine responses and central adiposity in young women. *Int J Obesity (Lond)* 2008;32(3):443–450.

20. Rosengren A, Skoog I, Gustafson D, Wilhelmsen L. Body mass index, other cardiovascular risk factors, and hospitalization for dementia. *Arch Int Med* 2005;165(3):321–326.

21. Resnick HE, Carter EA, Aloia M, Phillips B. Cross-sectional relationship of reported fatigue to obesity, diet, and physical activity: results from the third national health and nutrition examination survey. *J Clin Sleep Med* 2006;2(2):163–169.

22. Casey DE. Metabolic issues and cardiovascular disease in patients with psychiatric disorders. *Am J Med* 2005;118(suppl 2):15–22.

23. Newcomer JW. Metabolic syndrome and mental illness. *Am J Manag Care* 2007;13(7 suppl):170–177.

24. Gearhardt AN, Corbin WR, Brownell KD. Preliminary validation of the Yale Food Addiction Scale. *Appetite* 2009;52(2):430–436.

25. Ifland JR, Preuss HG, Marcus MT, et al. Refined food addiction: a classic substance use disorder. *Med Hypotheses* 2009;72(5):518–526.

26. Tekol Y. Salt addiction: a different kind of drug addiction. *Med Hypotheses* 2006;67(5):1233–1234.

27. Byrnes MC, McDaniel MD, Moore MB, Helmer SD, Smith RS. The effect of obesity on outcomes among injured patients. *J Traum* 2005;58(2):232–237.

28. McGee DL. Body mass index and mortality: a meta-analysis based on person-level data from twenty-six observational studies. *Ann Epidemiol* 2005;15(2):87–97.

29. Teachman BA, Brownell KD. Implicit anti-fat bias among health professionals: is anyone immune? *Int J Obes Relat Metab Disord* 2001;25(10):1525–1531.

30. Wang SS, Brownell KD, Wadden TA. The influence of the stigma of obesity on overweight individuals. *Int J Obes Relat Metab Disord* 2004;28(10):1333–1337.

31. Durso LE, Latner JD. Understanding self-directed stigma: development of the weight bias internalization scale. *Obesity* 2008;16(suppl 2):80–86.

32. Friedman KE, Reichmann SK, Costanzo PR, Zelli A, Ashmore JA, Musante GJ. Weight stigmatization and ideological beliefs: relation to psychological functioning in obese adults. *Obes Res* 2005;13(5): 907–916.

33. Chen EY, Brown M. Obesity stigma in sexual relationships. *Obes Res* 2005;13(8):1393–1397.

34. Lemon SC, Zapka J, Li W, Estabrook B, Magner R, Rosal MC. Perceptions of worksite support and employee obesity, activity, and diet. *Am J Health Behav* 2009;33(3):299–308.

35. Han E, Norton EC, Stearns SC. Weight and wages: fat versus lean paychecks. *Health Econ* 2009;18(5): 535–548.

36. Daniels SR. The consequences of childhood overweight and obesity. *Future Child* 2006;16(1):47–67.

37. Graf C, Rost SV, Koch B, et al. Data from the StEP TWO programme showing the effect on blood pressure and different parameters for obesity in overweight and obese primary school children. *Cardiol Young* 2005;15(3):291–298.

38. MacLean PS, Higgins JA, Johnson GC, et al. Enhanced metabolic efficiency contributes to weight regain after weight loss in obesity-prone rats. *Am J Physiol* 2004;287(6):R1306–R1315.

39. Avena NM, Rada P, Hoebel BG. Evidence for sugar addiction: behavioral and neurochemical effects of intermittent, excessive sugar intake. *Neurosci Biobehav Rev* 2008;32(1):20–39.

40. Blass EM, Shide DJ, Weller A. Stress-reducing effects of ingesting milk, sugars, and fats. A developmental perspective. *Ann NY Acad Sci* 1989;575:292–305.

41. Buda-Levin A, Wojnicki FH, Corwin RL. Baclofen reduces fat intake under binge-type conditions. *Physiol Behav* 2005;86(1–2):176–184.

42. Kaasinen V, Aalto S, Nagren K, Rinne JO. Dopaminergic effects of caffeine in the human striatum and thalamus. *Neuroreport* 2004;15(2):281–285.

43. Zhang M, Kelley AE. Intake of saccharin, salt, and ethanol solutions is increased by infusion of a mu opioid agonist into the nucleus accumbens. *Psychopharmacol* 2002;159(4):415–423.

44. Fantino M, Hosotte J, Apfelbaum M. An opioid antagonist, naltrexone, reduces preference for sucrose in humans. *Am J Physiol* 1986;251(1 pt 2):R91–R96.

53

From the Front Lines

A Clinical Approach to Food and Addiction

PHILIP WERDELL

This chapter provides a brief history of food addiction treatment; the key differences between obesity, eating disorders, and chemical dependency on food; five principles of effective treatment for food addiction; and a vision for integrated food addiction recovery services.

Since 1986, I have worked professionally with over 4,000 late-stage food addicts, first at the residential food addiction program of Glenbeigh Psychiatric Hospital of Tampa, then at the outpatient program of Rader Institute of Washington. Over the last 15 years, I have developed ACORN Food Dependency Recovery Services and, most recently, the Food Addiction Institute.

BRIEF HISTORY OF FOOD ADDICTION TREATMENT

In the 1980s, with few published peer-reviewed articles on the science of food addiction,[1] there were dozens of hospital-based programs and thousands of individual health professionals who used the Minnesota chemical dependency model for treating food addiction.[2,3] Outcome research showed that this model of treatment worked as effectively for food addiction as it did for alcoholism and drug addiction.[4,5]

Although scientific research validating food addiction was growing exponentially, private and public insurance programs in the 1990s began to refuse treatment using the addiction model for the obese. Almost all residential programs closed or shifted to the behavioral or psychotherapeutic model, and most private practitioners stopped taking chemical dependency on food seriously. Major academic texts claimed, "There is no convincing empirical support" that physical craving results from ingesting a particular food or food in general.[6,7] For the past two decades, most health professionals have been taught to disregard food as an addiction. As a result, most doctors, dietitians, and therapists discount or minimize chemical dependency on food. This is, without a doubt, one of the contributing factors to the growing obesity epidemic.

In 2009, the Food Addiction Institute posted 2,745 peer-reviewed articles and books on the science of food addiction. The Refined Food Addiction Foundation listed 35 review articles showing specific areas of scientific consensus regarding a biochemical basis of food as a substance use disorder. There is presently more evidence of chemical dependency on food than there was on alcohol and other drugs when they were formally declared substances of abuse.[8]

Over the last 25 years, the food-related 12-step fellowships have continued to flourish—though not as vibrantly as when they were getting regular alumni from food addiction treatment programs. A few clinicians who saw the positive results of using the addiction model for food have continued to successfully work with food addicts. They have developed new models of professional service, mostly outside the private and public health insurance systems.[9,10]

OBESITY, EATING DISORDERS, AND CHEMICAL DEPENDENCY ON FOOD— THREE SEPARATE DISEASES

Our single most important learning—and the first thing I teach both clients and professionals in training—is that obesity, eating disorders, and chemical dependency on food are three very different and distinct diseases.[11] This is often confusing to the inexperienced practitioner because all three of these diseases frequently appear concurrently. Understanding these differences is critical to effective treatment.

There are many "normal eaters" who are overweight or obese, and yet are able to reduce and maintain a healthy weight based upon the simple principle, "less calories in, more calories out."[12,13] These overweight and obese people, as measured by the body mass index (BMI), are able to control their eating and weight through diet and exercise alone. This is because they have coping skills other than eating to deal with difficult feelings and/or they are not chemically dependent on food. Many of these normal eaters are able to diet successfully on their own. Others may need a doctor-supervised or commercial weight loss program, though only 10% to 30% of these individuals maintain a weight loss of more than 25 pounds for more than a year.[14] Those who successfully lose and maintain their weight loss are, by this definition, normal eaters.

"Emotional eaters"—some obese and some a normal weight—may be binge eaters, bulimics, and/or anorexics. Many are able through intensive therapy to develop a healthy practice of eating all foods in moderation.[7,15] They learn to identify irrational thinking about food, their bodies, and sense of self, and they learn healthier ways of coping with difficult feelings and resolving old trauma. This is difficult work, often requiring professional help, but they find that their problem is "not the food they are eating, but rather what is eating them."[16] There are thousands of professionals trained to help those with eating disorders as defined by *The Diagnostic and Statistical Manual of Mental Disorders*, fourth edition, text revision (*DSM-IV-TR*),[17] and most are quite successful in helping their emotional eating clients if they are not chemically dependent on food.

Those we have come to call "food addicts" have an entirely different medical condition. When they ingest certain foods—or sometimes any foods in excess volume—there is a biochemical change in their brain, and they develop a physical craving for food(s) beyond ordinary physical hunger.[18] Over time, the progression of this chemical dependency leads them to desire their addictive foods more than other foods and, later, more than other things in their lives. They are unable to diet effectively, and talk therapy alone does not stop their out-of-control eating.[19] To heal, food addicts need to abstain completely from their chemically offending food(s), learn more about the nature of food addiction, avail themselves of help from others to maintain abstinence and break food-addictive denial, and replace the addictive experience of food with something better—sometimes this is a spiritual experience.[20,21] The fact that there are thousands of food addicts whose physical cravings disappeared only when they abstained from their food drug(s) of choice[22,23] is the main reason we need to diagnose food addicts as having a substance use disorder.

These three distinct diseases—obesity, eating disorders, and chemical dependency on food—are co-occurring in many individuals, particularly in the most difficult cases. Combined treatment is complex, and sometimes paradoxical. This important problem is beyond the scope of this chapter.

FIVE PRINCIPLES OF TREATING FOOD ADDICTION

Effective treatment for food addiction is based upon five principles, each addressing one of five universally accepted characteristics of addiction: physical craving, loss of control, withdrawal, tolerance or progression, and biochemical denial.

Food Addicts Need to Abstain to Eliminate Physical Craving

There is scientific consensus that specific foods can cause physical craving.[8,24–30] First defined by Overeaters Anonymous (OA) in the 1960s,[31] food abstinence has become a key part of food addiction literature[32–35] and professional treatment programs for food addiction.[9,36–40]

Effective treatment for food addiction puts physical abstinence first and teaches the food addict the reasons for this priority. For almost 50 years, recovery in OA—and other 12-step fellowships focusing on food addiction—has been built on the principle, "We practice abstinence by staying away from all eating between planned meals and all individual binge foods."[41] Clinical treatment of late-stage food addicts generally begins with a food plan that eliminates all commonly addictive foods: sugar, flour, excess fat, caffeine, and alcohol.[39,42–46] There are many such food plans; one is the Glenbeigh Healthy Eating plan, which is a good place to start for most late-stage food addicts who do not have a food plan that works.[47] It is also important to eliminate specific personal binge foods[48] and to address a client's distorted sense of satiation and portion size.[49,50] Unlike in alcoholism and drug addiction, as food addiction progresses, abstinence sometimes needs to become more rigorous.[51] All plans for food abstinence should be reviewed by the food addict's doctor or dietitian and by someone who understands food addiction.

Food Addicts Need to Ask for and Accept Help to Address Loss of Control

Loss of control from food dependency has been firmly established for animals[52] and humans.[53] In all addictions, loss of control or powerlessness arises at three levels: physical craving, mental obsession, and distortion of will and self.[20,54] Physical craving creates an experience of "false starving"; changes in the conscious part of the brain create "false thoughts"— euphoric recall, minimization, and rationalizations that are believed; and late-stage food addicts develop a "false self," believing that they are the addiction.[50] Thus, as with other substance use disorders, food addiction is a disease that makes you believe that you do not have a disease.

Treatment regarding loss of control begins with education about the science of food addiction[34,55,56]; however, knowledge is seldom sufficient. A deeper practice addressing loss of control is for food addicts to commit what they eat to a recovering peer or professional. In this way, progressed food addicts do not make decisions about their food plan or specific meals by themselves. In food-related 12-step fellowships, this is called surrendering your food to a sponsor, and it includes being rigorously honest about food secrets and any problems encountered in the food commitment process. It helps late-stage food addicts to inventory breaks in abstinence physically, emotionally, mentally, and spiritually.[50] The easiest way to find other food addicts to help with this process is in food-related 12-step fellowships.[i] At a local level, it is important to find meetings with members who have solid food abstinence and recovery or to use phone meetings and long-distance sponsors.

Food Addicts Need Varying Levels of Support for Withdrawal and Detoxification

Withdrawal has been established in sugar-addicted animals.[20,57,58] Clinical observation of humans during detoxification shows classic symptoms of biochemical withdrawal from food. Some of these observed symptoms include fatigue, dizziness, irritability, depression, fainting spells, insomnia, night sweats, suicidal tendencies, shaking, crying spells, poor memory, mood swings, temper outbursts, indigestion, and headaches.[33]

Physical withdrawal from addictive foods requires sufficient structure and support—and the food addict's willingness to accept the help—to maintain physical abstinence throughout the pain and difficulties of detoxification. We can use what we know in supporting detoxification from alcoholism through diet, nutritional supplements, and medication to help food addicts detoxify when appropriate.[59] Some are able to detoxify by themselves.[36,60] Others need support from a professional and/or mutual support group. For those unable to achieve stable abstinence, even with the help of a professional or by using a 12-step fellowship, a residential workshop or treatment center is advised. In addition to ACORN workshops, there are some residential programs that have a history of success with food addicts.[ii]

If They Cannot Maintain Abstinence, Food Addicts Need Progressive Levels of Intervention

Animal research has documented physical tolerance and progression regarding sugar.[61] Progression charts from case histories of clients in food treatment centers show increased tolerance for addictive foods.[62] These charts are almost identical to the Jellinek curve for alcoholism.

Food addiction treatment needs to be appropriate to the stage of disease progression, for example: preventive education for those in the pre-addictive stage; assessment and prescribed food plan for those in early food addiction; referral to 12-step work for middle-stage food addicts; support for detoxification, developing cognitive and feeling skills, and breaking denial for those in late stage[50]; hospitalization and long-term treatment for final stage food addicts with coaddictions[63] and with other co-occurring illnesses.[iii]

Food Addicts Need a Process for Challenging and Breaking Denial

Food addiction, like all chemical dependency, is a disease of denial. Addictive denial is different from common or conscious denial and from psychological denial.[50] Common denial is where people deny something while being fully conscious of whether what they are saying is true. Psychological denial is when an emotional trauma is repressed in part or completely into the subconscious. Addictive denial is a condition created by the interaction of an addictive substance and the brain. Ultimately, food addiction denial supports continued use of a food substance even with the person's full knowledge that it is dangerous physically, emotionally, and/or spiritually.[9,50,53]

Treatment of food addiction over the long term is effective only to the extent that it successfully breaks food addiction denial. The process of breaking denial typically begins with lectures and literature. Successful treatment almost always needs an experiential process of challenging denial, especially for those in late-stage food addiction. This process usually begins with reality-based feedback from peers in recovery and/or from professionals experienced in doing this work. Next, the food addict writes a detailed descriptive history of his or her powerlessness over food. This is not a list of binge foods or an analysis of the reason why one overeats; it is a description of specific incidents of powerlessness over food and the progressive negative consequences.[64] For late-stage food addicts, presenting this writing to another person or a recovering community is often the culmination of treatment.

In summary, residential programs and professionals working with food addicts are most effective when they include all five of the aforementioned treatment principles. Following treatment and once abstinence is achieved, success is measured by whether the food addict continues to put food abstinence first and works on underlying mental, emotional, and spiritual issues that remain. Sometimes called "stage II recovery," this topic is also beyond the scope of this chapter.

A VISION OF INTEGRATED FOOD ADDICTION RECOVERY

There is a need for a comprehensive health policy and strategy to manage treatment in the food addiction aspect of the obesity epidemic in the United States and the world. Currently in the United States, there is almost no food addiction prevention at a national level. Few professionals are trained to work with late-stage food addicts. Treatment is scarce and scattered, and there is not one primary hospital-based treatment program for food addiction. Food has yet to be recognized as a substance use disorder by the *DSM*, and professionals wanting to offer effective help to food addicts find it

virtually impossible to be reimbursed by insurance. There is only one in-depth experiential training program and no degree programs for food addiction professionals.

Efforts under way in Iceland, a small country of 300,000, might serve as a model. There is regular public education about food addiction in the major media. Members of the Icelandic government's obesity task force understand the role of chemical dependency on food. At the center of the food addiction recovery community are two vital food-related 12-step programs, OA and Grey Sheeters Anonymous. For those needing food addiction assessment and support, there is the Matarfíkn counseling center. They are developing intensive workshops, a residential treatment program, and a recovery house specializing in food addiction. Doctors, nurses, dietitians, physical trainers, therapists, and other health professionals receive continuing education units for education about chemical dependency on food. A major Icelandic university is considering a degree program in addiction studies including an emphasis on food addiction recovery.

This private-public health strategy for food addiction is currently functioning on a small scale. The Icelandic program provides a vision of integrated food addiction recovery services for any small country or large metropolitan area of the United States. The next step is to serve a larger percentage of active food addicts.

NOTES

i. Overeaters Anonymous (OA) is by far the oldest, largest, and most diverse of the food-related 12-step fellowships. Within OA, there have been three movements—OA-HOW, 90 Day Meetings, and Grey Sheet—which focus on the food addiction model. The remainder of OA encompasses a wide variety of compulsive eaters, including those with anorexia, bulimia, and other psychologically based eating disorders. In the last decade, several groups have split off from OA to focus more on recovery from food addiction. Those seeing themselves more as food addicts have created Food Addicts Anonymous (FAA), Compulsive Eaters Anonymous-HOW (CEA-HOW), Food Addicts in Recovery Anonymous (FA), Recovering Food Addicts Anonymous (RFA), and Grey Sheeters Anonymous (GSA).

ii. Milestones in Recovery, Turning Point of Tampa, Shades of Hope, The Willough.

iii. Also, Dr. Lefevre developed multiaddiction assessments for his all-addiction treatment program, PROMIS, in Kent, England.

REFERENCES

1. Wilson J. The great addiction challenge. *The Food Addiction Newsletter* July 1989;1–3.

2. Owen P. Minnesota model: description of counseling approach. In: Carroll KM, ed. *Approaches to Drug Abuse Counseling.* Bethesda, MD: National Institute on Drug Abuse; 2000: 117–126. NIH publication no. 00–4151.

3. Danowski D. *Locked Up for Eating Too Much: Diary of a Food Addict in Rehab.* Center City, MN: Hazelden, 2004.

4. Carroll MT. *The Eating Disorder Inventory and Other Predictors of Successful Symptom Management in Bulimic and Obese Women Following an Inpatient Treatment Program Employing an Addictions Paradigm* [dissertation]. Tampa, FL: University of South Florida; 1993.

5. Hillock C, Prager M, Werdell PR. Survey of ACORN outcomes. In: Foushi M, Weldon C, Werdell PR. *Food Addiction Recovery: A New Model for Professional Service—The ACORN Primary Intensive.* Sarasota, FL: Evergreen; 2007: 94–98.

6. Wilson GT. Binge eating and addictive disorders. In Fairburn CG, Wilson GT, (eds). *Binge Eating: Nature Assessment and Treatment.* New York: Gilford Press; 1993: 97–120.

7. Fairburn, CG. *Overcoming Binge Eating.* New York: Guilford Press, 1995.

8. Cheren M, Hillock C, Gold M, et al. *Physical Craving and Food Addiction.* Sarasota, FL: The Food Addiction Institute, 2009.

9. Foushi M, Weldon C, Werdell PR. *Food Addiction Recovery: A New Model for Professional Service—The ACORN Primary Intensive.* Sarasota, FL: Evergreen; 2007.

10. Ifland, J. How can work places, hospitals and faith-based organizations help educate workers in the addiction model? Promising Practices in Food Addiction conference Society of Food Addiction Professionals. January 22-23 2009; Houston, TX.

11. Werdell PR. *Food Addiction: Beyond Ordinary Eating Disorders.* Pekin, IL: The Clinical Forum of the International Association of Eating Disorders Professionals, 1994.

12. Das S, Gilovly CH, Golden JK, et al. Long term effects of high and low glycemic load diets at different levels of calorie restriction on dietary adherence, body composition and metabolism in CALERIE. *Am J Clin Nutr* 2007;85(4):1023–1034.

13. DeNoon D. Calories count most in weight loss. 2007. Available at: http://www.cbsnews.com/stories/2007/04/09/health/webmd/main2666013.shtml. Accessed October 22, 2010.

14. Editors. Losing weight: what works, what doesn't. Rating the diets. *Consumer Rep* 1993;June:347–357.

15. Kouimtsidis C, Reynolds M, Drummond C, Davis P, Tarrier N. *Cognitive-Behavioral Therapy in the Treatment of Addiction: A Treatment Plan for Clinicians.* West Sussex, England: John Wiley and Sons, 2007.

16. Roth G. *Breaking the Bonds of Compulsive Eating.* New York: Macmillan Publishing, 1984.

17. American Psychiatric Association. *Diagnostic and Statistical Manual of Mental Disorders.* 4th ed. Washington, DC: American Psychiatric Association, 2000.

18. Glenbeigh Clinical Services. *Self-Study Guide for Glenbeigh Clinical Staff.* Tampa, FL: Glenbeigh Inc., 1987.

19. Goodrick GK, Foreyt JP. The business of weight loss: why treatments for obesity don't last. *J Am Diet Assoc* 1991;91(10):1243–1248.

20. May G. *Addiction and Grace: Love and Spirituality in the Healing of Addictions.* San Francisco, CA: HarperCollins, 1982.

21. Overeaters Anonymous. *Overeaters Anonymous Stories of Recovery.* Rio Rancho, NM: Overeaters Anonymous World Service, 1980.

22. Kriz KLM. *The Efficacy of Overeaters Anonymous in Fostering Abstinence in Binge-Eating Disorder and Bulimia and Nervosa* [dissertation]. Blacksburg, VA: Virginia Polytechnic Institute; 2002.

23. Overeaters Anonymous. *Membership Survey Report.* Rio Rancho, NM: Overeaters Anonymous World Service, 2004.

24. Nobel EP, Noble RE, Ritchie T, et al. D2 Dopamine receptor gene and obesity. *Int J Eat Disorder* 1994;15:205–219.

25. Katz DL, Gonzales MH. *The Way We Eat: A Six Step Path to Weight Control.* Naperville, IL: Sourcebooks, 2002.

26. Wang GJ, Volkow ND, Thano PK, Fowler JS. Similarity between obesity and drug addiction as assessed by neurofunctional imagining: a concept review. In: Gold M, ed. *Eating Disorders, Overeating, and Pathological Attachment to Food: Independent of Addictive Disorders?* Binghamton, NY: The Haworth Medical Press; 2004: 39–53.

27. Avena NM, Rada P, Hoebel BG. Evidence for sugar addiction: behavioral and neurochemical effects of intermittent, excessive sugar intake. *Neurosci Biobehav Rev* 2008;32(1):20–39.

28. Ifland J, Preuss M. Marcus M, et al. Refined food addiction: a classic substance use disorder. *Med Hypotheses* 2009;72(5):518–526.

29. Wang GJ. Inside our brain: obesity and dopamine deficiency. Presented at: Summit on Food Addiction: The Obesity Epidemic Connection; April 24–26 2009; Bainbridge Island, WA.

30. Kessler DA. *The End of Overeating: Taking Control of the Insatiable American Appetite.* New York: Rodale Press, 2009.

31. Rozanne S. Abstinence enters OA. In: Overeaters Anonymous, eds. *Abstinence: Members of Overeaters Anonymous Share Their Experience, Strength, and*

Hope. Rio Rancho, NM: Overeaters Anonymous World Service; 1994: 2–4.

32. Dufty W. *Sugar Blues.* New York: Warner Books; 1975: 22–23.

33. Hollis J. *Fat is a Family Affair.* Center City, MN: Hazelden Publishing Group, 1985.

34. Sheppard K. *Food Addiction: The Body Knows.* Deerfield Beach, FL: Health Communications, 1989.

35. Ifland J. *Sugars and Flours: How They Make Us Crazy, Sick and Fat and What to Do About It.* Bloomington, IN: 1st Books Library, 2000.

36. Kline M. *The Junk Food Withdrawal Manual.* Bellevue, WA: Total Living, 1978.

37. Katherine A. *Anatomy of a Food Addiction: The Brain Chemistry of Overeating.* Carlsbad, CA: Gurze Books, 1991.

38. Danowski D, Lazaro P. *Why Can't I Stop Eating? Recognizing, Understanding and Overcoming Food Addiction.* City Center, MN: Hazelden Publishing, 2000.

39. Bernard N. *Breaking the Food Seduction: The Hidden Reasons Behind Food Cravings—and 7 Steps to End Them Naturally.* New York: St. Martin's Press, 2003

40. Foushi M, Weldon C, Werdell PR. *Food Addiction Recovery: A New Model for Professional Service—The ACORN Primary Intensive.* Sarasota, FL: Evergreen, 2007.

41. Overeaters Anonymous. *Stories of Recovery.* Rio Rancho, NM: Overeaters Anonymous World Service, 1980.

42. Appleton N. *Lick the Sugar Habit.* New York: Avery Publishing Group, 1988.

43. Sheppard K. *From the First Bite: A Complete Guide to Recovery from Food Addiction.* Deerfield Beach, FL: Health Communications, 2000.

44. Leibowitz SH. Over consumption of fats: a vicious cycle from the start. Paper presented at: Seattle Summit on Food Addiction: The Obesity Epidemic Connection; April 24–26 2009; Bainbridge Island, WA.

45. Drewnowski A, Krahn DD, Demitrack MA, Nairn K, Gosnell BA. Taste responses and preferences for sweet high-fat food: evidence for opioid involvement. *Physio Behav* 1992;51:371–379.

46. Colantuoni C, Pedro R, McCarthy J, et al. Evidence that intermittent, excessive sugar intake causes endogenous opioid dependence. *Obes Res* 2002;10:478–488.

47. Staff. Glenbeigh healthy eating plan. In: Foushi MJ, Werdell PR, eds. *Handbook for Primary Intensive.* Sarasota, FL: ACORN Food Dependency Services.; 2010: 67–79.

48. Wright T. *Your Personal Food Plan: A Basic Food Plan for Recovery from Addictive and Compulsive Eating Behaviors.* Plymouth Meeting, PA: Renaissance Nutrition Center, 2004.

49. Shell EP. *The Hungry Gene: The Science of Fat and the Future of Thin.* New York: Atlan Month Press, 2002.

50. Werdell PR. *Bariatric Surgery and Food Addiction: Preoperative Considerations.* Sarasota, FL: Evergreen, 2009.

51. Staff. Dosages of psychoactive medications compared to calibrated levels of sugar abstinence. In: *ACORN Handbook.* Sarasota, FL: ACORN Food Dependency Recovery Services, 2008.

52. Avena NM, Rada P, Hoebel BG. Evidence for sugar addiction: behavioral and neurochemical effects of intermittent, excessive sugar intake. *Neurosci Biobehav Rev* 2008;32:20–39.

53. Gold M. *Eating Disorders, Overeating, and Pathological Attachment to Food: Independent of Addictive Disorders?* Binghamton, NY: The Haworth Medical Press, 2004.

54. Silkworth W. Doctor's opinion. In: *Alcoholics Anonymous: The Story of How Many Thousands of Men and Women Have Recovered from Alcoholism.* 4th ed. New York: Alcoholics Anonymous World Service; 2004: xxv–xxxii.

55. Werdell PR. *An Introduction to Food Addiction.* [2 DVD set]. Sarasota, Fl: ACORN Food Dependency Recovery Services; 2006.

56. Summit on Food Addiction: The Obesity Epidemic Connection; April 24–26, 2009; Bainbridge Island, WA.

57. Drewnowski A, Krahn DD, Demitrack MA, Nairn K, Gosnell BA. Taste responses and preferences for sweet high-fat food: evidence for opioid involvement. *Physio Behav* 1992;51:371–379.

58. Alcoholics Anonymous. *Alcoholics Anonymous: The Story of How Many Thousands of Men and Women Have Recovered from Alcoholism.* 4th ed. New York: Alcoholics Anonymous World Service, 2004.

59. Larson JM, Sehnert KW. *Seven Weeks to Sobriety: The Proven Program to Fight Alcoholism through Nutrition.* New York: Fawcett Columbine, 1992.

60. Dufty W. *Sugar Blues.* New York: Warner Books, 1975.

61. Avena NM, Rada P, Hoebel BG. Evidence for sugar addiction: behavioral and neurochemical effects of intermittent, excessive sugar intake. *Neurosci Biobehav Rev* 2008;32(1):20–39.

62. Schneider F. Food addiction and recovery chart. In: *Patient Handbook: Glenbeigh Eating Disorder and Food Addiction Program.* Tampa, FL: Glenbeigh, Inc.; 1987: III, 1.

63. Lefever R, Shafe M. Brain chemistry: combinations of foods in blood trigger effects similar to alcohol. *Employee Assistance* 1991; Volume 3, Issue 4.

64. Werdell PR. Writing incidents of powerlessness. In: *ACORN, Handbook for Primary Intensive.* Sarasota, FL: ACORN Food Dependency Services; 2008: 221–236.

54

Food and Addiction

A Personal Story

ANNE ROSENBERG

I was born to parents who absolutely adored me. In fact, my father told me he cried when I was born. He thought he had the perfect family—two boys and two girls. My mother said the nurses in the hospital loved my curly hair, combing it all into a banana curl before they brought me to her, looking just like a cherub. I was a chubby baby girl weighing over nine pounds. My arms had rings or rolls of fat, and so did my legs. In those days this was a sign of a very healthy baby. I went home to my three older siblings. In the years to come my parents had three more children—eventually making me the middle child of seven.

For some reason, by the time I was in kindergarten, my parents and paternal grandparents had become concerned about my weight. I was taken to a pediatrician and put on an extremely restricted diet. I think that was the first of many attempts to make me thinner. I was sent to Cape Cod to spend summers at a camp for fat girls. I was put on Metrecal. I was given Cott's diet drinks while on some kind of gluten-free diet. The problem with all of these attempts to make me thinner was that I continued to sneak candy from my Nana Esther's crystal candy bowl or wherever else I could find it. I had an uncanny ability to locate anything with sugar in it. As I got a little older, I would purchase it from the candy store. I couldn't seem to get enough.

I remember eating package after package of Metrecal cookies and one after the other of those chocolate caramel Aydes that were supposed to suppress your appetite. I would eat Aydes while chewing special gum that was also supposed to magically make me thinner. By the time I entered high school I was putting myself on extreme diets. The number on the scale always meant more to me than the number on my exams. I dieted and binged my way through high school.

Once away at university, I started to experience depression and anxiety. After graduating with my social work degree, I found myself in my doctor's office pleading for help with my uncontrollable bingeing. I could not get through a day without a binge. The doctor seemed to understand, and she suggested I try a recovery program designed for compulsive overeaters. My first meeting was on a Friday, in Vancouver's West End. I had no idea what I was walking into. There was a man who told his story—and to this day, decades later, I remember almost every single word that man said. I wasn't alone anymore, and I knew it.

After that first meeting, I made this group a significant part of my life. Yet I couldn't quite find the relief I was searching for. I embraced the spiritual part of the program, but I wasn't able to find support for the physical problem of craving and bingeing. At that time, the suggested food plan was three meals a day and nothing in between—or you could decide on your own food plan.

I joined Weight Watchers numerous times during those years. I can remember bingeing on their "legal" ice-cream bars. ("Legal" meant permitted on their food plan.) I would starve myself the day before my weekly weigh-ins and then binge the moment I stepped off the scale. I also tried the Jenny Craig Program and even binged on their food.

At one point I had an expensive food delivery company deliver prepared "diet" meals to our home, thinking I would just eat their three meals and the measured snack every day. I wouldn't have to think about food during the rest of the day—or so I thought. You had to sign up for a month in advance. On the first day, when the bin arrived,

I ate the snack first—and I was off and bingeing by 10:00 a.m. The food kept being delivered every morning for the next month, even though there was no way I could stay on that plan. I tried the Atkins Diet, the Cabbage Soup Diet, and every other diet I read about in the line-up at the grocery store—and I kept going to support meetings and praying.

One of the terribly embarrassing moments for me during that period was when my husband and daughter returned to the house after playing soccer and discovered that a beautifully wrapped gift we were supposed to send off to Japan had been opened and consumed. They had carefully selected some exquisite handmade chocolates to give to our houseguest, who was leaving to fly home to Japan that afternoon. She flew home empty-handed, and I was left full of shame.

In 2003, I hit yet another low. My bingeing was horrific. I was depressed and anxious. I felt that I wasn't there as a mother and wife. Chocolate cake was more important. After my husband and daughter went to bed, I ended most days with a container of ice cream. I wanted to die. This probably doesn't sound like a person who had created and founded a very successful global company. But I had. I was very capable in one part of my life and out of control in another.

I continued to search the Internet for help. I wanted to go somewhere where they would keep me safe from myself. I couldn't find anywhere; however, I did find an organization that instructed me over the phone to consider completely eliminating all sugar and flour from my diet. This was the first time I had heard anyone recommend that. The woman in their office told me about someone in this program who could come to stay in our home and help me. It seemed strange, but I was desperate—so I agreed. My husband and daughter knew I needed help and were willing to try anything. My pockets were full of candy when I greeted this stranger at the Vancouver airport.

This woman moved in and immediately began to help me to prepare weighed and measured meals that were free of sugar, flour, and wheat. She explained the food plan and why it was essential that I follow it so closely. She took me grocery shopping, cooked with me, and planned menus. Within 4 days I began to experience clarity of mind I had never felt before. It was as if a cloud had lifted.

As time went on and I followed the suggested food plan, my depression and anxiety cleared, and so did my cravings, irritability, and shame.

This lasted for 2 years—and then I started to binge again. It began with a passing thought that I was obviously fine now and could return to a "normal" way of eating. There was no need to be so careful. That thought led me back to a very abnormal way of eating and the depression that accompanied it. My daughter, who was 16 years old at the time, wrote me a letter that began: "Why did you show me what a real mother could be and then take it away from me?" My heart was broken and I sobbed—and I still couldn't find any peace. I kept eating.

After Halloween 2007 I had gained a significant amount of weight. Every day ended with a binge, and I felt that life was not worth living. I set out across the border to a workshop advertised for "food addicts." I'm not sure whether I was actually looking for help or just wanted to escape. As I was filling up my Smart Car with diesel, I was filling up myself with petroleum-tasting stale candy from the convenience store at the gas station. I felt sick. I started my drive, not really having any idea where I was going—but I knew it had to be better than where I was.

As I drove down the highway eating bags of rock-solid, stale Licorice Allsorts, I realized that people driving on either side of me were staring. I wanted to be invisible while I binged, but I was in a car many Americans hadn't seen yet (the Smart Car came out in the United States the following year). I couldn't disappear. I tried to chew and discreetly put the food in my mouth when no one was beside me. It was difficult to eat, watch the road, and change gears. I was also getting physically ill from the amount of candy I was consuming. The stormy weather and the sixteen-wheeler trucks passing me made the drive even more nerve racking.

I arrived safely and found that there were nine of us at this workshop. After just 5 days of being fed well, and being with others who really understood, I was happy to be alive again. My drive home was very different from my ride down. Now when people looked at me in my car, I smiled—and they seemed to smile back. While stopped at a gas station, I even answered some questions about my car and the fuel consumption. I felt that I had returned to who I was meant to be. The most obvious shift was that I could see beauty again, in people, places, and things. The drive north along the coast was magnificent, and I was filled with gratitude.

I appreciated the way we had been encouraged to make our food look attractive. It had been suggested in the previous program that I not glorify my food. Now I was given permission to prepare my meals with beauty in mind. The way things look has always been very important to me, and to be encouraged to make our plates of healthy food look appealing opened up a whole new way of looking at the food I eat. I was inspired.

Today I enjoy preparing my food. I travel a lot, and I am always trying to create the most exquisite and delicious meals for the plane. I take time, and it gives me great pleasure to mix colors—garnet yams, mixed greens, purple cabbage, and red quinoa, for instance—in with a main course. I use attractive containers and of course a cloth napkin. I treat myself well. In a certain way, I enjoy when other passengers look longingly at my sugar-, flour-, and wheat-free home-prepared creations.

I have a healthy relationship with food, now that I have eliminated those foods that destroyed all the real pleasure. My family immediately began to benefit from this new appreciation of food. We began to take more time to plan and prepare meals and our kitchen became a much more inviting place. I believe this has had a very positive impact on our relationships. Both my daughter and husband are excellent cooks, and prepare food creatively, using ingredients we can all enjoy.

On any given weekend you can find us at our local farmers' market, filling our bags with organic produce, farm-fresh eggs, and bunches of flowers for the kitchen counter. Once we get home, after we've put everything out for our eyes to feast on, our kitchen becomes a flurry of activity. My husband can make eggs, new potatoes, and rainbow Swiss chard look like a work of art and taste better than anything in a competition on the cooking channel. My daughter has the same talent as my husband and, thank goodness, has always enjoyed a healthy relationship with food.

Recently my husband and I were invited to a formal sit-down dinner party at an acquaintance's home. I knew that this would be a meal that contained many of the foods I choose not to eat. My first reaction was to stay home—and then I decided that I wanted to enjoy everyone's company. So I prepared my own meal to take with me. I had missed out on far too many social occasions in my life.

I was nervous about bringing out my own prepared food. I tried to not be noticed as I tiptoed to the fridge and took out my glass container and quietly took it to my seat at the dinner table. A man sitting beside me said in a very loud voice, so that everyone seated at the table could hear, "You brought your own dinner?" Without missing a beat, my husband rescued me by saying: "She loves my cooking so much she won't eat anything else." There were smiles all around, and no one said a word after that. I told my husband later that night that he had just made me fall in love with him all over again.

Will I ever find myself bingeing and depressed again? I hope not. There are a lot of land mines out there. I was recently reading a magazine in the dentist's office and came across this ad for Nestlé Coffee Crisp Singles:

Nestlé's Coffee Crisp Singles: Instructions for use when one is engulfed by a chocolate craving…remain calm. 1. Locate Coffee Crisp Singles. 2. Ensure your chair is in the reclined position. 3. Breathe normally…enjoy your nice light snack.

Nestlé's is now adding Aero Singles to that line:

In the event of a chocolate craving, please take care of your craving first before helping others with theirs. Remove bar. Bite to release bubbles. Enjoy normally. Be prepared! Ensure Aero Singles are stowed in close proximity.

It is noteworthy that chocolate maker Nestlé owns Jenny Craig. These are certainly interesting times.

So, am I really and truly a "food addict"? I am not a scientist, and I am not too concerned with the exact label. But I do know that I could not eat just *one* of those Nestlé's Singles—Aero or Coffee Crisp. Not if my life depended on it. I've done that type of experiment with various items out of bags and boxes—more often than I care to acknowledge—and I have never ever been able to eat just one. And I am not alone. Nestlé is banking on that.

So, what is working for me right now? What are some of the ingredients that make my life so worth living? Today I take the time to feed myself well. To me, it is a simple equation: what I eat affects how I feel. I've learned how to prepare and enjoy aesthetically pleasing and delicious meals. I have a daily meditation practice that is important for me, because when my internal landscape is at peace it seems I am more likely to make healthy choices in my external landscape. I have very close family and friends who understand food addiction and make it much easier for me to eat well in their company. I know I can go to their homes for dinner and they will have prepared food we can enjoy together. I am in a women's group with five other women; we meet once a week and go away a few times a year. I believe there are health benefits for women who have close friendships with each other.

I have a husband and a daughter who encourage me to take the time to eat well. I attend support meetings. I'm very involved in the arts. I love to dance, and I have a number of other passions I pursue wholeheartedly. I think one of the most important ingredients in all of this is that I have found my niche. Today I choose to work on projects that are meaningful to me and inspire me.

Most important, I remember from moment to moment to appreciate this one precious life I have. From the time I was 5 years old, I always felt that somewhere inside of me I had the resilience that would help me eventually find my way to a life I can fully enjoy. People have asked me what I would change from my past. I can honestly say: "Not a thing."

PART V

Public Health Approaches and Implications

55

Taxes on Energy-Dense Foods to Improve Nutrition and Prevent Obesity

JOHN CAWLEY

INTRODUCTION

As the developed world has wrestled with how to respond to the rapid rise in the prevalence of obesity, there has been increasing recognition that successful, long-term behavior modification may be possible only by incentivizing change. This has led to calls for taxing energy-dense foods.[1-7] The purpose of this chapter is to provide the economic perspective on strategies for taxing foods in order to improve nutrition and prevent or reduce obesity.

Economics recognizes a rationale for government intervention (such as taxes to change behavior) when there are market failures, which occur when the operation of private free markets fails to maximize social welfare.[8,9] One market failure relevant for obesity is external costs: obese individuals do not bear the full cost of their condition—some costs are paid by taxpayers, employers, and coworkers. For example, Finkelstein et al. calculate that the medical costs of obesity in the United States in 2006 totaled $85.7 billion, of which $19.7 billion was paid by Medicare, $8.0 billion was paid by Medicaid, and $49.4 billion was paid by private sources such as health insurance.[10] The costs covered by Medicare and Medicaid are ultimately paid by taxpayers. In addition, healthy-weight individuals subsidize obese individuals in the same health insurance pool. Employers may also bear some of the costs of obesity-related work absenteeism, which totals $4.3 billion annually,[11] and some of the costs of obesity-related work "presenteeism"—lower productivity while at work.[12]

The typical fiscal solution to the problem of external costs is to use taxes to "internalize" the costs: that is, force decision makers to face the full social costs of their actions. A straightforward way to internalize the external costs associated with obesity would be to tax people on the basis of their body weight; however, that raises concerns about fairness (e.g., because about half of variation in weight across individuals is genetic[13]) and political feasibility, so attention has focused on taxing consumption of foods and beverages that contribute to obesity.

This chapter discusses each of the steps by which a tax on food would affect consumption and weight, which are the following: (1) a tax is levied; (2) producers adjust down or up their "pre-tax" price; (3) a new after-tax price is determined ("tax pass-through"); (4) consumers respond to the after-tax price by decreasing consumption of the taxed food; (5) consumers may respond to the tax by increasing consumption of untaxed substitutes; and (6) consumer weight responds to these changes in consumption.

This chapter is organized according to those steps. Section 2 discusses public opinion regarding taxes on energy-dense foods and Section 3 notes practical considerations for the design of food taxes. Section 4 discusses the possibility that producers will lower (or even raise) the pre-tax price in order to influence the amount of the tax that gets passed on to consumers. Section 5 reviews own-price and cross-price elasticities of demand, which indicate how taxes will affect consumption of the taxed goods and substitute foods. Section 6 discusses proposals to earmark revenue from food taxes for related public health efforts. Section 7 describes how state and local food taxes may to some extent be evaded through cross-border shopping in certain areas. Section 8 presents estimates of how taxes on specific energy-dense foods can affect weight. The chapter concludes with a discussion of future research needs and policy implications.

PUBLIC OPINION REGARDING TAXES ON ENERGY-DENSE FOODS

Divided public opinion and outright industry opposition are obstacles to enacting or raising taxes on energy-dense foods. In recent years I have added questions to Cornell University's Empire State Poll of New York State residents to measure support for specific antiobesity policies, including taxes on energy-dense foods. The Empire State Poll surveys a sample that is representative of New York State residents, and the sample size each year is 800. In the 2006, 2008, and 2009 surveys, respondents were asked the extent to which they agreed or disagreed with the following statement: "The government should raise taxes on candy, chips, and soda pop." Table 55.1 presents the percentage of respondents that strongly disagree, disagree, are neutral, agree, or strongly agree with that statement. In each year, a clear majority (roughly 60%) disagrees with raising taxes on energy-dense foods, and less than a quarter agree with raising the tax. Even among those who answered that they think youth obesity in the United States is a "major problem" (which in each year is slightly more than 80% of the overall sample), a majority is opposed to higher taxes on these foods.

These results are from a sample of New York State residents, but nationally representative surveys have also found that only a minority of the public support taxes on energy-dense food; for example, in a 2005 phone survey,[14] 26.7% agreed with "raising taxes on unhealthy food, e.g., fast food" and in a 2006 Internet survey[15] 28.4% supported a policy to "impose a tax on junk food similar to existing government taxes on cigarettes and alcohol." Many other surveys on support for antiobesity policies have been conducted, and there is a need for a literature review or meta-analysis that investigates how poll results differ by location, demographics, the framing of questions, and whether the food or restaurant industry is running antitax ads in respondents' areas of residence.

The public is not simply opposed to all anti-obesity policies. For example, in the 2009 Empire State Poll, 64.37% agreed with the statement, "The government should ban candy, chips, and soda pop from schools" and 65.62% agreed with the statement, "The government should require that restaurants list calorie and nutritional information on menus and menu boards." There are some antiobesity policies that are supported by a clear majority of the public, but raising taxes on energy-dense foods is opposed by a clear majority.

A majority of economists is also opposed to taxes on energy-dense foods. A 2007 survey of a random sample of members of the American Economic Association (response rate, 41.8%) asked respondents to indicate their level of agreement with the statement: "The U.S. should impose taxes on unhealthy foods."[16] Of the 130 respondents, 27.7% strongly disagreed, 33.1% disagreed, 14.6% were neutral, 21.5% agreed, and 3.1% strongly agreed. Summing without regard to strength of feeling, more than twice as many economists disagreed as agreed with taxing unhealthy foods (60.8% versus 24.6%), numbers that are quite similar to those from the Empire State Poll.

Efforts to enact taxes on energy-dense foods have historically faced opposition from lobbyists working on behalf of, for example, the Grocery Manufacturers of America.[17] The power of this lobby explains why many food taxes enacted by states were quickly repealed.[18]

Despite opposition by the public, economists, and industry to taxes on energy-dense foods, sales

TABLE 55.1. PERCENT AGREEING WITH STATEMENT THAT GOVERNMENT SHOULD RAISE TAXES ON ENERGY-DENSE FOODS

Year	Strongly Disagree	Disagree	Neutral	Agree	Strongly Agree
2006	21.91	37.03	6.42	18.14	14.74
2008	17.19	40.90	6.02	24.47	11.42
2009	24.00	42.13	5.63	18.88	9.38

Data: Empire State Poll of New York State residents, selected years. Author's calculations. Sample sizes: N = 794 in 2006, N = 797 in 2008, and N = 800 in 2009. Notes: Respondents were presented with the following statement: "The government should raise taxes on candy, chips, and soda pop" and were asked to indicate their level of agreement. Cells contain the percent expressing the level of agreement indicated in the column heading among respondents surveyed in the year indicated in the row heading. Totals do not sum to 100 because respondents also had the option of saying that they did not know.

tax is currently assessed on food (as a category) in 14 states (see Table 55.2). In addition, 20 states tax grocery sales of soft drinks at a higher rate, and 16 states tax grocery sales of candy at a higher rate, than food as a category.[19] Additional states levy a higher tax on energy-dense food than on food as a category when it is sold through vending machines.[19] No states currently impose a tax on fast food.[17] The state taxes on soda pop and other energy-dense foods that do exist are relatively low; for example, the average sales tax on soft drinks was 3.43% for units sold in grocery stores and 4.02% for units sold in vending machines, and the average sales tax on snacks is even lower: 1.2% for units sold in grocery stores and 3.13% for units sold in vending machines; no state is explicitly using such taxes as an antiobesity policy.[19,20]

Other countries have enacted taxes, sometimes substantial, on energy-dense foods. In France, food in general is taxed at a rate of 5.5%, but sweets, chocolates, margarines, and vegetable fats are taxed at a rate of 20.6%.[4] In Canada, sales tax does not apply to most food, but it is levied on soft drinks, sweets, and snack foods.[6]

PRACTICAL CONSIDERATIONS FOR TAXES ON ENERGY-DENSE FOODS

One challenge for a policy of using taxes and subsidies to prevent excess weight gain is how to define the scope of what should be taxed and what should be subsidized. For example, should apple juice be taxed because it is energy dense, or subsidized because it is 100% fruit and sometimes contains added vitamins, or neither taxed nor subsidized? Recently, public health researchers and advocates have called for taxes on full-calorie soda pop in particular.[2,3] The risk of taxing too narrow a set of energy-dense foods is that consumers may substitute away from the taxed items toward energy-dense items that are not taxed. Another difficult question is whether diet soft drinks should be taxed; although they do not themselves contain calories, they may promote the habit of consuming sweets or be complements with other energy-dense foods.[3]

One concern is that food taxes would be regressive, falling more heavily on poor families who spend a larger percentage of their income on food than do wealthier families. (Low-income families

TABLE 55.2. STATE TAX RATES ON FOOD AS OF JANUARY 1, 2008

State	Tax Rate (%) on Food
Alabama	4
Alaska	0
Arizona	0
Arkansas	3
California	0
Colorado	0
Connecticut	0
Delaware	0
Dist. of Columbia	0
Florida	0
Georgia	0
Hawaii	4
Idaho	6
Illinois	1
Indiana	0
Iowa	0
Kansas	5.3
Kentucky	0
Louisiana	0
Maine	0
Maryland	0
Massachusetts	0
Michigan	0
Minnesota	0
Mississippi	7
Missouri	1.225
Montana	0
Nebraska	0
Nevada	0
New Hampshire	0
New Jersey	0
New Mexico	0
New York	0
North Carolina	0
North Dakota	0
Ohio	0
Oklahoma	4.5
Oregon	0
Pennsylvania	0
Rhode Island	0
South Carolina	0
South Dakota	4
Tennessee	5.5
Texas	0
Utah	1.75
Vermont	0
Virginia	2.5
Washington	0
West Virginia	4
Wisconsin	0
Wyoming	0

Source: Federation of Tax Administrators.[24]

not only spend a higher fraction of their income on food, they spend disproportionately more on energy-dense foods in particular.[4,21]) However, because obesity is negatively correlated with socio-economic status for women[22,23] and children,[24] it could be argued that one *wants* this tax to be felt more strongly by the low-income because it is precisely their behavior one most wants to change. In addition, there is a way to use taxes to influence behavior while protecting the low-income from a loss of purchasing power: it is to combine the tax with an income tax credit. In economics jargon, this combination of policies allows for a substitution effect, but reduces the income effect, of a price change.[25] In fact, several states (HI, ID, KS, OK, SD, WY) have implemented such a combination of policies—they both tax food and provide a rebate or income tax credit to low-income households to compensate them for the loss of their purchasing power.[26]

"PASS-THROUGH" OF TAXES TO CONSUMER PRICES

Assuming that a tax on energy-dense foods is politically feasible, it is important to know how much of the tax would be "passed-through" to consumers in the form of higher prices. The price after the tax is not simply equal to the former price plus the amount of the new tax because producers may respond to the tax legislation by reducing their pre-tax price. Such a reduction in pre-tax price might be optimal for producers if consumer demand was extremely sensitive to price (i.e., highly price elastic), implying that purchases would plummet if the entire tax were passed on to consumers.

In a perfectly competitive market, the percentage of a tax that is passed on to consumers in the form of higher prices is equal to $S/(S—D)$, where S is the price elasticity of supply and D is the price elasticity of demand.[25] This formula has the striking implication that *the impact of a tax on consumer after-tax price is independent of whether the tax is levied on producers or consumers*; no matter on which party the tax is levied, who actually pays the tax is determined by the relative elasticities of supply and demand.

However, in imperfectly competitive markets, prices can actually rise by *more* than the amount of the tax; that is, taxes can be "overshifted."[27] Studies have confirmed that tax pass-through rates sometimes exceed 100% so that, for example, a tax of 5% could raise prices by more than 5%. Besley and Rosen[27] find that, for sales tax rates ranging from 0% to 8.25%, the tax pass-through rate is 100% for fast food hamburgers and exceeds 100% for Coca-Cola. In other words, taxing Coca-Cola has historically increased its price by *more* than the amount of the tax.

One possible reason that prices may rise by more than the amount of the tax is that, particularly in food markets, there is a tradition of "psychological pricing": vendors tend to set prices that end in a 5 or 9. For example, Kreul[28] analyzed menu prices from 242 restaurants and found that the terminal digit for meals priced at or below \$6.99 was most commonly a 9 (58%), followed by 5 (35%); in the 242 restaurant menus, there was not a single case of a meal price ending in a 1, 2, 3, 4, 6, or 7![28] Vendors may use psychological pricing because they believe that consumers round prices down (e.g., think that a \$1.99 item costs basically a dollar rather than basically two dollars) or view prices ending in 9 as a signal of a price discount.[29] The widespread use of psychological pricing can explain the overshifting of taxes—a small increase in tax may not lead to a small movement along the price line; it may instead lead to a substantial jump in price as the vendor moves to the next psychological price (e.g., from \$0.99 to \$1.49). This is particularly relevant for proposed taxes on fast food and soda pop, as both of those products are characterized by psychological pricing: their prices tend to end with 99 cents.

Psychological pricing is common in retail but not wholesale markets. Thus, psychological pricing is likely to affect pass-through of a sales tax on bottled or canned soda pop (which is purchased by consumers), but it may not affect the pass-through of a tax on soft drink syrup (which is purchased by, e.g., fast food restaurants).

PRICE ELASTICITIES OF DEMAND

Information about how a change in after-tax consumer price affects consumer demand is provided by the statistic called the price elasticity of demand, which is equal to the percentage change in quantity demanded in response to a 1% change in price. According to the Law of Demand, which states that quantity demanded falls with price, price elasticities of demand should be negative.

Andreyeva et al. (2010) summarize published estimates of the price elasticity of demand for various categories of food.[30] They locate 14 estimates of the price elasticity of demand for soft drinks, which range from −0.13 to −3.18, with a mean of −0.79. (Recall that the price elasticity of demand indicates the percentage change in quantity demanded associated with a 1% change in price; this wide range of estimates implies that a 1% increase in the price of soft drinks could decrease the quantity of soft drinks demanded by anywhere from 0.13% to 3.18%.) They find 13 estimates of the price elasticity of demand for food away from home which range from −0.23 to −1.76 with a mean of −0.81. They also locate 13 estimates of the price elasticity of demand for sweets and sugars, which range from −0.05 to −1.00 with a mean of −0.34. The Economic Research Service at the US Department of Agriculture maintains an online database of price elasticities of demand by nation and type of food (http://www.ers.usda.gov/Data/Elasticities/Query.aspx).

Estimates of price elasticity are also available for specific branded food items. (Although taxes are unlikely to vary by brand, it is interesting to see how taxes would affect demand for specific branded food items.) Table 55.3 lists price elasticities of demand for four major brands of full-calorie soda pop: Coke, Sprite, Pepsi, and Mountain Dew.[31] These estimates suggest that demand for branded full-calorie soft drinks is highly elastic to price; for example, a 10% increase in the price of Coke will decrease the quantity of Coke demanded by 37.948%.

It is also useful to know the *cross-price* elasticity of demand, which tells us how an increase in the price of one food affects consumption of a related food. In other words, cross-price elasticities of demand can tell us what people buy more of when they buy less of the taxed goods. Table 55.4 lists the own-price and cross-price elasticities of demand for varieties of milk.[21] The estimates indicate that taxes on whole and 2% milk lead consumers to switch to lower-fat milk varieties. Specifically, a 10% tax on whole milk (assuming all other prices held constant) would decrease consumption of whole milk by 6.52% and would raise consumption of 1% milk by 1.68%. A 10% tax on 2% milk (all other prices held constant) would reduce consumption of 2% milk by 7.42% and would raise consumption of nonfat milk by 0.84%. However, taxes on 1% and nonfat milk lead consumers to substitute toward higher-fat milk varieties. Specifically, a 10% tax on 1% milk (all other prices held constant) would decrease consumption of 1% milk by 20.52% and would raise consumption of whole milk by 1.81% (it would also raise consumption of nonfat milk by 1.15%). A 10% tax on nonfat milk (all other prices held constant) would reduce consumption of nonfat milk by 6.28% and would raise consumption of 2% milk by 0.79% and would raise consumption of 1% milk by 1.1%. Thus, the total effects of tax policy depend critically on not just own-price elasticities of demand but also cross-price elasticities of demand. An important gap in the research literature is that it is not well understood what people would switch to eating and drinking when they switch away from energy-dense foods and drinks that are taxed.

There are few studies of children's price elasticity of demand for energy-dense foods, but the studies that have been conducted suggest that youth purchases of energy-dense foods are at least somewhat sensitive to price.[32]

EARMARKING OF TAX REVENUE FOR RELATED PUBLIC HEALTH EFFORTS

Proposals for taxes on energy-dense foods sometimes include that the revenue collected be used to fund related public health initiatives, such as counteradvertising or information campaigns, in order to further reduce consumption of the good.[2,4,5,18] From the perspective of economics, this is linking the size of two things that should be determined separately: the optimal tax to internalize externalities and the optimal budget for a public health campaign. The optimal size of each is determined by different criteria: the optimal amount of the tax is that which forces the consumer to internalize the external costs he or she

TABLE 55.3. OWN-PRICE ELASTICITY OF DEMAND FOR SELECTED SOFT DRINKS

Product	Price Elasticity of Demand
Coke	−3.7948
Sprite	−2.8400
Pepsi	−3.9384
Mountain Dew	−4.3877

Source: Dhar et al., Table VII.[34] Reprinted with permission from Journal of Economics & Management Strategy, T. Dhar, et al, An Econometric Analysis of Brand-Level Strategic Pricing Between Coca-Cola Company and PepsiCo, 905–931, Copyright (2005), John Wiley and Sons.

TABLE 55.4. OWN-PRICE AND CROSS-PRICE ELASTICITY OF DEMAND FOR
VARIETIES OF MILK

		Percentage Change in Price			
		Whole Milk	2% Milk	1% Milk	Nonfat Milk
Percentage change in quantity demanded	Whole milk	−0.652*	0.025	0.181*	−0.022
	2% milk	0.022	−0.742*	0.018	0.079*
	1% milk	0.168*	0.019	−2.052*	0.110*
	Nonfat milk	−0.022	0.084*	0.115*	−0.628*

Asterisks indicate that the authors reject the null hypothesis that the elasticity is zero at the 5% significance level. Notes: the diagonal elements in the matrix list the own-price elasticities of demand (e.g., the upper-left cell indicates that a 1% increase in the price of whole milk will decrease the quantity of whole milk demanded by 0.652%). The off-diagonal elements in the matrix list cross-price elasticities of demand (e.g., the cell in the first column, third row indicates that a 1% increase in the price of whole milk will increase the quantity demanded of 1% milk by 0.168%).
Source: Chouinard et al., Table 4.[19]

would otherwise impose on others, while the optimal budget for a public health campaign is determined by its cost effectiveness. Proposing that revenue be earmarked for specific programs may sound like it generates twice the benefit from one tax, but such a linkage does not have an economic rationale or justification.

Moreover, there is a tradeoff between a tax's effectiveness in decreasing consumption and its ability to raise revenue. For example, a high elasticity of demand implies that the tax will greatly reduce consumption, but it also implies less tax revenue than if demand was relatively inelastic. At the extreme, taxing an unhealthy good could be a victory for public health if it led to a complete cessation of all purchases (i.e., if the good was infinitely price elastic), but this same tax would raise zero revenue. Of course, this is an extreme example—it is highly doubtful that any food tax that could be enacted would be so high as to drive consumption to zero—but the example illustrates the tradeoff between changing behavior and raising revenue that has been underappreciated in discussions about food taxes.

EVASION OF LOCAL FOOD TAXES THROUGH CROSS-BORDER SHOPPING

One challenge to taxing energy-dense foods at the state or local level is tax evasion through cross-border shopping. Tosun and Skidmore (2007) examine the case of West Virginia, which in 1990 raised its food tax from 0% to 6%.[33] West Virginia's neighboring states taxed food at a lower rate or exempted food from sales taxation altogether. The authors find evidence that consumers responded to the increased

food taxes by increasingly crossing the state border to shop; they estimate that the six percentage point increase in food taxes decreased food sales in West Virginia border counties by about 8%. More generally, they estimate that for every one percentage point increase in relative food prices due to increases in sales tax, per capita food sales decreased by about 1.38%. The extent to which these estimates generalize to other states depends on how close state residents are to other states with lower tax rates. For most people in Texas, cross-border shopping may not be economical because of the time and travel costs involved. On the other end of the spectrum, the District of Columbia is so small that if food prices are higher there than in neighboring Virginia and Maryland, it is relatively easy to shop across the border. As a result, food demand in D.C. is highly elastic to local taxes; it has been estimated that for each one percentage point increase in the sales tax of the District of Columbia relative to neighboring states, food sales in D.C. fall 7%.[34] Crossing state borders to shop is not a concern for a federal tax on energy-dense foods, but it is relevant for individual state and local governments that consider raising their food taxes above those of their neighbors.

ESTIMATES OF EFFECTS OF FOOD TAXES ON CONSUMPTION AND WEIGHT

Several recent papers have estimated the effect of specific kinds of food taxes on consumption and weight. Kuchler et al. (2005) estimate that a 20% tax on all salty snacks would decrease purchases by

5.57 ounces per person and would raise $7.08 per household.[18] Fletcher and colleagues estimate that, for adults, a one-percentage point increase in soft drink tax would lower body mass index (BMI) by 0.003 units,[35] and that for youths, a 6% soft drink tax would not significantly affect BMI or obesity prevalence.[36] They conclude that, as currently practiced, soda taxes are an ineffective antiobesity policy. Chouinard et al. (2007) estimate that a 10% tax on the fat content of dairy products (the largest source of fat in the American diet) would reduce fat consumption by less than one percentage point. They estimate that it would take a 50% tax to reduce fat intake by just 3%. The authors note that, because the demand for dairy is relatively price inelastic, such a tax would be an effective way to raise revenue, though it would be highly regressive.[21] Schroeter et al. (2008) simulate a 10% tax on food away from home and conclude that it would lead to a decrease in consumption of food away from home but a more than offsetting increase in food at home, with a net effect of *increasing* the body weight of the average person by a third of a pound. They also estimate that a 10% tax on full-calorie soft drinks would decrease weight by an average of 0.2 pounds.[37]

Kim and Kawachi (2006) note that the six states that repealed a tax on soft drinks or snack foods between 1991 and 1998 were more than 13 times as likely than states that retained their soft drink tax to experience a relatively high increase in the prevalence of obesity (given the small number of units being compared and the endogeneity of tax policy this should be considered merely suggestive).[17] More generally, Powell and Chaloupka (2009) survey the literature on weight and obesity elasticities with respect to food prices and conclude that small taxes are unlikely to produce significant changes in BMI but that nontrivial taxes might have a measurable impact on weight.[20]

In general, a challenge for estimating the impact of a substantial tax on energy-dense foods is that none currently exists. One can extrapolate its effects based on the effects of existing taxes, but this requires projecting out of sample. If tax effects are nonlinear—for example, rise dramatically with the magnitude of the tax—then such extrapolations may be highly inaccurate.

DIRECTIONS FOR FUTURE RESEARCH

Better data are needed in order to more accurately estimate own-price and cross-price elasticities

of demand. Frequently, elasticities are calculated using data of expenditures or purchases, not consumption. Moreover, the data are often repeated cross-sections rather than longitudinal; the latter are preferable because we would like to see how the same individuals decrease their consumption when price increases. Moreover, elasticities are most frequently reported in large categories (e.g., "dairy," "fats and oils"), but it would also be useful and interesting to see own-price and cross-price elasticities of demand for specific branded food items within each broad category. It would also be useful to have elasticities calculated for specific subgroups: for example, by income, by education, by age, and by gender, race, and ethnicity. Elasticities calculated using large and diverse samples may mask important differences across population subgroups. Finally, data should be collected that will allow researchers to go beyond studying impacts on consumption to studying impacts on body weight and body composition.

POLICY IMPLICATIONS

External costs of obesity, such as the medical costs of treating obesity-related illness that are paid by public health insurance programs such as Medicare and Medicaid, represent an economic rationale for government intervention to reduce or prevent obesity.[38] Taxes on energy-dense foods are one economic tool for internalizing such external costs. Price elasticities of demand suggest that (e.g.) full-calorie soda pop is price elastic, implying that every 1% of tax on such beverages reduce demand by more than 1%. However, estimates of the effect of such taxes on body weight indicate mixed results, with many showing little impact on weight, though it is difficult to simulate the effect of substantial food taxes because none have been implemented. All else equal, taxes at the federal level are preferable to those at the state or local level because the former cannot be evaded by crossing state borders to shop. Such taxes could be combined with income tax credits to protect the welfare of low-income families while still creating disincentives to consuming energy-dense foods. Policy challenges include divided public opinion, industry opposition, and defining the optimal scope of such a tax. Given the importance of obesity for public health, and the appeal of economic policy levers such as taxes, it is certain that there will be ongoing interest among researchers and policy makers in taxes on energy-dense foods to improve nutrition and prevent obesity.

ACKNOWLEDGMENT

The author thanks Tatiana Andreyeva for helpful comments and suggestions.

REFERENCES

1. Popkin B. *The World is Fat: The Fads, Trends, Policies, and Products That are Fattening the Human Race.* New York: Avery, 2009.

2. Brownell KD, Frieden TR. Ounces of prevention: the public policy case for taxes on sugared beverages. *N Engl J Med* 2009;360(18):1805–1808.

3. Brownell KD, Farley T, Willett WC, et al. The public health and economic benefits of taxing sugar-sweetened beverages. *N Engl J Med* 2009;361:1599–1605.

4. Leicester A, Windmeijer F. *The "Fat Tax": Economic Incentives to Reduce Obesity.* London: Institute for Fiscal Studies, 2004. Briefing note 49.

5. Nestle M. *Food Politics: How the Food Industry Influences Nutrition and Health.* Los Angeles: University of California Press, 2002.

6. Jacobson MF, Brownell KD. Small taxes on soft drinks and snack foods to promote health. *Am J Public Health* 2000;90(6):854–857.

7. Marshall T. Exploring a fiscal food policy: the case of diet and ischaemic heart disease. *Brit Med J* 2000;320: 301–305.

8. Cawley J. An economic framework for understanding physical activity and eating behaviors. *Am J Prev Med* 2004;27(suppl 3):117–125.

9. Cawley J. Markets and childhood obesity policy. *Future Child* 2006;16(1):69–88.

10. Finkelstein EA, Trogdon JG, Cohen JW, Dietz W. Annual medical spending attributable to obesity: payer- and service-specific estimates. *Health Affair* 2009; 28(5):w822–w831.

11. Cawley J, Rizzo JA, Haas K. Occupation-specific absenteeism costs associated with obesity and morbid obesity. *J Occup Environ Med* 2007;49(12): 1317–1324.

12. Gates DM, Succop P, Brehm BJ, Gillespie GL, Sommers BD. Obesity and presenteeism: the impact of body mass index on workplace productivity. *J Occup Environ Med* 2008;50(1):39–45.

13. Comuzzie AG, Allison DB. The search for human obesity genes. *Science* 1998;280:1374–1377.

14. Hilbert A, Rief W, Braehler E. What determines public support of obesity prevention? *J Epidemiol Commun H* 2007;61(7):585–590.

15. Barry CL, Brescoll VL, Brownell KD, Schlesinger M. Obesity metaphors: how beliefs about the causes of obesity affect support for public policy. *Milbank Q* 2009;87(1):7–47.

16. Whaples R. The policy views of American Economic Association members: the results of a new survey. *Econ J Watch* 2009;6(3):337–348.

17. Kim D, Kawachi I. Food taxation and pricing strategies to "thin out" the obesity epidemic. *Am J Prev Med* 2006;30(5):430–437.

18. Kuchler F, Tegene A, Harris JM. Taxing snack foods: manipulating diet quality or financing information programs? *Rev Agr Econ* 2005;27(1):4–20.

19. Chriqui JF, Eidson SS, Bates H, Kowalczyk S, Chaloupka FJ. State sales tax rates for soft drinks and snacks sold through grocery stores and vending machines, 2007. *J Public Health Pol* 2008;29(2): 226–249.

20. Powell LM, Chaloupka FJ. Food prices and obesity: evidence and policy implications for taxes and subsidies. *Milbank Q* 2009;87(1):229–257.

21. Chouinard HH, Davis DE, LaFrance JT, Perloff JM. Fat taxes: big money for small change. *Forum Health Econ Pol* 2007;10(2):Article 2.

22. McLaren L. Socioeconomic status and obesity. *Epidemiol Rev* 2007;29:29–48.

23. Sobal J, Stunkard A. Socioeconomic status and obesity: review of the literature. *Psychol Bull* 1989;105: 260–275.

24. Murasko JE. Socioeconomic status, height, and obesity in children. *Econ Hum Biol* 2009;7(3):376–386.

25. Perloff JM. *Microeconomics.* New York: Pearson Addison-Wesley, 2009.

26. State sales tax rates January 1, 2008. Washington, DC: Federation of Tax Administrators, 2009. Available at: http://www.taxadmin.org/FTA/rate/sales. html. Accessed October 19, 2009.

27. Besley T, Rosen H. Sales taxes and prices: an empirical analysis. *Natl Tax J* 1999;52(2):157–178.

28. Kreul LM. Magic numbers: psychological aspects of menu pricing. *Cornell Hotel Rest Admin* 1982;23: 70–75.

29. Stiving M, Winer RS. An empirical analysis of price endings with scanner data. *J Consum Res* 1997;24(1):57–67.

30. Andreyeva T, Long MW, Brownell KD. The impact of food prices on consumption: a systematic review of research on the price elasticity of demand for food. *Am J Public Health* 2009;100(2):216–222.

31. Dhar T, Chavas JP, Cotterill RW, Gould BW. An econometric analysis of brand-level strategic pricing between Coca-Cola Company and PepsiCo. *J Econ Manage Strat* 2005;14(4):905–931.

32. Epstein LH, Handley EA, Dearing KK, et al. Purchases of food in youth: influence of price and income. *Psychol Sci* 2006;17(1):82–89.

33. Tosun MS, Skidmore ML. Cross-border shopping and the sales tax: an examination of food purchases in West Virginia. *BE J Econ Anal Poli* 2007;7(1, topics):Article 63.

34. Fisher RC. Local sales taxes: tax rate differentials, sales loss, and revenue estimation. *Public Financ Rev* 1980;8(2):171–188.

35. Fletcher JM, Frisvold D, Tefft N. Can soft drink taxes reduce population weight? *Contemp Econ Policy* 2010;28(1):23–35.

36. Fletcher JM, Frisvold D, Tefft N. Taxing soft drinks and restricting access to vending machines to curb child obesity. *Health Affair* 2010;29(5): 1059–1066.

37. Schroeter C, Lusk J, Tyner W. Determining the impact of food price and income changes on body weight. *J Health Econ* 2008;27(1):45–68.

38. Cawley J. The economics of childhood obesity. *Health Affair* 2010; 29(3):364–371.

56

Addressing Disparities Related to Food Intake and Obesity

SHIRIKI KUMANYIKA

INTRODUCTION

Obesity increases risks of diabetes, cardiovascular diseases, and certain cancers. Cardiovascular diseases and cancer risks are also increased by dietary pattern variables such as fruit and vegetable, dietary fiber, fat, and sodium intake.[1] There are marked disparities in these health outcomes by ethnic minority and socioeconomic status (SES). For example, diagnosed diabetes prevalence is estimated at 12% for Black Americans, 10% in Hispanic/Latino Americans, 16.5% in American Indians/Alaska Natives, 7.5% in Asian Americans, and is even higher in some subgroups within these populations, compared to 6.6% in White Americans.[2] Death rates from heart disease, stroke, and cancer are higher for Blacks than Whites.[3] The prevalence of diabetes, hypertension, and serious heart conditions is higher in the low-income population.[3]

This chapter reviews ethnic and SES group differences in obesity prevalence and food intake and highlights public health nutrition approaches to address related health disparities. "Ethnic minorities" refers to non-Hispanic Black Americans, Hispanic Americans, American Indians and Alaska Natives, Asian Americans, Native Hawaiians, and Pacific Islanders, based on the current US Census Bureau classifications of race and ethnicity.[4] The focus is on US populations. Most data cited relate to Blacks and Mexican Americans.

BACKGROUND

Ethnic minority populations are diverse in many respects that relate to health profiles, ways of living, and perspectives in relation to society at large.[5] Relevant variables include cultural and regional origins, place of birth and length of residence in the United States, family structures and household composition,

place of residence, political status, and interactions with the health care system, media, and other social institutions. However, on average, poverty and lower educational attainment are more common among ethnic minority populations compared to Whites. For example, among Black Americans, 35% of children and 20% of adults (ages 18 to 64) are in low-income households (defined as less than 100% of the federal poverty level) and 29% of Hispanic children and 18% of adults are in low-income households, compared with 10% of White children and 8% of White adults. Therefore, risks related to ethnicity or minority status and SES may overlap.

ETHNIC AND SOCIOECONOMIC STATUS DIFFERENCES IN OBESITY AND FOOD INTAKE

Obesity

US National Health and Nutrition Examination Survey (NHANES) data show substantial disparities in obesity prevalence by ethnicity among adults and children, particularly for Black women and girls compared to Whites of both sexes and also to Black men (see Table 56.1).[6,7] Among children and adolescents, Black girls and Hispanic boys have the highest prevalence of obesity. National Health Interview Survey data, which provide estimates (based on self-reported weight and height) for a broader set of ethnic groups, indicate higher obesity prevalence among American Indians/Alaska Natives than Whites in both sexes and, in men, higher obesity prevalence among Native Hawaiian or Pacific Islanders compared to Whites.[8] Similar patterns are observed for children, that is, higher in American Indian/Alaska Native, Hispanic, and Black children than in White children based on

TABLE 56.1. PREVALENCE (%) OF OBESITY IN U.S. BLACK, WHITE, AND HISPANIC ADULTS AND CHILDREN, 2007–2008

	Females		Males	
	Ages 6 to 19 Years BMI ≥ 95th Percentile*	Ages ≥ 20 Years BMI ≥ 30 kg/m²	Ages 6 to 19 Years BMI ≥ 95th Percentile	Ages ≥ 20 Years BMI ≥ 30 kg/m²
Black	25.9	49.6	18.9	37.3
White	15.6	33.0	18.2	31.9
Hispanic	19.5	43.0	26.7	34.3

*Centers for Disease Control BMI reference.
BMI, body mass index.
Sources: Flegal, K. M., Carroll, M. D., Ogden, C. L., & Curtin, L. R. (2010). Prevalence and trends in obesity among US adults, 1999–2008. *JAMA, 303*(3), 235–41; and Ogden, C. L., Carroll, M. D., Curtin, L. R., Lamb, M. M., & Flegal, K. M. (2010). Prevalence of high body mass index in US children and adolescents, 2007–2008. *JAMA, 303*(3), 242–9.

measurements of 4-year-old children in the Early Childhood Longitudinal Study.[9] Obesity prevalence estimates for Asian American adults and children are usually lower than for Whites when the conventional body mass index (BMI) cutoffs are used.[9] However, Asian Americans are also at risk of obesity, especially when abdominal fat is considered.[10] Definitions of obesity are adjusted to consider that excess health risks such as type 2 diabetes are often observed in adults of Asian descent at lower BMI levels than in Whites or other ethnic minority populations.

Low SES is sometimes associated with higher obesity prevalence in adults and children, although this is not consistent across gender, age, ethnicity, over time, or with different SES indicators.[11] No association or a positive gradient in obesity with increasing income has been reported in NHANES data for Black children[11,12] and also for Mexican American and Black men.[13] In data for 2- to 19-year-old children, obesity prevalence is generally higher in Black and Mexican American compared to White children at all income levels.[12]

Energy Intake

The ability to link ethnic or SES-related disparities in obesity to differences in energy intake is limited because, in general, energy balance cannot be directly estimated from reports of total calories in survey data. Some evidence indicates higher consumption in minority or low-income populations of food categories that are associated with excess weight gain and less healthful diets, specifically sugar-sweetened beverages (SSBs) and fast food.[14–17]

In 1999–2004 NHANES data, 76% and 70% of Blacks and Mexican Americans, respectively, reported consuming SSBs at least once a day compared with 60% of Whites.[18] In 2005 National Health Interview Survey data, added sugar intake was inversely related to income and education, was highest in African Americans, also high in Whites and American Indians/Alaska Natives, and lowest in Asian Americans and Hispanics.[19] From 1988–1994 to 1999–2004, per capita calories from SSB increased significantly more in Black and Mexican American compared to White adolescents.[20] Also, SSB calories were higher among preschool children and adolescents in households with incomes <130% versus 130% or more of the poverty line. Nearly a third of children surveyed in 1994–1996 consumed fast food on a typical day, with significantly higher consumption in Black compared to White, Hispanic, and other children, adjusting for income and other demographic variables, and among poor children.[14]

Major contributors to intakes of calories, fat, and added sugar show more similarities than differences across ethnicity and income.[21,22] For example, among children in the population overall, almost 40% of energy came from solid fats and added sugars (termed "empty calories"), and about half of added sugars were from sodas and fruit drinks—substantially exceeding upper limits of recommended intakes. Grain desserts and pizza were in the top five contributors to energy intake across ethnicity.[21] For Black children only, fruit drinks rather than soda and pasta/pasta dishes were in the top five contributors to energy intake, and fried potatoes were in the top five contributors to solid fat intake. Whole milk and Mexican mixed dishes were in the top five contributors to energy intake, and Mexican mixed dishes were in the top five contributors to solid fat intake only for Mexican American children. In the data for adults, grain-based desserts and SSBs (soda, energy, and sports drinks combined), and chicken and chicken mixed dishes were in the top five for all ethnic and income subgroups, and yeast breads were in the top five for all except Mexican Americans.[22] In both adults and children, most of the top five contributors to energy intake were similar across income levels. SSB calories were higher among the lowest income subgroup.

Dietary Quality

Dietary quality can be assessed by scores on the Healthy Eating Index (HEI), a metric based on adherence to national dietary recommendations.[23,24] Ethnic comparisons of HEI scores, estimated from 1999–2000 NHANES data, showed lower scores for Blacks (61.1), slightly higher scores for Mexican Americans (64.5) than Whites (64.2), and intermediate scores for Asian, Pacific Islander, American Indian, and Alaska Native Americans (63.4). HEI scores increased with income and education in the 1999–2000 data.

The HEI has been revised to assess diet quality on a per calorie basis.[24] This approach allows for assessing the quality of the mix of foods consumed as opposed to the quantity of food consumed. The revised index (HEI-2005) has nine components for adequacy of intake (total fruit, whole fruit, total vegetables, dark green and orange vegetables and legumes [DGOLs], total grains, whole grains, milk, meat and beans, and oils [expressed as amounts per 1,000 kcal]) and three for moderation (saturated fat, sodium, and calories from solid fats, alcoholic beverages, and added sugars [SoFAAS; expressed as percent of energy or g/1,000 kcal]). Analyses of 2003–2004 NHANES data indicate an overall mean total HEI-2005 score of 57.5 on a scale of 100; scores were less than 50% of the maximum value for DGOLs, whole grains, sodium, and SoFAAS calories.[25] Scores for total vegetables, DGOLs, and whole grains were significantly lower among people with incomes <130% of the poverty line. In 2- to 18-year-old children, those in households with incomes <185% of the poverty line had a higher score for total vegetables, possibly reflecting higher levels of school lunch program participation.

Similar to the findings for the original HEI in 1999–2000, HEI-2005 total scores for adults age 18–64 years in 2003–2004 were highest for Hispanics (59), and higher for Whites (56) than Blacks (53).[22] Relative to Whites, Blacks had lower scores for total fruit and total vegetables, DGOLs, whole grains, and milk and higher scores for saturated fat and sodium. Diets of Hispanics had higher scores for total fruit, total vegetables, DGOLs, saturated fat and sodium, and lower scores for whole grains, milk, and oils relative to Whites. Hispanics also had higher scores than Blacks for whole fruit and SoFAAS calories.

The lower HEI scores for Blacks in 1999–2000 as well as 2003–2004 apparently reflect persistent differentials between Black and White Americans.[26] Together with the greater overall burden of heart disease, stroke, and cancers in Blacks, this suggests a particular need for improving dietary patterns in the Black population. Data are insufficient to draw broad conclusions about how dietary change priorities for other ethnic groups differ from those in the population at large. Also, priority issues for other groups will vary by region and ethnic subgroup. For example, among Black Americans, dietary profiles vary among those who are Caribbean versus US born.[27] In Hispanic Americans, diet-related risks differ for Mexican American men in Texas versus men in other Hispanic ethnic groups and regions.[28]

Food Insecurity

With respect to low SES populations, concerns about *excess* consumption of calories, saturated fat, and salt are in addition to concerns about food security.[29] Food insecurity affects as many as 15% of US households.[30] Having inadequate resources to buy food may limit purchases of fruits and vegetables and lead to reliance on high-calorie, low-nutrient, processed foods that are low in cost.[31] More than half of food insecure households participate in federal nutrition assistance programs such as the Supplemental Nutrition Assistant Program (SNAP), the Supplemental Nutrition Program for Women, Infants, and Children (WIC), and the National School Lunch Program, which may mitigate some of the effects of food insecurity, particularly on children. However, food insecurity is associated with obesity among women.[32]

INTERVENTION PERSPECTIVES

When asking what circumstances of diverse ethnic minority and low SES populations predispose to obesity and diet-related disease at rates greater than for other populations, a typical focus is on cultural or social class influences on attitudes and beliefs, with excess risks attributed to an excess of adverse personal health behaviors. Given negative stereotypes, it becomes especially critical to recognize the extent to which environmental influences may constrain and discourage healthful food choices, as a counter to explanations that blame individuals for factors that are largely outside of their control. Deterrents to healthful eating that are more pervasive and more difficult to overcome in ethnic minority and low-income populations include higher neighborhood availability of fast food and lower availability of supermarkets and large grocery stores that sell a wide variety of healthful foods[33,34] and ethnically targeted advertising of high-calorie, low-nutrient foods and beverages through television and other channels.[33,35–38]

Given the overall epidemic of obesity, the similarity of many contributors to energy intake across ethnicity and SES, and the low levels of adherence to dietary recommendations in the US population at large, broadly based interventions will be needed to provide an infrastructure that can support further, focused efforts to reduce disparities. The challenge with respect to addressing disparities is how to ensure that initiatives reach and are effective with high-risk ethnic and SES groups and, to close gaps, what specially targeted initiatives might also be undertaken for specific groups. Current examples of targeted initiatives include efforts to increase the availability of healthful foods through locating supermarkets in underserved neighborhoods[39] and the development of new guidelines for the foods provided through federal nutrition programs that restrict eligibility to low-income populations, for example, WIC and the free and reduced price options for school breakfast and school lunch.[40,41] Efforts to discourage SSB consumption through taxation may also have a particular impact on populations that are high SSB consumers (e.g., Black Americans) or are more price sensitive (e.g., low-income consumers).[42] Using taxes to generate revenue to support obesity prevention programs targeted to high-risk populations is another strategy.[43]

Initiatives to regulate food marketing to children will have a disproportionate benefit for both ethnic minority and low-income children, who have higher exposure to such marketing.[44] Improving access to farmers' markets that accept electronic benefit cards from SNAP enrollees and providing financial incentives for SNAP participants who purchase healthful foods[45] will also selectively benefit the low-income population. Effective social marketing programs for the general population, with approaches designed to reach specific high-risk population segments, will be a critical complement to these strategies as will policies to improve routine access to dietary and weight loss counseling in health care settings that reach high-risk populations. These strategies will help to increase receptivity to improved food marketing environments and, ultimately, the likelihood of healthier food choices.

REFERENCES

1. *Dietary Guidelines for Americans.* Washington, DC: US Department of Health and Human Services and US Department of Agriculture, 2005. DHHS publication no. HHS-ODPHP-2005-01-DGA-A.
2. Centers for Disease Control and Prevention. National diabetes data fact sheet. 2007. Available at: http://www.cdc.gov/Features/dsDiabetes/. Accessed July 9, 2008.
3. *Health, United States, 2009: With Special Feature on Medical Technology.* Hyattsville, MD: National Center for Health Statistics, 2010. DHHS publication no. 2010–1232.
4. Grieco EM, Cassidy RC. *Overview of Race and Hispanic Origin. Census 2000 Brief.* Washington, DC: US Census Bureau, 2001. Publication no. C2KBR/01-1.
5. Pollard K, O'Hare W. America's racial and ethnic minorities. *Popul Bull* 1999;54:1–34.
6. Flegal KM, Carroll MD, Ogden CL, Curtin LR. Prevalence and trends in obesity among US adults, 1999–2008. *JAMA* 2010;303(3):235–241.
7. Ogden CL, Carroll MD, Curtin LR, Lamb MM, Flegal KM. Prevalence of high body mass index in US children and adolescents, 2007–2008. *JAMA* 2010;303(3):242–249.
8. Schoenborn CA, Adams PE. Health behaviors of adults: United States, 2005–2007. *Vital Health Stat* 2010;10(245):1–132.
9. Anderson SE, Whitaker RC. Prevalence of obesity among US preschool children in different racial and ethnic groups. *Arch Pediatr Adolesc Med* 2009; 163(4):344–348.
10. Smith SC Jr, Clark LT, Cooper RS, et al. Discovering the full spectrum of cardiovascular disease: Minority Health Summit 2003: report of the Obesity, Metabolic Syndrome, and Hypertension Writing Group. *Circulation* 2005;111(10):e134–e139.
11. Wang Y, Beydoun MA. The obesity epidemic in the United States—gender, age, socioeconomic, racial/ethnic, and geographic characteristics: a systematic review and meta-regression analysis. *Epidemiol Rev* 2007;29:6–28.

12. Freedman DS, Ogden CL, Flegal KM, Khan LK, Serdula MK, Dietz WH. Childhood overweight and family income. *Med Gen Med* 2007;9(2):26.

13. Ogden CL, Yanovski SZ, Carroll MD, Flegal KM. The epidemiology of obesity. *Gastroenterol* 2007;132(6):2087–2102.

14. Bowman SA, Gortmaker SL, Ebbeling CB, Pereira MA, Ludwig DS. Effects of fast-food consumption on energy intake and diet quality among children in a national household survey. *Pediatrics* 2004;113 (1 Pt 1):112–118.

15. Malik VS, Popkin BM, Bray GA, Despres JP, Hu FB. Sugar-sweetened beverages, obesity, type 2 diabetes mellitus, and cardiovascular disease risk. *Circulation* 2010;121(11):1356–1364.

16. Palmer JR, Boggs DA, Krishnan S, Hu FB, Singer M, Rosenberg L. Sugar-sweetened beverages and incidence of type 2 diabetes mellitus in African American women. *Arch Intern Med* 2008;168(14):1487–1492.

17. Pereira MA, Kartashov AI, Ebbeling CB, et al. Fast-food habits, weight gain, and insulin resistance (the CARDIA study): 15-year prospective analysis. *Lancet* 2005;365(9453):36–42.

18. Bleich SN, Wang YC, Wang Y, Gortmaker SL. Increasing consumption of sugar-sweetened beverages among US adults: 1988–1994 to 1999–2004. *Am J Clin Nutr* 2009;89(1):372–381.

19. Thompson FE, McNeel TS, Dowling EC, Midthune D, Morrissette M, Zeruto CA. Interrelationships of added sugars intake, socioeconomic status, and race/ethnicity in adults in the United States: National Health Interview Survey, 2005. *J Am Diet Assoc* 2009;109(8):1376–1383.

20. Wang YC, Bleich SN, Gortmaker SL. Increasing caloric contribution from sugar-sweetened beverages and 100% fruit juices among US children and adolescents, 1988–2004. *Pediatrics* 2008;121(6):e1604–e1614.

21. Reedy J, Krebs-Smith S. Dietary sources of energy, solid fats, and added sugars among children and adolescents in the United States. *J Am Diet Assoc* 2010;110(10):1477–1484.

22. National Cancer Institute, Risk Factor Monitoring and Methods Branch. Sources of energy among the US population, 2005–06. 2010. Available at: http://riskfactor.cancer.gov/diet/foodsources/energy/. Accessed May 21, 2010.

23. Basiotis PP, Carlson A, Gerrior SA, Juan WY, Lino M. *The Healthy Eating Index: 1999–2000*. Washington, DC: US Department of Agriculture, Center for Nutrition Policy and Promotion, 2002. CNPP publication no. CNPP-12.

24. Guenther PM, Reedy J, Krebs-Smith SM. Development of the Healthy Eating Index-2005. *J Am Diet Assoc* 2008;108(11):1896–1901.

25. Guenther PM, Juan WY, Lino M, Hiza HA, Fungwe T, Lucas R. *Diet Quality of Low-Income and Higher Income Americans in 2003–2004 as Measured by the Healthy Eating Index-2005*. Washington, DC: US Department of Agriculture Center for Nutrition Policy and Promotion, 2008. Nutrition insight no. 42.

26. Kant AK, Graubard BI, Kumanyika SK. Trends in black-white differentials in dietary intakes of U.S. adults, 1971–2002. *Am J Prev Med* 2007;32(4): 264–272.

27. Lancaster KJ, Watts SO, Dixon LB. Dietary intake and risk of coronary heart disease differ among ethnic subgroups of black Americans. *J Nutr* 2006; 136(2):446–451.

28. Ramirez AG, Suarez L, Chalela P et al. Cancer risk factors among men of diverse Hispanic or Latino origins. *Prev Med* 2004;39(2):263–269.

29. Bowman S. Low economic status is associated with suboptimal intakes of nutritious foods by adults in the National Health and Nutrition Examination Survey, 1999–2002. *Nutr Res* 2007;27:515–523.

30. Nord M, Andrews M, Carlson S. *Household Food Security in the United States, 2008*. Washington, DC: US Dept. of Agriculture, Economic Research Service, 2009. ERR-83.

31. Drewnowski A. Obesity, diets, and social inequalities. *Nutr Rev* 2009;67(suppl 1):S36–S39.

32. Larson N, Story M. Food insecurity and risk for obesity among children and families. Is there a relationship? Princeton, NJ: Healthy Eating Research, A National Program of the Robert Wood Johnson Foundation, 2010.

33. Grier SA, Kumanyika SK. The context for choice: health implications of targeted food and beverage marketing to African Americans. *Am J Public Health* 2008;98(9):1616–1629.

34. Powell LM, Chaloupka FJ, Bao Y. The availability of fast-food and full-service restaurants in the United States: associations with neighborhood characteristics. *Am J Prev Med* 2007;33(4 suppl): S240–S245.

35. Bell RA, Cassady D, Culp J, Alcalay R. Frequency and types of foods advertised on Saturday morning and weekday afternoon English- and Spanish-language American television programs. *J Nutr Educ Behav* 2009;41(6):406–413.

36. Grier S. African American & Hispanic youth vulnerability to target marketing: implications for understanding the effects of digital marketing. Berkeley, CA: NPLAN Marketing to Children Learning Community, 2009.

37. Powell LM, Szczypka G, Chaloupka FJ. Trends in exposure to television food advertisements among children and adolescents in the United States. *Arch Pediatr Adolesc Med* 2010;164(9):794–802.

38. Yancey AK, Cole BL, Brown R, et al. A cross-sectional prevalence study of ethnically targeted and

general audience outdoor obesity-related advertising. *Milbank Q* 2009;87(1):155–184.

39. Obama administration details Healthy Food Financing Initiative. Washington, DC: White House Press Release, 2010. Available at: http://www.hhs.gov/news/press/2010pres/02/20100219a.html. Accessed February 19, 2010.

40. Committee on Nutrition Standards for National School Lunch and School Breakfast Programs. *School Meals: Building Blocks for Healthy Children*. Washington, DC: National Academies Press, 2009.

41. Committee to Review the WIC Food Packages. *WIC Food Packages: Time for a Change*. Washington, DC: National Academies Press, 2005.

42. Sturm R, Powell LM, Chriqui JF, Chaloupka FJ. Soda taxes, soft drink consumption, and children's body mass index. *Health Affair* 2010;29(5): 1052–1058.

43. Brownell KD, Frieden TR. Ounces of prevention—the public policy case for taxes on sugared beverages. *N Engl J Med* 2009;360(18):1805–1808.

44. Kumanyika S, Grier S. Targeting interventions for ethnic minority and low-income populations. *Future Child* 2006;16(1):187–207.

45. US Department of Agriculture, Food and Nutrition Service. Healthy Incentives Pilot. 2010. Available at: http://www.fns.usda.gov/snap/HIP/qa-s.htm#HIP. Accessed May 21, 2010.

57

Is Food Advertising Feeding Americans' Sugar Habit?

An Analysis of Exposure to Television Advertising for High-Sugar Foods

JENNIFER L. HARRIS

❝ I'm cuckoo for Cocoa Puffs," "Get your chocolate fix without undoing your day" with Special K Chocolatey Delight or "Crave those crazy [Cinnamon Toast Crunch] squares." These cereal advertising slogans imply addictive properties of highly sweetened foods. Americans consume too much sugar, and this chapter explores the possibility that food advertising contributes to this sugar habit. Increasing evidence that sugar and other caloric sweeteners have addictive properties, together with skyrocketing obesity rates, indicates that limiting sugar consumption should be a beneficial public health initiative. However, the enormous volume of advertising for foods high in sugar provides a continuous reminder of the rewards of consuming highly sweetened products. Young people's exposure to advertising for these foods is of special concern as it likely increases their preferences for high levels of sugar, influences beliefs about how much sugar consumption is normal, and potentially fuels an addictive process.

AMERICANS' SUGAR HABIT

Coinciding with the rapid rise in obesity rates in the United States since the 1970s,[1] consumption of added sugar has also increased.[2] The American Heart Association recommends that individuals consume no more than half of their daily discretionary calories in added sugar: a maximum of 100 calories for women and 150 for men.[2] The average American, however, consumes two to almost four times that amount, or 355 calories every day. Sugar consumption peaks in adolescence, with 9- to 13-year-old boys consuming 467 calories of added sugar per day and 14- to 18-year-old boys consuming 549 calories

per day. Consumption among girls is somewhat lower, but still problematic: 371 calories per day for 9- to 13-year-olds and 403 for 14- to 18-year-olds. These average consumption levels far exceed the recommended amounts of 100–180 calories for the most physically active girls and 200–325 calories for boys.[3] Therefore, sugar consumption likely contributes to rising obesity rates directly.

In addition, overconsumption of added sugars is associated with other health risks, including cardiovascular disease, diabetes, and reduced intake of calcium, vitamin A, iron, and zinc.[2] Increasing evidence suggests that sugar consumption may also lead to addiction or psychological dependence. Sugar consumption has been linked to food reward pathways in the brain.[2] Symptoms of addiction, including bingeing, withdrawal, craving, and sensitization, have been documented in animals fed high-sugar diets.[4] A recent study of human response to a novel sweet high-carbohydrate food demonstrates the potential for overconsumption of such foods to enhance mood.[5]

Over 90% of Americans' intake of added sugar comes from just a few food categories: regular soft drinks and fruit drinks (43%), sweetened grains (including cereal and cookies/cakes/snack bars, 23%), sweets and sweeteners (16%), and milk products (9%).[6] Relative consumption of each category varies somewhat by age and gender. For example, children consume more sugar calories from sweetened cereals, milk products, and cakes and cookies than other age groups; and adolescent males consume over 50% of their sugar calories in beverages. Overall, however, these categories comprise the vast majority of sugar consumed by all age groups.

FOOD ADVERTISING FOR HIGH-SUGAR PRODUCTS

An important strategy to improve public health would be to discourage consumption of high-sugar foods and beverages, especially those that are consumed most often. However, research on the prevalence of advertising for products with high levels of added sugar indicates that the categories of packaged foods most commonly featured in television and other forms of advertising mirror the high-sugar foods and beverages most often consumed. For example, 51% of all food ads seen by children[7] and 45% seen by adolescents[8] in 2006 were for sweets (including candy, cookies, and desserts), sugar-sweetened beverages, and cereals. Over one-quarter of all food ads seen by children were for just one type of food: breakfast cereals. Although the cereal category contains both high and low sugar varieties, the majority of those marketed to children contain high levels of sugar.[9,10] The average calories from sugar for all products advertised to children and adolescents on television was 46% and 49%, respectively.[11] Although the nutrition quality of products advertised to adults has not been extensively documented, general audience programming also commonly features advertising for candy, other sweets, and soft drinks.[12]

High-sugar foods are also frequently promoted in other types of marketing targeted to children. For example, added sugar comprised 40% of calories of products in the supermarket that featured child- and adolescent-targeted promotions.[13] The majority of elementary schools (59%) engage in at least one type of corporate agreement to market foods high in fat and sugar and/or foods of minimal nutritional value (e.g., soft drinks or candy) to children in their schools.[14] On the Internet, 90% of products featured on children's advergaming sites were high in sugar, fat, and/or sodium and included candy, sugared cereals, and soft drinks.[15]

Potential Improvements in Advertising for High-Sugar Foods

Through the Children's Food and Beverage Advertising Initiative (CFBAI), sponsored by the Council of Better Business Bureaus, many of the largest food marketers pledged to reduce marketing for unhealthy foods targeted to children.[16] Since 2006, 16 food marketers, including cereal, beverage, candy, and snack food manufacturers, have documented how they will comply with their pledges.

Players in the different food categories have taken different approaches. For example, participating beverage (i.e., Coca-Cola and PepsiCo) and some confectionary companies (i.e., Mars, Hershey, and Cadbury-Adams) pledged that they will not advertise their products at all in child-directed media. In other high-sugar categories, including cereals and snack foods, participants pledged to advertise only "better-for-you" foods to children. Unfortunately, the criteria they have established to define "better-for-you" often permit high levels of added sugar. For example, cereals and fruit snacks may contain up to 12 g (i.e., 3 tsp) of added sugar per serving, as much as 44% of the total calories in some cereals (e.g., Cocoa Puffs or Cap'n Crunch) and 92% in fruit snacks. In addition, company pledges do not apply to advertising that appears in adolescent-targeted or general audience programming viewed by large numbers of children.

Given these potential changes in children's exposure to food advertising and the need for additional data on adolescent and adult exposure to advertising for high-sugar products, it is important to reexamine exposure to high-sugar foods and beverages in television advertising.

2008 Exposure to Television Advertising for High-Sugar Foods

The following analysis presents 2008 advertising expenditures and exposure to advertising on television for packaged foods using data licensed from The Nielsen Company.[17] Total advertising spending (including television, magazines, radio, and newspaper) and exposure to television advertising for children (ages 2–11 years), adolescents (ages 12–17 years), and younger adults (ages 18–34 years) are reported for the seven food categories that comprise 90% of Americans' sugar consumption.[6] For the cereal category, only high-sugar products, defined as those containing 25% or more of total content from added sugar, are included in the analysis. For dairy products, only advertising in the yogurt category is reported. This category represents the majority of dairy ads seen by children and adolescents, and yogurts typically contain high levels of sugar.[11]

Table 57.1 presents 2008 advertising data for the seven high-sugar categories examined. Approximately $2.4 billion was spent to advertise these products, and the average adult viewed 3.2 television ads per day for high-sugar products. Exposure was even higher among young people: children

TABLE 57.1. ADVERTISING FOR HIGH-SUGAR CATEGORIES IN 2008

High-Sugar Categories	Advertising Spending	Television Ads Viewed Per Year		
	($1000s)	Children	Adolescents	Adults
Fruit and sports drinks	471,455	184	246	233
Candy	425,357	209	296	287
Cookies, cakes, pastries, and snack bars	372,619	179	184	180
Yogurt and yogurt drinks	372,133	215	171	173
Regular soft drinks	336,566	29	62	69
High-sugar cereals	225,418	568	297	157
Other desserts, toppings, and sweeteners	189,155	56	63	70
Total	2,392,707	1,439	1,319	1,168

Source: ©The Nielsen Company.[17]

viewed 3.9 ads per day and adolescents viewed 3.6; 23% and 13% more ads (respectively) than adults.

Examination of television advertising for individual categories reveals some differences by age of viewer. In the candy and beverage categories, food marketers pledged to stop advertising to children, and children did view approximately one-third fewer advertisements for these categories than adults and adolescents. In fact, the average child saw only 29 ads in total for regular soft drinks in 2008. However, children continued to view approximately 200 ads per year for both candy and other sweetened beverage products (i.e., sports and fruit drinks). These numbers were comparable to those for other high-sugar categories, including yogurt and cookies/cakes/snack bars, categories in which many food marketers did not pledge to stop advertising to children. Therefore, self-regulatory pledges by these companies have not substantially reduced child exposure to ads for highly sweetened products.

The cereal category remained the predominant marketer of highly sweetened products to children and continues to disproportionately promote high-sugar products. Children viewed 260% more ads for high-sugar cereals, and adolescents viewed almost twice as many ads than did adults. High-sugar cereals represented 39% of all advertising exposure for high-sugar products for children and 23% of all exposure for adolescents. Even very young children view significant numbers of these ads: the *average* 2- to 5-year-old saw over 500 television ads in 2008 for high-sugar cereals.[18] If advertising for high-sugar cereals was eliminated, adolescents' greater exposure

to advertising for high-sugar-foods would not exist, and children would view 14% fewer high-sugar ads as compared to adults.

Figure 57.1 presents the proportion of packaged food ads by age group for the combined categories of sugar-sweetened beverages, candy and other sweets, sweetened grains (including cookies and cereals), and yogurt, as well as other categories. Highly sweetened products continue to represent a large proportion of television food advertising. Additionally, young people are exposed to disproportionately more ads for high-sugar categories; these categories represent 49% of ads viewed by children, 44% of those viewed by adolescents, and 37% of ads viewed by adults. Sweetened beverages and sweets together comprise 16% of packaged food ads to children and 21%–22% of ads to adolescents and adults. The largest difference by age was found in sweetened grains: cereals and cookies represent one-quarter of all ads seen by children versus only 11% of those seen by adults. Therefore, despite food industry self-regulatory pledges to reduce unhealthy marketing to children, children continue to view many ads for high-sugar products on a daily basis, and they view more of these ads as compared to both adults and adolescents.

CONSEQUENCES OF EXPOSURE TO ADVERTISING FOR HIGH-SUGAR FOODS

Research has established that food advertising increases children's preferences and requests to parents for the high-sugar products commonly advertised [19–21] and,

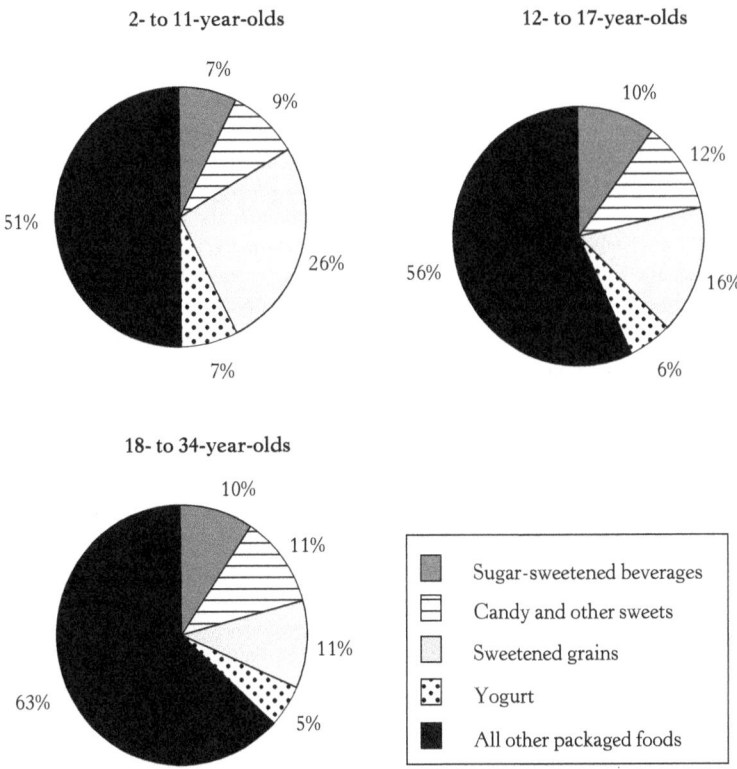

FIGURE 57.1. Percentage of exposure to television advertising for packaged foods by category.
Source: Nielsen, 2009.

therefore, likely contributes to childhood obesity. Newer research on effects of advertising on older children, adolescents, and adults, as well as potential addictive properties for high-sugar foods, raises additional concerns about the predominance of advertising for these foods among all age groups.

The effects of exposure to advertising for high-sugar foods may be most damaging to young children. Although humans prefer sweet tastes from birth, taste preferences are highly malleable and develop early, primarily through learning processes.[22,23] Therefore, a taste for highly sweetened foods that develops at a very early age likely affects a person's diet throughout his or her lifetime. Young children whose mothers routinely added sugar to their food preferred apple juice with added sugar and cereals with higher sugar content as compared to children whose mothers did not add sugar to their foods.[24] In addition, young children may be more influenced by advertising because they cannot understand the persuasive intent of marketing.[25,26]

Moreover, messages commonly presented in children's food advertising likely reinforce beliefs that children should be fed highly sweetened foods and, therefore, increase these practices. For example, children's food advertising, including advertising for cereals and other high-sugar foods, typically promotes the message that consuming these foods is fun, rewarding and, perhaps most problematic, normal.[18,27,28] Unfortunately, repeated advertising messages that children will not eat healthy foods unless the taste is hidden by large amounts of sugar likely influences children's and parents' normative beliefs about what children should eat. Cereal manufacturers reinforce this message to parents with claims that a bowl of cereal with 2–3 tsp of sugar is healthy because it contains whole grains, calcium, or added fiber and the sugar helps encourage children to eat breakfast.[29] A recent study demonstrates, however, that children will eat low-sugar cereal when served.[30] In fact, children consumed one serving of low-sugar cereals as compared to almost two servings of sugared varieties, or 6 tsp of sugar in total. As a result, advertising not only encourages preferences for highly sweetened foods, but it may also reduce preferences for the true taste of healthy foods.

Research in the alcohol and tobacco advertising literature suggests that repeated exposure to advertising also negatively affects older children and adolescents. For example, alcohol advertising creates positive expectancies about product consumption that increases trial in young people and contributes to alcohol addiction.[31,32] Similarly, food advertising messages commonly associate food consumption with exaggerated pleasure and mood enhancement and even depict addictive properties of foods directly as something the child cannot live without.[33] It is therefore likely that, as with alcohol advertising exposure, exposure to food advertising creates expectancies about positive outcomes from consuming the high-sugar foods commonly advertised.

Alcohol and tobacco research also highlights increased vulnerability among adolescents due to their reduced ability to inhibit impulsive behaviors and resist immediate gratification for longer term rewards, as well as susceptibility to peer pressure.[34,35] As a result, adolescents are more influenced by advertising for alcohol and tobacco as compared to adults, and these same developmental processes are also likely to increase their vulnerability to frequent advertising exposure for extremely tempting foods that should be consumed only occasionally and in small quantities.[36] The evidence of potential addictive properties of high-sugar foods raises even greater concern about adolescent exposure to advertising for these foods. Neurological research demonstrates that exposure to addictive substances during adolescence, before the brain is fully developed, increases the potential for long-term addiction.[34]

A troubling consequence of repeated exposure to advertising for high-sugar foods among age groups is the barrier it presents to effectively reduce consumption. Avoiding cues associated with consumption of a desired substance is essential to overcome any addiction. However, food advertising is a powerful consumption cue. Exposure to unhealthy food advertising increases snacking, and these effects may be most pronounced among children and regular dieters who wish to limit consumption.[37] As long as the food industry continues to feed our sugar habit with substantial levels of advertising for high-sugar products, it is unlikely that Americans will be able to kick this unhealthy habit.

REFERENCES

1. Ogden CL, Carroll MD, Curtin LR, McDowell MA, Tabak CJ, Flegal KM. Prevalence of overweight and obesity in the United States, 1999–2004. *JAMA* 2006;295:1549–1555.
2. Johnson RK, Appel LJ, Brands M, et al. Dietary sugars intake and cardiovascular health. A scientific statement from the American Heart Association. *J Am Heart Assoc* 2009;120:1011–1020.
3. US Department of Agriculture. Inside the pyramid: discretionary calories. 2008. Available at: http://www.mypyramid.gov/pyramid/discretionary_calories. Accessed December 6, 2009.
4. Avena NM, Rada P, Hoebel BG. Evidence of sugar addiction: biobehavioral and neurochemical effects of intermittent, excessive sugar intake. *Neurosci Biobehav Rev* 2009;32(1):20–39.
5. Spring B, Schneider K, Smith M, et al. Abuse potential of carbohydrates for overweight carbohydrate cravers. *Psychopharmacol* 2008;197:637–647.
6. Guthrie JF, Morton JF. Food sources of added sweeteners in the diets of Americans. *J Am Diet Assoc* 2000;100(1):43–51.
7. Powell LM, Szczpka G, Chaloupka FJ. Exposure to food advertising on television among US children. *Arch Pediat Adol Med* 2007;161:553–560.
8. Powell LM, Szczpka G, Chaloupka FJ. Adolescent exposure to food advertising. *Am J Prev Med* 2007;33:S251–S256.
9. Schwartz MB, Vartanian L, Wharton C, Brownell KD. Examining the nutritional quality of breakfast cereals marketed to children. *J Am Diet Assoc* 2008;108:702–705.
10. Schwartz MB, Ross C, Harris JL, et al. Cereal industry pledges to self-regulate advertising to youth: will they improve the marketing landscape? *J Public Health Pol* 2009;31:59–73.
11. Powell LM, Szczpka G, Chaloupka FJ, Braunschweig CL. Nutritional content of television food advertisements seen by children and adolescents. *Pediatrics* 2007;120:576–583.
12. Harrison K, Marske AL. Nutritional content of foods advertised during the television programs children watch most. *Am J Public Health* 2005;95:1568–1574.
13. Harris JL, Schwartz MB, Brownell KD. Marketing foods to children and youth: licensed characters and other promotions on packaged foods in the supermarket. *Public Health Nutr* 2010;13:409–427.
14. Molnar A, Garcia DR, Boninger F, Merrill B. Marketing of foods of minimal nutritional value to children in schools. *Prev Med* 2008;47:504–507.
15. Moore ES, Rideout VJ. The online marketing of food to children: is it just fun and games? *J Public Policy Mark* 2007;26(2):202–220.
16. Kolish E, Peeler L. The children's food and beverage advertising initiative: a progress report. 2008. Available at: http://www.bbb.org/us/storage/16/documents/CFBAI/ChildrenF&BInit_Sept21.pdf. Accessed December 3, 2009.

17. The Nielsen Company. Ratings and other data contained herein are the copyrighted property of The Nielsen Company. Unauthorized use of this copyrighted material is expressly prohibited. Violators may be subject to criminal and civil penalties under Federal Law (17 USC 101 et seq.). All rights reserved. 2009.

18. Harris JL, Schwartz MB, Brownell KD, et al. Cereal FACTS: evaluating the nutrition quality and marketing of children's cereals. Available at: http://www.cerealfacts.org. Accessed December 3, 2009.

19. Institute of Medicine. National Academy of Sciences, Committee on Food Marketing and the Diets of Children and Youth. In: McGinnis JM, Gootman J, Kraak VI, eds. *Food Marketing to Children and Youth: Threat or Opportunity?* Washington, DC: National Academies Press; 2006.

20. Hastings G, Stead M, McDermott L, Forsyth A. *Review of Research on the Effects of Food Promotion to Children*. Glasgow, Scotland: Center for Social Marketing, University of Strathclyde, 2003.

21. Harris JL, Pomeranz JL, Lobstein T, Brownell KD. A crisis in the marketplace: how food marketing contributes to childhood obesity and what can be done. *Ann Rev Publ Health* 2009;30:211–225.

22. Birch LL. Development of food preferences. *Ann Rev Nutr* 1999;19:41–62.

23. Rozin P. Sociocultural influences on food selection. In: Capaldi ED, ed. *Why We Eat What We Eat: The Psychology of Eating*. Washington, DC: American Psychological Association; 1996: 233–263.

24. Liem DG, Mennella JA. Sweet and sour preferences during childhood: role of early experiences. *Dev Psychobiol* 2002;41:388–395.

25. John DR. Consumer socialization of children: a retrospective look at twenty-five years of research. *J Consum Res* 1999;26:183–213.

26. Kunkel D, Wilcox BL, Cantor J, Palmer E, Linn S, Dowrick P. Report of the APA task force on advertising and children. Available at: http://www.apa.org/releases/childrenads.pdf. Accessed November 22, 2004.

27. Reece BB, Rifon NJ, Rodriguez K. Selling food to children. Is fun part of a balanced breakfast? In: Machlin LC, Carlson L, eds. *Advertising to Children:*

Concepts and Controversies. Thousand Oaks, CA: Sage Publications; 1999: 189–208.

28. Warren R, Wicks JL, Wicks RH, Fosu I, Chung D. Food and beverage advertising to children on U.S. television: did national advertisers respond? *Journalism Mass Comm* 2007;84(4):795–810.

29. Clark C, Crockett SJ. Concern over ready-to-eat breakfast cereals: letter to the editor. *J Am Diet Assoc* 2008;108(10):1618–1619.

30. Schwartz MB, Harris JL, Ustjanauskas A, Brownell KD. The influence of high versus low-sugar cereal on children's breakfast consumption. Paper presented at: Obesity Society Annual Meeting; October 26, 2009; Washington, DC.

31. Austin EW, Knaus C. Predicting the potential for risky behavior among those "too young" to drink as the result of appealing advertising. *J Health Commun* 2000;2:17–42.

32. Dunn ME, Goldman MS. Empirical modeling of an alcohol expectancy memory network in elementary school children as a function of grade. *Exp Clin Psychopharm* 1996;4(2):209–217.

33. Page RM, Brewster A. Depiction of food as having drug-like properties in televised food advertisements directed at children: portrayals as pleasure enhancing and addictive. *J Pediatr Health Car* 2009;23(3): 150–157.

34. Pechmann C, Levine L, Loughlin S, Leslie F. Impulsive and self-conscious: adolescents' vulnerability to advertising and promotion. *J Public Policy Mark* 2005;24(2):202–221.

35. Pechmann C, Knight SJ. An experimental investigation of the joint effects of advertising and peers on adolescents' beliefs and intentions about cigarette consumption. *J Consum Res* 2002;29:5–19.

36. Leslie FM, Levine LJ, Loughlin SE, Pechmann C. Adolescents' psychological and neurobiological development: implications for digital marketing. Paper presented at: Second NPLAN/BMSG Meeting on Digital Media and Marketing to Children; June 29–30, 2009; Berkeley, CA.

37. Harris JL, Bargh JA, Brownell K. The direct effects of television food advertising on eating behavior. *Health Psychol* 2009;28:404–413.

58

Environmental Interventions to Reduce Overeating in Children

THOMAS N. ROBINSON AND DONNA M. MATHESON

Most interventions to change eating behaviors and weight focus on exerting cognitive control over food choices and amount of consumption—intentionally consuming less of some foods and more of others and less overall energy.[1-3] These interventions are designed to elicit behavioral self-regulatory skills such as self-monitoring, goal setting, and rewarding successful behavior change.[2] Relatively less attention has been paid to the environmental factors that influence what and how much is eaten. Recently, researchers have started to identify environmental factors that influence intake without requiring conscious, cognitive control[4]—what food marketing researcher Brian Wansink has called "mindless eating."[5] Evidence is mounting that environmental manipulations may alter food choices and consumption to an extent that will produce substantially reduced energy intake.

Reviewing the extant literature, five such environmental strategies seem most promising for the purpose of reducing children's energy intake: (1) replacing short and wide and large-volume glasses with tall and thin and small-volume glasses; (2) replacing larger diameter and volume plates, bowls, and utensils with smaller diameter and volume plates, bowls, and utensils; (3) keeping foods targeted for less consumption inconveniently stored and less visible while keeping food targeted for more consumption conveniently placed and more visible; (4) reducing the total time children spend watching screen media; and (5) eliminating eating while watching television and other screen media.

PORTION SIZE AND OVEREATING

Portion sizes, including portions of foods eaten in the home, have increased along with increased obesity in the United States.[6,7] It has been consistently demonstrated that adults and children consume more food and total energy when served larger portions. For example, Wansink has demonstrated that when packages are doubled in size, consumption increases by 18%–25% for meal-related food and 30%–45% or more for many snack-related foods.[8,9] These effects persist over time, without caloric compensation, at subsequent meals. Rolls et al. demonstrated, among adults, that increasing portions by 50% at all meals for 11 days resulted in increased average energy intake of more than 400 kcals per day, sustained over the entire duration without decline.[10]

In children, the influence of portion size on consumption appears to emerge as early as the toddler and preschool years.[11-13] For example, when preschool children and their mothers were given double-sized portions of entrees as part of their meals and an afternoon snack, children and mothers increased their energy intake from the entrees by 23% and 21%, respectively, and their total energy intakes by 12% and 6%, respectively.[14] As in adults, young children's increased intakes due to increased portion sizes are not compensated for by decreased consumption of other foods during the same meal or during the remainder of the day.

So why not just tell people to eat smaller portions? Humans, both adults and children, are not very good at estimating the amount of food they serve themselves and consume.[4,15] Our study of portion size estimates in preadolescent girls is a good example.[16] Eight- to twelve-year-old African American girls (*n* = 54) were served a weighed test meal of spaghetti, salad, bread, and a drink. They were allowed to eat ad libitum, and plate waste was measured to calculate actual consumption. Within

10 minutes of completing the meal, dietitians collected recalls from the girls. The percent ± standard deviation errors based on absolute value differences between actual and estimated consumption were 32.8% ± 72.8% for total grams of food and 54.3% ± 96.2% for total energy. For individual foods the absolute value errors varied from 48% ± 90% for the beverage to 222% ± 524% for bread. In addition to the large errors, the large standard deviations indicated the very wide variations in the (in) accuracies of the intake estimates.

If people are not aware of precisely how much they consume, how do they know how much to eat? Environmental cues to portion size, like plate or glass size, may serve as cognitive and/or visual clues to how much to serve and when to stop eating.[17,18] Visual illusions in geometry are very well known. Piaget and colleagues showed that children perceive that taller, thinner containers hold more than shorter but wider containers.[19] This bias is evident for adults as well and can produce dramatic impacts on beverage consumption.[17] For example, 12- to 17-year-olds at a weight loss camp consumed 74% more calories from juice and soft drinks when they poured these beverages into a short, wide glass than when they poured into a tall, narrow glass holding the same volume, but afterward they estimated drinking significantly less.[20] This illusion also appears to be resistant to practice. Even college students practicing pouring and bartenders with an average of 6 years of experience poured about 20% more into short, wide glasses than tall, thin glasses.[21] *These results suggest that replacing short, wide glasses and cups with taller and thinner glasses and cups may result in reduced consumption of drinks.*

A similar visual illusion occurs with plates, bowls, and spoons. The amount of error in estimating the portion size of food depends on the relative difference between the sizes of the food and the surrounding plate, bowl, and/or spoon. People overestimate portion size when the food covers more of the area of the surface, and they underestimate the portion size when the food covers a smaller proportional area.[17] In studies in all-you-can-eat cafeterias, both overweight children and normal weight adults unknowingly served themselves more cereal using a larger bowl than a smaller bowl, while underestimating the amount served and eaten from the larger bowl and overestimating the amount from the smaller bowl.[17] Even nutrition experts[22] and adults educated about these biases[23] are unable to

cognitively overcome these visual illusions. *These results suggest that people will serve themselves and consume less without being aware of it when eating from smaller plates, bowls, and serving utensils.*

Will children and parents adjust their intake upward because they know they are drinking from taller glasses and eating from smaller plates and bowls? Most of the prior research has been limited to a single meal up to just a small number of days. To assess the real-world feasibility of substituting smaller plates, bowls, cups, glasses, and utensils, we conducted a 6-week pilot study with five families (six children) participating in the Stanford Pediatric Weight Control Program, a family-based, group, behavioral program for obese children. At an initial home visit, a research assistant inventoried and measured each family's current dishware. We then asked parents and children to (1) serve themselves their usual portions of cereal, soup (colored water), and ice cream (yogurt) into the bowls they typically use for these foods; (2) serve their usual portions of meat (formed from Play-Doh) and mixed vegetables onto their typical dinner plate; and (3) pour their usual portion of juice (colored water) into their typical drinking glass. The amounts were measured with a calibrated measuring cup and kitchen scale. Participants also responded to three questions about hunger after meals and taking second and third helpings. Families were then shown samples of smaller dishware and selected new plates, bowls, cups, and glasses to replace their current dishware.

Three to seven days later, the research assistant delivered new dishware and used the inventory completed at the first visit to collect and pack all existing dishware. Comparing the sizes of the original dishware to the replacement dishware, average bowl size reduced from 20.3 oz to 11.1 oz (−45%), glasses from 15.9 oz to 9.0 oz (−43%), cups/mugs from 12.8 oz to 7.3 oz (−43%), and dinner plate diameters from 24.9 cm to 20.8 cm (16%). Families were also instructed to use tablespoons (instead of serving spoons) for serving and teaspoons for eating.

Over the subsequent 6 weeks, the research assistant called families about weekly to monitor their reactions to the smaller dishware and encourage their continued use. For the first 1–2 weeks, the families were somewhat resistant to the smaller dishware, particularly the bowls and glasses, which looked smaller to them. After about 2 weeks, however, they all became more accustomed to the smaller dimensions. Parents reported that their children easily adapted with few complaints or comments after the first week. All families said it was helping them eat less, even when they took extra helpings. No families asked for their original dishware to be returned or reported buying additional new dishware (this was confirmed at the final visit).

After 6 weeks, the data collector made a final home visit. She repeated the same serving measurements as the first visit, asking parents and children to serve their usual portions using their current dishware. The results are shown in Figure 58.1. Compared to baseline, both parents and children substantially reduced the portions they served themselves for cereal, soup, and drinks, by about 20%–35% on average. Parents also substantially reduced their meat portions (34%) and children their ice cream portions (31%). Lesser reductions were seen in vegetable helpings on the mixed plate with meat (12.5% for both adults and children). Participants were also asked the same three hunger questions from baseline to see whether they experienced increased hunger or took more helpings with the smaller dishware. Results are shown in Figures 58.2 (parents) and 58.3 (children), demonstrating either no change or an apparent decrease in reported hunger after meals and second and third helpings.

Parents also were asked about the acceptability and helpfulness of the smaller dishware. Some of their comments included the following: "We had to make different choices and think about which foods we really wanted to eat because everything wouldn't fit on the plate," "Even when we assumed that we would go back for seconds, we would often forget and be done after the first serving," "I didn't have to have so much control over what my daughter ate because she couldn't really put too much food in the dish," "It made it so much easier…we could just pour the cereal or snacks into a bowl and know it wasn't too much," "When eating cereal I eat slower with the spoons and then get full faster," and "Rice and pasta—I definitely had to take less because of the plates." All five families said they would continue using their new smaller dishware. Only one family wished to keep their old dishware (only for entertaining), but the other four families did not want their original (larger) dishware back.

This short-term pilot test demonstrated (1) the feasibility and acceptability of substituting smaller bowls, plates, cups, glasses, and serving utensils for families participating in a weight control program, and (2) that smaller dishware appeared to result in serving smaller portions without evidence of increased hunger or additional servings.

AVAILABILITY, VISIBILITY, AND CONVENIENCE

The visual availability, visibility, and convenience (ease of access) of foods and drinks also influence whether they are consumed. In epidemiological studies, availability and accessibility of fruits and vegetables are associated with children's fruit and vegetable consumption.[24,25] Studies in cafeterias have found that people eat more ice cream when the lid of the ice cream cooler is left open, drink more milk when the dispenser is in closer proximity to the dining area, and drink more water when a water pitcher is on the dining table.[4] Office workers also eat progressively fewer chocolate kisses when they are in a container on top of their desk (convenient and visible), in a desk drawer (convenient but not visible), and on a shelf 2 meters away (visible but not convenient),[26] and fewer in clear than opaque covered bowls.[27] *These results suggest that making foods available, visible, and convenient may increase their consumption and making foods less visible and inconvenient may decrease their consumption.*

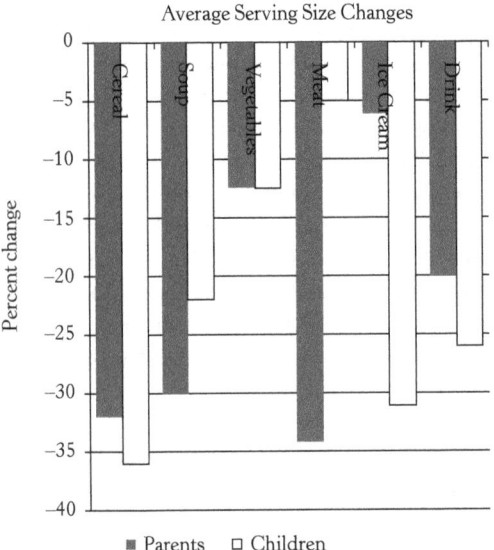

FIGURE 58.1. Serving size reductions in parents and children after 6 weeks of smaller dishware.

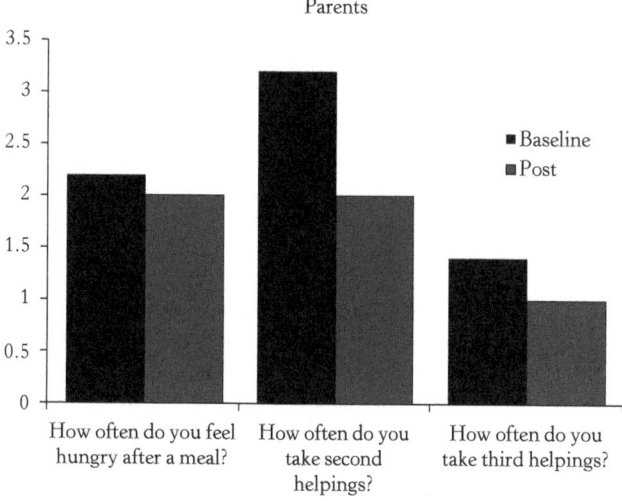

FIGURE 58.2. Parents' reports of hunger and multiple servings at baseline and after 6 weeks of smaller dishware (response scale: 1 = never to 5 = always).

SCREEN MEDIA VIEWING AND OVEREATING

National data indicate US children spend about one-third of their waking hours watching a television screen.[28] In a randomized, controlled school-based study among third and fourth graders we demonstrated the effects of reducing screen time alone for preventing weight gain.[29] Over the course of a school year, the 18-lesson screen time reduction intervention (Stanford SMART, Student Media Awareness to Reduce Television; http://noTV.stanford.edu) decreased children's screen time (relative reductions of about one-fourth to one-third), meals eaten with TV, BMI, triceps skinfold thickness, waist circumference, and waist-to-hip ratio, compared to controls. In another recent study

manipulating screen time alone, we randomized 4- to 7-year-old children with BMI ≥ 75th percentile for age and sex to a 2-year intervention to reduce their screen time by 50%, using an electronic television time manager, or to an assessments-only control group.[30] Children in the screen time reduction group showed greater reductions in their screen time, energy intake, and age- and sex-adjusted BMI (zBMI) compared to controls, maintained over the entire 2-year period.

Food advertising is one of the factors linking screen time with eating. Television advertising has been demonstrated to influence children's food and brand preferences and choices.[31-33] Another factor is increased eating while viewing. In population-based studies we have found that elementary school

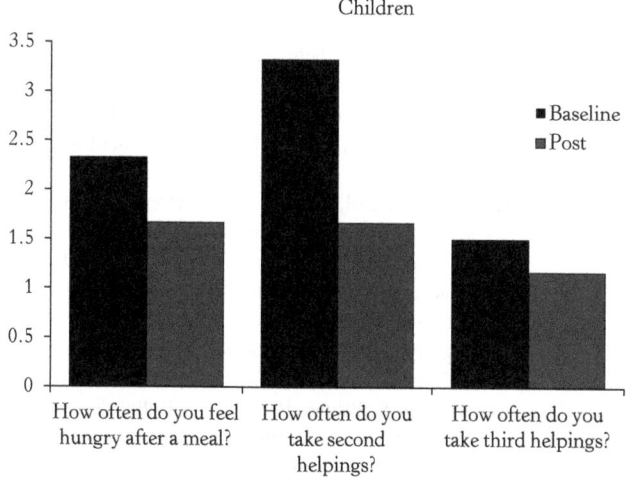

FIGURE 58.3. Children's reports of hunger and multiple servings at baseline and after 6 weeks of smaller dishware (response scale: 1 = never to 5 = always).

children consume an average 17%–27% of their total weekday calories while watching television and 26%–32% on weekends.[34,35] Eating while watching television may increase energy intake by triggering eating independent of hunger (by the association of television viewing with eating), extending the duration of eating (eating until the show is over), and obscuring awareness of eating and satiety cues.[4] The latter may occur by interfering with habituation to gustatory and olfactory cues.[36–38] For example, when 9- to 12-year-old children were shown a television show concurrently with ad libitum access to a favorite snack food, they spent more time eating and consumed more grams and more energy of food than children spending the same time not watching television or watching repeated 1.5-minute segments of the same television show, to control for the audiovisual stimulation but requiring less attention (i.e., less distraction).[38] *These studies suggest reducing total television viewing and eating while watching television may reduce excessive energy intake.*

CONCLUSION

The evidence summarized in this chapter indicates that environmental manipulations can have a substantial impact on what and how much we eat. These effects are observed in children as well as adults. As a result, relatively small environmental manipulations may alter food choices and consumption, without cognitive awareness, to an extent that will produce meaningful reductions in energy intake. Five environmental strategies seem most promising for purposes of reducing children's energy intake: (1) replacing short, wide, large-volume glasses with tall, thin, small-volume glasses; (2) replacing larger diameter and volume plates, bowls, and utensils with smaller diameter and volume plates, bowls, and utensils; (3) keeping food targeted for less consumption inconveniently placed and less visible while keeping food targeted for more consumption conveniently placed and more visible; (4) reducing the total time children spend watching screen media; and (5) eliminating eating while watching television and other screen media.

ACKNOWLEDGMENTS

We thank Tracy White for her assistance with the dishware replacement pilot study. This work was supported in part by Award Number R01HL096015 from the National Heart, Lung, and Blood Institute, National Institutes of Health. The content is solely the responsibility of the authors and does not necessarily represent the official views of the National Heart, Lung, and Blood Institute or the National Institutes of Health.

REFERENCES

1. Stuart RB. Behavioral control of overeating. *Behav Res Ther* 1967;5:357–365.
2. Dietz WH, Robinson TN. Overweight children and adolescents. *N Engl J Med* 2005;352:2100–2109.
3. Summerbell CD, Ashton V, Campbell KJ, Edmunds L, Kelly S, Waters E. Interventions for treating obesity in children. *Cochrane Database Syst Rev* 2003;3: CD001872.
4. Wansink B. Environmental factors that increase the food intake and consumption volume of unknowing consumers. *Annu Rev Nutr* 2004;24:455–479.
5. Wansink B. *Mindless Eating: Why We Eat More Than We Think.* New York: Bantam Dell, 2006.
6. Young LR, Nestle M. The contribution of portion sizes to the US obesity epidemic. *Am J Public Health* 2002;92:246–249.
7. Nielsen SJ, Popkin BM. Patterns and trends in food portion sizes, 1977–1998. *JAMA* 2003;289:450–453.
8. Wansink B. Can package size accelerate usage volume? *J Market* 1996;60:1–14.
9. Wansink B, Kim J. Bad popcorn in big buckets: portion size can influence intake as much as taste. *J Nutr Educ Behav* 2005;37:242–245.
10. Rolls BJ, Roe LS, Meengs JS. The effect of large portion sizes on energy intake is sustained for 11 days. *Obesity* 2007;15:1535–1543.
11. Rolls BJ, Engell D, Birch LL. Serving portion size influences 5-year-old but not 3-year-old children's food intakes. *J Am Diet Assoc* 2000;100:232–234.
12. Fisher JO, Rolls BJ, Birch LL. Children's bite size and intake of an entree are greater with large protions than with age-appropriate or self-selected portions. *Am J Clin Nutr* 2003;77:1164–1170.
13. Fisher JO. Effects of age on children's intake of large and self-selected food portions. *Obesity* 2007;15: 403–412.
14. Fisher JO, Arreola A, Birch LL, Rolls BJ. Portion size effects on daily energy intake in low-income Hispanic and African American children and their mothers. *Am J Clin Nutr* 2007;86:1700–1716.
15. Thompson FE, Byers T. Dietary assessment resource manual. *J Nutr* 1994;124:2245s–2317s.
16. Matheson DM, Hanson KA, McDonald TE, Robinson TN. Validity of children's food portion estimates: a comparison of 2 measurement aids. *Arch Pediatr Adolesc Med* 2002;156:867–871.
17. Van Ittersum K, Wansink B. Do children really prefer large portions? Visual illusions bias their estimates and intake. *J Am Diet Assoc* 2007;107:1107–1110.
18. Wansink B, Painter JE, North J. Bottomless bowls: why visual cues of portion size may influence intake. *Obes Res* 2005;13:93–100.

19. Piaget J, Inhelder B, Szeminska A. *The Child's Conception of Geometry*. New York: Harper Torchbooks, 1960.
20. Wansink B, van Ittersum K. Bottom's up! The influence of elongation on pouring and consumption volume. *J Cons Res* 2003;30:455–463.
21. Wansink B, van Ittersum K. Shape of glass and amount of alcohol poured: comparative study of effect of practice and concentration. *BMJ* 2005;331:1512–1514.
22. Wansink B, van Ittersum K, Painter JE. Ice cream illusions: bowls, spoons and self-served portions. *Am J Prev Med* 2006;31:240–243.
23. Wansink B. Can package size accelerate usage volume? *J Market* 1994;60:1–14.
24. Hearn MD, Baranowski T, Baranowski JC, et al. Environmental influences on dietary behavior among children: availability and accessibility of fruits and vegetables enable consumption. *J Health Educ* 1998;29:26–32.
25. Cullen KW, Baranowski T, Owens E, Marsh T, Rittenberry L, de Moor C. Availability, accessibility, and preferences for fruit, 100% fruit juice, and vegetables influence children's dietary behavior. *Health Educ Behav* 2003;30:615–626.
26. Painter JE, Wansink B, Hieggelke JB. How visibility and convenience influence candy consumption. *Appetite* 2002;38:237–238.
27. Wansink B, Painter JE, Lee Y-K. The office candy dish: proximity's influence on estimated and actual consumption. *Int J Obes Relat Metab Disord* 2006;30:871–875.
28. Robinson TN. Television viewing and childhood obesity. *Pediatr Clin North Am* 2001;48:1017–1025.
29. Robinson TN. Reducing children's television viewing to prevent obesity. *JAMA* 1999;282:1561–1567.
30. Epstein LH, Roemmich JN, Robinson JL, et al. A randomized trial of the effects of reducing television viewing and computer use on body mass index in young children. *Arch Pediatr Adolesc Med* 2008;162:239–245.
31. Borzekowski DLG, Robinson TN. The 30-second effect: an experiment revealing the impact of television commercials on food preferences of preschoolers. *J Am Diet Assoc* 2001;101:42–46.
32. Robinson TN, Borzekowski DLG, Matheson DM, Kraemer HC. Effects of fast food branding on young children's taste preferences. *Arch Pediatr Adolesc Med* 2007;161:792–797.
33. Institute of Medicine Committee on Food Marketing and the Diets of Children and Youth. *Food Marketing to Children and Youth: Threat or Opportunity?* Washington, DC: National Academies Press; 2006.
34. Matheson DM, Killen JD, Wang Y, Varady A, Robinson TN. Children's food consumption while watching television. *Am J Clin Nutr* 2004;79:1088–1094.
35. Matheson DM, Wang Y, Klesges LM, Beech BM, Kraemer HC, Robinson TN. African-American girls' dietary intake while watching television. *Obes Res* 2004;12:32S–37S.
36. Epstein LH, Paluch R, Smith JD, Sayette M. Allocation of attentional resources during habituation to food cues. *Psychophysiol* 1997;34:59–64.
37. Epstein LH, Rodefer JS, Wisniewski L, Caggiula AR. Habituation and dishabituation of human salivary response. *Physiol Behav* 1992;51:945–950.
38. Temple JL, Giacomelli AM, Kent KM, Roemmich J, Epstein LH. Television watching increases motivated responding for food and energy intake in children. *Am J Clin Nutr* 2007;85:355–361.

59

Nutrition Practices in Schools

MARLENE B. SCHWARTZ AND NICOLE L. NOVAK

The mounting evidence that food, especially food of low nutritional value, has addictive properties underscores the importance of healthy food environments in schools. As with any addiction, a child's susceptibility to the addictive properties of food hinges not only on genetics but also on the child's environment.[1] Monitoring and reforming the food environment of schools is critical to ensure that children are offered nutritious food choices and develop tastes and habits that will support their health. The importance of schools is emphasized by the White House Task Force on Childhood Obesity, which identifies "Healthy Food in Schools" as one of the four priority areas for childhood obesity prevention.[2] This chapter will review (a) the importance of school food for student nutrition, (b) the current status of the school food landscape, and (c) current efforts to improve school food by the federal government, state governments, and segments of the food industry.

THE IMPORTANCE OF SCHOOL FOOD FOR STUDENT NUTRITION

There are several reasons to invest in better food at school. First, 95% of children attend schools and a significant proportion of children's caloric intake takes place in schools.[3,4] Second, the school environment shapes student eating behavior both explicitly (as an educational environment) and implicitly (as the environment in which students form food and physical activity habits). Finally, regulation of the school environment (as evidenced by early school antismoking policies[5]) has greater political feasibility because the primary audience is children.

Cross-sectional studies have found that school food practices and policies are significantly linked to student diet. Students with access to à la carte foods sold in competition with the national school lunch program report lower intakes of fruits and vegetables, and higher calories from total and saturated fat.[6-8] Young adolescents who attend schools with vending machines have lower intakes of fruit.[6] Other research has demonstrated that school-wide food practices that support frequent snacking such as greater access to vending and snacks permitted in class are adversely associated with body mass index (BMI), with student BMI increasing 10% for every additional food practice allowed.[9]

Improving Food at School Improves Students' Diets

In addition to the studies documenting the co-occurrence of poor student diet and exposure to unhealthy foods at school, there is an emerging literature of intervention studies designed to prevent and reduce childhood obesity. Recent reviews of this body of work suggest that well-designed and well-implemented school-based programs can improve physical activity and eating behaviors in children. A 2008 systematic review of school-based obesity interventions found that combined diet and physical activity interventions in schools may help prevent childhood overweight, and a 2010 review of interventions in Europe found that interventions may be more effective when combined with nutrition and physical activity education.[10,11]

WHAT DOES THE SCHOOL FOOD LANDSCAPE LOOK LIKE?

Current Status of School Breakfast and Lunch

Over 101,000 schools in the United States participate in the National School Lunch Program (NSLP), and 87,000 also provide breakfast through the National School Breakfast Program (NSBP). The number of children who depend on these programs is significant: 31 million children participated in the NSLP in 2009, and 11.1 million children participated in the school breakfast program. [12,13] Because of their vast reach, any change to the nutrition regulations of these programs has the potential to influence tens of millions of American children every day.

The foods that are offered through these programs are federally regulated, but the standards are quite lenient. To qualify as a reimbursable school breakfast using the traditional menu planning approach, the meal must include (a) a serving of milk, (b) a fruit or juice serving, and (c) either two meat/meat alternates, two grains, or one of each. For lunch, the meal pattern requires (a) a serving of milk, (b) a meat/meat alternate, (c) a grain, and (d) two fruits, two vegetables, or one of each. The breakfast should provide 25% and lunch should provide 30% of a child's calories for the day. The only limits are that fewer than 30% of the calories should be from fat, and fewer than 10% of the calories should be from saturated fat.

Research on the nutrition quality of school meals provides a complex picture. The first national study to examine the nutrition quality of school meals (the School Nutrition Dietary Assessment) found a very surprising and disturbing result: only 1% of all school meals met all of the federal requirements for nutrition due to an excess of saturated fat.[7] This study has been repeated twice to date, and findings from the School Nutrition Dietary Assessment III study suggest that the NSLP and NSBP have improved. The meals typically meet nutrition standards for protein, vitamins, and minerals; nevertheless, a quarter of breakfast meals and two-thirds of lunch meals still exceed the limits placed on fat and saturated fat.[14] The dietary quality of school lunches is reflected in the nutritional status of students. The majority of students (and especially those who participate in school food programs) have nutritionally adequate diets; however, 80% of students have excessive saturated fat intake and 92% of students consume excess sodium.[15]

Competitive Foods

While the federally reimbursable meals must follow some nutrition standards, the major problem that has evolved in the last two decades is the increasingly large number of competitive foods offered to children at school. Competitive foods are defined as any foods sold outside of the reimbursable meals. The only federal regulation that exists at this time is that the food service cannot sell foods of minimal nutritional value (FMNV). The definition of FMNVs, however, was created over 30 years ago and includes only a few categories: soda water, chewing gum, water ices, and certain candies (e.g., hard candies, licorice, fondant). Among the allowable foods are many items that are inconsistent with the dietary recommendations for Americans, such as noncarbonated sugary drinks, potato chips, ice cream, cookies, and brownies.

Over 30% of elementary schools and 60% of middle and secondary schools have an à la carte program at lunchtime.[16] The snacks and beverages most commonly offered à la carte are baked goods, juices, juice drinks, ice cream, and chips.[17] Only 4% of à la carte foods are fruits and vegetables.[4] On a given day, approximately one-third of NSLP participants and nearly half (46%) of nonparticipants consume one or more competitive foods.[18] The most commonly consumed à la carte items are candy, cookies, cakes, and brownies, and beverages other than milk.[18]

In addition to the competitive foods sold by the food service during lunch, many schools also sell food and beverages through vending machines, school stores, or fundraising activities. All of these sources of food are not regulated by the FMNV rules as long as they are not sold during the lunch period. Currently, 97% of high schools, 82% of middle schools, and 17% of elementary schools have vending machines.[18] These machines can include FMNV items such as sugar-sweetened soft drinks and all types of candy.

Finally, another source of unhealthy foods can be classroom parties and food used as a reward by the teacher. Food in class is most common in elementary schools, where many communities have developed the ritual of bringing cupcakes in to celebrate birthdays, as well as having parties with candy and treats for Halloween, Valentine's Day, other holidays, and the end of the year. Because the food is not being sold, the items given to children in class by either the teacher or other parents are the most difficult to regulate with federal or state laws.

CURRENT EFFORTS TO IMPROVE THE SCHOOL FOOD ENVIRONMENT

It is critical that school districts accurately track and understand the policies that are regulating the school environment; however, this can be difficult because federal, state, and local policies have all been used to improve the nutrition of food and beverages at school. At the same time, in the case of sugary drinks, the beverage industry has attempted to self-regulate and change the mix of beverages delivered to schools. Each of these actions has the potential to improve children's diets.

Federal Policies

At the federal level, the NSLP and the NSBP must meet nutrition standards in order to receive federal reimbursement for meals. Encouragingly, much progress has been made in the effort to improve the nutrition standards for school meals. The Institute of Medicine released a report in 2009 recommending a number of important changes to school meals, including (a) setting not only a minimum but also a maximum number of calories per meal, (b) increasing the amount and variety of fruits, vegetables, and whole grains, and (c) clearer methods for reducing the amounts of fat and saturated fat.[19] In 2011, the US Department of Agriculture (USDA) released its planned changes for the school meal programs, which are closely aligned to the Institute of Medicine recommendations.[20]

Two key nutrients—sodium and sugar—are treated quite differently in the proposed rule. There are very aggressive standards for reducing the amount of sodium in meals over the next decade. In contrast, there are no specific and direct limits on added sugars; instead the rule appears to rely on the calorie limits to effectively reduce the amount of allowable sugar. In other words, the food service meal planner must choose the low-sugar versions of foods in order to meet all the nutrient requirements without going over the calorie limit. This strategy may work, or the result may replicate the current problem with fat levels, which also requires mathematic calculations for every possible meal to determine the calories per meal and then the percentage of calories from fat and saturated fat. To the extent that sugar emerges as a nutrient with potentially addictive properties, this indirect method to regulate sugar may emerge as a problem area to address in the future.

Another important component of the new federal legislation on school food gives USDA the power to regulate not just the federal food programs but also competitive foods. This is a significant victory, as the regulation of competitive foods has previously fallen to the states.

State Policies

Many states regulate the school food environment above and beyond the policies set at the federal level. As of 2010, 20 states and Washington, D.C. implemented additional nutritional standards for school meals. Much of this policy change has been recent; 14 of these states have only added standards in the past 6 years. For example, D.C. passed legislation requiring that school meals be free of trans fat and that saturated fat constitute less than 10% of total calories. The legislation also prescribed sodium reductions by 2020 and required that all school meals meet or exceed the standards set by the USDA's HealthierUS School Challenge program at the Gold Award Level.[21] Twenty-eight states and Washington, D.C. have also developed nutritional standards for competitive foods. Similarly, most of these standards are new; 22 of these states have only added standards in the past 6 years. For example, Louisiana recently revised nutrition standards to limit competitive beverages to bottled water, 100% fruit juice, milk, and low-calorie or no-calorie beverages with less than 66 calories per 8 ounces. Twenty-nine states and Washington, D.C. limit access to competitive foods by prohibiting them from being sold at certain times of day or in certain places.[21]

District Policies

Regulation of the school food environment also occurs at the district level. The Child Nutrition and WIC Reauthorization Act of 2004 (Public Law 108–265) required that each of 14,000 school districts participating in USDA child nutrition programs develop a school wellness policy by 2006. Some districts used wellness policies to improve school meals and limit the range and availability of competitive foods.

The Child Nutrition and WIC Reauthorization Act of 2004 required all district wellness policies to ensure that school meal nutritional guidelines would meet or exceed the federal school meal standards. A 2010 review of school wellness policies found that over half of students nationwide attend school in a district that uses the 2005 Dietary Guidelines as its nutritional standard, a stricter standard than the federal guidelines.[22] Approximately 20% of students were enrolled in a district that required meals to *exceed* the 2005 Dietary Guidelines or meet even stricter standards such as the 2009 Institute of Medicine standards.

While some school districts have used wellness policies to limit access to or prohibit certain competitive foods, many districts continue to have weak policies in this area, especially for middle and high schools. Only 7% of policies banned competitive foods at the elementary school level, and no policies prohibited competitive foods in middle or high schools. Districts were much more likely to limit the nutritional content of competitive foods in vending machines or à la carte sales than in school fundraisers, classroom parties, or the use of food as a reward.

District wellness policies can also be used to regulate vending machines and marketing within schools, but few districts have done so. Just 22% of students nationwide attend school in a district that requires vending contracts to comply with the district's nutrition standards.[22]

One of the challenges districts face in restricting sales of competitive foods is their belief that they will lose much of their income. There is very little research on this topic, but several studies have shown that limiting access to competitive foods has increased participation in NSLP, which in turn can compensate for lost revenue and in some cases increase the revenue for the local foodservice.[23]

The Special Case of Sugar-Sweetened Beverages

As of 2006, most schools (58% elementary schools, 84% middle schools, 94% of high schools) sold sugar-sweetened beverages.[4] School systems can sign contracts with soft drink bottlers, which typically commit to exclusive sale of one company's products and advertising rights in exchange for lump-sum and ongoing payments.[4] This practice has become extremely controversial in the face of mounting evidence of the negative health consequences of these beverages.[24] Both sugar and caffeine have been demonstrated to have addictive properties.[25] Sugar-rich diets activate reward centers in the brain, a process that has the potential to override self-control mechanisms and may lead to addiction.[26] Although some reviews argue against the idea of food addiction,[27] the growing body of evidence for the addictive properties of sugary beverages highlights the need for a more careful consideration of the implications of offering sugar-sweetened beverages to children and adolescents while they are at school.

Some steps have been taken by the industry itself to reduce access to sugar-sweetened beverages in schools. In 2006, the American Beverage Association (the trade association of the soft drink industry, including Coca-Cola, PepsiCo, and Cadbury Schweppes) announced a voluntary commitment to remove sugar-sweetened soft drinks and many other sugar-sweetened beverages from all elementary, middle, and high schools by 2009–2010. While American Beverage Association reports indicate that many schools have reduced or eliminated the availability of soft drinks, the plan has been criticized for its lack of clear oversight or binding commitments.[28] It also leaves some high-calorie drinks, like sports drinks or sugar-sweetened "light juices" in schools, and continues to provide branding opportunities in schools.

While the achievements to date in improving the school food environment are not to be discounted, there is progress left to be made. Fortunately, there are opportunities to strengthen school food policies using district, state, and federal regulatory mechanisms. Over the past few years, the groundwork has been laid to restrict in-school access to potentially habit-forming foods and beverages and improve the diet of the nation's children. As a result, there is much greater awareness and public acceptance of the importance of improving food at school. The dream of having a school environment where every food and beverage choice is a healthy choice is getting closer to reality each year.

REFERENCES

1. Merlo LJ, Klingman C, Malasanos TH, Silverstein JH. Exploration of food addiction in pediatric patients: a preliminary investigation. *J Addict Med* 2009;3:26–32.
2. *Report to the President: Solving the Problem of Childhood Obesity within a Generation*. Washington, DC: White House Task Force on Childhood Obesity, 2010.
3. Wechsler H, Devaraux RS, Davis M, Collins J. Using the school environment to promote physical activity and healthy eating. *Prev Med* 2000;31:S121–S137.
4. Story M, Kaphingst KM, French S. The role of schools in obesity prevention. *Future Child* 2006;16:109–142.
5. Leads from the MMWR. School policies and programs on smoking and health—United States, 1988. *JAMA* 1989;261:2488.
6. Kubik MY, Lytle LA, Hannan PJ, Perry CL, Story M. The association of the school food environment with dietary behaviors of young adolescents. *Am J Public Health* 2003;93:1168–1173.
7. Burghardt J, Gordon A, Fraker T. Meals offered in the National School Lunch Program and the School Breakfast Program. *Am J Clin Nutr* 1995;61:187S–198S.
8. US Department of Agriculture. *Nutrition Standards in the National School Lunch and School Breakfast*

Programs; Proposed Rule. Washington, DC: The Federal Register, 2011.

9. Kubik MY, Lytle LA, Story M. Schoolwide food practices are associated with body mass index in middle school students. *Arch Pediat Adol Med* 2005;159:1111–1114.

10. Brown T, Summerbell C. Systematic review of school-based interventions that focus on changing dietary intake and physical activity levels to prevent childhood obesity: an update to the obesity guidance produced by the National Institute for Health and Clinical Excellence. *Obes Rev* 2009;10:110–141.

11. De Bourdeaudhuij I, Van Cauwenberghe E, Spittaels H, et al. School-based interventions promoting both physical activity and healthy eating in Europe: a systematic review within the HOPE project. *Obes Rev* 2011;12:205–216.

12. Food and Nutrition Service. *School Lunch Program Fact Sheet*. Washington, DC: US Department of Agriculture, 2010.

13. Food and Nutrition Service. *School Breakfast Program Fact Sheet*. Washington, DC: US Department of Agriculture, 2010.

14. Crepinsek MK GA, McKinney PM, Condon EM, Wilson A. Meals offered and served in US public schools: do they meet nutrient standards? *J Am Diet Assoc* 2009;109:S31–S43.

15. Clark MA, Fox MK. Nutritional quality of the diets of US public school children and the role of the school meal programs. *J Am Diet Assoc* 2009;109: S44–S56.

16. Fox MK, Gordon A, Nogales R, Wilson A. Availability and consumption of competitive foods in US public schools. *J Am Diet Assoc* 2009;109: S57–S66.

17. Lytle LA, Kubik MY, Perry C, Story M, Birnbaum AS, Murray DM. Influencing healthful food choices in school and home environments: results from the TEENS study. *Prev Med* 2006;43:8–13.

18. Gordon A, Fox MK. *School Nutrition Dietary Assessment Study-III: Summary of Findings*. Washington, DC: US Department of Agriculture, 2007.

19. Institute of Medicine of the National Academy of Science. *School Meals: Building Blocks for Healthy Children*. Washington, DC: National Academies Press, 2009.

20. US Department of Agriculture. *Nutrition Standards in the National School Lunch and School Breakfast Programs; Proposed Rule*. Washington, DC: The Federal Register, 2011.

21. Levi J, Vinter S, St. Laurent R, Segal LM. *F as in Fat: How Obesity Threatens America's Future*. Washington, DC: Trust for America's Health: 2010.

22. Chiriqui JF, Schneider L, Chaloupka FJ, et al. *School District Wellness Policies: Evaluating Progress and Potential for Improving Children's Health Three Years after the Federal Mandate. School years 2006–07, 2007–08 and 2008–09*. Chicago, IL: Bridging the Gap Program, Health Policy Center, Institute for Health Research and Policy, University of Illinois at Chicago, 2010.

23. Long MW, Henderson KE, Schwartz MB. Evaluating the impact of a Connecticut program to reduce availability of unhealthy competitive food in schools. *J Sch Health* 2010;80:478–486.

24. Vartanian LR, Schwartz MB, Brownell KD. Effects of soft drink consumption on nutrition and health: a systematic review and meta-analysis. *Am J Public Health* 2007;97:667–675.

25. Satel S. Is caffeine addictive?—a review of the literature. *Am J Drug Alcohol Abuse* 2006;32:493–502.

26. Lenoir M, Serre F, Cantin L, Ahmed SH. Intense sweetness surpasses cocaine reward. *PLoS ONE* 2007;2:e698.

27. Drewnowski A, Bellisle F. Is sweetness addictive? *Nutr Bull* 2007;32:52–60.

28. Mello MM, Pomeranz J, Moran P. The interplay of public health law and industry self-regulation: the case of sugar-sweetened beverage sales in schools. *Am J Public Health* 2008;98:595–604.

PART VI

Legal and Policy Implications

60

Legal and Policy Implications

Litigation

STEPHEN P. TERET AND LAINIE RUTKOW

There are many types of litigation—such as lawsuits that seek injunctive relief to forestall harm, or lawsuits brought by governmental authorities like attorneys general who are seeking compensation for the expenditure of public funds—that can be relevant to damage caused by addiction to harm-producing products. The type of litigation discussed in this chapter is an individual's lawsuit, founded upon tort law, which seeks monetary damages based on the alleged improper conduct of the defendant that resulted in injury to the plaintiff. The essential elements to be proven in a successful lawsuit of this type are that (1) the defendant owed a duty of care to the plaintiff; (2) the duty was breached; and the breach (3) was causally related to (4) damage suffered by the plaintiff.

The duty of a product manufacturer is to make the product reasonably safe for its intended use. When a consumer product, due to its faulty design or manufacture or marketing, causes an injury, that duty has arguably been breached, and an ensuing lawsuit based on this is generally referred to as product liability litigation. Such lawsuits can involve a defect in the product, but they may also involve concepts such as failure to warn of an inherent danger or the overpromotion of a dangerous product.

A product that has the potential to cause harm, such as cigarettes that cause cancer, exposes the maker of the product to being liable to the user of the product. Such liability may be enhanced if the product, in addition to being hazardous to one's health, is also addictive. If the addictive qualities of the product result from the manufacturer knowingly modifying the product, and if the harmful and addictive properties of the product were not clearly called to the user's attention through effective warnings, then the risk of liability will be even greater.

Some food products have the ability to cause harm. Calorie-dense products can cause obesity, and obesity is linked to damaging illnesses such as diabetes. If a food product is addictive, and if that addictive quality is a result of intentional product manipulation by the manufacturer, and if there was a failure to warn the user of the addictive nature of the product even though the manufacturer knew or should have known that overuse of the product could result in damage, then one could argue that the manufacturer should be held liable to the damaged consumer.

This chapter considers efforts to impose liability on the makers of other potentially addictive products, and what that teaches us about the likelihood that liability may be imposed on manufacturers and marketers of unhealthy foods that can be addictive.

CIGARETTES

Every year in the United States, tobacco products are associated with more than 400,000 deaths.[1] For decades, researchers have consistently documented the addictive properties of nicotine, a key component of tobacco products.[2] Yet addiction has only recently emerged as a prominent theme in tobacco-related litigation.

Legal scholars divide tobacco litigation into three waves.[3,4] The first wave of litigation was sparked by research that demonstrated an association between smoking and lung cancer.[5] During this wave, from the 1950s to the 1970s, individuals brought hundreds of lawsuits against tobacco manufacturers, with almost no success.[6] Tobacco manufacturers dominated this period, through the use of several strategies, such as arguing that smokers knew there was some risk associated with smoking and claiming that scientific evidence did not conclusively link smoking to negative health outcomes.[7]

During the second wave of tobacco litigation, in the 1980s and 1990s, the tobacco industry continued to triumph, despite mounting evidence that linked smoking to multiple forms of cancer. In the second wave of litigation, the tobacco industry lost only a single case.[8,9] When faced with this loss, the tobacco industry aggressively pursued multiple rounds of appeals. Ultimately, the plaintiffs were forced to end the litigation, because they could no longer afford to participate in the prolonged appellate process.[5]

In recent years, the third wave of tobacco litigation has focused more on the industry's deceptive conduct regarding its knowledge about the addictive nature of nicotine and its deliberate efforts to cause individuals to become addicted to cigarettes. Two major lawsuits have paved the way for future tobacco litigation that employs arguments related to addiction.

In 2006, Federal District Court Judge Gladys Kessler issued a nearly 1,800-page opinion in *United States v. Philip Morris*. The litigation began in 1999, when the US government sued the major tobacco manufacturers and alleged that they had violated the Racketeer Influenced and Corrupt Organizations (RICO) Act.[10] RICO, a federal law, can be used to bring charges against businesses that impact commerce among the states through conspiracies and racketeering. Among its many allegations, the US government claimed that the major tobacco manufacturers had conspired to deny nicotine's addictive qualities and had deliberately concealed information about the dangers associated with smoking.[11]

In the *Philip Morris* decision, Judge Kessler concluded that the major tobacco manufacturers had indeed violated RICO. She explained that the tobacco manufacturers had, in part, broken the law by denying the addictive qualities of nicotine despite much evidence to the contrary. The opinion's vast factual findings about nicotine and addiction reveal the extent of the tobacco manufacturers' knowledge:

> Since the 1950s, [the tobacco manufacturers] have researched and recognized…that nicotine is an addictive drug, that cigarette manufacturers are in the drug business, and that cigarettes are drug delivery devices.[11]
>
> [The tobacco manufacturers] have intentionally maintained and coordinated their position on addiction and nicotine as an important

part of their overall efforts to…persuade people that smoking was not dangerous…[11]

> For approximately forty years, [the tobacco manufacturers] publicly, vehemently, and repeatedly denied the addictiveness of smoking and nicotine's central role in smoking.[11]

The *Philip Morris* opinion contains several remedies intended to punish the major tobacco manufacturers, such as requiring the companies to issue statements about the harmful health effects associated with smoking. The tobacco manufacturers appealed the decision, and litigation surrounding *Philip Morris* is ongoing. Regardless of the ultimate outcome, lessons can be drawn from this lawsuit for future addiction-based tobacco litigation.[7] First, the *Philip Morris* opinion contains hundreds of pages of factual findings that explain what the tobacco manufacturers knew about nicotine's addictive qualities and the steps they took to conceal this information. This information is now publicly available and can be used in future litigation. Second, the opinion provides a roadmap for how to bring litigation against an industry that has allegedly engaged in fraud or conspiracy to conceal its products' addictive qualities.

A second recent lawsuit, *Engle v. Liggett Group, Inc.*, has also had profound ramifications for tobacco litigation that involves the addictive qualities of nicotine. The *Engle* litigation began in 1994, when several individuals in Florida sued the major cigarette manufacturers as representatives of the class of people "who have suffered, presently suffer or who have died from diseases and medical conditions caused by their addiction to cigarettes that contain nicotine."[12] In this class action lawsuit, the plaintiffs asked for compensatory damages for themselves, in light of the medical conditions that arose from their addiction to cigarettes, and they asked for punitive damages, which were intended to punish the tobacco industry's outrageous conduct.

After a 2-year trial, the jury determined that the plaintiffs had proven certain facts related to their case. These findings included the acknowledgment that nicotine is addictive, and went on to explain that the tobacco manufacturers "agreed to misrepresent information relating to the health effects of cigarettes or the addictive nature of cigarettes with the intention that smokers and the public would rely on this information to their detriment."[12] In addition, the jury awarded compensatory damages to the plaintiffs along with $145 billion in punitive damages. Ultimately, after several years of appeals, the punitive damages award was overturned. Despite this, in 2006, the Florida Supreme Court affirmed the factual findings concerning nicotine's addictive qualities and the steps that tobacco manufacturers took to misrepresent their knowledge about nicotine and addiction.[12]

Engle has already served as a catalyst for additional addiction-based litigation against the tobacco industry in Florida. *Engle*'s factual findings about nicotine, addiction, and the tobacco manufacturers' conduct can be used by other individuals who sue the tobacco industry. Individuals no longer have to reestablish this general information each time a lawsuit is brought against the tobacco industry, though they still must prove that tobacco products were responsible for their own illness.[7] In the 3 years since *Engle* was decided, thousands of lawsuits have been filed against the tobacco industry by individuals in Florida.[13] Several have already been decided in favor of plaintiffs who relied on *Engle*'s factual findings about smoking and addiction.[14]

OTHER PRODUCTS
Some consumer products in addition to cigarettes have addictive qualities—for example, alcoholic beverages and pharmaceuticals—and one might therefore surmise that litigation involving those products has followed the same path as tobacco litigation. This, however, is not the case.

Alcoholic beverages, like cigarettes, can be legally marketed and sold to adults, even though they are associated with considerable excess morbidity and mortality, and are generally considered to be addictive. The federal Centers for Disease Control and Prevention estimated that more than 75,000 alcohol-attributable deaths occurred in the United States in 2001 due to excessive alcohol consumption.[15]

Most lawsuits brought by individuals against the makers of alcoholic beverages for harm suffered have not resulted in liability being imposed upon the defendants. James Mosher, a leading scholar of alcohol policy and alcohol-related litigation, has reviewed potential and actual alcohol lawsuits and speculated as to whether the same theories that resulted in winning tobacco lawsuits might work in alcohol-related lawsuits.[16] Mosher's conclusions include the following:

Both products are addictive and use begins at very young ages; neither can be supplied

legally to young people, yet the two industries use similar youth-oriented marketing strategies; and both industries have been highly successful in blocking public health reforms through the legislative process. Litigation appears to be an important tactic for addressing the contribution of alcohol marketing practices to alcohol problems in society.[16]

But, even though there are clear similarities between the two products, and attempts have been made to bring tobacco-like lawsuits against alcoholic beverage makers, the defendants have largely avoided liability. The explanation for this may be that the public (i.e., judges and jurors) have not yet experienced the type of anger against alcoholic beverage makers that they feel against cigarette makers based on many decades of antitobacco research and advocacy.

A rare appellate opinion that commented favorably about the possibility of imposing liability on an alcoholic beverage maker for damages sustained by a drinker is *Hon v. Stroh Brewery Co.*, 835 F.2d 510 (3rd Cir. 1987).[17] In that case, a 26-year-old drinker of the defendant's beer died of pancreatitis, and medical evidence was presented that there was a causal relationship between the consumption of the beer and the fatal disease. There was no warning by the defendant that use of its product could result in this type of illness and death. The court found that "there is a material dispute of fact as to whether Stroh's beer without a warning is safe for its intended purpose," and therefore the case should be tried.[17]

Another addictive product that has been involved in litigation is the painkiller oxycodone, marketed under the brand name of OxyContin by Purdue Pharma. Oxycodone is a particularly addictive drug that has caused considerable damage to its users.[18]

According to *The New York Times*, there have been hundreds of lawsuits brought against Purdue for its failure to adequately warn users of OxyCodone that the product is addictive and can cause harm, but none of the lawsuits brought by individuals have succeeded.[19] West Virginia brought a case against Purdue based on alleged violations of the state's consumer protection laws, and the claim was settled by payment of $10 million. Again, a possible explanation for the failure of these lawsuits from the plaintiffs' perspective may be that society is more willing to blame the product user, in these cases, than the product manufacturer because of the legitimate need and demand for the product.

Thus, lawsuits other than those against tobacco companies, which have been based on the addictive qualities of a product and the damage that results from overuse of that product, have not generally been successful for the individual plaintiffs.

OTHER CONSIDERATIONS

Litigation in general, and product liability litigation specifically, has been hailed as a powerful tool for protecting the public's health.[20–23] Successful litigation can cause product makers to pay greater attention to the safety of their products so that they do not have to pay a financial penalty for neglect. It can also unearth important, new information about products through the discovery phase of litigation, and it can attract media and public attention to the risks posed by unsafe products. Litigation against food makers and marketers based on the addictive qualities of their products and the damage caused by overconsumption can be an important factor in stimulating companies to provide healthier foods.

A few cautionary notes are in order, however, about a rush to such litigation. First, if this type of litigation is to be successful, there must be and should be a strong basis in science for proving that a breach of duty and causally related damage has occurred. Litigation of this type should not be brought prematurely, before the science is well enough developed and scientists who are willing and able to serve as expert witnesses have been identified. Second, it is to be expected that the food industry, anticipating such litigation, will try to acquire immunity to litigation through the legislative process. This, for example, was done by the gun manufacturers when gun litigation was becoming prevalent.[24] In some states, similar legislation, euphemistically known as "cheeseburger laws," already exists; these laws were intended to grant immunity from certain types of litigation to the restaurant industry.[25] Whether immunity should be granted to food makers and marketers who may have intentionally made their products addictive, analogously to adding nicotine to cigarettes, while knowing of the health consequences of overconsumption of such foods, is a matter of public policy that will be influenced by advocacy.

REFERENCES

1. Centers for Disease Control and Prevention. Tobacco-related mortality. 2009. Available at: http://www.cdc.gov/tobacco/data_statistics/fact_sheets/health_effects/tobacco_related_mortality/. Accessed November 1, 2009.
2. Kluger R. *Ashes to Ashes: America's Hundred-Year Cigarette War, the Public Health, and the Unabashed Triumph of Philip Morris.* New York: Knopf, 1997.
3. Rabin RL. A sociolegal history of the tobacco tort litigation. *Stanford Law Rev* 1992;44(4):853–878.
4. Rabin RL. The third wave of tobacco tort litigation. In: Rabin RL and Sugarman SD, eds. *Regulating Tobacco.* New York: Oxford University Press; 2001: 176–206.
5. Douglas CE, Davis RM, Beasley JK. Epidemiology of the third wave of tobacco litigation in the United States, 1994–2005. *Tobacco Control* 2006;15(supp. 4):iv9–iv16.
6. LaFrance AB. Tobacco litigation: smoke, mirrors, and public policy. *Am J Law Med* 2000;26(2–3):187–202.
7. Vernick JS, Rutkow L, Teret SP. Public health benefits of recent litigation against the tobacco industry. *JAMA* 2007;298(1):86–89.
8. *Cipollone v Liggett Group, Inc.,* 505 U.S. 504 (1992).
9. Alderman J, Daynard RA. Applying lessons from tobacco litigation to obesity lawsuits. *Am J Prev Med* 2006;30(1):82–88.
10. Tobacco Control Legal Consortium. *The Verdict is in: Findings from United States v. Philip Morris Collection.* St. Paul, MN: Tobacco Control Legal Consortium, 2006.
11. *United States v Philip Morris USA, Inc.,* 449 F Supp 2d 1 (DDC 2006).
12. *Engle v Liggett Group, Inc.,* 945 So.2d 1246 (Fla 2006).
13. Loney J. Smokers, tobacco both winners in early Engle cases. *Reuters,* August 20, 2009. Available at: http://www.reuters.com/article/reutersEdge/idUS-TRE57J63F20090820. Accessed November 1, 2009.
14. Tobacco Control Resource Center. Plaintiffs have won verdicts in 7 of 9 post-Engle individual trials so far. Boston, MA: Tobacco Control Resource Center, 2009.
15. MMWR. Alcohol-attributable deaths and years of potential life lost—United States, 2001. *Morb Mort Wkly Rep* 2004;53(37):866–870.
16. Mosher JF. Litigation and alcohol policy: lessons from the U.S. tobacco wars. *Addiction* 2009;104 (suppl 1):27–33.
17. *Hon v Stroh Brewery Co.,* 835 F.2d 510 (3rd Cir. 1987).
18. Cicero TJ, Inciardi JA, Munoz A. Trends in use in OxyContin and other opioid analgesics in the United States: 2002–2004. *J Pain* 2005;6(10):662–672.
19. Associated Press. Drug maker named in lawsuits over OxyContin. *New York Times,* Aug. 27, 2005.
20. Teret SP. Injury control and product liability. *J Public Health Pol* 1981;2(1):49–57.

21. Teret SP. Litigating for the public's health. *Am J Public Health* 1986;76(8):1027–1029.

22. Vernick JS, Mair JS, Teret SP, Sapsin JW. Role of litigation in preventing product-related injuries. *Epidemiol Rev* 2003;25:90–98.

23. Vernick JS, Sapsin JW, Teret SP, Mair JS. How litigation can promote product safety. *J Law Med Ethics* 2004;32(4):551–555.

24. Vernick JS, Rutkow L, Salmon DA. Availability of litigation as a public health tool for firearm injury prevention: comparison of guns, vaccines, and motor vehicles. *Am J Public Health* 2007;97(11):1991–1997.

25. CNN. "Cheeseburger bill" puts bite on lawsuits. Oct. 20, 2005. Available at: http://www.cnn.com/2005/POLITICS/10/20/cheeseburger.bill/index.html. Accessed November 1, 2009.

61

Legal Implications

Regulating Sales and Marketing

JENNIFER L. POMERANZ

INTRODUCTION

As science continues to reveal the addictive properties of certain foods and beverages, government regulation of the sale and marketing of such products may become necessary. In the United States, both the federal and state governments have regulatory authority over food and beverages (hereinafter "food"). The Food and Drug Administration (FDA) has the primary authority over the safety and labeling of both food and added ingredients, such as sugar, caffeine, and chemicals to enhance shelf-life, color, and other physical properties.[1] State governments (via their legislatures, state agencies, and attorneys general) can regulate consumer goods, including food, to the extent not preempted by federal law. State and local governments also have the authority to act to protect public health, safety, and welfare under their traditional police powers, and they can use this power to regulate the sale of food.[2]

Although not a food, tobacco products are highly addictive and legally available for sale in the United States. Federal and state regulation of tobacco products provides valuable insight into potential avenues to regulate the sale and marketing of food if it is found to be addictive. Government regulation of tobacco includes restrictions on advertisements for such products; however, the First Amendment of the Constitution protects marketers from government interference with their right to advertise. This constitutional protection of "commercial speech" has proven to be a barrier to some restrictions on marketing and will be explored in this chapter in the context of tobacco products.

A review of federal and state regulation of addictive substances and products reveals gaps in the current regulatory framework and the potential for future government intervention in response to scientific advances in the field of food and addiction. This chapter will review the FDA's regulatory framework for food and the government's regulation of caffeine, sugar, and tobacco products to suggest legally permissible regulations in the realm of food and addiction.

THE FDA'S REGULATORY FRAMEWORK FOR FOOD

The FDA has the primary regulatory responsibility over food, which is defined as "articles" or "components" of articles used for "food or drink" (including chewing gum).[3] Because this definition is vague, the judiciary provided a guiding clarification that food includes "articles used by people in the ordinary way most people use food—primarily for taste, aroma, or nutritive value."[4]

The Nutrition Labeling and Education Act of 1990 (NLEA) requires that all food regulated by the FDA must have a nutrition facts panel and ingredient list on the product's packaging. The Food Allergen Labeling and Consumer Protection Act of 2004 requires that such labels also identify the source of ingredients that are, or are derived from, the eight most common food allergens (milk, eggs, fish, crustacean shellfish, tree nuts, peanuts, wheat, and soybeans).[5]

Under the Federal Food, Drug, and Cosmetic Act, substances classified as food are presumed to be safe unless the FDA can prove "by a preponderance of the evidence" that the food is "injurious to health."[6] On the other hand, food additives, which are substances intentionally added to food, are presumed to be unsafe unless premarket safety testing leads the FDA to conclude they are safe. If a food additive is not proven safe by the entity seeking to introduce it into the food supply, the food containing such additive is considered "adulterated" and may be condemned.[7] If an additive is approved but new information emerges that indicates that it is unsafe, the Secretary of Health and Human Services can withdraw its safe status and all food products produced with it would be considered adulterated.[8]

Adulterated food is food that contains "any poisonous or deleterious substance which may render it injurious to health."[8] In order for the food to qualify as adulterated, such a substance must be "artificially introduced, or attributable in some degree to the acts of man."[9,10] Any quantity of the deleterious substance is considered unsafe unless it could not be avoided by good manufacturing practices. In this latter case, the FDA sets a level under which producers must still limit the substance in their foods.[11,12]

The final category of substances added to food is ingredients that have been generally recognized as safe (GRAS) by the agency.[13] Substances such as salt, pepper, sugar, and caffeine have been GRAS for decades. It is rare for a substance considered GRAS to lose this status; however, if new information subsequently reveals that it is actually unsafe, the Secretary has the statutory authority to declare it unsafe or prescribe conditions under which it may safely be used.[14,15]

As indicated earlier, the regulatory framework applies to substances added to food by humans, rather than those that are naturally occurring. The best science reveals that caffeine and sugar are both addictive substances. Both occur naturally in some foods, but manufacturers also add them to enhance certain properties of their products. A review of FDA regulation of the latter provides insight into gaps in the current regulatory framework and the potential for future regulation.

Caffeine

Caffeine is added to cola-type beverages, energy drinks, some foods, and over-the-counter stimulant products (e.g., NoDoz). In 1978, the Select Committee on GRAS substances concluded that "no evidence in the available information on caffeine demonstrates a hazard to the public when it is used in cola type beverages at levels...in the manner now practiced."[16] The FDA thus granted caffeine GRAS status when added to cola-type beverages up to a level of 0.02% of the product.[17] The Committee expressed concern over the lack of evidence

on long-term use and larger doses of caffeine,[16] but caffeine remains a GRAS substance today. It is noteworthy that the consumption of soft drinks has more than doubled since the Committee's original conclusion.[18,i]

In the context of stimulant drug products, the FDA recognized that the "chronic ingestion of caffeine in larger than recommended doses can lead to 'habituation,' which is a mild form of addiction."[19] Thus, when caffeine is added to stimulant drug products, the product's package must bear a specific warning label stating that the product is for "occasional use only" and not intended for children under 12 years of age.[20]

Despite this recognition, when caffeine is added to stimulant beverages, or "energy drinks," FDA regulation is absent. Companies are free to add as much caffeine to such products without warning. Energy drinks are marketed to and consumed by youth and can contain exponentially more caffeine than soft drinks.[21] For example, one 12-ounce bottle of soda contains less than 40 mg of caffeine, but one 24-ounce container of an energy drink has up to 500 mg of caffeine.[21] Furthermore, there is no requirement that manufacturers of energy drinks, or soft drinks for that matter, disclose the amount of caffeine in their products. These regulatory gaps remain an area where FDA action is outstanding.

Sugar

In the mid-1970s the FDA declared added sugar in the form of dextran, sucrose, corn sugar (dextrose), invert sugar, and corn syrup to be GRAS.[22-26] Although at this time, the FDA recognized a potential association between increased consumption of added sugars and obesity, diabetes, and coronary heart disease, the Select Committee on GRAS substances found there was no evidence that demonstrated a hazard to the public when added sugar was used at levels consumed at that time.[22-26] The FDA confirmed this finding when it approved the final rule that added sugar was a GRAS substance in 1988,[27] and subsequently found high fructose corn syrup to be GRAS in 1996.[28]

The NLEA requires that total sugar be listed on the nutrition facts panel. However, beyond this labeling there are no other requirements or limits on manufacturers adding sugar to their products. In fact, the FDA formulated daily recommended values of most nutrients on the fact panel but excluded sugar from its recommendations.

For purposes of future regulations, it is noteworthy that in addition to scientific advances revealing addictive properties of sugar, consumption of added sugar has doubled[29] and almost tripled for teens,[18] since the time the FDA originally reviewed the science for GRAS purposes. At that time, the Committee did say that it was "not possible to determine, without additional data, whether a significant increase in consumption would constitute a dietary hazard."[30] As for caffeine, it would be prudent for the agency to review and revise its earlier recommendations in light of scientific advances and modern consumption patterns.

TOBACCO

In 1988, the Surgeon General's report concluded that tobacco is addicting, nicotine causes addiction, and the pharmacologic and behavioral processes that determine tobacco addiction are similar to those of drugs such as heroin and cocaine.[31] Government regulation of tobacco is stronger than that for food perhaps due to its recognition of these addictive properties.

Congress enacted several laws to regulate tobacco products, including conditioning the receipt of federal funds on states prohibiting the sale of tobacco products to minors,[32] instituting federal excise taxes,[33] and requiring mandatory warning labels on cigarette packages, advertisements, and billboards.[34] Federal control of tobacco is divided among several agencies, and until recently, there was not a formal regulatory regime for tobacco products.[ii]

In 1996, the FDA attempted to regulate tobacco products by designating nicotine a drug within the meaning of the Food, Drug, and Cosmetic Act to bring nicotine-containing products within its jurisdiction.[37] The agency sought to reduce consumption among youth and proposed rules restricting the sale and distribution of cigarettes and smokeless tobacco.[38] However, the Supreme Court ruled that the FDA exceeded its jurisdiction (i.e., Congress did not grant the agency this authority) and it nullified the regulations.[39]

In the absence of a federal regulatory regime, many states stepped in to regulate tobacco products and the Supreme Court confirmed that the states are free to enact zoning regulations and regulate conduct with respect to tobacco use and sales[40] Thus, all 50 states and the District of Columbia impose excise taxes on cigarettes and prohibit the sale or distribution of

tobacco products to minors.[41] Forty-six states and the District of Columbia restrict the placement of tobacco products in vending machines and twenty states prohibit consumers from having direct access to tobacco products (e.g., bans on self-service displays).[41]

In June 2009, President Obama signed the Family Smoking Prevention and Tobacco Control Act, granting the FDA extensive authority to regulate tobacco products.[42] Notable provisions include banning flavored tobacco products,[43] strengthening warning labels,[44] and granting the FDA the authority to reduce the nicotine or other addictive substances in tobacco products (but not to zero).[45] Several of the major tobacco companies sued the FDA to prevent enforcement of the Act.[46] Some advertising restrictions in the Act may be controversial; however, the prohibitions on sales to children and restrictions on vending machine placement have not been challenged by industry. Regardless of whether the FDA regulations withstand judicial scrutiny, current federal, state, and local regulations of tobacco products remain in force and are legally viable in the realm of food and addiction.

The government has also attempted to restrict tobacco advertising. As mentioned earlier, the constitution protects against government restrictions on truthful advertising for products legally purchasable by a segment of the population. As a result, the Supreme Court struck down state advertising restrictions even though the regulations were promulgated to shield children, who cannot legally purchase tobacco products, from seeing the advertisements.[47] Nevertheless, as the law stands advertising restrictions that directly advance a substantial government interest and are not more extensive than necessary should pass constitutional review.[48] Eight states and the District of Columbia have restrictions on tobacco advertising.[41] Among these, the most constitutionally viable restrictions include prohibiting such ads in state-owned buildings[49] and transit systems,[41] and prohibiting billboards within 200–500 feet of schools.[50,51]

LESSONS FOR FOOD AND ADDICTION
Advertising

Restricting advertising of addictive food products that are legally purchasable by any segment of the population will be met with constitutional challenges. Permissible restrictions would include narrowly tailored limitations on advertising near child-oriented facilities or in schools, school buses, government buildings, and transit systems. Because the First Amendment is a barrier to restricting speech, the courts often suggests the government require factual disclosures, warning labels, or counter advertising to rectify the information imbalance for the marketing of unhealthy products. These options are available in the realm of food.

Labeling

Manufacturers and distributors of consumer products can be required to provide factual disclosures about their products. This would include highlighting a problematic ingredient like under the Food Allergens Act, and also requiring warnings similar to those on tobacco packaging, advertisements, and billboards, stating that a food product may pose health risks, including the risk of addiction. State and local (hereinafter "state") governments are preempted from regulating food products' packaging but can require warnings to be placed on billboards and signs posted at the point of purchase.

Conduct

State government can also regulate conduct associated with the purchase of food products as part of their police power to protect public health, and it may choose to do so based on the science of food and addiction. States can prohibit the purchase of specified items by minors, as has been done for tobacco and alcohol. States can enact zoning and conditional licensing requirements or otherwise restrict where products are sold within their communities. For example, San Francisco banned the sale of tobacco in pharmacies,[52] and the same can be done for certain foods. States can also institute per capita restrictions on the purchase of certain items,[53] as has been done in several states for pseudoephedrine-containing drug products.[54]

States are authorized to regulate minors' possession of unhealthy products; however, the American Cancer Society reported that penalizing children for possessing tobacco products has "not been proven to be an effective technique to reduce underage tobacco usage."[41]

Ingredients

Finally, the government can regulate food products themselves. As the Tobacco Control Act of 2009 allows the FDA to reduce addictive ingredients in tobacco products, the government can limit the permissible quantity of a problematic ingredient in food.[55] Even if caffeine and sugar remain GRAS substances, the FDA could revisit its earlier conclusions and determine a safe limit of these substances permitted to be added to food. On the other hand, if science emerges that any food additive is unsafe or actually added to induce addiction, the Secretary of Health can declare it unsafe and all such food products produced with them can be regulated.[56]

States can also enact regulations that do not conflict with federal law. If, for example, sugar was found to be addictive in certain quantities, states and locales could enact regulations restricting the percent of sugar allowed in food processed at food service establishments because these venues are not preempted by FDA regulation. New York City's ban on *trans* fat is an example of such a law.[57]

CONCLUSION

The government has many options to regulate the sale and marketing of addictive ingredients and additives in the food supply. In light of modern science and consumption patterns, the FDA should revisit some of its earlier conclusions, and all levels of government may need to consider the various options available to them to regulate addictive food products in order to protect the public's health.

NOTES

i. In terms of quantities consumed, from 1970 to 2000, the per-person daily consumption of regular soft drinks increased from 7.8 to 13.2 ounces, which is an increase of 70%.

ii. The Alcohol and Tobacco Tax and Trade Bureau enforces Chapter 52 of the Internal Revenue Code (Title 26 of the United States Code), which addresses Federal excise taxes on tobacco products. The Federal Cigarette Labeling and Advertising Act 35 and the Comprehensive Smokeless Tobacco Health Education Act of 1986[36] require that each person who manufactures, packages, or imports tobacco products to submit to the Department of Health and Human Services a list of ingredients added to tobacco in the manufacture of cigarettes. The Centers for Disease Control and Prevention, Office on Smoking and Health, has been delegated the responsibility of implementing these provisions. The Federal Trade Commission enforces laws concerning accurate information shown on packages and labels for the benefit of the consumer in general and has administrative responsibilities for the Surgeon General's health warnings required for cigarettes and smokeless tobacco products.

REFERENCES

1. The Federal Food, Drug, and Cosmetic Act of 1938; 21 U.S.C. § 301 et seq.
2. *Hutchinson Ice Cream Co. v Iowa*, 242 U.S. 153, 157 (1916).
3. 21 U.S.C. § 321(f).
4. *Nutrilab, Inc. v Schweiker*, 713 F.2d 335, 338 (7th Cir. 1983).
5. Title II of Public Law 108–282 (August 2, 2004).
6. *United States v 29 Cartons [Oakmont Investment Co.]*, 987 F.2d 33, 35 (1st Cir. 1993).
7. *United States v An Article of Food, Coco Rico*, 752 F.2d 11, 14–15 (1st Cir. 1985).
8. 21 U.S.C. § 342 (a)(1).
9. *United States v Anderson Seafoods, Inc.*, 622 F.2d 157, 160 (5th Cir. 1980).
10. *United States v Coca Cola*, 241 U.S. 265, 284 (1915).
11. *Young v Community Nutrition Institute*, 476 U.S. 974, 977 (1986).
12. 21 U.S.C. § 346.
13. 21 C.F.R. 182.1.
14. 21 U.S.C. 348(d).
15. *California Canners & Growers Assn v United States*, 9 Cl. Ct. 774, 782 (Cl. Ct. 1986).
16. US Food and Drug Administration. Database of Select Committee on GRAS Substances reviews: caffeine. Report no. 89. I.D. code 58-08-2. Available at: http://www.accessdata.fda.gov/scripts/fcn/fcnDetailNavigation.cfm?rpt=scogsListing&id=42. Accessed October 1, 2009.
17. 21 C.F.R. § 182.1180.
18. American Heart Association Nutrition Committee of the Council on Nutrition, Physical Activity, and Metabolism and the Council on Epidemiology and Prevention. Dietary sugars intake and cardiovascular health: a scientific statement from the American Heart Association. *Circulation* 2009;120:1011–1020.
19. US Food and Drug Administration. FDA response to comments on Labeling of Stimulant Drug Products. 53 FR 6100. February 29, 1988.
20. 21 C.F.R. § 340.50.
21. Reissig CJ, Strain EC, Griffiths RR. Caffeinated energy drinks—a growing problem. *Drug Alcohol Depen* 2009;99:1–10.
22. 21 C.F.R. § 186.1275.
23. 21 C.F.R. § 184.1854.
24. 21 C.F.R. § 184.1857.
25. 21 C.F.R. § 184.1859.
26. 21 C.F.R. § 184.1865.
27. 53 *Federal Register* 44863 (1988).
28. 61 *Federal Register* 43447 (1996).
29. Bray GA, Nielsen SJ, Popkin BM. Consumption of high-fructose corn syrup in beverages may play a role in the epidemic of obesity. *Am J Clin Nutr* 2004;79(4):537–543.
30. US Food and Drug Administration. GRAS Substances (SCOGS) Database. Available at: http://www.fda.gov/Food/FoodIngredientsPackaging/Generally RecognizedasSafeGRAS/GRASSubstancesSCOGS-Database/default.htm. Accessed October 1, 2009.
31. US Department of Health and Human Services. The health consequences of smoking: nicotine addiction. Report of the Surgeon General. 1988. Available at: http://profiles.nlm.nih.gov/NN/B/B/Z/D/_/nnbbzd.ocr. Accessed October 2, 2009.
32. 42 U.S.C. § 300x-26.
33. The Children's Health Insurance Program Reauthorization Act of 2009 (CHIPRA, Public Law 111–3) (February 4, 2009)
34. 15 U.S.C. § 1333.
35. 15 U.S.C 1331–1341
36. 15 U.S.C. 4401–4408
37. *Food and Drug Administration v Brown & Williamson Tobacco Corp.*, 529 U.S. 120, 125–127 (2000).
38. *Food and Drug Administration v Brown & Williamson Tobacco Corp.*, 529 U.S. 120, 127 (2000).
39. *Food and Drug Administration v Brown & Williamson Tobacco Corp.*, 529 U.S. 120 (2000).
40. *Lorillard v Reilly*, 533 U.S. 525, 550 (2001).
41. American Lung Association. State Legislated Actions on Tobacco Issues. 2011. Available at: http://www.lungusa2.org/slati/slatiOverview.php. Accessed April 9, 2012.
42. Family Smoking Prevention and Tobacco Control Act, Public Law 111–31, 123 Stat. 1776 (June 22, 2009).
43. Family Smoking Prevention and Tobacco Control Act, Public Law 111–31, 123 Stat. 1776, Title I, Chapter IX. § 907(a)(1)(A) (2009).
44. Family Smoking Prevention and Tobacco Control Act, Public Law 111–31, 123 Stat. 1776, Title II, Section 4 Labeling (2009).
45. Family Smoking Prevention and Tobacco Control Act, Public Law 111–31, 123 Stat. 1776, Title I, Chapter IX. § 907(a)(3), (d)(3) (2009).
46. Complaint: *Commonwealth Brands, Inc. v United States*, in the W.D. KY (August 31, 2009).
47. *Lorillard v Reilly*, 533 U.S. 525 (2001).
48. *Central Hudson Gas & Electric Corp. v Public Service Commission of New York*, 447 U.S. 557, 566 (1980).
49. CA Govt. Code § 19994.35 (1993).
50. Del. Code Ann. tit. 6, § 2507 (2000).
51. KY Rev. Stat. Ann. § 438.047 (1992).
52. *Philip Morris USA, Inc. v San Francisco*, 2009 U.S. App. 9th Cir. (2009). LEXIS 20142.
53. *44 Liquormart v Rhode Island*, 517 U.S. 484, 507 (1996).
54. Code of Ala. § 20-2-190 (2009); Cal Health & Saf Code § 11100 (2009); 16 Del. C. § 4740 (2009); Idaho Code § 37-3303 (2009).
55. *Rubin v Coors Brewing Co.*, 514 U.S. 476, 490–491 (1995).
56. 21 U.S.C. § 342.
57. New York City Health Code § 81.08 (2006).

62

What Lessons for Food Policy Can Be Learned from Alcohol Control?

IAN GILMORE AND KARISHMA CHANDARIA

Alcohol has become part of the social and cultural fabric of many countries and is associated with pleasure and relaxation. It is now consumed by almost half the world's population, although there is a large degree of variation between and within countries.[1] Alcohol has been shown to confer some health benefits—for instance, in men over 40 years and postmenopausal women moderate consumption leads to decreased risk of myocardial infarction. However, it is also a toxic and psychoactive substance that can induce dependence and addiction and cause a significant amount of harm to public health. There are some similarities between the public health approaches that have been used to tackle alcohol misuse and obesity, but one important difference exists: the fact that alcohol, like tobacco, is not essential to life, whereas food is.[2]

THE HEALTH AND SOCIAL COSTS OF ALCOHOL MISUSE

For nearly all types of alcohol-related health harm, the more an individual drinks, the greater the risk of harm.[3] The World Health Organization estimates that around 2 billion people around the globe drink alcohol, over 76 million of whom have ill health as a result. Worldwide alcohol causes 1.8 million deaths (3.2% of total) and 58.3 million disability-adjusted life years (DALYs) (4% of total).[1] In 2004, 4.6% of the global burden of disease and injury were attributable to alcohol: 7.6% for men and 1.4% for women.[4] Alcohol is linked to psychiatric, liver, neurological, gastrointestinal, and cardiovascular conditions and several types of cancer. Unintentional injuries alone account for about one-third of the 1.8 million deaths, while neuropsychiatric conditions account for close to 40% of the 58.3 million DALYs.[4] Alcohol is also an important cause of health inequalities. Poorer populations and

low-income countries have a relatively higher burden than do high-income countries.[4]

The consequences of drinking go far beyond just the health and well-being of individuals. Alcohol-use disorders are associated with large unmeasured social costs such as relationship breakdown, domestic violence and aggression, poor parenting, unsafe and regretted sex, truancy, delinquency, antisocial behavior, and homelessness. It is vitally important to record these social costs because the externalities they can impose on society are a central justification for government intervention and action.[5]

ACCESS TO ALCOHOL

The consumption data indicate that there has been increased access to alcohol across three dimensions; real price, availability, and the social acceptability of drinking.[5] Globally, alcohol consumption has increased in recent decades, with all or most of that increase in developing countries. The overall rise in consumption has been accompanied by a marked decrease in the overall price of alcohol. This is important because evidence shows that alcohol responds to price increases like most consumer goods on the market, that is, when other factors remain constant an increase in the price of alcohol generally leads to a decrease in consumption.[6] In the United States and the United Kingdom, despite the fact that taxes on alcohol are heavier than on many other products, alcoholic drinks are still cheaper relative to income.[7]

Alcohol has also become much more readily available in many countries, with huge increases in the number and density of licensed premises especially in urban areas, which has been shown to lead to an increase in consumption among young people.[8] Increasing availability coupled with the liberalization of licensing laws means alcohol can be accessed at almost any time of the day and at more affordable prices. Supermarkets and all-purpose convenience stores have now become the main sources for off-sales, and they have frequently used low prices of alcoholic beverages to attract customers.

There is also much more social access to alcohol through aggressive marketing and promotions. This, in turn, has generated the conditions for increasing levels of drinking and alcohol-related problems, particularly among poorer populations. In 2003 the World Health Organization review concluded that "The promotion of alcohol is an enormously well-funded, ingenious and pervasive aspect of modern life…Exposure to repeated high-level alcohol promotion initiates pro-drinking attitudes and increases the likelihood of heavier drinking."[9]

THE CURRENT POLICY LANDSCAPE

Many countries are experiencing a rising tide of alcohol-related problems as the globalization and industrialization of alcohol production has meant higher volumes of alcohol being produced at a lower unit cost, along with aggressive advertising and promotions.[4] Some are responding by implementing policies and packages of measures aimed at reducing the health and social harms from the use of alcohol. These include measures to tackle price, availability, advertising, and awareness of health harms. There are also a variety of other policies that can reduce or increase alcohol-related problems, but they are not described specifically as alcohol policies, since they are not implemented solely to reduce alcohol-related harm. These include general road safety measures.[4] To some extent, the strategies adopted will depend upon locations. In developed countries the focus may be on tackling binge drinking, as is the case in the United Kingdom and the United States, whereas introducing drunk-driving laws may be more important in developing countries, where ownership of cars and access to alcohol is increasing.

EFFECTIVENESS OF DIFFERENT STRATEGIES OF PREVENTION

Here we review the effectiveness of different types of interventions that have been used in alcohol policy.

Information and Education

Information and education strategies have been used to raise awareness and increase the general public's knowledge about the risks and health consequences of drinking and overeating and to prepare the public for the introduction of more effective measures. The problem with information and education campaigns, however well thought out and targeted, is that evidence shows that their impact is largely ineffective.[10] Here we come across an apparent contradiction: while many governments are convinced of the impact and efficacy of public health messages to change unhealthy eating and drinking habits, they refuse to acknowledge that the large volume of advertising and promotions used by the drinks and food industries to market their products might have the same ability to affect behavior and consumption levels, thus counterbalancing their efforts.[11,12]

Advertising and Marketing Restrictions

There is growing evidence to show a link between exposure to advertising and increases in alcohol consumption. Behavioral studies show that the more aware and appreciative young people are of alcohol advertising, the more likely they are to drink now and in the future. A recent systematic review to assess the impact of alcohol advertising and media exposure on future adolescent alcohol consumption found that exposure to media and commercial communications on alcohol are linked to increased likelihood of drinking in adolescents and baseline drinkers.[13] The Science Group of the European Commission's Alcohol and Health Forum recently concluded that "there was consistent evidence to demonstrate an impact of alcohol advertising on the uptake of drinking among non-drinking young people, and increased consumption among their drinking peers."[14]

Across Europe and in the United States there is a strong reliance on self-regulation or voluntary systems, often implemented by the drinks industry trade bodies. However, these types of codes do not deal with the volume of marketing, which is seen to be of major importance in influencing behavior, or with what young people find appealing in advertisements, such as humor.[15] Robust external governance of alcohol advertising is needed to tackle both the volume as well as the nature of advertising.[16]

Limiting Availability through Taxes and Other Influences on Price

There is a clear relationship between price and the consumption of alcohol.[6] In order to reduce overall consumption and the resulting health harms, the issue of price must be addressed. Alcohol can currently be bought in the off trade at a very low price. A recent review of alcohol price, promotion, and harm showed that there is a strong relationship between pricing and consumption and that pricing policies can be effective in reducing harm related to health, crime, and unemployment. It also demonstrated that pricing policies can be targeted, so that people who drink within recommended limits are hardly affected, whereas very heavy drinkers, who cause by far the most alcohol-related harm, pay the most.[17]

Taxation has been used by governments to increase alcohol prices with the aim of reducing consumption. Recent research from Finland showed that when taxes on alcohol were reduced by an average of 33% in 2004, researchers estimated a 10% increase in consumption and recorded a rise in alcohol-related mortality of 16% for men and 31% for women.[18] The problem with using modest increases in taxation as a policy lever is that they may not be passed on to customers by the large retailers, including supermarkets, who will try to squeeze the profits of suppliers and producers instead.

Another option that is currently being explored is setting a minimum unit price for alcohol in a response to growing concern about the availability and consumption of very low-priced forms of alcohol. Recent research suggests that minimum pricing targets heavy drinkers the most as they consume the cheapest forms of alcohol. In the United States, surveys have reported the top 20% of drinkers accounted for 90% of self-reported consumption.[19] While minimum pricing has not been implemented in many countries and has not been evaluated extensively, there has been a generally positive experience in countries that have introduced these types of measures. For example, in Canada the minimum pricing of beer (sometimes referred to as "social reference pricing") and the implementation in some Australian localities of bans on the sale of the cheapest form of alcohol (which amounts to raising the minimum price) have resulted in reductions in alcohol problems.[20]

Health Interventions

There is currently limited access to professional support and advice for those who want to drink less in both the primary and secondary health care systems in many countries. However, there is growing evidence to show that early intervention with a provision of relevant health information can play a

part in reducing alcohol-related health harms. For example, "brief advice" or "brief interventions" have been shown to have an effect on reducing alcohol consumption on people who are drinking above sensible amounts but have not developed a dependency on alcohol.[21] These interventions are low-cost, effective, and can reduce mortality.[22] More needs to be done to ensure the implementation of brief interventions in primary care and hospital settings. This includes training and support for staff to deliver these interventions, which can help to reduce alcohol-related liver mortality and reduce costs to health systems.

FRAMING OF ALCOHOL CONSUMPTION AND OVEREATING DEBATES

Policy makers have framed debates around alcohol and food addiction in similar ways. The most common frame emphasizes the role of individual and personal responsibility. The personal responsibility frame is deeply rooted in a libertarian political tradition that champions individualism and aims to keep regulation and state intervention in the lives of individuals to a minimum. It argues that interventions in addressing alcohol misuse and overeating should be focused on encouraging and educating people to change their behavior. For example, the idea of encouraging a "responsible" drinking culture has been the key message underpinning policies and public health campaigns in England for some time. This focuses on individuals taking responsibility for their drinking behavior and patterns, helped by public education and information on risks. The personal responsibility approach has been popular with both the alcohol and food industries in the Western world because it deflects attention away from their practices.

What is increasingly becoming clear in the development of both alcohol and obesity policy is that personal choices are always made in the context of wider social and environmental determinants. These influence and shape people's lifestyles, the range of choices they can make, and the uptake, or more usually lack of uptake, of health-promoting behaviours.[23] For example, poor diet can be a consequence of affordability and availability, and alcohol consumption is often related to stress and coping in particular situations.

The acknowledgment of the role of wider determinants of health on individual choices in alcohol and food consumption are encapsulated in the "stewardship" model that implies that the state has a duty to look after important needs of people individually and collectively.[23] It emphasizes the role of the state in fostering conditions that allow individuals to make healthy choices and, in particular, to ameliorate health inequalities. The stewardship-guided state sees the health of the nation as an asset and higher levels of health corresponding to greater well-being and productivity.

It is increasingly becoming clear that prevention policies must address both ends of the spectrum, the individual and the environment. Only by addressing these wider determinants of health operating in the lives of individuals and communities can we hope to improve the health of populations. There is a need to reframe thinking around food and nutrition from an individual focus to an environmental perspective.[23]

IMPLICATIONS FOR POLICY

Alcohol is enjoyed and drunk by many people, but it is not essential to life and its consumption is down to individual behavior. While many people understand superficially that consumption comes with risks and those with serious "drinking problems" are more at risk of health harm, the link between excess alcohol and subsequent mortality and morbidity is not well understood or effectively communicated in public health campaigns. However, newspaper reports of alcohol- related violence and crime, visible drunken behavior, and growing availability of cheap alcohol are beginning to raise awareness in the general public about the social costs of alcohol misuse, especially around domestic violence and mental health.

In obesity and overeating the issues are more complex. It is self-evident that food is essential to life, and there is no choice about whether we consume it, only about how much and what kind. The public currently appreciates no immediate harms from consuming too much food and since food is not a dangerous substance in and of itself, there is much less acceptance that food could be addictive. The message that obesity leads to increased mortality and morbidity might be promoted as a population problem, but many individuals deny the risk factors that their excess weight gives them. For those with a weight problem there is a focus on drugs and surgery to suggest a quick answer rather than a long-term significant change to lifestyle.

These differences in public perception of the links between consumption and harm caused by alcohol and obesity affect what policy interventions will be used by governments and deemed acceptable by the public. In the United Kingdom we are seeing the beginning of the tipping point where the social harm caused by a growing tide of alcohol-related disorder and violence has begun to filter into the public psyche and generate disquiet; as a result, the government is beginning to consider restrictions on availability and tackling below-cost sales. It is difficult to see this happening in the case of obesity, where the public does not yet fully understand the immediate harms caused by overeating and where restrictions on the availability of fatty and sugary foods would be hard to gain support for. These foods also form a large part of the diets of the least well-off and a price rises could serve to increase, rather than decrease, inequalities. As with alcohol, tackling the availability of unhealthy foods would not only be politically arduous but would also face opposition from both producers and retailers alike.[23]

As the evidence base around the impacts of advertising on alcohol and food consumption continues to grow, restricting both the volume and the content of advertising of alcohol and unhealthy foods must be considered. This will help to shore up school-based education programs and targeted public health campaigns that are needed to disseminate information about health risks.[23]

The preconditions that allowed the development of a strong global and national response to the health harm from smoking and tobacco are now also beginning to emerge for alcohol. These conditions include evidence for the health harm caused by alcohol misuse and the cost-effectiveness of interventions; a greater understanding about the motivations of and strategies and tactics used by industry; and pressure for change from the public health community. The World Health Organization has begun the process of developing a global strategy to reduce the use of alcohol; therefore, taking action on alcohol remains a matter of political will.[24] In the case of food, it is likely that there is a need for more work from scientists and health professionals to help create the conditions in society that would enable politicians to be bold.

REFERENCES

1. World Health Organization. Alcohol. Available at: http://www.who.int/substance_abuse/facts/alcohol/en/index.html. Accessed November 18, 2009.

2. Gilmore I. What lessons can be learned from alcohol control for combating the growing prevalence of obesity? *Obes Rev* 2007;8(s1):157–160.

3. Anderson P. The risk of alcohol [dissertation]. Nijmegen, The Netherlands: Nijmegen University; 2003.

4. Rehm J, Mathers C, Popova S, Thavorncharoensap M, Teerawattananon Y, Patra J. Global burden of disease and injury and economic cost attributable to alcohol use and alcohol-use disorders. *Lancet* 2009; 373:2223–2231.

5. Anderson P, Chisholm D, Fuhr D. Effectiveness and cost-effectiveness of policies and programmes to reduce the harm caused by alcohol. *Lancet* 2009;373: 2234–2246.

6. *Second report of the Expert Committee on Problems related to Alcohol Consumption.* Geneva, Switzerland: World Health Organisation, 2007. Technical report series no. 944.

7. Coghlan A. WHO launches worldwide war on booze. *New Scientist* 2009;2730:8–9.

8. Chikritzhs T, Catalonao P, Pascal R. Predicting alcohol-related harms from licensed outlet density: a feasibility study. National Drug Law Enforcement Research Fund, monograph, series no. 28, 2007. Available at: http://www.ndlerf.gov.au/pub/Monograph_28.pdf. Accessed December 20, 2009.

9. Barbor T, Caetano R, Edwards G, et al. *Alcohol: No Ordinary Commodity: Research and Public Policy.* Oxford, England: Oxford University Press, 2003.

10. Room R, Babor T, Rehm J. Alcohol and public health. *Lancet* 2005;365:519–530.

11. Shaw E. New Labour: A party for whom? The case of obesity and alcohol misuse. Paper presented at: 2008 Annual Meeting of the Political Studies Association; April 1–4, 2008; Swansea, Wales. Available at: http://www.psa.ac.uk/journals/pdf/5/2008/Shaw.pdf. Accessed October, 14, 2009.

12. McKee M, Raine R. Choosing health? First choose your philosophy. *Lancet* 2005;365:9457.

13. Anderson P, Bruijn de A, Angus K, Gordon R, Hastings G. Impact of alcohol advertising and media exposure on adolescent alcohol use: a systematic review of longitudinal studies. *Alcohol Alcohol* 2009;44(3): 229–243.

14. Science Group of the European Alcohol and Health Forum. Does marketing communication impact on the volume and patterns of consumption of alcoholic beverages, especially by young people?—a review of longitudinal studies. Available at: http://ec.europa.eu/health/ph_determinants/life_style/alcohol/Forum/docs/science_o01_en.pdf. Accessed December 17, 2009.

15. Anderson P. Is it time to ban alcohol advertising? *Clin Med* 2009;9(2):121–124.

16. Rigaud A, Craplet M. The "Loi Evin": a French exception. Available at: http://www.ias.org.uk/btg/conf0604/papers/rigaud_craplet.pdf. Accessed December 17, 2009.

17. Brennan A, Booth A, Meier P. *The Independent Review of the Effects of Alcohol Pricing and Promotion. Summary of Evidence to Accompany Report on Phase 1: Systematic Reviews.* Sheffield, England: School of Health and Related Research, University of Sheffield, 2008.

18. Herttua K, Mäkelä P, Martikainen, Herruta P. Changes in alcohol-related mortality and its socioeconomic differences after a large reduction in alcohol prices: a natural experiment based on register data. *Am J Epidemiol* 2008; 168(10):1110–1118.

19. Greenfield TK, Rodger JD. Who drinks most of the alcohol in the US? The policy implications. *J Stud Alcohol* 1999;60(1):1110–1118.

20. Alcohol Policy Coalition. Alcohol taxation and pricing. 2009. Position Statement. Available at: http://www.cancervic.org.au/downloads/cpc/alcohol/position_statements/pricing_and_taxation_position_statement.pdf. Accessed December 5, 2009.

21. Royal College of Physicians. *Alcohol: Can the NHS Afford It?* London, England: Royal College of Physicians, 2001.

22. Sheron N, Olsen N, Gilmore I. An evidence-based alcohol policy. *Gut* 2008;57(10):1341–1344.

23. Dorfman L, Wilbur P, Lingas E, Woodruff K, Wallack L. Accelerating policy on nutrition: lessons from tobacco, alcohol, firearms, and traffic safety. Berkeley Media Studies Group, 2005. Available at: http://www.reportingonrace.org/documents/Acceleration-MtgReportPrelim.pdf. Accessed December 18, 2009.

24. Casewell S, Thamarangsi T. Reducing harm from alcohol: a call to action. *Lancet* 2009; 373:2246–2256.

63

Policy Lessons Learned from Tobacco

KENNETH E. WARNER

Early in the twentieth century, then medical student Alton Ochsner observed a surgery for a lung carcinoma, a disease so rare, his instructors insisted, he might never see another case. He did not encounter another case for almost two decades as a prominent surgeon. Then, in the short space of 6 months, he observed eight cases, all men who had started smoking during World War I.[1] Shortly thereafter Dr. Ochsner coauthored one of the first articles linking cigarette smoking to lung cancer.[2]

Today lung cancer is by far the most important cancer cause of death for both men and women in the United States. The rise of lung cancer closely mirrors the phenomenal growth in cigarette smoking during the first six decades of the twentieth century, with cancer prevalence lagging smoking prevalence by two to three decades. As important as the growth in smoking has been its subsequent decline. Smoking prevalence has fallen by more than half since 1964, the year of publication of the first Surgeon General's report on smoking and health,[3] an event commonly denoted as the beginning of our national "antismoking campaign." After 1991 lung cancer prevalence among men started to fall steadily, a reflection of the decline in smoking that began in the mid-1960s. Women's smoking started declining later; women's lung cancer prevalence will follow suit in the not too distant future.[4]

The rise and fall of smoking during the twentieth century may well prove to be one of the most significant, and fascinating, stories in the history of public health. The story gains relevance today as we find ourselves in the midst of an epidemic of obesity and its disease sequelae. What lessons might we derive from the experience with smoking?

THE ROLE OF POLICY IN TOBACCO CONTROL

If one examines the data analytically, while exhortations not to smoke have played a role (occasionally a key role) in reversing the direction of the smoking epidemic, especially at its inception,[i] formal policy measures are most closely associated with decreases in smoking. Some of those measures have an apparent "visible" impact on smoking: you can see them in contemporaneous movements in aggregate tobacco consumption data. As seen in Figure 63.1, adult per capita cigarette consumption[ii] fell by nearly 5% in 1964, the year of the original Surgeon General's report. Antismoking messages on the broadcast media, required by the Federal Communications Commission's Fairness Doctrine policy, produced a 4-year decline in smoking from 1967 through 1970. The congressional broadcast advertising ban, which took effect in January 1971, reversed that unprecedented decline by eliminating the need for the Fairness Doctrine ads.[8] The inception of statewide restrictions on smoking in public places, beginning in 1973, marked the beginning of the nearly annual declines in smoking since then. The doubling of the federal cigarette excise tax in 1983 instantly steepened the decline that year. The Master Settlement Agreement between the major tobacco companies and the states in 1998[iii,9] created a large cigarette price increase that caused the decline to accelerate.

These visible associations between tobacco control policies and decreases in smoking are just that: temporal (albeit striking) associations. Compelling evidence of policy impact comes from the now-extensive body of tobacco control policy research. In summary form, major findings include the following[10]:

- Increases in cigarette prices, typically resulting from increases in cigarette excise taxes, have a statistically strong and important effect in decreasing smoking. On average, an increase of 10% in cigarette price is associated with a

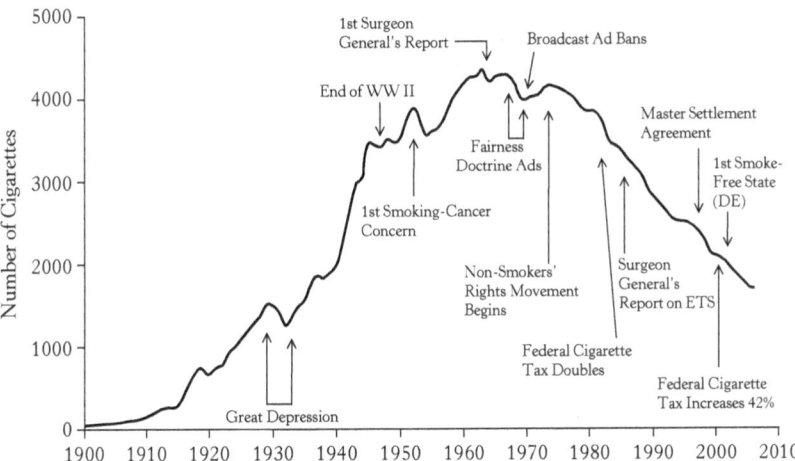

FIGURE 63.1. US adult per capita cigarette consumption and major antismoking "events," 1900–2006.

decrease in cigarette consumption of 3%–4%. Long-run effects may be larger. About half the effect reflects quitting smoking; the other half reflects decreases in daily consumption by continuing smokers. Poor smokers are more price-responsive than affluent smokers. Children are 2–3 times more responsive to price increases than are adults (and younger adults are correspondingly more price responsive than older adults). The impact of taxation (through cigarette price) has the most substantial research base of any tobacco control policy.

- Research on smoke-free workplace policies, by now quite substantial, presents convincing evidence that such policies:
  - Dramatically reduce workers' exposure to the toxins in secondhand smoke (by 80%–90%)
  - Increase quitting among workers (by an estimated 3.8%)
  - Decrease daily smoking among continuing smokers (by 3.1 cigarettes per day)
  - Do not harm business in hospitality industry enterprises, specifically restaurants and bars[iv]
  - Most important, significantly reduce the incidence of myocardial infarctions[11]
- When well-financed, professionally produced, and sustained, mass media counteradvertising campaigns reduce smoking among both youth and adults.
- A comprehensive ban on all forms of advertising and promotion of cigarettes reduces smoking (by an estimated 6%).

- The impact of the cigarette package warning labels in the United States today is negligible. However, early research on novel warning labels in many countries suggests that more prominent and graphic warnings can discourage smoking.
- The evidence on the "motherhood and apple pie" of smoking education strategies—school health education—indicates that while some programs demonstrate efficacy under best-practice conditions, they do not produce sustained reductions in smoking among students in everyday-practice conditions. Typically, such programs are poorly funded, are a low priority among school boards, and teachers are neither well prepared nor motivated to deliver them effectively. "Booster" programs—further education regarding smoking in later grades—are rare.
- Unless thoroughly enforced, legal prohibitions against selling cigarettes to minors are rarely very effective in reducing youth smoking.
- Based on very limited evidence, comprehensive state tobacco control programs, promoted by the Centers for Disease Control and Prevention,[12] may reduce smoking modestly, beyond the impacts of individual policies.

All told, the aggregate impact of the antismoking campaign has been quite dramatic, if painful in the time it has taken. Absent the campaign—the policies that have defined it and the knowledge that underlies their development—the number of cigarette smokers and the number of cigarettes they consume could be three times higher than is the case today. Through campaign-induced decisions to quit smoking or not to start, the antismoking campaign in the United States has avoided quite literally millions of premature deaths. On average, each individual who has avoided a smoking-produced death has gained 15 years of life.[10] It is a remarkable public health legacy.

APPLICATION OF LESSONS FROM TOBACCO CONTROL POLICY FOR OBESITY CONTROL

While smoking is hardly "cured," it is gradually on the wane. Such is not the case with obesity, now rapidly becoming a pandemic. Lessons from the experience with tobacco control can and should be applied to the effort to reduce obesity and its toll.

Lessons are of two types. First are the specific applications regarding individual policies; what, for example, can we learn for obesity control from knowledge about the role of taxes in controlling tobacco? Second are the general lessons. To illustrate, what is the role of policy in creating norm changes and, vice versa, what is the role of norm changes in creating policies? How does the emergence of policy reflect societal attitudes toward industry behavior? Here, to begin, are a few of the most important specific policy lessons:

1. Raising prices discourages consumption. Increasing the prices of foods most responsible for delivering "empty calories," such as soft drinks and other "junk food," will decrease their consumption. Econometric research can establish exactly how much. Conversely, lowering prices of more desirable foods will increase their consumption. Thus, using mechanisms like produce-specific food stamps, government could decrease the cost of fresh produce for low-income population groups. With their ability to pay significantly enhanced, supply—now frequently a problem in inner cities—will follow. Additionally, junk food taxes raise revenues that can be targeted toward other obesity control efforts, such as media campaigns. Many cigarette excise tax increases have been earmarked, at least in part, for tobacco control. Junk food taxes are obviously controversial and they require

occasionally challenging administrative changes. But a serious, substantial national effort to address obesity almost certainly will have to include them.[13]

2. Mass media campaigns work. They require professional design, sufficient exposure, and staying power to achieve maximal effect. That, in turn, requires a substantial financing source, such as earmarked taxes. Media campaigns can educate, activate the public, and ultimately contribute to norm change. The American Legacy Foundation's multimedia truth campaign has reduced youth smoking.[14] A well-financed and sustained "truth campaign" targeting kids' attitudes toward eating could make a difference in the health of the next generation. A similar campaign addressing adult eating (and exercising) behaviors could do the same for the current generation. Obesity control crusaders should also take advantage of free media opportunities. Over the years, news stories on tobacco grabbed the attention of many Americans.

3. In the aggregate, the evidence suggests that strong and effective advertising and promotion restrictions can reduce smoking. The most obvious application in obesity control relates to the advertising of sweetened breakfast cereals to kids.

4. While school health education regarding smoking appears not to have altered smoking behaviors, well-designed and -implemented educational programming has the potential to have an important impact. Although such programming never achieved currency in school systems regarding smoking, growing recognition of the roles of schools in obesity control might foster serious attention to school health education.

5. The tobacco experience indicates that the size, nature, and placement of product labeling matters a great deal. Creative new food labeling might attract the attention of consumers not now inclined to read the small print on contemporary nutrition labels.

6. Last but decidedly not least, are lessons that derive from experience with smoke-free workplace and public place policies. These have played a central role in tobacco

control, changing norms about public smoking while protecting nonsmokers from the dangers of secondhand smoke. The relationship between public attitudes toward smoking and the adoption of such policies is itself instructional. Research suggests that while laws alter norms, policy adoption often *follows* norm change. Legislatures follow the will of their constituents. Smoke-free laws become increasingly viable as the voting public demands the removal of smoke from their workplaces and other public places. The lesson for obesity control is less obvious, unfortunately. Long well-established, the effects of secondhand smoke make the case for smoke-free policies compelling. There is no obvious parallel for obesity control. It is hard to make the case for the adverse health effects of "secondhand obesity," and "obesity-free zones" are difficult to conceptualize. But recent research demonstrates that obesity may have elements of contagion, spreading among friends and associates.[15] And policies restricting employment of the obese are not inconceivable,[v] although issues regarding protection of the disabled inevitably arise. While defining the equivalent of smoke-free workplace policies to deal with obesity is perplexing at a minimum, smoke-free policies are so central to tobacco control that further contemplation of the obesity equivalent seems advisable.

The more general lessons of the tobacco control experience are critical to sustaining the obesity control crusader's motivation, momentum, and ultimately success. They include the following:

1. The accomplishments of the antismoking campaign derived from a mix of policy and nonpolicy interventions. In its simplest form, one can characterize the dynamic of the campaign as follows: In its first decade information on smoking's hazards significantly impacted smoking among the most educated segment of the population. As they renounced smoking, this politically engaged group pressured their legislators to "do something" about the problem. Legislators leaped at the opportunity to increase cigarette taxes—they could "do good" for

public health while "doing well" for state coffers, with only limited opposition. Evidence on the hazards of secondhand smoke led the educated, politically enfranchised to lobby for restrictions on smoking in public places. The adoption of such policies—modest restrictions at first, today comprehensive—impeded smoking among the less educated and heavier smoking population. Gradually the shift toward a nonsmoking norm spread toward the less educated. Today smoking is concentrated disproportionately among marginalized groups: the poor and less educated and, increasingly, people suffering from comorbid mental illness and substance abuse conditions.[16] The obesity control community will have to find their own lessons in this experience. It does suggest, however, a major role for education in the early going. Increasingly more stringent policy measures will come with norm change and political activation among a politically engaged subset of the population.

2. The tobacco control experience offers one obvious but critically important lesson: Major social norm change takes time—a lot of it. Significant evidence on the dangers of smoking arose in the early 1950s. Smoking continued to rise for a decade thereafter. It roughly stabilized for another decade before beginning its now annual decline. More than 45 years after publication of the first Surgeon General's report, a fifth of adults continue to smoke and smoking continues to exact an incredible toll from the public's health. Smoking, and its toll, will be with us for decades to come.[17] Obesity control campaigners must be in it for the long haul, seeking gratification in small and partial victories, while keeping their eyes on the ultimate prize.

3. As with tobacco, obesity control will require nimble thinking and constant adaptation to circumstances. A major lesson of tobacco control—one not yet fully applied—is that once-effective interventions may diminish in value over time. Finding the next generation of interventions, which must target the hard-to-convert remaining smokers, becomes

increasingly challenging.[18] What should tobacco control do (if anything) to assist hard-core smokers once all workplaces and public places are smoke-free? One study characterized the prototypical hard-core smoker as a relatively poor, undereducated White male retiree living by himself.[19] How do we reach him? *Should* we try to reach him? At some point we must respect that some people derive sufficient pleasure (solace, etc.) from smoking that they rationally accept the health consequences. Are we our brother's keeper? Tobacco control's opponents often refer to the public health community as "the nanny state." We are on solid ground when we are protecting nonsmokers from the hazards of second-hand smoke and educating children and adults about the dangers of direct smoking and the fact and implications of addiction. How far beyond that obvious public health mandate do we have the right to go? The relevance for obesity control is self-evident.

4. Throughout tobacco control history, activists have been spurred on, and their progress often impeded, by the pronouncements and behaviors of the once all-powerful tobacco industry. For decades, its own knowledge to the contrary, the industry claimed that the disease-causation case against smoking was not "closed" and invariably called for "more research." Similarly, the industry denied that smoking was addictive, while having relied on the fact of addiction in marketing its product.[vi] The 1988 Surgeon General's report on nicotine addiction[21] brought the issue to the public's attention and began unraveling the industry's arguments. And as industry documents reveal, an industry that professed to offer adults the "choice" of smoking, in fact early on targeted children.[vii] From the beginning, the industry used its economic might and the derivative political power to fight tobacco control policy initiatives at all levels of government.[23] Industry behavior undoubtedly stalled progress against tobacco; but once revealed, it also motivated the tobacco control community and shifted public attitudes in a direction that facilitated the adoption of increasingly stringent tobacco control policies.

Although the comparison is imperfect, experience with the tobacco industry has important implications for obesity control. The parallels between the behavior of the tobacco and food industries are often quite striking. In its damage-control rhetoric, the food industry often relies on the same individual-choice theme that long worked so well for the tobacco industry. Major companies target children through marketing campaigns for sugared breakfast cereals and soda pop. Like their tobacco counterparts, the food companies wield enormous economic power and hence political influence, utilizing it to block policy measures.[7] As discussed throughout this volume, eating may even have an addiction component that a savvy industry may be exploiting. The industry parallels recommend that the obesity control community carefully study how the tobacco industry employed devious tactics, often behind the scenes, to derail productive tobacco control policy initiatives.[23] Obesity control activists will approach working with the food industry with a healthy skepticism and a sophisticated appreciation of industry motives and methods.

This said, and in striking contrast with the tobacco experience, the obesity control community may well find it profitable to work with the food industry, or at least with segments of it. The differences between the tobacco and food industries are as numerous as the similarities. To start, the far more complicated structure and product and service mix of the food industry makes referring to "the" industry far less compelling than it does in the case of the tobacco industry, and it makes the issue of working with the industry to address the obesity problem far more complicated. Tobacco control activists see nothing but risk in working with the tobacco industry. But some food companies exist by selling healthy food options to the health-conscious public. Even companies that promote calorie-dense, nutritionally empty foods often have product lines that nutrition experts would endorse. Many farmers, food distributors, food product manufacturers, and restaurateurs genuinely *want* to be a part of the solution. So while tobacco offers lessons about industry behavior and dealing with the industry, they almost certainly will not translate directly into the most productive industry-engagement strategies for the obesity control community. The approach that develops over time should be informed by the experience with Big Tobacco but not defined by it.

CONCLUSION

There are many parallels between the growing epidemic of obesity in the United States and the now-declining epidemic of smoking. The situations are far from identical, however. The obesity situation is far more complicated. Humans must eat to live; they do not need to smoke. Many foods are health promoting; no tobacco product meets that standard. The same companies that sell junk food produce healthy foods. The often antisocial behaviors of leading companies in both industries have many similarities; but food companies exhibit some behaviors, and have many opportunities to demonstrate others, that are not practically available to tobacco companies.[7]

Both similarities and differences dictate the need for the obesity control community to learn from tobacco control. Tobacco experiences will allow obesity control professionals to anticipate and avoid problems that afflicted the tobacco control community, which lacked similar experiences from which to draw important strategic insights. In the process, the attack on obesity may follow a more logical, effective, and efficient path toward a healthier future.

NOTES

i. Education regarding the disease toll of smoking played a critical role in the early phase of the antismoking campaign. However, much of the education resulted from policies, ranging from many school districts requiring health education on smoking to the production and release of Surgeon General's reports. Likely the best example of the impact of "mere words," not deriving from policy, preceded the period here labeled as the antismoking campaign. In 1950 Wynder and Graham published the first significant empirical study strongly associating smoking with lung cancer.[5] Two years later, in December 1952, an article in the *Reader's Digest*, provocatively entitled "Cancer by the Carton," broadcast the implications of that scientific study to the general public.[6] As seen in Figure 63.1, per capita consumption took a 2-year nosedive, the only one since the Great Depression. The damage to smoking was reversed only when the

tobacco industry began marketing filtered cigarettes, advertised with the message, either explicit or implicit, that filters trapped the dangerous substances in cigarette smoke and "let the flavor through." The public bought the message. As seen in Figure 63.1, adult per capita cigarette consumption resumed its sharply upward half-century-long trend until the Surgeon General's report initiated the antismoking campaign. The tobacco companies' response to the setback in the early 1950s is itself an object lesson in the creativity and resilience of American industry, offering obvious and important parallels to recent food industry response to national concern with the epidemic of obesity.[7]

ii. Total cigarette consumption, measured by production and excise tax data, divided by the population >17 years of age.

iii. The Master Settlement Agreement (MSA) settled lawsuits brought by the states against the tobacco industry, with the states wanting the industry to pay for Medicaid costs associated with smoking. The MSA was what one might call a quasi-policy. Although it was a legal settlement, the plaintiffs were the states, represented by their elected top legal officers, the attorneys general, and the provisions of the MSA have distinct policy characteristics, such as banning cigarette ads in publications read by youth, and impacts, such as the cigarette price increase necessitated by the financial penalties payable to the states.

iv. There is a dearth of studies on the impact on the revenues of casinos, the last bastion of smoke-filled workplaces. The most evidence applies to restaurants.

v. There is an important distinction here, of course. Smoke-free workplaces do not prohibit smokers; rather, they prohibit the activity of smoking in the workplace. It does not seem plausible to prohibit being obese only in the workplace.

vi. One of the most infamous quotations demonstrating the industry's knowledge of the addictiveness of its product was an executive's direct admission, in a confidential memo to colleagues written in 1963, that "We are, then, in the business of selling nicotine, an addictive drug."[20]

vii. As one example, in 1972 Brown & Williamson discussed flavorings for their new "youth cigarette" that children would like: cola, apple, and sweet.[22]

REFERENCES

1. Ochsner A. *Smoking and Cancer, a Doctor's Report.* New York: Messner, 1954.
2. Ochsner A, DeBakey M. Primary pulmonary malignancy. *Surg Gynecol Obstet* 1939;48:433–451.
3. Public Health Service. *Smoking and Health. Report of the Advisory Committee to the Surgeon General of the Public Health Service.* Atlanta, GA: US Department of Health, Education, and Welfare, Public Health Service, Center for Disease Control, 1964. PHS Publication 1103.
4. National Cancer Institute. SEER Cancer Statistics Review, 1975–2006, Table 15.5, cancer of the lung and bronchus. Available at: http://seer.cancer.gov/csr/1975_2006/browse_csr.php?section=15&page=sect_15_table.05.html. Accessed January 23, 2010.

5. Wynder EL, Graham EA. Tobacco smoking as a possible etiologic factor in bronchiogenic carcinoma: a study of 684 proved cases. *JAMA* 1950;143:329–396

6. Norr R. Cancer by the carton. *Reader's Digest.* December 1952, 7–8.

7. Brownell KD, Warner KE. The perils of ignoring history: how big tobacco lied and millions died. How similar is big food? *Milbank Q* 2009;87:259–294.

8. Warner KE. Clearing the airwaves: the cigarette ad ban revisited. *Policy Anal* 1979;5:435–450.

9. National Association of Attorneys General. Master settlement agreement. 1998. Available at: http://web.archive.org/web/20080625084126/http://www.naag.org/backpages/naag/tobacco/msa/msa-pdf/1109185724_1032468605_cigmsa.pdf. Accessed April 2, 2012.

10. Warner KE. Tobacco policy research: insights and contributions to public health policy. In Warner KE, ed., *Tobacco Control Policy.* San Francisco, CA: Jossey-Bass; 2006: 3–86.

11. Lightwood JM, Glantz SA. Declines in acute myocardial infarctions after smoke-free laws and individual risk attributable to secondhand smoke. *Circulation* 2009;120:1373–1379.

12. Centers for Disease Control and Prevention. *Best Practices for Comprehensive Tobacco Control Programs—2007.* Atlanta, GA: US Department of Health and Human Services, Centers for Disease Control and Prevention, National Center for Chronic Disease Prevention and Health Promotion, Office on Smoking and Health, 2007.

13. Brownell KD, Farley T, Willett WC, et al. The public health and economic benefits of taxing sugar-sweetened beverages. *N Engl J Med* 2009;361:1599–1605.

14. Farrelly MC, Davis KC, Haviland ML, et al. Evidence of a dose-response relationship between "truth" antismoking ads and youth smoking prevalence. *Am J Public Health* 2005;95:425–431.

15. Christakis N, Fowler J. The spread of obesity in a large social network over 32 years. *N Engl J Med* 2007;357:370–379.

16. Lasser K, Boyd JW, Woolhandler S, Himmelstein DU, McCormick D, Bor DH. Smoking and mental illness: a population-based prevalence study. *JAMA* 2000;284:2606–2610.

17. Mendez D, Warner KE. Commissioned simulation modeling of smoking prevalence as an outcome of selected tobacco control measures. In: Bonnie RJ, Stratton K, Wallace RB, eds. *Ending the Tobacco Problem: A Blueprint for the Nation.* Washington, DC: National Academies Press; 2007: 599–640.

18. Warner KE, Mendez D. Tobacco control policy in developed countries: Yesterday, today, and tomorrow. *Nicotine Tob Res* 2010;12:876–887.

19. Emery S, Gilpin EA, Ake C, Farkas, AJ, Pierce JP. Characterizing and identifying "hard-core" smokers: implications for further reducing smoking prevalence. *Am J Public Health* 2000;90:387–394.

20. Yeaman A. Implications of Battelle Hippo I & II and the Griffith filter. Philip Morris internal memo, July 17, 1963. University of California, San Francisco, Legacy Tobacco Documents Library. Available at: http://legacy.library.ucsf.edu/tid/xrc72d00/pdf. Accessed January 24, 2010.

21. US Department of Health and Human Services, Public Health Service, Centers for Disease Control, Center for Health Promotion and Education. *The Health Consequences of Smoking: Nicotine Addiction. A Report of the Surgeon General.* Washington, DC: U.S. Government Printing Office, 1988.

22. Marketing Innovations Inc. Youth cigarette-new concepts. Brown & Williamson Tobacco Corporation project report. September 1972. University of California, San Francisco. Legacy Tobacco Documents Library. Available at: http://legacy.library.ucsf.edu/tid/oyq83f00/pdf. Accessed on January 24, 2010.

23. Advocacy Institute. *Smoke & Mirrors: How the Tobacco Industry Buys & Lies Its Way to Power & Profits.* Washington, DC: Advocacy Institute, 1998.

64

Lessons from Drug Policy

ROBERT L. DUPONT

INTRODUCTION

Drug abuse has been called "the American disease" because of the prominent role drug abuse has played in the United States for more than a century.[1] Over this time there have been two distinctive epidemics of drug abuse, the first at the end of the nineteenth and the first decade of the twentieth century and the second beginning in the late 1960s and continuing to the present.[2] In recent years the modern drug abuse epidemic has become global, leading to fierce debates over drug policy that have flourished especially in Europe as well as in the United States, Canada, and Latin America.[3]

Consideration of addiction in the context of food and eating has been encouraged by the prominence of the issue of addiction in modern culture and by the remarkable developments in brain science that can both be traced to the high level of public concern over the drug abuse epidemic.[4–7] In this chapter I explore some of the lessons to be learned from the drug abuse experience.[8,9]

Looking to addiction to alcohol and other drugs for useful lessons for dealing with food addiction can be problematic not only because of the differences between addictions to drugs and to food but also because dealing with alcohol and drugs is often characterized as one of the signal failures of contemporary public health policy. American drug policies are sometimes ridiculed as failures and worse, they are seen to be dehumanizing. I do not share those negative views. Contemporary American drug policy, the result of four decades of bipartisan development, is characterized as a balance of law enforcement and treatment aimed at reducing the use of illegal drugs and promoting recovery from addiction.[3] The annual economic cost of illegal drug use in the United States is astounding, totaling over $193 billion.[10] The annual *National Drug Control Strategy*, published by the Office of National Drug Control Policy (ONDCP), presents the federal government's comprehensive strategy. The latest *Strategy* can be accessed at ONDCP.gov.

I proceed to a discussion of drug policy with several key assumptions: (1) drug abuse treatment has been characterized as futile, but data support a more positive conclusion; (2) addiction is a merciless teacher, labeled "cunning, baffling and powerful" by Alcoholics Anonymous[11]; (3) recovery from addiction is characterized by not merely a return to premorbid condition, but to greatly enhanced lives; (4) a great achievement of drug abuse research has been the identification of disordered brain reward as the sine qua non of addiction, not withdrawal[12]; (5) although the risk of addiction varies with the substance, the route of administration, and many other factors, the risk of addiction is universal to all individuals who use brain-rewarding substances or behaviors repeatedly and intensely; (6) changes in biology and thinking brought about by substances of abuse make the concepts of choice and personal responsibility of limited relevance when it comes to the continuation of drug use, as the brain reward from drugs of abuse is produced by a sledgehammer effect on the delicate brain reward mechanism; and (7) addictive disorders are often lifelong, hence the term "chronic relapsing brain diseases."

After this short introduction let us explore five lessons from drug abuse that have relevance to food addiction.

LESSON ONE—THE EPIDEMIC NATURE OF THE PUBLIC HEALTH THREAT

While many behavior-related disorders are relatively stable over time, this has not been the case with drug abuse, which has seen a dramatic increase in recent decades. In 1962—before the modern drug abuse epidemic—only 4% of Americans 18 to

25 years old had ever used an illegal drug. This is the age group that has the highest rate of use of addictive substances. By l979, the peak of the drug abuse epidemic, this figure had risen to 69% for this age group.[13] It has since fallen to 58%.[14] Neither the rise nor the fall in this number can be attributed to brain biology or to characteristics of the drugs of abuse. Not only did brain biology not change over this relatively short period of time but the most commonly used drugs are almost all old if not ancient.

Over these same few decades there has been a dramatic increase in food-related problems such as obesity. Why would those two behavioral shifts occur over the span of time? Biology cannot explain that timing. The only way to understand that change is to focus on the environment in which these behaviors occur. Over the past few decades there has been a profound global culture shift to a greater emphasis on personal, individual control of behavior and a shift to immediate pleasure. This shift has been magnified by massive increases in the availability of brain-rewarding substances (drugs and high-intensity foods). This shift has had major economic drivers. This lesson is clear: drug addiction and food issues are both epidemic problems that are rooted in brain biology. Their prevalence is strongly influenced by the environment in which use occurs.

LESSON TWO—FIRST THINGS FIRST: DEFINING THE PROBLEM AND SEEKING SOLUTIONS

Drug abuse policy continues to suffer from confusion in defining the problem. Some see it as a moral failing while on the other extreme drug abuse is seen to be the result of legal prohibition of drugs and drug use. Neither of these definitions is close to correct—but neither is entirely wrong. The new brain biology that locates the common site of action of all abused drugs as brain reward provides a solid, scientific definition of the drug abuse. Human beings in their restless exploration of their environments have discovered, and more recently invented, a relatively small number of chemicals that provide unnaturally intense stimulation of brain reward. Repeated chemical stimulation of brain reward produces changes in the brain that are long-lasting and that powerfully shape not only behavior, but also thoughts. In this new view, the source of the drug abuse problem is the universal innate and inescapable

vulnerability of the human brain to the seductive call of direct chemical stimulation of brain reward. The solution to the drug problem, when understood in this way, is to develop policies and programs that reduce drug use while being compatible with contemporary culture, laws, and values.

Experience with drug abuse during the modern epidemic—and earlier—has shown that while drug use cannot be extinguished, the damage drug use produces in individuals and in society as a whole can be contained. This biological view highlights the enormous potential of the drug problem to get very much worse very fast. This is true because the vulnerability to brain-rewarding chemicals is universal. Drug traffic functions to meet the "demand" for drugs. Real demand reduction involves not only limiting the supply of drugs, but also raising their prices. Demand reduction also includes changing the environments in which drugs and human brains interact to encourage people not to use drugs. Furthermore, when people do use drugs, demand reduction encourages them to stop using drugs. These approaches to demand reduction are defined, respectively, as prevention and treatment.

Messages about drug use are complex in part because there are many drug users who have no problems as a result of their drug use, especially, but not only, early in their history of drug use when they are most likely to spread the drug-using behavior like an infectious disease. There is a robust body of opinion that drug use is normal and even desirable. In this view, the appropriate public health strategy is not to stop drug use but to teach people, including youth, to use drugs moderately and safely. This more tolerant movement has gained strength in the past two decades under the banner of "harm reduction."[15]

So what are the lessons for food addiction from this complex and confusing discussion of the definition of the drug abuse problem? First, the problem of drug addiction is us, all of us. It rests in the vulnerability of our brains to the stimulation of the specific chemicals we call drugs. Second, there is no silver bullet, no one grand action or program that will stop the problem of drug addiction. Third, the drug addiction problem is not going to go away—it cannot be eliminated. Those three observations apply directly to food and addiction. Is that pessimistic? I don't think so. However, this short summary does orient public health efforts to focus on the long haul and to use a wide range of complementary strategies rather than relying on, or even seeking, any one solution.

Because brain biology cannot be changed and because the drugs of abuse are not going to go away, the major public health opportunity is to focus on efforts on the environment in which decisions are made to use or not to use drugs of abuse. This is the primary focus of both prevention and treatment since both drug addiction and food addiction are encouraged or discouraged by cultural and economic factors that characterize the environments in which human brains have access to these brain-rewarding—addicting—substances.

LESSON THREE—THE POWER AND THE LIMITS OF THE LAW

Drugs laws are of preeminent importance both in affecting the supply of drugs and the acceptability of drug use. In relation to food and addiction, it has only recently become clear that laws can play a useful public health role in reducing risk.

For all disorders of brain reward except those of illegal drugs, laws relate to the suppliers but not to the individuals engaged in the unhealthy behaviors. For example, drunk driving is illegal and severely punished but drinking by adults is not, even when the drinking is clearly unhealthy. For illegal drugs the criminal law applies not only to the suppliers of the drugs but also to the users of the drugs. The criminal penalties for users as well as for suppliers are often severe, especially for repeat offenders, in contrast to other disordered behaviors.

The use of drugs such as marijuana, heroin, and cocaine has been illegal for decades in the United States and around the world for so long that some critics of modern drug policy claim that it is "prohibition" that has created and now sustains the modern drug problem. A look at history shows the fallacy of this view: it was the earlier epidemic in drug use during the free market for drugs that led to legal restrictions on the access to and use of these drugs. Furthermore, for those who are not persuaded by this history, there is unmistakable contemporary evidence that the drug problem is not caused by legal restrictions, by making certain drugs illegal. The fastest growing and in many ways the largest drug problem in the United States today is the nonmedical use of prescription-controlled substances, especially opioid analgesics. Every year since 2005 as many or more Americans first used

prescription opioids nonmedically than first used marijuana. I did not imagine that in my lifetime I would see any drug of abuse more widely used than marijuana. The emergence of the prescription drug problem illuminates the fallacy of the argument that it is the illegality of drugs that creates the drug problem. When it comes to the nonmedical use of prescription opioids, there is little illegal market and a small law enforcement role. The current focus on prescription drug abuse returns drug prevention efforts to the biology of the drug itself, to the availability of the drug, and to the circumstances in which decisions to use and not to use drugs occur.

On the other hand, and just as important, it is clear that making a drug illegal does not eliminate the use of that drug or the problems that flow from its use. There is a clear public health benefit from keeping the use and sale of these drugs illegal. The issue of the role of legal status in the rates of use in the United States is easily seen in the numbers of Americans who have used each of the most commonly used addictive substances in the prior 30 days: alcohol, 131.3 million; tobacco, 69.6 million; and all illegal drugs combined, 22.6 million.[14] It is impossible to argue that this huge contrast in prevalence is the result of biology when many of the currently illegal drugs are much more intensely brain rewarding than alcohol or tobacco. The far lower level of use of the currently illegal drugs compared to the level of use of the two legal drugs reflects not their capacity to produce brain reward but their legal status and the willingness of the society to tolerate their use.

When asked what the major issue was for voters in the 1992 election, Bill Clinton said, "It's the economy, stupid." We can conclude that when it comes to drug abuse, "It's the drug, stupid," with the caveat that the problem is not only drugs. It is also the environment in which the human brain is exposed to drugs.

For food addiction, the drug experience suggests both the power and the limits of the law when it comes to reducing the damage from the brain's pell-mell pursuit of brain reward. Surely in both drug and food addiction, experience has shown that a totally "free market" is a major health hazard for powerful biological reasons.

The public policy challenge for drug policy, like food policy, is to find better strategies to limit the damage of disordered function of brain reward that are cost-effective and compatible with modern values as they minimize the negative public health consequences of these behaviors.[3]

The new idea in recovery for both drugs and alcohol use disorders focuses on the drug user with zero tolerance for any use. This standard is actively enforced with random drug and alcohol tests. Any violation of the no-use standard leads to prompt, certain, and meaningful consequences in what has been labeled the "new paradigm" for the management of people with significant alcohol and drug problems.[16] Programs using this approach are found in the criminal justice system[17,18] and elsewhere, including in the management of the nation's physicians in the state Physician Health Programs.[19-24] The new paradigm is entirely outside the range of public health options now used for eating disorders and for virtually all other areas of medicine. The fact that this approach produces remarkably good long-term results encourages a more thoughtful consideration of this approach in other areas of public health—for example, in the management of some psychotic disorders where noncompliance with treatment has profoundly negative consequences for the patients and for others. There may be ways that this new paradigm can be used in the management of eating disorders.

LESSON FOUR—THE UNIQUE ROLES OF COMMUNITY FELLOWSHIPS

One of the most distinctive aspects of the contemporary drug scene is the role of the 12-step fellowships: Alcoholics Anonymous (AA), Narcotics Anonymous (NA), and Al Anon, the program for family and for other people who are concerned about addicts.[25-27] These fellowships are uniquely effective in overcoming the central problem of addiction: the lifelong risk of relapse. They began when AA was born June 10, 1935. AA now reaches more than 1 million American addicts each year.[28] Worldwide estimates show the number of AA members to be over 2 million while there are over 250,000 members of NA around the world.[29] They are without precedent in the world and without precedent in health care. Not only are these fellowships not treatment, but they do not compete with any form of substance abuse treatment. There is no money involved in these fellowships and, surprising to many, no religion. The only requirement for membership is the desire to stop alcohol and drug use. The defining discovery of the founders was

that the only way they could stay sober was to help other suffering alcoholics—the 12th step.[30]

It is no accident that a companion organization focused on food and addiction has emerged in recent decades, Overeaters Anonymous (OA), which like AA and NA is a spiritually based but nonreligious organization. OA held its first meeting on January 19, 1960 and has adopted the 12-step program to food addiction. Many in health care are baffled and even repelled by the ubiquitous roles of these fellowships in contemporary culture. A simple way to think about them sympathetically is to recognize that treatment for addiction to drugs and to food is often relatively brief, even when prolonged. Compare that duration with the lifelong risk of relapse to these addictive disorders. The genius of the so-called Minnesota Model of substance abuse treatment, which began in the late 1940s, was to make the 12 steps the foundation of the treatment program and then to add the most sophisticated professional treatment available to create a seamless continuum that starts with treatment, residential or outpatient, followed by prolonged, and often lifelong, participation in one or more of the 12-step fellowships.[31,32]

It cannot be surprising that there has grown over recent years similar 12-step programs to deal not only with sexual disorders but other related disorders of brain reward, including gambling and debt. Science has shown that brain reward is the common characteristic of abused drugs, and what distinguishes these chemicals from all others—including many that are psychoactive. Similarly, modern brain science has shown that brain reward is the common characteristic of all of the problems that are dealt with by the 12-step fellowships. Those problems are rooted in disordered brain reward that has resulted from excessive and intense stimulation, often for many years.

All of the 12-step programs have grown in local communities by incorporating what is useful and by discarding what is not. None are funded by the government, by health insurance, or by health care institutions. There are no professionals in charge and no licensees or regulations. They are entirely voluntary. They exist only to the extent that they provide benefits to their members. There are several modern competitors of the 12-step programs. It is easy to see how relatively successful each of these programs is by seeing how many members they have since they all function based on attraction and not promotion.

One of the more important lessons from drug abuse is that AA and NA have not approached alcohol and drug addiction as substance-specific the way the modern science of addiction medicine has in its diagnostic manual. In this official manual there are separate diagnoses for each individual substance of abuse.[33] Since its origin, a person in AA was not considered to be "sober," let alone in recovery, if he or she stopped alcohol use and continued to use marijuana, heroin, or other drugs. NA has the same standard with respect to alcohol use; no use of alcohol is required before the fellowship member can be considered abstinent or "clean."

One apparent difference of AA and NA, on the one hand, and OA, on the other, is that AA and NA focus on complete abstinence from the use of addicting substances. OA, while not promoting abstinence from eating, takes a similar approach when it counsels abstinence from the most brain-rewarding ("addictive") foods and from the most addictive eating patterns (binge eating, for example).[34] Another difference is that AA and NA both emphasize that the sobriety date of every member is the last day the member used alcohol or other drugs nonmedically. There is no similar tradition in OA.

LESSON FIVE—BRAIN MANAGEMENT

Professionals working in the field of addiction are used to working with people who have been defeated, if not destroyed, by their addictions. They commonly see people in denial about their problems and the relationship of those problems to their use of addicting substances. The alcoholic and the drug addict are in the grip of an abusive chemical love affair. They are highly ambivalent about giving up their chemical lovers. They want to go back to that lover but not to suffer the painful and humiliating consequences of the love affair, thinking that "next time it will be different." The task of treatment includes helping the addict see that "next time it will not be the same—next time it will be worse." The process of recovery almost always begins only when repeated, often severe, and painful consequences from drug use are linked to strong and sustained measures from those around the addicted person insisting that the drug use stop.

Addiction is a disorder of brain reward, caused by repeated excessive stimulation of brain reward. In the brain there is an "addiction switch" that transforms an alcohol or a drug user into an addict.

Once turned "on," the addiction switch stays on, creating the distinctive problems of addiction, including denial, dishonesty, and the enduring risk of relapse even after prolonged abstinence from the addicting behavior.[2]

The work of the therapist and the doctor in dealing with addiction is to help the patient identify a path to recovery and to help the addict get on and stay on that path. This requires not only a sense of urgency, since the issues are quite literally life and death, but it also requires patience since few suffering alcoholics and addicts get the message right away.

There is a major role for humility in addiction treatment because the patient needs to hear the message, "You alone can do it; but you cannot do it alone." With all addictions it is often helpful and even necessary not only to use professional help, but also to work with other addicts who can share their "experience, strength, and hope" with those newer on the path to recovery.

Drug prevention, treatment, and even relapse prevention can all be understood as efforts to promote healthy management of brain reward, or more simply, "brain management." There are sound public health reasons not to start behaviors that can lead to addiction. For illegal drugs there is the warning not to use these drugs because of the risk of addiction. For cigarettes the same message is appropriate: don't even start smoking cigarettes because you have no way of knowing where that habit will end. It often ends in premature death. The risk is not worth the reward. For alcohol, and even more for food, the sound prevention message is more nuanced; however, it can be simply stated: don't drink under age because the risk of addiction is greatest for those who begin drinking alcohol early. The legal drinking age provides a bright line with a clear public health value. For adults who choose to drink alcohol the simple message is not to drink to excess. Excess is defined as drinking more than two or three drinks in a day for a man and one or two drinks in a day for a woman. Drinking more than this is a high-risk behavior that prudent people avoid.

For eating, the prevention message is similar to that for alcohol use by adults: eat healthy foods and do not eat excessively. Eating unhealthy foods is a high-risk behavior as is excessive eating.

For people who experience a disorder of brain reward known as addiction, the single prevention message is equally clear for drugs, cigarettes, alcohol, and food: stop using illegal drugs, stop smoking cigarettes, stop drinking excessively, and stop eating unhealthy foods and eating to excess. There is a caveat here: stopping is easy for all of these behaviors. At some point, all addicts have stopped their addictive behaviors, but the defining attribute of addiction is relapse even after prolonged abstinence.

For addicted people who cannot maintain abstinence, the message is also clear: get help. Get professional help and get help from the fellowship of addicts in recovery. That usually means 12-step programs. Comply with your professional treatment. After treatment ends, stick with your recovery fellowship.

A final word on brain management to deal with addiction: sufferers benefit from working not only to regain their premorbid health but from aiming far higher. They are most likely to succeed in their struggle with addiction when they work to achieve real and lasting recovery. Recovery is robust good health. It includes not only physical well-being but also mental health and spiritual health.

Brain management is both necessary and difficult. It is not something someone can do alone. It takes a network of relationships in the family and the community precisely because our brains are vulnerable to addiction and because we are the last to recognize our problems. This is true because hijacking our thinking is part of addiction. That is why in the 12-step fellowships, the sponsor and the group are so important. They have objectivity that the addicts lack about themselves. Brain management is an important part of responsible stewardship for our bodies and for our lives. Brain management can mean doing things our brains tell us not to do and not doing things are brains tell us to do. We can sort those distinctions out best in relationship to others who care about us. It is striking that one of the key features of addiction is dishonesty. This is just as true in food and addiction as it is in addiction to alcohol and other drugs. Honesty is the one-word antidote for addiction because those who care about us do not want us to engage in addictive behavior because they clearly see that it harms us.

Recovery is the hard-earned gift of addiction for the addicted person. This relatively new use of the very old word "recovery" comes from the past three-quarters of a century of dealing with addiction to alcohol and other drugs. The concept of recovery is the ultimate lesson from the people

dealing with addiction to alcohol and other drugs for our new colleagues in food addiction.

CONCLUSION

Although disordered brain reward is not new, the modern world provides more potent brain rewards in an environment that encourages their uses. This new reality requires new strategies to protect the public health. Drugs are part of this new challenge, as is food.

REFERENCES

1. Musto DF. *The American Disease.* New York: Oxford University Press, 1999.
2. DuPont RL. *The Selfish Brain: Learning from Addiction.* Center City, MN: Hazelden, 2000.
3. DuPont RL, Madras BK, Johansson P. Drug policy: a biological science perspective. In: Lowinson JH, Ruiz P, eds. Substance Abuse: A Comprehensive Textbook. 5th ed. Philadelphia, PA: Lippincott Williams & Wilkins; 2011: 998–1010.
4. Schwartz MB, Brownell KD. Action necessary to prevent childhood obesity: creating the climate for change. *J Law Med Ethics* 2000;35(1):78–89.
5. Randolph TG. The descriptive features of food addiction: addictive eating and drinking. *Q J Stud Alcohol* 1956;17(2):198–224.
6. Wang GJ, Volkow ND, Thanos PK, Fowler JS. Imaging of brain dopamine pathways: implications for understanding obesity. *J Addict Med* 2009;3(1):8–18.
7. Hoebel BG, Avena ME, Bocarsly ME, Rada P. Natural addiction: a behavioral and circuit model based on sugar addiction in rats. *J Addict Med* 2009;3(1):33–41.
8. Gold MS, Graham NA, Cocores JA, Nixon SJ. Food addiction? *J Addict Med* 2009;3(1):42–45.
9. Kessler D. *The End of Overeating: Taking Control of the Insatiable American Appetite.* Emmaus, PA: Rodale Books, 2009.
10. US Department of Justice, National Drug Intelligence Center. The economic impact of illicit drug use on American society. 2011. Available at: http://www.justice.gov/ndic/pubs44/44731/44731p.pdf. Accessed March 25, 2012.
11. Alcoholics Anonymous World Service. *Alcoholics Anonymous: Big Book.* 4th ed. Center City, MN: Hazelden Publishing & Educational Services, 2001.
12. Volkow ND, Li TK. Drug addiction: The neurobiology of behavior gone awry. In: Ries RK, Fiellin D, Miller C, Saitz R, eds. *Principles of Addiction Medicine.* 4th ed. Chevy Chase, MD: American Society of Addiction Medicine; 2009: 3–12.
13. Substance Abuse and Mental Health Services Administration. 1998 National household survey on drug abuse: detailed tables. 1999. Available at: http://www.oas.samhsa.gov/NHSDA/98DetailedTables.htm. Accessed October 30, 2009.

14. *Results from the 2010 National Survey on Drug Use and Health: National Findings.* Rockville, MD: Substance Abuse and Mental Health Services Administration, 2011. Office of Applied Studies, NSDUH Series H-41, HHS Publication No. (SMA) 11-4658.

15. Caulkins JP, Reuter PH. Setting goals for drug policy: harm reduction or use reduction? *Addiction* 1997;92(9):1145–1150.

16. DuPont RL, Humphreys K. A new paradigm for long-term recovery. *Subst Abus* 2011;32(1):1–6.

17. Hawken A, Kleiman M. *Managing Drug Involved Probationers with Swift and Certain Sanctions: Evaluating Hawaii's HOPE.* Washington, DC: US Department of Justice, National Institute of Justice, 2009.

18. Long, L. The 24/7 Sobriety Project. *The Public Lawyer* 2009; 17(2):2–5.

19. DuPont RL, McLellan AT, White WL, Merlo L, Gold MS. Setting the standard for recovery: Physicians Health Programs evaluation review. *J Subst Abuse Treat* 2009;36(2):159–171.

20. DuPont RL, McLellan AT, Carr G, Gendel M, Skipper GE. How are addicted physicians treated? A national survey of Physician Health Programs. *J Subst Abuse Treat* 2009;37:1–7.

21. Skipper GE, Campbell MD, DuPont RL. Anesthesiologists with substance use disorders: a 5-year outcome study from 16 state Physician Health Programs. *Anesth Analg* 2009;109(3):891–896.

22. McLellan AT, Skipper GE, Campbell MG, DuPont RL. Five year outcomes in a cohort study of physicians treated for substance use disorders in the United States. *BMJ* 2008;337:a2038.

23. Skipper GE, DuPont RL. Substance abuse among physicians and other health professionals. In: Korsmeyer P, Kranzler HR, eds. *Encyclopedia of Drugs, Alcohol & Addictive Behaviors.* 3rd ed. Farmington Hills, MI: Gale; 2008: 242–251.

24. White WL, DuPont RL, Skipper GE. Physician Health Programs: what counselors can learn from these remarkable programs. *Counselor* 2007;8(2):42–47.

25. Schulz JE, Williams V, Galligan JE. Twelve step programs in recovery. In: Ries RK, Fiellin D, Miller SC, Saitz R, eds. *Principles of Addiction Medicine.* 4th ed. Chevy Chase, MD: American Society of Addiction Medicine; 2009: 911–922.

26. McCrady BS, Tonigan JS. Recent research into twelve step programs. In: Ries RK, Fiellin D, Miller SC, Saitz R, eds. *Principles of Addiction Medicine.* 4th ed. Chevy Chase, MD: American Society of Addiction Medicine; 2009: 923–937.

27. Galanter M. Spirituality in the recovery process. In: Ries RK, Fiellin D, Miller SC, Saitz R, eds. *Principles of Addiction Medicine.* 4th ed. Chevy Chase, MD: American Society of Addiction Medicine; 2009: 939–942.

28. Alcoholics Anonymous World Services. Estimates of A.A. groups and members. Available at: http://www.aa.org/subpage.cfm?page=74. Accessed November 3, 2009.

29. Babor TF, Caulkins JP, Griffiths E et al. *Drug Policy and the Public Good.* New York: Oxford University Press, 2009.

30. DuPont RL, McGovern JP. *A Bridge to Recovery: An Introduction to 12-Step Programs.* Washington, DC: American Psychiatric Press, 1994.

31. Anderson DJ, McGovern JP, DuPont RL. The origins of the Minnesota model of addiction treatment: a first-person account. *J Addict Dis* 1999;18(1):107–110.

32. White WL. *Slaying the Dragon: The History of Addiction Treatment and Recovery in America.* Bloomington, IL: Chestnut Health Systems, 1998.

33. American Psychiatric Association. *Diagnostic and Statistical Manual of Mental Disorders.* 4th ed. Washington, DC: American Psychiatric Association, 1994.

34. Merlo LJ, Stone AM, Gold MS. Co-occurring addiction and eating disorders. In: Ries RK, Fiellin D, Miller SC, Saitz R, eds. *Principles of Addiction Medicine.* 4th ed. Chevy Chase, MD: American Society of Addiction Medicine; 2009: 1263–1274.

65

Global Policies Affecting Diet and Obesity

TIM LOBSTEIN

INTRODUCTION

Other sections of the present book will describe the obesity epidemic and its extraordinary increase, especially among children in the developing as well as the developed world in the last two decades. Other sections will also describe some of the drivers that appear to be causing this unprecedented threat to human health: the changes in diet and physical activity experienced by populations and subgroups as a result of changing agricultural production, changing food processing and pricing, changes in urbanization and industrialization, and changes in work routines as well as transport and leisure activities. This chapter considers whether there are opportunities at the highest, global level to change the rules.

WHY GLOBAL?

The discourse on obesity has for many years focused upon individuals and their unhealthy behavior patterns. Interventions to prevent obesity are most frequently targeted at those who are already obese or likely to become so, and techniques of persuasion, exhortation, education, and inducement are used to try to change behavior. They have been found to have little effect, for reasons explained elsewhere in this book but that might be summarized in the notion that behavior is largely determined by the setting in which the behavior is likely to happen: change the environment and you change the behavior. If obesity-enhancing food products are cheap to buy and easily obtained by picking up a phone, they will be purchased and consumed. Only if healthier foods are easier to obtain than obesogenic foods will you have a reasonable chance of changing behavior.

In reality, the last half-century has seen an extraordinary "nutrition transition," which has led to fatty, sugary, energy-dense foods becoming widely available to developed and urbanized populations around the globe. The agricultural, trade, and investment policies that led to this change in dietary patterns have been driven by forces with little regard for obesity or chronic disease consequences.

In its crudest sense, it can be argued that the aim of agriculture and food trade policies internationally has been to ensure adequate supplies of food energy to prevent starvation and to feed the global community—primarily the workforce in the globalized marketplace—and the primary commercial aim has been to extend the market for branded products to meet the requirement placed on corporations to provide increasing returns to their shareholders, to grow the corporation, and to reduce the competition. The two main mechanisms are (1) trade in commodities and branded goods, and (2) foreign investment in local production. This drastically oversimplifies the complex web of drivers that shape globalized food supplies, but it serves to help understand the unfolding history of nutritional transitions and the rules that now control them.

International trade can be traced back millennia, to the shipment of goods by boat and packhorse and camel caravan, but the wholesale shipment of long-shelf-life bulk food commodities over long distances can be traced back almost exactly 500 years to the establishment of sugar plantations in the New World, and the rapid growth of sugar consumption among the wealthier classes in Europe and elsewhere in subsequent decades. Sugar epitomizes the health issues raised by globalized trade, being a highly desired and highly saleable commodity, with a very long shelf life and low risk of contamination, but virtually devoid of nutritional benefits. It also depended on slavery for its low production costs. A similar story can be told for cotton, tobacco, and for the development of the Asian palm oil industry to supply edible fats (and soap) to the West.

An equivalent example from history of the problems with foreign direct investment could be the introduction to southern Africa of American corn (maize) as a hardy crop, able to supply a staple food to the farm, plantation and mining workforce being developed in the 1800s in the region. Cheap and plentiful, maize was more useful to land and mine owners than the less productive indigenous millet and labor-intensive vegetable plots. It was, though, like sugar, a less nutritious crop, being low in protein and B vitamins.

We can dip into these major historical developments and see the rise of international food trade in refined food-related commodities (sugar, vegetable oil, starchy grains) and the gradual process by which cheaply supplied food ingredients, transported long distances from their sources or introduced as new staple foods, came to dominate food manufacturing by offering long shelf-life, calorie-rich products at low cost. As a footnote, a valuable history could be written of military rations, such as the ship's biscuit and grog, as precursors for processed foods today—they were designed to be resistant to spoilage, easily transported, and energy dense to serve as fuel for servicemen

The twentieth century saw immense developments: the technology of refrigerated transport allowed an international trade in higher value perishable foods (mainly meat but also fish and cheese). The intensification of agriculture and the exploitation of a few crops—corn and soya are obvious examples—to supply a basic range of long-shelf-life refined ingredients—starches, oils, sugars—has kept down the price of processed foods made from these refined globalized commodities,

even when transport costs have risen. Lastly, the extension of markets by branded goods has seen the colonization of local food supplies by imported foods and food technologies: a process that may be less visible in the United States, which has been the source of much globalization, than it is in Asia, Latin America, or Africa, where the local cuisines have been replaced by the Western pattern within a single generation. The growth of the McDonald's fast food chain is a helpful reminder of the nature of the change in food supplies—not simply for its own sake but because it represents a shifting pattern in the market, with rising domination by branded confectionery, soft drinks, snack foods, and fast food stores, and declining fresh fruit, green vegetables, whole grains and pulses, and plain drinking water (see Fig. 65.1).

This remarkable change in food and nutrition patterns demonstrates the cross-border, international nature of the problem, and it shows that intervening at the national level, using small taxes or subsidies, for example, is likely to have little impact on the globalized food supply. A country wanting to protect its people from these changes in food supplies would need to isolate itself from trends in economic development experienced around much of the globe. The only alternative is to change the trends in a more favorable direction.

GLOBAL INTERVENTION

How do we change the policies in order to improve the opportunities for health? What tools of governance are available that can allow us to control the terms of operation of the global food market? Recognizing that commercial policies have driven

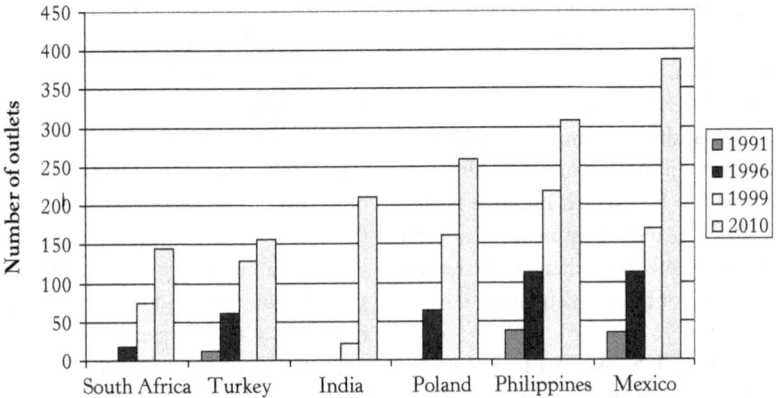

FIGURE 65.1. Changing food supply patterns, as indicated by the rise in McDonald's stores in non-US markets.
Source: McDonald's company reports.

much of the expansion and globalization of food supplies, supported by political moves for economic development, we need to examine opportunities for intervention in order to improve public health. Short of some form of revolutionary movement, we must focus on the rules that are in place, or need to be in place, and that can be used to lever the food trade.

In classical economic theory, interventions in the operations of a freely operating market are only justified under certain circumstances. Market interventions in order to tackle obesity are discussed in several documents,[1-3] and these focus on traditional market problems, including externalities (costs borne by nonconsumers, including the costs of ill health to community-funded health programs) and failures of informed rationality (arising, for example, from a lack of adequate information or the presence of addictive ingredients). These market problems justify intervention through mechanisms such as taxation on supplies, levies on producers, or subsidizing the price or distribution of alternative products. As it is, the food markets of many countries are distorted through agricultural support polices—that might be increasing the risk of chronic disease in the population—so that a pro-health market intervention might consist of the removal of a subsidy or levy.

In the global arena there are different levers available to control trade. Interventions in international free trade (including direct investment in foreign states to provide facilities to produce new goods, such as fast food chains or soft drink bottling plants) may be justified in order to harmonize markets or remove preexisting barriers, or to set standards for the quality of goods being exchanged, but for present purposes the main levers available are interventions that permit controlling the market in order to protect the health of a population or—as in the case of the Framework Convention on Tobacco Control—tackling a common threat to the health of populations in many countries. Although not always designed to be used to improve health, the international trade and investment rules offer some scope for implementing changes to reduce the obesogenic nature of the marketplace.

INSTRUMENTS AVAILABLE

The current rules of engagement were set in place in the late 1940s following an international conference held in Bretton Woods, New Hampshire, in 1944. The principal institutions established at that time were the International Monetary Fund, The International Bank for Reconstruction and Development (later to become the World Bank) and the General Agreement on Tariffs and Trade (GATT). GATT became the main forum for trade negotiations and the settling of disputes, and in 1995 it was replaced by a more powerful body, the World Trade Organization, whose main task has been to reduce or eliminate trade barriers between countries.

The erosion of trade barriers has led to an unprecedented rise in globalized trade, matched by the concentration of power in a few very large companies, or transnational corporations (TNCs). By the early 1990s it was estimated that TNCs controlled a third of the world's private sector production.[4] Their purchasing power gives them the ability to control and coordinate production, processing, and supply chains in many countries even if they do not own all the links in a chain. In food manufacturing, companies develop brand name products to a uniform standard and use high levels of promotion so the branded products achieve global recognition, which in turn commands a higher profit margin than would be obtained from unbranded foods, leading to further investment and market expansion.

What tools are available to counter these commercial imperatives? In a review of the commitments made by a meeting of ministers of health to counteract obesity in Europe, David Fidler[5] suggests there are several opportunities for intervention, included in Table 65.1. In addition, the European ministers made a number of recommendations[6] that had trading and foreign investment implications, also shown in Table 65.1.

Countries may take further steps against imports and foreign investment if they can show that the measures they are taking are necessary to protect human health: for example, France successfully banned the sale of asbestos products as this was recognized by the WTO as meeting France's objective of eliminating human exposure to asbestos fibres.[5,7] A more explicit statement of the use of health as a means of restricting trade is made in the WTO's Sanitary and Phytosanitary (SPS) agreement,[8] and this is generally used to prevent the importation of food, beverages, or animal feed that could cause a risk to health arising from "additives, contaminants, toxins or disease-causing organisms." It is usually assumed that the SPS does not cover

TABLE 65.1. INTERNATIONAL TRADE ISSUES RAISED BY OBESITY POLICIES

Charter Proposals	Trade Issues
"ensuring access to and availability of healthier food, including fruit and vegetables"	Subsidies may be deemed to give an unfair advantage to domestic *versus* imported produce, triggering a trade dispute. This might be avoided if subsidies are applied equally to both domestic and imported foods in a given sector (e.g., fruit and vegetables).
"economic measures that facilitate healthier food choices" and *"affordable pricing for healthier foods"*	As above, taxes or subsidies should be applied equally to imported and domestic products in a given sector.
"reduction of fat, free (particularly added) sugars and salt in manufactured products"	As above, any formulation requirements should apply equally to imports and domestic products. Also, foreign-owned companies may complain that their proprietary products are no longer saleable, triggering a claim for compensation: this might be avoided by giving sufficient notice of intention to legislate.
"adequate nutrition labeling"	As above, labeling regulations should be applied without discrimination. Also, due warning of intention to legislate may help avoid claims for compensation for lost sales.
"increasing access to healthier foods at workplaces and in areas of socioeconomic deprivation"	As above, subsidies for distributing food should not favour domestically produced foods over imported ones.
"reduction of marketing pressure, particularly to children" and *"the adoption of regulations to substantially reduce the extent and impact of commercial promotion of energy-dense foods and beverages, particularly to children, with the development of international approaches, such as a code on marketing to children in this are"*	As above, marketing controls should not discriminate against imported products or products produced by foreign-owned companies. Similarly, the controls should not discriminate against foreign-owned services affected by the controls (advertising agencies, media) and adequate notice should be given regarding changes in legislation.

Sources: Table inspired by Fidler[5] with text from European Charter for Counteracting Obesity.[6]

nutrition-related standards for food imports.[9] However, Fidler argues that ingredients added to foods, including salt, sugar, and fats, could be considered "additives" that are included within the SPS rules, especially as it was accepted in 2006 that added genetic material constituted an "additive" under the SPS rules.[5,10] However, the proof required to link the presence of salt, sugar, or fats in a food to resulting disease may render the SPS approach too difficult.

Another arena for action on obesity prevention is the food standards-setting body Codex Alimentarius, set up jointly by the World Health Organization and the UN Food and Agricultural Organization. Codex sets standards and publishes guidelines on the nature and quality of food-related goods that are traded internationally, but it also sets standards for labeling and related issues such as nutrient declarations and health claims. Codex standards are voluntary and nonbinding.

In international trade disputes, Codex standards and guidelines may be cited as reference texts at the World Trade Organization (WTO). A government can adopt a higher level of protection, but in the event of a trade dispute, it may be required to justify its chosen level of protection on scientific, health, or other legitimate grounds. In 2004 the WHO commissioned a consultant to assess the role that Codex could play in implementing the recommendations of the WHO Global Strategy on Diet, Physical Activity and Health, and the subsequent report suggested that Codex should set maximum limits on the fat and salt content of foods, develop codes to limit food and drink commercials during children's television programming, and establishing a new Codex Task Force for Good Nutrition Practices.[11] There appears to have been little subsequent movement on these proposals.

The World Health Organization might be thought to be able to regulate international trade in order to protect health, but in fact its powers are remarkably limited. The strongest power it has is to issue *International Health Regulations,* which are primarily designed to deal with contamination and disease outbreaks, but could potentially be used to improve surveillance of chronic disease, food consumption, and food marketing and might even be used to issue international standards for nutrition labeling and advertising practices, including regulating cross-border advertising.[9,11] This has not been tried or even proposed by any of the member state governments, so its validity is untested.

An alternative approach available to the WHO is to formulate *codes of practice* that set a standard for member countries to adopt into legislation and that also, crucially, set a standard for transnational corporation activity. An example is the International Code of Marketing of Breastmilk Substitutes, a joint WHO and UNICEF document that has been adopted in part or in full by many member states and that producer companies state they adhere to. The weakness of this approach, clearly shown in the case of breastmilk substitutes, is that companies may break the codes of practice and only receive some bad publicity if they are exposed. There are no legal sanctions unless the code is enshrined in local law.

Finally, the WHO has shown it is possible to introduce one other type of instrument, namely a *convention* that is virtually an international treaty. The Framework Convention on Tobacco Control (FCTC)[12] was introduced following the recognition that some form of international agreement was essential to control the global marketing of tobacco products. A framework convention is a compromise between purely recommended measures and a full convention. A convention approach is a slow and difficult one requiring several rounds of international negotiation and national ratification, and a two-thirds majority from member states in the World Health Assembly. Although a convention appears an attractive approach to controlling the supply and marketing of, say, fatty, sugary, and salty foods, the long delay in achieving a workable convention might actually lead to a worsening of health if other, more immediate measures are abandoned in the process.

WHAT NEXT?

The WHO has developed a set of recommendations for member states on limiting the advertising of energy-dense foods to children, which was adopted at the World Health Assembly of 2010. The development of adequate marketing standards has been hampered by an unwillingness to make recommendations on controlling cross-border marketing—such as marketing through the Internet, through satellite TV channels and other forms of marketing originating outside a national jurisdiction, and the current set of recommendations are aimed at member states.[13] Advocacy organizations have urged the WHO to issue a strong code of practice,[14] at least as a first step to tougher measures.

Several factors came together to bring about the FCTC, which have yet to happen with food marketing. First, there was increasing frustration that tobacco TNCs were effectively challenging regulation at the national level; second, there was increasing evidence that tobacco was causing widespread health costs; third, there was concern that governments might be held liable for compensation for failing to protect their populations, especially children, from harm; and fourth, tobacco products and their manufacturers were relatively easy to identify and define. With food products, these factors are not so apparent: national controls have barely been tried, governments are unlikely to be held liable for damages to health from foods, and although there are many large and easily identified TNCs in the food sector there are also thousands upon thousands of smaller ones. Lastly, although there are various models being proposed to define the foods that need to be controlled, these are highly disputed and potentially the source of much litigation. That said, several models have now been adopted by government agencies, including one officially adopted in regulations controlling marketing to children.[15]

What is clear from the discussion thus far is that the institutions for controlling global trade and investment are not adequately attuned to health. The institutions were established to open up markets for commercial exploitation, and the rules they set are primarily designed to maintain the status quo and to set some standards for how the trade relations operate. The promotion of public health is not a commercial goal, and the mechanisms for governance at the international level are simply not adequate to force global traders to adopt public health as a new priority.

Meanwhile other priorities are emerging that might have a profound influence on trading patterns and their governance. Global warming is forcing industry to envisage new priorities and forcing governments to intervene in production. Food price rises and food shortages are likely to lead to government interventions in food supply chains, while developments in biotechnology may bring unexpected benefits as much as they may bring new problems. In 2009, the World Economics Forum ranked *chronic disease* as the most pressing societal issue for the next 10 years, in terms of likelihood of occurrence and economic cost when it occurs.[16] Next down the list comes *global governance gaps*. Global political structures are changing rapidly, and opportunities for introducing rational, health-promoting interventions into uncontrolled markets may emerge in unexpected circumstances. When such opportunities do emerge, public health advocates need to be ready to seize them.

REFERENCES

1. Suhrcke M, Nugent RA, Stuckler D, Rocco L. Chronic disease: an economic perspective. Oxford Health Alliance. 2006. Available at: http://archive. oxha.org/knowledge/publications/oxha-chronic-disease-an-economic-perspective.pdf. Accessed April 10, 2012.

2. Lobstein T. Obesity policy: the next steps. In: Branca F, Nikogosian H, Lobstein T, eds. *The Challenge of Obesity in the WHO European Region and the Strategies for Response.* Copenhagen, Denmark: World Health Organization Regional Office for Europe; 2007: 293–303.

3. Sassi F, Hurst J. *The Prevention of Lifestyle-Related Chronic Diseases: An Economic Framework.* Paris: Organization for Economic Co-operation and Development, 2008. OECD Health Working Paper no. 32 DELSA/HEA/WD/HWP(2008)2.

4. Gereffi G. The global economy: organization, governance and development. In: Smelser N, Swedberg R, eds. *Handbook of Economic Sociology.* Princeton, NJ: Princeton University Press and Russell Sage Foundationl 2005: 160–182.

5. Fidler DG. International trade and investment rules in the context of obesity prevention and management: case study of obesity intervention recommended in the European Charter for Counteracting Obesity. In: Hawkes C, Blouin C, Henson S, Drager N, Dubé L, eds. *Trade, Food, Diet and Health: Perspectives and Policy Options.* Oxford, England: Wiley Blackwell; 2010: 279–298.

6. Akdag R, Danzon M. *European Charter for Counteracting Obesity.* Copenhagen, Denmark: World Health Organization Regional Office for Europe, 2006. Document no. EUR/06/5062700/8.

7. *European Communities: Measures Affecting Asbestos and Asbestos-Related Products.* Geneva, Switzerland: World Trade Organization, 2001. Document no. WT/DS135/AB/R.

8. World Trade Organization. Agreement on the application of sanitary and phytosanitary measures. 1998. Available at: http://www.wto.org/english/tratop_e/sps_e/sps_e.htm. Accessed April 10, 2012.

9. Lee E. The World Health Organization's global strategy on diet, physical activity and health: Turning strategy into action. *Food Drug Law J* 2005;60(4):569–601.

10. *European Communities: Measures Affecting the Approval and Marketing of Biotech Products.* Geneva, Switzerland: World Trade Organization, 2006. Document nos. WT/DS201, WT/DS292, WT/DS293.

11. Topp, R. Codex Alimentarius vis-à-vis the WHO Global Strategy on Diet, Physical Activity and Health. Prepared under contract for the World Health Organization. 2004. Available at: http://www.cspinet.org/reports/WHOGlobalStrategyCODEX.pdf. Accessed April 10, 2012.

12. World Health Organization. Framework convention on tobacco control. 2003. Available at: http://www.who.int/fctc/publications/en/. Accessed April 10, 2012.

13. World Health Organization. Set of recommendations on the marketing of foods and non-alcoholic beverages to children. 2010. Available at: http://www.who.int/dietphysicalactivity/publications/recs-marketing/en/index.html. Accessed April 10, 2012.

14. Consumers International, the International Obesity Task Force and the International Association for the Study of Obesity. Recommendations for an international code for marketing food and non-alcoholic beverages to children. 2008. Available at: http://www.consumersinternational.org/news-and-media/publications/recommendations-for-an-international-code-on-marketing-of-foods-and-non-alcoholic-beverages-to-children. Accessed April 10, 2012.

15. Ofcom. New restrictions on the television advertising of food and drink products to children. 2006. Available at: http://media.ofcom.org.uk/2006/11/17/new-restrictions-on-the-television-advertising-of-food-and-drink-products-to-children/. Accessed April 10, 2012.

16. World Economics Forum. Global risk report 2009. 2009. Available at: http://www.weforum.org/pdf/globalrisk/2009.pdf. Accessed April 10, 2012.

PART VII

Concluding Comments

66

Food and Addiction

Scientific, Social, Legal, and Legislative Implications

KELLY D. BROWNELL AND MARK S. GOLD

IS FOOD AND ADDICTION A VIABLE CONCEPT?

Whether food and addiction is a viable concept is scarcely in question. This book has marshaled the world's top experts in nutrition, addiction, and the intersection of these fields. The work is impressive in quality and scope, joins together studies using animal models with highly sophisticated human research, and converges on clear conclusions.

Food can act on the brain as an addictive substance. Certain constituents of food, sugar in particular, may hijack the brain and override will, judgment, and personal responsibility, and in so doing create a public health menace. The foods most likely to trigger an addictive process appear to be those marketed most aggressively by industry, which manipulates its products to maximize palatability. Just like drugs of abuse, brain-rewarding effects or reinforcement from food can lead to loss of control. Vast numbers of people are likely to be affected, particularly those most vulnerable, such as youth. The addictive impact of food may be a contributor to the global health crises created from obesity and diabetes, to the point where legislative and legal efforts might be informed by advances in this field, much as they were with tobacco.

We expect the concept of food and addiction to enter the public and public policy limelight shortly—the evidence is too strong to do otherwise. The implications could be significant in the way the public views nutrition and disease, in matters such as culpability for health problems related to food, and in the way nations work to prevent diet-related problems. Given the potential importance of this concept, it is essential that the work be robust, adequately funded, and communicated in accurate and effective ways.

A KEY DISTINCTION

An important distinction in this field is whether the emphasis should be on individuals who are "food addicts," or whether food should be the focus and the primary concern should be the health of large populations. Both medical and public health models can be applied, each creating different targets and potential outcomes. A traditional medical approach might focus on individuals with extreme eating patterns in hopes of intervening to provide relief. Relatively small numbers of people might merit the label "food addict"; thus, intervention can be seen as helping those in need but not having a public health impact on large populations.

Adopting a public health perspective changes the emphasis to food *and* addiction, that is, whether food acts on the brain as an addictive substance with sufficient strength in a sufficient number of people to affect the world's diet. For instance, intake of sugar-sweetened beverages is linked to risk for obesity and diabetes. Population consumption has risen dramatically in the past several decades, a trend rued by nutrition experts. To the extent high intake is driven by the addictive effect of sugar, and caffeine, is it reasonable to adopt the metaphor from drug addiction to say that food can hijack the brain?

MAPPING BIOLOGY ON TO HUMAN EXPERIENCE

In their chapter on the genetics of obesity, Chung and Leibel state, "The fact that apparently voluntary activities—eating and physical activity—strongly influence energy balance has led to the notion, still prevalent in many quarters, that individuals become obese solely by acts of free will and choice. While there may be some perverse righteous satisfaction in this formulation, the biology does not suggest this." Biological vulnerabilities, apparently shared by most humans given high rates of obesity, intersect with a toxic food and activity environment to produce disease. How important is the addictive effect of food?

If one simply listens to people, the addiction concept seems plausible. It is common for people to use addiction-like terms to describe their eating. Cravings for specific foods are often described, people speak of withdrawal when they stop using products with caffeine and sugar, and there is clear evidence that eating can map on to the diagnostic criteria for substance abuse (e.g., of use of food beyond the point where harm occurs). It is informative to examine such observations and then to determine how these are supported or not by available science.

The food industry exploits this colloquial use of addiction terms by advertising products to satisfy cravings and by depicting addiction at work ("chocoholics"). Examples are an ad campaign run by Dunkin Donuts for its cookies saying, "Craving, Meet Your Maker," and a McDonald's campaign for the Angus Third Pounder Deluxe said, "Crafted for Your Craving." This may be no more than marketing moxie, but it would be extremely interesting to obtain internal industry documents to see how often the language of addiction is used in consideration of both marketing and product formulation.

DISPATCHES FROM THE FIELD

Several chapters in this book are written by professionals who direct food addiction programs, and another is written by a person who defines herself as a food addict, sought help for it, and saw her life change dramatically as a consequence. It is unusual in a scholarly book to have such chapters.

We consider these chapters to be dispatches from the field. They provide clues based on observation and personal experience that hint at underlying biology, suggest clusters of symptoms that may have clinical meaning, and might possibly form the basis for treatment programs that can be tested in clinical trials. Our belief is that useful information comes from such experience and should not be overlooked.

These chapters tell stories and provide observations of individuals who have lives governed by their relationship with food. These stories read like those of people addicted to classic substances of abuse, with similar powerlessness over a substance, similar problems controlling use, and similar consequences on relationships, work life, and more. It is not known how common such patterns are in the population, and exactly how strong such addiction might be, but such stories suggest that more basic research is warranted.

COMPELLING BIOLOGICAL ADVANCES

Clearly, the field has made substantial progress in understanding and proving that drugs of abuse hijack the brain and that addiction is a disease of the brain.[1] Our group (Gold and colleagues) has worked since the 1970s on heroin and the locus coeruleus, cocaine and dopamine, and addictions in general. During this work, it became clear that drugs of abuse caused changes in eating and weight and that withdrawal caused the opposite changes.[2] Food is very appealing to a person in early withdrawal, almost irresistible.

While we posited the food addiction hypothesis,[3] we had little data.[4,5] Clinical data from pre-bariatric surgery cases confirmed that drugs and alcohol interfered with appetite and that withdrawal caused increased appetite, increased eating, and weight gain. Bart Hoebel and Nicole Avena showed animals will avidly self-administer glucose and, more striking, naloxone administration caused opiate withdrawal-like symptoms in these glucose-bingeing rats.[6] So, if we just follow the definition of the day for addiction—self-administration by lab animals—glucose is a drug and addiction is possible.[7] Also, withdrawal is provoked by opiate blockade. It was a remarkable series of studies by this Princeton group with self-administration, withdrawal, bingeing, and cross-tolerance to other drugs of abuse demonstrated in short order.[8-11]

Major advances followed Nora Volkow's and Brookhaven building a positron emission tomography (PET) facility capable of scanning obese and morbidly obese patients. First, they showed that these patients had D2 down-regulation like alcoholics and other addicts.[12] They also showed brain-stomach connections,[13] as well as changes in the somatosensory cortex in obese individuals after bariatric surgery. The work of Drs. Gene-Jack Wang and Nora Volkow led to the conclusion that overeating and obesity changed the brain, as if food were a drug.[14]

WHICH SUBSTANCES MIGHT BE ADDICTIVE AND WHY?

Thus far research has focused primarily on sugar. This is justified based on biological plausibility but also because sugar is an important player in the overconsumption of calories. The intake of added sugar in US adolescents, for instance, is two to three times higher than recommended. The evidence suggests that sugar acts on the brain in ways similar to substances of abuse, strengthening the case for making foods high in added sugar a top priority for public policy.

Added sugar is already targeted as a policy priority. A great many organizations have called for reductions in sugar or sugared beverage intake, including the American Heart Association, the American Medical Association, the American Academy of Pediatrics, and the World Health Organization. Cities around the country, including New York, Los Angeles, Boston, Seattle, Philadelphia, and Cleveland, among others have launched aggressive antisoda campaigns or have moved to ban the sales of such beverages in municipal facilities.

An emphasis on sugar is justified, but foods contain much more than sugar. Fat, because it is so highly palatable and caloric, would be a logical ingredient to examine, but it has been the focus of relatively little work thus far. Individuals who direct food addiction programs often speak of refined flour as a problem, but again, relatively little research has been done.

Processed foods contain a great many ingredients with entirely unknown effects on the brain. Listed here, as an example, is the ingredient list for a common food, a Frosted Chocolate Fudge Pop Tart made by Kellogg, which shows the stunning array of chemicals involved in the manufacture of foods.

ENRICHED FLOUR (WHEAT FLOUR, NIACIN, REDUCED IRON, THIAMIN MONONITRATE [VITAMIN B1], RIBOFLAVIN [VITAMIN B2], FOLIC ACID), SUGAR, DEXTROSE, SOYBEAN AND PALM OIL (WITH TBHQ FOR FRESHNESS), CORN SYRUP, WHEY, CRACKER MEAL, HIGH FRUCTOSE CORN SYRUP, CONTAINS 2% OR LESS OF CORNSTARCH, COCOA, COCOA (PROCESSED WITH ALKALI), SALT, CALCIUM CARBONATE, MODIFIED CORN STARCH, LEAVENING (BAKING SODA, SODIUM ACID PYROPHOSPHATE, MONOCALCIUM PHOSPHATE), MONO-AND DIGLYCERIDES, SODIUM STEAROYL LACTYLATE, GELATIN, EGG WHITES, DATEM, XANTHAN GUM, PARTIALLY HYDROGENATED SOYBEAN OIL†, CARAMEL COLOR, SOY LECITHIN, COLOR ADDED, VANILLA EXTRACT, VITAMIN A PALMITATE, NIACINAMIDE, TRICALCIUM PHOSPHATE, REDUCED IRON, PYRIDOXINE HYDROCHLORIDE (VITAMIN B6), RIBOFLAVIN (VITAMIN B2), THIAMIN HYDROCHLORIDE (VITAMIN B1), FOLIC ACID.

Industry's aim is to maximize sales by enhancing the reinforcing properties of its products. A great many colorings, preservatives, fragrances, and "flavor enhancers" (including caffeine, said by industry to enhance flavor) are added to food. Industry is not required to test its products for addictive effects on the brain or the extent to which constituents of its food provoke overeating. The Food and Drug Administration requires that food additives be generally regarded as safe (GRAS), but addictive effects on the brain have not been considered in the purview of safety. We suspect this may change.

Why foods are addictive could have teleological or strictly environmental explanations. With food needed to survive, foods with greatest survival value (i.e., those highest in energy), become most desirable and would be consumed in large amounts when the environment provided them. Because such foods would be abundant only occasionally, mechanisms to protect against overuse would not be necessary and eating beyond the satisfaction of short-term hunger would be adaptive in an attempt to maximize energy stores.

Innate drives to consume calorie-rich foods have gone from adaptive to destructive because of changing food conditions. Industrial processing by the food industry has created "foods" that do not appear in nature and are stripped of ingredients that might slow their reinforcing properties. Much like mildly reinforcing coca leaves being processed into highly and immediately reinforcing cocaine, foods are made to be as immediately reinforcing as possible, creating a biological drive for more, withdrawal, and chaos with the body's ability to regulate eating and weight.

WHO IS MOST VULNERABLE?

It is essential to know whether certain segments of the population might be especially sensitive to the addictive properties of food. Exposure early in life to drugs of abuse is an especially serious problem; hence, the age at which children consume foods with addictive potential might be an important consideration. This would be especially important if exposure to such foods alters the brain, perhaps permanently, such that tolerance and cross-sensitization occur. Policies to protect youth from such foods may be justified.

Other demographic variables may make certain groups more vulnerable, thus making targeting such groups with the marketing of unhealthy foods highly problematic. The chapters by Kumanyika and Harris (Chapters 56 and 57), for instance, show that some demographic groups are at particularly high risk for obesity and related diseases such as diabetes, and that these very groups appear to have greatest exposure to the marketing of unhealthy foods.

WHAT IS TO BE DONE AND DOES GOVERNMENT HAVE A ROLE?

Society sees a central role for government in regulating access to and the price and marketing of products with addictive properties. There are strict rules about sales to youth of legal but addictive products, taxes are high, there are restrictions on marketing, and government uses its authority for compelled speech (when business is forced to speak for the common good even when contrary to its self-interest, such as adding warning labels to packages).

At this moment it might seem far-fetched to think of warning labels on foods or restrictions on sales to minors, but these strategies once seemed far-fetched with tobacco and alcohol. The political power of the food industry might seem a daunting obstacle to policy change, but the tobacco industry was once considered invincible. There are many indications that the United States and many other countries view policy change, in some cases directly confronting industry interests, as the hallmark of an obesity prevention strategy.

It is our belief that there will soon be common public awareness of the concept of food and addiction and that attention to the issue by policy makers will generate a number of new legislative and regulatory debates. It is instructive, therefore, to examine the policies that have been developed in areas such as tobacco, alcohol, and drugs.

POLICY LESSONS FROM OTHER AREAS

A great deal is known about public policy and addictive substances, learned from years of lessons with tobacco, alcohol, and drugs. Chapters in this book by leaders in these areas point to the legitimate and productive role government can play. In his chapter on tobacco (Chapter 63), for instance, Warner states, "The rise and fall of smoking during the twentieth century may well prove to be one of the most significant, and fascinating, stories in the history of public health."

Access and Cost

It is instructive to identify the conditions that promote problems with addictive substances. Gilmore and Chandaria in their chapter on alcohol policy (Chapter 62) note, "The consumption data indicate that there has been increased access to alcohol across three dimensions; real price, availability, and the social acceptability of drinking." The widespread access to, and low costs of, unhealthy foods is a hallmark of the modern food environment.

There has already been work on limiting access to unhealthy foods, particularly among youth. School policies have changed dramatically, at local, state, and federal levels. Restricting foods that compete with school meals, and banning sugared beverages and snack foods as a la carte items or in vending machines, is quite common. Hence, schools have become a safer nutrition environment.[15] The mayors of Cleveland and Boston have proposed ordinances banning the sale of sugared beverages in municipal buildings. We expect to see more policies aimed at access issues.

In their chapters on tobacco, alcohol, and drugs, respectively, Warner, Gilmore and Chandaria, and DuPont (Chapters 63, 62, and 64, respectively) mention the importance of price. DuPont states, "Real demand reduction involves not only limiting the supply of drugs but also raising their prices." Gilmore and Chandaria point out that when Finland reduced alcohol taxes by 33% in 2004, there was a 10% increase in consumption and 16% and 31% increases in alcohol-related mortality for men and women, respectively. Warner, an economist who has done pioneering work on tobacco taxes, notes a direct relationship between increasing taxes and lower consumption.

Due in part to agriculture subsidies and trade policies, there is an unfortunate divide between the costs of healthy and unhealthy foods. It certainly makes sense for government agriculture policy to align with health and nutrition policy, such that economic influences on food systems favor healthier foods. The reverse is true now.

It is likely that attention to food taxes will only increase. There has been considerable discussion in the United States on taxes on sugar-sweetened beverages.[16,17] The beverage companies have launched massive campaigns to fight such taxes. Demark has a comprehensive tax program designed to raises prices on foods with added sugar and saturated fat, Hungary has taxes designed to affect consumption patterns, and a number of other countries are considering such approaches.

An issue related to both price and access is whether government food assistance programs should pay for or provide foods linked to risk for diseases such as obesity and diabetes that government largely pays for through programs like Medicare and Medicaid.[18] Whether certain foods have addictive potential may have a strong influence on this debate.

Marketing

There is a large literature on food marketing. It is powerful, pervasive, and pernicious.[19] The well-known report on children's food marketing by the Institute of Medicine begins with the statement "Marketing works."[20] Gilmore and Chandaria note the same is true for alcohol: "In 2003 the World Health Organization review concluded that 'The promotion of alcohol is an enormously well-funded, ingenious and pervasive aspect of modern life…Exposure to repeated high-level alcohol promotion initiates pro-drinking attitudes and increases the likelihood of heavier drinking.'" They note further that "Robust external governance of alcohol advertising is needed to tackle both the volume as well as the nature of advertising."

In her chapter on food marketing (Chapter 57), Harris notes how much marketing there is, how it circumvents cognitive defenses and parental authority, how sophisticated it has become, and how many forms of media deliver it (e.g., social media such as Facebook). There is much debate about the role of federal regulatory bodies such as the Federal Trade Commission and the Food and Drug Administration in addressing this problem. There is also some

authority at the state level, particularly through the state attorneys general.[21]

The science on food and addiction might well have an important role to play in decisions about how far government might move to restrict marketing. Knowledge that foods can be injurious to health is the current impetus for marketing restrictions, but if that is joined by concerns with the effects of foods on the brain, more aggressive restrictions might be possible.

THE LEGAL IMPORTANCE OF FOOD AND ADDICTION

If some foods or their constituents affect the brain to the extent that judgment and responsibility are overridden, are the companies that make and market them accountable for the negative consequences? This is a complicated issue that will likely take years to clarify and would involve public attitudes, scientific input, and of course interpretation of the law by the courts, but the chapter by Teret and Rutkow (Chapter 60) notes that there is a basis in legal theory for addressing this issue.

If attributions of harm are made to companies, an important issue is who knew what when and hence when culpability would begin. This is yet another example of an action, litigation perhaps, that might seem far-fetched at the moment, but at one point it was far-fetched to hold the tobacco companies responsible for addiction and health damages. It was as recently as 1994 when top executives of seven leading tobacco companies swore under oath before Congress that nicotine is not addictive. Internal industry documents later showed that the companies knew full well about nicotine and addiction, with some of the studies being done by their own scientists. When the public and legislators discovered that the tobacco companies were intentionally manipulating nicotine levels, outrage resulted.

Society cares about the negative impacts of food on health. It is why schools are kicking out junk foods, the Food and Drug Administration is beginning to crack down on health claims, the Federal Trade Commission is looking seriously into food marketing directed at children, and more. There may be different culpability timetables for the health consequences of food and the addictive nature of food. If outrage builds about companies manipulating ingredients such as sugar, and a solid case is made about food hijacking the brain, companies may have an entire new level of legal exposure to confront.

LIKELY FOOD INDUSTRY RESPONSE

Surprisingly, the food industry has not begun a vigorous effort to address the issue of food and addiction. It is just a matter of time. Once such work becomes more public, but more important, is discussed in policy circles, the industry will be put in a defensive posture and will likely act in predictable ways. The behavior of the tobacco industry, as well as the response of the food industry, to damaging evidence thus far on other fronts (e.g., links of sugar-sweetened beverage intake with negative health outcomes) suggests that a likely script will follow. Industry is likely to:

- ignore the food and addiction issue until it begins to enter public discourse;
- dismiss the idea and lampoon any suggestions of its validity;
- through its trade associations and front groups characterize available studies as "junk science";
- through these same groups, attack scientists, in some cases personally, claiming they are biased against industry;
- pay scientists who will then do studies to plant doubt;
- call in favors from community groups and professional associations it has supported to discount the concept;
- begin a public relations campaign to counter the concept;
- make self-regulatory pledges to care for the public good and issue promises to change business practices such as marketing certain foods to children;
- spend massive amounts to lobby against policy changes that would alter its ability to continue business as usual; and
- work to have industry figures or supportive political figures installed in key regulatory agencies in order to stall, subvert, or weaken regulatory action.

The food industry has reacted much like the tobacco industry as evidence has emerged about the damaging impact of some products.[22,23] In the case of tobacco, industry misbehavior delayed and even prevented public policy actions that could have saved millions of lives. It is essential this history not be repeated with food.

CHANGING DEFAULTS AND GOVERNMENT'S RIGHTFUL ROLE

A number of chapters in this book make clear that a bad food environment is driving poor diets. There is genetic variability in who responds most adversely when dietary conditions become problematic, but patterns of unhealthy eating rampant in all parts of the world are driven by food environments that offer high access to, heavy promotion of, and low costs for, diets high in constituents that make people unhealthy, particularly sugar, fat, and salt. Conditions such as poverty leave some segments of the population at especially high risk.

Unhealthy conditions exist as the default,[24] and consequently, bad health is the default. Attempts to portray problems such as obesity as personal failing and individual irresponsibility will, in our belief, be no more successful than attempts by the tobacco industry to make the same claim about tobacco-related diseases. Discoveries that certain foods affect the brain in ways akin to the impact of classic drugs of addiction, and clear knowledge these very foods are the most heavily promoted, particularly to children, could become a key impetus for changes in social norms, attitudes about the food industry, and bold policy changes.

As mentioned earlier, there is no better example than the schools. As Schwartz and Novak point out in their chapter (Chapter 59), children in schools with worse food policies eat worse. When policies improve, children's diets improve. Opponents argue against improving foods in schools with statements like, "Kids will then just eat more of these foods after school," as if children have a "junkostat" that keeps the intake of unhealthy foods constant. Research shows the opposite: when children's diets improve as schools clean up the junk food, they do *not* react by eating more of these foods outside school.

This concept of improving health by changing defaults in the environment is consistent with elementary principles of public health and has also been used by addictions experts. In his chapter on drug policy, DuPont notes, "Because brain biology cannot be changed and because the drugs of abuse are not going to go away, the major public health opportunity is to focus on efforts in the environment in which decisions are made to use or not to use drugs of abuse."

Gilmore and Chandaria, speaking of alcohol policy, take this concept a step further and emphasize the role of government:

> The acknowledgment of the role of wider determinants of health on individual choices in alcohol and food consumption are encapsulated in the "stewardship" model that implies that the state has a duty to look after important needs of people individually and collectively. It emphasizes the role of the state in fostering conditions that allow individuals to make healthy choices and, in particular, to ameliorate health inequalities. The stewardship-guided state sees the health of the nation as an asset and higher levels of health corresponding to greater well-being and productivity.

We agree that government has a role, in fact a responsibility, to exert stewardship over an environment that fosters good health. When the environment becomes toxic in ways that predict and create high levels of disease, government has the opportunity to act for the collective benefit of its citizens, but it must sometimes have the courage to resist corporate interests determined to protect the status quo.

Discourse about food and addiction may well play a pivotal role in determining how government will deal with diet, nutrition, and problems such as obesity. The public now believes that foods can act in addictive ways (see Chapter 41 by Barry), and this is without widespread knowledge of the available science. It is a short jump to then become angry with the food industry for manufacturing such foods and promoting them so aggressively. This can mobilize groups like parents, health professionals, and nongovernmental organizations to work with government officials for change. Elected leaders, aware of public sentiment and concerned with high rates of obesity and diabetes, may be less likely to yield to industry pressures and create policies to foster a better food environment.

We believe it is critically important to connect science with public policy such that science is communicated effectively with policy makers and scientists can respond rapidly to the need for studies that can inform policy. There are many positive signs that this is occurring, but more can be done.

We hope we have succeeded in fostering these connections with the publication of this book.

REFERENCES

1. Blumenthal DM, Gold MS. Neurobiology of food addiction. *Curr Opin Clin Nutr* 2010;13:359–365.
2. Gold MS. Eating disorders, overeating, and pathological attachment to food: independent or addictive disorders? *J Addict Dis* 2004;23:1–3.
3. Gold MS. Are eating disorders addictions? *Adv Biosci* 1993;90:455–463.
4. Jonas JM, Gold MS. The use of opiate antagonists in treating bulimia: a study of low-dose versus high-dose naltrexone. *Psychiatry Res* 1988;24:195–199.
5. Jonas JM, Gold MS. Cocaine abuse and eating disorders. *Lancet* 1986;1:390–391.
6. Avena NM. Examining the addictive-like properties of binge eating using an animal model of sugar dependence. *Exp Clin Psychopharm* 2007;15:481–491.
7. Gold MS. From bedside to bench and back again: a 30-year saga. *Physiol Behav* 2011;104:157–161.
8. Avena NM, Bocarsly ME, Rada P, Kim A, Hoebel BG. After daily bingeing on a sucrose solution, food deprivation induces anxiety and accumbens dopamine/acetylcholine imbalance. *Physiol Behav* 2008;94:309–315.
9. Avena NM. Binge eating: neurochemical insights from animal models. *Eat Disord* 2009;17:89–92.
10. Avena NM. The study of food addiction using animal models of binge eating. *Appetite* 2010;55:734–737.
11. Avena NM, Gold MS. Food and addiction—sugars, fats and hedonic overeating. *Addiction (Abingdon, England)* 2011;106:1214–1215; discussion 9–20.
12. Wang GJ, Volkow ND, Logan J, et al. Brain dopamine and obesity. *Lancet* 2001;357:354–357.
13. Wang GJ, Tomasi D, Backus W, et al. Gastric distention activates satiety circuitry in the human brain. *Neuroimage* 2008;39:1824–1831.
14. Volkow ND, Wang GJ, Baler RD. Reward, dopamine and the control of food intake: implications for obesity. *Trends Cogn Sci* 2011;15:37–46.
15. Story M, Nanney MS, Schwartz MB. Schools and obesity prevention: creating school environments and policies to promote healthy eating and physical activity. *Milbank Q* 2009;87:71–100.
16. Brownell KD, Farley T, Willett WC, et al. The public health and economic benefits of taxing sugar-sweetened beverages. *N Engl J Med* 2009;361:1599–1605.
17. Brownell KD, Frieden TR. Ounces of prevention—the public policy case for taxes on sugared beverages. *N Engl J Med* 2009;360:1805–1808.
18. Brownell KD, Ludwig DS. The Supplemental Nutrition Assistance Program, soda, and USDA policy: who benefits? *JAMA* 2011;306:1370–1371.
19. Harris JL, Pomeranz JL, Lobstein T, Brownell KD. A crisis in the marketplace: how food marketing

contributes to childhood obesity and what can be done. *Annu Rev Public Health* 2009;30:211–225.

20. Institute of Medicine. *Food Marketing to Children and Youth: Threat or Opportunity?* Washington, DC: National Academies Press, 2006.

21. Pomeranz JL, Brownell KD. Advancing public health obesity policy through state attorneys general. *Am J Public Health* 2011;101:425–431.

22. Brownell KD, Warner KE. The perils of ignoring history: Big Tobacco played dirty and millions died. How similar is Big Food? *Milbank Q* 2009;87:259–294.

23. Koplan JP, Brownell KD. Response of the food and beverage industry to the obesity threat. *JAMA* 2010;304:1487–1488.

24. Brownell KD, Kersh R, Ludwig DS, et al. Personal responsibility and obesity: a constructive approach to a controversial issue. *Health Aff (Millwood)* 2010;29:379–387.

INDEX